The Law
and
Public School
Operation

The Law
and
Public School
Operation

The Law and Public School Operation

SECOND EDITION

LEROY J. PETERSON
University of Wisconsin
RICHARD A. ROSSMILLER
University of Wisconsin
MARLIN M. VOLZ
University of Louisville

Harper & Row, Publishers, Inc.
New York, Hagerstown, San Francisco, London

Sponsoring Editor: George A. Middendorf
Project Editor: David Nickol
Designer: Michel Craig
Production Supervisor: Kewal K. Sharma
Compositor: David E. Seham Assoc. Inc.
Printer and binder: Halliday Lithograph Corporation

THE LAW AND PUBLIC SCHOOL OPERATION, Second Edition

Library of Congress Cataloging in Publication Data

Peterson, LeRoy James, Date-
  The law and public school operation.

  Bibliography: p.
  Includes indexes.
  1. Educational law and legislation—United States.
I. Rossmiller, Richard A., joint author. II. Volz,
Marlin M., Date- joint author. III. Title.
KF4119.P4   1978   344'.73'071   77-17037
ISBN 0-06-045143-2

To our wives, without whose tolerance,
encouragement, and assistance
the original publication and the revision
would have been impossible

CONTENTS

PREFACE

Recent years have witnessed an upsurge in the magnitude of school-related statutory enactments, federal legislation, and court decisions. These legal enactments and interpretations are having a far-ranging influence on the lives of all who are associated with the schools—children, parents, teachers, supervisors, administrators, and members of boards of education as well as municipal, county, state, and national authorities and persons conducting business with school districts in an extensive variety of capacities. Civil rights acts, both federal and state, extension of the concept of due process, vesting of property and other rights in the expectation of continued employment, and extension of rights through judicial interpretation of constitutional guarantees have expanded the boundaries of legal contention.

An understanding of these legislative enactments and judicial interpretations within a framework of legal principles is basic to sound operational practice and to effective decision making in classrooms, administrative circles, board meetings, and communities as well as in intermediate districts and at state and federal levels.

It is the purpose of this publication to present in nontechnical language understandable to educational practitioners without legal training well-documented legal information, identified as legal principles, on all major facets of school operation. The development of this manuscript required judicious selection from an extensive array of legal information. In making selections the authors attempted to identify broad issues of maximum educational and legal import and to select material descriptive of principles identifying the legal rights, privileges, duties, and responsibilities of school-connected personnel. While generalizations have been made, it must be understood that they are circumscribed by statutes enacted in individual states. Reference to specific state statutes and to interpretations of them are minimal.

The book, although extensively documented, is not intended to be only a report of cases on the several legal topics. Rather, it attempts to develop legal principles that will serve as guides in analyzing future educational situations and making judgments. It is aimed at the development of principles of the living law applicable to prospective educational operations. While describing the present, it looks to the future.

The book projects a comprehensive outlook. It is designed to serve as a source book of classified court decisions and judicial interpretations on all major educational topics. Its potential value to teachers, administrators, and school board members justifies a place in the professional library of all local school systems.

Dealing with a recognized discipline, this volume is suitable for use as a textbook for courses in school law in colleges and universities. The information presented has been drawn from materials utilized in more than twenty years of school law teaching. The inclusion of sections directly related to pupils and teachers should make the book a valuable supplementary text in teacher preparation programs. The final chapter, which presents a comprehensive array of legal sources and explains their uses, should be particularly helpful to educators desiring to research problems in school law.

The active development of the original publication spanned five years and the revision a three year period. To the many people who have assisted in the production—attorneys, school administrators, teachers, students of law and school law, research and secretarial assistants—the authors are deeply grateful for insightful criticism and invaluable suggestions. Professor Volz is especially grateful to Assistant Professor Linda S. Ewald for her assistance. Any errors of omission or commission that remain are the sole responsibility of the authors.

LeRoy J. Peterson
Richard A. Rossmiller
Marlin M. Volz

The Law
and
Public School
Operation

The Legal Framework of Education

1.0 INTRODUCTION

Education in the United States operates within a well-defined legal structure, and each unit of government exercises designated functions. Specific functions are the established province of the federal government, the state government, and local governmental units, and limitations are imposed on each unit. Within a framework of constitutional provisions and statutory enactments the guidelines for educational operation are established.

In overall authority and direction the United States Constitution is the supreme law of the land. It is superior to the constitutional provisions of each of the states and superior to federal or state legislative enactments. Although legally education is the responsibility and primary concern of the individual states, such responsibility must be exercised in a manner consistent with federal constitutional requirements.[1] In the interpretation of the United States Constitution and the guarantees contained therein and in the interpretation of legislation enacted by the Congress, the United States Supreme Court is the highest authority. Decisions of the United States Supreme Court concerning the provisions of the Constitution must be followed by federal and state courts regardless of whether they concur in the correctness of the decisions.[2]

In education, as in other matters, interference with the power of the states is not a constitutional criterion for determination of the power of Congress. If a power is not granted to Congress, it cannot exercise that power; if a power is granted to Congress, it may be exercised even though it interferes with state laws or even with provisions of the state constitution.[3]

Where there are no federal constitutional or statutory enactments the state has exclusive jurisdiction in education. The constitution of the state is controlling, and statutes which are in violation of the state constitution are invalid. Statutes which do not violate the federal Constitution or statutes, or the state constitution, are a valid exercise of the legislative power of the state. Such statutes delineate the broad boundaries within which public schools operate and establish policies which govern the state's educational activities.

Most states have vested control of the day-by-day operation of schools in local school districts either by specific statutes or by clear implication of statutes. Since many of these statutes convey a broad grant of power, local boards of education generally have considerable leeway in excercising broad discretion in the development and operation of local educational programs. Their activities, however, must be in accord with the powers granted them and must not be in violation of the state constitution, congressional action, or the federal Constitution. If a rule adopted by a local board of education is in violation of state law, the state law will prevail.

All units of government—federal, state, intermediate unit, municipality, and school district—exercise some degree of control and direction over education. All units except local school districts will be discussed briefly in this chapter. The operation of local school districts will be treated in detail in subsequent chapters.

1.1 RELATIONS OF THE FEDERAL GOVERNMENT TO EDUCATION

The powers of the federal government are delegated and enumerated and not inherent powers. This is clearly discerned in the Tenth Amendment to the United States Constitution, which provides that "the powers not delegated to the United States by the Constitution, nor prohibited by it to the States, are reserved to the States respectively, or to the people."

Since powers relating to education are neither delegated to the United States by the Constitution nor prohibited to the states, it might be assumed that federal relations to education would be minimal. The opposite is true, and the federal government has and is exerting profound and far-reaching influence on state educational systems, through the impact of the provisions of the federal Constitution, decisions of the United States Supreme Court, and congressional enactments relative to civil rights and financial support to public schools.

The United States Supreme Court has described the lines of authority as follows:

It is, of course, quite true that the responsibility for public education is primarily the concern of the States, but it is equally true that such responsibilities, like all other state activity, must be exercised consistently with federal constitutional requirements as they apply to state action.[4]

[1]Cooper v. Aaron, 358 U.S. 1, 78 S.Ct. 1401, 3 L.Ed.2d 3 (Ark. 1958).

[2]Davis v. East Baton Rouge Parish School Board, 214 F.Supp. 624 (La. 1963); Acree et al. v. County Board of Education, 301 F.Supp. 1285 (Ga. 1969); American Civil Liberties Union v. Albert Gallatin Area School District, 307 F.Supp. 637 (Pa. 1969).

[3]Annals of Congress 1897 (1791). Views of James Madison.

[4]Cooper v. Aaron, 358 U.S. 1, 78 S.Ct. 1401, 3 L.Ed.2d 3 (Ark. 1958).

1.1a Provide for the general welfare

Article I, Section 8 of the United States Constitution provides that "the Congress shall have power to lay and collect Taxes, Duties, Imposts and Excises, to pay the Debts and provide for the common Defence and general Welfare of the United States. . . ."

Arguments relative to the role of the federal government under the "general welfare" clause have been long and heated outside as well as within educational circles. James Madison and Alexander Hamilton intensely debated the meaning of this clause. In the view of Madison the framers of the Constitution had adopted Article I, Section 8 without any thought that it would extend the authority of or grant any substantive power to the federal government. Hamilton maintained that it conferred upon Congress the power to tax and spend for purposes other than those specifically enumerated and extended to any purpose which would "promote the general welfare."

Congress early acted upon Hamilton's interpretation and made appropriations for a wide array of internal improvements,[5] without having an interpretation of the meaning of the "general welfare" clause by the United States Supreme Court. Finally, in a case decided in 1896, the Court sustained[6] the right of the federal government to acquire land within a state for use as a national park, invoking the power of taxation for the general welfare. In a later case the Court in its dicta endorsed Hamilton's views.[7] The following year the United States Supreme Court was called upon to answer directly the question of the authority of the Congress to levy taxes and spend money for another aspect of general welfare—social security legislation. In this decision the power of the federal government to provide for the general welfare was directly sustained.[8] This point of view was also expressed in later decisions.[9] As a result of these decisions it is now well settled that the Congress may tax and spend for general welfare purposes. Furthermore, the decision as to whether or not a given expenditure is for the general welfare is within the discretion of the Congress, for

the United States Supreme Court has declared that the discretion of the Congress in regard to such matters is not to be interfered with unless it is "clearly wrong, a display of arbitrary power, not an exercise of judgment."[10]

While none of the above cases involved an educational issue, the decisions leave no doubt of the authority of the federal government to levy and collect taxes for educational purposes. This conclusion is buttressed by the widespread legal acceptance of the variety of federal grants for educational purposes on the assumption that a high level of education is essential for the civic and economic well-being of the country. To improve education is to "provide for the general welfare" in the view of many.

Although there appears to be no question of the authority of Congress to levy taxes for educational purposes, an early interpretation does establish some guidelines. In this discussion the scope and power of the "general welfare" clause was stated as follows:

> . . . They [Congress] are not to lay taxes ad libitum for any purpose they please but only to pay the debts or provide for the general welfare of the Union. In like manner they are not to do anything they please for the general welfare but only to lay taxes for that purpose.[11]

This interpretation is easily applicable to education, if not to other areas. The federal Congress is authorized to levy taxes for the purpose of providing financial support for education, but it is not authorized to direct or control education.

In a previously cited case it was held[12] that a federal law which attempted to use the federal taxing power to regulate and control agricultural production was unconstitutional because this authority was not within the powers delegated to the federal government. Since the Tenth Amendment clearly makes education a state function, educational matters appear to come within the same category. However, participation in cooperative educational programs is a different matter. Where a state or school district has a clear option of accepting or rejecting federal funds offered under a given program, the federal government is within its authority in prescribing the framework within which the program will operate.

[5]1 U.S.C. 229 (1792); 2 U.S.C. 257 (1806).
[6]United States v. Gettysburg Electric Ry., 160 U.S. 668, 16 S.Ct. 427, 40 L.Ed. 576 (Pa. 1896).
[7]United States v. Butler, 297 U.S. 1, 56 S.Ct. 312, 80 L.Ed. 477 (Mass. 1936).
[8]Helvering v. Davis, 301 U.S. 619, 57 S.Ct. 904, 81 L.Ed. 1307 (Mass. 1937).
[9]Steward Machine Co. v. Davis, 301 U.S. 548, 57 S.Ct. 883, 81 L.Ed. 1279 (Ala. 1937); City of Cleveland v. United States, 323 U.S. 329, 65 S.Ct. 280, 89 L.Ed. 274 (Ohio 1945).

[10]Helvering v. Davis, 301 U.S. 619, 57 S.Ct. 904, 81 L.Ed. 1307 (Mass. 1937).
[11]Writings of Thomas Jefferson, 147–149 (Library Edition 1904).
[12]United States v. Butler, 297 U.S. 1, 56 S.Ct. 312, 80 L.Ed. 477 (Mass. 1936).

Thus, it has been held[13] that if any state, school district, or other agency receiving federal funds fails to comply with the statutes the federal government may terminate all future aid and assistance to the program. If a school board accepts federal funds for the maintenance and operation of schools after the passage of the Civil Rights Act of 1964, it is bound by the provisions of the act.[14] To hold that the federal government did not have this authority would violate accepted principles of fiscal accountability. Sound fiscal administration requires that the unit of government responsible for allocating tax revenue must exercise some responsibility for determining the objectives to be attained by the expenditure and the procedures by which such objectives are to be reached.

1.1b Obligation of contracts

Article I, Section 10 of the United States Constitution reads in part: "No State shall ... pass any Bill of Attainder, ex post facto Law, or Law impairing the Obligation of Contracts...." This article guaranteeing the sanctity of contracts has been tested in many directions. An early United States Supreme Court case tested the authority of the legislature to alter a charter granted by a sovereignty to a private college. In this instance it was held[15] that a charter was a contract within the meaning of the federal Constitution and that the rights guaranteed under the terms of the charter could not be abrogated. In later cases, however, the Court held[16] that a state could insert a provision in a charter to the effect that the charter could be revoked and that if such a clause were inserted the authority to revoke would be sustained. Since this provision becomes part of the contract, there is no impairment of the contract when the option provided for in the contract is exercised.

It is clear from the Dartmouth College case and others[17] that the constitutional prohibition against the impairment of contracts applies to both public and private

contracts. Numerous court decisions have made it clear that contracts entered into by school districts, including teaching contracts, are fully protected under Article I, Section 10 of the United States Constitution.

There are, however, restrictions on the type of contracts which may be consummated and guaranteed against impairment. Contracts which are in violation of constitutional provisions, statutes, or public policy are prohibited. Thus, contracts may not be entered into legally which will make state laws inoperative. Nor do the obligations of contracts prohibit the state from enacting statutes outlawing undesirable practices.[18]

The prohibition against impairment of contracts expressed in the United States Constitution applies to both teacher tenure and teacher retirement legislation when such legislation is drawn in a manner which gives it contractual status. For example, in a Wisconsin case the statute provided for a retirement payment from funds contributed by the teacher and a death benefit paid entirely from state funds. The death benefit portion of the statute was later repealed. Upon the death of a teacher, his wife brought action to recover the benefit established in the original act. The court permitted recovery and concluded that "one engaged in teaching in this state and whose services are to be paid for in whole or part by the state school fund is not a public officer and his valid contracts cannot lawfully be destroyed or impaired by subsequent legislation...."[19] Other cases in Wisconsin[20] and New Jersey[21] were to the same effect.

A teacher tenure case in Indiana also revealed the influence of the "impairment of contract" clause of the federal Constitution. In this case it was held[22] that statutes could contain provisions which, when accepted by individuals, would establish contracts between such individuals and the state. Thus the Indiana Teacher Tenure Act was deemed to be contractual, and the United States Supreme Court refused to permit the legislature to amend the law to exclude rural teachers from the coverage of the ten-

[13]LeBeauf v. State Board of Education, 244 F.Supp. 256 (La. 1965).

[14]Lemon v. Bossier Parish School Board, 240 F.Supp. 709 (La. 1965).

[15]Trustees of Dartmouth College v. Woodward, 17 U.S. (4 Wheat.) 518, 4 L.Ed. 629 (N.H. 1819).

[16]Denny v. Bennett, 128 U.S. 489, 9 S.Ct. 134, 32 L.Ed. 491 (Minn. 1888); Railway Co. v. Philadelphia, 101 U.S. 528, 25 L.Ed. 912 (Pa. 1879); Spring Valley Water Co. v. Schottler, 110 U.S. 347, 4 S.Ct. 48, 28 L.Ed. 173 (Cal. 1884).

[17]Sliosberg v. New York Life Insurance Co., 216 N.Y.S., 215, 217 App. Div. 67 (1947); Board of Education of City of Lincoln Park v. Board of Education of City of Detroit, 222 N.W. 763 (Mich. 1929).

[18]Myers v. Irwin, 2 S&R 368, 372 (Pa. 1816); Brown v. Penobscot Bank, 8 Mass. 445 (1812); Manigault v. Springs, 199 U.S. 473, 26 S.Ct. 127, 50 L.Ed. 274 (S.C. 1905).

[19]State ex. rel. O.Neil v. Blied, 206 N.W. 213 (Wis. 1925).

[20]State ex. rel. Stafford v. State Annuity and Investment Board, 261 N.W. 718 (Wis. 1935).

[21]Ball v. Board of Trustees of Teachers Retirement Fund, 58 Atl. 111 (N.J. 1904).

[22]Indiana ex. rel. Anderson v. Brand, 303 U.S. 95, 58 S.Ct. 443, 82 L.Ed. 685, 113 A.L.R. 1482 (Ind. 1938).

ure act. The Alabama and Colorado tenure laws[23] are another example of contractual status.

1.1c The establishment of a religion

One of the major guarantees of individual rights found in the United States Constitution is contained in the First Amendment. This amendment, having far-reaching influence both upon private individuals and upon the educational system of the several states, provides that "Congress shall make no law respecting an establishment of religion, or prohibiting the free exercise thereof. . . ." It should be noted that originally the provisions of the amendment applied only to Congress and not to state legislatures; i.e., "Congress shall make no law." However, the Fourteenth Amendment, which provides that "no State shall make or enforce any law which shall abridge the privileges and immunities of citizens of the United States," has been held[24] by the United States Supreme Court to make all provisions of the federal Constitution applicable to the citizens of all states.

A large array of cases involving education has come before the United States Supreme Court under the First Amendment. Most of these cases will be discussed as they bear upon specific topics treated in other chapters. However, two cases are reported here as examples of the influence of the First Amendment on education.

After the practice of released time for religious instruction conducted in public school facilities in Champaign, Illinois, had been declared unconstitutional[25] by the United States Supreme Court, a related case from New York involving a somewhat different set of facts came to the Supreme Court. In this instance the pupils were released from school to attend religious services in their own places of religious worship. No pupil was compelled to go to any place of religious worship, and public school teachers did not assist in the program. Since no public school funds, facilities, or staff time was used, the majority of the Supreme Court held[26] that in these

circumstances there was neither the "establishment of religion" nor any prohibition against the "free exercise" thereof. The minority argued that the First Amendment was in fact abridged and that there were no material distinctions between the facts of the case under consideration (Zorach) and the McCollum (Champaign, Illinois) case in which a released-time program was held to be unconstitutional.

The influence of the First Amendment on educational practice was evident in another New York case that was appealed to the United States Supreme Court. In this instance the state board of regents adopted the following prayer to be repeated by pupils in the presence of a teacher at the beginning of each school day at the option of the local district: "Almighty God, we acknowledge our dependence upon Thee, and we beg Thy blessings upon us, our parents, our teachers and our country." Parents of several pupils objected to this prayer. It was charged that the prayer violated that part of the First Amendment which forbids an establishment of religion, made applicable to the states by the Fourteenth Amendment. The United States Supreme Court sustained[27] the objection and prohibited the use of the prayer. Again, there was a vigorous dissent by three justices.

1.1d A witness against oneself

In recent years considerable controversy has centered on the first provision of the Fifth Amendment which provides that: "No person . . . shall be compelled in any criminal case to be a witness against himself. . . ." Under this constitutional guarantee it has been held[28] that in any proceedings in which testimony is legally required persons may refuse to answer any questions the answers to which might be used against them in any future criminal proceedings or might uncover further evidence against them. A person may refuse to answer such a question on the grounds that by answering, one would expose one's self to prosecution by the state.[29]

This particular provision of the United States Constitution has been the subject of extensive litigation, especially in state courts. Two cases will be cited to demonstrate its influence. Both involved refusal of an individual to answer questions regard-

[23]Faircloth v. Folmer, 40 So.2d 697 (Ala. 1949); Ebbe v. Julesburg School District No. R.E-1, 550 P.2d 355 (Col. 1976).

[24]Cantwell v. Connecticut, 310 U.S. 296, 60 S.Ct. 900, 84 L.Ed. 1213 (Conn. 1940); Everson v. Board of Education, 330 U.S. 1, 67 S.Ct. 504, 91 L.Ed. 711 (N.J. 1947).

[25]Illinois ex. rel. McCollum v. Board of Education, 333 U.S. 203, 68 S.Ct. 461, 92 L.Ed. 649, 2 A.L.R.2d 1338 (Ill. 1948).

[26]Zorach v. Clauson, 343 U.S. 306, 72 S.Ct. 679, 96 L.Ed. 954 (N.Y. 1952).

[27]Engel v. Vitale, 370 U.S. 421, 82 S.Ct. 1261, 8 L.Ed.2d 601, 86 A.L.R.2d 1285 (N.Y. 1962).

[28]McCarthy v. Arndstein, 266 U.S. 34, 45 S.Ct. 16, 69 L.Ed. 158 (N.Y. 1924).

[29]Murphy v. N.Y. Waterfront Commission, 378 U.S. 52, 84A S.Ct. 1594, 12 L.Ed.2d 678 (N.J. 1964).

ing alleged communistic affiliations and/or activities. In one case the defense was based upon the Fifth Amendment; in the other case the Fifth Amendment was disclaimed as a defense.

In the first case a man who had taught in the Philadelphia public school system for twenty-two years refused on two occasions to answer questions put to him by the superintendent of schools regarding his alleged past communistic activities. Several months later—and five days after the teacher asserted the privilege against self-incrimination during a televised hearing conducted by a subcommittee of the Committee on Un-American Activities of the House of Representatives—the teacher was notified by the superintendent that he had been given an "unsatisfactory" rating because of his failure to answer the superintendent's questions and had been charged with being incompetent. After a formal hearing before the board of education, the teacher was found to be incompetent and was discharged from his employment as a teacher. The United States Supreme Court upheld his discharge and stated:

> By engaging in teaching in the public schools, petitioner did not give up his right to freedom of belief, speech or association. He did, however, undertake obligations of frankness, candor and cooperation in answering inquiries made of him by his employing Board examining into his fitness to serve it as a public school teacher.[30]

It would appear from this decision that a teacher may, under certain circumstances, be compelled either to give up his constitutional right to plead the Fifth Amendment or to give up his means of earning a livelihood. Obviously, there were vigorous dissents from the majority opinion in this case.

In the second case, also decided by a divided court, the defendant decided not to rely on the Fifth Amendment in defending his refusal to answer questions put to him by a subcommittee of the House Committee on Un-American Activities. Rather, the defendant, who was a teaching fellow at the University of Michigan, maintained that inquiry into his present and past affiliations was a violation of the freedom of speech, religion, and association guaranteed him by the First Amendment. The Supreme Court, however, affirmed his conviction of con-

tempt of Congress for failure to answer questions put to him and commented:

> . . . broadly viewed, inquiries cannot be made into the teaching that is pursued in any of our educational institutions. When academic teaching-freedom and its corollary learning-freedom, so essential to the well-being of the Nation, are claimed, this Court will always be on the alert against intrusion by Congress into this constitutionally protected domain. But this does not mean that the Congress is precluded from interrogating a witness merely because he is a teacher. An educational institution is not a constitutional sanctuary from inquiry into matters that may otherwise be within the constitutional legislative domain merely for the reason that inquiry is made of someone within its walls. . . .[31]

From these and other cases involving a teacher's rights against furnishing self-incriminating information it would appear that teachers may not avoid answering questions put to them by their employers which bear upon their qualifications of fitness for teaching in a public school. They are obligated to be frank, candid, and cooperative in responding to such inquiries. It also would appear that a state may, under certain circumstances, provide that membership in specific organizations will disqualify a teacher from obtaining or holding a teaching position, for, as the United States Supreme Court has said, "It is clear that such persons have the right under our law to assemble, speak, think and believe as they will. . . . It is equally clear that they have no right to work for the State in the school system on their own terms. . . ."[32]

1.1e Deprivation of property without due process of law

The Fourteenth Amendment to the Constitution of the United States provides that no state shall "deprive any person of life, liberty, or property without due process of law. . . ." A large number of educational cases involving this guarantee have come to the courts. Perhaps the most important, at least in terms of its influence upon the development of American education, was *Pierce v. Society of Sisters.*[33] The basis of this case was an Oregon statute which provided that children between the ages of eight and sixteen must, with a few limited

[30]Beilan v. Board of Education, 357 U.S. 399, 78 S.Ct. 1317, 2 L.Ed.2d 1414 (Pa. 1958). See also Garner v. Bd. of Pub. Works, 341 U.S. 716, 71 S.Ct. 909, 95 L.Ed. 1317 (Cal. 1951); Adler v. Board of Education, 342 U.S. 485, 72 S.Ct. 380, 96 L.Ed. 517, 27 A.L.R.2d 472 (N.Y. 1952).

[31]Barenblatt v. United States, 360 U.S. 109, 79 S.Ct. 1081, 3 L.Ed.2d 1115 (D.C. 1959).
[32]Adler v. Board of Education, 342 U.S. 485, 72 S.Ct. 380, 96 L.Ed. 517, 27 A.L.R.2d 472 (N.Y. 1952).
[33]Pierce v. Society of Sisters, 268 U.S. 510, 45 S.Ct. 571, 69 L.Ed. 1070, 39 A.L.R. 468 (Ore. 1925).

exceptions, attend public schools exclusively. The Society of Sisters and the Hill Military Academy objected to this statute as depriving them of property without due process of law. They also claimed that the statute interfered unreasonably with the liberty of parents to direct the education of their children. The United States Supreme Court held the statute unconstitutional, agreeing with both of these contentions. On the basis of this decision no state may enforce legislation that requires children to attend public schools exclusively.

1.1f Equal protection of the laws

The Fourteenth Amendment also provides that no state shall "deny to any person within its jurisdiction the equal protection of the laws." The "equal protection" clause has been subjected to virtually continuous court action in recent years. In 1954 the United States Supreme Court interpreted this clause to mean that segregation of pupils in the public schools on the basis of race was unconstitutional.[34] Thus, since 1954 the racial segregation of public school pupils has been outlawed. Earlier cases distinguished desegregation from intergration with the courts holding that integration was not required. The distinction between desegregation and integration now appears to be without meaning. Recent cases designed to eliminate racial imbalance appear to require both desegregation and intergration regardless of the terms applied.

It should be understood that the "equal protection" clause of the Fourteenth Amendment does not take from the legislature the authority to classify subjects, including pupils. What it does do is prohibit arbitrary and unreasonable classifications of subjects or persons.[35]

The Fourteenth Amendment requires that protection of the law be extended equally to all persons, clearly implying that unequal application of the law is prohibited.[36] The United States Supreme Court will enforce this prohibition in education, as elsewhere, regardless of the regulations of local boards of education, the provisions of state statutes and state constitutions, or the decisions of state courts.

1.1g Eminent domain

No provision for exercising the right of eminent domain is found in the United States Constitution. Such a provision is unnecessary, however, for the right of eminent domain requires no consitutional recognition. It is a right of sovereignty possessed by both the federal and state governments.[37] The Constitution simply requires that just compensation be granted for property taken in the exercise of eminent domain. As stated in the Fifth Amendment, "nor shall private property be taken for public use without just compensation." This requirement acts as a limitation on the exercise of an existing power of government[38] to which all private property is subject.[39]

1.1h Ex post facto laws

Whenever laws are passed and made applicable retroactively, it is commonly charged that they are ex post facto laws in violation of federal and state constitutions. The federal government has a "cognate restriction" clause directly prohibiting ex post facto laws.[40] However, it is not generally understood that this section of the Constitution relates only to penal and criminal legislation and not to civil laws which could adversely affect private rights.[41] Thus, obviously neither school personnel nor school districts are assured that they will be protected against adverse civil laws made effective retroactively.

1.1i Exercise of police power

Police power is defined as the power to enact laws for the comfort, health, and prosperity of the state, i.e., for the common welfare of all the people. Such laws may be enacted by either state legislatures or the Congress and they are enforceable even if some individual rights are abrogated. The United States Supreme Court is the final authority in determining whether or not an attempted exercise of police power is proper. The United States Supreme Court determines whether individual rights guaranteed by the Constitution shall be denied in the interest of the greatest good for the greatest number. Where it is not necessary to abrogate individual rights in the interest of the greater good of society, it is the function of

[37]United States v. Jones, 109 U.S. 513, 518, 3 S.Ct. 346, 27 L.Ed. 1015 (Wis. 1883).

[38]United States v. Lynah, 188 U.S. 445, 465, 23 S.Ct. 349, 47 L.Ed. 539 (S.C. 1903).

[39]Kohl v. United States, 91 U.S. 367, 374, 23 L.Ed. 449 (Ohio 1875).

[40]U.S. Const. Article I, Section 9.

[41]Calder v. Bull, 3 U.S. (3 Dall.) 386, 390, 1 L.Ed. 648 (Conn. 1798); Watson v. Mercer, 33 U.S. (8 Pet.) 88, 110, 8 L.Ed. 876 (Pa. 1834); Orr v. Gilman, 183 U.S. 278, 285, 22 S.Ct. 213, 46 L.Ed. 196 (N.Y. 1902); Kentucky Union Co. v. Kentucky, 219 U.S. 140, 31 S.Ct. 171, 55 L.Ed. 137 (Ky. 1911).

[34]Brown v. Board of Education, 347 U.S. 483, 74 S.Ct. 686, 98 L.Ed. 873, 38 A.L.R.2d 1180 (Kan. 1954).

[35]Clein v. City of Atlanta, 139 S.E. 46 (Ga. 1927); McCullers v. Williamson, 144 S.E.2d 911 (Ga. 1965).

[36]Evans v. Buchanan, 207 F.Supp. 820 (Del. 1962).

the United States Supreme Court to restrain state legislatures and the Congress from taking away individual rights guaranteed by national and state constitutions.

Two cases will be cited as examples of the exercise of police power in educational matters. One case[42] tested the constitutionality of a state statute requiring vaccination against smallpox as a condition of school attendance. In this instance the United States Supreme Court held that such statutes were within the police power of a state and were enforceable.

In the other case[43] the Supreme Court was required to rule on the legality of a statute making it unlawful to teach foreign languages to any pupils in private, parochial, or public schools unless they previously had completed the work of the eighth grade. The Supreme Court of Nebraska held that this statute was a legitimate exercise of the police power in view of the general educational level of the children of foreign-speaking parents at that time. However, the United States Supreme Court pointed out that a state legislature does not have final or conclusive jurisdiction in determining whether or not police power should be exercised. This is a function of the courts, and since the United States Supreme Court is the final judicial authority, the United States Supreme Court is the body which *finally* determines whether or not the police power may properly be exercised. In this instance it was decided that the situation did not justify the invocation of police power or the abrogation of guaranteed individual rights.

1.1j Civil rights acts

The Congress of the United States has attempted to delineate the dimensions of equal protection under the law as provided in the U.S. Constitution in a number of civil rights acts. The earlier acts of 1866 and 1871 were designed and enacted largely for protection of blacks. However, the terms of the 1871 act were sufficiently broad to guarantee equal protection to all. Major provisions of this act are embodied in the following quotation:

> *Every person who, under color of any statute, ordinance, regulation, custom or usage of any state or territory, subjects or causes to be subjected any citizen of the United States or any other person within the jurisdiction thereof to the deprivation of any rights,*

> *privileges or immunity secured by the Constitution and laws shall be liable to the party injured in an action at law, suit in equity or other proper proceedings for redress.* [44]

The Civil Rights Act of 1964, with subsequent acts and amendments, explicated and/or extended the rights granted in 1871. It guaranteed the right to be free from discrimination because of race, color, national origin, religion or sex.[45] Subsequent enactments have spelled out equal protection of the law in specific areas, principally in public accomodations, public facilities, public education, federally assisted programs and equal employment opportunities. The Equal Employment Opportunity Act of 1972, which amended Title VII of the federal Civil Rights Act of 1964, brought public employees within its purview.[46]

The civil rights statutes now provide the basis for extensive court action by pupils and teachers in an expansive array of cases. These cases will be presented in subsequent chapters under the appropriate titles.

1.2 STATE GOVERNMENT AND EDUCATION

Since the Tenth Amendment to the United States Constitution provides that "the powers not delegated to the United States by the Constitution, nor prohibited by it to the States, are reserved to the States respectively, or to the people," the control and direction of education is clearly vested in the states and the people. It is an inherent power of state government. In contrast with the federal government, where Congress must find constitutional authority for all its educational acts, a state legislature may enact any educational legislation not expressly or by implication forbidden by fundamental law.[47]

1.2a Authority and responsibility of the state

The authority of a state to provide for an educational activity is not found exclusively in the state constitution. It may or may not be provided in the state constitution. The constitution of a state may mandate certain educational and other obligations, but it is not an exclusive grant of state power. The state constitution does not represent a measure of the extent of the power

---

[42]Zucht v. King, 260 U.S. 174, 43 S.Ct. 24, 67 L.Ed. 194 (Tex. 1922).

[43]Meyer v. Nebraska, 262 U.S. 390, 43 S.Ct. 625, 67 L.Ed. 1042; 29 A.L.R. 1446 (1923).

[44]42 U.S.C. § 1983.

[45]42 U.S.C. § 1981–1995.

[46]42 U.S.C. § 12000a, 2000b-2, 2000c-8, 2000d, 2000c –2000c-17.

[47]City of Manitowoc v. Town of Manitowoc Rapids, 285 N.W. 403 (Wis. 1939); Board of Education v. Upham, 191 N.E. 876, 94 A.L.R. 813 (Ill. 1934).

of the legislature. Rather, it is a restraining instrument which prohibits the legislature from enacting laws at variance with state constitutional provisions.[48] Those who challenge a statute must show that it is forbidden by either the state or the federal Constitution. If this showing cannot be made, the statute will remain in full force and effect.

If constitutional provisions are not violated, the state legislature has plenary power in education and in the establishment of educational policy. It has been asserted that the educational power of the state is absolute in all respects, limited only by constitutional provisions.[49] This power entends to complete control over school property.[50] When property is transferred from one district to another, it is only the owner (the state) designating a new trustee for its own property.[51] However, the state may not act in an arbitrary and capricious manner. The courts will restrain the legislature from so acting[52] although they will not question the judgment of the legislature in the exercise of its discretion.

The state not only has the right and power to provide an educational program for its youth; it is the state's duty[53] and obligation to do so at public expense.[54] Courts hold that it is the function of the state to provide and promote an efficient educational program[55] and that school laws are to be liberally construed to effect a beneficial purpose.[56]

1.2b Delegation of legislative authority

Given the American framework of decentralization of educational operation, it is obvious that most state legislatures have chosen to delegate the actual administration of the schools to other agencies. When administrative functions are delegated, there is no problem,[57] but attempts to delegate legislative authority have resulted in extensive litigation. The rule is clear: The state may not delegate legislative power to other agencies but must exercise this power itself. The state may direct another agency to carry on certain functions, and if it establishes guideposts, standards, and directions for the discharge of the task, the courts will hold that administrative functions, not legislative functions, have been delegated. However, the degree of direction required varies widely from state to state. The Supreme Court of Kansas has held[58] that the guidelines of action which are established for an agency carrying on a state function must be clearly and specifically stated. In spite of the legislature's providing that a school reorganization committee should consider such factors as assessed valuations, geographical features of the district, number of pupils attending school, location and condition of school buildings, centers for children to attend high school, and any other factors concerning adequate high school facilities, the court held that the statute was an illegal delegation of legislative power. The reasoning of the court was that nowhere could it find standards upon which the committee was authorized to act or refrain from acting in the reorganization of a school district.

In Wisconsin the court upheld[59] a statute authorizing the state superintendent to consolidate school districts having an equalized value of less than $100,000. No other standards or directions were given. The Wisconsin Supreme Court held that the statute was constitutional against a wide range of charges, including that of illegal delegation of legislative authority. In a more recent Wisconsin case the court specifically declared[60] that the legislature may delegate authority over school district boundaries to the state superintendent without prescribing standards for him to follow.

A liberal attitude toward delegation of authority by the legislature has been taken recently by the courts in a number of states. In North Carolina it was held[61] that, while the

[48]City of Newport News v. Elizabeth City County, 55 S.E.2d 56 (Va. 1949).

[49]State ex. rel. Eagleton v. Van Landuyt, 359 S.W.2d 773 (Mo. 1962); De Jonge v. School District, 139 N.W.2d 296 (Neb. 1966); Silver City Consolidated School District v. Board of Regents, 401 P.2d 95 (N.M. 1965).

[50]Fawcett v. Ball, 251 Pac. 679 (Cal. 1926); Newt Olson Lumber Co., v. School District No. 8, 263 Pac. 723 (Col. 1928); Waddell v. Board of Directors, 175 N.W. 65 (Iowa 1919).

[51]Pass School District v. Hollywood School District, 105 Pac. 122 (Cal. 1909).

[52]Hepner v. County Board of School Trustees, 133 N.E.2d 39 (Ill. 1956).

[53]State ex. rel. Board of Education v. D'Aulesa, 52 A.2d 636 (Conn. 1947).

[54]Wichita Falls Junior College District v. Battle, 204 F.2d 632 (5th Cir. 1953).

[55]State ex. rel. Thomson v. Giessel, 61 N.W.2d 903 (Wis. 1953).

[56]State ex. rel. Reorganized School District R-2 v. Robinson, 276 S.W.2d 235 (Mo. 1955); Matlock v. Board of County Commissioners, 281 P.2d 169 (Okla. 1955).

[57]Latham v. Board of Education, 201 N.E.2d 111 (Ill. 1964); Lobelville Special School District v. McCanless, 381 S.W.2d 273 (Tenn. 1964).

[58]State ex. rel. Donaldson v. Hines, 182 P.2d 865 (Kan. 1947).

[59]School District No. 3 v. Callahan, 297 N.W. 407 (Wis. 1941).

[60]School Board v. State Superintendent, 121 N.W.2d 900 (Wis. 1963). See also Joint School District No. 1 v. State, 203 N.W.2d 1 (Wis. 1973).

[61]Peacock v. County of Scotland, 136 S.E.2d 612 (N.C. 1964).

legislature cannot delegate its power to make a law, it can enact a law delegating power to determine whether or not there exist some facts or situations upon which action is dependent.

In South Dakota it was held[62] that the legislature may delegate authority to administrative boards, commissions, and officers to create, enlarge, consolidate, alter, and dissolve school districts; in the exercise of such delegated authority the board was acting as the agent of the legislature, with the exercise of some legislative power.

The Minnesota Supreme Court recently held[63] that the legislature could delegate its legislative power to reorganize school districts to a board or boards. The only apparent restriction was that such boards could not redelegate the power.

Some states, while less liberal than those described above, permit some delegation of authority by the legislature. Pennsylvania, for example, has held[64] that delegating to the state superintendent a reasonable amount of discretion to determine individual fact situations and to issue rules governing his administration is not an unconstitutional delegation of authority. In Illinois it was held[65] that, even though the responsibility was of a discretionary nature, the legislature could delegate its authority as long as it established broad guides for the operation of the program. In Tennessee it was held[66] that, if the legislature conferred power on a board and created machinery for the execution of an act by the board, the legislation was not invalid despite the fact that the legislature had also granted to such board the option of not exercising its authority. Provisions of the State School Building Authority Act and provisions of the Minimum Foundation Act which vested the state board of education in Georgia with wide discretion did not violate constitutional provisions placing all legislative power in the General Assembly and commanding that legislative, executive, and judicial powers remain forever separate and distinct.[67] In cases arising in New Jersey the courts have said that "the exigencies of modern government have increasingly dictated the use of general rather than minutely

detailed standards in regulatory enactment."[68] Nebraska, after noting the complexity of distinguishing clearly between the delegation of administrative and legislative functions, arrived at the same conclusion.[69]

A perusal of court decisions over a period of time shows an increasingly liberal interpretation of the degree of delegation of legislative power which is permitted to the state. This is particularly apparent in decisions in Illinois,[70] Nebraska,[71] and Pennsylvania.[72]

1.2c Delegation of local control

The large degree of local control of education which prevails in the United States leads many people to assume that local school districts have been granted the right of continued control of education and that the state, by granting substantial control to the local district, has relinquished its authority over the operation of local school districts. There is no legal basis for this assumption. The state does not relinquish any of its control over education when it permits local districts to exercise it.[73] The taxpayers of a city, village or town have no vested interests in education or the operation of the local schools.[74] The state may withdraw any power or authority it has granted local districts at will; it may create school districts, alter the boundaries of existing school districts, or even destroy them.[75]

No constitutional limitation is placed on the legislature relative to the agencies to which it may delegate control of the school.[76] It may change these agencies from time to time as it desires. The state's discretion is not exhausted by use.[77]

1.3 STATE BOARDS OF EDUCATION

The Council of State Governments reported that, in 1975, 48 states had state

[62]Sunnywood Common School District v. County Board of Education, 131 N.W.2d 105 (S.D. 1964).

[63]Lego v. Rolfe, 129 N.W.2d 811 (Minn. 1964).

[64]Commonwealth v. Smoker, 110 A.2d 740 (Pa. 1955).

[65]Schreiber v. County Board of School Trustees, 198 N.E.2d 848 (Ill. 1964).

[66]Lobelville Special School District v. McCanless, 381 S.W.2d 273 (Tenn. 1964).

[67]Sheffield v. State School Building Authority, 68 S.E.2d 590 (Ga. 1952).

[68]Ward v. Scott, 93 A.2d 385 (N.J. 1952); Schinck v. Board of Education, 159 A.2d 396 (N.J. 1960).

[69]School District v. State Board of Education, 127 N.W.2d 458 (Neb. 1964).

[70]Board of Education v. Page, 211 N.E.2d 361 (Ill. 1965).

[71]De Jonge v. School District, 139 N.W.2d 296 (Neb. 1965).

[72]Chartiers Valley Jt. Schools v. County Board of School Directors, 211 A.2d 487 (Pa. 1965).

[73]Halstead v. Rozmiarek, 94 N.W.2d 37 (Neb. 1959).

[74]Zawerschnik v. Joint County School Committee, 73 N.W.2d 566 (Wis. 1955).

[75]Barrett v. Haas, 62 Dauph. 118 (Pa. 1951).

[76]Smith v. Board of Education, 89 N.E.2d 893 (Ill. 1950).

[77]Hasbrouk v. School Committee, 128 Atl. 449 (R.I. 1925); Vaughan v. McCartney, 115 So. 30 (Ala. 1927); Reams v. McMinnville, 284 S.W. 382 (Tenn. 1926).

boards of education for the common system;[78] Illinois and Wisconsin did not. Provisions were reported underway in Illinois for the establishment of such a board, and though Wisconsin had a state board for schools of vocational, technical and adult education, it had none for elementary and secondary schools. In 12 of the states the board is elected by the people, an increase of nine over the past 28 years, and in 31 states appointed by the governor, an increase of one in that time. Five states employ other methods, three less than 28 years ago. Regardless of the method employed, once it is established the board operates as an independent agency and the appointing agency has no veto power over the board's actions.

State boards of education have responsibilities varying from extremely comprehensive to quite limited. Extensive regulatory powers are vested in the state boards of education in Kansas, New Jersey, Pennsylvania, Tennessee, and Virginia.

1.3a Method of establishment

The method of establishment and the authority under which a state board of education may be established vary markedly. A state board of education may be established by provisions of statute, constitution, or special charter. When it is established by statute, its powers and functions are defined by the legislature. Even when the state constitution provides for a state board of education, the establishment and operation of the board in most aspects is subject to the will of the legislature.[79] However, legislative control is subject to specific limitations when a state board of education is established by special charter. The legislature must recognize and permit the continued existence of the board and has no reserve power to abolish it.[80]

1.3b Nature of

While authorities in educational administration generally hold that policy making should be the major function of a state board of education and that the executive function should be vested in the state superintendent or state commissioner of education, no such division of tasks is found in many states. In fact, the combination of policy making and executive author-

ity has legal sanction. The courts have declared[81] that the state board of education is part of the executive department of state government and that it is an administrative body.[82] The board also has been held[83] to be a quasi-judicial body in a number of its functions and has been authorized to exercise limited judicial power as well as to formulate policy.

1.3c Power of

A state board of education may have very broad or very limited powers depending on the breadth of legislative authorization. It may be placed in control of the state's public school system[84] and have power to determine general educational policy,[85] particularly policy related to teachers, curriculum, and supervision.[86] When a statute authorizes a state board of education to decide all controversies and disputes, it confers visitorial powers which are summary and conclusive.[87] In some states the state board of education is vested with final and conclusive authority in all school matters which may be appealed to it from county or city boards of education.[88] It may not, however, exercise those functions which the legislature has specifically conferred on county and city boards of education.[89] Where the decisions of state boards of education are final and conclusive and not subject to review, the courts are not deprived of jurisdiction on the many purely legal questions which may arise in connection with the educational statutes.[90] It is always a function of the courts to decide legal questions and interpret education statutes. It is also a court function to determine whether or not a board has exceeded its powers, has exercised its powers fraudulently or in bad faith, or has breached its trust.[91] The courts do so through the use of one of the extraor-

[78]Council of State Governments, *Book of the States 1976–77* (Lexington, Ky., 1976).

[79]State *ex. rel.* Holt v. State Board of Education, 112 S.W.2d 18 (Ark. 1938).

[80]Fitzsimmons v. State Board of Education, 153 N.E. 749 (Ill. 1926).

[81]State *ex. rel.* School District No. 29 v. Cooney, 59 P.2d 48 (Mont. 1936).

[82]Blair v. Board of Trustees, 161 S.W.2d 1030 (Tex. 1942); *In re* Advisory Opinion to Governor, 39 So. 63, 64 (Fla. 1905).

[83]State *ex. rel.* School District No. 29 v. Cooney, 59 P.2d 48 (Mont. 1936).

[84]Bell v. Board of Education, 215 S.W.2d 1007 (Ky. 1948).

[85]Board of Education v. Goodpaster, 84 S.W.2d 55 (Ky. 1935).

[86]Board of Education v. Rogers, 15 N.E.2d 401 (N.Y. 1938).

[87]Wiley v. Allegany County School Commissioners, 51 Md. 401 (1879).

[88]Mayor etc. of Union Point v. Jones, 78 S.E.2d 348 (Ga. 1953).

[89]Opinion of the Justices, 160 So.2d 648 (Ala. 1964).

[90]McCormick v. Board of Education, 274 P.2d 299 (N.M. 1954).

[91]Wilson v. Board of Education, 200 A.2d 67 (Md. 1964).

dinary remedies such as mandamus, prohibition, or injunction, which exist even in the absence of a right of appeal. The courts do not, however, have power to review or evaluate the sociological, psychological, or educational assumptions upon which educational policies are formulated or administrative decisions are based.[92] They are not empowered to question the wisdom of decisions of state boards of education.[93]

State boards of education may not shirk the obligations placed on them by law where they are charged with the duties of public instruction[94] or the determination of all educational matters,[95] including aspects of district and high school operation.[96] They must accept their responsibilities and carry on the functions related to them unless the decision of whether to act or not to act is within their discretion.

A constitutional provision vesting the power of supervision of schools in a state board of education has been held[97] to be a grant of power, and not a limitation. Thus, additional powers may be conferred upon state boards of education by the legislature, and they are not restricted to those directly involving elementary and secondary education.[98] The legislature also may grant to state boards of education power to supervise normal schools and colleges even though there is no constitutional authorization to do so.[99]

State officers may be given power to sue and to be sued.[100] However, the constitution may provide that the state board of education is not subject to suit unless consent is given. Where no consent has been given, the state board cannot be sued, but members of the board may be sued in their individual capacity.[101]

Like other state boards or agencies, a state board of education must exercise the authority vested in it by the constitution and statutes and may not delegate its authority to others. Thus it has been held that a state board of education cannot delegate to a state director of vocational education the right to decide whether or not to continue vocational training of prisoners of war upon termination of the federal war production program.[102]

It should be noted that discretion cannot be compelled. Where the state board of education is authorized to accredit schools, a local board cannot compel approval of an application for accreditation unless it can be shown that the denial of accreditation was an unreasonable and capricious act.[103] In a similar case it was held[104] that the state board of education was exercising its discretion in denying accreditation to a high school with less than thirty-six pupils in average daily attendance. Since this was the exercise, not of a judicial function, but of an administrative function, the Superior Court was held to have no power to review that state board's action.

1.3d Operation of

A state board of education has power to adopt its own rules of procedure and this power is not subject to narrow and limited construction.[105] Where members serve without compensation, they are not required to assemble the facts necessary for the exercise of their supervisory power.[106] They may require the assembling of such data for them by other state officers.[107]

Proceedings of a state board of education may be informal. The minutes need not embody all the elements essential in court of law procedures.[108] All that is necessary is that the minutes clearly disclose the intent and the actions of the board.

In its operations a state board of education is not bound by the findings of the commissioner of education but may make its own inquiry and determination. This principle was substantiated in a case involving the right to discharge employees.[109] Any member of the state board of education

---

[92]Etter v. Littwitz, 262 N.Y.S.2d 924 (1965).

[93]Padberg v. Martin, 357 P.2d 255 (Ore. 1960); State Board of Education v. Fasold, 445 P.2d 489 (Ore. 1968); School District of Omaha v. State Board of Education, 181 N.W.2d 861 (Neb. 1970).

[94]Rankin v. Board of Education, 51 A.2d 194 (N.J. 1947).

[95]State ex. rel. School District No. 29 v. Cooney, 59 P.2d 48 (Mont. 1936).

[96]Ibid.

[97]School District No. 25 v. Hodge, 183 P.2d 575 (Okla. 1947).

[98]State ex. rel. Porterie v. Louisiana State Board of Education, 182 So. 676 (La. 1938).

[99]Board of Education v. Elliott, 29 N.W.2d 902 (Mich. 1947).

[100]Fitzsimmons v. State Board of Education, 153 N.E. 749 (Ill. 1926).

[101]McCoy v. Louisiana State Board of Education, 229 F.Supp. 735 (La. 1964).

[102]State ex. rel. R. R. Crow & Co. v. Copenhaver, 184 P.2d 594 (Wyo. 1947).

[103]State ex. rel. School District No. 29 v. Cooney, 59 P.2d 48 (Mont. 1936).

[104]Okanogan County School District v. Andrews, 363 P.2d 129 (Wash. 1961).

[105]Jones v. Merrimack Valley School District, 218 A.2d 55 (N.H. 1966).

[106]State ex. rel. School District No. 29 v. Cooney, 59 P.2d 48 (Mont. 1936).

[107]Ibid.

[108]Gragg v. Hill, 58 S.W.2d 150 (Tex. 1933).

[109]Quinlan v. Board of Education, 179 A.2d 161 (N.J. 1962).

has a right of reasonable access to the records of the board of education and may request access at any reasonable time.[110]

1.4 THE STATE SUPERINTENDENT

A chief state school officer, known variously as the state superintendent, superintendent of public instruction, state commissioner of education, education commissioner, etc., functions in each of the fifty states. In the balance of the present chapter this officer will be referred to as the state superintendent.

While state superintendents have great potential influence on education in their states and can directly affect the quality of the instruction received by more children than any other educational worker, they are nearly always paid less than superintendents in the larger cities of their respective states. In almost every case their offices are understaffed and underpaid considering the responsibilities involved and the magnitude of the tasks performed.

As late as 1920 approximately 70 percent of all state superintendents were elected by popular vote. In 1975 only 40 percent of the superintendents attained office by this method. There also has been a trend away from appointment by the governor. On the other hand, the number appointed by a state board of education has increased markedly, from 23 percent in 1947 to 50 percent in 1975.

Although in the past the functions of the state superintendent were largely regulatory—enforcement of laws, formulation of regulations and standards, supervision of schools, and distribution of and accounting for school funds—in recent years other activities have come to occupy a major role. Research, planning and development, and the assertion of educational leadership have become significant aspects of the office. It is largely within the realm of these activities that the high potential for leadership inherent in the office will be realized. While in all states the superintendents are responsible for education in the state, the extent of authority and the areas of responsibility are varied. In some states they are responsible only for elementary and secondary education; in others, for elementary, secondary, and vocational education; in still others, for elementary, secondary, vocational, and junior college education; and in some states, for the entire educational program of the state.

1.4a Legal powers

The courts tend to interpret the authority of the state superintendent broadly in both the operational aspects of the office and the promulgation of regulations. For example, it has been held[111] that the state superintendent has implied power to make regulations for the operation of the schools even when such power is not expressly granted. Such regulations must, of course, be in conformity with the public policy of the state. When a statute authorizes the state superintendent, with approval of the state board of education, to prescribe rules and regulations, reasonable rules which he or she prescribes obviously will be upheld. For example, under a statute of this kind the state superintendent was upheld[112] in requiring that a minimum number of students be enrolled in a high school to permit its continued operation.

The grant of general legislative power to supervise schools extends to schools not yet in existence when the power was granted and to those established by special legislative acts. It has been determined, for example, that the general supervisory power extends to union-free school districts created by special legislative acts and permits the removal of a school board member there in the same manner as in other districts.[113] It has also been held[114] that the legislature may confer legislative power on the state superintendent, as permitted in an instance in which the constitution placed the responsibility for the general supervision of education in the state superintendent.

The state superintendents may require information as needed from school districts and they must comply with this request. Thus they may ask for information reporting children as white and nonwhite, provided that the purpose is not to promote segregation.[115] The state superintendent may request data from school districts in addition to what is specified in the statutes.[116] The proper procedure for obtaining this information is by mandamus, not by withholding state aid as was being attempted.

In all aspects of racial problems the state

---

[110]State *ex. rel.* Hopkins v. Wooster, 208 Pac. 656 (Kan. 1922).

[111]O'Connor v. Hendrick, 77 N.E. 612 (N.Y. 1906).
[112]Dicken v. State Board of Education, 199 S.W.2d 977 (Ky. 1947).
[113]*Matter of Light*, 49 N.Y.S. 345 (1897), *reversed on other grounds,* 51 N.Y.S. 743 (1898), 30 App. Div. 50 (1898).
[114]Tecumseh School District v. Throckmorton, 403 P.2d 102 (Kan. 1965).
[115]School Committee of New Bedford v. Commissioner of Education, 208 N.E.2d 814 (Mass. 1965).
[116]*Ibid.*

superintendents are vested with broad authority to deal with state policy in such a manner as to alleviate racial discrimination.[117] They are also vested with powers to review acts of individuals and boards and, in areas under their jurisdiction, to substitute their judgment relative to actions they are reviewing.[118]

Where state superintendents are required to give their consent to a school district's plan for increased borrowing, they have the power to ascertain which methods are most economical. They may also ascertain the quality of education which might be provided under the various methods of financing.[119]

However, as substantial as the power of state superintendents is, there are a number of actions which are beyond the scope of their authority. It has been held,[120] for example, that they have no right to issue publications not authorized by statutes. Nor have they power to impound the funds of an independent school district in order to pay an assessment of a county superintendent's salary.[121] It also is clear that state superintendents cannot require their orders to be carried out when the orders are not authorized by statute.[122] They may not legally carry on activities based on erroneous conceptions of what laws actually are.[123] When a state superintendent has proceeded under a misapprehension of the impact of a constitutional provision on a problem, that decision will be annulled and the matter will be remitted to that superintendent for a new determination, free of the erroneous views of the constitutional provisions which had influenced the previous decision and actions.[124]

1.4b Nature of the position

The nature of the position of state superintendent varies considerably from state to state. The state superintendent has been held[125] to be a state officer with power to sue. Where elected, the state superinten-

dent has been held[126] to be a public officer and not a public employee. However, where the state superintendent is the executive officer of the state board of education and is appointed by that body, he or she may be regarded as a public employee. The superintendent also has been held[127] to be a quasi-judicial officer who exercises discretionary powers, thus combining in one position both judicial and administrative functions. In practice, the position carries with it the authority to exercise judicial functions as they relate to controversies within a common school system.[128] As administrative officers, state superintendents have wide authority in dealing with educational matters and in individual fact situations governing their administrations.[129]

1.4c Compensation

Since state superintendents, at least those elected to the office, are public officers, their compensation in many states is fixed and may not be changed during their term of office. As a result many devices have been employed in an effort to increase the state superintendent's compensation, especially during inflationary periods. In almost every case such efforts have been held illegal. In Michigan and South Dakota, for example, it was held[130] that an extra office could not be created through which the state superintendent could be paid for carrying on responsibilities germane to his regular office. In Michigan the state superintendent was not permitted to receive pay for serving as director of the Smith-Hughes Program, nor could his compensation be increased by granting him fees which he collected in connection with his office. Where the statutes provide that the state superintendent shall have the use of certain fees, such revenue may be used for support of the office but is not the personal property of the superintendent.[131] Subterfuges such as payment of added compensation from clerk hire and expenses[132] and payment from a general salary appropriation[133] are not permitted. Compensation for performance of extra duties, however, has

[117]Booker v. Board of Education, 212 A.2d 1 (N.J. 1965).

[118]Harrison v. Allen, 258 N.Y.S.2d 233 (1965).

[119]Durgin v. Brown, 180 A.2d 136 (N.J. 1962).

[120]Vansant v. Commonwealth, 224 S.W. 367 (Ky. 1920).

[121]Austin Independent School District v. Marrs, 41 S.W.2d 9 (Tex. 1931).

[122]Howell School Board District No. 9 v. Hubberth, 70 N.W.2d 531 (Iowa 1955).

[123]Trujillo v. State, 352 P.2d 80 (N.M. 1960).

[124]Abramson v. Commissioner of Education, 150 N.Y.S.2d 270 (1956), *rehearing motion denied*, 152 N.Y.S.2d 426 (1956).

[125]Fitzsimmons v. State Board of Education, 153 N.E. 749 (Ill. 1926).

[126]Francis v. Iowa Employment Security Commission, 98 N.W.2d 733 (Iowa 1959).

[127]Craig v. Board of Education, 27 N.Y.S.2d 993 (1941).

[128]Application of Bowen, 230 N.Y.S.2d 578 (1962).

[129]Commonwealth v. Smoker, 110 A.2d 740 (Pa. 1955).

[130]People v. Coffey, 213 N.W. 460 (Mich. 1927); State ex. rel. McMaster v. Reeves, 184 N.W. 1007 (S.D. 1921).

[131]State v. Stockwell, 134 N.W. 767 (N.D. 1912).

[132]State ex. rel. Raymer v. Cunningham, 51 N.W. 1133 (Wis. 1892).

[133]State ex. rel. Russell v. Barnes, 5 So. 698 (Fla. 1889).

been held[134] to be permissible under certain circumstances. The state superintendent is also entitled to reimbursement for travel expenses, including travel to conferences outside the state. This is implied even though not specifically provided by statutes.[135]

1.4d Election and removal

Statutory or constitutional provisions relating to the manner of election of the state superintendent must be followed. For example, when *election* is specified, the selection of the state superintendent by a state board of education is unconstitutional,[136] since election means election by the people, not election by a state board of education.

The election of a state superintendent to the office does not appear to establish a contractual relation with the state according to dicta in a Utah case.[137] It was declared that a superintendent elected for a four-year term was not entitled to serve the full four-year period, unless the statutes so provided, when the constitution was changed and the office was made appointive rather than elective.

As is true of other public officers and employees, a state superintendent may be removed from office on the grounds of misconduct and inefficiency. Withholding information from members of the state board of education and failing to make recommendations which would facilitate the board's work are also justification for dismissal.[138] On a related issue it was held[139] that the director of vocational education had an unqualified right of access to the books pertaining to his duties in the position.

1.4e Appeal to

By the nature of the position the state superintendent must adjudicate many educational controversies. In some states this authority, expressed in the constitution and statutes, is extremely far reaching. In other instances the statutes grant him only limited authority. Obviously, court decisions regarding the state superintendent's actions are influenced and circumscribed by the authority granted to the position by the constitution and legislature. However, a number of general principles are basic to all jurisdictions.

Where an appeal to the state superintendent is provided, an appeal to the courts will not lie until appeal to the state superintendent is exhausted, unless statutory or constitutional provisions are challenged.[140] Thus, an administrative remedy must be exhausted, when one is provided, before an appeal can be taken to the courts. Nevertheless, when the interpretation of statutes or constitutional provisions affecting a valuable right is involved, the administrative remedy of appeal to the state superintendent is not exclusive and does not oust the courts of jurisdiction,[141] especially with regard to rights guaranteed by the United States Constitution. Courts will assume jurisdiction in the first instance where constitutionally guaranteed rights are in dispute.[142] In actions involving the interpretation of statutes the courts do not relegate aggrieved parties to proceedings before the state superintendent.[143]

Adherence to strict rules of pleading and proof is not required or expected in hearings before the state superintendent and/or the state department of education.[144] It is essential only that rules of good procedure be followed and that everyone has a fair opportunity to be heard.

On an appeal taken from a decision of the state superintendent the courts will not consider the wisdom or expediency of the decision.[145] Unless determinations of the state superintendent which are authorized by educational law are arbitrary or capricious,[146] they will not be interfered with by the courts. An example of what the courts deem arbitrary is found in a Montana case, in which, by the decision of the state superintendent, children were required to travel fourteen miles farther each way to attend overcrowded schools instead of being permitted to attend contiguous adequate schools.[147]

---

[134]McElderry v. Abercrombie, 104 So. 671 (Ala. 1925).
[135]State *ex. rel.* Lamkin v. Hackmann, 204 S.W. 513 (Mo. 1918).
[136]State *ex. rel.* Musa v. Minear, 401 P.2d 36 (Ore. 1965).
[137]State Board of Education v. Commission of Finance, 247 P.2d 435 (Utah 1952).
[138]State *ex. rel.* Rockwell v. State Board of Education, 6 N.W.2d 251 (Minn. 1942).
[139]State *ex. rel.* Hopkins v. Wooster, 208 Pac. 656 (Kan. 1922).

[140]Stinson v. Graham, 286 S.W. 264 (Tex. 1926).
[141]McMaster v. Owens, 81 N.Y.2d 564 (1948).
[142]Levert v. Gavin, 241 N.Y.S.2d 300 (1963).
[143]Szendy v. Board of Education, 197 N.Y.S.2d 810 (1960).
[144]Board of Education of Independent School District v. County Board of Education, 121 N.W.2d 137 (Iowa 1963).
[145]Craig v. Board of Education, 19 N.Y.S.2d 293 (1940), *affirmed*, 27 N.Y.S.2d 993 (1941).
[146]Gable v. Raftery, 65 N.Y.S.2d 513 (1945); Board of Education v. Allen, 264 N.Y.S.2d 813 (1965). *See also* Bermingham v. Commissioner of Education, 266 N.Y.S.2d 700 (1966); Application of Board of Education, 223 N.Y.S.2d 347 (1960), *reversing* 221 N.Y.S.2d 587.
[147]Potter v. Miller, 399 P.2d 994 (Mont. 1965).

The state superintendent must, of course, act within the jurisdiction of the position if such actions are to be sustained. This includes jurisdiction both over the parties involved and over the subject matter under consideration.

When issues are appealed to state superintendents, their review[148] is not limited to a review of the record (unless the statutes so provide); facts outside the record may be obtained and utilized, as was determined[149] in a case on appeal to the state superintendent from the decision of a county superintendent involving the dismissal of a district superintendent.

As is true of state boards of education. state superintendents may be required to carry out specific functions within their orbits of responsibility. For example, they may be required to file affirmative action programs under the Civil Rights Act of 1964[150] or may be compelled to take action concerning sending-receiving of secondary school students.[151]

1.5 COUNTY AND
INTERMEDIATE BOARDS OF EDUCATION

County and intermediate boards of education, hereafter referred to as county boards of education for brevity, are difficult to describe legally. In some states they serve as local boards of education with jurisdiction over the geographical area of the county; in other states they serve as an intermediate unit of school government between the local district and the state. When they serve as local boards of education, they are subject to the same legal controls as other school districts, described in subsequent chapters. This section is concerned with county boards of education as intermediate school units and with the principles of law applicable to them.

1.5a Nature of

Members of county boards of education have been variously described. For some purposes they appear to be local or county officers whose jurisdiction is confined to a given county. This interpretation seems particularly appropriate as it relates to a requirement that a person be a resident of the county in order to be eligible for office. In line with this interpretation, it has been ruled[152] that a member of a county board of education who acquired residency in another county was no longer eligible to serve in the first county.

More frequently members of county boards of education have been found[153] to be state officers. This interpretation represents the predominant point of view, since there is almost unanimous agreement that they are discharging a state function—education—even in states considering them local officers for residency and related purposes. Thus, county boards of education have been held to be an agency of the county for the operation and maintenance of its schools[154] and an agency of the state for the administration of a public school system—a state function.[155]

The functions of a county board of education are of an exclusively public character, performed solely for public benefit.[156] Thus, members of county boards of education are held to be public officers, and laws governing public officials apply to them unless specific statutes applicable to county board members have been enacted.[157]

County boards of education may be constitutional boards, statutory boards, or both, depending on the legal basis of their establishment. Where their offices are established by the state's constitution, members are considered constitutional, not statutory officers.[158] Constitutional offices may not be abolished by legislative acts, although they are controlled by statutory enactments. Statutory boards, i.e., boards established by the legislature, may be abolished by the body that created them.

1.5b Powers of

Whether county boards are established by constitution or statute, they may exercise only such powers as are conferred upon them either expressly or by implication.[159] In some states these powers must be expressed or necessarily implied, and the powers granted may be exercised only in

---

[148]County Board of Education v. Parker, 45 N.W.2d 567 (Iowa 1951).

[149]Appeal of Black, 287 P.2d 96 (Wash. 1955).

[150]United States v. State of Texas, 447 F.2d 441 (5th Cir. 1971).

[151]Jenkins v. Township of Morris School District, 27 A.2d 619 (N.J. 1971).

[152]Baker v. Conway, 108 So. 18 (Ala. 1926).

[153]Benton County Council v. State ex. rel. Sparks, 65 N.E.2d 116 (Ind. 1946); State ex. rel. Osborne v. Eddington, 195 N.E. 92 (Ind. 1935); Phelps v. Witt, 201 S.W.2d 4 (Ky. 1947); Stokes v. Harrison, 115 So.2d 373 (La. 1960).

[154]Reed v. Rhea County, 225 S.W.2d 49 (Tenn. 1949).

[155]Kirby v. Stokes County Board of Education, 55 S.E.2d 322 (N.C. 1949).

[156]Andrews v. Claiborne Parish School Board, 189 So. 355 (La. 1939).

[157]Howard v. Cornett, 1 S.W. 1 (Ky. 1886).

[158]Saxon v. Bell, 41 S.W.2d 536 (Ga. 1947).

[159]Reeves v. Been, 228 S.W.2d 609 (Ark. 1950); State Line Consolidated School District No. 6 v. Farwell Independent School District, 48 S.W.2d 616 (Tex. 1932).

the manner authorized.[160] The powers of the boards may not be extended by construction,[161] and where the right is doubtful it may not be exercised.[162] The situation was well summarized by the Florida court in a 1959 case in which it was held[163] that county board members are part of the machinery of government, operating at the local level, as an agency of the state, in the performance of public functions. Their powers rest exclusively in legislative discretion and constitutional provisions.

Operating within the constitutional and statutory powers granted it, the county board of education has wide discretionary powers as well as powers of an administrative and ministerial nature.[164] The county board itself must exercise its discretionary powers.[165] However, duties of a ministerial nature and administrative functions may be delegated by the board.

1.5c Court review of decisions of

When a county board of education is vested with authority in the establishment, management, administration, and supervision of schools, in the absence of arbitrary action the courts will not substitute their judgment for that of the board nor interfere in the discharge of the board's functions.[166] The courts will act only when there is a clear abuse of discretion,[167] a violation of law,[168] or an act beyond the legal authority of the board.[169] Acts of fraud and bad faith are reviewable by the courts and subject to redress.[170]

The courts always have a right to review a case to determine whether an order was supported by substantial evidence, whether it was arbitrary, capricious, or beyond the power of the board, or whether some statutory or constitutional right was violated.[171] No agreement entered into by the county board of education can bar the state courts from the right of review prescribed by statute.[172] While the county board of education has broad educational authority, it is not vested with the power of legal interpretation. The construction and interpretation of a statute is not within the competency of a county board of education but is a function of the courts.[173]

In determining whether an action taken by a county board of education is a valid exercise of discretionary power the courts generally apply the "substantial evidence" rule; i.e., Was the action supported by substantial evidence? Application of this rule calls for consideration of the evidence as a whole.[174] Motives are irrelevant unless they result in abuse of discretion.[175] Findings must be based on established facts presented in evidence, and county board members may not rely on their own information unsupported in fact as a basis for action.[176]

1.5d Operational capacity of

A county board of education operates in many capacities. In a number of activities it functions as an administrative agency,[177] as when it administers free textbooks or school-lunch programs. Some of its acts are legislative,[178] as when it formulates rules and regulations for the operation of schools. Acts of this nature are not subject to collateral attack. In other instances the county board of education acts in a quasi-judicial capacity,[179] as in hearings on issues and controversies involving local school districts, determining the location of consolidated schools and providing transportation of pupils. All of the above described functions have been held to be proper spheres of activities of county boards of education.

---

[160]Sugar Grove School District No. 19 v. Booneville Special School District No. 65, 187 S.W.2d 339 (Ark. 1945); Sunnywood Common School District No. 46 v. County Board of Education, 131 N.W.2d 105 (S.D. 1964).

[161]Harvey v. Board of Public Instruction, 133 So. 868 (Fla. 1931).

[162]*Ibid.*

[163]Buck v. McLean, 115 So.2d 764 (Fla. 1959).

[164]Warner Independent School District No. 230 Brown County v. Board of Education of Brown County, 179 N.W.2d 6 (S.D. 1970).

[165]Johnson v. Sabine Parish School Board, 140 So. 87 (La. 1932).

[166]Mullins v. Board of Education, 29 So.2d 339 (Ala. 1947); Hodges v. Board of Education, 16 So.2d 97 (Ala. 1943); County Board of Education v. Parent and Custodians of Students, 168 So.2d 814 (Miss. 1964); School District No. 106 v. County Board of School Trustees, 198 N.E.2d 164 (Ill. 1964).

[167]Wilson v. Graves County Board of Education, 210 S.W.2d 350 (Ky. 1948); Williams v. Ragsdale, 53 S.E.2d 339 (Ga. 1949).

[168]Boney v. County Board of Education, 45 S.E.2d 442 (Ga. 1947); Bedingfield v. Parkerson, 94 S.E.2d 714 (Ga. 1956).

[169]Bell County Board of Education v. Lee, 39 S.W.2d 492 (Ky. 1931).

[170]Mullins v. Board of Education, 29 So.2d 339 (Ala. 1947); Hodges v. Board of Education, 16 So.2d 97 (Ala. 1943).

[171]Loftin v. George County Board of Education, 183 So.2d 621 (Miss. 1966).

[172]*In re* Varner, 146 S.E.2d 401 (N.C. 1966).

[173]Hobbs v. Hodges, 5 A.2d 842 (Md. 1939).

[174]Neill v. Cook, 365 S.W.2d 824 (Tex. 1963).

[175]*Ibid.*

[176]Wheeler v. County Board of School Trustees, 210 N.E.2d 609 (Ill. 1965).

[177]State Line Consolidated School District No. 6 v. Farwell Independent School District, 48 S.W.2d 616 (Tex. 1932); Board of Education v. County Board of School Trustees, 142 N.E.2d 742 (Ill. 1957).

[178]Morris v. Vandiver, 145 So. 228 (Miss. 1933).

[179]Lauderdale County Board of Education v. Alexander, 110 So.2d 911 (Ala. 1959).

1.5e Eligibility for office

A state may set eligibility requirements of various types for the office of member of a county board of education. Educational requirements are mandatory.[180] A requirement that a candidate must have an eighth-grade education is an example.

The state also may fix the method by which compliance with eligibility requirements shall be shown,[181] or the state may set the requirement and leave the method of determining compliance with it to some other agency. When the state does not indicate the specific method of determining compliance with eligibility requirements, more than one method may be used. For instance, in establishing that a candidate is an eighth-grade graduate, graduation records may be preferred, but affidavits from previous teachers certifying that the person has completed the work of the eighth grade are acceptable.[182] However, such affidavits are the weakest kind of proof, and other evidence of achievement may be required.[183]

When the eligibility of a candidate for public office is challenged, it is the candidate's responsibility to establish eligibility for the office.[184] There is no presumption that the candidate is qualified, as is true of certified professional workers.

1.5f Attainment of the office

The members of a county board of education are either elected or appointed depending on statutory provisions. When they are appointed, the power of the appointing board is exhausted with the appointment; it may not control the actions of board members after their appointment.[185] When the law provides for the appointment of one person from each district in the county, the law is mandatory, and two candidates from the same district may not serve even though they have been elected or appointed.[186]

The legislature has been held competent to provide a complete plan for nominating, electing, or filling vacancies on boards of education.[187] Statutory provisions for appointment of the county board of education must be complied with unless the statute is declared void[188] or unconstitutional.[189] When an appointment is made by the proper board, it is valid regardless of whether the appointment results in creating a *de jure* or a *de facto* officer.[190] A person who has been elected or appointed as a *de facto* member has the same authority to act in the office as does a *de jure* officer, and all his acts are valid as regards a third party.[191]

When the elected member receiving the highest number of votes is ineligible to hold the office, the person receiving the next highest number of votes is not elected.[192]

The office of county school board member is incompatible with certain other offices. For example, it has been held[193] that a person may not serve as a local school board member and a member of the county board of education with terms running concurrently. Nor may a person serve concurrently as postmaster and as a member of the county board of education where the state constitution prohibits the holding of two offices at the same time, and that person may not act as either a *de jure* or a *de facto* officer.[194]

1.5g. Resignation and removal from office

When individuals resign from county boards of education they must do so directly. Resignation will not be inferred from their acts. For example, the affirmative vote of a member of the county school board for his or her own removal from office is not a resignation and does not estop that member from later challenging the legality of the procedure.[195] In most instances a resignation is effective when it is accepted by the official or body to whom it is addressed. Sometimes, however, the resignation of a member of the county board of education is not effective until a successor has qualified.[196] This interpretation is based on the reasoning that a person should continue in

[180]Commonwealth *ex. rel.* Dummit v. Mullins, 211 S.W.2d 133 (Ky. 1948); Whittaker v. Commonwealth *ex. rel.* Attorney General, 115 S.W.2d 355 (Ky. 1938).

[181]Commonwealth *ex. rel.* Meredith v. Norfleet, 115 S.W.2d 353 (Ky. 1938).

[182]Commonwealth *ex. rel.* Breckinridge v. King, 343 S.W.2d 139 (Ky. 1961).

[183]Commonwealth *ex. rel.* Ferguson v. Coffee, 329 S.W.2d 203 (Ky. 1959).

[184]Spurlock v. Commonwealth *ex. rel.* Breckinridge, 350 S.W.2d 472 (Ky. 1961).

[185]State *ex. rel.* Wolfe v. Henegar, 175 S.W.2d 553 (Tenn. 1943).

[186]Clarke v. Long, 111 S.E. 31 (Ga. 1922).

[187]Advisory Opinion to Governor, 19 So.2d 198 (Fla. 1944).

[188]State *ex. rel.* Norquist v. Glennon, 149 So. 257 (Ala. 1933); State *ex. rel.* Norquist v. Evans, 149 So. 260 (Ala. 1933).

[189]Treadway v. Carter County, 118 S.W.2d 222 (Tenn. 1938).

[190]Owen v. Reynolds, 1 S.E.2d 316 (Va. 1939).

[191]Hazelton-Moffit Special School District No. 6 v. Ward, 107 N.W.2d 636 (N.D. 1961).

[192]Marshall v. Walker, 187 S.E. 81 (Ga. 1936).

[193]State *ex. rel.* Le Buhn v. White, 133 N.W.2d 903 (Iowa 1965).

[194]State *ex. rel.* Atkins v. Fortner, 72 S.E.2d 594 (N.C. 1952).

[195]State *ex. rel.* Leighley v. Eikenberry, 121 N.E. 823 (Ohio 1918).

[196]Gearhart v. State Board of Education, 355 S.W.2d 667 (Ky. 1962).

public office until a successor to that person is elected and qualifies. Members of a county board of education do not automatically vacate their office by committing acts contrary to the statutes, and county residents and taxpayers cannot declare that the office is vacant on these grounds[197] and prohibit a member from performing official acts.

County board members have been removed from office for a variety of reasons. The most common are misconduct in office,[198] neglect of duty,[199] absence from meetings,[200] illegal expenditure,[201] and financial interest in contracts entered into by the board.[202] Grounds for removal from office may be specified by statutes,[203] and when causes are specified, attempts to remove a member from office for other causes are illegal.[204] When specific causes for removal are listed, they are assumed to be exhaustive. When the statutes specify that absence from office for ninety days constitutes cause for removal, the ninety days are to be counted from the first meeting not attended, not from the last meeting attended.[205]

There must be substantial reason for the removal of a member of a county board of education from office. For example, the state board of education cannot validly remove from office a member of the county board of education one day after she took office without charges against her simply because of a desire to change the entire membership of the board.[206] Statutory requirements that charges against a member of the county board of education be reduced to writing are mandatory, and compliance with them is necessary to give the court jurisdiction.[207]

1.5h Compensation
As a general rule members of county boards of education are not paid an amount sufficient to make the subject of compensation a frequent issue. However, in a case

which came before the courts it was held[208] that a county officer was not estopped from later claiming the full amount to which he was entitled by the fact that he had agreed to accept less and actually had accepted less compensation.

1.5i Effect of changes in law
Since the legislature has plenary power in education, in the absence of constitutional restrictions it is free to change the composition and operation of the county board of education at will. In this respect vested rights do not accrue to members of county boards of education. Thus, an act abolishing a county board of education and creating in lieu thereof a county school commission was not unconstitutional on the basis that it violated vested rights or destroyed uniformity of the system of public schools.[209] When such a change is made, the terms of office of county school board members may be terminated and the usual method for removal from office need not be followed.[210]

1.5j Financial interest in educational contracts
County school board members by statutes and/or court decisions almost universally have been prohibited from having any financial interest in contracts entered into by the county board of education. To permit otherwise obviously would be in violation of public policy and create a conflict between personal interest and interest as a board member. A law which made ineligible a person who, at the time of his election, had a financial interest in the sale of school supplies purchased at his store or in providing transportation was equally applicable after his election.[211] No other interpretation would eliminate the conflict of interest which the law sought to prevent. However, statutes prohibiting a direct or indirect interest in contracts on the part of a member of the county board of education apply only to a financial or monetary interest; they do not apply to an emotional interest.[212]

1.5k Meetings and records
The county board of education can act only as a body,[213] at a meeting properly

[197]Griffey v. Board of Education, 385 S.W.2d 319 (Ky. 1964).

[198]Haislip v. White, 22 S.E.2d 361 (W. Va. 1942).

[199]Howard v. Bell County Board of Education, 57 S.W.2d 466 (Ky. 1933).

[200]Martin v. Cassell, 220 S.W.2d 552 (Ky. 1949).

[201]Wysong v. Walden, 52 S.E.2d 392 (W. Va. 1938).

[202]Hunt v. Allen, 53 S.E.2d 509 (W.Va. 1948).

[203]Wysong v. Walden, 52 S.E.2d 392 (W.Va. 1938).

[204]State ex. rel. Harvey v. Stanly, 138 So. 845 (La. 1931).

[205]State ex. rel. Leighley v. Eikenberry, 121 N.E. 823 (Ohio 1918).

[206]Gearhart v. State Board of Education, 355 S.W.2d 667 (Ky. 1962).

[207]Swim v. Leeber, 105 S.E.2d 136 (W.Va. 1958).

[208]Lee v. Macomb County, 284 N.W. 892 (Mich. 1939).

[209]Tucker v. State ex. rel. Poole, 165 So. 249 (Ala. 1935).

[210]Ibid.

[211]Commonwealth ex. rel. Matthews v. Coatney, 396 S.W.2d 72 (Ky. 1965).

[212]Chadwell v. Commonwealth ex. rel. Meredith, 157 S.W.2d 280 (Ky. 1941).

[213]Ellis v. Acadia Parish School Board, 29 So.2d 461 (La. 1946).

called.[214] It has no power to transact business except at regular and special meetings.[215] To transact business a quorum must be present.[216] Unless otherwise provided, a majority of the board constitutes a quorum. All members must have had notice of the meeting and an opportunity to be present.[217] When special meetings are held, everyone must be notified of the meeting; otherwise any action taken is void.[218]

Records and minutes of the meetings of county school boards must be kept.[219] It is not required or expected that they contain all the elements of legal reporting. Nor are the procedures expected to be as refined as those in courts of record. The only requirement is that they show the true intent of the board and of the individual members.[220]

A board may order its clerk to amend the record of a previous meeting to show the facts, even though the personnel of the board has changed.[221] Executive sessions may be held when not prohibited by law.[222] A board is not required to follow its past policies in matters within its jurisdiction[223] since discretion is not consumed by use and may be exercised in changing policies as well as in other actions. The discretion vested in the board must be exercised by it and may not be delegated. However, ministerial and administrative acts may be delegated to others.[224]

1.5l Integrity and liability of members

County school board members are held to the same degree of integrity and liability as other individuals or boards.[225] For example, a county board of education may not reduce a school district to a substandard basis and then use that as the reason for eliminating it.[226] As a general rule, school board members are not liable as individuals for acts carried on in their official capacity.[227] Yet if an act is of a ministerial nature, board members may be held personally liable for its wrongful consequences. Thus it was held[228] that board members were personally liable when they wrongfully prevented a teacher with "continuing service status" from teaching. The basis of judgment was that the board members were conducting a ministerial function under which liability legally could be assessed. County school board members may also be held liable under civil right laws.

1.6 THE COUNTY SUPERINTENDENT

Any discussion of the legal status of the county superintendent is likely to appear repetitive of the discussion of the legal status of county board of education members. They are all public officers, and, for the most part, have the same legal status. However, to relieve the reader of the necessity of cross-checking to ascertain whether the principles of law already presented for the county board of education member are also applicable to the county superintendent, those bearing on the superintendent are presented separately.

Like members of county boards of education, county superintendents serve both in intermediate units and as heads of local school systems consisting of the geographical area of a county. Since the local district superintendency is dealt with elsewhere in this book, the following discussion is concerned only with county superintendents in intermediate units and with the principles of law relating to their activities. The intermediate county superintendent is currently being replaced in several states by intermediate district superintendents designed to carry on similar functions but serving a geographical area much more extensive than a county. While little judicial opinion is available on the operation of such districts, it is assumed that a substantial number of the legal principles relating to the county superintendency will be applicable to the officers of other intermediate units.

1.6a Provision for the office

The office of county superintendent may be provided for by constitution, by statutes, or by both. When the office is established by the constitution, the county superintendent is a constitutional officer, and the office cannot be eliminated by direct legislative

[214]Wysong v. Walden, 52 S.E.2d 392 (W.Va. 1938).
[215]Kistler v. Board of Education, 64 S.E.2d 403 (N.C. 1951).
[216]Hopkins v. Dickens, 222 S.W. 101 (Ky. 1920).
[217]Ozark School District No. 6 v. Wicker Consolidated School District No. 79, 49 S.W.2d 373 (Ark. 1932); Hopkins v. Dickens, 222 S.W. 101 (Ky. 1920).
[218]Palmer v. District Trustees, 289 S.W.2d 344 (Tex. 1956).
[219]Hartford Graded Schools v. Ohio County Board of Education, 189 S.W. 433 (Ky. 1916).
[220]Holcombe v. Board of Education, 4 So.2d 503 (Ala. 1941); Bridgeport Township High School District No. 3-12 v. Shank, 129 N.E.2d 264 (Ill. 1955).
[221]Board of Education v. Township 42, 51 N.E. 656 (Ill. 1898).
[222]Kistler v. Board of Education, 64 S.E.2d 403 (N.C. 1951).
[223]Neill v. Cook, 365 S.W.2d 824 (Tex. 1963).
[224]Johnson v. Sabine Parish School Board, 140 So. 87 (La. 1932).
[225]Board of Public Instruction v. Connor, 4 So.2d 382 (Fla. 1941); 78 C.J.S. Schools and School Districts, P. 854, § 100.
[226]Wooley v. Spalding, 293 S.W.2d 563 (Ky. 1957).

[227]Williams v. Ragsdale, 53 S.E.2d 339 (Ga. 1949).
[228]Moore v. Babb, 343 S.W.2d 373 (Ky. 1961).

action.[229] However, when the office is established by statutes, it may be abolished by the legislature, or the salary may be reduced to a point where it is, in fact, not an office of employment but an office of honorary public service. In New Mexico, where the constitution provided that the legislature should determine the salaries of all county offices, a statute was enacted whereby a county superintendent who had no rural schools under his direction could be paid a salary of $1.00 per year. It was held[230] that the law was constitutional and that the county superintendent was entitled to no compensation beyond the $1.00 per year.

In the absence of constitutional restrictions, a statute may empower the county commissioner's court to abolish the office of the county superintendent when this action is deemed advisable. Such an action was held[231] not to be an unconstitutional delegation of power by the legislature. The legislature also may abolish the office of county superintendent, if it is not established in the constitution, and transfer the duties to another office.[232] Even though the term for which the person was elected had not expired, the county superintendent's office ceased to exist when the transfer of functions was made.[233]

1.6b Status of

The legal status of county superintendents is difficult to describe. For certain purposes they have been held to be local or county officers. In North Dakota, for example, it was held[234] that the county superintendent was a local officer whose duties were within the county from which he was elected. While in this case the central issue was whether or not a school district could be compelled to accept a tuition pupil against its wishes, the question of whether the county superintendent was an officer having statewide jurisdiction was also raised. The court declared he was not, holding him to be a local officer with only countywide jurisdiction.

In Florida also it was held[235] that the county superintendent was a county officer. In this instance the court determined that the office of county superintendent was a county office created by the constitution and that the legislature was prohibited from adding to or taking away from the specific regulations prescribed in the constitution. It was decided that, where the constitution declared the qualifications for an office, the legislature had no authority to change the qualifications. In this instance the only constitutionally required qualification was that the county superintendent be a "qualified elector."

The county superintendent also has been held[236] to be a county officer in instances relating to the requirement that he be a resident of the county to be eligible to hold the office. However, where statute or constitution provides that a person must be a resident of the county to be eligible for election to the office, one does not become disqualified by residing temporarily in another county for the purpose of teaching while the contest is pending.[237]

The courts have held[238] that in the performance of duties county superintendents are limited to their counties. They are responsible for looking after the educational and personal qualifications of persons teaching or desiring to teach in their counties. The extent to which their authority is limited to their counties is seen in a decision which held[239] that, though authorized to remove school directors for cause in their own county, a superintendent was not authorized to remove those who were elected in part by the people of another county.

The more persuasive authority has held[240] that the office of county superintendent is in no sense local, and that functions pertaining to the office are those of state government.[241] These decisions are in line with the many decisions declaring education to be a state function and educational officers to be state officers. However, this interpretation is not completely at odds with decisions holding that for certain regulatory purposes and certain residency requirements the county superintendent is a local or county officer.

While there is some evidence to the contrary, county superintendents generally have been held[242] to be public officers

[229]Thomas v. State *ex. rel.* Cobb, 58 So.2d 173 (Fla. 1952).

[230]Thomson v. Board of County Commissioners, 344 P.2d 171 (N.M. 1959).

[231]Stanfield v. State *ex. rel.* McAllister, 18 S.W. 577 (Tex. 1892).

[232]Bunch v. Woods, 115 Pac. 76 (Ariz. 1911).

[233]*Ibid.*

[234]Kessler v. Board of Education, 87 N.W.2d 743 (N.D. 1958).

[235]Thomas v. State *ex. rel.* Cobb, 58 So.2d 173 (Fla. 1952).

[236]Bower v. Avery, 158 S.E. 10 (Ga. 1931).

[237]People *ex. rel.* McCarty v. Wilson, 91 Pac. 661 (Cal. 1907).

[238]Tanner v. Stevenson, 128 S.W. 878 (Ky. 1910).

[239]People v. Harris, 164 Ill. App. 136 (1911).

[240]Benton County Council v. State, 65 N.E.2d 116 (Ind. 1946).

[241]Harrison County School Board v. State Highway Commission, 284 So.2d 50 (Miss. 1973).

[242]State *ex. rel.* Smith v. Theus, 38 So. 870 (La. 1905).

rather than public employees. As such they may be proceeded against under statutes providing for the removal of public officers when there are no specific statutes relative to the removal of the county superintendent.

In Kentucky the county superintendent was held[243] not to be an officer within the meaning of the constitution which prohibited changes in compensation after election. In this instance, not only was additional compensation paid, but authorization was granted to pay the county superintendent an additional amount for serving as secretary of the county board education.

As with other officers, the actions of *de facto* county superintendents are valid as regards a third party.[244] They are not valid, however, in matters in which there is a personal interest.[245] *De facto* officers holding over after expiration of their terms of office are not entitled to recover compensation for the period for which they hold office against the legal claim of duly elected and qualified *de jure* officers.[246]

1.6c Qualification of

Qualifications of county superintendents are set in the constitution or provided in statutes. Qualifications may include such items as holding a Class A certificate for administrators, or graduate work in school administration, or five years of actual administrative experience in a public school, or a certificate of eligibility from the state department of education.[247] Rules of the board of education requiring a county superintendent to hold a first-class teacher's certificate are not to be applied retroactively.[248] A "grandfather" clause giving current holders of the office continued eligibility regardless of whether they meet the higher requirements is not terminated at age seventy even though the retirement system is intended to accommodate retirement at that age.[249] The principle of exemption from current statutes under the "Grandfather Clause" also was upheld[250] in Georgia in 1971.

In some instances it has been held[251] that a person who has been elected or appointed to the office is not affected by subsequent acts imposing additional qualifications. In one state a holder of the office was not disqualified from reelection although he did not meet the higher requirements.[252] This, however, is usually not the case unless there is a "grandfather" clause in the law.

In Tennessee it was held[253] that the qualifications for county superintendent must be uniform and that the establishment of qualifications for the office in one county which were higher and different from those in other counties was invalid. But the constitutional requirement that the legislature must establish a uniform system of education does not mean that there must be a uniform system of appointment or election of all county superintendents.[254]

A candidate who had qualified for the certificate required of county superintendents but had not actually received it was ruled eligible to file for the office.[255] Having filed for the office and having been elected, persons are entitled to serve if they hold the certificate at the time of their induction.[256]

A statute which requires a candidate to file a certificate is directory only; failure to file does not make the candidate ineligible for the office.[257] The certificate of a county superintendent, like that of a teacher, is not subject to collateral attack.[258] If it is charged that a certificate is irregular or illegal, it must be attacked directly and not indirectly.

1.6d Authority and exercise of power

The powers and duties of a county superintendent, except for those which are found in the state constitution, are derived entirely from statutory enactments and must be exercised within the terms and conditions set forth in the statutes.[259] County superintendents can exercise only the powers specifically granted and those necessary to carry them into effect.[260] In the exercise of their functions they necessarily must use wide discretion.[261] Their powers

[243]Board of Education v. De Weese, 343 S.W.2d 598 (Ky. 1961).
[244]Hazelton-Moffit Special School District No. 6 v. Ward, 107 N.W.2d 636 (N.D. 1961).
[245]Rowan v. Board of Education, 24 S.E.2d 583 (W.Va. 1943).
[246]Edington v. Board of Commissioners, 13 N.E.2d 895 (Ind. 1938).
[247]State ex. rel. Patterson v. Land, 95 So.2d 764 (Miss. 1957).
[248]State ex. rel. Lynch v. Board of County Commissioners, 296 P.2d 986 (Wyo. 1956).
[249]State ex. rel. Vossbrink v. Carpenter, 388 S.W.2d 823 (Mo. 1965).
[250]Black v. Blanchard, 179 S.E.2d 288 (Ga. 1971).

[251]Callahan v. Lyman, 227 S.W.2d 964 (Ark. 1950).
[252]State ex. rel. Derricks v. Swails, 142 N.E. 706 (Ind. 1924).
[253]Gallien v. Miller, 92 S.W.2d 403 (Tenn. 1936).
[254]Wynn v. State ex. rel. District Attorney, 7 So. 353 (Miss. 1890).
[255]Martin v. County Election Board, 245 P.2d 714 (Okla. 1952).
[256]Murphy v. Darnell, 268 P.2d 860 (Okla. 1954).
[257]Huffines v. Gold, 288 S.W. 353 (Tenn. 1926).
[258]Wilkins v. Large, 141 So. 585 (Miss. 1932).
[259]Reserve Rural High School District No. 4 v. Hanika, 339 F.2d 788 (8th Cir. 1964).
[260]Morris v. Vandiver, 145 So. 228 (Miss. 1933).
[261]School District No. 5 v. Community High School, 69 P.2d 1102 (Kan. 1937).

are largely administrative or executive in nature,[262] and hence their actions are not subject to collateral attack.[263]

They also may exercise quasi-judicial functions—as when the statutes provide for appeals to them from actions of local school officials[264] or to settle controversies among local districts.[265] When cases are appealed to them they are given broad powers of investigation on items necessary for a sound decision.[266] In some states an appeal from the decision of a local school board in a matter involving exercise of discretion must be taken to the county superintendent before recourse can be had to the state or to the courts. However, an appeal may be taken directly to the courts in cases involving duties imposed by law.[267] In Oklahoma it was held[268] that a statute providing for appeal to the court from an action of the county superintendent applied only when his actions were judicial or quasi-judicial, not when they were purely ministerial. Of course, for ministerial acts the remedies of mandamus, prohibition, or injunction normally would be available.

While the county superintendent has broad discretionary power and may carry out such acts as shortening the school year, that authority does not extend to closing schools unless the superintendent is specifically vested with this authority.[269] Unless so authorized by statutes a county superintendent has no right to decide a contested election between school district trustees.[270] Nor can the superintendent withhold the names and addresses of pupils in certain schools from the parish (county) board of education,[271] even when the police and FBI agents warn that this information should be kept secret.

County superintendents have no authority to contract debts on behalf of the county boards of education without previous authorization, nor can they contract with the state board of education on behalf of their counties without previous authorization.[272]

However, in a Mississippi case[273] it was decided that the county superintendent could employ part-time clerical help for his office without previous authorization. The court stated that although the minutes of the county board of education did not authorize this act, it was not such an irregularity as to impose personal liability on the county superintendent. It also has been held[274] that the fees paid to an attorney who was retained to compel the board of county commissioners to provide necessary funds for the operation of the county superintendent's office were properly charged as an expense of his office.

1.6e Court review of actions

Although county superintendents enjoy wide latitude in their educational operations and in exercising the discretion vested in the office, they must act on all occasions within reason and on the basis of evidence. The "substantial evidence" rule in discretionary acts applies to county superintendents as well as to other officers. Arbitrary and unwarranted actions by a county superintendent are subject to review and correction by the courts.[275] A court will intervene to prevent fraudulent action or arbitrary abuse of discretion when such abuse is established by clear and convincing evidence.[276]

1.6f Liability of

As a general rule, county superintendents are not liable for errors in judgment, such as turning over unexpended funds of a school district to another agency.[277] However, they may be liable personally to teachers where their wrongful misapplication of funds prevents payment of the teachers' salaries.[278] They also may be liable for failure to properly perform ministerial acts.[279]

County superintendents are immune from liability to a district superintendent for their acts insofar as they relate to a district superintendent's fitness for office but they are not immune from liability for defamatory statements made to the public or to the press which do not constitute official action but are based on personal knowledge.[280]

Under statutes imposing criminal liabil-

[262]State Board of Education v. Elbert County Board of Education, 146 S.E.2d 344 (Ga. 1965).

[263]Sloan v. Hawkins, 86 N.E.2d 117 (Ill. 1949).

[164]Ibid.; Jackson School Township v. State, 183 N.E. 657 (Ind. 1932).

[265]Okfuskee County v. Okfuskee County School District No. 27, 293 Pac. 1078 (Okla. 1930).

[266]Sloan v. Hawkins, 86 N.E.2d 117 (Ill. 1949).

[267]Altman v. Independent School District, 32 N.W.2d 392 (Iowa 1948); Riecks v. Independent School District, 257 N.W. 546 (Iowa 1934).

[268]In re Consolidation of School Districts Nos. 14 and 20, 69 P.2d 365 (Okla. 1937).

[269]Peterson v. Pratt, 167 N.W. 101 (Iowa 1918).

[270]Mershon v. Baldridge, 7 Watts 500 (Pa. 1838).

[271]Wager v. Redmond, 127 So.2d 275 (La. 1961).

[272]State Board of Education v. Elbert County Board of Education, 146 S.E.2d 344 (Ga. 1965).

[273]Golding v. Latimer, 121 So.2d 615 (Miss. 1960).

[274]Bierman v. Campbell, 124 N.W.2d 918 (Neb. 1963).

[175]Measles v. Owens, 46 S.W.2d 40 (Ark. 1932).

[276]Sloan v. Hawkins, 86 N.E.2d 117 (Ill. 1949).

[277]Gridley School District v. Stout, 66 Pac. 785 (Cal. 1901).

[278]Powell v. Mathews, 280 S.W. 903 (Tex. 1926).

[279]Bronaugh v. Murray, 172 S.W.2d 591 (Ky. 1943).

[280]Lipman v. Brisbane Elementary School District, 359 P.2d 465 (Cal. 1961).

ity on a county superintendent who willfully fails to make a settlement of an account, the interpretation of "willfull" is important. In Kentucky it was held[281] that *willful* meant *voluntarily*. The county superintendent's indicating that he would make a settlement as soon as he could obtain duplicate receipts for those which had been lost was no defense.

1.6g Appointment or election of

A vacancy in the office of county superintendent must exist before an appointment can be made or an election held. A vacancy exists when a post is unoccupied or unfilled. However, this definition is not applicable when a public officer enters the military service of the United States. Decisions on this issue have been rendered in several jurisdictions.[282] One directly relating to a county superintendent was handed down in Florida, where it was held[283] that when a county superintendent joined the armed forces no vacancy was created that was within the power of the governor to fill. Rather, he was, in effect, having a leave of absence, with a deputy authorized to carry on his functions. Obviously an appointment is invalid where no vacancy exists.[284]

Where a county superintendent has been elected illegally at a "called" meeting, that appointment may be ratified at a subsequent meeting where all members are present and voting.[285] Town trustees may not legally vote for themselves for the office of county superintendent.[286]

A county superintendent of schools may be appointed for any period of time which does not exceed that provided by statutes. The fact that the term of the county superintendent exceeds terms of a majority of the members of the appointing board has no legal effect.[287]

1.6h Compensation and expenses

While there is some minor conflict among the courts, the following statement is descriptive of the county superintendent's right to compensation: County superintendents are entitled to a salary as established by law and may collect the difference between what has been paid and the statutory amount;[288] they are not entitled to retain fees or payments for duties associated with the office, or to retain overpayments for their services; they may not be paid for performing the duties of another office;[289] they are not entitled to additional compensation as ex officio members of the county board of education.[290] It has been held[291] in Missouri, however, that where the state appropriated funds to pay county superintendents additional compensation for supervision of transportation and preparation of budgets this money could legally be paid. In this instance the additional compensation was authorized even in counties where the superintendent had no responsibility for transportation and budget making.

A lawfully elected county superintendent holding over after expiration of the term of office and continuing to perform the duties thereof is entitled to the compensation of the office.[292] The salary of the county superintendent is to be fixed by whatever agency is designated by statute as having this duty, and the county boards of education can be compelled to fix the salary where the statutes vest such authority in them.[293]

Reimbursement is usually provided for actual expenses incurred in discharging the duties of the office, including visitation of schools.[294] However, unless the law so provides, reimbursement may not cover expenses incurred in attending out-of-state meetings and national conventions. Nor does it cover commencement addresses to graduating classes of county normal schools when the county superintendent is ex officio a member of the board employing the speaker.[295] Where traveling expenses are to be paid only on an itemized and verified claim, a county board is not authorized to pay a lump sum for salary and traveling expenses.[296] For example, a lump sum allowance of $50.00 per month was not permitted to be paid where payments on the

[281]Tracy v. Commonwealth, 76 S.W. 184 (Ky. 1903).

[282]State *ex. rel.* Thomas v. Wysong, 24 S.E.2d 463, 467 (W.Va. 1943); Gullickson v. Mitchell, 126 P.2d 1106, 1110, 1111, 1114 (Mont. 1942); In re Advisory Opinion to the Governor, 8 So.2d 26, 140 A.L.R. 1481 (Fla. 1942).

[283]*In re* Advisory Opinion to the Governor, 8 So.2d 26, 140 A.L.R. 1481 (Fla. 1942).

[284]Wooten v. State *ex. rel.* Butler, 230 P.2d 889 (Okla. 1951).

[285]Marshall v. Walker, 187 S.E. 81 (Ga. 1936).

[286]Hornung v. State *ex. rel.* Gamble, 19 N.E. 151, 2 L.R.A. 510 (Ind. 1888).

[287]Moore v. Johnson, 32 S.W.2d 353 (Ky. 1930).

[288]Clarke v. Milwaukee County, 9 N.W. 782 (Wis. 1881).

[289]Shelton v. State *ex. rel.* Caldwell, 162 Pac. 224 (Okla. 1917).

[290]Carrico v. Couch, 146 Pac. 447 (Okla. 1915).

[291]State *ex. rel.* Vossbrink v. Carpenter, 388 S.W.2d 823 (Mo. 1965).

[292]State *ex. rel.* Bickford v. Fabrick, 112 N.W. 74 (N.D. 1907).

[293]Peachy v. Calaveras County, 59 Cal. 548 (1881).

[294]Dodge County v. Kaiser, 11 N.W.2d 348 (Wis. 1943).

[295]*Ibid.*

[296]Van Loh v. Waseca County, 265 N.W. 298 (Minn. 1936).

basis of itemized claims were required by statute.[297] When the county superintendent files and verifies his claim for compensation and mileage, a *prima facie* case for payment is established and the burden of proof is on the person or agency attacking the correctness of the claim.[298]

1.6i Resignation and removal

When a county superintendent resigns from office and that resignation has been accepted, it cannot be withdrawn. In Indiana when a county superintendent who had resigned attempted to withdraw his resignation after the election of his successor, he was unsuccessful.[299]

A county superintendent may be removed from office for a variety of reasons. The following occur most frequently:

1. Misconduct in office.[300]
2. Neglect of duty.[301]
3. Insubordination.[302]
4. Immorality.[303]
5. Misappropriation of funds.[304]

Where the county superintendent may be removed for cause, an error in judgment is not sufficient cause for removal—at least it has been so held[305] in regard to another county officer (county board member). It also has been held[306] that a county superintendent of schools may be required to be of good moral character and that such a requirement is not an arbitrary exercise of power. Where a county superintendent was convicted of false claims against the United States in violation of federal statutes—an act punishable by a fine of not more than $10,000 or imprisonment for not more than five years, or both—he was guilty of "moral turpitude" making him ineligible to hold his office, and the fact that the sentence was suspended was immaterial.[307] A statute providing for forfeiture of the office if the county superintendent engages in certain conduct is self-executing; if such conduct is proved he or she is automatically removed

from office. However, the board of education is not competent to make this determination. It must be made by a judicial tribunal.[308] Failure of a county superintendent to perform the duties as prescribed by law is a "cause for removal" from office.[309] County superintendents cannot question the motives actuating removal proceedings against them, since such motives are immaterial.[310]

1.6j Action on surety bonds

A substantial number of cases have involved actions against county superintendents under which they and their sureties were sued. In some actions sureties were liable for payment; in others county superintendents were acquitted and their sureties relieved of liability. In some cases diametrically opposed decisions were rendered on similar sets of facts.

The surety generally was held liable when technicalities such as failure to file the bond with the state superintendent as the law required prevailed.[311] It is the purpose of bonds to cover losses or defaults related to school funds[312] and good faith and mistaken judgment in issuing teacher pay certificates in excess of the amount authorized is no defense against action on a surety bond.[313] County superintendents and their sureties are also liable for salaries paid in excess of those contracted and for payments for services not rendered.[314] When county superintendents appropriate for unauthorized purposes funds borrowed on behalf of the county school board, their sureties become liable.[315] Recovery from a county superintendent was permitted where there was no evidence that the county board had approved the expenditures of the county superintendent and little evidence that the material for which the money had been spent was actually received.[216]

In any action against county superintendents and their sureties the burden of proof is on the county to show that money is due before the county is entitled to an accounting.[317] County superintendents (and/or their

[297]Board of Education v. DeWeese, 343 S.W.2d 598 (Ky. 1961).

[298]Garfield County v. White, 66 Pac. 682 (Col. 1901).

[299]McGee v. State *ex. rel.* Axtell, 3 N.E. 139 (Ind. 1885).

[300]Graham v. Jewell, 263 S.W. 693 (Ky. 1924).

[301]Hunter v. Board of Education, 96 S.W.2d 265 (Ky. 1936).

[302]State *ex. rel.* Rogers v. Board of Education, 25 S.E.2d 537 (W.Va. 1943).

[303]Hufford v. Conover, 38 N.E. 328 (Ind. 1894).

[304]State *ex. rel.* Ten Citizens v. Smith, 11 S.W.2d 897 (Tenn. 1928).

[305]Wysong v. Walden, 52 S.E.2d 392 (W.Va. 1938).

[306]People *ex. rel.* Odell v. Flaningam, 179 N.E. 823 (Ill. 1932).

[307]Huff v. Anderson, 90 S.E.2d 329 (Ga. 1955).

[308]Arnett v. DeWeese, 304 S.W.2d 784 (Ky. 1957).

[309]Hoskins v. Keen, 350 S.W.2d 467 (Ky. 1961).

[310]Hunter v. Board of Education, 96 S.W.2d 265 (Ky. 1936).

[311]Reed v. Summers, 79 Ala. 522 (1885).

[312]Powell v. Mathews, 280 S.W. 903 (Tex. 1926).

[313]Trantham v. Russell, 158 So. 143 (Miss. 1934).

[314]Golding v. Latimer, 121 So.2d 615 (Miss. 1960).

[315]Citizens' Bank v. American Surety Company, 164 S.E. 817 (Ga. 1932); American Surety Company v. Citizens' Bank, 172 S.E. 801 (Ga. 1934).

[316]Golding v. Latimer, 121 So.2d 615 (Miss. 1960).

[317]Warren County v. Elmore, 93 N.W.2d 756 (Iowa 1959).

sureties) were held not to be liable for decisions made in good faith involving a judicial or quasi-judicial function and not a ministerial function.[318] Such acts may extend in many directions and include the issuance of pay certificates when there are no statutes giving directions.[319] Sureties on a general bond are not liable on funds covered by a special bond.[320] Bonds given by county superintendents are intended to cover loss of school funds, not damages in other actions against the county superintendent.[321]

1.7 TOWN OR TOWNSHIP SCHOOL BOARDS AND OFFICERS

In most instances town or township schools are under direction of a local board of education. In these cases the same legal principles apply to the operation of the town schools as apply to any other school districts, and no discussion of them is included here. In a few states town or township officials are responsible for some or all aspects of the operation of the schools in the town and serve in the dual capacity of municipal officers and school board members. In such instances a paucity of judicial opinions relative to this dual responsibility exists, with only minor direction from courts of record. A few pertinent cases are presented in the following section, together with some principles related to town or township schools under the direction of a town officer.

1.7a Operational Aspects

As is true in other types of school districts, the power of town officials over schools is purely statutory.[322] When authorized by statute, they may build schools, equip and operate them, employ staff, and carry on all activities necessary to promote a sound educational program. In carrying out their educational functions town officers are considered to be public officers,[323] carrying out a state function[324] and performing a governmental rather than a proprietary activity.[325]

In their role as school board members it is their responsibility to employ legally qualified teachers. When they do so, they may not be impeached for refusal to consider for employment certain applicants who refused to make contributions to political campaign funds as allegedly was required by the trustee.[326]

Where statutes so provide, the township officer has no option but must assume responsibilities for and carry out the duties of the school officer.[327] This is an integral part of the responsibility of a township officer. Like most officers handling public funds, township treasurers are insurers of the safety of school funds which are in their hands.[328] In the management of school funds the township school board may authorize the creation of a consolidated account to finance all school activities. Such an account may include class dues, income from student activities, etc. The fund may be augmented by the school board as needed. When such a fund is established and operated, it is a public fund subject to audit by the town auditor.[329]

1.8 SCHOOL DISTRICTS AND MUNICIPALITIES

Questions persist regarding the relationship of boards of education to cities, villages, towns, and counties, and to the governing boards of such municipalities. The concept that the board of education is an agency of the state rather than a subdivision of the state is fundamental in answering these questions.[330] The general rule followed by the courts is that a board of education is a legal entity separate and distinct from the municipalities which include the school district within their boundaries,[331] regardless of whether the school district and the municipality are coterminous. Nor

---

[318]Barnett v. Lollar, 19 So.2d 748 (Miss. 1944).

[319]Trantham v. Russell, 158 So. 143 (Miss. 1934).

[320]Glade District Board of Education v. Rader, 24 S.E. 680 (W.Va. 1896).

[321]Powell v. Mathews, 280 S.W. 903 (Tex. 1926).

[322]Corley v. Montgomery, 46 S.W.2d 283 (Mo. 1932).

[323]Maitland v. Town of Thompson, 27 A.2d 160 (Conn. 1942).

[324]Board of Education v. Board of Finance, 16 A.2d 601 (Conn. 1940).

[325]Norwalk Teachers Association v. Board of Education, 83 A.2d 482 (Conn. 1951).

[326]State ex. rel. Ayer v. Ewing, 106 N.E.2d 441 (Ind. 1952).

[327]Weatherholt v. State, 199 N.E. 713 (Ind. 1936).

[328]People v. Farmers State & Savings Bank, 170 N.E. 236 (Ill. 1930).

[329]Petition of Auditors, 63 Mont'g, 25 (Pa. 1946), affirmed 161 Pa. Super. 388 (1947).

[330]Norwalk Teachers Association v. Board of Education, 83 A.2d 482 (Conn. 1951); Wauconda Township High School District v. County Board of School Trustees, 129 N.E.2d 177 (Ill. 1955); People ex. rel. Gibson v. Peller, 181 N.E.2d 376 (Ill. 1962); Board of Education v. Board of Finance, 16 A.2d 601 (Conn. 1940); State v. Conlon, 3 So.2d 241 (La. 1941); Herman v. Board of Education, 137 N.E. 24 (N.Y. 1922); Kellem v. School Board, 117 S.E.2d 96 (Va. 1960).

[331]Bodecker v. Community Unit District, 100 N.E.2d 573 (Ill. 1951); Huffman v. School Board, 41 N.W.2d 455 (Minn. 1950); Kelso v. Board of Education, 109 P.2d 29 (Cal. 1941); Board of Education v. D'Aulisa, 52 A.2d 636 (Conn. 1947); McCurdy v. Board of Education, 194 N.E. 287 (Ill. 1934).

does the fact that some members of the board of education serve by virtue of being officers of a municipality alter this conclusion. The school board is an instrumentality of the state, and its members, in their corporate capacities, are engaged in the discharge of a state and not a local function. The legal rule with respect to the separate identity of school districts and municipalities has been aptly stated by the Supreme Court of Ohio:

Whether the lines of the political subdivisions are, or are not coextensive with the school district, the administration and control of the schools is not vested in the officer of that political subdivision but in the board of education for each school district. [332]

Such boards are agencies of the state for the organization, administration and control of the public school system of the state, separate and apart from the usual political and governmental functions of other subdivisions of the state. The fact that certain officers of other subdivisions may be delegated some duties or authority in relation thereto does not change the status or destroy the separate identity of the school district. [333]

Complications and controversies frequently arise in the relationships between school districts and municipalities because of wide variation in the degree of control over education granted to municipal governments via statutes, city charters, and constitutional provisions. It is a well-established principle that education is not inherently a municipal function. [334] Consequently, statutes or charters conferring upon municipalities powers over education are strictly construed by the courts. That is, if any doubt exists as to whether a particular power has been granted to a school district or to a municipality, the doubt will be resolved in favor of the school district. Any power that a municipality may exercise in

educational matters must be conferred specifically by statutes or by a charter. [335] Action by a city council to control the amount of the school budget when provided in law is obviously upheld. However, attempts to control the expenditure of funds once the budget has been approved have been consistently rejected. [336]

1.8a Effect of home-rule charters

States occasionally grant "home-rule" charters to municipalities giving them a large measure of freedom to determine their local affairs. This was true in an Alaska case where the municipality (borough) demanded that the school district participate in its centralized accounting system. The court held[337] that since education was a state function, the school district was not subject to local control and could not be required to participate. Municipalities frequently attempt to exercise control over educational activities, claiming that education falls within the sphere of "local affairs." The general rule is that education is a matter of statewide concern governed by statutory and constitutional provisions and does not come within the control of a municipality operating under a home-rule charter. [338] However, in some charter arrangements school committees clearly become a department of city government and function as such. [339] A California court, while recognizing education as a state function, held that where educational matters are not governed by statute they may be subject to regulation by a municipality. [340] Where such charters have been granted, they do not prohibit the legislature from passing other laws for the government and management of local schools. [341] A New York court, in a 1952 decision, ruled[342] that the provisions of the New York City charter were applicable to school employees,

[332]Durgin v. Brown, 180 A.2d 136 (N.J. 1962); Terrebonne Parish School Board v. St. Mary Parish School Board, 131 So.2d 266 (La. 1961); Bohley v. Patry, 159 N.E.2d 252 (Ohio 1958); Perritt v. Carter, 325 S.W.2d 233 (Tenn. 1959); Hogan v. Glasscock, 324 S.W.2d 815 (Ky. 1959).
[333]Cline v. Martin, 115 N.E. 37 (Ohio 1916).
[334]James Duckworth, 170 F.Supp. 342 (Va. 1959); Mountain View Union High School District v. City Council, 335 P.2d 957 (Cal. 1959); Opinion of the Justices, 145 A.2d 250 (Me. 1958); Barth v. School District, 143 A.2d 909 (Pa. 1958); Nelson v. Mayor, et al., of Town of Homer, 19 So. 271 (La. 1896); Board of Education v. Alton Water Company, 145 N.E. 683 (Ill. 1924); Board of Education v. City of Corbin, 192 S.W.2d 951 (Ky. 1946); Board of Education v. Houghton, 233 N.W. 834 (Minn. 1930).

[335]Conzonetti v. City of New Britain, 162 A.2d 695 (Conn. 1960); Van Fleet v. Oltman, 221 N.W. 299 (Mich. 1928); Mayor and Council of Wilmington v. State, 57 A.2d 70 (Del. 1947); O'Connell v. School Committee, 158 N.E.2d 868 (Mass. 1959).
[336]Board of Education v. King, 110 N.E.2d 895 (N.Y. 1953); Divisich v. Marshall, 22 N.E.2d 327 (N.Y. 1939).
[337]Macauley v. Hildebrand, 491 P.2d 120 (Alaska, 1971).
[338]State ex. rel. Harbach v. Mayor, etc., of City of Milwaukee, 206 N.W. 210 (Wis. 1925); Lansing v. Board of Education, 45 P.2d 1021 (Cal. 1935); Board of Education v. State, 109 Pac. 563 (Okla. 1910).
[339]Eastern Massachusetts Street Railway v. Mayor of Fall River, 31 N.E.2d 543 (Mass. 1941).
[340]Butterworth v. Boyd, 82 P.2d 434 (Cal. 1938).
[341]Zane-Cetti v. Fort Worth, 269 S.W. 130 (Tex. 1924).
[342]Daniman v. Board of Education, 118 N.Y.S.2d 487 (1952).

reasoning that the city school board was both a city and a state agency.

1.8b Effects of municipal regulations related to school buildings

Several cases have come before the courts in which boards of education have refused to conform to municipal building codes or ordinances relating to health or safety. From the decisions which were handed down it is apparent that the courts are not in agreement on this issue.

As a general rule the power to select sites for school buildings is vested in the board of education. This power is usually explicitly granted by statute, but even where the statutes are silent school boards have this authority because the power to build schools necessarily implies the power to procure sites. In some cases the power to select school sites may be vested in an annual meeting of the electors or in municipalities. Normally, authority to select school sites is vested in municipalities when they must produce the funds to pay for the site. In some states the board of education selects the site, and it is then purchased by the city, which holds title to the property.

In the selection of a site questions are often raised as to whether the location of schools must conform to an overall municipal community plan and whether local zoning ordinances are applicable to schools. The Superior Court of California handed down a decision which bears directly on the control of a municipal plan over the location of school buildings. It was here decided[343] that citywide planning is advisory only in relation to school buildings and not binding on school districts. In the absence of clear statutory provisions local zoning restrictions cannot be applied to schools.[344] However, if the type of school which is planned has a bad community effect, its construction can be controlled by zoning laws in at least one state.[345]

Bonds to pay for new buildings are usually issued upon approval of the electors of a school district in a referendum election, but in some states other methods are provided by statutes. In some city school districts bonds may be issued only on approval of the city board of estimates or the city council.[346]

Whether school districts are subject to municipal building codes is a point of legal disagreement. There are, however, some principles which appear to be accepted. It seems clear that municipal building codes are not applicable to the state itself[347] and are not applicable to school districts when the state so provides.[348] Constitutional provisions giving any county or city power to enforce within its limits all local police, sanitary, and other regulations do not confer upon local units power to regulate construction of school buildings.[349]

Where plans and specifications are approved by the state board of education, they need not be filed with the municipality, and municipal and town building codes do not apply.[350] However, where the state has not "occupied the field," power to control school building construction is permitted to municipalities.[351] For example, a city was entitled to collect a building permit fee for erection of a public school building, which was constructed in compliance with the municipal building code and was inspected by the municipal building inspector.[352] Inspections by municipalities of boilers and other possible areas of hazard in schools have been permitted in a number of instances.[353] Control over sanitary fixtures, sanitary conditions, ventilation, and proper repair of a building housing a cafeteria was held[354] to be within the province of the municipal building inspector and municipal ordinances.

An analysis of cases appears to point to three different views of municipal-school district relationships. One line of decision is based on the idea that since education is a state function the police power of the state must be presumed to be vested in the board

[347]City of Milwaukee v. McGregor, 121 N.W. 642 (Wis. 1909); Kentucky Institution for the Blind v. City of Louisville, 97 S.W. 402 (Ky. 1906).

[348]N.J. Statutes Annotated, 18:11-11; Smith v. Board of Education, 113 A.2d 187 (N.J. 1955); Kaveny v. Board of Commissioners, 173 A.2d 536 (N.J. 1961).

[349]Hall v. City of Taft, 302 P.2d 574 (Cal. 1956).

[350]Kaveny v. Board of Commissioners, 173 A.2d 536 (N.J. 1961).

[351]Cedar Rapids Community School District v. City of Cedar Rapids, 106 N.W.2d 655 (Iowa 1960); City of Groves v. Port Arthur Independent School District, 366 S.W.2d 849 (Tex. 1963); State ex. rel. Audrain County v. City of Mexico, 197 S.W.2d 301 (Mo. 1946).

[352]Corder v. City of Milford, 196 A.2d 406 (Del. 1963); Contra: R.G.H. Plumbing, Inc. v. City of Syracuse, 339 N.Y.S.2d 329 (1972).

[353]Cedar Rapids Community School District v. City of Cedar Rapids, 106 N.W.2d 655 (Iowa 1960); City of Kansas City v. School District, 201 S.W.2d 930 (Mo. 1947); Community Fire Protection District v. Board of Education, 315 S.W.2d 873 (Mo. 1958).

[354]Bredeck v. Board of Education, 213 S.W.2d 889 (Mo. 1948).

[343]Town of Atherton v. Superior Court, 324 P.2d 328 (Cal. 1958).

[344]State ex. rel. Ohio Turnpike Comm. v. Allen, 107 N.E.2d 245 (Ohio 1952); State ex. rel. St. Louis Union Trust Co. v. Ferriss, 304 S.W.2d 896 (Mo. 1957).

[345]Shields v. School District, 196 P.2d 352 (Wash. 1948).

[346]N.J. Statutes Annotated, 18:7-118.

of education unless it has been specifically vested in the municipality by statute or charter.[355] A second line, followed principally by the Missouri courts, reasons that the police power of a municipality applies to all within its boundaries, including boards of education.[356] A third line of decisions holds that the police power of the board of education must give way to the police power of a municipality when public health or safety is involved.[357]

1.8c Fiscal relationships

The fact that school districts and municipalities are separate and distinct corporate entities does not preclude the state's delegating to municipalities or to municipal officers certain powers with respect to education, or requiring them to perform certain duties in this area. It is not uncommon for school district budgets to be subject to approval by municipal bodies, for school taxes to be levied and/or collected by a municipal agency, or for school funds to be disbursed by a municipal officer.[358] The rationale for the establishment of fiscally dependent school districts has been stated clearly by the Supreme Court of Appeals of Virginia:

It has been the policy of the state, under present laws and for many years past, to repose in one board only, the power and authority to raise money by taxation for local purposes. . . . The reasons for this are obvious. One board can take a comprehensive view of all local tax needs, and can control the total amount of taxes to be raised and can fix the rate of taxation at such an amount as in their judgment the people can and ought to pay. It can examine and weigh the needs and importance of the various functions of government to be supported by local taxation and can make a final apportionment amongst the various agencies and functions of government.[359]

It should be emphasized, however, that because education is a state function

municipalities have no inherent right to exercise control over the fiscal affairs of school districts. Any authority which a municipality possesses in this area must expressly be conferred by statutes or by municipal charter.[360] Because the rule of strict construction is generally applied when interpreting statutes or charters which confer upon municipalities control over the affairs of school districts, where doubt exists as to whether the authority in question has been granted to a municipality the issue will be resolved in favor of the school district.

The board of education of a fiscally dependent school district is commonly required to submit to the municipality which appropriates the money an annual budget or an estimate of the revenue it will need during the next fiscal year. Questions occasionally arise concerning the interpretation which is to be given statutory directions concerning the preparation of such a document. It was held,[361] for example, that the word *purpose*, as used in an Arizona statute pertaining to school district budgets, referred to six general budget categories, not to forty-one subitems listed in the budget.

It generally has been held[362] that a budget does not become final at the time it is filed but may be altered after the date of filing. Once the proposed budget has been adopted or approved, however, it may not be altered in such a manner as to negate previous action of responsible boards.[363]

Questions frequently arise relative to the extent of the authority of a municipal body which reviews the school district budget. Under some statutes the appropriating body has no authority to alter the budget submitted by school officials but must appropriate the amount requested if it does not exceed statutory or constitutional limitations.[364] Under other statutes the municipal body which appropriates the funds may exercise

[355]Kentucky Institute for the Blind v. City of Louisville, 97 S.W. 402 (1906); Salt Lake City v. Board of Education, 175 Pac. 654 (Utah 1918); Kaveny v. Board of Commissioners, 173 A.2d 536 (N.J. 1961).

[356]Community Fire Protection District v. Board of Education, 315 S.W.2d 873 (Mo. 1958); Smith v. Board of Education, 221 S.W.2d 203 (Mo. 1949); Kansas City v. School District, 201 S.W.2d 930 (Mo. 1947).

[357]Pasadena School District v. City of Pasadena, 134 Pac. 985 (Cal. 1913); People v. Board of Education, 195 N.W. 95 (Mich. 1923).

[358]Whiteville City Administrative Unit v. Columbus County Board of County Commissioners, 112 S.E.2d 539 (N.C. 1960); Divisich v. Marshall, 22 N.E.2d 327 (N.Y. 1939); Kennedy v. Miller, 32 Pac. 558 (Cal. 1893).

[359]Board of Supervisors v. County School Board, 28 S.E.2d 698 (Va. 1944).

[360]Mayor and Council of Wilmington v. State ex. rel. Du Pont, 57 A.2d 70 (Del. 1947); Board of Education v. Board of Finance, 16 A.2d 601 (Conn. 1940); City of El Paso v. Carroll, 108 S.W.2d 251 (Tex. 1937).

[361]Isley v. School District No. 2, 305 P.2d 432 (Ariz. 1956).

[362]Gualano v. Board of School Estimate, 177 A.2d 580 (N.J. 1962), 188 A.2d 569 (N.J. 1963); Marsh v. Erhard, 47 A.2d 713 (Pa. 1946); Board of Education v. Board of Finance, 16 A.2d 601 (Conn. 1940).

[363]Young v. City of Worcester, 133 N.E.2d 211 (Mass. 1956); Board of School Trustees v. Benner, 24 S.E.2d 259 (N.C. 1943).

[364]Board of Education v. City of Hackensack, 165 A.2d 33 (N.J. 1960); City of Franklin v. Hinds, 143 A.2d 111 (N.H. 1958); Mayor and Council of Wilmington v. State ex. rel. Du Pont, 57 A.2d 70 (Del. 1947); Hayes v. City of Brockton, 48 N.E.2d 683 (Mass. 1943); Williamson v. Board of Education, 117 P.2d 120 (Okla. 1941).

discretion as to the funds granted for school purposes and may appropriate less than the sum requested by school officials.[365] However, even in the latter situation there are limitations on the authority of the appropriating agency to reduce the sum requested by school officials. It may not arbitrarily refuse to appropriate the funds requested, particularly when such an action would have the effect of overruling the judgment of school officers in matters under their jurisdiction.[366] The circumstances under which a reviewing agency may reduce the budget requested by a board of education have been spelled out as follows:

> When a town board of education includes in the estimates it submits to a board of finance expenditures for a purpose which is not within statutory provisions imposing a duty upon it nor within one which vests it with a discretion to be independently exercised, the board of finance may, if in its judgment, considering not only the educational purposes to be served but also the financial condition of the town, if it finds the expenditure is not justified, decline to recommend an appropriation for it; where, however, the estimate is for an expenditure for a purpose which the statutes make it the duty of the board of education to effectuate or they vest in the board of education a discretion to be independently exercised as to the carrying out of some purpose, the town board of finance has not the power to refuse to include any appropriation for it in the budget it submits and can reduce the estimate submitted by the board of education only when that estimate exceeds the amount reasonably necessary for the accomplishment of the purpose, taking into consideration along with the educational needs of the town, its financial condition and other expenditures it must make. The board of finance in such a case must exercise its sound judgment in determining whether or to what extent the estimates of the board of education are larger than the sums reasonably necessary. . . .[367]

Although the question seldom has been posed, an authority indicates that an appropriating agency may not appropriate more money than has been requested by school authorities.[368] Some statutes provide that supplementary appropriations may be made, but any restrictions placed upon the

power to make supplementary appropriations must be observed.[369] In an Oklahoma case it was held[370] that, where the specified conditions under which a supplemental appropriation could be made existed, the appropriating agency had no discretion to refuse to make a supplemental appropriation when requested to do so by school authorities.

The approval of a proposed budget or the acceptance of the estimates of revenue required has been held[371] to constitute an appropriation. Once an appropriation has been made, the appropriating agency has neither the power to exercise item control over the school district's budget nor the power to exercise control over the specific use of money appropriated to the school district unless the statutes expressly give it such powers.[372] Control over the specific expenditures to be made by the school district is within the discretion of the board of education and will not be interfered with unless the board exercises its discretion in an arbitrary or unreasonable manner.[373] The law on this point has been stated concisely:

> After the Common Council has adopted the budget and the educational monies have been set off to the Board of Education, there is no further duty or responsibility or authority in the Board of Estimate over the educational funds. How, when, and in what amount these funds are disbursed is solely the prerogative and responsibility of the Board of Education so long as they are spent for the educational purposes appropriated and within the limits of the appropriation.[374]

However, it has been held that boards of education may not set salary scales independent of municipal control where the city is responsible for providing the revenue. In this instance it was held[375] that the ne-

[365]Board of Education v. Carlo, 131 A.2d 217 (Conn. 1957); Board of Supervisors v. County School Board, 28 S.E.2d 698 (Va. 1944); Board of Education v. Rogers, 15 N.E.2d 401 (N.Y. 1938).

[366]Board of Education v. Board of Finance, 16 A.2d 601 (Conn. 1940); Washington Township Advisory Board v. State ex. rel. Whaley, 73 N.E. 700 (Ind. 1905).

[367]Board of Education v. Board of Finance, 16 A.2d 601 (Conn. 1940).

[368]Stanolind Pipe Line Company v. Payne County Excise Board, 91 P.2d 767 (Okla. 1939).

[369]Young v. City of Worcester, 133 N.E.2d 211 (Mass. 1956); Threadgill v. Coalgate Board of Education, 204 Pac. 1100 (Okla. 1922).

[370]Excise Board v. Board of Education, 61 P.2d 693 (Okla. 1936).

[371]Board of School Trustees v. Benner, 24 S.E.2d 259 (N.C. 1943); State ex. rel. McHose v. District Court, 26 P.2d 345 (Mont. 1933); Excise Board v. School District No. 34, 10 P.2d 643 (Okla. 1932).

[372]Board of Education v. Carlo, 131 A.2d 217 (Conn. 1957); Board of Education v. King, 114 N.Y.S.2d 329 (1952); Board of Supervisors v. County School Board, 28 S.E.2d 698 (Va. 1944); Board of School Trustees v. Benner, 24 S.E.2d 259 (N.C. 1943); Divisich v. Marshall, 22 N.E.2d 327 (N.Y. 1939).

[373]Atkins v. McAden, 51 S.E.2d 484 (N.C. 1949); Board of Education v. Board of Finance, 16 A.2d 601 (Conn. 1940); McCollom v. City of Richardson, 121 S.W.2d 423 (Tex. 1938).

[374]Board of Education v. King, 114 N.Y.S.2d 329 (1952).

[375]Waterbury Teachers' Association v. Furlong, 294 A.2d 546 (Conn. 1972).

gotiated level of salaries was not necessary to maintain good public education. The fact that school funds are raised and disbursed by a municipal agency is not persuasive, since school funds are universally regarded as state funds. It has been said that school funds held by municipalities are to be regarded as trust funds to be used for educational purposes and for the benefit of school children.[376]

1.8d Boards of education created as part of municipality

Additional complications arise when municipal charters or state statutes create local boards of education which are not separate legal entities. It was held,[377] for example, that statutes creating a city board of education as a corporate entity do not create a corporate entity independent of the municipality. It also was held[378] that a board of education may be a separate corporate entity and at the same time a branch of city government. City boards of education, even though bodies corporate, have been regarded by the courts as departments of city government for certain purposes.[379] However, a board of education has been held[380] not to be a mere agency of the municipality, even though the legislation under which it was created did not make it a corporate body.

1.8e Relationships reviewed

While the foregoing sections indicate that a variety of relationships exist between school districts and municipalities, the prevailing view is that they are separate corporate entities. With some exceptions school districts are not subject to municipal control. They cannot be controlled in any manner unless the state so provides. The state's desire may be expressed either by statutory enactment or by silence. In connection with school buildings particularly, municipalities are permitted to enforce regulations when the state "has not occupied the field." Expressed in another way, the state determines by its action or inaction who shall control education and to what extent each unit of government shall exercise control.

[376]Williams v. State *ex. rel.* Attorney General, 46 So.2d 591 (Miss. 1950); Love v. City of Dallas, 40 S.W.2d 20 (Tex. 1931).
[377]City of Albany v. Lipsey, 34 S.E.2d 513 (Ga. 1945).
[378]Tanner v. Civil Service Commission, 1 N.W.2d 602 (Minn. 1941).
[379]McCabe v. Gross, 9 N.E.2d 269 (N.Y. 1937); Huettner v. City of Eau Claire, 9 N.W.2d 583 (Wis. 1943).
[380]City of Blakely v. Singletary, 75 S.E. 1054 (Ga. 1912).

1.9 SUMMARY

Education in the United States functions within a clearly defined framework of constitutional, statutory, and charter provisions, and no authority exists to carry on school activities except as the power is granted by specific enactments or by clear implications. Within the boundaries of these provisions the several levels of government—federal, state, county, municipal, and school district—must conduct their designated educational functions.

The United States Constitution is the supreme law of the land. All aspects of the educational enterprise must conform to it even if state constitutional provisions are violated by this conformity. Any congressional or state statutory enactments violative of the federal Constitution are void. When no federal constitutional prohibitions exist, the state is assumed to have exclusive jurisdiction in educational affairs.

The role of the federal government in education stems from provisions of the "general welfare" clause and the protection of constitutional rights as defined by the United States Supreme Court and by Civil Rights legislation. The "general welfare" clause has provided authority to levy taxes to support an extensive array of educational functions as well as activities outside the field of education. In a wide variety of cases the United States Supreme Court has assiduously upheld all rights guaranteed by the federal Constitution against all manner of intricate charges. More recently major judicial action by both pupils and teachers has evolved from civil rights enactments prohibiting discrimination and guaranteeing equal protection under the law.

By silence on the subject of education the United States Constitution has designated education as a state function, and the state has plenary legislative power except as constrained by state or federal constitutional provisions. The state, however, must exercise its legislative powers and may not delegate them to other agencies. Administrative functions may be delegated, and they normally are delegated to state boards of education and state superintendents at the state level and to local school boards and municipal bodies at the local level. But state and local boards of education must exercise the authority vested in them and may not delegate it to others. State superintendents are usually given extensive power in educational matters. Courts tend to interpret their status so as to confer extensive authority on them both in the operational aspects of their position and in the promulgation of regulations and policy.

County boards of education function either as local boards of education with jurisdiction over the geographical area of a county or as intermediate district boards. Intermediate district boards as well as local boards may exercise only such powers as are specifically granted or clearly implied. Their functions, too, are circumscribed by legislative prescription. Unless the boards are established in the constitution they may be abolished by legislative decree.

County superintendents are held to be both county and state officers. For residency and related purposes they generally are deemed to be county officers. For educational purposes they are state officers carrying on the state function of education. Their powers are found exclusively in the state constitution and in statutes, expressly declared or clearly implied.

Town or township officers are sometimes vested with the responsibility of managing the schools as well as conducting local governmental activities. Their authority in the control and operation of schools must be found in constitutional and statutory enactments, and they have no authority beyond that extended by these documents.

In limited circumstances the state has vested control of some aspects of school operation in municipal bodies such as city councils. Since education is a state function, municipal control generally is not extended beyond that specially granted by statutes, strictly interpreted by the courts.

A major exception is found in the application to school districts of local building ordinances and related regulations. In this instance municipal regulations generally are applicable to school property if the state "has not occupied the field," i.e., if the state has not enacted statutes placing such authority in the board of education. In any case the state has plenary power, within constitutional provisions, to place the control of any aspect of education in whatever body it desires. Almost universally this has been achieved by positive legislative action, but in a few instances it has been conferred by legislative silence and lack of action.

CHAPTER 2

The Board of Education

2.0 INTRODUCTION

In this chapter attention is focused on the board of education as a corporate body. The term *board of education* will refer to the corporate body responsible for managing the affairs of a local school district and for administering the laws of the state which govern the public schools within the district. The term is used generically and refers to the governing board of a local school district whether this body is designated as a board of trustees, a board of directors, a school board, a school committee, or some other similar title.

2.1 THE BOARD OF EDUCATION AS A CORPORATION

Although the board of education may be viewed as indistinguishable from the school district itself in many respects, it also may be regarded as a corporation, separate and distinct from the district, which exists to furnish the method and machinery for the government and management of the district's schools.[1] Even where the statutes provide for their incorporation, boards of education generally are not considered corporations in the usual sense. Rather, they are regarded as public or quasi-public corporations,[2] and also have been referred to as municipal corporations[3] and as quasi-municipal corporations.[4] The distinction between the terms *municipal corporation* and *quasi-municipal corporation* is of importance, since statutes frequently confer certain powers and place certain limitations upon municipal corporations. Consequently, questions frequently arise in regard to whether or not a board of education may properly be categorized as belonging to a given class of corporation and thus come within the coverage of a statute.

When strictly interpreted, the term *municipal corporation* is properly applied to a governmental unit incorporated primarily for purposes of self-government. Its orientation is essentially local; it serves mainly as a vehicle which enables citizens to govern their local affairs. To accomplish this purpose, municipal corporations are necessarily granted substantial regulatory and legislative power.

The primary function of a quasi-municipal corporation, on the other hand, is to execute state policy; its duties are not essentially local in nature. In view of this distinction, there can be little doubt that boards of education are quasi-municipal corporations under a strict definition of the term. They are created by the state to perform what is clearly a state function, namely, to provide for the education of the children living in the school district. In practice, the distinction between a municipal corporation and a quasi-municipal corporation is of concern, since the powers possessed by quasi-municipal corporations are much more limited than those possessed by municipal corporations; quasi-municipal corporations possess only such powers as are conferred upon them by statutes, either directly or by clear implication.

The courts have rather consistently held[5] that school districts and school boards are quasi-municipal corporations, not municipal corporations. Their reasoning is illustrated by the following statement by a Michigan court:

> Not only is no authority given to the school board to exercise municipal functions, but its limited powers are exclusively restricted to purposes of education. Although invested with certain corporate characteristics to more efficiently serve the purpose for which they are created, school districts are not municipalities, nor public corporations in the full sense, but because of their very restricted powers are distinguished and recognized as quasi corporations.[6]

In interpreting constitutional provisions and statutory enactments, however, the courts not infrequently have decided that boards of education and school districts are municipal corporations, thus bringing them within the coverage of the statute or con-

---

[1]Wauconda Township High School District No. 118 v. County Board of School Trustees, 129 N.E.2d 177 (Ill. 1955); People v. Community Unit District No. 316, 100 N.E.2d 573 (Ill. 1951).

[2]Stokes v. Harrison, 115 So.2d 373 (La. 1959); In re Consolidation of School Districts, 74 N.W.2d 410 (Minn. 1956); Yow v. Tishomingo County School Board, 172 So. 303 (Miss. 1937); Dickson v. Brewer, 104 S.E. 887 (N.C. 1920); Wilson v. Abilene Independent School District, 190 S.W.2d 406 (Tex. 1945).

[3]Smith v. Board of Education of Ludlow, 23 F.Supp. 328 (Ky. 1938); City of Louisville v. Board of Education of Louisville, 195 S.W.2d 291 (Ky. 1946); Board of Education v. Stoddard, 60 N.E.2d 757 (N.Y. 1945).

[4]Chicago City Bank & Trust Co. v. Board of Education of City of Chicago, 54 N.E.2d 498 (Ill. 1944); Board of Education of Kenyon County v. Talbott, 151 S.W.2d 42 (Ky. 1941); Rose v. Board of Education of Abilene, 337 P.2d 652 (Kan. 1959).

[5]Driskell v. Independent School District No. One, 323 P.2d 964 (Okla. 1958); Barth v. School District of Philadelphia, 143 A.2d 909 (Pa. 1958); Town of Atherton v. Superior Court, 324 P.2d 328 (Cal. 1958); Zawerschnik v. Joint County School Committee, 73 N.W.2d 566 (Wis. 1955); Andrews v. Claiborne Parish School Board, 189 So. 355 (La. 1939); Dickson v. Brewer, 104 S.E. 887 (N.C. 1920); Daniels v. Board of Education, 158 N.W. 23 (Mich. 1916).

[6]Daniels v. Board of Education, 158 N.W. 23 (Mich. 1916).

stitutional provision in question.[7] In these cases it appears that the courts have attempted to determine the intent of the framers of the statute in question, i.e., whether the lawmakers meant to use the term *municipal corporation* generically so as to include quasi-municipal corporations within the scope of the statute. The Supreme Court of Kansas, in interpreting a statute providing that eight hours would constitute a workday for all laborers employed by the state of Kansas, or by or on behalf of any county, city, township or other municipality of said state," said:

Strictly speaking, cities are the only real municipal corporations in this state. We have no doubt, however, that the lawmakers, by the use of the word "municipality" in the connection in which it is employed . . . intended to include school districts.[8]

It would appear that whether a school board will be considered a municipal corporation is heavily dependent on the specific wording of the statute or constitutional provision in question. If the courts are able to determine that the framers of a measure intended to bring quasi-municipal corporations within its purview, they will generally hold the board of education or school district to be a municipal corporation. If such intent on the part of the framers of a measure is not discernible, inclusion of boards of education within the coverage of such provisions will be denied.

2.2 CONTINUING NATURE OF THE BOARD OF EDUCATION

Fundamental to an understanding of the nature of the board of education is recognition of the fact that it is a continuing body which exists separate and apart from its individual members.[9] A school board has been described as a corporation representing the district.[10] Although its membership may change, the board of education continues as a corporate body unchanged.[11]

The acts of the board of education are those of the corporation, not the acts of the individual members of the board; and the district is bound by the board's acts, so long as the acts are legal.[12] This is true even if the membership of the board should be changed.[13]

It also must be recognized that a board of education legally may act only in its corporate capacity. This rule has been judicially stated as follows:

The board of directors of a school district is an entity which can act and speak only as such. The separate and individual acts and decisions of the director members, even though they may be in complete agreement with each other, have no effect. They must be assembled and act as a board.[14]

The individual members of the board of education are not the corporation. As individuals, they can neither exercise the corporate powers of the board nor enforce its corporate rights.[15] The board of education may act in its corporate capacity only when its individual members are meeting together in a legally called session.[16] Power to act is vested in the board, not in its individual members, and in matters requiring the exercise of discretion members of the board of education, as individuals, have no more power to act for the board than does any other citizen.

Minor exceptions to the above rule should be noted. Individual members have been permitted to act for the board in matters which are ministerial in nature, i.e., acts which do not require the exercise of

---

[7]Halstead v. Rozmiarek, 94 N.W.2d 37 (Neb. 1959); Hall v. Ira Township, 83 N.W.2d 443 (Mich. 1957); Sims v. Board of Education, 290 S.W.2d 491 (Ky. 1956); Curry v. District Township of Sioux City, 17 N.W. 191 (Iowa 1883); Caldwell v. New York Board of Education, 216 N.Y.S. 501 (1926); City of Louisville v. Board of Education of Louisville, 195 S.W.2d 291 (Ky. 1946).

[8]State v. Wilson, 69 Pac. 172 (Kan. 1902).

[9]King City Union High School District v. Waibel, 37 P.2d 861 (Cal. 1934); McLaughlin v. Beasley, 108 S.E.2d 226 (N.C. 1959).

[10]Appeal of Black, 287 P.2d 96 (Wash. 1955).

[11]King City Union High School District v. Waibel, 37 P.2d 861 (Cal. 1934); Appeal of Black, 287 P.2d 96 (Wash. 1955); Funchess v. Lindsey, 133 So.2d 357 (La. 1961).

[12]Arehart v. School District No. 8, 289 N.W. 540 (Neb. 1940), Taylor v. District Township of Wayne, 25 Iowa 447 (1868).

[13]Appeal of Black, 287 P.2d 96 (Wash. 1955); Stokes v. Newell, 165 So. 542 (Miss. 1936); State v. Board of Education of Loudon District, 118 S.E. 877 (W.Va. 1923); Cleveland v. Amy, 50 N.W. 293 (Mich. 1891); State v. Winchell, 23 N.E.2d 843 (Ohio 1939).

[14]State v. Consolidated School District No. 3, 281 S.W.2d 511 (Mo. 1955).

[15]State v. Cooney, 59 P.2d 48 (Mont. 1936); Grubbs v. White Settlement Independent School District, 390 F.Supp. 895 (Tex. 1975).

[16]Lynn School District No. 76 v. Smithville School District No. 31, 211 S.W.2d 641 (Ark. 1948); Pratt v. Board of Education of District No. 61, 63 N.E.2d 275 (Ill. 1945); McLaughlin v. Board of Education of Fordson School District, 239 N.W. 374 (Mich. 1931); State v. Cooney, 59 P.2d 48 (Mont. 1936); Landers v. Board of Education of Town of Hot Springs, 116 P.2d 690 (N.M. 1941); Talbot v. Board of Education, 14 N.Y.S.2d 340 (1939); Lewis v. Board of Education of Johnson County, 348 S.W.2d 921 (Ky. 1961); Toyak Independent School District v. Pecos-Barstow Independent School District, 466 S.W.2d 377 (Tex. 1971); Busboom v. Southeast Nebraska Technical Community College, 232 N.W.2d 24 (Neb. 1975).

judgment or discretion.[17] There also is judicial support for the view that a single board member, or a group of board members, may take action which binds the district in the face of an extreme emergency where failure to act may jeopardize the lives or health of pupils or result in serious damage to the district's property.[18] Acts of individual members may also obligate the district under the law of agency.

2.3 THE BOARD OF EDUCATION AND THE STATE

Each of the fifty states has provided for the establishment and maintenance of a system of public schools. Determination of the state's educational policies generally has been vested in the legislative arm of state government. Rather than manage the operation of public schools directly, in most states the legislature has chosen to create local school districts and to make provision for governing boards which are charged with responsibility for the day-to-day operation of the public schools in these districts. In view of the fact that local school districts may be created, altered, and dissolved at the discretion of the legislature, it follows that the existence of local boards of education is dependent upon state constitutional or statutory provisions. Boards of education have no existence save as constitutional or statutory enactments provide for them, and they must be created in conformity with such enactments.[19]

2.4 THE BOARD OF EDUCATION AND THE SCHOOL DISTRICT

The board of education legally is regarded as the governing body of a school district, and its powers and duties are essentially those possessed by the school district. Only the board of education can act for the district and exercise its powers. The courts generally have applied the same principles of law to boards of education as they have to school districts, particularly when considering their powers and duties. For example, in cases questioning the authority to employ legal counsel the courts have attached no particular significance to whether a school district or a school board was involved in the case.[20]

In addition to being dependent upon the legislature for its existence, a board of education cannot exist apart from a school district. Since it serves as the administrative body of a local school district, there is no need for a board of education unless there is a district for the board to administer. It has been held[21] in this regard that there can be no valid election of a board of education until a school district is legally in existence. Barring specific statutory provision to the contrary, it would appear that a board of education may not be elected to act for the district until the date on which the school district legally is organized. Similarly, when a school district is dissolved, the board of education charged with management of affairs of that district ceases to exist. In short, the powers and duties of a board of education—in fact, its very existence—are inextricably related to the school district which it serves.

2.5 RELATIONSHIP BETWEEN BOARDS OF EDUCATION

Disputes between boards of education occur from time to time, particularly in states where separate elementary and high school districts have been established to serve the same area. A board of education has no authority over the affairs of other school districts; it has jurisdiction only within the territorial area of the district which it serves.[22] It may not exercise control over the affairs of other school districts even when the latter are partially or totally within the geographic area of the district it serves.[23]

In recent years decision-making has been decentralized in a number of large urban school districts by establishing subdistricts. In New York, for example, the legislature directed the board of education of New York City to divide the city into several local school board districts. The New York City Board of Education was given power to either appoint or provide for the election of, and removal at its pleasure, a school board for each subdistrict. In a case contesting the authority of the New York City Board of Education, it was held[24] that the board could legally suspend the governing board

---

[17]Kinney v. Howard, 110 N.W. 282 (Iowa 1907).

[18]Smith Laboratories v. Chester School Board, 33 Del.Co. 97 (Pa. 1944); In re Chester School District's Audit, 151 Atl. 801 (Pa. 1930).

[19]People v. Wabash Railway Co., 28 N.E.2d 119 (Ill. 1940); State v. Coulon, 3 So.2d 241 (La. 1941); People v. Rosenblum, 54 N.Y.S.2d 295 (1945); City of Beaumont v. City of Beaumont Independent School District, 164 S.W.2d 753 (Tex. 1942).

[20]See 75 A.L.R.2d 1341.

[21]People v. Community Unit School District No. 316, 100 N.E.2d 573 (Ill. 1951).

[22]Hagunin v. Madison School Township, 27 N.E.2d 926 (Ind. 1940); Chastain v. Mauldin, 32 S.W.2d 235 (Tex. 1930); Guyer v. Stutt, 191 Pac. 120 (Col. 1920); Kryger v. Board of Education, 323 N.Y.S.2d 777 (N.Y. 1971).

[23]Chastain v. Mauldin, 32 S.W.2d 235 (Tex. 1930).

[24]Ocean-Hill Brownsville Governing Board v. Board of Education of City of New York, 294 N.Y.S.2d 134 (N.Y. 1968).

of a subdistrict where the local board failed and refused to obey lawful directions given it by the New York City Board of Education. It was further held[25] that, since the enabling statute provided for neither a fixed term of office for the members of a subdistrict board nor tenure terminable only for cause, the members of such a board could be suspended without notice, charges, or a hearing.

In some states statutes provide for an annual meeting of all qualified electors in certain school districts. The voters who attend these meetings are empowered to deal with various matters affecting the welfare of the district, such as adoption of the district's annual budget, election of school board members, and similar activities. The annual school district meeting frequently is granted certain powers which are separate and distinct from those conferred upon the board of education. Questions occasionally arise as to which body has ultimate authority when controversies develop. It was decided[26] in a case in which this issue was raised that a school district board is not inherently superior to the annual school district meeting which elects the board. As a consequence, the board of education was without power to overrule decisions made by the electors at the district meeting on any matter which the statutes did not specifically place within the control of the board of education.

In the course of school district reorganization, responsibility for the administration of a school district is frequently transferred from one board of education to another. In such cases the powers and duties which have been lodged with the existing board of education are usually transferred to the board which succeeds it. It has been ruled,[27] for example, that contracts which legally have been entered into by a previous board must be honored by the succeeding board. Unless statutes provide otherwise, the succeeding board generally has the same powers and duties as its predecessor.[28]

2.5a Power to bind succeeding boards

As a rule, a school board cannot bind a future board to take a specific action on a question which may come before it at some future date.[29] However, if statutes specifically grant authority to a board of education to perform an act or enter into a contract covering a period of time extending into the future, succeeding boards will be bound by the act if it was done in good faith and without fraudulent intent. Although the membership of the board may later change, the board may not repudiate an action which was lawfully taken under a specific grant of power.[30]

Although the courts are not in complete agreement on the question, the weight of authority indicates that a board of education may enter into a contract extending beyond the term of office of its individual members even without specific statutory authority.[31] It is reasoned that since the board is a continuing body it would be contrary to public policy to limit the board's contractual power to the official life of its individual members. However, contracts tinged with fraud, collusion, or bad faith are void, and contracts covering an unreasonably long period of time may be regarded as constituting evidence of fraud or bad faith. Courts in several jurisdictions have held[32] that contracts of employment for a period wholly within the term of office of a succeeding board are invalid. The power of a board to bind its successors may be restricted by constitutional or statutory restrictions on debt.[33] In view of variations in state statutes, as well as conflicting court decisions on this question, school board members should check the law of their state relative to their power to bind succeeding boards on actions which extend beyond their term of office.

2.6 THE BOARD OF EDUCATION AND MUNICIPAL BOARDS

Disputes frequently arise relative to the power of a board of education and the power of a municipal board. Except as its

[25]Ocean Hill-Brownsville Governing Board v. Board of Education of City of New York, 245 N.E.2d 219 (N.Y. 1969).

[26]State v. Anderson, 22 N.W.2d 516 (Wis. 1946).

[27]McClure v. Princeton Reorganized School District R-5, 307 S.W.2d 726 (Mo. 1957).

[28]Zimmerman v. Board of Education of Buncombe County, 154 S.E. 397 (N.C. 1930); Nelson v. Board of Education of Williamsburg, 284 S.W. 386 (Ky. 1926).

[29]Miller v. Alsbaugh, 2 S.W.2d 208 (Mo. 1928); Murphy v. City of Cambridge, 173 N.E.2d 616 (Mass. 1961); School District No. 69 of Maricopa County v. Altherr, 458 P.2d 537 (Ariz. 1969); City and County of San Francisco v. Cooper, 534 P.2d 403 (Cal. 1975).

[30]State v. Winchell, 23 N.E.2d 843 (Ohio 1939).

[31]Taylor v. School District No. 7, 47 Pac. 758 (Wash. 1897); State v. Board of Education of Loudon District, 118 S.E. 877 (W.Va. 1923); Reubelt v. School Town of Noblesville, 7 N.E. 206 (Ind. 1886); Cleveland v. Amy, 50 N.W. 293 (Mich. 1891); State v. Winchell, 23 N.E.2d 843 (Ohio 1939); King City Union High School District v. Waibel, 37 P.2d 861 (Cal. 1935); Stokes v. Newell, 165 So. 542 (Miss. 1936); Tate v. School District, 23 S.W.2d 1013 (Mo. 1930).

[32]Maynard v. Gilbert, 140 S.W.2d 1064 (Ky. 1940); Shores v. Elmore County Board of Education, 3 So.2d 14 (Ala. 1941).

[33]Independent School District of Liberty v. Pennington, 165 N.W. 209 (Iowa 1917); Independent School District No. 1 v. Howard, 336 P.2d 1097 (Okla. 1959).

power is restricted by statute, a board of education enjoys full and exclusive authority to manage and control the educational affairs of the district it serves.[34] Local municipal authorities are without authority to limit or control the exercise of those powers which have expressly been granted to a board of education by the legislature.[35] While municipal authorities have plenary power in their realm, their realm does not include management of the educational affairs of a school district.[36] Consequently, boards of education are subject to the control of municipal authorities only to the extent prescribed by the law.[37]

Thus, it has been held[38] that members of a district school committee, although selected by the towns joining to form the school district, serve the district, not the towns, and their authority is determined by statutes, relating to such districts. It also has been decided that it is not the function of a city council to determine what schools or grades should be operated where this function is reserved exclusively to the school board,[39] and that a school committee exercises a portion of the state's sovereignty and is not bound by a city home-rule charter provision requiring the award of all purchases of goods and services to the lowest responsible bidder.[40]

2.7 POWERS AND DUTIES OF THE BOARD OF EDUCATION

Boards of education frequently are confronted with the question of whether or not a given act is within their power. It is virtually impossible for the constitution and statutes of a state to cover in detail every question which may confront a board of education. Such innovations as programmed

instruction, the application of electronic devices to educational tasks, and the use of "lay readers" to read and comment on themes written by students in English classes are illustrative of areas seldom, if ever, specifically covered by legislation. Faced with deciding whether or not it may employ noncertificated persons to read English themes, a board of education must resolve the question in terms of whether such an action is within its authority.

It is worth noting that many innovations in American education have not specifically been authorized by statutes. They have been incorporated into school programs by boards of education on the assumption that their action was within the power granted to them by the constitution and statutes. It has been quite common, after innovations have been adopted widely, for legislation to be enacted authorizing such programs and outlining general requirements and procedures. School-lunch services, guidance and counseling services, and pupil health services are typical of the activities which have been the subject of legislation after their relatively widespread incorporation into public school programs. When viewed in retrospect, many elements of modern educational programs appear to have been originally incorporated into the educational programs of a few districts by boards of education operating under the assumption that the innovation was within their authority.

2.8 SOURCE AND NATURE OF THE BOARD OF EDUCATION'S POWERS

As a creature of the state, a local board of education enjoys only such powers as it may derive from the state constitution and statutes. In general, a board of education may exercise only those powers which are expressly conferred upon it by statute or which are clearly implied from those expressly conferred.[41] The powers of a local school board have been judicially defined as follows:

[34]Beard v. Board of Education of North Summit School District, 16 P.2d 900 (Utah 1932); School Town of Milltown v. Adams, 65 N.E.2d 635 (Ind. 1946); Smith v. City of Dallas, 36 S.W.2d 547 (Tex. 1931); Crowell v. Jackson Parish School Board, 28 So.2d 81 (La. 1946); See also Carroll v. City of Malden, 320 N.E.2d 843 (Mass. 1974).

[35]Fleischmann v. Graves, 138 N.E. 745 (N.Y. 1923); City of New Haven v. Town of Torrington, 43 A.2d 455 (Conn. 1945).

[36]Chrestman v. Tompkins, 5 S.W.2d 257 (Tex. 1928).

[37]Hirshfield v. Cook, 125 N.E. 504 (N.Y. 1919); Waterbury Teachers Association v. Furlong, 294 A.2d 546 (Conn. 1972).

[38]Knapp v. Swift River Valley Community School District, 129 A.2d 790 (Me. 1957).

[39]James v. Duckworth, 170 F.Supp. 342 (Va. 1959); School District No. 69 of Maricopa County v. Altherr, 458 P.2d 537 (Ariz. 1969); Reeves v. Orleans Parish School Board 264 So.2d 243 (La. 1972); Cook v. Griffin, 364 N.Y.S.2d 632 (1975); Board of Education of City of Chicago v. Chicago Teachers Union, 326 N.E.2d 158 (Ill. 1975).

[40]Dawson v. Clark, 176 A.2d 732 (R.I. 1962).

[41]Superior Oil Company v. Harsh, 39 F.Supp. 467 (Ill. 1941); Kellam v. School Board of the City of Norfolk, 117 S.E.2d 96 (Va. 1960); Barth v. School District of Philadelphia, 143 A.2d 909 (Pa. 1958); Rosenheim v. City of Chicago, 139 N.E.2d 856 (Ill. 1956); Maddox v. Neal, 45 Ark. 121 (1885); State v. Haworth, 23 N.E. 946 (Ind. 1890); Andrew v. Stuart Savings Bank, 215 N.W. 807 (Iowa 1927); Mathews v. Board of Education, 86 N.W. 1036 (Mich. 1901); Wright v. Board of Education of St. Louis, 246 S.W. 43 (Mo. 1922); McNair v. School District No. 1, 288 Pac. 188 (Mont. 1930); Batty v. Board of Education of City of Williston, 269 N.W. 49 (N.D. 1936); Board of Education v. Best, 39 N.E. 694 (Ohio 1894); Crawford v. District School Board, 137 Pac. 217 (Ore. 1913).

The school board has and can exercise those powers that are granted in express words, those fairly implied in or necessarily incidental to the powers expressly granted, and those essential to the declared objects and purposes of the corporation.[42]

All power and authority enjoyed by a board of education spring either from the constitution or from enactments of the legislature. Powers granted by the constitution may be changed only through amendment of that instrument. Powers granted by the legislature, however, may be modified by that body as it deems appropriate.[43] The legislature may enlarge the powers of the board of education and it may impose restrictions on powers it previously has granted.

The courts will not question the authority of a board of education to engage in a particular activity when that activity has been given express legislative approval. As for activities which have not been given express approval, the courts must determine whether existing statutes clearly imply authority to engage in the particular activity or whether the activity is necessary to accomplish the purposes for which the school district was created. A multitude of cases may be found in which innovations instituted by boards of education have been challenged as being beyond the power of the board. The courts generally have been disposed to interpret the implied powers of boards of education quite liberally. It has been held, for example, that a statute placing upon school district trustees the duty of caring for and managing the school property carries the necessary implication that they may procure insurance to protect it against loss as a result of fire;[44] that a board of education has implied authority to employ legal counsel as a result of the express grant of power to manage and control the affairs of the district, to sue and be sued, and to enter into and enforce contractual obligations;[45] and that a board of education has implied authority to require physical examination of pupils attending the district schools.[46]

It should be noted, however, that courts

are not in complete agreement as to whether statutes which confer a power or impose a duty on boards of education are to be construed strictly or liberally. Courts in some states have indicated that statutes conferring power or imposing duties of regulation and administration of the schools upon boards of education must be construed strictly,[47] and that such statutes must be viewed not only as grants of power but also as limitations of power.[48] Courts in other jurisdictions have ruled that such statutes should be given a liberal construction and that the view of the court should be toward a construction which will expedite accomplishment of the purpose for which the statute was enacted. As a general rule, where there exists any doubt as to whether a board of education possesses a given power, the courts will deny the existence of the power in question.[49] They will do the same if the terms of the statute cited as granting the power are ambiguous.[50]

It should be noted that in cases dealing with the authority of a board of education the courts usually follow the rule of *ejusdem generis;* i.e., a general grant of power following an enumeration of specific powers is to be interpreted as applying to the same general kind of powers as those which are specifically mentioned.[51] Thus, a blanket provision granting to boards of education authority to do all things necessary for the maintenance, prosperity, and success of the schools and the promotion of education does not enlarge upon the powers which have specifically been conferred upon it.[52]

In contrast to situations in which a board of education is charged with attempting to go beyond the powers granted it are those in which the board attempts to divest itself of a power or duty. A board of education has no authority to divest itself of the powers and duties imposed upon it by the law, nor can a board, through its own action, preclude it-

[42]Board of Education of Oklahoma City v. Cloudman, 92 P.2d 837 (Okla. 1939).

[43]People v. Trustees of Schools, 4 N.E.2d 16 (Ill. 1936); Bopp v. Clark, 147 N.W. 172 (Iowa 1914); Morris v. Vandiver, 145 So. 228 (Miss. 1933); Love v. City of Dallas, 40 S.W.2d 20 (Tex. 1931).

[44]Clark School Township v. Home Insurance & Trust Company, 51 N.E. 107 (Ind. 1898).

[45]Arrington v. Jones, 191 S.W. 361 (Tex. 1917).

[46]Streich v. Board of Education, 147 N.W. 779 (S.D. 1914).

[47]Smith v. School District of the Township of Darby, 130 A.2d 661 (Pa. 1957); Union High School District No. 2 v. Paul, 95 P.2d 5 (Col. 1939); Conley v. Brophy, 60 S.E.2d 122 (Ga. 1950); Batty v. Board of Education of City of Williston, 269 N.W. 49 (N.D.1936).

[48]Abshire v. School District, 220 P.2d 1058 (Mont. 1950); Batty v. Board of Education of City of Williston, 269 N.W. 49 (N.D. 1936).

[49]Yeates v. School Directors, 26 N.E.2d 748 (Ill. 1940); Batty v. Board of Education of City of Williston, 269 N.W. 49 (N.D. 1936); Caldwell v. Bauer, 99 N.E. 117 (Ind. 1912); Andrew v. Stuart Savings Bank, 215 N.W. 807 (Iowa 1927).

[50]Wright v. Board of Education of St. Louis, 246 S.W. 43 (Mo. 1922).

[51]Vansant v. Commonwealth, 224 S.W. 367 (Ky. 1920).

[52]Hansen v. Board of Education, 116 P.2d 936 (Utah 1941).

self from exercising powers or duties imposed by law.[53] Boards of education have been created to perform a state function and granted the authority necessary to fulfill this function in anticipation that their responsibilities will properly be discharged. Thus, courts have held that a board of education may not waive by contract the authority imposed upon it by law,[54] that it may not abdicate the powers and duties imposed upon it by law despite a pledge to the contrary made to the electors,[55] and that it may not restrict or diminish its powers by its own rule or bylaw.[56] On the other hand, a school board cannot, by its own rules or bylaws, increase its powers or jurisdiction beyond that granted by the constitution and statutes.[57] School boards exist to serve public purposes and may exercise such powers, and only such powers, as are conferred upon them by law. Furthermore, when the occasion arises for the board to exercise its powers, the board must act.[58]

2.9 MODE OF SCHOOL BOARD ACTION

In exercising the powers which it has been granted, a board of education must act only in the manner prescribed or authorized by statute.[59] The rule in such cases is that the mode is the measure of power. The Oregon Supreme Court has put it this way:

It is a principle settled by numerous decisions that where a power is given to a corporation to do an act, and the particular method by which that power is to be exercised is pointed out by

the statute, the mode is the measure of power.[60]

When statutes prescribe the procedure to be followed in contracting with employees, advertising for bids, giving notice of meetings, or any other aspect of school board operation, the board must operate in the manner prescribed or run the risk that its acts will be held invalid. However, it has been ruled[61] that, where a school district has power to bind itself, it will be bound despite the fact that its board of education proceeded irregularly and in disregard of statutory directions.

Boards of education should always follow the direction of statutes since failure to do so may result in legal action contesting the validity of the board's act. Even if the board's action is upheld, legal proceedings are costly and time consuming and create suspicion that the board is incompetent or dishonest.

The general rule that a board of education can act only as a body at a meeting legally called and held has already been noted. It follows that only when the board is assembled in a legal meeting and acting as a board will its actions be held valid.[62] An individual member of the board has no power to act for or bind the board.[63] Furthermore, a majority of the board's membership does not have power to act for the board except when assembled in a legal meeting.[64] Actions taken by an individual member of the board, or by a group of members when the board is not meeting in legal session, are invalid and have no effect unless power to take such action has validly been delegated[65] or unless the action is required by an extreme emergency.[66] It also should be noted that mere concurrence on the part of

[53]Smith v. Board of Education of Ludlow, 94 S.W.2d 321 (Ky. 1936); Conley v. West Deer Township School, 32 Pa. 194 (1858); Boice v. Board of Education, 160 S.E. 566 (W.Va. 1931); Board of Education v. Rockford Education Association, 280 N.E.2d 286 (Ill. 1972).

[54]Farley v. Board of Education of City of Perry, 162 Pac. 797 (Okla. 1917); Smith v. Ouzts, 103 S.E.2d 567 (Ga. 1958).

[55]Molacek v. White, 122 Pac. 523 (Okla. 1912).

[56]Smith v. Board of Education of Ludlow, 94 S.W.2d 321 (Ky. 1936); Short-Conrad Company v. School District of Eau Claire, 69 N.W. 337 (Wis. 1896).

[57]Verberg v. Board of Education, 20 N.E.2d 368 (Ohio 1939); School District No. 69 of Maricopa County v. Altherr, 458 P.2d 537 (Ariz. 1969); Kerns v. School District, 515 P.2d 121 (Col. 1973); Busboom v. Southeast Nebraska Technical Community College, 232 N.W.2d 24 (Neb. 1975).

[58]Stetson v. Board of Education of City of New York, 112 N.E. 1045 (N.Y. 1916).

[59]Lewis v. Board of Education of Johnson County, 348 S.W.2d 921 (Ky. 1961); Farrell v. School District No. 54, 84 N.W.2d 126 (Neb. 1957); Jayton Rural High School District v. Girard Independent School District, 301 S.W.2d 80 (Tex. 1957); Lynn School District No. 76 v. Smithville School District No. 31, 211 S.W.2d 641 (Ark. 1948); Landers v. Board of Education of Town of Hot Springs, 116 P.2d 690 (N.M. 1941); In re Cochran, 43 A.2d 84 (Pa. 1945); Huettner v. City of Eau Claire, 9 N.W.2d 583 (Wis. 1943).

[60]Barton v. School District No. 2, 150 Pac. 251 (Ore. 1915).

[61]Hatch v. Maple Valley Township Unit School, 17 N.W.2d 735 (Mich. 1945).

[62]McLaughlin v. Beasley, 108 S.E.2d 226 (N.C. 1959); Moore v. Babb, 343 S.W.2d 373 (Ky. 1960); State v. School City of Anderson, 142 N.E.2d 914 (Ind. 1957); Lynn School District No. 76 v. Smithville School District No. 31, 211 S.W.2d 641 (Ark. 1948); Pratt v. Board of Education of District No. 61, 63 N.E.2d 275 (Ill. 1945); State v. Cooney, 59 P.2d 48 (Mont. 1936).

[63]McLaughlin v. Beasley, 108 S.E.2d 226 (N.C. 1959); Marting v. Groff, 162 N.E.2d 186 (Ohio 1959); State v. Cooney, 59 P.2d 48 (Mont. 1936).

[64]Lynn School District No. 76 v. Smithville School District No. 31, 211 S.W.2d 641 (Ark. 1948); Landers v. Board of Education of Town of Hot Springs, 116 P.2d 690 (N.M. 1941); McBee v. School District No. 48, 96 P.2d 207 (Ore. 1939).

[65]Kinney v. Howard, 110 N.W. 282 (Iowa 1907).

[66]Smith Laboratories v. Chester School Board, 33 Del.Co. 97 (Pa. 1944).

its members does not constitute official action by the board of education.[67] For a board action to be valid and binding, a formal vote on a motion or resolution,[68] or on the adoption of an ordinance, bylaw, or rule[69] is required. In short, the board of education must act at the time, in the place, and in the manner prescribed by law if its actions are to be valid.

2.10 DELEGATION OF AUTHORITY

Corollary to the rule that a board of education may act only when its members are deliberating together at a legal board meeting is the rule that the board cannot delegate to a committee of board members, an officer of the board, or an employee of the board any act requiring the exercise of discretion.[70] A distinction is made between discretionary acts, which require the attention, counsel, and deliberation of the entire board, and ministerial acts, which are relatively mechanical in nature and do not require the exercise of judgment or discretion. As a general rule, ministerial acts and duties may be delegated; discretionary acts and duties may not be delegated.[71]

2.10a Committees

The question of what constitutes a discretionary act is of importance. Many boards of education have standing committees to expedite the work of the board by dealing with the minutiae of activities requiring the board's attention. Obviously, care must be taken lest the committee attempt to act for the entire board on a matter which requires the exercise of discretion. For example, the board of education may not delegate to a committee the authority to disburse school funds.[72] It follows, therefore, that a board of education's finance committee has no power to authorize the expenditure of district funds. Its proper course of action is to bring recommendations on expenditures to the full board for formal approval. Similarly, a school board's building committee cannot be delegated complete responsibility for carrying out a program of school construction.[73] The committee may make recommendations after investigating sites, screening architects, studying new school plants, and the like, but final approval of a site, selection of an architect, and approval of a contract for construction require the exercise of discretion and must involve the entire board.

The rule relating to delegation of authority to a committee is aptly demonstrated in a North Carolina case in which a board of education attempted to delegate to its property committee authority to sell certain district property. The property committee, through its chairman, contracted to sell the property to a particular buyer. A second buyer, who was willing to pay a higher price for the property, brought suit claiming that the sale of district property required the exercise of discretion and could not be delegated to a committee. The North Carolina Supreme Court agreed with this contention, holding:

This is an allegation and admission that the Trustees attempted to delegate a non-delegable power and responsibility. It means that they attempted to abdicate their solemn trust by a delegation of their authority. The principle is a plain one that the public powers or trusts devolved by law or charter upon the council or governing body, to be exercised by it when and in such manner as it shall deem best, cannot be delegated to others. This principle may not prevent the delegation of duties which are ministerial, but where the trust committed to the governing body involves the exercise of functions which partake of a judicial character, it may not be delegated.[74]

As noted previously, the board of education may delegate ministerial duties to its committees, or to an officer, agent, or employee. For example, a board may direct its chairman to execute a contract in the name of the board.[75] In this case the board

[67]Butler v. School District of Borough of Lehighton, 24 Atl. 308 (Pa. 1892); Kerns v. School District, 515 P.2d 121 (Col. 1973).
[68]Cowley v. School District No. 3 90 N.W. 680 (Mich. 1902). Sheahan v. School Committee of Worcester, 270 N.E.2d 912 (Mass. 1971).
[69]McBee v. School District No. 48, 96 P.2d 207 (Ore. 1939).
[70]School City of Crawfordville v. Montgomery, 187 N.E. 57 (Ind. 1933); Garber v. Central School District, 295 N.Y.S. 850 (1937); State v. Jones, 224 S.W. 1041 (Tenn. 1920); In re German Township School Directors, 46 Pa. Dist. & Co. 562 (1942); Mulhall v. Pfannkuch, 221 N.W. 833 (Iowa 1928); Kinney v. Howard, 110 N.W. 282 (Iowa 1907); Big Sandy School District No. 100-J v. Carroll, 433 P.2d 325 (Col. 1967); Board of Education v. Rockford Education Association, 280 N.E.2d 286 (Ill. 1972); Quality Education for All Children, Inc. v. School Board, 385 F.Supp. 803 (Ill. 1975).
[71]Kinney v. Howard, 110 N.W. 282 (Iowa 1907); Wright v. Jones, 120 S.W. 1139 (Tex. 1909).
[72]Petition of Auditors of Hatfield Township School District, 54 A.2d 833 (Pa. 1947); In re German Township School Directors, 46 Pa. Dist. & Co. 562 (1942).

[73]Kinney v. Howard, 110 N.W. 282 (Iowa 1907).
[74]Bowles v. Fayetteville Graded Schools, 188 S.E. 615 (N.C. 1936).
[75]Eddy v. City of Omaha, 101 N.W. 25 (Neb. 1904).

exercises its discretion in deciding to enter into the contract and may delegate to one of its members the mechanical act of affixing a signature. Discretion is involved in determining whether to enter into the contract; no discretion is involved in signing the contract.

In questions involving the amount of power delegated to a committee, both the language and the purpose of the appointment are considered. Thus, it has been held[76] that a committee appointed to investigate claims against the district, and to hire an attorney, has power to institute an appeal from a judgment rendered against the district where the time for the appeal would have expired before the next regular meeting of the board of education.

2.10b Ratification

Occasionally an agent or a committee of the board oversteps its authority and takes actions which have not been authorized by the board of education. The general rule in such cases is that the board may ratify any act which it could have authorized in advance.[77] Once an act has been ratified, it becomes binding on the board of education.[78] Ratification will not validate acts which the board was without authority to perform in the first place.

2.11 RIGHTS OF THIRD PARTIES

One is tempted to conclude that those who deal with a school board or school district do so at their own peril. The courts have consistently held[79] that all persons who deal with school boards are presumed to have knowledge of the law and to be aware of the extent of the powers of the board of education, as well as how such powers must be exercised. Unfortunately, boards of education sometimes misjudge the extent or scope of their power and become involved in activities which are beyond their power. Such activities are said to be *ultra vires*. Activities may be *ultra vires* in the primary sense, in that they are

expressly forbidden, or in the secondary sense, in that, while not expressly forbidden, they are outside the scope of the powers conferred upon the board of education either expressly or by implication. In any event, an activity which is beyond the power of the board is invalid and does not bind the district.[80] In most cases it has been held[81] that those who deal with a board of education have no right of recovery under an *ultra vires* contract.

The doctrine that one who misjudges the power of a board of education does so at one's own peril is based on the fact that school districts are quasi corporations and possess very limited powers. Furthermore, the extent of a school board's power is a matter of public record. Those who deal with school districts and boards of education are held responsible for determining that a board of education does, in fact, have authority to engage in a particular activity, agreement, or contract. By way of illustration, it has been held that where textbooks were purchased for the free use of pupils without specific statutory authority the district was under no obligation to pay for them,[82] that a district could not recover its losses under an insurance policy with a county mutual fire insurance company where the constitution made it illegal for school districts to take out insurance with such companies,[83] and that a district would not be required to repay money borrowed from a bank where the only statutory mode of borrowing money was by issuance of bonds.[84]

2.12 AUTHORITY OF A BOARD OF EDUCATION TO MAKE AND ENFORCE RULES AND REGULATIONS

It has been established clearly that a board of education may adopt and enforce reasonable rules and regulations to facilitate administration of the schools and conduct

[76]Byrne & Read v. Board of Education of City of Covington, 131 S.W. 260 (Ky. 1910).
[77]*Ibid.*; Wysong v. Walden, 196 S.E. 573 (W.Va. 1938); Ryan v. Humphries, 150 Pac. 1106 (Okla. 1915); Frank v. Board of Education of Jersey City, 100 Atl. 211 (N.J. 1917).
[78]Wysong v. Walden, 196 S.E. 573 (W.Va. 1938).
[79]Brown v. Gardner, 334 S.W.2d 889 (Ark. 1960); State v. Stewart, 326 S.W.2d 688 (Tenn. 1959); Dunfield v. School District No. 72, 28 P.2d 987 (Kan. 1934); Morris v. Vandiver, 145 So. 228 (Miss. 1933); Harris v. Joint School District No. 6, 233 N.W. 97 (Wis. 1930); School District No. 69 of Maricopa County v. Altherr, 458 P.2d 537 (Ariz. 1969).

[80]First National Bank v. Adams School Township, 46 N.E. 832 (Ind. 1897); A. H. Andrews Company v. Delight Special School District, 128 S.W. 361 (Ark. 1910); Fletcher v. Board of Education, 88 Atl. 834 (N.J. 1913); Seaborn v. School District No. 42, 146 S.E. 675 (S.C. 1929); Special Tax School District No. 1 v. Hillman, 179 So. 805 (Fla. 1938).
[81]First National Bank v. Adams School Township, 46 N.E. 832 (Ind. 1897); Powell v. Bainbridge State Bank, 132 S.E. 60 (Ga. 1926); Reams v. Cooley, 152 Pac. 293 (Cal. 1915); First National Bank of Waldron v. Whisenhunt, 127 S.W. 968 (Ark. 1910).
[82]Honey Creek School Township v. Barnes, 21 N.E. 747 (Ind. 1889).
[83]School District No. 8 v. Twin Falls County Mutual Fire Insurance Co., 164 Pac. 1174 (Ida. 1917).
[84]Powell v. Bainbridge State Bank, 132 S.E. 60 (Ga. 1926).

of the district's business.[85] The right to make and enforce rules and regulations is inherent in every corporation.[86] In some states authority to enact rules and regulations has expressly been conferred upon boards of education by statute, but the authority exists even without specific statutory enactment.[87]

It should be emphasized, however, that a board of education's power to enact and enforce rules and regulations is not unlimited. Rules or regulations of a board of education are invalid if they conflict with constitutional provisions or statutes.[88] The enactment of a statute which conflicts with a rule or regulation adopted by a board of education automatically repeals such a rule.[89] Furthermore, a board of education, by its own rule, can neither expand its powers beyond those granted by statute nor restrict its own power.

The courts have recognized that it is virtually impossible for a board of education to foresee every emergency and meet in advance every requirement through enactment of rules and regulations. Consequently, it has been held[90] that any reasonable rule adopted by a teacher or a school administrator which is not inconsistent with state statutes or with rules promulgated by a higher authority is binding on pupils. It also has been held[91] that not all

rules and regulations pertaining to the management of the schools have to be authorized or confirmed by an official vote. However, if the legislature directs boards of education to "establish" rules, this mandate, it has been held,[92] implies more than writing the rules in a book. It implies that, in addition to establishing rules, the board must make a reasonable effort to communicate and enforce rules governing the administration and management of the schools. It is not necessary, however, for the board to assume direct responsibility for enforcing rules affecting each of the classrooms and classes of a complex school system, nor is it necessary to provide in detail for the types of activities to be conducted.[93] When statutes require the rules and regulations enacted by a board of education to be entered in its records and read to the teachers of the schools affected, a rule which has not been recorded and read has been found not to be valid and binding.[94]

It should be emphasized that a school board has no authority to make and enforce rules governing matters over which it has no jurisdiction. Rules and regulations of boards of education must bear a direct relationship to the management and government of the schools. This principle is illustrated by an early Wisconsin case[95] in which a pupil was expelled from school for refusal to obey a rule requiring that pupils bring in a stick of wood suitable for use in the school stove when they returned from the playground at recess. The court held that this rule could not be enforced since it did not directly concern the education of pupils or the discipline of the school. The court said:

> The rules and regulations made [by a board of education] must be reasonable and proper, or, in the language of the statute, "needful," for the government, good order, and efficiency of the schools,—such as will best advance the pupils in their studies, tend to their education and mental improvement, and promote their interest and welfare. But the rules and regulations must relate to these objects. The boards are not at liberty to adopt rules relating to other subjects according to their humor or

---

[85]Smith v. School District of the Township of Darby, 130 A.2d 661 (Pa. 1957); Richardson v. Board of Education of Los Angeles City School District, 59 P.2d 1285 (Cal. 1936); School City of East Chicago v. Sigler, 36 N.E.2d 760 (Ind. 1941); Parrish v. Moss, 106 N Y S 2d 577 (1951); Batty v. Board of Education of City of Williston, 269 N.W. 49 (N.D. 1936); Verberg v. Board of Education, 20 N.E.2d 368 (Ohio 1939); McCormick v. Burt, 95 Ill. 263 (1880); Ferriter v. Tyler, 21 Am.Rep. 133 (Vt. 1876); State v. District Board, 116 N.W. 232 (Wis. 1908); Ginther v. Park School District R-3, 511 P.2d 520 (Col. 1973).

[86]Fertich v. Michener, 11 N.E. 605 (Ind. 1887); Richardson v. Braham, 249 N.W. 557 (Neb. 1933).

[87]Montenegro-Riehm Music Co. v. Board of Education of Louisville, 145 S.W. 740 (Ky. 1912); Kane v. School Committee of Woburn, 59 N.E.2d 10 (Mass. 1944); Greco v. Roper, 61 N.E.2d 307 (Ohio 1945); Jones v. School District of Borough of Kulpmont, 3 A.2d 914 (Pa. 1939).

[88]Adkins v. Rogers, 303 S.W.2d 820 (Tex. 1957); Kane v. School Committee of Woburn, 59 N.E.2d 10 (Mass. 1944); Wilson v. Abilene Independent School District, 190 S.W.2d 406 (Tex. 1945); Birkbeck v. Wadsworth Board of Education, 245 N.E.2d 746 (Ohio 1969).

[89]People v. Van Siclen, 43 Hun 537 (N.Y. 1887).

[90]Deskins v. Gose, 55 Am.Rep. 387 (Mo. 1885); Patterson v. Nutter, 7 Atl. 273 (Me. 1886); Fertich v. Michener, 11 N.E. 605 (Ind. 1887); Tanton v. McKenney, 197 N.W. 510 (Mich. 1924); State v. District Board, 116 N.W. 232 (Wis. 1908); Guernsey v. Pitkin, 76 Am. Dec. 171 (Vt. 1859).

[91]Fertich v. Michener, 11 N.E. 605 (Ind. 1887); Tanton v. McKenney, 197 N.W. 510 (Mich. 1924); State v. District Board, 116 N.W. 232 (Wis. 1908).

[92]Germond v. Board of Education, 197 N.Y.S.2d 548 (1960).

[93]Luce v. Board of Education, 159 N.Y.S.2d 965 (1957); Pierce v. Lake Stevens School District No. 4, 529 P.2d 810 (Wash. 1974).

[94]Horne v. School District of Chester, 75 Atl. 431 (N.H. 1910).

[95]State v. Board of Education of City of Fond du Lac, 23 N.W. 102 (Wis. 1885).

fancy, and make a disobedience of such a rule by a pupil cause for his suspension or expulsion.

The courts will determine whether or not a rule is reasonable. In fact, final determination as to the reasonableness of rules enacted by a board of education is a matter of law to be decided by the courts.[96] The reasonableness of board rules, regulations, and actions can be determined only by consideration of the facts surrounding the particular case. For example, rules which are reasonable if applied to high school pupils may be quite unreasonable if applied to kindergarten pupils. In any event, the local school board is the final authority on rules and regulations so long as the board acts within its power, in good faith, without malice, and refrains from adopting rules and regulations which are clearly arbitrary and unreasonable.

When the validity of an action or rule of a board of education is attacked, the courts will always presume that the board acted within its powers and followed the requirements of the law. Unless there is evidence to the contrary, the court will presume that the act or rule in question is reasonable and proper, that the board acted in good faith, and that its decision was correct.[97] In regard to board procedure, the presumption in any case challenging an action taken by a board of education is that the act was taken at a meeting properly called and held, that due notice of the meeting was given where notice was required, that a quorum of the board was present at the meeting, and that the proceedings of the board were not irregular.[98] Consequently, those who claim that the board has acted irregularly or illegally or has abused its discretion must establish these facts by clear and convincing evidence.[99]

Since the test to determine the validity of a rule or regulation is its reasonableness, care should be exercised to create a history or a record establishing this fact. Except in an emergency, action should normally be preceded by study of pertinent facts, by discussion and/or consultation with persons having special knowledge of or interest in the problem, by obtaining and considering actions taken by or experiences of other boards of education in coping with the same or a similar matter, by holding a public hearing where appropriate, and finally and most important, by making certain that the proposed rule or regulation relates to a proper educational purpose, i.e., is reasonably calculated to promote the educational program, to advance the pupils in their studies, or to promote their education, mental improvement, welfare, morals, safety, or health.

2.13 THE BOARD OF EDUCATION AND THE COURTS

Courts take the view that, since the legislature has delegated to school boards power to exercise judgment and discretion in matters affecting the schools, they will not interfere unless the board exercises its power in an unreasonable, arbitrary, capricious or unlawful manner.[100] The Wisconsin Supreme Court has identified the scope of review by a court over the action of an administrative body as follows:

. . . a court in reviewing the action of an administrative board or agency in certiorari will go no further than to determine: (1) whether the board kept within its jurisdiction, (2) whether it acted according to law, (3) whether its action was arbitrary, oppressive, or unreasonable and represented its will and not

---

[96]School City of Evansville v. Culver, 182 N.E. 270 (Ind. 1932); Coggins v. Board of Education of City of Durham, 28 S.E.2d 527 (N.C. 1944); Trustees v. Bagsby, 237 S.W.2d 750 (Tex. 1950); Fertich v. Michener, 11 N.E. 605 (Ind. 1887); Tanton v. McKenney, 197 N.W. 510 (Mich. 1924); Foley v. Benedict, 55 S.W.2d 805 (Tex. 1932).

[97]Goodman v. School District, 32 F.2d 586 (8th Cir. 1929); Christian v. Jones, 100 So. 99 (Ala. 1924); People v. Witte, 146 N.E. 178 (Ill. 1924); Kinzer v. Directors of Independent School District of Marion, 105 N.W. 686 (Iowa 1906); Morse v. Ashley, 79 N.E. 481 (Mass. 1906); McLeod v. State, 122 So. 737 (Miss. 1929); Foley v. Benedict, 55 S.W.2d 805 (Tex. 1932); O'Neal v. School District No. 15 School Board, 451 P.2d 791 (Wyo. 1969).

[98]Fiedler v. Eckfeldt, 166 N.E. 504 (Ill. 1929); Waters v. Boone County School District, 59 Mo.App. 580 (1894); Hanna v. Wright, 89 N.W. 1108 (Iowa 1902).

[99]Safferstone v. Tucker, 357 S.W.2d 3 (Ark. 1962); Board of Education v. Stevens, 88 S.W.2d 3 (Ky. 1935); Board of Commissioners of City of Bayonne v. Board of Education of City of Bayonne, 36 A.2d 594 (N.J. 1944); Commonwealth v. School District of City of Sunbury, 6 A.2d 279 (Pa. 1939); Warner Independent School District No. 230 v. County Board of Education of Brown County, 179 N.W.2d 6 (S.D. 1970); Brownsville Area School District v. Lucostic, 297 A.2d 516 (Pa. 1972).

[100]Nichols v. Aldine Independent School District, 356 S.W.2d 182 (Tex. 1962); Magenheim v. Board of Education, 347 S.W.2d 409 (Mo. 1961); Detch v. Board of Education, 117 S.E.2d 138 (W.Va. 1960); Kopera v. Board of Education, 158 A.2d 842 (N.J. 1960); White v. Jenkins, 209 S.W.2d 457 (Ark. 1948); Gazaway v. Godfrey, 163 S.E. 480 (Ga. 1932); Security National Bank of Mason City v. Bagley, 210 N.W. 947 (Iowa 1926); McLeod v. State, 122 So. 737 (Miss. 1929); Beard v. Board of Education of North Summit School District, 16 P.2d 900 (Utah 1932).

its judgment, and (4) whether the evidence was such that it might reasonably make the order or determination in question.[101]

Courts have no authority to control the discretion vested by statute in the board of education unless the board exercises its discretion in an arbitrary or unreasonable manner.[102] A court will not substitute its judgment for that of the school board on any question which the board is authorized by law to determine.[103] The courts are not inclined to pass judgment upon the wisdom of rules and regulations enacted by boards of education,[104] nor will they interfere with a board's determination of whether or not a rule has been violated unless the board acts with malice or in bad faith.[105]

2.14 BOARD OF EDUCATION HEARINGS

Although the board of education is primarily an administrative body, it also may be required to perform duties of a quasi-judicial nature. Statutes frequently require boards of education to hold hearings on such matters as budgets, proposed bond issues, school district reorganization, and dismissal or transfer of personnel. Some states specify in detail the procedure to be followed in school board hearings. More commonly, however, the statutes specify only that hearings be held and do not prescribe the procedure which is to be observed. The following statement by the Supreme Court of Alabama in a case involving a teacher tenure law identifies the generally accepted procedural requirements

for a hearing in the absence of specific statutory requirements:

No particular form of procedure is prescribed for hearings under the statutes here in question but of course due process must be observed. . . . The Teacher Tenure Law in its provisions clearly contemplates the rudimentary requirements of fair play with reasonable notice and opportunity to be present, information as to charges made and opportunity to controvert such charges, the right to examine and cross-examine witnesses and submit evidence and to be heard in person and by counsel.[106]

Hearings before boards of education need not follow the usual formalities observed in court proceedings. The courts agree, however, that the right to a hearing includes the right to be represented by legal counsel.[107] The court in a West Virginia case said, "In America, the very word 'hearing,' both in common and legal parlance, implies some kind of trial, formal or informal, and presupposes permission to have legal aid if desired."[108] But whether witnesses called at a hearing need to be sworn is a matter of disagreement. Some jurisdictions have held[109] that failure to swear in witnesses nullifies the hearing; others have held[110] that since hearings before boards of education are informal the testimony need not be taken under oath.

When holding hearings it is important that the board maintain an accurate record of the hearing, including a clear statement of the facts on which its findings are based. A statement of the supporting facts is particularly important when required by statutes. A plain record of the hearing provides the basis for review of the board's ruling by a court in the event of appeal. Without a clear summary of the facts upon which the board's decision was based, the court has no ground for judging the validity of the board's findings.[111]

In general, the right to judicial review of the action of a school board following a hearing depends on statutory provisions.[112]

[101]State v. Board of School Directors, 111 N.W.2d 198 (Wis. 1961).

[102]Leeds v. Board of Education, 190 N.Y.S.2d 127 (1959); Kissick v. Garland Independent School District, 330 S.W.2d 700 (Tex. 1959); Coggins v. Board of Education of City of Durham, 28 S.E.2d 527 (N.C. 1944); Blair v. City of Fargo, 171 N.W.2d 236 (N.D. 1969); School District of City of Pittsburg v. Zebra, 325 A.2d 330 (Pa. 1974).

[103]Mapp v. Board of Education, 203 F.Supp. 843 (Tenn. 1962); Roberts v. Board of Directors of School District of City of Scranton, 341 A.2d 475 (Pa. 1975).

[104]Scott County Board of Education v. McMillen, 109 S.W.2d 1201 (Ky. 1937); Richardson v. Braham, 249 N.W. 557 (Neb. 1933); State v. Bruno, 367 P.2d 995 (Wash. 1962); Pugsley v. Sellmeyer, 250 S.W. 538 (Ark. 1923); Wilson v. Board of Education of Chicago, 84 N.E. 697 (Ill. 1908); Tanton v. McKenney, 197 N.W. 510 (Mich. 1924); Foley v. Benedict, 55 S.W.2d 805 (Tex. 1932); Flory v. Smith, 134 S.E. 360 (Va. 1926); State v. Judges, 181 N.E.2d 261 (Ohio 1962); O'Neal v. School District No. 15 School Board, 451 P.2d 791 (Wyo. 1969); Blair v. City of Fargo, 171 N.W.2d 236 (N.D. 1969); White v. Board of Education, 344 N.Y.S.2d 564 (1973).

[105]Kinzer v. Directors of Independent School District of Marion, 105 N.W. 686 (Iowa 1906); Board of Education of City of Covington v. Booth, 62 S.W. 872 (Ky. 1901).

[106]Board of Education v. Kennedy, 55 So.2d 511 (Ala. 1951).

[107]*Ibid.*; State v. Board of Education of Lewis County, 25 S.E.2d 537 (W.Va. 1943).

[108]State v. Board of Education of Lewis County, 25 S.E.2d 537 (W.Va. 1943).

[109]*Ibid.*

[110]Anthony v. Phoenix Union High School District 100 P.2d 988 (Ariz. 1940); School District No. 1 v. Thompson, 214 P.2d 1020 (Col. 1950).

[111]Laney v. Holbrook, 8 So.2d 465 (Fla. 1942).

[112]Downs v. Bruce Independent School District No. 49, 216 N.W. 949 (S.D. 1927).

In some jurisdictions it has been held[113] that all administrative appeals must be exhausted before judicial proceedings can be maintained. Thus, where statutes provide that decisions of boards of education may be appealed to a higher jurisdiction, such as a state superintendent or state board of education, the courts will not hear the case until all administrative remedies have been exhausted. It has been stated, however, that when the issue to be decided is solely a question of law, the doctrine of exhaustion of administrative remedy is not applicable with respect to judicial review of a school board's decision.[114] The courts are reluctant to set aside the findings of a board of education unless the record clearly contains no substantial evidence supporting the board's findings.[115]

It goes without saying that a hearing before a board of education must be fair and impartial. In a case[116] involving dismissal of a tenure teacher, evidence presented before the Michigan Supreme Court indicated that the hearing was held in a room completely inadequate to accommodate those who wished to attend; that only friends and witnesses of the school board were allowed in the hearing room besides the teacher, his wife, his attorney, and one witness; that between seventy-five and a hundred people were kept from the room by two armed policemen; and that a request to adjourn the meeting to a room where adequate seating facilities could be had for all was refused. In view of these circumstances, the court overruled the dismissal of the teacher. In conducting hearings, as in its other activities, good faith and fair dealing should be the objectives of the board of education.

2.15 SCHOOL BOARD MEETINGS

The fact that a board of education legally can act only when its members are meeting together in a properly called session has previously been emphasized. Thus the importance of the school board meeting is readily apparent. It is at legal school board meetings, and only at such meetings, that the board of education may transact business. The procedures followed in calling and conducting the meetings determine their legality. Failure to follow statutory and common-law requirements may cause a meeting to be ruled illegal and all actions taken at the meeting declared invalid. It is imperative that those responsible for calling and conducting school board meetings be aware of the law on this subject if they are to avoid the possibility that actions taken at such meetings will be void and meaningless.

2.15a Call or notice of

One criterion employed in determining the legality of a school board meeting is the manner in which it is called and the manner in which notice of the meeting is given to those entitled to receive it. The Supreme Court of Maine has commented in this regard:

> It is of course essential that there be some definite requirement of notice for meetings of school boards, since such a board is a deliberative body, every member of which is entitled to be present at every meeting to counsel and advise on any and every action which the committee is required or authorized by law to take. . . .[117]

Since the law contemplates that actions taken by a board of education shall be the result of the members' deliberating together, a basic rule is that each member of the board must receive either actual or constructive notice of the meeting in advance of the time at which the meeting is scheduled.[118] If a member of a board of education fails to receive notice of a meeting and does not attend, any action taken by the board at the meeting will be invalidated should the matter come before the courts.[119]

2.15b Regular

A distinction is drawn between regular and special meetings of a board of education, and the requirements for giving notice of these two types of meetings generally differ. The term *regular meeting* is customarily

[113]Daniel v. Dallas Independent School District, 351 S.W.2d 356 (Tex. 1961); Betterson v. Stewart, 121 S.E.2d 102 (S.C. 1961); Chastain v. Mauldin, 32 S.W.2d 235 (Tex. 1930); Griffith v. Red Oak Community School District, 167 N.W.2d 166 (Iowa 1969); Ken Stanton Music, Inc. v. Board of Education of City of Rome, 181 S.E.2d 67 (Ga. 1971); Silverman v. Board of Education of Millburn Township, 339 A.2d 233 (N.J. 1975).
[114]Silverman v. Board of Education of Millburn Township, 339 A.2d 233 (N.J. 1975).
[115]Board of Education v. Shockley, 155 A.2d 323 (Del. 1959); Leach v. Board of Education of New Castle County Vocational-Technical School District, 295 A.2d 582 (Del. 1972).
[116]Rehberg v. Board of Education of Melvindale, 77 N.W.2d 131 (Mich. 1956).

[117]Elsemore v. Inhabitants of Town of Hancock, 18 A.2d 692 (Me. 1941).
[118]Turner v. Wellford Special Consolidated School District, 91 S.W.2d 285 (Ark. 1936); Hlavka v. Common School District No. 83, 255 N.W. 820 (Minn. 1934); State v. Commercial State Bank of Crawford, 253 N.W. 692 (Neb. 1934); Holton v. Board of Education, 169 S.E. 239 (W.Va. 1933).
[119]Palmer v. District Trustees of District No. 21, 289 S.W.2d 344 (Tex. 1956).

applied to a meeting of a board of education which is convened at a stated time and place pursuant either to statutes or to action of the board itself. Since, by definition, regular meetings are held at a stated time and place, it is presumed that all members of the board have constructive notice of them. Consequently, no other notice is required to make them legal unless it is so specified by statutes.[120] A school board has authority to prescribe the requisites of regular or special meetings by appropriate resolution or motion.[121]

An Oregon case[122] illustrates the application of the rule regarding notice of regular meetings. In this instance four teachers had entered into teaching contracts with the board of education at one of its regular meetings. Later there was a change in the membership of the board, and the new board refused to honor the contracts. The teachers brought suit to recover on their contracts. The board contended that the contracts were illegal, claiming that the meeting at which they were authorized was not a legal meeting since notice thereof had not been given. The Supreme Court of Oregon upheld the validity of the contracts, stating that under the statutes of that state no notice of regular school board meetings need be given to members.

2.15c Special

The term *special meeting* is applied to a school board meeting called for a special purpose. In the case of special meetings it cannot be assumed that members of the board of education have knowledge of the time and place of the meeting without notice. Statutes which specify the procedure to be followed in holding special meetings are mandatory. However, notice of special meetings is required even in the absence of a statute.[123]

A Wyoming case[124] serves to illustrate the rule regarding notice of special school board meetings. The plaintiffs contended that the school board had agreed to reimburse them for certain expenses incurred in sending their children to an elementary school in another district in lieu of main-

taining a special school for the children. Evidence indicated that two of the three members of the board of education met and signed a paper, purported to be the minutes of their meeting, which ordered payment to the parents of the amount then due, as well as ordering that further payments be paid as they came due. The third member of the board had not been notified and was not present at the meeting at which this action was taken. The Wyoming Supreme Court held that action taken by two members of the board, where the third member was absent and had not been notified of the meeting, was their individual act and was not binding upon the school district.

2.15d Waiver of notice

Although the rule that all board members must receive notice of special meetings is strictly enforced, the courts are in agreement that this rule may be waived if all members of the board of education are present and all agree to act.[125] The purpose of the requirement that notice be given of meetings, the courts reason, is to insure that all members have an opportunity to be present and to participate. If all members are present and all agree to act, there is no point in requiring notice, since the purpose of the rule has been achieved.[126]

It is important to note that two requirements must be met if the rule regarding formal notice of meetings is to be waived. First, all members must be present, and second, all members must agree to act. If any member of the board refuses to act, the other members of the board can take no legal action. It has been held,[127] for example, that, when two of the three members of the board of trustees went to the home of a third to consider a contract with a teacher and the third member refused to discuss the matter, no valid contract could be entered into. Similarly, it has been decided[128] that the mere presence at the place of the board meeting of a member to whom no notice

[120]Board of Education v. Carolan, 55 N.E. 58 (Ill. 1899); Stoddard v. District School Board, 12 P.2d 309 (Ore. 1932).
[121]Stoddard v. District School Board, 12 P.2d 309 (Ore. 1932).
[122]*Ibid.*
[123]Green v. Jones, 108 S.E.2d 1 (W.Va. 1959); Elsemore v. Inhabitants of Town of Hancock, 18 A.2d 692 (Me. 1941); State v. Ellis, 259 Pac. 812 (Wyo. 1927); Center Hill School District No. 32 v. Hunt, 110 S.W.2d 523 (Ark. 1937).
[124]State v. Ellis, 259 Pac. 812 (Wyo. 1927).

[125]District Trustees v. Pleasanton Independent School District, 362 S.W.2d 122 (Tex. 1962); Green v. Jones, 108 S.E.2d 1 (W.Va. 1959); Butler v. Joint School District No. 4, 145 N.W. 180 (Wis. 1914); Lawrence v. Trainer, 27 N.E. 197 (Ill. 1891); School District No. 68 v. Allen, 104 S.W. 172 (Ark. 1907); Johnson v. Dye, 127 S.W. 413 (Mo. 1910); Anti-Administration Association v. North Fayette County Community School District, 206 N.W.2d 723 (Iowa 1973); Barnhart Independent School District v. Mertzon Independent School District, 464 S.W.2d 197 (Tex. 1971).
[126]People v. Frost, 32 Ill.App. 242 (1889).
[127]Rice v. School District No. 20, 159 S.W. 29 (Ark. 1913).
[128]School District No. 49 v. Adams, 61 S.W. 793 (Ark. 1901).

was given does not waive the requirement of notice or validate action taken at the meeting if the member was present for another purpose and did not participate in the meeting.

Exceptions to the rule that all members of the board of education must receive notice of special meetings also have been made where there was knowledge that a board member would be unable to attend the meeting because of illness or absence from the district.[129] In an Iowa case,[130] for example, the court sustained the validity of a special meeting of a board of education despite the fact that one member of the board was not notified because it was known that at the time of the meeting he would be in another state and obviously would be unable to attend the meeting had he been given notice. As was said by the Supreme Court of New York:

> The object of notice is to give the person notified an opportunity to attend. There is no other virtue in the notice. Now when a person, elected as a trustee, is at the time of his election in a distant State and continues there all the time until after the meeting in question, never having had any formal notice of his election, it would be unreasonable to say that a meeting was made invalid by a failure to give him notice thereof. Must a personal notice be served on him in Minnesota? Or if a notice left at his house is sufficient, of what use would it be to one who was beyond its reach? It cannot be necessary to do an act which, when done, would be of no use.[131]

2.15e Notice to the public

In the absence of statutes requiring that the public be given notice of all school board meetings, there is no obligation to inform the public as to the time, date, and place of such meetings. It has been said that notice of school board meetings is for the benefit of the members of the board, not the public.[132] Similarly, it has been ruled[133] that a statute which requires board members to be given notice of school board meetings does not require the public to be notified of them.

A legislature may require that all meetings of a school board at which official actions are to be taken must be open to the public[134] and statutes requiring that the public be given notice of all meetings of the board of education are enforced by the courts.[135] There has been a substantial amount of litigation concerning so-called "Sunshine Laws" which require that the meetings of public bodies such as boards of education be open to the public. There is some disagreement concerning the validity of the actions of a board of education taken at a meeting held in violation of the requirements of such a statute. It has been held[136] that the failure of a county board of education to give advance notice of its meeting, despite a statutory provision requiring such notice, did not invalidate the action taken at the meeting. On the other hand, it has been ruled[137] that a school board's failure to comply with the requirements of an open meeting law in dismissing a principal invalidated the board's action. It also has been held[138] that a teachers' strike did not constitute an "emergency" within the meaning of an open meeting statute, and that a resolution to seek an injunction to halt the strike passed at a meeting held without the required 24-hour notice was unauthorized.

Questions have arisen concerning what constitutes adequate notice to the public. In a California case[139] the board of education, acting at a regular meeting, fixed the date of a special meeting. It was held that the action taken at the regular meeting constituted adequate notice to the public and no other notice was required. In an Iowa case[140] it was ruled that adequate notice to the public was given where the school district superintendent relayed to the news media information concerning the upcoming school board meeting. In another case,[141] notice that the school board would meet on June 18 to adopt a resolution concerning an occupa-

[129]Consolidated School District of Glidden v. Griffin, 206 N.W. 86 (Iowa 1925); Porter v. Robinson, 30 Hun 209 (N.Y. 1883); Russell v. Wellington, 157 Mass. 100 (1892); Barnhart Independent School District v. Mertzon Independent School District, 464 S.W.2d 197 (Tex. 1971).

[130]Consolidated School District of Glidden v. Griffin, 206 N.W. 86 (Iowa 1925).

[131]Porter v. Robinson, 30 Hun 209 (N.Y. 1883).

[132]Green v. Jones, 108 S.E.2d 1 (W.Va. 1959); Knickerbocker v. Redlands High School District, 122 P.2d 289 (Cal. 1942); Capehart v. Board of Education, 95 S.E. 838 (W.Va. 1918).

[133]Alva v. Sequoia Union High School District, 220 P.2d 788 (Cal. 1950).

[134]Canney v. Board of Public Instruction of Alachua County, 278 So.2d 260 (Fla. 1973).

[135]Lipscomb Independent School District v. County School Trustees of Lipscomb County, 498 S.W.2d 364 (Tex. 1973); Stoneman v. Tamworth School District, 320 A.2d 657 (N.H. 1974); Mead School District No. 354 v. Mead Education Association, 530 P.2d 302 (Wash. 1975).

[136]Dobrovolny v. Reinhardt, 173 N.W.2d 837 (Iowa 1970).

[137]Stoneman v. Tamworth School District, 320 A.2d 657 (N.H. 1974).

[138]Mead School District No. 354 v. Mead Education Association, 530 P.2d 302 (Wash. 1975).

[139]Ibid.

[140]Widmer v. Reitzler, 182 N.W.2d 177 (Iowa 1970).

[141]Taylor v. Coatesville Area School District, 279 A.2d 90 (Pa. 1971).

tional tax was advertised in a newspaper having general circulation in the district on May 28, June 4, and June 11, in compliance with a statutory requirement. It then became necessary to postpone until June 25 the meeting originally scheduled for June 18. The postponement of the meeting was publicized in a front page news item in the same paper in which the meeting had been advertised. It was held that the advertisement requirements of the statute had been fulfilled because the public had ample information and opportunity to express opposition to the resolution.

2.15f Who should receive notice

It is obvious that all members of the board of education are entitled to receive notice of regular and special meetings. However, questions sometimes arise as to whether other parties also are entitled to receive notice of school board meetings, particularly where certain officials, by virtue of their office, serve as ex officio members of a board of education.

This question was before the courts in Minnesota where a statute made the superintendent of schools an ex officio member of the board of education, but without a vote. When the board desired to consider the superintendent's contract, it did not notify him of the meeting, and an action was brought to test the legality of the meeting. The court held the meeting to be valid and said:

> At best, his function as member ex officio is limited by statute to that of a counsellor. It was certainly not the intention of the statute that school board meetings could not be held without notice to the superintendent. To hold otherwise, to say that absence of such notice would nullify all proceedings of the meeting, would be to reach an absurdity of conclusion such as it can not be supposed the legislature could have intended.[142]

It should be noted that in the above case the special meeting was held to consider the superintendent's contract. In view of the fact that the court referred to the superintendent as a "counsellor," it is logical to conclude that had the meeting been called to consider some other subject, notice to the superintendent as an ex officio member would have been required. Considering the uncertainty in this area, it appears that the wisest course of action is to notify all members of the board, whether they are regular or ex officio members, of meetings.

2.15g Form of notice

Questions relative to the form in which notice of school board meetings is to be given have frequently been before the courts. The great majority of these cases have involved the question of whether written or oral notice of a meeting is required. In states where statutes specify that written notice is required, an oral notice of the meeting will not suffice.[143] The only time an exception is made to this rule is when all members of the board are present and all agree to act.

Where the statutes require notice but are silent as to the form of the notice, or are ambiguous, the courts disagree on whether oral or written notice is required. Some have held[144] that the notice must be in writing; others,[145] that oral notice is sufficient. An Iowa case illustrates the reasoning applied where oral notice has been held effective. According to statute, special school board meetings could be called "upon notice specifying the time and place, delivered to each member." One board member was notified by telephone of the time and place of a special school board meeting but failed to attend. The validity of business transacted at the meeting was challenged on the ground that the statute required written notice. In sustaining the validity of the notice given by telephone, the Iowa Supreme Court said:

> . . . notice by word of mouth may be delivered quite as effectually as one in writing. What this exacts is that it actually reach the several members, so that each shall be informed of the time and place of meeting. . . . For this purpose, oral notice would be as effective as written, and there is nothing in the context indicating that one was intended rather than the other.[146]

The Arkansas Supreme Court, on the other hand, has held that written notice is required where the statutes do not specify the form. In its opinion the court said:

> Our statute is silent on the question whether a notice of the called meeting of a municipal corporation shall be in writing. But we are of the opinion that, when an official notice is required to be given of such a meeting, it is

[142]Gilbertson v. Independent School District No. 1, 293 N.W. 129 (Minn. 1940).

[143]Kattman v. New Knoxville School District Board of Education, 15 Ohio Cir. Ct. (N.S.) 232 (1911); State v. Tucker, 166 N.W. 820 (N.D. 1918).
[144]Burns v. Thompson, 43 S.W. 499 (Ark. 1897); Vreeland v. School District No. 2, 249 N.W. 829 (Mich. 1933).
[145]Gallagher v. School Township of Willow, 154 N.W. 437 (Iowa 1915); Board of Education v. Stevens, 88 S.W.2d 3 (Ky. 1935).
[146]Gallagher v. School Township of Willow, 154 N.W. 437 (Iowa 1915).

contemplated that it shall be in writing, and that it shall state the time, place, and purpose of the meeting.[147]

When all members of the board of education reach an oral agreement to meet at a specified time and place, the necessity for a formal notice is eliminated.[148] Thus, if all members of the board, while meeting in a properly called session, agree to meet at a specified time and place, they may be assumed to have constructive notice of the meeting and need not receive formal notice.

Where the public is entitled to receive notice of school board meetings, the notice should be given in the manner specified by the statutes. It has been held[149] that statutory requirements concerning the giving of notice of meetings of a school board are mandatory and at least substantial compliance with the provisions of such statutes is required. Thus it has been held[150] that newspaper publicity cannot replace the proper posting of an agenda of a school board meeting.

2.15h Service of notice

Questions occasionally arise as to whether the notice of a meeting of the board of education must be served upon members of the board personally or may be served by telephone or via the mails. If the method by which notice of board meetings is to be given is specified by statute, the statute must be strictly observed.[151] It has been held,[152] for example, that where a statute required that notice of special meetings be written or printed, notice delivered to a member of the board by telephone did not fulfill the statutory requirement. Similarly, where statutes required that notice be delivered in person, notice by mail has been ruled insufficient.[153]

If statutes do not specify the procedure to be followed in serving notice, the courts have generally approved the practice of sending notice by mail.[154] Thus, the legality of a special meeting of an Arkansas board of education, when all members of the board were notified of the meeting by mail, was upheld.[155] The practice of giving notice of meetings by telephone, in the absence of statutes requiring otherwise, also has been given judicial approval.[156]

2.15i Time of notice

If a statute requires that notice of meetings be given a specified period of time prior to the date of the meeting, strict adherence to the statute is essential.[157] Meetings held before the required amount of time has elapsed are illegal. It has been held[158] that, where a statute required seven days' notice and only six days elapsed between the date of the notice and the date of the meeting, the meeting was illegal and actions taken thereat were void. As in other aspects of notice of meetings, the time requirement may be waived if all who are entitled to be present are present and all agree to act.[159]

When the statutes do not establish the time at which notice of meetings is to be given, the courts generally require that each member of the board receive notice of the meeting a reasonable period of time prior to the date set for the meeting.[160] The question of what constitutes a reasonable period of time is difficult to answer and must be determined by examining the circumstances surrounding each case. A West Virginia case contesting the validity of action taken by a board of education at a special meeting is illustrative. The president of the board of education called a special meeting to be convened at 7:00 P.M. for the purpose of accepting the resignation of a member of the board. Two members of the board were notified personally by telephone between 2:00 and 3:00 P.M. and were served with written notice of the meeting at 4:30 P.M. while at work at a plant twenty miles from the site of the meeting. Neither member attended the special meeting at 7:00 P.M., and the plaintiff contended that the meeting was illegal for want of reasonable notice. The West Virginia Supreme Court refused this contention, saying:

[147]Burns v. Thompson, 43 S.W. 499 (Ark. 1897).

[148]Olney School District v. Christy, 81 Ill.App. 304 (1898); Johnson v. Dye, 127 S.W. 413 (Mo. 1910).

[149]Carlson v. Paradise Unified School District, 95 Cal.Rptr. 650 (1971); Lipscomb Independent School District v. County Board of School Trustees of Lipscomb County, 498 S.W.2d 364 (Tex. 1973).

[150]Santa Barbara School District v. Superior Court of Santa Barbara County, 530 P.2d 605 (Cal. 1975).

[151]Burns v. Thompson, 43 S.W. 499 (Ark. 1897); State v. Tucker, 166 N.W. 820 (N.D. 1918).

[152]State v. Tucker, 166 N.W. 820 (N.D. 1918).

[153]Barclay v. School Township of Wapsinonoc, 138 N.W. 395 (Iowa 1912).

[154]Schmutz v. Special School District of City of Little Rock, 95 S.W. 438 (Ark. 1906); Russell v. Wellington, 157 Mass. 100 (1892).

[155]Schmutz v. Special School District of City of Little Rock, 95 S.W. 438 (Ark. 1906).

[156]Independent School District of Switzer v. Gwinn, 159 N.W. 687 (Iowa 1916); Gallagher v. School Township of Willow, 154 N.W. 437 (Iowa 1915).

[157]Schafer v. School District No. 1, 74 N.W. 465 (Mich. 1898); Hunt v. School District, 14 Vt. 300 (1842).

[158]Hunt v. School District, 14 Vt. 300 (1842).

[159]Knickerbocker v. Redlands High School District, 122 P.2d 289 (Cal. 1942).

[160]Wood v. School District No. 73, 162 N.W. 1081 (Minn. 1917); Board of Education v. Stevens, 88 S.W.2d 3 (Ky. 1935); Green v. Jones, 108 S.E.2d 1 (W.Va. 1959).

When a statute or rule or regulation does not prescribe the period for which notice of a meeting shall be given a notice given a reasonable time before the meeting is sufficient. A reasonable time within which notice of a meeting must be given before such meeting means sufficient time to the party notified for preparation and attendance at the time and place of such meeting. . . . What constitutes reasonable notice with respect to the period of time depends upon the facts and circumstances of each particular case and is not determined by any fixed rule or formula.[161]

The court also noted that the fact that a meeting is called for at a time which makes it difficult or inconvenient for board members to attend is not germane to the reasonableness of notice and does not excuse their absence.

A Kentucky court refused to hold a board meeting illegal even though one member of the board received only fifteen minutes' notice of the meeting.[162] In this case, however, the board member made no objection when he received the notice and testified that his reason for not attending was that he was not interested in the matter to be considered.

It has been held[163] that notice will be considered reasonable if board members make no objection at the time they receive it regarding the shortness of time between receipt of the notice and the time set for the meeting.

In a Minnesota case[164] involving the validity of a teacher's contract the evidence indicated that a candidate for a teaching position had called upon one member of a three-member board early in the morning. The board member hurriedly called a meeting to be held at her home between 7:00 and 8:00 A.M. Two of the three members of the board attended the meeting and voted to employ the teacher, but the third member, who had been in his barn when he received notice of the meeting, did not attend. In ruling the teacher's contract invalid, the court held that in view of the facts of the case the time of notice was unreasonable.

2.15j Authority to give notice

In general, it may be said that the call or notice of a school board meeting must be issued by one who has been authorized to issue it.[165] Thus, where a statute requires

school board meetings to be called by the chairman or presiding officer, other members of the board of education have no authority to call a meeting.[166] Similarly, where the notice is required to be signed by the presiding officer of the board, it may not lawfully be signed by any other member of the board.[167] However, when all members of the board are present and agree to act, the legality of the meeting will be upheld despite the fact that the notice of the meeting was given by one not qualified to do so.[168]

It has been decided[169] that a rule established by the state board of education making it the duty of the secretary of a local board of education to call a special meeting when requested to do so by the president or by a petition signed by a majority of the board is directory rather than mandatory.

2.15k Receipt of notice

Notice of a board meeting must be personal in the sense that it must actually reach the member who is entitled to receive it.[170] It appears that the requirement of notice will be met, however, if the notice reaches the board member through a third party. Thus, notice of a board meeting given by telephone to the wife of a board member who was ill and delivered to him prior to the time of the meeting was held sufficient.[171] In a somewhat similar case it was decided[172] that delivery of notice to the son of a board member, who failed to relay it to his father until after the meeting had been held, did not constitute legal notice. In a Maine case,[173] on the other hand, the court held that adequate notice had been given where the notice of a meeting was left at the home of a board member who was out of town, despite the fact that he did not receive the notice until after the meeting had been held.

From the above cases it seems that the courts are primarily concerned with whether or not the notice is actually received by a member of the board. Apparently giving notice of school board meetings to third parties for delivery to board members frequently is not sufficient. Every precaution must be taken to insure that the

---

[161]Green v. Jones, 108 S.E.2d 1 (W.Va. 1959).
[162]Board of Education v. Stevens, 88 S.W.2d 3 (Ky. 1935).
[163]*Ibid.*; Mullins v. Eveland, 234 S.W.2d 639 (Mo. 1950).
[164]Wood v. School District No. 73, 162 N.W. 1081 (Minn. 1917).
[165]*Ibid.*

[166]Johnson v. Dye, 127 S.W. 413 (Mo. 1910).
[167]Riggs v. Polk County, 95 Pac. 5 (Ore. 1908).
[168]District Trustees v. Pleasanton Independent School District, 362 S.W.2d 122 (Tex. 1962).
[169]Cullum v. Board of Education of North Bergen Township, 104 A.2d 641 (N.J. 1954).
[170]Wood v. School District No. 73, 162 N.W. 1081 (Minn. 1917).
[171]Independent School District of Switzer v. Gwinn, 159 N.W. 687 (Iowa 1916).
[172]Barton v. Hines, 185 S.W. 455 (Ark. 1916).
[173]Elsemore v. Inhabitants of Town of Hancock, 18 A.2d 692 (Me. 1941).

notice is actually received by the board member.

2.15l Contents of notice

The statutes of some states are explicit concerning the nature of the information to be included in the notice of school board meetings. In general, such statutes require that the notice state the time and place of the meeting and the nature of the business to be transacted. When statutes are silent on the subject, the courts usually require that the notice contain all information necessary to properly inform the board member about the meeting. Clearly, the notice of the meeting must, at the very least, state the time and place of the meeting and it should identify the business to be transacted.[174] It has been held[175] that a notice stating the hour at which the meeting was to be convened, but not the day, was insufficient. Obviously, if a change in the date or time of a previously called meeting is necessary, all members of the board are entitled to receive notice of it. A notice which is ambiguous or misleading in regard to the matters to be considered will invalidate action taken at the meeting if any member of the board fails to attend or refuses to participate.

Only business mentioned in the notice of the meeting may be transacted at a special meeting.[176] The courts are occasionally called upon to determine what matters may come before a special meeting when the notice of the meeting includes a broad category such as "miscellaneous business" in the description of the business to be transacted. In a New Jersey case,[177] for example, the call for a special meeting of the board of education stated that the purpose of the meeting was to adopt the budget, to adopt rules and regulations, and to take up "other matters that may come before the board." At the meeting the board accepted a teacher's resignation. The teacher later wished to withdraw her resignation and questioned the legality of its acceptance by the board on the ground that accepting a teacher's resignation was not included within the general language of the notice. No statute or rule specifically covered the practice of transacting miscellaneous items of business under a general-purpose notice. However, it was the local board of education's practice, of many years' standing, to hold special meetings between regular meetings and to transact miscellaneous business under a general-purpose notice. The court attached great weight to the board's long-standing practice in ruling that the board's action in accepting the teacher's resignation was valid.

Irregularities in the information included in the notice will be overlooked if all board members are present at the meeting and are willing to act. Also, if all members are present and willing to act, business in addition to that specifically mentioned in the notice may be transacted. In the absence of evidence that anyone was misled by the notice, a minor irregularity in the notice will not invalidate a meeting held pursuant to it.[178]

2.15m Place of

If statutes prescribe the place at which meetings of a board of education are to be held, meetings held elsewhere are illegal and actions taken at them are void.[179] In the absence of a statute specifying the location at which school board meetings are to be held the board is free to choose its own meeting place so long as it meets within the geographical boundaries of the district.[180] Unless specifically authorized by statute, a school board meeting cannot be held outside the geographical limits of the district.[181]

The legislature can, of course, authorize a board of education to hold meetings outside the district. For example, an Iowa statute provided that meetings of school boards could be held anywhere within the civil township in which the district was situated. In interpreting this statute, it was held[182] that a board of education of a district lying partly within each of two or more townships could meet in any of these townships.

2.15n Quorum

It frequently happens that all members of the board are not present at a legally called meeting. Assuming that the meeting has been properly called and that all members of the board have received sufficient notice

---

[174]Burns v. Thompson, 43 S.W. 499 (Ark. 1897); In re Redstone Township School District, 131 Atl. 226 (Pa. 1925); Carlson v. Paradise Unified School Board, 95 Cal.Rptr. 650 (1971).

[175]Shepherd v. Gambill, 75 S.W. 223 (Ky. 1903).

[176]In re Redstone Township School District, 131 Atl. 226 (Pa. 1925).

[177]Evaul v. Board of Education of the City of Camden, 167 A.2d 39 (N.J. 1961).

[178]Joint School District No. 5 v. Waupaca, Winnebago and Outagamie County School Committees, 72 N.W.2d 909 (Wis. 1955).

[179]Crawford v. School Township of Beaver, 166 N.W. 702 (Iowa 1918).

[180]State v. Rural High School District, 220 P.2d 164 (Kan. 1950); Dunfield v. School District No. 72, 28 P.2d 987 (Kan. 1934); State v. Kessler, 117 S.W. 85 (Mo. 1909).

[181]State v. Kessler, 117 S.W. 85 (Mo. 1909).

[182]Crawford v. School Township of Beaver, 166 N.W. 702 (Iowa 1918).

of the meeting, the question may arise as to how many members of the board must be present if the board is legally to transact business. The universal rule in this regard is that a simple majority of the membership of a school board constitutes a legal quorum unless the statutes provide otherwise.[183] A statute specifying the number of board members which shall constitute a quorum is controlling.[184] In either case, no legal action may be taken unless the required number of members is present. When a quorum is present, the act of a majority of the quorum is regarded as the act of the entire board.[185] The United States Supreme Court has said in this regard:

> . . . the general rule of all parliamentary bodies is that, when a quorum is present, the act of a majority of the quorum is the act of the body. This has been the rule for all time, except so far as in any given case the terms of the organic act under which the body is assembled have prescribed specific limitations.[186]

In the absence of a quorum, any action taken is merely the action of the individual members and does not bind the district.[187]

While the legislature may determine the number of members required to constitute a quorum, a board of education has no authority to define its own quorum by rule or bylaw.[188] The courts reason that the law establishes the board's power and this power cannot be enlarged or diminished by the board itself. In a Maryland case a city council passed a rule defining a quorum as a number greater than the majority. In ruling this action illegal, the court said:

> . . . it seems to us that if we concede to that branch the power to fix the quorum at a greater number than the majority, then we must concede to it the power to fix it at less than a majority, and fix the legal body at

one-third. . . . But a majority, being the legal body, cannot delegate its rights and powers to a minority. Such would be the practical effect of this two-third rule. It would give to one more than a third of the whole number of councilmen elected the power to prevent the passage of every ordinance, and thus entirely block the business of the council.[189]

The number of members required to constitute a quorum is not reduced by vacancies on the board of education, nor do vacancies prevent the board from acting as long as a quorum remains.[190] However, if vacancies reduce the number of board members to below that required for a quorum as the board was originally constituted, the remaining members are without power to take action.[191] A Montana case[192] illustrates this point. The father, mother, and uncle of the only pupils in the school district were elected as trustees. But the mother chose to act as clerk rather than to qualify as a trustee, and the uncle later moved from the district. The court ruled that the mother could not act as a trustee, having failed to qualify as such, and the father could not conduct the affairs of the district under a statute providing that the board of trustees was to consist of three members and that a majority of the board would constitute a quorum.

2.15o Conduct of
Since the meetings of a board of education constitute the vehicle through which it exercises its corporate rights, it is obvious that school board meetings should be conducted in an orderly manner and should observe the usual rules of parliamentary procedure. However, the courts do not insist upon strict adherence to technical rules of order, and the fact that parliamentary procedures have not been followed scrupulously will not necessarily void a school board's action.[193]

In the interest of orderly and efficient conduct of school district business, it is desirable for boards of education to adopt and publish rules of procedure. Statutes in

[183]Bray v. Barry, 160 A.2d 577 (R.I. 1960); In re Walters' Appeal, 72 N.W.2d 535 (Wis. 1955); In re Wells Township School District's Directors, 146 Atl. 601 (Pa. 1929); Turner v. Wellford Special Consolidated School District, 91 S.W.2d 285 (Ark. 1936); State v. School District No. 13, 151 P.2d 168 (Mont. 1944); Decker v. School District No. 2, 74 S.W. 390 (Mo. 1903).

[184]State v. School District No. 13, 151 P.2d 168 (Mont. 1944); Talbot v. Board of Education, 14 N.Y.S.2d 340 (1939).

[185]Turner v. Wellford Special Consolidated School District, 91 S.W.2d 285 (Ark. 1936); Jensen v. Independent Consolidated School District No. 85, 199 N.W. 911 (Minn. 1924); Trustees of Slaughterville Graded School District v. Brooks, 173 S.W. 305 (Ky. 1915); State ex rel. Broussard v. Gauthe, 265 So.2d 828 (La. 1972).

[186]United States v. Ballin, 144 U.S. 1, 12 S.Ct. 507, 36 L.Ed. 321, (N.Y. 1892).

[187]Ball v. Jones, 102 So. 563 (Miss. 1925).

[188]In re Walters' Appeal, 72 N.W.2d 535 (Wis. 1955); Heiskell v. City of Baltimore, 4 Atl. 116 (Md. 1886).

[189]Heiskell v. City of Baltimore, 4 Atl. 116 (Md. 1886).

[190]Trustees of Slaughterville Graded School District v. Brooks, 173 S.W. 305 (Ky. 1915); Knickerbocker v. Redlands High School District, 122 P.2d 289 (Cal. 1942).

[191]State v. School District No. 13, 151 P.2d 168 (Mont. 1944); Glass v. City of Hopkinsville, 9 S.W.2d 117 (Ky. 1928); Gearhart v. Kentucky State Board of Education, 355 S.W.2d 667 (Ky. 1962).

[192] State v. School District No. 13, 151 P.2d 168 (Mont. 1944).

[193]Lamb v. Danville School Board, 162 A.2d 614 (N.H. 1960); Huntley v. North Carolina State Board of Education, 493 F.2d 1016 (4th Cir. 1974).

many states either require or permit boards of education to establish rules of procedure, but boards have such authority even in the absence of statutes.[194] In a Louisiana case[195] where the school board had adopted a motion that "meetings be conducted under Roberts Rules of Order" over 14 years prior to the meeting in question, and the motion had never been revoked or amended, it was decided that Roberts Rules of Order constituted the rules of parliamentary procedure of the school board except where they were inconsistent with the statutes or the regulations of the State Board of Education. In New Jersey, however, it was decided[196] that since a board of education is a noncontinuous body, the rules and regulations adopted by a board of education generally expire with the annual reorganization meeting of the board unless they are adopted anew by the next board.

Where no rules have been adopted, ordinary rules of parliamentary procedure are deemed to govern school board meetings. Thus, the New Mexico Supreme Court has said, "In the absence of the adoption of rules of procedure and in the absence of statutory regulation, the generally accepted rules of parliamentary procedure would control."[197]

In states where statutes expressly authorize or require boards of education to adopt rules and bylaws, it is imperative that great care be exercised in complying with them, since it has been decided[198] that the regulations and bylaws of a board of education made under statutory authority have the force of law and are binding upon the board. In Kentucky, for example, a statute provided that a board of education adopt rules and bylaws within thirty days after its organization following each election. Further, once the board had adopted rules and bylaws, they could not be amended, suspended, or repealed except by affirmative vote of at least two-thirds of the board members in office at the time. The Louis-

ville Board of Education adopted a rule to the effect that no purchase in excess of $500 could be made without first advertising for bids. In spite of this rule a contract was entered into for the purchase of pianos in the amount of $2500 without advertising for bids. Later, after a change in its membership, the board refused to execute the contract, and the seller brought suit to force the board to accept and pay for the pianos. The Court of Appeals of Kentucky, in upholding the board's position, commented:

We are only concerned with the effect of the rules and by-laws adopted by public corporations to enable them to better carry out the purpose of their creation and existence, and we have no doubt that the material reasonable rules and by-laws of a public corporation made and adopted in pursuance of legislative authority and within the scope of the powers of the public corporation to aid it in the discharge of its public duties have the same binding force and effect upon it and all persons with whom it does business as the statute under which it derives its power.[199]

It should be noted, however, that bylaws of a school board which are inconsistent with statutory requirements are without force or effect.[200]

2.15p Noncompliance with established procedures

In some jurisdictions it has been held that under certain conditions a board of education may ignore its own rules and regulations. Although the courts are in some disagreement on this point, a board apparently may disregard its own rules and regulations where no rights have accrued to third parties or where the rule has to do only with parliamentary procedure. Thus, it has been held that a board of education may ignore its own rule requiring all applications for teaching positions to be made in writing,[201] may disregard its regulation concerning procedure to be followed in amending or repealing any rule adopted by the board,[202] need not comply with its own rule that all school building contracts be let to the lowest and best bidder,[203] and need not follow its own rule fixing the time each year when

[194]Holman v. Glasgow Graded Common School District, 34 S.W.2d 733 (Ky. 1931).

[195]State ex rel. Broussard v. Gauthe, 265 So.2d 828 (La. 1972).

[196]Rall v. Board of Education of City of Bayonne, 249 A.2d 616 (N.J. 1969).

[197]McCormick v. Board of Education, 274 P.2d 299 (N.M. 1954).

[198]United States v. Callahan, 294 Fed. 992 (D.C. 1924); Rodman v. Lofaso, 196 N.Y.S.2d 509 (1960); Bear v. Donna Independent School District, 85 S.W.2d 797 (Tex. 1935); Montenegro-Riehm Music Co. v. Board of Education of Louisville, 145 S.W. 740 (Ky. 1912); Valentine v. Independent School District of Casey, 183 N.W. 434 (Iowa 1921); Frates v. Burnett, 87 Cal.Rptr. 731 (1970); Anbrose v. Community School Board No. 30, 367 N.Y.S.2d 550 (1975).

[199]Montenegro-Riehm Music Co. v. Board of Education of Louisville, 145 S.W. 740 (Ky. 1912).

[200]Channel 10, Inc. v. Independent School District No. 709, 215 N.W.2d 814 (Minn. 1974).

[201]Weatherly v. Mayor of City of Chattanooga, 48 S.W. 136 (Tenn. 1898).

[202]Grosjean v. Board of Education, 181 Pac. 113 (Cal. 1919).

[203]Anderson v. Board of Public Schools, 27 S.W. 610 (Mo. 1894).

the board would elect the superintendent of schools.[204]

2.15q Executive sessions

In view of the fact that a board of education is a public body transacting public business, it would seem that citizens should be entitled to attend meetings of the board. The Supreme Court of Utah has clearly put the case for holding open to the public the meetings of a board of education:

> It would seem that, unless matters were of such a delicate nature or of the type where public policy dictates non-dissemination, the meeting itself should be open to the public and press, and information concerning what transpired there should be made available at least in a general way, to both at any time thereafter, by him whose duties require its recordation. There is nothing unreasonable in that under our free and democratic way of life. The truth about the official acts of public servants always should be displayed in the public market place, subject to public appraisal.[205]

Many states have enacted statutes requiring that meetings of the board of education be open to the public and providing for private or executive sessions of the board when certain matters or transactions are being considered. (An executive session is one at which the public is excluded and only such persons as the school board may invite are permitted to be present.)[206]

A board of education must comply with a statute requiring its meetings to be open to the public.[207] This is illustrated by a case decided by the Supreme Court of New Jersey under such a statute. A meeting of the board had been called for 8:00 P.M. to consider the appointment of a superintendent

of schools. Three of the five members of the board met in caucus at 7:00 P.M., ostensibly to consider applicants for the position. At 7:55 P.M. they signed a resolution appointing a superintendent. The regular meeting convened at 8:00 P.M., and the resolution appointing a superintendent was adopted without discussion and over an objection from the floor that the appointment had not been considered as provided in the notice of the meeting. The Supreme Court of New Jersey held the appointment to be invalid and, in discussing the requirement of a public meeting, said:

> The Legislature has unmistakably and wisely provided that meetings of boards of education shall be public; if a public meeting is to have any meaning or value, final decision must be reserved until fair opportunity to be heard thereat has been afforded. This in nowise precludes advance meeting during which there is free and full discussion, wholly tentative in nature; it does, however, justly preclude private final action such as that taken by the majority in the instant matter.[208]

Statutes which require that school board meetings be open to the public generally permit the board to meet in executive session when certain topics are discussed, for example, consideration of the acquisition of property[209] or discharge or nonrenewal of an employee.[210] It has been ruled,[211] however, that an executive session conducted for the purpose of evaluating teachers and/or administrators violates open meeting laws.

A school board is not precluded by open meeting laws from meeting in private with its administrative staff to discuss school matters, but such meetings may not be used as a subterfuge to circumvent the purposes of such laws.[212] Thus it has been ruled[213] that "superintendent's conferences" which were held regularly at a designated time and place, and which generally were followed by regularly scheduled board meetings at which little discussion of the issues

[204]State v. Sinclair, 175 Pac. 41 (Kan. 1918).

[205]Conover v. Board of Education of Nebo School District, 267 P.2d 768 (Utah 1954).

[206]Dathe v. Wildrose School District No. 91, 217 N.W.2d 781 (N.D. 1974).

[207]Lipman v. Brisbane Elementary School District, 4 Cal.Rptr. 8 (1960); Application of Flinn, 154 N.Y.S.2d 124 (1956); Cullum v. Board of Education of North Bergen Township, 104 A.2d 641 (N.J. 1954). Canney v. Board of Public Instruction of Alachua County, 278 So.2d 260 (Fla. 1973); Carlson v. Paradise Unified School Board, 95 Cal.Rptr. 650 (1971); Hennessy v. Grand Forks School District No. 1, 206 N.W.2d 876 (N.D. 1973); Reeves v. Orleans Parish School Board, 281 So.2d 719 (La. 1973); Lipscomb Independent School District v. County School Trustees of Lipscomb County, 498 S.W.2d 364 (Tex. 1973); Board of School Directors v. Wisconsin Employment Relations Commission, 168 N.W.2d 92 (Wis. 1969); Bagby v. School District No. 1, 528 P.2d 1299 (Col. 1974); Goodwin v. District of Columbia Board of Education, 343 A.2d 63 (D.C. 1975); See also Griswold v. Mt. Diablo Unified School District, 134 Cal.Rptr. 3 (1976).

[208]Cullum v. Board of Education of North Bergen Township, 104 A.2d 641 (N.J. 1954).

[209]Collinsville Community Unit School District No. 10 v. Witte, 283 N.E.2d 718 (Ill. 1972).

[210]Hennessy v. Grand Forks School District No. 1, 206 N.W.2d 876 (N.D. 1973); Lucas v. Board of Trustees of Armijo Joint Union High School District, 96 Cal.Rptr. 431 (1971).

[211]Stoneman v. Tamworth School District, 320 A.2d 657 (N.H. 1974); Peters v. Bowman Public School District No. 1, 231 N.W.2d 817 (N.D. 1975).

[212]Reeves v. Orleans Parish School Board, 264 So.2d 243 (La. 1972).

[213]Bagby v. School District No. 1, 528 P.2d 1299 (Col. 1974).

occurred before a formal vote was taken, were "meetings" within the meaning of the public meeting law and must be publicly scheduled and open to the public and news media. Neither the public nor the press, however, has a right to enter into the deliberations of a board of education.[214]

Where the statutes do not require open board meetings, action taken at an executive session of the board, regardless of the wisdom of such a procedure, has the same force and effect as action taken at a public meeting.[215] The only requirement is that the meeting be properly called and conducted.

2.15r Voting

The courts agree that, when a quorum is present, a majority of those actually voting is sufficient to pass a measure unless the statutes provide otherwise.[216] It is the duty of each board member present at a meeting to vote for or against any proposition which is presented.[217] Refusal to vote on the part of some members who are present will not defeat the action of those who do vote, because a member of a board of education who fails to vote when given the opportunity to do so is regarded as acceding to the decision of the majority.[218] A Missouri case[219] illustrates the point. Two of the three members of a school board were present at the meeting in question. A petition to call an election to vote on the question of school district consolidation was presented to the board by its president, who voted in favor of calling the election. The other member of the board refused to vote. The call for the election was issued and the validity of action on the petition was questioned on the ground that acceptance of the petition had not been approved by a majority of the board. The court, however, held the action to be legal, saying, "When a member of a

school board sits silently by when given an opportunity to vote, he is regarded as acquiescing in, rather than opposing, the measure, and is regarded in law as voting with the majority. . . ."

Members of a board of education cannot destroy a quorum and avoid the necessity of voting by withdrawing from the meeting if they remain in the immediate vicinity of the meeting. This unique situation arose in an Indiana case[220] in which six township trustees assembled for the purpose of electing a county superintendent of schools. After 236 rounds of balloting had been completed without any candidate's receiving a majority, three of the members claimed it was useless to continue voting, left the immediate area where the meeting was in progress, and mingled with bystanders who were observing the meeting. On the 237th ballot all votes were cast for a single candidate, who was declared elected. One trustee protested, and action was taken to determine the legality of the election. The court held that since all six trustees were present when the election took place, a quorum still existed and a majority of those voting was sufficient to culminate the election.

If statutes require that certain types of measures be approved by a specified fraction of the votes of the entire board, or of those present, any action receiving less than the specified number of votes is defeated.[221] An exception to the general rule that one who fails to vote is considered as acquiescing with the majority is found where the statutes require an affirmative vote of all present. In such cases a refusal to vote will not be regarded as an affirmative action; rather, it will be considered a negative vote.[222]

Questions sometimes arise concerning how the officer presiding at a school board meeting is to cast his vote. It has been ruled[223] that where the vote is a tie the announcement of the presiding officer that the measure has carried is tantamount to casting a deciding vote and a formal declaration of that officer's vote is unnecessary. Similarly, it has been held[224] that where the chairperson's vote was necessary to establish a majority as required by law the chairperson had cast the decisive vote when he declared that the motion had passed. How-

[214]Canney v. Board of Public Instruction of Alachua County, 231 So.2d 34 (Fla. 1970).

[215]School District No. 9 v. District Boundary Board, 351 P.2d 106 (Wyo. 1960).

[216]Parish v. Moss, 106 N.Y.S.2d 577 (1951); Montgomery v. Claybrooks, 281 S.W. 469 (Ky. 1926); Lenhart v. Newton Township Board of Education, 5 Ohio N.P. (n.s.) 129 (1907); Board of Education of Town of Carney v. News Dispatch Printing & Audit Company, 245 Pac. 884 (Okla. 1926); Collins v. Janey, 249 S.W. 801 (Tenn. 1923); Board of Education of City of New York v. Alonso, 303 N.Y.S.2d 932 (1969).

[217]Mullins v. Eveland, 234 S.W.2d 639 (Mo. 1950); Bonsack & Pearce v. School District, 49 S.W.2d 1085 (Mo. 1932).

[218]Montgomery v. Claybrooks, 281 S.W. 469 (Ky. 1926); Collins v. Janey, 249 S.W. 801 (Tenn. 1923); Bonsack & Pearce v. School District, 49 S.W.2d 1085 (Mo. 1932); Rushville Gas Co. v. City of Rushville, 23 N.E. 72 (Ind. 1889); State ex rel. Broussard v. Gauthe, 265 So.2d 838 (La. 1972).

[219]Mullins v. Eveland, 234 S.W.2d 639 (Mo. 1950).

[220]State v. Vanosdal, 31 N.E. 79 (Ind. 1892).

[221]Parish v. Moss, 106 N.Y.S.2d 577 (1951).

[222]Somers v. Bridgeport, 60 Conn. 521 (1891); Launtz v. People, 113 Ill. 137 (1885).

[223]Jensen v. Independent Consolidated School District No. 85, 199 N.W. 911 (Minn. 1924).

[224]Keyes v. Class "B" School District No. 421, 261 P.2d 811 (Ida. 1953).

ever, where 14 of 15 board members were present at a legally called meeting and 7 members voted for and 6 voted against a motion to appoint an applicant as superintendent he was elected. The president of the board who abstained from voting then announced that the applicant had not been elected. It has held[225] that the president's announcement had no effect, particularly in view of the fact that a motion to overrule the chair passed by a vote of 7 for and 6 against.

Blank Ballots

According to the weight of authority, a blank ballot is a nullity; i.e., it cannot be counted for or against a measure, nor can it be counted in determining the total number of ballots cast.[226] A Maryland court has commented on the common-law rule governing blank ballots as follows:

> To denominate such a paper a "ballot" would seem to miscall it. It is in fact nothing; it cannot be expressive of any intention; no rule or method of interpretation can relieve it of its dumbness. It no more indicates a preference for one of the candidates than for another. . . . A ballot is a form of expression for a candidate to be voted for. If the paper falls short of expressing such a wish, it is defective; certainly, if it expresses nothing, it lacks all of the essential elements of a ballot.[227]

While this case dealt with the election of a candidate to a particular position, the common-law rule applies to a blank ballot of any kind.

It should be noted, however, that courts in two states—Ohio and Minnesota—have ruled[228] that, where a statute required a favorable vote by a majority of the votes cast, blank ballots had to be counted in determining the number of votes cast.

2.15s Recess or adjournment of

From the general rule that the acts of members of a board of education are not binding on the district unless the board is meeting in legal session it follows that any action taken after a school board meeting has been adjourned is invalid.[229] It is not unusual, however, for a board of education

to discover, after adjournment of the meeting has already been moved and voted, that some necessary action has been overlooked. This raises the question of what constitutes adjournment of a meeting. The rule has been stated as follows: "An adjournment is an act, not a declaration. It is an act of separation and departure, and, until this takes place, the adjournment is not complete."[230] The mere fact that a motion to adjourn has been passed does not prevent the board from taking subsequent action where the adjournment has not become effective.[231] Adjournment becomes effective when a quorum of the members of the board depart, and any action taken after a quorum is destroyed is invalid.

Unless restricted by statute, boards of education have the same power to adjourn meetings as is possessed by all similar bodies.[232] Where a meeting is recessed, or breaks up without an adjournment, members of the board may subsequently reassemble on the same day to continue the meeting, and action taken under these circumstances has been ruled valid.[233]

2.16 SCHOOL BOARD MINUTES AND RECORDS

It is difficult to overstate the importance of maintaining a clear and accurate record of school board proceedings. As has often been held,[234] a board of education speaks through its records, which constitute prima facie evidence of its actions. Although legally it is not necessary for a board of education to keep minutes of its proceedings in the absence of a statute requiring such records,[235] an accurate and complete record of its actions should be considered essential by every school board. It has been said that a board of education should keep proper minutes and records so that citizens who are carrying the tax load in support of the schools may make reference to them, and so that future boards may know how their predecessors acted on questions

[225]State ex rel. Broussard v. Gauthe, 265 So.2d 838 (La. 1972).
[226]Murdoch v. Strange, 57 Atl. 628 (Md. 1904); Attorney General v. Bickford, 92 Atl. 835 (N.H. 1914); State v. Roper, 66 N.W. 539 (Neb. 1896); Bonsack & Pearce v. School District, 49 S.W.2d 1085 (Mo. 1932).
[227]Murdoch v. Strange, 57 Atl. 628 (Md. 1904).
[228]Wellsville v. Connor, 109 N.E. 526 (Ohio 1914); Smith v. Board of Commissioners of Rensville County, 65 N.W. 956 (Minn. 1896).
[229]State v. Orr, 184 N.W. 326 (Iowa 1921).

[230]Beatle v. Roberts, 137 N.W. 1006 (Iowa 1912).
[231]Gallagher v. School Township of Willow, 154 N.W. 437 (Iowa 1915).
[232]Donough v. Hollister, 46 N.W. 782 (Mich. 1890); People v. Nelson, 96 N.E. 1071 (Ill. 1911).
[233]State v. Powell, 70 N.W. 592 (Iowa 1897).
[234]Lone Jack Graded School District v. Henderson, 200 S.W.2d 736 (Ky. 1947); Lewis v. Board of Education of Johnson County, 348 S.W.2d 921 (Ky. 1961); Botts v. Prentiss County School Board, 166 So. 398 (Miss. 1936); Bartlett v. Kinsley 15 Conn. 327 (1843); State v. Smith, 80 S.W.2d 858 (Mo. 1935); Lawrence v. Trainer, 27 N.E. 197 (Ill. 1891); Commonwealth ex rel. Matthews v. Ford, 444 S.W.2d 908 (Ky. 1969).
[235]Bellmeyer v. Independent District of Marshalltown, 44 Iowa 564 (1876); Tufts v. State, 21 N.E. 892 (Ind. 1889); Smith v. Johnson, 178 N.W. 835 (Neb. 1920).

which came before the board for decision.[236]

Many states have statutes requiring boards of education to keep a record of their proceedings. Courts frequently are asked to determine the precise meaning of such statutes and, in so doing, have distinguished between those which are directory and those which are mandatory. Statutes which specify that a record is to be kept of certain types of action, or those which require that a roll call show the vote cast by each member of the board, generally have been held to be mandatory.[237] Failure to comply with the requirements of mandatory statutes will invalidate any action taken by the board. In Pennsylvania, for example, a statute provided that an agreement between school districts to establish a joint vocational school was to be recorded in the minutes of the respective districts. The Supreme Court of Pennsylvania held[238] this requirement to be mandatory, ruling that, where the minutes were not recorded, actions taken were not valid and the district was not bound by them. In Illinois, Ohio, Pennsylvania, and Colorado it has been held[239] that failure to record in the minutes the name of each member voting "aye" and "nay," as required by statute, was fatal to any action the board took.

Statutes which impose a general requirement that records of school board meetings be kept usually have been held to be directory in nature, and failure to keep records under such statutes will not invalidate actions taken by the board.[240] In a Massachusetts case it was held[241] that a school board rule excluding children under seven years of age from school unless they entered within four weeks after the opening of the fall term was not void because it did not appear in the board's minutes, despite the fact that a statute required a record of all orders and proceedings of the board. An Iowa case[242] also affirmed the position that a statute requiring an official record of board proceedings to be kept is directory only. In a suit to enjoin the county treasurer from paying tuition to a school district for pupils whose own school had been closed and later reopened, it was contended that the school had not been closed by legal board action because no record of the action appeared in the official records of the board. The court, however, upheld the validity of the action.

It is becoming increasingly common for statutes to require that proceedings of school board meetings be published. A Minnesota statute, for example, required publication of school board proceedings but did not specify in detail what was to be published. The court held[243] that the statute was directory and that it left the decision as to what should be published to the sound discretion of the board of education. The court also indicated that a statute requiring publication of school board proceedings carried the implication that minutes of the board's proceedings were to be kept.

2.16a Form and nature of

In general, the minutes of a school board meeting need not be formal or technical in nature.[244] As the court remarked in an early Iowa case:

Too strict rules should not be adopted with reference to records of the proceedings of school boards. They are usually kept by persons not versed in the law, and are generally quite informal in character. If they show the action in fact taken, although not conventionally or formally expressed, they should be held sufficient.[245]

The minutes of the board of education should show what actions were taken by the board and should show that the board acted

[236]Hankenson v. Board of Education, 134 N.E.2d 356 (Ill. 1956).

[237]Ready v. Board of Education, 17 N.E.2d 635 (Ill. 1938); Bituminous Casualty Corp. v. Folkerts, 27 N.E.2d 670 (Ill. 1940); Schafer v. Board of Education, 94 N.E.2d 112 (Ohio 1950); School District of Borough of Appollo v. School District of Township of Kiskiminetas, 159 A.2d 705 (Pa. 1960); Kerns v. School District, 515 P.2d 121 (Col. 1973).

[238]School District of Borough of Appollo v. School District of Township of Kiskiminetas, 159 A.2d 705 (Pa. 1960).

[239]Ready v. Board of Education, 17 N.E.2d 635 (Ill. 1938); Lippincott v. Board of Education, 97 N.E.2d 566 (Ill. 1951); Tate v. School District, 23 S.W.2d 1013 (Mo. 1929); School District No. 49 v. School District No. 65-R, 66 N.W.2d 561 (Neb. 1954); Union School Township v. Moon, 187 N.E. 332 (Ind. 1933).

[241]Alvord v. Inhabitants of Town of Chester, 61 N.E. 263 (Mass. 1901).

[242]School District of Soldier Township v. Moeller, 73 N.W.2d 43 (Iowa 1955).

[243]Ketterer v. Independent School District No. 1, 79 N.W.2d 428 (Minn. 1956).

[244]Cheatham v. Smith, 92 So.2d 203 (Miss. 1957); McClure v. Princeton Reorganized School District R-5, 328 S.W.2d 65 (Mo. 1959); Trustees of Slaughterville Graded School District v. Brooks, 173 S.W. 305 (Ky. 1915); Kinney v. Howard, 110 N.W. 282 (Iowa 1907); Quisenberry v. School District No. 6, 105 N.W. 982 (Neb. 1905).

[245]Kinney v. Howard, 110 N.W. 282 (Iowa 1907).

within the requirements of the law. They also ought to show that the required number of votes were cast in favor of each proposal adopted or approved[246] and, when statutes require, should list the names of the members casting affirmative and negative votes.[247]

The general rule is that statutes which require school board records to show "ayes" and "nays" are mandatory, and a statement that the measure was carried unanimously does not meet the requirements of such a statute.[248] Two reasons are advanced in support of this position. First, the public is entitled to know how each individual member of the board voted; second, a record of the "ayes" and "nays" is necessary to establish that a quorum was present at the time the vote was taken. Thus, under a Kentucky statute providing that a board of education could enter into contracts only with the approval of a majority of the members of the board, and that "ayes" and "nays" were to be entered upon its record, it was held that a record showing a contract had been entered into by unanimous vote was not sufficient. The court said:

> It is true the minute shows that at the opening of the board there were present a sufficient number of the members to constitute a quorum, and if they unanimously voted in favor of the acceptance of the bank's proposition the requirements of the statute would be substantially complied with so far as the requisite number was concerned. But it does not follow that, because there was a statutory quorum at the opening of the board, all these members remained until the proposition of the bank came up for acceptance or rejection. Common experience teaches that the contrary is usually true. The members of deliberative bodies come and go, and often, when there is not a call for the "yeas and nays," business is transacted with less than a quorum present.[249]

Under a statute requiring the clerk of the board to call the role of members publicly and to enter the names of those voting "aye"

and "nay," it has been held[250] that a record showing the vote cast by each member is sufficient even if the record does not explicitly state that the roll was called. However, omission from the record of the names of those voting "aye" and "nay" is fatal to the validity of the action.[251] It also has been ruled[252] that a record showing that all members of the board were present and that all voted affirmatively meets the requirements of such a statute.

The question of what constitutes an official record also has been raised. In keeping with the view that the records of a board of education need not be formal and technical, it has been held that a record consisting of sheets fastened into a record book with clips or pins is sufficient,[253] that minutes made on a piece of paper and not transcribed into the record book because of the illness of the clerk are sufficient,[254] and that records kept on half-sheets and quarter-sheets of paper, but not bound in book form, will suffice.[255]

2.16b Conclusiveness of

In general, it may be said that since a board of education speaks through its records, the official records of the board are prima facie evidence of its action. Consequently, parol evidence will not be admitted to deny, disprove, alter, or contradict the written record of the board.[256] In commenting on this rule a Michigan court said:

> When the law requires municipal bodies to keep records of their official action in the legislative business conducted at their meetings, the whole policy of the law would be defeated if they could rest partly in writing and partly in parol, and the true official history of their acts would perish with the living witnesses, or fluctuate with their

[246]Mathewson v. Factoryville School, 23 Pa.Co. 121 (1899).

[247]Price v. School District of Borough of Taylor, 42 A.2d 99 (Pa. 1945); Lippincott v. Board of Education, 97 N.E.2d 566 (Ill. 1951); Schafer v. Board of Education, 94 N.E.2d 112 (Ohio 1950); Kerns v. School District, 515 P.2d 121 (Col. 1973).

[248]Board of Education of City of Newport v. Newport National Bank, 90 S.W. 569 (Ky. 1906); Board of Education v. Best, 39 N.E. 694 (Ohio 1894); Steckert v. City of East Saginaw, 22 Mich. 103 (1870); Potts v. School District of Penn Township, 193 Atl. 290 (Pa. 1937).

[249]Board of Education of City of Newport v. Newport National Bank, 90 S.W. 569 (Ky. 1906).

[250]Beck v. Board of Education, 81 N.E. 1180 (Ohio 1907).

[251]Board of Education v. Best, 39 N.E. 694 (Ohio 1894).

[252]Burke v. Wilkes-Barre School District, 28 Pa.Super. 16 (1905).

[253]Trustees of Slaughterville Graded School District v. Brooks, 173 S.W. 305 (Ky. 1915).

[254]Foreman v. School District No. 25, 159 Pac. 1155 (Ore. 1916).

[255]Higgins v. Reed, 74 Am.Dec. 305 (Iowa 1859).

[256]Whaley v. Nocona Independent School District, 339 S.W.2d 265 (Tex. 1960); Schreiner v. City of Chicago, 92 N.E.2d 133 (Ill. 1950); Everts v. District Township of Rose Grove, 41 N.W. 478 (Iowa 1889); Cowley v. School District No. 3, 90 N.W. 680 (Mich. 1902); Cameron v. School District, 42 Vt. 507 (1869); Brooks v. School District of Franconia, 61 Atl. 127 (N.H. 1905); Vaughn v. School District No. 31, 39 Pac. 393 (Ore. 1895); Strine v. School District of Upper Merion Township, 27 A.2d 552 (Pa. 1942); Lewis v. Board of Education of Johnson County, 348 S.W.2d 921 (Ky. 1961); Commonwealth ex rel. Matthews v. Ford, 444 S.W.2d 908 (Ky. 1969).

conflicting memories. No authority was found, and we think none ought to be, which would permit official records to be received as either partial or uncertain memorials. That which is not established by the written records, fairly construed, cannot be shown to vary them. They are intended to serve as perpetual evidence, and no unwritten proofs can have this permanence.[257]

It has been held[258] that the official record of the meeting of a board of education imparts verity and is conclusive as to the matters set forth unless fraud or a mistake can be shown. The rule that the official record of the board cannot be contradicted or enlarged by parol evidence is designed to protect those whose rights are fixed or whose actions are governed by their dealings with public bodies, as well as to avoid the problems which would arise if evidence of board action were left to shifting sources.

The courts generally will admit parol evidence to supply omissions in the record, to clarify ambiguities in the record, or to provide information needed to establish the contents of records which have been lost or destroyed.[259] Parol evidence has been admitted to clarify the terms of a contract where the records of the board were ambiguous,[260] and to establish the action taken on a contract when no record of the action appeared in the minutes of the meeting.[261] The rule that parol evidence may be admitted to supply omissions in the record is illustrated by an Illinois case.[262] A statute provided that the school directors should appoint a clerk to keep a "record of all the official acts of the board in a well-bound book." Tho minutes of the board did not contain any record of the board's action in employing a teacher. Nevertheless, the court ruled that parol evidence could be admitted to supply the omission, stating, ". . . unless the law expressly and imperatively requires all matters to appear of rec-

ord, and makes the record the only evidence, parol proof is admissible to prove things omitted to be stated on the record." It should be noted, however, that, where statutes make the official record of the acts and proceedings of school boards the only record of what transpired, parol evidence will not be admitted.[263]

2.16c Time of recording
It is not necessary that the official record of board transactions be made at the time of the meeting. Notes may be taken and later transcribed into the official record book. It has been held[264] that a statute requiring a record to be kept of the proceedings of a board meeting does not mean that the record must be made or the minutes prepared before adjournment of the meeting; a record made after the meeting will meet the statutory requirement. It should be noted that the duties of the secretary or clerk of a board of education are purely clerical unless otherwise provided by statute.[265] Where statutes call for election or appointment of a clerk of the board and require that a person qualify for the office by taking a prescribed oath, it is necessary only that the clerk be duly qualified before preparing the official minutes. The fact that a clerk prepared the official minutes from notes made before the prescribed oath of office had been taken did not invalidate minutes prepared from such notes.[266] An action by a board of education is not invalidated because its clerk is absent from the meeting.[267]

2.16d Amendment of
The general rule in regard to the amendment of school board minutes or records is that a board of education has the power to correct, amend, or change a record to make it speak the truth.[268] Moreover, when a record has been properly amended, it

[257]Stevenson v. Bay City, 26 Mich. 44 (1872).

[258]Smith v. Board of Education of Ludlow, 23 F.Supp. 328 (Ky. 1938); Fiedler v. Eckfeldt, 166 N.E. 504 (Ill. 1929); Creech v. Board of Trustees of Common School District No. 15, 102 S.W. 804 (Ky. 1907).

[259]Tolleson Union High School District v. Kincaid, 85 P.2d 708 (Ariz. 1938); Hankenson v. Board of Education, 141 N.E.2d 5 (Ill. 1957); School District No. 9 v. District Boundary Board, 351 P.2d 106 (Wyo. 1960); Joint School District No. 7 v. Walworth County School Committee, 94 N.W.2d 695 (Wis. 1959); Cagle v. Wheeler, 242 S.W.2d 338 (Tenn. 1951); Kinney v. Howard, 110 N.W. 282 (Iowa 1907); People v. Hubble, 38 N.E.2d 38 (Ill. 1941); Higgins v. Reed, 74 Am.Dec. 305 (Iowa 1859).

[260]School District No. 2 v. Clark, 51 N.W. 529 (Mich. 1892).

[261]German Insurance Co. v. Independent School District, 80 Fed. 366 (8th Cir. 1897).

[262]School Directors v. Kimmel, 31 Ill.App. 537 (1889).

[263]*Ibid.*; State v. Scott, 86 N.E. 409 (Ind. 1908); Tucker v. McKay, 111 S.W. 867 (Mo. 1908); Callahan v. Mayor, 54 N.Y.S. 279 (1898).

[264]Kent v. School District No. 28, 233 Pac. 431 (Okla. 1925).

[265]Lowland School District No. 32 v. Wooldridge School District No. 34, 216 S.W.2d 545 (Mo. 1948).

[266]Bartlett v. Kinsley, 15 Conn. 327 (1843).

[267]Crabtree v. Board of Education, 270 N.E.2d 668 (Ohio 1970).

[268]Rogers & Tracy v. Board of Education, 99 F.2d 773 (7th Cir. 1939); Peter v. Kaufmann, 38 S.W.2d 1062 (Mo. 1931); Lingle v. Slifer, 131 N.E.2d 822 (Ill. 1956); State v. Board of Education, 101 N.E.2d 137 (Ohio 1952); State v. Smith, 80 S.W.2d 858 (Mo. 1935); Kent v. School District No. 28, 233 Pac. 431 (Okla. 1925); Harris v. School District, 28 N.H. 58 (1853); Williams v. Longtown School District No. 71, 468 S.W.2d 673 (Mo. 1971); Haight v. Board of Education of Community Unit School District No. 205, 329 N.E.2d 442 (Ill. 1975).

speaks as of the day on which the proceedings were taken.[269] It is not necessary that amendment of the record occur at the next meeting, or even during the next year. It has been held[270] that a record may be amended after a substantial period of time has elapsed and personnel on the board have changed. In an Illinois case[271] an action was brought against the board of education by a former music teacher to obtain reinstatement under a teacher tenure law after the position of music teacher was abolished. The teacher's contention was that the position had never been abolished by board action. A year after the incident the board had amended its records to show the action taken by the board in authorizing the dismissal. In approving the board's authority to amend its records in this case, the court said that "the record of a school board may be amended at any time to show what was in fact done at such proceeding."

The courts are in some disagreement as to the authority of the clerk of a board of education to change entries in the official proceedings of board meetings after expiration of that clerk's term of office. An Ohio court has held[272] that the clerk of a board cannot, by an independent act, amend or correct official entries in the minutes after expiration of the term of office. However, a Missouri court has ruled[273] that the clerk who wrote the original minutes had power to amend them to make them speak the truth in spite of the fact that the clerk had ceased to hold office several years before.

Restrictions upon

It is important to recognize that the right of a board of education to correct its record is not unlimited. Approval by a board of education of false or inaccurate minutes does not validate them.[274] Nor can the minutes or records be amended to suit the pleasure and convenience of the board. Records must be amended within a reasonable period of time. The determination of what constitutes a reasonable period of time must be made on the basis of the facts in each case. In an Illinois case,[275] for example,

an attempt was made to amend a record nineteen years after it was originally made. The court refused to uphold the board's action after the passage of this long period of time, pointing out that a record cannot be amended if parol testimony is uncertain, since facts cannot be established on the basis of uncertain memory.

An important restriction on the authority of a board of education to amend its records is found in the rule that a record may not be amended to the prejudice of third parties.[276] This rule is based on the principle that a board of education speaks through its records, and that third parties dealing with a board should not be required to look beyond the official account of its proceedings. The rule that the records of a board of education cannot be amended to the disparagement of the rights of innocent third parties is illustrated by a case[277] decided in a federal court. A board of education accepted a bid on tax anticipation warrants which were to be issued by the board. The successful bidder later sold the tax anticipation warrants to the appellee and received payment for them. However, he did not pay the board of education for thirty warrants, and the board refused to honor these warrants when they were presented for payment. The board later attempted to amend its minutes to show that the successful bidder had agreed to *sell* the bonds for the board rather than to *buy* them from the board. The court refused to permit the board to amend its minutes in this case, saying, "We have no doubt of the Board's power to correct its record so that it will speak the truth, but it cannot be done to the disparagement of rights of innocent third parties which have previously intervened."

2.16e Public nature of

Courts follow the general rule that the records and proceedings of boards of education are public documents and are open to inspection by the public.[278] The principles involved in this position are clearly illustrated in an Illinois case. A group of residents and taxpayers sought to inspect the

[269]Phenicie v. Board of Education, 157 N.E. 34 (Ill. 1927).

[270]Board of Education v. Trustees of Schools, 51 N.E. 656 (Ill. 1898); Lingle v. Slifer, 131 N.E.2d 822 (Ill. 1956).

[271]Lingle v. Slifer, 131 N.E.2d 822 (Ill. 1956).

[272]Beck v. Board of Education, 81 N.E. 1180 (Ohio 1907).

[273]State v. Smith, 82 S.W.2d 61 (Mo. 1935).

[274]Board of Education of City of Shawnee v. American National Co., 275 Pac. 285 (Okla. 1928).

[275]People v. Chicago Heights Terminal Transfer Railroad Co., 32 N.E.2d 161 (Ill. 1941).

[276]Rogers & Tracy v. Board of Education, 99 F.2d 773 (7th Cir. 1939); Sawyer v. Manchester & Keene Railroad Co., 62 N.H. 135 (1882); California Improvement Co. v. Moran, 60 Pac. 969 (Cal. 1900).

[277]Rogers & Tracy v. Board of Education, 99 F.2d 773 (7th Cir. 1939).

[278]People v. Peller, 181 N.E.2d 376 (Ill. 1962); Lehrman v. Board of Examiners, 195 N.Y.S.2d 478 (1959); Conover v. Board of Education of Nebo School District, 267 P.2d 768. (Utah 1954); see also Ravenna Education Association v. Ravenna Public Schools, 245 N.W.2d 562 (Mich. 1976).

financial records of the district and to make photographic reproductions of them. The board gave the group permission to examine the records but refused them permission to make photographic reproductions. The taxpayers brought action to compel the board to permit them to photograph the records, basing their suit on common law and also on the state records act. The board of education contended that the state records act did not apply to boards of education and, while conceding the taxpayers the right to examine the records, claimed that they had no right to make photographic reproductions of them. The court refused to accept the board of education's contentions. It ruled that the state records act did apply to boards of education and said further:

> The right of relators to reproduce the public records is not solely dependent upon statutory authority. There exists at common law the right to reproduce, copy and photograph public records as an incident to the common law right to inspect and use public records. Good public policy requires liberality in the right to examine public records.[279]

Questions occasionally arise as to the point in time at which notes taken by the secretary at board meetings become minutes and thus public documents. A Utah case dealt specifically with this question. The day following a board meeting a group of citizens requested permission to examine and copy the secretary's notes from which the minutes of the meeting were to be transcribed, but the secretary denied them permission to do so. In holding that the secretary's untranscribed notes were not "public writings" under the statute, the court observed that there appears to be no infallible rule of thumb by which one may determine when the notes of board proceedings become minutes. The court commented:

> . . . between two extremes, not necessarily midway, there is a point where reason shows brightest, dimming as the point shifts in one direction or the other. To hold that a public writing includes the unexpurgated scribbled notes of a Clerk, legible, perhaps, to him alone, would be unreasonable, we think, and even might deify doodling. It would be unreasonable also to hold that any record made by the Clerk short of approval by a board and placement in a Journal, is not a public writing. Such conclusion might deify dawdling. We hold, therefore, that the Clerk's untranscribed notes reasonably are not classifiable as a public writing under the statute, whereas the transcribed minutes, in final form, but awaiting only approval and placement in the Journal, are a public writing in contemplation of the statute.[280]

The court went on to state that, in its opinion, board minutes should be made available for public inspection within a reasonable time after the meeting. Obviously, what constitutes a reasonable time will vary according to the facts in a specific case.

2.17 SUMMARY

A board of education is a corporate body and exists separate and apart from its individual members. The individual members of a board of education cannot act or speak for the board in matters requiring the exercise of judgment and discretion. Only when the members of the board are meeting together in legal session are they empowered to act in such matters. It must be emphasized that an individual school board member is without power to commit the school district to a particular course of action.

A board of education has no inherent powers. All authority enjoyed by it is derived from the state through constitutional provisions and legislative enactments. Furthermore, all powers granted a board of education may be expanded, altered, or withdrawn by the people acting through their elected representatives. Any action attempted by it must be authorized by the state, either expressly or by clear implication. Where its authority to engage in a particular activity is questioned, the board must be able to point to statutes authorizing that activity. In practice, however, statutes seldom authorize specific activities. They usually are general in nature, authorizing by implication a broad range of activities. Faced with this dilemma, a board of education must determine whether or not a given activity falls within the scope of those activities which are authorized by clear implication.

In exercising its powers a board of education must adhere strictly to the methods prescribed by statutes. Failure to do so will invalidate the action. For example, if statutes require written contracts, oral contracts will not suffice; if competitive bidding is required, contracts awarded without competitive bidding will not be upheld.

It is important to recognize that a board of education may not delegate to a member, to a committee of members, or to its employees responsibility for decision or action in mat-

---

[279]People v. Peller, 181 N.E.2d 376 (Ill. 1962).

[280]Conover v. Board of Education of Nebo School District, 267 P.2d 768 (Utah 1954).

ters requiring the exercise of discretion. Boards of education may establish standing committees to give closer attention to specific operational areas, but the committees cannot legally act for the board. They may prepare reports and submit recommendations for action; final action must be taken by the full board. Furthermore, a board of education cannot delegate responsibility for decisions in matters requiring the exercise of the board's discretion to the superintendent or to other administrative officers of the district. The superintendent may bring recommendations to the board, but may not act for the board where exercise of the board's discretion is required.

The relationship between school boards and municipal officers and boards is often misunderstood, particularly where school district boundaries are coterminous with those of cities or villages. Fundamental to an understanding of their relationship is recognition of the fact that school districts and school boards are agencies of the state created to carry out a state function, while municipalities are political subdivisions of the state created for the purposes of local self-government. A board of education has jurisdiction only over the educational affairs of the district it serves. Its power to manage the district's affairs is complete and final, and it is subject to the control of municipal authorities only to the extent specified in the statutes.

When confronted with disputes involving actions taken by a board of education, the courts will inquire as to whether the action complained of was within the board's power; whether the board acted in the manner required by law; and whether the board's action was reasonable and not capricious, arbitrary or fraudulent. If these questions can be answered affirmatively, the courts will uphold the board's action; if not, they will declare the action invalid. A court will not substitute its judgment for that of a board of education, nor will it rule on the wisdom of a board's action. The courts will assume that a board of education acted legally and in good faith. Those who claim that a board acted irregularly or illegally or abused its discretion must establish their claim by clear and convincing evidence.

Since a board of education legally can act only when its members are meeting together in a properly called session, it is imperative that school board meetings be properly called and conducted. One important requirement is that each member receive notice of a school board meeting. Every board member should have knowl-

edge of the date, time, and place of each meeting and of the business to be transacted at the meeting. Notice of the meeting should be given far enough in advance of the meeting to enable board members to prepare for and to attend the meeting. If statutes give directions regarding the time at which notice is to be given, the content of the notice, or the method to be used in giving notice, such directions must be followed strictly. Failure in this regard will invalidate the meeting and any actions taken thereat. In general, formal notice of regularly scheduled meetings held at an established date, time, and place is unnecessary. However, formal notice of special meetings is required. Written notice of meetings is preferable. Regardless of how the notice is given, the person responsible for giving it should make certain that the notice is actually received by each board member.

It is essential that a quorum be present if business is legally to be transacted. Unless statutes specify otherwise, a majority of the membership of the board constitutes a quorum. When a quorum of the membership is present, a majority of those voting is sufficient to pass a measure. As in other matters, however, statutes which specify the number of members necessary to constitute a quorum, or which specify the percentage of votes required to pass a given measure, are controlling.

While strict adherence to technical rules of order is not required of boards of education, it is desirable that accepted rules of parliamentary procedure be followed. Boards of education should adopt and follow written rules and regulations for their own guidance, as well as for the guidance of those who deal with the board.

A clear and accurate written record of school board proceedings should be kept. The minutes and records of a board of education evidence its actions. Statutes which specify the content of school board minutes must be followed. Even in the absence of statutory requirements, however, the board's record should include an exact statement of all motions submitted for vote and should show the vote cast by each member. Unless an accurate written record of board proceedings is kept, the record of the board's actions must rest upon the memories of those present—an unreliable source at best.

The relationship between a board of education and the public is best summarized by stating that school board business is public business and school board records are public records. Many states have enacted legislation requiring that school board meetings be open to the public but permitting executive sessions to be held when the nature of the business or the public interest demands that a matter be kept confidential. Such statutory requirements must be followed explicitly. It is clear that the cause of education is best served when boards of education act openly and in good faith in transacting the business of the district.

The School Board Member

3.0 INTRODUCTION

Although a board of education legally may act only as a corporate body, nevertheless, the decisions of the board reflect the decisions of its individual members. Attention in this chapter is directed to matters of concern to the school board member as an individual—the nature of the office, legal aspects of obtaining and holding the office, and relinquishing the office.

3.1 NATURE OF THE OFFICE

School board members function as officers of the school district in administering the laws relating to the public schools. Their status as school officers is, to a large degree, derived from the fact that the board of education legally is regarded as an agency of the state which has been created by the state to perform a state function. Just as the local board of education is regarded as a state agency, so are its members regarded as state[1] or public[2] officers. A public officer is one who, by virtue of the office, is invested with the authority and duty to exercise some portion of the sovereign functions of government for the benefit of the public.[3]

The courts are in some disagreement, however, as to whether a member of a board of education is also to be regarded as a municipal officer. In some jurisdictions members of a board of education have been ruled[4] to be municipal officers, at least for certain purposes. Among such purposes are application of civil service rules,[5] compensation,[6] tenure,[7] recall,[8] and removal.[9] In other cases, however, members of boards of education have been held[10] not to be municipal officers and have been regarded as state or public officers only.[11] Although some courts regard the board of education as an arm of the municipal government,[12] courts in most jurisdictions do not consider school board members to be municipal officers[13] or to be mere agents of the school district.[14] Rather, school board members usually are considered officers of the school district, not officers of the municipality in which the district is located.[15] They act for the district in a public, governmental capacity.[16] Whether school board members will be held to be municipal officers depends primarily on the specific wording and intent of the statute or constitutional provision in question. The weight of authority, however, indicates that unless the statutes show a clear intent to the contrary, school board members are public or state officers.

3.1a Effect of appointment by mayor or city council

The fact that school board members are appointed by a mayor, city council, or municipal board does not subordinate them to the appointing officer or agency,[17] nor does it alter their status as state officers.[18] It

[1]Becker v. City of Albany, 118 P.2d 924 (Cal. 1941); City of New Haven v. Town of Torrington, 43 A.2d 455 (Conn. 1945); Norton v. Letton, 111 S.W.2d 1053 (Ky. 1937).
[2]Cobb v. City of Malden, 105 F.Supp. 109 (Mass. 1952); Conley v. Brophy, 60 S.E.2d 122 (Ga. 1950); Norton v. Letton, 111 S.W.2d 1053 (Ky. 1937); Sweeney v. City of Boston, 34 N.E.2d 658 (Mass. 1941); McKittrick v. Whittle, 63 S.W.2d 100 (Mo. 1933); Talbot v. Board of Education, 14 N.Y.S.2d 340 (1939); Gray v. Wood, 64 A.2d 191 (R.I. 1949); People v. Peller, 181 N.E.2d 376 (Ill. 1962); Ogden v. Raymond, 22 Conn. 379 (1853); Komyathy v. Board of Education, 348 N.Y.S.2d 28 (1973); Dayton Classroom Teachers Association v. Dayton Board of Education, 323 N.E.2d 714 (Ohio 1975).
[3]Floyd R. Mecham, *A Treatise on the Law of Public Offices and Officers* (Chicago: Callaghan & Co., 1890), pp. 1–2.
[4]Huettner v. City of Eau Claire, 9 N.W.2d 583 (Wis. 1943); Lansing v. Board of Education, 45 P.2d 1021 (Cal. 1935); Bonner v. Belsterling, 137 S.W. 1154 (Tex. 1911).
[5]Tanner v. Civil Service Commission of Minneapolis, 1 N.W.2d 602 (Minn. 1941).
[6]Stern v. Council of City of Berkeley, 145 Pac. 167 (Cal. 1914).
[7]Lansing v. Board of Education, 45 P.2d 1021 (Cal. 1935).
[8]Akerman v. Moody, 176 Pac. 696 (Cal. 1918); Blue v. Stockton, 355 P.2d 395 (Alaska 1960).
[9]Fowler v. Thomas, 275 S.W. 253 (Tex. 1925).

[10]Kirwan v. Speckman, 232 S.W.2d 841 (Ky. 1950); Warburton v. City of Quincy, 34 N.E.2d 661 (Mass. 1941); Frans v. Young, 46 N.W. 528 (Neb. 1890); People v. Rosenblum, 54 N.Y.S.2d 295 (1945); Chalfant v. Edwards, 33 Atl. 1048 (Pa. 1896).
[11]City of New Haven v. Town of Torrington, 43 A.2d 455 (Conn. 1945); Board of Education v. Society of Alumni, 239 S.W.2d 931 (Ky. 1951); Conley v. Brophy, 60 S.E.2d 122 (Ga. 1950); Sweeney v. City of Boston, 34 N.E.2d 658 (Mass. 1941); McKittrick v. Whittle, 63 S.W.2d 100 (Mo. 1933); Gray v. Wood, 64 A.2d 191 (R.I. 1949); Talbot v. Board of Education, 14 N.Y.S.2d 340 (1939); State v. Loechner, 91 N.W. 874 (Neb. 1902).
[12]State v. Board of School Directors, 111 N.W.2d 198 (Wis. 1961); Huettner v. City of Eau Claire, 9 N.W.2d 583 (Wis. 1943); Blue v. Stockton, 355 P.2d 395 (Alaska 1960).
[13]City of New Haven v. Town of Torrington, 43 A.2d 455 (Conn. 1945); Frans v. Young, 46 N.W. 528 (Neb. 1890); State v. Board of Commissioners of Elk County, 58 Pac. 959 (Kan. 1899); Lanza v. Wagner, 183 N.E.2d 670 (N.Y. 1962); Waterbury Teachers Association v. Furlong, 294 A.2d 546 (Conn. 1972).
[14]Morse v. Ashley, 79 N.E. 481 (Mass. 1906); Ogden v. Raymond, 22 Conn. 379 (1853); Agar v. Pagin, 79 N.E. 379 (Ind. 1906); State v. Fasse, 88 S.W. 1 (Mo. 1905); Schwing v. McClure, 166 N.E. 230 (Ohio 1929); State v. Jones, 224 S.W. 1041 (Tenn. 1920); Kimbrough v. Barnett, 55 S.W. 120 (Tex. 1900).
[15]Becker v. City of Albany, 118 P.2d 924 (Cal. 1941).
[16]Common School District v. Twin Falls Bank & Trust Co., 4 P.2d 342 (Ida. 1931).
[17]Ham v. Mayer *et al.* of New York, 70 N.Y. 459 (1877).
[18]Barnes v. District of Columbia, 91 U.S. 540, 23 L.Ed. 440 (D.C. 1875); City of Louisville v. Commonwealth, 121 S.W. 411 (Ky. 1909); Ward v. San Diego School District, 265 Pac. 821 (Cal. 1928).

has been held[19] that, when they appoint school board members, municipal officers are acting as ex officio state officers rather than as representatives of the municipality. The authority of the mayor or city council over school board members ceases with the act of appointment unless statutes make express provision to the contrary.

3.2 SELECTION OF SCHOOL BOARD MEMBERS

The method by which school board members are chosen is largely within the control of the state legislature. A state legislature, within such limitations as may be imposed upon it by the constitution of the state, has broad discretion in determining how members of boards of education are to be chosen.[20] The residents of a school district have no inherent right to choose the members of the district's board of education.[21] Any right to participate in the selection of school board members which the electors of a district may enjoy is the result of legislative action. The legislature may, if it chooses, name school board members directly, or it may provide for their appointment by some other officer or agency.[22] Furthermore, the legislature may designate the number of members which shall constitute a board of education,[23] may establish the qualifications which members of the board must have to be eligible for the office, and may through legislation determine the general character and composition of a board of education.[24]

The virtually complete authority of a state legislature over local boards of education is evident in a case challenging the constitutionality of a statute enacted by the New York State legislature, which peremptorily terminated the terms of office of members of the existing New York City Board of Educa-

tion and altered the method by which new board members were to be selected. The plaintiffs, incumbents who were removed from office, argued that the statute was unconstitutional under the home-rule provision of New York's constitution, that it constituted a bill of attainder, and that the establishment of a "selection board" to nominate candidates for the board of education constituted impermissible delegation of legislative authority. The court found no merit in these contentions. Home-rule restrictions were inapplicable since, as the court noted, "Education is a State, not a local function and members of New York City's Board of Education are state, not local, officers. . . ." The legislation was not a bill of attainder since it was aimed solely at the office, not at the incumbent officeholders. Vesting power to nominate candidates for a board was not an improper delegation of legislative authority because the state constitution granted the legislature authority to prescribe the method by which all officers, other than those provided for by the constitution, were to be chosen. After noting that each plaintiff held an office created by the legislature, the court said:

Absent any express constitutional limitation, the Legislature has full and unquestionable power to abolish an office of its creation or to modify its term, or other incidents attending it, in the public interest, even though the effect may be to curtail an incumbent's unexpired term.[25]

3.2a Eligibility for office

Obviously, in order legally to hold the office of school board member, a person must possess the prescribed qualifications for that office. It usually is necessary to search the statutes of the state to determine the qualifications which have been established for the office of school board member. Save as its authority is limited by the state constitution, it is the prerogative of the legislature to establish the qualifications which one must possess to be eligible for membership on a board of education.[26] The legislature may not, however, modify or contradict constitutional provisions relative to the qualifications required of persons who aspire to public office. Consequently, it has been held[27] that, where the constitution makes all persons who possess specified qualifications eligible to hold office, a stat-

[19]McDonnell v. City of New Haven, 121 Atl. 824 (Conn. 1923); School District v. Ryker, 68 Pac. 34 (Kan. 1902); Kuhn v. Thompson, 134 N.W. 722 (Mich. 1912).

[20]State v. Hine, 21 Atl. 1024 (Conn. 1890); State v. Board of Commissioners of Elk County, 58 Pac. 959 (Kan. 1899); Tate v. School District, 23 S.W.2d 1013 (Mo. 1930); Harris v. Burr, 52 Pac. 17 (Ore. 1898); Minsinger v. Rau, 84 Atl. 902 (Pa. 1912); Lorang v. High School District, 247 P.2d 477 (Mont. 1952); School District of Seward Education Association v. School District of Seward, 199 N.W.2d 752 (Neb. 1972).

[21]State v. Hine, 21 Atl. 1024 (Conn. 1890).

[22]Minsinger v. Rau, 84 Atl. 902 (Pa. 1912); Wilson v. School District of Philadelphia, 195 Atl. 90, 113 A.L.R. 1401 (Pa. 1937); Campbell v. Area Vocational-Technical School No. 2, 159 N.W.2d 817 (Neb. 1968).

[23]Kreiser v. Groenwald, 86 P.2d 990 (Okla. 1939); Smith v. Morton Independent School District, 85 S.W.2d 853 (Tex. 1935).

[24]Craig v. Bell, 46 S.E.2d 52 (S.C. 1948); Commonwealth v. King, 343 S.W.2d 139 (Ky. 1961); Adams v. Cisco, 107 N.W.2d 873 (Mich. 1961).

[25]Lanza v. Wagner, 183 N.E.2d 670 (N.Y. 1962).

[26]Wood v. Board of Election Commissioners, 168 N.E. 181 (Mass. 1929).

[27]Lacey v. State, 192 So. 576 (Miss. 1940).

ute which imposes additional requirements is invalid. For example, if a state constitution provided that all qualified electors shall be eligible to hold office, the legislature would have no authority to prescribe additional eligibility requirements.

In general, the various states impose relatively few qualifications for school board membership. However, when the legislature has prescribed the qualifications, only those persons possessing them may hold the office and discharge its duties.[28] There is also precedent supporting the position that only a real person may serve as a school board member, since it has been held[29] that a corporation, such as a bank or trust company, is not legally qualified to hold the office of treasurer of a school district.

Illustrative of qualifications which may be required of school board members are requirements that board members be residents of the district, that they own property within the district, that they pay taxes within the district, or that they possess a minimum level of education. In Michigan, for example, a statute was found to be valid which required that school board membership be limited to persons whose names appeared on the assessment roll and who owned the property assessed.[30] However, a person who owned property but whose name did not appear on the assessment role because of an error on the part of the assessor was held[31] to be qualified and could not be denied the office because of an omission by clerical error.

Payment of Taxes

Occasionally statutes require that a candidate must have paid school taxes for a specified period of time before becoming eligible to hold the office of school board member. Under such a statute it has been held[32] that a candidate for the office must show payment of the required taxes for the identical period specified in the statute. The candidate must also be able to show that the taxes were assessed against property in which there was a taxable interest at either the date of assessment or the date of payment. Nor is the requirement met where taxes are paid under a fraudulent scheme designed to show compliance.[33] However,

these decisions may be replaced by a recent case which held that a statute requiring ownership of property to be eligible to be a school board member was in violation of the equal protection clause of the Fourteenth Amendment.[34] In light of this and other recent cases declaring invalid the requirement of ownership of property or payment of taxes for eligibility to vote, these requirements for holding office are now probably invalid.

Residence in the District

A constitutional or statutory requirement that a public officer reside in the district to be served is quite common, and a candidate who does not satisfy the requirement is not eligible to serve.[35] If residence within the district is a necessary qualification for office, removal from the district with the intent to establish a home and residence elsewhere renders a candidate ineligible to hold the office. Moreover, an incumbent member becomes disqualified to continue to serve when that member becomes a permanent nonresident of the district.[36] However, it has been held[37] that the fact that a school board candidate resided in a trailer across a highway which formed a boundary of the district while awaiting the reconstruction of his home in the district where he had lived for many years did not make him ineligible for the office of school board member.

Questions occasionally arise when the statutes governing eligibility for school board membership are in conflict with those governing eligibility for public office in a city which is part of the school district. In such situations the statutes governing eligibility for school board membership control. Thus, persons who meet the statutory residence provisions for school board membership are eligible for the office even though they may not meet the requirement regarding residence in the city.[38]

Minimum Education

Several cases have arisen under a Kentucky statute which specified that candidates for the office of school board member must have at least an eighth-grade educa-

[28]State v. McSpaden, 39 S.W. 81 (Mo. 1897); Spencer v. Board of Education of City of Schenectady, 334 N.Y.S.2d 783 (1972); Blassman v. Markworth, 359 F.Supp. 1 (Ill. 1973).
[29]In re Treasurers of School Districts, 13 Pa. Dist. & Co. 395 (1930).
[30]Brady v. Weissenstein, 245 N.W. 798 (Mich. 1932).
[31]Adams v. Cisco, 107 N.W.2d 873 (Mich. 1961).
[32]State v. Macklin, 41 Mo.App. 335 (1890).
[33]State v. Rebenack, 36 S.W. 893 (Mo. 1896).

[34]Williams v. Lansing Board of Education, 245 N.W.2d 365 (Mich. 1976).
[35]Harris v. People, 81 P.2d 383 (Col. 1938); Oser v. Cullen, 435 S.W.2d 896 (Tex. 1968); State ex rel. Askew v. Thomas, 293 So.2d 40 (Fla. 1974); DeHond v. Nyquist, 318 N.Y.S.2d 650 (1971).
[36]Whitmarsh v. Buckley, 324 S.W.2d 298 (Tex. 1959); State ex rel. Askew v. Thomas, 293 So.2d 40 (Fla. 1974).
[37]Robinson v. Atkins, 275 So.2d 444 (La. 1973).
[38]People v. Mertz, 39 P.2d 422 (Cal. 1934).

tion in order to qualify to hold the office.[39] It is apparent from these cases that the burden of proving that the education requirement has been met rests with the candidate. In the absence of contradictory evidence, the courts generally have accepted a teacher's affidavit as evidence that the education requirement has been met.[40]

Age

Adoption of the Twenty-Sixth Amendment conferring on eighteen-year-olds the right to vote has resulted in several cases involving the question of whether or not a person who has attained the age of eighteen is eligible to hold the office of school board member. It has been held[41] that a state statute which fixes the minimum age for school board membership at twenty-one is not unreasonable or irrational, and that it violates neither the First Amendment right of free association nor the Fourteenth Amendment right to equal protection. In a New York case,[42] it was ruled that the Twenty-Sixth Amendment conferred only the right to vote at age eighteen and did not extend a concurrent right to hold a public office; therefore, an eighteen-year old was not eligible to serve on a board of education where the state's Public Officers Law stated that persons would not be eligible to hold a civil office unless they had attained the age of twenty-one.

A New Jersey statute which established the qualifications for school board membership did not include a minimum age qualification. In a case involving a sixteen-year-old student, it was held[43] that the legislature intended that one not old enough to vote was not qualified for the office of school board member and thus a sixteen-year old could not be a candidate for the office. High school students have been permitted to serve on the school board in other states.

Other

A person who has been convicted of a crime may be precluded from being a candidate for election to the position of school board member, whether or not the sentence was suspended.[44] It also has been decided[45] that school board members who violate a statute prohibiting them from voting on the appointment or reemployment of any person who is related to them are ineligible for reelection to the school board.

3.2b Time for meeting eligibility requirements

The legislature has full power to specify the time at which a candidate for the office of school board member must meet the qualifications established for the office. If a statute, either expressly or by necessary implication, prescribes the time at which a candidate must possess the requisite qualifications, any person who does not meet them at that time is ineligible to hold office[46] For example, if statutes provide that one must meet eligibility requirements at the time of election, a person who fails to do so at that time is not eligible for office even if that disqualification is removed prior to the time of taking office.[47]

In the absence of precise statutory direction the courts are in disagreement as to the time when eligibility requirements must be met. Court decisions have hinged on the interpretation given the word *eligible* in statutes relating to qualifications for office. In a majority of the cases it has been held[48] that the term is to be construed as the capacity of holding office rather than the capacity of being elected to office. Courts which have followed this line of reasoning have ruled that disqualification at the time of election is immaterial if the reason for the disqualification is removed before the candidate is inducted into office.[49] In *Bradfield v. Avery* the court was called upon to determine whether the eligibility requirements prescribed in a statute could be met after election but prior to induction into office, or

[44]Cardon v. Dauterive, 264 So.2d 806 (La. 1972).
[45]Commonwealth ex rel. Breckinridge v. Winstead, 430 S.W.2d 647 (Ky. 1968).
[46]Seals v. State, 51 So. 337 (Ala. 1910); Hummelshime v. Hirsch, 79 Atl. 38 (Md. 1910); People v. Board of State Canvassers, 29 N.E. 345 (N.Y. 1891); Bowring v. Dominguez, 44 P.2d 299 (Cal. 1935).
[47]Seals v. State, 51 So. 337 (Ala. 1910); People v. Board of State Canvassers, 29 N.E. 345 (N.Y. 1891).
[48]See 23 L.R.A. (n.s.) 1228; 88 A.L.R. 1026; 143 A.L.R. 1026.
[49]Bradfield v. Avery, 102 Pac. 687 (Ida. 1909); Demaree v. Scates, 32 Pac. 1123 (Kan. 1893); State v. Murray, 28 Wis. 96 (1871); People v. Hamilton, 24 Ill.App. 609 (1887); Hoy v. State, 81 N.E. 509 (Ind. 1907); State v. Huegle, 112 N.W. 234 (Iowa 1907); Jones v. Williams, 156 S.W. 876 (Ky. 1913); Powell v. Hart, 61 So. 233 (La. 1913); State v. Breuer, 138 S.W. 514 (Mo. 1911); State v. Breckenridge, 126 Pac. 806 (Okla. 1912); State v. Edwards, 130 Atl. 276 (Vt. 1925); Mosby v. Armstrong, 139 Atl. 151 (Pa. 1927); In re Kilburn, 284 N.Y.S. 748 (1936).

[39]Commonwealth v. Coffee, 329 S.W.2d 203 (Ky. 1959); Commonwealth v. King, 343 S.W.2d 139 (Ky. 1961); Spurlock v. Commonwealth, 350 S.W.2d 472 (Ky. 1961).
[40]Spurlock v. Commonwealth, 350 S.W.2d 472 (Ky. 1961).
[41]Blassman v. Markworth, 359 F.Supp. 1 (Ill. 1973); Human Rights Party of Ann Arbor v. Secretary of State, 370 F.Supp. 921 (Mich. 1973).
[42]Spencer v. Board of Education of City of Schenectady, 334 N.Y.S.2d 783 (1972).
[43]Vittoria v. West Orange Board of Education, 300 A.2d 356 (N.J. 1973).

whether it was necessary for them to be met prior to the time of the election. In holding that it was sufficient to meet the prescribed requirements prior to induction into office, the court said:

We are satisfied that the better reason is with the proposition that where the word "eligibility" is used in connection with an office, and there are no explanatory words indicating that such word is used with reference to time of election, it has reference to the qualification to hold the office rather than the qualification to be elected to the office. . . . "Eligible to the office" clearly implies the qualification or capacity to hold the office, and clearly indicates the intent of the Legislature to use the word "eligible" in the sense that it applies to the capacity or qualification of the person to the office.[50]

The interpretation of eligibility requirements is particularly important in states in which persons may not hold two or more specified public offices concurrently. Thus, under a New York statute which provided that "no trustee of a school district . . . shall be eligible to the office of supervisor of any town or ward in this state," it was held[51] that a school district trustee was qualified to be a candidate for the office of town supervisor and that the school trustee could qualify for that office by resigning his position as school trustee after election but before taking office as a town supervisor.

In some jurisdictions, however, it has been ruled[52] that one must possess the prescribed qualifications for the office at the time of election. In these jurisdictions it is not sufficient for a school board member to meet the qualifications prior to taking office; he must have them when he is elected. The fact that he may remove his disqualification after his election but prior to the time he takes office is of no consequence and does not qualify him for the position.

3.2c Election
Legal provisions governing school board elections will be found in Chapter 5.

3.2d Appointment
It is quite common for statutes to provide for the appointment of school board members by a designated officer or agency. This procedure frequently is followed in larger cities. The power to prescribe the procedure to be followed in the appointment of school board members rests with the legislature, not with the city council, mayor, or other governmental agency. It may be exercised only by the officer or agency so authorized, and the appointment must be made in conformity with statutory requirements.[53] That is, if the statutes specify the method and procedures to be used when school board members are appointed, the appointing authority has no power to alter the method. The situation is illustrated by a Wisconsin case in which the commissioners of a city attempted to change the way the members of the city board of education were appointed. According to state statutes, the school board members were to be appointed by the mayor, subject to confirmation by the city council. When a change was made to a commissioner form of city government, the commissioners attempted, by passing an ordinance, to provide for election of the members of the board of education by the city commissioners. In holding this ordinance invalid, the Wisconsin Supreme Court said:

The commissioners [of the city] had no power to provide by ordinance for the election of commissioners of education. The statutes then required that the commissioners of education should be appointed by the mayor, subject to confirmation of the council. That being so, the action of the commissioners in attempting to pass the ordinance and in attempting to select . . . a commissioner of education was wholly void and of no effect.[54]

In city school districts where members of the board of education are appointed by the mayor, confirmation by the city council is commonly required. It is clear that the city council has full authority to reject the mayor's appointment, but it has also been held[55] that a city council has power, after initially confirming a mayor's appointee, to reconsider its action and disapprove the appointment.

A judge or a court occasionally is given power to appoint school officers. When this power is vested in a court consisting of two or more judges, the court must exercise it as a whole. Thus, an appointment of a school board member made by one of several

[50]Bradfield v. Avery, 102 Pac. 687 (Ida. 1909).

[51]People v. Kenyon, 136 N.Y.S. 525 (1912), *affirmed* 101 N.E. 117.

[52]Finklea v. Farrish, 49 So. 366 (Ala. 1909); Searcy v. Grow, 15 Cal. 118 (1860); Shaw v. DeVane, 151 S.E. 347 (Ga. 1930); State v. Sullivan, 47 N.W. 802 (Minn. 1891); Roane v. Matthews, 21 So. 665 (Miss. 1897); State v. Wait, 146 N.W. 1048 (Neb. 1914); State v. Clark, 3 Nev. 566 (1867); State v. Powell, 126 Pac. 954 (Wash. 1912); Rasin v. Leaverton, 28 A.2d 612 (Md. 1942).

[53]People v. Rosenblum, 54 N.Y.S.2d 295 (1945); State v. Carlson, 199 N.W. 70 (Wis. 1924).

[54]State v. Carlson, 199 N.W. 70 (Wis. 1924).

[55]People v. Davis, 120 N.E. 326, 2 A.L.R. 1650 (Ill. 1918).

judges acting independently has been held[56] invalid.

As in the case of elections, strict compliance with statutory procedures concerning the appointment of school board members is required only where the provisions of the statutes are mandatory. Slight irregularities in complying with the directory provisions of statutes generally will not invalidate the appointment of a school board member in the absence of evidence of fraud or abuse.[57] It is advisable, however, to follow closely the procedures prescribed by the statutes to avoid the need for litigation to determine the validity of the appointment.

3.2e Evidence of election or appointment

Questions sometimes are raised concerning the point in time when a candidate is regarded as legally elected. It has been held[58] that a member of a board of education is considered elected when returns of the election have been canvassed and the result of the election has been declared by an agent authorized by law to do so, and that a candidate has not been elected until these acts are completed. The duty of a canvassing board in declaring the results of a school board election is purely ministerial.[59] Such a board may not refuse to perform its duty and, if necessary, its performance may be enforced by a mandamus action.

When a certificate of election is required, one who claims to have been elected to an office but who does not have a certificate of election has no claim upon the office.[60] A certificate of appointment or election is regarded as prima facie evidence of title to office, unless, of course, the election was held without statutory or constitutional authority.[61] When statutes provide that the record of the meeting at which an election takes place is to be the sole and conclusive evidence of what transpired, the courts will not accept parol evidence to prove the result of an election.[62] In fact, it has been held[63] that absence from the official record of the fact of the election to office is proof that the

claimant was not elected. Oral testimony regarding the outcome of a school election will be accepted, however, when the statutes do not require that the record of the meeting be the sole and conclusive evidence of what happened at the election.[64]

3.3 OFFICIAL OATHS AND BONDS—QUALIFYING FOR OFFICE

School officers are frequently required, either by constitutional or by statutory provisions, to qualify for office by taking an oath, giving a bond, or both. Where an oath or bond is required, a person who has been elected or appointed a school board member must meet the requirement before that person is legally entitled to hold office.[65] Although their language may be quite explicit, statutes fixing the time within which school officers must qualify by taking an oath or giving a bond are generally regarded as directory, and a delay in qualifying does not, in itself, create a vacancy in the office.[66] The Supreme Court of Ohio has said in this regard.

The law does not look with favor upon declaring a forfeiture in an office to which one has been elected in a legal manner, and where the office has not been declared vacant, and no other rights or title have intervened, such irregularities as failure to give bond, or take the oath of office within a certain time, have not generally been held to be sufficient grounds for declaring a forfeiture of the office.[67]

Even where statutes provide that a vacancy will exist if school officers have failed to qualify within a prescribed period of time, the courts are in disagreement as to whether the failure of elected officers to qualify within the prescribed time results ipso facto in a forfeiture. Some jurisdictions have held[68] that a vacancy is created in such a

---

[56]*In re* Hanover Township School Directors, 137 Atl. 811 (Pa. 1927).

[57]Price v. School District of Borough of Taylor, 42 A.2d 99 (Pa. 1945).

[58]Green v. Jones, 108 S.E.2d 1 (W.Va. 1959); State v. Meder, 38 Pac. 668 (Nev. 1895).

[59]Stearns v. Twin Butte Public School District No. 1, 185 N.W.2d 641 (N.D. 1971).

[60]Chapman v. Freeman, 179 S.W. 450 (Ky. 1915).

[61]Jewitt v. West, 127 Pac. 476 (Okla. 1912).

[62]Otey v. Westerman, 276 Ill.App. 395 (1934).

[63]*Ibid.*

[64]State v. Cahill, 105 N.W. 691 (Iowa 1906).

[65]Meadors v. Patrick, 56 S.W. 652 (Ky. 1900); School District of Omaha v. Adams, 39 N.W.2d 550 (Neb. 1949); Edgemont Independent School District v. Wickstrom, 223 N.W. 948 (S.D. 1929); Scherz v. Telfer, 74 S.W.2d 327 (Tex. 1934).

[66]State v. Heath, 132 S.W.2d 1001 (Mo. 1939); State v. Stratte, 86 N.W. 20 (Minn. 1901); Howland v. Luce, 16 John. 135 (N.Y. 1819); State v. Cave, 26 Ohio C.C.R. 301 (1904); Buchanan v. Graham, 81 S.W. 1237 (Tex. 1904); Commissioners of Knox County v. Johnson, 24 N.E. 148 (Ind. 1890); City of Chicago v. Gage, 95 Ill. 593 (1880); State v. Falconer, 44 Ala. 696 (1870); State v. Churchill, 41 Mo. 27 (1867).

[67]State v. Turner, 144 N.E. 599 (Ohio 1924).

[68]School District of Omaha v. Adams, 39 N.W.2d 550 (Neb. 1949); Ashby v. Patrick, 28 S.W.2d 55 (Ark. 1930); Chiles v. Todd, 43 Ky. 126 (1843).

situation; others have ruled[69] that failure to qualify within the prescribed time results merely in ground for forfeiture of the office.

Although one may not necessarily forfeit one's office by failing to qualify within the prescribed time, delay in taking the oath of office or filing the required bond should be avoided. Unless substantial compliance with statutory requirements has taken place, a person is not duly qualified and is not legally entitled to hold office.[70] Furthermore, when delay persists beyond the time fixed by statute for qualifying, and the authority in whom the law lodged the power to fill a vacancy has appointed another to the office, a person who neglected to qualify as required has absolutely forfeited any title to the office and cannot regain title by qualifying thereafter.[71] However, a person who has been prevented from qualifying for the office to which that person was elected by a conspiracy between the qualifying officer and an incumbent of the office becomes the lawful holder of the office.[72]

The courts are reluctant to declare that an office has been forfeited by an inadvertent act on the part of a school officer. A Kentucky case illustrates their reasoning. Three members of a county school board were elected to office and took the constitutionally required oath prior to taking office. However, they inadvertently failed to take an additional oath required by statute until five months later, when, upon discovering their omission, they took the oath in writing and entered it in the records of the board. Action was brought by the attorney general to remove them from office because of their failure to take the statutory oath prior to taking office. The court ruled[73] that their failure to take the statutory oath did not cause them to forfeit the office, stating that "the innocent and inadvertent omission of a public officer who has taken the Constitutional oath to take some further oath prescribed by statute does not forfeit his office or authorize his removal from it."

3.4 INCOMPATIBLE OFFICES

Questions arise occasionally as to whether or not a school board member may concurrently hold some other public office. It is a well-accepted principle of law that a public officer cannot hold two incompatible public offices at the same time. The basis of this principle is that it is not in the public interest for a person to hold two public offices the duties of which might conflict, with the result that performance of the duties of one office would interfere with or be compromised by performance of the duties required of the other office. Many states have enacted constitutional or statutory provisions which expressly declare certain offices to be incompatible. However, even in the absence of such provisions, common law forbids the holding of incompatible offices. The distinction between the two was noted by the Court of Appeals of Kentucky in an action brought by the attorney general to determine whether the office of member of a county board of education was incompatible with the office of county election commissioner. In holding that the two offices were incompatible, the court said:

> There are two kinds of incompatibility between offices which have been recognized and applied in declaring the first office vacant upon acceptance of the latter. The first is a constitutional or statutory incompatibility, which is one so declared by the Constitution or legislative enactment. The second is a common-law or functional incompatibility, which is declared by courts without the aid of specific constitutional or statutory prohibition, when the two offices are inherently inconsistent or repugnant, or when the occupancy of the two offices is detrimental to the public interest.[74]

It is often difficult, in the absence of specific statutory or constitutional direction, to determine whether two public offices are, in fact, incompatible. It is often impossible to predict how the courts will rule in a given instance. In general, public offices are incompatible if one of the offices is subordinate to the other in one or more particulars, e.g., being subject to appointment or removal power, or if the performance of the duties of one office conflicts with the performance of the duties of the other so as to be incompatible with full and complete performance of the duties of both offices by the same officer.[75] Some direction is provided by a New York case in which the court said:

[69]State v. Stewart, 135 Pac. 1182 (Kan. 1913); Sprowl v. Lawrence, 33 Ala. 674 (1859); City of Chicago v. Gage, 95 Ill. 593 (1880); State v. Ring, 11 N.W. 233 (Minn. 1882).

[70]Minnick v. State, 56 N.E. 851 (Ind. 1900).

[71]State v. Board of Education of Curry District, 115 S.E. 726 (W.Va. 1923); Minnick v. State, 56 N.E. 851 (Ind. 1900); Owens v. O'Brien, 78 Va. 116 (1883).

[72]Culver v. Armstrong, 43 N.W. 776 (Mich. 1889).

[73]Commonwealth v. Marshall, 361 S.W.2d 103 (Ky. 1962).

[74]Adams v. Commonwealth, 268 S.W.2d 930 (Ky. 1954).

[75]People v. Green, 58 N.Y. 295 (1874); State v. Bus, 36 S.W. 636 (Mo. 1896); Polley v. Fortenberry, 105 S.W.2d 143 (Ky. 1937); Tucci v. Nyquist, 322 N.Y.S.2d 476 (1971).

Where one office is not subordinate to the other, nor the relations of the one to the other such as are inconsistent and repugnant, there is not that incompatibility from which the law declares that the acceptance of the one is the vacation of the other. The force of the word, in its application to this matter is, that from the nature and relations to each other, of the two places, they ought not to be held by the same person, from the contrariety and antagonism which would result in the attempt by one person to faithfully and impartially discharge the duties of one, toward the incumbent of the other. . . . The offices must subordinate, one the other, and they must, per se, have the right to interfere, one with the other, before they are incompatible in common law. [76]

Clearly, a school board member may simultaneously hold another public office if the duties as a school board member and the duties of the other public office do not conflict. It has been held,[77] for example, that the position of deputy sheriff is not incompatible with the position of school director. Consequently, a person could hold both offices at the same time. Teachers are not eligible to serve as school board members for districts in which they are employed because of conflict of interest.[78] Teachers, supervisors or administrators may, unless prohibited by statute, serve as school board members in school districts other than the one in which they are employed.[79]

Under the common-law rule, as well as under statute, a public officer who accepts another office incompatible with the office held currently automatically relinquishes the right to the original office.[80] This is illustrated by a Texas case in which a person who had been appointed tax collector for a school district about two weeks later was elected sheriff and tax collector for the county. He later defaulted, and suit was brought against his sureties for the amount lost by the district as a result of his defalcation. In holding that his sureties were not liable, the court ruled that under Texas statutes the district collector had immediately vacated his office as tax collector for the school district when he accepted the office of sheriff and county tax collector. The court said:

If a person holding an office is elected or appointed to another (where the two offices cannot be legally held by the same person) and he accepts and qualifies as to the second, such acceptance and qualification operate, ipso facto, as a resignation of the former office. [81]

An exception to the rule that acceptance of an incompatible office automatically vacates the first office is to be found in states where statutory or constitutional provisions specify that an officer shall hold office until a successor is elected and qualified. In these cases acceptance of an incompatible office does not vacate the first office.[82] In interpreting such a statute, the Supreme Court of New Mexico ruled[83] that, while the offices of school board member and clerk of the board of education were, under New Mexico law, incompatible, a school board member did not create a vacancy in that office by accepting the position of clerk of the board; the school board member merely lost the right to continue to hold that office when a properly elected and qualified successor was presented. The courts reason that under statutes of this type incumbents have no authority to remove themselves from positions by their own act.

In some states the statutes provide that an incumbent who accepts certain other offices automatically vacates the first office held. In the state of New York, for example, a statute specified that acceptance of the office of either district superintendent or town supervisor by a member of a board of education would vacate the office. Thus, when a school board member accepted the office of town supervisor, he was held[84] automatically to have vacated his office as school board member. Under statutes like this the question of whether the offices are incompatible is not an issue. Rather, the act of accepting a specified office automatically terminates the incumbent's tenure in the previous office.

3.5 DETERMINING TITLE TO OFFICE—QUO WARRANTO ACTION

Disputes sometimes arise as to whether school board members legally are entitled to their offices. It may be claimed that they did not possess the qualifications required of candidates, that their elections were irregular, or that they did not properly qualify for

[76]People v. Green, 58 N.Y. 295 (1874).

[77]State v. Bus, 36 S.W. 636 (Mo. 1896).

[78]Visotcky v. City Council of City of Garfield, 273 A.2d 597 (N.J. 1971); Haskins v. State ex rel. Harrington, 516 P.2d 1171 (Wyo. 1973).

[79]Commonwealth ex rel. Waychoff v. Tekavec, 319 A.2d 1 (Pa. 1974).

[80]People v. Brooklyn, 77 N.Y. 503 (1879); Edwards v. Board of Education of Yancey County, 70 S.E.2d 170 (N.C. 1952); Pruitt v. Glen Rose Independent School District No. 1, 84 S.W.2d 1004 (Tex. 1935).

[81]Pruitt v. Glen Rose Independent School District No. 1, 84 S.W.2d 1004 (Tex. 1935).

[82]Badger v. United States, 93 U.S. 599, 23 L.Ed. 991 (Ill. 1876); State v. Nobles, 85 N.W. 367 (Wis. 1901); People v. Supervisor, 100 Ill. 332 (1881); Haymaker v. State, 163 Pac. 248 (N.M. 1917).

[83]Haymaker v. State, 163 Pac. 248 (N.M. 1917).

[84]Application of Cole, 115 N.Y.S.2d 751 (1952).

office after election. Regardless of the reason for the protest, the public interest requires that a public officer, in active possession of office and performing its duties, be recognized as that officer until such time as that person has been removed from office by a proper legal proceeding.[85] It would not be in the public interest to permit reckless attacks on the acts of public officials or to permit their authority to perform the duties of their office to be questioned indiscriminately. Consequently, it has been widely held[86] that the title to office of a school board member is not subject to collateral attack. In practice, this means that an injunction will not be granted to prevent persons holding school offices from exercising the duties thereof,[87] nor can a school board member's title to office be questioned in a mandamus action.[88] It has been held, for example, that the title to office of a school board member cannot be tried in a suit for an injunction to restrain the collection of taxes levied by the board,[89] and that in an action for breach of contract it cannot be shown that a school board treasurer lacks title to office because of failure to file a bond.[90]

The proper method of contesting an alleged school board member's title to office is by a quo warranto action.[91] Such an action is brought to determine directly the right by which an officer is exercising the duties of the office of which possession is claimed. The action is instituted in the name of the state by the attorney general or some other officer representing the state. In speaking of the remedy of quo warranto, the Supreme Court of Pennsylvania has said:

Quo warranto is the Gibralter of stability in government tenure. Once a person is duly elected or duly appointed to public office, the continuity of his services may not be interrupted and the uniform working of the governmental machinery disorganized or disturbed by any proceeding less than a formal challenge to the office by that action which is now venerable with age, reinforced by countless precedent, and proved to be protective of all parties involved in a given controversy, namely, quo warranto.[92]

It is for the state to question the title of those who claim to be its officers, and if the state is satisfied, private citizens may not complain. In fact, a private citizen cannot bring a quo warranto action if there is no interest in the matter which differs from that of the public at large.[93] The reasoning of the courts has been stated concisely by the Supreme Court of the United States:

Offices are created for the benefit of the public, and private parties are not permitted to inquire into the title of persons clothed with the evidence of such offices and in apparent possession of their powers and functions. For the good order and peace of society their authority is to be respected and obeyed until in some regular mode prescribed by law their title is investigated and determined. It is manifest that endless confusion would result if in every proceeding before such officers their title could be called into question.[94]

Whether a private citizen has sufficient special interest to institute quo warranto proceedings to determine the title to office of a school board member will depend upon the facts of the specific case although it has been held[95] that a person who claims title to an office may institute quo warranto proceedings to oust the incumbent. It should be noted, however, that a school board cannot pass on the qualifications of its members, question their title to office, or refuse to seat a person who has been duly elected unless the board has been given specific authority to do so.[96]

[85]State v. Board of Commissioners of Warrick County, 25 N.E. 10 (Ind. 1890); State v. Foxworthy, 256 S.W. 466 (Mo. 1923); In re Vacancy in Board of School Directors of Carroll Township, 180 A.2d 16 (Pa. 1962).

[86]Roberts v. Bright, 133 So. 907 (Ala. 1931); State v. Board of Commissioners of Warrick County, 25 N.E. 10 (Ind. 1890); Schmohl v. Williams, 74 N.E. 75 (Ill. 1905); DeLoach v. Newton, 68 S.E. 708 (Ga. 1910); State v. Hart, 61 S.W. 780 (Tenn. 1901); Griffin v. Thomas, 206 Pac. 604 (Okla. 1922).

[87]Brady v. Sweetland, 13 Kan. 37 (1874); Hagner v. Heyberger, 7 Watts v. Serg. 104 (Pa. 1844); Coleman v. Glenn, 30 S.E. 297 (Ga. 1898); School District No. 116 v. Wolf, 98 Pac. 237 (Kan. 1908).

[88]People v. Askins, 200 Ill.App. 621 (1915).

[89]Brown v. Fouts, 138 N.E. 721 (Ill. 1923).

[90]Martin v. Common School District No. 3, 204 N.W. 320 (Minn. 1925).

[91]Olsen v. Merrill, 5 P.2d 226 (Utah 1931); In re Vacancy in Board of School Directors of Carroll Township, 180 A.2d 16 (Pa. 1962); State v. Whitford, 233 S.W.2d 694 (Mo. 1950); Awalt v. Beeville Independent School District, 226 S.W.2d 913 (Tex. 1949); Board of Education of Martin v. Cassell, 220 S.W.2d 552 (Ky. 1949); Romine v. Black, 25 N.E.2d 404 (Ill. 1939); Green Mountains School District No. 103 v. Durkee, 351 P.2d 525 (Wash. 1960).

[92]In re Vacancy in Board of School Directors of Carroll Township, 180 A.2d 16 (Pa. 1962).

[93]Norton v. Shelby County, 118 U.S. 425, 6 S.Ct. 1121, 30 L.Ed. 178 (Tenn. 1885); Connine v. Smith, 157 N.W. 450 (Mich. 1916); Miller v. Feather, 195 S.W. 449 (Ky. 1917).

[94]Norton v. Shelby County, 118 U.S. 425, 6 S.Ct. 1121, 30 L.Ed. 178 (Tenn. 1885).

[95]See annotation at 21 L.R.A. (N.S.) 685.

[96]Dando v. Lord, 71 Pa. Dist. & Co. 370 (1950); Stearns v. Twin Butte Public School District No. 1, 185 N.W.2d 641 (N.D. 1971).

3.6 DE FACTO SCHOOL OFFICERS

The legality of the actions of a board of education occasionally is questioned on the ground that the entire board or one or more of its individual members are not legally holding office. In situations of this type the law relating to *de facto* officers is usually invoked. A *de facto* officer is one who appears to be the officer claimed to be, and is accepted as such by the public, but who is not legally entitled to hold the office claimed. A *de jure* officer, on the other hand, is one who has the lawful right of title to be office. It has been said:

To constitute a person an officer de facto, he must be in the actual possession of the office, and in the exercise of its functions, and in the discharge of its duties. . . . The distinction, then, which the law recognizes, is that an officer de jure is one who has the lawful right or title, without the possession, of the office; while an officer de facto has the possession, and performs the duties, under the color of right, without being actually qualified in law so to act, both being distinguished from the mere usurper, who has neither lawful title nor color of right.[97]

To be considered a *de facto* officer, one must be in actual possession of the office and exercising its functions under some color of title and with the acquiescence of the public.[98]

3.6a Examples of

A school board member whose title to office is defective often attains the status of a *de facto* officer. One common cause of defective title to office is an election or appointment which is irregular or illegal. However, a school officer whose acts are accepted by the public is regarded as a *de facto* officer in spite of the fact that the election or appointment was void.[99] For example, school trustees who were elected at an election called by one without authority to do so, but who were approved, recognized, and issued commissions by a county board of education which had authority to call the election, were held[100] to be *de facto* officers.

One also may attain the status of a *de facto* school officer, even though ineligible for the office, if one is elected or appointed and exercises the functions of the office.[101] Thus, a member of a township board of assessors who was appointed a school trustee and performed the duties of both offices was held[102] to be a *de facto* officer despite the fact that according to the constitution of South Carolina no person may hold two offices of honor or trust at the same time. In this case, it should be noted, a school trustee was held to be a *de facto* officer even though at the time of his appointment he was disqualified from legally holding the office. This point is also illustrated by a Michigan case in which two justices of the peace were elected school board members despite the fact that a statute made justices of the peace ineligible to hold membership on a board of education and stipulated that any votes cast for justices of the peace should be void. The two men served as school board members for practically a year, during which time it was voted to issue bonds. Later an action was brought to enjoin the issuance of the bonds, on the ground that the two board members in question had acted without authority. The court, however, ruled[103] that their acts were valid, since they were *de facto* officers.

A person who has failed to qualify for the office of school board member because of failure to take an oath or give a bond also may be regarded as a *de facto* officer.[104] Consequently, it was held[105] that, despite school board members' violation of a loyalty oath requirement in filing their loyalty oaths in the office of the county superintendent rather than in the office of the county clerk as the statutes required, they were *de facto* officers.

A school board member who has vacated the office by moving to another school district may be regarded as a *de facto* officer if that person continues to serve with the ac-

---

[97]Hamlin v. Kassafer, 15 Pac. 778 (Ore. 1887).

[98]Bishop v. Fuller, 110 N.W. 715 (Neb. 1907); School Town of Milford v. Zeigler, 27 N.E. 303 (Ind. 1891); State v. Hart, 61 S.W. 780 (Tenn. 1901); Awalt v. Beeville Independent School District, 226 S.W.2d 913 (Tex. 1949); Rhodes v. McDonald, 24 Miss. 418 (1852); Center Hill School District No. 32 v. Hunt, 110 S.W.2d 523 (Ark. 1937); Hazelton-Moffit Special School District No. 6 v. Ward, 107 N.W.2d 636 (N.D. 1961); Green Mountain School District No. 103 v. Durkee, 351 P.2d 525 (Wash. 1960); Hatfield v. Jimerson, 365 P.2d 980 (Okla. 1961).

[99]Awalt v. Beeville Independent School District, 226 S.W.2d 913 (Tex. 1949); Gardner v. Goss, 227 S.W. 25 (Ark. 1921); Miller v. Feather, 195 S.W. 449 (Ky. 1917); Howard v. Burke, 93 N.E. 775 (Ill. 1910); Hazelton-Moffit Special School District No. 6 v. Ward, 107 N.W.2d 636 (N.D. 1961).

[100]DeLoach v. Newton, 68 S.E. 708 (Ga. 1910).

[101]Connine v. Smith, 157 N.W. 450 (Mich. 1916); State v. Carroll, 38 Conn. 449 (1871); Rowan v. Board of Education of Logan County, 24 S.E.2d 583 (W.Va. 1943).

[102]Dove v. Kirkland, 75 S.E. 503 (S.C. 1912).

[103]Connine v. Smith, 157 N.W. 450 (Mich. 1916).

[104]Rhodes v. McDonald, 24 Miss. 418 (1852); Hatfield v. Jimerson, 365 P.2d 980 (Okla. 1961); State v. Carroll, 38 Conn. 449 (1871).

[105]Hatfield v. Jimerson, 365 P.2d 980 (Okla. 1961).

quiescence of the public.[106] Also, a school officer who forfeits the office by accepting an incompatible office but continues to serve as a school officer may be considered a *de facto* officer.[107]

3.6b When no de facto relationship exists

Not everyone who claims title to a school office will be regarded as a *de facto* officer. A person cannot become a *de facto* officer by merely claiming title to the office.[108] One must possess some color of title to the office, such as an election or appointment. This principle of law is clearly illustrated in a case brought by a teacher to recover damages for the alleged breaching of a contract of employment negotiated by one who claimed to be a school trustee. In holding that the person who claimed to be a trustee could not be regarded as a *de facto* officer the court said:

> . . . to constitute a de facto officer, it is essential that his acts of official character be founded upon some colorable right to the office, having the form of election or appointment, or that he has acted as such, with the acquiescence of the public, for a sufficient length of time to permit the presumption of an election or appointment. . . . The mere claim of a person that he is an officer does not relieve his acts from the character of usurpation, and give him the character of an officer de facto, unless he has notoriously performed them for such length of time, with the acquiescence of the public, as to give him the general reputation in the official district of being in that respect what he thus assumes to be.[109]

It is also clear that there cannot be a *de facto* officer unless there exists a *de jure* office.[110] In fact, there can be no officer, either *de facto* or *de jure*, unless there is an office to fill. It was held,[111] for example, that a school trustee elected under a statute which had not yet gone into effect had no status as

an officer, either *de facto* or *de jure*. Similarly, when more school board members are elected than the number specified by the statute creating the district, those elected cannot be given the status of *de facto* officers.[112] It has been held[113] that, under a statute entitling an area to representation on a district school board only when the area contained a certain population and a certain amount of taxable property, an area which did not meet these requirements had no *de jure* office to fill, and a member of the board of education elected from that area was not a *de facto* school officer.

A *de jure* officer and a *de facto* officer cannot be in simultaneous possession of the same office; neither can there be both a *de jure* and a *de facto* board of education in office at the same time.[114] Since one who contracts with a board of education does so at one's own risk, one who contracts with a *de facto* board of education when a *de jure* board of education exists cannot recover under the contract.[115] However, when two persons claim the same office, and the *de jure* officer fails to perform the functions of the office, the acts of a *de facto* officer who does perform them are binding. Thus, when two high school boards were elected in the same district and the *de jure* board failed to act pending the outcome of the controversy whereas the irregularly elected board issued bonds, employed teachers, and levied taxes, an injunction to prevent the collection of taxes levied by the *de facto* board was refused.[116] The court reasoned that, while *de jure* officers did exist, they made no attempt to exercise the functions of their office and consequently those who were in possession of the office and acted must be regarded as a *de facto* board of education. In fact, in an Ohio case it was held[117] that where there was a *de facto* school board in possession of the office the acts of the *de jure* board which was not in possession of the office were invalid.

A *de facto* body cannot appoint a *de jure* officer. This principle is illustrated by a case in which a school board, by a vote of four to two, named a seventh member to the

---

[106]Center Hill School District No. 32 v. Hunt, 110 S.W.2d 523 (Ark. 1937); Hardrick v. State, 185 S.E. 577 (Ga. 1936); Graham v. School District No. 69, 54 Pac. 185 (Ore. 1898).

[107]Privett v. Board of Education, 138 S.E. 461 (W.Va. 1927).

[108]Hand v. Deady, 29 N.Y.S. 633 (1894); Brown v. Lunt, 37 Me. 423 (1854).

[109]Hand v. Deady, 29 N.Y.S. 633 (1894).

[110]Norton v. Shelby County, 118 U.S. 425, 6 S.Ct. 1121, 30 L.Ed. 178 (Tenn. 1885); People v. Welsh, 80 N.E. 313 (Ill. 1907); Smith v. Morton Independent School District, 85 S.W.2d 853 (Tex. 1935); School District of Kirkwood R-7 v. Zeibig, 317 S.W.2d 295 (Mo. 1958).

[111]Gray v. Ingleside Independent School District, 220 S.W. 350 (Tex. 1920).

[112]Smith v. Morton Independent School District, 85 S.W.2d 853 (Tex. 1935).

[113]Jay v. Board of Education of City of Emporia, 26 Pac. 1025 (Kan. 1891).

[114]Day v. McCandless, 142 So. 486 (Miss. 1932); School Directors v. National School Furnishing Co., 53 Ill.App. 254 (1893); School District No. 13 v. Smith, 32 Atl. 484 (Vt. 1895); White v. School District of Borough of Archbald, 8 Atl. 443 (Pa. 1887).

[115]White v. School District of Borough of Archbald, 8 Atl. 443 (Pa. 1887).

[116]Howard v. Burke, 93 N.E. 775 (Ill. 1910).

[117]Caldwell v. Marvin, 8 Ohio N.P. (N.S.) 387 (1909).

board. However, two of the four members who voted with the majority had not been properly elected to their positions. When the title to office of the seventh member was questioned, the court ruled[118] that since the board making the appointment was a *de facto* board its attempted appointment of a *de jure* officer was a nullity. After a board of education has been ousted in a *quo warranto* proceeding, it is neither a *de jure* nor a *de facto* body, and any subsequent acts of an ousted board are invalid.[119]

3.6c Protection of third parties

The doctrine of *de facto* officers is intended to protect the public and third parties who deal in good faith with one who claims to be a public officer. As the Supreme Court of Ohio put it:

> It has been said that the doctrine of de facto officers rests on the principle of protection to the interests of the public and third parties, not to protect or vindicate the acts or rights of the particular de facto officer or the claims or rights of rival claimants to the particular office. The law validates the acts of de facto officers as to the public and third persons on the ground that, although not officers de jure, they are, in virtue of the particular circumstances, officers in fact whose acts public policy requires should be considered valid.[120]

Obviously, if the public or third parties are aware that an officer has not been properly elected or appointed, the doctrine of *de facto* officers cannot be applied. Insofar as the acts of a *de facto* officer involve the interest of the public and third persons, and are within the authority of the officer's position, they are just as valid and binding as are the acts of a *de jure* officer.[121] The fact that the acts of a *de facto* officer are performed while a court test is pending to determine the right to office does not alter the binding nature of that officer's acts.[122] However, the acts of a person who is neither a *de jure* nor a *de facto* school officer are absolutely void and under no circumstances can they bind the school district.

3.7 COMPENSATION TO SCHOOL BOARD MEMBERS

The right of school board members to receive compensation for their services is sometimes questioned. A school board member's right to compensation rests upon statutory provisions; no claim to compensation for services can be made where none is provided for or authorized by the statutes.[123] School board members may not receive compensation where statutes expressly provide that they shall serve without compensation,[124] nor can a school board compensate its members indirectly by electing them to school board offices for which compensation is provided, or by employing them in some other capacity.[125] In Texas, for example, a board of education attempted to vote compensation to its secretary and treasurer, who were also members of the board. The statute in point provided that school board members were to serve without compensation. In upholding an injunction against payment of compensation to the secretary and treasurer, the Court of Civil Appeals of Texas said:

> School trustees, and the secretary and treasurer elected by them, are public officers. No public officer can receive compensation from the public funds unless the same has been allowed and fixed by law. . . . If the secretary and treasurer of the appellant board are entitled to receive salaries, authority must be found in the law for the board to fix them.[126]

When statutes provide for the payment of compensation to school board members, they are entitled to the amount specified in the statutes and no more. However, if the statutes do not specify a fixed sum, they are entitled to reasonable compensation for their services,[127] and if a salary is provided for the board as a whole, each member of the board is entitled to a pro rata portion of the

[118]Application of Stephan, 150 N.Y.S.2d 359 (1956).
[119]People v. Cleveland, C., C. & St. Louis Railway Co., 143 N.E. 425 (Ill. 1924); School District of Kirkwood R-7 v. Zeibig, 317 S.W.2d 295 (Mo. 1958).
[120]State v. Russell, 122 N.E.2d 780 (Ohio 1954).
[121]Norton v. Shelby County, 118 U.S. 425, 6 S.Ct. 1121, 30 L.Ed. 178 (Tenn. 1885); State v. Langlade County, 236 N.W. 125 (Wis. 1931); DeLoach v. Newton, 68 S.E. 708 (Ga. 1910); School Town of Milford v. Zeigler, 27 N.E. 303 (Ind. 1891); Graham v. School District No. 69, 54 Pac. 185 (Ore. 1898); Hatfield v. Jimerson, 365 P.2d 980 (Okla. 1961).
[122]Gardner v. Goss, 227 S.W. 25 (Ark. 1921); Howard v. Burke, 93 N.E. 775 (Ill. 1910).

[123]Stone v. Towne, 29 Atl. 637 (N.H. 1892); Hinman v. Battle Creek School District No. 1, 4 Mich. 168 (1856); Moore v. Independent District of Toledo City, 8 N.W. 631 (Iowa 1881); Mertz v. City of Los Angeles, 61 P.2d 346 (Cal. 1936).
[124]Lehigh Coal and Navigation Co. v. Mauch Chunk Township School District, 75 Pa.Super. 428 (1921); Board of Trustees of Independent School District of Houston v. Dow, 63 S.W. 1027 (Tex. 1901).
[125]Board of Trustees of Independent School District of Houston v. Dow, 63 S.W. 1027 (Tex. 1901); De Bell v. Goodall, 161 S.E. 612 (W.Va. 1931).
[126]Board of Trustees of Independent School District of Houston v. Dow, 63 S.W. 1027 (Tex. 1901).
[127]City of Manchester v. Potter, 30 N.H. 409 (1855).

total salary.[128] Where the school board has been given authority to fix the salary of its members or officers, it is well settled that a member of the board cannot cast the deciding vote on a motion or resolution fixing that member's own salary.[129] A Pennsylvania case in which the secretary of the school board was voted an increase in salary by a four-to-three vote, with the secretary voting with the majority, illustrates this point. In approving the issuance of an injunction to prevent payment of the increase in compensation to him, the Pennsylvania Supreme Court noted:

. . . a thorough study of the statute fails to reveal any indication whatsoever that it was the legislative intent to abrogate the well-founded and long-established public policy that one who has a direct personal interest in a matter under consideration by a representative public agency of which he is a member is disqualified from voting thereon, and if his vote is determinative, the action taken is void.[130]

3.8 REIMBURSEMENT TO SCHOOL BOARD MEMBERS

School board members are entitled to receive reimbursement for their personal expenditures made in the interest of the district, provided that such expenditures are authorized and are properly made.[131] It has been held,[132] for example, that where a statute expressly required school directors to appear on behalf of the district a school district director was entitled to recover the amount of any necessary expenses incurred in prosecuting a suit brought by or against the district. A school board member's right to reimbursement for personal expenditures made in behalf of the district is also illustrated by an Indiana case in which a school district trustee, acting within the scope of his authority, contracted with teachers and paid the balance of their salaries with his personal funds when district receipts were inadequate. He then sought reimbursement from the district. In upholding his right to reimbursement the court said:

That a public officer may not contract with himself is not to be doubted; but, like any other agent or trustee, he may, within the scope of his agency, when a necessity arises, advance money to save his principal or cestui que trust from inevitable loss or damage, or to pay just liabilities growing out of his agency; and for such advances, upon the same principle that any other agent may be reimbursed, he may be.[133]

School board members cannot receive reimbursement, however, when they have acted beyond the scope of their authority, or when they have failed to comply with statutory requirements.[134]

It should be remembered that statutes which grant the power to levy taxes and to spend public funds are strictly construed. Consequently, it has been held[135] that a board of education has no authority to spend school district funds to reimburse the expenses incurred by some of its members in attending a conference on school hygiene where such authority was not specifically granted by the statutes. Moreover, school board members are not entitled to reimbursement for expenses incurred in defending themselves in a suit charging them with improper expenditure of school funds where such reimbursement is not authorized by statute.[136] Where the reimbursement of school board members is illegal, payment may be enjoined,[137] or, if payment has been made, it may be recovered by the district.[138] Several New Jersey cases have involved questions concerning statutory provisions with regard to the reimbursement of school board members for expenses incurred in defending themselves in legal actions. It was held,[139] for example, that a board of education has the power and duty to pay or reimburse its members for legal expenses incurred in defending themselves against any act of omission or commission "arising out of and in the course of the performance of their duties as board members." However, it also has been held[140] that a board of education need not indemnify a member for expenses incurred in defense against criminal charges arising

[128]Stone v. Towne, 29 Atl. 637 (N.H. 1892).
[129]Reckner v. School District of German Township, 19 A.2d 402 (Pa. 1941); Price v. School District of Borough of Taylor, 42 A.2d 99 (Pa. 1945).
[130]Reckner v. School District of German Township, 19 A.2d 402 (Pa. 1941).
[131]Kiefer v. Troy School Township, 1 N.E. 560 (Ind. 1885); Kingman v. North Bridgewater School District No. 13, 2 Cush. 426 (Mass. 1848); City of Manchester v. Potter, 30 N.H. 409 (1855).
[132]Fobes v. School District, 10 Wis. 101 (1859).

[133]Kiefer v. Troy School Township, 1 N.E. 560 (Ind. 1885).
[134]Tolman v. Marlborough, 3 N.H. 57 (1824).
[135]Smith v. Holovtchiner, 162 N.W. 630 (Neb. 1917).
[136]Bruce v. Sykesville Borough School District, 96 Pa.Super. 346 (1929).
[137]Smith v. Holovtchiner, 162 N.W. 630 (Neb. 1917).
[138]School Directors v. Parks, 85 Ill. 338 (1877).
[139]Errington v. Mansfield Township Board of Education, 241 A.2d 271 (N.J. 1968); Jones v. Kolbeck, 291 A.2d 378 (N.J. 1972).
[140]Powers v. Union City Board of Education, 308 A.2d 71 (N.J. 1973).

out of alleged acts of extortion and "kickbacks" paid by persons contracting with the board while that member was serving on the board.

3.9 PERSONAL INTEREST IN SCHOOL CONTRACTS

It must always be recognized that members of boards of education cannot legally place themselves in such positions that their personal interests and the interests of the districts they serve are in conflict. To do so would be in opposition to public policy. This principle is illustrated by an Oklahoma case. A member of a board of education brought suit to recover funds due him under a contract with the school district for services which he rendered in constructing a schoolhouse. His claim for compensation was denied, the court asserting:

In the regular order of things, the claim upon which the plaintiff sued should have been presented to and passed upon by the district board, and it is against public policy for an officer of such board to become personally interested in the allowance or disallowance of such claims; he cannot properly serve two masters, his own personal interest on the one hand, and the interest of the district, of which he is an officer, on the other.[141]

Although a school board member may be required to forfeit office as a result of having a direct interest in a contract with the school district, a school officer who is a salaried employee of a company doing business with the school district is not disqualified from office so long as that officer receives no direct or indirect personal benefit from the company's business with the district.[142] Neither is a person who has an outstanding claim against a school district disqualified from seeking election to its school board.[143] It has been held[144] that a person who has entered into a contract with a school district and has only partially performed the contract is not ineligible for election to the district's board, but any contractual relationship with the district must be severed before one is entitled to hold office.

3.9a Contracts with relatives

School districts occasionally contract with relatives of members of the school board to teach in the district's school or to perform other services. In such circumstances a question naturally arises as to whether such a contract violates public policy by virtue of the fact that a member of the school board has a direct personal interest in the contract. Neither public policy nor statutory provisions forbidding contracts between a school district and its officers are violated by the mere fact that a person employed by or contracting with the school board is related to a member of the school board. The determining factor is whether the school board member does, in fact, have a pecuniary interest in the contract or agreement. It has been held,[145] for example, that a school board may legally employ as a teacher a close relative of two of the three members on the board. It also has been held[146] that a school director may employ his minor daughter to teach in the schools of the district, since he would be estopped from claiming the wages he had contracted to pay. However, the courts will not enforce a contract in which a school board member does have a direct financial interest. For example, a New Jersey court refused to enforce a contract between the son of a school board member and the board of education where the father had a pecuniary interest in the contract.[147]

There is some difference of opinion among the courts as to whether a board of education may contract with the spouse of a school board member. In general, the decision turns on whether, under the laws of the state, the other member has a financial interest in the earnings of the spouse. Such a contract was not upheld in an Idaho case because under the laws of that state the earnings of the wife constituted a part of the common property of the husband and wife.[148] However, where under the laws of the state a school board member has no financial interest in the earnings of the spouse the courts have generally upheld the legality of the employment.[149] In an Arkansas case, for example, the wives of certain members of the district board of education were employed as teachers and in other capacities. A group of taxpayers sought to recover district funds which had been paid to the wives of board members, claiming such payments were illegal. The court

[141]Youngblood v. Consolidated School District No. 3, 230 Pac. 910 (Okla. 1924).
[142]Waddle v. Hughes, 84 S.W.2d 75 (Ky. 1935); Commonwealth v. Ilgenfritz, 26 Pa. Dist. & Co. 418 (1936); Brewer v. Howell, 299 S.W.2d 851 (Ark. 1957); State v. Anthony, 335 S.W.2d 832 (Tenn. 1960).
[143]In re Ziegler, 194 Atl. 911 (Pa. 1937).
[144]Weston v. Lane, 20 Pac. 260 (Kan. 1889).

[145]Dolan v. Joint School District No. 13, 49 N.W. 960 (Wis. 1891).
[146]State v. Burchfield, 80 Tenn. 30 (1883).
[147]Ames v. Board of Education of Montclair, 127 Atl. 95 (N.J. 1925).
[148]Nuckols v. Lyle, 70 Pac. 401 (Ida. 1902).
[149]Thompson v. District Board of School District No. 1, 233 N.W. 439 (Mich. 1930); Board of Education v. Boal, 135 N.E. 540 (Ohio 1922).

held[150] that the funds could not be recovered where no fraud was involved, where there was no contention that the wives were overpaid, and where it appeared that the parties had acted in good faith.

3.10 TENURE IN OFFICE

School board members invariably are elected or appointed for a specific term of office—typically three to six years. A board member may fail to complete the term in office for any one of several reasons. Tenure in office may be terminated by death, resignation, abandonment of the position, or removal from office. In any of these eventualities, general rules of law as well as specific statutory or constitutional provisions will determine a person's status as a school officer.

3.11 RESIGNATION OF SCHOOL BOARD MEMBERS

American courts have followed the general rule that public officers, including school district officers, may resign their offices, but that such a resignation is without effect unless it has been accepted by the proper authorities.[151] There are also cases in which it has been held[152] that the right of a public officer to resign is absolute; that acceptance of that resignation is not necessary. Although the right of a local school officer to resign from office is well recognized, certain limitations on the exercise of this right must also be considered. For example, if the resignation of a school officer is to be effective, it must be made at the proper time, in the proper manner, and in keeping with the method prescribed by statute.[153] Furthermore, unless there is an unequivocal act or statement which shows an absolute intention to effect a resignation, there can be no resignation.[154] A verbal statement indicating an intention to resign at some unspecified future time does not constitute a resignation.[155]

3.11 Time of

Although it may appear obvious, it should be noted at the outset that one cannot resign an office to which one has not yet been elected or appointed.[156] This situation may obtain, however, if a school board member is required to sign an undated resignation as a condition of appointment to the office. In one such situation it was held[157] that an undated resignation was invalid and could not later be accepted by the appointing official. It also has been held[158] that a public officer may not resign an office prior to induction into that office, and that a resignation tendered prior to the time the officer is duly qualified is void. The court in this case reasoned that one who had not become an incumbent of an office had no office to resign.

3.11b Procedure

A statute which prescribes how a resignation is to be made must be followed. When a statute requires that the resignation of a school officer be made in writing, a verbal resignation is invalid and has no effect.[159] Also, a resignation must be tendered to the authority designated by statute to receive it. Where statutes do not specify the authority to whom a school officer shall tender a resignation, the rule has been expressed as follows: "Where there is no definite provision in a statute directing to whom the resignation of a public officer may properly be given, it is the general rule that such public officer should tender his resignation to the power authorized to fill the vacancy or to call an election for that purpose."[160]

3.11c Time of taking effect

The time at which a resignation takes effect is determined by both the intent of the person resigning and the acceptance of resignation by the proper authority. The resignation of a school district officer is governed by the common-law principle that a public officer cannot resign from office without the consent of the body which appointed that officer or which has power to

[150]Brewer v. Howell, 299 S.W.2d 851 (Ark. 1957).

[151]Edwards v. United States, 103 U.S. 471, 26 L.Ed. 314 (Mich. 1880); Hoke v. Henderson, 15 N.C. 1 (1883); Clark v. Board of Education of City of Detroit, 71 N.W. 177 (Mich. 1897); State v. Webster Parish School Board, 150 So. 446 (La. 1933); Vaughn v. School District No. 31, 39 Pac. 393 (Ore. 1895).

[152]State v. Fowler, 48 So. 985 (Ala. 1909); Reiter v. State, 36 N.E. 943 (Ohio 1894).

[153]Ellis v. Van Horn, 53 S.W.2d 367 (Ky. 1932); People v. Reinberg, 105 N.E. 715 (Ill. 1914); Terry v. Terry, 117 S.W. 284 (Ky. 1909).

[154]Giles v. School District No. 14, 31 N.H. 304 (1855).

[155]Hunlock v. Jones, 9 Kulp 278 (Pa. 1898).

[156]People v. Reinberg, 105 N.E. 715 (Ill. 1914); In re Corliss, 11 R.I. 638 (1876).

[157]People v. Reinberg, 105 N.E. 715 (Ill. 1914).

[158]Miller v. Board of Supervision of Sacramento County, 25 Cal. 94 (1864).

[159]Graham v. Jackson, 66 S.W. 1009 (Ky. 1902).

[160]State v. Talick, 201 N.W. 144 (Neb. 1924); See also Vaughn v. School District No. 31, 39 Pac. 393 (Ore. 1895); State v. Popejoy, 74 N.E. 994 (Ind. 1905); Hoke v. Henderson, 15 N.C. 1 (1883).

fill the vacancy.[161] Consequently, a resignation by a school board member is not effective unless it has been accepted by the proper authority.[162] The rule has been judicially put as follows: ". . . to be effective the resignation of a public officer must be accepted by competent authority and . . . without acceptance the resignation is of no effect and the officer remains in office."[163] It is not necessary, however, that there be formal acceptance of the resignation. Conduct on the part of the officer or agency responsible for filling the vacancy which indicates an intent to accept the resignation—for example, the appointment of a successor—is sufficient to make it effective.[164] Nevertheless, some statutes provide that a school board member whose resignation has been accepted has a duty to continue to exercise the functions of that office until a successor is inducted.[165]

3.11d Withdrawal of

In determining the right of a school board member to withdraw a resignation which has been tendered, it is necessary to distinguish between an unconditional resignation, i.e., one to take effect immediately, and a prospective resignation, i.e., one to take effect at some future date. In a majority of cases it has been held[166] that a voluntary resignation, given unconditionally and tendered to the proper authority, may not later be withdrawn. For example, under a statute providing that the resignation of a school officer shall constitute a vacancy in that office, a school board member who left a signed written statement of resignation with the secretary of the board of education created an immediate vacancy in his office and could not later withdraw his resignation.[167] Some courts, however, have ruled[168] that an unconditional resignation may be withdrawn prior to the time it has been accepted or acted upon by the proper author-

ity. In any event, once an unconditional resignation has been accepted, it cannot be withdrawn, even if the officer or agency authorized to accept it consents to the withdrawal.[169]

In regard to a prospective resignation, it has generally been held[170] that a resignation which is to become effective on a specified future date may be withdrawn at any time prior to its acceptance by the proper authority. The courts are not in agreement, however, on the right of a school board member to withdraw a prospective resignation which has been accepted, but which has not yet taken effect, without the consent of the accepting officer or agency. In some cases it has been held[171] that consent of the accepting authority is not necessary if the resignation is withdrawn prior to the date fixed for it to become effective. In fact, it has even been held[172] that the resignation may be withdrawn against the will of the body which accepted it. In other cases it has been decided[173] that a prospective resignation which has been accepted cannot be withdrawn without the consent of the body empowered to accept it.

3.12 ABANDONMENT OF OFFICE OR REMOVAL FROM DISTRICT

A school board member may forfeit that office by abandoning the position through failure to attend meetings or failure to discharge the responsibilities of the office, and vacancies may occur when a school board member moves from the district of which that person is an officer. Questions occasionally arise as to what constitutes abandonment of the office of school board member. A school board member does not abandon the position merely by being absent from some school board meetings,[174] nor does failure to perform some duties of the office constitute abandonment. However, it has been held[175] that a school district trustee who refused to act in his official capacity for a long period of time, claiming

---

[161]Townsend v. Essex County School District No. 12, 41 N.J. Law 312 (1879).

[162]Ellis v. Van Horn, 53 S.W.2d 367 (Ky. 1932); Gearhart v. Kentucky State Board of Education, 355 S.W.2d 667 (Ky. 1962).

[163]Green v. Jones, 108 S.E.2d 1 (W.Va. 1959).

[164]State v. Board of Education of City of Council Grove, 189 Pac. 915 (Kan. 1920).

[165]State v. Webster Parish School Board, 150 So. 446 (La. 1933).

[166]Pace v. People, 50 Ill. 432 (1869); State v. Fitts, 49 Ala. 402 (1873); State v. Clarke, 3 Nev. 566 (1867); State v. Hauss, 43 Ind. 105 (1873).

[167]Board of Directors of Menlo Consolidated School District v. Blakesley, 36 N.W.2d 751 (Iowa 1949).

[168]Ellis v. Van Horn, 53 S.W.2d 367 (Ky. 1932); State v. Stickley, 61 S.E. 211 (S.C. 1908).

[169]State v. Grace, 82 S.W. 485 (Tenn. 1904); Gates v. Delaware County, 12 Iowa 405 (1861).

[170]Biddle v. Willard, 10 Ind. 62 (1857); Clark v. Board of Education of City of Detroit, 71 N.W. 177 (Mich. 1897); State v. Boecker, 56 Mo. 17 (1874); State v. Clarke, 3 Nev. 566 (1867); Schafer v. Board of Education, 94 N.E.2d 112 (Ohio 1950).

[171]State v. Beck, 49 Pac. 1035 (Nev. 1897).

[172]Schafer v. Board of Education, 94 N.E.2d 112 (Ohio 1950).

[173]Board of Education of Wolfe County v. Rose, 147 S.W.2d 83 (Ky. 1940); State v. Webster Parish School Board, 150 So. 446 (La. 1933).

[174]Hunlock v. Jones, 9 Kulp 278 (Pa. 1898).

[175]Grawunder v. Stravoski, 254 S.W. 655 (Tex. 1923).

that the district was no longer in existence, had abandoned his office. It must be shown clearly that a school board member intended to relinquish the office before the office will be declared vacant. Temporary removal from the district does not constitute evidence of such intent.[176] It has been said in this regard:

> It is true that the incumbent of the office can abandon the office and thus create a vacancy, and such abandonment may occur through resignation or removal from the district. The authorities seem to be in accord in holding that an office cannot be abandoned without the actual intention on the part of the officer to abandon and relinquish the office. The relinquishment of the office must be well defined, and it is not produced merely by non-user or neglect of duty. The officer must clearly intend an absolute relinquishment of the office; and a removal from the district, if only temporary, would not evince such intention. The non-user or neglect of duty or removal from the district in order to amount to a vacation of the office must be not only total and complete, but of such a continuance as to make it permanent, and under such circumstances so clearly indicating absolute relinquishment as to preclude all future questions of fact.[177]

Whether removal from the district constitutes clear evidence of an intent to abandon the position of school board member depends upon the facts of the case. If it appears from the facts that the member intended to establish residence elsewhere, and had no intent to return to the district at a definite future time, that member will generally be held to have abandoned the position.[178] However, there must be some action indicative of intent to change residence. For example, it has been held[179] that selling a home and moving from it to another district constituted abandonment of the office of school board member.

3.13 REMOVAL FROM OFFICE

Just as the legislature has power to provide for the election or appointment of school board members, it also has the power to remove them from office, or to delegate the power to do so.[180] When the legislature delegates to some other officer or agency the power to remove school board members from office, there must be a clear grant of power to do so, and such power may be exercised only by the designated officer or agency.[181] The power of the legislature to delegate its authority to remove school officers is also limited by constitutional provisions. For example, a statute providing that a board of education could remove school officers only for cause after a hearing had been conducted was held[182] unconstitutional because it conflicted with a constitutional provision stipulating the removal of appointed officers at the pleasure of the appointing power.

According to the weight of authority, a school officer whose term of office is fixed and definite may not be removed from office without cause before expiration of the term,[183] but a school officer appointed for an indefinite term to serve at the pleasure of the appointing power may arbitrarily be removed by it without notice and hearing.[184] The rule regarding removal of school board members from office has been put as follows by the Supreme Court of Kansas:

> Where an office is held at the pleasure of the appointing power, and also where the power of removal may be exercised at its discretion, it is well settled that the officer may be removed at any time without notice or hearing. The defendant holds his office by virtue of an election, and is chosen for a definite time. Nothing in the law warrants the implication that a school-district officer who has been elected and qualified, and entered upon his duties, may be removed at the will or pleasure of any officer. The statute prescribes the causes for which a removal may be had, and fairly implies that the cause must be shown, and that the party charged with negligence and wrong is entitled to notice, and a right to be heard in his own defense. It is well established by the great weight of authority that an officer elected by the people for a definite term, and provision is made for his removal for cause, the power of removal cannot, in the absence of the positive mandate of statute, be exercised without notice and hearing.[185]

[176]School District No. 54 v. Garrison, 119 S.W. 275 (Ark. 1909); State v. Board of Education of City of Council Grove, 193 Pac. 1074 (Kan. 1920); Hodgkins v. Sansom, 135 S.W.2d 759 (Tex. 1939).

[177]School District No. 54 v. Garrison, 119 S.W. 275 (Ark. 1909).

[178]Prince v. Inman, 280 S.W.2d 779 (Tex. 1955).

[179]Major v. Loy, 155 S.W.2d 617 (Tex. 1941).

[180]Lanza v. Wagner, 183 N.E.2d 670 (N.Y. 1962); Bonner v. Belsterling, 137 S.W. 1154 (Tex. 1911); School District No. 20 v. Walden, 293 Pac. 199 (Okla. 1930).

[181]Matthews v. Rogers, 53 S.W. 413 (Ky. 1899); Blado v. Knoll, 90 N.W.2d 176 (Wis. 1958).

[182]Buell v. Union Township School District, 150 A.2d 852 (Pa. 1959).

[183]State v. State Board of Education, 6 N.W.2d 251 (Minn. 1942); Jacques v. Little, 33 Pac. 106 (Kan. 1893); Coleman v. Glenn, 30 S.E. 297 (Ga. 1898); Field v. Commonwealth, 32 Pa. 478 (1859).

[184]State v. Mitchell, 33 Pac. 104 (Kan. 1893); Potts v. Morehouse Parish School Board, 150 So. 290 (La. 1933); Coleman v. Glenn, 30 S.E. 297 (Ga. 1898).

[185]Jacques v. Little, 33 Pac. 106 (Kan. 1893).

However, where the constitution or statutes so provide, school officers may be removed without cause by the appointing power even though they are serving a fixed term of office.[186] Although in a few cases it has been held[187] that officers serving fixed terms, but subject to removal for cause, may be removed without notice or hearing, the weight of authority holds that such officers are entitled to notice of the charges against them and opportunity to be heard in their own defense.[188]

The power to remove school board members may be lodged either with a court or with some other public agency, e.g., a state board of education. Where the authority to remove school board members is lodged with an administrative officer or agency, it is not necessary that strict rules of judicial procedure be followed, but officers should be notified of the charges against them and given full and fair opportunity to defend themselves.[189] This includes the right to the assistance of an attorney and the swearing in of witnesses.[190]

In some states the removal of school district officers is entrusted to the discretion of a court. A court is restricted in exercising such discretion by the specific grant of authority conveyed by the statutes. Consequently, when a statute specifies the grounds for removal of school officers, such a listing is generally considered to be restrictive, and a school officer cannot be removed on any grounds other than those authorized.[191] It has been said that removal from office is a "drastic step" and that hearings on the removal of a school board member must safeguard that person's constitutional rights.[192] For example, a school board member cannot be removed from office for incompetence, neglect of duty, or malfeasance in office simply by a showing that the affairs of the district are in a deplorable condition.[193]

Malfeasance or misconduct in office are among the most common bases for removal of school board members. It has been held,[194] for example, that private use of school facilities for personal gain by school board members constitutes strong evidence of malfeasance and is ground for their removal from office. Similarly, reelection of a school board member did not "whitewash" his misconduct during a previous term of office in violating a statute which prohibited board members from conducting business with the school district and thus he was subject to removal from office.[195] It also has been held[196] that a member of a board of education who voted for the employment of another board member in violation of the statutes is guilty of misconduct and subject to removal from office. In another case it was held[197] that where the president of a board of education directed employees of the board to do work on a home owned by his relatives, and ordered the payment of such employees from public funds, he was guilty of "gross misconduct in office" sufficient to justify his removal from office. A Texas case is also illustrative of official misconduct by school board members which was sufficient to justify their removal from office. The school trustees in this case had approved a tax rate of $1.35 knowing that this amount was insufficient to operate the schools of the district for the entire school year, and when additional financing was made available they refused to permit the schools to reopen. In holding that the trustees were guilty of official misconduct the court noted:

> [The] voluminous record shows without dispute that this school district could not be operated and maintained on a tax rate of $1.35. Each of the trustees knew this fact . . . and they further knew . . . that it would take the sum of $1.59 tax rate to properly maintain and support the schools. Surely their statutory duty was plain and clear, yet, they wholly disregarded their duty. . . . What clearer and more convincing evidence is required to show incompetency, gross ignorance or gross carelessness, and failure of a duly elected officer to discharge his duty to the office with which he has been entrusted.[198]

Some statutes provide that a school officer may be removed from office for failure

[186]Bradford v. Coughlin, 154 Atl. 880 (N.J. 1931).

[187]People v. Mays, 7 N.E. 660 (Ill. 1886); Hertel v. Boismenue, 82 N.E. 298 (Ill. 1907).

[188]Jacques v. Little, 33 Pac. 106 (Kan. 1893); Coleman v. Glenn, 30 S.E. 297 (Ga. 1898); Field v. Commonwealth, 32 Pa. 478 (1859); State v. Maroney, 90 S.W. 141 (Mo. 1905); Miles v. Stevenson, 30 Atl. 646 (Md. 1894); Commissioners of Knox County v. Johnson, 24 N.E. 148 (Ind. 1890).

[189]State v. State Board of Education, 6 N.W.2d 251 (Minn. 1942); Komyathy v. Board of Education of Wappingers Central School District No. 1, 348 N.Y.S.2d 28 (1973).

[190]State v. Board of Education of Lewis County, 25 S.E.2d 537 (W.Va. 1943).

[191]Bell County Board of Education v. Collett, 61 S.W.2d 902 (Ky. 1933).

[192]Komyathy v. Board of Education of Wappingers Central School District No. 1, 348 N.Y.S.2d 28 (1973).

[193]State v. Cyr, 50 So. 595 (La. 1909).

[194]Evans v. Hutchinson, 214 S.E.2d 453 (W.Va. 1975).

[195]Stringer v. Commonwealth ex rel. Matthews, 428 S.W.2d 403 (Ky. 1968).

[196]Cimino v. Board of Education of Marion County, 210 S.E.2d 485 (W.Va. 1974).

[197]Antoine v. McCaffery, 335 S.W.2d 474 (Mo. 1960).

[198]Tautenhahn v. State, 334 S.W.2d 574 (Tex. 1960).

84 The School Board Member

to perform a mandatory duty. They do not, however, authorize the removal of a school officer who fails to perform a duty which lies wholly within one's personal discretion.[199] Illustrative of this view is a case in which suit was brought to remove school trustees from office because they had refused to place on the election ballot the name of a candidate for the office of school trustee. The court refused[200] to remove the trustees from office because the decision was within their discretion, they had relied on the advice of a reputable lawyer, and there was no evidence to show that they had acted willfully or curruptly in failing to place the candidate's name on the ballot.

3.13a Recall

Another method of removing school officers from office is the recall election. When this method is employed, the removal from office of a school board member rests with the electorate rather than with a court or with some other public officer or agency.

A recall is commonly initiated by a petition signed by the requisite number of voters and filed with the board of education or other body which is authorized to call such an election. The petition for recall need not state the precise technical proof of the allegations contained therein, but the allegations should be sufficiently definite to justify bringing the matter before the people.[201] The sufficiency of the charges is a matter to be determined by the electorate through the ballot box. In *Skidmore v. Fuller*,[202] for example, a teacher petitioned for an election to recall members of the board of education. The petition charged that the school directors, acting in concert and with malice, made untrue statements ascribing to teachers in the district evil designs and charging them with being unworthy of public trust and confidence. The statements were alleged to have been made in connection with an investigation of personnel relationships within the district which was being conducted by a committee appointed by the Washington Education Association. When the board of education refused to prepare a ballot synopsis for the recall election, suit was brought to compel their action. The court required the board to pre-

pare the ballot synopsis and noted that, while the truth or falsity of allegations in a petition for recall is a political question to be answered by the voters, the legality of the proceedings for a recall election is a judicial question and may be reviewed by the courts. In a Michigan case[203] involving the attempted recall of school board members, two of the members were reelected to the board subsequent to the filing of the petitions for their recall. It was held that the petitions were void in this circumstance and that new petitions would have to be filed.

3.14 HOLDING OVER IN OFFICE

Many states, either by constitution or by statute, provide that public officers shall hold office until their successors are elected and qualified. Under such provisions a school board member is entitled to remain in office until replaced by a qualified successor.[204] In fact, it has been held[205] that a public officer may hold over in office until replaced by a qualified successor despite the fact that that officer is ineligible for reelection. Where there is no constitutional or statutory provision for an officer to remain in office until a successor has qualified, it generally has been held[206] that a public officer may remain in office until a successor is elected and qualified unless such holding over is forbidden, either expressly or by implication. The rule has been stated as follows by the Supreme Court of South Dakota:

> . . . the general rule seems to be that, in the absence of a statute or constitutional provision in terms prohibiting an officer from holding over after the expiration of his term, such officer may continue to retain and perform the duties of his office after the expiration of his term until his successor is elected or appointed and qualified. Mr. Mecham on Public Officers, Section 397, says: "It is usually provided by law that officers elected or appointed for a fixed term shall hold not only for that term but until their successors are elected and qualified. . . . Where, however, no such provision is made the question of the right of the incumbent to hold over is not so clear, but the prevailing opinion in this country seems to be that, unless such holding over be expressly

[199]*In re Kline Township School Directors*, 44 A.2d 377 (Pa. 1945).

[200]State v. Reyna, 333 S.W.2d 832 (Tex. 1960).

[201]Eaton v. Baker, 55 N.W.2d 77 (Mich. 1952); Skidmore v. Fuller, 370 P.2d 975 (Wash. 1962); State ex rel. Citizens Against Mandatory Bussing v. Brooks, 492 P.2d 536 (Wash. 1972); Bocek v. Bayley, 505 P.2d 814 (Wash. 1973).

[202]Skidmore v. Fuller, 370 P.2d 975 (Wash. 1962).

[203]Anchor Bay Concerned Citizens v. People ex rel. Kelly, 223 N.W.2d 3 (Mich. 1974).

[204]State v. Harrison, 16 N.E. 384 (Ind. 1888); Jenness v. Clark, 129 N.W. 357 (N.D. 1910); State v. Tallman, 64 Pac. 759 (Wash. 1901); Haymaker v. State, 163 Pac. 248 (N.M. 1917).

[205]Jones v. Roberts County, 131 N.W. 861 (S.D. 1911).

[206]Ibid.; State v. Harrison, 16 N.E. 384 (Ind. 1888); Thomas v. Owens, 4 Md. 189 (1853); People v. Oulton, 28 Cal. 45 (1865).

or impliedly prohibited, the incumbent may continue to hold until some one else is elected and qualified to assume the office."[207]

It has been held[208] that one who holds over in office pending qualification of a successor is entitled to such compensation as the law may provide for services.

3.15 SUMMARY

School board members legally are considered to be state officers and frequently are referred to as public officers. They generally are not regarded as municipal officers even though they may have been appointed to office by a municipal official or by a municipal board.

The legislature, subject to constitutional limitations, has broad discretion to determine how school board members shall be selected. The legislature may choose them directly, or it may provide for their election by the people or for their appointment by some other official or agency. The residents of a school district have no inherent right to choose school board members, although the legislature may permit them to participate in their selection.

Subject to constitutional limitations, the legislature also may specify the qualifications which school board members shall possess, such as being a resident of the district or possessing a minimum level of education. In the absence of legislation specifying the time when such qualifications are to be met, the courts are not in agreement as to when one must possess the requisite qualifications. Some courts have ruled that the qualifications must be met at the time of election; others have decided that it is sufficient if they are met prior to the time the person actually takes office.

Statutes which provide for the appointment of school board members should be followed strictly. The appointing authority has no power to alter the method of appointment from that specified in the statutes. However, slight irregularities in complying with the directory provisions of such statutes will not invalidate an appointment.

Having been declared elected or appointed by the proper officer or agency, persons may still be required to file a bond or take an official oath before they can legally hold the office of school board member. Some courts have ruled that failure to fulfill this requirement within the specified time results in forfeiture of the office; others have

ruled that such failure is ground for forfeiture.

School board members cannot concurrently hold two public offices which are incompatible; i.e., performance of the duties of one office may conflict with performance of the duties of the other. However, unless prohibited by statute, school board members may simultaneously hold other public offices which are not incompatible with that of school board member. School board members who accept incompatible public offices automatically forfeit their office on the school board, although the statutes may provide that they shall continue to hold office until successors have qualified.

The public interest demands that the title to office of one who is in possession and performing the duties of a public office should not be questioned indiscriminately. Consequently a school board member's title to office cannot be attacked collaterally; it can be attacked only in a *quo warranto* action brought by an officer representing the state, e.g., the attorney general.

The acts of a *de facto* school officer, i.e., one who appears to be a school officer and is accepted by the public as such but who is not legally entitled to the office, are valid and binding so far as the public and third parties acting in good faith are concerned. One may be a *de facto* school board member as a result of an irregular or illegal election or appointment, through failure to give a bond or take an oath as the law requires, or because of some other action which prevents one from meeting fully the requirements for holding the office. One cannot become a *de facto* officer by merely claiming title to an office; there must be some basis for claiming the office, e.g., an apparent election or appointment. It should be emphasized that when a *de jure* officer, i.e., one who has legal title to the office, is occupying the office and exercising its functions, another person who claims the office cannot acquire *de facto* status and is a mere pretender.

School board members are entitled to receive the amount of compensation the statutes specify and no more. If the statutes do not fix the amount school board members are to receive, they are entitled to reasonable compensation. School board members generally are entitled to reimbursement for personal expenditures made on behalf of the district if the reimbursement is authorized and if the expenditures are properly made.

A school board member may not have a direct pecuniary interest in a contract with the district of which that member is an of-

[207]Jones v. Roberts County, 131 N.W. 861 (S.D. 1911).
[208]State v. Fabrick, 112 N.W. 74 (N.D. 1907); Jones v. Roberts County, 131 N.W. 861 (S.D. 1911).

ficer. To permit such contracts would not be in the public interest for it would place the school board member in a position where personal interests and those of the district could conflict. Unless prohibited by statute a school board generally may contract with or employ a relative of one of its members if the board member does not have a pecuniary interest in the contract or agreement.

Subject to certain limitations, a school board member may resign an office. One cannot resign an office which one does not yet hold. Therefore, an undated resignation signed as a condition of appointment to the office is invalid. All statutory requirements relative to resignations must be followed. If a written resignation is called for, a verbal resignation is invalid. Unless the statutes provide otherwise, a resignation is not effective until it has been accepted by the proper authority. The weight of authority indicates that an unconditional resignation voluntarily tendered to the proper authority cannot later be withdrawn, although in some cases it has been ruled that such a resignation may be withdrawn prior to the time it is accepted. In regard to a prospective resignation, i.e., one to become effective at a specified future date, the weight of authority indicates that it may be withdrawn prior to the time it is to take effect, although the courts disagree as to whether the consent of the body empowered to accept it is necessary before the resignation can be withdrawn.

It must be shown that a school board member intended to relinquish the office before it can be declared vacant. Temporary removal from the district does not constitute evidence of such intent, nor does absence from some school board meetings.

A school officer whose term of office is fixed and definite generally may not be removed from office without cause and is entitled to notice and a hearing. However, a school board member whose term of office is indefinite, and who serves at the pleasure of the appointing officer, generally may be removed from office without notice and a hearing. A statutory listing of the grounds for removal of school officers is considered restrictive, and a school officer cannot be removed from office on grounds other than those specified. Statutes may also provide for removal from office by a recall election.

In some states the statutes provide that a school board member shall continue to serve until a successor has qualified for the office. Where the statutes do not provide for holding over in office, it generally has been held that a school board member may remain in office until a successor has qualified unless holding over is either expressly or impliedly forbidden.

Creation and Alteration of School Districts

4.0 INTRODUCTION

Although education is universally recognized as a state function, it does not follow that public schools must be administered directly by the state. State legislatures have usually chosen to create local school districts and delegate to them responsibility for the day-to-day operation of the schools. Consequently, the local school district is the basic unit of educational organization, at least from a legal viewpoint.

4.1 NATURE OF SCHOOL DISTRICTS

School districts are created by the state and legally are regarded as agencies or instrumentalities of the state.[1] In fact, no school district can exist unless statutes provide for its creation.[2] School districts are formed for one purpose only—to discharge the state's duty to provide for the establishment and maintenance of the public schools.[3] Thus a school district has no sovereign power but derives all of its power from the state. Furthermore, a state, through its legislature, may modify or abrogate the power of a school district as it sees fit, subject only to such limitations as the state or federal constitutions may impose.[4] The status of a school district has been aptly described by the Supreme Court of Pennsylvania:

> . . . our entire school system is but an agency of the State Legislature–maintained by them [sic] to carry out a constitutional duty. . . . The school system, or the school district, then, are but agencies of the state legislature to

administer this constitutional duty. . . . Within that school system, a school district is an agency of the State, created by law for the purpose of promoting education, deriving all of its powers from the statute, and discharging only such duties as are imposed on it by statute. . . .[5]

A school district, then, may be defined as a subordinate agency of the state which has been created to supervise the operation of one or more public schools. The term *school district* is also used in reference to a geographic area. Thus, it has been used to denote the territory under the jurisdiction of a single school board[6] and has been applied to the territory included within the boundaries of the district.[7]

Because of the nature of their functions and duties, school districts are usually regarded as public corporations.[8] The courts are in substantial agreement that a school district is not a true corporation, in the sense of a private corporation, because the only powers it may exercise are those expressly granted by or necessarily implied from the statutes.[9] As to the exact corporate nature of a school district, however, the courts seem to be in hopeless disagreement, as is illustrated by the fact that school districts have been referred to as quasi corporations,[10] quasi-public corporations,[11]

---

[1]De Levay v. Richmond County School Board, 284 F.2d 340 (4th Cir. 1960); County Board of Education v. Slaughter, 160 So. 758 (Ala. 1935); Independent School District No. 1 v. Common School District No. 1, 55 P.2d 144 (Ida. 1936); City of Chicago v. Board of Education of City of Chicago, 246 Ill.App. 405 (1927); Board of Education of City of Detroit v. Campbell, 239 N.W. 370 (Mich. 1931); State v. School District No. 70, 283 N.W. 397 (Minn. 1939); Barth v. School District of Philadelphia, 143 A.2d 909 (Pa. 1958); Kellam v. School Board of City of Norfolk, 117 S.E.2d 96 (Va. 1960); Lanza v. Wagner, 183 N.E.2d 670 (N.Y. 1962); City of Bloomfield v. Davis County Community School District, 119 N.W.2d 909 (Iowa 1963); Hadley v. Junior College District of Metropolitan Kansas City, 432 S.W.2d 328 (Mo. 1968); State ex rel. Dix v. Board of Education, 527 P.2d (Kan. 1974).

[2]State v. District No. 2, 209 Pac. 665 (Kan. 1922).

[3]Prescott Community Hospital Commission v. Prescott School District No. 1, 115 P.2d 160 (Ariz. 1941); Ridge v. Boulder Creek Union Junior-Senior High School District, 140 P.2d 990 (Cal. 1943); Board of Education of Louisville v. Board of Education of Jefferson County, 458 S.W.2d 6 (Ky. 1970).

[4]Kramer v. Renville County, 175 N.W. 101 (Minn. 1919); Fitzpatrick v. State Board of Examiners, 70 P.2d 285 (Mont. 1937); School District No. 74 v. School District of City of Grand Island, 186 N.W.2d 485 (Neb. 1971).

[5]Barth v. School District of Philadelphia, 143 A.2d 909 (Pa. 1958).

[6]Board of Education of City of Detroit v. Elliott, 29 N.W.2d 902 (Mich. 1947).

[7]Kellogg v. School District No. 10, 74 Pac. 110 (Okla. 1903).

[8]Baldwin v. Board of Education of City of Fargo, 33 N.W.2d 473 (N.D. 1948); Bertagnoli v. Baker, 215 P.2d 626 (Utah 1950); School District of Oakland v. District of Joplin, 102 S.W.2d 909 (Mo. 1937); State v. School District No. 1 of Silver Bow County, 34 P.2d 522 (Mont. 1934); Schmutz v. Special School District, 95 S.W. 438 (Ark. 1906); Funchess v. Lindsey, 133 So.2d 357 (La. 1961); State v. Bilyeu, 346 S.W.2d 221 (Mo. 1961).

[9]Travelers Insurance Co. v. Township of Oswego, 59 Fed. 58 (8th Cir. 1893); Appeal of Bowers, 280 A.2d 632 (Pa. 1971); Moses Lake School District No. 161 v. Big Bend Community College, 503 P.2d 86 (Wash. 1972); Cannot v. Monroe, 227 N.W.2d 827 (Neb. 1975).

[10]Silver Lake Consolidated School District v. Parker, 29 N.W.2d 214 (Iowa 1947); Board of Education of Bowling Green v. Simmons, 53 S.W.2d 940 (Ky. 1932); Baldwin v. Board of Education of City of Fargo, 33 N.W.2d 473 (N.D. 1948); Heller v. Stremmel, 52 Mo. 309 (1873); Ford v. Independent School District of Shenandoah, 273 N.W. 870 (Iowa 1937); Regional High School District No. 3 v. Town of Newton, 59 A.2d 527 (Conn. 1948); Butler v. Compton Junior College District of Los Angeles County, 176 P.2d 417 (Cal. 1947); Egan Independent Consolidated School District No. 1 v. Minnehaha County, 270 N.W. 527, 108 A.L.R. 572 (S.D. 1936); Morgan v. Cherokee County Board of Education, 58 So.2d 134 (Ala. 1952).

[11]Wilson v. Abilene Independent School District, 190 S.W.2d 406 (Tex. 1945).

municipal corporations,[12] quasi-municipal corporations,[13] and corporations.[14] It should be noted that this apparent confusion on the part of the courts is largely the result of different interpretations of specific statutes as they apply to school districts. In making such interpretations the courts attempt to determine the intent of the legislature; i.e., they try to determine whether the legislature intended the statute in question to apply to school districts and, if so, to what extent. If it is clear that the legislature intended a given measure to apply to school districts, the courts will attempt to define the corporate nature of a school district in such a way as to bring it within the purview of the statute in question.

4.2 THE STATE AND THE SCHOOL DISTRICT

The state has full and complete power over local school districts by virtue of the fact that education is a state function. This power is exercised by the state legislature and is limited only by such restrictions as may be imposed upon the legislature by the constitution of the state or by the United States Constitution. Since state constitutions are generally silent in regard to the creation and alteration of school districts, it is apparent that the legislature has virtually unlimited authority in such matters.

It has been said that the legislature has full and complete power to provide for the creation of local school districts.[15] It may

create local school districts by its own act, or it may provide for their creation by a subordinate officer or agency.[16] Its power does not cease with the formation of school districts, for the legislature may provide, either directly or indirectly, for the alteration of existing districts or for their dissolution.[17] It also may change the form of organization of existing districts and may alter their functions.[18] The power of the legislature over local school districts is clearly shown in the following statement by a Texas court:

The Legislature has the power to create school districts at will without any kind of notice. It also has the power to change the boundaries of or to abolish school districts, to consolidate them, to group them for high school purposes, to annex school districts to other school districts and to provide the mode and agencies for effecting such action.[19]

Citizens in local school districts occasionally express the belief that they are entitled to decide all questions relating to school district reorganization. From the foregoing statements it should be apparent that the citizens of a school district have no vested rights in the existence of the district.[20] Unless required to do so by the

[12]Juntila v. Everett School District No. 24, 35 P.2d 78 (Wash. 1934); Ladd v. Higgins, 50 A.2d 89 (N.H. 1946); Bertagnoli v. Baker, 215 P.2d 626 (Utah 1950); Joint School District No. 132 v. Dabney, 260 Pac. 486 (Okla. 1927); State v. Wilson, 69 Pac. 172 (Kan. 1902); Curry v. District Township of Sioux City, 17 N.W. 191 (Iowa 1883); Brown v. Board of Education, 57 S.W. 612 (Ky. 1900); Halstead v. Rozmiarek, 94 N.W.2d 37 (Neb. 1959); School District of Kirkwood R-7 v. Zeibig, 317 S.W.2d 295 (Mo. 1958).

[13]Love v. City of Dallas, 40 S.W.2d 20 (Tex. 1931); Chicago City Bank & Trust Co. v. Board of Education, 54 N.E.2d 498 (Ill. 1944); Frazier v. East Baton Rouge Parish School Board, 128 So.2d 250 (La. 1961); Kellam v. School Board of City of Norfolk, 117 S.E.2d 96 (Va. 1960); Garrison v. Community Consolidated School District No. 65, 181 N.E.2d 360 (Ill. 1962); Ludwig v. Board of Education, 183 N.E.2d 32 (Ill. 1962); Noe v. Edmonds School District No. 15, 515 P.2d 977 (Wash. 1973).

[14]Attorney General v. Lowrey, 199 U.S. 233, 26 S.Ct. 27, 50 L.Ed. 167 (Mich. 1905); Stokes v. Harrison, 115 So.2d 373 (La. 1959); In re Opinion of the Justices, 145 A.2d 250 (Me. 1958).

[15]State v. Smith, 121 S.W.2d 160 (Mo. 1938); Independent School District of Danbury v. Christiansen, 49 N.W.2d 263 (Iowa 1951); Ross v. School District No. 16, 130 P.2d 914 (Ariz. 1942); Common School District No. 42 v. Stuttgart Special School District No. 22, 58 S.W.2d 680 (Ark. 1933); Moore v. Board of Education of Iredell County, 193 S.E. 732 (N.C. 1937); Associated Schools of

Independent District No. 63 v. School District No. 83, 142 N.W. 325 (Minn. 1913); City of Groves v. Port Arthur Independent School District, 366 S.W.2d 849 (Tex. 1963); Kosmicki v. Kowalski, 171 N.W.2d 172 (Neb. 1969); Appeal of Wickstrum, 454 P.2d 660 (Okla. 1969); Fairview Independent School District v. County Board of Education, 197 N.W.2d 413 (S.D. 1972).

[16]Moore v. Board of Education of Iredell County, 193 S.E. 732 (N.C. 1937); School District No. 3 of Town of Adams v. Callahan, 297 N.W. 407, 135 A.L.R. 1081 (Wis. 1941); Common School District No. 42 v. Stuttgart Special School District No. 22, 58 S.W.2d 680 (Ark. 1933); Regional High School District No. 3 v. Town of Newton, 59 A.2d 527 (Conn. 1948); State v. Common School District No. 87, 185 P.2d 677 (Kan. 1947); School District No. 25 of Woods County v. Hodge, 183 P.2d 575 (Okla. 1947); Keiner v. Brule County Board of Education, 166 N.W.2d 833 (S.D. 1969).

[17]State v. Common School District No. 87, 185 P.2d 677 (Kan. 1947); State v. Smith, 121 S.W.2d 160 (Mo. 1938); Moore v. Board of Education of Iredell County, 193 S.E. 732 (N.C. 1937); School District No. 3 of Town of Adams v. Callahan, 297 N.W. 407, 135 A.L.R. 1081 (Wis. 1941); Wheeler School District No. 152 of Grant County v. Hawley, 137 P.2d 1010 (Wash. 1943); School District No. 25 of Woods County v. Hodge, 183 P.2d 575 (Okla. 1947); School District No. 74 v. School District of City of Grand Island, 186 N.W.2d 485 (Neb. 1971).

[18]Independent School District of Danbury v. Christiansen, 49 N.W.2d 263 (Iowa 1951).

[19]Neill v. Cook, 365 S.W.2d 824 (Tex. 1963).

[20]School District No. 3 of Town of Adams v. Callahan, 297 N.W. 407, 135 A.L.R. 1081 (Wis. 1941); State v. Common School District No. 87, 185 P.2d 677 (Kan. 1947); Board of Education v. Wilson, 100 N.E.2d 159 (N.Y. 1951); Alanreed Independent School District, 354 S.W.2d 232 (Tex. 1962).

constitution, the legislature is under no obligation to obtain the consent of persons residing in a district before altering its boundaries. In fact, the legislature may, if it chooses, create, alter, or destroy school districts against the wishes of persons residing in them.[21] A Nebraska court has commented:

> . . . the state may change or repeal all powers of a school district, take without compensation its property, expand or restrict its territorial area, unite the whole or part of it with another subdivision or agency of the state, or destroy the district with or without the consent of the citizens.[22]

4.3 DELEGATION OF POWER BY THE LEGISLATURE—ADMINISTRATIVE V. LEGISLATIVE

Although a state legislature has authority to act directly to create, alter, or destroy school districts, the authority is rarely exercised. State legislatures generally are not in a position to handle the specifics of each situation and seldom have either the time or the inclination to deal directly with the creation or alteration of every local school district. The usual practice is for the legislature to delegate its authority in such matters to some other officer or agency.

Frequently questions arise concerning the extent to which a legislature may delegate its authority to create or alter school districts. It is an almost universally accepted principle of law that while the legislature may delegate *administrative* authority to a subordinate officer or agency[23] it may not delegate *legislative* authority.[24] This principle means that the legislature is responsible for establishing the law, i.e., the policies and standards, which governs the creation and alteration of school districts. Having established the law, it may delegate authority

to administer the law to a subordinate body. In practice, however, the line which separates legislative authority and administrative authority is often difficult to discern. Although this issue has frequently come before the courts, no infallible rule has been established enabling one to determine in advance whether the legislature has delegated administrative power or legislative power.

4.4 THE NEED FOR STANDARDS GUIDING THE EXERCISE OF DELEGATED POWER

One criterion employed by the courts in judging whether legislative power has been delegated is whether the legislature has established definite standards and policies limiting the discretion of the agency to which it has delegated authority to create or alter school districts. This is clearly illustrated by a case in which the constitutionality of a law was challenged. The statute authorized the county superintendent, upon petition of the requisite number of voters, to call an election to determine whether a high school district should be established if in the superintendent's judgment the proposed district was satisfactory. In holding the statute unconstitutional, the court stated:

> . . . it delegates legislative power to the county superintendent of schools. . . . It is silent as to the area, assessed valuation, and number of prospective high school pupils, as well as the form and size of the proposed district requisite to the formation of a satisfactory and efficient high school district. Those questions are delegated to the several county superintendents, with direction to them, before calling an election, to consider the form, size, and assessed valuation of the proposed district and the proposed number of high school pupils, "and if in his judgment the proposed district does not meet the requirements heretofore specified," he may refer the petition back to the petitioners with recommendations or may deny the prayer of it altogether. . . . This statute was not complete when it left the Legislature. It attempted to confer on county superintendents, a discretion as to what the law should be. That cannot be done. . . . The law does not define or specify the requisite of a satisfactory and efficient community high school district, but leaves that matter to the discretion of the county superintendent without any rules of limitation for the exercise of such discretion. Until that official acts it cannot be known what the law is. . . . It is an arbitrary discretion and renders the section invalid because it delegates legislative powers to the county superintendent. . . .[25]

[21]Fisher v. Fay, 122 N.E. 811 (Ill. 1919); Wheeler School District No. 152 of Grant County v. Hawley, 137 P.2d 1010 (Wash. 1943); Halstead v. Rozmiarek, 94 N.W.2d 37 (Neb. 1959); Blackstone v. Rollins, 170 A.2d 405 (Me. 1961).

[22]Halstead v. Rozmiarek, 94 N.W.2d 37 (Neb. 1959).

[23]Gardner v. Ginther, 250 N.Y.S. 176 (1931); Zawerschnik v. Joint County School Committee, 73 N.W.2d 566 (Wis. 1955); Trustees of Slaughterville Graded School District v. Brooks, 173 S.W. 305 (Ky. 1915); Landis v. Ashworth, 31 Atl. 1017 (N.J. 1895); Irons v. Independent School District No. 2, 137 N.W. 303 (Minn. 1912); Thies v. Renner, 106 N.W.2d 253 (S.D. 1960); Alanreed Independent School District v. McLean Independent School District, 354 S.W.2d 232 (Tex. 1962); Marathon Oil Co. v. Welch, 379 P.2d 832 (Wyo. 1963); Opinion of the Justices, 246 A.2d 90 (Del. 1968).

[24]Kenyon v. Moore, 122 N.E. 548 (Ill. 1919); School District Joint No. 71 v. Throckmorton, 370 P.2d 89 (Kan. 1962).

[25]Kenyon v. Moore, 122 N.E. 548 (Ill. 1919).

The Supreme Court of Kansas followed similar reasoning in holding[26] a statute unconstitutional on the ground that it unlawfully delegated legislative authority to county boards of school planning. The court held that standards contained in the law were not sufficiently explicit to permit the county boards of school planning to act as administrative bodies.

Courts in other states have been more lenient in interpreting statutes delegating authority to create or alter school districts.[27] The decision in the case of *School District v. Callahan*[28] illustrates the position that the legislature may delegate authority to establish or alter school districts without specifying any standard whatsoever. A Wisconsin statute authorized the state superintendent of public instruction, by his own order, to attach districts with less than $100,000 valuation to contiguous districts. The statute was contested as unconstitutional by a school district which had been attached to a contiguous city school district. In upholding its constitutionality, the Wisconsin Supreme Court said that "the power to exercise discretion in determining whether such districts shall be altered . . . may be delegated without any standard whatsoever to guide in the exercise of the power delegated."

The dynamism of the law relative to delegation of legislative power is apparent from the statement by a New Jersey court that "recent years have witnessed an increasing liberality in the approach of our courts toward the construction of legislative delegations of power."[29] The court noted that changes in the nature of modern government have made it necessary for the legislature increasingly to delegate functions to administrative agencies.

One of the clearest statements of the principle governing the delegation of power to an administrative agency or official by a legislative body is found in a New York case.[30] The court quoted with approval the statement by the United States Supreme Court that a legislative body

> . . . does not abdicate its functions when it describes what job must be done, who must do it, and what is the scope of his authority. In our complex economy that indeed is frequently the only way in which the legislative process can go forward.[31]

The distinction between the delegation of legislative and the delegation of administrative powers is difficult to make. General guidelines can be identified, but the final determination rests upon the interpretation given specific statutes by the courts. Interpretations will probably differ from one jurisdiction to another. It would appear, however, that statutes delegating authority to create or alter school districts should prescribe as clearly as possible the standards and policies which are to be employed by subordinate officers or agencies in exercising the discretion vested in them.

4.5 LIMITATIONS ON DELEGATED POWER

Although the legislature may delegate to a subordinate agency power to create or alter school districts, such a body can exercise only those powers which have been expressly conferred upon it by statute.[32] Furthermore, the power which has been delegated may be exercised only under the circumstances described in the statute and only in the manner prescribed.[33] If statutes establish the time at which a meeting is to be held and the manner in which action is to be taken, the statutory requirements must be followed if the action is to be valid.[34] In a Wisconsin case,[35] for example, a statute required that a decision involving the consolidation of school districts be made at a conference of county school committees and school district boards. Where the decision to consolidate certain school districts

[26]School District Joint No. 71 v. Throckmorton, 370 P.2d 89 (Kan. 1962).

[27]Board of Education of Jefferson Local School District v. Board of Education of Columbus City School District, 180 N.E.2d 576 (Ohio 1962); Drouin v. Board of Directors, 67 So. 191 (La. 1915); Irons v. Independent School District No. 2, 137 N.W. 303 (Minn. 1912); School District No. 3 of Town of Adams v. Callahan, 297 N.W. 407, 135 A.L.R. 1081 (Wis. 1941); State v. Brechler, 202 N.W. 144 (Wis. 1925).

[28]School District No. 3 of the Town of Adams v. Callahan, 297 N.W. 407, 135 A.L.R. 1081 (Wis. 1941); *See also* School Board of Joint School District No. 2 v. State Superintendent of Public Instruction, 121 N.W.2d 900 (Wis. 1963).

[29]Schinck v. Board of Education of Westwood Consolidated School District, 159 A.2d 396 (N.J. 1960).

[30]Jokinen v. Allen, 182 N.Y.S.2d 166 (1958).

[31]Bowles v. Willingham, 321 U.S. 503, 64 S.Ct. 641, 88 L.Ed. 892 (Ga. 1944).

[32]State v. Brooks, 163 P.2d 414 (Kan. 1945); School District No. 3 of Town of Adams v. Callahan, 297 N.W. 407, 135 A.L.R. 1081 (Wis. 1941); Moore v. Board of Education of Iredell County, 193 S.E. 732 (N.C. 1937); State v. School Trustees of Shelby County, 239 S.W.2d 777 (Tex. 1951); Wheeler School District No. 152 of Grant County v. Hawley, 137 P.2d 1010 (Wash. 1943).

[33]Mesquite Independent School District v. Gross, 67 S.W.2d 242 (Tex. 1934); Ross v. School District No. 16, 130 P.2d 914 (Ariz. 1942); Moore v. Board of Education of Iredell County, 193 S.E. 732 (N.C. 1937).

[34]Ozark School District No. 56 v. Wickes Consolidated School District No. 79, 49 S.W.2d 373 (Ark. 1932); Webber v. Stover, 62 Me. 512 (1871).

[35]Joint School District No. 7 v. Walworth County School Committee, 94 N.W.2d 695 (Wis. 1959).

was reached at a meeting of county school committees immediately after the adjournment of the conference, it was decided that the order issued as a result of the decision was invalid because the procedure followed was not in accord with statutory requirements.

While the courts require strict compliance with statutory requirements in all important matters relating to the creation or alteration of school districts, they tend to be quite lenient with minor irregularities in proceedings, particularly when such irregularities do not affect the outcome. The question to be decided in such cases is whether the requirements contained in the statute are mandatory or directory. Statutes dealing with the creation or alteration of school districts will not be construed to impose severe restrictions unless the wording of the statutes clearly requires them.[36] For example, it has been ruled[37] that a provision for holding a meeting to fix or alter school district boundaries prior to a specified date each year was directory and that action taken at a meeting held after the specified date was not invalid for that reason. Furthermore, it has been held[38] that when a hearing on a petition for a change in district boundaries was held on the sixtieth day after receipt of the petition, rather than more than sixty days after such receipt as required by statute, the hearing was legal since those contesting the legality of the hearing had not suffered as a result of the irregularity.

An agency which has been delegated power to create or alter school districts may not, in turn, delegate this power to some other agency or individual. It can, however, employ subordinates to investigate and report the facts, make recommendations, and perform administrative duties.[39]

The discretion vested in an agency or officer relative to the creation or alteration of school districts must be exercised in a reasonable manner and not in a malicious, arbitrary, or discriminatory fashion.[40] For example, it has been found[41] to be an abuse of discretion if schools are consolidated in such a way as to destroy an effective school system and to require many pupils to reach school by walking over mountain passes. Another example of what has been considered unreasonable and arbitrary action is revealed by a South Dakota case[42] in which a county board of education approved a petition for school district reorganization which left one district with few children, inadequate financial resources, and a school building unsuited to its needs.

In reviewing the actions taken by administrative bodies, the courts will not interfere with the actions of a legally constituted body so long as it has not abused its discretion or failed to comply with the law.[43] A court will ascertain whether or not the determinations of such a body are supported by evidence, but it will not substitute its judgment for that of the body empowered to act on the matter.[44] The general rule governing review by the courts of the actions of administrative bodies has been stated as follows:

A court of review cannot substitute its judgment for the judgment of the administrative tribunal. The question is not simply whether the court of review agrees or disagrees with the finding below. It has been said that courts should not disturb administrative findings unless such findings

No. 9 v. District Boundary Board, 351 P.2d 106 (Wyo. 1960); Elementary School District No. 77 v. Gardner, 183 N.E.2d 307 (Ill. 1962); Neary v. Allen, 227 N.Y.S.2d 1015 (1962).

[41]Bell County Board of Education v. Wilson 92 S.W.2d 821 (Ky. 1936).

[42]Glenham Independent School District v. Walworth County Board of Education, 98 N.W.2d 348 (S.D. 1959).

[43]Knox County Board of Education v. Fultz, 43 S.W.2d 707 (Ky. 1931); Merritt School District No. 50 v. Kimm, 157 P.2d 989 (Wash. 1945); Lyerley v. Manila School District No. 15, 215 S.W.2d 733 (Ark. 1948); Board of Education v. County Board of School Trustees, 166 N.E.2d 472 (Ill. 1960); Allely v. Board of Education, 110 N.W.2d 410 (Iowa 1961); Detroit Edison Co. v. East China Township School District No. 3, 115 N.W.2d 298 (Mich. 1962); Marathon Oil Co. v. Welch, 379 P.2d 832 (Wyo. 1963); Canutillo Independent School District v. Anthony Independent School District, 442 S.W.2d 916 (Tex. 1969); Common School District No. 899 v. Independent School District No. 784, 177 N.W.2d 775 (Minn. 1970); Appeal of School District of Borough of Braddock Hills, 285 A.2d 880 (Pa. 1971); Joint School District No. 1 v. State, 203 N.W.2d 1 (Wis. 1973); Fairview Independent School District v. State Commission on Elementary and Secondary Education, 215 N.W.2d 831 (S.D. 1974).

[44]Board of Education v. County Board of School Trustees, 176 N.E.2d 633 (Ill. 1961); Common School District No. 899 v. Independent School District No. 784, 177 N.W.2d 775 (Minn. 1970); Appeal of School District of Borough of Braddock Hills, 285 A.2d 880 (Pa. 1971); Locher v. County Board of School Trustees, 330 N.E.2d 282 (Ill. 1975).

[36]State v. Acom, 236 S.W.2d 749 (Mo. 1951).

[37]State v. Watts, 78 So. 515 (Miss. 1918).

[38]DeWitt v. Board of Supervisors of County of San Diego, 348 P.2d 567 (Cal. 1960).

[39]School District No. 3 of Town of Adams v. Callahan, 297 N.W. 135, 407, A.L.R. 1081 (Wis. 1941).

[40]Board of District Trustees v. Board of County School Trustees, 232 S.W.2d 100 (Tex. 1950); Felker v. Roth, 178 N.E. 381 (Ill. 1931); In re Consolidated School District No. 25, 59 P.2d 1137 (Wash. 1936); Read v. Stephens, 193 P.2d 626 (Mont. 1948); Myers v. Board of Supervisors, 125 So. 718 (Miss. 1930); Glenham Independent School District v. Walworth County Board of Education, 98 N.W.2d 348 (S.D. 1959); School District

*are arbitrary, or constitute an abuse of
discretion, or are without substantial
foundation in evidence, or are obviously and
clearly wrong, or unless an opposite
conclusion is clearly evident.*[45]

Whether an agency has exercised its power
in an arbitrary or unreasonable manner
cannot be determined by applying a simple
rule. It can be determined only from the
facts surrounding a specific case, which
must be decided by the courts.

4.6 CONSTITUTIONAL CONSIDERATIONS
As those who have been involved in
school district reorganization will attest,
any consideration of the issues involved is
much more likely to be dominated by pas-
sion than by reason. The constitutionality of
legislation concerned with school district
reorganization has often been contested.
Frequently it has been claimed that statutes
providing for the creation or alteration of
school districts are unconstitutional because they impair the obligation of contracts or because they constitute the taking
of property without due process of law.

4.6a Impairment of
the obligation of contracts
Article I, Section 10 of the United States
Constitution provides that no state shall
enact any law which impairs the obligation
of contracts. It has been claimed that statutes providing for the reorganization of
school districts do impair the obligation of
contracts. This claim has been rejected,
however, since nothing in the nature of a
contract exists between a school district and
the state,[46] as has been affirmed emphati-
cally by the United States Supreme Court:

*. . . [school districts] are the auxiliaries of the
State in the important business of municipal
rule, and cannot have the least pretension to
sustain their privileges or their existence upon
anything like a contract between them and the
legislature of the State, because there is not
and cannot be any reciprocity of stipulation,
and their objects and duties are utterly
incompatible with everything of the nature of
compact.*[47]

The situation is somewhat different
where bondholders are involved. A contract
does exist between a bondholder and the
district which issued the bonds. A case[48]
arising in Michigan involved a statute permitting territory to be detached from one
school district and added to another and re-
lieving the detached territory from liability
for the indebtedness of the district to which
it formerly belonged. In ruling the statute
unconstitutional, the court declared:
"While the Legislature possesses the power
to detach a part of the territory from one
school district and attach it to another . . . it
may not impair the obligation in the bondholders' contract by taking such action
without making provision for the payment
thereof."

4.6b Taking property
without due process of law
It has been universally held that statutes
providing for the creation or alteration of
school districts, either with or without the
consent of the voters in the area affected, are
not in conflict with the "due process"
and "equal protection" clauses of the
Fourteenth Amendment.[49] School district
property is public property, not private
property.[50] It also has been held[51] that the
Fourteenth Amendment does not apply to
governmental agencies and that a school
district is not a "person" within the meaning of the Constitution.[52] Basically, the creation and alteration of school districts rest
exclusively within the discretion of the
legislature and, as the Supreme Court of
Wisconsin has said:

[45]Board of Education v. County Board of School Trustees, 176 N.E.2d 633 (Ill. 1961).
[46]Attorney General v. Lowrey, 199 U.S. 233, 26 S.Ct.
27, 50 L.Ed. 167 (Mich. 1905); *In re* School Committee of
North Smithfield, 58 Atl. 628 (R.I. 1904); Ross v. Adams
Mill Rural School District, 149 N.E. 634 (Ohio 1925);
Opinion of the Justices, 246 A.2d 90 (Del. 1968).
[47]Attorney General v. Lowrey, 199 U.S. 233, 26 S.Ct.
27, 50 L.Ed. 167 (Mich. 1905).

[48]Board of Education of City of Lincoln Park v. Board
of Education of City of Detroit, 222 N.W. 763 (Mich.
1929).
[49]State v. Brooks, 249 S.W. 73 (Mo. 1923); *In re*
School Committee of North Smithfield, 58 Atl. 628 (R.I.
1904); Ross v. Adams Mill Rural School District, 149
N.E. 634 (Ohio 1925); School District No. 3 of Town of
Adams v. Callahan, 297 N.W. 407, 135 A.L.R. 1081 (Wis.
1941); Pass School District v. Hollywood City School
District, 105 Pac. 122 (Cal. 1909); Kramer v. Renville
County, 175 N.W. 101 (Minn. 1919); Thies v. Renner,
106 N.W.2d 253 (S.D. 1960); McGary v. Barrows, 163
A.2d 747 (Me. 1960); Casmalia School District v. Board
of Supervisors, 4 Cal. Rptr. 656 (1960); Padberg v. Martin, 357 P.2d 255 (Ore. 1960); School District of City of
Lansing v. State Board of Education, 116 N.W.2d 866
(Mich. 1962); Webb v. Dixon, 447 P.2d 268 (Ariz. 1968);
State *ex rel.* Apodaca v. New Mexico State Board of
Education, 484 P.2d 1268 (N.M. 1971).
[50]*In re* School Committee of North Smithfield, 58 Atl.
628 (R.I. 1904).
[51]Kramer v. Renville County, 175 N.W. 101 (Minn.
1919).
[52]Lincoln Township School District v. Redfield Consolidated School District, 283 N.W. 881 (Iowa 1939).

. . . it is well established that the alteration or abolition of school districts in such manner and through such instrumentalities as the Legislature prescribes is not the taking of property nor does it deprive any person of his property within the meaning of the constitutional inhibitions in these respects; and that statutes in authorizing such changes in school districts do not deny equal protection of the laws or due process of law.[53]

4.7 TWO SCHOOL DISTRICTS IN SAME TERRITORY

The legal principle is well established that two corporate entities performing the same functions cannot simultaneously occupy the same territory.[54] In a number of states, however, statutes have been enacted which provide for the creation of two or more school districts occupying the same territory. It is possible in these states to have an elementary school district, a high school district, and a junior college district serving the same geographic area. Although such statutes would appear to violate this legal principle, they have been upheld by the courts on the ground that the districts do not perform the same functions.[55] In upholding the legality of a union high school district which embraced the same territory occupied by three elementary districts the Oregon Supreme Court stated:

The plaintiffs argue that it is impossible for two corporations with like purposes to exist in the same territory. This principle, sound as it may be, does not apply to the present contention. The high school is not concerned with the primary branches of education taught in the common schools. Its field of activity is enlarged and different in scope from that of the ordinary districts. . . . The two classes of districts complement one another, but do not conflict in their organization.[56]

This issue also has been before the courts quite frequently in Illinois. The courts there have gone so far as to uphold the legality of a community high school district which in-cluded within its boundaries a common school district maintaining an accredited high school.[57] They have also permitted a common school district and a high school district which occupied part of the same geographic area to each levy the maximum tax permitted by the law.[58] Similarly, the Arizona Supreme Court has ruled[59] that high school and common school districts may be identical in territory and that each may tax the property therein. It also has been held[60] that the existence of a *de facto* school district which is exercising its functions does not prevent the establishment of a *de jure* school district occupying the same territory.

4.8 TYPES OF SCHOOL DISTRICTS

Even the most cursory review of statutes and court decisions reveals the wide assortment of names which are applied to school districts. There are, for example, independent districts, special districts, municipal independent districts, common school districts, high school districts, graded school districts, community school districts, rural high school districts, union school districts, and consolidated school districts. This bewildering array of names is explained by the fact that state legislatures have the authority to create different kinds of school districts to serve different purposes.[61] Legislatures frequently have provided for the creation of new types of districts as needs in the various states have changed. As a result, the names applied to different types of school districts, and the characteristics of the districts, are likely to be unique to each state. Consequently, if one desires specific information on a particular type of school district, it is necessary to refer to the statutes of that state.

4.8a Independent School Districts

As its name implies, an independent school district is independent of the regular township or county system of school districts, as well as separate and distinct from any municipality which it encompasses.[62] An independent school district may include

[53]School District No. 3 of Town of Adams v. Callahan, 297 N.W. 407, 135 A.L.R. 1081 (Wis. 1941).
[54]People v. Fairchild Community High School, 73 N.E.2d 292 (Ill. 1947); Kelly v. Brunswick School District, 187 Atl. 703 (Me. 1936); Clardy v. Winn, 258 S.W. 333 (Ark. 1924); Stewart v. Thorn Valley Joint Union School District, 121 P.2d 49 (Cal. 1942).
[55]Splonskofsky v. Minto, 126 Pac. 15 (Ore. 1912); People v. Woodward, 120 N.E. 496 (Ill. 1918); Welsh v. Getzen, 67 S.E. 294 (S.C. 1910); People v. Pinari, 163 N.E. 385 (Ill. 1928); Union High School District No. 2 v. Paul, 95 P.2d 5 (Col. 1939).
[56]Splonskofsky v. Minto, 126 Pac. 15 (Ore. 1912).

[57]People v. Woodward, 120 N.E. 496 (Ill. 1918); People v. Pinari, 163 N.E. 385 (Ill. 1928).
[58]People v. Henkle, 100 N.E. 175 (Ill. 1912).
[59]Glendale Union High School District v. Peoria School District No. 11, 78 P.2d 141 (Ariz. 1938).
[60]People v. Militzer, 112 N.E. 57 (Ill. 1916).
[61]Regional High School District No. 3 v. Town of Newton, 59 A.2d 527 (Conn. 1948).
[62]State v. Rodriguez, 213 S.W.2d 877 (Tex. 1948); Independent School District of Alexandria v. Independent School District No. 2, 152 N.W. 706 (S.D. 1915).

only such territory as is authorized by the statutes under which it is created.[63]

The courts are not in agreement as to whether an independent school district may be created from territory already embraced by another independent school district. Some jurisdictions have held that independent school districts cannot be created from territory which is already included in some other independent school district;[64] other jurisdictions have held to the contrary.[65]

4.8b Municipal independent school districts

Municipal independent school districts, which are comprised of the territory of a city, village, or other municipality, are found in some states. The fact that the boundaries of such a school district are coterminous with those of a municipality does not make it a part of a municipal government,[66] nor does the granting of "home-rule" privileges to the municipality affect a municipal independent school district.[67]

As a general rule, all territory of the municipality must also be included in the municipal independent school district unless statutes provide to the contrary.[68] In some jurisdictions territory annexed by a municipality automatically comes within the jurisdiction of the municipal independent school district;[69] in others, additional specified steps must be taken if any change in school district boundaries is to be effected.[70]

4.8c Community school districts

The statutes of some states authorize the creation of community school districts. The territory of such districts is usually limited to a community of people with common interests and having a community center where people customarily gather.[71] The territory included in the district should comprise a natural school community which is compact and contiguous. The territory of two or more separate and distinct communities cannot be included in a single community school district.[72] However, the "community" may exist for school purposes only, and the fact that some residents of the district go to other places for purposes of business, worship, or pleasure does not necessarily establish that the area in which they live is not part of the school community.[73]

4.8d Consolidated school district

The term *consolidated school district* is applied to a school district formed by the union of two or more adjacent school districts or portions thereof.[74] The legislature may act directly to consolidate school districts;[75] it may delegate authority to consolidate school districts to the state superintendent, to a local board of education, or to some other subordinate agency;[76] or it may provide for consolidation by vote of the electors in the territory involved.[77] Legislation authorizing the consolidation of school districts may be permissive, in which case it has no effect on the status of existing districts other than giving them the power to unite if they choose.

When a consolidated school district is formed, each of the districts from which it was formed loses its separate identity unless statutes provide otherwise.[78] The consolidated district assumes jurisdiction over all of the territory within its boundaries.[79] A consolidated district may be added to, divided, or combined with other districts to form a still larger consolidated district.[80]

---

[63]Rural Special School District No. 85 v. Tatum, 211 S.W. 923 (Ark. 1919).

[64]*Ibid.;* Elk Point Independent School District No. 3 v. State Commission on Elementary and Secondary Education, 187 N.W.2d 666 (S.D. 1971).

[65]School District of Township of Union v. Independent School District of Stockpool, 128 N.W. 848 (Iowa 1910).

[66]Mayor and Council of Wilmington v. State, 57 A.2d 70 (Del. 1947); State v. Mitchell, 245 N.W. 640, 86 A.L.R. 1361 (Wis. 1932).

[67]City of Fort Worth v. Zane-Cetti Co. 278 S.W. 183 (Tex. 1925).

[68]State v. Carroll, 234 N.W. 875 (Wis. 1931); Missouri, Kansas & Texas Railroad Co. v. City of Whitesboro, 287 S.W. 904 (Tex. 1926).

[69]City of Beaumont Independent School District v. Broadus, 182 S.W.2d 406 (Tex. 1944).

[70]Thomas v. Spragens, 213 S.W.2d 452 (Ky. 1948).

[71]People v. Cowen, 137 N.E. 836 (Ill. 1922).

[72]People v. Hurst, 81 N.E.2d 491 (Ill. 1948).

[73]People v. Deatherage, 81 N.E.2d 581 (Ill. 1948); People v. Baird, 139 N.E. 132 (Ill. 1923).

[74]Rice v. Gong Lum, 104 So. 105 (Miss. 1925), *affirmed,* 275 U.S. 78 (1927); Wall v. State, 103 P.2d 925 (Okla. 1940).

[75]Tindall v. Byars, 59 S.E.2d 337 (S.C. 1950).

[76]Stokes v. New Mexico State Board of Education, 230 P.2d 243 (N.M. 1951); Keever v. Board of Education of Gwinnett County, 3 S.E.2d 886 (Ga. 1939); Audas v. Logan County Board of Education, 55 S.W.2d 341 (Ky. 1932).

[77]Audas v. Logan County Board of Education, 55 S.W.2d 341 (Ky. 1932); Rhea Common School District v. Bovina Independent School District, 214 S.W.2d 660 (Tex. 1948).

[78]Stewart v. Thorn Valley Joint Union School District, 121 P.2d 49 (Cal. 1942); Bramlett v. Callaway, 14 S.E.2d 454 (Ga. 1941); Harris v. State, 8 N.E.2d 594 (Ind. 1937).

[79]State v. Scott, 270 S.W. 382 (Mo. 1925).

[80]Consolidated Eagle Lake Independent School District v. Columbus Independent School District, 219 S.W.2d 741 (Tex. 1949); State v. Thompson, 181 N.W. 434 (Iowa 1921).

4.9 PROCEDURAL REQUIREMENTS IN CREATING AND ALTERING SCHOOL DISTRICTS

Before discussing procedural requirements in creating and altering school districts, we must sound a note of caution. The fact that school district organization and reorganization is preeminently a matter of legislative concern and responsibility has already been emphasized. Each state legislature, in providing for the creation and/or alteration of school districts, has produced a substantial body of law. Much of the litigation in this area involves the interpretation and application of specific statutes. Because many of these laws are unique, and must be interpreted in the context of other related laws, it is difficult to extract legal principles and to formulate broad generalizations. Consequently, one must turn to the statutes and court decisions in each of the states for precise information about the law relative to the creation and alteration of school districts.

4.9a In general

The procedure to be followed in creating or altering school districts is usually spelled out in some detail in the statutes, and the courts generally require at least substantial compliance with statutory requirements in actions to create or alter school districts.[81] Statutes which deal with the creation and alteration of school districts generally are construed liberally and in accordance with the intent of the legislature.[82] The courts will not read into the statutes any requirement which is not clearly expressed or implied and will presume that the legislature intended the law to be reasonable and effective.[83]

According to the weight of authority, substantial compliance with statutory requirements is sufficient to validate the creation or alteration of school districts.[84] Minor irregularities in proceedings which do not materially affect the outcome will be overlooked. However, some courts have required strict compliance with statutory requirements and have refused to uphold the validity of school districts in situations where procedural irregularities have occurred in the process of creation or alteration.[85]

4.9b Shape and physical characteristics

The only restrictions on the amount of territory which may be encompassed by a school district are those imposed by the constitution or statutes.[86] In the absence of express constitutional or statutory restrictions one or several counties may be included in a single school district.[87]

Although a school district of any desired shape may be created, a district may not be gerrymandered in a prejudicial manner, nor can it be laid out so as to exclude certain persons.[88] It is not necessary that school facilities be equally convenient to all children residing within the district, but all must be given reasonable opportunity to enjoy the benefits of the school.[89]

Whether all territory in a school district must be contiguous is a matter of some dispute. Courts in some jurisdictions have ruled[90] that a school district must be composed of contiguous territory unless the statutes make express provision to the contrary. Other courts have taken the view that territory need not be contiguous unless so required by statute.[91]

Some statutes specify that school districts shall be "compact." This requirement has been interpreted to mean that the territory embraced by a school district should be such that all children may travel to and from school in a reasonable period of time and in reasonable comfort.[92]

[81]Heid v. Hartline, 73 N.E.2d 524 (Ohio 1946); Peter v. Board of Supervisors of Kern County, 178 P.2d 73 (Cal. 1947); Perkins v. Lenora Rural High School Joint District No. 1, 237 P.2d 228 (Kan. 1951); Lipscomb Independent School District v. County School Trustees, 498 S.W.2d 364 (Tex. 1973).

[82]Cook v. Consolidated School District of Truro, 38 N.W.2d 265 (Iowa 1949); Elliott Common School District No. 48 v. County Board of School Trustees, 76 S.W.2d 786 (Tex. 1934); Goren v. Buena High School District of Cochise County, 372 P.2d 692 (Ariz. 1962); Branderhorst v. County Board of Education, 99 N.W.2d 433 (Iowa 1959); State ex rel. Fisher v. Fisher, 433 S.W.2d 63 (Mo. 1968).

[83]Elliott Common School District No. 48 v. County Board of School Trustees, 76 S.W.2d 786 (Tex. 1934); State v. McKinney, 132 N.W. 600 (Wis. 1911); Driskel v. O'Conner, 15 A.2d 366 (Pa. 1940).

[84]Leasure v. Beebe, 83 A.2d 117 (Del. 1951); Sloan v. Hawkins, 86 N.E.2d 117 (Ill. 1949); State v. McKinney, 132 N.W. 600 (Wis. 1911); Clement v. Everest, 29 Mich. 19 (1874); In re Cleveland, 19 Atl. 17, 7 L.R.A. 431 (N.J. 1890); State v. Langlie, 67 N.W. 958, 32 L.R.A. 723 (N.D. 1896).

[85]State v. Robinson, 1 So.2d 621 (Fla. 1941).

[86]State v. Board of School Directors, 95 So. 104 (La. 1922).

[87]Crook v. Bartlett, 159 S.W. 826 (Ky. 1913).

[88]Elliott v. Garner, 130 S.W.2d 997 (Ky. 1910); Bradley v. Milliken, 484 F.2d 215 (6th Cir. 1973).

[89]People v. Kinsey, 147 N.E. 408 (Ill. 1925); Krause v. Thompson, 211 S.W. 925 (Ark. 1919).

[90]Petitioners of School District No. 9 v. Jones, 140 P.2d 922 (Okla. 1943).

[91]Weeks v. Batchelder, 41 Vt. 317 (1868).

[92]People v. Young, 139 N.E. 894 (Ill. 1923); People v. Gardner, 96 N.E.2d 551 (Ill. 1951); Board of Education v. County Board of School Trustees, 166 N.E.2d 472 (Ill. 1960).

4.9c Number of inhabitants

Statutes which specify the minimum number of inhabitants, families, or school-age children that must be contained in any school district are controlling.[93] Failure to meet such requirements, however, does not invalidate or destroy an existing school district.[94] Where the statutes impose no such requirements, school districts may be created without regard to the number of inhabitants or school-age children residing therein.[95]

4.9d Consent of residents

As noted previously, unless it is required by the constitution of the state, the residents of a school district need not assent to its creation or alteration. The legislature may create or alter school districts and it may do so without notice to residents of the districts affected, or even against their will.[96]

Although the legislature is under no obligation to obtain the consent of the residents of a school district prior to its creation or alteration, it may make any action to create or alter a district contingent upon the consent of the residents or electors of the territory affected. Where statutes require the consent of the residents before a school district can be created or altered, no valid action can be taken without such consent.[97]

Although statutes requiring that the consent of the residents of a school district be obtained prior to its creation or alteration are many and varied, it is possible to group such statutes into two categories. One type requires that the consent of a specified proportion of the residents in the territory affected be obtained prior to the creation or alteration of school districts; the other type authorizes the creation or alteration of school districts unless a remonstrance against the contemplated action is filed by a designated proportion of the residents within a specified period of time. Thus, one

type of statute requires approval of the proposed action by the residents of the area affected; the other requires disapproval of the proposed action.

Court decisions interpreting these statutes are not always consistent. This is to be expected, since the wording of such statutes varies considerably from state to state and even within a state over a period of time. While it has been held,[98] for example, that consent must be specific and definite in terms of the action to be taken, it has also been held[99] that the action may be described in general terms. Further, in some jurisdictions any conditions which are attached in consenting to a proposed action are regarded as purely advisory;[100] in other jurisdictions they are regarded as mandatory, and failure to comply with them nullifies the consent.[101] There is general agreement, however, that the consent must be given or a remonstrance entered within the period of time specified by the statute, or, if none is specified, within a reasonable time,[102] and that a consent or remonstrance signed by less than the required number of persons is ineffective.[103]

4.10 PETITIONS CONCERNING THE CREATION OR ALTERATION OF SCHOOL DISTRICTS

Many states have enacted legislation which permits citizens to petition for the creation or alteration of a school district. Such petitions must be presented to a designated officer or agency having authority to act on the request of the petitioners. The legal principles which are generally applicable to petitions are also applicable to petitions concerning the creation or alteration of school districts.

It is not uncommon for statutes to require the submission of a petition signed by a specified number of voters as a condition precedent to any action to create or alter school districts. When this is the case, a petition must be presented before any valid action can be taken. Any action taken with-

---

[93]Allen v. District Township of Bertram, 30 N.W. 684 (Iowa 1886); Cheshire v. Kelley, 6 N.E. 486 (Ill. 1886).
[94]Griggs v. School District No. 76 of Wayne County, 40 N.W.2d 859 (Neb. 1950).
[95]People v. Painter, 108 N.E. 683 (Ill. 1915).
[96]Boughton v. Shears, 172 N.E.2d 497 (Ill. 1961); Fruit v. Metropolitan School District of Winchester, 172 N.E.2d 864 (Ind. 1961); Thies v. Renner, 106 N.W.2d 253 (S.D. 1960); Padberg v. Martin, 357 P.2d 255 (Ore. 1960); Blackstone v. Rollins, 170 A.2d 405 (Me. 1961); Alanreed Independent School District v. McLean Independent School District, 354 S.W.2d 232 (Tex. 1962); Wheeler School District No. 152 of Grant County v. Hawley, 137 P.2d 1010 (Wash. 1943); School District No. 74 v. School District of City of Grand Island, 186 N.W.2d 485 (Neb. 1971).
[97]Neal v. Lewis, 46 N.H. 276 (1865).

[98]Ibid.
[99]Grindle v. Brooksville School District No. 1, 64 Me 44 (1874).
[100]State v. Rowe, 175 N.W. 32 (Iowa 1919).
[101]State v. Campbell, 103 So. 471 (Ala. 1925).
[102]Valley Center School District No. 20 v. Hansberger, 237 Pac. 957 (Ariz. 1925); Munn v. Lentz, 239 N.W. 298 (Mich. 1931).
[103]Board of Education of Berea Rural School District v. Board of Education of Hamilton County. 31 N.E.2d 702 (Ohio 1940); School District No. 10 v. County Board of Education, 47 S.W.2d 606 (Ark. 1932); Petercheff v. City of Indianapolis, 178 N.E.2d 746 (Ind. 1961).

out the filing of such a petition is void.[104] When statutes grant the right to petition for the creation or alteration of school districts, this right is not exhausted by exercise; i.e., the fact that the action requested in a petition has previously been denied does not prevent the submission of a similar petition—unless, of course, further action is prohibited by the statute.[105]

4.10a Form and content

Obviously, when the statutes specify the form and content of petitions, the safest procedure is to follow such statutory requirements to the letter. In any event, a petition must be in writing regardless of whether statutes so specify. It has been held[106] that use of the word *petition* in a statute carries the clear implication that a written document, not an oral request is contemplated. If statutes are silent as to the form and content of petitions, no special form need be followed.[107] Insofar as form and content are concerned, the primary consideration is that the petition be worded in such a way that the electors comprehend clearly the question which is involved.[108] The petition should identify fully, clearly, and specifically the action sought by the petitioners.[109]

It is also important that the petition contain an accurate description of the territory involved in the action which is sought by the petitioners.[110] Absolute accuracy is generally not required since the primary consideration is that the intent of the petition be evident.[111] It has been held,[112] for example, in the absence of a statute forbidding such action, that when preparing election

notices and ballots a school board secretary may elaborate on the description of the area contained in a petition in order to clarify the changes sought by the petitioners. Similarly, it has been decided[113] that statements which clarify a petition or make it more definitive may be added after the petition has been signed. If any material changes are made in a petition after it has been signed, however, the petition is invalidated.[114]

4.10b Signatures

Statutes providing for the submission of petitions to create or alter school districts usually specify the qualifications which must be possessed by those who sign such petitions. Adherence to statutory requirements in this regard is essential, since without it the petition may be invalidated.[115] Many courts, however, will overlook minor irregularities in signatures so long as they do not change or affect the outcome of the petition. An illustration is afforded by an Oklahoma case[116] in which the validity of an election was contested on the basis that the signatures of some persons on the petition under which the election was called actually had been affixed to the petition by their spouses. However, it was evident that most of the nonsigning spouses ratified their signatures. The court upheld the validity of the election because it considered the irregularities to be minor and because it was not shown that they had altered the results of the election.

The intent of a petition should be clear from its wording. Those who circulate the petition must avoid misrepresenting the petition, making improper promises, or employing fraud or duress in order to obtain signatures. Signatures which are obtained by fraud invalidate a petition.[117] While those who sign a petition should do so voluntarily and with full knowledge of the facts, misapprehension or misunderstanding of the facts by some persons who have signed it does not necessarily invalidate a petition. Such signatures may be withdrawn, but if not withdrawn they may be counted if there is no evidence that they

---

[104]Peter v. Board of Supervisors of Kern County, 178 P.2d 73 (Cal. 1947); Gilbert v. Scarborough 131 So. 876 (Miss. 1931); Mesquite Independent School District v. Gross, 67 S.W.2d 242 (Tex. 1934); School District No. 2 v. Pace, 87 S.W. 580 (Mo. 1905); In re Change of Boundaries of School Districts, 91 N.W.2d 164 (Minn. 1958); Dansby School District No. 34 v. Haynes School District No. H, 197 S.W.2d 30 (Ark. 1946); Appeal of Wickstrum, 454 P.2d 660 (Okla. 1969).
[105]Wallace School District No. 1 v. Board of Education, 216 S.W.2d 790 (Ark. 1949); Hopkins v. Dickens, 222 S.W. 101 (Ky. 1920); Hightower v. Overhaulser, 21 N.W. 671 (Iowa 1884).
[106]State v. Compton, 44 N.W. 660 (Neb. 1890).
[107]Smith v. Blairsburg Independent School District, 159 N.W. 1027 (Iowa 1916).
[108]State v. School District No. 30 of Independence, 333 S.W.2d 36 (Mo. 1960); State v. Mohr, 199 N.W. 278 (Iowa 1924); England v. Eckley, 330 S.W.2d 738 (Mo. 1959).
[109]Botts v, Prentiss County School Board, 166 So. 398 (Miss. 1936).
[110]State v. Lensman, 88 P.2d 63 (Mont. 1939).
[111]Baker v. Brown, 165 S.W.2d 522 (Tex. 1942); Johnson v. Schrader, 507 P.2d 814 (Wyo. 1973).
[112]England v. Eckley, 330 S.W.2d 738 (Mo. 1959).

[113]Kelly v. Board of Trustees, 172 S.W. 1047 (Ky. 1915).
[114]Chitty v. Parker, 90 S.E. 17 (N.C. 1916).
[115]Peter v. Board of Supervisors of Kern County, 178 P.2d 73 (Cal. 1947); Caston v. Wilkinson County School Board, 154 So. 714 (Miss. 1934).
[116]Arterburn v. Summers, 372 P.2d 614 (Okla. 1962). See also Rural Special School District v. Hatfield Special School District, 47 S.W.2d 790 (Ark. 1932); State v. Tillatson, 304 S.W.2d 485 (Mo. 1957).
[117]Oakland School District No. 17 v. Board of Education of City of Humboldt, 163 Pac. 800 (Kan. 1917).

were obtained through fraud or misrepresentation.[118]

Unless statutes so specify, it is not necessary that all signatures appear on one petition. Several identical petitions may be circulated and will be accepted as sufficient if the total number of signatures equals the number required by the statute.[119]

4.10c Withdrawal of signatures

Occasionally persons who have signed petitions will change their minds and seek to withdraw their signatures. The right to withdraw signatures from a petition, in the absence of a statute governing the matter, depends largely on the extent to which subsequent action on the petition has taken place. After final action on a petition has taken place a signature cannot be withdrawn.[120] On the other hand, a signature may be withdrawn from a petition at any time before it is filed.[121]

Whether a signature may be withdrawn after a petition has been filed with the individual or agency to whom it is addressed, but before it has been acted upon, is a matter of some debate. The weight of authority[122] supports the view that a signature may be withdrawn from a petition at any time before it has been acted upon by the individual or agency to whom it is addressed. It has been said in this regard that "where the petition has not been acted upon . . . a signer has an absolute right to withdraw his name from the petition" and that "it is not within the province of any court to inquire into the psychology of his mind or the sufficiency of his reasons. . . ."[123] Courts in some

jurisdictions, however, have held[124] that, once a petition has been filed, signatures may no longer be withdrawn. They reason that the filing of the petition confers jurisdiction upon the individual or agency to which it is addressed and that signatures may not be withdrawn without the consent of this individual or agency.

4.10d Action on

To be effective a petition must be filed with the officer or agency specified by the statute.[125] This point is illustrated by an Ohio case[126] in which a petition requesting that certain territory be transferred from one school district to another was filed with the county board of education rather than with the county superintendent of schools as the statute required. The court ruled that all acts taken upon the petition were invalid because it had not been properly filed.

The action taken subsequent to the filing of a petition for the creation or alteration of school districts will vary according to the requirements of the statute under which it is submitted. Under some statutes the filing of a properly executed petition will accomplish the requested action and no further action on the part of the officer or agency with which it is filed is required. Under other statutes the officer or agency with which a properly executed petition is filed is required to initiate certain specified activities—e.g., a notice, hearing, or election—leading to the action sought by the petitioners. Under still other statutes the officer or agency with which a petition is filed is required to exercise discretion in determining whether the petitioners' plea should be granted. Where the exercise of such discretion is required, it has been said that the primary consideration should be the best interests of the schools in the area and the educational welfare of the people.[127]

Occasionally two or more petitions involving the same territory, but seeking different courses of action, are circulated and filed at nearly the same time. The question in such cases is which petition confers

[118]Dappen v. Weber, 184 N.W. 952 (Neb. 1921), rehearing. 187 N.W. 230 (Neb. 1922); Webb v. Dixon, 447 P.2d 268 (Ariz. 1968).

[119]Hopkins v. Dickens, 222 S.W. 101 (Ky. 1920); Jordan v. Overstreet, 352 S.W.2d 296 (Tex. 1961); Rural Special School District v. Hatfield Special School District, 47 S.W.2d 790 (Ark. 1932).

[120]School District No. 9 v. Dickson Consolidated School District No. 77, 72 P.2d 508 (Okla. 1937); Zilske v. Albers, 29 N.W.2d 189 (Iowa 1947).

[121]Zilske v. Albers, 29 N.W.2d 189 (Iowa 1947); Perry v. Gill, 44 S.W.2d 1084 (Ark. 1932).

[122]Heppe v. Mooberry, 183 N.E. 636 (Ill. 1932); School District No. 24 v. Renick, 201 Pac. 241 (Okla. 1921); State v. Boyden, 108 N.W. 897 (S.D. 1906); Territory v. Mayor and City Council of Roswell, 117 Pac. 846 (N.M. 1911); State v. Morrison, 51 N.W.2d 626 (Neb. 1952); Valley Center School District No. 20 v. Hansberger, 237 Pac. 957 (Ariz. 1925); State v. Mercer County Board of Education, 175 N.E.2d 305 (Ohio 1959); Petercheff v. City of Indianapolis, 178 N.E.2d 746 (Ind. 1961); Hendricks v. McCreary, 467 P.2d 478 (Okla. 1970); Board of Education of Metropolis County v. County Board of School Trustees of Massac County, 341 N.E.2d 10 (Ill. 1976).

[123]School District No. 24 v. Renick, 201 Pac. 241 (Okla. 1921).

[124]Nathan Special School District No. 4 v. Bullock Springs Special School District No. 36, 38 S.W.2d 19 (Ark. 1931); In re Mercersburg Independent School District, 85 Atl. 467 (Pa. 1912); Zilske v. Albers, 29 N.W.2d 189 (Iowa 1947).

[125]School District No. 28 v. Larson, 260 Pac. 1042 (Mont. 1927); State v. Mercer County Board of Education, 175 N.E.2d 305 (Ohio 1959).

[126]State v. Mercer County Board of Education, 175 N.E.2d 305 (Ohio 1959).

[127]Welch v. County Board of School Trustees, 160 N.E.2d 505 (Ill. 1959); Newman v. County Board of School Trustees, 312 N.E.2d 35 (Ill. 1974).

jurisdiction to proceed. The general rule is that the proceeding which was first initiated has priority.[128] Furthermore, any action to create or alter a school district while a prior proceeding is pending is invalid.[129] It is often difficult, however, to determine precisely when a proceeding begins and when it is ended. This can be determined only from a consideration of the facts of the case and the procedural requirements of the pertinent statutes.

4.11 ELECTIONS CONCERNING THE CREATION OR ALTERATION OF SCHOOL DISTRICTS

Since the residents of a school district have no inherent right to participate directly in decisions regarding its creation or alteration, submission of a proposal to create or alter school districts to a popular vote of the electors of the area involved is not necessary unless required by statute.[130] However, statutes which require that such an election be held are mandatory, and any proposed action which has not been approved by the requisite number of electors in an election held for that purpose is void and without force.[131]

Elections concerning the creation or reorganization of school districts are governed by the same rules as govern other school elections. The legal requirements governing school elections are discussed in Chapter 5.

4.12 CURATIVE LEGISLATION CONCERNING THE CREATION OR ALTERATION OF SCHOOL DISTRICTS

Occasionally a school district will be created and begin operation only to find later that it was not legally created, either as a result of irregularities in procedure or because the act under which it was created has been declared unconstitutional. In such circumstances a state legislature may attempt to pass a law validating the district's creation rather than requiring it to undergo the inconvenience and confusion which would otherwise result. Legislation of this type is commonly termed *curative legislation*. The general rule is that, if the defect consists of something which the legislature could have authorized in the first place, it may enact legislation which "cures" the defect by validating proceedings which would otherwise be illegal or void.[132] It has been said that "the legislature may validate, reconstitute and establish a school district, the original organization of which may be clouded with failure of strict compliance with statutory provisions relating to procedure."[133] It has been held,[134] for example, that a curative act may remedy such defects as an improper petition for the calling of an election, the failure of petitions to bear the required number of signatures, the use of improper ballots, and the casting of illegal votes. It also has been ruled[135] that the legislature may validate school districts organized under a law declared invalid by the courts and that it may validate a district which failed to meet statutory requirements regarding the number of inhabitants.[136]

A legislature cannot validate a district which it was without power to authorize in the first place. There is also authority indicating that curative legislation cannot render void proceedings valid.[137] Thus, it has been decided[138] that, where no election notice was given, a district could not later be validated by curative legislation. Among other restrictions on curative legislation are the following: Curative legislation cannot impair the obligation of contracts or a district's vested rights;[139] curative legislation cannot validate school districts created under proceedings which were tainted with fraud;[140] and curative legislation cannot validate school districts for which no statutory authority existed at the time of their creation.[141] It should also be noted that

---

[128]Rural Independent School District of Osprey v. County Board of Education, 111 N.W.2d 691 (Iowa 1961); Balson v. Joint County School Committee, 119 N.W.2d 438 (Wis. 1963); State v. Bilyeu, 346 S.W.2d 221 (Mo. 1961); State v. Board of Education of Hardin County, 176 N.E.2d 174 (Ohio 1959); In re Township 143 North, Range 55 West, 183 N.W.2d 520 (N.D. 1971).

[129]Turnis v. Board of Education of Jones County, 109 N.W.2d 198 (Iowa 1961); Balson v. Joint County School Committee, 119 N.W.2d 438 (Wis. 1963).

[130]People v. Keechler, 62 N.E. 525 (Ill. 1901).

[131]State v. Robinson, 1 So.2d 621 (Fla. 1941); State v. Underhill, 46 N.E.2d 861 (Ohio 1943); Gazaway v. Godfrey, 163 S.E. 480 (Ga. 1932); State v. Hawk, 228 S.W.2d 785 (Mo. 1950).

[132]Peavey v. Nickerson, 185 A.2d 309 (Me. 1962); State v. Common School District No. 87, 185 P.2d 677 (Kan. 1947); Smith v. Lexington School District No. 1, 64 S.E.2d 534 (S.C. 1951); Regional High School District No. 3 v. Town of Newton, 59 A.2d 527 (Conn. 1948); Marfa Independent School District v. Wood, 141 S.W.2d 590 (Tex. 1940); Hendrickson v. Powell County, 112 P.2d 199 (Mont. 1941); State v. Squires, 26 Iowa 340 (1868); People v. Community High School District No. 233, 77 N.E.2d 154 (Ill. 1948).

[133]Peavey v. Nickerson, 185 A.2d 309 (Me. 1962).

[134]People v. Birdsong, 76 N.E.2d 185 (Ill. 1947).

[135]Hodges v. Snyder, 261 U.S. 600, 43 S.Ct. 435, 67 L.Ed. 819 (S.D. 1923); State v. Common School District No. 87, 185 P.2d 677 (Kan. 1947); Marfa Independent School District v. Wood, 141 S.W.2d 590 (Tex. 1940).

[136]State v. Squires, 26 Iowa 340 (1868).

[137]Peter v. Board of Supervisors of Kern County, 178 P.2d 73 (Cal. 1947).

[138]People v. McCoy, 56 N.E.2d 393 (Ill. 1944).

[139]People v. Stitt, 117 N.E. 784 (Ill. 1917).

[140]Cleveland v. Gainer, 184 S.W. 593 (Tex. 1916).

[141]Isaacson v. Parker, 176 N.W. 653 (S.D. 1920).

curative legislation is purely retrospective in nature; it will not validate districts created or altered after its passage.[142]

4.13 STATUS OF DISTRICTS PENDING COMPLETION OF ALTERATION

In view of the remarkable decrease in the number of school districts in the United States in recent years brought about as a result of school district reorganization and consolidation, it is not surprising that several cases have come before the courts in which the status of school districts involved in alteration proceedings has been at issue. The point in time at which the alteration becomes effective and the legal rights of the school districts involved pending and following alteration are especially important. It has generally been held that the creation or alteration of a school district takes effect upon completion of the required proceedings,[143] or upon issuance of the proper order,[144] unless statutes provide that the creation or alteration shall become effective on some other specified date. It has been held that where the statutes make no provision to the contrary, an order creating or altering a school district becomes effective at the time it is signed;[145] that an annexation is completed when the vote at an election favors it;[146] and that where alteration of a district is mandatory upon presentation of a petition to a specified officer or board, the alteration is effective upon the day on which such a petition is presented.[147]

The same general rule applies where school districts are dissolved. The dissolution of a school district is effective immediately upon completion of the proceedings specified in the statutes.[148]

Statutes may, of course, prescribe the time or date on which the creation or alteration of school districts is to become effective. Under such statutes the organization and operation of the districts affected continue unchanged until the time fixed by statute for the alterations to become effective.[149] That is, the schools in an area which is to be annexed to another district remain under the control of the district from which they are being detached until the date the annexation becomes effective.[150]

Disputes occasionally arise when a school district becomes involved in a second annexation proceeding before action on the first has been completed. It has generally been held that priority belongs to the first proceeding initiated and that territory included in one proceeding cannot be included in another until action on the first has been completed.[151]

It is quite common for statutes to provide for appeal of a decision by an officer or agency concerning the creation or alteration of school districts, and numerous cases have dealt with the effect of an appeal on further proceedings. It has been held[152] that the taking of an appeal suspends further proceedings pending the outcome of the appeal. For example, in an unusual Oklahoma case[153] the consolidation of two school districts was appealed. While the appeal was pending, one of the districts was annexed to a third district. The court ruled that the appeal stayed the proceedings in the original annexation, thus permitting the annexation of one of the districts involved to a third district. In Wisconsin, however, it has been held[154] that a school district in-

[142]Roberts v. Caddo Parish School Board, 34 So.2d 916 (La. 1948); Cleveland v. Gainer, 184 S.W. 593 (Tex. 1916). Contra, Clark v. Allen, 177 N.Y.S.2d 180 (1958).

[143]People v. Community Unit School District No. 316, 100 N.E.2d 573 (Ill. 1951); State v. Pence, 31 N.E.2d 841 (Ohio 1941); Turnis v. Board of Education of Jones County, 109 N.W.2d 198 (Iowa 1961); Rutter v. Board of Education, 102 N.W.2d 192 (Mich. 1960); Hazelton-Moffit Special School District No. 6 v. Ward, 107 N.W.2d 636 (N.D. 1961); Lewis County C-1 School District v. Normile, 431 S.W.2d 118 (Mo. 1968).

[144]Weasel Head v. Armstrong, 43 P.2d 243 (Mont. 1935); Portland School District No. 4 v. Drew County Board of Education, 233 S.W.2d 66 (Ark. 1950); Beam v. Wilson, 110 N.Y.S.2d 94 (1952); Hunt v. Trimble, 145 S.W.2d 659 (Tex. 1940).

[145]Lundt v. School Board of Joint School District No. 1, 86 N.W.2d 452 (Wis. 1957); Board of Education of Southgate Independent School District v. Board of Education of Campbell County School District, 293 S.W.2d 568 (Ky. 1956).

[146]State v. Bilyeu, 351 S.W.2d 457 (Mo. 1961).

[147]State v. Summit County Board of Education, 155 N.E. 505 (Ohio 1926).

[148]Causey v. Guilford County, 135 S.E. 40 (N.C. 1926); State v. Goff, 218 Pac. 556 (Ore. 1923).

[149]Smith v. Canyon County, 226 Pac. 1070 (Ida. 1924); Goren v. Buena High School District of Cochise County, 372 P.2d 692 (Ariz. 1962); School District of Bellevue v. Strawn, 176 N.W.2d 42 (Neb. 1970).

[150]Board of Trustees of Demossville Graded Common School District v. Board of Education of Kenton County, 236 S.W. 1038 (Ky. 1922); Independent School District No. JI-69 v. Independent School District No. D-45, 363 P.2d 835 (Okla. 1961).

[151]Turnis v. Board of Education of Jones County, 109 N.W.2d 198 (Iowa 1961); State v. Board of Education of Hardin County, 176 N.E.2d 174 (Ohio 1959); Palmer v. Sawyer County School Committee, 96 N.W.2d 810 (Wis. 1959); Tryon Dependent School District No. 125 v. Carrier, 474 P.2d 131 (Okla. 1970).

[152]Weasel Head v. Armstrong, 43 P.2d 243 (Mont. 1935); State v. Mettler, 89 N.W.2d 168 (Minn. 1958); In re Walter's Appeal, 72 N.W.2d 535 (Wis. 1955); Sheridan Rural Independent School District v. Guernsey Consolidated School District, 100 N.W.2d 418 (Iowa 1960); State v. Cainsville Reorganized School District, 331 S.W.2d 629 (Mo. 1960).

[153]Independent School District No. JI-69 v. Independent School District No. D-45, 363 P.2d 835 (Okla. 1961).

[154]Palmer v. Sawyer County School Committee, 96 N.W.2d 810 (Wis. 1959).

volved in one reorganization plan cannot become involved in another, pending the outcome of an appeal from the first.

The fact that a school district's boundaries have been altered does not, of itself, mean that the district loses its name or identity, or that it immediately ceases to exist as a legal corporate entity.[155] Statutes may provide for the continuance for certain purposes, such as the payment of its debts or the enforcement of its legal rights, of a district which has been dissolved.[156] It also has been held[157] that even without specific statutory provision a school district which has been annexed to another district may retain its corporate entity long enough to terminate its affairs.

4.14 EFFECT OF ALTERATION OR DISSOLUTION OF SCHOOL DISTRICTS

Although it would appear to be self-evident, a number of cases have reinforced the conclusion that territory legally transferred from one school district to another becomes part of the district to which it has been attached and that its legal relationship to the district to which it formerly belonged is terminated.[158] The residents of such territory become electors of the district to which the territory is attached and lose their right to vote on matters relating to the district to which the territory formerly belonged.[159] Jurisdiction over such territory is transferred from the officers of the district to which it previously belonged to the officers of the district to which it is attached.[160]

A school district which has been dis-

solved in the process of school district reorganization or consolidation ceases to have legal existence.[161] Not only does dissolution revoke the rights and privileges of a school district;[162] it also revokes all power and authority held by others to act in the district's behalf.[163]

4.15 EFFECT OF EXTENSION OF MUNICIPAL BOUNDARIES ON SCHOOL DISTRICT BOUNDARIES

It has been emphasized repeatedly that a state legislature has full and complete control over the creation, alteration, and dissolution of school districts. The legislature may attach territory to a municipality for school purposes only, or it may create school districts whose boundaries coincide with those of a municipality.[164] Furthermore, it may place the schools in such districts directly under the control of the municipality, or it may make them completely independent of the municipality.

Where school district boundaries are coterminous with those of a municipality, questions as to whether changes in municipal boundaries automatically result in changes in school district boundaries frequently arise. In viewing them one must recognize that the relationship between a school district and a municipality is defined by the legislature through statutes and city charters; i.e., school districts and municipalities are separate and distinct legal entities established by the state. Having created them, the state is responsible for specifying the relationship, if any, of one to the other.

The extension of municipal boundaries does not *ipso facto* change the boundaries of school districts unless the statutes specifically affirm or clearly imply that such is the intent of the legislature.[165] The courts

[155]Hughes v. Ewing, 28 Pac. 1067 (Cal. 1892); Halstead v. Rozmiarek, 94 N.W.2d 37 (Neb. 1959); Schroeder v. Oeltjen, 165 N.W.2d 81 (Neb. 1969).

[156]Rogers v. People, 68 Ill. 154 (1873); Leone v. Hunter, 191 N.Y.S.2d 334 (1959).

[157]Board of Education v. Presque Isle County Board of Education, 97 N.W.2d 734 (Mich. 1959).

[158]Nishna Valley Community School District v. Malvern Community School District, 121 N.W.2d 646 (Iowa 1963); Shirley v. School Board of School District No. 58, 332 P.2d 267 (Kan. 1958); Heinze v. St. Joseph Township School District No. 1, 58 N.W.2d 920 (Mich. 1953); Chisena v. Central High School District No. 2, 136 N.Y.S.2d 598 (1954); State v. Appleton City Board of Education, 53 Mo. 127 (1873); Lewis County C-1 School District v. Normile, 431 S.W.2d 118 (Mo. 1968); Elementary School Districts 1, 3, and 10 v. District Boundary Board of Campbell County, 454 P.2d 237 (Wyo. 1969); School District of Bellevue v. Strawn, 176 N.W.2d 42 (Neb. 1970).

[159]Board of Education v. Campbell, 143 N.E. 273 (Ohio 1924).

[160]People v. Board of Education, 99 N.E. 659 (Ill. 1912); Ranier v. Board of Education of Prestonburg Independent School District, 273 S.W.2d 577 (Ky. 1954); Farley v. Lawton School District No. 41, 137 N.W. 821 (N.D. 1912); Pass School District v. Hollywood City School District, 105 Pac. 122 (Cal. 1909).

[161]Garrett v. Folsom, 357 P.2d 130 (Ariz. 1960); Padberg v. Martin, 357 P.2d 255 (Ore. 1960); Follett v. Sheldon, 144 N.E. 867 (Ind. 1924).

[162]People v. Calloway, 160 N.E. 834 (Ill. 1928); Garrett v. Folsom, 357 P.2d 130 (Ariz. 1960).

[163]People v. Calloway, 160 N.E. 834 (Ill. 1928); Robertson v. Town of Englewood, 123 S.W.2d 1090 (Tenn. 1939).

[164]School District No. 84 v. Asher School District No. 112, 32 P.2d 897 (Okla. 1934); State v. Hine, 21 Atl. 1024 (Conn. 1890); State v. Haworth, 23 N.E. 946 (Ind. 1890); State v. Board of Commissioners of Elk County, 58 Pac. 959 (Kan. 1899); Harrison School District No. 2 v. City of Minot, 189 N.W. 338 (N.D. 1922); Associated Schools of Independent District No. 63 v. School District No. 83, 142 N.W. 325 (Minn. 1913).

[165]Pleasant Hill Independent School District v. Norris, 94 N.W.2d 765 (Iowa 1959); Ross v. City of Crandon, 290 N.W. 587 (Wis. 1940); Tukwila School District v. Burrows, 190 Pac. 1010 (Wash. 1920); School District

reason that the statutes relating to the public schools prescribe the methods by which school district boundaries may be changed and that education is a matter of state, not municipal concern.[166] Consequently, a change in municipal boundaries does not result in a change in school district boundaries in the absence of a specific legislative provision to this effect. Unfortunately, since legislatures are not always explicit in this regard, a number of cases have arisen in which the courts have been required to determine a legislature's intent. Where legislative enactments specifically say or clearly imply that the boundaries of a school district serving a municipality shall be coterminous with those of the municipality, the courts have consistently ruled that changes in municipal boundaries result *ipso facto* in changes in school district boundaries.[167]

In the absence of specific legislative direction, however, changes in municipal boundaries, either by incorporation or by annexation, have no effect on school district boundaries.[168] It should also be noted that the granting of "home-rule" privileges to a city does not place the schools under the jurisdiction of the city government and does not affect the status of a school district comprised of the city.[169]

Questions may arise in regard to the effect on existing school districts of the establishment of a city school system. The same legal principles applicable in situations in which municipal boundaries are altered apply here. Thus, where the statutes provide that incorporation of a city automatically establishes it as an independent school district, all territory within the corporate limits of the municipality becomes

part of the city school district.[170] In the absence of clear statutory provision, however, the incorporation of a city does not thereby create a city school district and does not affect the status of school districts comprising the area included within the corporate boundaries of the city.[171] Some statutes provide that the area comprising a city may become an independent or city school district if other specified requirements, e.g., petition, referendum, etc., are met. Such requirements are mandatory and must be followed if a valid city school district is to be created.[172]

4.16 DISPOSITION OF ASSETS AND LIABILITIES

4.16a Where no controlling statutes exist

One of the most perplexing problems which arises when school districts are altered or dissolved is that of determining what disposition is to be made of the district's assets and/or liabilities where the statutes make no provision for their disposition. That is, who holds title to the property and funds of the district and who is responsible for its debts and the contracts into which it has entered?

Application of the basic concept that education is a state function is apparent in the decisions of the courts in such cases. The courts reason that school property in reality is state property, held in trust for the state by the school district it has created and used by such districts to carry out a state function.[173] Thus, ultimate title to school property rests with the state, not with the local school district. Since school district property is state or public property, it is clear that the citizens and/or taxpayers of a school district can claim no private property rights in it.[174] Furthermore, because school district property is state property held in trust and used for the purposes of

No. 7 v. School District of St. Joseph, 82 S.W. 1082 (Mo. 1904); Hays v. City of Beaumont, 190 S.W.2d 835 (Tex. 1945); Collins v. City of Detroit, 161 N.W. 905 (Mich. 1917).

[166]School District No. 7 v. School District of St. Joseph, 82 S.W. 1082 (Mo. 1904); Collins v. City of Detroit, 161 N.W. 905 (Mich. 1917).

[167]Winona v. School District No. 82, 41 N.W. 539, 3 L.R.A. 46 (Minn. 1889); Common School District No. 126 v. City of Fargo, 51 N.W.2d 364 (N.D. 1952); Jones v. Humphrey, 199 N.W. 772 (S.D. 1924); Harp. v. Consolidated School District No. 1, 241 Pac. 787 (Okla. 1925); Special School District No. 2 v. Special School District of Texarkana, 163 S.W. 1164 (Ark. 1914).

[168]Village of Brown Deer v. City of Milwaukee, 79 N.W.2d 340 (Wis. 1956); Thomas v. Spragens, 213 S.W.2d 452 (Ky. 1948); Appeal of School District of City of Bethlehem, 41 A.2d 713 (Pa. 1945); Fort Wayne Community Schools v. State, 159 N.E.2d 708 (Ind. 1959); State v. Henderson, 46 S.W. 1076 (Mo. 1898); Collins v. City of Detroit, 161 N.W. 905 (Mich. 1917).

[169]City of Fort Worth v. Zane-Cetti Co., 278 S.W. 183 (Tex. 1925).

[170]Common School District No. 126 v. City of Fargo, 51 N.W.2d 364 (N.D. 1952); Ross v. City of Crandon, 290 N.W. 587 (Wis. 1940); Harp v. Consolidated School District No. 1, 241 Pac. 787 (Okla. 1925); Jones v. Humphrey, 199 N.W. 772 (S.D. 1924); Franklin v. Goodrich, 108 Pac. 685 (Cal. 1910).

[171]Pleasant Hill Independent School District v. Norris, 94 N.W.2d 765 (Iowa 1959); Tukwila School District v. Burrows, 190 Pac. 1010 (Wash. 1920).

[172]Cook v. Consolidated School District of Truro, 38 N.W.2d 265 (Iowa 1949).

[173]Pass School District v. Hollywood City School District, 105 Pac. 122 (Cal. 1909); In re School Committee of North Smithfield, 58 Atl. 628 (R.I. 1904); School District of Oakland v. District of Joplin, 102 S.W.2d 909 (Mo. 1937).

[174]In re School Committee of North Smithfield, 58 Atl. 628 (R.I. 1904).

the state, the legislature may, in the absence of constitutional prohibition, transfer legal title to such property from one school district to another school district, or make any other disposition of the property as it may deem proper.[175] The California Supreme Court, in a case in which it was claimed that the transfer of property from one school district to another deprived the former district of its property without due process of law, stated concisely the legal principles involved:

> To the contention that a transfer of ownership thus accomplished works the taking of property without due process of law, it should be sufficient to point out that in all such cases the beneficial owner of the fee is the state itself, and its agencies and mandatories—the various public and municipal corporations in whom the title rests—are essentially nothing but trustees of the state, holding the property and devoting it to the uses which the state itself directs. The transfer of title without due process of law, of which appellant so bitterly complains, is nothing more, in effect, than the naming by the state of other trustees to manage property which it owns and to manage the property for the same identical uses and purposes to which it was formerly devoted. In point of law, then, the beneficial title to the estate is not affected at all. All that is done is to transfer the legal title under the same trust from one trustee to another.[176]

In the absence of statutes providing for the division of property and debts when school district boundaries are altered, the weight of authority is that school property belongs to the district in which it is located after the alteration but that liability for any existing indebtedness remains with the district in which the property was originally situated.[177] The courts reason that the problem of providing for the equitable adjust-ment of assets and liabilities when school districts are altered should be resolved by the legislature, not by the courts.[178] There is some authority, however, that school property located within territory which has been attached to another school district remains the property of the district in which it was originally located.[179] In a few cases, too, it has been held that territory which is attached to another district remains liable for its proportionate share of the existing debt of the district to which it originally belonged.[180]

In regard to the disposition of cash on hand and accounts receivable, it must be recognized that when a school district is altered, but not dissolved, the altered district retains its corporate identity and all of its rights and privileges. Thus, where there is no statutory provision to the contrary, it has been held[181] that the original district retains all cash on hand as well as any funds which are receivable.

Where no part of the original corporate entity remains, however, different principles of law must be applied in determining the disposition of its assets and liabilities. In the absence of a controlling statute, the general rule is that when an entire school district is annexed to or consolidated with one or more other school districts, the new districts are entitled to all of the property and assets of the old district and are liable for all of its existing debts and obligations.[182] If a school district is absorbed in its

---

[175]Attorney General v. Lowrey, 199 U.S. 233, 26 S.Ct. 27, 50 L.Ed. 167 (Mich. 1905); Common School District No. 2 v. District No. 1, 227 P.2d 947 (Ida. 1951); People v. Bartlett, 136 N.E. 654 (Ill. 1922); Pass School District v. Hollywood City School District, 105 Pac. 122 (Cal. 1909); State v. Hine, 21 Atl. 1024, 10 L.R.A. 83 (Conn. 1890).

[176]Pass School District v. Hollywood City School District, 105 Pac. 122 (Cal. 1909).

[177]School District of Oakland v. District of Joplin, 102 S.W.2d 909 (Mo. 1937); People v. Bartlett, 136 N.E. 654 (Ill. 1922); Board of Education of Barker Dist. v. Board of Education of Valley Dist., 4 S.E. 640 (W.Va. 1887); Pass School District v. Hollywood City School District, 105 Pac. 122 (Cal. 1909); Livingston v. School District No. 7, 68 N.W. 167 (S.D. 1896); Lovejoy v. School District No. 46 of Sedwick County, 269 P.2d 1067 (Col. 1954); Duffee v. Jones, 68 S.E.2d 699 (Ga. 1952); Zawerschnik v. Joint County School Committee, 73 N.W.2d 566 (Wis. 1955); Ridgeland School District No. 14 v. Biesmann, 21 N.W.2d 324 (S.D. 1946).

[178]People v. Bartlett, 136 N.E. 654 (Ill. 1922).

[179]Board of Education v. School District No. 7, 26 Pac. 13 (Kan. 1891); Board of Education of Campbell County v. Board of Education of Newport, 146 S.W.2d 30 (Ky. 1940); School Board of Consolidated District No. 36 v. Edwards, 87 P.2d 692, 121 A.L.R. 820 (Okla. 1939); Whittier v. Sanborn, 38 Me. 32 (1854).

[180]Board of Education v. Board of Education, 222 N.W. 763 (Mich. 1929); Walpole v. Wall, 149 S.E. 760 (S.C. 1929); Manahan v. Adams County, 110 N.W. 860 (Neb. 1906).

[181]School District No. 14 v. School District No. 21, 71 P.2d 137 (Wyo. 1937); Gamble v. Dubose, 54 S.E.2d 803 (S.C. 1949); People v. Trustees of Schools, 106 N.E.2d 892 (Ill. 1952); Cooke v. School District No. 12, 21 Pac. 496 (Col. 1889); Rice v. McClelland, 58 Mo. 116 (1874). Contra, Towle v. Brown, 10 N.E. 626 (Ind. 1887).

[182]San Francisco Unified School District v. City & County of San Francisco, 128 P.2d 696 (Cal. 1942); Rapp v. Bethel-Tate Consolidated School District, 16 N.E.2d 224 (Ohio 1937); Wilson v. Wilson, 50 S.W.2d 48 (Ky. 1932); Board of Education of McDowell County v. Burgin, 174 S.E. 286 (N.C. 1934); Independent School District No. 1 v. Williamson, 262 P.2d 701 (Okla. 1953); Rocky Mount Independent School District v. Jackson, 152 S.W.2d 400 (Tex. 1941); Independent School District No. 7 v. Barnes, 228 P.2d 939 (Ida. 1951); Las Animas County High School District v. Raye, 356 P.2d 237 (Col. 1960); Slabosheske v. Chikowske, 77 N.W.2d 497 (Wis. 1956); Ingram v. Doss, 124 S.E.2d 87 (Ga. 1962); State v. Smith, 121 S.W.2d 160 (Mo. 1938); Fulton

entirety by another district, its assets and liabilities are automatically assumed by the new district. If, however, the district is divided between two or more districts, each is entitled to the property located within its boundaries following the division.[183] The weight of authority indicates that in such a situation each district is liable for its proportionate share of the debts of the old district,[184] although there is also authority indicating that each district is liable for the entire indebtedness of the district which has gone out of existence.[185]

A school district which is attached to or consolidated with another district frequently will have entered into teaching contracts, school building contracts, or contracts for materials and supplies. Such contracts, if entered into in good faith, must be honored by the successor district to which the contracting district is attached.[186] It has been ruled,[187] for example, that a school district may be held liable for construction contracts entered into by a district which it later absorbed. Similarly, it has been decided[188] that a school district absorbing another district must honor any contracts with teachers which that district had entered into prior to its absorption.

School district reorganization is sometimes accomplished by merely changing from one type of school district to another with no change in boundaries involved. In such cases the successor district retains the property of its predecessor and is liable for the debts of its predecessor.[189]

4.16b Where statutes exist

Most states have enacted legislation aimed at securing an equitable distribution of assets and liabilities when school districts are altered or dissolved. Since school districts are creatures of the state, the legislature has complete authority in this regard except as limited by constitutional provisions. The principal constitutional clause which may be involved relates to impairment of the obligation of contracts. It has been held[190] that a statute providing for the apportionment of assets and liabilities when school districts are reorganized is not void as impairing the obligation of contracts. It is reasoned that persons who contract with a school district are obligated to know that it may be dissolved or altered.[191] The legislature must, however, make some provision for the payment of an outstanding indebtedness when a district is altered or dissolved. It may not relieve territory originally obligated for the payment of indebtedness of such an obligation unless it also makes adequate provision for repayment of the debt.[192] This is illustrated by a Michigan case contesting the constitutionality of a statute which provided that where territory of one school district was attached to another district the territory remaining in the original district would remain liable for any bonds it had issued. In holding the statute to be unconstitutional, the court noted that a contractual relationship exists between a school district and its bondholders. The court stated:

If a district consisting of nine sections may be dismembered by act of the Legislature, and one section detached therefrom, any number of sections less than the whole might be detached, and the security of the bondholder

Township School District v. School District No. 4, 5 N.W.2d 467 (Mich. 1942); Smythe v. Stroman, 162 S.E.2d 168 (S.C. 1968).

[183]Winona v. School District No. 82, 41 N.W. 539 3 L.R.A. 46 (Minn. 1889); Whitmore v. Hogan, 22 Me. 564 (1843).

[184]Mount Pleasant v. Beckwith, 100 U.S. 514, 25 L.Ed. 699 (Wis. 1879); Board of Education of Barker District v. Board of Education of Valley District, 4 S.E. 640 (W.Va. 1887); Halbert v. School Districts, 36 Mich. 421 (1877).

[185]Hughes v. School District No. 29, 72 Mo. 643 (1880); Welch v. Getzen, 67 S.E. 294 (S.C. 1910).

[186]Chidester School District No. 59 v. Faulkner, 235 S.W.2d 870 (Ark. 1951); McClure v. Princeton Reorganized School District R-5, 307 S.W.2d 726 (Mo. 1957); Martin v. Board of Education of Bath County, 146 S.W.2d 12 (Ky. 1940); Lippincott v. Board of Education, 97 N.E.2d 566 (Ill. 1951); Sweeney v. Lakeland School District, 319 A.2d 207 (Pa. 1974).

[187]Hatch v. Maple Valley Township Unit School, 17 N.W.2d 735 (Mich. 1945).

[188]Stroud v. Stevens Point, 37 Wis. 367 (1875); People v. Deatherage, 81 N.E.2d 581 (Ill. 1948); Rocky Mount Independent School District v. Jackson, 152 S.W.2d 400 (Tex. 1941); Chidester School District No. 59 v. Faulkner, 235 S.W.2d 870 (Ark. 1951); Shirley v. School Board of School District No. 58, 332 P.2d 267 (Kan. 1958); McClure v. Princeton Reorganized School District R-5, 307 S.W.2d 726 (Mo. 1957); Lakeland Joint School District v. Gilvary, 283 A.2d 500 (Pa. 1971); Knapp v. School District No. 109 R, 207 N.W.2d 223 (Neb. 1973); But see, Beckett v. Roderick, 251 A.2d 427 (Me. 1969).

[189]Breathitt County Board of Education v. Back, 283 S.W. 99 (Ky. 1926); Causey v. Guilford County, 135 S.E. 40 (N.C. 1926); Board of Education for Pike County v. A. H. Andrews Co., 122 S.W. 207 (Ky. 1909); School District No. 12 v. School District No. 33, 139 Pac. 136 (Ida. 1914).

[190]Tindall v. Byars, 59 S.E.2d 337 (S.C. 1950); Coble v. Board of Commissioners of Guilford County, 114 S.E. 487 (N.C. 1922); In re School Committee of North Smithfield, 58 Atl. 628 (R.I. 1904); Rawson v. Spencer, 113 Mass. 40 (1873).

[191]Curtis v. Haynes Special School District No. H, 193 S.W. 523 (Ark. 1917).

[192]Board of Education of City of Lincoln Park v. Board of Education of City of Detroit, 222 N.W. 763 (Mich. 1929); Hill v. Smithville Independent School District, 251 S.W. 209 (Tex. 1923); Excise Board of Lincoln County v. St. Louis-San Francisco Railway Co., 93 P.2d 1081 (Okla. 1939).

be thereby seriously impaired, if not entirely destroyed. The constitutional right of the Legislature to enact such a law cannot be made dependent upon whether the bondholder is sufficiently protected by the balance of the property not detached. He purchased the bonds, relying on the security afforded him; the right to enforce collection by a tax on the property of the district as it existed at the time the bonds were issued. [The act in question] relieves a considerable part of the territory then in the district from the payment of such tax without making any provision therefor, and for that reason it violates the constitutional provision [forbidding any law impairing the obligation of contracts].[193]

Other constitutional provisions may also limit a legislature's authority in apportioning the assets and liabilities of a school district. For example, a state's constitution may prohibit the levying of a tax or the incurring of indebtedness without first securing the approval of a majority of the taxpayers in the area involved. Under such a constitutional provision it has been held[194] that a statute making a school district to which another district is attached liable for the bonded indebtedness of the attached territory is void unless the taxpayers of the original district have voted to assume the indebtedness of the attached territory. Similarly, it has been held[195] that, under a constitutional provision forbidding the incurrence of debt without a vote of the taxpayers concerned, a district to which territory is attached is not liable for the indebtedness of the attached territory.

In regard to the liability of taxpayers in territory which has been attached to a school district for the existing indebtedness of the district to which they are attached, the situation is somewhat different. Territory which is attached to a school district is generally held to be liable for any obligations incurred by that district prior to the attachment,[196] particularly when the an-

nexed territory has petitioned or voted for the annexation.[197] It is reasoned that by voluntarily petitioning for or voting for annexation the taxpayers of the territory involved have automatically chosen to share in the obligations of the district to which they were attached.[198]

As a general rule, the rights and liabilities of districts involved in reorganization and consolidation are determined by statutes, subject always to constitutional restrictions. Statutes which provide for apportionment of assets and liabilities among the districts affected by alteration or consolidation are common. They typically provide for appraisal of the school property involved and a cash settlement among the districts involved based on the appraised value of the property and any outstanding indebtedness on the property. The constitutionality of such statutes has been upheld against the contention that they result in an unfair distribution of the burden of taxation,[199] and against the contention that they impose a tax for the benefit of private persons.[200] A statute requiring the district to which territory has been attached to pay the debts of the attached territory in proportion to its valuation has been upheld against the contention that it results in the taking of property without due process of law.[201]

Statutes which prescribe the steps to be followed in apportioning assets and liabilities are generally held to be directory, not mandatory, and minor irregularities will not invalidate the proceedings.[202] Obviously, the rules prescribed by the statute should be followed in apportioning assets and liabilities. The actual determination of assets and liabilities, however, usually requires the exercise of discretion on the part of the officer or agency responsible. As a general rule, the courts will not substitute their judgment for that of the officer or agency responsible for the apportionment unless there is clear evidence that the action

[193]Board of Education of City of Lincoln Park v. Board of Education of City of Detroit, 222 N.W. 763 (Mich. 1929).

[194]Gerhardt v. Yorktown Independent School District, 252 S.W. 197 (Tex. 1923); Burns v. Dilley County Line Independent School District, 295 S.W. 1091 (Tex. 1927).

[195]Protest of Missouri-Kansas-Texas Railroad Co., 73 P.2d 173 (Okla. 1937).

[196]Southern Pacific Co. v. Maricopa County, 129 P.2d 312 (Ariz. 1942); Excise Board of Lincoln County v. St. Louis-San Francisco Railway Co., 93 P.2d 1081 (Okla 1939); Linke v. Board of County Commissioners of Grand County, 268 P.2d 416 (Col. 1954); Watertown Independent School District No. 1 v. Thyen, 159 N.W.2d 122 (S.D. 1968).

[197]Board of County Commissioners v. Carpenter, 303 P.2d 1104 (Col. 1956); Wilcox v. County of Olmstead, 104 N.W.2d 297 (Minn. 1960).

[198]Wilcox v. County of Olmstead, 104 N.W.2d 297 (Minn. 1960).

[199]In re School Committee of North Smithfield, 58 Atl. 628 (R.I. 1904).

[200]Brown v. Bunselmeyer, 167 N.Y.S. 993 (1917); Arsenal School District v. Consolidated Town and City of Hartford, 180 Atl. 511 (Conn. 1935).

[201]School District No. 3 v. School District of City of Pontiac, 246 N.W. 145 (Mich. 1933); Ross v. Adams Mill Rural School District, 149 N.E. 634 (Ohio 1925).

[202]Follett v. Sheldon, 144 N.E. 867 (Ind. 1924); Johann v. Milton Township Rural Board of Education, 26 Ohio Cir.Ct. (N.S.) 209 (1915).

taken was arbitrary, or that it constituted an abuse of discretion.[203] The courts will not interfere in cases involving the apportionment of assets and liabilities unless the officer or agency involved was without jurisdiction, failed to comply with statutory requirements, or acted in an arbitrary or capricious manner.[204]

Questions occasionally arise as to what may properly be included within the categories of funds, property, or indebtedness under statutes providing for the apportionment of assets and liabilities. "Funds" have been defined as all moneys in the possession of the original district and all moneys to which it is entitled at the time of the transfer; "indebtedness' has been defined as all liabilities incurred prior to the date of the transfer, including bonded indebtedness and contractual obligations.[205] "Property" has been defined as anything which is owned or which is subject to legal ownership.[206] It should be noted, however, that the actual assets and liabilities which are to be apportioned must be determined by reference to the statutes and court decisions of the state involved. Although as a general rule only such assets as exist at the time of the action may be apportioned,[207] a number of cases have arisen concerning what constitutes an asset and when an asset legally exists. It has been decided,[208] for example, that funds derived from bonds sold to finance the construction of a schoolhouse are assets and must be apportioned, as are funds derived from a special tax levied to finance construction of a schoolhouse.[209] Although there is some authority to the contrary,[210] the general rule is that taxes which have been levied but not

yet collected must be included in the assets to be apportioned.[211]

4.16c Bases

A number of bases for apportioning assets and liabilities have been employed. One is the proportion of taxable property in the territory which is being transferred from one district to another compared to the proportion of taxable property which remains within the old district.[212] Apportionment has also been based on the number of pupils in the area affected[213] and on the needs of the respective districts.[214] Some statutes vest an officer or agency with broad discretionary power to make an "equitable" division of the assets and liabilities of school districts involved in reorganization or consolidation. The constitutionality of such a statute has been contested on the ground that it provided no standards for the agency to follow.[215] The statute was upheld on the basis that it established the broader test that the division of assets and liabilities must be equitable under the unique circumstances of each situation. It would appear that, if maximum equity in apportioning the assets and liabilities of districts involved in reorganization or consolidation is to be achieved, the apportionment should be based on the total appraised value of the school property and other assets of the district involved, the bonded indebtedness and other obligations of the district concerned, and the proportion of the taxable property of the original district which is involved in the alteration proceedings.

4.17 COLLECTION OF TAXES WHEN DISTRICTS ARE ALTERED OR DISSOLVED

When school districts are altered or dissolved, confusion is likely to arise in regard to the collection and distribution of taxes. Insofar as the district from which territory is detached is concerned, its power to tax such territory terminates at the time the detach-

[203]State v. Board of Commissioners of Wright County, 148 N.W. 53 (Minn. 1914); In re White Township School District, 150 Atl. 744 (Pa. 1930); School District No. 3 v. School District of City of Pontiac, 246 N.W. 145 (Mich. 1933).

[204]In re White Township School District, 150 Atl. 744 (Pa. 1930); In re School Directors of Borough of Aliquippa, 33 Atl. 236 (Pa. 1895).

[205]State v. Board of Education, 151 N.E. 669 (Ohio 1926). See also Board of School Directors of Mifflinburg Area School District v. Dock, 318 A.2d 370 (Pa. 1974).

[206]Las Animas County High School District v. Raye, 356 P.2d 237 (Col. 1960).

[207]Derry Township School District v. Derry Borough School District, 164 Atl. 802 (Pa. 1932).

[208]State Board of Education, 151 N.E. 669 (Ohio 1926).

[209]School District No. 61 v. School District No. 32, 98 Pac. 523 (Ore. 1908).

[210]School District No. 9 v. School District No. 5, 95 N.W. 148 (Wis. 1903); Rice v. McClelland, 58 Mo. 116 (1874).

[211]Las Animas County High School District v. Raye, 356 P.2d 237 (Col. 1960); Manchester v. Reserve Township, 4 Pa. 35 (1846); Towle v. Brown, 10 N.E. 626 (Ind. 1887); Banquet Independent School District v. Agua Dulce Independent School District, 241 S.W.2d 192 (Tex. 1951); Town of Barre v. School District No. 13, 30 Atl. 807 (Vt. 1894); Lewis County C-1 School District v. Normile, 431 S.W.2d 118 (Mo. 1968).

[212]Spring Township School District v. West Reading School District, 19 Pa.Dist. 519 (1910).

[213]Inhabitants of Needham v. Inhabitants of Wellesley, 31 N.E. 732 (Mass. 1885).

[214]District Township of Algona v. District Township of Lott's Creek, 6 N.W. 295 (Iowa 1880).

[215]State v. Board of Education of Columbus City School District, 179 N.E.2d 347 (Ohio 1961).

ment is effected.[216] However, it is entitled to collect taxes which have been levied prior to the time of the detachment.[217] The mere voting of a tax is not sufficient; the tax must actually be levied. Thus, if prior to the detachment a tax has been voted, but not levied, the detached territory is not liable for the tax.[218] If an appeal from an order for the alteration of school districts is taken, the status quo is maintained until final disposition of the appeal is made and the district in which the disputed territory was originally located retains power to levy a tax on the territory for school purposes.[219]

Unless the statutes make other provisions, territory which is attached to another school district may be taxed by the new district as soon as the attachment is effected.[220] The general rule in such cases is that a school district may levy a tax on all of the taxable property within its boundaries at the time the levy is made. However, property may not be taxed for the same purpose by two school districts within the same fiscal year.[221] Consequently, if the territory which is attached to another school district has already been taxed by the school district from which it was detached, it may not be taxed again by the district to which it is attached. It has been held[222] that, where a new school district recovers taxes wrongfully levied and collected by the old district on territory which had been detached from it, the funds recovered should be divided between the new district and any other districts formed from the area from which the tax was collected. Similarly, it has been decided[223] that, where taxes have been collected by a school district from territory attached to it through an inadvertent error,

the district to which the tax should have been paid may recover the proceeds from the district which received them.

4.18   THE COURTS AND CREATION OR ALTERATION OF SCHOOL DISTRICTS

The authority of the courts in matters related to school district reorganization extends to determining the constitutionality of legislation pertaining to the creation or alteration of school districts, interpreting legislation pertaining to the creation or alteration of school districts, and reviewing the acts of administrative officers or agencies responsible for carrying out the provisions of such legislation. The courts are not permitted to exercise discretion in determining whether or not a school district should be created or altered, nor can the legislature delegate to the courts authority to determine or fix the boundaries of school districts.[224] Legislation which delegates to a court the authority to determine school district boundaries has been held unconstitutional as a violation of the principle of separation of the powers of government.[225]

While the decisions of an officer or agency empowered to create or alter school districts may be made subject to review by another officer or agency, or by the courts,[226] the right to appeal such decisions is not absolute and frequently has been described as purely statutory.[227] The right of appeal is limited to those who have been granted that right by statute, or, in the absence of statute, to one who is aggrieved by the decision.[228] When the right of appeal is governed by statute, an appeal must be taken to the officer, agency, or court designated by statute to hear such appeals; in the absence of statutory provision for further appeal, the decision of the body designated to hear and determine appeals is final.[229]

[216]People v. New York Central Railroad Co., 60 N.E.2d 228 (Ill. 1945); Board of Education of City of Wichita v. Barrett, 167 Pac. 1068 (Kan. 1917).

[217]Prohm v. Non-High School District No. 216, 130 N.E.2d 917 (Ill. 1955); Marsh v. Early, 86 S.E. 303 (N.C. 1915); Independent District of Union v. Independent District of Cedar Rapids, 17 N.W. 895 (Iowa 1883); Dyer v. School District No. 1, 17 Atl. 788 (Vt. 1889).

[218]Hughes v. Ewing, 28 Pac. 1067 (Cal. 1892); State v. Burford, 82 Mo.App. 343 (1899); Pierce v. Whitman, 23 Vt. 626 (1851).

[219]Trico Community Unit School District v. Steeleville Community Unit School District, 159 N.E.2d 507 (Ill. 1959).

[220]Missouri-Kansas-Texas Railroad Co. v. Cowden, 86 P.2d 776 (Okla. 1939); Groul v. Illingworth, 108 N.W. 528 (Iowa 1906); Adriaansen v. Union Free School District No. 1, 226 N.Y.S. 145 (1927); Fifield v. Swett, 56 N.H. 432 (1876); State ex rel. Fort Osage School District v. Conley, 485 S.W.2d 469 (Mo. 1972).

[221]Board of Education v. Givens, 146 S.W. 16 (Ky. 1912).

[222]School District No. 9 v. School District No. 6, 12 N.W. 921 (Neb. 1882).

[223]Joint School District No. 1 v. Joint School District of Rice Lake, 109 N.W.2d 658 (Wis. 1961).

[224]In re Community School District of Malvern, 98 N.W.2d 737 (Iowa 1959); Turnis v. Board of Education of Jones County, 109 N.W.2d 198 (Iowa 1961).

[225]In re Community School District of Malvern, 98 N.W.2d 737 (Iowa 1959).

[226]Church v. Purcell, 196 S.E. 806 (Ga. 1938); Husser v. Fouth, 53 N.E.2d 949 (Ill. 1944); Board of Education of Central School District No. 1 v. Spaulding, 75 N.Y.S.2d 583 (1947); Schweigirt v. Abbott, 142 N.W. 723 (Minn. 1913).

[227]In re Durant Community School District, 106 N.W.2d 670 (Iowa 1960); In re Apportionment and Adjustment of Indebtedness, 169 A.2d 774 (Pa. 1961); Langland v. Joint County School Committee, 107 N.W.2d 503 (Wis. 1961).

[228]Ozark School District No. 56 v. Jackson, 145 S.W.2d 732 (Ark. 1941); Mason v. People, 56 N.E. 1069 (Ill. 1900).

[229]Perkins v. Lenora Rural High School Joint District No. 1, 237 P.2d 228 (Kan. 1951); Read v. Stephens, 193 P.2d 626 (Mont. 1948); In re Consolidated School District No. 25, 59 P.2d 1137 (Wash. 1936).

Such decisions are not subject to review by the courts unless they are arbitrary or fraudulent or constitute an abuse of discretion.[230] It should also be noted that before one may appeal to the courts, all other remedies provided by the statutes must be exhausted.[231]

The concerns of a court in reviewing the actions taken by an administrative officer or agency have been stated succinctly by the Supreme Court of Wisconsin:

> ... a court in reviewing the action of an administrative board or agency in certiorari will go no further than to determine: (1) whether the board kept within its jurisdiction, (2) whether it acted according to law, (3) whether its action was arbitrary, oppressive, or unreasonable and represented its will and not its judgment, and (4) whether the evidence was such that it might reasonably make the order or determination in question.[232]

It should be emphasized that the courts will not pass judgment on the wisdom or merit of a particular plan of school district reorganization, nor will they substitute their judgment for that of an administrative officer or agency unless the evidence clearly shows an abuse of discretion or utter failure to comply with statutory requirements.[233] Again, the principle of separation of powers is involved, substituting the judgment of a court for that of a legislative or administrative agency designated to make the decision would violate this principle.

It is firmly established that when an agency acts beyond its jurisdiction, its acts

will not be upheld by the courts.[234] While this principle is perhaps obvious, questions occasionally arise as to whether jurisdiction over the creation or alteration of school districts has been conferred upon an officer or agency. Such cases involve questions of fact; that is, was there compliance with statutory requirements? For example, in Ohio it has been ruled[235] that a petition which was filed with the county board of education, rather than with the county superintendent of schools as the statute required, did not confer jurisdiction upon the county board and that all subsequent acts taken on the petition were invalid.

The courts will require an administrative officer or agency to adhere to statutory requirements concerning procedural matters. However, as noted earlier, in procedural matters the courts are generally satisfied with substantial compliance with the statutes. Strict compliance is necessary only where the statutory requirements are mandatory.

As a general rule, when the legality of a school district is challenged, it is presumed that a district which has been established under statutory authority has been validly organized.[236] Thus, the burden of proving that the district has been illegally organized rests upon those who challenge its legal existence.[237] A record of proceedings showing substantial compliance with the procedures prescribed by statute constitutes prima facie evidence that a district has been validly organized.[238] Furthermore, where a complete record of the proceedings exists, parol evidence, e.g., oral testimony, ordinarily is not admitted.[239] Parol evidence is admissible, however, where there is no record of the proceedings.[240] It is also generally assumed that a public officer or agency involved in the creation or alteration of school districts has acted in substantial com-

[230]Read v. Stephens, 193 P.2d 626 (Mont. 1948); Wilsey v. Cornwall, 82 Pac. 303 (Wash. 1905); Givden v. Trustees of Common School District No. 54, 102 S.W. 1191 (Ky. 1907); Canutillo Independent School District v. Anthony Independent School District, 442 S.W.2d 916 (Tex. 1969); Fairview Independent School District No. 115-69 v. County Board of Education of Hand County, 176 N.W.2d 742 (S.D. 1970); Appeal of School District of Borough of Braddock Hills, 285 A.2d 880 (Pa. 1971).
[231]Laughlin v. Columbiana County Board of Education, 189 N.E.2d 726 (Ohio 1959); Stanberry v. Smith, 377 P.2d 8 (Ore. 1962); Board of Education v. Board of Education, 104 N.W.2d 590 (Iowa 1960).
[232]State v. Board of School Directors of Milwaukee, 111 N.W.2d 198 (Wis. 1961).
[233]In re Joint School District No. 2, 113 N.W.2d 141 (Wis. 1962); Board of Education v. County Board of School Trustees, 166 N.E.2d 472 (Ill. 1960); State v. Eckley, 347 S.W.2d 704 (Mo. 1961); Allely v. Board of Education, 110 N.W.2d 410 (Iowa 1961); Neary v. Allen, 227 N.Y.S.2d 1015 (1962); Board of Education v. County Board of School Trustees, 176 N.E.2d 633 (Ill. 1961); State v. Board of Education of Hardin County, 176 N.E.2d 174 (Ohio 1959); Common School District No. 899 v. Independent School District No. 784, 177 N.W.2d 775 (Minn. 1970); Appeal of School District of Borough of Braddock Hills, 285 A.2d 880 (Pa. 1971).

[234]Springville Community School District v. Iowa Department of Public Instruction, 109 N.W.2d 213 (Iowa 1961); Balson v. Joint School Committee, 119 N.W.2d 438 (Wis. 1963); State v. Mercer County Board of Education, 175 N.E.2d 305 (Ohio 1959).
[235]State v. Mercer County Board of Education, 175 N.E.2d 305 (Ohio 1959).
[236]Palmer v. Sawyer County School Committee, 96 N.W.2d 810 (Wis. 1959); People v. Gardner, 96 N.E.2d 551 (Ill. 1951).
[237]Majerus v. School District No. 52, 299 N.W. 178 (Neb. 1941); Magnolia Springs Common School District v. Kirbyville Independent School District, 255 S.W.2d 326 (Tex. 1953); Goodnoe Hills School District No. 24 v. Forry, 329 P.2d 1083 (Wash. 1958).
[238]Clark v. State, 189 S.W. 84 (Tex. 1916); Ralls v. Sharp's Administrator, 131 S.W. 998 (Ky. 1910).
[239]State v. School District No. 7, 33 N.W. 266 (Neb. 1887); Whitmore v. Hogan, 22 Me. 564 (1843).
[240]Barnes v. Barnes, 6 Vt. 338 (1834).

pliance with statutory requirements.[241] This assumption may be disproved, however, by a record which shows that the proceedings were improper or ineffective or that the required procedures were not followed.[242]

Occasionally statutes provide that, when a newly organized school district has exercised the powers conferred upon it by the state, it will be presumed to have been legally created. It has been held[243] that the presumption of legal creation under such statutes is conclusive; that the validity of a school district which has exercised its statutory powers cannot be questioned. This is the case even where there is no evidence of its legal creation, or where there is evidence that statutory requirements were ignored.[244]

Another factor which the courts will consider in reviewing the acts of an agency which has been empowered to create or alter school districts is whether the agency has acted in an arbitrary or capricious manner or has abused its discretion. The courts will not hesitate to interfere with or negate the acts of such a body when there has been a clear abuse of discretion, or where discretion has been exercised in an arbitrary, fraudulent, corrupt, or oppressive manner.[245] It has been said that "arbitrary action" or "capricious action" on the part of an agency authorized to reorganize school districts occurs when it can be said that such action is unreasonable or does not have a rational basis, and that "arbitrary action" is the result of an unconsidered, will-

ful and irrational choice of conduct and not the result of the winnowing and sifting process.[246] Thus, it has been held[247] that a county committee acted in an arbitrary and capricious manner when it approved the transfer of territory from one school district to another when the transfer would thereafter make the district in which the territory originally was located dependent on excess tax levies. Similarly, it has been held[248] that the action of a county board of education, in approving a change of school district boundaries which left one district with few children and limited financial resources, was unreasonable and arbitrary.

Finally, the courts will examine whether the actions taken by an administrative officer or agency relative to the creation or alteration of school districts were justified by the evidence. In general, the test employed by the courts is whether, given the available evidence, a reasonable person could have arrived at the same conclusion as that reached by the administrative officer or agency.[249] It has been decided,[250] for example, that, where the sole reason for a proposed alteration of school district boundaries was the desire of the petitioners to have their children attend a particular high school, the evidence was insufficient to justify a change in school district boundaries.

4.19 DE FACTO SCHOOL DISTRICTS

It is not unusual for irregularities such as failure to comply with statutory requirements to occur during the creation or alteration of school districts. It also is possible for school districts to be created or altered in full compliance with the requirements of a statute which is later declared unconstitutional. Such districts frequently enter into contracts for construction or personal services, issue bonds, levy taxes, and exercise all powers granted to school districts by the state. The legality of these acts may later be challenged on the ground that the district was created illegally and its acts are therefore void. Here the legality of the district's acts depends upon whether it has attained

[241]Casterline v. Meyers, 197 N.W. 561 (Mich. 1924); State v. Andrae, 116 S.W. 561 (Mo. 1909); Trustees of Princeton Graded Common Schools v. Stone, 135 S.W. 307 (Ky. 1911); Worthington School District v. Eureka School District, 159 Pac. 437 (Cal. 1916); Board of Education v. Boyer, 47 Pac. 1090 (Okla. 1897); Independent School District of Liberty Township v. Independent School District of Clemons, 134 N.W. 75 (Iowa 1912).

[242]Sioux City Bridge Co. v. Miller, 12 F.2d 41 (8th Cir. 1926); Townsend v. Garrett, 152 N.W. 565 (Iowa 1915).

[243]Smith v. Joint School District No. 3, 295 Pac. 794 (Col. 1931); Griggs v. School District No. 76 of Wayne County, 40 N.W.2d 859 (Neb. 1950); State v. Melstrand, 195 N.W. 314 (Wis. 1923); Bricelyn School District No. 132 v. Board of County Commissioners, 55 N.W.2d 602 (Minn. 1952).

[244]Collins v. Liberty School District No. 7, 52 Me. 522 (1864); State v. School District No. 152 of Blue Earth County, 55 N.W. 1122 (Minn. 1893); Griggs v. School District No. 76 of Wayne County, 40 N.W.2d 859 (Neb. 1950).

[245]Knox County Board of Education v. Fultz, 43 S.W.2d 707 (Ky. 1931); Lyerley v. Manila School District No. 15, 215 S.W.2d 733 (Ark. 1948); Glenham Independent School District v. Walworth County Board of Education, 98 N.W.2d 348 (S.D. 1959); School District No. 9 v. District Boundary Board, 351 P.2d 106 (Wyo. 1960); Elementary School District No. 77 v. Gardner, 183 N.E.2d 307 (Ill. 1962); State v. Allen, 350 P.2d 465 (Wash. 1960).

[246]Joint School District No. 1 v. State. 203 N.W.2d 1 (Wis. 1973).

[247]State v. Allen, 350 P.2d 465 (Wash. 1960).

[248]Glenham Independent School District v. Walworth County Board of Education, 98 N.W.2d 348 (S.D. 1959).

[249]Neary v. Allen, 227 N.Y.S.2d 1015 (1962); State v. County Board of School Trustees, 334 S.W.2d 588 (Tex. 1960); Armstrong Township High School District v. County Board of School Trustees, 161 N.E.2d 607 (Ill. 1959).

[250]Armstrong Township High School District v. County Board of School Trustees, 161 N.E.2d 607 (Ill. 1959).

de facto status. The conditions which must be met in order to attain *de facto* status have been set forth as follows:

> A corporation de facto exists when there is (1) a charter or statute under which a corporation with the powers assumed might have been organized; (2) a bona fide attempt to organize a corporation under such a charter or statute; (3) an actual user of the corporate powers, or some of them, which might have been rightfully used by such an organization.[251]

There is general agreement among the courts that, where an attempt to create a school district is made in good faith under the provisions of a valid statute, and where the district has actually exercised some of the powers granted to school districts, the district will be regarded as a *de facto* district despite the fact that the proceedings under which the district was created failed to conform to statutory requirements,[252] particularly if the district has acted with the acquiescence of the public.[253] It should be emphasized that an attempt to create the district under a valid statute is not sufficient; there must also be an actual exercise of corporate powers before the district can gain *de facto* status.[254]

The acts of a *de facto* school district are just as valid and binding as those of a *de jure* school district, i.e., one that is legally organized in every respect, as far as the rights of third parties and the public are concerned.[255] Public policy requires that this principle be followed. To do otherwise would result in severe impairment of the educational system, since few persons would be willing to contract with a school district or purchase its bonds until the legality of its existence had been established beyond the shadow of a doubt. The law provides adequate opportunity for one to question the legality of a school district while it is being organized. Those who remained silent when they should have spoken are not looked upon with favor by the courts.

The courts are divided on the question of whether a school district created under an unconstitutional statute can gain *de facto* status. The better-reasoned line of decisions holds that a corporation can acquire *de facto* status even though created under an unconstitutional statute.[256] The courts holding this view argue that laws must be presumed to be valid until such time as the courts declare them invalid, that people must act on the assumption that the law is valid, and that it is in the public interest that their acts prior to the time the law is declared unconstitutional be treated as valid and lawful. Another line of decisions, however, holds that a school district created under an unconstitutional statute has neither *de jure* nor *de facto* status.[257] The courts holding this view reason that a corporation can have no existence unless it is organized under a law authorizing its creation and that an unconstitutional statute is not a law.

A district cannot gain *de facto* status where there is no statute authorizing its creation.[258] Furthermore, there must be a bona fide attempt to create a school district under the statutory provisions which authorize its creation before a district can acquire *de facto* status.[259]

4.20 ATTACKING
THE LEGALITY OF SCHOOL DISTRICTS

The procedure which must be employed in attacking the legality of a school district is dependent upon the point in time when

---

[251]Splonskofsky v. Minto, 126 Pac. 15 (Ore. 1912). *See also* Evens v. Anderson, 155 N.W. 1040 (Minn. 1916); School District of Agency v. Wallace, 75 Mo.App. 317 (1898); DeBerg v. County Board of Education of Butler County, 82 N.W.2d 710 (Iowa 1957).

[252]Stewart v. Thorn Valley Joint Union School District, 121 P.2d 49 (Cal. 1942); State v. Gardner, 204 S.W.2d 319 (Mo. 1947); Gwynne v. Board of Education of Union Free School District, 181 N.E. 353 (N.Y. 1932); Cowley v. Wilkins, 174 P.2d 257 (Okla. 1946); State v. School District No. 23, 172 P.2d 655 (Ore. 1946); Wilson v. Reed, 74 S.W.2d 415 (Tex. 1934); People v. Newman Community Unit School District No. 303, 115 N.E.2d 606 (Ill. 1953); State v. Community School District of St. Ansgar, 78 N.W.2d 86 (Iowa 1956); Hazelton-Moffit Special School District No. 6 v. Ward, 107 N.W.2d 636 (N.D. 1961); Pickett v. Board of Commissioners, 133 Pac. 112 (Ida. 1913); Dappen v. Weber, 184 N.W. 952 (Neb. 1921), *rehearing*, 187 N.W. 230 (Neb. 1922); Board of Trustees of School District No. 3 v. District Boundary Board of Natrona County, 489 P.2d 1393 (Wyo. 1971).

[253]Speer v. Board of County Commissioners, 88 Fed. 749 (8th Cir. 1898); Pickett v. Board of Commissioners, 133 Pac. 112 (Ida. 1913).

[254]School District of Agency v. Wallace, 75 Mo.App. 317 (1898); Evens v. Anderson, 155 N.W. 1040 (Minn. 1916); School District No. 28 v. Larson, 260 Pac. 1042 (Mont. 1927).

[255]Coler v. Dwight School Township, 55 N.W. 587, 28 L.R.A. 649 (N.D. 1893); Reynolds v. Moore, 9 Wend. 35 (N.Y. 1832); Clement v. Everest, 29 Mich. 19 (1874).

[256]McCain v. Des Moines, 174 U.S. 168, 19 S.Ct. 644, 43 L.Ed. 936 (Iowa 1899); Speer v. Board of County Commissioners, 88 Fed. 749 (8th Cir. 1898); School District No. 25 v. State, 29 Kan. 57 (1882).

[257]Norton v. Shelby County, 118 U.S. 425, 6 S.Ct. 1121, 30 L.Ed. 178 (Tenn. 1886); People v. Wiley, 124 N.E. 385 (Ill. 1919); Wilson v. Brown, 145 S.W. 639 (Tex. 1912).

[258]DeBerg v. County Board of Education of Butler County, 82 N.W.2d 710 (Iowa 1957); State v. Smith, 86 S.W.2d 943 (Mo. 1935); Dean v. Board of Education of Harrodsburg, 57 S.W.2d 477 (Ky. 1933).

[259]Maricopa County v. Southern Pacific Co., 148 P.2d 824 (Ariz. 1944); People v. New York Central Railroad Co., 119 N.E. 299 (Ill. 1918).

the attack is mounted. Prior to the time a district formed under the color of law has exercised its corporate powers, an injunction may be secured to restrain any illegal or improper acts on the part of the officers or agencies responsible for its creation.[260] There is some disagreement, however, in regard to whether a private individual can challenge the legality of a school district. It has been held in some jurisdictions that a private individual,[261] or taxpayer,[262] cannot bring an action contesting the legality of a school district; that such an action must be brought by the state.[263] Nevertheless, the weight of authority indicates that a private individual may bring action to enjoin or set aside the actions of an officer or agency empowered to create school districts where such actions are unreasonable, unjust, or oppressive,[264] or where the actions have no constitutional or statutory basis.[265] The latter appear to be the better-reasoned cases, since, prior to the time a school district actually begins operation, challenges to its legality are not likely to impair the educational system unduly. It is also in the public interest to clarify questions relative to the legality of a school district prior to the time it begins operation.

Once a district organized under a valid statute has exercised its corporate powers, its legal existence cannot be attacked collaterally.[266] That is, an injunction to restrain the operation of the district on the basis that it was created illegally cannot be obtained.[267] Whether a school district operating under the color of law was legally created can be determined only in a direct action in *quo warranto* brought in the name of the state by a proper officer of the state, e.g., the attorney general.[268] The concepts underlying this principle of law have been aptly summarized as follows:

> *Some courts give as the reason . . . that corporate franchises are grants of sovereignty only, and, if the state acquiesces in their usurpation, individuals will not be heard to complain. Others base the rule upon consideration of public policy, emphasizing the importance of stability and certainty in such matters, and the serious consequences which might follow if the existence of a public corporation could be called in question by persons who do not have an interest in the matter separate and distinct from that of the State itself. But, whatever reason is advanced, the rule is unanimous that where a public body has, under color of authority, assumed to exercise the power of a public corporation of a kind recognized by law, the validity of its organization can only be challenged by the State. The same rule applies where such public corporation extends its authority, under color of law, over additional territory.*[269]

The courts are especially reluctant to declare a school district which has been in operation for a number of years invalid. Thus, it has been held[270] that a court has discretion to declare a district valid despite the invalidity of its creation where the district has been in operation for several years and where its dissolution would disrupt the educational system of the community.

Persons may be estopped from attacking the validity of the organization of school districts if they have acquiesced in the actions of the district whose validity they seek

[260]Coler v. Dwight School Township, 55 N.W. 587, 28 L.R.A. 649 (N.D. 1893); Fritter v. West, 65 S.W.2d 414 (Tex. 1933); Kennedy v. Broughton, 70 S.W.2d 500 (Tex. 1934).

[261]Laughlin v. Columbiana County Board of Education, 189 N.E.2d 726 (Ohio 1959); Spilker v. Bethel Special School District, 235 S.W.2d 78 (Mo. 1950); Kirts v. Board of County Commissioners, 215 P.2d 642 (Kan. 1950).

[262]Halstead v. Rozmiarek, 94 N.W.2d 37 (Neb. 1959); Kirts v. Board of County Commissioners, 215 P.2d 642 (Kan. 1950).

[263]Kirts v. Board of County Commissioners, 215 P.2d 642 (Kan. 1950); Gwynne v. Board of Education of Union Free School District, 181 N.E. 353 (N.Y. 1932); Spilker v. Bethel Special School District, 235 S.W.2d 78 (Mo. 1950).

[264]Felker v. Roth, 178 N.E. 381 (Ill. 1931); Tucker v. Daniels, 50 So.2d 896 (Miss. 1951); Blackstone v. Rollins, 170 A.2d 405 (Me. 1961); Gates School District Committee v. Board of Education, 72 S.E.2d 429 (N.C. 1952); Thies v. Renner, 106 N.W.2d 253 (S.D. 1960).

[265]Fritter v. West, 65 S.W.2d 414 (Tex. 1933); Madeo v. McGuire, 192 N.Y.S.2d 936 (1959); School District of Gering in Scotts Bluff County v. Stannard, 228 N.W.2d 600 (Neb. 1975).

[266]School District No. 116 v. Wolf, 98 Pac. 237 (Kan. 1908); Dappen v. Weber, 184 N.W. 952 (Neb. 1921), rehearing, 187 N.W. 230 (Neb. 1922); Reynolds v. Moore, 9 Wend. 35 (N.Y. 1832); Coler v. Dwight School Township, 55 N.W. 587, 28 L.R.A. 649 (N.D. 1893); Crabb v. Celeste Independent School District, 146 S.W. 528 (Tex. 1912); Evens v. Anderson, 155 N.W. 1040 (Minn. 1916); County Board of School Trustees v. Leon Independent

School District, 328 S.W.2d 928 (Tex. 1959); Williams v. Rolfe, 101 N.W.2d 923 (Minn. 1960); Board of Trustees of School District No. 3 v. District Boundary Board of Natrona County, 489 P.2d 1393 (Wyo. 1971).

[267]School District No. 116 v. Wolf, 98 Pac. 237 (Kan. 1908); Dappen v. Weber, 184 N.W. 952 (Neb. 1921), rehearing, 187 N.W. 230 (Neb. 1922).

[268]Evens v. Anderson, 155 N.W. 1040 (Minn. 1916); Coler v. Dwight School Township, 55 N.W. 587, 28 L.R.A. 649 (N.D. 1893); Board of Education v. Board of Education, 137 N.E.2d 721 (Ill. 1956); Detroit Edison Co. v. East China Township School District No. 3, 115 N.W.2d 298 (Mich. 1962); Wilkins v. County Board of Education, 102 N.W.2d 924 (Iowa 1960); Green Mountain School District No. 103 v. Durkee, 351 P.2d 525 (Wash. 1960).

[269]Spilker v. Bethel Special School District, 235 S.W.2d 78 (Mo. 1950).

[270]Gosney v. Butler Graded School, 292 S.W. 781 (Ky. 1927).

to challenge.[271] One who fails to exercise one's legal rights seasonably is guilty of laches and loses them. One who is so guilty will not later be allowed to complain that a school district was invalidly organized.[272] It has been said that "those who are silent, when in conscience they should have spoken, have no claim upon the equity" of the court.[273] It has been ruled[274] that, where action has been taken in accord with the results of an election, neither the officer nor the board which called the election can later claim the election was invalid for want of compliance with jurisdictional or procedural requirements. Participation in an election, however, does not estop one who voted in the election from later attacking the validity of a district created thereby.[275]

Questions have arisen as to whether or not a school district may attack the legality of a school district reorganization which results in changes in its own boundaries. It has been held[276] that a school district cannot attack the legality or question the boundaries of another district, nor can it challenge the validity of changes made in its boundaries by an officer or agency empowered to make such changes.[277]

When the creation or alteration of a school district is absolutely void—for example, where no statutory authority for the attempted action exists—the validity of the district is subject to collateral attack.[278] A school district which has been created under utterly void proceedings cannot be validated by acquiescence, nor does ac-

quiescence estop one from later challenging its legality.[279]

Finally, it should be noted that when a judgment of ouster is entered in a *quo warranto* proceeding the effect is to terminate the corporate existence of a school district. As stated by the Supreme Court of Illinois:

The effect of a judgment of ouster against a school district in quo warranto proceedings is to immediately dissolve the corporation, whether it existed de jure or de facto, and work its dissolution, and take away all its rights, liberties, privileges, and franchises. The dissolution of a municipal corporation by the judgment of the court on quo warranto, as in the death of a natural person, operates as an absolute revocation of all power and authority on the part of others to act in its name or in its behalf.[280]

However, a court, in its discretion, may allow a school district to continue in operation for a limited period of time in order to avoid complete disruption of the educational program of the pupils involved.[281]

4.21 SUMMARY

School districts are created by the state to provide for the operation of the state's public schools. As agencies of the state they have no inherent powers; rather, they have only such powers as are conferred upon them by the state. A state legislature can create, alter, or dissolve a school district with or without the consent of its residents, subject only to such limitations as the constitution may impose. A legislature also may delegate to a subordinate agency authority to reorganize and/or consolidate school districts if it establishes definite standards and policies which that agency is to follow. Statutes providing for the alteration of school districts have been upheld against the contention that they are in conflict with the "due process" and "equal protection" clauses of the Fourteen Amendment, and against the contention that they impair the obligation of contracts (if the interest of bondholders is protected).

It is not necessary that the residents of a school district consent to proposed changes unless, of course, the state's constitution so requires. However, the legislature may, if it chooses, require that the residents of the

[271]Peterson v. School District No. 91 of Hamilton County, 246 N.W. 728 (Neb. 1933); Magnolia Special School District v. Rural Special School District No. 3, 149 S.W.2d 579 (Ark. 1941); State v. Union High School District No. 1, 53 P.2d 1047 (Ore. 1936); Driskel v. O'Connor, 15 A.2d 366 (Pa. 1940).

[272]Howell v. Howell, 66 S.E. 571 (N.C. 1909); Weiderholt v. Lisbon Special School District No. 19, 178 N.W. 432 (N.D. 1920); State v. Union High School District No. 1, 53 P.2d 1047 (Ore. 1936); Dominic v. Davis, 262 P.2d 143 (Okla. 1953).

[273]Coler v. Dwight School Township, 55 N.W. 587, 28 L.R.A. 649 (N.D. 1893).

[274]Walker v. Hall, 131 S.E. 160 (Ga. 1925).

[275]People v. Buesinger, 155 N.E. 473 (Ill. 1927); State v. Potter, 191 S.W. 57 (Mo. 1916); Grant v. Norris, 85 N.W.2d 261 (Iowa 1957).

[276]School District No. 14 v. Board of County Commissioners, 110 P.2d 744 (Kan. 1941); School District of City of Lansing v. State Board of Education, 116 N.W.2d 866 (Mich. 1962); Halstead v. Rozmiarek, 94 N.W.2d 37 (Neb. 1959).

[277]School District No. 67 v. School District No. 24, 76 N.W. 420 (Neb. 1898); Board of Education v. Wilson, 100 N.E.2d 159 (N.Y. 1951).

[278]Mesquite Independent School District v. Gross, 67 S.W.2d 242 (Tex. 1934); Thompson v. Freeny, 170 P.2d 233 (Okla. 1946); Gwynne v. Board of Education of Union Free School District, 181 N.E. 353 (N.Y. 1932); Gilbert v. Scarbrough, 131 So. 876 (Miss. 1931).

[279]Gabbart v. Johnson, 118 S.W. 883 (Tex. 1909); Carter Special School District v. Hollis Special School District, 293 S.W. 722 (Ark. 1927); County Board of School Trustees v. Leon Independent School District, 328 S.W.2d 928 (Tex. 1959).

[280]People v. Calloway, 160 N.E. 834 (Ill. 1928).

[281]State v. Community School District of St. Ansgar, 78 N.W.2d 86 (Iowa 1956).

area which would be affected by proposed changes in school district boundaries give their consent to the changes. Legislation which permits citizens to petition for creation or alteration of a school district also may be enacted. Such petitions are subject to the same legal principles as are other petitions. Signatures generally may be withdrawn from a petition prior to the time official action upon it has taken place, although in some jurisdictions signatures may not be withdrawn after a petition has been filed.

Elections concerning the creation or alteration of school districts generally are subject to the same legal principles as apply to all other school elections. Where an election is required, any action taken which has not been approved at a legal election is void.

A school district which was not legally created can be validated by the enactment of "curative" legislation. A legislature may validate any district whose creation it could have authorized in the first place.

School districts and municipalities legally are regarded as separate and distinct corporate entities. Thus, a change in the boundaries of a municipality does not automatically change the boundaries of a school district which is associated with that municipality unless the legislature so provides.

The state may transfer title to school property from one trustee to another, i.e., from one school district to another, or may make such other disposition of school property as it deems proper. Statutes concerning the disposition of the assets and liabilities of a school district that has been altered or dissolved are controlling so long as they do not violate constitutional restrictions or guarantees. Where no statute governing the disposition of assets and liabilities exists, it is generally agreed that (1) where a school district is altered, school property belongs to the district in which it is located following the alteration, and liability for any existing indebtedness remains with the district which incurred the debt, and (2) where a district goes out of existence, the new district(s) is entitled to all property and assets of the old district and is liable for all of its existing debts and obligations.

The courts may pass on the constitutionality of statutes concerning the creation and/or alteration of school districts, may interpret such statutes, and may review the actions of officers and/or agencies who are responsible for carrying out such legislation. The courts may not determine whether school districts should be created or altered, nor may they fix the boundaries of school districts. The right of appeal from the decisions of those who are responsible for the creation or alteration of school districts may be controlled by statute, and, in any event, all administrative remedies must be exhausted before one may appeal to the courts. In reviewing cases of this kind the courts will not interfere with the decisions of those responsible for the creation or alteration of school districts unless they have abused their discretion or have failed to adhere to statutory requirements.

An illegally created school district may attain *de facto* status if the attempt to create it was made in good faith and if it has actually exercised some of the powers granted to school districts, e.g., entered into contracts, issued bonds, or levied taxes. As far as third parties are concerned, the acts of a *de facto* school district are just as valid and binding as those of a *de jure* school district. As a general rule, any interested person may challenge the legality of a school district prior to the time it is organized and has exercised some of its corporate powers. After it has exercised its corporate powers, however, only the state may challenge its legality by a direct action in *quo warranto*.

School Elections

5.0 INTRODUCTION

School elections have been devised to permit voters to express their preference and to secure the consensus of the voters on educational issues. They are held for a wide array of purposes including election of school board members, bond issues, tax or millage levy approval and school district alteration and consolidation. Generally, but not universally, general election statutes are applicable to school elections. This specific issue was before the courts in both Arizona and Michigan. In the Arizona case the court stated[1] specifically that not all statutes related to general elections are applicable in school elections. The Michigan decision was somewhat more restricted. In this instance it was held[2] that the general statute prohibiting the use of paper ballots in precincts of over 800 was not applicable in school district reorganization elections.

Courts repeatedly have held[3] that the power to hold school elections must be found in the statutes and statutory provisions must be followed. The degree of adherence required is dependent on whether the statutory provisions are considered mandatory or directory.

An array of general principles has evolved from judicial decisions related to school elections for various purposes. These principles will be presented as a unit regardless of the area from which they were derived. In addition, cases applicable only to specific areas will be considered.

5.1 GENERAL PRINCIPLES IN SCHOOL ELECTIONS

Among the principles applicable to all elections are determination of which statutory provisions are mandatory and which are directory, the one-man one-vote principle, requirement of supermajority for approval, ownership of property to vote in bond and levy elections, discrimination against minorities, residency requirements, polling places, counting of absentee ballots, time of elections and challenges, effect of unclear and misleading statements, irregularities in elections, and miscellaneous issues. Each of these issues will be presented in the following sections.

5.1a Mandatory and directory statutory provisions

Some provisions of the statutes are mandatory and must be strictly followed or the election will be declared void. It is difficult to determine in advance of a court decision just which provisions will be held mandatory but a number of helpful guidelines are set forth in an Illinois case.[4] Provisions interpreted as mandatory were:

1. Where statutes expressly or implicitly provide that failure to follow the provisions shall render the election void
2. Where the failure to follow provisions interferes in any way with the results of the election
3. Where a person who was legally entitled to vote was not permitted to do so
4. Where a person who voted was not a resident of the district
5. Where the polling places were chosen from improper motives
6. Where fraud occurred

When the courts are called upon to determine whether a statute is mandatory or directory they will attempt to determine the intent of the legislature when the statute was enacted. If it is decided that the legislature intended to require strict compliance it will be held mandatory; if not it will be considered directory. A provision of a statute may be mandatory or directory depending on the time of the protest. Provisions may be ruled mandatory if action is taken prior to an election but directory after an election has been held.[5] Generally, provisions of statutes are considered directory after the election is held. Substantial compliance is all that is required as long as the will of the people prevails. This type of decision has been rendered[6] under a wide range of circumstances and facts. Any person contesting an election on the basis that all statutory provisions were not fulfilled must carry the burden of proving that the results of the election would have been changed if all provisions had been rigidly followed.[7] The

---

[1]Webb v. Dixon, 455 P.2d 447 (Ariz. 1969).

[2]Penn School District No. 7 v. Board of Education of Lewis-Cass Intermediate School District, 165 N.W.2d 464 (Mich. 1968).

[3]Crowe v. Wheeler, 439 P.2d 50 (Colo. 1968); Harney v. Clear Creek Community School District, 154 N.W.2d 88 (Iowa 1967); Walker v. Thetford, 418 S.W.2d 276 (Tex. 1967); Bruhn v. Azle Independent School District, 423 S.W.2d 617 (Tex. 1968).

[4]Gann v. Harrisburg Community Unit School District, 218 N.E.2d 833 (Ill. 1966).

[5]Rutter v. Board of Education, 102 N.W.2d 192 (Mich. 1960); Phillips v. Stern, 252 N.E.2d 267 (Ind. 1969); Hood v. State, 539 P.2d 931 (Ariz. 1975).

[6]Douglas v. Williams, 405 S.W.2d 259 (Ark. 1966); Marler v. Board of Public Instruction, 197 So.2d 506 (Fla. 1967); Masheter v. Vining, 426 P.2d 149 (Kan. 1967); Royalty v. Nicholson, 411 S.W.2d 565 (Tex. 1967).

[7]West v. Unified School District, 460 P.2d 103 (Kan. 1969); Kimsey v. Board of Education of Unified School District 273, 507 P.2d 180 (Kan. 1973); Karker v. Board of Unified School District No. 1, 187 N.W.2d 160 (Wis. 1971).

courts will assume elections to be valid and anyone charging invalidity has the burden of proof that the will of the voters did not obtain.[8] In the absence of evidence that someone was misled or the rights of voters were prejudiced the election results will stand.

5.1b One-man one-vote principle

One of the most highly contested issues in recent years has been the one-man one-vote principle. This principle has come to mean that if public officials are selected by popular vote the equal protection clause applies and all voters must have equal influence in the selection of persons to represent them.[9] The one-man one-vote principle has been held applicable in election of school boards, school directors, and school trustees.[10] Earlier cases attempted to draw a distinction between legislative and administrative bodies, with the one-man one-vote applying only to legislative bodies. A New York case in 1971 was to this effect.[11] However, the Supreme Court of the United States failed to recognize this type of distinction and held[12] instead that the one-man one-vote principle applied to all elected governmental officials. It does not, however, apply to appointed officials nor does it require that all officials be elected.[13]

It is recognized that when school officials are elected from sub-districts, or areas which represent certain populations, the apportionment may not be exactly equal and small variations are permitted.[14] However, variations of 52.781 percent of the voters for two members and 10.447 percent for one member was considered malapportionment,[15] as was a situation where a vote in one district was equal to approximately ten votes in another district.[16] Existence of so-called "communities of interest" was found not to justify a deviation of 37.45 percent in voting strength of individual voters.[17]

Voting for seats at large is legal,[18] as is electing half the school directors from a designated district and half at large, if the voting is by all electors of the district.[19] School directors may be permitted to represent districts in which the population is of varying size without violation of the one-man one-vote principle as long as the voting is at large, according to a decision of the U.S. Supreme Court.[20]

The courts are in some disagreement as to whether a school board member elected from a malapportioned district may be permitted to serve. Some courts hold that the board is abolished when the district is judicially declared malapportioned.[21] Others hold that elected school board members should be permitted to serve out their terms.[22] This is particularly true when the majority will be replaced in a relatively short period of time.[23] While such members are serving, acts of the board are completely legal.

Federal courts are now reluctant to rule on the one-man one-vote principle in school board elections holding that the issue should be adjudicated at the state level. However, if substantial federal constitutional questions are involved federal courts will take jurisdiction.[24]

5.1c Supermajority requirement

With the principle well established that every person's vote must be equal under the one-man one-vote principle many people assumed that each vote for a bond issue, tax levy, etc. would be required to be equal whether a person voted for or against the proposition. Thus, requiring of a supermajority, e.g., 60 percent vote, for approval would be unconstitutional since 40 plus any fraction percent of "no" votes would be

[8]Millet v. Board of Supervisors, 429 P.2d 508 (Ariz. 1967); Harney v. Clear Creek Community School District, 154 N.W.2d 88 (Iowa 1967).

[9]Hadley v. Junior College District, 397 U.S. 50, 90 S.Ct. 791, 25 L.Ed.2d 45 (Mo. 1970); Leopold v. Young, 340 F.Supp. 1014 (Vt. 1972); Rosenthal v. Board of Education of Central H.S. District No. 3, 385 F.Supp. 223 (N.Y. 1974).

[10]Dunham v. Sauter, 201 N.W.2d 75 (Iowa 1972).

[11]Board of Education v. Board of Cooperative Educational Services, 325 N.Y.S.2d 592 (1971).

[12]Hadley v. Junior College District, 397 U.S. 50, 90 S.Ct. 791, 25 L.Ed.2d 45 (Mo. 1970).

[13]Sailors v. Board of Education 387 U.S. 105, 87 S.Ct. 1549, 18 L.Ed.2d 650 (Mich. 1967); Egan v. Wisconsin State Board, 332 F.Supp. 964 (Wis. 1971).

[14]Adams v. School Board, 332 F.Supp. 982 (Pa. 1971); Chargois v. Vermilion Parish School Board, 348 F.Supp. 478 (La. 1972).

[15]Peper v. Jackson Parish Police Jury, 429 F.2d 39 (5th Cir. 1969); LeBlanc v. Rapides Parish Police Jury, 315 F.Supp. 783 (La. 1969), case remanded 431 F.2d 502 (5th Cir. 1970).

[16]Fahey v. Laxalt, 313 F.Supp. 417 (Nev. 1970).

[17]Panior v. Iberville Parish School Board, 498 F.2d 1232 (5th Cir. 1974).

[18]Zimmer v. McKeithen, 467 F.2d 1381 (5th Cir. 1972).

[19]Dunham v. Sauter, 201 N.W.2d 75 (Iowa 1972).

[20]Ibid.; Mayes v. Teague, 341 F.Supp. 254 (Tenn. 1972); Dusch v. Davis, 387 U.S. 112, 87 S.Ct. 1554, 18 L.Ed.2d 656 (Va. 1967).

[21]Fetterman v. Cope, 364 F.Supp. 70 (Tenn. 1973).

[22]Johnson v. Iberville Parish School Board, 498 F.2d 1232 (5th Cir. 1974), rehearing denied (Aug. 13, 1974).

[23]Visnich v. Sacramento County Board of Education, 112 Cal.Rptr. 469 (1974).

[24]Powers v. Maine School Administrative District No. 1, 359 F.Supp. 30 (Me. 1973).

as powerful as any percent less than 60 of "yes" votes.

The courts, while recognizing this argument, have not been persuaded by it and have upheld the supermajority requirement. A California court[25] did reject the supermajority requirement prior to a ruling by the U.S. Supreme Court upholding the requirement.[26] An Iowa court held[27] that the fiscal stability and continued solvency of local government provided sufficient justification either under the rational basis test or the compelling interest test for requiring a 60 percent affirmative vote. A federal district court in Missouri held[28] that the constitution does not either explicitly or implicitly prohibit a state from establishing a rule whereby more than a simple majority is required to approve certain propositions.

5.1d Ownership of property requirement

Several states have at various times enacted statutes requiring that one own property or pay taxes to be eligible to vote in an election for school bonds, special tax levies, and other fiscal matters. Although over a period of time most of these requirements had been eliminated, they persist in a few states. Since 1969, as a result of decisions of the U.S. Supreme Court in several cases, this type of requirement has been struck down.[29] On the basis of these decisions it should now be assumed that any requirement of ownership of property, evidence of taxes paid, and similar fiscal restraints upon voting rights has been eliminated in all states, although remnants of these requirements are still being contested.

5.1e Discrimination against minorities

Courts have guarded assiduously the rights of minorities in school elections. A 1974 Pennsylvania case held[30] discrimination against minorities in any way operated to void the election. Where bilingual ballots, placards, and instructions, were inadequately given and the interpretations of

inspectors and interpretors were discriminatory, i.e., unfair and inconsistent, the election was void.[31] Statutes limiting the number of candidates and vacancies for which voters can cast their ballots to secure minority representation are constitutional. The basis of the holding was that all voters were treated alike in the election.[32] However, there is no constitutional requirement that a county board of education reflect the racial composition of the county.[33]

5.1f Residency requirements

Typically a person who has achieved residency for purposes of voting in general elections is entitled to vote in school elections. However, what constitutes "residence" for voting purposes is often difficult to determine. In most cases it is essential to ascertain the domicile of a person to establish eligibility to vote in school elections. A domicile is where a person's residence is located and if that person is absent, it is the place to which a return is planned. Intent is a very important aspect in the establishment of domicile, as was made clear in an Arkansas case.[34] The court established two criteria for the determination of residency for purposes of voting in school elections: (1) What was the intent of the voter regarding residency? and (2) Was the conduct of the voter reasonably consistent with the asserted intent of residency? In this instance the voter lived with her parents in the school district while her husband was overseas, and at the time they intended to live in the district upon his return. However, after her husband's return and four days after the election they moved to another state where her husband had found employment. They left their personal belongings in the district and voted by absentee ballot. Several months later they returned to the original school district. The courts held they were legal voters of the district at all times when their ballots were cast. In an Illinois case[35] a family moved to a neighboring district when their home was destroyed by fire. Their new residence was a temporary abode, since they intended to move back to the original district as soon as the construction of their new house was completed. Thus, they were

[25]Westbrook v. Michaly, 471 P.2d 487 (Cal. 1970).

[26]Gordon v. Lance, 403 U.S. 1, 91 S.Ct. 1889, 29 L.Ed.2d 273 (W.Va. 1971).

[27]Adams v. Fort Madison Community School District, 182 N.W.2d 132 (Iowa 1970).

[28]Brenner v. School District of Kansas City, 315 F.Supp. 627 (Mo. 1970).

[29]Kramer v. Union Free School District No. 15, 395 U.S. 621, 89 S.Ct. 1886, 23 L.Ed.2d 583 (N.Y. 1969); Cipriano v. City of Houma, 395 U.S. 701, 89 S.Ct. 1897, 23 L.Ed.2d 647 (La. 1969); Phoenix v. Kolodziejski, 399 U.S. 204, 90 S.Ct. 1990, 26 L.Ed.2d 523 (Ariz. 1970).

[30]Carlynton School District v. James, 314 A.2d 891 (Pa. 1974).

[31]Coalition for Education in District No. 1 v. Board of Education of City of New York, 495 F.2d 1090 (2nd Cir. 1974).

[32]Lo Frisco v. Schaffer, 341 F.Supp. 743 (Conn. 1972).

[33]Locklear v. North Carolina State Board of Elections, 379 F.Supp. 2 (N.C. 1974).

[34]Pike County School District v. County Board of Education, 444 S.W.2d 72 (Ark. 1969).

[35]Stein v. County Board of School Trustees, 240 N.E.2d 668 (Ill. 1968).

and continued to be residents of the original district. Their adult daughter, however, who lived with them both in the original district and the adjoining district, planned to marry and to live with her husband in another district. She moved some of her furniture to the apartment of her prospective husband and later married and lived in a district other than the one in which the family had lived. As a result she was not a resident of the original district after the family moved out and was not entitled to vote in school elections after she moved out of the district.

A school district may legally deviate from a 60-day residence requirement for voting in general elections by setting a 30-day requirement as qualification for voting in school elections. In the absence of showing a compelling reason for the 60-day requirement the election was not invalidated in a Wyoming case.[36]

5.1g Polling places

Where statutes prescribe the polling place to be used in school elections they generally have been held to be mandatory. Where an election, such as in a reorganization proceeding, involves more than one district it is not necessary to have multiple polling places unless required by statutes.[37] If the statutes require that polling places be within the district they must obviously be so located. However, in the absence of such a statutory requirement, a polling place may be established outside the district if it is convenient and accessible to the electorate and there is no evidence of fraud or abuse.[38] Where statutes do not provide for the location of the polling place it may be changed. Use of three places for original voting and one for reconsideration is permissable.[39] In fact it has been ruled[40] that an election held in an unauthorized polling place did not void the election as long as the voters were not misled or deprived of an opportunity to vote.

5.1h Absentee ballots

Provisions of statutes relating to absentee ballots are considered in the same category as mandatory provisions in that statutes are to be strictly construed and explicitly followed.[41] This interpretation was given in a case where absentee ballots were not endorsed on the back by an election officer as required by statute. In this circumstance the absentee ballots were void. Where signatures on absentee ballots were not compared with those on the ballot envelopes and names were not announced when the envelopes were opened all the absentee ballots were invalid. However, since these ballots in no way effected the result of the election it was not invalidated.[42] Absentee ballots were excluded because of numerous irregularities in another case. Since the irregular ballots could be identified with certainty and proof of irregularity did not extend to other ballots the legal ballots were counted to determine the results of the election.[43]

5.1i Time of elections and challenges

In posting notice of election a time span between the posting of notice and the election is nearly universal. How this time is to be computed was the issue in a Texas case. In this instance the court, after indicating that this was the general rule, held[44] that the day of posting is included in the time period and the day of the election is excluded. A school election is not void because it is held on Saturday[45] or on a Jewish holiday[46] in the absence of statutory prohibition. Such prohibition may be direct, or it may be indirect by the designation of another day. When statutes provide that an election be held on Tuesday or Wednesday an election on Friday is illegal.[47] However, a regular meeting on the required date may be adjourned to another day and all the business, including the election, may be held on the new date. Where there has been a change in the district's boundaries, the time between notice and election must begin anew with the change in boundaries

---

[36]Torres v. Laramie County School District No. 1, 506 P.2d 817 (Wyo. 1973).

[37]State v. Goodwin, 243 S.W.2d 353 (Mo. 1951); State v. Independent Consolidated School District No. 160, 92 N.W.2d 70 (Minn. 1958); Wall v. County Board of Education of Johnson County, 86 N.W.2d 231 (Iowa 1957); Board of Education of Burbank Independent School District No. 20 v. Allen, 156 P.2d 596 (Okla. 1945).

[38]Turnis v. Board of Education, 109 N.W.2d 198 (Iowa 1961).

[39]Town of Groton v. Union School District No. 21, 241 A.2d 332 (Vt. 1968).

[40]State v. Community School District of St. Ansgar, 78 N.W.2d 86 (Iowa 1956); Miely v. Metzger, 156 Pac. 753 (Kan. 1916); School District No. 49 v. School District No. 65-R, 66 N.W.2d 561 (Neb. 1954).

[41]Mommsen v. School District, 147 N.W.2d 510 (Neb. 1966).

[42]Webb v. Benton Consolidated H.S. District No. 103, 264 N.E.2d 415 (Ill. 1970).

[43]Ibid.

[44]Royalty v. Nicholson, 411 S.W.2d 565 (Tex. 1967).

[45]Kimsey v. Board of Education of Unified District No. 273, 507 P.2d 180 (Kan. 1973).

[46]Board of Education of Tri-Valley v. Board of Cooperative Educational Services, 343 N.Y.S.2d 901 (1973).

[47]N.Y. Commissioner of Education Decision No. 8941 (1974).

so *all* voters have the required number of days notice of the election.[48]

Often some voters are displeased with the results of an election, or with the procedures followed, and wish to contest the election. However, they do not have this right unless it is found in the statutes or constitution.[49] Nor may a court prohibit the holding of an election which is provided in the statutes.[50] Frequently a time limit for contesting an election is set by statutes. This must be rigidly observed even when a constitutional question is at issue.[51] The number of days permitted varies considerably, e.g., from ten days[52] to sixty days.[53] In cases in which the specified time has elapsed the decision is always the same— failure to bring a suit within the time specified is fatal and extinguishes any right to contest the election. In these situations the courts have declared themselves without jurisdiction. However, a ten day limit placed on general elections is not applicable to special tax levies in school districts.[54]

5.1j Unclear or misleading statements

Occasionally voters are misled, or claim to be misled, by the proposition on which they are asked to cast their vote. In such cases, the court, after a careful review based on the statements and evidence presented, makes a determination which either validates or voids the election. In a Kansas case it was asserted that the proposal presented to the voters was unclear. The proposition indicated that the cost of the entire program would not exceed $810,000 and that if a federal grant were received the amount raised locally would be reduced by the amount of the federal grant. The court held[55] this proposition clear and the election valid.

While a definite proposal must be submitted so the exact proposition to be voted on is clear to the voter, proposals for varying amounts of funds or tax rates may be sub-

mitted. In a Kentucky case it was held[56] that a proposition to vote a levy of not less than 5 cents and not more than 15 cents per $100 of valuation was sufficiently clear to disclose the effect of an affirmative vote.

Unclear statements void the election, e.g., as when a board used the term "for school purpose" when it should have used the term "purpose of the tax increase" in the legal notice.[57] In a Kansas case the wording of a resolution for providing capital funds indicated that the proposition was to spend $15 million, whereas the board in fact proposed to spend $15 million plus building fund balances, plus future building fund levies and governmental allotments. The court held[58] the voters were not properly informed and the election void.

Occasionally false statements are made in speeches and published statements or promises are made to obtain a favorable vote. The disappointed voter may later attempt to secure relief by judicial action. However, the results to date have been disappointing for the voter. Courts have held that an election is not void because of misleading statements.[59] Promises made before an election are simply that—promises which are unenforceable at law.[60]

5.1k Irregularities in elections

The courts have repeatedly held that mere irregularities do not invalidate an election. Every reasonable presumption will be made in favor of the validity of an election once it has been held and one who asserts irregularities bears the burden of proof.[61] Where irregularities are not questioned until after an election has taken place, the election will not be invalidated if the will of the people has been expressed.[62] Unless there exists the possibility that the results of the election would have changed by elimination of illegal votes the results will stand.[63] However, statutory provisions for

[48]Lambert v. Unified School District, 461 P.2d 744 (Kan. 1969).

[49]State v. Consolidated School District, 417 S.W.2d 657 (Mo. 1967).

[50]Metropolitan School District v. Vaught, 233 N.E.2d 155 (Ind. 1968).

[51]Andrieux v. East Baton Rouge Parish School Board, 227 So.2d 370 (La. 1969).

[52]Bagley v. Beaverton School District No. 48, 507 P.2d 39 (Ore. 1973).

[53]Andrieux v. East Baton Rouge Parish School Board, 227 So.2d 370 (La. 1969); See *also* Webster v. Board of Education, 437 S.W.2d 956 (Ky. 1969); Independent School District v. State Board of Education, 451 P.2d 684 (Okla. 1969).

[54]LaVergne v. Boysen, 513 P.2d 547 (Wash. 1973).

[55]Knapp v. Unified School District No. 449, 496 P.2d 1400 (Kan. 1972).

[56]Mullen v. Board of Education of Harrodburg Independent School District, 440 S.W.2d 261 (Ky. 1969).

[57]Street v. Maries County R-1 School District, 511 S.W.2d 814 (Mo. 1974).

[58]Unified School District No. 259 v. Hedrick, 454 P.2d 536 (Kan. 1969).

[59]Stelzer v. Huddleston, 526 S.W.2d 710 (Tex. 1975).

[60]Grant v. School District, 415 P.2d 165 (Ore. 1966).

[61]Reitveld v. Northern Wyoming Community College District, 344 P.2d 986 (Wyo. 1959). *See also* Stanley v. Southwestern Community College Merged Area, 184 N.W.2d 29 (Iowa 1971); Kimsey v. Board of Education of Unified School District No. 273, 507 P.2d 180 (Kan. 1973); Harberson v. Lawhon, 518 S.W.2d 840 (Tex. 1975).

[62]DeJong v. Pasadena Unified School District, 70 Cal.Rptr. 913 (1968).

[63]Boyer v. Allen, 301 N.Y.S.2d 664 (1969).

notice are mandatory[64] and the defective publication of notice is not a mere irregularity. Publication of notice prescribed by statute is a condition precedent to holding a valid election. Deviation from statutes or where the issue to be voted on is not intelligibly presented to the voters, is fatal to an election.[65]

When a person attacks an election as being illegal, that person must be given the opportunity to show sufficient irregularities to invalidate the election. However, a recanvassing of ballots will not be ordered on unsupported allegations.[66]

Several types of irregularities have been considered by the courts and ruled insufficient to invalidate an election. These include:

1. Where precinct workers failed to deface unused ballots and did not keep the unused ballots unopened in the custody of the county superintendent[67]
2. Where fewer voting booths than required by the statute were provided[68]
3. Where notice of election was brought to the newspaper in ample time but because of delay in publication and mailing missed the time requirement by one day[69]
4. Where the U.S. Supreme Court declared unconstitutional the requirement of ownership or lease of real estate for voter eligibility nine days before the election; the election was valid even though fourteen days notice of an election was required.[70] (This decision appears at variance with the decision in *Lambert* cited in footnote 64.)
5. Where members of the board of canvassers carried the poll books to the autos to accommodate three voters and ten votes were cast by ineligible voters. Under these circumstances the presumption of validity of the election was rebutted according to the lower court.[71] However, the decision was reversed on appeal[72]
6. Where the board illegally paid a public relations firm $100 to conduct a workshop to promote an election. The court did, however, indicate board members might be personally liable for the money paid.[73]

In a number of instances the courts have held that a deviation from statutory requirements was sufficient to void the election. Instances of this type include:

1. Where the number of ballots was less than required by statutes and there were not sufficient ballots for everyone to vote[74]
2. Where a candidate received a plurality of only three votes, and there was an unexplained discrepancy of two votes between the public counter and the protective counter on the voting machine, and there was the possibility that the candidate was credited with two votes not cast for him and three persons were improperly disenfranchised[75]

5.1l Miscellaneous issues

Miscellaneous directives in school elections vary from cases on board responsibility to effects of agreements under which a district has committed itself financially to perform an obligation. These cases have held that:

School directors have the responsibility not only to determine the need for operating and construction money but also for placing it on the ballot for approval or rejection.[76]

Boards of education may not hold an advisory referendum unless such a referendum has been authorized by statute, since it would be an unlawful expenditure of school funds.[77]

Boards of education are not required to follow the views of residents of the district under statutes that require that the views of residents be considered.[78]

Statutes that require a majority vote of the electors for approval of a proposition require a majority of the electors voting, not a majority of all electors in the school district.[79]

Blank ballots or those otherwise illegible are to be disregarded in determining whether a proposition has been approved or rejected. Such votes are not counted in determining the majority of votes cast.[80]

[64]Lambert v. Unified School District No. 232, 461 P.2d 744 (Kan. 1969).
[65]Cohen v. Ketchum, 344 A.2d 387 (Me. 1975).
[66]Tenore v. Feuer, 370 N.Y.S.2d 74 (1975).
[67]DeJong v. Pasadena Unified School District, 70 Cal.Rptr. 913 (1968).
[68]Town of Groton v. Union School District, 241 A.2d 332 (Vt. 1968).
[69]Widmer v. Reitzler, 182 N.W.2d 177 (Iowa 1970).
[70]Coffee v. Commissioner of Education, 308 N.Y.S.2d 660 (1970).
[71]Boyes v. Allen, 301 N.Y.S.2d 664 (1968).
[72]Boyes v. Allen, 302 N.Y.S.2d 440 (1968).
[73]Eustace v. Speckhart, 514 P.2d 65 (Ore. 1973).

[74]In re Gorham-Fayette Local School District, 250 N.E.2d 104 (Ohio 1969).
[75]Berard v. Nyquist, 304 N.Y.S.2d 403 (1969).
[76]Henry v. Stuart, 473 S.W.2d 165 (Ark. 1971).
[77]Murray v. Egan, 256 A.2d 844 (Conn. 1969); See also Waterbury Homeowners Association, Inc. v. City of Waterbury, 259 A.2d 650 (Conn. 1969).
[78]Templeton Independent School District v. Carroll County Board of Education, 228 N.W.2d 1 (Iowa 1975).
[79]Kuhrt v. Sully County Board of Education, 176 N.W.2d 479 (S.D. 1970).
[80]Hornsby v. Hilliard, 189 So.2d 361 (Fla. 1966).

Where a school district enters an agreement with another district for cooperative use of school facilities and the second district obligates itself for new facilities, the first district may not later vote to withdraw from the agreement. Such an agreement is a legal contract from which one district may not withdraw unilaterally.[81]

5.2 ELECTION OF SCHOOL BOARD MEMBERS

There is some difference of opinion as to whether elections to fill school board offices fall within the jurisdiction of general election laws. The weight of authority indicates that the general election laws of a state will apply in school board elections unless the statutes make special provision for the election of school officers.[82] However, in an Oklahoma case it was held[83] that a school election is not governed by a requirement in the general election laws of the state that all voters be registered. Although the courts are not agreed as to whether general election laws govern school elections, there is no question that the conduct of school elections is an appropriate matter for legislative regulation. Thus, an election at which school board members are named must be held under the cloak of some legal authority, and an election held contrary to or in disregard of the provisions of the law is null and void.[84]

That school board members must be elected in accordance with the requirements of statutes is illustrated by a Texas case. The appellant had been hired on February 16, 1934, as superintendent of schools for the 1934-1935 school year by the existing three-member board of education. On April 7, 1934, six new members were added to the board and one incumbent was retained. The statutes provided, however, that districts of the type in question should have a board of trustees consisting of three persons. On April 14, 1934, the new seven-member board of education voted to discharge the appellant and hired a new superintendent in his place. The appellant sued for breach of contract, claiming that the board which discharged him was not legally constituted. The court held[85] that the seven-member board was illegal, since a board consisting of more than three trustees was not authorized by the statutes under which the district was organized.

Since the legislature has full power to prescribe the methods and procedures to be followed in school elections, it may from time to time, prescribe a new mode of election. Also, alteration of the boundaries of a school district, or creation of a new school district from several districts already in existence, may *ipso facto* change the method by which school board members are elected. Under some statutes school board members are elected to represent certain areas of the district, rather than being elected at large, and such statutes have been held[86] valid.

To be eligible for office a candidate must be qualified by age and residency. In Illinois the age for serving on the school board was set by statute at 21 years. The court did not find this unreasonable or irrational nor did it believe that it denied equal protection of the law or the right of free association.[87] A New Jersey Court upheld[88] a constitutional requirement that office-holders must be of voting age. An extended residency requirement was also sustained by the Court where a three-year residency requirement was in force. The Court held[89] that this requirement bore a reasonable relationship to the legislative objective of obtaining for public office people who were knowledgeable in local governmental affairs.

School board members are often required to run as nonpartisan candidates, at nonpartisan elections. However, this does not prevent a political party from endorsing a candidate and working for the candidate's election.[90] When a candidate inadvertently fails to file an application with the correct agency that candidate is not barred from seeking the office.[91] However, if the winner of an election is an ineligible candidate the person receiving the next highest number of votes is not declared elected.[92] A vacancy exists until procedures for filling the vacancy have been consummated. Where the

---

[81]Plymouth School District v. Rumney School District, 250 A.2d 831 (N.H. 1969).

[82]Hoskins v. Ramsey, 247 S.W. 371 (Ky. 1923); Findley v. Sorenson, 276 Pac. 843 (Ariz. 1929); Glover v. Henry, 328 S.W.2d 382 (Ark. 1959).

[83]Jones v. Burkett, 346 P.2d 338 (Okla. 1959).

[84]Smith v. Morton Independent School District, 85 S.W.2d 853 (Tex. 1935); State v. Holmes, 231 S.W.2d 185 (Mo. 1950).

[85]Smith v. Morton Independent School District, 85 S.W.2d 853 (Tex. 1935).

[86]Snelling v. Franklin County Board of Education, 142 S.W.2d 147 (Ky. 1940); Fowler v. Turner, 26 So.2d 792 (Fla. 1946).

[87]Blassman v. Markworth, 359 F.Supp. 1 (Ill. 1973); *See also* Human Rights Party of Ann Arbor v. Secretary of State of Michigan, 370 F.Supp. 921 (Mich. 1973).

[88]Vittoria v. West Orange Board of Education, 300 A.2d 356 (N.J. 1973).

[89]DeHond v. Nyquist, 318 N.Y.S.2d 650 (1971).

[90]Boone v. Taylor, 256 A.2d 411 (D.C. 1969).

[91]Perez v. Alarcon, 491 S.W.2d 688 (Tex. 1973), re-hearing denied 1973.

[92]State v. Robinson, 108 S.W.2d 901 (Ark. 1937); Diaz v. Valadez, 20 S.W.2d 458 (Tex. 1975).

notice to voters stated they were to vote for three candidates when, in fact, there were only two vacancies the election was sufficiently defective to invalidate it and a new election was required.[93]

Obviously, it is important that school elections be held in conformity with the statutes. When the state statutes specifically prescribe the methods and procedures to be followed in school elections, they should be followed closely. If the statutes do not make specific provision for school elections, it would appear that the general election laws of the state should be followed to avoid the necessity for litigation to establish the title to office of those who are elected.

5.2a Calling of

The call for school elections must be made by an officer authorized to make it and must be issued in accordance with statutory requirements.[94] There can be no voluntary school election, and one called by an unauthorized body is a nullity in the eyes of the law.[95] When statutes place upon an officer or agency the clear and mandatory duty to call school elections, the officer or agency may be compelled to do it,[96] regardless of whether the district school board or some other governmental agency has been given authority to call school elections.

5.2b Notice and time of

The notice of a school election should specify the time and place at which the election is to be held. It is particularly important that the notice contain any information which is required by statutes. It was held,[97] for example, that, under a statute requiring a notice of a school district meeting to specify the time and place of the meeting and the business to be transacted thereat, failure to state in the notice that a district officer was to be elected at the meeting voided the election and invalidated the officer's title to office.

It is elementary, of course, that no valid election of school board members can take place until a school district is legally in existence.[98] It is especially important that this legal principle be recognized in newly created school districts. A board of education elected prior to the time a school district legally exists is a nullity, and its acts are not binding upon the district.

Statutes which lodge the authority to fix the time and place of school elections with some governmental agency are not uncommon. Frequently, the board of education is given this power. In such cases the board must cause the election to be held at a time reasonably close to the expiration of the terms of office of the incumbents.[99] When a public body, such as a board of education, is authorized to fix the time for election of school officers, subsequent elections need not be held at the same time. The board does not exhaust its power by exercising it and may, if it chooses, fix different times for future elections.[100]

5.2c Place of

The place at which school elections are to be held may be specified by statutes or designated by an officer or agency acting under statutory authorization.[101] As in other aspects of school elections, the statutes are controlling. If they require that school elections be held within the district, elections held elsewhere are invalid.[102] However, if statutes do not require school elections to be held within the district, an election held at a polling place outside the geographical boundaries of the district is legal if the polling place is convenient and accessible to the electorate and if there is no evidence of fraud or abuse.[103]

5.2d Ballots and voting

The election of school board members need not be by ballot unless ballots are required by statute.[104] Where the statutes contain no provision requiring election by ballot, school board members may be elected either by ballot or by acclamation.[105] It has been held,[106] however, that an election of school directors is an election by the people and thus comes within a constitutional pro-

[93]New Jersey Commissioner of Education Decision (1973).
[94]Leslie v. Barnes, 208 N.W. 725 (Iowa 1926); People v. Thomas, 198 N.E. 363 (Ill. 1935); Keyker v. Watson, 291 S.W. 957 (Tex. 1927).
[95]Leslie v. Barnes, 208 N.W. 725 (Iowa 1926); Ison v. Watson, 183 S.W. 468 (Ky. 1916).
[96]State v. St. Louis School Board, 33 S.W. 3 (Mo. 1895); People v. Board of Education, 65 N.E.2d 825 (Ill. 1946).
[97]School District No. 13 v. Smith, 32 Atl. 484 (Vt. 1895).
[98]People v. Community Unit School District No. 316, 100 N.E.2d 573 (Ill. 1951).
[99]State v. St. Louis School Board, 33 S.W. 3 (Mo. 1895).
[100]State v. Foley, 94 Atl. 841 (Vt. 1915).
[101]People v. Brown, 60 N.E. 46 (Ill. 1901); Smith v. Kelley, 58 S.W.2d 621 (Ky. 1933).
[102]School Directors v. National School Furnishing Co., 53 Ill.App. 254 (1893).
[103]Myer v. Crispell, 28 Barb. 54 (N.Y. 1858); Turnis v. Board of Education, 109 N.W.2d 198 (Iowa 1961).
[104]Bernier v. Russell, 89 Ill. 60 (1878); City of Cynthiana v. Board of Education, 52 S.W. 969 (Ky. 1899).
[105]Keithley v. Haney, 69 P.2d 352 (Okla. 1937).
[106]State v. Foxworthy, 256 S.W. 466 (Mo. 1923).

vision requiring that all elections by the people be by ballot. When required, ballots must be printed or written and oral voting is not permissible.[107]

When ballots are used in school elections, they must comply in every way with statutory requirements. Votes cast on ballots which do not do so are invalid.[108] In fact, it has been held[109] that an election must be set aside if the ballots used were sufficiently defective to affect the result of the election and to mislead the voters. When the statutes do not prescribe the form of ballot to be employed in school elections, any form may be used so long as the voters are not misled or deprived of their right to participate in the election.[110]

Frequently, two or more officers are elected at the same time, sometimes for differing terms of office. In such cases the ballot should designate the term of office for each candidate.[111]

Questions frequently arise over the marking of ballots and the counting of votes. Obviously, there must be compliance with any statutory directions concerning the manner in which voters are to indicate their choice. Voters are generally permitted to write in the name of a candidate if that name is not printed on the ballot, and the writing in of the name has been ruled to be sufficient to indicate the candidate for whom they wish to vote even if no cross mark is placed on the ballot.[112] In fact, under a statute which authorizes write-ins, pasting stickers bearing the name of a candidate on ballots containing no names has been held[113] proper in the absence of fraud.

Only those persons who are legally qualified to vote in a school district election may vote for school officers.[114] The election of school district officers will not be invalidated simply because unqualified persons were allowed to vote in the election, although obviously their votes cannot be counted in determining the winner.[115]

Questions occasionally arise relative to the number of votes which a candidate must receive in order to be duly elected. When a majority vote is required, the lawful number of votes is indicated by the number of ballots cast, and a candidate must receive a majority of the votes cast in order to be elected.[116] Where two candidates receive the same number of votes, neither is validly elected.[117] In such cases a vacancy results unless a statute directs the manner in which the tie is to be broken.[118]

5.2e Recall election

Even when school board members are qualified and properly elected the electorate may desire their recall. This may be done through the courts, or if a statute so provides, by a recall election.

A recall election is commonly initiated by a petition signed by the requisite number of voters and filed with the board of education or other body which is authorized to call such an election. The petition for recall need not state the precise technical proof of the allegations contained therein, but the allegations should be sufficiently definite to justify bringing the matter before the people.[119] Their truth or falsity is a matter to be determined by the electorate through the ballot box.[120] For additional information on this topic, see Chapter 3, 3.13a.

5.3 ELECTIONS CONCERNING CREATION OR ALTERATION OF SCHOOL DISTRICTS

Since the residents of a school district have no inherent right to participate directly in decisions regarding its creation or alteration, submission of a proposal to create or alter school districts to a popular vote of the electors of the area involved is not necessary unless required by statute[121] or constitution.[122] However, statutes which require that such an election be held are mandatory, and any proposed action which has not been approved by the requisite number of electors in an election held for that purpose is void and without force.[123]

[107]Watson v. Trotter, 66 S.W.2d 634 (Ark. 1933).

[108]State v. Aalgaard, 78 P.2d 596 (Wash. 1938).

[109]In re Danville Election Contest, 48 Pa.Co. 445 (1919).

[110]Ashby v. Patrick, 28 S.W.2d 55 (Ark. 1930).

[111]Watson v. Trotter, 66 S.W.2d 634 (Ark. 1933); Commonwealth v. Whitlock, 12 Pa.Dist. 791 (1903).

[112]Findley v. Sorenson, 276 Pac. 843 (Ariz. 1929); Thompson v. Roberts, 263 N.W. 491 (Iowa 1935); Rollyson v. Summers County Court, 167 S.E. 83 (W.Va. 1932).

[113]Bennett v. Miller, 53 S.W.2d 853 (Ark. 1932).

[114]Gentry v. Hornung, 15 P.2d 445 (Kan. 1932); Allen v. Haddix, 198 S.W. 1155 (Ky. 1917); McKinnon v. Union High School District No. 1, 241 Pac. 386 (Ore. 1925); Blue v. State, 188 N.E. 583, 91 A.L.R. 334 (Ind. 1934); People v. Birdsong, 76 N.E.2d 185 (Ill. 1947).

[115]Boesch v. Byrom, 83 S.W. 18 (Tex. 1904).

[116]State v. Fagan, 42 Conn. 32 (1875); Cleveland v. Amy, 50 N.W. 293 (Mich. 1891); Grimsrud v. Johnson, 202 N.W. 72 (Minn. 1925).

[117]Ison v. Watson, 183 S.W. 468 (Ky. 1916).

[118]Commonwealth v. Meanor, 31 Atl. 552 (Pa. 1895).

[119]Eaton v. Baker, 55 N.W.2d 77 (Mich. 1952); Skidmore v. Fuller, 370 P.2d 975 (Wash. 1962).

[120]Skidmore v. Fuller, 370 P.2d 975 (Wash. 1962).

[121]People v. Keechler, 62 N.E. 525 (Ill. 1901).

[122]United States v. Board of School Commissioners of City of Indianapolis, 368 F.Supp. 1191 (Ind. 1973).

[123]State v. Robinson, 1 So.2d 621 (Fla. 1941); State v. Underhill, 46 N.E.2d 861 (Ohio 1943); Gazaway v. Godfrey, 163 S.E. 480 (Ga. 1932); State v. Hawk, 228 S.W.2d 785 (Mo. 1950).

A state legislature may determine by what manner school districts are to be altered and reorganized. They may consolidate schools on their own motions.[124] They may enact statutes providing that each district is to vote separately on reorganization[125] and that each district shall retain its own indebtedness or that the indebtedness may be assumed by the new district upon a favorable vote of all voters in the new district.[126]

5.3a Notice of

Frequently the statutes will require that notice of elections be posted in a "public place." Questions inevitably arise relative to what constitutes a public place. One such came before the court in Missouri.[127] After noting that "a 'public place' within the meaning of the statute is a relative and not an absolute term, and the determination of what is a 'public place' is a question partly of fact and partly of law," the court went on to state that "a public place is any place where the public is permitted or invited to go or congregate, a place of common resort, a place where the public has the right to go and be. . . ." Among the locations which have been held to be public places within the meaning of a statute requiring the notice of election be posted in a public place are a schoolhouse;[128] a store or retail shop;[129] and a tree, pole, or rock.[130]

Statutes sometimes require that notice be posted in each district which would be affected by a proposal to alter existing school district boundaries. It has been held[131] under such a statute that failure to post notice in each district voids any subsequent action. However, if a statute requires only that a specified number of notices be posted, or that notices be posted in specified places, it is not necessary that notices be posted in each district which would be affected so long as the requisite number of notices are posted at the places specified.[132]

Although the statutes may specify that a particular officer shall post notices, it has been held[133] sufficient if the actual posting of notices is done by another person acting under that officer's direction. It also has been held[134] that where a school district board acting within its authority determined to hold an election and post notices thereof "as soon as possible," the subsequent election was not void because the president of the board, rather than the secretary, signed and posted notices of an election on the question of transferring a portion of the district to another district. While it is essential that notices be posted in the places specified and for the number of days specified in the statute, apparently it is not essential that the notices remain legible. Thus, it has been ruled[135] that the fact that posted typewritten notices later became illegible did not invalidate subsequent proceedings.

5.3b Calling of

An election on a question having to do with the creation or alteration of school districts must be called by the officer or agency authorized by law to do so. There is no such thing as a voluntary school election in the eyes of the law. Consequently, an election called by one who has no authority to call it, or who is without jurisdiction in the matter, is invalid.[136]

In general, substantial compliance with statutory requirements which govern the calling of elections will suffice.[137] It has been decided,[138] for example, that an inaccurate description of the territory to be included in a proposed alteration of school district boundaries will not invalidate the election if the voters are not misled or the results of the election are not prejudiced by the error. Furthermore, it has been decided[139] that an election called after expira-

[124]United States v. Board of School Commissioners of City of Indianapolis, 368 F.Supp. 1191 (Ind. 1973).
[125]Keane v. Golka, 304 F.Supp. 331 (Neb. 1969).
[126]Detroit Edison Company v. East China Township School District, 167 N.W.2d 332 (Mich. 1969).
[127]Montgomery v. Reorganized School District No. 1, 339 S.W.2d 831 90 A.L.R.2d 1201 (Mo. 1960).
[128]Ibid.; Wilson v. Bucknam, 71 Me. 545 (1880).
[129]Montgomery v. Reorganized School District No. 1, 339 S.W.2d 831, 90 A.L.R.2d 1201 (Mo. 1960); Onion v. Moreland, 97 S.W.2d 726 (Tex. 1936).
[130]State v. School Board of Jefferson Joint School District, 91 N.W.2d 219 (Wis. 1958); Baker v. Scranton Independent School District, 287 S.W.2d 210 (Tex. 1956); Wann v. Reorganized School District No. 6, 293 S.W.2d 408 (Mo. 1956).
[131]Lewis v. Young, 171 S.W. 1197 (Ark. 1914); Fractional School District No. 1 v. Metcalf, 53 N.W. 627 (Mich. 1892).

[132]Townsend v. Garrett, 152 N.W. 565 (Iowa 1915).
[133]Kelly v. Board of Trustees, 172 S.W. 1047 (Ky. 1915).
[134]Rutter v. Board of Education, 102 N.W.2d 192 (Mich. 1960).
[135]Lacock v. Miller, 160 N.W. 291 (Iowa 1916).
[136]State v. Hall, 144 Pac. 475 (Ore. 1914); State v. Crow, 172 N.W. 451 (Iowa 1919).
[137]Taylor v. Cundiff, 118 S.W. 379 (Ky. 1909); People v. Goodrich, 135 N.E.2d 610 (Ill. 1956); State v. Miskimins, 72 N.W.2d 571 (Iowa 1955); Duncan v. Willis, 302 S.W.2d 627 (Tex. 1957); State v. Allen, 237 S.W.2d 489 (Mo. 1951).
[138]Ralls v. Sharp's Administrator, 131 S.W. 998 (Ky. 1910).
[139]State v. Lamar, 291 S.W. 457 (Mo. 1927).

tion of the time period specified by statute is not for that reason invalid.

5.3c Time and place of

Statutes prescribing the time and/or place of elections on the question of creating or altering school districts have been held to be mandatory.[140] Failure to comply with such requirements will render the election void.[141] If statutes do not prescribe the time or place at which an election concerning the creation or alteration of school districts is to be held, it may be held at the same time as a general election, or at a time fixed by the officer or agency authorized to call such an election.[142] Unless required by statute, an election affecting two or more school districts need not be held on the same day in each district;[143] nor is it necessary that a polling place be established in each of the districts unless required by statute.[144] In fact, it has been held[145] that so long as the voters were not misled or deprived of an opportunity to vote, an election was valid even though it was held at an unauthorized polling place.

5.3d Conduct of

Statutes in some states require that separate ballot boxes be provided for persons residing in each of the school districts which would be affected by a proposal to alter school boundaries. The courts are in some disagreement as to whether such a provision is to be considered mandatory or directory. If the statutory requirement is held to be mandatory, failure to comply with the requirement is fatal to the validity of the election;[146] if directory, noncompliance does not invalidate the election.[147] The distinction appears to rest on whether the question must pass in all districts affected

or whether a majority of the total number of persons voting in the election is sufficient for passage. It is in the former case that the statutory requirement has been held to be mandatory.

5.3e The election ballot

In preparing ballots to be used in elections involving the creation or alteration of school districts it is imperative that the question be stated in a manner which is clear, concise, and subject to only one interpretation. It has often been said that the primary objective in such elections is to elicit the full and free expression of the will of the voters.[148] Again, substantial compliance with statutory requirements is required. For example, it has been held[149] that a statute requiring that ballots in an election involving consolidation of school districts give the alternatives as "For organization" and "Against organization" was substantially complied with by a ballot which presented the alternatives as for and against "consolidation."

A Montana case[150] illustrates a situation in which irregularities sufficient to invalidate a school district consolidation election occurred. Among other irregularities, ballots which did not follow the precise form specified by the statute were prepared by the board. This irregularity was sufficient to invalidate the election.

Questions occasionally arise relative to the effect of a defect in the election ballot—for example, an error in the description of the area involved in the proposal. While the description should clearly identify the area involved, strict technical accuracy is generally not required so long as voters are not misled.[151] It has been held,[152] for instance, that an error in the name of the district which appeared on the ballot would not invalidate an election in the absence of evidence that any voter was misled thereby or

[140]State v. Goodwin, 243 S.W.2d 353 (Mo. 1951); State v. Independent Consolidated School District No. 160, 92 N.W.2d 70 (Minn. 1958); Wall v. County Board of Education of Johnson County, 86 N.W.2d 231 (Iowa 1957); Board of Education of Burbank Independent School District No. 20 v. Allen, 156 P.2d 596 (Okla. 1945).
[141]Bunch v. Chaffin, 153 S.W. 255 (Ark. 1913); State v. Doepke, 51 N.W.2d 10 (Wis. 1952).
[142]State v. Underhill, 46 N.E.2d 861 (Ohio 1943); Walker v. Hall, 131 S.E. 160 (Ga. 1925); School District No. 49 v. School District No. 65-R, 66 N.W.2d 561 (Neb. 1954); State v. Schmiesing, 66 N.W.2d 20 (Minn. 1954).
[143]Molyneaux v. Molyneaux, 106 N.W. 370 (Iowa 1906).
[144]Walker v. Hall, 131 S.E. 160 (Ga. 1925); State v. Schmiesing, 66 N.W.2d 20 (Minn. 1954).
[145]State v. Community School District of St. Ansgar, 78 N.W.2d 86 (Iowa 1956); Miely v. Metzger, 156 Pac. 753 (Kan. 1916); School District No. 49 v. School District No. 65-R, 66 N.W.2d 561 (Neb. 1954).
[146]State v. Community School District of St. Ansgar, 78 N.W.2d 86 (Iowa 1956).
[147]State v. Lockwood, 165 N.W. 330 (Iowa 1917).

[148]Woolsey v. Carney, 378 P.2d 658 (Mont. 1963); State v. Independent Consolidated School District No. 88, 61 N.W.2d 410 (Minn. 1953); People v. Birdsong, 76 N.E.2d 185 (Ill. 1947); Wilds v. Golden, 330 P.2d 373 (Okla. 1958); Polk v. State, 103 So. 114 (Fla. 1925).
[149]State v. Stouffer, 197 S.W. 248 (Mo. 1917).
[150]Woolsey v. Carney, 378 P.2d 658 (Mont. 1963).
[151]State v. Independent Consolidated School District No. 88, 61 N.W.2d 410 (Minn. 1953); In re Sugar Creek Local School District, 185 N.E.2d 809 (Ohio 1962); People v. Birdsong, 76 N.E.2d 185 (Ill. 1947); Blue v. Board of Education of Oakland County, 36 N.W.2d 222 (Mich. 1949); Burns v. Roberts, 128 A.2d 545 (Conn. 1956); Wall v. County Board of Education of Johnson County, 86 N.W.2d 231 (Iowa 1957); Grindle v. Brooksville School District No. 1, 64 Me. 44 (1874).
[152]People v. Birdsong, 76 N.E.2d 185 (Ill. 1947); See also In re Sugar Creek Local School District, 185 N.E.2d 809 (Ohio 1962).

that the results of the election were affected. When two or more districts are affected by a proposed alteration of school district boundaries, identical propositions must be presented to the voters in each district.[153]

The requirement of a secret ballot is usually applicable in school elections. However, if it appears that the result of the election may have been affected by their ballots, ineligible voters may be required to disclose how they voted and their votes shall be disregarded.[154] Again, the courts are reluctant to upset the results of an election unless it is impossible to ascertain the true will of the voters.

5.4 SCHOOL BOND ELECTIONS

The residents of a school district have no inherent right to vote on the question of whether school bonds should be issued. However, many states require that this question be submitted to the voters. Where such requirements exists, bonds are void if they are issued without submission of the question to the voters,[155] even if the bonds are in the hands of a bona fide holder for value.[156] In such cases the courts follow the familiar principle that, since the powers of school officials are a matter of public record, all persons who deal with them are assumed to be aware of any restrictions upon their powers.

In general, substantial compliance with all statutory requirements is necessary,[157] but mere irregularities in the proceedings will not invalidate a school bond election unless it is shown that the results have been affected thereby.[158] Once the issuance of school bonds has been approved at an election called for that purpose, the voters of a school district may not later rescind the authority to issue bonds unless specific statu-

tory authority for them to do so exists.[159] Where the voters of a school district approve the issuance of school bonds in an amount in excess of that permitted by law, the election is not invalid for that reason, and the issuing authority may issue bonds in any amount within the statutory limits.[160]

Questions sometimes arise as to whether a board of education may call repeated school bond elections in the hope of eventually obtaining an affirmative vote. Unless their authority to call school bond elections is limited by statute, successive elections on a school bond proposition may be called at the discretion of district officers even though the same proposition was defeated at an earlier election.[161] It was held[162] that a school bond election was not necessarily invalid simply because repeated elections were called until consent of the voters was obtained.

To avoid the "vice of doubleness," i.e., requiring voters to vote for something they do not want in order to secure something they do want, a separate proposal must be submitted on each proposition.[163] However, courts have become very lenient in interpreting this principle in recent years. For example, an issue of school bonds to provide funds for "schoolhouses, lunchrooms, vocational and physical education buildings and facilities, purchasing sites therefor and acquiring other property, real or personal," was considered one proposition. The court upheld[164] this election, indicating it was clearly a vote on a single proposition—the improvement of education facilities. In another case it was held[165] that issuance of bonds to pay for acquiring, constructing and equipping school buildings and facilities; adding to, improving and repairing existing educational facilities; and acquiring necessary property and paying incidental expenses was considered one proposition. In a similar situation it was held[166] that a board of education was not

[153]Gardner v. State, 95 Pac. 588 (Kan. 1908); Farber Consolidated School District No. 1 v. Vandalia School District No. 2, 280 S.W. 69 (Mo. 1926).

[154]Powers v. Harten, 167 N.W. 693 (Iowa 1918); Wehrung v. Ideal School District No. 10, 78 N.W.2d 68 (N.D. 1956).

[155]Behrle v. Board of Education, 200 N.E. 523 (Ohio 1935); Parker v. Seward School Township, 159 N.E.2d 575 (Ind. 1959).

[156]Robertson v. Rural Special School District No. 9, 244 S.W. 15 (Ark. 1922).

[157]Henson v. School District No. 92, 95 P.2d 346 (Kan. 1939); Board of Public Instruction v. State, 164 So. 516 (Fla. 1935); Appeal of Lush, 185 N.Y.S.2d 195 (1957); In re Special Election in School District No. 68, 237 N.W. 412 (Minn. 1931).

[158]Cacheville Elementary School District v. Hiddleson, 233 P.2d 57 (Cal. 1951); King v. Independent School District, 272 Pac. 507 (Ida. 1928); Nordby v. Dolan, 78 N.W.2d 689 (N.D. 1956); Holt v. Vernon Parish School Board, 45 So.2d 745 (La. 1950); State v. Maxwell, 60 N.E.2d 183 (Ohio 1945).

[159]Independent School District No. 68 v. Rosenow, 240 N.W. 649 (Minn. 1932); Orr v. Marrs, 47 S.W.2d 440 (Tex. 1932).

[160]Shover v. Buford, 208 Pac. 470 (Col. 1922); Pittsburg Board of Education v. Davis, 245 Pac. 112 (Kan. 1926).

[161]Luzader v. Sargent, 30 Pac. 142 (Wash. 1892); McKinney v. Board of Trustees, 137 S.W. 839 (Ky. 1911).

[162]Taylor v. Brownfield, 41 Iowa 264 (1875).

[163]Berrie v. State of Georgia 166 S.E.2d 631 (Ga. 1969); See also Miles v. State of Georgia, 101 S.E.2d 173 (Ga. 1957).

[164]Ibid.

[165]Lilly v. Crisp County School System, 162 S.E.2d 456 (Ga. 1968).

[166]Kimsey v. Board of Education Unified School District 273, 507 P.2d 180 (Kan. 1973).

required to decide in advance whether one building or more than one building was to be constructed and construction money without building specifications legally could be voted. It has also been held[167] that misleading statements concerning the tax effect of a bond election do not invalidate an election.

The question of whether a bond issue, once voted, is inviolable has been before the courts on a number of occasions with contrary results. In some, but not all cases, the explanation is found in the party desiring to void the results. It has been held[168] that a board may void an election where bonds carrying six percent interest could not be sold and call a new election to vote on bonds carrying eight percent interest. However, where a minority group attempted to rescind a bond issue approved at a prior election the court refused to grant authority to hold an election on rescinding of the bonds and indicated this decision represented the weight of authority.[169]

A board of education may not avoid a vote on bonds for school building purposes by leasing a school building under an agreement by which the building would become the property of the school district.[170] A board is, however, authorized to use capital reserve funds to replace outmoded buildings without an affirmative vote.[171] This was considered a "necessary expense" for which expenditures were permitted without approval of the voters.

5.5 TAX LEVY ELECTIONS
In most states the board of education is authorized to determine the amount needed to finance the school program and to order the amount of taxes needed to be spread on the tax rolls. In some states municipal authorities must approve the budget in some or all districts before the tax can be levied. In these cases there are no elections on the tax levy. In a limited number of states school districts must secure the approval of the voters for at least some of their local tax revenue. In some instances a favorable vote of at least 60 percent of the voters is required for approval and a certain percent of the total number of votes in a previous election is required for validation. In these cases the general principles and most of the statutes related to other elections apply.

Where some levies are voted and some are not voted, the money from those voted may be applied to payment of accumulated operating deficits as well as principal and interest on bonds.[172] A referendum of voters is not required under a statute authorizing county commissioners to make a levy. In this situation the Constitution provided that no county shall levy and tax except for necessary expense, unless approved by the majority of voters.[173]

To secure the necessary favorable votes for approval of school tax levies committees often are established. In some states a determination must be made relative to whether such a committee is political and subject to the regulation of political committees. The State of Washington recently held that a "Levy Pass Committee" was a political committee within meaning of the statutes and subject to its provisions.[174]

5.6 SUMMARY
School elections are designed to permit the voters to express their preference on educational issues and to arrive at a consensus on proposals. The legal principles and statutes which govern general elections are usually applicable to school elections unless specific statutes have been enacted. The power to hold a school election must be found in the statutes. Provisions of a statute may be interpreted as mandatory or directory. If they are regarded as mandatory, the provisions must be strictly followed or the election will be void. Statutory provisions are almost universally held mandatory before an election has been held. If the statutory provisions are considered directory, substantial compliance with them is all that is required. However, irregularities will not be permitted to prohibit a full and fair expression of the will of the voters.

One-man one-vote is now a clearly established legal principle. It applies to all elected governmental bodies whether their function is legislative or administrative. School officials may represent specific areas of the district as long as each one represents the same (approximate) numbers of voters. Areas of the districts may be of unequal voter population if the vote for the office is

---

[167]Stelzer v. Huddleston, 526 S.W.2d 710 (Tex. 1975).

[168]Hanson v. Harrisburg Independent School District No. 91, 190 N.W.2d 843 (S.D. 1971); *See also* Cohen v. Ketchum, 344 A.2d 387 (Me. 1975).

[169]Members of the Board of Education Pearce Union H.S. District v. Leslie, 526 P.2d 773 (Ariz. 1974), *rehearing denied* (Oct. 30, 1974).

[170]Schull Construction Company v. Webster Independent School District No. 101, 198 N.W.2d 512 (S.D. 1972).

[171]Yoder v. Board of Commissioners of Burke County, 173 S.E.2d 529 (N.C. 1970).

[172]*In re* Advisory Opinion Constitutionality of P.A. 1 and 2, 211 N.W.2d 28 (Mich. 1973).

[173]Harris v. Board of Commissioners, 161 S.E.2d 213 (N.C. 1968).

[174]Bare v. Gorton, 526 P.2d 379 (Wash. 1974).

by the district at large. Federal courts are now reluctant to rule on the one-man one-vote issue unless a federal constitutional question is involved, holding that this issue should be adjudicated in the state courts.

The one-man one-vote principle does not prohibit states from requiring a supermajority, e.g. a favorable vote by 60 percent of the voters, for passage of bond issues, tax levies, etc. Thus, more than a simple majority vote may legally be required for approval as long as every voter has equal opportunity to vote. This requirement has been upheld under the rational basis test and the compelling interest test. Nothing in the U.S. Constitution either explicitly or implicitly prohibits a state from establishing a supermajority requirement.

Statutes which require ownership of property or payment of taxes as a condition for voting are unconstitutional. Fiscal requirements of this type have been held to violate the due process and equal protection provisions of the U.S. Constitution.

A person who has achieved residency for purposes of voting in general elections is usually also qualified to vote in school elections. Whether a person is entitled to vote in an election is dependent on that person's domicile. This is determined by the voter's expressed intent and by whether the voter's actions are consistent with the expressed intent. Temporary absence from the school district does not preclude a person from voting if the person plans to return to the district to live.

Courts vigorously guard the rights of minorities in school elections. If bilingual ballots and explanations are employed, they must be clear and fair to all groups or the election will be set aside. All voters, regardless of their race, origin, or ethnic background must be accorded equal treatment.

A strict compliance rule is applied in counting absentee ballots. Unless the statutory provisions are rigidly followed such ballots may be declared void. Even when absentee ballots are declared void, the election results will stand if mandatory regulations have been adhered to, if there has been substantial compliance with directory provisions, and if the absentee ballots would not have changed the results.

The day an election must be held, as well as the time period within which the election must be held, are often specified by statute. Elections are not void because they are held on Saturday or on a Jewish holiday unless other days are required by statutes, either directly or indirectly. When district boundaries are changed, the time for holding an election must be counted anew so that all the voters will have the prerequisite number of days notice of the election. A statute which specifies the number of days within which the result of an election may be challenged is considered mandatory and no deviations are permitted. Failure to file a challenge within the specified time is fatal and courts are without jurisdiction.

Misleading claims, false statements and promises made during an election campaign do not void an election. However, unclear statements of the propositions upon which the electors are to vote will void an election. For the election to be valid, the court must find the proposition clearly stated.

The courts have been faced with a multitude of cases in which irregularities of various types were alleged. However, if it appears that the will of the voters is fully expressed the courts will not void an election unless some mandatory provision has not been followed. There must exist the possibility that the results of an election would have been changed as a result of the irregularities before an election will be declared void, since the presumption of validity of election results always exists.

School districts may not hold elections which could result in repudiating agreements with another district which has expended money based on the agreement. A new election may be called by the school board when school bonds approved in a prior election cannot be sold. However, a disgruntled minority may not force a new election on a bond issue.

To qualify for the office of school board member a person must meet the age, residency, and other requirements established by the statutes. The courts have upheld an age requirement of 21 years and a requirement that the candidate be of voting age. A three-year residency requirement also has been upheld.

When a person seeks the office of school board member in a non-partisan election he may legally be endorsed by a political party. Members of the party also may work for that person's election. When the winner of a school election is an ineligible candidate a new election must be called. The person receiving the second highest number of votes cannot be declared elected unless the statute so states. In case of a tie vote, the tie must be broken as the statute provides and deciding a tie vote by the flip of a coin is illegal unless the statute so provides.

The legislature may determine the manner of altering and reorganizing school districts. There is no constitutional requirement that district residents be permitted to vote on reorganization. The legislature may consolidate schools on its motion if it chooses to do so.

In balloting on school funds or school bonds each proposal must be stated as a separate proposition to avoid the "vice of doubleness." However, the courts are permitting several aspects of questions relative to provisions for educational facilities to be submitted as a single proposition.

A board of education may not avoid a vote on a bond issue by entering into a long term lease of a school building which ultimately becomes the property of the district. Special tax levy elections legally may require a supermajority of the votes cast or a specified percentage of the total vote cast in a previous election for validation. A committee organized to work for the passage of the levy has been held to be a political committee subject to the statutes applicable to political committees in the state.

Contracts and Contract Liability

6.0 INTRODUCTION

The subject of contracts is one of the largest in the field of law. In the normal course of their responsibilities school authorities enter into numerous contracts. In fact, most disbursements made by school districts are made under the terms of contracts for such things as the professional services of teachers and administrators, the furnishing of supplies, equipment, and materials, or the construction of school facilities. The discussion in this chapter is confined primarily to a consideration of the legal principles which are common to most contracts. Specific problems relating to contracts for personal services, supplies, and building construction will be treated as they arise in other chapters.

6.1 ELEMENTS OF A VALID CONTRACT

Five elements are essential to all contracts: capacity or authority of the parties to contract, mutual assent of the contracting parties, valid and adequate consideration, definiteness, and lawful subject matter. Each element will be discussed in succeeding sections.

6.2 AUTHORITY OF A SCHOOL DISTRICT TO CONTRACT

It should be emphasized at the outset that a school district has no inherent power to contract.[1] As an entity established by the state to exercise the governmental function of providing a system of public schools, it must look to the state for all of its powers. The state acts through its legislature. Therefore, a school district is empowered to enter into contracts only to the extent authorized by legislative enactments.[2] It has been said, for example, that "a school district has only such power and authority as is granted by the legislature and its power to contract . . . is only such as is conferred either expressly or by necessary implication."[3] There is a further limitation. In contracting, a school district must act through its board of education. State laws may impose restrictions

upon this authority[4]—by prohibiting the board from entering into contracts in which one of its members has a financial interest, for instance.

Contracts which are within the scope of authority of a school district, or of its board of education, and which have been entered into in accordance with all statutory requirements as to mode and procedure of contracting, are valid and binding upon the district.[5] Under them the district is liable for such payments as it has agreed to make. It is where a school district has contracted beyond its authority, or has failed to comply with statutory requirements concerning contracting, that questions of the liability of the school district most frequently arise.

Teaching services are undoubtedly proper subject matter for contracts by boards of education. However, the contracting may be done in such a manner as to render the contract invalid, as where a board fails to follow the procedure prescribed by the statutes. The board of education and the teacher must be legally qualified to enter into a contract if it is to be binding on both parties. Problems arise when a teacher has not yet received a teacher's certificate or is under the legal age for contracting. In states where contracts may be entered into only with legally qualified teachers, a teacher who has not received a certificate lacks legal capacity to contract.[6] An underage teacher also lacks such capacity, unless joined by a guardian or some other authorized adult and or the contract is signed by such a person on the teacher's behalf. Where the statutes do not otherwise specify, a contract signed by a minor will be binding on the school district but normally not on the teacher if he or she elects to rescind it. However, if the statutes prescribe a minimum age as a prerequisite for teaching, a contract with a person below that age is unenforceable and such person will be unable to collect a salary for teach-

[1]Wichita Public Schools Employees, Local 513 v. Smith, 397 P.2. 357 (Kan. 1964); Barth v. School District of Philadelphia, 143 A.2d 909 (Pa. 1958).

[2]Brown v. Gardner, 334 S.W.2d 889 (Ark. 1960); State ex rel. Blair v. Gettinger, 105 N.E.2d 161 (Ind. 1952); Farrell v. School District No. 54, 84 N.W.2d 126 (Neb. 1957); Rose v. Board of School Directors, 179 P.2d 181 (Kan. 1947); Dvorak v. School District, 22 N.W.2d 238 (Iowa 1946); Cray v. Howard-Winneshiek Community School Dist., 150 N.W.2d 84 (Iowa 1967).

[3]Wichita Public Schools Employees, Local 513 v. Smith, 397 P.2d 357 (Kan. 1964); See also School District No. 1 of Pima County v. Lohr, 498 P.2d 512 (Ariz. 1972); Grasko v. Los Angeles City Board of Education, 107 Cal.Rptr. 334 (1973).

[4]Yoder v. School District of Luzerne Township, 160 A.2d 419 (Pa. 1960); Sheffield v. State School Building Authority, 68 S.E.2d 590 (Ga. 1952); City of Cincinnati v. Board of Education, 30 Ohio N.P. (N.S.) 595 (1933).

[5]Hamilton v. Oakland School District, 26 P.2d 296 (Cal. 1933); Carter Oil Co. v. Liggitt, 21 N.E.2d 569 (Ill. 1939); Bansack & Pearce v. School District of Marceline, 49 S.W.2d 1085 (Mo. 1932); Sleight v. Board of Education, 170 Atl. 598 (N.J. 1934); Rogers v. Butler, 92 S.W.2d 414 (Tenn. 1936); Dawson v. Clark, 176 A.2d 732 (R.I. 1962); Southwestern Broadcasting Co. v. Oil Center Broadcasting Co., 210 S.W.2d 230 (Tex. 1947); Lynch v. Webb City School Dist. No. 92, 418 S.W.2d 608 (Mo. 1967).

[6]Board of School Commissioners v. Wagaman, 35 Atl. 85 (Md. 1896).

ing services, except where recovery on a *quantum meruit*[7] basis is permitted.[8]

6.2a Limitations upon

One very important limitation upon the power of a school district to contract has already been noted: It may contract only within the authority conferred upon it by statute, either expressly or by implication. A school district's power to contract may also be limited by constitutional and/or statutory provisions which place specific restrictions upon such authority. Some examples of such limitations are: a requirement that the contract be authorized by a vote of the district's electors;[9] a restriction upon the amount of indebtedness which a school district may incur under a contract;[10] and a requirement that funds must be appropriated before a contract obligating payment may be entered into.[11]

Another type of restriction frequently placed upon a school district's power to contract is to be found in statutes which specify the mode and method of contracting. For example, statutes may establish procedural requirements such as that a contract be let on the basis of competitive bids or that a bid bond be filed with each bid. The form of the contract may also be specified by statute—e.g., a requirement that school district contracts be reduced to written form. The courts consistently have held[12] that the statutory mode of contracting is the measure of power, and that a contract is invalid which is let in violation of statutory requirements as to the mode and method of contracting.

A school district contract which is against public policy also is invalid.[13] It has been held,[14] for example, that a contract to pay a member of a school board for superintending the construction of a schoolhouse created a conflict of interest on the part of the school board member and therefore was void because it was against public policy. Likewise, it has been held[15] that a contract for the purchase of land which would bind the board of education to a particular line of action in the future was against public policy and therefore invalid. The requirement that the contract bear a relationship to the purpose for which the district was created is another limitation that has been placed upon the authority of a school district to contract. It has been held,[16] for example, that a contract unrelated to the purpose for which the district was created was void.

Questions occasionally arise as to whether or not a contract entered into by a school board for a term exceeding the tenure of the board is binding upon succeeding boards. There is general agreement that a school district contract is binding if it was valid at the time it was made and does not extend for an unreasonable length of time.[17]

Of course, as is generally true of all contracts involving school districts, a contract made with fraudulent intent is invalid. It should also be noted that, because contracting requires the exercise of discretion, a school board may not delegate to an officer or an employee of the board authority to contract on behalf of the board. Contracts made in violation of this rule are invalid.[18]

A board of education sometimes misjudges its authority to contract, or is unaware of restrictions upon its authority, and attempts to make a contract which is beyond its authority. Contracts beyond the authority of a school district or board of education are commonly termed *ultra vires* contracts. The liability of a school district under such contracts will be discussed in Section 6.13 of this chapter.

6.3 MUTUAL ASSENT OF THE CONTRACTING PARTIES

A contract is an agreement wherein the parties promise to do or to refrain from

---

[7]See Section 6.14 for discussion of recovery on *quantum meruit.*

[8]Floyd County Board of Education v. Slone, 307 S.W.2d 912 (Ky. 1957).

[9]Hatfield v. School District No. 58, 10 S.W.2d 374 (Ark. 1928).

[10]Union Graded School District No. 5 v. Ford, 37 P.2d 258 (Okla. 1934).

[11]Campbell v. School District, 195 Atl. 53, 113 A.L.R. 841 (Pa. 1937).

[12]Barton v. School District No. 2, 150 Pac. 251 (Ore. 1915); Miller v. McKinnon, 124 P.2d 34 (Cal. 1942); Board of School Commissioners v. State *ex rel.* Wolfolk, 199 N.E. 569 (Ind. 1936); A. H. Andrews Co. v. Delight Special School District, 128 S.W. 361 (Ark. 1910); Carpenter v. Yeadon Borough, 57 A.H. 837 (Pa. 1904); Vandenberg v. Board of Education, 230 Pac. 321 (Kan. 1924).

[13]Modesto Investment Co. v. Modesto City School District, 2 P.2d 387 (Cal. 1931); County of Pima v. School District No. 1, 278 P.2d 430 (Ariz. 1954); Spearman v. City of Texarkana, 24 S.W. 883 (Ark. 1894); Youngblood v. Consolidated School District No. 3, 230 Pac. 910 (Okla. 1924); Seim v. Independent District of Monroe, 17 N.W.2d 342 (S.D. 1945).

[14]Youngblood v. Consolidated School District No. 3, 230 Pac. 910 (Okla. 1924).

[15]Modesto Investment Co. v. Modesto City School District, 2 P.2d 387 (Cal. 1931).

[16]Prescott Community Hospital Commission v. Prescott School District No. 1, 115 P.2d 160 (Ariz. 1941).

[17]School District No. 54 v. Garrison, 119 S.W. 275 (Ark. 1909); V. L. Dodds Co. v. Consolidated School District, 263 N.W. 522 (Iowa 1935); Detweiler v. School District, 104 A.2d 110 (Pa. 1954), Reinken v. Keller, 280 N.Y.S.2d 253 (1967).

[18]Johnson v. Sabine Parish School Board, 140 So. 87 (La. 1932); Consolidated School District No. 6 v. Panther Oil & Grease Mfg. Co., 168 P.2d 613 (Okla. 1946); Big Sandy School Dist. No. 100-J v. Carroll, 433 P.2d 325 (Col. 1967).

doing certain acts upon the occurrence of specified conditions and terms. An agreement requires a meeting of the minds between the parties, or a mutual understanding and concurrence, upon all the essential elements of their contract. Without a meeting of the minds there can be no agreement. Ordinarily, where the terms of the contract are discussed, reduced to writing, and read by both parties, their mutual assent will be presumed. If the parties do not agree upon the terms or upon one of the essential items of the contract, there has been no mutual assent, no meeting of the minds, and therefore no valid contract.[19] Of course, under such circumstances the dissenting party should not sign the contract until the differences have been resolved.

6.4 ADEQUATE AND VALID CONSIDERATION

To be legally binding a contract cannot require one party to do all the giving without requiring something of adequate value in return. This is called "consideration," without which a contract is unenforceable. What constitutes the consideration should be specified in the contract.[20] It may be money, goods, services, or any other thing of value. Whenever a school district bargains for and receives a *quid pro quo*, the lack of adequate consideration is not a legal issue. In a teacher's contract, for example, the consideration for the payment of a salary and other benefits is the services rendered by the teacher.

6.5 DEFINING THE TERMS WITH DEFINITENESS

In drafting the contract all anticipated matters should be covered as specifically as the circumstances permit. The rights and obligations of each party should be set out with certainty. If a person is to be compensated for performing services, the amount to be paid should be specified.[21] If that person is to work for a given period of time, the beginning and ending time should be stated.[22] An indefinite promise of employment may be too vague to be enforceable.[23]

However, a contract is not invalid where all possible matters are not covered in the agreement. Some items may be left for later negotiation or will be implied by the law.

6.6 LAWFUL SUBJECT MATTER

In a contract the parties in effect write their own law. The law encourages maximum freedom in this regard. However, if they step outside the bounds of the law, their contract may be invalid as being contrary to public policy or in violation of a prohibition found in the constitution, a statute, or the common law. Four examples illustrate this point: First, a contract which requires an employee to forgo rights under the workmen's compensation laws is held to be against public policy. Second, a teacher who signs a contract agreeing to teach for less than the state minimum salary.[24] Since it has been held[25] that a state has full authority to prescribe minimum salaries, teachers may collect their full salary even though they have agreed to teach for less than the minimum. Third, contracts in restraint of marriage are usually found to be contrary to public policy although, because of the special circumstances involved, they have been upheld[26] in the past in some instances as applied to teachers. Fourth, the school board's use of a substitute contract to avoid giving tenure to a married woman has been held to frustrate the purposes of the tenure law and is against public policy.[27]

Contracts between a school district and a member of its governing board pose a special problem. As a general rule, a contract in which a school board member has a direct pecuniary interest is contrary to public policy and therefore unenforceable.[28] Contracts of the district with spouses of board members are valid if the board member has no financial interest in the spouse's earnings.[29] However, in "community property" states a husband has an interest in his wife's property and earnings (and vice versa), and in such states contracts with the wife are con-

[19]Brewington v. Mesker, 51 Mo.App. 348, 356 (1892); Kirby v. Stokes County Board of Education, 55 S.E.2d 322 (N.C. 1949).
[20]State *ex rel.* Melvin v. Board of Education, 34 N.E.2d 285 (Ohio 1940); Mingo v. Trustees of Colored Common School District No. A, 68 S.W. 483 (Ky. 1902).
[21]Fairplay School Township v. O'Neal, 26 N.E. 686 (Ind. 1891).
[22]Atkins v. Van Buren School Township, 77 Ind. 447 (1881); State v. Bauman, 260 N.W. 523 (Minn. 1935).
[23]Lost Creek School Township v. York, 21 N.E.2d 58, 127 A.L.R. 1287 (Ind. 1939).

[24]Bopp v. Clark, 147 N.W. 172, 52 L.R.A. (N.S.) 493 (Iowa 1914).
[25]McMinn County Board of Education v. Anderson, 292 S.W.2d 198 (Tenn. 1956).
[26]People *ex rel.* Templeton v. Board of Education, 102 N.E.2d 751 (Ill. 1951). *Contra*, State, *ex rel.* Wood v. Board of Education, 206 S.W.2d 566 (Mo. 1947).
[27]Perry v. Independent School District, 210 N.W.2d 283 (Minn. 1973).
[28]Currie v. School District No. 26, 27 N.W. 922 (Minn. 1886); Bissell Lumber Co. v. Northwestern Casualty & Surety Co., 207 N.W. 697 (Wis. 1926). *See also:* Ann.Cas. 1912 D 1132.
[29]Thompson v. School District, 233 N.W. 439, 74 A.L.R. 790 (Mich. 1930).

sidered in the same category as contracts with the husband (board member) and are therefore illegal. Contracts in which the board member has a pecuniary interest, except to the extent permitted by statutes, are voidable in all states as violative of public policy.[30]

6.7 ORAL CONTRACTS

Unless the statutes require that a contract be in writing, an oral agreement is as valid as a written one, except that it is usually more difficult to prove its terms.[31] Statutes normally require that a teacher's contract be in writing, and some specify that contracts with school districts involving expenditures over a stated amount also must be written. Where the statutes require a contract to be in writing, an oral contract is unenforceable, at least prior to the time that there has been performance of it.[32] To meet the legal requirements of a written contract it is not necessary that all provisions be contained in one formal written document. The terms thereof may be found in several different writings, such as in letters, in minutes of school board meetings, and the like. If the essential elements of a contract are contained therein, the contract is considered to be a written one.[33]

There are cases in which a school employee has been able to collect salary under an oral contract where the statutes required it to be in writing—even where the contract has been for services beyond those specified in the written contract. In one case the teacher began teaching under an oral contract and it later was reduced to writing. In this instance the school district was held[34] to be estopped from denying the va-

lidity of an oral contract. The acceptance of services also was found[35] to ratify the contract. Recovery was permitted where the school board was held[36] to be guilty of laches by accepting the services of the teacher for five months before objecting to the oral contract. However, as a rule the teacher must show more than the mere rendition of services in order to collect salary. The theory of *quantum meruit*, i.e., payment for value of service rendered, generally has been held[37] not to apply where the teacher is under an oral contract and the law requires a written one.

In view of the uncertainties involved and the decisions holding oral contracts void or voidable when written contracts are required, it is desirable for a teacher who agrees to render additional service, after the original contract has been signed, to have the supplemental agreement evidenced by writing. This advice appears warranted although one court upheld[38] the validity of an oral contract for additional compensation for extra services where the original contract was in writing.

It is not uncommon for all of the terms of the contract to be negotiated orally before being reduced to writing. This is entirely permissible.[39] The writing should be executed before performance of the contract begins although, as stated above, this may not be strictly necessary for its enforcement. Often the parties will rely upon standard forms of written contracts.

6.8 WRITTEN CONTRACTS

Organizations of teachers and school boards have expended considerable effort to improve the forms of teacher contracts. Several state departments of education have adopted uniform contract forms which are mandatory; many other states use an approved form which is discretionary with each school district. Most states now re-

[30]Pickett v. School District No. 1, 25 Wis. 551, 3 Am.Rep. 105 (1870); Smith v. Dandridge, 135 S.W. 800, 34 L.R.A. (N.S.) 129 (Ark. 1911); School District No. 98 v. Pomponi, 247 Pac. 1056 (Col. 1926).

[31]Jackson School Township v. Shera, 35 N.E. 842 (Ind. 1893); Pearson v. School District No. 8, 129 N.W. 940 (Wis. 1911); Robinson v. Board of Education, 73 S.E. 337 (W.Va. 1911); Kapustic v. School District, 111 A.2d 169 (Pa. 1955).

[32]Hoevelman v. Reorganized School District R2 of Crawford County, 452 S.W.2d 298 (Mo. 1970); Wenders v. White Mills Independent School District, 90 A.2d 318 (Pa. 1952); Board of Trustees v. Ohio County Board of Education, 189 S.W. 433 (Ky. 1916); County Board of Education v. Dudley, 157 S.W. 927 (Ky. 1913); Hutchins v. School District No. 1, 87 N.W. 80 (Mich. 1901).

[33]Edwards v. School District No. 73, 297 S.W. 1001 (Mo. 1927); Bailey v. Jamestown School District, 77 S.W.2d 1017 (Mo. 1934); Hall v. Deer Creek Township, 189 N.E. 527 (Ind. 1934); State ex rel. Foster v. Griffin, 246 S.W.2d 396 (Mo. 1952); Lynch v. Webb City School Dist. No. 92, 418 S.W.2d 608 (Mo. 1967).

[34]Edgecomb v. Traverse City School District, 67 N.W.2d 87 (Mich. 1954).

[35]Davis v. White, 284 S.W. 764 (Ark. 1926); Bald Knob Special School District v. McDonald, 283 S.W. 22 (Ark. 1926); Cook v. Independent School District, 40 Iowa 444 (1873).

[36]Williams v. Board of Education, 31 S.E. 985 (W.Va. 1898).

[37]Leland v. School District No. 28, 80 N.W. 354 (Minn. 1899); Metz v. Warwick, 269 S.W. 626 (Mo. 1925); Taylor v. School District No. 3, 60 Mo.App. 372 (1894); Perkins v. Independent School District of Ridgeway, 74 S.W. 122 (Mo. 1903).

[38]Joint Consolidated School District No. 2 v. Johnson, 203 P.2d 242 (Kan. 1949).

[39]Faulk v. McCartney, 22 Pac. 712 (Kan. 1889); School District No. 68 v. Allen, 104 S.W. 172 (Ark. 1907); Corum v. Common School District No. 21, 47 P.2d 889 (Ida. 1935); Hugunin v. Madison Township, 27 N.E.2d 926 (Ind. 1940).

quire that teachers be employed by written contracts. Generally, state-adopted contract forms provide for annual employment. Even in tenure states, where no written contracts are issued to teachers on permanent tenure, annual contracts are entered into with probationary teachers.

Court decisions upholding oral contracts for teachers cannot be relied upon since statutes have been enacted in most states requiring written contracts. A written contract may be required by the application of some other statute. For example, a statutory requirement that all contracts over a specified amount be in writing applies to teachers' contracts as well as to contracts for other purposes.

6.9 GENERAL PROVISIONS OF TEACHERS' CONTRACTS

The teacher's contract is the beginning point for determining the rights, duties, and responsibilities of the teacher. However, it is more inclusive than the formal statement signed by the board and the teacher since it also incorporates all reasonable rules adopted by the board, either before or after the employment of the teacher,[40] and all relevant statutes of the state, unless illegal or unconstitutional.[41]

Tenure teachers, too, are subject to reasonable rules, including those enacted after their employment or after the acquisition of tenure.[42] Since relevant rules of the board are considered part of a teacher's contract, they should be made known to the teacher before or upon employment.[43]

As both local regulations and state statutes are part of a teacher's contract, there is a possibility of conflict between the two and also between the terms of the formal contract and state law. In such cases state law takes precedence, unless it applies only in the absence of local regulation or contract.[44]

6.10 REASONS WHICH EXCUSE PERFORMANCE[45]

When contracts contain the essential elements of a valid contract enumerated above, they generally are enforceable. However, under certain circumstances their performance may be excused on one or more of the following grounds:

1. Where performance is impossible because of an "act of God" or of a public enemy.
2. Where a change in the law renders the contract illegal.
3. Where the person who agrees to render personal services dies, thus preventing the fulfillment of the contract.
4. Where the specific subject matter required in the contract is destroyed and is irreplaceable, as an original oil painting.
5. Where there has been a mutual mistake of fact, a fraudulent misrepresentation of a material fact, or duress.[46]

The courts are hesitant to excuse a party from performing the agreed bargain because of an "act of God." An "act of God" is an excuse only when it makes performance impossible;[47] it is not sufficient if it only makes performance difficult or inconvenient. Neither is an "act of God" a justification for nonperformance where it was reasonably foreseeable at the time the contract was entered into.[48]

Contracts may be rendered impossible of performance because of war conditions or the public enemy. In this circumstance a party is excused from performance and there is no liability for nonperformance.[49] But the mere fact that performance may be more difficult than the parties contemplated will not excuse performance. For example, in the absence of a waiver provision in the agreement, a strike or other event which interferes with the performance of a transportation contract will not excuse performance.[50]

A contract in violation of some superior law, such as a provision of the United States

---

[40]School City of East Chicago v. Sigler, 36 N.E.2d 760 (Ind. 1941); Rible v. Hughes, 150 P.2d 455 (Cal. 1944); Finot v. Pasadena City Bd. of Educ., 58 Cal.Rptr. 520 (Cal. 1967).
[41]Malone v. Hayden, 197 Atl. 344 (Pa. 1938); Canfield v. Board of Education, 235 A.2d 470 (N.J. 1967).
[42]Richard v. Board of Education, 171 N.E.2d 37 (Ill. 1960).
[43]School City of East Chicago v. Sigler, 36 N.E.2d 760 (Ind. 1941); Fursman v. Chicago, 116 N.E. 158 (Ill. 1917); Backie v. Cromwell Consolidated School District, 242 N.W. 389 (Minn. 1932).
[44]Crabb v. School District No. 1, 93 Mo.App. 254 (1902); Alexander v. School District No. 1, 164 Pac. 711 (Ore. 1917); Everett v. Fractional School District No. 2, 30 Mich. 249 (1874).

[45]For an excellent presentation of reasons justifying nonperformance of contracts see 84 A.L.R.2d 12.
[46]Edwards, Newton, *The Courts and the Public Schools* (Chicago. University of Chicago Press, rev. ed., 1955), p. 464.
[47]Dewey v. Union School District, 5 N.W. 646, 38 Am.Rep. 206 (Mich. 1880).
[48]84 A.L.R.2d 42, Excuse for Nonperformance of Contracts. 158 A.L.R. 1446.
[49]Carvel v. John Kellys (London), 53 N.Y.S.2d 640 (1945).
[50]Board of Education v. United Bus Corporation, 310 N.Y.S.2d 749 (1970).

or state constitution, cannot be enforced.[51] However, the prohibition in the federal Constitution against the passage of laws impairing the obligation of contracts does not invalidate state laws prescribing the mode of contracting by school districts or reasonably regulating contracts entered into by them.[52]

It is, of course, impossible to require personal service from a deceased person. The decedent's estate is under no obligation to attempt to perform the contract. The duty to perform terminates with death or a disabling illness or injury.

Another condition justifying the nonperformance of contracts for property or supplies is that in which the subject matter of the contract is unique and is destroyed and cannot be replaced. The excuse for failure to perform the terms of the contract because of destruction of unique property is sometimes available to building contractors.[53]

In some cases a contract may be reformed or rescinded where one or both of the parties were mistaken as to material facts regarding the agreement. While textwriters and courts frequently refer to "mutual mistake of fact," in reality relief is frequently granted where the mistake is unilateral.[54] For example, a contractor was permitted to cancel a contract where he mistakenly omitted a $22,000 item in a $225,000 construction bid. The contract would have resulted in a loss to the bidder and the court concluded that the mistake was fundamental and a substantial part of the whole consideration and consequently there was no meeting of the minds.[55] It is the absence of this fundamental element of the contract, the meeting of the minds rather than the mutuality of the mistake, which generally serves as a basis for rescision in such cases.

6.11 INTERPRETATION OF CONTRACTS

The clear drafting of a written contract minimizes the possibilities of misinterpretation by the parties. However, differences do arise and often find their way into the courts for resolution. Over the years the courts have developed helpful rules to guide them in the interpretation of contracts, the objective in each instance being to ascertain and apply the intent of the parties.

1. This intent is sought first in the written language used by the parties in setting forth the terms of their agreement. If the terms of the writing are clear and unmistakable, the courts will interpret the contract as written, it being presumed that the parties intended to accord to the words their ordinary meaning unless a contrary intent is disclosed, as in a definition of terms. It is immaterial that one of the parties has assumed that they were agreeing to something different. No parol or outside evidence is permitted where the language used is clear and unambiguous.[56] However, extrinsic aids to interpretation are permitted where a choice must be made between several "clear" but inconsistent provisions in the same contract. It is assumed that the parties intended to give some weight to each part of their agreement.

2. If terms of the contract are not clear on their face, evidence is admissible to clarify them. Sometimes the substance of the discussions leading to the execution of the agreement, or the minutes recording negotiations, or the general nature of the subject matter will assist in clarifying and establishing the intent of the parties on the point in issue. In ascertaining such intent the courts will assume that the parties intended to achieve a realistic and workable arrangement, and one reasonably related to an educational function or operation. While the court attempts to avoid a harsh result, concluding that such a result could not have been intended, it will, where it so finds, enforce a contract even though it may produce hardship on one of the parties. In an extreme case the court may relieve against unusually severe hardship by granting equitable relief.[57]

3. The status of omitted items, which were discussed but not included in the writing, is sometimes at issue. Normally, they are considered to be merely part of the discussions during negotiations and not matters of contractual agreement.[58] Ordinarily, all oral understandings are deemed to have been merged in the written agreement, and neither party may hold the other to such

[51]Stamey v. State Highway Commission, 76 F.Supp. 946 (Kan. 1948).
[52]Trustees of Dartmouth College v. Woodward, 4 Wheat, (U.S.) 518, 4 L.Ed. 629 (1819).
[53]74 A.L.R. 1292, Destruction of Specific Subject Matter.
[54]*Corbin on Contracts*, p. 556 (One Volume Edition, 1952).
[55]Board of Regents of Murray State Normal School v. Cole, 273 S.W. 508 (Ky. 1925); See also Board of School Commissioners of City of Indianapolis v. Bender, 72 N.E. 154 (Ind. 1904).

[56]Howland v. Prentice, 106 N.W. 1105 (Mich. 1906).
[57]Hanna v. Wright, 89 N.W. 1108 (Iowa 1902); Lee v. Percival, 52 N.W. 543 (Iowa 1892).
[58]Western Publishing House v. Murdick, 56 N.W. 120 (S.D. 1893).

"understandings" omitted therefrom. Where the omission was due to mutual mistake of fact, the parties may wish to amend their agreement or to enter into a supplemental contract. Where the matter was of sufficient importance, an action to reform the contract to make it conform to the real intent of the parties may be brought. As stated earlier, parol evidence normally is not admissible to alter the terms of an unambiguous written instrument.

4. If a teacher has been sent a contract for signature which already has been signed by the designated members of the board, and the teacher has objections to it, the contract should be returned with a statement of the objections. The teacher should not attempt to correct the matter by striking out or rewriting objectionable provisions. To do so may render the contract void. In an instance of this type the court ruled[59] that there had never been a meeting of the minds and mutual assent. The terms had been altered by one party unilaterally without the acquiescence of the other. Clauses prohibiting smoking, participating in cocktail hours, or leaving communities on weekends may be examples of provisions which a teacher finds objectionable and may wish to modify.

5. Doubts in a contract are usually resolved against the party who has drafted the language. This rule of interpretation is based on the premise that the party writing the contract has had an opportunity to study it carefully and therefore to be protected from any liability or obligation which that party does not intend to assume. Since a school board normally writes the contract, any doubtful section is generally interpreted more favorably to the teacher than to the board. However, where the provision is clear, it will be construed and applied as written, even though it may prove unfavorable to the teacher.

6. Handwritten or typed provisions of a contract take precedence over printed matter where the two are in conflict.[60] It is an assumption of the courts that what is interlineated or added to a printed contract expresses the intent of the parties more exactly than any conflicting printed statement which was not specifically written to deal with the situation. However, any material added to a printed contract which is in violation of law or public policy is void and does not have the effect of amending the printed agreement.

7. Unless the statutes otherwise provide, a board of education may enter into a contract the term of which extends into the term of a succeeding board.[61] While there are some cases holding to the contrary, the weight of modern authority approves contracts for periods of time which exceed the term of current board members.[62] However, if the law is to the contrary, or if there is evidence of bad faith, fraud, or malicious action, such contracts are invalid.[63]

8. Contractual agreements with individual board members are generally not binding on the school district.[64] A teacher should be employed at a regular or properly called special meeting of the board in order to be certain of a valid contract.[65] However, ratification of an employment contract is possible at a subsequent meeting of the board, and it becomes validated upon ratification.[66]

9. When a contract is legalized by ratification, it becomes valid for the full length of the time specified in the contract, not just for the period still remaining.[67]

6.12 VOIDABLE AND VOID CONTRACTS

Defective contracts are commonly classified as either voidable or void. Voidable contracts are those containing all of the essential elements of a contract but at the same time embracing some irregularity which permits a party to take action to have it set aside. The irregularity is often correctable. Void contracts are so defective that it is impossible to validate them. The courts have held the following to be voidable:

[59]Harris v. Manning Independent School District, 66 N.W.2d 438 (Iowa 1954).

[60]Fairbanks, Morse and Co. v. Consolidated Fisheries Company, 190 F.2d 817 (3rd Cir. 1951); Miravalle Supply v. El Campe Rice Mill Co., 181 F.2d 679 (8th Cir. 1950), *certiorari denied*, 340 U.S. 822, 71 S.Ct. 56, 95 L.Ed. 604; School District Number 1 of Pima Co. v. Hastings, 466 P.2d 395 (Ariz. 1970).

[61]Parker v. School District of Maplewood, 271 S.W.2d 860 (Mo. 1954).

[62]State *ex rel.* Rees v. Winchell, 23 N.E.2d 843 (Ohio 1939).

[63]*Ibid.*

[64]Cloverdale Union High School District v. Peters, 264 Pac. 273 (Cal. 1928); School District No. 39 v. Shelton, 109 Pac. 67 (Okla. 1910).

[65]McNolty v. Board of School Directors, 78 N.W. 439 (Wis. 1899).

[66]Crane v. Bennington School District, 28 N.W. 105 (Mich. 1886); School District No. 56 v. Jackson, 161 S.W. 153 (Ark. 1913); School District No. 36 v. Gardner, 219 S.W. 11 (Ark. 1920); Hermance v. Public School District No. 2, 180 Pac. 442 (Ariz. 1919); Parrick v. School District No. 1, 164 Pac. 1172 (Kan. 1917); Graham v. School District No. 69, 54 Pac. 185 (Ore. 1898); Landers v. Board of Education, 116 P.2d 690 (N.M. 1941).

[67]Ryan v. Humphries, 150 Pac. 1106 (Okla. 1915).

1. Contracts entered into with prospective teachers who at the time of contract did not hold a license but later secured one.[68]
2. Contracts by teachers with individual members of the school board and not with the board.[69]
3. Employment of a teacher at a meeting not properly called, e.g., one in which some members of the board were absent for lack of notice.[70]
4. Employment of a teacher by the superintendent or some committee of the board through erroneous delegation of power to employ.[71]

The irregularities in the above contracts could be cured by ratification. The board could have made the contract in the first instance and therefore it possessed the power of ratification. However, in ratifying a contract a school board must follow any specifically prescribed procedure for adopting the contract in the first instance.[72] When a contract is ratified, it is ratified for the full period and for the full amount of salary or other consideration designated in the original contract. When a contract has been ratified, the board may not later claim that the contract was invalid because of previous irregularities.[73]

Contracts which are void are impossible to ratify. A number of contracts of this nature are listed:

1. Contracts with teachers without certificates.[74]
2. An oral contract where the state requires that the particular contract be in writing.[74]
3. Contracts which create obligations in excess of statutory or constitutional debt limits.[76]

4. Contracts which exceed the amount that a district is permitted to spend in any one year.[77]
5. Contracts in which conditions precedent have not been met, such as the requirement that all teachers be recommended by the superintendent.[78]
6. Contracts which are *ultra vires* (outside the authority of the board to make) or are prohibited by statute, constitution, or public policy.[79]
7. Contracts by the board with one of its own members where such is prohibited by law.[80]
8. Contracts by board where statutory bidding procedure was not followed.[81]

Contracts of the above types cannot be ratified. Persons rendering service under contracts of this nature generally cannot be paid, even if the board is willing to pay for the service. The board is without legal authority to validate the contracts, nor may persons recover on a *quantum meruit* theory for reasonable value of their services.

6.13 SCHOOL DISTRICT LIABILITY ON ULTRA VIRES CONTRACTS

When a school board enters into a contract which is beyond its power to make, questions frequently arise as to whether the school district is liable under the contract. The authorities are in agreement[82] that an *ultra vires* contract is invalid and unenforceable.

One who enters into a contract with a school district is obligated to inform himself or herself on whether the school district has authority to make the contract in question.[83] The courts reason that the power of a school district is a matter of public record. Consequently, those who contract with a school district do so at their own peril, and if the contract proves to be *ultra vires*, they

---

[68]Jenness v. School District No. 31, 12 Minn. 337 (1867); *See also* Rase v. Southeast Nebraska Consolidated School District, 212 N.W.2d 629 (Neb. 1973), involving school bus driver's failure to obtain permit prior to execution of contract.

[69]Watkins v. Special District, 183 S.W. 168 (Ark. 1916); Smith v. School District No. 57, 42 Atl. 368 (Pa. 1898).

[70]School District No. 39 v. Shelton, 109 Pac. 67 (Okla. 1910).

[71]State *ex rel.* Kenny v. Jones, 224 S.W. 1041 (Tenn. 1920).

[72]Commonwealth *ex rel.* Ricapito v. School District, 25 A.2d 786 (Pa. 1942).

[73]Crane v. Bennington School District, 28 N.W. 105 (Mich. 1886).

[74]Goose River Bank v. Willow Lake School Township, 44 N.W. 1002 (N.D. 1890); Perkins v. Inhabitants of Town of Standish, 62 A.2d 321 (Me. 1948).

[75]Leland v. School District No. 28, 80 N.W. 354 (Minn. 1899); Metz v. Warwick, 269 S.W. 626 (Mo. 1925); Taylor v. School District No. 3, 60 Mo.App. 372 (1894); Bankston v. Tangipahoa Parish School Board, 190 So. 177 (La. 1939).

[76]Boydstun v. Rockwell County, 23 S.W. 541 (Tex. 1893); Riesen v. School District No. 4, 208 N.W. 472 (Wis. 1926); Grady v. Pruit, 63 S.W. 283 (Ky. 1901).

[77]Collier v. Peacock, 54 S.W. 1025 (Tex. 1900).

[78]Board of Education v. Watts, 95 So. 498 (Ala. 1922); Ratcliff v. Buna Independent School District, 46 S.W.2d 459 (Tex. 1932).

[79]Westun Publishing House v. District Township of Rock, 50 N.W. 551 (Iowa 1891).

[80]Scott v. School District, 31 Atl. 145, 27 L.R.A. 588 (Vt. 1894).

[81]Schull v. Webster Independent School District No. 101, 198 N.W.2d 512 (S.D. 1972).

[82]Powell v. Bainbridge State Bank, 132 S.E. 60 (Ga. 1926); Fulk v. School District No. 8 of Lancaster County, 53 N.W.2d 56 (Neb. 1952); McAtee v. Gutierrez, 146 P.2d 315 (N.M. 1944); Honey Creek School Township v. Barnes, 21 N.E. 747 (Ind. 1889); Seim v. Independent District, 17 N.W.2d 342 (S.D. 1945); A. H. Andrews Co. v. Delight Special School District, 128 S.W. 361 (Ark. 1910); Charles R. McCormick Lumber Co. v. Highland School District, 147 Pac. 1183 (Cal. 1915).

[83]School District No. 1 of Pima County v. Lohr, 498 P.2d 512 (Ariz. 1972); Hoevelman v. Reorganized School District R2 of Crawford Co., 452 S.W.2d 298 (Mo. 1970).

have no right of recovery upon the contract for legally no contract exists.[84]

As a general rule, a contract which is clearly beyond the power of a school district, or which is expressly prohibited by statute, or which violates public policy is held[85] to be void and unenforceable. Thus, a school district generally will not be held liable under a contract which is *ultra vires* because it is prohibited or against public policy even if the contract is fully executed and the school district has benefited by the performance of the contract.[86] The reverse is also true; the other party to such a contract may refuse to fulfill any contractual obligation because a contract of this nature is unenforceable.[87] However, where a contract is not expressly prohibited but is *ultra vires* because it is beyond the power granted the district or is in violation of the statutory mode of contracting, one who has benefited from the contract generally cannot avoid the obligation which was assumed under the contract by claiming as a defense that the contract was *ultra vires*.[88] The courts in these cases have reasoned that the intent of the law was to protect the public, not private parties, and that a private party who had benefited from a contract with a public corporation should not be allowed to avoid the contractual obligation simply because the contract in question was beyond the power of the corporation.

6.14 RECOVERY ON QUANTUM MERUIT

The courts occasionally permit recovery on *quantum meruit* where goods or services are supplied to a school district under an *ultra vires* contract. Recovery under *quantum meruit* is based on the equitable principle that one who receives a substantial benefit from another should be required to pay just compensation for it. It should be emphasized, however, that any recovery had under *quantum meruit* is for the actual

value of the goods or services received; it is not based on the contract. In regard to recovery under *quantum meruit*, it has been said that "recovery is not upon the theory that the contract was a valid one, but upon the theory that it would be inequitable and unconscionable to permit the retention of the benefits and permit a division of the government to avoid payment therefor."[89]

As a general rule, recovery on the basis of *quantum meruit* is permitted only in cases where the contract would have been within the power of the school district if properly made; the defect must be in the exercise of the power only.[90] Thus, recovery under *quantum meruit* has been allowed where a school board, acting in good faith, altered a contract and thus rendered it unenforceable.[91] Again, a statute may provide that the district can obligate itself only through action of the board of education at a legal meeting. An attempt to contract by a majority of board members acting individually would be void in the face of such a statute, but *quantum meruit* has been allowed.[92] The remedy also has been granted where a contract for construction of a school building was executed despite the fact that the notices of a meeting of the electors to consider the question of erecting a new building were not posted for a sufficient length of time and there was not sufficient publication of the notice calling for bids.[93]

The weight of authority indicates that recovery may not be had on *quantum meruit* for contracts which are clearly beyond the power of the school district,[94] contracts which violate statutory requirements concerning the mode of contracting,[95] contracts which violate constitutional or statutory restrictions regarding the amount of indebt-

[84]Powell v. Bainbridge State Bank, 132 S.E. 60 (Ga. 1926); Reams v. Cooley, 152 Pac. 293 (Cal. 1915); First National Bank v. Adams School Township, 46 N.E. 832 (Ind. 1897); Charleroi Lumber Co. v. District of Borough of Bentleyville, 6 A.2d 88 (Pa. 1939); Beckley-Cardy Co. v. West Point Special School District, 192 S.W.2d 540 (Ark. 1946).

[85]First National Bank v. Adams School Township, 46 N.E. 832 (Ind. 1897); Riesen v. School District No. 4, 208 N.W. 472 (Wis. 1926); City of Pittsburg v. Goshorn, 79 Atl. 505 (Pa. 1911).

[86]Goose River Bank v. Willow Creek School Township, 44 N.W. 1002 (N.D. 1890); City of Pittsburg v. Goshorn, 79 Atl. 505 (Pa. 1911); Honey Creek School Township v. Barnes, 21 N.E. 747 (Ind. 1889).

[87]School District No. 8 v. Twin Falls County Mutual Fire Insurance Co., 164 Pac. 1174 (Ida. 1917).

[88]Baumann v. City of West Allis, 204 N.W. 907 (Wis. 1925); City of Belfast v. Belfast Water Co., 98 Atl. 738 (Me. 1916).

[89]Scheschy v. Binkley, 245 N.W. 267 (Neb. 1932).

[90]Schaut v. Joint School District No. 6, 210 N.W. 270 (Wis. 1926); Fulk v. School District No. 8, 53 N.W.2d 56 (Neb. 1952); State *ex rel.* Kuhn v. Smith, 194 N.E.2d 186 (Ohio 1963); Hatch v. Maple Valley Township Unit School, 17 N.W.2d 735 (Mich. 1945); Sebastian v. School Directors, 40 N.E.2d 565 (Ill. 1942).

[91]Schaut v. Joint School District No. 6, 210 N.W. 270 (Wis. 1926).

[92]Sebastian v. School Directors, 40 N.E.2d 565 (Ill. 1942).

[93]Charles R. McCormick Lumber Co. v. Highland School District, 147 Pac. 1183 (Cal. 1915).

[94]First National Bank v. Adams School Township, 46 N.E. 832 (Ind. 1897); Fulk v. School District No. 8 of Lancaster County, 53 N.W.2d 56 (Neb. 1952); McAtee v. Gutierrez, 146 P.2d 315 (N.M. 1944); Richland County Bank v. Joint School District No. 2, 250 N.W. 407 (Wis. 1933).

[95]Reams v. Cooley, 152 Pac. 293 (Cal. 1915); Taylor v. School District No. 3, 60 Mo.App. 372 (1894); Oberwarth v. McCreary County Board of Education, 121 S.W.2d 716 (Ky. 1938); Price v. School District, 42 A.2d 99 (Pa. 1945).

edness a school district may incur,[96] and contracts which are contrary to public policy.[97] Statutes requiring that contracts be let to the lowest responsible bidder are to be regarded as mandatory, and one who furnishes labor or materials on a contract let in violation of such requirements will not be allowed to recover on *quantum meruit*.[98] Similarly, the weight of authority indicates that where the statutes require school district contracts to be made in writing no recovery on *quantum meruit* can be had on oral contracts,[99] although some authority to the contrary does exist.[100]

The courts have tended to be more liberal in granting equitable relief in situations in which an invalid contract has been executed and the district retains the benefits of the contract. In an Indiana case, for example, a school township trustee, acting without authority, borrowed money to complete a school building, and the court permitted[101] recovery of the amount loaned. In a Florida case where school trustees, acting without authority, gave promissory notes in payment for a school site, the holders of the notes were permitted to secure payment of the actual value of the property.[102] In a Louisiana case an architect was permitted to recover the money due him for services rendered in planning and supervising the erection and repair of school property despite the fact that no legal contract for the architectural services had been made.[103] In these and similar cases, the courts have reasoned[104] that principles of equity and justice require that a school district should not be allowed to accept the benefits of a contract and then repudiate its obligations.

6.15 RECOVERY OF PROPERTY FURNISHED UNDER AN INVALID CONTRACT

The courts generally have permitted[105] the recovery of money or property furnished to a school district under an illegal contract if it can be identified and if its return can be accomplished without damage to the property of the district. Recovery is permitted, however, only when the contract is one which is not prohibited by law or which does not violate public policy. Again, the principles of equity have been given great weight. It has been held,[106] for example, that, where a school district purchased electric heaters without advertising for bids and later refused to pay for the heaters claiming that the contract was void, the company which supplied the heaters was entitled to recover them from the school district. Similarly, in a case involving school bonds sold without the assent of the voters as required by the constitution, the court said[107] that, if the money derived from the sale of the illegal bonds could be identified, a court of equity would require the district to pay it back to the bondholders.

It is important to note the limitation that property furnished under an invalid contract can be removed only if its removal can be accomplished without material damage to the property of the district. Where property furnished under an invalid contract cannot be removed without damaging the district's property, the courts will not permit its recovery.[108] In a North Dakota case, for example, a school building was constructed under a contract which created an indebtedness in excess of the constitutional debt limit. After the building was completed and placed in use by the district, a taxpayer brought suit to enjoin the district from paying the balance due the contractor. The contractor then sought to recover the property. The court refused[109] to permit recovery of the property because it could not be recovered without destroying the property of the school district. In a Utah case a

[96]McGillivray v. Joint School District No. 1, 88 N.W. 310 (Wis. 1901); Superior Manufacturing Co. v. School District No. 63, 114 Pac. 328 (Okla. 1910); Goose River Bank v. Willow Creek School Township, 44 N.W. 1002 (N.D. 1890); Wayne County v. Hopper, 75 So. 766 (Miss. 1917).
[97]Seim v. Independent District, 17 N.W.2d 342 (S.D. 1945); Toler v. Love, 154 So. 711 (Miss. 1934).
[98]Reams v. Cooley, 152 Pac. 293 (Cal. 1915); Seim v. Independent District, 17 N.W.2d 342 (S.D. 1945); Contra: Williams v. National Contracting Co., 199 N.W. 919 (Minn. 1924).
[99]Taylor v. School District No. 3, 60 Mo.App. 372 (1894); Oberwarth v. McCreary County Board of Education, 121 S.W.2d 716 (Ky. 1938); Leland v. School District No. 28, 80 N.W. 354 (Minn. 1899); City School Corporation v. Hickman, 94 N.E. 828 (Ind. 1911).
[100]Tolleson Union High School District v. Kincaid, 85 P.2d 708 (Ariz. 1938).
[101]White River School Township v. Dorrell, 59 N.E. 867 (Ind. 1901).
[102]Special Tax School District No. 1 v. Hillman, 179 So. 805 (Fla. 1938).
[103]Burk v. Livingston Parish School Board, 182 So. 656 (La. 1938).
[104]Sutton v. Board of Education, 266 N.W. 447 (Minn. 1936); Craig v. Bell, 46 S.E.2d 52 (S.C. 1948).

[105]Strauch v. San Mateo Junior College District, 286 Pac. 173 (Cal. 1930); State v. Smith, 194 N.E.2d 186 (Ohio 1963); Board of Trustees v. Postel, 88 S.W. 1065 (Ky. 1905); Moe v. Millard County School District, 179 Pac. 980 (Utah 1919); Superior Manufacturing Co. v. School District No. 63, 114 Pac. 328 (Okla. 1910).
[106]Strauch v. San Mateo Junior College District, 286 Pac. 173 (Cal. 1930).
[107]Board of Trustees v. Postel, 88 S.W. 1065 (Ky. 1905).
[108]Bartelson v. International School District No. 5, 174 N.W. 78 (N.D. 1919); Moe v. Millard County School District, 179 Pac. 980 (Utah 1919).
[109]Bartelson v. International School District No. 5, 174 N.W. 78 (N.D. 1919).

heating plant was installed in a school building under a contract which created an indebtedness in excess of that permitted by the constitution; the court permitted[110] removal of the heating plant because it could be easily identified and removed without material injury to the building.

6.16 RECOVERY OF MONEY PAID OUT ON INVALID CONTRACTS

The courts are in disagreement as to whether a school district may recover funds paid out on illegal contracts. In a number of cases it has been held[111] that a school district may recover money paid out on contracts made in violation of constitutional or statutory restrictions or on contracts which were beyond the power of the district to make. The reasoning in these cases is exemplified by the following statement by the Supreme Court of Wisconsin:

> To hold that, when public officers have paid out money in pursuance of an illegal and unwarranted contract, such monies cannot be recovered in a proper action brought upon behalf of the public, merely because the payment has been voluntarily made for services actually rendered, would be to introduce a vicious principle into municipal law, and a principle which would necessarily sweep away many of the safeguards surrounding the administration of public affairs. Were this, in fact, the law, it can readily be seen that public officials could at all times, with a little ingenuity, subvert and nullify that wholesome principle of the law which prohibits their spending the public funds for illegal purposes. All that would be necessary to be done would be to make the contract, have the labor performed, pay out the money, and the public would be remedyless.[112]

Accordingly, it has been held[113] that a school district may recover funds paid out for an insurance contract which was *ultra*

vires, that it may recover money paid out on a contract with a school board member where such a contract was prohibited by statutes,[114] and that it may recover money paid out on a contract for transportation of pupils which the district had no authority to make.[115]

In a number of jurisdictions, however, it has been held[116] that money paid out by a school district on an illegal contract cannot be recovered where the contract was made in good faith and the district has benefited from the contract. For example, no recovery was permitted of money paid out on a contract in which a school board member was personally interested,[117] of money paid out under a contract with a teacher who did not possess the teaching certificate required by statute,[118] and of money paid out as interest on bonds which created an indebtedness in excess of the specified debt limit.[119]

The decisions concerning the right of a school district to recover money it has paid out under an illegal contract are impossible to harmonize. Whether recovery will be permitted on such contracts appears to depend upon the state involved and upon the specific facts of each case. The decisions which have permitted a school district to recover money paid out on illegal contracts generally have been based upon the concept that school funds are trust funds which must not be diverted to illegal purposes. Decisions which have denied recovery usually have been based on the principle of equity, which precludes recovery where the contract was made in good faith and the district has benefited therefrom.

6.17 RATIFICATION OF ILLEGAL OR IRREGULAR CONTRACTS

Ratification, as it applies to contracts, refers to the act of adopting or confirming a contract which was invalid at the time of its making. The courts are in general agree-

[110]Moe v. Millard County School District, 179 Pac. 980 (Utah 1919).
[111]Vick Consolidated School District v. New, 187 S.W.2d 948 (Ark. 1945); Independent School District No. 5 v. Collins, 98 Pac. 857 (Ida. 1908); Board of Education v. Commercial Casualty Insurance Co., 182 S.E. 87 (W.Va. 1935); Milquet v. Van Straten, 202 N.W. 670 (Wis. 1925); Burke v. Wheeler County, 187 S.E. 246 (Ga. 1936); School District No. 9 v. McLintock, 237 N.W. 539 (Mich. 1931); School Directors v. Parks, 85 Ill. 338 (1877); Directors of School District No. 302 v. Libby, 237 Pac. 505 (Wash. 1925).
[112]Frederick v. Douglas County, 71 N.W. 798 (Wis. 1897).
[113]Board of Education v. Commercial Casualty Insurance Co., 182 S.E. 87 (W.Va. 1935).

[114]Independent School District No. 5 v. Collins, 98 Pac. 857 (Ida. 1908).
[115]Milquet v. Van Stratten, 202 N.W. 670 (Wis. 1925).
[116]Culver v. Brown, 243 N.W. 10 (Mich. 1932); Ryszka v. Board of Education, 214 N.Y.S. 264 (1926); Kagy v. Independent District, 89 N.W. 972 (Iowa 1902); Witmer v. Nichols, 8 S.W.2d 63 (Mo. 1928); School District No. 46 v. Johnson, 143 Pac. 264 (Col. 1914); Ohio National Life Insurance Co. v. Board of Education, 55 N.E.2d 163 (Ill. 1944).
[117]Culver v. Brown, 243 N.W. 10 (Mich. 1932); Ryszka v. Board of Education, 214 N.Y.S. 264 (1926).
[118]School District No. 46 v. Johnson, 143 Pac. 264 (Col. 1914).
[119]Ohio National Life Insurance Co. v. Board of Education, 55 N.E.2d 163 (Ill. 1944).

ment[120] that a school district contract which was made in an irregular or informal manner may be ratified. On the other hand, contracts which are void because they are beyond the power of the board, or because they violate constitutional or statutory requirements or prohibitions, or because they are in violation of public policy may not be ratified.[121] As a rule, a school district may ratify any contract which it legally could have made initially.[122] The Supreme Court of Nebraska has stated that "it is a rule subject to few, if any, exceptions, that a corporate authority may ratify and confirm any act or contract in its behalf or for its benefit which it might have lawfully done or made originally."[123]

Ratification is most commonly employed to validate contracts which were entered into in an irregular manner or which were made by an agent of the board acting without authority. It has been held,[124] for example, that a school district may ratify a contract made by school board members acting individually, contracts made at an improperly called school board meeting,[125] and contracts made by an unauthorized agent of the board.[126] On the other hand, it has been held[127] that a contract may not be ratified if it creates an indebtedness in excess of constitutional or statutory limits.

Questions sometimes arise as to what actions are necessary to constitute ratification of a contract.[128] The ratification of an invalid contract by a school district may be either expressed or implied,[129] but it will not be implied from mere silence on the part of the district.[130] The ratification of an invalid contract must be unequivocal,[131] and done in compliance with the law relative to the original contract.[132] Ratification of a contract is accomplished when a school district, with full knowledge of all the facts, accepts and retains the benefits of the contract. Ratification of an invalid school contract is most frequently accomplished by either accepting and paying for services received under the contract or accepting and using material furnished under the contract. It has often been held,[133] for example, that where a qualified teacher whose contract is invalid is allowed to teach and is paid for services the contract has been ratified. Similarly, it has been held[134] that acceptance of services or use of property by a school district is sufficient to constitute ratification of a contract, although in some cases it has been established[135] that there must be affirmative corporate action to constitute valid ratification. Where athletic equipment was insured by a school principal who acted without authority, for example, and the school district collected proceeds from the insurance after the equipment was destroyed by fire and used the proceeds to purchase other equipment, the actions of the district constituted ratification of the act of the principal in purchasing the insurance.[136]

Ratification will not be implied from temporary or necessary use of property where the school district did not have full

[120]Lowe & Campbell Athletic Goods Co. v. Tangipahoa Parish School Board, 20 So.2d 422 (La. 1944); Farmers' State Bank v. School District No. 100, 4 P.2d 404 (Kan. 1931); Beck v. Independent Consolidated School District, 241 N.W. 427 (Iowa 1932); Ryan v. Humphries, 150 Pac. 1106 (Okla. 1915); Saline County v. Gage County, 92 N.W. 1050 (Neb. 1902).

[121]First National Bank v. Whisenhunt, 127 S.W. 968 (Ark. 1910); Murry v. Union Parish School Board, 185 So. 305 (La. 1938); Morse v. Inhabitants of Montville, 99 Atl. 438 (Me. 1916); Richards v. School Township of Jackson, 109 N.W. 1093 (Iowa 1906); Ketterer v. Independent School District No. 1, 79 N.W.2d 428 (Minn. 1956).

[122]Beckley-Cardy Co. v. West Point Special School District, 192 S.W.2d 540 (Ark. 1946); Ryan v. Humphries, 150 Pac. 1106 (Okla. 1915); State ex rel. Blair v. Gettinger, 105 N.E.2d 161 (Ind. 1952); Frank v. Board of Education, 100 Atl. 211 (N.J. 1917); Glidden State Bank v. School District No. 2, 128 N.W. 285 (Wis. 1910).

[123]Saline County v. Gage County, 92 N.W. 1050 (Neb. 1902).

[124]Union School Furniture Co. v. School District No. 60, 32 Pac. 368 (Kan. 1893).

[125]Board of Education v. News Dispatch Printing & Audit Co., 245 Pac. 884 (Okla. 1926).

[126]Frank v. Board of Education, 100 Atl. 211 (N.J. 1917).

[127]Rusin v. School District No. 4, 208 N.W. 472 (Wis. 1926).

[128]Richards v. School Township, 109 N.W. 1093 (Iowa 1906).

[129]Township Board of Education v. Carolan, 55 N.E. 58 (Ill. 1899).

[130]Caxton Co. v. School District No. 5, 98 N.W. 231 (Wis. 1904).

[131]Goin v. Board of Education, 183 S.W.2d 819 (Ky. 1944).

[132]Knott County Board of Education v. Martin, 76 S.W.2d 601 (Ky. 1934); St. Paul Foundry Co. v. Burnstad School District No. 31, 269 N.W. 738 (N.D. 1936).

[133]Athearn v. Independent District, 33 Iowa 105 (1871); Ryan v. Humphries, 150 Pac. 1106 (Okla. 1915); Crane v. Bennington School District, 28 N.W. 105 (Mich. 1886); Hermance v. Public School District No. 2, 180 Pac. 442 (Ariz. 1919); Parrick v. School District No. 1, 164 Pac. 1172 (Kan. 1917).

[134]Board of Education v. News Dispatch Printing & Audit Co., 245 Pac. 884 (Okla. 1926); Springfield Furniture Co. v. School District No. 4, 54 S.W. 217 (Ark. 1899); Frank v. Board of Education, 100 Atl. 211 (N.J. 1917).

[135]Caxton Co. v. School District No. 5, 98 N.W. 231 (Wis. 1904); Taylor v. District Township, 25 Iowa 447 (1868); Pehrson v. School District No. 334, 77 P.2d 1022 (Wash. 1938); School Administrative District No. 3 v. Maine School District Commission, 185 A.2d 744 (Me. 1962).

[136]Lowe & Campbell Athletic Goods Co. v. Tangipahoa Parish School District, 20 So.2d 422 (La. 1944).

knowledge of the invalid contract.[137] Also, ratification will not be implied when a school district retains benefits which it has no option to reject.[138] It has been held,[139] for example, that where a contract for construction of a schoolhouse on land owned by a town exceeded the amount of money which had been authorized for the cost of the building, the fact that the town took possession of and used the schoolhouse did not ratify the contract for its construction.

An important limitation on the authority of a school district to ratify an invalid contract is the requirement that where the statutes specify the mode of contracting, ratification can be accomplished only by following the procedure prescribed for making such contracts.[140] Thus, it has been held[141] that where school directors, without being authorized by the electors to do so as required by statute, contracted to purchase a set of charts which were used in the school, the use of the charts did not constitute ratification of the contract.

Once ratified, a contract is just as legal and binding as it would have been had the initial contract been properly made.[142] Furthermore, the act of ratification validates the entire contract, because it is not possible to ratify one part of a contract and reject another part. Thus, if an invalid contract with a teacher is ratified by a school district, the district is obligated for the entire amount stipulated in the contract.[143] Concerning the effect of ratification of a contract, it has been said, "By the very nature of the act of ratification, the party ratifying becomes a party to the original contract. He that was not bound becomes bound by it, and entitled to all the proper benefits of it."[144]

[137]Beckley-Cardy Co. v. West Point Special School District, 192 S.W.2d 540 (Ark. 1946).

[138]Turney v. Town of Bridgeport, 12 Atl. 520 (Conn. 1887); Young v. Board of Education of Independent School Dist., No. 47, 55 N.W. 1112 (Minn. 1893); Allen County Board of Education v. Scottsville Builders' Supply Co., 259 S.W. 39 (Ky. 1924).

[139]Turney v. Town of Bridgeport, 12 Atl. 520 (Conn. 1887).

[140]First National Bank v. Whisenhunt, 127 S.W. 968 (Ark. 1910); Caxton Co. v. School District No. 5, 98 N.W. 231 (Wis. 1904); Boydstun v. Rockwell County, 23 S.W. 541 (Tex. 1893).

[141]First National Bank v. Whisenhunt, 127 S.W. 968 (Ark. 1910).

[142]Hill v. City of Indianapolis, 92 Fed. 467 (7th Cir. 1899); Jones v. School District No. 144, 51 Pac. 927 (Kan. 1898); Athearn v. Independent District, 33 Iowa 105 (1871); Ryan v. Humphries, 150 Pac. 1106 (Okla. 1915).

[143]Jones v. School District No. 144, 51 Pac. 927 (Kan. 1898); Athearn v. Independent District, 33 Iowa 105 (1871).

[144]Hill v. City of Indianapolis, 92 Fed. 467 (7th Cir. 1899).

6.18 SUMMARY

A board of education has only such authority to contract as the state legislature has conferred upon it. Everyone contracting with a school board should be aware of this general principle and should realize that one may be acting at one's peril whenever the board has no authority to enter into the particular contract. Where it has authority to contract and where it follows the statutory procedures for doing so, contracts entered into by the board will be enforceable provided the other elements of a valid contract are present.

No teacher should start teaching without a written contract signed by the required members of the board of education. Even if oral contracts are valid, the terms thereof are too difficult to establish in case of differences of opinion. Agreements to render additional services for extra compensation also should be reduced to writing in order to minimize difficulty.

Since all reasonable rules and regulations of a board of education form part of a teacher's contract, the teacher should become familiar with board policies affecting teachers. Any teacher handbook or school policy handbook should be studied by the teacher. Where available, minutes of school board meetings should be examined from time to time. All teachers should keep current on school board action since all reasonable regulations passed after a teacher's employment also become part of the contract.

State statutes and regulations relating to teachers are considered part of their contract too. Therefore, a teacher should be acquainted with all statutes, attorney general rulings, and court decisions relating to teachers. Teachers should know the legal provisions in their state relating to sick leave, retirement, social security, workmen's compensation, continuing contract, tenure, etc.

All agreements between the board of education and the teacher made in advance of signing a contract should be embodied in the contract. Otherwise, omitted understandings will be considered as "mere negotiations" and of no effect.

Voidable contracts may be validated by ratification. Void contracts may not. The latter are frequently contracts which are beyond the authority of boards of education to make. Since the authority of a board is dependent upon state law, it varies from state to state. So does the liability of a school district under a void or voidable contract. Many states hold to the view that any person contracting with a school district must be held to know of the limitations placed upon the powers of the board to contract. Hence, in these states persons act at their peril in entering into contracts which exceed the authority of the board to make. Other states examine the equities involved and permit recovery for the reasonable value of services rendered, or for supplies or property furnished in good faith and accepted without objection by the school district. As a general rule any money or property furnished a school district under an invalid contract may be recovered if it can be identified and can be recovered without damage to other property of the school district.

CHAPTER 7

School Funds and Their Administration

7.0 INTRODUCTION

Current expenditures for public elementary and secondary schools are now approximately 50 billion dollars. Most of this money is expended by local school districts. They purchase the personal services of teachers and administrators and the supplies and materials employed directly in the instructional programs of the schools; they also finance such related services as pupil transportation and school-lunch programs. In view of the magnitude of the expenditures made in support of the public schools, and the importance of these expenditures in maintaining effective instructional programs, the legal questions involved in securing and administering school funds are a matter of vital concern.

7.1 SCHOOL TAXES

Taxes levied by local school districts constitute a major source of revenue for the public schools. Considering this heavy reliance on revenue from local taxes, the authority of local school districts to levy taxes is of the utmost importance to school board members and school administrators.

It should be emphasized at the outset that neither a school district nor a board of education has any inherent power to levy taxes.[1] Since education is a state function, responsibility for providing financial support for the operation of public schools rests with the state and may be met through either constitutional or legislative provisions.[2] Within such limits as the constitution may impose, a state legislature has broad power to provide for the financial support of the public schools and may exercise much discretion in determining how the public schools are to be financed, as witnessed by the following statement by the Supreme Court of Indiana:

The legislature may, in their discretion, support all the schools of the state by means of a general levy directly made by a legislative act, or they may thus provide for part of the expense of maintaining the schools, or they may delegate to local officers the power to levy

such taxes as in their judgment may be needed to supply the wants of the local schools and make them useful and effective.[3]

7.1a Constitutional considerations

Statutes providing for taxation to support the public schools have been attacked on various constitutional grounds. It occasionally has been claimed that a tax for support of the schools is unconstitutional because those who will be required to pay the tax will derive no direct benefit from it. When confronted with this contention, the courts consistently have held that school taxes need not bear a direct relationship to the benefits received by those who pay them. Their reasoning is typified by the following statement by a federal court:

When . . . the tax is levied upon all property for public use, such as schools, . . . the tax need not, and in fact seldom does, bear a just relationship to the benefits received. . . . The benefits are intangible and incapable of pecuniary ascertainment, but it is constitutionally sufficient if the taxes are uniform and are for public purposes in which the whole city has an interest.[4]

In the same vein, it has been held[5] that the residents of a school district may be required to pay taxes to support an educational institution which is open to all residents of the state.

Neither the legislature nor a local school district may levy school taxes for the benefit of private schools, and any statute which authorizes such a tax is unconstitutional.[6] Constitutional provisions which prohibit the use of public funds for sectarian purposes apply to school funds, and the courts have held[7] unconstitutional a number of efforts which would, in effect, have provided financial support for sectarian instruction.

The U.S. Supreme Court has identified

[1]Weyerhauser Timber Co. v. Roessler, 99 P.2d 1070, 126 A.L.R. 882 (Wash. 1940); Marion & McPherson Railway Co. v. Alexander, 64 Pac. 978 (Kan. 1901); Opinion of the Justices, 280 So.2d 97 (Ala. 1973).

[2]Salem Independent School District v. Circuit Court, 244 N.W. 373 (S.D. 1932); Bull v. Read, 13 Gratt. 78 (Va. 1855); State v. Board of Commissioners of Elk County, 58 Pac. 959 (Kan. 1899); Associated Schools v. School District No. 83, 142 N.W. 325 (Minn. 1913); See also 113 A.L.R. 1416, 1419, 1422. LeRoy v. Special Independent School District No. 1, 172 N.W.2d 764 (Minn. 1969); Lund v. Schrader, 492 P.2d 202, (Wyo. 1971); Bradley v. School Board of City of Richmond, 462 F.2d 1058 (4th Cir. 1972).

[3]Robinson v. Schenck, 1 N.E. 698 (Ind. 1885).

[4]Morton Salt Co. v. City of South Hutchinson, 177 F.2d 889 (10th Cir. 1949).

[5]Ransom v. Rutherford County, 130 S.W. 1057 (Tenn. 1910).

[6]Curtis's Administrator v. Whipple, 24 Wis. 130 (1869); Lemon v. Kurtzman, 403 U.S. 602, 91 S.Ct. 2105, 29 L.Ed.2d 745 (Pa. 1971).

[7]Synod of Dakota v. State, 50 N.W. 632 (S.D. 1891); Zellers v. Huff, 236 P.2d 949 (N.M. 1951); People v. Board of Education, 13 Barb. 400 (N.Y. 1851); Otken v. Lamkin, 56 Miss. 758 (1879); State v. Switzler, 45 S.W. 245 (Mo. 1898); Lemon v. Kurtzman, 403 U.S. 602, 91 S.Ct. 2105, 29 L.Ed.2d 745 (Pa. 1971); Johnson v. Sanders, 319 F.Supp. 421 (Conn. 1970); But see Wolman v. Walter, 45 U.S. L.W. 4861 (1977). Committee for Public Education and Religious Liberty v. Levitt, 342 F.Supp. 439 (N.Y. 1972); Sloan v. Lemon, 413 U.S. 825, 93 S.Ct. 2982, 37 L.Ed.2d 939 (Pa. 1973); Meek v. Pittinger, 421 U.S. 349, 95 S.Ct. 1753, 44 L.Ed.2d 217 (Pa. 1975).

three evils against which the establishment clause of the First Amendment was intended to afford protection—sponsorship, financial support, and active involvement of the sovereign in religious activity. The Court also enunciated the following three-part test which is to be applied in determining whether state financing programs that directly or indirectly aid sectarian educational institutions violate the establishment clause of the First Amendment:

First, the statute must have a secular legislative purpose; second, its principal or primary effect must be one that neither advocates nor inhibits religion; finally, the statute must not foster an excessive governmental entanglement with religion. [8]

The courts have universally recognized that the education of children is a public duty which may properly be supported by taxation. Of course, school taxes are subject to the same constitutional restrictions as are taxes for any other purpose. Among these restrictions is the requirement that taxes be uniform. Although uniformity in school taxes is to be sought, exact uniformity is not essential. Thus, the uniformity requirement generally is satisfied by that degree of equality of burden which may reasonably be attained. [9]

7.1b Delegation of authority to tax

It generally has been held[10] that, in the absence of constitutional provisions to the contrary, a legislature may designate a school district as a taxing district and may delegate to a school district the power to levy and collect a tax for school purposes. Furthermore, it may compel school districts to levy a school tax without the consent, or even against the wishes, of those who are to be taxed.[11] Authority to levy a tax for school

purposes may also be delegated to local school authorities such as boards of education.[12]

Statutes which authorize or require local school districts or other governmental bodies to levy taxes for school purposes often have been the subject of litigation. As noted above, the weight of authority supports the power of the legislature to delegate to local units of government the power to levy and collect school taxes. In some jurisdictions, however, it has been held[13] that constitutional restrictions make it impossible for the legislature to delegate to certain political subdivisions its authority to levy a school tax. On the other hand, some courts have held[14] that in requiring a political subdivision to levy a tax for school purposes the legislature has not, in fact, delegated the right to levy the tax; it has merely placed responsibility for levy and collection of the tax.

A substantial amount of litigation has involved the question of whether a school district is to be regarded as a municipal corporation for purposes of taxation. Although the courts are by no means in agreement on this question, school districts frequently have been held[15] to be municipal corporations within the meaning of a constitutional provision that the taxing power may be delegated to municipal corporations for municipal purposes. Some state constitutions prohibit the legislature from imposing upon municipal corporations a tax for a municipal or corporate purpose. It has been held[16] that such a provision does not prevent the legislature from imposing school taxes upon a municipality, since such taxes are for state purposes, not for municipal or corporate purposes. Also, it has been held[17] that a school district is not a municipal corporation within the meaning of such a constitutional prohibition. Even where school taxes are viewed as being for municipal or

---

[8]Lemon v. Kurtzman, 403 U.S. 602, 91 S.Ct. 2105, 29 L.Ed.2d 745 (Pa. 1971).

[9]Independent School District No. 35 v. Borgen, 246 N.W. 119 (Minn. 1932); Brennan v. Black, 104 A.2d 277 (Del. 1954); In re 1969-70 County Tax Levy, 186 N.W.2d 729 (Neb. 1971).

[10]Fruit v. Metropolitan School District of Winchester, 172 N.E.2d 864 (Ind. 1961); Brennan v. Black, 104 A.2d 277 (Del. 1954); State v. Board of Commissioners of Elk County, 58 Pac. 959 (Kan. 1899); Smith v. Board of Trustees, 53 S.E. 524 (N.C. 1906); Atchison, Topeka & Santa Fe Railway Co. v. State, 113 Pac. 921 (Okla. 1911); Hartman v. Columbia Malleable Castings Corp., 63 A.2d 406 (Pa. 1949); Independent School District No. 12 v. Manning, 185 Pac. 723 (Ida. 1919); Village of West Milwaukee v. Area Board of Vocational, Technical and Adult Education, 187 N.W.2d 387 (Wis. 1971).

[11]State v. Board of Commissioners of Elk County, 58 Pac. 959 (Kan. 1899).

[12]School District No. 88 v. Kooper, 43 N.E.2d 542 (Ill. 1942); School Board of Carroll County v. Schockley, 168 S.E. 419 (Va. 1933).

[13]Williamson v. McClain, 249 S.W. 811 (Tenn. 1923); Hamrick v. Special Tax School District No. 1, 178 So. 406 (Fla. 1938); Willis v. Owen, 43 Tex. 41 (1875).

[14]Saul v. Williams County Board of Education, 29 N.E.2d 907 (Ohio 1940); State v. City of Racine, 236 N.W. 553 (Wis. 1931).

[15]Smith v. Board of Trustees, 53 S.E. 524 (N.C. 1906); Atchison, Topeka & Santa Fe Railway Co. v. State, 113 Pac. 921 (Okla. 1911); Wilkinson v. Lord, 122 N.W. 699 (Neb. 1909).

[16]Atchison, Topeka & Santa Fe Railway Co. v. State, 113 Pac. 921 (Okla. 1911); Lamar v. Board of Education of Hancock County School District, 467 S.W.2d 143 (Ky. 1971).

[17]See 46 A.L.R. 652.

corporate purposes and thus within the purview of such a prohibition, it has been held[18] that the legislature is prohibited only from assessing and collecting the tax, not from imposing a burden which must be met by local tax levies.

The fact that the legislature has delegated to a school district or municipal corporation the power to levy a tax for school purposes does not exhaust its authority in this regard. The legislature may exercise the power itself if a local body fails or refuses to levy or collect school taxes.[19] It may also change or repeal statutes relating to school taxes,[20] withdraw the power to levy school taxes,[21] or impose an increase in school taxes.[22]

One important restriction on the authority of the legislature to delegate to local school officials its authority to levy taxes for public school purposes is that such authority may not be delegated to an appointed body. It was held[23] that a school board which was appointed, rather than elected by the people, was a "special commission" within the context of a constitutional provision prohibiting the delegation of taxing authority to special commissions.

Any power to levy taxes which a school district may possess must be conferred upon it by the state.[24] The state may confer taxing power upon local school districts by either constitutional provision or legislative enactment. It should be noted, however, that any delegation of taxing power is subject to the rule of strict construction.[25] That is, the power must be either expressly granted or necessarily implied by powers which have been expressly granted. Any doubt as to the existence of the authority to levy taxes will be resolved against the existence of such authority and it will be de-nied.[26] This rule has been stated concisely by the Supreme Court of Kansas as follows:

The authority to levy taxes is an extraordinary one. It is never left to implication, unless it is a necessary implication. Its warrant must be clearly found in the act of the legislature. Any other rule might lead to great wrong and oppression, and when there is a reasonable doubt as to its existence the right must be denied. Therefore to say that the right is in doubt is to deny its existence.[27]

7.1c Nature of

A school tax ordinarily is regarded as a state tax regardless of whether it is levied by a school district or a municipality.[28] The reasoning of the courts on this question is illustrated by the following statement by a federal court:

Providing funds by taxation for common schools, and providing for their organization and government, are inherently legislative in character, and by the provisions . . . of the Constitution of Kentucky are expressly committed to the legislative department. All taxes imposed for common school purposes in this state are state taxes, although the fund raised by any particular common school tax may be designed to be devoted exclusively to schools located in the territory affected by the tax. So the levying of taxes for common school purposes, . . . are state legislative acts, performed either by the General Assembly directly, or by some subordinate legislative body expressly authorized by the Legislature to perform this legislative duty in the local territory within its jurisdiction.[29]

Because school taxes are legally regarded as state taxes, the legislature may require a municipality to levy a tax for school purposes with or without the consent of the municipality. Thus, it has been held that a county can be compelled to levy a tax for the purpose of building and maintaining a high school.[30] and that a city can be com-

[18]MacMillan Co. v. Clarke, 194 Pac. 1030, 17 A.L.R. 288 (Cal. 1920).

[19]Wilkinson v. Lord, 122 N.W. 699 (Neb. 1909).

[20]Berrier v. Board of Commissioners of Davidson County, 120 S.E. 328 (N.C. 1923); People v. New York Central Railroad Co., 141 N.E.2d 38 (Ill. 1957); Board of Education v. Hanchett, 167 Pac. 686 (Utah 1917).

[21]People v. Cleveland, C., C. & St. L. Railway Co., 122 N.E. 792 (Ill. 1919).

[22]Malone v. Hayden, 197 Atl. 344 (Pa. 1938).

[23]Wilson v. School District of Philadelphia, 195 Atl. 90, 113 A.L.R. 1401 (Pa. 1937); See also Lund v. Schrader, 492 P.2d 202 (Wyo. 1971).

[24]Mann v. Board of Education, 92 N.E.2d 743 (Ill. 1950); School District v. Cambria County Legion Recreation Association, 192 A.2d 149 (Pa. 1963); Saul v. Williams County Board of Education, 29 N.E.2d 907 (Ohio 1940); In re Bunker Hill Urban Renewal Project 1 B, 389 P.2d 538 (Cal. 1964).

[25]Mann v. Board of Education, 92 N.E.2d 743 (Ill. 1950); State v. Board of Education, 69 S.E. 378 (W.Va. 1910); Randall v. School District No. 44, 205 Pac. 748 (Wash. 1922); Gilberton Borough School District v. Morris, 137 Atl. 864 (Pa. 1927).

[26]Glendale Heights Ownership Association v. School District, 143 A.2d 386 (Pa. 1958); Marion & McPherson Railway Co. v. Alexander, 64 Pac. 978 (Kan. 1901).

[27]Marion & McPherson Railway Co. v. Alexander, 64 Pac. 978 (Kan. 1901).

[28]Paducah-Illinois Railroad Co. v. Graham, 46 F.2d 806 (6th Cir. 1931); Board of Education v. City of Louisville, 157 S.W.2d 337 (Ky. 1941); Pullman Car & Mfg. Corp. v. Hamilton, 181 So. 244 (Ala. 1938); Richardson v. Liberty Independent School District, 22 S.W.2d 475 (Tex. 1929); City Board of Education of Athens v. Williams, 163 So. 802 (Ala. 1935); Robinson v. Cahill, 287 A.2d 187 (N.J. 1972); State ex rel. Woodahl v. Straub, 520 P.2d 776 (Mont. 1974).

[29]Paducah-Illinois Railroad Co. v. Graham, 46 F.2d 806 (6th Cir. 1931).

[30]State v. Board of Commissioners of Elk County, 58 Pac. 959 (Kan. 1899).

pelled to issue bonds to raise funds for the purpose of constructing a schoolhouse.[31]

7.1d Purposes for which levied

In view of the fact that the authority to levy school taxes must be expressly granted, or necessarily implied from powers expressly granted, it is not surprising that questions frequently have arisen concerning the authority of a school district to levy a tax for a specific purpose. Such questions are complicated by the fact that the power to levy a tax for school purposes may be conveyed by a state constitution, a municipal charter, or a state statute[32] and are further complicated by the fact that many states authorize school taxes to be levied for a variety of specific purposes, e.g., education, building, or debt retirement.

Where school taxes are authorized for a specific purpose, they may be used only for that purpose.[33] A tax levied for educational purposes may be used only for educational purposes, and a tax levied for building purposes may be used only for building purposes; they may not be used interchangeably. As noted by a Texas court:

It is too well settled to require citation, or any extended discussion, that a public fund collected and allocated for a particular public purpose cannot be lawfully diverted to the use of another particular public purpose. Under that wise rule . . . when the taxpayer pays a certain tax for the specific purpose of liquidating a particular public bonded indebtedness of his school district, the funds derived therefrom cannot lawfully be used for the purpose of paying teachers' salaries, chargeable under law to a different public fund. . . .[34]

Educational

When a grant of power to levy a tax for educational purposes is made, the question of whether a given activity may legitimately be considered an educational purpose invariably arises. The answer depends upon the interpretation given specific statutes and is likely to vary from state to state. It has been held, for example, that a tax may be levied to support kindergartens,[35] furnish transportation for children,[36] and provide pension or retirement payments to teachers.[37] On the other hand, it was held in some early cases that a tax may not be levied to provide free medical treatment for pupils,[38] employ a football coach,[39] or provide transportation for pupils.[40] Obviously, there is no single criterion which can be applied to answer the question of whether a given activity has an educational purpose. It is likely that the answer will vary over time and also will vary according to specific statutes and how the courts interpret them in the several states.

The historic Kalamazoo case[41] involved the authority of a school district to levy a tax for the support of a high school where such authority was not expressly granted by statute. The Supreme Court of Michigan in a well-reasoned decision held that the power of school district officials to determine the grades and branches of knowledge in which instruction was to be given was not limited if the voters consented to raise the necessary taxes. However, it also has been held[42] that a school district cannot levy a tax for the purpose of maintaining a high school unless the power to do so has been conferred upon it by statute.

There can be no doubt that a state legislature may delegate to local school districts or municipalities the power to levy a tax to support a high school or a junior college.[43] Furthermore, the legislature may, if it chooses, direct that high schools be supported by methods different from those used to support other schools.[44]

---

[31]Revell v. Mayor, etc., of City of Annapolis, 31 Atl. 695 (Md. 1895).

[32]Rathjen v. Reorganized School District R-II, 284 S.W.2d 516 (Mo. 1955); Brooks v. One Motor Bus, etc., 3 S.E.2d 42 (S.C. 1939); Thorp v Board of Education, 90 N.E.2d 71 (Ill. 1950); Inhabitants of School District No. 1 v. Bailey, 12 Me. 254 (1835).

[33]Yarger v. Raver, 143 N.E.2d 662 (Ind. 1957); San Benito Independent School District v. Farmers' State Bank, 78 S.W.2d 741 (Tex. 1935); People v. Bell, 141 N.E. 187 (Ill. 1923); Russell v. Frank, 154 S.W.2d 63 (Mo. 1941).

[34]San Benito Independent School District v. Farmers' State Bank, 78 S.W.2d 741 (Tex. 1935).

[35]Wall v. State, 167 P.2d 740 (Cal. 1946).

[36]People v. Graves, 153 N.E. 49 (N.Y. 1926).

[37]Board of Education v. City of Louisville, 157 S.W.2d 337 (Ky. 1941); People v. Hayes, 148 N.E.2d 428 (Ill. 1958); Bridges v. City of Charlotte, 20 S.E.2d 825 (N.C. 1942).

[38]McGilvra v. Seattle School District No. 1, 194 Pac. 817 (Wash. 1921).

[39]Rockwell v. School District No. 1, 220 Pac. 142 (Ore. 1923).

[40]Hendrix v. Morris, 191 S.W. 949 (Ark. 1917).

[41]Stuart v. School District No. 1 of Village of Kalamazoo, 30 Mich. 69 (1874).

[42]Morton Salt Co. v. School District No. 136, 31 F.2d (10th Cir. 1929).

[43]Powell v. Hargrove, 134 S.E. 380 (S.C. 1926); McHenry v. Ouachita Parish School Board, 125 So. 841 (La. 1929); Shepherd v. San Jacinto Junior College District, 363 S.W.2d 742 (Tex. 1962); Moses Lake School District No. 161 v. Big Bend Community College, 503 P.2d 86 (Wash. 1972).

[44]People v. Lodi High School District, 57 Pac. 660 (Cal. 1899).

Building

If they do not contravene constitutional or statutory provisions, it is well established that taxes may be levied for the purpose of erecting,[45] purchasing,[46] or equipping school buildings.[47] Furthermore, a grant of authority to levy a tax for school buildings has been held[48] to authorize a tax levy to finance the purchase of land for a school site. A grant of authority to levy a tax for "school purposes" does not necessarily convey authority to levy a tax for the purpose of erecting school buildings.[49] Such authority must be expressly granted. Similarly, where a tax is authorized specifically for "building purposes," the revenue therefrom cannot be used to rent a school building or classrooms, since such expenditures are for "educational purposes."[50]

Debt Retirement

A school district may seek to levy a tax for the purpose of repaying indebtedness which it has legitimately incurred. The general rule is that school officials have power to levy and collect taxes for the payment of school district bonds.[51] In many states the state constitution or statutes impose upon school officials a duty to levy the tax needed to retire bonded indebtedness, but even without such specific authority it has been held[52] that a grant of power to issue bonds necessarily implies a grant of power to levy a tax to redeem them. Where school taxes are classified according to purpose, it has been held[53] that a tax levied for building purposes may be used to redeem

bonds if the proceeds from sale of the bonds were used for building purposes, but a bonded indebtedness incurred for educational purposes must be paid from a tax levied for educational purposes.[54]

Boards of education occasionally are in doubt as to whether or not they have authority to accumulate a cash reserve or establish a reserve for contingencies. It has been held[55] that a board of education may levy taxes which provide sufficient revenue for it to operate on a cash basis, i.e., avoid short-term borrowing. The board has no authority, however, to accumulate a fund which will be used at some undetermined future date.[56]

Finally, it should be emphasized that a school tax levy for a purpose which is not authorized either expressly or by necessary implication is void.[57] Similarly, a tax may not be levied to repay a debt which has been illegally incurred,[58] or to redeem a bond which is void.[59]

7.1e Procedural requirements in levying

The citizens of a school district have no inherent right to vote on the question of whether a school tax shall be levied. Unless such an election is required by a state's constitution or statutes, it is not necessary to submit a proposed school tax levy to a vote of the people.[60] However, in a number of states the constitution or statutes do require that school tax levies be approved by the citizens of the school district in an election held for that purpose. In this situation the question must be submitted to the voters and a favorable response received before the tax can validly be levied.[61] Failure to hold

---

[45]Rathjen v. Reorganized School District R-II, 284 S.W.2d 516 (Mo. 1955); People v. First National Bank of Amboy, 187 N.E. 518 (Ill. 1933); Lone Star Gas Co. v. Bryan County Excise Board, 141 P.2d 83 (Okla. 1943).

[46]Madeley v. Trustees of Conroe Independent School District, 130 S.W.2d 929 (Tex. 1939).

[47]*Ibid.*; People v. Illinois Central Railroad Co., 9 N.E.2d 310 (Ill. 1937).

[48]People v. Reilly Tar and Chemical Corp., 59 N.E.2d 843 (Ill. 1945); City of Rockdale v. Cureton, 229 S.W. 852 (Tex. 1921).

[49]State v. Wabash, St. L. & P. Railway Co., 2 S.W. 275 (Mo. 1886); Rathjen v. Reorganized School District R-II, 284 S.W.2d 516 (Mo. 1955).

[50]People v. Cummins, 169 N.E. 188 (Ill. 1929).

[51]State v. Underwood School District No. 16, 250 S.W.2d 843 (Mo. 1952); State v. Rasmusson, 300 N.W. 25 (N.D. 1941); Wilson v. School District of Philadelphia, 195 Atl. 90, 113 A.L.R. 1041 (Pa. 1937); Bell v. Board of Education of Barren County School District, 343 S.W.2d 804 (Ky. 1961); Mann v. Board of Education, 92 N.E.2d 743 (Ill. 1950); Storie v. Norman, 130 S.W.2d 101 (Tenn. 1939).

[52]State v. Board of Public Instruction of Brevard County, 64 So.2d 659 (Fla. 1953); State v. Rasmusson, 300 N.W. 25 (N.D. 1941); State v. Allison, 66 S.W.2d 547 (Mo. 1933).

[53]Moyer v. Board of Education, 62 N.E.2d 802 (Ill. 1945).

[54]People v. Illinois Central Railroad Co., 169 N.E. 178 (Ill. 1929).

[55]People v. Roth, 59 N.E.2d 643 (Ill. 1945).

[56]Board of Education v. Board of Education, 52 N.E.2d 274 (Ill. 1943); Cleveland, C., C. & St. L. Railway Co. v. People, 69 N.E. 832 (Ill. 1904).

[57]Whiteville City Administrative Unit v. Columbus County Board of County Commissioners, 112 S.E.2d 539 (N.C. 1960); People v. Buena Vista Building Corp., 71 N.E.2d 10 (Ill. 1947).

[58]Howard v. Trustees of School District No. 27, 102 S.W. 318 (Ky. 1907); Lowden v. Stephens County Excise Board, 126 P.2d 1023 (Okla. 1942); People v. Toledo, P. & W. Railway Co., 82 N.E. 420 (Ill. 1907).

[59]Hamrick v. Special Tax. School District No. 1, 178 So. 406 (Fla. 1938); Sinclair Prairie Pipe Line Co. v. Excise Board, 49 P.2d 114 (Okla. 1935).

[60]Larue v. Redmon, 182 S.W. 622 (Ky. 1916); School District No. 1 v. Gleason, 168 P.2d 347 (Ore. 1946); Bridges v. City of Charlotte, 20 S.E.2d 825 (N.C. 1942); People v. Bell, 141 N.E. 187 (Ill. 1923); Bancroft v. Randall, 87 Pac. 805 (Cal. 1906).

[61]State v. Robinson 1 So.2d 621 (Fla. 1941); Commissioners of Chatham County v. Savannah Electric & Power Co., 112 S.E.2d 655 (Ga. 1960); Wingate v. Whitney Independent School District, 129 S.W.2d 385 (Tex. 1939).

such an election is fatal to the validity of the proposed levy.[62]

7.1f Effect of alteration of district boundaries

The creation or alteration of school districts often presents special problems in states where school tax levies must be submitted to a vote of the people. In several cases involving territory which was annexed to an existing school district it was held[63] that taxpayers in the annexed territory cannot be required to pay the tax rate prevailing in the district to which the territory has been annexed until it has been approved by the voters in the annexed territory.

The provision for a separate election in the added or contiguous territory is not only a fair and just one, but is required to protect those living in the new territory from the levy of a tax imposed upon them virtually without their consent, or when, because of the differences in population and voting strength, they had no fair opportunity to be heard upon the question whether they should . . . be taxed for support and maintenance [of the enlarged district].[64]

A school tax voted by the electorate in a district which has been altered by consolidation or reorganization supersedes any tax voted before the change.[65] It should be cautioned, however, that a new school district must legally be in existence before a school tax election is held,[66] since any election for which there is no authority is void. The legislature may, of course, choose to make specific provision for the financial support of schools where school district boundaries have been altered.

7.1g Elections

Considerable care must be taken in the calling and conducting of school tax elections, since failure to comply with any mandatory requirements of the statutes governing such elections can render the election and any tax levy made pursuant to it null and void.[67] In general, the legal requirements which apply to other school elections are applicable to school tax elections. The rules which apply to school elections are discussed in Chapter 5.

7.1h Amount of

Limitations upon the amount or rate of tax which may be levied for school purposes may be found in a state constitution or statutes, or in municipal charters. In the absence of such restrictions the authorities responsible for determining the amount or rate of the tax to be levied for school purposes may set the tax at any level which, in their judgment, is needed to operate the schools,[68] and, unless they grossly abuse their discretion, the courts will uphold the tax levy they set.[69] In fact, in the absence of constitutional or statutory restrictions there is no limit to the amount of tax which may be levied for school purposes, although the courts will not allow school officials to abuse their discretion.[70] Both minimum and maximum limits for school tax levies may be established,[71] but the establishment of a maximum does not mean that the maximum amount must be levied. Limitations on school taxes are generally controlling, and any tax in excess of the limit specified is illegal and void.[72] The general rule is that the entire tax is not illegal but only the amount of the levy which exceeds the limitation.[73]

Limitations on school tax levies may be

---

[62]Auditor General v. Duluth, S.S. & A. Railway Co., 74 N.W. 505 (Mich. 1898); People v. Chicago & N.W. Railway Co., 108 N.E.2d 22 (Ill. 1952).

[63]Hicks v. Board of Education of Wayne County, 112 S.E. 1 (N.C. 1922); Register v. Colter, 155 S.E. 767 (Ga. 1930); School District No. 1 v. McCormick, 93 N.W. 956 (Neb. 1903).

[64]Hicks v. Board of Education of Wayne County, 112 S.E. 1 (N.C. 1922).

[65]Hope v. Shelby County Board of Education, 281 S.W. 815 (Ky. 1926).

[66]Howard v. County Board of Education, 127 S.E. 704 (N.C. 1925); Blackman v. Dowling, 89 So.829 (Ala. 1921).

[67]People v. Chicago, Milwaukee, St. P. & P. Railroad Co., 97 N.E.2d 463 (Ill. 1951); Knowles v. School District No. 10, 63 Me. 261 (1873); Cain v. Vernon Parish School Board, 77 So. 584 (La. 1918); Union Pacific Railroad Co. v. Troupe, 155 N.W. 230 (Neb. 1915).

[68]Parr v. United States, 363 U.S. 370, 80 S.Ct. 1171, 4 L.Ed.2d 1277 (Tex. 1960); Griffin v. Board of Supervisors of Prince Edward County, 124 S.E.2d 227 (Va. 1962); People v. Illinois Central Railroad Co., 9 N.E.2d 310 (Ill. 1937); Superior Oil Company v. Sinton Independent School District, 431 S.W.2d 383 (Tex. 1968); Kemp v. Jefferson Parish School Board, 305 So.2d 744 (La. 1974).

[69]State v. County of Moore, 341 S.W.2d 746 (Tenn. 1960); Community Unit School District No. 6 v. County Board of School Trustees, 132 N.E.2d 584 (Ill. 1956).

[70]Fisher v. Fay, 122 N.E. 811 (Ill. 1919); Mathews v. City of Chicago, 174 N.E. 35 (Ill. 1930).

[71]School District No. 4 v. Bayly, 235 P.2d 911 (Ore. 1951); Missouri Pacific Railway Co. v. Kuehle, 482 S.W.2d 505 (Mo. 1972); Baker v. Strode, 348 F.Supp. 1257 (Ky. 1972).

[72]People v. Thompson, 35 N.E.2d 335 (Ill. 1941); Marathon Oil Co. v. Welch, 379 P.2d 883 (Wyo. 1963).

[73]Kiowa County Excise Board v. St. Louis-San Francisco Railway Co., 301 P.2d 677 (Okla. 1956); People v. Chicago & N.W. Railway Co., 108 N.E.2d 22 (Ill. 1952); School Board of Carroll County v. Shockley, 168 S.E. 419 (Va. 1933); Moore-Norman Area Vocational-Technical School District No. 17 v. Board of Trustees of South Oklahoma City Junior College, 519 P.2d 497 (Okla. 1974).

expressed in a variety of ways. Although they are commonly stated so as to prohibit tax levies in excess of specified rates or amounts, they also may be put so as to guarantee a prescribed amount of money per pupil. In this regard, a statute requiring county commissioners to levy a tax sufficient to provide a certain amount of tax revenue per pupil has been held[74] to be mandatory. Limitations may also be in terms of the amount or rate of tax which may be levied for specific purposes, e.g., erection of school buildings or retirement of bonded indebtedness.

In addition to placing a limitation on taxes for school purposes, a legislature may provide for exceptions to the limitations. It usually has been held[75] that general limitations may be exceeded when the taxes are levied for a special purpose such as retiring bonded indebtedness, purchasing school sites, or constructing school buildings.

Double taxation, e.g., simultaneous taxing by two jurisdictions for the same purpose, is sometimes an issue, particularly when two or more school districts levy a tax on the same person or property. Illegal double taxation must be avoided, but the mere fact that two or more school districts levy school taxes on the same property does not constitute illegal double taxation unless both are taxing for the same purpose. Thus, since they are taxing for different purposes, an elementary school district and a high school district which occupy all or part of the same territory may each levy school taxes on the same property without being guilty of illegal double taxation.[76] It has been held that no illegal double taxation exists where only one school tax is paid annually,[77] or when an increase in taxes is imposed on all taxable property in a district for a new or different purpose.[78]

7.1i Time of levy

Questions occasionally arise concerning the actions which constitute the levying of a tax and the time at which school tax levies must be made. Any provisions in the law relative to the procedure to be followed in levying a school tax obviously should be observed. Substantial compliance with constitutional or statutory requirements is usually deemed sufficient, since the courts are not inclined to invalidate a school tax levy merely because of minor irregularities.[79] The courts will not overlook mandatory requirements, however, and will invalidate levies not made in the manner prescribed.[80]

Legal requirements governing the levy of school taxes are not always found in the school code. However, since school taxes are not legally different from taxes levied for other purposes, general rules governing tax levies are applicable unless specific statutory or constitutional provisions have been made for school taxes.[81]

There is considerable disagreement among the courts as to whether statutes specifying the time at which a school tax is to be levied are to be regarded as mandatory or directory. In some jurisdictions it has been held[82] that a school tax levied after the date set by statute is void. In such cases the courts have reasoned that, since all powers of a school district are derived from the statutes, compliance with the statutes is required. The better-reasoned cases, however, have ruled that, unless the statute specifying the time at which school taxes are to be levied also clearly specifies that taxes levied after the prescribed date are invalid, the statute should be regarded as directory and that taxes levied after the prescribed date are valid.[83] Invalidating taxes levied after the date fixed by statute could seriously impair the operation of public schools, or even force their closing. It should not be presumed that this is the intent of the legislature in the absence of a clear expression of such intent. In ruling on the validity of a school tax levied after the date set by statute, the Supreme Court of Kansas has supported this line of reasoning:

---

[74]State v. Clark County, 31 P.2d 897 (Wash. 1934).

[75]Maricopa County v. Southern Pacific Co., 162 P.2d 619 (Ariz. 1945); Board of Education v. Stillman, 184 Pac. 159 (Utah 1919).

[76]Glendale Union High School District v. Peoria School District No. 11, 78 P.2d 141 (Ariz. 1938); People v. Henkle, 100 N.E. 175 (Ill. 1912).

[77]Thoman v. City of Lansing, 24 N.W.2d 213 (Mich. 1946).

[78]Independent School District v. Iowa Employment Security Commission, 25 N.W.2d 491 (Iowa 1946).

[79]Kiowa County Excise Board v. St. Louis-San Francisco Railway Co., 301 P.2d 677 (Okla. 1956); State v. Keyes, 246 N.W. 547 (Minn. 1933); Beckman v. Gallemore, 93 S.E. 884 (Ga. 1917); Holland v. Davies, 36 Ark. 446 (1880); Crosson v. Downington Area School District, 270 A.2d 377 (Pa. 1970); Watkins v. Jackson, 179 S.E.2d 747 (Ga. 1971).

[80]Howard v. Jensen, 219 N.W. 811 (Neb. 1928); Myers v. Board of Education, 192 N.E. 393 (Ohio 1933).

[81]State v. Keyes, 246 N.W. 547 (Minn. 1933); State v. W. J. Dennis & Co., 74 N.E.2d 542 (Ill. 1947).

[82]People v. Pennsylvania Railroad Co., 162 N.E.2d 350 (Ill. 1959); Smith v. Canyon County Consolidated School District No. 34, 226 Pac. 1070 (Ida. 1924).

[83]In re Haines Independent School District's Delinquent Taxes, 12 Alaska 662 (1950); School Board v. Rupp, 106 P.2d 669 (Kan. 1940); Walker v. Edmonds, 47 Atl. 867 (Pa. 1901); Crosson v. Downington Area School District, 270 A.2d 377 (Pa. 1970); Watkins v. Jackson, 179 S.E.2d 747 (Ga. 1971).

Provisions of this nature specifying the time in which public officers shall perform their duties are generally regarded as directory "unless the nature of the act to be performed, or the phraseology of the statute, is such that the designation of time must be considered as a limitation of the power of the officer." Sutherland on Statutory Construction, 448. The provisions with respect to time are, under such circumstances, considered merely as a direction with a view simply to orderly and prompt conduct of official business. . . .

. . . in view of the general principles upon which the reason for the rule of interpretation referred to rests, and the interests of the public in a case like the present, we are fully warranted in holding that the provisions in respect to time in which officers shall act are directory only, and not mandatory. [84]

The action which must be taken to constitute the levying of a tax ordinarily is described in either general tax laws or statutes relating specifically to school taxes. Usually, when the officer or agency authorized by statute to do so determines the amount of money needed to operate the schools and certifies this amount to the authorities responsible for the assessment and collection of the tax, such action constitutes the levying of a tax.[85]

7.1j Levied on basis of budget

The requirement that school taxes be levied on the basis of a budget or estimate of the amount of tax revenue required to operate the schools during the forthcoming year is quite common. Frequently the budget or estimate must be submitted to a municipal agency or board which is authorized to assess and/or collect taxes as a condition precedent to the levy of a school tax.[86]

Strict adherence to all of the procedural requirements contained in the statutes is essential. It has been held, for example, that failure to submit the estimate to the proper agency or officer will negate the proceedings,[87] as will failure to specify the period of

time for which the levy is required.[88] Unless the law specifies that a budget or estimate be submitted in a particular form, any written communication between the designated authorities that contains the necessary facts on which the requested tax levy is based is acceptable.[89] Such necessary facts would generally include, at the very minimum, an estimate of the amount of revenue which will be required to operate the schools and an estimate of the amount of revenue which is anticipated from sources other than the tax levy.[90] Where a budget or estimate must be submitted by school officials to another officer or agency, a school tax levied in the absence of such a budget or estimate is void.[91] It should be noted, however, that an estimate may be modified, or withdrawn and replaced by a new estimate, up until the time it is acted upon by the agency or officer with whom it is filed.[92]

7.1k Apportionment between taxing jurisdictions

In many states school district boundaries are not coterminous with the boundaries of the municipalities which are responsible for the assessment and collection of school taxes. Where school districts have territory in two or more political subdivisions, statutes commonly provide for apportionment of the school tax among the various taxing jurisdictions. It has been ruled[93] that the duty to apportion school taxes is administrative in nature and that irregularities in the apportionment procedure will not invalidate the tax unless the proper amounts were not apportioned.[94] Even where a political subdivision not part of the school district was erroneously included in making the apportionment of school taxes, it has been found[95] that the apportionment was not invalidated by the error.

[84]Rural High School District No. 93 v. Raub, 176 Pac. 110 (Kan. 1918).
[85]People v. Wabash Railroad Co., 85 N.E.2d 14 (Ill. 1949); Board of Education v. Board of County Commissioners, 81 S.E.2d 256 (N.C. 1954); State v. Hunter, 96 N.W. 921 (Wis. 1903); Board of Education v. Brown, 42 Pac. 1109 (Utah 1895).
[86]Lowden v. Woods, 284 N.W. 155 (Iowa 1939); State v. City of Racine, 236 N.W. 553 (Wis. 1931); Clements v. Starbird, 12 So.2d 578 (Fla. 1943); Board of Education v. Coleman, 130 P.2d 277 (Utah 1942); Baldwin v. City of Martinsburg, 56 S.E.2d 886 (W.Va. 1949); Sanders v. Folsom, 451 P.2d 612 (Ariz. 1969).
[87]State v. Burke, 123 N.W. 110 (Wis. 1909); Vanzandt v. Town of Braxton, 14 So.2d 222 (Miss. 1943).

[88]Smith v. Board of Education, 113 S.E. 147 (Ga. 1922).
[89]Bancroft v. Randall, 87 Pac. 805 (Cal. 1906); Dent v. Bryce, 16 S.C. 1 (1881).
[90]Jackson v. Joint Consolidated School District No. 1, 255 Pac. 87 (Kan. 1927); Johnson v. Marrow, 44 S.E.2d 468 (N.C. 1947); People v. Crear, 133 N.E. 287 (Ill. 1921).
[91]State v. Young, 38 S.W.2d 1021 (Mo. 1931); Powell v. Board of Supervisors, 50 N.W. 1013 (Wis. 1879); St. Louis, R.I. & C. Railroad Co. v. People, 52 N.E. 364 (Ill. 1898).
[92]State v. Phipps, 49 S.W. 865 (Mo. 1899); Board of Education of Town of Stamford v. Board of Finance of Town of Stamford, 16 A.2d 601 (Conn. 1940); Gualano v. Board of School Estimates, 177 A.2d 580 (N.J. 1962).
[93]School District of City of Lansing v. City of Lansing, 249 N.W. 848 (Mich. 1933).
[94]Board of Education of Alpena Public Schools v. Township Board, 179 N.W.2d 691 (Mich. 1970).
[95]State v. Lamont, 57 N.W. 369 (Wis. 1893).

7.1l What may be taxed?

Since school districts possess no inherent taxing power, one must look to the constitution and statutes to determine what persons and property may be taxed for school purposes.[96] One point is clear: the fact that no direct benefit will be derived from school taxes does not exempt one from paying them.[97] This principle has been affirmed by the Supreme Court of Iowa in a case in which the constitutionality of a statute providing tax relief for agricultural land holdings of ten acres or more was contested. In rejecting the claim that certain taxpayers would receive no benefit from school taxes, the court stated:

It is no defense to the collection of a tax for school or other purposes that the person or property taxed is not actually benefitted by the expenditure of the proceeds of the tax nor as much benefitted as others. Accordingly a childless, nonresident or corporate owner of property may be taxes for school purposes.[98]

Taxes levied on property have always constituted the most important source of tax revenue for local school districts. The rapidly growing revenue needs of the schools have led several states to seek additional bases against which local school districts may levy taxes. By way of illustration, poll taxes have been utilized as a source of revenue for schools, as have taxes on bank stocks, merchants' licenses, and liquor licenses. Problems of administration and enforcement, however, make it difficult for most school districts to use extensively taxes other than those levied on property.

Pennsylvania's so-called "Tax Anything Act," which gives school districts in that state relatively broad power to tax for school purposes—subject to certain procedural requirements—has led to considerable litigation. In regard to the question of what constitutes a "business" which is subject to taxation by a school district under the law,

it was held[99] that a corporation actively engaged in any business beyond the mere holding of property is a "business" within the meaning of the statute. Concerning a tax on business transactions, it was decided[100] that not every ingredient of the transaction need take place within the school district but only the phase of the transaction upon which the tax is based. It also was decided[101] that, under the requirement that every person engaged "in any business in any school district" pay a tax on the annual receipts of the business, receipts from work done outside the direct but directed from a business office within the district may be taxed. A school district resolution imposing a tax on the wages of residents and on the net profits derived from businesses and professions has been upheld.[102] The validity of an "occupation tax" levied by a school district also has been upheld.[103] The court distinguished between an occupation tax, a property tax and an income tax by noting that an occupation tax is not a tax on property but upon a pursuit followed in order to acquire property, and that an occupation tax is a tax on income only in the same sense that every other tax is a tax upon income; that is, it reduces a person's disposable income by the amount of the tax.

7.1m Property, where taxed

The general rule is that the place at which property is taxable, and the governmental unit which is legally entitled to levy and collect a tax on property, is determined by the situs of the property involved.[104] Property usually acquires a situs for tax purposes at either the domicile of the owner or the place where it is located, although in some cases it may acquire a taxable situs at both. Insofar as the property located within its boundaries is concerned, a state may fix the situs of such property for tax purposes,[105] but it may not fix the taxable situs of prop-

---

[96]City of Fort Worth v. Southwestern Bell Telephone Co., 80 F.2d 972 (5th Cir. 1936); Glendale Heights Ownership Association v. School District, 143 A.2d 386 (Pa. 1958).

[97]Dickinson v. Porter, 35 N.W.2d 66 (Iowa 1948); County Board of Education of Meade County v. Bunger, 41 S.W.2d 931 (Ky. 1931); Board of Trustees v. Board of County Commissioners, 359 P.2d 635 (Ida. 1961); Duncan v. Town of Jaffrey, 100 A.2d 163 (N.H. 1953); Opinion of the Justices, 259 N.E.2d 564 (Mass. 1970); Brusca v. State of Missouri, 332 F.Supp. 275 (Mo. 1971).

[98]Dickinson v. Porter, 35 N.W.2d 66 (Iowa 1948).

[99]Bankers Security Corp. v. School District of Philadelphia, 149 A.2d 545 (Pa. 1959).

[100]Glendale Heights Ownership Association v. School District, 143 A.2d 386 (Pa. 1958).

[101]Albright and Friel v. School District of Philadelphia, 144 A.2d 745 (Pa. 1958).

[102]Farmington Township School District v. Yeskey, 185 A.2d 516 (Pa. 1962).

[103]Crosson v. Downington Area School District, 270 A.2d 377 (Pa. 1970).

[104]First National Bank v. Maine, 284 U.S. 312, 52 S.Ct. 174, 76 L.Ed. 313 (Me. 1932); Archer-Daniels-Midland Co. v. Board of Equalization, 46 N.W.2d 171 (Neb. 1951); Westinghouse Electric & Mfg. Co. v. Los Angeles County, 205 Pac. 1076 (Cal. 1922).

[105]Schaffer v. Carter, 252 U.S. 37, 40 S.Ct. 221, 64 L.Ed. 445 (Okla. 1920); Wheeling Steel Corp. v. Fox, 298 U.S. 193, 56 S.Ct. 773, 80 L.Ed. 1143 (W.Va. 1936).

erty which is located outside its bound-aries.[106]

Questions have frequently arisen con-cerning the definition and interpretation of domicile. One's domicile is the place where one resides or to which one intends to re-turn.[107] Absence, even for a prolonged period of time, does not necessarily change one's domicile; there must be a positive ac-tion to establish a residence elsewhere coupled with an intention not to return to one's former domicile in order to effect a change.[108] As for corporations, the domicile of a corporation is the place where it main-tains its main office or principal place of business, or where its governing body func-tions and its records are kept.[109]

7.1n Taxes on real estate

Real estate may be taxed only in the state in which it is located.[110] Where school dis-tricts are authorized to levy a tax on real estate, all real property within the bound-aries of the school district which has not specifically been exempted is subject to school taxes,[111] regardless of whether the person responsible for payment of the tax has children in school[112] and even if the owner is not a resident of the district.[113] On the other hand, a school district may not levy a tax on real property which is not lo-cated within its boundaries unless the state has specifically authorized such a levy.[114]

Although real estate is ordinarily taxed where it is located, a state may provide by statute that real property located within its boundaries shall be taxed at the domicile of the owner.[115]

As a general rule, it is unlawful for two school districts to levy taxes against the same property for the same purpose.[116] Thus, in the absence of specific statutory provision to the contrary, where a tract of real estate lies in two or more school dis-tricts, each may tax only that portion of the real estate within its borders.[117] To avoid confusion some states have enacted statutes which provide that in such cases the entire tract of real estate shall be taxed by one school district, and the legality of the stat-utes has been upheld.[118]

7.1o Taxes on tangible personal property

For many years the ancient maxim *mobilia personam sequuntur*, "movables follow the person," governed the taxation of personal property. It was invariably held that tangible personal property—property having value in its own right—was to be taxed at the domicile of the owner regard-less of its physical location. This rule is not well adapted to modern-day commerce, for tangible personal property may be moved rapidly and may be located permanently many miles from the state where its owner has a domicile. Consequently, the rule evolved that tangible personal property could acquire taxable situs at the place where it was permanently located.[119] With the evolution of this rule it became possible for such property to be taxed at both the domicile of the owner and the location of the property.[120] In 1905, however, the United States Supreme Court ruled that if tangible personal property has acquired taxable situs in another state if cannot be taxes in the state of the owner's domicile, less the "due process" clause of the Four-

[106]McCulloch v. Maryland, 4 Wheat. 415, 4 L.Ed. 579 (Md. 1819); Curry v. McCanless, 307 U.S. 357, 59 S.Ct. 900, 83 L.Ed. 1339 (Tenn. 1939).

[107]Mitchell v. United States, 21 Wall. 350, 22 L.Ed. 584 (1874); Holt v. Hendee, 93 N.E. 749 (Ill. 1911); Croop v. Walton, 157 N.E. 275 (Ind. 1927).

[108]Holt v. Hendee, 93 N.E. 749 (Ill. 1911).

[109]In re Hillmark Associates, 47 F.Supp. 605 (N.Y. 1942); Tennessee Coal, Iron & Railroad Co. v. State, 193 So. 143 (Ala. 1940).

[110]First National Bank v. Maine, 284 U.S. 312, 52 S.Ct. 174, 76 L.Ed. 313 (Me. 1932); Great Atlantic and Pacific Tea Co. v. Grosjean, 301 U.S. 412, 57 S.Ct. 772, 81 L.Ed. 1193 (La. 1937).

[111]Visalia Savings Bank v. City of Visalia, 94 Pac. 888 (Cal. 1908); Foscato v. Byrne, 87 N.W.2d 512 (Wis. 1958); People v. Chicago, B. & Q. Railroad Co., 111 N.E.2d 509 (Ill. 1953); Board of Education of Meade County v. Bunger, 41 S.W.2d 931 (Ky. 1931).

[112]Sioux City Bridge Co. v. Miller, 12 F.2d 41 (8th Cir. 1926); Dickinson v. Porter, 35 N.W.2d 66 (Iowa 1948); Berkeley Heights Township v. Board of Education, 128 A.2d 857 (N.J. 1957); Brusca v. State of Missouri, 332 F.Supp. 275 (Mo. 1971).

[113]State v. Van Winkle, 25 N.J. Law 73 (1855); Inde-pendent District of Ottumwa v. Taylor, 69 N.W. 1009 (Iowa 1897); Allen v. Gleason, 4 Day 376 (Conn. 1810).

[114]People v. Barry, 142 N.E.2d 33 (Ill. 1957); Linke v. Board of County Commissioners of Grand County, 268 P.2d 416 (Col. 1954); Board of Education v. City of Louisville, 268 S.W.2d 707 (Ky. 1953); McAtee v. Gutier-rez, 146 P.2d 315 (N.M. 1944); American Liberty Oil Co. v. State, 125 S.W.2d 1107 (Tex. 1939).

[115]Curry v. McCanless, 307 U.S. 357, 59 S.Ct. 900, 83 L.Ed. 1339 (Tenn. 1939); Walton County v. Morgan County, 48 S.E. 243 (Ga. 1904); Great Southern Life In-surance Co. v. City of Austin, 243 S.W. 778 (Tex. 1922).

[116]People v. Illinois Central Railroad Co., 118 N.E. 495 (Ill. 1917); State v. Lost Springs Rural High School Dis-trict, 271 P.2d 812 (Kan. 1954). *Contra,* People v. Pinari 163 N.E. 385 (Ill. 1928).

[117]Shaw v. Lockett, 60 Pac. 363 (Col. 1900); Lessee of Barger v. Jackson, 9 Ham. 163 (Ohio 1839).

[118]Jackson v. Brewer, 66 S.W. 396 (Ky. 1902); Blackstone Mfg. Co. v. Town of Blackstone, 85 N.E. 880 (Mass. 1908).

[119]Southern Pacific Co. v. Kentucky, 222 U.S. 63, 32 S.Ct. 13, 56 L.Ed. 96 (Ky. 1911).

[120]Battle v. Corporation of Mobile, 9 Ala. 234 (1846).

teenth Amendment be violated.[121] Thus, tangible personal property now may be taxed either at the domicile of the owner or at the place where it is located in another state, but not at both places.

It is sometimes difficult to determine whether tangible personal property has actually acquired a taxable situs in another state. The usual criterion is whether the property is there for an indefinite period of time and is used in the same manner as similar property at that location is used.[122] Clearly, property which is in transit, or which is located within the state temporarily pending transfer to another location, does not acquire taxable situs.[123] Tangible personal property which has not acquired taxable situs in another state may be taxed by the state in which the owner of the property has a domicile.[124]

Of particular interest to school officials is the law which governs the taxation of tangible personal property located within the boundaries of a state. A legislature, subject to such limitations as may be imposed by the state's constitution, may fix the taxable situs of all tangible personal property under its jurisdiction at either the domicile of the owner or the place where the property is located.[125] Thus, a school district's right to tax the tangible personal property of persons domiciled in the district, or property owned by nonresidents but permanently located in the district, must be found in state statutes. Where the statutes make no specific provision concerning the taxation of tangible personal property, it has been held[126] that such property is to be taxed at the domicile of the owner and not elsewhere. The question of whether tangible personal property has acquired taxable situs in the school district is answered by application of the criterion previously dis-

cussed. Accordingly, tangible personal property which remains in the district indefinitely has been held[127] subject to school taxes; when it is in transit or temporarily in the district, generally it may not be taxed.[128]

7.1p Taxes on intangible personal property

The rules governing taxation of intangible personal property—property which is not intrinsically valuable in its own right—are similar to those governing taxation of tangible personal property with one major exception: Intangibles may be taxed both by the state in which the owner has a domicile and by another state in which such property has attained a business situs.[129] Intangible personal property can attain a business situs at a location other than the domicile of the owner by virtue of being permanently located and used in the conduct of business there.[130] However, the maxim *mobilia personam sequuntur* generally applies in the taxation of intangible personal property, and the only taxable situs of such property is at the domicile of the owner unless a business situs also can be shown to exist.[131]

The legislature may fix the taxable situs of intangible person property within a state at either the domicile of the owner or the place where the property is located.[132] As in the case of tangible personal property, it is necessary to examine the statutes of a state to determine a school district's authority to levy taxes on intangible personal property.

7.1q Exemption of property from

Some categories of property typically are granted exemption from school taxes. For example, public property or property which is used for public purposes is ordinarily

---

[121]Union Refrigerator Transit Co. v. Kentucky, 199 U.S. 194, 26 S.Ct. 36, 50 L.Ed. 150 (Ky. 1905).

[122]Standard Paving Co. v. County Board of Equalization, 273 Pac. 201 (Okla. 1928); Nacogdiches Independent School District v. McKinney, 504 S.W.2d 832 (Tex. 1974).

[123]Coe v. Errol, 116 U.S. 517, 6 S.Ct. 475, 29 L.Ed. 715 (N.H. 1886); City Bank Farmers' Trust Co. v. Schnader, 8 F.Supp. 815 (Pa. 1934).

[124]Central Railroad Co. of Pennsylvania v. Pennsylvania, 370 U.S. 607, 82 S.Ct. 1297, 8 L.Ed.2d 720 (Pa. 1962); Johnson Oil Co. v. Oklahoma, 290 U.S. 158, 54 S.Ct. 152, 78 L.Ed. 238 (Okla. 1933).

[125]Town of Cady v. Alexander Construction Co., 107 N.W.2d 267 (Wis. 1961); Lewis & Holmes Motor Freight Corp. v. City of Atlanta, 25 S.E.2d 699 (Ga. 1943); Lee v. Atlantic Coast Line Railroad Co., 200 So. 71 (Fla. 1941).

[126]Lewis & Holmes Motor Freight Corp. v. City of Atlanta, 25 S.E.2d 699 (Ga. 1943); Crocker v. City of Malden, 118 N.E. 527 (Mass. 1918).

[127]Gulf Refining Co. v. Phillips, 11 F.2d 967 (5th Cir. 1926); Mills v. Thornton, 26 Ill. 300 (1861); Clark v. Cedar Hill Independent School District, 295 S.W.2d 671 (Tex. 1956); Brown v. City of Dallas, 508 S.W.2d 134 (Tex. 1974).

[128]Hawley v. Malden, 232 U.S. 1, 34 S.Ct. 201, 58 L.Ed. 477 (Mass. 1914); Commonwealth v. American Dredging Co., 15 Atl. 443 (Pa. 1888); State v. Shepperd, 117 S.W. 1169 (Mo. 1909).

[129]Curry v. McCanless, 307 U.S. 357, 59 S.Ct. 900, 83 L.Ed. 1339 (Tenn. 1939).

[130]Safe Deposit and Trust Co. v. Virginia, 280 U.S. 83, 50 S.Ct. 59, 74 L.Ed. 180 (Va. 1929); First Bank Stock Corp. v. Minnesota, 301 U.S. 234, 57 S.Ct. 677, 81 L.Ed. 1061 (Minn. 1937); Akron Trading Co. v. Bowers, 188 N.E.2d 583 (Ohio 1963).

[131]Greenough v. Tax Assessors, 331 U.S. 486, 67 S.Ct. 1400, 91 L.Ed. 1621 (R.I. 1947); Curry v. McCanless, 307 U.S. 357, 59 S.Ct. 900, 83 L.Ed. 1339 (Tenn. 1939).

[132]General Motors Acceptance Corp. v. Hulbert, 125 P.2d 975 (Okla. 1942).

exempt from local school taxes.[133] A legislature may, however, make state-owned property subject to local school taxes.[134] It has been held[135] that land owned by the federal government may not be taxed for school purposes unless its immunity from taxation has been waived, but persons residing on federal property are not exempt from occupation and per capita taxes levied by a school district.[136] Similarly, it has been decided[137] that state bonds are exempt from school taxes. However, personal property owned by one using and operating it in the conduct of a private business located on land owned by the government may be taxed by a school district,[138] as may land held by a private owner with an option to purchase is held by the federal government but not yet exercised.[139]

The taxation of property owned by a public utility or by a public corporation sometimes presents problems. Several states have made special provisions for taxing public utilities because of the difficulties in administration of taxes on such property. In the absence of special provisions, however, there is general agreement that property owned by a public utility may be taxed for school purposes.[140] Conversely, it has been decided[141] that property essential to the functions of a public or quasi-public corporation is exempt from school taxes unless specifically made subject to them by the statutes.

Most states also grant exemption from school taxes to religious and charitable institutions. The U.S. Supreme Court has

ruled[142] that exempting from taxation property owned by religious organizations, and used solely for religious purposes, does not violate the First Amendment. The Court determined that:

> The legislative purpose of a property tax exemption is neither the advancement nor the inhibition of religion; it is neither sponsorship nor hostility . . . . (New York) has not singled out one particular church or religious group or even churches as such; rather, it has granted exemption to all houses of religious worship with a broad class of property owned by nonprofit, quasi-public corporations.

After considering the question of entanglement, the Court concluded that granting tax exemptions to religious property would result in less entanglement than would taxing such property. Thus a place of religious worship may be exempted from payment of school taxes, and that exemption extends to the property necessary to occupancy and enjoyment of the place of worship.[143] Although the issue has seldom arisen, it appears that a cemetery association may also be granted exemption from school taxes.[144]

Most states have constitutional or statutory provisions exempting from taxation property used for educational purposes. To qualify for such exemptions an institution must meet all conditions specified in the constitution or statutes.[145] Questions occasionally arise as to what is meant by educational purposes. It has been held[146] that property of the University of Vermont used to house members of the faculty and staff was subject to local property taxes because it did not provide a direct and immediate benefit to the university's educational purposes; the benefit provided was indirect. In Wisconsin, it was held[147] that a statute permitting the taxation of state-owned agricultural land did not authorize the City of Madison to levy property taxes upon a biological research center operated by the University of Wisconsin and located on a

[133]Town of Williston v. Pine Ridge School, Inc., 321 A.2d 24 (Vt. 1974); Canutillo Independent School District v. City of El Paso, 514 S.W.2d 466 (Tex. 1974); Southeastern Pennsylvania Transportation Authority v. Board for the Assessment and Revision of Taxes, 319 A.2d 10 (Pa. 1974)

[134]State v. City of Madison, 198 N.W.2d 615 (Wis. 1972).

[135]School District of Warminster Township v. Reconstruction Finance Corp., 72 F.Supp. 149 (Pa. 1947); Port Neches Independent School District v. Reconstruction Finance Corp., 121 F.Supp. 561 (Tex. 1954).

[136]United States v. Lewisburg Area School District, 398 F.Supp. 948 (Pa. 1975).

[137]Preston v. Clements, 232 S.W.2d 85 (Ky. 1950).

[138]Phillips Chemical Co. v. Dumas Independent School District, 316 S.W.2d 382 (Tex. 1958); Prior Aviation Service, Inc. v. Board of Assessors, 362 N.Y.S.2d 623 (1974).

[139]United States v. Certain Parcels of Land in Philadelphia, 130 F.2d 782 (3d Cir. 1942).

[140]City of Fort Worth v. Southwestern Bell Telephone Co., 80 F.2d 972 (5th Cir. 1936); City of Anchorage v. Chugach Electric Association, 252 F.2d 412 (9th Cir. 1958).

[141]In re Baltimore & Philadelphia Steamboat Co., 153 Atl. 559 (Pa. 1931); Philadelphia Rural Transit Co. v. City of Philadelphia, 159 Atl. 861 (Pa. 1932).

[142]Walz. v. Tax Commission of the City of New York, 397 U.S. 664, 90 S.Ct. 1409, 25 L.Ed.2d 697 (N.Y.1970).

[143]Second Church of Christ Scientist v. City of Philadelphia, 157 A.2d 54, 75 A.L.R.2d 1103 (Pa. 1959); Mayor and Council of Wilmington v. Saint Stanislaus Kostka Church, 108 A.2d 581 (Del. 1954).

[144]Laureldale Cemetery Association v. Matthews, 47 A.2d 277 (Pa. 1946).

[145]In re Ogontz School, 65 A.2d 150 (Pa. 1949); Regents of University of New Mexico v. Board of Revenue, 304 P.2d 878 (N.M. 1956).

[146]University of Vermont v. Town of Essex, 285 A.2d 728 (Vt. 1971).

[147]State v. City of Madison, 198 N.W.2d 615 (Wis. 1972).

portion of one of the university's experimental farms.

In general, property owned by private schools and used for educational purposes will be exempt from property taxes where a state's constitution or statutes so provide.[148] Property owned by private schools which is not used for educational purposes will be subject to taxation even if the income from the property is used to support educational activities.[149]

Practices such as granting tax exemptions, partial exemptions, or a "freeze" on assessments as incentives to attract new industrial development, or to encourage the redevelopment of run-down property, occasionally are employed by taxing jurisdictions. Whether or not such exemptions apply to school taxes appears to depend upon the relationship between the school district and the municipality granting the exemption. It has been held[150] that school district taxes were not included in an exemption from county and township taxes. On the other hand, it has been ruled[151] that a tax exemption granted by a city to a housing developer applied to the property tax levied by the city school district where the city acted on behalf of the district in assessing property. It also has been ruled[152] that a tax exemption contract entered into by owners of commercial property and a town was binding upon the town's school district.

7.1r Taxes on income

A state has authority to tax the income from a property and/or a business located or conducted within its boundaries by a resident of another state. In holding that taxation of income derived within a state by a citizen of another state does not violate the Constitution, the United States Supreme Court said:

That the State, from whose laws property and business and industry derive the protection and security without which production and gainful occupation would be impossible, is

debarred from exacting a share of those gains in the form of income taxes for the support of the government, is a proposition so wholly inconsistent with fundamental principles as to be refuted by its mere statement. That it may tax the land but not the crop, the tree but not the fruit, the mine or well but not the product, the business but not the profit derived from it, is wholly inadmissible.[153]

A state may, if it chooses, authorize local school districts to levy a tax on the income earned by its residents or on income earned within its boundaries by nonresidents. It is worthy of note that the Pennsylvania Supreme Court has upheld[154] the validity of a tax imposed by a school district on wages earned by inhabitants while working outside the state.

7.1s Enforcement of school tax levies

Many school districts encounter the problem of delinquent taxes, and questions regarding the procedure for their collection occasionally arise. Statutes may provide, either expressly or by necessary implication, that a school tax, when properly levied, constitutes a lien on the property against which it is levied.[155] Penalties and interest on the delinquent tax have been held[156] to be included in a school tax lien. Once perfected, such a lien becomes a vested right and is payable from funds derived from the sale of the property.[157]

Statutes may provide for the collection of delinquent school taxes by sale of the real estate against which the tax constitutes a lien. When land is sold to satisfy school tax claims, the lien on the property is discharged once the required sum of money has been paid to the school district.[158] A taxpayer has no right to later redeem the property unless such a right is granted by the statutes; but when property offered at a tax sale is purchased by a political subdivision, the former owner usually may redeem the property by payment of the delinquent taxes as long as title to the property remains with the political subdivision.[159]

[148]State Board of Tax Commissioners v. Professional Photographers of America, 268 N.E.2d 617 (Ind. 1971); Rabun Gap-Nacoochee School v. Thomas, 184 S.E.2d 824 (Ga. 1971); Town of Williston v. Pine Ridge School, Inc., 321 A.2d 24 (Vt. 1974); Trustees of Columbia University v. Taylor, 351 N.Y.S.2d 928 (1974).

[149]Rabun Gap-Nacoochee School v. Thomas, 184 S.E.2d 824 (Ga. 1971).

[150]Bowaters Carolina Corp. v. Smith, 186 S.E.2d 761 (S.C. 1972).

[151]Housing Development Fund Corp. v. Buckley, 347 N.Y.S.2d 125 (1973).

[152]Lewis v. Town of Brandon, 313 A.2d 673 (Vt. 1973).

[153]Shaffer v. Carter, 252 U.S. 37, 40 S.Ct. 221, 64 L.Ed. 445 (Okla. 1920).

[154]Farmington Township School District v. Yeskey, 185 A.2d 516 (Pa. 1962).

[155]Bentley v. Kirbo, 169 F.Supp. 38 (Alaska 1958); Lubbock Independent School District v. Owens, 217 S.W.2d 186 (Tex. 1948); Toothaker v. Moore, 9 Iowa 468 (1859); Stein v. Lewisville Independent School District, 481 S.W.2d 436 (Tex. 1972)

[156]Getman v. Niferopulos, 11 N.E.2d 713 (N.Y. 1937).

[157]Keystone State Building & Loan Association v. Butterfield, 74 Pa.Super 582 (1920)

[158]Braun v. De Rosa, 194 Atl. 514 (Pa. 1937).

[159]School District of Blythe Township v. Mary-D Coal Mining Co., 47 A.2d 535 (Pa. 1946)

Another remedy for the enforcement of school tax levies is afforded by statutes which provide for the seizure and sale of the personal property of delinquent taxpayers. It has been held[160] that all conditions concerning such an action must be complied with fully. For example, there must be an actual demand to pay the tax and a refusal by the taxpayer before such a statute may be invoked.

7.1t Remedies against illegal school taxes

In view of the school district's very limited powers of taxation, and in view of the strict construction given statutes regarding taxation, it is not surprising that school taxes occasionally have been declared illegal. School taxes may be declared illegal because of failure to comply with mandatory requirements concerning procedure in levying taxes, because they were levied under the authority of a statute later declared unconstitutional, or because of some other legal defect. Two major questions regarding illegal school taxes are of concern: (1) What remedies may be used to prevent the collection of an illegal tax? and (2) May a taxpayer recover illegal taxes which have been paid?

7.1u Preventing wrongful collection

As a general rule, the collection of an illegal school tax may be enjoined.[161] The right to an injunction in such cases is not absolute, however, for ordinarily only a taxpayer may seek an injunction against the collection of school taxes.[162] Furthermore, an injunction may be refused because the person seeking it has been guilty of laches,[163] or has acquiesced in the levy of the tax.[164] Taxpayers who seek an injunc-

tion to stay the collection of school taxes have the burden of proving that the plan of taxation is arbitrary, discriminatory, erroneous, and/or illegal and that they actually have been injured by the taxing plan of which they complain.[165] The courts are not likely to grant an injunction because of mere procedural irregularities which do not affect the validity or justice of the tax levy in question.[166] Nevertheless, injunctions have been issued to restrain the collection of school taxes in a variety of situations. For example, an injunction has been issued to restrain the collection of a tax where the election held for voting the tax was void,[167] where no school tax levy was made,[168] where the school district was not lawfully established,[169] where the tax was levied for the purpose of paying an illegal bond issue,[170] where the tax was levied on the wrong property,[171] and where the tax was levied on territory not subject to taxation.[172]

Other remedies which may be invoked against the collection of a wrongful tax include an appeal, a tax protest, and an action to set aside or cancel the levy. In both the appeal and the tax protests actions the burden of proving that the tax is illegal or excessive rests with the person seeking relief from the tax.[173] The proper remedy for wrongful use of school taxes does not lie in preventing their collection.[174] Hence, a tax levy will not be canceled simply because school officials indicate they intend to use the taxes for a purpose other than that for which they were raised. No matter what legal remedy is sought to prevent the wrongful collection of taxes, only a person who has a direct and personal interest in the

[160]Gearhart v. Dickson, 1 Pa. 224 (1845); Atkison v. Amick, 25 Mo. 404 (1857).
[161]Shaffer v. Carter, 252 U.S. 37, 40 S.Ct. 221, 64 L.Ed. 445 (Okla. 1920); Wilson v. School District of Philadelphia, 195 Atl. 90, 113 A.L.R. 1401 (Pa. 1937); Pickett v. Russell, 28 So. 764 (Fla. 1900); Moss v. Board of Education, 50 N.E. 921 (Ohio 1898); Southern Railway Co. v. Hamblen County, 222 S.W.2d 9 (Tenn. 1949); Tefft v. Lewis, 60 Atl. 243 (R.I. 1905); Hanselman v. Humboldt County, 173 N.W.2d 75 (Iowa 1969).
[162]Board of Education v. Guy, 60 N.E. 573 (Ohio 1901); State v. McLaughlin, 15 Kan. 179 (1875); Kerr v. Woolley, 24 Pac. 831 (Utah 1866).
[163]Searfoss v. School District of Borough of White Haven, 156 A.2d 841 (Pa. 1959); Griffin v. Beasley, 151 S.E. 481 (Ga. 1930); Jones v. Oxford Area School District, 281 A.2d 188 (Pa. 1971).
[164]Wilson v. School District of Philadelphia, 195 Atl. 90, 113 A.L.R. 1401 (Pa. 1937); Wilson v. Dunn, 85 S.E. 198 (Ga. 1915); Hawthorne v. Hillin, 463 S.W.2d 266 (Tex. 1971).

[165]Superior Oil Co. v. Sinton Independent School District, 431 S.W.2d 383 (Tex. 1968); Duffey v. Union Hill Independent School District, 490 S.W.2d 201 (Tex. 1973); Bynum v. Alto Independent School District, 521 S.W.2d 656 (Tex. 1975).
[166]Yarger v. Raver, 143 N.E.2d 662 (Ind. 1957); Creech v. Board of Trustees, 102 S.W. 804 (Ky. 1907); Gray v. Board of School Inspectors, 83 N.E. 95 (Ill. 1907).
[167]DuPre v. Cotton, 67 S.E. 876 (Ga. 1910).
[168]Gerhardt v. Yorktown Independent School District, 252 S.W. 197 (Tex. 1923).
[169]Palmer v. Elizaville Graded Common School District, 29 S.W.2d 648 (Ky. 1930).
[170]Martin v. Bennett, 122 S.W. 779 (Mo. 1909).
[171]Robinson v. Board of Commissioners of Brunswick County, 109 S.E. 855 (N.C. 1921).
[172]Menagh v. Elvira School District No. 4, 210 N.W. 51 (S.D. 1926).
[173]People v. Chicago, B. & Q. Railroad Co., 111 N.E.2d 509 (Ill. 1953); Stanolind Pipe Line Co. v. Jefferson County Excise Board, 114 P.2d 925 (Okla. 1941); In re 1969-1970 County Tax Levy, 186 N.W.2d 729 (Neb. 1971).
[174]Lyons v. School District of Joplin, 278 S.W. 74 (Mo. 1925).

tax, e.g., a taxpayer, may question the legality of the tax.[175]

7.1v Recovery of taxes paid

The rules governing recovery of school taxes which already have been paid are stringent; recovery is difficult. A taxpayer who knowingly and willingly pays an illegal tax may not later recover the tax unless the statutes specifically provide for its recovery.[176] This rule has been followed even in cases where the tax was collected under an unconstitutional law.[177] Furthermore, usually a tax paid under protest may not later be recovered unless the statutes make specific provision for its recovery.[178] The courts reason that everyone is presumed to know the law, and one who knowingly pays an invalid tax will not later be heard to claim ignorance in order to recover taxes there was no obligation to pay. It should further be noted that a taxpayer who fails to take advantage of an adequate remedy to test the validity of a school tax levy prior to its collection cannot later recover any invalid taxes that may have been paid.[179]

If illegal school taxes are paid under duress or compulsion, on the other hand, they may later be recovered.[180] It should be emphasized, however, that merely protesting the tax at the time it is paid is not enough; there must be actual duress or compulsion involved. What constitutes duress and compulsion is a difficult question, although it has been said that duress or compulsion exists where taxes are collectible by the summary process of fine or imprisonment.[181] The general rules which govern the recovery of illegal tax levies have been stated as follows by the Supreme Court of Pennsylvania.

This court has uniformly adhered to the well-established rule, that "money voluntarily paid out on a claim of right, where there has been no mistake of fact, cannot be recovered back on the ground that the party supposed he was bound in law to pay it when in truth he was not." . . . Justice Mercur set forth the requisites to the maintenance of an action to recover back tax payments: The tax must have been void, the money received by the municipal corporation, and the payment by the plaintiff made under compulsion. Unless these elements are present, mere protest is of no avail in the absence of a statutory right permitting recovery on a different basis.[182]

Although it has been held[183] that a taxpayer may recover illegal school taxes which were paid under duress—as where the district levying the tax legally did not exist—mere irregularities in the tax do not justify recovery. There must be an act of omission or commission which violates a mandatory statute or deprives taxpayers of a fundamental legal right before recovery will be permitted.[184]

Statutes may provide for the recovery of taxes paid in error. Under such a statute it has been decided[185] that, where property not within a school district has been taxed by mistake, the taxes paid as a result thereof can be recovered. There is also authority for the view that taxes paid in error may not be recovered where the situation is such that the taxpayer should have discovered that the property was not in the district prior to the time the taxes were paid.[186] It has been held[187] that taxes paid in error may not be recovered once they have been disbursed for school purposes.

It also is common for statutes to provide for the recovery of taxes paid under protest. Obviously, if one wishes to base recovery on such a statute, the tax must actually be paid under protest. Taxpayers must exhaust all other statutory remedies before they will be allowed to bring suit for the recovery of taxes paid under protest[188] and must com-

---

[175]Chalupnik v. Savall, 263 N.W. 352 (Wis. 1935).

[176]Columbia Casualty Co. v. Westmoreland County, 52 F.Supp. 788 (Pa. 1943); Eichman v. Anderson, 162 N.E.2d 673 (Ill. 1959); Wilson v. School District of Philadelphia, 195 Atl. 90, 113 A.L.R. 1401 (Pa. 1937); Monteith v. Alpha High School District of Chase County, 251 N.W. 661 (Neb. 1933); First National Bank of Scottsboro v. Jackson County, 150 So. 690 (Ala. 1933); School District No. 8 v. School District No. 15, 164 N.W.2d 438 (Neb. 1969).

[177]City National Bank of Lincoln v. School District of City of Lincoln, 236 N.W. 616 (Neb. 1931); Wilson v. School District of Philadelphia, 195 Atl. 90, 113 A.L.R. 1401 (Pa. 1937).

[178]Harding v. Wiley, 219 Ill.App. 1 (1920); Wilson v. School District of Philadelphia, 195 Atl. 90, 113 A.L.R. 1401 (Pa. 1937).

[179]Pittsburgh Coal Co. v. School District of Forward Township, 78 A.2d 253 (Pa. 1951).

[180]Board of Education v. Louisville & Nashville Railroad Co., 134 S.W.2d 219 (Ky. 1939); Haines v. School District No. 6, 41 Me. 246 (1856); Brown v. LeSuer, 27 A.2d 754 (Pa. 1942).

[181]Board of Education v. Louisville & Nashville Railroad Co., 134 S.W.2d 219 (Ky. 1939).

[182]Wilson v. School District of Philadelphia, 195 Atl. 90, 113 A.L.R. 1401 (Pa. 1937).

[183]Isaacson v. Parker, 178 N.W. 139 (S.D. 1920).

[184]Public Service Co. of Oklahoma v. Parkinson, 143 P.2d 125 (Okla. 1943); Lowden v. King, 78 P.2d 29 (Kan. 1938).

[185]Churchill v. Board of Trustees, 89 S.W. 122 (Ky. 1905); Frost v. Fowlerton Consolidated School District No. 1, 111 S.W.2d 754 (Tex. 1937).

[186]San Diego Land & Town Co. v. La Presa School District, 54 Pac. 528 (Cal. 1898); Cornell v. Board of Education for High School District No. 99, 3 N.E.2d 717 (Ill. 1936).

[187]Wilson v. Board of Commissioners, 162 Pac. 1158 (Kan. 1917); Edwards v. Board of Commissioners, 36 P.2d (Okla. 1934).

[188]Republic Steel Corp. v. School District of West Deer Township, 99 F.Supp. 190 (Pa. 1951).

ply with all conditions precedent to recovery.[189] The burden of proving the illegality of a school tax rests with the party seeking to recover taxes which have been paid under protest,[190] since it will be presumed that all statutory requirements have been followed unless there is evidence to the contrary.[191] In a case[192] where taxpayers were able to show that the burden of taxation was not distributed with a reasonable degree of uniformity over all taxpayers in the school district they were able to obtain a refund of a portion of the taxes they had paid under protest.

7.1w Recovery of damages by taxpayer
Taxpayers who have been subjected to an illegal school tax may bring an action in trespass to recover from the collecting officer the value of the property which was taken from them to satisfy the tax. It was held[193] that a taxpayer could bring an action in trespass against the collecting officer where a tax was assessed on nontaxable property, and also where a tax was levied by an illegally formed school district.[194] A trespass action may also be employed to compensate a taxpayer for the expenses incurred in recovering such property.[195] In this instance the burden of proving that the tax complained of was legal rests with the officer responsible for assessment or collection of the tax.[196]

7.1x Right of school district to recover taxes
School district boundaries frequently are changed as a result of consolidation and reorganization, but public records may not immediately reflect the changes. As a result, it is entirely possible for school taxes to be paid to the wrong district. If such an error is discovered, the question arises as to whether the school district which is entitled to the taxes may recover them from the district which actually received them. The courts are not in agreement on this question. The better-reasoned decisions hold

that the district which is entitled to receive the taxes may recover them from the district which collected them on the basis that the money was received by mistake.[197] Other courts have not permitted the district in which the property was located to recover taxes mistakenly paid to another district on the principle that a tax paid voluntarily may not later be contested.[198] It is to be noted, however, that taxes erroneously paid to a school district by a county through a mistake by a county assessor in listing property may be recovered by the district which was entitled to receive them.[199]

Some confusion also exists as to the amount of tax which may be recovered. There is some authority for the view that, when a tax is assessed in the wrong district, the district entitled to the tax may recover the full amount of tax collected by the wrong district, even if this amount exceeds the amount which would have been collected had the tax been levied by the proper district.[200] According to another view, however, in no event will a district be permitted to recover an amount greater than it would have received had no error occurred.[201] The fact that property has been taxed illegally by another district, it should be noted, does not prevent the district in which the property is located from levying and collecting a tax on it.[202]

7.2 STATE SUPPORT FOR SCHOOLS
Although taxes levied by local school districts are still the largest single source of revenue for the public schools, aids paid to local school districts by the state have become an increasingly important source of school revenue in recent years. The legislature of each state has complete power to control school funds and to determine how

[189]City National Bank of Lincoln v. School District of City of Lincoln, 236 N.W. 616 (Neb. 1931).
[190]Albuquerque Broadcasting Co. v. Bureau of Revenue, 184 P.2d 416 (N.M. 1947); Parker v. Grenada County, 11 So.2d 446 (Miss. 1943).
[191]St. Louis-San Francisco Railway Co. v. Saterfield, 27 F.2d 586 (8th Cir. 1928); McComb v. Dutton, 122 Atl. 81 (Del. 1923).
[192]People ex rel. Skidmore v. Anderson, 307 N.E.2d 391 (Ill. 1974).
[193]Suydam v. Keys, 13 John. 444 (N.Y. 1816).
[194]Withington v. Eveleth, 7 Pick. 106 (Mass. 1828); Tucker v. Wentworth, 35 Me. 393 (1853).
[195]Baker v. Freeman, 9 Wend. 36 (N.Y. 1832).
[196]Bassett v. Porter, 10 Cush. 418 (Mass. 1852); Rogers v. Bowen, 42 N.H. 102 (1860).

[197]Independent School District v. School Township of Washington, 143 N.W. 837 (Iowa 1913); State v. Beale, 90 Mo.App. 341 (1901); Board of Education v. Board of Education, 293 S.W.2d 568 (Ky. 1956); School District No. 6 v. School District No. 5, 238 N.W. 214 (Mich. 1931); Alfred Vail Mutual Association v. Borough of New Shrewsbury, 274 A.2d 801 (N.J. 1971).
[198]School Directors District No. 153 v. School Directors District No. 154, 83 N.E. 849 (Ill. 1908); Walser v. Board of Education, 43 N.E. 346 (Ill. 1895); Carter Special School District v. Hollis Special School District, 293 S.W. 722 (Ark. 1927); School District of Gering v. Stannard, 228 N.W.2d 600 (Neb. 1975).
[199]School District No. 8 v. Board of Education, 224 Pac. 892 (Kan. 1924); State ex rel. Board of Education of Kanawha County v. Johnson, 190 S.E.2d 483 (W. Va. 1972).
[200]School District No. 6 v. School District No. 5, 238 N.W. 214 (Mich. 1931).
[201]Walser v. Board of Education, 43 N.E. 346 (Ill. 1895).
[202]Arthur v. School District of Polk Borough, 30 Atl. 299 (Pa. 1894).

the public schools are to be financed subject only to such restrictions as the federal and state constitutions may impose. Where a constitution indicates the method to be employed in apportioning state aid to local school districts, the legislature has no power to prescribe some other method.[203]

7.2a Permanent school funds

One must distinguish between two types of state aid: aid paid under specific constitutional provisions and aid paid pursuant to statutory provisions. Many state constitutions provide for the establishment of a permanent school fund for public school purposes. The general rule is that such funds must be kept inviolate and used only for public school purposes.[204] This rule, however, applies only to the principal of the permanent school fund; the income from the fund is usually apportioned to the schools either as the constitution stipulates or, if the constitution makes no provision, as the legislature may direct.[205]

7.2b Other state school funds

In addition to any revenue which school districts may receive from a permanent state school fund, all states provide additional funds to local school districts either by appropriation from the general revenues of the state or by the levy of taxes earmarked for school purposes. Frequently such funds are distributed in a manner designed to equalize educational opportunity and tax burden among the school districts of the state.

7.2c Constitutionality of

The constitutionality of some of the early state statutes which provided for the unequal apportionment of revenue raised for school purposes was attacked on the grounds that citizens are deprived of property without due process of law, that constitutional provisions concerning uniformity of taxation are violated, or that public funds are being diverted to a private purpose. Such contentions have uniformly

been rejected.[206] In Ohio, for example, the court upheld[207] the constitutionality of a tax the proceeds of which were to be apportioned among various classes of school districts according to a statutory formula designed to reflect their respective needs.

In more recent years a number of state school support programs have been attacked in the federal courts on the basis that they violate the due process and/or equal protection clauses of the Fourteenth Amendment, and in the state courts on the basis that they violate state constitutional provisions concerning education. Plaintiffs in these cases have alleged that the state aid systems fail to equalize educational opportunity among school districts in the state; that they enable wealthy districts, i.e., those with a large tax base, to spend substantially more per pupil than poor districts, i.e., those with a small tax base; and that pupils residing, through no fault of their own, in poor districts are deprived of educational opportunities equivalent to those available to pupils in rich districts.

One line of reasoning is that children vary considerably in their educational needs and therefore the state should take into account the educational needs of the pupils in each district in determining the allocation of state aid. It has been argued that state aid should be distributed in a manner which permits all children to have equal access to the educational programs they need, and that failure to do so is a violation of their rights under the Fourteenth Amendment. This argument has been rejected by the federal courts in cases arising in Illinois[208] and Virginia.[209] In each case the courts refused to place limitations on a state legislature's power to allocate funds for education as that legislature sees fit. With regard to educational need as a criterion for allocation of state aid, the court in *Burriss* noted that, while equalization of educational opportunity is a worthy goal:

> . . . the courts have neither the knowledge, nor the means, nor the power to tailor the public moneys to fit the varying needs of these students throughout the state. We can only see

[203]Board of Education of City of Detroit v. Fuller, 218 N.W. 764 (Mich. 1928).

[204]Teachers' Retirement System of Idaho v. Williams, 374 P.2d 406 (Ida. 1962); Board of Education of Memphis City Schools v. Shelby County, 339 S.W.2d 569 (Tenn. 1960); Taylor v. Board of Public Instruction of Lafayette County, 26 So.2d 180 (Fla. 1946); Moon v. Investment Board, 525 P.2d 335 (Idaho, 1974).

[205]Walls v. State Board of Education, 116 S.W.2d 354 (Ark. 1938); State v. Blind, 105 N.E. 225 (Ind. 1914); Watt v. Town of Chelmsford, 104 N.E.2d 419 (Mass. 1952).

[206]Knights v. Jackson, 260 U.S. 12, 43 S.Ct. 1, 67 L.Ed. 102 (Mass. 1922); Sawyer v. Gilmore, 83 Atl. 673 (Me. 1912); Miller v. Korns, 140 N.E. 773 (Ohio 1923); Mumme v. Marrs, 40 S.W.2d 31 (Tex. 1931); Kleen v. Porter, 23 N.W.2d 904 (Iowa 1946); State v. Mathews, 50 N.E. 572 (Ind. 1898); Dean v. Coddington, 131 N.W.2d 700 (S.D. 1964).

[207]Miller v. Korns, 140 N.E. 773 (Ohio 1923).

[208]McInnis v. Shapiro, 293 F.Supp. 327 (Ill. 1968), *affirmed* 394 U.S. 322, 89 S.Ct. 1197 (1969).

[209]Burris v. Wilkerson, 310 F.Supp. 572 (Va. 1969), *affirmed* 397 U.S. 44, 90 S.Ct. 812 (1970).

to it that the outlays on one group are not invidiously greater or less than that of another.[210]

A second line of cases has been based on the rationale that permitting the quality of a child's education to be contingent on the wealth of the school district in which the child happens to reside is a violation of the equal protection clause of the Fourteenth Amendment. It is claimed that because most state school finance systems rely heavily on local property taxes, they result in wide disparities in the amount of revenue per pupil available among the school districts of a state, thus discriminating among districts on the basis of wealth and permitting citizens living in wealthy districts to provide a higher quality of education for their children than those living in poor districts while paying lower taxes. It is argued that state aid should be distributed in a manner which assures that the level of spending for a child's education will not be a function of wealth other than the wealth of the state as a whole. This line of reasoning was accepted in both state and federal courts in cases in which the state school finance systems in California,[211] Minnesota,[212] Texas,[213] and New Jersey[214] were declared to be in violation of the equal protection clause of the Fourteenth Amendment. The United States Supreme Court, however, rejected (in a 5-4 decision) this line of reasoning in its decision reversing the lower court ruling in *Rodriguez* and held[215] that the Texas system of school finance did not violate the equal protection clause of the Fourteenth Amendment. The Texas system for financing public elementary and secondary education relied upon property taxes levied by local school districts to raise approximately half of the funds, thus creating substantial disparities in revenue available among local school districts which were not equalized by state aid. The Court found that the Texas system did not create a "wealth classification" of the kind that had been found "suspect" in other cases. Furthermore, the Court reasoned, the wealth discrimination complained of did not result in an absolute deprivation of education but only reduced the quality of the education to some undetermined degree. The Court also rejected the contention that education is a "fundamental interest" on the basis that no right to education is either "explicitly or implicitly guaranteed by the Constitution."

The argument that the level of spending for a child's education should not be a function of wealth other than the wealth of the state as a whole and other related arguments have been advanced in a number of cases in which the constitutionality of state school finance programs has been contested on state constitutional grounds. The landmark case is *Serrano v. Priest*[216] in which the California Supreme Court held that California's system of school finance violated the equal protection provisions of the California Constitution. Of equal importance is *Robinson v. Cahill*[217] in which the Supreme Court of New Jersey upheld the trial court's decision that the New Jersey system of school finance violated that state's constitutional mandate to provide a "thorough and efficient" education and established a deadline within which the legislature should establish a state school finance program which would meet the constitutional test. The Montana Supreme Court ruled[218] constitutional a statute requiring counties raising more revenue than needed to fund the state's "foundation program" with a 40 mill tax levy to pay the excess to the state for redistribution to counties which raised less than the amount required for the foundation program with a 40 mill tax levy.

Not all state court cases alleging "wealth discrimination" have been successful. The constitutionality of Washington's state school finance program has been upheld[219] against a charge that it violated the equal protection and education provisions of the state constitution. In a slightly different case a lower court held the state support program unconstitutional. In Idaho and Oregon courts have upheld[220] the constitutionality of the state school finance program of those states. It should be noted that the courts have been divided in most of the cases, with strong dissenting opinions presented in both the federal and state decisions. The issues in this area are far from settled; at the close of 1975 cases involving the constitutionality of procedures em-

---

[210]*Ibid.*

[211]Serrano v. Priest, 487 P.2d 1241 (Cal. 1971).

[212]Van Dusartz v. Hatfield, 334 F.Supp. 870 (Minn. 1971).

[213]Rodriguez v. San Antonio Independent School District, 337 F.Supp. 280 (Tex. 1971).

[214]Robinson v. Cahill, 287 A.2d 187 (N.J. 1972).

[215]San Antonio Independent School District v. Rodriguez, 411 U.S. 1, 93 S.Ct. 1278, 36 L.Ed.2d 16 (Tex. 1973).

[216]Serrano v. Priest, 487 P.2d 1241 (Cal. 1971).

[217]Robinson v. Cahill, 303 A.2d 273 (N.J. 1973).

[218]State *ex rel.* Woodahl v. Straub, 520 P.2d 776 (Mont. 1974).

[219]Northshore School District v. Kinnear, 530 P.2d 178 (Wash. 1974).

[220]Thompson v. Engelking, 537 P.2d 635 (Ida. 1975); Olsen v. State , 554 P.2d 139 (Ore. 1976).

ployed in state school finance programs were before the courts in eleven states. Wisconsin has now declared its state support program unconstitutional on a different basis [*Busé* v. *Smith*, 247 N.W.2d 141 (Wis. 1976)]. Decisions from the other states are expected soon.

7.2d Funds for
special education programs

Cases involving the allocation of state funds for special education programs are of relatively recent origin. In 1971 a federal district court in Pennsylvania enjoined[221] the state from denying mentally retarded children equal educational opportunity in violation of their rights under the Fourteenth Amendment. A federal district court in the District of Columbia ordered that each child termed mentally retarded or otherwise "exceptional" be provided with a publicly supported educational program suited to his or her needs.[222] In rejecting the argument that there were insufficient funds to pay for the education of the plaintiffs, the court stated:

> If insufficient funds are available to finance all of the services and programs that are needed and desirable in the system, then the available funds must be expended equitably in such a manner that no child is entirely excluded from a publicly supported education. . . .
> The inadequacies of the District of Columbia Public School System, whether occasioned by insufficient funding or administrative inefficiency, certainly cannot be permitted to bear more heavily on the "exceptional" or handicapped child than on the normal child.

Decisions such as these have considerable import for state school finance programs, since educational programs for exceptional children tend to be considerably more expensive than regular school programs.

Most states have enacted legislation concerning the education of handicapped children. A Wisconsin statute is typical. The stated purpose of the statute is to insure that all children who have exceptional educational needs are provided comparable educational benefits without charge. The statute provides that if no local public program exists a child must be placed in a public agency program as close as possible to the child's home; if no public agency program is available and no such program can be procured from a public agency in another state,

the local school board may contract for educational services with a private educational agency, the governing board, faculty, student body, and teachings of which must not be chosen or determined by any religious organization or for any sectarian purpose. The Wisconsin Supreme Court using the three-part test established by the U.S. Supreme Court, ruled[223] that the statute, on its face, did not violate the First Amendment because (1) it had a clear secular purpose, (2) the primary effect was not to advance religion, and (3) there was no need for the continuing state surveillance that would constitute excessive entanglement. The court commented as follows concerning the secular nature of special education:

> While the educators and staff involved in such a laudable endeavor as the providing of special educational services may generally be of a singular religious denomination, such is insufficient to characterize their conscious or subconscious attitudes as necessarily religiously directed.

Most state constitutional provisions concerning education use words such as "free" or "without charge" in describing the system of public education which the state is to provide. In New York it has been ruled[224] that the state will be required to pay the expenses for special training for handicapped children where there are no suitable public facilities. It has been held,[225] however, that a parent may, if financially able, be required to contribute to the *maintenance* expenses but not the *educational* expenses for an exceptional child attending a private institution at state expense. A Wisconsin case involved a class action brought to establish the entitlement of handicapped children to special education at public expense. The court stated that:

> While the state must provide each child with an equal educational opportunity, it is not necessarily required to do so in the context of "neighborhood" or a conveniently accessible setting, especially where . . . a virtually infinite range of special educational needs must be met with limited resources.[226]

---

[221]Pennsylvania Association for Retarded Children v. Pennsylvania, 334 F.Supp. 1257 (Pa. 1971).

[222]Mills v. Board of Education of the District of Columbia, 348 F.Supp 866 (D.C. 1972).

[223]State *ex rel.* Warrenv. Nusbaum, 219 N.W.2d 577 (Wis. 1974).

[224]Diana L. v. State, 335 N.Y.S.2d 3 (1972); *In re* Borland, 340 N.Y.S.2d 745 (1973); *In re* Downey, 340 N.Y.S.2d 687 (1973).

[225]*In re* Claire, 355 N.Y.S.2d 399 (1974); *In re* Logel, 356 N.Y.S.2d 775 (N.Y. 1974).

[226]Panitch v. State of Wisconsin, 390 F.Supp. 616 (Wis. 1974).

7.2e Apportionment of state funds

The criteria employed in apportioning state aid among the school districts of a state may be found in either its constitution or its statutes. Constitutional provisions concerning the apportionment of state aid are usually considered mandatory only in regard to the distribution of income from the common school fund; they do not apply to money appropriated for school aid from other sources.[227] However, the specific wording of the state constitution must be studied to determine how state aid is to be apportioned. Some state constitutions make no provision for apportionment, others provide for the apportionment of specific funds, and still others specify the basis for apportioning all state school funds.

Several criteria have been used in apportioning state aid to local school districts: school-age population in the district, average daily attendance or average daily membership of pupils in the district's public schools, assessed or equalized valuation of property in the district, an "economic index" reflecting the district's ability to raise money from local taxes, and the educational services provided by the district.

A state legislature enjoys wide discretion in determining how school funds shall be apportioned as long as the basis for the apportionment is just and not arbitrary.[228] In discussing the authority of the legislature regarding the apportionment of school funds, the Supreme Judicial Court of Maine said:

> The method of distributing the proceeds of . . . [a school tax] . . . rests in the wise discretion and sound judgment of the Legislature. If this discretion is unwisely exercised, the remedy is with the people, and not with the court. Such distribution might be according to population or according to the number of scholars of school age, or according to school attendance, or according to valuation, or partly on one basis and partly on another.[229]

A legislature, if it chooses to do so, may even provide that school funds raised by taxation in one school district may be appropriated to the use of other school districts in an effort to equalize educational opportunities throughout the state.[230]

Furthermore, a legislature's discretion is not exhausted by exercise; it may change the basis for apportionment of school funds from time to time, as noted by the Supreme Court of Colorado:

> The fact that the Legislature adopted a method of apportioning said income fund to the various counties and school districts based upon the registration of the school population thereof does not deprive the Legislature of thereafter . . . changing uniformly the method of such apportionment. . . . If the prescription adopted by the Legislature is not unreasonable, not discriminatory, and not in contravention of constitutional mandates, it cannot be assailed.[231]

Where state aids are distributed on the basis of population, the enumeration must be performed by the agency or individual designated by the statutes. It was ruled[232] that a board of education was without power to alter the census made by enumerators appointed as the statute directed, even though the census was obviously in error. Also, the accuracy of a census made pursuant to statutory authority is not subject to collateral attack.[233] Statutory provisions concerning the time the enumeration is to be made are considered directory unless from their wording it is clear that the provisions were intended to be mandatory.[234] Questions occasionally arise as to who shall be counted in the school census. In general, all residents who fall within the specified age span are to be included, whether or not they attend a school within the district.[235] Children in orphanages are to be included in such a census if they are entitled to attend public school within the district; otherwise they are to be excluded.[236]

Where state aid is apportioned according to school attendance or membership, statutory provisions govern the procedure to be folowed in computing the attendance or membership and determine the amount of

---

[227]Kleen v. Porter, 23 N.W.2d 904 (Iowa 1946); Mumme v. Marrs, 40 S.W.2d 31 (Tex. 1931); State v. Warren, 57 So.2d 337 (Fla. 1951).

[228]Dickinson v. Edmondson, 178 S.W. 930 (Ark. 1915); Craig v. People, 299 Pac. 1064 (Col. 1931).

[229]Sawyer v. Gilmore, 83 Atl. 673 (Me. 1912).

[230]Miller v. Korns, 140 N.E. 773 (Ohio 1923); State v. Hauge, 164 N.W. 289 (N.D. 1917); State ex rel. Woodahl v. Straub, 520 P.2d 776 (Mont. 1974).

[231]Craig v. People, 299 Pac. 1064 (Col. 1931). Accord, Cox v. Bates, 116 S.E.2d 828 (S.C. 1960) Board of School Trustees v. Bray, 109 P.2d 274 (Nev. 1941).

[232]Board of Education of Alpine School District v. Board of Education of Salt Lake City, 219 Pac. 542 (Utah 1923).

[233]State v. Evans, 145 S.W. 40 (Mo. 1912).

[234]Board of Education of Alpine School District v. Board of Education of Salt Lake City, 219 Pac. 542 (Utah 1923).

[235]Pickett v. Smith, 182 Pac. 680 (Okla. 1919).

[236]Board of Education of Louisville v. County Board of Education, 97 S.W.2d 11 (Ky. 1936); State v. Dovey, 12 Pac. 910 (Nev. 1887).

state aid to which a district is entitled.[237] Specific provisions usually are made for computing state aid for summer school sessions, but in a Tennessee case it was held[238] that a summer term was not to be considered a portion of the regular school year and that attendance in the summer term was to be excluded in computing average daily attendance in the absence of specific legislative direction to the contrary. If the statutes do not specify the minimum number of hours necessary to constitute a school day for purposes of computing attendance, a school board has authority to make such a determination.[239]

The state may recognize differences in costs of programs, or the need for additional financial resources for handicapped or disadvantaged children in its apportionment of funds to local school districts.[240] Neither state nor local officials will be permitted to circumvent the legislature's intent in appropriating funds for state aid.[241]

7.2f Withholding of state funds

That a state legislature has the power to specify reasonable conditions which must be met by school districts in order to receive certain types of state aid is beyond question. In a Texas case, for example, it was claimed that a statute which provided for apportionment of state aid on an equalization basis, and which required school districts to meet certain standards as a condition precedent to receiving aid, violated the constitutional guarantees of due process and equal protection of the law. The Texas Supreme Court rejected these contentions and stated:

Nor are the requirements exacted of those who apply for aid arbitrary or unreasonable. Those sections of the law regulating the type of schoolhouse required, the equipment necessary, the courses of study to be pursued, and which require obedience to the lawful rulings of the state superintendent and the board of education, are certainly reasonable requirements, and clearly within the legislative power.[242]

To insure compliance with the standards it has established, the legislature may authorize the state superintendent, or some other designated official to withhold state aid from a school district which has violated state laws or refused to comply with the legitimate orders of state school officers.[243] Where notice of the intention to withhold state aid is required, the district affected must be given the opportunity to be heard and the fact that a violation of the law has occurred must be established.[244] In addition to providing for the withholding of state aid unless certain requirements are met, the legislature may provide that state aid may not be refused a district which has met certain requirements.[245]

Questions sometimes arise regarding the authority of the state to recover funds which have been paid improperly to a school district and the procedure to be followed in adjusting inadvertent overpayment or underpayment of state aid. A school district does not obtain a proprietary right to school aid paid to it by the state; the money remains public money belonging to the state.[246] Consequently, it has been held[247] that the state may recover aid paid to a school district whose organization was held invalid after the aid had been paid, and that excess aid paid to a district because of a mistake in enumerating the school population may be recovered by the state.[248] Where school districts receive more or less than their proper share of state aid, the error is ordinarily adjusted, in the absence of statutory provisions for adjustment, at the time of the next apportionment by adding to or deducting from the shares due those school districts which received an underpayment or overpayment of the aid to which they were entitled.[249] Statutes also may provide for an adjustment of this type, and such a statute has been held[250] to be mandatory. The courts are not agreed as to whether one school district may recover

---

[237]State v. Dietrich, 21 N.E.2d 597 (Ohio 1939); Harkins v. School District No. 4, 288 P.2d 777 (Ariz. 1955); Young v. State , 103 N.E.2d 431 (Ind. 1952); State v. State Board of Education, 256 P.2d 446 (Okla. 1953).

[238]Board of Education of City of Nashville v. Dodson, 11 S.W.2d 265 (Tenn. 1928).

[239]City and County of San Francisco v. Hyatt, 125 Pac. 751 (Cal. 1912).

[240]Robinson v. Cahill, 303 A.2d 273 (N.J. 1973); Board of Education v. Assessor of Worcester, 333 N.E.2d 450 (Mass. 1975).

[241]Board of Education of Cleveland City School District v. Gilligan, 311 N.E.2d 529 (Ohio 1974); Board of Education v. Assessor of Worcester, 333 N.E.2d 450 (Mass. 1975).

[242]Mumme v. Marrs, 40 S.W.2d 31 (Tex. 1931).

[243]State v. State Board of Education, 112 S.W.2d 18 (Ark. 1937); Joint School District No. 1 v. Security State Bank, 90 N.W.2d 389 (Wis. 1958); Harwell v. Sheffield, 112 So.2d 377 (Fla. 1959).

[244]State v. Johnson, 65 N.W.2d 668 (Minn. 1954).

[245]Christman v. State, 187 N.E. 584 (Ohio 1932).

[246]Garner v. Scales, 194 S.W.2d 452 (Tenn. 1946); Butler v. Compton Junior College District, 176 P.2d 417 (Cal. 1947); Joint School District No. 1 v. Security State Bank, 90 N.W.2d 389 (Wis. 1958).

[247]Joint School District No. 1 v. Security State Bank, 90 N.W.2d 389 (Wis. 1958).

[248]State v. Mayor, etc. of City of Knoxville, 90 S.W. 289 (Tenn. 1905).

[249]Board of Education of Alpine School District v. Board of Education of Salt Lake City, 219 Pac. 542 (Utah 1923).

[250]State v. Lee, 262 S.W. 344 (Mo. 1924).

from another district state aid received by the latter which should have been paid to the former. Although it has been held[251] that the district entitled to the aid may recover it from the district which received it, there also is authority to the contrary.[252]

7.3 FEDERAL SUPPORT FOR SCHOOLS

Federal funds for support of elementary and secondary school programs have increased markedly since the passage of the Elementary and Secondary Education Act of 1965 (Public Law 89-10). Most federal funds are provided either through categorical aids designed to stimulate or support programs for specified target groups, e.g., vocational education, compensatory education, and education of the handicapped, or through payments in lieu of taxes designed to offset the impact of concentrated federal activities or the creation of federal installations which are exempt from property taxes, e.g., federal aid to local school districts under the provisions of Public Laws 815 and 874. As the amount of federal funds flowing to local school districts has increased, questions concerning eligibility for and the administration of federal funds, and the purposes for which such funds may be expended, also have increased. In one of the earliest cases concerning federal aid it was held[253] that a school district which accepts a grant of funds from the federal government is subject to the terms of the grant and to all federal regulations relative to the administration and expenditure thereof. Where inconsistent with state law, such regulations generally supercede state law.

A number of questions have arisen concerning that portion of Title I of the Elementary and Secondary Education Act which provides for federal funding of special programs for educationally disadvantaged children in both public and private schools. Regulations promulgated pursuant to the Act require that programs in private schools be "comparable" to those in public schools. The U. S. Supreme Court has ruled[254] that "comparability" does not require identical programs, and that the fact that public school children receive on-site instruction does not require the provision of on-site instruction for children who attend parochial schools. The Court noted that the Congress

evidenced strong intent that responsibility for these programs be lodged at the state and local level. The Court emphasized the importance of local control of schools and directed the district court to "make every effort" to defer to the judgment of state and local agencies. The Court also pointed out that it is the role of state and local agencies, not that of the district court, to formulate a plan for providing comparable services.

In a New Mexico case[255] it was alleged that a local school district had discriminated against Native American school children on the basis of race, that the district had misused Johnson-O'Malley funds, and that contrary to the law, Title I funds had been used for support of basic educational services. The court ruled that the district had indeed discriminated against the Native American students. It also found that the district had used both Johnson-O'Malley and Title I funds for health and administrative services in the Native American schools—services that were considered basic services in New Mexico—and enjoined such use of the funds.

The federal legislation providing "impact aid" to districts in which the school age population has been substantially enlarged by the children of federal employees is intended to supplement local funds, not to substitute for them.[256] In California a state statute which provided for the deduction from the state aid due local school districts of an amount equal to a portion of the funds they received under P.L. 874 was held[257] invalid under the supremacy clause of Article VI of the U. S. Constitution. Payments by the federal government in lieu of taxes on national forest lands, however, may be considered in determining how much state aid a district is to receive where the federal statutes neither prescribe how a state is to allocate such funds nor prohibit the state from considering such funds in allocating state aid to local districts.[258]

In a case involving the Emergency School Aid Act, it has been ruled[259] that a local school district has the burden of establishing its eligibility for funds provided under

[251]Independent School District No. 1 v. Common School District No. 1, 55 P.2d 144 (Ida. 1936).

[252]School City of Terre Haute v. Harrison School Township, 112 N.E. 514 (Ind. 1916).

[253]Montana State Federation of Labor v. School District No. 1, 7 F.Supp. 82 (Mont. 1934).

[254]Wheeler v. Barrera, 417 U.S. 402, 94 S.Ct. 2274, 41 L.Ed.2d 159 (Mo. 1974).

[255]Natonabah v. Board of Education, 355 F.Supp. 716 (N.M. 1973).

[256]Shepheard v. Godwin, 280 F.Supp. 869 (Va. 1968); Hergenreter v. Hayden, 295 F.Supp. 251 (Kan. 1968); Douglas Independent School District No. 3 v. Jorgenson, 293 F.Supp. 849 (S.D. 1968).

[257]Carlsbad Union School District v. Rafferty, 429 F.2d 337 (9th Cir. 1970).

[258]Carroll v. Bruno, 499 P.2d 876 (Wash. 1972).

[259]Board of Education v. Department of Health, Education, and Welfare, 396 F.Supp. 203 (Ohio 1975).

the terms of the Act. It has also been held[260] that rejection of a proposed "open enrollment plan" of desegregation by the Office of Civil Rights was sufficient reason for the Department of Health, Education and Welfare to deny assistance under terms of the Act.

7.4 USER FEES AS A SOURCE OF SCHOOL REVENUE

While user fees do not constitute a major source of school revenue, whether they may legitimately be charged—and if so, for what purposes—often perplexes school administrators and boards of education. For purposes of discussion, user fees may be grouped into two categories: those charged pupils and those charged other individuals and groups for the use of school facilities or property.

7.4a Fees charged pupils

Since state constitutions typically provide for the establishment of a system of free public schools, the principal point at issue in considering the legality of fees charged pupils is whether or not such fees are in violation of the constitution. It has generally been held[261] that the charging of a tuition fee violates the constitutional guarantee of free public schools but that the charging of an incidental fee does not.[262] The difficulty comes in distinguishing between a tuition fee and an incidental fee. It would appear that a tuition fee is one which will be used to support the school in general, pay teachers' salaries, or extend the school term. It has been held, for example, that if the state constitution provides for free public education, a statute authorizing a school district to charge tuition fees is unconstitutional,[263] that a matriculation fee may not be charged in order to keep the schools open an additional three months,[264] and that a pupil may not be excluded from school for refusal to pay a monthly fee, part of which was to be used to pay the teacher's salary.[265] If such illegal fees are charged, the

courts will issue a writ of mandamus to compel the admission of a pupil who has been refused admission or who has been expelled because of failure to pay the fee.

The authority of a board of education to charge a fee for the use of textbooks, for supplies consumed by a student, or for incidental items such as towels or insurance coverage hinges on the specific wording of the state constitution or statutes. When confronted with cases in which the constitutionality of a student fee is being contested, the courts will attempt to ascertain the intent of the framers of the state's constitution.[266] Thus, the extent to which incidental fees for textbooks, school supplies, and other items may legally be charged varies considerably from state to state depending upon how the state's constitution is interpreted. A Wisconsin case[267] in which the defendant challenged the authority of a school district to charge fees for book rental, incidental educational supplies, and insurance premiums is illustrative. The Wisconsin Supreme Court based its decision upon a historical analysis of the practices that were in existence in 1848 (the year the state's constitution was adopted) and the practices that may reasonably be presumed to have been known to the framers of the constitution. The court concluded that:

> . . .when the framers of our constitution used the phrase "free and without charge for tuition to all children. . .," the word "free" meant without charge for physical facilities and equipment; "without charge for tuition" meant there should be no fee charged for instruction; and "to all children. . ." meant such schools were equally available to all children within the district.

The court therefore ruled that sale or rental of textbooks, workbooks, or similar items did not violate the state's constitution, and that items such as pencils, pens, notebooks and paper customarily furnished for their own use need not be provided free to pupils. The court also stated:

> . . . similar items, not specifically contemplated in 1848 but of the same nature, in the sense of being individually used, need not be furnished free; such items as gym suits

---

[260]Northeast Community Organization, Inc. v. Weinberger, 378 F.Supp. 1287 (Md. 1974).

[261]Dowell v. School District No. 1, 250 S.W.2d 127 (Ark. 1952); Batty v. Board of Education of Williston, 269 N.W.49 (N.D. 1936); Morris v. Vandiver, 145 So. 228 (Ala. 1933); Claxton v. Stanford, 128 S.E. 887 (Ga. 1925).

[262]Bryant v. Whisenant, 52 So. 525 (Ala. 1910); State v. Regents of the University of Wisconsin, 11 N.W. 472 (Wis. 1882); Connell v. Gray, 127 Pac. 417 (Okla. 1912); Vincent v. County Board of Education, 131 So. 893 (Ala. 1931).

[263]Special School District No. 65 v. Bangs, 221 S.W. 1060 (Ark. 1920).

[264]Claxton v. Stanford, 128 S.W. 887 (Ga. 1925).

[265]Roberson v. Oliver, 66 So. 645 (Ala. 1914).

[266]Bond v. Ann Arbor School District, 178 N.W.2d 484 (Mich. 1970); Paulson v. Minidoka County School District No. 31, 463 P.2d 935 (Idaho 1970); Hamer v. Board of Education of School District No. 109, 265 N.E.2d 616 (Ill. 1970); Granger v. Cascade County School District, 499 P.2d 780 (Mont. 1972); Board of Education v. Sinclair, 222 N.W.2d 143 (Wis. 1974).

[267]Board of Education v. Sinclair, 222 N.W.2d 143 (Wis. 1974); See also Hamer v. Board of Education of School District No. 109, 265 N.E.2d 616 (Ill. 1970).

and towels and band instruments would be in this category, and if rented, such rental must be reasonable and tied to cost. On the other hand, electronic listening devices, microfilm readers and similar devices, used by individual pupils are comparable in nature to the "apparatus" . . . which the school must furnish without charge to the individual pupil.

In Michigan, on the other hand, it was found that the term "free," as used in the provisions of Michigan's constitution relating to free schools, meant without cost or charge. Consequently, it was held[268] that imposition of a fee for books and school supplies violated the constitutional guarantee of free schools, since books and school supplies were found to be an essential part of a system of free public schools. In Montana it has been ruled[269] that no fee may be charged for a course or activity that is reasonably related to a recognized academic and educational goal of a particular school system. Fees imposed for school supplies, but not for textbooks, have also been upheld.[270] It has been ruled[271] that a lump sum fee imposed on all students for extracurricular activities, whether or not they participated in such activities, is unconstitutional. A fee for materials and supplies used by students based solely upon the grade in which the student is enrolled has been upheld.[272]

It has been held[273] that a statute permitting school authorities to fix reasonable incidental fees did not violate a constitutional provision directing the establishment of a liberal system of schools. There is general agreement that a school board must be granted specific authority to do so before it can make the payment of incidental fees a condition precedent to school attendance.[274] In *Morris v. Vandiver*[275] the court,

in holding that a school board could assess fees, distinguished between the authority to assess athletic, literary, and library fees and the authority to require the payment of such fees as a condition precedent to entering school. It has been held[276] that pupils may be required to make a deposit for the use of free textbooks which will be forfeited if the textbooks are mishandled or are not returned. A student's transcript may not be withheld for failure to pay an unconstitutional fee.[277]

It should be noted that a constitutional provision for free public education generally applies only to pupils who reside in the district.[278] However, the legislature may grant to nonresident pupils the privilege of attending school in another district subject to the payment of tuition.[279] Such tuition may be paid by the school district in which the pupil resides, or by the pupil's parents, depending upon the terms of the statute. A local school board has no authority to alter the statutory scheme[280] where it provides a complete plan for the payment of nonresident tuition.

7.4b Fees charged for use of school property

Whether fees have been received for the use of school property by nonschool organizations has not been a significant issue in cases involving the use of school property. Although in early decisions it was generally held that school property could be used only for purposes directly related to the instruction of pupils,[281] more recent decisions have tended to allow the use of school property for temporary, casual, or incidental nonschool purposes as long as such usage does not interfere with the instruction of pupils.[282] Of course, the question of whether permitting the use of school property for specific nonschool purposes is

[268]Bond v. Ann Arbor School District, 178 N.W.2d 484 (Mich. 1970).

[269]Granger v. Cascade County School District, 499 P.2d 780 (Mont. 1972); see also Norton v. Board of Education of School District No. 16, 553 P.2d 1277 (N.M. 1976).

[270]Paulson v. Minidoka County School District No. 31, 463 P.2d 935 (Ida. 1970); Beck v. Board of Education of Harlem Consolidated School District No. 122, 325 N.E.2d 640 (Ill. 1975).

[271]Paulson v. Minidoka County School District No. 31, 463 P.2d 935 (Ida. 1970).

[272]Beck v. Board of Education of Harlem Consolidated School District No. 122, 325 N.E.2d 640 (Ill. 1975).

[273]Vincent v. County Board of Education, 131 So. 893 (Ala. 1931); Shirey v. City Board of Education of Fort Payne, 94 So.2d 758 (Ala. 1957).

[274]Young v. Trustees of Fountain Inn Graded School, 41 S.E. 824 (S.C. 1902); Connell v. Gray, 127 Pac. 417 (Okla. 1912); Morris v. Vandiver, 145 So. 228 (Ala. 1933).

[275]Morris v. Vandiver, 145 So. 228 (Ala. 1933).

[276]Segar v. Rockford Board of Education, 148 N.E. 289 (Ill. 1925).

[277]Paulson v. Minidoka County School District No. 31, 463 P.2d 935 (Ida. 1970).

[278]Eisenberg v. Corning, 179 F.2d 275 (4th Cir. 1949); Cape Girardeau School District No. 63 v. Frye, 225 S.W.2d 484 (Mo. 1949); Town School District v. Town School District, 169 A.2d 352 (Vt. 1961); Logan City School District v. Kowallis, 77 P.2d 348 (Utah 1938).

[279]Logan City School District v. Kowallis, 77 P.2d 348 (Utah 1938); Rogers v. Trustees Graded School, 13 S.W. 587 (Ky. 1890).

[280]State v. School District of City of Jefferson, 74 S.W.2d 30 (Mo. 1934).

[281]School District v. Arnold, 21 Wis. 657 (1867); George v. School District, 47 Mass. 497 (1843); Spencer v. Joint School District, 15 Kan. 259 (1875).

[282]Simmons v. Board of Education, 237 N.W. 700 (N.D. 1931); Ralph v. Orleans Parish School Board, 104 So. 490 (La. 1925).

within the discretion of school authorities must be answered affirmatively before such use will be allowed.

The fact that a school district will derive additional revenue as a result of permitting nonschool organizations to use its facilities has seldom been a major factor in court decisions. In a few cases, however, the question has received judicial attention. In an early Kansas case the court stated that the fact that adequate rental would be received was immaterial in determining whether school property could be used for a nonschool purpose.[283] In more recent decisions—in which the use of school facilities by nonschool organizations has been upheld—the fact that the revenue derived from such usage would improve the district's financial position has been noted with approval.[284]

7.5 ADMINISTERING SCHOOL DISTRICT FUNDS

Just as it can in other matters concerning school district operation, a state legislature can exercise a great deal of control over the business affairs of a school district. The legislature has power to determine the procedures which are to be followed in safeguarding and disbursing school district funds and to specify the board or officers who are to be responsible for the administration thereof.[285] It has been said that school funds are trust funds for educational purposes and are to be used for the benefit of school children by the agency entrusted with their custody.[286] Thus, school district officers legally are regarded as trustees of the school funds under their control and may spend such funds only for school purposes. Within the limits of the authority granted them by statutes the administration of school district funds rests within the sound discretion of the officers who are responsible for them.[287] Their discretion will

not be interfered with by the courts if it is reasonably exercised.[288]

Statutes or charters in many states provide that municipalities or counties are to keep and disburse school funds. In such cases, however, the municipality or county has only as much control over school district expenditures as is specifically granted to it by the statutes. Unless it has been granted specific statutory authority to do so, a municipality or county may not exercise control over the use of money appropriated to a school district.[289]

7.5a Depository

School funds ordinarily may be deposited in a bank, and in most states statutory authorization therefor will be found. The statutes usually specify the procedure to be followed in selecting the depository and the qualifications which the depository must meet. It has been ruled[290] that unless the statutes make specific provision to the contrary, school funds may be deposited in a bank prior to the time a depository has been chosen as required by statute. To hold otherwise obviously would not be in the interest of properly safeguarding school funds. It should be noted that, where a district officer placed school funds in a bank without authorization to do so and the bank became insolvent, the court held[291] that the school board had a preferred right to the assets of the bank which was superior to the rights of the bank's general creditors. Despite these cases, sound operating procedure requires that every reasonable effort be made to see that school funds are deposited in a properly designated depository.

7.5b Budgets

It is generally acknowledged that a school district budget represents an indispensable instrument of fiscal control. In many states the importance of a budget has been recognized by the enactment of statutes requiring school authorities to prepare an annual budget which must be submitted for approval either to the electorate or to a designated appropriating agency, e.g., a city

[283]Spencer v. Joint School District, 15 Kan. 259 (1875).

[284]Royse Independent School District v. Reinhardt, 159 S.W. 1010 (Tex. 1913); Cost v. Shinault, 166 S.W. 740 (Ark. 1914); Simmons v. Board of Education, 237 N.W. 700 (N.D. 1931).

[285]City of Franklin v. Hinds, 143 A.2d 111 (N.H. 1958); Branch v. Board of Education of Robeson County, 65 S.E.2d 124 (N.C. 1951); Fiscal Court v. Board of Education, 127 S.W. 527 (Ky. 1910).

[286]Dickinson v. Edmondson 178 S.W. 930 (Ark. 1915); Conley v. Rogers, 149 S.E. 699 (Ga. 1929); Love v. City of Dallas, 40 S.W.2d 591 (Tex. 1931); Board of Education of City of Syracuse v. King, 114 N.Y.S.2d 329 (1952).

[287]McCauley v. Hampton, 196 F.Supp. 123 (Tenn. 1961); Regional High School District No. 3 v. Town of Newton, 59 A.2d 527 (Conn. 1948); Carter v. Taylor, 231 S.W.2d 601 (Ky. 1950); City State Bank v. Wellington Independent School District, 178 S.W.2d 114 (Tex. 1944); People ex rel. Hamer v. Board of Education of School District No. 113, 316 N.E.2d 820 (Ill. 1974).

[288]Williams v. Holt, 303 P.2d 208 (Kan. 1956); Munderville v. Nichols, 183 N.Y.S.2d 428 (1959); McCollum v. City of Richardson, 121 S.W.2d 423 (Tex. 1938); Pearce v. Wisdom, 165 S.E. 574 (Ga. 1932).

[289]Dawson v. Clark, 176 A.2d 732 (R.I. 1962); Board of Education of West Haven School District v. Carlo, 131 A.2d 217 (Conn. 1957); Board of Education of City of Syracuse v. King, 114 N.Y.S.2d 329 (1952); Wilson County Board of Education v. Wilson County Board of Commissioners, 215 S.E.2d 412 (N.C. 1975).

[290]Farmers' and Merchants' State Bank v. Consolidated School District No. 3, 219 N.W. 163 (Minn. 1928).

[291]Myers v. Board of Education, 32 Pac. 658 (Kan. 1893).

council or county board. Statutes concerning school budgets vary in their specificity; some call for rather detailed estimates of expenditures and revenue in various categories and subcategories while others require only an estimate of the total amount to be expended.

In preparing a school budget it is imperative that all statutory requirements be met. It was held,[292] for example, that a statute expressly providing that a school district's annual budget was not to exceed the amount of funds which would be available for school purposes, including the proposed tax levy and state subventions, prohibited the adoption of a budget exceeding the anticipated revenue. Similarly, it is illegal to eliminate an appropriation for evening schools from a school budget when a statute requires that such schools be maintained.[293]

Where a school district's budget must be submitted to a separate appropriating agency for approval, questions regarding that agency's authority to alter the budget frequently have arisen. In general, unless the appropriating agency has explicitly been granted statutory authority to reduce or eliminate specific items in the school district budget, its authority extends only to determining the amount of the total budget.[294] That is, the appropriating agency may reduce the total budget; it may not eliminate specific items from the budget. This principle recognizes that, while an appropriating agency may be able to evaluate the overall public needs and revenue potential of a taxing jurisdiction, a board of education is better able to assign priorities to the fiscal needs of the schools. Where statutes so authorize, an appropriating authority may consider on a line-by-line basis the budget submitted by a board of education,[295] and is not required to approve a budget in its entirety.[296] It has been ruled,[297] however, that a municipality is obligated to supply sufficient funds for a board of education to perform its essential duties whether or not such funds have been approved by the municipality's legislative or financial

body. It also has been held[298] that where a city council was vested with authority to appropriate funds for a school district, its power was subject to the limitation that it must appropriate sufficient funds to finance services and programs mandated by statute and enable the district to meet minimum standards established by the state board of education.

Adoption or approval of the school budget constitutes an appropriation of funds for the programs and services contained within the budget.[299] A school budget or estimate which has been filed with an appropriating agency may be withdrawn for amendment or correction prior to the time it has been accepted or adopted.[300] Once accepted, however, it may not be withdrawn.[301]

Transferring Funds between Categories

Questions sometimes arise concerning the authority of a board of education to transfer funds between budget categories after a budget has been adopted. That is, may a board of education transfer funds from one category to another within the operating budget after it has been approved? A statute which answers this question is controlling, of course, but it would appear that in the absence of specific statutory prohibition a board of education may transfer funds from one budget category to another provided the total appropriation is not exceeded.[302] For example, the transfer of excess appropriations from one budget item to make up deficiencies in another budget item has been allowed.[303]

Planned Surplus or Contingency Fund

The question of whether a school board may include in its budget a planned surplus or contingency fund is occasionally raised. As in other aspects of fiscal operation the

[292]Marsh v. Erhard, 47 A.2d 713 (Pa. 1946).

[293]Talbot v. Board of Education, 14 N.Y.S.2d 340 (1939).

[294]City of Franklin v. Hinds, 143 A.2d 111 (N.H. 1958); Board of Education of West Haven School District v. Carlo, 131 A.2d 217 (Conn. 1957); Board of School Trustees v. Benner, 24 S.E.2d 259 (N.C. 1943); Divisich v. Marshall, 24 N.E.2d 327 (N.Y. 1939); Laconia Board of Education v. City of Laconia, 285 A.2d 793 (N.H. 1971).

[295]Wilson County Board of Education v. Wilson County Board of Commissioners, 215 S.E.2d 412 (N.C. 1975).

[296]Board of Public Education v. Zimmerman, 203 S.E.2d 178 (Ga. 1974).

[297]Board of Education v. Butler, 343 A.2d 657 (Conn. 1974).

[298]Laconia Board of Education v. City of Laconia, 285 A.2d 793 (N.H. 1971).

[299]Board of School Trustees v. Benner, 24 S.E.2d 259 (N.C. 1943); Excise Board of Marshall County v. School District No. 34, 10 P.2d 643 (Okla. 1932); State v. District Court of Fourteenth Judicial District, 26 P.2d 345 (Mont. 1933).

[300]Lowden v. Caddo County Excise Board, 55 P.2d 472 (Okla. 1936); City of Paducah v. Board of Education of Paducah, 158 S.W.2d 615 (Ky. 1942).

[301]Young v. City of Worcester, 133 N.E.2d 211 (Mass. 1956); Board of School Trustees v. Benner, 24 S.E.2d 259 (N.C. 1943).

[302]State v. District Court of Fourteenth Judicial District, 26 P.2d 345 (Mont. 1933); Isley v. School District No. 2 of Maricopa County, 305 P.2d 432 (Ariz. 1956); Rodman v. Lofaso, 196 N.Y.S.2d 509 (1960); Board of Selectmen v. School Board of Pittsfield School District, 311 A.2d 124 (N.H. 1973).

[303]State v. District Court of Fourteenth Judicial District, 26 P.2d 345 (Mont. 1933).

statutes are controlling, but where there is no specific statutory authorization for a contingency fund or budget surplus, the courts are not in agreement as to whether such an item may legally be included in a school budget. In Massachusetts it has been held[304] that, since a regional school district is a corporate body, it may maintain a budget surplus subject to appropriate statutory and constitutional safeguards. In New York, on the other hand, a school budget must be confined to school purposes for the ensuing year, and a school district has no authority to raise money for a planned surplus.[305] In Illinois an appropriation for contingent expenses is permissible if the sum is small and reasonable in relation to the wealth and population of the district.[306]

Unforeseen contingencies may arise after a school budget has been adopted. In such a situation it was held[307] that a board of education had power to increase the district budget to cover "ordinary contingent expenses" without first procuring approval of the voters of the school district. Ordinary contingent expenses were defined as those which could not reasonably have been foreseen or expected at the time the budget was adopted and state mandated expenses which were not contained in the budget.

7.5e Purposes for which expended

A cardinal principle of school finance is that school funds may be expended only for those purposes authorized either expressly or by necessary implication by the statutes.[308] The difficulty, of course, arises when one attempts to determine whether authority to engage in a particular activity is necessarily implied by those powers which have expressly been granted. The answer in any case will hinge on the interpretation given the statutes by the courts, and it is here that jurists differ. In considering whether a board of education has implied authority to spend school funds for a particular purpose one must remember that the power to tax is an extraordinary one and that statutes conveying it are strictly con-

strued. School taxes constitute the revenue side of the budget; school expenditures represent the disbursement side. Consequently, the rule of strict construction also will normally apply to statutes authorizing expenditures.

The area of health services for pupils has generated considerable litigation and illustrates the determinations a court must make when confronted with the question of whether or not a given expenditure is authorized. The courts have generally agreed that a board of education has implied power to employ doctors, dentists, and nurses to inspect children to insure that health regulations are met.[309] They are also agreed, however, that such implied power extends only to diagnostic and inspectorial health services; a board of education may not provide medical, surgical, or dental care for pupils at district expense unless such expenditures are specifically authorized.[310]

Other expenditures which have been held to be necessarily implied by statutes granting boards of education broad authority to establish educational programs include the purchase of band uniforms,[311] the purchase of athletic facilities and equipment,[312] the operation of cafeterias (so long as the purpose is educational, not pecuniary profit),[313] the retention of legal counsel,[314] the purchase of life and disability insurance for teachers,[315] the conduct of research and development activities,[316] and the advertising

---

[304]Regional District School Committee v. Town of Bridgewater, 197 N.E.2d 688 (Mass. 1964).

[305]Leone v. Hunter, 191 N.Y.S.2d 334 (1959); Contra: People ex rel Walgenbach v. Chicago and N.W.R. Co., 354 N.E.2d 42 (Ill. 1976).

[306]People v. New York Central Railroad Company, 72 N.E.2d 821 (Ill. 1947).

[307]Raffone v. Pearsall, 333 N.Y.S.2d 316 (1972).

[308]Smith v. Holovtchiner, 162 N.W. 630 (Neb. 1917); Shanklin v. Boyd, 142 S.W. 1041 (Ky. 1912); Protest of Chicago, Rock Island and Pacific Railway Co., 25 P.2d 690 (Okla. 1933); State v. Albright, 20 N.J. Law 644 (1846).

[309]Hallett v. Post Printing and Publishing Co., 192 Pac. 658 (Col. 1920); State v. Brown, 128 N.W. 294 (Minn. 1910); Board of Education of Bowling Green v. Simmons, 53 S.W.2d 940 (Ky. 1932). Contra, Protest of Chicago, Rock Island and Pacific Railway Co., 25 P.2d 690 (Okla. 1933).

[310]McGilvra v. Seattle School District No. 1, 194 Pac. 817 (Wash. 1921); Jarrett v. Goodall, 168 S.E. 763 (W. Va. 1933).

[311]Kay County Excise Board v. Atchison, Topeka and Santa Fe Railway Co., 91 P.2d 1087 (Okla. 1939).

[312]Galloway v. School District of Borough of Prospect Park, 200 Atl. 99 (Pa. 1938); McNair v. School District No. 1, 288 Pac. 188 (Mont. 1930); Alexander v. Phillips, 254 Pac. 1056 (Ariz. 1927); Young v. Linwood School District No. 17, 97 S.W.2d 627 (Ark. 1936). Contra, Brine v. City of Cambridge, 164 N.E. 619 (Mass. 1929).

[313]Goodman v. School District No. 1, 32 F.2d 586 (8th Cir. 1929).

[314]Arrington v. Jones, 191 S.W. 361 (Tex. 1917); Fleischmann v. Graves, 138 N.E. 745 (N.Y. 1923); Board of Education v. Thurman, 247 Pac. 996 (Ariz. 1926); Ward v. San Diego School District, 265 Pac. 821 (Cal. 1928); Rural Independent School District v. Daly, 207 N.W. 124 (Iowa 1926); Broome County v. Board of Education of Central School District No. 1, 317 N.Y.S.2d 486 (1971).

[315]Nohl v. Board of Education, 199 Pac. 373, 16 A.L.R. 1085 (N.M. 1921); Kerrigan v. City of Boston, 278 N.E.2d 387 (Mass. 1972).

[316]California School Employees Association v. Sunnyvale Elementary School District, 111 Cal.Rptr. 433 (1973).

of courses in cosmetology offered at a vocational school operated by the district.[317]

7.6 ADMINISTRATION OF PARTICULAR FUNDS

7.6a School activity funds

School officials have sometimes assumed that funds derived from admission charges paid by spectators who attend such school activities as athletic contests, concerts, and theatrical productions are not subject to the control of the board of education. This assumption is completely erroneous. School activity funds are subject not only to the control of the board of education but to the same accounting requirements as other school funds. The legal principles involved were clearly identified by the Superior Court of Pennsylvania in a case in which it held that school activity fund accounts were subject to audit.

The monies derived from the sale of admissions to witness the event in question comes into being because of (1) the use and wear of the school building and grounds; (2) the use and wear of personal property owned by the district; (3) the payment to employees such as coaches for their services; (4) the payment by the district for light, heat and various maintenance charges, including janitorial service. By reason of the use of these public funds the event takes place, and from it are reaped the admission fees paid to witness the performance.

. . . where monies or property are derived directly or indirectly through the use of school buildings, or from the expenditure of public funds of the district, the monies thus derived are public property, must be handled exactly as tax monies and be paid to the district treasurer.[318]

7.6b Special school funds

Statutes frequently provide for the establishment of special funds to be used for specific purposes, e.g., constructing and equipping school buildings, paying teachers' salaries, or retiring debt. Where special funds are established, each fund must be administered separately and a separate accounting made for each fund.[319] The general rule is that the money in each school fund must be used for the purposes for which it was raised. Constitutional or statutory provisions concerning the expenditure of such funds are strictly enforced.[320] Accordingly, money collected for one fund cannot be diverted to another unless the statutes so provide.[321] It has been held,[322] for example, that money in a teachers' fund may not be transferred to an incidental fund, and that revenue raised for the purpose of building, equipping, or repairing a school constitutes a trust fund for the specific purpose for which it was raised and cannot be used for other purposes.[323]

The restrictions concerning transfer of money from a special fund without specific statutory authorization apply despite the fact that a surplus remains in the fund after the purposes for which it was established have been accomplished.[324] However, there is also authority which holds that a surplus remaining in a special fund after all obligations of the fund have been met may be used for general school purposes.[325] Where authorized by statute, money may temporarily be transferred from one special fund to another, or to a general fund.[326]

7.7 GENERAL SCHOOL FUNDS

Revenue raised for the general support and maintenance of the schools may, as a rule, be used for any general school purpose.[327] Not only may a general school fund be used for general school purposes, but the same is true of any school fund not raised

---

[317]Board of Public Instruction of Bay County v. Jeter, 277 So.2d 69 (Fla. 1973).

[318]Petition of Auditors of Hatfield Township School District, 54 A.2d 833 (Pa. 1947).

[319]McPhail v. Tax Collector, 280 S.W. 260 (Tex. 1925); People v. Chicago & N.W. Railway Co., 108 N.E.2d 22 (Ill. 1952).

[320]Union Trust Company v. Board of Education, 66 F.Supp 88 (Ill. 1037); Ewing v. Peak, 266 S.W.2d 300 (Ky. 1954); Tuttle v. Beem, 24 P.2d 12 (Ore. 1933); Lakeside Special School District v. Gaines, 153 S.W.2d 149 (Ark. 1941).

[321]Rector v. Consolidated School District No. 3, 58 S.W.2d 785 (Mo. 1933); State v. Board of Equalization of Hall County, 90 N.W.2d 421 (Neb. 1958); State v. City of Racine, 236 N.W. 553 (Wis. 1931); Board of Education v. Strausser, 251 N.E.2d 515 (Ohio 1969); People ex rel. Redfern v. Penn Central Co., 266 N.E.2d 334 (Ill. 1971).

[322]Cleveland Village School District No. 118 v. Zion, 190 S.W. 955 (Mo. 1916).

[323]Dodge County Board of Education v. Dykes, 155 S.E. 489 (Ga. 1930); Southern v. Beeler, 195 S.W.2d 857 (Tenn. 1946).

[324]George S. Chatfield Co. v. City of Waterbury, 91 Atl. 436 (Conn. 1914); Hull v. Board of Education, 300 Pac. 775 (Okla. 1931); People v. Chicago & N.W. Railway Co., 108 N.E.2d 22 (Ill. 1952).

[325]Oak Grove Consolidated School District No. 9 v. Fitzgerald, 129 S.W.2d 223 (Ark. 1939).

[326]Fawcett v. Ball, 251 Pac. 679 (Cal. 1926); Stinson v. Thorson, 158 N.W. 351 (N.D. 1916).

[327]State v. Cave, 52 Pac. 200 (Mont. 1898); Dodge v. Jefferson County Board of Education, 181 S.W.2d 406 (Ky. 1944); Neal v. Board of Education, 52 P.2d 614 (N.M. 1935).

for a special purpose.[328] The determination of whether a given expenditure is necessary for the proper support and maintenance of the schools rests in the discretion of the school board, unless, of course, the statutes afford other explicit directions. The authority to spend money for general school purposes ordinarily is interpreted to include only expenditures for current operation. Thus, it was held[329] that revenue raised for the general support and maintenance of the schools may not be used to finance capital outlay projects like the purchase of a school site or the erection of a school building unless the statutes specifically authorize such use.

7.8 APPROPRIATION AND DISBURSEMENT OF SCHOOL FUNDS

The authority to appropriate school funds for particular purposes may rest with a board of education or with some other governmental body. Regardless of the governmental body involved, appropriations for school purposes must be made in accordance with the procedure established in the statutes and must not exceed statutory or constitutional limits.[330]

Before an appropriation is made, funds to cover its amount must be available or provision must be made to obtain them.[331] When another governmental body is responsible for appropriating funds to the use of the school district, its control over the funds ceases once the appropriation has been made. The appropriating body may not interfere with the school board's discretion concerning the use of the money appropriated to the schools.[332]

For an appropriation from a special fund to be valid, the item for which the appropriation was made must have a direct and legitimate connection with the purpose for which the fund was created. For instance, it has been ruled[333] improper to charge such items as coal, electricity, and window shade

repairs against a building fund. Also, when the appropriation for a given item is to be made from a particular fund, the board of education may not appropriate other funds in the district treasury for the purpose.[334]

The rule bears repeating that an appropriation from school funds may be made only for purposes expressly authorized or necessarily implied by the statutes. In keeping with this rule, an appropriation for an illegal or unauthorized purchase is void, as is an appropriation to pay a claim which the school district is not legally obligated to pay.[335]

Obviously all statutory requirements regarding the procedure to be followed in disbursing school district funds should be observed scrupulously. Since statutes concerning the disbursement of school moneys frequently are not particularly explicit, it is imperative that sound business procedures designed to safeguard school funds and to account for each expenditure be followed. Disbursements from school funds should be made only on warrants or orders drawn on the appropriate fund and countersigned by the officers whose signatures are required by law.[336]

7.9 DELEGATION OF AUTHORITY IN FISCAL MATTERS

In view of the size and complexity of present-day school operations, and in view of the wide variety of goods and services purchased almost continuously by the schools, the question of whether a board of education may legally delegate to an employee the authority to make purchases on behalf of the board is an important one. It is a well-settled principle of law that a board of education may not delegate its discretionary powers to an employee, to a member of the board of education, or to a committee composed of members of the board.[337] Since the purchase of goods and services clearly requires the exercise of discretion, one must conclude that in most states a board of education has no right to delegate to an employee the authority to make purchases on its behalf. In fact, several decisions hold that a board of education is not bound by purchases made for the dis-

[328]Rector v. Consolidated School District No. 3, 58 S.W.2d 785 (Mo. 1933); Sleight v. Board of Education of City of Paterson, 170 Atl. 598 (N.J. 1934); Wyckoff v. Force, 214 Pac. 489 (Cal. 1923).

[329]Crabbe v. Board of Trustees, 116 S.W. 706 (Ky. 1909); Pledger v. Cutrell, 74 S.W.2d 646 (Ark. 1934); Davis v. City of Tuscumbia, 183 So. 657 (Ala. 1938).

[330]Short-Conrad Co. v. School District, 69 N.W. 337 (Wis. 1896); Divisich v. Marshall, 22 N.E.2d 327 (N.Y. 1939); Protest of Chicago, Rock Island and Pacific Railway Co., 25 P.2d 690 (Okla. 1933).

[331]Morley v. State, 47 P.2d 170 (Okla. 1934).

[332]Board of Education of Town of Stamford v. Board of Finance of Town of Stamford, 16 A.2d 601 (Conn. 1940); Parker v. Anson County, 74 S.E.2d 338 (N.C. 1953).

[333]People v. Reilly Tar & Chemical Corp., 59 N.E.2d 843 (Ill. 1945).

[334]State v. Albright, 20 N.J. Law 644 (1846).

[335]People v. Buena Vista Building Corp., 71 N.E.2d 10 (Ill. 1947); Fowler v. Town of Enfield, 86 A.2d 662 (Conn. 1952).

[336]Andrus v. Board of Directors, 32 So. 420 (La. 1902).

[337]School City of Crawfordsville v. Montgomery, 187 N.E. 57 (Ind. 1933); Mulhall v. Pfannkuch, 221 N.W. 833 (Iowa 1928); Garber v. Central School District No. 1, 295 N.Y.S. 850 (1937); Sebastian v. School Directors of District No. 17, 40 N.E.2d 565 (Ill. 1942).

trict by a school superintendent, a school principal, or an individual school board member.[338]

It would be virtually impossible to operate schools if all purchases had to receive prior approval from the board of education, and, in practice, school administrators often do make purchases for the schools which are later ratified by the board of education. Ratification takes place when the board accepts and pays for the goods or services which the administrator purchased. The salient point is that final approval rests with the board of education. The board may refuse to ratify the administrator's purchases, in which case, unless the supplier can establish the principle of agency or recover the goods, the supplier is without legal recourse save what may be recovered on *quantum meruit*. This situation illustrates forcefully the importance of the adoption by a board of education of clearly stated policies concerning purchasing procedures which will insure that the day-to-day needs of the schools are met, that school administrators are given guidance concerning purchases, that suppliers are protected to the fullest extent possible, and that all concerned recognize that final approval of all purchases rests with the board of education.

7.10 FINANCIAL REPORTS AND AUDITS

In order to insure that school funds are properly safeguarded and that they are devoted to the purposes for which they were appropriated, most states have enacted statutes requiring school district officers to publish, or to file with a designated agency, reports or statements of the district's financial accounts. Such statutes have been held[339] to be mandatory. In Utah, for example, a statute required boards of education to publish an annual statement showing the amount of money paid out, the purpose for which the money was paid, and to whom it was paid. It was held[340] that publication of the general expenditure categories (and under each category a long list of persons, followed by the total sum expended in each category) did not comply with the statute,

which was designed to inform taxpayers as to whether the financial affairs of the district had properly been conducted by the board of education.

In addition to any reports which may be published by school officials, it is wise to have an audit of the school district's financial transactions performed annually. It has been decided[341] that the grant of power to control and manage school funds necessarily implies that a board of education may employ an accountant to conduct a general audit of the district's records. A statute requiring the audit creates an absolute duty to have the audit performed.[342] While the requirement that an audit be made has been held mandatory, a provision that the audit report be filed within a designated time was held[343] directory and the report was permitted to be filed at a later date. Also, it has been decided[344] that, once the auditors have filed their report, they may not make a second audit, although they may make such further examinations as are necessary to complete the report. School officers are accountable only for money which actually comes into their hands and are entitled to credits only for legal disbursements.[345] Ordinarily, a school officer may appeal from the findings of an audit, but the burden of proving that the audit is in error rests with the one who makes the appeal.[346]

7.11 SUMMARY

A school district has no inherent power to levy taxes; any authority which it possesses in this area must specifically be delegated to it by the state and must be exercised in compliance with any procedural requirements established by the state. A school tax is regarded as a state tax whether it is levied directly by the state or by a school district or a municipality. School taxes may be used only for the purposes for which they were levied, and a school tax levied for one purpose may not be used for another purpose.

A school district may levy any tax which the statutes specifically authorize it to levy. In most states, however, school districts are authorized to levy a tax only on property. As a general rule, the state may determine who shall tax the property within its bor-

[338]Consolidated School District v. Panther Oil and Grease Mfg. Co., 168 P.2d 613 (Okla. 1946); Hammond & Stephens v. Christian County, 62 S.W.2d 844 (Mo. 1933); Lowe & Campbell Sporting Goods Co. v. Tangipahoa Parish School Board, 15 So.2d 98 (La. 1943); Johnson v. Sabine Parish School Board, 140 So. 87 (La. 1932).

[339]Conover v. Board of Education, 175 P.2d 209 (Utah 1946); Crockett v. Board of Education, 199 Pac. 158 (Utah 1921); Lewis v. Morgan, 252 S.W.2d 691 (Ky. 1952).

[340]Conover v. Board of Education, 175 P.2d 209 (Utah 1946).

[341]Lewis v. Morgan, 252 S.W.2d 691 (Ky. 1952).

[342]*Ibid.*

[343]Scranton District Audit, 51 Pa. Dist. & Co. 1 (1944).

[344]*In re* Washington Township Auditors' Report, 18 Pa. Dist. & Co. 455 (1933).

[345]Wise v. Bull, 141 N.Y.S. 917 &1913); People v. Edwards, 109 N.E.2d 754 (Ill. 1952).

[346]Appeal of Winters, 105 Atl. 293 (Pa. 1918); Bruce v. School District of Sykesville Borough, 96 Pa.Super. 346 (1929).

ders. Real estate, which comprises the great bulk of the property-tax base, is taxed by the school district in which it is located regardless of whether the person responsible for paying the tax has children in school or is a resident of the district.

The collection of an illegal school tax may be enjoined, but usually only a person who has a direct and personal interest in the tax—such as a taxpayer—may question its legality. Once a tax has been paid, the rule is that an illegal school tax may be recovered by the taxpayer only if it was paid under duress or compulsion.

Generally, a constitutionally established permanent school fund must be kept inviolate and used only for public school purposes, although the income from the fund may be apportioned to the schools. The general revenues of the state, or the revenue from "earmarked" taxes, may be apportioned to local school districts by the legislature in a manner designed to equalize educational opportunity and tax burden among the districts of the state, or may be apportioned among local school districts according to such other criteria as the legislature shall establish.

The U. S. Constitution does not demand that the amount of money available per pupil be equalized among the school districts of a state or that funds be distributed in accordance with the educational needs of pupils. State constitutions may, however, be interpreted to require that the level of spending for a child's education may not be a function of the wealth of the district in which the child resides; it may be a function only of the wealth of the state as a whole.

A school district which accepts funds from the federal government is obligated to comply with the terms of the grant and with any regulations established concerning the administration of such funds.

Pupils apparently may be required to pay incidental fees for locker rental, towels, and the like. However, the charging of a tuition fee for general support of the school program is regarded as a violation of the constitutional guarantee of free public schooling.

School officers legally are regarded as trustees of the school funds under their control and may use them only for public school purposes. It is imperative that all statutory directions be followed in such matters as selection of a depository for school funds and the preparation and administration of the district budget. School funds may be expended only for the purposes which are authorized by statute. Funds derived from school activities are subject to the same controls and accounting requirements as are funds derived from other sources; they do not "belong" to the teacher (or club) sponsoring the activity. School money collected for one purpose may not be diverted to another without specific statutory authorization.

A board of education cannot delegate to an employee, to a member of the board, or to a committee of the board its discretionary power to expend school funds unless the statutes specifically authorize such delegation. However, the board of education may ratify purchases made by employees or board members by accepting and paying for goods or services purchased by them on behalf of the school district.

Statutes requiring financial reports and/or audits are generally regarded as mandatory and require strict compliance. Even without specific statutory authority a board of education may employ an accountant to audit its records.

School District Bonds and Other Indebtedness

8.0 INTRODUCTION

School districts frequently find it necessary to incur debt. Indebtedness may be incurred on a long-term basis to finance capital expenditures or on a short-term basis to finance day-to-day operation of the schools. Because the restrictions on the authority of a school district to incur indebtedness are relatively stringent, it is important that school officials be familiar with the statutes and legal principles governing this area of school operation.

8.1 SCHOOL DISTRICT INDEBTEDNESS

It should be emphasized at the outset that in the absence of express constitutional or statutory authorization to do so, a school district has no authority to incur indebtedness.[1] In all states school districts have been granted such authority, but the specific grant varies considerably from state to state. Therefore, it is necessary to study the statutes and constitution of the state in question to determine the circumstances under which a school district may incur indebtedness. As a general rule, statutory provisions concerning the creation of indebtedness by school districts are strictly construed.[2] Consequently, the provisions of such statutes concerning the purposes for which a debt may be incurred, the procedures to be followed in incurring indebtedness, and the amount of indebtedness which may be incurred must be carefully observed.[3] It has been said, for example, that a legislature may impose whatever limitations it deems necessary to prevent deficit spending and the issuance of bonds or other evidence of indebtedness.[4]

8.2 SCHOOL BONDS

The great bulk of school building construction is financed through the issuance of school district bonds. It must be recognized, however, that a school district has no inherent power to issue bonds.[5] In fact, in several cases, it has been held[6] that the power to issue bonds must be specifically conferred and cannot be implied from other powers which have been expressly granted; that even the express power to borrow money does not imply power to issue bonds. In discussing the authority of a school district to issue bonds, the Supreme Court of South Dakota has said:

It is elementary that a school district cannot issue bonds excepting by statutory permission. The Legislature, which alone can grant the power, is entitled to prescribe the terms and conditions of its exercise, and it is the undoubted general rule that a compliance with all the requirements of the provisions of law conferring the power is essential to a valid exercise of such power.[7]

The legislature, having once exercised its right to authorize school districts to issue bonds, may at any time remove, modify, or limit the power it initially granted. The only limitation on the legislature's authority in this regard is that it may not infringe constitutional rights which have become vested under the initial legislation.[8] Thus, the legislature may alter the procedure to be followed in issuing school bonds; it may modify the purposes for which school bonds may be issued; it may limit the amount of bonds which may be issued to a specified percentage of the value of property in the district; or it may make other changes as desired.

The courts are not in agreement as to whether or not a grant of power to borrow money carries with it by implication the power to issue bonds. In some jurisdictions it has been held[9] that a grant of power to borrow money necessarily implies a grant of power to issue bonds. In other jurisdictions it has been held[10] that authority to issue bonds cannot be implied from a grant of power to borrow money.

[1]Union School Township v. First National Bank, 2 N.E. 104 (Ind. 1885).

[2]Pennock v. State, 54 So. 1004 (Fla. 1911); Middleton v. Greeson, 5 N.E. 755 (Ind. 1886).

[3]Day v. City of Newton, 174 N.E.2d 426 (Mass. 1961); New Mexico Bus Sales v. Michael, 360 P.2d 639 (N.M. 1961); Manning v. Van Buren District Township, 28 Iowa 332 (1869); Wright v. Compton Unified School District, 120 Cal.Rptr. 115 (1975).

[4]*In re* Advisory Opinion, 211 N.W.2d 28 (Mich. 1973).

[5]Hewitt v. Board of Education, 94 Ill. 528 (1880); People v. Thompson, 36 N.E.2d 351 (Ill. 1941); Reuland v. Independent District of White Lake, 269 N.W. 484 (S.D. 1936); State v. Johnson County High School, 5 P.2d 255 (Wyo. 1931); Lakeside Special School District v. Gaines, 153 S.W.2d 149 (Ark. 1941).

[6]Brenham v. German-American Bank, 144 U.S. 173, 12 S.Ct. 559, 36 L.Ed. 390 (Tex. 1892); Ashuelot National Bank v. School District No. 7, 56 Fed. 197 (8th Cir. 1893).

[7]Reuland v. Independent District of White Lake, 269 N.W. 484 (S.D. 1936).

[8]State v, Clausen, 186 Pac. 319 (Wash. 1919).

[9]People v. Sisson, 98 Ill. 335 (1881); Russell v. Middletown City School District, 125 Atl. 641 (Conn. 1924); Schmutz v. Little Rock Special School District, 95 S.W. 438 (Ark. 1906); Orchard v. School District No. 70, 15 N.W. 730 (Neb. 1883); Union School District Board of Education v. Goodrich, 175 N.W. 1009 (Mich. 1920).

[10]Merrill v. Monticello, 138 U.S. 673, 11 S.Ct. 441, 34 L.Ed. 1069 (Ind. 1890); Brenham v. German-American Bank, 144 U.S. 173, 12 S.Ct. 559, 36 L.Ed. 390 (Tex. 1892); Ashuelot National Bank v. School District No. 7, 56 Fed. 197 (8th Cir. 1893).

8.2a Purposes for which issued

School bonds typically are issued for a variety of purposes, including borrowing money generally,[11] purchasing school sites and schoolhouses,[12] improving school sites and school grounds[13] constructing new school buildings or remodeling old ones,[14] furnishing and/or equipping school buildings,[15] purchasing transportation vehicles,[16] and refunding existing indebtedness.[17] It should be noted, however, that school bonds which are issued without authority or for an unauthorized purpose are void, even in the hands of an innocent purchaser.[18]

8.2b Procedure for issuance

The procedure to be followed when issuing school bonds is determined by the statutes and constitutional provisions which deal with this matter. Statutes may vest authority to issue school bonds in a specified officer or board, or may require that the question of whether or not to issue school bonds be submitted to a vote of the people. Where authority to issue school bonds is vested in a particular officer or board, the courts will not interfere with their exercise of discretion unless it is abused.[19] Thus, such a board may refuse to issue bonds when it believes that their issuance is unnecessary.[20] Under some statutes the officer or board which is empowered to issue school bonds must issue them if certain jurisdictional requirements have been met.[21] The board may be required to determine whether certain jurisdictional facts exist—for example, whether the district is legally organized, whether the amount of bonds will exceed statutory limitations, or whether the bonds are to be issued for purposes authorized by law. If the essential jurisdictional facts are found to exist, the issuing board has no authority to refuse to issue the bonds. It also has been held[22] that, where a county fiscal court is the issuing authority for bonds, it cannot refuse to issue bonds as requested by a board of education simply because it disagrees with the board as to the need therefor.

Another procedure, which is followed in some states, makes the submission of a petition by the taxpayers of a district a condition precedent to the issuance of school bonds. In some jurisdictions it is the absolute duty of the school board to issue bonds in compliance with such a petition;[23] in others, the question of whether or not to issue bonds must be submitted to the voters of the district.[24] Persons who sign a petition to issue bonds have the right to withdraw their names therefrom prior to the time the agency designated to act on the petition has acted.[25] It also should be noted that, where statutes provide for the filing of a petition in opposition to the issuance of school bonds, school district authorities have no power to issue or sell school bonds if a valid petition in opposition has been filed.[26]

8.2c Elections

The residents and taxpayers of a school district have no inherent right to vote on the question of whether school bonds should be issued. However, many states require that this question be submitted to the voters. Where such requirement exists, bonds are void if they are issued without submission of the question to the voters,[27] even if the bonds are in the hands of a bona fide holder for value.[28] In such cases the courts follow the familiar principle that, since the powers of school officials are a matter of public record, all persons who deal with them are assumed to be aware of any restrictions upon their powers. The legal principles which

---

[11]Folsam v. McLean County District No 5, 91 Ill. 402 (1879).

[12]State v. State Board of Education, 89 So.2d 31 (Fla. 1956); Evans v. Mecklenburg County, 172 S.E. 323 (N.C. 1934).

[13]King v. Independent School District, 272 Pac. 507 (Ida. 1928); Van Arden v. Cache County School District, 191 Pac. 230 (Utah 1920).

[14]State v. Smith, 75 S.W.2d 574 (Mo. 1934); Johnson v. City of Sheffield, 183 So. 265 (Ala. 1938); Guffee v. Crockett, 315 S.W.2d 646 (Tenn. 1958).

[15]Ashcroft v. Board of Supervisors, 36 So.2d 820 (Miss. 1948).

[16]Bodine v. Johnson, 222 Pac. 993 (Okla. 1924).

[17]Mann v. Board of Education, 92 N.E.2d 743 (Ill. 1950); Wall v. Eudora Special School District, 154 S.W.2d 12 (Ark. 1941).

[18]Ashuelot National Bank v. School District No. 7, 56 Fed. 197 (8th Cir. 1893).

[19]Connelly v. Earl Frazier Special School District, 279 S.W. 13 (Ark. 1926); State v. Saffley, 112 S.W.2d 831 (Tenn. 1938).

[20]Good v. Howard, 92 N.E. 115 (Ind. 1910).

[21]Board of Supervisors of Quitman County v. State, 38 So.2d 314 (Miss. 1949).

[22]Fyfe v. Hardin County Board of Education, 205 S.W.2d 165 (Ky. 1947).

[23]Price v. Sims, 77 So. 649 (Miss. 1918).

[24]McCord v. Marsh, 189 N.W. 386 (Neb. 1922).

[25]Parker v. Seward School Township, 159 N.E.2d 575 (Ind. 1959); See also Board of Education of Metrolpolis County v. County Board of School Trustees of Massac County, 341 N.E.2d 10 (Ill. 1976).

[26]Wallace v. Simpson, 27 N.E.2d 130 (Ind. 1940).

[27]Behrle v. Board of Education, 200 N.E. 523 (Ohio 1935); Parker v. Seward School Township, 159 N.E.2d 575 (Ind. 1959).

[28]Robertson v. Rural Special School District No. 9, 244 S.W. 15 (Ark. 1922).

apply to school bond elections are similar to those which govern other school elections.

8.2d Issuance of

Once the authority to issue school bonds has been ascertained, questions may arise as to the procedure which should be followed in issuing the bonds. In some states it is necessary to register school bonds with a designated official before they may be issued. Since it is the duty of this official to make certain that all requirements of law have been met before registering the bonds, the school board must furnish the records necessary to show that there has been compliance with all legal requirements.[29]

Obviously, bonds must be issued for the purpose for which they were voted. However, bonds need not be issued in the same year in which they were voted,[30] and all bonds need not be issued at the same time.[31] Thus, it has been held[32] that a lapse of time between the authorization and the issuance of bonds does not defeat the right to issue them unless the purpose for which they were to be issued has ceased to exist. It also has been decided[33] that school bonds may be issued at a lower rate of interest than the rate authorized in the election at which their issuance was approved.

It is not necessary to provide for payment of the principal and interest on bonded indebtedness prior to issuance of the bonds unless the statutes specifically require it.[34] However, where this requirement is imposed by statutes or the constitution, any bonds issued without such provision are void.[35]

8.2e Sale of

Although the state may vest authority to sell school bonds in any appropriate officer or agency, such authority is usually vested in a school district's board of education. As is true in other areas of school bond management, there must be compliance with any statutory provisions relative to the method or procedures to be employed in disposing of school bonds. Where statutes provide that school bonds must be registered or approved by a designated official in order to give them validity, such approval must be obtained prior to the time the bonds are delivered.[36] However, it has been held[37] that a board of education may advertise for and accept bids on bonds, or enter into a contract for the sale of bonds prior to their registration, but prior to such approval it may not deliver them to the purchaser.

Competitive Bids

A common requirement is that school bonds be sold on the basis of competitive bids after they have been publicly advertised for sale. As it relates to school bond sales, the word *sold* does not necessarily mean that title to the bonds has passed; it does mean that there has been agreement on terms and conditions of the sale.[38] It should be noted, moreover, that no "sale" of bonds occurs when a district exchanges new bonds for outstanding bonds.[39]

A bid is simply an offer to purchase school bonds.[40] When accepted, the bid, together with the acceptance, constitutes a complete contract and obligates the bidder to accept delivery of the bonds and to pay for them under the terms of the contract.[41]

Statutes in a number of states require that school bonds be sold to the highest and best bidder. Where such statutes exist, questions are likely to arise relative to their interpretation. Where bonds must be sold to the highest and best bidder, a contract has not been completed until a bid has officially been accepted even though a notice inviting bids may have been published. It has been held[42] that a district is not liable for damages if it refuses to accept a bid even though it may be the highest one made, particularly where the advertisement for bids reserves the right to reject any and all bids.

Advertisements for the sale of school bonds may call for the submission of unconditional bids. Where such a specification is made, it has been held[43] that a bid

[29]State v. Smith, 80 S.W.2d 858 (Mo. 1935).

[30]Fisherdick v. San Juan County Board of Education, 236 Pac. 743 (N.M. 1925).

[31]Shadow v. Rapides Parish School Board, 56 So.2d 555 (La. 1951); State v. Special Tax School District No. 14, 161 So. 410 (Fla. 1935).

[32]Shadow v. Rapides Parish School Board, 56 So.2d 555 (La. 1951); Covington v. McInnis, 142 S.E. 650 (S.C. 1928).

[33]Brown v. Truscott Independent School District, 20 S.W.2d 214 (Tex. 1929).

[34]Montpelier Savings Bank & Trust Co. v. School District No. 5, 92 N.W. 439 (Wis. 1902); Davis v. Orland Consolidated School District, 108 S.E. 466 (Ga. 1921).

[35]Montpelier Savings Bank & Trust Co. v. School District No. 5, 92 N.W. 439 (Wis. 1902).

[36]State v. Gordon, 133 S.W. 44 (Mo. 1910).

[37]Seabrook Independent School District v. Brown, 195 S.W.2d 828 (Tex. 1946).

[38]*Ibid.*

[39]Wall v. Eudora Special School District, 154 S.W.2d 12 (Ark. 1941).

[40]Joint School District No. 132 v. Dabney, 260 Pac. 486 (Okla. 1927).

[41]Gates v. First National Bank, 188 N.W. 571 (Minn. 1922).

[42]Coquard v. Joplin Independent School District, 46 Mo.App. 6 (1891).

[43]Grant v. Wake County Board of Education, 100 S.E. 522 (N.C. 1919); State v. Patton, 142 N.E. 239 (Ohio 1923).

may properly be conditioned upon approval of the legality of the bond issue by a competent attorney. In fact, a bid which required the school district to furnish a certified transcript showing that the bonds had been issued in compliance with statutory requirements has been ruled not to be a conditional one.[44] If a bid is made subject to approval of the validity of the bond issue by a competent attorney, approval by necessary implication is sufficient; expressed approval is not necessary.[45] A bidder whose conditional bid has been accepted is relieved of obligation to purchase the bonds if the bidder's attorney, acting honestly, in good faith, and without fraud or collusion, gives an opinion questioning the legality of the bonds regardless of whether, as a matter of law, they are valid or invalid.[46] Where a contract for the purchase of school bonds provided that the purchaser was to be furnished with a complete transcript of "all proceedings leading up to the issue evidencing the legality of same to the satisfaction of our attorney," failure to provide satisfactory evidence regarding the notice of the election held to authorize the school bond issue was ruled[47] to be a breach of the contract which entitled the purchaser to the return of his deposit.

Rights and Duties of Purchaser

Questions occasionally arise as to when the purchaser of bonds is entitled to receive them. It has been held[48] in this regard that a school bond purchaser must actually pay the purchase price before becoming entitled to receive delivery of the bonds. Delivery of the purchase price to a financial institution which is acting as the district's agent in the transaction is usually sufficient to entitle the purchaser to receive the bonds. For example, in one case[49] the officer of a bank which was a depository of the district's funds acted as the district's agent in negotiating the sale of school bonds. It was held in this case that money delivered to the bank by a bond purchaser and placed in a "bond account" was sufficient to entitle the purchaser to possession of the bonds, which

had been turned over to the bank for delivery to the purchasers.

A purchaser of school district bonds is required to accept only such bonds as are called for by the particular contract. When a bid to purchase school bonds in a definite amount has been accepted, the purchaser is not obligated to accept bonds in a smaller amount than called for by the contract. In fact, in such instance the purchaser is entitled to the return of any deposit.[50] One who has contracted to purchase school district bonds may also be relieved of contractual obligation by the district's failure to comply with statutory requirements. For example, it has been held[51] that a purchaser does not have to accept bonds which are invalid because the district failed to give the required notice of a school bond election, or invalid because a district failed to reserve the right to redeem the bonds.[52] It has also been decided[53] that a contract for the sale of school bonds is unenforceable if it was executed prior to the time the required proceedings for authorizing the issuance of the bonds took place.

The protection given to school bond purchasers by the law is generally quite limited. The courts reason that one who enters into a contract for the purchase of school district bonds is bound to know the law under which they are issued. If one neglects to familiarize oneself with the law or misjudges the power of a school board in issuing bonds, one does so at one's own peril. A contract to purchase school bonds is not necessarily invalidated by material mistakes on the part of either the purchaser or the district. It has been held,[54] for example, that a school bond purchaser cannot void a contract to purchase bonds on the ground that false representations were made by district officers where the officers' statements were literally true and could readily have been understood by one having knowledge of the law.

Payment of Broker's Fee

The sale of school district bonds usually involves a financial institution which serves as the school district's agent in the transaction. In regard to paying for the services of agents and brokers who

[44]State v. Patton, 142 N.E. 239 (Ohio 1923).
[45]Spitzer v. Board of Trustees, 267 Fed. 121 (6th Cir. 1920).
[46]School District of Kirksville v. Mississippi Valley Trust Co., 116 S.W.2d 146 (Mo. 1938); Grant v. Wake County Board of Education, 100 S.E. 522 (N.C. 1919).
[47]Koontz v. Iowa City State Bank, 166 N.W. 709 (Iowa 1918).
[48]Keeler v. Sheridan County School District No. 3, 205 Pac. 217 (Mont. 1922).
[49]McCurdy v. West Branch Township School District, 86 N.W. 803 (Mich. 1901).

[50]Compton Bond, etc., Co. v. Barbourville Graded School District No. 1, 181 S.W. 179 (Ky. 1916).
[51]Aldrich v. Gallup State Bank, 182 Pac. 863 (N.M. 1919).
[52]Dupont v. Mills, 196 Atl. 168 (Del. 1937).
[53]Keeler v. Sheridan County School District No. 3, 205 Pac. 217 (Mont. 1922).
[54]Spitzer v. Board of Trustees, 267 Fed. 121 (6th Cir. 1920).

negotiate the sale of school bonds, it was held[55] that a statute which authorized the sale of school bonds at no less than par value also authorized by implication the payment of a reasonable broker's fee for assisting the district in the sale of its bonds where such assistance is deemed necessary. On the other hand, it was decided[56] that, where a statute authorized a school district to advertise its bonds for sale, and to re-advertise as necessary until they had been sold, the district was without authority to pay anyone a commission for selling the bonds. In general, expenses incurred in selling school bonds may be paid from the proceeds of the sale.[57]

Damages for Breach of Contract

If a contract to purchase school district bonds is breached, the district is entitled to recover compensatory damages.[58] A common requirement is that a bidder on an issue of school bonds must place on deposit a sum of money as evidence of good faith. If the purchaser of the bonds later defaults, the school district is entitled to retain such deposits in compensation for the damage it has sustained, at least where the loss is equal to or in excess of the amount of the deposit.[59]

8.2f Form and content of

Statutes may require that school bonds (1) specify the purpose for which they are issued, (2) be of specific denominations, and/or (3) be signed by designated officers. Where these and similar statutes exist, school bonds must be issued in compliance with them.[60] For example, there must be compliance with any constitutional or statutory restrictions concerning the period of time for which bonds may be issued[61] or

the amount of interest which they may earn.[62] Authority to fix the rate of interest on school bonds may be delegated to school officers, who may exercise discretion in determining the term of the bonds where no limitations are imposed by statute in this regard.[63] Minor irregularities in the issuance and sale of school bonds generally will not invalidate them.[64]

8.2g Validity of

As has been noted previously, school bonds issued in contravention of constitutional requirements are void and unenforceable. School bonds issued or sold in violation of statutory provisions also may be unenforceable. Not only must a school district possess authority to issue bonds; it must follow all prescribed procedures in securing authorization for and in issuing and selling the bonds. For example, bonds have been held[65] invalid and were not to be issued and sold when they were authorized at an election called and conducted by the board of education rather than by the mayor and city council as required by statute. Bonds which created an indebtedness in excess of constitutional or statutory limitations also have been found[66] to be void and unenforceable. However, the courts have generally ruled that substantial compliance with all requirements surrounding the issuance of school bonds is sufficient to give them validity.[67] If bonds are otherwise valid, minor irregularities in their issuance will not invalidate them.[68] Likewise, school bond elections will not be declared void unless it can be shown that the irregularity

[55]Park v. Rural Special School District No. 26, 293 S.W. 1035 (Ark. 1927).

[56]Walla Walla County Consolidated School District No. 20 v. Union Trust Co., 215 Pac. 28 (Wash. 1923).

[57]Goren v. Buena High School District, 372 P.2d 692 (Ariz. 1962).

[58]Board of Trustees v. Spitzer, 255 Fed. 136 (6th Cir. 1919).

[59]Gates v. First National Bank, 188 N.W. 571 (Minn. 1922); Sapulpa Board of Education v. Broadwell, 245 Pac. 60 (Okla. 1925).

[60]Atchison Board of Education v. DeKay, 148 U.S. 591, 13 S.Ct. 706, 37 L.Ed. 573 (Kan. 1893); School District No. 11 v. Chapman, 152 Fed. 887 (8th Cir. 1907); Southwest Securities Co. v. Board of Education, 54 P.2d 412 (N.M. 1936); State v. Clausen, 217 Pac. 712 (Wash. 1923); Pawnee County School District No. 42 v. Xenia First National Bank, 26 N.W. 912 (Neb. 1886).

[61]Jewett v. School District No. 25, 54 P.2d 546 (Wyo. 1936); Shamblin v. Board of Supervisors, 5 So.2d 675 (Miss. 1942).

[62]Brownlee v. Brock, 92 S.E. 477 (S.C. 1917).

[63]Amey v. Pittsburgh School District, 64 A.2d 1 (N.H. 1949).

[64]Jewett v. School District No. 25, 54 P.2d 546 (Wyo. 1936); State v. Special Tax School District No. 14, 161 So. 410 (Fla. 1935); Southwest Securities Co. v. Board of Education, 54 P.2d 412 (N.M. 1936); Cacheville Elementary School District v. Hiddleson, 233 P.2d 57 (Cal. 1951).

[65]Barry v. Board of Education, 169 Pac. 314 (N.M. 1917).

[66]School District No. 1 v. Whiting, 107 P.2d 1075 (Ariz. 1940); Crow v. Burnett Independent School District, 304 S.W.2d 439 (Tex. 1957); Innes v. School District of City of Nanticoke, 20 A.2d 225 (Pa. 1941).

[67]County School Board of Hanover County v. Shelton, 93 S.E.2d 469 (Va. 1956); Hoffman v. Pounds, 173 N.E. 622 (Ohio 1930); State v. State Board of Education, 89 So.2d 31 (Fla. 1956); Graham v. Miller, 84 N.W.2d 46 (Mich. 1957); Baker v. Scranton Independent School District, 287 S.W.2d 210 (Tex. 1956).

[68]Cacheville Elementary School District v. Hiddleson, 233 P.2d 57 (Cal. 1951); Southwest Securities Co. v. Board of Education, 54 P.2d 412 (N.M. 1936); Jewett v. School District No. 25, 54 P.2d 546 (Wyo. 1936).

complained of actually affected the results of the election.[69]

It should be noted that the validity of proceedings pursuant to the issuance of school bonds is not subject to collateral attack.[70] Questions regarding the validity of school bonds must be raised in a direct action, and any defects or irregularities in the proceedings attendant to the bond issue must be material, or harmful, or both, if the proceedings are to be successfully attacked.[71] Of course, if the statutes make mandatory a particular procedure, substantial compliance will not suffice and the prescribed procedure must be adhered to strictly for the bonds to be held valid.[72]

Some states provide for special proceedings to determine the validity of school bonds prior to their issuance. Ordinarily, the judgment obtained in such a proceeding is conclusive as to the validity of the bonds in any subsequent action in which their validity is question.[73]

8.2h Ratification of illegal bond issues

As a rule, a school district or board of education may ratify any bonds which were within its authority to issue but which are invalid because of failure to secure the necessary approval for the bond issue or to follow the necessary procedures.[74] Ratification will not, however, validate an indebtedness which was incurred in violation of a specific statutory provision, nor will it validate an indebtedness exceeding constitutional or statutory debt limits.[75]

8.2i Curative legislation

A state legislature may, by passing appropriate legislation, "cure" any defects which impair the validity of school district bonds.[76] Such action might be termed ratification of defective school bonds by legislative action. It is limited to that which the legislature could originally have passed.[77] Accordingly, it has been held[78] that a curative statute may be used to validate all bonds issued by a new school district regardless of whether the district was validly created. Curative legislation cannot be used in violation of a constitutional provision, or the issuance of bonds which were completely beyond the authority of the district.[79]

8.2j Recitals in

School bonds commonly contain statements reciting that the bonds are issued in accordance with the law and that there has been compliance with all statutory requirements and conditions precedent to their issuance. Questions frequently arise as to the confidence which a prospective purchaser may place in such recitals and as to whether they estop the district from later contesting the validity of the bonds. The wide variety of statutory provisions which relate to the issuance of school bonds, and the variety of language employed in recitals, dictate that attention be given to the specific requirements of the particular state involved.

In general, where school officials are empowered to determine whether or not statutory and constitutional requirements concerning the issuance of school bonds have been met, a recital that the bonds have been issued in accordance with all requirements and conditions precedent will estop the school district from later denying the validity of the bonds held by bona fide purchasers, even if the recitals are in fact false.[80] A Michigan case is illustrative. Bonds issued by a school district contained a recital, signed by the director and moderator of the district, that the bonds had

[69]Strawn v. Independent School District of Indianola, 203 N.W. 12 (Iowa 1925); Dye v. Brewton, 80 So. 761 (Miss. 1919); McKinnon v. Union High School District No. 1, 241 Pac. 386 (Ore. 1925).

[70]In re Savannah Special Consolidated School District, 44 So.2d 545 (Miss. 1950).

[71]Williams v. Holt, 303 P.2d 208 (Kan. 1956); State v. Holmes, 245 S.W.2d 882 (Mo. 1952); State v. Maxwell, 60 N.E.2d 183 (Ohio 1945).

[72]Edwards v. Board of Supervisors, 87 So. 8 (Miss. 1921); Horsefall v. School District of City of Salem, 128 S.W. 33 (Mo. 1910).

[73]Vanzandt v. Braxton, 115 So. 557 (Miss. 1928); Weinberger v. Board of Public Instruction, 112 So. 253 (Fla. 1927); Cox v. Georgia Education Authority, 170 S.E.2d 240 (Ga. 1969).

[74]School District No. 3 v. Western Tube Co., 38 Pac. 922 (Wyo. 1895); O'Loughlin v. Dorn, 169 N.W. 572 (Wis. 1918).

[75]Riesen v. School District, 212 N.W. 783 (Wis. 1927); Superior Grade School District No. 110 v. Rhodes, 75 P.2d 251 (Kan. 1938).

[76]Osage National Bank v. Oakes Special School District, 7 N.W.2d 920 (N.D. 1943).

[77]Brown v. Truscott Independent School District, 34 S.W.2d 837 (Tex. 1931).

[78]Young v. Edna Independent School District, 34 S.W.2d 857 (Tex. 1931).

[79]Sechrist v. Guilford County, 107 S.E. 503 (N.C. 1921); People v. Thompson, 36 N.E.2d 351 (Ill. 1941).

[80]Town of Coloma v. Eaves, 92 U.S. 484, 23 L.Ed. 579 (Ill. 1875); Southwest Securities Co. v. Board of Education, 54 P.2d 412 (N.M. 1936); Gibbs v. School District, 50 N.W. 294 (Mich. 1891); Hoffman v. Pounds, 173 N.E. 622 (Ohio 1930); Loomis v. Fifth School District, 145 Atl. 571 (Conn. 1929); Bonsack & Pearce v. School District of Marceline, 49 S.W.2d 1085 (Mo. 1932); Coler v. Dwight School Township, 55 N.W. 587 (N.D. 1893); Citizens Bank v. City of Terrell, 14 S.W. 1003 (Tex. 1890).

been authorized by a two-thirds vote of the qualified voters as required by statute. The district later attempted to avoid payment on the bonds, claiming that its records failed to show that the required election had been held. In holding that the district was estopped from denying that the bonds had been properly authorized, the Michigan Supreme Court said:

> Purchasers of municipal bonds are bound to know the extent and limitations upon the authority of the corporation to issue the bonds. They are bound, in other words, to know the law under which the authority is exercised. Purchasers of such securities have a right to rely upon all facts asserted or appearing upon the face of the bonds made by any person or body authorized by law to pass upon and determine the facts. . . . The recitals in this bond are made by the director and moderator, who compose a majority of the school board. Neither the school board nor the moderator and director are authorized to issue the bonds unless voted by the district at a lawful meeting; and . . . before the board can act, they have a function to perform, in its nature somewhat judicial, and that is as to their own authority to issue the bonds. The statute limits that authority to bonds voted by the school district, and consequently the question whether the proceedings to vote such bonds are such as will authorize the board to issue them must be passed upon by the board. A purchaser of the bonds, therefore, need look no further back than the face of the bonds for the facts which show a compliance with the law. We think the assertion appearing upon the face of the bond is sufficient evidence to an innocent purchaser that the board ordered and directed the bond to be issued. . . .
>
> The law under which these bonds were issued authorized the school board to issue them, and made the board the body to determine when such facts existed; and hence when the bonds were issued by their orders, that fact appearing upon the face of the bond, a bona fide holder is entitled to recover, and, as against him, the district is not allowed to defend upon the ground that the law was not complied with previous to their determination to issue the bonds. The law having placed that responsibility with the district board, the school district, if defrauded, must seek their remedy against such board.[81]

It has been held[82] that a recital in school bonds estopped the district from denying that a petition had been filed with the board as required by statute. Similarly, it has been held[83] that a recital to the effect that the schoolhouse site was owned by the district prevented it from later contending that it was not owned by the district.

Estoppel

The doctrine of estoppel prevents one from alleging or denying a certain thing because of previous conduct or statements; that is, a person's own act "stops or closes his mouth to allege or plead the truth."[84] As it relates to the validity of recitals in school bonds, the doctrine of estoppel may be invoked only where a particular officer or agency has been authorized to determine that all requirements surrounding the issuance and sale of school bonds have been met. A district is estopped from denying the validity of a recital in a school bond only when the recital is made by one who is authorized by law to determine the existence of the fact in question. The doctrine of estoppel does not apply to recitals made by a person unauthorized to make such a determination.[85] A recital made by one not so authorized will not prevent a school district from denying the validity of its bonds. As stated by the United States Supreme Court:

> If the officers authorized to issue bonds, upon a condition, are not the appointed tribunal to decide the fact, which constitutes the condition, their recital will not be accepted as a substitute for proof. In other words, where the validity of the bonds depends upon an estoppel, claimed to arise upon the recitals of the instrument, the question being as to the existence of power to issue them, it is necessary to establish that the officers executing the bonds had lawful authority to make the recitals and to make them conclusive. The very ground of the estoppel is that the recitals are the official statements of those to whom the law refers the public for authentic and final information on the subject.[86]

It is not necessary that authority to determine the facts asserted in a recital be specifically conferred by statute; it may be conferred by necessary implication. Con-

---

[81]Gibbs v. School District, 50 N.W. 294 (Mich. 1891).

[82]Coler v. Dwight School Township, 55 N.W. 587 (N.D. 1893).

[83]Flagg v. School District No. 70, 58 N.W. 499 (N.D. 1894).

[84]*Black's Law Dictionary* (St. Paul, Minn.: West Publishing Co., 1951), p. 648.

[85]Dixon County v. Field, 111 U.S. 83, 4 S.Ct. 315, 28 L.Ed. 360 (Neb. 1884); National Life Insurance Co. v. Board of Education, 62 Fed. 778 (8th Cir. 1894); Coler v. Dwight School Township, 55 N.W. 587 (N.D. 1893); Thornburg v. School District No. 3, 75 S.W. 81 (Mo. 1903).

[86]Dixon County v. Field, 111 U.S. 83, 4 S.Ct. 315, 28 L.Ed. 360 (Neb. 1884).

sequently, a purchaser of school bonds must ascertain that a recital contained in a school bond has been made by one authorized either expressly or by necessary implication to determine that all requirements have been met concerning the issuance of the bonds. The rule on the content of the recital is that it need not be exhaustive; a general statement that all things required by law to be done have been done is sufficient if it is made by one authorized to so determine.[87]

Clearly, the protection afforded a purchaser of school bonds by the doctrine of estoppel is not complete. It does not apply where a school district is completely lacking in authority to issue bonds.[88] Those who purchase school bonds are expected to have knowledge of the district's authority or lack of authority to issue them, for "every man is charged with notice of that which the law requires him to know, and that which, after being put upon inquiry, he might have ascertained by the exercise of reasonable diligence."[89] A recital in a school bond to the effect that the bond is issued in conformity to the statutes cannot validate the bond when, in fact, no authority for its issuance exists.[90] It has been held,[91] for example, that where a county issued bonds only six months after its creation, rather than waiting until twelve months had elapsed as required by the statutes, a recital in the bonds that all things had been done as required by law could not render the bonds valid because a purchaser was bound to know that the county had no authority to issue them. Bonds containing a recital that they were being issued pursuant to the authority of a named statute have been invalidated where the named statute conferred no such authority.[92] Bonds issued under the authority of an unconstitutional statute also have been invalidated in spite of a recital they contained.[93] Thus, a district cannot be estopped from asserting its total lack of authority to

issue bonds,[94] nor can it be estopped by recitals in bonds when the bonds show upon their face that they were issued without authority or for an unauthorized purpose.[95] Even the fact that a school district has paid interest on bonds does not estop it from denying their validity where the bonds were void for want of authority and the district did not have full knowledge of the facts surrounding their sale.[96]

Although bonds issued in excess of a constitutional or statutory debt limit usually are void, there is general agreement that, where a recital states that the bonds are not in excess of the district's debt limit and do not show on their face the total indebtedness or the total issue in question, the district is bound by them, especially if the recital is made by one authorized to determine whether the debt limit would be exceeded.[97] Where the recital does not specifically state that the issue is not in excess of the district's debt limit, the purchaser is bound to ascertain that the district's debt limit was not exceeded and the recital could not be relied upon.[98]

8.2k Redemption of

When a school district issues bonds, it enters into a contract promising to pay principal and interest to bondholders at specified dates until the debt is retired. Under this contract the district is obligated to provide the funds necessary to make principal and interest payments as they become due. Payments may be made either from special funds earmarked for the purpose or from the general revenue of the district. Where principal and interest payments are made from funds earmarked specifically therefor, the money in such funds may not be diverted to any other purpose. Likewise, funds ear-

[87]Town of Coloma v. Eaves, 92 U.S. 484, 23 L.Ed. 579 (Ill. 1875); Township of Bernards v. Morrison, 133 U.S. 523, 10 S.Ct. 333, 33 L.Ed. 726 (N.J. 1890); Coler v. Dwight School Township, 55 N.W. 587 (N.D. 1893).

[88]Dixon County v. Field, 111 U.S. 83, 4 S.Ct. 315, 28 L.Ed. 360 (Neb. 1884); National Life Insurance Co. v. Board of Education, 62 Fed. 778 (8th Cir. 1894).

[89]Livingston v. School District No. 7, 69 N.W. 15 (S.D. 1896).

[90]First Trust Co. of St. Paul v. County Board of Education, 78 F.2d 114 (6th Cir. 1935).

[91]Coffin v. Board of Commissioners of Kearny County, 57 Fed. 137 (8th Cir. 1893).

[92]Read v. Abe Rosenblum & Sons, 58 N.E.2d 376 (Ind. 1944).

[93]Town of South Ottawa v. Perkins, 94 U.S. 260, 24 L.Ed. 154 (Ill. 1876).

[94]Dixon County v. Field, 111 U.S. 83, 4 S.Ct. 315, 28 L.Ed. 360 (Neb. 1884); Nesbit v. Riverside Independent District, 144 U.S. 610, 12 S.Ct. 746, 36 L.Ed. 562 (Iowa 1892); State v. School District No. 50, 120 N.W. 555 (N.D. 1909); Board of Education v. Blodgett, 40 N.E. 1025 (Ill. 1895); Livingston v. School District No. 7, 69 N.W. 15 (S.D. 1896).

[95]State v. School District No. 4, 20 N.W. 209 (Neb. 1884).

[96]Ashuelot National Bank v. School District No. 7, 56 Fed. 197 (8th Cir. 1893).

[97]Chaffee County v. Potter, 142 U.S. 355, 12 S.Ct. 216, 35 L.Ed. 1040 (Col. 1892); Sutliff v. Lake County Commissioners, 147 U.S. 230, 13 S.Ct. 318, 37 L.Ed. 145 (Col. 1893).

[98]School District v. Stone, 106 U.S. 183, 1 S.Ct. 84, 27 L.Ed. 90 (Iowa 1882); Dixon County v. Field, 111 U.S. 83, 4 S.Ct. 315, 28 L.Ed. 360 (Neb. 1884); Doon Township v. Cummins, 142 U.S. 366, 12 S.Ct. 220, 35 L.Ed. 1044 (Iowa 1892); First National Bank v. District Township of Doon, 53 N.W. 301 (Iowa 1892).

marked for other specific purposes cannot be used to pay principal and interest on school bonds.[99]

Where permitted to do so by constitutional or statutory provisions, a school district may, by agreement with the holder, "call" a bond, i.e., refund it rather than redeem it.[100] School bonds may not be called without the consent of the holder, however, unless a provision for calling them is contained either in the bonds themselves or in a statute.[101] Where bonds may be called, it has been held[102] that they may be called only when sufficient money for such purpose is available in an appropriate fund.

In some states the statutes provide for the establishment of a sinking fund for the redemption of school bonds as they mature. In general, money which has been placed in a sinking fund may be used only for such purposes as are permitted by statute.[103] It was held,[104] for example, that, where a de facto school district had issued bonds and deposited money in a sinking fund to redeem them, the accumulated fund could not be paid to the district legally organized to replace the de facto district but had to be used to redeem the bonds.

8.21 Rights of holders

In considering the rights enjoyed by holders of school bonds the fundamental principle to be recognized is that purchasers of school bonds are assumed to have knowledge of all statutory and constitutional requirements concerning their issuance. One who purchases school bonds is expected to determine whether the authority to issue the bonds exists, regardless of what recitals contained in the bonds may state.[105] As a general rule, school bonds which are issued without authority or for an unauthorized purpose, or which are in excess of statutory or constitutional debt limits, do not bind the district; no recovery

on them can be had even when they are held by innocent purchasers for value.[106]

A purchaser of school bonds is expected to note all recitals contained on the face of the bonds and all facts concerning the bonds which are a matter of public record; the purchaser is also charged with knowledge of the financial condition of the district insofar as it affects the validity of the bonds.[107] However, where a bond is regular on its face and the recitals contained thereon show compliance with the statutes under which it was issued, a purchaser may usually rely on its validity.[108] Inconsequential irregularities in the issuance of school bonds will not affect their validity in the hands of an innocent holder for value.[109] Furthermore, bonds issued by a de facto board of education are just as valid and binding in the hands of bona fide purchasers as are bonds issued by a de jure board.[110]

In most states the only way bondholders may be paid is by the levy and collection of a tax. It has been held[111] that a holder of school bonds may insist on the levy and collection of the amount of tax which was authorized at the time the bonds were sold. It is important to note in this regard that in the absence of a statute so providing, a bondholder cannot obtain a lien on the property of the district, nor can the district's property be sold to satisfy a judgment awarded to a bondholder.[112] Where a district whose organization is declared illegal is holding the proceeds of a bond issue, it has been held[113] that purchasers of the district's bonds are entitled to recover the price they paid for them. A bondholder's right to recover on the bonds held is not defeated by a change in the school district's boundaries,[114] nor is

[99]State v. Indian River County Board of Education, 125 So. 357 (Fla. 1929); First National Bank v. School District No. 64, 278 Ill.App. 190 (1934); McKinley v. Alamagordo Municipal School District Authority, 465 P.2d 79 (N.M. 1969).

[100]Wall v. Eudora Special School District, 154 S.W.2d 12 (Ark. 1941).

[101]Kansas City Life Insurance Co. v. Evangeline Parish School Board, 58 F.Supp. 39, affirmed, 153 F.2d 611 (La. 1944).

[102]School District No. 78 v. Miley, 220 Pac. 281 (Kan. 1923).

[103]State v. Lewis, 27 P.2d 250 (Kan. 1933).

[104]Hamilton v. San Diego County, 41 Pac. 305 (Cal. 1895).

[105]State v. School District No. 50, 120 N.W. 555 (N.D. 1909).

[106]Hewitt v. Board of Education, 94 Ill. 528 (1880); Board of Education v. Blodgett, 40 N.E. 1025 (Ill. 1895); First National Bank v. District Township of Doon, 53 N.W. 301 (Iowa 1892); State v. School District No. 50, 120 N.W. 555 (N.D. 1909).

[107]Board of Education v. McLean, 106 Fed. 817 (8th Cir. 1901); Nesbit v. Independent School District of Riverside, 25 Fed. 635, affirmed 144 U.S. 610, 12 S.Ct. 746, 36 L.Ed. 562 (Iowa 1885); Thornburg v. School District No. 3, 75 S.W. 81 (Mo. 1903).

[108]Grater v. Logan County High School District, 173 Pac. 714 (Col. 1918).

[109]Heard v. Calhoun School District, 45 Mo.App. 660 (1891).

[110]State v. School District No. 13, 14 N.W. 382 (Neb. 1882).

[111]State v. Boring, 164 So. 859 (Fla. 1935); Perry v. Cox, 112 S.E. 6 (N.C. 1922).

[112]Lincoln Park Board of Education v. Detroit Board of Education, 222 N.W. 763 (Mich. 1929).

[113]Calloway Bank v. Ellis, 238 S.W. 844 (Mo. 1922).

[114]Rapp v. Bethel-Tate Consolidated School District, 16 N.E.2d 224 (Ohio 1937); Ranier v. Board of Education, 273 S.W.2d 577 (Ky. 1954).

it defeated because proceeds from the bond issue were misapplied.[115]

Questions occasionally arise concerning the right of a bondholder to recover on invalid bonds. In general, where a school district's bonds are invalid and unenforceable, a purchaser may recover the money if it has not been spent or lost and if it can be identified.[116] Furthermore, if a school district has already purchased property with revenue derived from the sale of invalid bonds, the holder of the bonds is entitled to recover such property if it can be identified and retrieved without injuring property belonging to the district.[117] However, if the money can no longer be identified, or if the property purchased with proceeds of the bond issue cannot be retrieved without injuring the property or prejudicing the rights of the district, the bondholder is left without recourse against the district.[118]

The courts will not imply a contract and permit a bondholder to recover on *quantum meruit* on bonds which are absolutely void. Recovery on *quantum meruit* has occasionally been permitted on bonds which are void because of failure to comply with procedural requirements.[119]

8.3 SCHOOL DISTRICT WARRANTS AND NOTES

Some states authorize boards of education to issue school district warrants. A warrant differs substantially from a bond.

A "warrant" is ordinarily the command of one duly authorized officer to another, whose duty it is to obey, to pay from public funds a specified sum to a designated person whose claim therefor has been allowed by the proper authorizing official or body. It has not the attributes of commercial paper and is not negotiable, being subject to the defenses it would be subject to in the hands of the original payee.

A "bond" is an obligation in writing to pay a sum of money. It imports a promise to pay a sum of money at a future date specified and *commonly bears no specific designation of the party in whose favor it runs. They are treated as commercial paper and as such are negotiable.*

The chief distinction between "warrants" and "bonds" is that warrants are payable in order of presentation when funds are available, while bonds are general obligations payable at a definite time, running through a series of years and are payable independently of any presentation.[120]

A school district warrant is an order issued by a board of education which directs the custodian of school funds to pay to the holder of the warrant, from a specified fund, money which is or will become available. It should be emphasized that, in contrast to school district bonds, school district warrants are not negotiable instruments, although they generally may be transferred by assignment.[121] It has been said that a school district warrant is a nonnegotiable written contract for the payment of money.[122] The fact that school district warrants are not considered negotiable instruments under the terms of the Uniform Negotiable Instruments Acts is rather significant. It means that while the title of a payee of a school district warrant may be assigned to another person, the district retains all defenses against the invalidity of the warrant that it could have employed against the original payee if the warrant was invalid for some reason.[123] If warrants were negotiable instruments, any holder other than the original payee would be considered an "innocent" purchaser and the district would be obligated to pay regardless of whether the warrant was invalid. This point is illustrated by a case[124] in which a teacher was paid by a warrant which she sold to a local bank. It was later discovered that she did not hold a proper teaching certificate, and when the bank presented the warrant for payment the district refused to pay. In refus-

[115]Page v. Sanson, 192 S.E. 203 (Ga. 1937).

[116]Board of Trustees v. Postel, 88 S.W. 1065 (Ky. 1905).

[117]Parkersburg v. Brown, 106 U.S. 487, 1 S.Ct. 442, 27 L.Ed. 238 (W.Va. 1882); Board of Trustees v. Postel, 88 S.W. 1065 (Ky. 1905).

[118]Litchfield v. Ballou, 114 U.S. 190, 5 S.Ct. 820, 29 L.Ed. 132 (Ill. 1885); Board of Trustees v. Postel, 88 S.W. 1065 (Ky. 1905); Powell v. Bainbridge State Bank, 132 S.E. 60 (Ga. 1926); Strickler v. Consolidated School District No. 1, 291 S.W. 136 (Mo. 1927).

[119]Geer v. School District No. 11, 111 Fed. 682 (8th Cir. 1901); Livingston v. School District, 76 N.W. 301 (S.D. 1898).

[120]County Board of Education v. Taxpayers and Citizens, 163 So.2d 629 (Ala. 1964).

[121]School District No. 9 v. First National Bank, 118 P.2d 78 (Ariz. 1941); School District 47 Joint v. United States National Bank, 211 P.2d 273 (Ore. 1949); First National Bank v. Consolidated School District No. 28, 240 N.W. 662 (Minn. 1932).

[122]Waverly Consolidated School District No. 1 v. Young, 253 N.W. 480 (S.D. 1934).

[123]Goose River Bank v. Willow Lake School Township, 44 N.W. 1002 (N.D. 1890); First Bank and Trust v. Dumas Independent School District, 527 S.W.2d 499 (Tex. 1975).

[124]Goose River Bank v. Willow Lake School Township, 44 N.W. 1002 (N.D. 1890).

ing to permit the bank to recover, the court stated:

> The plaintiff cannot claim protection as an innocent purchaser for value. That such instruments are not negotiable in the sense that their negotiation will cut off all defenses is the voice of all the decisions. . . . The purchaser buys at his peril.

Whereas indebtedness is generally incurred when school bonds are issued, school district warrants are likely to be issued after a debt has been incurred as a means of satisfying the obligation. Warrants are usually issued in payment of general school debts and expenses. In some states, however, warrants may be issued to borrow money and thus create a debt.[125]

As in the case of school bonds, a school district has no inherent power to issue warrants and may issue them only when it has been granted express or implied statutory authorization to do so.[126] Not only must statutory authority to issue warrants exist, but the warrant must follow the form prescribed by statute, must bear the required signatures, must specifically identify the school district on which it was issued, and must show on its face the purpose for which it was drawn.[127] It generally has been held that minor irregularities in the issuance of a school district warrant will not affect its validity and that such irregularities may be cured by ratification.[128] It should be emphasized, however, that to be valid, a school warrant must be authorized properly and it must be issued in payment of a valid debt.[129]

It is not necessary that money be on hand to pay for warrants at the time they are issued unless this is required by statute. Where a warrant is drawn against a tax levy, it is not necessary that the taxes be collected prior to its issuance. Under some statutes it is permissible to issue warrants in anticipation of funds to be raised.[130]

It is worth reemphasizing that one who purchases school district warrants takes them subject to all defects and defenses regarding their validity.[131] Whether the warrants are in the hands of the original payee or of one who has purchased them from a previous holder matters not. As a rule, the fact that a warrant appears to be regular on its face constitutes prima facie evidence of its validity. Such a warrant will be presumed to be issued legally unless evidence to the contrary is presented.[132] However, the presumption of validity is not conclusive and evidence may be presented by the district to show that it is invalid.[133]

School district warrants may contain recitals attesting to their validity. It has been held[134] that the recitals are binding on the issuing authorities and may be relied upon by bona fide purchasers. Unless they have expressly agreed to be individually liable, school officers who issue invalid warrants will not be held personally liable for the instrument, since the purchaser is expected to know the limit of the school board's authority.[135]

If a warrant does not specify the time when payment is due, it ordinarily is payable on demand regardless of how long it may have been outstanding.[136] School district warrants usually may be paid only out of the fund established for the purpose for which the warrant was issued. Thus, it was held[137] that, where a warrant was given for general school purposes but drawn against a special fund whose use was restricted to a particular purpose, the warrant could not be

[125]McBee v. School District No. 48 of Clackamus County, 96 P.2d 207 (Ore. 1939); State v. Board of Public Instruction, 164 So.2d 6 (Fla. 1964).

[126]Vanzandt v. Town of Braxton, 14 So.2d 222 (Miss. 1943).

[127]Clark v. School District No. 1, 78 Ill. 474 (1875); Brashears v. State, 160 S.W.2d 505 (Ark. 1942); Kane v. Calhoun School District, 48 Mo.App. 408 (1892); Glidden v. Hopkins, 47 Ill. 525 (1862).

[128]School District No. 3 v. Western Tube Co., 38 Pac. 922 (Wyo. 1895); Gray v. Board of School Inspectors, 83 N.E. 95 (Ill. 1907); School District No. 9 v. First National Bank, 118 P.2d 78 (Ariz. 1941).

[129]Board of Public Instruction v. Lexington Co., 90 F.2d 83 (5th Cir. 1937); Pratt v. Board of Education, 63 N.E.2d 275 (Ill. 1945); Isley v. School District No. 2, 305 P.2d 432 (Ariz. 1956).

[130]Savage v. Board of Public Instruction, 133 So. 341 (Fla. 1931).

[131]Kellogg v. School District No. 10, 74 Pac. 110 (Okla. 1903); Goose River Bank v. Willow Lake School Township, 44 N.W. 1002 (N.D. 1890); School District No. 9 v. First National Bank, 118 P.2d 78 (Ariz. 1941); First National Bank v. Whisenhunt, 127 S.W. 968 (Ark. 1910).

[132]Meyer v. School District No. 31, 57 N.W. 68 (S.D. 1893).

[133]Ibid.; Axt v. Jackson School Township, 90 Ind. 101 (1883).

[134]Board of Public Instruction v. Lexington Co., 90 F.2d 83 (5th Cir. 1937).

[135]Oppenheimer v. Greencastle School Township, 72 N.E. 1100 (Ind. 1905); Germania Bank v. Trapnell, 45 S.E. 446 (Ga. 1903); First National Bank v. Whisenhunt, 127 S.W. 968 (Ark. 1910).

[136]Bernstein v. School Directors, 49 N.E.2d 314 (Ill. 1943); First National Bank v. Consolidated School District No. 28, 240 N.W. 662 (Minn. 1932); Dubard v. Nevin, 10 S.W.2d 875 (Ark. 1928).

[137]Merritt v. M. W. Elkins Investment Co., 65 S.W.2d 15 (Ark. 1933).

paid from such a fund but had to be paid from general funds.

School district warrants customarily bear no interest until after they have been presented for payment and payment has been refused.[138] It should be noted, however, that in some jurisdictions they may draw no interest; in others they may not draw interest in excess of the legal rate in that state.

8.4 TAX ANTICIPATION WARRANTS

A tax anticipation warrant differs from the usual school district warrant in that it directs the custodian or collector of tax money to pay the holder of the warrant out of the funds which will be collected from the anticipated tax levy. A school district may not issue tax anticipation warrants unless it has been given statutory authority to do so.[139] It has been held[140] that a tax anticipation warrant does not create a debt or obligation on the part of the issuing district. In effect, such a warrant is an assignment of the tax money and creates no liability on the part of the school district to pay the warrant if it cannot be paid from the revenue derived from the tax levy. The warrant is payable solely from taxes collected from the levy against which it is issued. If the total amount of warrants presented for payment exceeds the amount of tax which has been collected, the available tax money must be prorated among all the warrants.[141]

8.5 SHORT-TERM LOANS

School districts are often confronted with the necessity of obtaining money to finance their day-to-day operation for a short period of time, particularly if they maintain only a small cash operating balance. The district may have to borrow money on a short-term basis to tide it over the period between the time a tax is levied and the time it is collected, or to obtain cash to meet a sudden and unexpected emergency. In such instances the authority of a district to borrow money on promissory notes is likely to be called into question.

A school district has no authority to issue bills or notes unless such authority is granted it by statute either expressly or by

necessary implication.[142] As is true of other financial instruments, bills and notes may be issued only for authorized purposes, and all constitutional and statutory requirements concerning their issuance must be observed. Notes issued without authority or for an unauthorized purpose are void and create no liability on the part of the district.[143] It has been held,[144] for example, that if the statutes require approval by the voters at an election, a loan made by a board of education without securing that approval is invalid.

In that they may be assigned to another person by the original holder, school district notes are similar to school district warrants. They are also similar to warrants in that they are not negotiable within the definition of Uniform Negotiable Instruments laws, and the assignee takes school district notes subject to all the defenses which the district may assert against the original holder concerning invalid notes.[145] Where an officer of the school board is authorized by statute to execute short-term notes on behalf of the district, such notes are binding upon the district, and the officer is not personally liable for them.[146]

The security afforded holders of school district notes generally depends upon the statutes. It is common for statutes to provide that a school district may incur short-term obligations only up to some prescribed percentage of its tax levy or anticipated revenue for the year. The taxes levied by the district or other income which it receives constitutes the security for the loan; in fact, some statutes provide that taxes levied by a school district are to be dedicated to repaying such a loan. Money in other funds, such as a building fund, cannot be used to retire short-term obligations without specific statutory authorization.[147] Nevertheless, in at least one case[148] a school district was permitted to use surplus or uncommitted funds to retire its short-term obligations. Under some statutes a person holding a

[138]Wright v. Board of Public Instruction, 77 So.2d 435 (Fla. 1955); Robertson v. Town of Englewood, 123 S.W.2d 1090 (Tenn. 1939).
[139]Pratt v. Board of Education, 63 N.E.2d 275 (Ill. 1945).
[140]Schreiner v. City of Chicago, 92 N.E.2d 133 (Ill. 1950).
[141]Union Trust Co. v. Board of Education, 66 F.Supp. 88 (Ill. 1937).

[142]Board of Public Instruction v. Barefoot, 193 So. 823 (Fla. 1939); Peers v. Madison County Board of Education, 72 Ill. 508 (1874).
[143]Board of Education v. Franklin, 49 S.E.2d 804 (Ga. 1948); Jasper School District v. Gormley, 196 S.E. 232 (Ga. 1938).
[144]Arkansas National Bank v. School District No. 99, 238 S.W. 630 (Ark. 1922).
[145]Stanton v. Shipley, 27 Fed. 498 (7th Cir. 1886).
[146]State v. Helms, 35 N.E. 893 (Ind. 1893).
[147]Felts v. Cherry Hill School District No. 10, 68 S.W.2d 467 (Ark. 1934); In re Stevenson's Estate, 47 N.E.2d 531 (Ill. 1943).
[148]State v. Consolidated School District No. 5, 233 S.W.2d 702 (Mo. 1950).

school district's note may sue the district and obtain a judgment against it if payment thereof is unreasonably delayed. More commonly, however, if a loan is secured only by a tax levy, which fails to yield sufficient money to repay the loan, the lender has no further recourse against the district.

8.6 LIMITATIONS ON SCHOOL DISTRICT INDEBTEDNESS

All states have established some type of limitation on the indebtedness which may be incurred by school districts. These limitations take a variety of forms, but regardless of their nature a school district may not incur indebtedness in excess of the prescribed limit. It matters not how pressing the need, or how convinced school officials are that exceeding the prescribed debt limit is justified; under no conditions do they have authority to exceed debt limitations.[149]

8.6a Types of

The most common type of debt limitation imposed upon school districts is one which directs that the aggregate indebtedness of the district shall not exceed a specified percentage of the value of the taxable property in the district. It has been held that limitations of this type are to be construed strictly and any doubt as to the authority of a school district to incur the indebtedness in question must be resolved against the district.[150] The Supreme Court of Montana has stated the rule as follows:

> The argument of need, necessity, hardship or inconvenience, cannot avail in the interpretation of the constitutional mandate relative to the limitations placed upon the power of school districts to contract indebtedness. The rule of strict construction must be applied, and any doubt of such power must be resolved against it. . . .
>
> It is also crystal clear that there is no provision in the Constitution authorizing the legislature in regard to school districts to extend the limit therein fixed. . . . The constitutional provision curbs equally the power of the legislature, the officials and the people themselves, and was designed to protect the taxpayer from the folly and improvidence of either, or of all combined.[151]

Questions have been raised concerning the property to be included when comput-

ing the valuation of property in the district for debt limit purposes. All property in the district, it would appear, except that which is exempt from taxation should be taken into consideration when determining the valuation of the district.[152] Although the types of property which may be included in determining the total valuation of the district will vary according to the property tax laws of the respective states, it has been held[153] that money and credits may properly be included in computing the district's valuation, as can the value of lands held by the state which are subject to redemption by the owners. Concerning the point in time at which the district's valuation is to be computed to determine the limit of the indebtedness it can incur, it has generally been held[154] that the assessment of property immediately preceding the issuance and sale of bonds is to be used.

A second type of limitation specifies that during any one year a school district may not incur indebtedness in excess of the income or revenue which will be available to it during that year. Thus a school district is prohibited from incurring debts which will be payable out of anticipated revenues from future years.[155] Restrictions of this type do not, however, require the funds actually to be on hand at the time indebtedness is incurred; it is sufficient if the income is provided within the year in which the debt is incurred.[156] Where such limitations are in effect, a district is permitted to anticipate its current revenue, and the fact that the amount of revenue which is realized is less than the amount anticipated will not violate the limitation so long as the estimated revenue is within the amount which might reasonably have been anticipated.[157]

Another type of limitation on school district indebtedness is found in statutes or constitutional provisions which limit indebtedness to an amount not exceeding the

---

[149]Riesen v. School District, 212 N.W. 783 (Wis. 1927); Farbo v. School District No. 1, 28 P.2d 455 (Mont. 1933); Green v. Mail, 200 N.E. 604 (Ill. 1936).

[150]Rankin v. Love, 232 P.2d 998 (Mont. 1951); Miles v. State, 101 S.E.2d 173 (Ga. 1957).

[151]Rankin v. Love, 232 P.2d 998 (Mont. 1951).

[152]State v. Hackmann, 241 S.W. 913 (Mo. 1922); Williams v. School District No. 32, 102 P.2d 48 (Wyo. 1940).

[153]Farrar v. Britton Independent School District, 32 N.W.2d 627 (S.D. 1948); State v. Barker, 167 So. 16 (Fla. 1936).

[154]Sutherland v. School District of Corbin, 272 S.W. 887 (Ky. 1925); Mistler v. Eye, 231 Pac. 1045 (Okla. 1924); Hebel v. School District, 279 P.2d 673 (Col. 1955).

[155]Consolidated School District v. Panther Oil and Grease Mfg. Co., 168 P.2d 613 (Okla. 1946); First National Bank of Stoutland v. Stoutland School District, 319 S.W.2d 570 (Mo. 1958); National Surety Corporation v. Friendswood Independent School District, 433 S.W.2d 690 (Tex. 1968).

[156]Wyckoff v. Force, 214 Pac. 489 (Cal. 1923).

[157]Fiscal Court v. Lincoln County Board of Education, 115 S.W.2d 891 (Ky. 1937); First National Bank of Stoutland v. Stoutland School District, 319 S.W.2d 570 (Mo. 1958).

budget adopted for a given year, or to the amount appropriated for a particular purpose. In a further variation indebtedness is limited to a designated percentage of the estimated revenue for a given year. Where such limitations exist it has been held[158] that any act on the part of school authorities increasing the amount of indebtedness beyond what is permitted is void. Occasionally limitations are phrased so as to permit a district to exceed the specified limit of indebtedness in the event of an emergency. The question of what constitutes an emergency sufficient to justify exceeding the limitation has not been answered satisfactorily, although it has been decided that a strike of professional employees which results in complete closing of the schools meets the definition of an emergency under such a statute.[159]

8.6b Computation of indebtedness

It is necessary to refer to constitutional and statutory provisions of the state in question, as well as to court decisions interpreting these provisions, to ascertain the procedure to be followed in computing the indebtedness of a school district. In determining whether the indebtedness limit of a school district has been reached or exceeded the courts generally hold that the limitation is upon net indebtedness, not gross indebtedness.

Gross indebtedness includes all valid obligations which a district may be called upon to pay.[160] Thus, it includes any liability which may become a legal obligation of the district. Among the liabilities to be included in computing gross indebtedness are bonds,[161] promissory notes,[162] outstanding warrants,[163] (although warrants issued in anticipation of tax levies already made may be excluded[164]), special assessments against

real estate owned by the district,[165] funds set aside for a special purpose which have been advanced to pay other obligations,[166] and any other money owed by the district.

Net indebtedness is computed by deducting from the gross indebtedness of the district any assets it holds, such as funds in the district's treasury which are available for the payment of liabilities,[167] cash on hand,[168] taxes which have been levied but not collected[169] (unless there is evidence showing that current expenses will consume such taxes[170]), money due from another district,[171] the value of property which the school district has authority to sell,[172] money in a sinking fund which is available to reduce indebtedness,[173] and any other assets of the district which are available to pay indebtedness.

Where a district's existing debt will be discharged prior to the time that new bonds are issued, the debt existing at the time the new bonds were authorized is not to be included in determining whether or not the district has exceeded its debt limit.[174] It also has been held[175] that annual lease payments required under the terms of a long-term lease are to be considered as ordinary expenses, not as a "debt" within the meaning of a constitutional debt limitation.

There is some disagreement as to whether delinquent taxes should be included as assets. Although it has been held[176] that delinquent taxes should be considered as as-

---

[158]Eason v. Hardin County Board of Education, 172 S.W.2d 816 (Tenn. 1943).
[159]Coal Township School District v. Coal Township Taxpayers Association, 59 Pa. Dist. & Co. 665 (1947).
[160]Jones v. Brightwood Independent School District No. 1, 247 N.W. 884 (N.D. 1933); Kansas City Southern Railway Co. v. Board of Education, 13 P.2d 115 (Okla. 1932).
[161]Mannsville Consolidated School District No. 7 v. Williamson, 49 P.2d 749 (Okla. 1935); School District No. 3 v. Western Tube Co., 38 Pac. 922 (Wyo. 1895).
[162]Rettinger v. School Board of City of Pittsburgh, 109 Atl. 782 (Pa. 1920).
[163]Mannsville Consolidated School District No. 7 v. Williamson, 49 P.2d 749 (Okla. 1935); Farbo v. School District No. 1, 28 P.2d 455 (Mont. 1933); Angola Brick & Tile Co. v. Millgrove School Township, 127 N.E. 855 (Ind. 1920).
[164]Jones v. Brightwood Independent School District No. 1, 247 N.W. 884 (N.D. 1933).

[165]Riesen v. School District, 212 N.W. 783 (Wis. 1927).
[166]Ibid.
[167]Jones v. Brightwood Independent School District No. 1, 247 N.W. 884 (N.D. 1933); Halldorson v. State School Construction Fund, 224 N.W.2d 814 (N.D. 1974).
[168]Ridgeland School District v. Biesmann, 21 N.W.2d 324 (S.D. 1946); School District No. 3 v. Western Tube Co., 38 Pac. 922 (Wyo. 1895).
[169]Jones v. Brightwood Independent School District No. 1, 247 N.W. 884 (N.D. 1933); Lollich v. Hot Springs Independent School District, 201 N.W. 354 (S.D. 1924); Edwards v. City of Clarksville, 133 S.E. 45 (Ga. 1926).
[170]Holst v. Consolidated Independent School District, 211 N.W. 398 (Iowa 1926).
[171]Dolan v. Lackawanna Township School District, 10 Pa. Dist. 694 (1901).
[172]Holst v. Consolidated Independent School District, 211 N.W. 398 (Iowa 1926).
[173]Mannsville Consolidated School District No. 7 v. Williamson, 49 P.2d 749 (Okla. 1935); Hendricks v. School District No. 1, 10 P.2d 970 (Wyo. 1932); Farrar v. Britton Independent School District, 32 N.W.2d 627 (S.D. 1948); Halldorson v. State School Construction Fund, 224 N.W.2d 814 (N.D. 1974).
[174]Torres v. Laramie County School District No. 1, 506 P.2d 817 (Wyo. 1973).
[175]Teperick v. North Judson-San Pierre High School Building Corporation, 275 N.E.2d 814 (Ind. 1971).
[176]Ridgeland School District v. Biesmann, 21 N.W.2d 324 (S.D. 1946); Raynor v. King County, 97 P.2d 696 (Wash. 1940).

sets, it has also been decided[177] that delinquent taxes in the process of collection do not constitute assets.

In some jurisdictions current revenue and current expense are not included when computing school district indebtedness. In these jurisdictions cash on hand which is not in a sinking fund and taxes which have been or will be levied are assumed to offset current obligations and are not considered in computing net indebtedness.[178] Where this method is employed, it has been held[179] that a short-term loan taken by a school district for operating purposes is not an indebtedness within the constitutional limitation.

Two Districts in Same Territory

Sometimes an elementary school district and a high school district occupy the same territory. In this situation questions have arisen as to whether constitutional or statutory debt limitations contemplate the combined indebtedness of the districts or whether the debt limitation is to be applied separately to each district. Although there are some decisions to the contrary,[180] the weight of authority holds that only the indebtedness of the district involved should be considered when determining whether debt limitations have been exceeded.[181] It has been held[182] that since they are separate corporate entities, the limitations apply separately to a grade school district and a high school district occupying the same territory. Following this reasoning, where a school district occupies the same territory as another municipality, the debt limitations apply separately to each of them.[183]

Refunding Existing Obligations

Although there is some conflict among the courts on the matter, the general rule is that a school district does not create a new debt or increase its indebtedness when it refunds existing indebtedness.[184] It is reasoned in such cases that the refunding of the debt does not create a new debt but merely changes the form of a preexisting debt. Also, total indebtedness is not increased merely by exchanging old obligations for new ones.[185]

This situation is most likely to occur when bonds are called before their maturity date. It is sometimes expedient to refund existing bonds by exercising the option to call them and exchange them for new bonds which bear lower interest rates. At some point during such a transaction there is often an interval when the number of old and new bonds outstanding will exceed the debt limit. The net result of the total transaction, however, constitutes no change in the district's indebtedness position. Under the rule noted above, the transaction does not violate debt limitations.

Debts Imposed by Law

Constitutional and statutory limitations on school district indebtedness do not apply to obligations which are imposed upon a school district by law or against its will.[186] Accordingly, it was held[187] that a constitutional debt limit did not preclude the annexation of elementary school districts to a high school district, since any additional indebtedness resulting from the merger would be imposed by law rather than by the voluntary act of the district. It also was held[188] that judgments against a school district are not void if they create a debt in excess of the legal limit of indebtedness because the judgment is not itself a debt; it is simply a recognition of a preexisting debt. In at least one case,[189] however, it has been held that certain limitations im-

---

[177]Mannsville Consolidated School District No. 7 v. Williamson, 49 P.2d 749 (Okla. 1935); Farbo v. School District No. 1, 28 P.2d 455 (Mont. 1933).

[178]Kansas City Southern Railway Co. v. Board of Education, 13 P.2d 115 (Okla. 1932); Wyckoff v. Force, 214 Pac. 489 (Cal. 1923); Trepp v. Independent School District of Pocahontas, 240 N.W. 247 (Iowa 1932).

[179]School District No. 6 v. Marine National Exchange Bank, 101 N.W.2d 112 (Wis. 1960).

[180]Rankin v. Love, 232 P.2d 998 (Mont. 1951); Ericksen v. School District No. 2, 217 Pac. 887 (Wyo. 1950).

[181]City of Louisville v. Board of Education of Louisville, 195 S.W.2d 291 (Ky. 1946); Board of Education v. Upham, 191 N.E. 876 (Ill. 1934).

[182]Morgan v. Board of Supervisors, 192 P.2d 236 (Ariz. 1948); Straw v. Harris, 103 Pac. 777 (Ore. 1909).

[183]Hamrick v. Special Tax School District No. 1, 178 So. 406 (Fla. 1938); McLain v. Phelps, 100 N.E.2d 753 (Ill. 1951); Grey v. Vaigneur, 135 S.E.2d 229 (S.C. 1964).

[184]Board of Education of Town of Carmen v. James, 49 F.2d 91 (10th Cir. 1931); Eaton v. St. Louis-San Francisco Railway Co., 251 Pac. 1032 (Okla. 1925); School District No. 3 v. Western Tube Co., 38 Pac. 922 (Wyo. 1895); National Life Insurance Co. v. Mead, 82 N.W. 78 (S.D. 1900); State v. Board of Public Instruction, 164 So.2d 6 (Fla. 1964); Prohm v. Non-High School District, 130 N.E.2d 917 (Ill. 1955). *Contra*, Doon Township v. Cummins, 142 U.S. 366, 12 S.Ct. 220, 35 L.Ed. 1044 (Iowa 1892); State v. Ross, 86 Pac. 575 (Wash. 1906).

[185]Taylor v. School District of Garfield, 97 Fed. 753 (8th Cir. 1898).

[186]People v. San Bernardino High School District, 216 Pac. 959 (Cal. 1923); Bales v. Holt, 109 S.W.2d 632 (Ky. 1937); Wilson v. City of Hollis, 142 P.2d 633 (Okla. 1943); Edmundson v. Independent School District of Jackson, 67 N.W. 671 (Iowa 1896).

[187]People v. San Bernardino High School District, 216 Pac. 959 (Cal. 1923).

[188]Edmundson v. Independent School District of Jackson, 67 N.W. 671 (Iowa 1896).

[189]Eaton v. St. Louis-San Francisco Railway Co., 251 Pac. 1032 (Okla. 1925).

posed by law, e.g., the salaries of school district officers, are to be considered when determining whether constitutional debt limitations have been exceeded.

Future Payments

Must a contract obligating a school district to pay a yearly rental fee over a period of future years be included in its entirety in determining whether a debt limit has been exceeded? With regard to this question, it should be noted that the nature of a debt is determined by the terms of the contract under which the debt is created.[190] Thus, it has been held[191] that an executory contract calling for the performance of personal services which may or may not be performed does not constitute an indebtedness until the services have actually been performed. It has also been decided[192] that a contract does not violate debt limitations when it covers work to be performed in the future and paid for in installments, no one of which will exceed the funds available to the school district at the time it is due. According to the weight of authority, under a long-term contract calling for payments at specified intervals over a number of years the debt increases only as each installment becomes due, not in the aggregate amount of the contract.[193]

Occasionally a school district approaching its limit of indebtedness attempts to secure additional school facilities by entering into a contract for construction of a school building which calls for the contract price to be paid in installments over a period of years. It has been held[194] in such a situation that the full amount of the contract price must be considered in computing the district's indebtedness. Also, a building lease which provided for rental payments to be divided into a series of yearly installments, with ultimate conveyance of the building to the school district, was found invalid where it created a total debt in excess of the revenue provided for the year in question.[195] However, such a contract has been ruled valid where the lease was renewed from year to year with the district bound for only one year at a time.[196] A self-liquidating project, such as a building which is leased to a school district in return for annual rental payments, has been found not to increase the indebtedness of the district where the rental is payable solely from its current revenue.[197]

8.6c Effect of debt in excess of limitations

The general rule is that a contract of indebtedness which exceeds constitutional or statutory debt limitations is void.[198] It frequently has been held,[199] however, that such a contract is void only insofar as it exceeds the debt limit and is valid and enforceable up to the amount of the debt limitation. For example, the fact that a contractor's duty to perform is not severable has been found not to defeat the right to enforce a contract up to the debt limit of the district,[200] although it also has been held[201] that where the debt has not yet been incurred the entire obligation is void. It should be noted, too, that a bond issue which exceeded the constitutional debt limitation was determined to be indivisible so that no part of it was valid.[202]

Questions inevitably have arisen concerning the point in time when school bonds or other obligations constitute an indebtedness which must be counted in ascertaining whether a school district has exceeded its permissible limit of indebtedness. The weight of authority indicates that it is the amount of debt outstanding at the time the bonds are sold, not the amount outstanding

---

[190]Ohio National Life Insurance Co. v. Board of Education, 55 N.E.2d 163 (Ill. 1944); Jones v. Brightwood Independent School District No. 1, 247 N.W. 884 (N.D. 1933); Trepp v. Independent School District of Pocahontas, 240 N.W. 247 (Iowa 1932).

[191]Pullum v. Consolidated School District No. 5, 211 S.W.2d 30 (Mo. 1948).

[192]Posz v. Taylor, 215 Pac. 107 (Cal. 1923).

[193]Walla Walla v. Walla Walla Water Co., 172 U.S. 1, 19 S.Ct. 77, 43 L.Ed. 341 (Wash. 1898); Becker v. Albion-Jefferson School Corporation, 132 N.E.2d 269 (Ind. 1956); Wyckoff v. Force, 214 Pac. 489 (Cal. 1923). *Contra*, Fiscal Court v. Board of Education of Jackson County, 104 S.W.2d 1103 (Ky. 1937); Teperick v. North Judson–San Pierre High School Building Corporation, 275 N.E.2d 814 (Ind. 1971).

[194]McKinnon v. Mertz, 73 Atl. 1011 (Pa. 1909).

[195]Fiscal Court v. Board of Education of Jackson County, 104 S.W.2d 1103 (Ky. 1937).

[196]Scott County Board of Education v. McMillen, 109 S.W.2d 1201 (Ky. 1937).

[197]Greenhalgh v. Woolworth, 64 A.2d 659 (Pa. 1949).

[198]Ohio National Life Insurance Co. v. Board of Education, 55 N.E.2d 163 (Ill. 1944); Riesen v. School District, 212 N.W. 783 (Wis. 1927); Angola Brick & Tile Co. v. Millgrove School Township, 127 N.E. 855 (Ind. 1920); Coberly v. Gainer, 72 S.E. 790 (W.Va. 1911); Howard v. Trustees of School District No. 27, 102 S.W. 318 (Ky. 1907); National Surety Corporation v. Friendswood Independent School District, 433 S.W.2d 690 (Tex. 1968).

[199]Trepp v. Independent School District of Pocahontas, 240 N.W. 247 (Iowa 1932); McGillivray v. Joint School District, 88 N.W. 310 (Wis. 1901); People v. Peoria, etc., Railroad Co., 74 N.E. 734 (Ill. 1905); Stockdale v. School District No. 2, 10 N.W. 349 (Mich. 1881).

[200]McGillivray v. Joint School District, 88 N.W. 310 (Wis. 1901).

[201]State v. Clausen, 119 Pac. 797 (Wash. 1911).

[202]Kansas City Southern Railway Co. v. Board of Education, 13 P.2d 115 (Okla. 1932).

at the time they are voted, which is to be considered.[203] In reaching this conclusion the courts have reasoned that there is no indebtedness actually incurred until the district has issued the bonds and received the money for them. It has been decided,[204] for example, that the computation of the amount of bonds a district may issue without exceeding its debt limit can be made as of the date the bonds are sold and delivered to purchasers. In at least one case, however, it was held[205] that the bonds which exceeded the constitutional debt limit at the time of the election authorizing their issuance were void despite the fact that at the time they were sold they did not exceed the debt limit.

8.7 SUMMARY

School districts have no inherent power to issue school bonds or other evidence of indebtedness; they have only such power in this regard as is granted them by the constitution and/or legislature of the state. Since statutes regarding school district indebtedness are strictly construed, it is of the utmost importance that their provisions be followed with care.

Unless the constitution or statutes of a state so require, the electors of a school district do not have to approve the issuance of school bonds. However, where it is provided that such approval must be obtained, bonds issued without securing the approval of the voters are void. The legal requirements governing a school bond election are substantially the same as those governing other school district elections. Bonds may be issued only for the purpose for which they were voted, but all the bonds authorized need not be issued at the same time.

School bonds generally are sold on the basis of competitive bids. A bid is simply an offer to buy at a specified price; when accepted, the bid and the acceptance constitute a binding contract. The purchaser is not entitled to receive school bonds until the agreed purchase price has actually been paid; it may be paid to the district's agent in the transaction, e.g., a financial institution.

One who purchases school bonds is assumed to know the law under which they are issued. If one neglects to inform oneself as to the law, or if one misjudges the authority of school officials, one does so at one's own peril should the bonds prove to be invalid.

School bonds issued in violation of constitutional or statutory requirements generally are invalid, although minor irregularities in their issuance usually will not invalidate them. The validity of school bonds may not be attacked collaterally; it must be attacked in a direct action. Where a failure to follow procedural requirements renders bonds invalid, the matter ordinarily may be cured by a ratification by the school district. A legislature may pass curative legislation to validate defective school bonds if the defect consists of something which the legislature could have authorized in the first place.

As a rule, a purchaser may rely on a recital attesting to the validity of school bonds *only* if the recital is made by an official authorized to ascertain that all constitutional and statutory requirements relative to their issuance have been met. A recital made by such an official, even if it is false, will usually estop the district from later denying the validity of the bonds. The doctrine of estoppel applies only to recitals made by an authorized person, not to recitals made by one unauthorized to make such determinations. Also, the doctrine does not apply where a school district is completely lacking in authority to issue bonds, regardless of what the recitals may state.

The general rule is that no recovery may be had on bonds invalid because they were issued without authority, or exceeding constitutional or statutory debt limits, even if they are held by innocent purchasers. However, the holder of an invalid bond may recover the money if it has not been spent and if it can be identified. Property purchased with the proceeds of the bond issue can also be recovered if such property can be retrieved without injuring the property or prejudicing the rights of the district.

In some states school districts are authorized to issue warrants. A warrant is an order issued by a school district (or its governing board) directing the custodian of the district's funds to pay to the holder of the warrant, from a specified fund, money which is or will become available. Although school district warrants may be assigned to another party by the original purchaser, they are not regarded as negotiable instruments, and subsequent holders take them subject to all defenses which the district could have asserted against the original holder should the warrants prove to be invalid. Warrants generally may be paid only from a fund established specifically for that

[203]Hebel v. School District, 279 P.2d 673 (Col. 1955); Sutherland v. Board of Education of Corbin, 272 S.W. 887 (Ky. 1925); Mistler v. Eye, 231 Pac. 1045 (Okla. 1924); Torres v. Laramie County School District No. 1, 506 P.2d 817 (Wyo. 1973).
[204]Hebel v. School District, 279 P.2d 673 (Col. 1955).
[205]State v. Holmes, 245 S.W.2d 882 (Mo. 1952).

purpose. In a few states school districts are permitted to issue tax anticipation warrants, which provide that the holder will be paid out of funds to be collected from a forthcoming tax levy.

School districts may negotiate short-term loans to obtain cash to meet emergency needs or to provide operating funds until the proceeds of a tax levy have been obtained only if they have been granted such authority either expressly or by necessary implication. Notes issued by a school district without this authority are void.

The amount of indebtedness a school district may incur commonly is limited by constitutional or statutory provisions. Such limitations are strictly construed. The most prevalent form of debt limitation is one which specifies that the aggregate indebtedness of a school district shall not exceed a certain percentage of the value of taxable property in the district. Because limitations on school district indebtedness vary greatly from state to state, one must consult the laws of the state and court decisions interpreting these laws to ascertain the procedure which is to be employed in computing a school district's indebtedness. Where a bond issue, or other contract of indebtedness, exceeds the debt limit of a school district, it has been held that the portion of the debt which does not exceed the debt limit is valid and the portion which exceeds the debt limit is void.

School Property

9.0 INTRODUCTION

The educational importance of a school district's physical plant is evident when one recognizes that the school plant is the largest piece of instructional equipment used. It can either hinder or facilitate the educational program and is first and foremost an educational tool.

The economic importance of a school district's physical plant also is readily apparent. The total investment in school property in the United States is well in excess of $100 billion. Thus, from both an educational and an economic viewpoint, the acquisition and management of school property is a major area of responsibility for school boards and school administrators.

9.1 OWNERSHIP OF SCHOOL PROPERTY

The principle that education is a responsibility of the state is the basic law relative to the ownership and control of school property. The overwhelming weight of authority clearly establishes that public school property is owned by the state, not by the local school district.[1] The ownership status of school property was concisely summarized by the Supreme Court of Illinois:

> The "property of the school district" is a phrase which is misleading. The district owns no property, all school facilities, such as grounds, buildings, equipment, etc., being in fact and law the property of the State and subject to the legislative will."[2]

Accordingly, it has been held that both school land[3] and school buildings[4] are the property of the state, or the people thereof.

9.1a School district as agency of the state

While a school district or board of education does not own school property in the sense of private or corporate ownership, title to school property frequently is held by an agency of the state such as a school district, board of education, or municipality. In holding title to school property, school officials or municipalities are serving as agents of the state.[5] It has been said,[6] for example, that public school officers are merely administrators of public school property, and that in holding public school property they act as trustees of the public for the sole purpose of promoting the education of the youth of the state.

Thus, where a statute allowed school directors to take property under a will or deed, when property was given to the school district it was held[7] that the school directors were acting only as agents to carry out the will of the testator or grantor of such property. As an agent of the state holding school property in a trusteeship capacity, neither a school district nor a board of education may acquire a vested interest in such property.[8] Furthermore, neither individual taxpayers nor voters have a proprietary interest or a vested right in public school property.[9]

9.1b Power of legislature

Since school property is owned by the state, it should be evident that the legislature may change trustees at its discretion.[10] Further, since local taxpayers and voters have no vested interest in public school property, the legislature is under no obligation to obtain the consent of the residents of a school district when the trustee is changed. Thus, it has been held[11] that the transfer of property from one school district to another does not deprive a school district or its inhabitants of property without due process of law. It also has been held[12] that

---

[1]People v. Deatherage, 81 N.E.2d 581 (Ill. 1948); School District of Oakland v. School District of Joplin, 102 S.W.2d 909 (Mo. 1937); McInnis v. Board of Education of Madison County, 135 So.2d 180 (Miss. 1961); Butler v. Compton Junior College District, 176 P.2d 417 (Cal. 1947); Young v. Board of Trustees of Broadwater County High School, 4 P.2d 725 (Mont. 1931); Board of Regents of Western Kentucky Normal School v. Engle, 5 S.W.2d 1062 (Ky. 1928); Yreka Union High School District v. Siskiyou Union High School District, 39 Cal.Rptr. 112 (1964).

[2]People v. Deatherage, 81 N.E.2d 581 (Ill. 1948).

[3]School District of Oakland v. School District of Joplin, 102 S.W.2d 909 (Mo. 1937); People v. Deatherage, 81 N.E.2d 581 (Ill. 1948).

[4]City of Grafton v. Otter Tail Power Co., 86 N.W.2d 197 (N.D. 1957); Low v. Blakeney, 85 N.E.2d 741 (Ill. 1949).

[5]McInnis v. Board of Education of Madison County, 135 So.2d 180 (Miss. 1961); State v. Board of Education of Cleveland City School District, 88 N.E.2d 808 (Ohio 1949); Young v. Board of Trustees of Broadwater County High School, 4 P.2d 725 (Mont. 1931).

[6]Love v. City of Dallas, 40 S.W.2d (Tex. 1931); State v. Board of Education of Cleveland City School District, 88 N.E.2d 808 (Ohio 1949); Seidel v. City of Seward, 133 N.W.2d 390 (Neb. 1965); State v. Besson, 266 A.2d 175 (N.J. 1970); United States v. Board of School Commissioners of City of Indianapolis, 368 F.Supp. 1191 (Ind. 1973).

[7]Carter Oil Co. v. Liggett, 21 N.E.2d 569 (Ill. 1939).

[8]State v. Tukey, 128 N.E. 689 (Ind. 1920).

[9]Gorrell v. Bevans, 179 Pac. 337 (Col. 1919); People v. Goodrich, 135 N.E.2d 610 (Ill. 1956).

[10]People v. Deatherage, 81 N.E.2d 581 (Ill. 1948); Hall v. City of Taft, 302 P.2d 574 (Cal. 1956); United States v. Board of School Commissioners of City of Indianapolis, 368 F.Supp. 1191 (Ind. 1973).

[11]Ross v. Adams Mill Rural School District, 149 N.E. 634 (Ohio 1925); Moses Lake School District No. 161 v. Big Bend Community College, 503 P.2d 86 (Wash. 1972).

[12]Love v. City of Dallas, 40 S.W.2d 20 (Tex. 1931); Pearson v. State, 19 S.W. 499 (Ark. 1892).

no contractual relationship exists between the state and a local school district which would protect the district's enjoyment of the school property to which it holds title. It has been said that "with or without the consent of the inhabitants of a school district, over their protests, even without notice or hearing, the State may take the school facilities in the district, without giving compensation therefor, and vest them in other districts or agencies."[13]

Let it be noted, however, that the power of a legislature in regard to public school property is not unlimited. A legislature is, of course, restricted by any limitations placed upon its power by the constitution. A legislature has also been said to have no power to devote public school property to any other purpose.[14] Moreover, where a legislative act constituted an absolute grant of land to a school corporation to be held in trust for the use of the school forever, the act was regarded as a contract and could not be revoked by a subsequent legislature.[15] Although its decision is not in accord with the weight of authority, a Texas court has held[16] that independent school districts in that state, although creatures of the state, are independent political entities and that their property is not state property.

9.2 ACQUISITION OF SCHOOL PROPERTY

In most states school districts and/or boards of education have been granted express statutory authority to acquire and hold property for public school purposes, but there is general agreement that even without statutory authority a board of education has implied power to acquire and hold school property.[17] Statutes which accord the authority to acquire and hold school property may also specify the manner in which school districts may acquire property and the purposes for which it may be used.[18]

School property may be acquired in several ways. Buildings and equipment, for example, are generally purchased through contracts based on competitive bids, although they may also be acquired through gift or bequest. School sites, on the other hand, are most frequently acquired through deed, bequest, gift, or condemnation.

9.3 SCHOOL SITES

A state legislature may itself purchase land for school sites,[19] or it may delegate to school districts or boards of education the power to purchase land for school purposes.[20] A specific grant of authority to buy school sites is not essential, however, since it has been held[21] that a grant of authority to construct school buildings necessarily implies the authority to purchase school sites. Furthermore, it has been held[22] that where a board of education has been granted authority to purchase land, it may do so for any school purpose, including sites for gymnasiums, playgrounds, and athletic fields. Such areas need not be adjacent to the land on which a school building is located. It has been decided,[23] for example, that a school board may buy land located two blocks away from the school building for use as an athletic field. Further, a statute authorizing a county board of education to acquire and hold title to all property which may be required for educational purposes authorizes the acquisition of land located outside the geographical limits of the district for use as a camp and recreation ground in conjunction with the school program.[24] On the other hand, according to an earlier decision,[25] authority to acquire land for school buildings, playgrounds, and the like does not authorize the purchase of land to be used in the teaching of agriculture. Likewise, in the absence of specific statutory authority, a school board cannot issue bonds to purchase land for a farm to be used for demonstration purposes.[26]

[13]People v. Deatherage, 81 N.E.2d 581 (Ill. 1948).

[14]Love v. City of Dallas, 40 S.W.2d 20 (Tex. 1931); San Francisco United School District v. City and County of San Francisco, 128 P.2d 696 (Cal. 1942).

[15]Franklin County Grammar School v. Bailey, 20 Atl. 820 (Vt. 1890).

[16]Port Arthur Independent School District v. City of Groves, 376 S.W.2d 330 (Tex. 1964).

[17]Orleans Parish School Board v. Brown, 154 So.2d 545 (La. 1963); Breeding v. Williams, 9 Tenn.App. 335 (1929); Hill v. Boston, 122 Mass. 344 (1877).

[18]Independent School District v. McClure, 113 N.W. 554 (Iowa 1907); McShann v. Richardson Independent School District, 341 S.W.2d 691 (Tex. 1960); Lincoln Parish School Board v. Ruston College, 162 So.2d 419 (La. 1964).

[19]Town of Atherton v. Superior Court, 324 P.2d 328 (Cal. 1958); Cain v. Lumsden, 204 S.W. 115 (Tex. 1918).

[20]Smith v. Maresh, 284 N.W. 390 (Iowa 1939); In re School District of Pittsburg, 244 A.2d 42 (Pa. 1968).

[21]State v. Board of Education, 76 S.E. 127 (W.Va. 1912); Sorenson v. Christiansen, 129 Pac. 577 (Wash. 1913); Board of Directors of Public Schools of Parish of Lincoln v. Ruston State Bank, 62 So. 492 (La. 1913).

[22]Sorenson v. Christiansen, 129 Pac. 577 (Wash. 1913); Trustees of Schools v. Sherman Heights Corp., 169 N.E.2d 800 (Ill. 1960); Reiger v. Board of Education, 122 N.E. 838 (Ill. 1919).

[23]Reiger v. Board of Education, 122 N.E. 838 (Ill. 1919).

[24]In re Board of Public Instruction of Alachua County, 35 So.2d 579 (Fla. 1948); See also Winslow Township v. Board of Education of City of Camden, 260 A.2d 529 (N.J. 1970).

[25]Board of Education of City of Nickerson v. Davis, 135 Pac. 604 (Kan. 1913).

[26]Hemler v. Richland Parish School Board, 76 So. 585 (La. 1917).

The authority to purchase school sites is, of course, restricted by any limitations on indebtedness which are imposed by statutes.[27] Thus, a school district may not exceed its statutory debt limit when purchasing land for a school site. In some states a further restriction is placed upon the authority of a school board to acquire sites: land cannot be purchased for school purposes except as directed by the voters of the district.[28]

9.3a Acquisition through condemnation

Most school sites are acquired by purchasing from the existing owner such land as is necessary to provide adequate space for the educational program. Occasionally, however, it is impossible to reach agreement on purchase terms, and a school district must acquire the necessary land through condemnation proceedings. The right of eminent domain, i.e., the right to take private land for a public use, with just compensation of the owner, is inherent in sovereignty. It is universally recognized that a state may exercise the power of eminent domain to acquire land for public uses. The United States Supreme Court has said, "The right of eminent domain, that is, the right to take private property for public uses, appertains to every independent government. It requires no constitutional recognition; it is an attribute of sovereignty."[29]

A local school district has no inherent right to exercise the power of eminent domain, i.e., to acquire property through condemnation. It may exercise such power only when it has expressly been granted the right to do so by statute.[30] While eminent domain may be exercised only to take land for a public purpose, the courts are in complete agreement that the taking of land for a public school site meets this criterion.[31] Courts have also upheld the exercise of eminent domain to acquire land for playgrounds,[32] athletic fields,[33] and gymnasium sites.[34] However, the courts have not permitted school districts to use the right of eminent domain in all situations. It has been held,[35] for example, that private land could not be taken through condemnation when the intended purpose was to erect a building which was to be used in large part to house the administrative offices of the district.

Amount and Location of Land

The amount of land which may be taken through condemnation is sometimes a subject of litigation. In some states the statutes specify the maximum amount of land which may be taken for a school site by condemnation. In a majority of cases it has been held[36] that such a statute does not limit the total size of the school sites but applies only to the amount of land which may be taken by condemnation. Where the statutes place no limit on the amount of land which may be taken through condemnation, the amount to be taken rests in the sound discretion of school officials; as a general rule, they may take whatever amount of land they consider necessary.[37] The determination by a board of education of the amount of land needed for school purposes will not be controlled by the courts unless discretion is abused. The rule followed by the courts in this regard has been put as follows:

Generally, the action of a public agency or a municipal corporation having the right of eminent domain in selecting land for a public use will not be controlled by the courts, except for a manifest abuse of discretion, violation of law, fraud, improper motives, or collusion. This court has frequently held that, in eminent domain proceedings, selections of land to be condemned by the proper public agency is conclusive in the absence of bad faith, or arbitrary, capricious, or fraudulent action.[38]

---

[27]Langford v. Odom, 81 So. 469 (Fla. 1919).

[28]Ladd v. School District No. 6, 97 N.W. 594 (Neb. 1903).

[29]Boom Co. v. Patterson, 98 U.S. 403, 25 L.Ed. 206 (Minn. 1878).

[30]State v. Stojack, 330 P.2d 567, 71 A.L.R.2d 1064 (Wash. 1958); Thompson v. Trustees of Schools, 218 Ill. 540 (1905); Lazarus v. Morris, 61 Atl. 815 (Pa. 1905); School District of Columbia v. Jones, 129 S.W. 705 (Mo. 1910).

[31]State v. Stojack, 330 P.2d 567, 71 A.L.R.2d 1064 (Wash. 1958); Long v. Fuller, 68 Pa. 170 (1871); Williams v. School District No. 6, 33 Vt. 271 (1860); Township Board of Education v. Hackmair, 48 Mo. 243 (1871); Richland School Township of Fulton County v. Overmeyer, 73 N.E. 811 (Ind. 1905).

[32]Board of Education of Orange County v. Forest, 130 S.E. 621 (N.C. 1925); Cousens v. School District, 67 Me. 280 (1877); Independent School District of Oakland v. Hewitt, 75 N.W. 497 (Iowa 1898).

[33]City of Binghamton v. Buono, 208 N.Y.S. 60 (1924); Board of Education of City of Minot v. Park District, 70 N.W.2d 899 (N.D. 1955); Wey v. Ben Avon Borough School District, 14 Pa. Dist. & Co. 690 (1930).

[34]Sorenson v. Christiansen, 129 Pac. 577 (Wash. 1913).

[35]Higginson v. Slattery, 99 N.E. 523 (Mass. 1912).

[36]State v. Stojack, 330 P.2d 567, 71 A.L.R.2d 1064 (Wash. 1958); Nelson v. School District No. 3, 164 Pac. 1075 (Kan. 1917); Bell's Committee v. Board of Education of Harrodsburg, 234 S.W. 311 (Ky. 1921). *Contra*, Schaefer v. School District No. 18, 141 P.2d 903 (Col. 1943).

[37]Board of Education of City of Minot v. Park District, 70 N.W.2d 899 (N.D. 1955); Spann v. Joint Board of School District of Darlington Township, 113 A.2d 281 (Pa. 1955); City of Waukegan v. Stanczak, 129 N.E.2d 751 (Ill. 1955); Williams v. School District No. 6, 33 Vt. 271 (1860).

[38]State v. Stojack, 330 P.2d 567, 71 A.L.R.2d 1064 (Wash. 1958); *accord*, Orleans Parish School Board v. Brown, 154 So.2d 545 (La. 1963).

The courts have usually recognized the right of school authorities to provide for future needs when taking land by condemnation and have given approval to taking an amount of land which is reasonably necessary for future expansion of school facilities.[39] However, the courts will not uphold the taking of land by condemnation where future plans are indefinite and future needs are vague.[40]

Not only may a board of education determine how much land is to be taken through condemnation; it may also determine the particular piece of property which is to be taken. The property to be condemned need not be contiguous to an existing school site. Where expressly authorized by statute, land beyond the corporate limits of the school district, and situated in a different district, may be condemned for school purposes.[41] The taking of improved city lots for school purposes by condemnation has also been upheld.[42]

A district which initiates condemnation proceedings may require that buildings on the property be left intact if they would serve the school district's interest. It has been held,[43] for example, that a property owner may not remove trees and fences on property which is the subject of a condemnation proceeding since they may be useful or necessary for a schoolhouse lot. Be it also noted that the power to condemn property for public school use is not exhausted by exercise. A school district may continue to exercise the right of eminent domain to enlarge an existing school site or to secure additional school sites.[44]

Compensation

The owner of property which is taken through condemnation proceedings is entitled to receive just compensation for the property. The taking of property without just compensation would violate constitutional provisions which forbid the taking of property without due process of law. The measure of the value of property taken through condemnation is the fair market value of that property based on the most profitable use to which it could be put at the date of its taking.[45] The fair market value of condemned property is that price which a willing buyer and a willing seller would agree upon, taking into consideration all uses to which the property may be put.[46]

Where only a portion of holdings are taken, the landowner is entitled to compensation for any depreciation in the value of the remaining property. The damage allowable in such cases is the difference between the market value of the property immediately before and immediately after its taking through condemnation.[47] Occasionally a district desires to take all but a small portion of a parcel of land. The remaining portion, because of its size or location, may be of little value to the original owner. In such cases the district may utilize "excess condemnation" and be permitted or required to take the entire property.[48]

Limitations on Power

Unless its taking is specifically authorized by statute, land which is being used for some other public purpose generally may not be taken for school purposes through condemnation on the basis that a particular location is usually not essential for school purposes. It has been held,[49] for example, that school authorities cannot acquire by eminent domain a public square. Following the same reasoning, school property may generally be taken by condemnation for some other public use which does require specific location. Thus, it has been held[50] that public school property may be taken by condemnation for highways, railroads, and the like. It would appear that, where two public bodies each desire the same property, the body having greatest necessity for that particular parcel of land will prevail.

The power to acquire land for school sites must be exercised in compliance with the

[39]Independent School District of Boise v. C. B. Lauch Construction Co., 264 P.2d 687 (Ida. 1953); City of Waukegan v. Stanczak, 129 N.E.2d 751 (Ill. 1955); State v. Stojack, 330 P.2d 567, 71 A.L.R.2d 1064 (Wash. 1958); Pike County Board of Education v. Ford, 279 S.W.2d 245 (Ky. 1955).

[40]Winger v. Aires, 89 A.2d 521 (Pa. 1952).

[41]Wey v. Ben Avon Borough School District, 14 Pa. Dist. & Co. 690 (1930); Norton Realty and Loan Co. v. Board of Education of Hall County, 200 S.E.2d 461 (Ga. 1973).

[42]Ferree v. Alleghany Sixth Ward School District, 76 Pa. 376 (1874).

[43]Eighth School District v. Copeland, 68 Mass. 414 (1854).

[44]Ferree v. Alleghany Sixth Ward School District, 76 Pa. 376 (1874); Board of Education of Wake County v. Pegram, 147 S.E. 622 (N.C. 1929).

[45]Orleans Parish School Board v. Brown, 154 So.2d 545 (La. 1963); Sargent v. Town of Merrimac, 81 N.E. 970 (Mass. 1907).

[46]Orleans Parish School Board v. Brown, 154 So.2d 545 (La. 1963).

[47]*Ibid.*

[48]Cincinnati v. Vester, 281 U.S. 439, 50 S.Ct. 360, 74 L.Ed. 950 (Ohio 1930).

[49]McCullough v. Board of Education of San Francisco, 51 Cal. 418 (1876).

[50]Easthampton v. Hampshire County Commissioners, 28 N.E. 298 (Mass. 1891); Rominger v. Simmons, 88 Ind. 453 (1882); State v. Ouachita Parish School Board, 138 So.2d 109 (La. 1961); Harrison County School Board v. State Highway Commission, 284 So.2d 50 (Miss. 1973).

statutes, and there must be at least substantial compliance with all statutory requirements concerning the acquisition of land for school purposes.[51] Thus, a statutory requirement that the owner must have either refused to sell or demanded an unreasonable price for the property has been held[52] to constitute a condition precedent to initiation of condemnation proceedings.

9.3b Acquisition through donation

It is an accepted principle of law that the owner of land may dedicate such land for public purposes and a school district or municipality may accept and hold in trust land which has been dedicated for public school use.[53] Such a dedication need not be in written form, for it has been held[54] that an express dedication may be made orally. Moreover, it is not necessary that there be in existence a corporation in which to vest title in order for a dedication of land for public school purposes to be made,[55] for "the public is an ever-existing grantee, capable of taking a dedication for public uses."[56] If necessary, a court of equity will appoint a trustee to hold property which has been dedicated for public school purposes.[57]

Land which has been dedicated for public school uses must be administered perpetually in accordance with the express wishes of the donor. It has been said that "the general rule of law is that money or property devoted to a charitable use where a trust is created must, if the gift is accepted, be irrevocably devoted to such use, and that in case of attempted diversion a court of equity will intervene, and if necessary name a new trustee to carry out the objects and purposes of the trust."[58]

A school district may also receive a gift of land for school purposes, since the term "purchase" has been said to include acquisition by gift.[59] It has been ruled[60] that stat-utes limiting the authority of a board of education to borrow money do not prevent the board from accepting as a gift the deed to a school site, even though it was alleged that the board had entered into an agreement to repay the citizen who made the gift.

9.3c Selection of

While the legislature itself may select the site of a school building,[61] in most states the legislature has chosen to delegate authority to select school sites either to local boards of education or to the electors in local school districts. Unless the statutes provide otherwise, it has generally been held that authority to select a school site rests with the board of education.[62] The discretion of the board of education in selecting school sites may be limited by statutory requirements concerning the location in which school buildings are to be placed. For example, the legislature may specify that a public school must be located on a public road or highway,[63] in a central location,[64] or at a location where the greatest number of pupils will be benefited.[65] Statutory limitations as to the location of school buildings may also be of a negative nature, such as a requirement that school buildings not be located within a certain distance of a railroad track.[66]

A board of education's discretion with regard to the selection of school sites may also be limited by the due process and equal protection clauses of the Fourteenth Amendment. School sites must be chosen so as to alleviate or prevent segregation of pupils on the basis of race.[67] It has been ruled[68] that all site selection and school construction in a school district must be done in a manner which will prevent recurrence of a dual

[51]Southworth v. Ogle County School District 131, 87 N.E. 403 (Ill. 1909); Application of Flinn, 154 N.Y.S.2d 124 (1956); Wayne Township School District v. Lantz, 13 Pa. Dist. & Co. 584 (1928).

[52]Harris v. Inhabitants of Marblehead, 76 Mass. 40 (1857); Detroit Board of Education v. Moross, 114 N.W. 75 (Mich. 1907).

[53]Vestal v. Pickering, 267 Pac. 821 (Ore. 1928).

[54]Hill v. Honk, 46 So. 562 (Ala. 1908).

[55]Bailey v. Kilburn, 10 Met. 176 (Mass. 1845); Board of Regents of Normal School District No. 3 v. Painter, 14 S.W. 938 (Mo. 1890).

[56]Board of Regents of Normal School District No. 3 v. Painter, 14 S.W. 938 (Mo. 1890).

[57]Bailey v. Kilburn, 10 Met. 176 (Mass. 1845).

[58]Maxcy v. City of Oshkosh, 128 N.W. 899 (Wis. 1910).

[59]Reiger v. Board of Education, 122 N.E. 838 (Ill. 1919); Ladd v. Higgins, 50 A.2d 89 (N.H. 1946).

[60]Crow v. Consolidated School District No. 7, 36 S.W.2d 676 (Mo. 1931).

[61]Attorney General v. Lowrey, 92 N.W. 289 (Mich. 1902).

[62]Bates v. Orr, 367 S.W.2d 122 (Ark. 1963); State v. Lally, 194 A.2d 252 (N.J. 1963); Ricker v. Board of Education, 396 P.2d 416 (Utah 1964); Board of Education of Blount County v. Phillips, 89 So.2d 96 (Ala. 1956); Painter v. Wake County Board of Education, 217 S.E.2d 650 (N.C. 1975).

[63]Salisbury v. Highland Township School District, 70 N.W. 706 (Iowa 1897).

[64]Hill v. Ralph, 265 S.W. 57 (Ark. 1924).

[65]State v. Smith, 254 S.W. 554 (Tenn. 1923).

[66]Temple v. State, 113 N.E. 233 (Ind. 1916).

[67]Swann v. Charlotte-Mecklenburg Board of Education, 402 U.S. 1, 91 S.Ct. 1267, 28 L.Ed.2d 554 (1971); Brewer v. School Board of City of Norfolk, 397 F.2d 37 (4th Cir. 1968); United States v. School District 151 of Cook County, 404 F.2d 1125 (7th Cir. 1968); Harris v. St. John the Baptist Parish School Board, 419 F.2d 1211 (5th Cir. 1969); United States v. Board of School Commissioners, 474 F.2d 81 (7th Cir. 1973); United States v. School District of Omaha, 521 F.2d 530 (8th Cir. 1975).

[68]Harris v. St. John the Baptist Parish School Board, 419 F.2d 1211 (5th Cir. 1969).

school system once a desegration plan is implemented. Questions concerning whether, where, and to what extent a public school should be built or improved are left primarily to the judgment and discretion of local school officials. Federal courts will not hesitate to interfere with the decisions of local school officials when it is clear that a particular project will work against the constitutional requirement of attaining or maintaining a racially nondiscriminatory school system.[69] A local school board has been found[70] to be guilty of de jure segregation where the board substantially contributed to the development or maintenance of segregation through its planning of school locations.

Power of the Electorate

Where authority to select school sites has been vested in the electors of a school district, their right to determine the location of a school must not be disregarded. Where such a requirement exists, it has been held[71] that a school site can be selected only by the voters at a regularly called meeting or election. The power vested in the voters to select a school site must be exercised in good faith and in the public interest.[72] Furthermore, the electorate may not delegate its authority to select school sites to the board of education.[73] In some jurisdictions statutes which vest school district electors with the power to select school sites have been construed to authorize the electors to select sites by general designation only, leaving the specific location of a school building on such designated land to be determined by the board of education.[74] In an Illinois case in which the voters were unable to decide on a school site, the district's board of education was allowed to participate in the selection of a site.[75]

There must be at least substantial compliance with all procedural requirements concerning district meetings or elections held for the purpose of selecting a school site.[76] It has been held,[77] for example, that failure to post notices as required by statute will invalidate an election.

Decisions by the courts concerning the propositions which may legitimately be combined with the question of purchasing a school site are difficult to harmonize. It has been held that an election to authorize the purchase of a public school site may be combined with an election to authorize the issuance of bonds to finance such a purchase,[78] and that an election to select a school site may be joined with an election to issue bonds for the purpose of building a schoolhouse thereon.[79] On the other hand, it has been held[80] that a proposition to authorize the purchase of a public school site may not be combined with one to erect a new school building or with the question of whether bonds should be issued to finance such a building.

Power of the Board of Education

In many states the legislature has vested authority to select school sites in the local board of education. Within such limitations as these statutes may impose, local boards of education may exercise a great deal of discretion in selecting locations for schools.[81] The courts will not interefere with a board's choice of school sites unless the board has clearly abused its discretion, violated the law, or been guilty of fraud or collusion.[82] The wisdom or expediency of

[69]Clark v. Board of Directors of Little Rock School District, 328 F.Supp. 1205 (Ark. 1971); Clark v. Board of Education of Little Rock School District, 449 F.2d 493 (8th Cir. 1971).

[70]Oliver v. Kalamazoo Board of Education, 346 F.Supp. 766 (Mich. 1972); affirmed Oliver v. School District of Kalamazoo County, 448 F.2d 635 (6th Cir. 1972). See also Oliver v. Kalamazoo Board of Education, 368 F.Supp. 143 (Mich. 1973) and United States v. School District of Omaha, 521 F.2d 530 (8th Cir. 1975).

[71]City of Waukegan v. Stanczak, 129 N.E.2d 751 (Ill. 1955); Nichols v. Ravallis County School District No. 3, 287 Pac. 624 (Mont. 1930).

[72]Iverson v. Union Free High School District, 202 N.W. 788 (Wis. 1925).

[73]Custer County School District No. 34 v. Stairs, 95 N.W. 492 (Neb. 1901).

[74]Petersburg School District v. Peterson, 103 N.W. 756 (N.D. 1905); Bates v. Orr, 367 S.W.2d 122 (Ark. 1963).

[75]Seely v. Green Valley Community High School District No. 306, 146 N.E. 187 (Ill. 1925).

[76]Application of Flinn, 154 N Y S 2d 124 (1956); Keime v. Community High School District No. 296, 180 N.E. 858 (Ill. 1932).

[77]Roberts v. Eyman, 136 N.E. 736 (Ill. 1922).

[78]Looney v. Consolidated Independent School District, 205 N.W. 328 (Iowa 1925).

[79]Matthews v. Rural High School District No. 5, 242 Pac. 1016 (Kan. 1926).

[80]O'Connor v. High School Board of Education, 123 N.E. 283 (Ill. 1919).

[81]Herr v. Board of Education of Newark, 83 Atl. 173 (N.J. 1912); Brown v. Hardin County Board of Education, 358 S.W.2d 488 (Ky. 1962); Board of Education of Blount County v. Phillips, 89 So.2d 96 (Ala. 1956); Painter v. Wake County Board of Education, 217 S.E.2d 650 (N.C. 1975).

[82]Sealy v. Department of Public Instruction of Pennsylvania, 159 F.Supp. 561 (Pa. 1957); Arthur v. Oceanside-Carlsbad Junior College District, 31 Cal.Rptr. 177 (1963); Brown v. Hardin County Board of Education, 358 S.W.2d 488 (Ky. 1962); Orleans Parish School Board v. Brown, 154 So.2d 545 (La. 1963); Gemmell v. Fox, 88 Atl. 426 (Pa. 1913); Pike Couny Board of Education v. Ford, 279 S.W.2d 245 (Ky. 1955); McInnish v. Board of Education of Hoke County, 122 S.E. 182 (N.C. 1924); Reams v. Board of Mayor and Aldermen, 284 S.W. 382 (Tenn. 1926).

the board's selection may not be challenged.[83] The courts recognize that it is virtually impossible to satisfy all constituents when school sites are selected and that it is seldom possible to locate schools so that they will be equally convenient to all pupils.[84] However, if it is apparent that a board of education has abused its discretion, has acted in bad faith, or has acted with fraudulent intent, the courts will not hesitate to interfere with the discretion of the board and, if necessary, enjoin its action.[85] Where authority to select school sites has been lodged with a board of education or some other designated body, that body cannot delegate to the voters its power to choose sites.[86]

It is difficult to determine when a board of education has abused its discretion in selecting a school site. It was held,[87] for example, that a board of education did not abuse its discretion despite the fact that a railroad track adjoined the site selected by the board, that an electric power line had been constructed over part of the site, and that a cotton gin was situated near the site. Similarly, it was held[88] that a school board did not abuse its discretion by selecting a site which was bounded on three sides by much-traveled roads, which was subject to an easement to maintain gas lines crossing it, and on which the right to enter and mine coal was reserved. On the other hand, where a taxpayer had offered to donate to the district a lot adjoining the existing school property and evidence showed that one additional schoolroom would meet the needs of the district for several years, it was held[89] to be an abuse of discretion for the board of education to attempt to purchase a site which would have required an expenditure of at least $5000 to protect the surface of the site.

The fact that a board of education has selected a given site does not prevent it from changing its mind and selecting some other site, assuming, of course, that no innocent third parties are injured by the change.[90] That is, a board of education, having exercised its discretion in selecting a school site, may, if it acts in good faith, change its mind and select another site since its discretion in the matter of selecting school sites is not exhausted by exercise. For example, a board of education which had selected a site for a school was allowed to rescind its action later and build the school on another site that had been donated to the district.[91]

School officials sometimes issue statements concerning the location at which a proposed school building will be constructed when campaigning for the approval of a school bond referendum. Under such circumstances questions occasionally arise concerning the extent to which a board of education may bargain away its discretion through promises or representations made to the public. The general rule is that a board of education's freedom to exercise discretion is not destroyed or limited by representations which it may make to the public.[92] The courts reason that a board of education which has been granted discretion to select sites for school buildings must always be free to act in what it considers the best interest of the district at the time the final action is taken. To illustrate, during a campaign for passage of a bond referendum the electorate was told that a new school building would be erected in one portion of the district, but the board of education later decided to build in another portion of the district. In holding that the board was not bound by any representations which might have been made relative to the location of the proposed school building, the court said:

> It would be contrary to public policy to allow public officers who are charged with the duty of exercising their judgment and discretion for the benefit of the whole district to bind or fetter themselves by promise or representation to individuals or to electors of a section of the district so that they could not, at all times, act freely and impartially for the benefit of the whole district. The power was conferred upon them for public purposes, and it could not be

[83]Arthur v. Oceanside-Carlsbad Junior College District, 31 Cal. Rptr. 177 (1963); Gemmell v. Fox, 88 Atl. 426 (Pa. 1913); Kramer v. Board of Education, 339 N.Y.S.2d 243 (1972).
[84]Cross v. Fisher, 177 S.W. 43 (Tenn. 1915).
[85]Wooley v. Spalding, 293 S.W.2d 563 (Ky. 1956); Gemmell v. Fox, 88 Atl. 426 (Pa. 1913); Iverson v. Union Free High School District, 202 N.W. 788 (Wis. 1925).
[86]Opinion of the Justices, 183 A.2d 909 (N.H. 1962); Sparks v. Cash, 88 S.E. 259 (S.C. 1916).
[87]McInnish v. Board of Education of Hoke County, 122 S.E. 182 (N.C. 1924).
[88]Gilfillan v. Fife, 109 Atl. 785 (Pa. 1920).
[89]Gemmell v. Fox, 88 Atl. 426 (Pa. 1913).

[90]Vaughan v. McCartney, 115 So. 30 (Ala. 1927); Parker v. Anson County, 74 S.E.2d 338 (N.C. 1953); Reams v. Board of Mayor and Aldermen, 284 S.W. 382 (Tenn. 1926); Bates v. Orr, 367 S.W.2d 122 (Ark. 1963).
[91]Vaughan v. McCartney, 115 So. 30 (Ala. 1927); Hasbrouck v. School Committee of Bristol, 128 Atl. 449 (R.I. 1925).
[92]Sarratt v. Cash, 88 S.E. 256 (S.C. 1916); Bates v. Orr, 367 S.W.2d 122 (Ark. 1963); Jennings v. Clearwater School District of Los Angeles County, 223 Pac. 84 (Cal. 1923); State v. Board of Education, 11 Ohio App. 146 (1919); Amity Township School District v. Daniel Boone Joint School System, 54 Berks. 215 (Pa. 1961).

lawfully bartered away to influence signatures to the petition or votes in the election. The electors are presumed to have known this. Therefore they had no legal right to rely upon the alleged representations, or to be influenced by them in signing the petition or in voting in the election.[93]

It also has been held[94] that, where several school districts had entered into an agreement that the site of a proposed school would be near the geographic center of a proposed consolidation, such an agreement was not mandatory and the school board did not abuse its discretion by later selecting a site 1.4 miles from the geographic center of the district. Likewise, it has been held[95] that acceptance by the electors of a proposition for consolidation of schools with the understanding that a new school plant was to be located on designated property on which an option had been taken did not obligate the board of education to locate new school facilities on that property and nowhere else. However, in at least one case it was held[96] that, where bonds were voted to erect a schoolhouse on a designated site, a board of education was without authority to erect the building on some other site.

9.3d Changing the location of

In some states a school site may be changed only when such a change is authorized by the electors of the district. In other jurisdictions authority to change the location of a school site is vested with the board of education. Where school officers are vested with authority to determine whether the location of a school should be changed, the decision rests within their sound discretion and the courts will not interfere unless the board has abused its discretion, violated the law, or been guilty of fraud, collusion, or misconduct.[97] Where a school board is vested with authority to change a school site, the fact that the existing site is located at the center of the district and that two-thirds of the patrons favor retaining the existing site has been ruled[98] not to prevent the board from relocating on another site. As is true in the initial selection of a site, there must be substantial compliance with any procedural require-

ments relative to changing a school site, e.g., approval by the electorate at an election held for that purpose.[99]

9.4 CONTROL AND MANAGEMENT OF SCHOOL PROPERTY

Since ownership of school property is vested in the state, it is clear that control of school property ultimately rests with the state. In most instances state legislatures have delegated authority to control school property to the local school district or to its board of education. However, any authority to control school property which a district or board of education possesses must be found in the state's statutes or in its constitution.

9.4a Care, maintenance, and repair

Although legally school property is state property, it usually is not feasible for the state to maintain such property and keep it in repair. State legislatures generally have delegated responsibility for the care, maintenance, and repair of public school buildings to local boards of education,[100] although responsibility may also be delegated to a municipality.[101] The powers and duties of school districts or boards of education relative to the maintenance and operation of school buildings are limited to those powers and duties created by statutes, either expressly or by implication.[102]

A duty imposed on school officials to preserve and care for the schoolhouse carries implied power to keep it in repair and to do all things which come within the scope of the term repair. It has been held[103] in this regard that repair means to restore to its previous state or condition after decay or injury. The authority to keep school buildings in proper repair does not convey the implied authority to remodel or improve them.[104] School authorities ordinarily have power to contract for repairs to school buildings,[105] but if they exceed their author-

---

[93]Sarratt v. Cash, 88 S.E. 256 (S.C. 1916).
[94]Amity Township School District v. Daniel Boone Joint School System, 54 Berks. 215 (Pa. 1961).
[95]Bates v. Orr, 367 S.W.2d 122 (Ark. 1963).
[96]Rodgers v. Independent School District of Colfax, 69 N.W. 544 (Iowa 1896).
[97]Venable v. School Committee, 62 S.E. 902 (N.C. 1908); Perry County Board of Education v. Deaton, 223 S.W.2d 882 (Ky. 1949).
[98]James v. Getturger, 98 N.W. 723 (Iowa 1904).

[99]Cunningham v. Ilg, 226 N.W. 333 (Neb. 1929); Willan v. Richardson, 98 N.E. 1094 (Ind. 1912); Routson v. Slater, 202 Ill.App. 487 (1916); Calkins v. Rice, 136 N.W. 481 (Mich. 1912).
[100]Murphy v. Duffy, 124 Atl. 103 (R.I. 1924); Molinari v. City of Boston, 130 N.E.2d 925 (Mass. 1955).
[101]Johnson v. City of Sheffield, 183 So. 265 (Ala. 1938).
[102]School Town of Milltown v. Adams, 65 N.E.2d 635 (Ind. 1946); Manders v. Consolidated Independent School District of Community Center, 43 N.W.2d 714 (Iowa 1950); Commonwealth v. Madison, 108 S.W.2d 519 (Ky. 1937).
[103]DeAngelis v. Laino, 252 N.Y.S. 871 (1931).
[104]Conklin v. School District No. 37, 22 Kan. 521 (1879).
[105]McAtee v. Gutierrez, 146 P.2d 315 (N.M. 1944).

ity when entering into such contracts, the contract is invalid.[106]

School equipment, although legally the property of the state, is generally placed under the control of the school district or its board of education. Thus, the board of education is responsible for keeping school equipment in proper repair. Since the equipment is held by the district as a trustee, it is clear that the legislature may transfer control of the equipment to some other trustee if it sees fit to do so. Statutes may provide, however, that school equipment which is purchased by the district becomes the property of the district. It has been held[107] that rental of such property to pupils attending the district's schools does not destroy its ownership.

9.5 USE OF SCHOOL PROPERTY

A state legislature may authorize the use of school property for any purpose not prohibited by the constitution. It is when the statutes are silent concerning the uses to which school property may be put, or where authority to permit the use of school property has been delegated to a school district or board of education, that questions are likely to arise. In most jurisdictions the school district or its board of education has been granted either specific or implied authority to manage and control school buildings and grounds.[108] Thus, it has been held[109] that management and control of an athletic field located on property owned by a school district are vested in the district's board of education. Likewise, where instruction in physical culture was authorized, it was held[110] that land deeded for purposes of public education could be used as a gymnasium site or as an athletic field and playground.

It must be recognized that school authorities do not enjoy as much control over school property as private individuals do over the property of which they are exclusive owners.[111] The public, including all citizens of the district, has the right to enter school property at all times for legitimate purposes.[112] At the same time, school authorities have a right to protect school property from disturbances and annoyances which will interfere with the orderly operation of the school, and to exclude from school property anyone who enters thereon for the purpose of disturbing the peace or interfering with the conduct of the school.[113] However, they cannot impose discriminatory individual restrictions so as to exclude some persons from public exhibitions or exercises to which all members of the public are invited.[114]

Within such limitations as the constitution may impose, a legislature has power to govern the use of school buildings.[115] It may utilize this power directly by enacting legislation specifying the uses which may be made of school buildings, or it may delegate its authority to control the use of school buildings and other property to local boards of education or local school district electors. As far as the use of school buildings is concerned, a school board may exercise only such power as has been conferred upon it by statute.[116] Furthermore, any rule or regulation of a board of education concerning the use of school buildings is invalid if it is in contravention of a statute.[117] It has been held,[118] for example, that a school board rule prohibiting the discussion of political subjects by organizations seeking the use of school facilities was invalid because it contravened a state statute which authorized boards of education to permit the use of school buildings and grounds by organizations formed for recreational, educational, political, economic, artistic, or moral activities.

---

[106]State v. Smith, 194 N.E.2d 186 (Ohio 1963); Leonard v. State, 93 N.W. 988 (Neb. 1903).

[107]Barry v. Phoenix Union High School, 197 P.2d 533 (Ariz. 1948).

[108]Peevy v. Carlile, 139 S.W.2d 779 (Tex. 1940); Owen v. New York, 126 N.Y.S. 38 (1910); City of Chicago v. Board of Education of City of Chicago, 246 Ill.App. 405 (1927); Scott County Board of Education v. McMillen, 109 S.W.2d 1201 (Ky. 1937); Day v. Greenfield, 124 N.E. 481 (Mass. 1919).

[109]Neiman v. Common School District No. 95, 232 P.2d 422 (Kan. 1951).

[110]Boney v. Board of Trustees, 48 S.E.2d 56 (N.C. 1948); City of Burlington v. Mayor of Burlington, 127 Atl. 892 (Vt. 1925).

[111]School District No. 100 v. Barnes, 202 Pac. 849 (Kan. 1921); LaGrange Reorganized School District No.

R-VI v. Smith, 312 S.W.2d 135 (Mo. 1958); School District No. 8 v. School District No. 15, 164 N.W.2d 438 (Neb. 1969); State v. Besson, 266 A.2d 175 (N.J. 1970).

[112]Hughes v. Goodell, 3 Pitts.R. 264 (Pa. 1870); Graves v. Walton County Board of Education, 300 F.Supp. 188 (Ga. 1968), affirmed 410 F.2d 1152 (5th Cir. 1968).

[113]Hughes v. Goodell, 3 Pitts.R. 264 (Pa. 1870); State v. Besson, 266 A.2d 175 (N.J. 1970); State v. Oyen, 480 P.2d 766 (Wash. 1971); State v. Kimball, 503 P.2d 176 (Hawaii 1972).

[114]Hughes v. Goodell, 3 Pitts.R. 264 (Pa. 1870); Graves v. Walton County Board of Education, 300 F.Supp. 188 (Ga. 1968); affirmed 410 F.2d 1152 (5th Cir. 1968).

[115]People v. Parker, 138 N.Y.S. 2d 2 (1955); State v. Board of Education of Richland Township, 6 Ohio Supp. 59 (1941).

[116]Ellis v. Dixon, 349 U.S. 458, 75 S.Ct. 850, 99 L.Ed. 1231 (N.Y. 1955); Warburton v. City of Quincy, 34 N.E.2d 661 (Mass. 1941); Goodman v. Board of Education of San Francisco, 120 P.2d 665 (Cal. 1941).

[117]Ellis v. Board of Education of San Francisco, 164 P.2d 1 (Cal. 1945); Goodman v. Board of Education of San Francisco, 120 P.2d 665 (Cal. 1941).

[118]Goodman v. Board of Education of San Francisco, 120 P.2d 665 (Cal. 1941).

The state is under no obligation to make school buildings or facilities available for public meetings. However, if it does so, it may not arbitrarily exclude members of the public from holding such meetings. This principle was clearly explicated in a case in which persons were denied the use of a public school building because they refused to sign an oath:

The state is under no duty to make school buildings available for public meetings. If it elects to do so, however, it cannot arbitrarily prevent any members of the public from holding such meetings. Nor can it make the privilege of holding them dependent on conditions that would deprive any members of the public of their constitutional rights. A state is without power to impose an unconstitutional requirement as a condition for granting a privilege even though the privilege is the use of state property.[119]

9.5a District control over

Considerable confusion exists concerning the extent to which local school districts or boards of education may control the use of school property for various activities. As noted previously, the legislature has complete power to determine the use which may be made of school buildings. Statutes have been enacted in a number of states authorizing the use of school buildings for a wide variety of specific activities. In some states, the statutes authorize local boards of education to exercise discretion in granting permission to use school property for other than school purposes. Other states, however, have either failed to identify by statute the activities for which school buildings may be used or not expressly granted local school boards authority to permit the use of school buildings for other than school purposes.

The weight of authority indicates that, where a school district or a board of education has been authorized to permit the use of school property for other than school purposes, it may do so for any purposes which are not inconsistent with its use for school purposes, or which do not interfere with the conduct of the school.[120] A statement by the Supreme Court of Rhode Island typifies the philosophy of those courts which have taken a liberal point of view to-

ward the use of school property for other than school purposes:

Our school system, with all the intellectual and material means for instruction provided by it, was designed to promote public education; and any use of the school property tending to this end, and which does not interfere with the regular schools, may be permitted by the trustees of a school district, as within the spirit of their trust.[121]

It should be noted, however, that in a number of early cases the courts refused to permit the use of school property for any purposes other than those directly related to the instruction of pupils.[122] These decisions were based primarily on the principle that money raised through taxation for school purposes may not be used, even indirectly, for private purposes.[123]

In considering the question of whether school property may be used for other purposes, the main concern of the courts has been whether the activity in question would interfere with the use of the property for school purposes. In a Florida case,[124] for example, it was held that a college, university, or public school authority may enact rules denying a campus group access to buildings, or denying an invitation to a speaker, if it reasonably appears that such a group or speaker would advocate or attempt violent overthrow of the government, destruction or seizure of the institution's property, disruption of classes or other educational functions, invasion of the rights of faculty members or students, or other disorders of a violent nature. Where it can reasonably be anticipated that the activity will interfere with the regular school program, the courts have denied the use of the property.[125] It has been held,[126] for example, that a school board was justified in denying the use of a school building for a mass meeting because the speaker was one whose appearances had frequently been attended by

[119]Danskin v. San Diego Unified School District, 171 P.2d 885 (Cal. 1946).
[120]Ristine v. School District, 26 Pa. Dist. & Co. 655 (1936); Royse Independent School District v. Reinhardt, 159 S.W. 1010 (Tex. 1913); Merryman v. School District No. 16, 5 P.2d 267 (Wyo. 1931); Appeal of Barnes, 6 R.I. 591 (1860); Carter v. Lake City Baseball Club, 62 S.E.2d 470 (S.C. 1950); Sugar v. Monroe, 32 So.961 (La. 1902).

[121]Appeal of Barnes, 6 R.I. 591 (1860).
[122]Bender v. Streabich, 37 Atl. 853 (Pa. 1897); School District No. 8 v. Arnold, 21 Wis. 665 (1867); Spencer v. Joint School District No. 6, 15 Kan. 259 (1875); Tyre v. Krug, 149 N.W. 718 (Wis. 1914).
[123]Spencer v. Joint School District No. 6, 15 Kan. 259 (1875); Lewis v. Bateman, 73 Pac. 509 (Utah 1903). Contra, Goodman v. School District No. 1 of Denver, 32 F.2d 586 (8th Cir. 1929).
[124]Lieberman v. Marshall, 236 So.2d 120 (Fla. 1970).
[125]Payroll Guarantee Association v. Board of Education, 163 P.2d 433 (Cal. 1945); Carter v. Lake City Baseball Club, 62 S.E.2d 470 (S.C. 1950); Sugar v. Monroe, 32 So. 961 (La. 1902); Ellis v. Allen, 165 N.Y.S.2d 624 (1957); Grayned v. Rockford, 408 U.S. 104, 92 S.Ct. 2294, 33 L.Ed.2d 222 (Ill. 1974).
[126]Payroll Guarantee Association v. Board of Education, 163 P.2d 433 (Cal. 1945).

picket lines, boisterous disturbances, noisy demonstrations, and public disorder. Similarly, permission to use a school athletic field for professional baseball games,[127] and to use school facilities for theatrical productions,[128] has been denied on the ground that such use would interfere with regular school activities.

The courts have exhibited little concern over the possibility of damage to school property in consequence of its use for a nonschool activity.[129] If a nonschool activity can be justified on other grounds, the fact that some incidental damage may result from the activity has not been regarded as a sufficient reason to deny the use of school property. In at least one case,[130] however, the possibility of damage to school property as a result of the proposed activity was considered a sufficient reason for denying the use of a school building for nonschool purposes.

In a number of cases the courts have permitted the use of school property for nonschool purposes on the ground that the proposed use was temporary, casual, and incidental and did not represent a total diversion of the property from its intended use.[131] Following this reasoning, it was held[132] that the occasional use of an assembly hall in a school building for outside meetings, lectures, and dances did not preclude a board's providing the assembly hall if it was for the primary use and benefit of students. It also has been held[133] that a school board may permit private individuals to sell lunches to pupils and teachers at a profit, since such a use of school facilities is merely incidental and complementary to the operation of the school system.

9.5b Discretion of school officials

Within the limits of the authority granted them by statutes, school officials may exercise discretion as to the use of school property for nonschool purposes.[134] Such discre-

tion must not be abused, however, and must not be exercised in an arbitrary or capricious fashion.[135] The courts will not interfere with decisions of school authorities regarding the use of school property unless they abuse their discretion.[136] It has been ruled within the discretion of a board of education to permit school buildings to be used for dances,[137] to authorize a cafeteria to be maintained on school premises,[138] to grant the use of school facilities for a vocal concert,[139] to permit the use of school facilities for athletic events,[140] and to allow a labor organization representing teachers to use school facilities.[141]

If a board of education permits the use of school facilities for certain nonschool purposes, it may not discriminate among users in a manner which will infringe their constitutional rights.[142] It has been said in this regard:

> ... school authorities may not deny to one organization the use of school buildings and permit such use to other organizations in the same category, all factors being reasonably equal. This appears to be plain common sense. School authorities may, if they choose, close the door to all outside organizations, but if they open the door they must treat alike all organizations in the same category. ... A school board of course is not a censor, and its duty so far as school buildings are concerned is merely to regulate and protect them. We do

[127]Carter v. Lake City Baseball Club, 62 S.E.2d 470 (S.C. 1950).

[128]Sugar v. Monroe, 32 So. 961 (La. 1902).

[129]Royse Independent School District v. Reinhardt, 159 S.W. 1010 (Tex. 1913); Cost v. Shinault, 166 S.W. 740 (Ark. 1914); Merryman v. School District No. 16, 5 P.2d 267 (Wyo. 1931).

[130]Ellis v. Allen, 165 N.Y.S.2d 624 (1957).

[131]Greenbanks v. Boutwell, 43 Vt. 207 (1870); Simmons v. Board of Education, 237 N.W. 700 (N.D. 1931); Ralph v. Orleans Parish School Board, 104 So. 490 (La. 1925).

[132]Greenbanks v. Boutwell, 43 Vt. 207 (1870).

[133]Ralph v. Orleans Parish School Board, 104 So. 490 (La. 1925).

[134]Goodman v. Board of Education of San Francisco, 120 P.2d 665 (Cal. 1941); American Civil Liberties Union of Southern California v. Board of Education, 379 P.2d 4

(Cal. 1963); State v. Grand Rapids Board of Education, 100 N.E.2d 294 (Ohio 1949); Velton v. School District of Slater, 6 S.W.2d 652 (Mo. 1928); McKnight v. Board of Public Education, 76 A.2d 207 (Pa. 1951); Beard v. Board of Education, 16 P.2d 900 (Utah 1932).

[135]Goodman v. Board of Education of San Francisco, 120 P.2d 665 (Cal. 1941); State v. Grand Rapids Board of Education, 100 N.E.2d 294 (Ohio 1949); Cannon v. Towner, 70 N.Y.S.2d 303 (1947); Trustees of Independent School District v. Johnson County Democratic Executive Committee, 52 S.W.2d 68 (Tex. 1932); Hennessey v. Independent School District No. 4, 552 P.2d 141 (Okla. 1976).

[136]State v. Grand Rapids Board of Education, 100 N.E.2d 294 (Ohio 1949); McKnight v. Board of Public Education, 76 A.2d 207 (Pa. 1951); Beard v. Board of Education, 16 P.2d 900 (Utah 1932).

[137]McClure v. Board of Education, 176 Pac. 711 (Cal. 1918); Brooks v. Elder, 189 N.W. 284 (Neb. 1922); Merryman v. School District No. 16, 5 P.2d 267 (Wyo. 1931).

[138]Goodman v. School District No. 1 of Denver, 32 F.2d 586 (8th Cir. 1929); Bozeman v. Morrow, 34 S.W.2d 654 (Tex. 1931).

[139]Cannon v. Towner, 70 N.Y.S.2d 303 (1947).

[140]Merryman v. School District No. 16, 5 P.2d 267 (Wyo. 1931).

[141]Dade County Classroom Teachers' Association v. Ryan, 225 So.2d 903 (Fla. 1969); Federation of Delaware Teachers v. De La Warr Board of Education, 335 F.Supp. 385 (Del. 1971).

[142]Ellis v. Allen, 165 N.Y.S.2d 624 (1957); American Civil Liberties Union v. Board of Education, 359 P.2d 45, 94 A.L.R.2d 1259 (Cal. 1961); Buckley v. Meng, 230 N.Y.S.2d 924 (1962).

not take it that it may discriminate against an organization simply because it, or even a part of the public, may be hostile to the opinions or program of such organization provided the same are not unlawful per se.[143]

9.5c Community Groups

The statutes in many states explicitly authorize the use of school property for public assemblies, community activities, political meetings, recreational activities, and social purposes. Even where the statutes do not specifically authorize the use of school property for such activities, many courts have allowed a local board of education to exercise considerable discretion in permitting school property to be used for nonschool purposes if the proposed use will not interfere with the proper maintenance and conduct of the school and if school property is not damaged or destroyed.

A distinction should be drawn between the use of school facilities by the community in connection with school-related activities and the use of school facilities by community groups for activities which are essentially unrelated to the school program. Sometimes it is claimed that school officials have no authority to charge admission fees, or otherwise restrict attendance, at school-related activities which are financed from public funds. It has been held[144] in this regard that a school district has a right to realize profits from games played on its premises and that it is within the power of a local board of education to enter into a contract with a radio station granting it the exclusive right to broadcast play-by-play accounts of football games played on the district's premises. Similarly, it has been held[145] that a board of education may permit the use of school buildings, without charge, for dances, lectures, shows, games, and other entertainments organized and sponsored by the student body of the school.

Decisions concerning the use of school property for community activities which are essentially unrelated to the school program are difficult to harmonize. Two reasons are readily apparent: differences in the philosophy of the courts and differences in the provisions of statutes pertaining to the use of school buildings for nonschool activities. For example, in some jurisdictions school authorities may permit fraternal organizations to use school facilities,[146] and they have even been allowed to lease the upper story of a school building to the Odd Fellows for use as a lodge.[147] In another jurisdiction, however, it was held[148] that despite the consent of a majority of the electors of the district the Sons of Temperance could not use a public schoolhouse as a meeting place.

School facilities are frequently in demand for dances, concerts, and plays. In a number of jurisdictions it has been held[149] that social dancing may be permitted in public school buildings. Concerts and theatrical presentations generally may take place in public school buildings, although it has been decided[150] that school officials may not lease the auditorium of a high school building for use as a public theater. It also has been held[151] that, under a statute permitting the use of school facilities for "charitable purposes," a board of education may permit the use of a school building for a meeting at which admission fees will be charged and the proceeds used as a legal defense fund for "freedom riders." A contract to use school facilities as a baseball park was upheld where it appeared there would be no interference with school activities.[152] In such cases two criteria are generally applied by the courts in determining whether school property may be used for nonschool purposes: First, there must be no interference with the regular school program, and second, there must be no damage to school property.

9.5d Political purposes

School property may be used for political meetings when authorized by statute, and an organization may not be denied the use of a school building merely because a board of education considers it subversive,[153] or because it thinks a meeting might result in violence and damage to the facilities.[154]

---

[143]Ellis v. Allen, 165 N.Y.S.2d 624 (1957).
[144]Southwestern Broadcasting Co. v. Oil Center Broadcasting Co., 210 S.W.2d 230 (Tex. 1947).
[145]Beard v. Board of Education, 16 P.2d 900 (Utah 1932).

[146]Lagow v. Hill, 87 N.E. 369 (Ill. 1909); Cost v. Shinault, 166 S.W. 740 (Ark. 1914).
[147]Cost v. Shinault, 166 S.W. 740 (Ark. 1914).
[148]School District No. 8 v. Arnold, 21 Wis. 665 (1867).
[149]Beard v. Board of Education, 16 P.2d 900 (Utah 1932); McClure v. Board of Education, 176 Pac. 711 (Cal. 1918); Young v. Board of Trustees of BroadwaterCounty High School, 4 P.2d 725 (Mont. 1931); Brooks v. Elder, 189 N.W. 284 (Neb. 1922).
[150]Sugar v. Monroe, 32 So. 961 (La. 1902).
[151]Dohrenwend v. Board of Education, 227 N.Y.S.2d 505 (1962).
[152]Royse Independent School District v. Reinhardt, 159 S.W. 1010 (Tex. 1913).
[153]Goodman v. Board of Education of San Francisco, 120 P.2d 665 (Cal. 1941).
[154]Healy v. James, 408 U.S. 169, 92 S.Ct. 2338, 33 L.Ed.2d 266 (Conn. 1972); National Socialist White People's Party v. Ringers, 473 F.2d 1010 (4th Cir. 1973).

Furthermore, a statute requiring those who apply for permission to use school buildings to submit a statement that the organization on behalf of which the application is made does not advocate overthrow of the government by force or other unlawful means and is not a communist or communist-front organization has been held[155] unconstitutional in that it infringes the right of assembly and free speech because of disapproval of an organization itself, not because of what the organization says or does. In another case with political overtones it was held[156] that, where a local board of education had granted a church organization permission to hold a concert in a school auditorium and subsequently learned that the featured singer had been named by a congressional committee as being a supporter of communist-front organizations, the board could not rescind its permission to use school facilities because a vested interest had developed prior to the board's attempt to rescind its permission.

In general, it would appear that, where political organizations may be granted permission to use school property, they cannot be singled out for special treatment. They must be allowed to use school facilities on the same basis as any other organization which may use them and may not be subjected to discriminatory regulations.

9.5e Commercial purposes generally

As previously noted, school facilities may be used for dances, athletic contests, plays, and concerts to which admission fees are charged. Such activities frequently are in direct conflict with private business enterprises. Potential conflicts also arise where the operation of a school cafeteria reduces the business of privately owned lunchrooms in the vicinity of the school. As a rule, the courts will not permit the use of public school property where the primary purpose of the activity in question is commercial gain.[157] Since public schools are supported primarily by tax funds, it is reasoned that a school board is without authority to engage in commercial ventures for financial gain unless it has been authorized to do so by statute, either expressly or by implication. This does not mean, however, that school districts may not derive income from fees charged spectators at school-sponsored activities. They may do so

if such revenue is incidental to the conduct of the activity and not its primary purpose.[158]

The use of school property for commercial purposes has been challenged on various constitutional grounds, particularly that permitting such use constitutes the diversion of public funds to a private purpose or the taking of property without due process of law. Early decisions limited the use of school property strictly to school purposes for the reasons that money raised through taxation for one purpose can be used for no other purpose and that tax money cannot be used to build a structure for private use.[159] More recent decisions, as will be seen in the following sections, have permitted the use of school property for private purposes so long as such use is incidental to its use for school purposes, does not interfere with its use for school purposes, and is not primarily for commercial gain.

Cafeteria

From the cases which have arisen questioning the authority of a board of education to either operate or permit the operation of a school cafeteria, it is clear that a board of education may authorize the operation of a cafeteria on school premises.[160] In fact, it has even been held[161] that a school board may permit a private enterprise to sell lunches to pupils and teachers at a profit on the ground that a safe and sanitary food service which facilitated the conduct of the school was thus provided. However, a ten-year lease of school property to a private individual who planned to operate a cafeteria on the premises for the convenience of pupils and teachers was ruled[162] invalid on the ground that it did not constitute an incidental and casual use of school property.

School Store

The operation of school stores occasionally has been questioned. It has been held[163]

---

[155]American Civil Liberties Union v. Board of Education, 359 P.2d 45, 94 A.L.R.2d 1259 (Cal. 1961).

[156]Cannon v. Towner, 70 N.Y.S.2d 303 (1947).

[157]Presley v. Vernon Parish School Board, 139 So. 642 (La. 1932); Sugar v. Monroe, 32 So. 961 (La. 1902).

[158]Greenbanks v. Boutwell, 43 Vt. 207 (1870); Hempel v. School District No. 329, 59 P.2d 729 (Wash. 1936); Southwestern Broadcasting Co. v. Oil Center Broadcasting Co., 210 S.W.2d 230 (Tex. 1947).

[159]Spencer v. Joint School District No. 6, 15 Kan. 259 (1875); Bender v. Streabich, 37 Atl. 853 (Pa. 1897).

[160]Goodman v. School District No. 1 of Denver, 32 F.2d 586 (8th Cir. 1929); Hempel v. School District No. 329, 59 P.2d 729 (Wash. 1936); Bozeman v. Morrow, 34 S.W.2d 654 (Tex. 1931).

[161]Ralph v. Orleans Parish School Board, 104 So. 490 (La. 1925).

[162]Presley v. Vernon Parish School Board, 139 So. 642 (La. 1932).

[163]Ristine v. School District, 26 Pa. Dist. & Co. 655 (1936).

that a board of education may properly permit pupils to operate school stores in buildings owned by the district. Also, while it is proper for a school official to sell school supplies to students at cost,[164] it is improper for school officials to permit the operation in a public school building of a store for the sale of books and supplies to pupils at a profit.[165]

Private Instruction

Public school property may, it seems, be used for the purpose of giving private instruction.[166] Thus, it was ruled[167] that a school board was acting within its authority when, after the district's funds were exhausted, it permitted a teacher to conduct a private school on public school premises and charge each pupil a monthly tuition fee. The use of public school facilities (outside of regular school hours) for the giving of private instruction in vocal music also has been upheld.[168] On the other hand, a board of education was deemed without authority to lease a schoolhouse for a term of eleven weeks for use as a private school.[169]

Leasing

Does a school district have authority to lease land for commercial purposes? The decisions on this question are in conflict. It has been held[170] that, where property is granted to a district to be used for school purposes, the district does not have a right to drill an oil well on the property. Also, where a school site was purchased subject to the right of reversion to the original owner, the school district was not permitted to develop mineral and gas deposits beneath the surface of the site despite the fact that it had occupied the property for a long period of time.[171] In an early West Virginia case it was held[172] that, since the board of education had not been given specific statutory authority to execute a lease for the

production of oil and gas, it could not execute such a lease because "the statute provides for the accomplishment of its object by taxation, not by negotiation in the business world." On the other hand, in Kentucky it was held[173] that, where boards of education had been granted statutory authority to hold and dispose of school property for the use and benefit of the district, they could execute an oil lease on school land. And in Pennsylvania it had been held[174] that land deeded to a school district "for school purposes only" could be leased for the production of oil and gas.

School officials have no authority to enter into a lease of school property which amounts to a gift to the other party.[175] Thus, it was held[176] that a school board could not lease a school building to a community hospital at a rental fee of one dollar per year, with the lessee to have the option of renewing the lease every five years, because the board, as the trustee of school property, could use it only for the educational advancement of youth. Similarly, a city council was judged[177] to have acted beyond its authority when it leased school premises constructed with the proceeds of a public bond issue to a private university rent free for a five-year term. On the other hand, a school board has been permitted to lease an otherwise unused school gymnasium to a civic group which conducted musical programs for which admission fees were charged.[178]

9.5f Religious purposes

Attempts to use school property for religious purposes have precipitated considerable litigation concerning the constitutionality of statutes specifically or impliedly authorizing such use or authorizing local school district officials to permit it. The great weight of authority holds that, in the absence of a statute authorizing the use of public school property for religious purposes or permitting local school officials or the school district electorate to authorize such use, religious services or meetings may not be held on public school prop-

[164]Cook v. Chamberlain, 225 N.W. 141 (Wis. 1929).
[165]Tyre v. Krug, 149 N.W. 718 (Wis. 1914).
[166]Chaplin v. Hill, 24 Vt. 528 (1852); Burrow v. Pocahontas School District No. 19, 79 S.W.2d 1010 (Ark. 1935); Appeal of Barnes, 6 R.I. 591 (1860).
[167]Burrow v. Pocahontas School District No. 19, 79 S.W.2d 1010 (Ark. 1935).
[168]Appeal of Barnes, 6 R.I. 591 (1860); *contra*: Hysong v. School District, 30 Atl. 482 (Pa. 1894).
[169]Weir v. Day, 35 Ohio St. 143 (1878).
[170]Board of Directors of School District No. 115 of Elk County v. Fleak, 245 Pac. 150 (Kan. 1926); United Fuel Gas Co. v. Morley Oil Co., 135 S.E. 399 (W.Va. 1926).
[171]Board of Directors of School District No. 115 of Elk County v. Fleak, 245 Pac. 150 (Kan. 1926).
[172]Herald v. Board of Education, 65 S.E. 102 (W.Va. 1909).

[173]Williams v. McKenzie, 262 S.W. 598 (Ky. 1924).
[174]Phillips Gas & Oil Co. v. Lingenfelter, 105 Atl. 888 (Pa. 1919).
[175]Prescott Community Hospital Commission v. Prescott School District No. 1, 115 P.2d 160 (Ariz. 1941); Sherlock v. Village of Winnetka, 68 Ill. 530 (1873).
[176]Prescott Community Hospital Commission v. Prescott School District No. 1, 115 P.2d 160 (Ariz. 1941).
[177]Sherlock v. Village of Winnetka, 68 Ill. 530 (1873).
[178]Hall v. Shelby County Board of Education, 472 S.W.2d 489 (Ky. 1971).

erty.[179] The rationale is exemplified by the following statement by the Supreme Court of Kansas:

> The public schoolhouse cannot be used for any private purposes. The argument is a short one. Taxation is invoked to raise funds to erect the building; but taxation is illegitimate to provide for any private purpose. Taxation will not lie to raise funds to build a place for a religious society, a political society, or a social club. What cannot be done directly cannot be done indirectly. As you may not levy taxes to build a church, no more may you levy taxes to build a schoolhouse and then lease it for a church. Nor is it an answer to say that its use for school purpose is not interfered with. . . . The use of a public schoolhouse for a single religious or political gathering is legally as unauthorized as its constant use therefor.[180]

It should be noted, however, that in some cases the use of public school property for certain religious purposes during times when school is not in session has been permitted, even though such usage was not specifically authorized by statute. It was held[181] that the occasional use of a public schoolhouse for Sunday school and religious meetings, occurring about four times per year over a five-year period, was not sufficient to constitute the schoolhouse a place of public worship and thus was not unconstitutional. It also has been held[182] that permitting the display of a nativity scene erected and maintained entirely at the expense of a private committee on the lawn of a junior-senior high school during the Christmas vacation period did not violate constitutional guarantees concerning freedom of religion. Some authority to the contrary is also found.

Statutes which expressly permit the use of public school property for religious purposes during times when school is not in session has been enacted in some states, and their constitutionality has been upheld by the courts.[183] Those who object to the use of public school premises for religious purposes frequently claim that such use violates constitutional provisions regarding the separation of church and state, or violates a constitutional provision that public funds are not to be used to support any religion or house of worship. Claims that the use of public school property for religious purpose violate constitutional guarantees have been rejected in several cases.[184] In upholding the constitutionality of a statute permitting the use of public schoolhouses for religious purposes, the Supreme Court of Illinois said:

> Religion and religious worship are not so placed under the ban of the constitution that they may not be allowed to become the recipient of any incidental benefit whatsoever from the public bodies or authorities of the State. That instrument itself contains a provision authorizing the legislature to exempt property used for religious purposes from taxation; and thereby, the same as is complained of here, there might be indirectly imposed upon the taxpayer the burden of increased taxation, and in that manner the indirect supporting of places of worship. In the respect of the possibility of enhanced taxation therefrom, this provision of the constitution is even more obnoxious to objection than this permission given by the school directors to hold religious meetings in the schoolhouse.[185]

In a number of states the statutes authorize the use of public school property for unspecified public purposes at the discretion of the board of education or the electors of the school district. Where such statutes have been enacted, questions have arisen as to whether they authorize the use of public school property for religious purposes. In several cases the statutes have been construed to authorize the use of a school building as a place for holding religious services at times when school is not in session and there is no interference with the regular activities of the school.[186] In Florida, for example, a statute authorized the use of school buildings during nonschool hours for "any legal assembly." When a board of education permitted several churches to hold religious services in school buildings on Sunday pending construction of church buildings, an injunction against the use of public schools as places of worship was sought. Since the record showed that no

[179]Scofield v. Eighth School District, 27 Conn. 499 (1858); Baggerly v. Lee, 73 N.E. 921 (Ind. 1905); Spencer v. Joint School District No. 6, 15 Kan. 259 (1875); Dorton v. Hearn, 67 Mo. 301 (1878); Hysong v. School District, 30 Atl. 482 (Pa. 1894); Resnick v. East Brunswick Township Board of Education, 343 A.2d 127 (N.J. 1975).

[180]Spencer v. Joint School District No. 6, 15 Kan. 259 (1875).

[181]State v. Dilley, 145 N.W. 999 (Neb. 1914).

[182]Baer v. Kolmorgen, 181 N.Y.S.2d 230 (1958); But see American Jurisprudence 2d Vol. 68 Section 297.

[183]Nichols v. School Directors, 93 Ill. 61 (1879); Hurd v. Walters, 48 Ind. 148 (1874).

[184]Nichols v. School Directors, 93 Ill. 61 (1879); State v. Dilley, 145 N.W. 999 (Neb. 1914); Southside Estates Baptist Church v. Trustees, 115 So.2d 697, 79 A.L.R.2d 1142 (Fla. 1959); Baer v. Kolmorgen, 181 N.Y.S.2d 230 (1958); Davis v. Boget, 50 Iowa 11 (1878).

[185]Nichols v. School Directors, 93 Ill. 61 (1879).

[186]Southside Estates Baptist Church v. Trustees, 115 So.2d 697, 79 A.L.R.2d 1142 (Fla. 1959); Baggerly v. Lee, 73 N.E. 921 (Ind. 1905); Townsend v. Hagan, 35 Iowa 194 (1872).

public financial assistance was given to the churches, other than inconsequential wear and tear on the buildings, and that no preference was given one sect or denomination over another, the Florida Supreme Court held that such use did not violate constitutional requirements:

While admittedly, there are some differences of view regarding the matter of religious meetings in schoolhouses during non-school periods, we think that logic, as well as our traditional attitudes towards the importance of religious worship, justifies our alignment with those courts which permit such use. The cases where this type of use of school property is permitted, usually involve the application of statutes. . . . The cases which deny such use customarily involve situations where there has been no such statutory authorization. . . .

In this instant case the Legislature has endowed the trustees of the school district with reasonable discretion to permit the use of school property during non-school hours "for any legal assembly." We think that the religious observances described in the complaint are well within the category of "legal assembly." . . .

We, therefore, hold that a board of trustees of a Florida School District has the power to exercise a reasonable discretion to permit the use of school buildings during non-school hours for any legal assembly which includes religious meetings, subject, of course, to judicial review should such discretion be abused to the point that it could be construed as a contribution of public funds in aid of a particular religious group or as the promotion or establishment of a particular religion.[187]

It is important to recognize that, while school boards in some states have authority to permit schoolhouses to be used for religious meetings, the decision as to whether such use will be permitted clearly lies within the discretion of the board of education. The courts have consistently upheld the authority of a school district or a board of education to deny applications for the use of school property for church services or religious observances.[188] In Ohio, for example, a statute permitted school boards to make school buildings available for educational, religious, and other meetings and "for such other purposes as may make for the welfare of the community." A board of

education refused to permit a group of Jehovah's Witnesses, none of whom were citizens residing in the district, to hold a series of Sunday meetings in the district's schoolhouse. When the action was questioned, it was held[189] that the board's power to permit the use of a schoolhouse for religious meetings was discretionary, not ministerial, and that the board had not abused its power where it had decided that use of the schoolhouse by the group in question would not be for the welfare of the community.

The United States Supreme Court has, of course, ruled that using public school classrooms during regular school hours to carry out a program of sectarian instruction for pupils is unconstitutional.[190] It has held that a program which utilized tax-established and tax-supported public schools to aid religious groups to spread their faith was a direct violation of the separation of church and state required by the First Amendment of the United States Constitution.

9.6 AUTHORITY TO INSURE SCHOOL PROPERTY

Boards of education may spend school funds only for those purposes specifically identified in or necessarily implied by the statutes. Consequently, the extent of the legal authority of a board of education to purchase insurance on school property is a matter of importance. When statutes clearly identify the property which is to be insured and the procedure which is to be followed in obtaining insurance coverage, a board of education is bound by the requirements.[191] In the absence of specific statutory requirements concerning school insurance, however, the courts have generally held that the determination of whether or not to insure school property, the amount of insurance to be taken, and the company from which it is to be procured is a discretionary function of a board of education.[192]

Where the statutes plainly specify the hazards to be insured against and/or the procedures to be employed in obtaining the required coverage, school board members may be held personally liable for any losses

[187]Southside Estate Baptist Church v. Trustees, 115 So.2d 697, 79 A.L.R.2d 1142 (Fla. 1959).
[188]State v. Grand Rapids Board of Education, 100 N.E.2d 294 (Ohio 1949); McKnight v. Board of Public Education, 76 A.2d 207 (Pa. 1951); Eckhardt v. Darby, 76 N.W. 761 (Mich. 1898); Boyd v. Mitchell, 62 S.W. 61 (Ark. 1901).

[189]State v. Grand Rapids Board of Education, 100 N.E.2d 294 (Ohio 1949).
[190]McCollum v. Board of Education, 333 U.S. 203, 68 S.Ct. 461, 92 L.Ed. 649 (Ill. 1948).
[191]People v. Stanley, 225 Pac. 1 (Cal. 1924); Bituminous Casualty Corp. v. Folkerts, 27 N.E.2d 670 (Ill. 1940).
[192]Fuller v. Lockhart, 182 S.E. 733 (N.C. 1935); Downing v. Erie City School District, 61 A.2d 133 (Pa. 1948); Dalzell v. Bourbon County Board of Education, 235 S.W. 360 (Ky. 1921).

which may result from their failure to comply with such requirements.[193] On the other hand, where the statutes do not contain specific instructions relative to the insurance to be procured or the procedures to be followed, a school board may exercise its discretion in these matters and its members will not be held personally liable so long as they act honestly and in good faith.

In the eyes of the courts, *property* is a generic term of a very broad and inclusive meaning.[194] Since the word may be used in a number of ways, the context must be considered in determining its meaning.[195] Thus, a clear definition of what constitutes school property under a statute authorizing the insurance of school property is difficult to establish. A perusal of statutes indicates that some states are quite specific in identifying what is to be insured while others stipulate only that insurance is to be taken on "school property." Clearly, the precise wording of relevant statutes must be considered in determining the extent of a school district's authority to procure insurance coverage. Furthermore, it will sometimes be found that insurance on specific items of school property is mandatory whereas insurance on other items is discretionary. It has firmly been established, however, that an express grant of power to control and manage school property carries with it by clear implication the authority to purchase insurance for the protection of the district's financial interest in such property.[196]

9.6a Self-insurance

A number of school districts have chosen to self-insure against the loss of property arising from fire, flood, earthquake, and the like. The possibility of self-insuring against losses immediately raises the questions of whether such a course of action is permissible and whether an insurance reserve fund to defray or assist in defraying the cost of any future loss can legally be established.

The legal authority of a school district to self-insure, either wholly or in part, has seldom been the direct subject of litigation despite the fact that some large school districts have for many years made use of self-insurance. Apparently, however, where a state has by statute directed school districts to place insurance with commerical com-

panies which meet certain qualifications, or has directed school districts to insure with a state insurance fund, the use of self-insurance as a method of protecting against monetary loss is of questionable legality. Nevertheless, when the statutes are silent on the subject, it may be assumed that the decision as to whether or not to self-insure is within the discretion of the board of education. In the absence of constitutional prohibition or statutory direction to the contrary, it appears that school boards do have authority to self-insure so long as their actions are reasonable.

The question of whether a school district legally may establish a reserve fund to absorb uncertain future losses is not easily answered. Some precedent indicates that a school board may not build up a fund to be used at an indefinite future date.[197] The cases involved, however, were decided in reference to the legality of establishing a reserve fund for school building purposes, not a reserve fund for insurance purposes. A closely related question is whether a board of education may levy taxes for the purpose of establishing such a reserve fund. There must be a clear implication of authority to levy a tax for the establishment of an insurance reserve fund or authority to levy such a tax will be denied.[198] Although many school districts have established insurance reserve funds without creating legal problems, it is wise to seek statutory authorization when the use of self-insurance through establishment of a reserve fund is contemplated.

9.6b Stock insurance company

The state's right to permit or compel school districts to procure insurance is well established. In fact, the state may specify the type of company in which insurance is to be taken and may even require some districts to take insurance while making it optional for others.[199] The Supreme Court of North Dakota has said in this regard:

> . . . we are wholly agreed that [in the absence of a specific constitutional inhibition] the legislature has power to either grant to, or withhold from, the officers of a school district authority to insure the property thereof against loss by fire. And it has equal power to direct

[193]Bronaugh v. Murray, 172 S.W.2d 591 (Ky. 1943).
[194]73 C.J.S., Property. sec. 1.
[195]Hunt v. Authier, 169 P.2d 913 (Cal. 1946).
[196]Clark School Township v. Home Insurance & Trust Co., 51 N.E. 107 (Ind. 1898); Hagan Lumber Co. v. Duryea School District, 121 Atl. 107 (Pa. 1923); American Insurance Co. v. Newberry, 112 So. 195 (Ala. 1927).

[197]Chicago & Alton Railway Co. v. People, 69 N.E. 72 (Ill. 1903); Cleveland, Cincinnati, Chicago & St. Louis Railway Co. v. People, 69 N.E. 832 (Ill. 1904).
[198]Marion & McPherson Railway Co. v. Alexander, 64 Pac. 978 (Kan. 1901).
[199]People v. Stanley, 225 Pac. 1 (Cal. 1924).

that the insurance be accomplished in a certain manner.[200]

The question of whether a board of education possesses implied authority to purchase insurance from a stock or nonassessable insurance company has been answered affirmatively by the courts in several cases.[201] While constitutional provisions in some states have been interpreted to prohibit the purchase of insurance contracts from which contingent liability may arise, insurance contracts issued by stock insurance companies do not contain such a provision. Thus, it is clearly within the discretion of a board of education to purchase insurance from a stock company even though the board may not be specifically authorized to do so by statute. Such authority is implied by statutes granting a board of education power to control and manage school property. This rule is illustrated by the following assertion by an Indiana court:

We are of the opinion that, under the statutory provisions placing upon the trustee the duty of caring for and managing the school property, he has such implied authority that, in the exercise of his discretion, he may make reasonable expenditures from the special school revenue, by way of procuring insurance on such property against fire.[202]

9.6c Mutual insurance company

The authority of a school district to purchase insurance from a mutual insurance company has frequently been contested on constitutional grounds. It has been claimed that the provision for contingent liability which is sometimes incorporated into insurance contracts issued by mutual companies violates a constitutional prohibition against school agencies' lending their credit. It has also been claimed that contracts with mutual insurance companies violate a constitutional prohibition against municipalities' becoming stockholders in a business, association, or corporation.

The weight of authority indicates that statutes which specifically authorize school districts to insure in a mutual insurance company are not unconstitutional so long as the contingent liability of the school district is limited. It has been held[203] that such insurance contracts do not constitute a lending of the district's credit if they provide for limited contingent liability, nor does the district become a stockholder in the company by virtue of its membership in a mutual insurance company. In a Pennsylvania case, for example, a school district requested bids for insurance on school property and a mutual insurance company submitted the low bid. Suit was brought to prevent the district from accepting the bid, contending that a statute giving municipalities the right to insure in mutual insurance companies was, in effect, permitting them to loan their credit and was thus unconstitutional. In holding that the statute in question was not unconstitutional, the court said:

Our constitutional provision was designed to prevent municipal corporations from joining as stockholders in hazardous business ventures, loaning its credit for such purposes, or granting gratuities to persons or associations where not in pursuit of some governmental purpose. Taking of insurance in a mutual company with limited liability is not within the inhibition, for the district does not become strictly a stockholder, nor is it loaning its credit.[204]

Although the courts are not in unanimous agreement on the question, the weight of authority supports the view that even without specific statutory permission school districts may purchase insurance from mutual companies if their contingent liability is limited. It has been found[205] that choosing to insure with a mutual company is within the discretion of a board of education, and that a district neither lends its credit nor becomes a stockholder in a private corporation or association by entering into such a contract.

---

[200]Minot Special School District No. 1 v. Olsness, 208 N.W. 968 (N.D. 1926).

[201]Clark School Township v. Home Insurance & Trust Co., 51 N.E. 107 (Ind. 1898); French v. Mayor, etc., of City of Millville, 49 Atl. 465 (N.J. 1901); Johnson v. School District No. 1, 270 Pac. 764 (Ore. 1928); King County v. United States Merchants & Shippers Insurance Co., 274 Pac. 704 (Wash. 1929); Downing v. Erie City School District, 61 A.2d 133 (Pa. 1948).

[202]Clark School Township v. Home Insurance & Trust Co., 51 N.E. 107 (Ind. 1898).

[203]Downing v. School District of City of Erie, 147 Atl. 239 (Pa. 1927); City of Macon v. Benson, 166 S.E. 26 (Ga. 1932); Miller v. Johnson, 48 P.2d 956 (Cal. 1935); Clifton v. School District No. 14 of Russellville, 90 S.W.2d 508 (Ark. 1936); Louisville Board of Insurance Agents v. Jefferson County Board of Education, 309 S.W.2d 40 (Ky. 1957). *Contra*, Lewis v. Independent School District of City of Austin, 161 S.W.2d 450 (Tex. 1942).

[204]Downing v. School District of City of Erie, 147 Atl. 239 (Pa. 1927).

[205]French v. Mayor, etc., of City of Millville, 49 Atl. 465 (N.J. 1901); Dalzell v. Bourbon County Board of Education, 235 S.W. 360 (Ky. 1921); McMahon v. Cooney, 25 P.2d 131 (Mont. 1933); Burton v. School District No. 19, 38 P.2d 610 (Wyo. 1934); Fuller v. Lockhart, 182 S.E. 733 (N.C. 1935).

On the other hand, when school districts have attempted to secure insurance from mutual insurance companies under contracts which impose unlimited contingent liability on policyholders, the courts have taken a different view of the situation. Such a contract was held to contravene a constitutional provision forbidding governmental units to lend their credit in an Idaho case that bore directly upon this question. The school district purported to have an insurance policy issued by a mutual insurance company covering a school building which had burned. The policy covering the building provided for the unlimited liability of the policyholders. The insurance company refused to indemnify the district for the loss of the building, claiming that no contract could exist because the school board was without authority to enter into such a contract. In holding for the insurance company the court said:

> It may be that a postponed contingent liability is not an indebtedness within the meaning of the Constitution until the contingency has occurred, but it is a liability which may become an indebtedness upon the happening of the contingency. Liabilities which are assumed by virtue of membership in a county mutual fire insurance company are not within the control of the member or limited in amount, and the contingency may occur at any time. The assumption of such liability by a school district is contrary to the provisions of . . . the Constitution.[206]

A similar view has been expressed by other courts in dicta.[207]

Although the courts have indicated that insurance may be taken from mutual companies under limited contingent liability contracts, but not when contingent liability is unlimited, they have not yet indicated the precise limit of contingent liability which a district may assume. Mutual insurance contracts have been approved in which there was no contingent liability,[208] in which liability was limited to one additional premium,[209] and in which liability was limited

to five times the annual premium.[210] Dicta in a Wyoming case[211] may provide some additional guidance. The court said that constitutional prohibitions against lending the district's credit, or against the district's becoming a stockholder in corporations or associations, were not violated where it was not shown that the ultimate liability which might be assumed by the district was disproportionate to the cost of ordinary insurance contracts.

9.6d State insurance fund

Some states—among them Alabama, North Carolina, North Dakota, South Carolina, and Wisconsin—have established a state insurance fund in which state property may be insured. Statutory authority to insure in such a fund is not a problem, since the groups which are eligible to insure in this way are identified in the statutes. Questions have been raised, however, concerning the constitionality of the statutes. The courts invariably have upheld the constitutionality of state insurance funds.[212] It should also be noted that the United States Supreme Court has upheld the power of a state to establish a workmen's compensation insurance fund[213] and power to enforce contributions to such a fund.[214]

9.7 USE OF PROCEEDS OF INSURANCE POLICIES

School funds are essentially of two kinds: general and special. General school funds may be used for any nonprohibited purpose; special funds are those authorized or allocated for a specific purpose and may be used only for that purpose. The extent to which a school board may exercise discretion in using the proceeds of insurance policies in the event of a loss depends upon whether the proceeds are regarded as general or special funds. This, in turn, depends upon the source from which the proceeds arise.

Money raised from the sale of bonds is

---

[206]School District No. 8 v. Twin Falls County Mutual Fire Insurance Co., 164 Pac. 1174 (Ida. 1917).

[207]Johnson v. School District No. 1, 270 Pac. 764 (Ore. 1928); Miller v. Johnson, 48 P.2d 956 (Cal. 1935).

[208]Johnson v. School District No. 1, 270 Pac. 764 (Ore. 1928); McMahon v. Cooney, 25 P.2d 131 (Mont. 1933).

[209]Burton v. School District No. 19, 38 P.2d 610 (Wyo. 1934); Fuller v. Lockhart, 182 S.E. 733 (N.C. 1935); Clifton v. School District No. 14 of Russellville, 90 S.W.2d 508 (Ark. 1936).

[210]Downing v. School District of City of Erie, 147 Atl. 239 (Pa. 1927); Miller v. Johnson, 48 P.2d 956 (Cal. 1935).

[211]Burton v. School District No. 19, 38 P.2d 610 (Wyo. 1934).

[212]Bryan v. Board of Education of City of Perry, 54 Pac. 409 (Okla. 1898); School District No. 5 v. Hopkins, 54 Pac. 437 (Okla. 1898); Minot Special School District No. 1 v. Olsness, 208 N.W. 968 (N.D. 1926).

[213]New York Central Railroad Co. v. White, 243 U.S. 188, 37 S.Ct. 247, 61 L.Ed. 667 (N.Y. 1917); Mountain Timber Co. v. State of Washington, 243 U.S. 219, 37 S.Ct. 260, 61 L.Ed. 685 (Wash. 1917).

[214]Mountain Timber Co. v. State of Washington, 243 U.S. 219, 37 S.Ct. 260, 61 L.Ed. 685 (Wash. 1917).

almost always designated for a specific purpose, e.g., constructing school buildings, and the proceeds of bond issues cannot be used for other purposes without statutory authority. It has been held[215] that proceeds of fire insurance policies on school buildings are to be regarded as trust funds; they must be used to replace the building which was destroyed and can be used for no other purpose. In this respect they are similar to the proceeds of the original bond issue.

It would appear that, when insurance proceeds arise from the loss of special funds or the loss or destruction of property which has been purchased with special funds, they must be used to replace such property. If, however, insurance proceeds arise from the loss of general funds or the loss or destruction of property purchased with general funds, the decision as to how they are to be used is within the discretion of the board of education. They may be used for any school purpose authorized by statute.

9.8 DISPOSITION OF SCHOOL PROPERTY

When property is no longer needed for school purposes, or when school equipment has outlived its usefulness, questions occasionally arise concerning the authority of a board of education or school district to dispose of it. Since public school property is legally regarded as state property, the legislature has complete power to control its disposition.[216] School property is subject to the general rule that property devoted to a public use can be disposed of only where express statutory authority to do so has been granted.[217] It has been found,[218] for example, that a statutory grant of authority to control and manage the public schools does not imply the existence of power to sell school property.

Statutes in a number of states grant authority to boards of education, or school district electors, to sell or otherwise dispose of school property. Where such statutes have been enacted they must be adhered to closely, for a conveyance of land or property

violating statutory requirements as to the procedure which is to be followed is invalid.[219] However, it generally has been held[220] that substantial compliance with the statutory requirements is sufficient.

Where a general grant of power to dispose of school property has been given, it is usually restricted to the disposition of property which is not needed for public school purposes.[221] Furthermore, the disposition which is made of school property must be for the benefit of the school district, and it is expected that good judgment will be exercised and sound business principles will be followed.[222] Thus, school property may not be conveyed as a gift or for a mere nominal consideration.[223] It has been held that public policy forbids the bartering of public school property, or its sale for other than money,[224] although in some cases the courts have permitted school property to be sold for other than cash.[225] Under a statute so permitting, a board of education may exchange land to acquire a school site and the exchange need not be limited to land of equal value.[226] As a rule, a school district cannot sell a schoolhouse merely for purposes of financial gain.[227] It also has been established that a school board may not sell or lease public school property for use as a racially segregated private school.[228] The

[215]Conley v. Rogers, 149 S.E. 699 (Ga. 1929); State v. Board of Trustees of Missoula County High School, 7 P.2d 543 (Mont. 1932).

[216]Kelley v. Brunswick School District, 187 Atl. 703 (Me. 1936); Orleans Parish School Board v. City of New Orleans, 90 So.2d 683 (La. 1956).

[217]Caldwell v. Bauer, 99 N.E. 117 (Ind. 1912); Lane v. Board of Education of Lincoln County, 131 S.E.2d 165 (W.Va. 1963).

[218]Weaver v. Board of Trustees of Wilson Independent School District, 184 S.W.2d 864 (Tex. 1944); Board of Education v. Unknown Heirs of Aughinbaugh, 134 N.E.2d 872 (Ohio 1955).

[219]State v. Zeidler, 66 N.W.2d 652 (Wis. 1954); Moore v. Wells, 93 S.E.2d 731 (Ga. 1956); Haskins v. Kelly, 78 N.Y.S.2d 912 (1948); Clemson Associates, Inc. v. Robinson, 190 S.E.2d 738 (S.C. 1972).

[220]Strathern v. Gilmore, 39 Atl. 83 (Pa. 1898); Ketterer v. Independent School District No. 1, 79 N.W.2d 428 (Minn. 1956); Hand v. School District of City of Sidney, 2 N.W.2d 313 (Neb. 1942).

[221]Weir v. Day, 35 Ohio St. 143 (1878); Lane v. Board of Education of Lincoln County, 131 S.E.2d 165 (W.Va. 1963); Duffee v. Jones, 68 S.E.2d 699 (Ga. 1952); State v. Zeidler, 66 N.W.2d 652 (Wis. 1954); Hayward Union High School District v. Madrid, 44 Cal.Rptr. 268 (1965).

[222]Harvey v. Board of Public Instruction, 133 So. 868 (Fla. 1931); Prescott Community Hospital Commission v. Prescott School District No. 1, 115 P.2d 160 (Ariz. 1941); Independent School District of Ionia v. DeWilde, 53 N.W.2d 256 (Iowa 1952); Blair v. City of Fargo, 171 N.W.2d 236 (N.D. 1969); School Board of Orange County v. Fechter, 309 So.2d 549 (Fla. 1975).

[223]Prescott Community Hospital Commission v. Prescott School District No. 1, 115 P.2d 160 (Ariz. 1941); Ketterer v. Independent School District No. 1, 79 N.W.2d 428 (Minn. 1956).

[224]Caldwell v. Bauer, 99 N.E. 117 (Ind. 1912).

[225]United States v. Finn, 127 F.Supp. 158 (Cal. 1954); King County School District No. 176 v. Sanford, 207 Pac. 1058 (Wash. 1922).

[226]Painter v. Wake County Board of Education, 217 S.E.2d 650 (N.C. 1975).

[227]Whitmore v. Hogan, 22 Me. 564 (1843); Abell v. Bell, 91 S.E.2d 548 (S.C. 1956).

[228]McNeal v. Tate County School District, 460 F.2d 568 (5th Cir. 1971); Graves v. Walton County Board of Education, 465 F.2d 887 (5th Cir. 1972); United States v.

courts will intervene to rescind such a sale,[229] or to enjoin the use of public school property sold or leased to another organization for the conduct of a segregated school.[230]

Concerning the disposition of personal property, it would appear that a school district may sell personal property when such an act is believed to be in the best interest of the district.[131]

9.8a Lease

Boards of education generally are allowed to exercise reasonable discretion in leasing for other purposes property held by the school district pending the time it is needed for school purposes.[232] However, a lease which in effect gives away the property of the district is *ultra vires* and void.[233] Also, it has been ruled[234] that a board of education may not enter into a long-term lease which diverts the district's property to a use entirely foreign to the purposes for which public funds may legally be expended.

9.8b Reversion of land to grantor

The question of whether school property which is no longer being used for school purposes should revert to the original owner or grantor, and the circumstances under which a reversion should occur, has generated considerable litigation. Occasionally the deed conveying property to a school district contains a provision to the effect that the land is to be used for school purposes, is to be used for school purposes only, or is to be held by the school district so long as it is used for school purposes. Where a deed contains language of this nature, should the property ever revert to the original grantor, or heirs or assigns, and if so, under what circumstances?

When a school district holds fee simple title to property, i.e., has absolute and indefeasible ownership, under no circumstances will the property revert to a previous owner or grantor; it may be disposed of by the district in any manner authorized by statute. It also is well established that, where the deed to the property in question contains no provision for reversion, and the statutes do not provide for reversion of the property to a previous owner, the property will not revert when it is no longer used for school purposes.[235]

Reversion of property may occur under statutes which provide that when land acquired by school authorities is abandoned for school purposes it will revert to the former owner.[236] It also has been ruled[237] that land acquired through the exercise of eminent domain shall revert to the original owner when it is no longer used for school purposes unless the statutes provide to the contrary. School property may also revert to a former owner by virtue of a provision for reversion contained in the deed that conveyed the property to the school district.[238]

The courts do not look with favor upon conditions in a conveyance of property which provide for a reversion to the grantor in the event of some future happening. Consequently, reversion clauses in deeds conveying title to school property are strictly construed on the theory that, since the deed is the act of the grantor, it should be construed most strongly against the grantor.[239] Unless it is clearly provided in the deed conveying property to a school district that

State of Mississippi, 499 F.2d 425 (5th Cir. 1974); Wright v. Baker County Board of Education, 501 F.2d 131 (5th Cir. 1974).

[229]Wright v. Baker County Board of Education, 501 F.2d 131 (5th Cir. 1974).

[230]McNeal v. Tate County School District, 460 F.2d 568 (5th Cir. 1971); United States v. State of Mississippi, 476 F.2d 941 (5th Cir. 1973).

[231]Board of Education of City of Muskogee v. Baldwin, 137 P.2d 932 (Okla. 1943); State v. Board of Education of Independent School "A," 152 P.2d 262 (Okla. 1944).

[232]Board of Education of City of Chicago v. Crilly, 37 N.E.2d 873 (Ill. 1941); Detweiler v. School District of Borough of Hatfield, 104 A.2d 110 (Pa. 1954); Madachy v. Huntington Horse Show Association, 192 S.E. 128 (W.Va. 1937); Silverman v. Board of Education of Millburn Township, 339 A.2d 233 (N.J. 1975).

[233]Prescott Community Hospital Commission v. Prescott School District No. 1, 115 P.2d 160 (Ariz. 1941).

[234]Madachy v. Huntington Horse Show Association, 192 S.E. 128 (W.Va. 1937).

[235]Smith v. School District No. 14, 94 S.W.2d 706 (Ark. 1936); Gladewater County Line Independent School District v. Hughes, 59 S.W.2d 351 (Tex. 1933); Board of Education of Taylor County v. Board of Education, 166 S.W.2d 295 (Ky. 1942).

[236]Maxwell v. Custer, 30 N.W.2d 177 (Iowa 1947); Lazarus v. Morris, 61 Atl. 815 (Pa. 1905).

[237]Mulligan v. School District, 88 Atl. 362 (Pa. 1913); Town of Brookline v. Carey, 245 N.E.2d 446 (Mass. 1969).

[238]Allemannia Fire Insurance Co. v. Winding Gulf Collieries, 60 F.Supp. 65 (W.Va. 1945); Board of Education of Louisville v. Society of Alumni, 239 S.W.2d 931 (Ky. 1951); Price v. Rowell, 159 A.2d 622 (Vt. 1960); Saletri v. Clark, 108 N.W.2d 548 (Wis. 1961); Board of Education v. Unknown Heirs of Aughinbaugh, 134 N.E.2d 872 (Ohio 1955); School District No. Six in County of Weld v. Russell, 396 P.2d 929 (Col. 1964); Duplin County Board of Education v. Carr, 190 S.E. 653 (N.C. 1972).

[239]Curtis v. Board of Education, 23 Pac. 98 (Kan. 1890); Board of Education of Borough of West Paterson v. Brophy, 106 Atl. 32 (N.J. 1919); Washington City Board of Education v. Edgerton, 94 S.E.2d 661 (N.C. 1956); Carroll County Academy v. Trustees of Gallatin Academy, 47 S.W. 617 (Ky. 1898).

it shall revert to the grantor in the event of some future occurrence, the property will not revert. It has been held,[240] for example, that, where property was deeded to a school district in return for a substantial consideration, reversion of the property will not occur unless the deed expressly provided for a reversion.

General statements in a deed conveying land to a school district to the effect that the property shall be used for school purposes do not create a possibility of reversion, and the property does not revert to the grantor when it is no longer used for school purposes.[241] It has been said that such phrases in a deed are merely descriptive of the nature of the use to which the property is to be put and do not create a limitation or condition subsequent on the title to the property.[242]

When a deed conveying land to a school district provides that it is to be used for school purposes only, and that when no longer so used it shall revert to the grantor, in most instances the property will revert when it is no longer used for the purposes specified. When the courts are called upon to interpret a conveyance of this type, their action will depend upon the precise wording of the deed. They generally take the position that a deed which contains such a clause creates a limitation or a condition subsequent. The distinction between the two terms has been put as follows:

In a limitation, the instrument creating the conditional estate marks its duration. Words of limitation restrict the continuance of the estate and denote the period which is to determine it. The happening of the named event ipso facto terminates the estate. In a condition subsequent, the instrument creating the conditional estate marks the event upon which the estate is liable to be defeated but some act of election on the part of the grantor or his

heirs is necessary to actually determine the estate.[243]

Thus, in a case in which title to one acre of land was conveyed by a corporation to a school district with the limitation that it would revert to the corporation and its assigns if the district ceased to use it for school purposes, it was held[244] that the land immediately reverted to the corporation when the school district discontinued use of the land for school purposes. Similarly, where land was conveyed to a school district by a warranty deed containing a provision that if the land was abandoned by the school district and not used for school purposes it would revert to the grantor, it was held[245] that when the school district abandoned use of the property for school purposes its interest in the land was automatically terminated.

Where the reversion clause in a deed establishes a condition subsequent, reversion of the property to the grantor is not automatic, and furthermore, the right to reversion can be exercised only by the grantor or heirs; it cannot be passed on to a third party.[246] It has been held,[247] for example, that, where the deed to school property provided that the grantor or heirs would have the right to repossess the property if it ceased to be used for school purposes, reversion of the property was not automatic, and that a third party who held the deed to the entire original tract could not exercise the condition subsequent created by the original deed.

In several cases it has been held[248] that with a deed to school property containing a reversion clause the right of reversion to the grantor may be overcome by the use of the property for school purposes for a long period of time. For instance, where a school had been maintained for ninety-seven years and was abandoned only because of construction of an interstate highway, a reversionary clause in the deed conveying the

[240]McElroy v. Pope, 154 S.W. 903 (Ky. 1913); Board of Education of Borough of West Paterson v. Brophy, 106 Atl. 32 (N.J. 1919); Hollomon v. Board of Education of Stewart County, 147 S.E. 882 (Ga. 1929); Raley v. County of Umalilla, 13 Pac. 890 (Ore. 1887).

[241]Board of Education of Taylor County v. Board of Education, 166 S.W.2d 295 (Ky. 1942); Brophy v. Board of Education of Borough of West Paterson, 172 Atl. 910 (N.J. 1934); Phillips Gas & Oil Co. v. Lingenfelter, 105 Atl. 888 (Pa. 1919); Herald v. Board of Education, 65 S.E. 102 (W.Va. 1909); Hagaman v. Board of Education of Woodbridge Township, 285 A.2d 63 (N.J. 1971).

[242]Board of Education of Taylor County v. Board of Education, 166 S.W.2d 295 (Ky. 1942); Boyd v. Ducktown Chemical & Iron Co., 89 S.W.2d 360 (Tenn. 1935); Fuchs v. Reorganized School District No. 2, 251 S.W.2d 677 (Mo. 1952); Hughes v. Gladewater County Line Independent School District, 76 S.W.2d 471 (Tex. 1934).

[243]Franks v. Sparks, 121 S.E.2d 27 (Ga. 1961). For a more extensive discussion of the conditions under which school property will revert to the grantor see 109 A.L.R. 1148, 28 A.L.R.2d 564, 45 A.L.R.2d 1154, and 53 A.L.R.2d 224.

[244]Saletri v. Clark, 108 N.W.2d 548 (Wis. 1961).

[245]School District No. Six in County of Weld v. Russell, 396 P.2d 929 (Col. 1964); See also Duplin County Board of Education v. Carr, 190 S.E.2d 653 (N.C. 1972).

[246]Franks v. Sparks, 121 S.E.2d 27 (Ga. 1961).

[247]Ibid.

[248]McArdle v. School District of Omaha, 136 N.W.2d 422 (Neb. 1965); Savannah School District v. McLeod, 290 P.2d 593 (Cal. 1955); Jordan v. Hendricks, 173 N.E. 288 (Ind. 1930); Board of Commissioners of Trego County v. Hays, 145 Pac. 847 (Kan. 1915).

property to the school district was held to have served its purpose and was obsolete, and title to the property was considered properly in the district.[249]

When the deed conveying property to a school district contains a reversion clause, questions may arise as to what actions constitute abandonment of the property. In such instances it is the use to which the property is being put, not the intent of the school authorities, that governs. So long as property granted for school purposes is used in good faith for such purposes, no abandonment has occurred.[250] The courts generally will not declare that property has been abandoned for school purposes unless the evidence clearly shows that failure to use the property in question was of such duration and character as to violate the purpose and spirit of the grant.[251] Thus, it has been held that a mere intent to change the site of a school does not constitute abandonment,[252] nor does failure to use the property for school purposes for a limited period of time constitute abandonment.[253] It also has been held that property has not been abandoned for school purposes when it is used as a way station for children riding a school bus to a consolidated school,[254] or where the school board has dedicated the land for park and playground purposes.[255]

9.8c Reversion of buildings to grantor

The courts are divided on the question of whether buildings erected on land which is subject to reversion belong to the school district or to the person to whom the land reverts. In a number of cases it has been held[256] that, where there is no statute governing title to buildings on land which is subject to reversion, and no provision in the deed conveying the land which authorizes their removal upon reversion, any buildings on the property revert to the original grantor along with the land in accordance with the general theory that improvements affixed to realty become a part thereof. Other courts in similar situations have ruled[257] that buildings erected on land which is subject to reversion do not revert with the land but remain the property of the school district. In the latter cases the courts based their rulings on the theory that the general rule of fixtures is inapplicable,[258] that school authorities have no power to give away public property,[259] and that a school building is not a fixture.[260] It should be noted, however, that, where the deed conveying the land contains a reversion clause and makes express provision for the removal or disposition of school buildings which have been erected on the land, the provisions of the deed are controlling.[261]

9.9 SUMMARY

Although local school districts may hold title to public school property, the ultimate ownership of school property rests with the state. Local school districts hold school property only in a trusteeship capacity; they have no vested interest in it. Thus, the state may, in its discretion, transfer school property from one trustee to another, e.g., through school district reorganization.

Even in the absence of specific statutory authority, it is generally agreed that a board of education has implied power to acquire and hold school property, including land for school sites. A grant of authority to construct school buildings carries with it implied authority to purchase land for school purposes, including land for use as a playground, athletic field, or the like.

[249]McArdle v. School District of Omaha, 136 N.W.2d 422 (Neb. 1965).

[250]Swink c. City of Dallas, 36 S.W.2d 222 (Tex. 1931); Shuster v. Board of Education, 86 A.2d 16 (N.J. 1951); Harris v. Consolidated School District No. 8C, 328 S.W.2d 646 (Mo. 1959); Ballantyne v. Nedrose Public School District No. 4, 177 N.W.2d 551 (N.D. 1970); School District RE-2 (J) v. Panucci, 490 P.2d 711 (Col. 1971).

[251]Clark v. Jones, 144 P.2d 498 (Ore. 1943); Conway v. San Miguel County Board of Education, 282 P.2d 719 (N.M. 1955); Harris v. Consolidated School District No. 8C, 328 S.W.2d 646 (Mo. 1959).

[252]Ritter v. Board of Education of Edmonson County, 151 S.W. 5 (Ky. 1912).

[253]Koonz v. Joint School District No. 4, 41 N.W.2d 616 (Wis. 1950); Clark v. Jones, 144 P.2d 498 (Ore. 1943); Board v. Nevada School District, 251 S.W.2d 20 (Mo. 1952); Board of Supervisors of Franklin County v. Newell, 56 So.2d 689 (Miss. 1952).

[254]McCullough v. Swifton Consolidated School District, 155 S.W.2d 353 (Ark. 1941).

[255]Koonz v. Joint School District No. 4, 41 N.W.2d 616 (Wis. 1950).

[256]Hand v. School District No. 1, 158 Pac. 315 (Mont. 1916); Malone v. Kitchen, 137 N.E. 562 (Ind. 1922); New Hebron Consolidated School District v. Sutton, 118 So.

303 (Miss. 1928); Williams v. Kirby School District No. 32, 181 S.W.2d 488 (Ark. 1944); Miller v. Common School District No. 10, 43 N.W.2d 102 (Minn. 1950).

[257]Allen v. Franks, 166 S.W. 384 (Tex. 1914); May v. Board of Education, 12 Ohio App. 456 (1920); Rose v. School District No. 94 of Miami County, 179 P.2d 181 (Kan. 1947); Low v. Blakeney, 85 N.E.2d 741 (Ill. 1949); Dickerman v. Town of Pittsford, 80 A.2d 529 (Vt. 1951); Board v. Nevada School District, 251 S.W.2d 20 (Mo. 1952); Gotheridge v. Unified School District No. 365, 512 P.2d 478 (Kan. 1973).

[258]Low v. Blakeney, 85 N.E.2d 741 (Ill. 1949); May v. Board of Education, 12 Ohio App. 456 (1920).

[259]Rose v. School District No. 94 of Miami County, 179 P.2d 181 (Kan. 1947).

[260]Sewell v. Reinhardt, 219 P.2d 996 (Okla. 1950).

[261]Werner v. Bennett, 31 Conn. 468 (1863); School District No. 42 of Cascade County v. Pribyl, 267 Pac. 289 (Mont. 1928); Milner v. New Edinburg School District, 200 S.W.2d 319 (Ark. 1947).

When it has expressly been granted such power, a school district may acquire property for school purposes through condemnation. All statutory requirements concerning the procedure to be followed in the taking of land through condemnation must be scrupulously observed. Unless the amount of property it may acquire through condemnation is specifically limited by statute, a board of education has discretion to determine the amount of land which is to be obtained and also to determine the particular piece of property which is to be secured. The owner of property taken through condemnation is entitled to receive just compensation for the property, i.e., the fair market value of the property at the date of its taking considering its present and potential use.

Authority to select school sites generally is delegated by the legislature to local boards of education or to the electorate. Where such authority is delegated to the electorate, school sites must be selected by the voters at a legally called meeting or election. Where such authority is vested in the board of education, it may exercise reasonable discretion in selecting sites and the courts will not interfere with its decision unless it has abused its discretion or has violated the law. A board, in selecting school sites, must choose them with the goal of alleviating or preventing racial segregation of pupils. A board of education may not bargain away its discretion in choosing school sites through promises or representations made to the public. Hence, the fact that it has announced its intention to build a school on a particular site does not prevent the board from later deciding to build the school on some other site.

The legislature may authorize the use of school property for any purpose not prohibited by the constitution. While the state is under no obligation to make public school property available for public meetings, if it does make such facilities available it may not arbitrarily exclude any person or group from using them. Although local school authorities may protect school property from disturbances and annoyances which interfere with the conduct of the school, they may not impose discriminatory restrictions on the use of or right to enter upon school property.

Where a board of education has been granted the authority to permit school property to be used for other than school purposes, usually it may permit school property to be used for any purpose which does not interfere with its use for school purposes and which is not specifically prohibited. The courts will not interfere with the discretion of school officials concerning the use of school property unless they abuse their discretion.

A school district may permit school property to be used for school-related activities to which an admission fee is charged and may derive revenue from such activities so long as the revenue is incidental to the conduct of the activity and not its primary purpose. In deciding whether school facilities may be used for nonschool-related activities, two criteria generally should be applied: (1) There must be no interference with the regular school program and (2) there must be no damage to school property.

School property may be used for political purposes if such use is authorized by statute. Where political organizations are permitted to use school property, they may not be singled out for special treatment but must use the property on the same basis as any other organization.

As a general rule, school districts may permit school property to be used for private purposes so long as such use is incidental to its use for school purposes and is not primarily for commercial gain. Thus, the use of school property for a cafeteria, for a school store, and for private instruction has been permitted. The courts are in some disagreement as to whether school property may be leased for commercial purposes. Such use has been permitted in some jurisdictions and denied in others.

The weight of authority indicates that unless a statute authorizes the use of school property for religious purposes, or permits local school officials to authorize such use, public school property may not be used for holding religious meetings and/or services. When local school officials are authorized to permit such use, they may exercise considerable discretion in deciding whether or not to permit it.

Specific statutory requirements concerning the insuring of school property must, of course, be followed. In the absence of such requirements a board of education may determine whether to insure school property, the amount of insurance to be taken, and the company from which it is to be procured. Unless there are statutory provisions to the contrary, school boards have authority to self-insure against potential losses so long as their actions are reasonable. A board of education may purchase insurance from a stock insurance company, and from a mutual insurance company if the contingent liability of policyholders is limited.

School property is subject to the general rule that public property can be disposed of only as the statutes provide. Statutory requirements concerning the disposition of school property must be adhered to closely, since a conveyance of property which violates statutory requirements is invalid. A board of education may not sell or lease public school property for use as a private segregated school.

Whether school property should revert to its original owner when it is no longer used for school purposes is dependent upon several factors. Property to which a school district holds fee simple title will not revert to a previous owner, nor will property revert to a previous owner where the deed to the property makes no provision for reversion. However, land acquired through condemnation will revert unless the statutes provide otherwise, and land will revert to the grantor when the deed conveying the land to the school district so provides. Reversion clauses in deeds conveying land to be used for school purposes are strictly construed. Unless the provision for reversion is clear and unmistakable, the right of reversion will be denied. Reversion clauses generally take the form of either a limitation or a condition subsequent. A limitation provides that upon the occurrence of a named event, e.g., abandonment of the property for school purposes, the property will immediately revert to the grantor. A condition subsequent, on the other hand, does not automatically result in reversion upon the occurrence of a certain event; it merely creates the possibility of reversion contingent upon some act by the grantor or heirs. In several cases it has been ruled that use of property for school purposes for a long period of time defeated the right of reversion contained in the deed conveying the land.

The courts are not in agreement on whether school buildings erected on land subject to reversion to the grantor become the property of the grantor when the land reverts. In some jurisdictions it has been ruled that they revert to the grantor along with the land; in other jurisdictions it has been held that they remain the property of the school district.

Construction of School Buildings

10.0 INTRODUCTION

In view of the fact that education is a state function, it is obvious that the duty to provide public school buildings rests with the state. The state customarily delegates authority to construct school facilities to local agencies, such as boards of education, municipalities, or local school district electors. The powers and duties of boards of education, municipalities, and school district electors relative to the construction of public school facilities are governed by the statutes, and only such authority as the statutes confer, either expressly or by implication, may be exercised by them.[1] It has been said that these statutes should be construed not only as a grant of power, but also as a limitation thereon,[2] although they are not to be given a narrow or limited construction.[3]

10.1 AUTHORITY FOR CONSTRUCTING SCHOOL BUILDINGS

Where the authority to determine the necessity for and the kind of school facilities to be constructed is vested with the voters of the school district, a board of education has no power to build a schoolhouse until the voters have authorized its construction.[4] While the district electorate may be empowered to determine the kind of schoolhouse to be constructed and the cost thereof, they cannot exercise this power in an arbitrary fashion. It has been held,[5] for example, that the power vested in the voters relative to the construction of school facilities is ministerial, and that it cannot be exercised to gratify a whim or caprice but must be exercised in good faith and in the public interest.

Where the district's electorate is empowered to authorize the construction of school facilities, such authorization is generally accomplished by means of an election. The general rules which govern school elections held for the purpose of electing school board members or of approving bond issues are applicable to elections held for the pur-pose of authorizing the construction of school facilities. There must also be compliance with any specific procedural requirements imposed by the statutes for such elections.

The more common and more desirable procedure is for the legislature to empower boards of education to determine the school facilities which are needed. Boards of education may be granted authority to determine where schools will be established,[6] how many will be established,[7] and the way an appropriation of money for the construction of school facilities will be spent.[8] Where a board of education has been granted authority to determine the necessity for and the kind of school facilities which are to be provided, decisions in regard to the construction of such facilities rest within the discretion of the board of education.[9] As a general rule, the courts will not interfere with the exercise of its discretion unless the board abuses its power or is guilty of misconduct or fraud.[10] It has been held,[11] for example, that the discretion vested in school authorities to determine whether to repair or rebuild an existing building or to construct a new building is not subject to judicial review in the absence of abuse of that discretion.

Where boards of education have been granted authority to determine school facility needs, they generally may provide any facility which is required for the teaching of any proper subject of instruction.[12] It frequently has been held,[13] for example, that under its general power to erect school buildings a board of education has implied authority to provide such facilities as gymnasiums, athletic fields, stadiums, and

[1]Commonwealth v. Madison, 108 S.W.2d 519 (Ky. 1937); Kretchman v. Burner County School District No. 12, 158 N.W. 993 (N.D. 1916).

[2]State v. Lyons, 96 Pac. 922 (Mont. 1908).

[3]Keime v. Community High School District No. 296, 180 N.E. 858 (Ill. 1932).

[4]Durgin v. Brown, 180 A.2d 136 (N.J. 1962); Henderson v. Long Creek School District No. 2, 171 N.W. 825 (N.D. 1919); Randall v. Hoff, 158 N.Y.S.2d 188 (1957); School District No. 3 of Norton Township v. Michigan Municipal Finance Commission, 62 N.W.2d 445 (Mich. 1954).

[5]Iverson v. Union Free High School District, 202 N.W. 788 (Wis. 1925).

[6]Corley v. Montgomery, 46 S.W.2d 283 (Mo. 1932); Pegale v. Oken, 324 P.2d 58 (Cal. 1958).

[7]Bartlett v. Board of Education of Miamisburg City School District, 128 N.E.2d 267 (Ohio 1955).

[8]State v. Board of Trustees of Stout Institute, 149 N.W. 205 (Wis. 1914).

[9]Smith v. Board of Education of Oswego Community High School District, 87 N.E.2d. 893 (Ill. 1950); Laing v. School District No. 10, 224 P.2d 923 (Ore. 1950); Ricker v. Board of Education, 396 P.2d 416 (Utah 1964).

[10]Carter v. Taylor, 231 S.W.2d 601 (Ky. 1950); Application of Kuhn, 152 N.Y.S.2d 813 (1956); Pickler v. Board of Education of Davis County, 62 S.E. 902 (N.C. 1908); De Angelis V. Laino, 252 N.Y.S. 891 (1931).

[11]Board of Education of Hancock County v. Moorehead, 136 N.E. 913 (Ohio 1922).

[12]Moyer v. Board of Education, 62 N.E. 2d 802 (Ill. 1945); Hoyt v. Trustees of State Normal School, 44 P.2d 513 (Col. 1935).

[13]Moyer v. Board of Education, 62 N.E.2d 802 (Ill. 1945); Perkins v. Trask, 23 P.2d 982 (Mont. 1933); Lowden v. Jefferson County Excise Board, 122 P.2d 991 (Okla. 1942); Nicholas v. Calhoun, 37 So.2d 313 (Miss. 1948); Juntila v. Everett School District No. 24, 35 P.2d 78 (Wash. 1934).

swimming pools. On the question of whether school boards have implied authority to build a residence for school employees the courts are in some disagreement. In some jurisdictions it has been decided[14] that a grant of authority to erect schoolhouses does not imply authority to build a teacherage; in other jurisdictions it has been held[15] that it does. A legislature may, of course, grant specific authority to construct and operate residences for teachers.[16]

In determining school facility needs, a school board not only is expected to consider the present needs of the district but may properly look beyond immediate necessity in its planning and make reasonable provisions to accommodate an increasing number of pupils where population growth is likely.[17] It is worth noting that provision of reasonable and convenient accommodations for all children in the school district has been referred to as a duty by some courts.[18] That is, not only do school authorities have power to provide the needed school facilities; it is their duty to provide them. Furthermore, it has been ruled[19] that permitting or requiring school children residing in the district to attend schools in other districts does not constitute compliance with a constitutional or statutory duty to provide schools.

A statutory grant of power to construct school buildings carries with it the implied power to provide school furniture, apparatus, and other ordinary and necessary equipment for the buildings.[20] Also, the authority to teach certain subjects or sponsor certain activities implies the authority to purchase the equipment or apparatus needed for such purposes.[21] In general, it may be said that school authorities have the power and duty to provide the furniture, equipment, apparatus, and supplies required to support the district's educational program.[22]

10.1a Employment of architects

It is well established that authority to erect a school building also conveys, by implication, authority to employ an architect to draw plans and specifications for it.[23] The courts reason that before school buildings can be constructed, detailed plans, specifications, and estimates must be prepared; that a board of education typically requires specialized professional assistance in this undertaking; and that an architect possessing the requisite technical competence and skill must be employed if the board of education is to discharge effectively its power to erect buildings. Where the board of education does not have the authority to erect school buildings it has no power to employ architects to design buildings; it may, however, employ architects for the purpose of obtaining expert advice concerning repairs if it has the duty to keep the buildings in proper repair.[24] The power to employ architects may be made subject to the limitation that the cost of the building designed by the architect must not exceed the sum of money which has been authorized for the buildings.[25] It may also be limited by a requirement that funds for the construction of the building to be designed by the architect must be authorized or available,[26] although there is some authority to the contrary on this point.[27] Finally, there are frequently statutory limitations on the architect's fee and any agreement for an

[14]Denny v. Mecklenburg County, 191 S.E. 26 (N.C. 1937); Fulk v. School District No. 8, 53 N.W.2d 56 (Neb 1952); Hansen v. Lee, 206 Pac. 927 (Wash. 1922).

[15]McNair v. School District No. 1 of Cascade County, 288 Pac. 188 (Mont. 1930); Alexander v. Phillips, 254 Pac. 1056 (Ariz. 1927); Taylor v. Board of Public Instruction of Lafayette County, 26 So.2d 180 (Fla. 1946).

[16]Adams. v. Miles, 300 S.W. 211 (Tex. 1927).

[17]Little v. State Board of Education, 142 Atl. 432 (N.J. 1928).

[18]Constantian v. Anson County, 93 S.E.2d 163 (N.C. 1956); Commonwealth v. Madison, 108 S.W.2d 519 (Ky. 1937).

[19]School District No. 26 v. Hards, 149 P.2d 651 (Col. 1944).

[20]Corley v. Montgomery, 46 S.W.2d 283 (Mo. 1932); Board of Trustees v. Pruden, 103 S.E. 369 (N.C. 1920); Connell v. Board of School Directors of Kennett, 52 A.2d 645 (Pa. 1947); Jewett v. School District No. 25, 54 P.2d 546 (Wyo. 1936).

[21]Knabe v. West Bay City Board of Education, 34 N.W. 568 (Mich. 1887); Galloway v. School District of Borough of Prospect Park, 200 Atl. 99 (Pa. 1938).

[22]Commonwealth v. Norfolk School Board, 63 S.E. 1081 (Va. 1909); Union District Township v. Meyers, 49 N.W. 1042 (Iowa 1891); School Committee of Gloucester v. City of Gloucester, 85 N.E.2d 429 (Mass. 1949); Constantian v. Anson County, 93 S.E.2d 163 (N.C. 1956).

[23]Harlingen Independent School District v. C. H. Page & Bro. 48 S.W.2d 983 (Tex. 1932); People v. Board of Education, 190 N.Y.S. 798 (1921); Wyckoff v. Force, 214 Pac. 489 (Cal. 1923); Barringer v. Guilford School Township of Hendricks County, 194 N.E. 651 (Ind. 1935); Sleight v. Board of Education of City of Paterson, 170 Atl. 598 (N.J. 1934); Pehrson v. School District No. 334, 77 P.2d 1022 (Wash. 1938).

[24]Simpson v. City of Marlborough, 127 N.E. 887 (Mass. 1920); William S. Drummey, Inc. v. City of Cambridge, 184 N.E. 458 (Mass. 1933).

[25]Laing v. School District No. 10, 224 P.2d 923 (Ore. 1950).

[26]Harlingen Independent School District v. C. H. Page & Bro., 48 S.W.2d 983 (Tex. 1932); Barton v. Tokio Independent School District, 49 S.W.2d 939 (Tex. 1932).

[27]Barringer v. Guilford School Township of Hendricks County, 194 N.E. 651 (Ind. 1935); Bonsack & Pearce v. School District of Marceline, 49 S.W.2d 1085 (Mo. 1932).

amount in excess of that amount is invalid.[28]

Contracts with

The architectural contract is primarily a contract for personal service. It calls for the rendering of personal service of a highly specialized professional nature which requires substantial technical skill. In view of the nature of the service called for by the contract, it generally has been held that statutes requiring that public contracts be let on the basis of competitive bids do not apply to contracts for architectural services.[29] The reasoning of the courts is aptly illustrated by a case in which it was claimed that a board of education must advertise for competitive bids before contracting for the professional services of an architect. The court denied the injunction which was sought and said:

> The contention here made has long since been denied judicially and legislatively. It has been held that because an architect is an artist, that his work requires taste, skill and technical learning and ability of a rare kind, it would be bad judgment to advertise and get many bids when the lowest bidder might also be the least capable and most inexperienced and his bid absolutely unacceptable and therefore "the employment of a person who is highly and technically skilled in his science or profession is one which may properly be made without competitive bidding." ... Where competitive proposals do not produce an advantage, a statute requiring competitive bidding does not apply.[30]

Contracts with architects are governed by the general rules relating to contracts. Since the selection of an architect requires the exercise of discretion, the general rule is that power to employ an architect may not be delegated.[31] In some instances, however, as where it is clear that employment of an architect is necessary, a committee of the board of education may enter into a valid contract with an architect. It has been held,[32] for example, that the building committee of a school board has the authority to hire an architect who will provide expert advice when it is needed. Since a contract with one who has no legal authority to enter into it is invalid, it is essential to the validity of architectural contracts that they be consummated with the body having power to contract.[33] Consequently, it is most desirable that a contract with an architect be entered into by action of the full board of education at a legally called meeting.

10.1b Relationship of architect and board of education

Architects whose services have been contracted for by boards of education are usually held to be agents of the board who possess limited powers.[34] Their powers are determined by the general rules of agency as well as by their contracts.[35] Since the architectural contract is one which calls for personal service, architects may not delegate the trust and confidence vested in them to other persons unless such delegation has been authorized by the board of education.[36] Also, as an agent of the board of education, architects have no power to enter into contracts in behalf of the board unless they have expressly been granted that power.

The school board cannot be bound by an architect to a contract for materials furnished for or work performed upon a structure for which the architect is responsible unless the architect has been given express authority to do so.[37] Similarly an architect cannot alter or change building plans and specifications so as to bind the parties to the building contract in the absence of express authority to do so.[38] An architect is not completely without power to change building plans and specifications, however, for it has been held that the architect has authority to make minor changes which do not entail additional cost and which are consistent with the purpose of the building.[39]

[28] Murphy v. City of Brockton, 305 N.E.2d 103 (Mass. 1973).

[29] Krohnberg v. Pass, 244 N.W. 329 (Minn. 1932); Cobb v. Pasadena City Board of Education, 285 P.2d 41 (Cal. 1955); State v. Brown, 21 S.W.2d 721 (Tenn. 1929).

[30] Cobb v. Pasadena City Board of Education, 285 P.2d 41 (Cal. 1955).

[31] Jameison v. City of Paducah, 241 S.W. 327 (Ky. 1922).

[32] William S. Drummey, Inc. v. City of Cambridge, 184 N.E. 458 (Mass. 1933).

[33] Dierks Special School District v. Van Dyke, 237 S.W. 428 (Ark. 1922); Harlingen Independent School District v. C. H. Page & Bro., 48 S.W.2d 983 (Tex. 1932).

[34] Union High School District No. 400 v. Pacific Northwest Construction Co., 269 Pac. 809 (Wash. 1928); Smith v. Board of Education of Parkersburg District, 85 S.E. 513 (W.Va. 1915).

[35] Weld v. First National Bank of Englewood, 166 Ill.App. 8 (1911); Fairbanks, Morse & Co. v. Merchants' and Consumers' Market Home Assocaition, 202 S.W. 596 (Mo. 1918).

[36] Smith v. Board of Education of City of Liberal, 222 Pac. 101 (Kan. 1924).

[37] Reifsnyder v. Dougherty, 152 Atl. 98 (Pa. 1930); Albert Steinfeld & Co. v. Broxholme, 211 Pac, 473 (Cal. 1922).

[38] Smith v. Board of Education of Parkersburg District, 85 S.E. 513 (W.Va. 1915); Hurley v. Kiona-Benton School District No. 27, 215 Pac. 21 (Wash. 1923).

[39] Hutchinson v. Bohnsack School District, 199 N.W. 484 (N.D. 1924).

Also, modifications in plans made by the architect are binding upon the school district so long as the action is within the scope of the architect's authority.[40]

Questions frequently arise concerning whether the architect or the school district owns the plans and specifications for a school building. As a general rule, a school district which employs an architect to prepare plans and specifications for a school building, and pays for them, becomes the owner of the plans.[41] But if the contract between the school board and the architect specifically states that all plans and specifications are the property of the architect, and are to be returned to the architect upon completion of the building, such a provision is binding and determines the ownership of the plans and specifications.[42]

10.1c Compensation of

The contract between the architect and the school district ordinarily embodies provisions governing the amount of compensation which the architect shall receive and/or the method to be used in computing such compensation. If the architect's contract is valid and enforceable such provisions govern compensation. A number of cases have arisen, however, in which the architect's compensation has been questioned either because the building designed was never built or because the contract was terminated prior to its completion or because the contract did not comply with statutory requirements.

Most architectural contracts are based on a standard contract form recommended by the American Institute of Architects with such modifications as are necessary to fit the contract to the job at hand. Where the contract involves the design of a building and supervision of its construction, a fixed percentage of the total cost of the building (or the work which is done), is regarded by the courts as the usual fair and reasonable method of determining the architect's compensation.[43] It has also been held[44] that standard charges which are based upon the scale recommended by the American Institute of Architects provide a suitable basis

for determining an architect's compensation.

Architectural contracts providing for compensation based upon a fixed percentage of the total cost of a building usually provide that regular payments based on the ratio of the value of the construction which has been completed to the total cost of the building shall be made to the architect. The right to terminate construction also is usually reserved in such contracts. When an architect's contract is terminated after bids on the proposed construction have been received and rejected, the architect is entitled to receive payment for the work of conducting preliminary studies and preparing working drawings and specifications in accordance with the terms of the contract.[45] Where all bids are rejected because they far exceed the budget and the architect makes revisions and a construction contract is finally let based on the revised plans, the architect's compensation is based on the cost of building the project, as revised. The architect is not entitled to payment for "additional services" for the revisions. The court reasoned[46] that where an architect agrees to provide working drawings, details, and specifications, this entails a duty to provide continuing services until a proposal satisfactory to the agency is reached. If the contract is terminated after some construction has taken place, the architect is entitled to compensation based upon the actual cost of the construction completed at the point of termination.[47]

When a school district breaches a contract with an architect, the architect is entitled to recover damages from the district. The rule governing recovery in such cases may be stated as follows: The damages for wrongfully discharging an architect who has undertaken to draw plans for and to superintend the construction of a building for a percentage of its cost are the difference between the contract price and what it would have cost the architect to complete the undertaking at the time of discharge.[48]

Where the architect's contract does not fix compensation, a school district is obligated to pay for the reasonable value of the services the architect has rendered. In determining the reasonable value of the architect's services in such cases, the courts have

[40]Sando v. Kalberg, 244 Pac, 576 (Wash. 1926).

[41]Hutton v. School City of Hammond, 142 N.F.E. 427 (Ind. 1924); McCoy v. Grant, 174 N.W. 728 (Minn. 1919); Tumey v. Little, 186 N.Y.S.2d 94 (1959).

[42]McCoy v. Grant, 174 N.W. 728 (Minn. 1919).

[43]People v. Board of Education, 210 N.Y.S. 686 (1925); Baylor University v. Carlander, 316 S.W.2d 277 (Tex. 1958).

[44]Llewellyn v. Board of Education, 154 N.E. 889 (Ill. 1926).

[45]Orth v. Board of Public Education of School District of Pittsburgh, 116 Atl. 366 (Pa. 1922).

[46]School District Number 1 of Pima County v. Hastings, 472 P.2d 44 (Ariz. 1970).

[47]Furst v. Board of Education of Highland Park High School District No. 113, 155 N.E.2d 654 (Ill. 1959).

[48]Page v. Harlingen Independent School District, 23 S.W.2d 829 (Tex. 1929).

deemed it appropriate to consider the customary charges of architects for similar services; the responsibility, training, ability, experience, and integrity of the architect involved; and any other pertinent facts or circumstances.[49]

Architects sometimes agree to design a building which can be built at a cost not in excess of a specified sum of money. If an architect enters into such an agreement and fails to provide plans for a building which can be erected for a cost no greater than the sum specified, the courts are agreed that the architect cannot recover for services rendered unless the increased cost is due to special circumstances or to a change in the plans made at the school board's direction.[50] It should be noted, however, that if the school district accepts and uses the plans, the architect is entitled to receive compensation for them despite the fact that the cost of the building exceeded the sum which has been agreed upon.[51]

In several cases the question at issue has been whether an architect is entitled to receive compensation for general drawings and specifications for a school building for which funds have not been authorized, or the construction cost of which would exceed the district's debt limit. Although the courts are not in complete agreement, the weight of authority indicates that an architect should be allowed to recover for services in such circumstances on the ground that preparation of plans and specifications is not a part of the construction of the building but a necessary preliminary step to determine whether construction should be undertaken.[52] The reasoning of the Supreme Court of Nebraska is illustrative:

The projected buildings were never erected; the preliminary plans and drawings could not be said to be a part of any construction of buildings; and, if not, the expense of them was not any part of a building, or necessarily to be

paid from a building fund. They were ordered for the use of the district, and were necessary as much so as many other articles or services which come within the general expenses of a school district, and must be paid for from the general fund.[53]

Other courts have held,[54] however, that, where the plans and specifications prepared by the architect pursuant to a contract with a school district call for a building costing more than the amount of money the district can legally spend, the contract is invalid, and the architect is not entitled to compensation. The courts in these cases reasoned that since the school district had no authority to construct such a building, it had no authority to contract with an architect to prepare plans and specifications for it. Similarly, where a statute specifically prohibits a municipal department from incurring liability in excess of its appropriations, an architect will be bound by the statute and cannot rely on the contract to recover more than was actually appropriated.[55] It also has been held[56] that a school district was not obligated to pay an architect for plans and specifications which were not accepted and for which the district had no money. Where the contract with the architect was entered into before an election was held to authorize the issuance of bonds to finance the building the district was not obligated.

10.2 BIDS ON SCHOOL CONSTRUCTION CONTRACTS

The authority of a board of education to contract for the construction of school buildings is seldom disputed. It has been granted either expressly or by implication in all states. However, the board's authority in letting contracts for the construction of school buildings may be restricted by a statutory requirement that the contracts be awarded on the basis of competitive bids, or by a requirement that certain procedures be followed in letting contracts.

Where the statutes do not demand that school construction contracts be let on the basis of competitive bids, the decision as to whether competitive bids will be secured rests in the sound discretion of the board of

[49]Davis v. South Omaha School District, 122 N.W. 38 (Neb. 1909); Hankin v. Board of Education of Hamilton Township, 135 A.2d 329 (N.J. 1957).

[50]Pierce v. Board of Education, 211 N.Y.S. 788 (1925); Rapp v. Board of Education of City of Las Vegas, 284 Pac. 761 (N.M. 1927); Johnson v. O'Neill, 150 N.W. 835 (Mich. 1915); Issenhuth v. Independent School District No. 22, 222 N.W. 494 (S.D. 1928); Ritter v. School District, 140 Atl. 126 (Pa. 1928).

[51]Bair v. School District No. 141, 146 Pac. 347 (Kan. 1915).

[52]Fiske v. School District, 80 N.W. 265 (Neb. 1899); People v. Board of Education, 190 N.Y.S. 798 (1921); Bonsack & Pearce v. School District of Marceline, 49 S.W.2d 1085 (Mo. 1932); Page v. Harlingen Independent School District, 23 S.W.2d 829 (Tex. 1929).

[53]Fiske v. School District, 80 N.W. 265 (Neb. 1899).

[54]Perkins v. Newark Board of Education, 161 Fed. 767 (3d Cir. 1908); Ritter v. School District, 140 Atl. 126 (Pa. 128); Bair v. School District No. 141, 146 Pac, 347 (Kan. 1915).

[55]Murphy v. City of Brockton, 305 N.E.2d 103 (Mass. 1973).

[56]Barton v. Tokio Independent School District, 49 S.W.2d 939 (Tex. 1932).

education.[57] That is, the board is under no obligation to advertise for bids and may or may not employ competitive bidding at its own discretion.

10.2a Competitive bids

In many states the statutes require that school districts secure competitive bids whenever contracts in excess of a specified sum of money are awarded. It usually has been held that such statutes are mandatory.[58]

Competitive bidding statutes are designed to protect the public interest. As the Supreme Court of Mississippi puts it:

> These statutes were born of experience. Their objects are to protect the public against wrongdoing, sometimes resulting from private and secret machinations; to secure to it the safeguards and benefits of public competitive bids, both in fairness and prices in contracts and in the paying out by county officials of the public funds.[59]

Where statutes call for competitive bidding, the board of education has no discretion in the matter; it must employ competitive bidding. Any contract let in violation of the competitive bidding procedures specified in the applicable statute is invalid.[60] A failure to comply with the requirements of such statutes is not excused by ignorance of the law or by the innocent motives of those involved.[61]

Some statutes requiring competitive bidding permit exceptions to be made when an emergency exists. In interpreting such statutes the courts have generally held that a school board has discretion to determine whether an emergency of the type envisioned by the statute does, in fact, exist.[62]

For example, an Ohio statute provided that the statutory competitive bidding requirements need not be followed in cases of "urgent necessity." In a case[63] involving the interpretation of this statute it was decided that the threat of overcrowded conditions in the schools as a result of the rapid construction of many new homes in the district constituted an "urgent necessity" for the construction of additional school facilities and was sufficient to justify a board of education's failure to advertise for bids for the period of time specified in the competitive bidding statutes. A true emergency must exist, however, before the courts will allow competitive bidding requirements to be ignored.[64]

School districts occasionally have attempted to avoid competitive bidding requirements by having the work performed by employees of the district, or to circumvent such requirements by awarding a number of contracts each of which is less than the sum beyond which competitive bids are required. It has been held[65] that competitive bidding statutes do not preclude the use of school employees to do repair work, regardless of its cost. On the other hand, it has been held[66] that repairs which exceed the amount specified in competitive bidding statutes can be made only on contracts awarded on the basis of competitive bids. In Ohio, for example, a board of education undertook a $20,000 repair job on a piecemeal basis using school janitors and additional laborers hired by the hour. A statute required that contracts for repairs costing in excess of $4,000 be awarded on the basis of competitive bids. The court ruled in this case[67] that the board had violated the competitive bidding statute. It is also clear that the board of education cannot evade competitive bidding requirements by entering into a number of contracts which in total exceed the statutory limit but which individually are each less than the specified sum.[68]

[57]People v. Busenhart, 193 N.E.2d 850 (Ill. 1963); Missoula County Free High School v. Smith, 8 P.2d 800 (Mont. 1932); Mayor and City Council of Baltimore v. Weatherby, 52 Md. 442 (1879).

[58]Commonwealth v. Zang, 16 A.2d 741 (Pa. 1940); State v. Smith, 194 N.E.2d 186 (Ohio 1963); Seim v. Independent District of Monroe, 17 N.W.2d 342 (S.D. 1945); Beall v. Board of Supervisors, 3 So.2d 839 (Miss. 1941); Hanna v. Board of Education of Wicomico County, 87 A.2d 846 (Md. 1952); East Side Construction Co. v. Town of Adams, 108 N.E.2d 659 (Mass. 1952).

[59]Beall v. Board of Supervisors, 3 So. 2d 839 (Miss. 1941).

[60]Randolph McNutt Co. v. Eckert, 177 N.E. 386 (N.Y. 1931); State v. Dugger, 111 S.W.2d 1032 (Tenn. 1938); Seim v. Independent District of Monroe, 17 N.W.2d 342 (S.D. 1945); St. Paul Foundry Co. v. Burnstad School District No. 31, 269 N.W. 739 (N.D. 1936).

[61]In re Audit of School District of City of Scranton, 47 A.2d 288 (Pa. 1946).

[62]Bolce v. Board of Education of Cincinnati, 5 Ohio Supp. 420 (1933); Commonwealth v. Zang, 16 A.2d 741 (Pa. 1940).

[63]Saunders v. Board of Education of Van Buren Township, 59 N.E.2d 936 (Ohio 1944).

[64]Commonwealth v. Zang, 16 A.2d 741 (Pa. 1940).

[65]Contracting Plumbers Association of St. Louis v. Board of Education of St. Louis, 194 S.W.2d 731 (Mo. 1946).

[66]In re Audit of School District of City of Scranton, 47 A.2d 288 (Pa. 1946); State v. Smith, 194 N.E.2d 186 (Ohio 1963).

[67]State v. Smith, 194 N.E.2d 186 (Ohio 1963).

[68]In re Audit of School District of City of Scranton, 47 A.2d 288 (Pa. 1946); California Motor Express, Ltd. v. Chowchilla Union High School District, 20 Cal.Rptr. 768 (1962).

When competitive bidding is employed, it is essential that all bidders be provided with plans and specifications sufficiently definite and precise to permit them to bid on the same basis.[69] Obviously, unless each bidder is provided with the same plans and specifications there can be no effective competitive bidding. Where the specifications set no date for completion of a construction project and each bidder is allowed to designate a date for completion, it has been held[70] that there has not been competitive bidding of the type contemplated by a statute requiring competitive bidding. Specifications concerning material to be used in the construction of a building must also be definite. It has been held,[71] for example, that where the specifications for a building called for either wrought iron or steel pipes, the specifications were not sufficiently precise to meet competitive bidding requirements because they did not make clear who was to decide which type of pipe would be used. There is general agreement that, while articles which may be obtained only from a particular firm, such as patented articles, cannot be specified to the exclusion of all others,[72] patented articles may be specified where the alternative of substituting other articles of similar quality is provided.[73]

Although it is essential that all bidders base their bids on a common standard, it is permissible for a board of education to request that bids be submitted on various alternates within the total construction project.[74] A board of education may request alternate bids based on the use of various construction materials, or alternate bids based on alternative arrangements of space. In effect, the board of education is inviting bidders to submit bids on several propositions rather than on a single proposition. When alternative bids are requested, it is imperative that each bidder be given the opportunity to bid on one, some, or all of the alternates, and that each bidder be provided with definite plans and specifications concerning each alternate. If alternate bids are to comply with competitive bidding statutes, each bidder must have an equal opportunity to submit bids on all of the alternates. It should be recognized, however, that each bidder is not required to submit bids on all alternates and may not be disqualified from the competition for failing to submit bids on all alternates.[75]

10.2b Procedural aspects of

Where competitive bidding is required, either by statute or by the bylaws of a board of education, the board must advertise its intention to receive bids so as to give due notice to all who may be interested in submitting bids. All statutory requirements concerning the methods or procedures to be used in securing competitive bids, the duration of the bidding period, and the media to be used in advertising for bids must be observed.[76] The courts require that prospective bidders be given reasonable notice and that the notice be given publicly.[77] It has been held[78] in this regard that if no newspaper is published in the district the advertisement for bids may be accomplished by posting notices in public places. As a general rule, advertising for competitive bids should be done by the board of education, although it has been ruled[79] that the responsibility of advertising for bids may be delegated to a committee of the board.

Bids submitted by those who wish to compete for school construction contracts must comply with statutory requirements concerning the form in which bids are to be submitted. Failure to conform to such requirements may void the bid. Thus, where statutes demand that the amount for labor and the amount for materials be stated separately in the bid, it has been ruled[80] that failure to comply with this requirement voids the bid. It is also imperative that bids be submitted in accordance with specifications.[81] It has been said that if a bid does not conform substantially to the specifications

---

[69]Homan v. Board of Education, 127 Atl. 824 (N.J. 1925); Edmundson v. Board of Education of Pittsburgh, 94 Atl. 248 (Pa. 1915); Warnock v. Wray, 194 N.Y.S. 396 (1922); Hannan v. Board of Education of City of Lawton, 107 Pac. 646 (Okla. 1909).
[70]Homan v. Board of Education, 127 Atl. 824 (N.J. 1925); Hibbs v. Arensberg, 119 Atl. 727 (Pa. 1923).
[71]Warnock v. Wray, 194 N.Y.S. 396 (1922).
[72]Wilkins v. Newkirk, 155 N.E. 516 (Ind. 1927); Cassel v. Board of Education Common School District No. 13, 220 N.Y.S.2d 262 (1961).
[73]Wilkins v. Newkirk, 155 N.E. 516 (Ind. 1927).
[74]Schwitzer v. Newark Board of Education, 75 Atl. 447 (N.J. 1910); Hannan v. Board of Education of City of Lawton, 107 Pac. 646 (Okla. 1909); Katterjohn & Son v. Board of Education of City of Paducah, 261 S.W. 257 (Ky. 1923).

[75]Warnock & Zahrndt v. Wray, 230 N.Y.S. 681 (1928).
[76]Prosper Contracting Corp. v. Board of Education of the City of New York, 341 N.Y.S.2d 196 (1973).
[77]Mays v. Bassett. 125 Pac. 609 (N.M. 1912); Taylor v. Parker, 302 S.W.2d 125 (Ky. 1957).
[78]In re Tremont Township School Directors, 34 Pa. Dist. & Co. 623 (1938).
[79]Schwitzer v. Newark Board of Education, 75 Atl. 447 (N.J. 1910).
[80]Perkins v. Bright, 141 N.E. 689 (Ohio 1923).
[81]Gunnip v. Lautenklos, 94 A.2d 712 (Del. 1953); Belousofsky v. Board of Education of City of Linden, 148 A.2d 632 (N.J. 1959).

which were advertised a public body has the right and duty to reject it.[82]

The overriding concern of the courts is that the objectives of competitive bidding can be accomplished. Consequently, minor irregularities which do not interfere with the principles of competitive bidding usually are disregarded.[83] Thus, failure of a bidder to submit the required noncollusive certificate with the bid was viewed as a technical noncompliance and he was allowed to provide it at a later date. The court concluded[84] that the irregularity did not materially affect the right of any bidder and it was in the best interest of the board to waive the requirement.

10.2c Bid bonds or deposits

It is customary to require bidders to file with their bids a certified check or a bond in a designated amount to assure that they will execute the contract if it is awarded to them. It has been held[85] that a board of education is justified in rejecting a low bid by a contractor where the security is not tendered in the required form. The purpose of requiring a bid bond or deposit is to protect the school district from any loss which it might incur should the successful bidder refuse to enter into a contract conditioned in accordance with the terms of the bid. Bid bonds should not be confused with surety bonds, which are given to insure that a contract will be fully performed after it has been signed.

The amount of the bid bond or deposit required usually depends on the size of the bid. Typically the amount of the bond or deposit must be a specified percentage of the total bid. When both base and alternate bids for a construction contract are submitted, the bid bond or deposit must be equal to the required percentage of the largest of the base and alternate bids.[86]

When a successful bidder refuses to enter into a contract in compliance with the terms of the bid, the bidder and/or the security become liable on the bid bond. In such situations the extent of the surety's liability frequently becomes an issue. The courts agree that the measure of a surety's liability on a bid bond is the difference between the successful contractor's bid and the bid of the

next lowest responsible bidder.[87] A second limitation on a surety's liability on a bid bond is that, where the bid bond is in a stated amount, the surety is not liable for any sum in excess of that amount plus any interest that may accrue from the time of the successful bidder's default.[88] Thus, the surety's liability is the smaller of two amounts—the amount specified on the bond plus interest, or the difference between the successful contractor's bid and that of the next lowest responsible bidder.

The successful bidder is entitled to the return of the deposit or bid bond when a contract has been entered into in accordance with the terms of the bid.[89] An unsuccessful bidder is, of course, entitled to the return of the bid bond or deposit, and where no contract results from the negotiation all bidders are entitled to the return of their bid bonds or deposits.[90]

Questions sometimes arise concerning whether a bidder is entitled to the return of the deposit or bid bond where a construction contract is canceled because of a fundamental mistake in the bid. In one case it was held[91] that the contractor was entitled to the return of the check he had deposited with his bid. In other cases, however, it has been decided that the contractor is entitled to the return of the deposit or bond only if the other party has not been disadvantaged by the bidder's mistake,[92] and on the condition that the bidder pay any damage suffered by reason of that mistake.[93] If the bidder's mistake is not fundamental, the bidder is not entitled to the return of the deposit or bond. Thus, the fact that a contractor made a mathematical error in computing the bid does not obligate the return of the bond.[94]

10.2d Modification or withdrawal of

In general, bids on school construction projects are to be submitted to the board of education unless the statutes specify that they are to be submitted to some other

---

[82]Application of Gottfried Baking Co., 257 N.Y.S.2d 833 (1964).

[83]Warnock & Zahrndt v. Wray, 230 N.Y.S. 681 (1928).

[84]Consolidated Sheet Metal Workers, Inc. v. Board of Education of the City of Watertown, 308 N.Y.S.2d 773 (1970).

[85]Menke v. Board of Education, Independent School District of West Burlington, 211 N.W.2d 601 (Iowa 1973).

[86]State v. Faust, 9 N.E.2d 912 (Ohio 1937).

[87]Independent School District No. 24 v. Weinmann, 68 N.W.2d 248 (Minn. 1955); Gaynor Construction Co. v. Board of Trustees, 233 S.W.2d 472 (Tex. 1950).

[88]Board of Education v. Maryland Casualty Co., 98 N.Y.S.2d 865 (1950); Gaynor Construction Co. v. Board of Trustees, 233 S.W.2d 472 (Tex. 1950).

[89]Tooele Building Association v. Tooele High School District No. 1, 134 Pac. 894 (Utah 1913).

[90]Smith v. St. Louis County Independent School District No. 12, 122 N.W. 173 (Minn. 1909).

[91]Kutsche v. Ford, 192 N.W. 714 (Mich. 1923).

[92]Federal Contracting Co. v. City of St. Paul, 225 N.W. 149 (Minn. 1929).

[93]Board of Regents of Murray State Normal School v. Cole. 273 S.W. 508 (Ky. 1925).

[94]Hedden v. Northampton Area Joint School Authority, 152 A.2d 463 (Pa. 1959).

agency. It has been held,[95] however, that an architect may receive bids on behalf of a school commmittee by which the architect has been employed. Questions occasionally arise as to whether the time limit for the reception of bids that was specified in the advertisement for bids must be observed strictly, and in regard to whether a bidder may alter a bid either prior to or after the time the bids are opened. It has been held[96] that a time limit for the reception of bids contained in the advertisement is not to be adhered to strictly and that school officers have a duty to receive bids submitted at any time prior to the awarding of the contract. After a bid has been filed, the bidder may correct it at any time prior to the formal opening of bids.[97] After the bids have been opened, however, a bidder cannot amend a bid because of an alleged mistake which does not appear on the face of the bid itself.[98]

Although decisions on the question are not unanimous, the weight of authority indicates that a bid may be withdrawn after it has been opened if the bidder erred in computing it, if there was no gross carelessness or negligence, and if the school district suffers no damage but loss of the bargain.[99] In a Kentucky case, for example, the low bidder on a construction contract discovered that he had inadvertently omitted a $12,000 item when computing his bid. When the low bidder refused to enter into a contract, the board of education entered into a contract with the next lowest bidder and sought to recover the amount of the low bidder's bond. In denying recovery the court said:

The rationale of the case is that even though the mistake is unilateral, the bidder may be relieved from his contract if the mistake is one of material substance and of such consequence that enforcement of the contract would be unconscionable; if the mistake involved mere ordinary negligence and not gross carelessness; if the other party will suffer no

damage other than the loss of the bargain; and if the bidder gives prompt notice of the mistake.[100]

In an Ohio case[101] involving a clerical error in computing a bid, however, the court refused to allow the contractor to withdraw his bid after it had been accepted. It was reasoned that to allow the contractor to withdraw would defeat the purpose of the bid bond which obviously was intended to compensate the public body, at least to some extent, for losses incurred in the case of default.

10.2e Changes in plans and specifications

A board of education occasionally will wish to change the plans or specifications for a building after bids have been received or after contracts for construction have been signed. Questions then arise as to whether such changes circumvent competitive bidding statutes. It has generally been held[102] that a board of education has no authority to change plans or specifications after bids have been opened, or to negotiate with the lowest bidder in order to bring the cost of the project within the amount of funds available. The courts reason that negotiated contracts violate competitive bidding requirements and also may violate implied contracts with taxpayers who have voted to issue bonds or levy taxes in certain amounts for specific purposes. In a Maryland case,[103] for example, the court refused to permit a school district to reduce the cost of construction by over $200,000 by eliminating a library building from the plans and then awarding the construction contract to the lowest bidder on the original plans.

It should be noted, however, that a board of education does have authority to change the plans and specifications for a building during the course of construction so long as the changes are made in good faith, do not substantially alter the character of the building, and do not markedly increase its

[95]Loranger v. Martha's Vineyard Regional High School District School Committee, 155 N.E.2d 791 (Mass. 1959).

[96]Zimmerman v. Miller, 22 Pa.Dist. 264 (1912).

[97]Klose v. Sequoia Union High School District, 258 P.2d 515 (Cal. 1953); Zimmerman v. Miller, 22 Pa. Dist. 264 (1912).

[98]Hotel China & Glassware Co. v. Board of Public Instruction, 130 So.2d 78 (Fla. 1961); McGreevy v. Board of Education of Toledo, 20 Ohio Cir.Ct. 114 (1900).

[99]Berkeley Unified School District v. James I. Barnes Construction Co., 123 F.Supp. 924 (Cal. 1954); Board of Education of Floyd County v. Hooper, 350 S.W.2d 629 (Ky. 1961); School District of Scottsbluff v. Olson Construction Co., 45 N.W.2d 164 (Neb. 1950); Elsinore Union Elementary School District v. Kastorff, 353 P.2d 713 (Cal. 1960); Kutsche v. Ford, 192 N.W. 714 (Mich. 1923).

[100]Board of Education of Floyd County v. Hooper, 350 S.W.2d 629 (Ky. 1961).

[101]Board of Education of Chillicothe City School District v. Sever-Williams Co., 258 N.E.2d 605 (Ohio 1970); See also Hotel China & Glassware Co. v. Board of Public Instruction, 130 So.2d 78 (Fla. 1961).

[102]Hanna v. Board of Education of Wicomico County, 87 A.2d 846 (Md. 1952); Charleroi Lumber Co. v. District of Borough of Bentlyville, 6 A.2d 88 (Pa. 1939); McAlexander v. Haviland School District, 7 Ohio N.P. (N.S.) 590 (1906); Seim v. Independent District of Monroe, 17 N.W.2d 342 (S.D. 1945).

[103]Hanna v. Board of Education of Wicomico County, 87 A.2d 846 (Md. 1952).

cost.[104] In discussing the authority of a board of education to change plans or specifications, the Supreme Court of Pennsylvania has remarked:

> Unforeseen contingencies or new ideas sometimes make it necessary to change the character or quality of material or a part of a structure from the original plans. A certain flexibility in the power of officials to take care of these matters is intended to be granted, that the law relating to public letting may not become an instrument of oppression through a too rigid construction. These officers must act honestly, reasonably, and intelligently, and a new departure must not so vary from the original plan or be of such importance as to constitute a new undertaking, which the act controls, and where fairness could only be reached through competitive bidding. Courts, however, will be slow to interfere unless it appears the officers are not acting in good faith.[105]

Accordingly, courts have permitted a board of education to reduce the cost of a building by eliminating ornamental columns and changing the location of the building from a hillside to more ground level,[106] to provide for a different kind of roofing from that called for in the original specifications,[107] and to use a more expensive type of brick than was originally specified.[108]

10.2f Right to reject

Advertisements for bids frequently contain a reservation of the right to reject any or all bids. If school authorities invite prospective contractors to submit bids when they are not legally required to do so, they need not award the contract to the lowest responsible bidder, or to any bidder, and may act independently of all bids in awarding the contract so long as they act in good faith and exercise reasonable discretion.[109]

When the statutes provide that school construction contracts are to be let to the lowest responsible bidder, it has been held[110] that school authorities are not at liberty to reject arbitrarily all bids submitted. In discussing the rationale of such holdings, it has been said:

> If bids are rejected arbitrarily or capriciously, contractors will not take the time and expend the money necessary to submit proposals. They will infer favoritism. This will result in few bidders and higher bids. The statute providing for the award of a contract for a public improvement to the lowest responsible bidder was enacted for the protection of the bidders. [Citing Paterson Contracting Co. v. Hackensack, 99 N.J.L. 260, 122 A. 741 (E. & A. 1923)].[111]

> The unbridled power to reject bids, even where such right is reserved in the invitation for bidding, if allowed would violate our public policy, contravene our Legislature's intention in enaction of the competitive bidding statute and, in fact, afford a means by which "the statute can be evaded under color of the rejection 'of any and all bids'." [citations omitted].[112]

Nevertheless, where a substantial factual basis for such an action exists, a board of education may disqualify certain contractors from bidding on contracts for school construction work.[113] Bids which are not in substantial compliance with statutory requirements may be rejected,[114] as may bids which do not comply with the conditions specified in the advertisement for bids.[115]

It has been held[116] in some jurisdictions that, where the right to reject any and all bids is reserved in the advertisement, school officers may reject any bid submitted. In fact, it has even been held[117] that such bids may be rejected arbitrarily.

10.2g Determining lowest responsible bidder

The requirement that contracts be awarded to the lowest responsible bidder (or to the "lowest and best bidder") has often resulted in litigation to determine the meaning of the term *responsible* and to establish criteria for the determination of the

[104]Hibbs v. Arensberg, 119 Atl. 727 (Pa. 1923); Criswell v. Everett School District No. 24, 75 Pac. 984 (Wash. 1904); Pung v. Derse, 162 N.W. 177 (Wis. 1917).
[105]Hibbs v. Arensberg, 119 Atl. 727 (Pa. 1923).
[106]Criswell v. Everett School District No. 24, 75 Pac. 984 (Wash. 1904).
[107]Pung v. Derse, 162 N.W. 177 (Wis. 1917).
[108]Hibbs v. Arensberg, 119 Atl. 727 (Pa. 1923).
[109]Kraft v. Weehawken Township Board of Education, 51 Atl. 483 (N.J. 1902).
[110]Arensmeyer-Warnock-Zandt v. Wray, 194 N.Y.S. 398 (1922).

[111]Cardell, Inc. v. Township of Woodbridge, 280 A.2d 203 (N.J. 1971).
[112]Ibid.
[113]Caristo Construction Corp. v. Rubin, 222 N.Y.S.2d 998 (1961).
[114]State v. Faust, 9 N.E.2d 912 (Ohio 1937); Haddock v. Board of Education in Wilmington, 84 A.2d 157 (Del. 1951); East Side Construction Co. v. Town of Adams, 108 N.E. 2d 659 (Mass. 1952); Menke v. Board of Education, Independent School District of West Burlington, 211 N.W.2d 601 (Iowa 1973).
[115]Gunnip v. Lautenklos, 94 A.2d 712 (Del. 1953); Wiltom Coach Co. v. Central High School District No. 3, 232 N.Y.S2d 876 (1962).
[116]Chandler v. Board of Education of City of Detroit, 62 N.W. 370 (Mich. 1895); Belousofsky v. Board of Education of City of Linden, 148 A.2d 632 (N.J. 1959).
[117]Anderson v. Public Schools, 27 S.W. 610 (Mo. 1894) Contra: Cardell, Inc. v. Township of Woodbridge, 280 A.2d 203 (N.J. 1971).

lowest responsible bidder. A responsible bidder is one who has the ability to perform the contract according to its terms.[118] Variables other than the bid itself must be considered in determining the lowest responsible bidder, and the one who submits the lowest bid on a construction project is not necessarily the lowest responsible bidder. While the financial standing of the bidder is one factor to be considered, the term *responsible* implies far more than mere financial standing. Thus, in determining who is the lowest responsible bidder, the board of education may consider such variables as the bidder's character, integrity, reputation, experience in similar projects, competence, skill, and efficiency, as well as the facilities and resources available to that bidder.[119] It has been said:

> The term "responsible" is not, however, limited to pecuniary ability . . . but pertains to many other characteristics of the bidder, such as his general ability and capacity to carry on the work, his equipment and facilities, his promptness, and the quality of the work previously done by him, his suitability to the particular task, and such other qualities as are found necessary to consider in order to determine whether or not, if awarded the contract, he could perform it strictly in accordance with its terms.[120]

As a general rule, the determination of who is the lowest responsible bidder on a contract is within the discretion of a board of education, and the courts permit a board wide latitude in making such a determination.[121] It has frequently been held[122] that a court will not interfere with the decision of the board of education as to who is, in fact, the lowest responsible bidder on a contract unless the decision was made arbitrarily, in bad faith, or with fraudulent intent. In reaching its decision, a board of education

is obligated to investigate the responsibility of all bidders who have filed bids before awarding a contract, but it generally is not obligated to afford bidders hearings on the matter of their responsibility.[123] However, in a New Jersey case it was held[124] that before rejecting a low bid, the bidder should be given notice of the basis of the proposed rejection and an opportunity to be heard.

When a board of education awards a contract to a bidder whose bid is not the lowest, its decision is final, providing it has exercised its discretions properly and in good faith.[125] The board's obligations under such circumstances have been aptly summarized by the Supreme Court of Pennsylvania:

> Though the directors were not bound in law to give the contract to the lowest bidder, who might be irresponsible, they were bound to investigate, and if a bidder measured up to the law's requirement as a responsible party, the board could not capriciously award the contract to another. . . . But there should be a sufficient reason, where a bidder is lowest and responsible, why the job was not given to him. And where such reason appears, the action of the board is generally conclusive.[126]

10.3 ACCEPTING BIDS AND AWARDING CONTRACTS

It is not essential that a bid be accepted at the same meeting at which bids are opened unless the statutes, the bylaws of the board of education, or the advertisement itself indicates that bids will be accepted at that time. However, a bid must be accepted within a reasonable period of time after the opening of bids.[127] This principle is illustrated by a Pennsylvania case[128] in which, after bids had been opened, the school authorities initially were of the opinion that all of them were too high but at a subsequent meeting decided to accept one of them. When their action in accepting the bid was questioned, the court ruled that a mere first opinion on the part of the board that all bids were too high did not preclude its subsequent acceptance of one of them.

Misunderstandings frequently arise concerning the actions which are necessary to

[118]Paccione v. Board of Education of City of New York, 195 N.Y.S.2d 593 (1959).

[119]Hibbs vs. Arensberg, 119 Atl. 727 (Pa. 1923); Ellingson v. Cherry Lake School District, 212 N.W. 773 (N.D. 1927); Hudson v. Board of Education, 179 N.E. 701 (Ohio 1931); Application of Caristo Construction Corp., 221 N.Y.S.2d 956 (1961); Culpepper v. Moore, 40 So.2d 366 (Fla. 1949); Parker Bros. v. Crawford, 68 So.2d 281 (Miss. 1953).

[120]Hudson v. Board of Education, 179 N.E. 701 (Ohio 1931).

[121]Somers Construction Co. v. Board of Education, 198 F.Supp. 732 (N.J. 1961); Schwitzer v. Newark Board of Education, 75 Atl. 447 (N.J. 1910); Parker Bros. v. Crawford, 68 So.2d 281 (Miss. 1953).

[122]Ellingson v. Cherry Lake School District, 212 N.W. 773 (N.D. 1927); Schwitzer v. Newark Board of Education, 75 Atl. 447 (N.J. 1910); Raymond v. Fresno City Unified School District, 267 P.2d 69 (Cal. 1954); Parker Bros. v. Crawford, 68 So.2d 281 (Miss. 1953).

[123]Hudson v. Board of Education, 179 N.E. 701 (Ohio 1931); Caristo Construction Corp. v. Rubin, 180 N.E.2d 794 (N.Y. 1962).

[124]Motorola Communications and Electronics, Inc. v. O'Connor, 279 A.2d 855 (N.J. 1971).

[125]Raymond v. Fresno City Unified School District, 267 P.2d 69 (Cal. 1954); Schwitzer v. Newark Board of Education, 75 Atl. 447 (N.J. 1910).

[126]Hibbs v. Arensberg, 119 Atl. 727 (Pa. 1923).

[127]Mulcahy v. Board of Education, 159 N.E. 324 (Ohio 1925); Hotel China & Glassware Co. v. Board of Public Instruction, 130 So.2d 78 (Fla. 1961).

[128]Hibbs v. Arensberg, 119 Atl. 727 (Pa. 1923).

constitute acceptance of a bid. It is important to remember that in order to have a valid contract all statutory formalities must be fulfilled. Where a statute requires that the contract be made in writing, it has been held that acceptance of the bid must be made in writing.[129] Similarly, in a Pennsylvania case[130] it was ruled that until a written contract had been signed by the school board no valid contract existed, and that although the school board had voted unanimously to award a contract and its secretary had verbally notified the low bidder to that effect, the board could still revoke its action in awarding a contract which had not yet been signed.

A second important principle is that there must be a bona fide and an unqualified acceptance before a contract can exist. In interpreting this principle a majority of the courts have ruled that the mere acceptance of a bid by a board of education does not result in a binding contract,[131] nor does passage of an action or resolution awarding a contract to a bidder produce a binding contract.[132] In fact, some courts have held[133] that no valid contract exists until the proposed contract has been duly executed by the contracting parties. It should be noted, however, that the federal courts have ruled that when a public body accepts a written bid submitted in response to an advertisement, a binding contract is formed.[134] They reason that a bid submitted in response to an advertisement by a school board constitutes an irrevocable offer and that acceptance of the bid by the school board is sufficient to complete a binding contract. Yet another interpretation is found in some jurisdictions, where it has been held[135] that a contract does not become binding until the successful bidder offi-

cially has been notified of the board's acceptance of the bid.

10.4 SCHOOL CONSTRUCTION CONTRACTS

Contracts for the construction of school buildings are subject to the general rules governing other types of school contracts. It has repeatedly been emphasized that a board of education has only such contractual powers as are conferred upon it by statute, either expressly or by implication. Its contracting power is also limited by any statutory directions concerning the methods and procedures which are to be used in contracting. The principle has been put succinctly by the Supreme Court of South Dakota:

> It is well settled that when by statute the mode and manner in which contracts of a school district or other local subdivision may be entered into is limited and any other manner of entering into a contract or obligation is expressly or impliedly forbidden a contract not made in compliance therewith is invalid and cannot ordinarily be ratified.[136]

It is well established that a contract which is beyond the power of a school district is *ultra vires* and void. As a general rule, a school district is not bound by an *ultra vires* contract, even if the district retains and enjoys the use of the property which is obtained under such a contract.[137] Property supplied a school district under a void contract can be recovered by the supplier only if it can be removed without injuring the property of the district.[138] If property supplied under a void contract cannot be removed without injury to the district's property the supplier generally has no remedy.[139]

10.4a Ratification of

A contract which a school board is expressly prohibited from entering into may not be ratified.[140] Thus, construction con-

[129]Metz v. Warrick, 269 S.W. 626 (Mo. 1925).

[130]Wayne Crouse, Inc. v. School District of Borough of Braddock, 19 A.2d 843 (Pa. 1941).

[131]Smith v. St. Louis County Independent School District No. 12, 122 N.W. 173 (Minn. 1909); Wayne Crouse, Inc. v. School District of Borough of Braddock, 19. A.2d 843 (Pa. 1941).

[132]Commonwealth v. School District of City of Bethlehem, 25 A.2d 786 (Pa. 1942); Cedar Rapids Lumber Co. v. Fisher, 105 N.W. 595 (Iowa 1906); Kutsche v. Ford, 192 N.W. 714 (Mich. 1923).

[133]Wayne Crouse, Inc. v. School District of Borough of Braddock, 19 A.2d 843 (Pa. 1941); Paterson v. Board of Trustees of Montecito Union School District, 321 P.2d 825 (Cal. 1958).

[134]United States v. Purcell Envelope Co., 249 U.S. 313, 39 S.Ct. 300, 63 L.Ed. 620 (Mass. 1919); Berkeley Unified School District v. James I. Barnes Construction Co., 112 F.Supp. 396 (Cal. 1953).

[135]Kutsche v. Ford, 192 N.W. 714 (Mich. 1923); Cedar Rapids Lumber Co. v. Fisher, 105 N.W. 595 (Iowa 1906); Johnston Heating Co. v. Board of Education, 161 N.Y.S. 867 (1916).

[136]Seim v. Independent District of Monroe, 17 N.W.2d 342 (S.D. 1945).

[137]Reams v. Cooley, 152 Pac. 293 (Cal. 1915); Honey Creek School Township v. Barnes, 21 N.E. 747 (Ind. 1889); Charleroi Lumber Co. v. District of Borough of Bentleyville, 6 A.2d 88 (Pa. 1939).

[138]Strauch v. San Mateo Junior College District, 286 Pac. 173 (Cal. 1930); State v. Smith, 194 N.E.2d 186 (Ohio 1963); Superior Manufacturing Co. v. School District No. 63, 114 Pac. 328 (Okla. 1910).

[139]Bartelson v. International School District No. 5, 174 N.W. 78 (N.D. 1919).

[140]Arkansas National Bank v. School District No. 99, 238 S.W. 630 (Ark. 1922); Turney v. Town of Bridgeport, 12 Atl. 520 (Conn. 1887); Ketterer v. Independent School District No. 1, 79 N.W.2d 428 (Minn. 1956); Murry v. Union Parish School Board, 185 So. 305 (La. 1938).

tracts which are in excess of constitutional or statutory debt limits are void and cannot be ratified. A contract may be ratified if it is within the power of a board of education but is void because of some irregularity in the mode of contracting, or void because it was made by an unauthorized party.[141] Such a contract may be ratified either expressly or by implication, but the ratification must be unequivocal and must be made in a manner which binds the ratifying board.[142] Ratification is not implied by mere silence,[143] although an invalid contract may be ratified by accepting and using property, or by retaining the benefits of the contract with a full knowledge of all of the facts.[144] Where a school district has no option to reject a school building—where it is built upon land owned by the district, for instance—it has been held[145] that ratification of a contract is not to be inferred from the fact that the district is using the building.

10.4b Modification or termination of

School boards occasionally find it necessary or desirable to modify the original contract during the course of school building construction projects. Attempts to modify a contract sometimes result in disputes over the authority of the board to make the modification which is sought. There can be no doubt that a board of education, acting within the limits of its authority, has power to modify a contract.[146] The power is not unlimited, however, for it must act in the same manner and follow the same procedures which were required in entering into the original contract. For example, a member of the board of education, as an individual, has no authority to modify a school construction contract.[147] Further,

changes in a contract must be supported by a consideration in order to be valid.[148] The right to modify a contract, it should be noted, does not authorize a district to let supplementary contracts for work which is independent of that covered by the original contract.[149]

School authorities have no right to terminate a contract which they have entered into unless they have adequate grounds for such action or have reserved the right to terminate the contract.[150] Where they possess authority to do so, a school board may terminate a contract.[151] For example, it has been ruled[152] that a contract may include a provision for cancellation where it appears that the cost of the construction under a guaranteed cost plus fixed fee plan may exceed the amount of money available to finance the building. If a school building contractor abandons the project and repudiates the contract, it has been held[153] that school authorities are justified in terminating the contract. A school district also may cancel a contract if the bid on which the contract was based contained a fundamental error.[154]

10.4c Defective performance of

Questions occasionally arise concerning the specific obligations of the contractor and the remedies which the district may employ if the contractor's work is unsatisfactory. The nature and extent of the work a contractor may be expected to perform depends upon the contract itself. One who contracts with school authorities to construct a school building is obligated to perform the contract according to its terms.[155] On the question of whether substantial performance of the contract will suffice the courts are in some disagreement. In some

[141]Richards v. Jackson School Township, 109 N.W. 1093 (Iowa 1906); Farmers' State Bank of Bonner Springs v. School District No. 100, 4 P.2d 404 (Kan. 1931); Board of Education of Lloyd County v. Hall, 353 S.W.2d 194 (Ky. 1962); St. Paul Foundry Co. v. Burnstad School District No. 31, 269 N.W. 739 (N.D. 1936).

[142]Goin v. Board of Education, 183 S.W.2d 819 (Ky. 1944); St. Paul Foundry Co. v. Burnstad School District No. 31, 269 N.W. 739 (N.D. 1936).

[143]Caxton Co. v. Spooner School District No. 5, 98 N.W. 231 (Wis. 1904).

[144]School District No. 38 of Brown County v. Sullivan, 29 Pac. 1141 (Kan. 1892); Farmers' State Bank of Bonner Springs v. School District No. 100, 4 P.2d 404 (Kan. 1931).

[145]Allen County Board of Education v. Scottsville Builders' Supply Co., 259 S.W. 39 (Ky. 1924); Arkansas National Bank v. School District No. 99, 238 S.W. 630 (Ark. 1922).

[146]Berger v. Sequoia Union High School District, 293 P.2d 467 (Cal. 1956); Ferkin v. Board of Education, 15 N.E.2d 799 (N.Y. 1938).

[147]State v. Tiedemann, 69 Mo. 515 (1879); Matevish v. School District of Borough of Ramey, 74 A.2d 797 (Pa. 1950).

[148]Wicker v. Board of Public Instruction of Dade County, 182 F.2d 764 (5th Cir. 1950); Martin, Ginter & Powers v. Liberty County Board of Education, 44 S.E.2d 462 (Ga. 1947).

[149]Seim v. Independent District of Monroe, 17 N.W.2d 342 (S.D. 1945); Hanna v. Board of Education of Wicomico County, 87 A.2d 846 (Md. 1952).

[150]Union School Township of St. Joseph County v. Moon, 187 N.E. 332 (Ind. 1933); Kingsbury v. Arcadia Unified School District, 271 P2d. 40 (Cal. 1954).

[151]Grande & Son. Inc. v. School Housing Committee, 135 N.E.2d 6 (Mass. 1956); Application of Caristo Construction Corp., 152 N.Y.S.2d 259 (1956).

[152]Lather v. School District No. 1, 219 N.W. 700 (Mich. 1928).

[153]Baumann v. City of West Allis, 204 N.W. 907 (Wis. 1925).

[154]Board of Regents of Murray State Normal School v. Cole, 273 S.W. 508 (Ky. 1925).

[155]Community School District of Eldorado v. Employers Mutual Casualty Co., 194 F.Supp. 733 (Iowa 1961); Pacific Coast Builders v. Antioch Live Oak Unified School District, 300 P.2d 309 (Cal. 1956).

cases[156] it has been ruled that substantial performance of a school building contract will not suffice, that the work must be completed in strict accord with the terms of the contract. In other cases[157] it has been held that where the contractor acted in good faith substantial performance of the contract is sufficient. *Substantial performance* means that the completed building must be such as to permit the full accomplishment of the purposes for which it was constructed. The principle followed by the courts in the latter cases is that "if a contractor has attempted in good faith to perform his contract and has substantially performed it—although by inadvertence he has failed to perform it literally according to its terms—he may recover under the contract, with a proper deduction to the owner for the imperfections or omissions in the performance."[158] Thus, the contractor is entitled to the contract price less deductions for any omissions in the performance of the contract.[159]

It must be recognized that a board of education is also bound by the terms of a construction contract. Where a school construction contract requires the board of education to maintain insurance on work and materials during the course of construction of a building, its failure to do so may make the district liable to the contractor in the event of the destruction of the building.[160] Moreover, where a construction contract requires a school district to pay insurance premiums, a contractor who pays the premiums may recover from the district the expense thus incurred.[161]

Disputes over whether the contractor or the school district is responsible for furnishing light and heat during the construction of a school building illustrate the problems which may arise in interpreting construction contracts. Where the contract so requires, light and heat must be furnished by the contractor without extra charge.[162] Where the matter is not expressly covered by the contract, however, the decisions

vary. It has been held[163] that if it is not customary for the owner to furnish heat for a building which is under construction the contractor must do so unless the matter is expressly covered in the contract. However, it also has been held[164] that where the contract does not require the contractor to furnish temporary heat during the course of construction, and the contractor does so under protest, the reasonable expense which was incurred furnishing the heat may be recovered.

When the contractor's work is defective, or the contractor defaults on the contract, a board of education is confronted with the question of how to remedy the defects or secure completion of the construction project. There is general agreement that a contractor is liable to the school district for defective workmanship or materials,[165] and where the district sustains injury due to a contractor's failure to perform according to the contract it may recover damages for a breach of contract by the contractor.[166] It has been held,[167] for instance, that the contractor must assume the risk of natural climatic conditions and at his own cost replace defective rubber tile flooring in a school building. The fact that a school building has been accepted and used does not constitute a waiver of defective construction where circumstances necessitate that the building be used.[168] Contractors who fail to complete a contract or who furnish inferior material forfeit their right to recover any money which may be due them under their contract.[169]

The obligation of a contractor to perform as the contract requires is illustrated by a Maine case[170] in which a board of education refused to accept and pay for a defective building. Members of the board of education had several times during the course of the construction of the building expressed to the contractor their displeasure with the

[156]Hill v. School District No. 2, 17 Me. 316 (1840); Pacific Coast Builders v. Antioch Live Oak Unified School District, 300 P.2d 309 (Cal. 1956).

[157]Kasbo Construction Co. v. Minto School District, 184 N.W. 1029 (N.D. 1921); J. E. Hollingsworth & Co. v. Leachville Special School District, 249 S.W. 24 (Ark. 1923); Dodge v. Kimball, 89 N.E. 542 (Mass. 1909).

[158]Dodge v. Kimball, 89 N.E. 542 (Mass. 1909).

[159]J. E. Hollingsworth & Co. v. Leachville Special School District, 249 S.W. 24 (Ark. 1923).

[160]Hagan Lumber Co. v. Duryea School District, 121 Atl. 107 (Pa. 1923).

[161]Lather v. School District No. 1, 219 N.W. 700 (Mich. 1928).

[162]Dance v. Board of Education of City of Middlesboro, 176 S.W.2d 90 (Ky. 1943); Millimet Construction Co. v. Board of Education of Town of Bloomfield, 30 A.2d 292 (N.J. 1943).

[163]Stewart-McGhee Construction Co. v. Caddo Parish School Board, 115 So. 458 (La. 128).

[164]Material Service Corp. v. School City of Hammond, 116 F.2d 98 (7th Cir. 1940).

[165]Pacific Coast Builders v. Antioch Live Oak Unified School District, 300 P.2d 309 (Cal. 1956); Vicknair v. Rapides Parish School Board, 123 So.2d 821 (La. 1961); Board of Education v. Matthew L. Carroll, Inc., 157 N.Y.S.2d 775 (1956).

[166]Decker v. Douglas County School District No. 2, 74 S.W. 390 (Mo. 1903).

[167]Stewart-McGhee Construction Co. v. Caddo Parish School Board, 115 So. 458 (La. 1928).

[168]Elliott Consolidated School District v. Busboom 227 F.Supp. 858 (Iowa 1964); Kasbo Construction Co. v. Minto School District. 184 N.W. 1029 (N.D. 1921).

[169]Continental Coal Co. v. United Fuel Co., 29 P.2d 395 (Wash. 1934); Dolben v. Duncan Construction Co., 177 N.E. 105 (Mass. 1931).

[170]Hill v. School District No. 2, 17 Me. 316 (1840).

workmanship being evidenced. The court ruled that, since the building had not been constructed according to the terms of the contract, the contractor was not entitled to payment for the building and, furthermore, could be required to remove it from the district's property.

When a contractor defaults on a contract and is unable or unwilling to complete it, school authorities may accept the uncompleted work and let another contract for its completion.[171] In a New Jersey case, for example, an unfinished school building was abandoned by a bankrupt contractor. In holding that the board of education had authority to enter into a contract with another contractor to finish the building, the court said:

Here the board of education owns an unfinished schoolhouse on its land. Whether it acquired it legally or illegally, whether it has paid for it or not, whether any one is liable to refund money already paid therefor or not, it cannot be required to destroy or remove the existing structure, nor can the public be required to suffer the loss of the land as the alternative or equivalent to keeping it as the site of a useless building. The board may accept the building as it stands and complete it. . . . To hold otherwise would put it in the power of a board of education to deprive the public of any beneficial use of public property, except at the cost of removing the building thereon.[172]

10.5 ACCEPTANCE OF COMPLETED CONSTRUCTION

Formal acceptance of a school building by the board of education signals satifactory completion of the building contract. Formal acceptance of a building ordinarily follows certification by the architect that all terms of the building contract have been fulfilled. Questions occasionally arise as to what actions constitute acceptance of a building. It has been held[173] that a formal resolution of acceptance is not required. Thus, in a case in which a school district made final payment to the contractor but did not adopt a formal resolution accepting the work until nearly seven months after that, it was

ruled[174] that the act of making final payment to the contractor clearly implied acceptance of the building.

Contracts for school building construction commonly contain a provision that certification by the architect that the construction project has satisfactorily been completed is required before a building will be accepted. It generally has been held[175] that the issuance of such a certificate by the architect is conclusive and binding as to completion of the contract unless the certificate is issued arbitrarily, fraudulently, or in bad faith. However, the adoption by a board of education of a resolution which unconditionally accepted a school building is binding, even though the architect had not certified that all work had been performed.[176] In discussing the relationship between the school board and the architect under a construction contract which provided that the architect had full power to reject all or any part of the work not conforming to the letter and spirit of the contract, the Supreme Court of Washington commented as follows:

As between the parties to the contract the decision of the architect is conclusive. But the delegation of the authority to represent the school board in the matter of the construction of the building is not a complete surrender of all power of the board. The architect is an agent of the board, to act in its behalf. If he refuses a certificate because the work is not done in accordance with the contract, the contractor is bound thereby, in the absence of willful, arbitrary, or capricious action on his part. If he issues such a certificate, it is likewise under the same conditions binding on the board. But this would not prevent the board from accepting the work in case they desired to do so. Certainly the board can waive any provision in the contract placed there for its benefit.

10.6 PAYMENT OF CONTRACTORS

Many school building contracts provide that pending satisfactory completion of the project the district is to retain a specified percentage of the money due the contractor as security for payment of laborers, material suppliers, and subcontractors. It has been said that money retained by the district as security for the payment of the liens of

[171]Holden v. Board of Education of Kearney, 91 Atl. 990 (N.J. 1913); Ludowici Caladon Co. v. Independent School District, 149 N.W. 845 (Iowa 1914); American Employers Insurance Co. v. School District of Town of Newport, 107 A.2d 684 (N.H. 1954).

[171]Holden v. Board of Education of Kearney, 91 Atl. 990 (N.J. 1913).

[173]Graybar Electric Co. v. Manufacturers Casualty Co., 122 A.2d 624 (N.J. 1956); Perkins Builders' Supply & Fuel Co. v. Independent School District, 221 N.W. 793 (Iowa 1928).

[174]Graybar Electric Co. v. Manufacturers Casualty Co., 122 A.2d 624 (N.J. 1956).

[175]Maryland Casualty Co. v. Board of Education, 34 F.2d 751 (3d Cir. 1929); Goerge H. Evans, Inc. v. School District of Darby Township, 164 Atl. 826 (Pa. 1933); Union High School District No. 400 v. Pacific Northwest Construction Co., 269 Pac. 809 (Wash. 1928).

[176]Union High School District No. 400 v. Pacific Northwest Construction Co., 269 Pac. 809 (Wash. 1928).

laborers, material suppliers, and subcontractors is to be regarded as a trust fund.[177] Where school authorities fail to retain the specified percentage of money due the contractor, they may become liable to laborers and material suppliers who have not been paid by the contractor.[178] If a board of education retains part of the money which is due the contractor pending final completion and acceptance of the building, it may deduct from such money any damage due it for deficient work or for damages resulting from the contractor's delay in completing the work.[179]

School building contracts frequently contain a clause providing that if the building is not finished by a designated date the contractor will forfeit a specified sum of money for each day of delay in completing it. A contractor will be held liable for delay in completing a building according to the terms of the contract.[180] It also should be noted that school authorities may become liable to a contractor if they unreasonably delay or impede the work.[181] It has been held,[182] for example, that under a school construction contract containing a clause penalizing a contractor for failure to complete the work by a specified date the district is, by implication, obligated to keep the building in a state which will enable the contractor to complete the work within the specified time and is liable to the contractor for damages if it fails to do so.

Disputes have arisen in regard to whether a contractor is entitled to receive additional compensation for any extra work which has been performed in constructing a school building. The contract itself may provide for extra work; if it does, a contractor who performs extra work is entitled to receive compensation for it according to the terms of the contract.[183] Where the contract requires that all work not called for in the contract be authorized in writing by the architect, a contractor cannot recover for extra work unless the required change order has been issued by the architect.[184] However, where it is impossible to perform a contract without doing additional work because of the architect's miscalculations in preparing plans and specifications, it has been held[185] that such additional work is not to be regarded as an extra and that a signed change order is not required in order for the contractor to receive compensation. A contractor may receive additional compensation for work and materials which are furnished in excess of the amount called for in the specifications for the project if they are required as a result of acts of the district, or if the specifications contained false representations on which the contractor was entitled to rely.[186]

School construction contracts sometimes provide for arbitration of disputes concerning the contractor's entitlement to additional compensation for extra work. Where such a provision is embodied in the contract, it has been held[187] that the report of the arbitrators selected to determine whether the contractor is entitled to extra compensation is conclusive and binding on all parties.

10.7 SURETY BONDS GIVEN BY CONTRACTORS

It is customary for school districts to require that those who contract with the district for the construction of school buildings (or for other materials or services) give a surety bond. In fact, most states require school districts to obtain surety bonds of various types from those who contract with the district to construct school buildings. Even in the absence of specific statutory direction it generally has been held[188] that a board of education may require bid, performance, and payment bonds. Bid bonds, dis-

[177]Key Agency v. Continental Casualty Co., 155 A.2d 547 (N.J. 1959); J. T. Jackson Lumber Co. v. Union Transfer & Storage Co., 55 S.W.2d 670 (Ky. 1932).
[178]W. A. Brockhurst Co. v. City of Yonkers, 268 N.Y.S. 637 (1933).
[179]National Loan & Exchange Bank of Greenwood v. Gustafson, 154 S.E. 167 (S.C. 1930).
[180]Stewart-McGhee Construction Co. v. Caddo Parish School Board, 115 So. 458 (La. 1928); Kelly v. Board of Education of City of New York, 168 N.E.2d 113 (N.Y. 1960).
[181]Morgan v. Town of Burlington, 55 N.E.2d 758 (Mass. 1944); John T. Brady & Co. v. Board of Education, 226 N.Y.S. 707 (1928); Byrne v. Bellingham Consolidated School District No. 301,108 P.2d 791 (Wash. 1941).
[182]Byrne v. Bellingham Consolidated School District No. 301, 108 P.2d 791 (Wash. 1941).
[183]Morgan v. Town of Burlington, 55 N.E.2d 758 (Mass. 1944); National Surety Co. v. Board of Education of Clifton, 170 Atl. 643 (N.J. 1934); Gellatly Construction Co. v. City of Bridgeport, 182 A.2d 625 (Conn. 1962).

[184]Dance v. Board of Education of City of Middlesboro, 176 S.W.2d 90 (Ky. 1943); Emporium Area Joint School Authority v. Anundson Construction and Building Supply Co., 156 A.2d 554 (Pa. 1959).
[185]Dance v. Board of Education of City of Middlesboro, 176 S.W.2d 90 (Ky. 1943).
[186]Mitchell & DeJersey v. Lincoln Parish School Board 8 So.2d 118 (La. 1942); Funk v. School District of Abington Township, 184 Atl. 659 (Pa. 1936).
[187]National Surety Co. v. Board of Education of Clifton, 170 Atl. 643 (N.J. 1934); Emporium Area Joint School Authority v. Anundson Construction and Building Supply Co., 156 A.2d 554 (Pa. 1959).
[188]N. O. Nelson Co. v. Stephenson, 168 S.W. 61 (Tex. 1914); Board of President and Directors of the St. Louis Public Schools v. Woods, 77 Mo. 197 (1883); Baker v. Bryan, 21 N.W. 83 (Iowa 1884); R. Connor Co. v. Olson, 115 N.W. 811 (Wis. 1908).

cussed in Section 10.2c, guarantee that the bidder, if awarded the contract, will enter into a contract as promised in the bid. Performance bonds guarantee that the contractor will faithfully execute the contract according to its terms. Payment bonds, frequently taken in association with performance bonds, guarantee that the contractor will pay all bills for labor and materials which are incurred in performing the contract with the school district. The difference between performance and payment bonds is shown in the following statement by a federal court:

The obligation of a surety on a performance bond, upon default of the principal or contractor, is to perform or finish the work agreed upon or pay the owner the cost of performing or finishing the work. The obligation of a surety on a payment bond is not to perform or finish the work or pay the cost of performing or finishing the work but is to pay any unpaid bills of the contractor or principal relating to the job.[189]

It should be noted at the outset that the precise meaning and scope of coverage of surety bonds ultimately are decided by the courts. Decisions by the courts depend upon the interpretation given the statutes of the state involved, the wording of the bond in question, and the contract for construction with which the bond is associated. Consequently, school officials must look to the statutes of their state, and to interpretations of such statutes by the courts, to determine the type and amount of bonds which they should require.

10.7a Performance bonds

In most states statutes require those who contract with local school districts to construct school buildings to give the district a performance bond guaranteeing the faithful performance of the contract. However, specific statutory authority to require such bonds is not necessary; the power to contract for the construction of school buildings carries with it by implication the authority to require the contractor to supply a bond conditioned for the faithful performance of the contract.[190] Where performance bonds are not required by statute, a board of education is under no obligation to insist that such a bond be furnished, for the decision as to whether it should be required

rests in the board's discretion.[191] Also, where the statutes demand a performance bond but do not specify its form or amount, such matters are left to the discretion of school authorities, and the courts will not interfere with their decision unless they grossly abuse their discretion.[192]

Construction of

The primary purpose of a performance bond is to protect a school district from losses which it might suffer as a result of a contractor's failure to perform the contract faithfully. When disputes arise, the courts will attempt to construe the bond in keeping with the intent of the parties to the contract. Ordinarily, a bond is read in conjunction with the contract it secures.[193] The principle involved has been expressed as follows:

. . . a bond given to guarantee the execution of a contract according to its terms becomes a part of such contract, and to that contract the sureties become parties the same as though they had actually made and executed the contract itself. Therefore, in interpreting the language of the undertaking for the purpose of gathering its scope or the measure of the liability of the sureties, we must do so by treating or viewing the contract and the undertaking as a whole or as constituting an indivisible contract. In other words, we must, in order to ascertain the nature and extent of the liability to which the sureties have bound themselves, examine the undertaking by the light of the agreement of whose terms it guarantees the faithful performance.[194]

Whereas an accommodation surety, i.e., a bond given by a person voluntarily and without pay, is strictly construed so that any deviation from the contract releases the surety from obligation,[195] bonds given by a surety company are given a liberal construction.[196] The principle is well established

[189]American Casualty Co. v. Board of Education, 228 F.Supp. 843 (Okla. 1964).
[190]N. O. Nelson Co. v. Stephenson, 168 S.W. 61 (Tex. 1914).
[191]Sundheim v. School District of Philadelphia, 166 Atl. 365 (Pa. 1933).
[192]Scranton School District v. Casualty & Surety Co., 98 Pa.Super. 579 (1930); St. Paul-Mercury Indemnity Co. v. Koppers Co., 99 S.E.2d 275 (Ga. 1957).
[193]Collins v. National Fire Insurance Co. of Hartford, 105 So.2d 190 (Fla. 1958); Texas Fidelity & Bonding Co. v. Rosenberg Independent School District, 195 S.W. 298 (Tex. 1917); Fuller & Co. v. Alturas School District, 153 Pac. 743 (Cal. 1915); Fodge v. Board of Education of Village of Oak Park, 32 N.E.2d 650 (Ill. 1941); Baumann v. City of West Allis, 204 N.W. 907 (Wis. 1925); Thomas Somerville Co. v. Broyhill, 105 S.E.2d 824 (Va. 1958).
[194]Fuller & Co. v. Alturas School District, 153 Pac. 743 (Cal. 1915).
[195]School District No. 18 v. McClure, 224 S.W. 831 (Mo. 1920); Maryland Casualty Co. v. Eagle River Union Free High School District, 205 N.W. 926 (Wis. 1925).
[196]Maryland Casualty Co. v. Fowler, 27 F.2d 421 (4th Cir. 1928); Texas Fidelity & Bonding Co. v. Rosenberg Independent School District, 195 S.W. 298 (Tex. 1917);

that one who gives surety for profit is not a favorite of the law.[197] Thus, a contract given by a surety company that is ambiguous in its terms will be construed against the surety and in favor of the school district.[198] Bonds given by a surety company for profit have all the features of an insurance contract and are construed accordingly. The rule governing the construction of such contracts has been spelled out by the Supreme Court of Wisconsin:

Due to the fact that modern corporations have undertaken the business of becoming sureties and indemnitors, that under such circumstances the applications and bonds are usually prepared by the surety, the same rule of law is applied to those contracts that is applied to other contracts which are prepared by and for the benefit of a party. While it is stated in many opinions that the rules of interpretation applicable to contracts of a gratuitous surety are not to be applied in a case of a surety for compensation, it is meant that a different rule of law is applicable because the changed situation makes it applicable. This court has held that where a bond is given for a money consideration it has all the essential features of an insurance contract and is therefore not to be construed according to the rules of law applicable to the contract of an ordinary accommodation surety. . . .

Such contracts are to be interpreted as are other contracts, with a view to ascertaining and giving effect to the true meaning and intention of the parties.[199]

Where the statutes require that a surety bond be taken, such a bond is to be construed in a manner which will make effective the intent of the legislature.[200] Where it is clear from the wording of the bond itself, or from circumstances surrounding the taking of the bond, that the parties intended to execute a bond which was in compliance with statutory requirements, the weight of authority indicates that the terms of the statute will be read into the bond despite the fact that the bond itself does not conform to the statute in all respects.[201] The reasoning of the courts which have reached this conclusion is illustrated by a Wisconsin case in which the statutes provided that no contract for the construction of public works could be made unless the contractor gave a bond conditioned for faithful performance of the contract and for payment of labor performed and material furnished in executing the contract. In this case a contract was let without the taking of a bond conditioned for the payment of laborers and material suppliers. Although this requirement was not met, the court held that it was a statutory bond and that the surety on the bond was liable to subcontractors for the value of the material and labor furnished by them. In the court's words:

It is the contention of appellants that the liability sought to be imposed by the statute does not arise unless the provision required by the statute is actually inserted in the contract. If this construction is correct, then the relief which the Legislature attempted to afford subcontractors and material men is very much like sounding brass. The remedy which the Legislature intended to extend may, under such a construction, be defeated if the parties to the contract do not insert the prescribed provision, and whether the remedy is available to subcontractors and material men depends, not upon the law, but upon the parties to the contract. If this be the proper construction of the law, then the statute might just as well not have been passed, because such was the law before. Such a statute will be construed in the light of the conditions and circumstances which give rise to the law and to effectuate the purpose which the Legislature sought to accomplish.[202]

In a number of decisions, however, it has been held[203] that a surety bond should be

Royal Indemnity Co. v. Northern Ohio Granite & Stone Co., 126 N.E. 405 (Ohio 1919); Maryland Casualty Co. v. Eagle River Union Free High School District, 205 N.W. 926 (Wis. 1925).

[197]Nye-Schneider-Fowler Co. v. Roeser, 173 N.W. 605 (Neb. 1919); Gill v. Paysee, 226 Pac. 302 (Nev. 1924); Maryland Casualty Co. v. Eagle River Union Free High School District, 205 N.W. 926 (Wis. 1925); Van Cor, Inc. v. American Casualty Co., 208 A.2d 267 (Pa. 1965).

[198]General Asbestos & Supply Co. v. Aetna Casualty & Surety Co., 198 N.E. 813 (Ind. 1935); Royal Indemnity Co. v. Northern Ohio Granite & Stone Co., 126 N.E. 405 (Ohio 1919); Maryland Casualty Co. v. Eagle River Union Free High School District, 205 N.W. 926 (Wis. 1925).

[199]Maryland Casualty Co. v. Eagle River Union Free High School District, 205 N.W. 926 (Wis. 1925).

[200]New Britain Lumber Co. v. American Surety Co., 154 Atl. 147 (Conn. 1931); Pan American Surety Co. v. Board of Public Instruction, 76 So2d 868 (Fla. 1955).

[201]Baumann v. City of West Allis, 204 N.W. 907 (Wis. 1925); Nye-Schneider-Fowler Co. v. Roeser, 173 N.W. 605 (Neb. 1919); Ceco Steel Products Corp. v. Tapager, 294 N.W. 210 (Minn. 1940); School District No. 30 v. Almeda Construction Co., 169 Pac, 507 (Ore. 1917); Metz v. Warrick, 269 S.W. 626 (Mo. 1925); MacDonald v. Calumet Supply Co., 19 N.E.2d 567 (Ind. 1939); Fodge v. Board of Education of Village of Oak Park, 32 N.E.2d 650 (Ill. 1941); Collins v. National Fire Insurance Co. of Hartford, 105 So.2d 190 (Fla. 1958).

[202]Baumann v. City of West Allis, 204 N.W. 907 (Wis. 1925).

[203]Tennessee Supply Co. v. Bina Young & Son, 218 S.W. 225 (Tenn. 1919); Acme Brick Co. v. Taylor, 223 S.W. 248 (Tex. 1920); J. N. McCausland & Co. v. R. A. Brown Construction Co., 90 S.E. 1010 (N.C. 1916); Massachusetts Bonding & Insurance Co. v. Hoffman, 130 S.E. 375 (Ga. 1925); Dillard v. Berry, 257 Pac. 772 (Okla. 1926).

strictly interpreted and that the terms of the statute will not be read into the bond. The courts which ruled in these cases refused to read into the bond the terms of the applicable statute. Consequently, in these jurisdictions the extent of protection afforded to the board of education, and to those who supply labor or material for school construction projects, must be determined from the wording of the bond itself, not from the wording of the statute.

Surety bonds occasionally are given which provide a coverage more comprehensive than that required by the statutes. Where such bonds have been given, questions have arisen as to whether the surety is liable only to the limits established by the statutes or to the limits established in the bond itself. The courts are in some disagreement. In Pennsylvania it has been held[204] that, where the bond is more comprehensive than the statutes require, the surety is bound by the terms of the bond, not by the statute. In Louisiana, however, it has been held[205] that the surety is liable only to the limit of the statutory requirement even though the terms of the bond may provide a more extensive coverage.

Liability of Surety

Surety bonds protect only those parties who are covered by the terms of the bond agreement itself, or who are required to be protected by state statutes. Thus, the extent of the surety's liability on a bond conditioned for faithful performance of a school building contract is usually dependent on the wording of the bond itself. It frequently has been held,[206] for example, that an agreement by a contractor to furnish labor and materials to be used in the construction of a school building does not bind the contractor to pay for such labor and materials. Also, it has been held[207] that a bond which is conditioned for faithful performance of the contract but which does not provide for payment of the claims of laborers and material suppliers does not afford them any security for their claims.

The first step in establishing a surety's liability on a bond conditioned for the faithful performance of a school building contract is to give the surety notice that the contractor has defaulted. In fact, where the bond contains a provision that the surety is to be given notice of the contractor's default, it has been held[208] that the giving of such notice is a condition precedent which must be fulfilled before the surety is liable on the bond. Unless the bond expressly requires it, written notice of a default is not generally demanded, and it has been said that notice to the surety's agent is equivalent to notice to the surety.[209]

In the event of default by a contractor who has given a bond conditioned for faithful performance of a contract the surety may choose either to complete the contract itself or to compensate the district for any loss the district has suffered as a result of the contractor's default. It should be noted that the surety is under no obligation to perform the contract.[210] However, if the surety chooses to complete the contract, it assumes all the rights and liabilities of the contractor and, in effect, stands in the contractor's shoes.[211] The position of a surety which undertakes to complete a contract after default of the contractor who gave the bond has been clearly stated by the Supreme Court of Indiana:

> When the surety took over the work it stood, for all practical purposes, in the shoes of the contractor. Its obligation was to perform his contract for him in terms, and to pay all subcontractors, materialmen, laborers, and those furnishing services which went into the building, and its right to compensation was limited by the statute. . . . The condition of the bond was that the contractor would perform his contract. The surety had bound itself that the contract would be performed, and when the contractor defaulted and the surety took over and undertook to complete the work it became the contractor, subject to all of the obligations, and entitled to all of the rights, of the original contractor in respect to the obligation under the contract to complete the building and to pay all subcontractors,

---

[204]School District v. B. A. Schrages Co., 9 A.2d 900 (Pa. 1939).

[205]Terrebonne Lumber & Supply Co. v. Favret, 2 So.2d 256 (La. 1941).

[206]Petrea v. Board of School Directors of School District No. 134, 226 Ill. App. 145 (1922); Hardison & Co. v. Yeaman, 91 S.W. 1111 (Tenn. 1906); Gill v. Paysee, 226 Pac. 302 (Nev. 1924); Warner v. Hallyburton, 121 S.E. 756 (N.C. 1924); Fodge v. Board of Education of Village of Oak Park, 32 N.E.2d 650 (Ill. 1941).

[207]American Radiator and Standard Sanitary Corp. v. Forbes, 259 F.2d 147 (9th Cir. 1958); Summerbell v. Weller, 294 Pac. 414 (Cal. 1930); Massachusetts Bonding & Insurance Co. v. United States Radiator Corp., 97 S.W.2d 586 (Ky. 1936).

[208]Maryland Casualty Co. v. Fowler, 31 F.2d 881 (4th Cir. 1929); United States Plywood Corp. v. Continental Casualty Co., 157 A.2d 286 (D.C. 1960); School District No. 1 v. A. G. Rushlight & Co., 375 P.2d 411 (Ore. 1962).

[209]Maryland Casualty Co. v. Fowler, 31 F.2d 881 (4th Cir. 1929).

[210]Van Cor. Inc. v. American Casualty Co., 208 A.2d 267 (Pa. 1965); Ludowici Caladon Co. v. Independent School District, 149 N.W. 845 (Iowa 1914).

[211]MacDonald v. Calumet Supply Co., 19 N.E.2d 567 (Ind. 1939); National Loan & Exchange Bank of Greenwood v. Gustafson, 154 S.E. 167 (S.C. 1930); Exchange Bank & Trust Co. v. Texarkana School District No. 7, 301 S.W.2d 453 (Ark. 1957); Wilson v. Moon, 270 N.Y.S. 859 (1934).

materialmen, and laborers who contributed to the construction of the building, regardless of whether the services or materials were furnished while the original contractor was in charge or afterward. In respect to such matters, the surety became the successor, by operation of law, the assignee, of the original contractor. [212]

Where the surety chooses to complete the contract, it is at liberty to choose whomever it pleases to finish the work.[213] Thus, it is under no obligation to subcontract with one of the original bidders, nor must the surety advertise for bids for completion of the work.

If the surety chooses not to complete the work, the board of education may proceed to do so.[214] The rules in such cases are aptly illustrated by an Iowa case[215] in which a contractor defaulted and his surety refused to complete the building. The board of education completed the building, applying the retained percentage of money which was due the contractor to finance the project. In discussing the board's right to complete the building, the court said:

By his insolvency and the assignment for the benefit of his creditors [the contractior] was unable to fully comply with the contract. . . . The sureties on his bond refused to complete the building. It was then in effect a breached contract. The owner was entitled to the benefit of its bargain and to have the building completed at no greater cost to it than the contract price. . . . The right to complete the building under such conditions cannot be made to depend upon a provision of the contract authorizing such to be done, but rests upon the elemental ground that a party to a contract not broken through his fault is entitled to its benefits; and when an expenditure of money is necessary in order to protect and complete that which is already in his possession, as the result of part performance, such expenditure may be made and recovery had for it. . . . We conclude that the fund held by the school district in excess of that paid on the contract was rightfully applied to the cost of completing the work.

Questions occasionally arise concerning the effect on the surety's liability of a change or alteration in the contract which is secured by a surety bond. The general rule

followed in early cases, where accommodation sureties were invariably involved, was that any material alteration or change in the contract which was prejudicial to the interest of the surety discharged the surety from any liability on that bond.[216] With the advent of bonding companies, which provide surety bonds with the intent of profiting from them, the courts have adopted the rule that a change or alteration in the work performed under the contract which is secured by the bond does not release the surety from liability unless the change materially increases the surety's chance of loss.[217] It has been held,[218] for example, that, where the surety was not damaged as a result of the granting of an extension of time for the performance of the contract, the surety was not discharged from liability on its bond; that prejudice in fact was necessary before the surety would be discharged. It also has been held[219] that a surety will be relieved only *pro tanto,* i.e., in part, by a variance in the performance of the contract, and should be relieved only to the extent of the damage it sustained as a result of acts prejudicial to its interests.

Construction contracts customarily contain provisions for changes and alterations. Where the original contract contains such provisions, a surety will not be released by changes and alterations affecting the performance of the contract, for such changes are assumed to have been contemplated by the surety when the bond was executed.[220] Of course, the alterations must not be of such scope as to constitute an entirely new and different contract.

Surety companies occasionally have attempted to evade liability on the basis of technicalities. The courts have been inclined to overlook technical irregularities which do not affect the surety's chance of loss. It has been held,[221] for example, that a failure on the part of school officials to comply with statutory provisions concerning building permits, sale of revenue bonds, and deposit of proceeds from bond sales

[212]MacDonald v. Calumet Supply Co., 19 N.E.2d 567 (Ind. 1939).
[213]Central Surety & Insurance Corp. v. Martin Infante Co., 272 F.2d 231 (3d Cir. 1959).
[214]Ludowici Caladon Co. v. Independent School District, 149 N.W. 845 (Iowa 1914); Garvey School District v. Southwest Surety Insurance Co., 194 Pac. 711 (Cal. 1920).
[215]Ludowici Caladon Co. v. Independent School District, 149 N.W. 845 (Iowa 1914).

[216]Reese v. United States, 76 U.S. 13, 19 L.Ed. 541 (Cal. 1869); Independent District of Mason City v. Reichard, 50 Iowa 98 (1878).
[217]Maryland Casualty Co. v. Fowler, 31 F.2d 881 (4th Cir. 1929); Rule v. Anderson, 142 S.W. 358 (Mo. 1911); Maryland Casualty Co. v. Eagle River Union Free High School District, 205 N.W. 926 (Wis. 1925).
[218]Maryland Casualty Co. v. Fowler, 31 F.2d 881 (4th Cir. 1929).
[219]Maryland Casualty Co. v. Eagle River Union Free High School District, 205 N.W. 926 (Wis. 1925).
[220]Cass v. Smith, 240 S.W. 778 (Tenn. 1922); American Surety Co. v. Lauber, 53 N.E. 793 (Ind. 1899); Hayden v. Cook, 52 N.W. 165 (Neb. 1892).
[221]Robstown Independent School District v. American Indemnity Co., 228 S.W. 105 (Tex. 1921).

does not affect the surety's liability. Similarly, it has been held[222] that the fact that a bond was made payable to the members of the school board rather than to the school district did not release the surety from liability if the bond was made payable to the school board members in their official representative capacity. It also has been held[223] that one who has the benefit of a contract with a school district is estopped from denying, in an action on one's bond, the authority of the school district to make the contract.

10.7b Payment bonds

Subcontractors on school construction projects, laborers who are employed on such projects, and those who supply materials for use in school construction projects have recourse only against the prime contractor unless they are granted additional protection by the statutes or by a bond conditioned to guarantee that they will be paid. While in private construction projects such persons can obtain a mechanic's lien against the property, the overwhelming weight of authority holds that no mechanic's lien can attach to public school property.[224] The reasoning of the courts in this regard is illustrated in the following statement by a Colorado court:

The right of a mechanic's lien has no existence, except by virtue of the statute. . . . The rights and remedies of a subcontractor are, to a certain extent, measured by those of the original contractor. The foundation of the right of either to a lien is the original contract, and if that is not such as the statute contemplates, and cannot, therefore, be made the basis of a lien in favor of the original contractor, a contractor under him is entitled to none. The original contract must be made with the owner of the land upon which the building is erected, or with some person authorized to act for him, and the resultant lien is coextensive with his interest or claim in the property. . . . By the terms of the statute all school property within the district is held by the school board in trust for the school district, for the benefit of the school, and the school is a state institution. We do not think that either the school board or the school district is, within the definition of the term, the "owner" of the school property; and, in our opinion, the provisions of the

mechanic's lien law cannot be applied to public school buildings.[225]

While no lien can be enforced against school property, statutes may permit subcontractors, laborers, or material suppliers to enforce a lien against money owed to the general contractor by the school district.[226] The right to obtain such a lien is, of course, subject to the rather severe limitation that there must be money due the contractor in order for the lien to be enforced.[227] Also, when one to whom the contractor owes money agrees to accept a pro-rata share of the money due the contractor which is being held by the board, that person is estopped from enforcing any lien claim.[228] It also should be noted that, where no statutory right to enforce liens against money due a contractor has been granted, it has been held[229] that subcontractors, laborers, and material suppliers cannot enforce such a lien.

Clearly, laborers, material suppliers, and subcontractors have no right of action against a school district for work they have performed or material they have furnished for a school building unless such right of action is afforded by the contract or by statute. The most common form of statutory protection afforded subcontractors, laborers, and material suppliers is the requirement that school authorities obtain from the contractor a bond conditioned for the payment of laborers and material suppliers. Even when not required by statute, such a bond may be required by school authorities.[230] One of the main purposes of statutes which require that a bond conditioned for the payment of laborers and material suppliers be taken is to afford a right of action to persons who would have a right to a mechanic's lien on the building if it were private property.[231]

[222]Finney v. Garner, 71 S.W. 592 (Tenn. 1902).
[223]Millville Board of Education v. Empire State Surety Co., 85 Atl. 223 (N.J. 1912).
[224]State v. Tiedermann, 10 Fed. 20 (8th Cir. 1881); Florman v. School District No. 11, 40 Pac, 469 (Col. 1895); Martin v. Holtville High School Building, 145 So. 491 (Ala. 1933); Board of Education of District No. 3 v. Neidenberger, 78 Ill, 58 (1875); Fatout v. Board of School Commissioners, 1 N.E. 389 (Ind. 1885); Board of Education v. Salt Lake Pressed Brick Co., 44 Pac. 709 (Utah 1896).

[225]Florman v. School District No. 11, 40 Pac. 469 (Col. 1895).
[226]Martin v. Holtville High School Building, 145 So. 491 (Ala. 1933); Barker-Lubin Co. v. Wanous, 167 N.E.2d 797 (Ill. 1960); Newburgh Nursery, Inc. v. Board of Education of Central School District No. 2, 247, N.Y.S.2d 74 (1964).
[227]Sioux Falls Pressed Brick Co. v. Board of Education, 125 N.W. 291 (S.D. 1910).
[228]Brittingham & Hixon Lumber Co. v. Board of Education of School District No. 71, 2 N.E.2d 172 (Ill. 1936).
[229]Martin v. Holtville High School Building, 145 So. 491 (Ala. 1933); Drinkwater v. D. Guschov Co., Inc., 196 N.E.2d 863 (Mass. 1964).
[230]Baker v. Bryan, 21 N.W. 83 (Iowa 1884); Jefferson County Board of Education v. Union Indemnity Co., 119 So. 837 (Ala. 1928); Board of President and Directors of the St. Louis Public Schools v. Woods, 77 Mo. 197 (1883).
[231]Royal School Laboratories, Inc. v. Town of Watertown, 236 F.Supp. 950 (Conn. 1965); Sundheim v. School District of Philadelphia, 166 Atl. 365 (Pa. 1933);

Construction of

Since the ultimate objective of payment bonds is to protect laborers and material suppliers, it has been said that such statutes are to be given a liberal construction,[232] and that a bond given under them is to be construed so as to make effective the intent of the parties and the purpose of the statute.[233] Thus, it has been held[234] that a slight difference in the language of the bond from that of the statute does not impair its validity as a statutory bond, nor is it necessary that the bond make specific reference to the statute in order to be considered a statutory bond.[235] Similarly, it has been ruled[236] that, where a statute requires a performance bond to be given but the construction contract, while requiring that a bond be given, does not specify its form, the court will assume the contractor intended to give the required statutory bond.

Questions sometimes arise concerning the persons who are entitled to the protection afforded by a payment bond. Where protection is afforded subcontractors, whether a person is to be regarded as a subcontractor is determined by whether it has been agreed that the original contract shall be the standard by which the performance of that person's contract is to be judged.[237] A material supplier has been defined as one who furnishes material which is used in the construction of a building.[238] Concerning claims by material suppliers, it is usually essential that the material for which compensation is sought be either consumed in use or incorporated in the actual structure. Thus, it has been ruled[239] that material which is neither consumed in construction activities nor incorporated in the structure is not entitled to the protection of a payment bond unless so provided by statutes.

Liability of Surety

To determine the extent of the surety's liability on a payment bond it is necessary to refer to the construction contract and the payment bond, as well as to any pertinent statutes. Where the coverage provided by the bond is broader than that required by statute, the weight of authority indicates that the liability of the surety is enlarged accordingly,[240] although in at least one case it has been held[241] that the surety's liability is limited to that provided by the statute.

The effect on the liability of the surety of additions to or alterations of the construction contract is occasionally questioned. It has been held[242] that a surety is not relieved of its liability if laborers and material suppliers did not participate in altering the contract on which the payment bond was given. It also has been held[243] that, where the construction contract makes provision for additions and alterations, changes made pursuant to the contract are binding on the surety unless they are so extensive as to substantially alter the original contract. In regard to the effect of an invalid contract on the liability of a surety the courts are in disagreement. The fact that the contract is invalid has been held[244] not to prevent material suppliers from recovering on a payment bond. But it also has been held[245] that material suppliers cannot recover on the bond if the contract is invalid.

As previously noted, statutory provisions are to be read into the bond. Where the statutes establish limitations on the time in which claims must be filed and actions taken on payment bonds, the limitations must be complied with strictly in order to establish a right of action on the bond.[246] A change in the statutory time limit does not affect bonds executed prior to the change. To do so would destroy the contractual statutory right which would clearly be an unconstitutional impairment of the obligation of the statutory payment bond.[247] There must also be substantial compliance with

Ingalls Iron Works Co. v. Standard Accident Insurance Co., 130 S.E.2d 606 (Ga. 1963); Ceco Steel Products Corp. v. Tapager, 294 N.W. 210 (Minn. 1940); American Mason's Supply Co. v. F. W. Brown Co., 280 A.2d 366 (Conn. 1971).

[232]Ingalls Iron Works Co. v. Standard Accident Insurance Co., 130 S.E.2d 606 (Ga. 1963); Baumann v. City of West Allis, 204 N.W. 907 (Wis. 1925).

[233]Hartford Accident & Indemnity Co. v. Board of Education, 15 F.2d 317 (4th Cir. 1926); Gill v. Paysee, 226 Pac. 302 (Nev. 1924).

[234]Continental National Bank v. Republic Casualty Co., 262 Pac. 300 (Cal. 1927).

[235]Miles v. Baley, 149 Pac. 45 (Cal. 1915).

[236]Nye-Schneider-Fowler Co. v. Roeser, 173 N.W. 605 (Neb. 1919).

[237]People v. Connell, 161 N.W. 844 (Mich. 1917).

[238]United States Fidelity & Guaranty Co. v. American Surety Co., 25 F.Supp. 280(Pa. 1938).

[239]School District v. B. A. Schrages Co., 9 A.2d 900 (Pa. 1939); Terrebonne Lumber & Supply Co. v. Favret, 2 So2d 256 (La. 1941); Board of Education in Wilmington v. Aetna Casualty & Surety Co., 159 Atl. 367 (Del. 1932).

[240]School District v. B. A. Schrages Co., 9 A.2d 900 (Pa. 1939); Board of Public Education in Wilmington v. Aetna Casualty and Surety Co., 152 Atl. 600 (Del. 1930).

[241]Terrebonne Lumber & Supply Co. v. Favret, 2 So.2d 256 (La. 1941).

[242]Cass v. Smith, 240 S.W. 778 (Tenn. 1922).

[243]Independent School District No. 41, v. Sloane, 224 N.W. 182 (S.D. 1929).

[244]Mississippi Fire Insurance Co. v. Evans, 120 So. 738 (Miss. 1929).

[245]Metz v. Warrick, 269 S.W. 626 (Mo. 1925).

[246]United States Fidelity & Guaranty Co. v. Tafel Electric Co., 91 S.W.2d 42 (Ky. 1935); Ceco Steel Products Co. v. Tapager, 294 N.W. 210 (Minn. 1940); Joseph F. Hughes & Co. v. George Robinson Corp., 175 S.E.2d 413 (Va. 1970).

[247]American Mason's Supply Co. v. F. W. Brown Co., 280 A.2d 366 (Conn. 1971).

any procedural requirements concerning the filing of claims and the bringing of actions against the surety which are contained in the building contract or in the surety bond itself.[248] Construction contracts and surety bonds customarily specify that claims may not be filed or actions taken against the surety until the contract work has been accepted. The courts have generally held that acceptance of the work must be unconditional. Acceptance of the work establishes the beginning of the period in which claims may be filed and actions taken. Consequently, it is important that laborers and material suppliers be made aware of the acceptance of the work in order that they may bring actions within any time limitations specified in the statutes, contract, or bond.

Liability for Failure to Require

Where the statutes require that payment bonds be taken and a board of education fails to secure them, a question as to the liability of the school district or the individual board members may arise. Where the statutes expressly stipulate that school districts will be liable if they fail to obtain the required bonds, they are, of course, liable. In the absence of express statutory provision for such liability, the courts disagree as to whether a school district will be held liable for its failure to obtain a bond conditioned for the payment of laborers and material suppliers where the statutes require that such a bond be taken. In some cases it has been held[249] that laborers and material suppliers have a right of action against the district; in others it has been held[250] that no right of action exists.

The courts also do not agree on whether school board members will be held indi-

vidually liable for their failure to take a performance bond as required by statute. In a number of cases the taking of a performance bond has been regarded as a mandatory duty, and failure to take such a bond will render school board members individually liable to those who are injured as a result of their failure.[251] In a majority of cases, however, it has been held[252] that school officers are not individually liable for losses resulting from their failure to take a performance bond unless such liability is imposed upon them by statute. Nevertheless, where statutes requiring school officers to take a bond have been interpreted as imposing upon such officers a ministerial duty, failure to take the required bond may make them personally liable to laborers and material suppliers who suffer loss as a result of that failure.[253]

10.8 SUMMARY

Authority to construct public school facilities is governed by statutes, and only such powers as the statutes confer, either expressly or by implication, can be exercised by local school officials. Where local boards of education are granted authority to construct school facilities, their decisions concerning the kind and amount of facilities needed will not be interfered with unless they abuse their discretion. Furthermore, they may provide any facilities and equipment required for the teaching of any proper subject of instruction.

A grant of authority to construct school buildings implies authority to employ an architect. As a general rule, such authority may not be delegated. Since architectural contracts call for the rendering of personal services of a highly specialized professional nature, it is not necessary that such contracts be let on the basis of competitive bids.

An architect is regarded as the agent of the board of education and possesses limited powers, the extent of which are determined by the contract. Unless expressly authorized to do so, an architect employed by a board cannot bind that board. The ar-

---

[248]Fidelity & Deposit Co. v. Herbert H. Conway, Inc., 128 P.2d 764 (Wash. 1942); *In re* Wilaka Construction Co., Inc., 2 N.Y.S.2d 251 (1937); General Asbestos & Supply Co. v. Aetna Casualty & Surety Co., 198 N.E. 813 (Ind. 1935).

[249]Royal School Laboratories, Inc. v. Town of Watertown, 236 F.Supp. 950 (Conn. 1965); Northwest Steel Co. v. School Dsitrict No. 16, 148 Pac. 1134 (Ore. 1915).

[250]Americna Casualty Co. v. Board of Education, 228 F.Supp. 843 (Okla. 1964); Phillips & Co. v. Board of Public Instruction of Pasco County, 122 So. 793 (Fla. 1929); Freeman v. City of Chanute, 66 Pac. 647 (Kan. 1901); New York Blower Co. v. Carbon County High School, 167 Pac. 670 (Utah 1917); Newt Olson Lumber Co. v. School District No. 8 in Jefferson County, 263 Pac. 723 (Col. 1928); *See also* Bolick v. Board of Education of Charles County, 260 A.2d 31 (Md. 1969); Higdon v. Board of Education of Charles County, 261 A.2d 783 (Md. 1970); Board of Education of Charles County v. Alcrymat Corporation of America, 266 A.2d 349 (Md. 1970) holding that a material supplier or laborer is barred from recovery because of governmental immunity.

[251]Warren v. Glen Falls Indemnity Co., 66 So.2d 54 (Fla. 1953); Staffon v. Lyon 68 N.W. 151 (Mich. 1896); Rupard Asphalt Co. v. O'Dell, 382 S.W. 2d 832 (Mo. 1964).

[252]Blanchard v. Burns, 162 S.W. 63 (Ark. 1913); Plumbing Supply Co. v. Board of Education of Independent School District of Canton, 142 N.W. 1131 (S.D. 1913); Sailling v. Morrell, 150 N.W. 195 (Neb. 1914); Hydraulic Press Brick Co. v. School District of Kirkwood, 79 Mo.App. 665 (1899); Noland Co. v. Board of Trustees of Southern Pines School, 129 S.E. 577 (N.C. 1925).

[253]Owen v. Hill, 34 N.W. 649 (Mich. 1887); C. A. Burton Machinery Co. v. Ruth, 186 S.W. 737 (Mo. 1916).

chitect's compensation usually is based on a fixed percentage of the total cost of the work which is done. If a building is designed but not constructed, the architect generally is entitled to compensation for his or her work according to the terms of the contract. If a district breaches the contract, the architect is entitled to damages based on the reasonable value of the work performed.

If the statutes require that school construction contracts be let on the basis of competitive bids, any contract let without taking such bids is invalid. If competitive bids are not required, they may or may not be taken, at the discretion of the board of education. Although it has been held that a board of education may have repair work done by its own employees regardless of cost, the courts generally will not permit a board of education deliberately to circumvent competitive bidding requirements by this method.

Where bids are required, all bidders must be provided with plans and specifications which are sufficiently definite and precise to permit all to bid on the same basis. Alternate bids may be taken; where they are, each bidder must be given an opportunity to bid on one, some, or all of the alternates, and a bidder may not be disqualified by failure to bid on all alternates. Prospective bidders are entitled to reasonable public notice that bids will be received.

Bidders are generally required to submit with their bids a deposit or a bond conditioned to insure that the bidder will enter into a contract if his or her bid is accepted. If the successful bidder refuses to enter into a contract, the surety is liable for either the amount specified on the bond plus interest or the difference between the successful bid and that of the next lowest bidder, whichever is less. Upon entering into a contract, the bidder is entitled to the return of the deposit or bond. A bid may be corrected prior to the time the bids are opened but not afterward. As a general rule, a bidder who makes a fundamental mistake in a bid is entitled to the return of his or her deposit or bond, although there are some decisions to the contrary.

Where school authorities are not legally required to obtain bids but choose to do so, they may reject all bids so long as they act in good faith and do not abuse their discretion. However, where bids are required, it is usually held that school authorities may not arbitrarily reject all bids, although in some cases they have been permitted to do so. The lowest bidder on a construction contract is not necessarily the lowest "responsible" bidder. In determining the lowest responsible bidder a board of education may consider all factors which bear upon the bidder's ability to perform the contract according to its terms, such as reputation, integrity, and experience in similar projects. If a contract is awarded to one other than the lowest bidder, it may not be done capriciously and without reasonable cause.

A bid must be accepted within a reasonable time after the opening of bids, although it generally need not be accepted at the time the bids are opened. If the statutes require that contracts be made in writing, the acceptance of a bid must be made in writing. Some courts have ruled that no valid contract exists until the contract document has been duly executed, but ordinarily an unqualified acceptance of a bid is regarded as constituting a valid contract.

School construction contracts are subject to the general rules which govern other types of school contracts. An *ultra vires* contract is void and cannot be ratified; a contract invalid because of an irregularity in the mode of contracting may be ratified. In some cases it has been ruled that substantial performance of a school construction contract is all that is required; in other cases it has been decided that the work must be performed in strict accord with the terms of the contract. A contractor is liable to the district for defective workmanship or materials.

Acceptance of the completed building, either expressly or by implication, indicates satisfactory completion of the contract. An architect's certificate of completion is generally determinative, although the board of education may accept the work without such certification.

A school district may deduct from money due the contractor damages due it for defective work, or for delay in completing the project if the contract contains a penalty clause. The contractor is entitled to additional compensation for extra work performed in accordance with the terms of the contract, or where the extra work results from errors or omissions in the plans and specifications upon which the contractor's bid was based.

When the statutes so provide, a board of education must obtain performance and payment bonds from the contractor, and it may require such bonds even if they are not called for by statute. Performance bonds insure that the contractor will perform the contract according to its terms; payment bonds guarantee that the contractor will pay all bills for labor and materials used in the construction. A bond ordinarily is read in conjunction with the contract it secures, and a bond given by a surety company will be construed in favor of the district if its terms are ambiguous. While the weight of authority indicates that a bond given in compliance with statutory requirements will be interpreted to conform with such requirements, in some cases it has been ruled that the bond should be interpreted strictly and the terms of the statute are not to be read into it.

If the contractor defaults, the contractor's surety may choose either to complete the project or to compensate the district for any loss it sustains as a result of the contractor's default. If the surety chooses to complete the project, it must assume all the obligations and rights of the original contractor. If the surety chooses not to complete the building, the school district may complete it and apply any money due the contractor at the time of default to the cost of completing the building. Changes in the contract ordinarily will not release the surety from liability unless they materially increase the surety's chance of loss; in some cases it has been held that such changes relieve the surety only to the extent of the damage it suffered through acts prejudicial to its interests.

No lien can attach to school property. Consequently, the only protection afforded laborers and material suppliers is that provided by a bond conditioned to guarantee their payment. As a rule, such bonds are liberally construed. However, there must be strict compliance with statutory requirements concerning the filing of claims on payment bonds.

If a district fails to secure a payment bond as the statutes require, the courts are in some disagreement as to whether the district will be liable to laborers and material suppliers. In some cases it has been held that such persons have a right of action against the district; in others, that they do not. Where the taking of a payment bond is regarded as a mandatory duty, school board members may be held individually liable if they fail to take such a bond. The weight of authority, however, indicates that they will not be held liable unless such liability is imposed upon them by statute.

Tort and Related Liability of School Districts, School Officers, and School District Employees

11.0 INTRODUCTION

Although school districts, school officers, and school employees may incur liability from several sources, a major source of concern is that liability which arises as a result of torts. A school district may be required to compensate a person for injury or loss resulting from a tort committed by an officer, agent, or employee of the district. Individual school officers or employees also may be liable personally for torts which they commit in the course of their activities or within the scope of their employment.

11.1 TORTS AND TORT LIABILITY

It is difficult to define a tort satisfactorily; in fact, Prosser stated that "a really satisfactory definition of a tort has yet to be found."[1] In general, a tort is a civil wrong for which a court will award damages. A tort may be committed against either a person or property and may range from direct physical injury to a person (assault or battery) to damage to an intangible asset such as a person's reputation (libel or slander). The purpose of the law of torts is to adjust losses arising out of human activities and "to afford compensation for injuries sustained by one person as the result of the conduct of another."[2] A civil action for a tort is brought by the injured person for the purpose of obtaining from the wrongdoer compensation for the damage suffered.

In determining whether a given act constitutes a tort, the following elements must be shown to exist to establish a legal cause of action:

1. A duty or obligation requiring one to conform to a certain standard of conduct so as to protect others against unreasonable risk.
2. A failure on one's part to act in a manner which conforms to the standard of conduct required.
3. Injury to another caused by one's failure to act in the manner required.
4. Actual loss or damage to the person or interest of another as a result of the injury.

Where a tort is alleged to have been committed, the person who claims to have been injured by the alleged tort must establish that:

1. The defendant had a duty to protect the complainant against unreasonable risk of injury.
2. The defendant breached the duty, i.e., failed to protect the complainant from injury.

3. The breach of duty by the defendant was the proximate cause of the complainant's injury, i.e., that a direct and unbroken chain of events existed between the breach of duty complained of and the injury to the complainant.[3]

Unless these three points can be proven, the defendant will not be held liable for injuries sustained by the complainant.

The concept of negligence is closely associated with the law of torts. Liability for torts arises from negligence, which may be defined as failure to exercise the degree of care for the safety and well-being of others that a reasonable and prudent person would have exercised under similar circumstances. Thus, the test for negligence is "What would a reasonable person have done?" For example, in discussing negligence the Supreme Court of Oregon said:

> Negligence, in the absence of statute, is defined as the doing of that thing which a reasonably prudent person would not have done, or the failure to do that thing which a reasonably prudent person would have done, in like or similar circumstances; it is the failure to exercise that degree of care and prudence that a reasonably prudent person would have exercised in like or similar circumstances.[4]

The burden of proving negligence rests with the plaintiff, while the existence of negligence and the amount of compensable damage arising therefrom are questions to be decided by the courts.

In view of the potential exposure of school districts and school employees to tort liability, it is important that school personnel be aware of some of the elements involved in cases in which torts are alleged to have been committed. It must be recognized that the law relating to torts is exceedingly complicated. Consequently, only a few of the major elements of tort actions can be noted.[5]

The legal principles which govern a tort action involving a school district or a school employee are identical to those which govern other tort actions. Tort actions generally involve both questions of law, which are answered by the court, and questions of fact, which are answered by a jury.

---

[1]William L. Prosser, *Handbook on the Law of Torts* (St. Paul, Minn.: West Publishing Co., 4th ed., 1971), p. 1.

[2]*Ibid.*, p. 6.

[3]Miller v. Griesel, 308 N.E.2d 701 (Ind. 1974). *See also: Restatement of Torts*, 281.

[4]Biddle v. Mazzocco, 284 P.2d 364 (Ore. 1955).

[5]For more comprehensive treatment see standard works such as Prosser, *op. cit.*, or a legal encyclopedia such as *Corpus Juris Secundum* or *American Jurisprudence 2d* series.

11.1a Standard of care required

The standard of care required of an officer or an employee of a school district is that degree of care which a person of ordinary prudence, charged with like duties, would exercise under similar circumstances.[6] It must be noted, however, that a standard of care which is adequate when dealing with adults generally will not be adequate when dealing with young children. As the Supreme Court of Indiana observed:

> . . . the relationship of school pupils and school authorities should call into play the well recognized duty in tort law that persons entrusted with children or others whose characteristics make it likely that they may do somewhat unreasonable things, have a special responsibility recognized by the common law to supervise their charges.[7]

The law is cognizant of the fact that children do not possess the same degree of foresight, caution, and knowledge as adults, and that children may not be judged according to the standard of care required of adults.[8] Furthermore, the amount of care due school children increases with the immaturity of the child.[9] In a California case, for example, a seventeen-year-old high school pupil suffered a brain concussion when struck by a car while he was crossing the street between the school's gymnasium and its athletic field. In discussing the amount of care due the pupil, the court said:

> It is well settled that the amount of care due to minors increases with their immaturity and consequent heedlessness to danger. The boy in this case was nearly eighteen, but we should not close our eyes to the fact that even boys of seventeen and eighteen years of age, particularly in groups where the herd instinct and competitive spirit tend naturally to relax vigilance, are not accustomed to exercise the same amount of care for their own safety as persons of more mature years.[10]

It should not be inferred, however, that someone necessarily is liable for all injuries sustained by pupils. It has been said[11] that a school board is not an insurer of the lives and safety of children but owes them only reasonable care. In dealing with pupils, officers and employees of a school district will be expected to observe that standard of conduct which a reasonable and prudent adult would adhere to when dealing with a child of the age, sex, health, and reputation of the pupil involved.

11.1b Licensees and invitees

The standard of care owed to a person who is on school premises is also dependent upon whether the individual is regarded as a licensee or an invitee. A person is a licensee if that person's entry upon or use of the premises is either expressly or impliedly permitted by the owner but has not been invited by the owner. An invitee, on the other hand, is one who enters the premises in answer to an express or implied invitation by the owner. Thus, a licensee differs from an invitee in that the former is on the premises only by permission or sufferance of the owner while the latter is on the premises at the invitation of the owner. The owner owes a licensee only a duty to abstain from injuring him willfully or wantonly. But the owner owes an invitee a duty of exercising reasonable care for safety commensurate with the circumstances involved and the age and capacity of the individual. As far as the invitee is concerned, the right to protection from injury is a positive one in that the owner not only must refrain from injurious acts but also must warn the invitee of any hidden or concealed perils which may be on the premises.

The question of whether an injured party was on school premises as a licensee or as an invitee generally has arisen either in cases involving adults injured while using school facilities or attending school functions or in cases involving pupils injured outside of regular school hours or functions. In a Delaware case, for example, an adult member of an amateur theatrical group that was using a school auditorium was injured when he fell while using a set of stairs alleged to be defective. The court refused to award damages, however, holding[12] that the person participated in the use of school facilities as a licensee, not as an invitee, and that the school board's only duty to such a person was to avoid trapping him or will-

---

[6]Luna v. Needles Elementary School District, 316 P.2d 773 (Cal. 1957); Briscoe v. School District No. 123, 201 P.2d 697 (Wash. 1949); Miller v. Griesel, 308 N.E.2d 701 (Ind. 1974); Pierce v. Norvath, 233 N.E.2d 811 (Ind. 1968).

[7]Miller v. Griesel, 308 N.E.2d 701 (Ind. 1974).

[8]Youngblood v. Newspaper Production Co., 158 So.2d 432 (La. 1963).

[9]Raymond v. Paradise Unified School District of Butte County, 31 Cal.Rptr. 847 (1963); Satariano v. Sleight, 129 P.2d 35 (Cal. 1942).

[10]Satariano v. Sleight, 129 P.2d 35 (Cal. 1942).

[11]Whitfield v. East Baton Rouge Parish School Board, 43 So.2d 47 (La. 1949); Miller v. Griesel, 308 N.E.2d 781 (Ind. 1974); Clary v. Alexander County Board of Education, 199 S.E.2d 738 (N.C. 1973).

[12]Slovin v. Gauger, 193 A.2d 452 (Del. 1963).

fully injuring him. It has also been held[13] that a child who entered the school grounds on a holiday when school was not in session was a licensee and took the premises as he found them.

In a number of cases involving school districts persons have been held to have had the status of invitees. The Court of Appeals of Louisiana has concluded[14] that a student basketball player participating in an invitational tournament was a business invitee. Under such circumstances the owner or occupier of the building must take reasonable and ordinary care to protect invitees from any dangerous conditions on the premises, and must also warn invitees against latent defects and inspect the premises for possible dangers. An adult spectator who was injured at a football game which had been advertised was held[15] to be an implied, if not an expressed, invitee. It also has been held[16] that an adult participating in a basketball game sponsored by a community recreation program, and held in a school gymnasium with the district's express approval and permission, was an invitee to whom the district owed the duty of reasonable care. A child who was attending a meeting of a Bluebirds group held in a school building, injured when a piano fell on her, was ruled[17] to be an invitee. Regarding invitees, it has been said[18] that a school district must observe that degree of care, precaution, and vigilance which circumstances demand in order to provide for their safety.

The question of whether pupils who are on a field trip as part of their regular school activities are to be accorded the status of licensees or regarded as invitees occasionally has arisen. The distinction is of considerable importance, since the standard of care owed to an invitee by the company being visited is higher than that owed to a licensee. In a majority of cases it has been found that a pupil injured while on a field trip was a licensee. In a Maryland case, for example, a high school pupil who fell into a vat of hot water and suffered severe burns while on a field trip brought an action for damages against the company. The principal of the school had written to the presi-

dent of the company seeking permission for the senior class to visit a power station and permission was granted. About thirty pupils participated in the field trip. They were conducted through a portion of the plant by an employee of the company, who warned them of the dangerous machinery. The employee then left the group, telling them they could look around for themselves. While doing so the pupil fell into a vat of hot water which was flush with the floor and located in a poorly lighted section of the plant. The court refused to hold the company liable on the ground that the pupil was present in the plant as a licensee and said:

> . . . a licensee who enters on premises by permission only, without any enticement, allurement, or inducement being held out to him by the owner or occupant, cannot recover damages for injuries caused by obstructions or pitfalls. He goes there at his own risk, and enjoys the license subject to its concomitant perils.[19]

Other cases in which pupils on field trips have been held to be licensees, and therefore not able to collect damages for their injuries, include the following: A high school pupil on a field trip to an ice plant was electrocuted when he inadvertently grabbed a charged copper wire to keep from falling when he slipped,[20] a pupil was injured while on a field trip to a knitting mill,[21] and a boy fell into a vat of hot water while visiting an ice plant on a field trip sponsored by a YMCA.[22]

In one case a company was held liable for injuries sustained by a pupil on the ground that it failed to show reasonable care to an invitee. The pupil, in a high school home economics class, had her arm so badly crushed in a machine that amputation was necessary. The defendant operated a bakery and creamery and had for some years encouraged inspection of his plant by the public; on one of its windows a sign invited inspection of the premises. It was customary for several classes from the local high school and from other schools in the area to visit the plant each year. The court said:

> From the long-established custom of bringing . . . classes [to the plant] . . . the jury would be justified in believing that such an arrangement

[13]Goldstein v. Board of Education of Union Free School District No. 23, 266 N.Y.S.2d 1 (1965).

[14]Nunze v. Isidore Newman High School, 306 So.2d 457 (La. 1975).

[15]Turner v. Caddo Parish School Board, 179 So.2d 702 (La. 1965).

[16]Stevens v. Central School District No. 1, 270 N.Y.S.2d 23 (1966).

[17]Kidwell v. School District No. 300, 335 P.2d 805 (Wash. 1959).

[18]Perry v. Seattle School District No. 1, 405 P.2d 589 (Wash. 1965).

[19]Benson v. Baltimore Traction Co., 26 Atl. 973 (Md. 1893).

[20]Myers v. Gulf Public Service Corp., 132 So. 416 (La. 1931).

[21]Castonguay v. Acme Knitting Machine & Needle Co., 136 Atl. 702 (N.H. 1927).

[22]Roe v. St. Louis Independent Packing Co., 217 S.W. 335 (Mo. 1920).

of long standing grew out of and was based upon some benefit to the defendants, and implied an invitation to the school authorities.[23]

11.1c Contributory and comparative negligence

One of the defenses commonly invoked by the defendant in a tort action is that of contributory negligence. Contributory negligence may be defined as failure by the injured party to exercise due care for his or her own safety. It is conduct on the part of the plaintiff which contributed to the injury, falling below the standard of care to which one is required to conform for one's own protection. The common-law rule is that one who is guilty of contributory negligence is barred from recovery and the defendant is relieved from all liability for the injury. The burden of proving that the injured person's negligence contributed to that injury rests with the defendant, who must establish a causal relationship between the injured person's negligence and the injury of which that person complains.

The defense of contributory negligence has been invoked in a number of cases involving schools. When determining liability, either at common law or under a statute, the usual rules of contributory negligence are applicable. However, a school child may not be charged with contributory negligence if the child is of such a tender age as to be incapable of appreciating danger.[24] It has been said[25] that in determining whether the conduct of a twelve-year-old child constituted contributory negligence the tests to be employed are whether there was a gross disregard of safety in the face of known, perceived, and understood dangers, and whether there was intentional exposure to obvious danger in a situation within the capacity of a twelve-year-old to appreciate and realize. A pupil may be guilty of contributory negligence if, while running to a school athletic field, there is a failure to be on the alert for the sudden appearance of a motor vehicle on a road through the school grounds.[26] It has been held that a pupil who was injured by a flare-up of certain chemicals which he mixed together was guilty of contributory negligence since he knew that the chemicals involved were dangerous;[27] that a high school student who was injured

while running in the dark after the lights went out in a school building was guilty of contributory negligence;[28] that a twelve-year-old pupil injured in a fall while walking on a properly maintained fence which was not intended or adaptable for that purpose was guilty of contributory negligence,[29] and that a senior basketball player who collided with a glass panel in the gym was guilty of contributory negligence.[30] In the latter case the court was influenced by the fact that the student had been a member of the team for three years, was familiar with the gym and was aware of the presence of the glass panel.

The defense of contributory negligence may be modified or abolished by statute. In several states "comparative negligence" statutes have been enacted. Their specific provisions vary from state to state. Under some statutes the right of the plaintiff to recover depends on the amount of negligence attributable to the plaintiff compared to that attributable to the defendant;[31] under other statutes recovery is permitted if the negligence of the plaintiff is slight and that of the defendant is gross;[32] other statutes permit recovery if the negligence of the plaintiff is less than that of the defendant;[33] and according to still others, the fact that the plaintiff was guilty of contributory negligence does not bar recovery but diminishes it in proportion to the amount of negligence attributable to the plaintiff.[34] Where a statute so provides, contributory negligence may not be invoked as a defense in a tort action. However, in accord with the general rule that statutes in derogation of common law are to be strictly construed, the intention to exclude the defense of contributory negligence must be clear. Comparative negligence usually permits one whose own negligence contributed only slightly to one's injury to obtain a proportionate recovery for the injury sustained rather than being completely barred from recovery, as is true where the common-law rule of contributory negligence is followed. This appears to be more equitable.

---

[23]Gilliland v. Bondurant, 59 S.W.2d 679 (Mo. 1933).
[24]Weems v. Robbins, 9 So.2d 882 (Ala. 1942).
[25]Cormier v. Sinegal, 180 So.2d 567 (La. 1965).
[26]Taylor v. Oakland Scavenger Co., 110 P.2d 1044 (Cal. 1941).
[27]Wilhelm v. Board of Education of City of New York, 227 N.Y.S.2d 791 (1962).

[28]Tannenbaum v. Board of Education, 255 N.Y.S.2d 522 (1964).
[29]Schuyler v. Board of Education, 239 N.Y.S.2d 769 (1963).
[30]Clary v. Alexander County Board of Education, 199 S.E.2d 738 (N.C. 1973).
[31]See, for example, Wisconsin Statutes 895.045 (1972).
[32]See, for example, Revised Statutes of Nebraska, 25–1151 (1975).
[33]See, for example, Arkansas Statutes, 27–1730.1 (Acts 1961, No. 61, sec. 1).
[34]See, for example, Mississippi Code annotated Chapter 71-3-1 to 71-3-111 (1972).

11.1d Assumption of risk

A second commonly involved defense in tort actions is that the injured party assumed the risk of injury. Under the doctrine of assumption of risk, one who voluntarily exposes oneself or one's property to a known danger may not recover for any injuries sustained as the result of the exposure. An essential requisite to invoking the assumption of risk doctrine is that there be not only knowledge of a physical defect in the premises but also appreciation of the danger produced by the physical defect.[35] Thus, it has been held[36] that a plaintiff who was injured when his arm went through a pane of glass in a door immediately behind a basketball backboard did not assume the risk of such an injury, particularly since he did not know that the glass in the door was not shatterproof. On the other hand, it has been held[37] that a nineteen-year-old boy who was injured when he collided with a doorjamb in a brick wall while playing as a voluntary member of a team in a basketball tournament held in a school gymnasium, and who had played on the court previously and knew the location of the basket, the wall, the door, etc., assumed the risk of such an injury.

Several cases involving injuries sustained while participating in intramural or interscholastic sports competition have come before the courts in which the matter of assumption of risk was at issue. It generally has been held that a pupil who voluntarily participates in sports competition assumes the risk of injury. It has been held that by registering and participating in football a pupil accepts the hazards regularly associated with the game,[38] that a child struck by a bat while sitting along the third base line at a baseball game assumes the risk of such injury,[39] and that players who voluntarily participate in a baseball game must accept the risk to which their roles expose them.[40]

The doctrine of assumption of risk relates only to those hazards and risks normally associated with the activity in question. By voluntarily participating in an activity, one does not assume the risk of the negligence of others, such as improper treatment of injuries, willful or wanton injury, or other risks not normally associated with the activity.

11.2 TORT LIABILITY OF SCHOOL DISTRICTS

Tort liability of a school district is dependent upon the common law, upon state statutes, and upon judicial interpretations of statutes. Statutes may be silent on the subject; they may specify that school districts are immune from tort liability; they may impose liability under certain conditions or subject to certain restrictions; or they may specifically make a school district liable for torts committed by its agents, officers, or employees. Judicial interpretations of statutes also have played an important role in establishing the extent to which a school district is subject to tort liability in a number of states.

Before specific aspects of the tort liability of school districts are discussed, a brief overview of the topic is in order. The common-law rule that an agency of government is not liable for torts was early applied to school districts, which legally are regarded as agencies of the state. In recent years, however, the common-law rule that school districts are immune from tort liability has been abrogated or modified in various ways.

Several states have enacted statutes which either completely or partially abrogate the common-law rule of immunity. Examples are "safe-place" laws; "save-harmless" laws; laws making school districts subject to liability for torts committed while engaged in certain activities—for example, transportation of pupils; and laws permitting recovery for damages but establishing a maximum limit of recovery.

Court decisions also have played an important role in either modifying or abrogating the doctrine of governmental immunity from tort liability. School districts in some states have been held liable for maintaining a nuisance, for torts committed while engaging in a proprietary function, and for damages to the extent of the district's liability insurance coverage for torts committed by the district. In recent years the courts in several states have overturned the common-law doctrine, ruling that henceforth governmental agencies, including school districts, would be held liable for their torts. Following such decisions, the legislatures in some of these states enacted statutes which either restored the immunity doctrine or placed limits on the amount of damages an injured party could recover.

---

[35] Stevens v. Central School District No. 1, 270 N.Y.S.2d 23 (1966).

[36] *Ibid.*

[37] Maltz v. Board of Education of New York City, 114 N.Y.S.2d 856 (1952).

[38] Vendrell v. School District No. 26C, 376 P.2d 406 (Ore. 1962).

[39] Benedetto v. Travelers Insurance Co., 172 So.2d 354 (La. 1965).

[40] McGee v. Board of Education of City of New York, 226 N.Y.S.2d 329 (1962).

11.2a Doctrine of governmental immunity

Originally, the status of school districts relative to their liability for torts rested primarily with the common law. While state statutes may specify that school districts shall be immune from tort liability,[41] most states, at least until recent years, had comparatively little legislation on the subject. When state statutes are silent, the tort liability of school districts generally rests on the common-law principle that a governmental agency is not subject to liability for injuries suffered by others as a result of torts committed by it through its officers, agents, or employees.[42]

The origin of the common-law doctrine of governmental immunity from tort liability, frequently expressed as "the King can do no wrong," generally has been traced to two early cases, one decided in England in 1788, the other in Massachusetts in 1812. The Supreme Court of Minnesota noted that:

All of the paths leading to the origin of governmental tort immunity converge on Russell v. The Men of Devon, *100 Eng. Rep. 359, 2 T.R. 667 (1788). This product of the English common law was left on our doorstep to become the putative ancestor of a long line of American cases beginning with* Mower v. Leicester, *9 Mass. 247 (1812).*[43]

In the United States the state was accorded the role of sovereign, there being no king, and could not be sued without its consent. Since school districts are created by the state to fulfill a state function, and legally are regarded as arms of the state, the doctrine of governmental immunity from tort liability also was applied to them.

Although the principal reason given for applying the doctrine of governmental immunity from tort liability to school districts is the fact that they are agencies of the state and perform a governmental function, but other reasons for retention of the doctrine also have been advanced. In some cases[44] it has been noted that a school district has no funds out of which damages can be paid; furthermore, in the absence of specific statutory authority, school districts have no power to establish a fund for such a purpose. In an Indiana case, for example, a laborer who was injured while repairing a schoolhouse sought to recover damages for his injury. The Supreme Court of Indiana, after reiterating the common-law rule that school districts could not be held liable for such injuries in the absence of statute, further stated that "school corporations in this state have no fund out of which such damages can be paid, nor have they any power, express or implied, to raise a fund for such purpose, by taxation or otherwise."[45]

The view that school funds are trust funds which have been set aside for the sole purpose of maintaining the schools and cannot be diverted to other purposes has been used in support of the doctrine of governmental immunity from tort liability.[46] It also has been rationalized that, since schools are organized and operated for the public benefit, the rule of immunity is justified.[47]

In states that still recognize the common-law rule, it does not matter whether the injured party is a student,[48] an employee,[49] or a member of the general public.[50] The school district is immune from liability re-

---

[41]Falcone v. Board of Education of Newark, 4 A.2d 687 (N.J. 1939).

[42]Freel v. School City of Crawfordsville, 41 N.E. 312 (Ind. 1895); Harris v. Salem School District, 57 Atl. 332 (N.H. 1904); Krutili v. Board of Education, 129 S.E. 486 (W.Va. 1925); School District No. 48 of Maricopa County v. Rivera, 243 Pac. 609 (Ariz. 1926); Smith v. Hefner, 68 S.E.2d 783 (N.C. 1952); Stephens v. Natchitoches Parish School Board, 115 So.2d 793 (La. 1959); Buck v. McLean, 115 So.2d 764 (Fla. 1959); Sayers v. School District No. 1, 114 N.W.2d 191 (Mich. 1962); Huff v. Northampton County Board of Education, 130 S.E.2d 26 (N.C. 1963); Campbell v. Pack, 389 P.2d 464 (Utah 1964); Koehn v. Board of Education of City of Newton, 392 P.2d 949 (Kan. 1964); Boyer v. Iowa High School Athletic Association, 127 N.W.2d 606 (Iowa 1964); Wayman v. Board of Education, 215 N.E.2d 394 (Ohio 1966).

[43]Spanel v. Mounds View School District, 118 N.W.2d 795 (Minn. 1962). For additional information concerning these two cases see Lee O. Garber, "Origin of the Governmental Immunity from Tort Liability Doctrine," *The Yearbook of School Law—1964* (Danville, Ill.: The Interstate Printers & Publishers, Inc., 1964), pp. 235–243.

[44]Freel v. School City of Crawfordville, 41 N.E. 312 (Ind. 1895); State v. Board of School Commissioners, 51 Atl. 289 (Md. 1902); Ernst v. City of West Covington, 76 S.W. 1089 (Ky. 1903); Weist v. School District No. 24, 137 Pac. 749 (Ore. 1914).

[45]Freel v. School City of Crawfordsville, 41 N.E. 312 (Ind. 1895).

[46]State v. Board of School Commissioners, 51 Atl. 289 (Md. 1902); Cochran v. Wilson, 220 S.W. 1050 (Mo. 1921); Krutili v. Board of Education, 129 S.E. 486 (W.Va. 1925).

[47]Bank v. Brainerd School District, 51 N.W. 814 (Minn. 1892); Harris v. Salem School District, 57 Atl. 332 (N.H. 1904); Krueger v. Board of Education of City of St. Louis, 274 S.W. 811 (Mo. 1925); Krutili v. Board of Education, 129 S.E. 486 (W.Va. 1925).

[48]Krutili v. Board of Education, 129 S.E. 486 (W.Va. 1925); Anderson v. Board of Education, 190 N.W. 807 (N.D. 1922); Perkins v. Trask, 23 P.2d 982 (Mont. 1933); Meyer v. Board of Education, 86 A.2d 761 (N.J. 1952).

[49]Freel v. School City of Crawfordsville, 41 N.E. 312 (Ind. 1895); McGraw v. Rural High School District No. 1, 243 Pac. 1038 (Kan. 1926); Krueger v. Board of Education of City of St. Louis, 274 S.W. 811 (Mo. 1925).

[50]McKenna v. Kimball, 14 N.E. 789 (Mass. 1888); Kellam v. School Board of the City of Norfolk, 117 S.E.2d 96 (Va. 1960).

gardless of its relationship to the individual.

11.2b Erosion and abrogation of the common-law doctrine

In recent years, there has been severe criticism of the common-law rule of governmental immunity. It has been observed that the basis on which such immunity was originally established—the prevention of pernicious dissipation of public funds—has become a myth under conditions of a modern enlightened society.[51] Opponents of the doctrine argue that elimination of immunity would mean "more equitable distribution of losses in society caused by the government unto members of society rather than forcing individuals to face the total loss of injury."[52] As a federal district court noted:

> Like gaslight of another time it [the doctrine of immunity] must give way to the brightened illumination of today, which chases the shadows and leaves exposed the inadequacy of such a Mid-Victorian concept.[53]

As a result of growing disenchantment with the common-law rule, courts and state legislatures have critically reexamined the doctrine; in some cases it has been abolished altogether and in others it has been severely limited. In some jurisdictions, the rule for state government is different than the rule for local governmental units. In other cases, it is the nature of the activity—governmental versus proprietary—that determines whether the rule of immunity applies. It must be recognized that the law relating to immunity is changing rapidly and is different in almost every jurisdiction. As the court pointed out in a recent Indiana case:

> The doctrine [of governmental immunity] has been amended and eroded until the most that remains is an abstract and confusing principle which finds literally no continuity between jurisdictions.[54]

Some of the general trends that have developed in the area of immunity will be discussed in the following sections.

Statutory Abrogation of
The courts frequently have held that changes in the common-law principle must be accomplished by constitutional amendment or by appropriate legislative enactment.[55] In an early Kansas case it was stated:[56]

> If the doctrine of state immunity in tort survives by virtue of antiquity alone, is an historical anachronism, manifests an inefficient public policy, and works injustice to everybody concerned . . . the Legislature should abrogate it. But the Legislature must make the change in policy, not the courts.

The severity of the doctrine has led several states to enact legislation which abrogates or modifies the common law. Some have removed governmental immunity from tort liability on a broad basis; others have removed immunity only in certain designated activities.

Broad Basis.   At the outset it must be recognized that any statute in derogation of the common law will be strictly construed. In a 1933 Oregon case, the Supreme Court of that state expressed the general rule:

> If the Legislature desires to impose liability upon a school district for tort while acting in any capacity whatsoever, it clearly has the power to do so. Statute in derogation of the common law must be strictly construed and the intention to impose such liability must, therefore, be clearly expressed.[57]

In a number of early cases, courts frequently relied on the above principle to deny recovery even where the statute appeared to allow it.[58] For example, a state statute which provided that:

> . . . an action or suit may be maintained against any of the other public corporations [school district] . . . for an injury to the rights of the plaintiff arising from some act or commission of such other public corporation . . .

was interpreted as allowing recovery only where the school district acted negligently

---

[51]Caporossi v. Atlantic City, 220 F.Supp. 508, (N.J. 1963), *affirmed,* 328 F.2d 620, *cert. denied,* 397 U.S. 825, 85 S.Ct. 51, 13 L. Ed.2d 35.
[52]Campbell v. State, 284 N.E.2d 733 (Ind. 1972).
[53]*Supra* note 51, at 518.
[54]*Supra* note 52, at 734.

[55]Krutili v. Board of Education, 129 S.E. 486 (W.Va. 1925); Bingham v. Board of Education of Ogden City, 233 P.2d 432 (Utah 1950); Buck v. McLean, 115 So.2d 764 (Fla. 1959); Tesone v. School District No. RE-2, 384 P.2d 82 (Col. 1963).
[56]McGraw v. Rural High School Dist. No. 1, 243 Pac. 1038, 1039 (Kan. 1926).
[57]Lovell v. School District No. 13, 143 Pac. 2d 236, (Ore. 1933).
[58]Bank v. Brainerd School District, 51 N.W. 814 (Minn. 1892); Allen v. Independent School District No. 17, 216 N.W. 533 (Minn. 1927); Spencer v. School District No. 1, 254 Pac. 357 (Ore. 1927); Antin v. Union High School District No. 2 of Clatsop County, 280 Pac. 664 (Ore. 1929).

in carrying out its non-governmental functions. As a result, recovery was denied where a pupil was injured on a negligently maintained sidewalk, since maintenance of school grounds was considered to be a governmental function.[59]

However, there have been several states which have enacted statutes which successfully abrogated the common-law rule. In 1923, California approached the problem directly by passing legislation explicitly making school districts liable for all injuries resulting from the negligent acts of the district, its officers, or its employees. In a case decided in 1930 it was ruled that this statute did indeed make school districts liable for injuries attributable to the negligence of the district.[60] The only question in California was whether the negligence complained of was, in fact, the cause of the injury.[61]

One of the most comprehensive statutes abolishing governmental immunity was enacted in 1967 in Iowa. It defined "municipality" to include school districts[62] and provided:

> Except as otherwise provided in this Chapter, every municipality is subject to liability for its torts and those of its officers, employees, and agents acting within the scope of their employment or duties, whether arising out of a governmental or proprietary function.

> A tort shall be deemed to be within the scope of employment or duties if the act or omission reasonably relates to the business or affairs of the municipality and the officer, employee, or agent acted in good faith and in a manner a reasonable person would have believed to be in and not opposed to the best interests of the municipality.[63]

It should be noted that in abolishing common-law immunity, states frequently provide that notice of the claim be given to the agency involved within a specified time after the accident.

Limited Basis. The so-called "safeplace" statutes afford one example of state legislation which has imposed limited liability on school districts. Such laws generally require that public buildings, including school buildings, be constructed and maintained so that they are safe for frequenters. The Michigan statute provides that:

> . . . governmental agencies are liable for bodily injury and property damage resulting from a dangerous or defective condition of a public building if the governmental agency has active or constructive knowledge of the defect. . . .[64]

As has been previously mentioned such statutes have been strictly construed by the courts. For example, it has been held[65] that a pupil injured by a falling flagpole could not sue the district under the safe-place statute because the flagpole, which was located on school grounds, was not a part of the school building. Similarly, it has been held[66] that sidewalks and structural approaches to public buildings which lie outside the lines of such buildings are not public buildings within the meaning of such statutes.

Several states have abrogated governmental immunity in a limited way by enacting legislation which makes school districts liable for injuries sustained by pupils while being transported by a school district and which establishes limits of recovery for such injuries. In Mississippi, for example, a statute limits to $10,000 recovery by a school pupil for accident or injury resulting from the negligent operation of a school bus.[67] In 1965 Utah enacted the Utah Governmental Immunity Act which waived its immunity in a number of areas. With limited exceptions, a school district may be sued for injuries that result from (1) the negligent operation of a motor vehicle,[68] (2) a dangerous or defective condition of a building,[69] or (3) the negligent acts or omissions of its employees.[70]

Other states have used a different approach. Rather than abrogating governmental immunity, they have created a state claims board to investigate claims and pay damages which result from the activities of public corporations and their employees. In North Carolina, for example, the North Carolina Industrial Commission is assigned the responsibility of hearing and passing

[59]Lovell v. School District No. 13, 143 Pac. 2d 236 (Ore. 1933).

[60]Ahern v. Livermore Union High School District, 284 Pac. 1105 (Cal. 1930).

[61]Taylor v. Oakland High School District, 83 P.2d 948 (Cal. 1938); Reithardt v. Board of Education of Yuba County, 111 P.2d 440 (Cal. 1941); Brown v. City of Oakland, 124 P.2d 369 (Cal. 1942).

[62]Iowa Code Annotated 1976 Supplement, 613A.1.

[63]Iowa Code Annotated 1976 Supplement, 613A.2.

[64]Michigan Common Laws Annotated, 691.1406 (1968).

[65]Lawver v. Joint School District No. 1, 288 N.W. 192 (Wis. 1939).

[66]Hemingway v. City of Janesville, 81 N.W.2d 492 (Wis. 1957); See also Pichette v. Manisitique Public Schools, 213 N.W.2d 784 (Mich. 1973).

[67]Mississippi Code Annotated, 1975 Supplement, 37-41-41.

[68]Utah Code Annotated, 63-30-7 (1975).

[69]Utah Code Annotated, 63-30-9 (1975).

[70]Utah Code Annotated, 63-30-10 (1975).

upon tort claims against departments, institutions, and agencies of the state. If the negligence of the agency involved is found to be the proximate cause of the injury, the Commission determines the amount of damages and directs payment of them by the agency concerned. Recovery is limited to a maximum of $10,000.[71]

Judicial Abrogation of

While the doctrine of governmental immunity from tort liability has been widely followed by the courts, it is by no means popular. It has been universally criticized by legal authorities and dissenting court opinions frequently advocate its abolition.[72] Despite widespread dissatisfaction with the doctrine, the courts have been reluctant to depart from precedent. They have generally taken the position that if the immunity doctrine is to be abrogated, it should be accomplished through legislative action rather than by judicial decree. Nevertheless, there have been numerous exceptions to the general rule over the years and in many jurisdictions the application of the doctrine has been severely restricted by judicial decision.

The first indication that school districts might be held liable for negligence in the absence of statute appeared in dicta in a New York case[73] in 1877. In a later case, in which a pupil was injured when plaster from the ceiling of a schoolroom fell on his head, it was held[74] that the school board was negligent, and therefore liable, despite the fact that no statute abrogating the immunity doctrine had been enacted. The courts in the state of New York have consistently ruled that negligence may be imputed directly to the board of education. It has been stated that "the board of education is a governmental agency of the state. . . . It is not liable for the torts of its agents. . . . It, however, remains liable for its own negligence."[75] Courts in New York have differentiated between the duties of a board of education which can be delegated and those which cannot be delegated. Only in connection with duties which cannot be delegated—e.g., provision and maintenance

of safe premises and equipment, provision of competent personnel, and provision of adequate supervision—may a school board be held liable for negligent performance.[76] The board is not held liable for negligence in the performance of duties which can be delegated, chief of which is instruction. However, under New York's save-harmless statute the district is required to pay judgments against an employee arising from the employee's negligence while acting within the scope of his or her assigned responsibilities. Thus, in New York the doctrine of governmental immunity from tort liability has been effectively circumvented.

Nuisance and Trespass. In a number of jurisdictions courts have, in a limited way, departed from the doctrine of governmental immunity by allowing recovery against school districts based on the theory of nuisance or trespass. The legal concept of nuisance has been defined as follows:

> . . . to constitute a nuisance there must have arisen a condition the natural tendency of which is to create danger or inflict injury upon person or property, . . . there must be more than an act or failure to act on the part of the defendant . . . the danger created must have been a continuing one. . . . [77]

Trespass is defined as:

> . . . the doing of an unlawful act or the doing of a lawful act in an unlawful manner to the injury of the person or property of another.[78]

Application of the theory of nuisance and trespass with regard to the tort liability of school districts was initially made in a Michigan case. Snow and ice had fallen from the roof of a school building onto an adjacent property, resulting in damage to the property and injury to the owner when he slipped and fell on a cake of ice. In holding the school district liable for damages, the court commented:

> The plaintiff had the right to the exclusive use and enjoyment of his property, and the defendant had no more right to erect a building in such a manner that the ice and

[71] North Carolina General Statutes, 1974 Replacement, 143-291.

[72] See, for example, dissenting opinions in Hoffman v. City of Bristol, 155 Atl. 499 (Conn. 1931), and Tesone v. School District No. RE-2, 384 P.2d 82 (Col. 1963).

[73] Bassett v. Fish, 75 N.Y. 303 (1877).

[74] Wahrman v. Board of Education, 97 N.Y.S. 1066 (1906), *affirmed*, 80 N.E. 192.

[75] Herman v. Board of Education, 137 N.E. 24 (N.Y. 1922). *See also:* Diamond v. Board of Education of City of New York, 171 N.Y.S.2d 703 (1958).

[76] Friedman v. Board of Education of City of New York, 186 N.E. 865 (N.Y. 1933); Garber v. Central School District No. 1, 295 N.Y.S. 850 (1937).

[77] Bush v. City of Norwalk, 189 Atl. 608 (Conn. 1937).

[78] Waco Cotton Oil Mill of Waco v. Walker, 103 S.W.2d 1071 (Tex. 1937).

snow would inevitably slide from the roof, and be precipitated upon the plaintiff's premises, than it would have to accumulate water upon its own premises, and then permit it to flow in a body upon his premises. . . .[79]

Cases involving similar issues have been adjudicated in several states.[80] School districts have been held liable for damages on the ground of nuisance or trespass when a boy was injured in a fall from a freshly varnished balance beam which was being used on a slippery floor,[81] when property adjoining a school playground was damaged by batted baseballs and trespassing pupils,[82] and when the water supply on adjacent private property was destroyed by grading of the site where a school building was under construction.[83]

Even where school boards are generally not immune from an action for injunctive relief and/or damages resulting from a school-related nuisance, situations arise where such relief is not granted because of public necessity. In an Iowa case, the court observed:

Nuisance claims of private owners must at times yield to public interest and convenience, and under the pressure of public necessity what would otherwise constitute a nuisance may be inflicted upon certain members of the community, subject to the limitation that if the creation or maintenance of the nuisance amounts to a taking of private property compensation therefor must be made. When the public welfare requires it a nuisance may, for special purposes, be permitted, and, as has been seen, public convenience or necessity may be taken into consideration in some cases in determining whether or not to grant equitable relief.[84]

In a number of jurisdictions the courts have refused to apply the theory of trespass or nuisance to school districts. In one case it was held[85] that nuisance was applicable only to property rights and no recovery was allowed for personal injury to a student. In other cases courts have refused to hold school districts liable under the theory of nuisance or trespass, reasoning that a board of education is never authorized to commit a tort of any kind and that if it does so it is acting beyond its power and consequently the district is not liable. Courts have refused to allow recovery on the theory of nuisance where a pupil died as a result of inhaling sewer gas,[86] where a child died as a result of being struck by a playground swing,[87] where a teacher contracted tuberculosis in an unfumigated schoolhouse,[88] where a child was severely burned by hot embers in an unguarded incinerator on the school grounds,[89] where a spectator slipped and fell on a highly polished gymnasium floor,[90] and where a child was bumped into a concrete pit on the school grounds.[91]

Proprietary Functions. In cases involving governmental agencies, courts have distinguished between governmental functions and so-called proprietary functions and held that an agency is not immune from liability if the injury resulted from the negligent performance of a proprietary function. In some jurisdictions this principle has been applied to school activities, primarily where admission fees have been charged or where there has been some financial benefit to the school, but courts generally have been very selective in the characterization of school-related functions as proprietary.

Some courts have held that a school district has no power to engage in a proprietary function; it has power only to operate schools, and all school activities must, therefore, be governmental functions. To engage in a proprietary function would be beyond the authority of a school district. A Tennessee case illustrates this point. A spectator at a high school football game at which admission fees were charged was injured when the bleachers collapsed. In refusing his claim for damages the court said:

The mere fact that an admission fee was charged by the High School does not make the

---

[79]Ferris v. Board of Education of Detroit, 81 N.W. 98 (Mich. 1899).

[80]Ness v. Independent School District of Sioux City, 298 N.W. 855 (Iowa 1941); Jones v. Kansas City, 271 P.2d 803 (Kans. 1954); Sestero v. Town of Glastonbury, 110 A.2d 629 (Conn. 1954); Eller v. Board of Education of Buncombe County, 89 S.E.2d 144 (N.C. 1955); Bartell v. School District No. 28, 137, P.2d 422 (Mont. 1943).

[81]Bush v. City of Norwalk, 189 Atl. 608 (Conn. 1937).

[82]Ness v. Independent School District of Sioux City, 298 N.W. 855 (Iowa 1941).

[83]Eller v. Board of Education of Buncombe County, 89 S.E.2d 144 (N.C. 1955).

[84]Kriener v. Turkey Valley Community School District, 212 N.W.2d 526, 530 (Iowa 1973) *citing* 58 Am.Jr.2d Nuisances, 214.

[85]Hardy v. Wernette, 114 S.W.2d 951 (Tex.Civ.App. 1938).

[86]Folk v. City of Milwaukee, 84 N.W. 420 (Wis. 1900).

[87]Anderson v. Board of Education, 190 N.W. 807 (N.D. 1922).

[88]Bang v. Independent School District No. 27, 255 N.W. 449 (Minn. 1929).

[89]Bingham v. Board of Education of Ogden City, 223 P.2d 432 (Utah 1950).

[90]Thompson v. Board of Education, 94 A.2d 206 (N.J. 1953).

[91]Barnett v. City of Memphis, 269 S.W.2d 906 (Tenn. 1954).

transaction an enterprise for profit. . . . The duties of a County Board of Education are limited to the operation of the schools. This is a governmental function. Therefore, in legal contemplation there is no such thing as such a Board acting in a proprietary capacity for private gain.[92]

Courts have refused to rule that school districts were engaged in proprietary functions by virtue of the fact that they charged admission fees for athletic contests,[93] sold articles made by students attending a vocational school,[94] charged tuition fees to students,[95] or leased an athletic field.[96]

In a number of states the courts have distinguished between governmental and proprietary functions of school districts and in some cases have held school districts liable for the negligent performance of proprietary functions.[97] In an Arizona case, for example, a school district had rented its football stadium to another district and a spectator was injured when a railing collapsed. The court awarded damages to the spectator on the grounds that the district owning the stadium was engaged in a proprietary function and liable for injuries resulting from negligent maintenance.[98] Similarly, a Pennsylvania school district conducting a recreation program for which admission was charged was held to have been engaged in a proprietary function and thus liable for damages when a child drowned as a result of negligence of the district's employees.[99]

Once a jurisdiction recognizes the principle that a school district is liable for negligence in connection with proprietary functions, the court then must determine which activities are proprietary and which are governmental. As a general rule, activities which relate to the educational purpose for which schools are established will be characterized as governmental. Thus,

maintenance of school buildings,[100] and school grounds,[101] transportation of pupils without charge,[102] and operation of school playground[103] have been held to be governmental fucntions.

Proprietary functions generally involve activities which are not related to the educational process and which involve some pecuniary benefit. The renting of school facilities is the most common example of a proprietary function.[104] The test for distinguishing between governmental and proprietary functions has been stated as follows:

The underlying test is whether the act is for the common good of all without the element of special corporate benefit or pecuniary profit.[105]

Complete Departure. Until recent years the courts in nearly all states in which the doctrine of governmental immunity has been accepted followed the principle of *stare decisis;* i.e., when a court has made a declaration of a legal principle, it is the law until changed by competent authority. In 1959, however, the Supreme Court of Illinois rendered its decision in the *Molitor* case and held[106] that henceforth school districts in that state would no longer enjoy the protection of governmental immunity. In that case a child had been injured when a school bus left the road, overturned, exploded, and burned, allegedly as a result of the driver's negligence. The suit brought to recover damages contended that the immunity rule was harsh, unfair, and outmoded and should be abolished. It is worth noting that the defendant school district carried liability insurance, and recovery might have been secured to the limit of the insurance coverage under precedent established in previous Illinois cases. Plaintiff, however, chose to base the appeal on the unjustness of the immunity rule, not on the existence of liability insurance covering the district.

---

[92]Reed v. Rhea County, 225 S.W.2d 49 (Tenn. 1949); see also Sims v. Etowah County Board of Education, 337 So.2d 1310 (Ala. 1976).

[93]*Ibid.;* Richards v. School District of City of Birmingham, 83 N.W.2d 643 (Mich. 1957).

[94]Kirchoff v. City of Janesville, 38 N.W.2d 698 (Wis. 1949).

[95]Daszkiewicz v. Board of Education of Detroit, 3 N.W.2d 71 (Mich. 1942).

[96]Smith v. Hefner, 68 S.E.2d 783 (N.C. 1952).

[97]Sawaya v. Tucson High School District No. 1, 281 P.2d 105 (Ariz. 1955); Morris v. Mt. Lebanon Township School District, 144 A.2d 737 (Pa. 1958); Shields v. School District of City of Pittsburgh, 184 A.2d 240 (Pa. 1962).

[98]Sawaya v. Tucson High School District No. 1, 281 P.2d 105 (Ariz. 1955).

[99]Morris v. Mt. Lebanon Township School District, 144 A.2d 737 (Pa. 1958).

[100]Coleman v. Beaumont Independent School District, 496 S.W.2d 245 (Tex. 1973).

[101]Braun v. Trustees of Victoria Independent School District, 114 S.W.2d 947 (Tex. 1938).

[102]Rankin v. School District No. 9, 23 P.2d 132 (Ore. 1933).

[103]Koehn v. Board of Education of City of Newton, 392 P.2d 949 (Kan. 1964); Pichette v. Manistique Public Schools, 231 N.W.2d 784 (Mich. 1973).

[104]Sawaya v. Tucson High School District No. 1, 281 P.2d 105 (Ariz. 1955).

[105]Rankin v. School District No. 9, 23 P.2d 132 (Ore. 1933).

[106]Molitor v. Kaneland Community Unit District No. 302, 163 N.E.2d 89 (Ill. 1959).

After considering the theory that "the King can do no wrong," the court concluded, "We are of the opinion that school district immunity cannot be justified on this theory." The contention that the immunity rule was necessary to protect public funds and public property was also considered by the court and disposed of as follows:

> We do not believe that in the present day and age, when public education constitutes one of the biggest businesses in the country, that school immunity can be justified on the protection-of-public-funds theory.

> If tax funds can properly be spent to pay premiums on liability insurance, there seems to be no good reason why they cannot be spent to pay the liability itself in the absence of insurance.

In abolishing the immunity from tort liability of Illinois school districts, the court said:

> We are of the opinion that none of the reasons advanced in support of school district immunity have any true validity today. . . .

> We conclude that the rule of school district tort immunity is unjust, unsupported by any valid reason, and has no rightful place in modern day society.

> Defendant strongly urges that if said immunity is to be abolished, it should be done by the legislature, not by this court. With this contention we must disagree. The doctrine of school district immunity was created by this court alone. Having found that doctrine to be unsound and unjust under present conditions, we consider that we have not only the power, but the duty, to abolish that immunity.

The decision of the Illinois Supreme Court in the *Molitor* case has engendered substantial litigation in other states to test the immunity doctrine. Courts in Wisconsin,[107] Minnesota,[108] and Arizona[109] were quick to follow the lead of the Illinois Supreme Court in abrogating the immunity rule. Although the decisions in the Wisconsin and Arizona cases did not involve school districts directly, it was clear that the immunity doctrine would no longer protect school districts in those states from tort liability. The school districts would in the future be held liable for injuries resulting

from the negligent actions of their officers, agents, and employees unless immunity was reinstated by legislative action. Rather than reinstate the immunity doctrine, however, legislatures generally have chosen to enact statutes limiting the amount of recovery which may be had by a party injured as a result of the negligence of the officers, agents, or employees of a school district. For example, in 1963 legislation was enacted in Wisconsin which (1) provided that an action founded in tort must be brought against a school district within 120 days of the action or damage causing the claim and (2) limited recovery to not more than $25,000 per person for any one accident.[110] In Minnesota, however, the legislature established a moratorium by reinstating the immunity doctrine as far as school districts were concerned until January 1, 1970, but provided that, if a school district procured liability insurance, immunity would be waived to the extent of $25,000 per person and $300,000 per occurrence.[111]

Waiver of Immunity. In those jurisdictions that recognize the doctrine of governmental immunity, the question sometimes arises as to whether or not a school district can waive its immunity. There is some disagreement among the courts on this issue and it appears to depend, to some extent, on the context in which the question arises. Occasionally a district will fail to assert its immunity and it will be argued that the failure results in a waiver. The Court of Appeals of Maryland disposed of such an argument by stating:

> . . . counsel for the State or one of its agencies may not either by affirmative action or by failure to plead the defense waive the defense of governmental immunity in the absence of express statutory authority. . . .[112]

But where a school district initiates an action, it may waive its immunity as to claims which the defendant has against the district. For example, where the board sought to recover wages from a former employee, it was held[113] that the board could not defeat the employee's counterclaim against the board by asserting its immunity. The Louisiana court observed:

---

[107]Holytz v. City of Milwaukee, 115 N.W.2d 618 (Wis. 1962).

[108]Spanel v. Mounds View School District, 118 N.W.2d 795 (Minn. 1962).

[109]Stone v. Arizona Highway Commission, 381 P.2d 107 (Ariz. 1963).

[110]Wisconsin Statutes, 895.43 (1973).

[111]Minnesota Statutes Annotated, 466.12 (1974).

[112]Board of Education of Charles County v. Alcrymat Corporation of America, 266 A.2d 349 (Md. 1970).

[113]Orleans Parish School Board v. Williams, 312 So.2d 647 (La. 1975). *Contra:* Independent School District No. 16 of Payne County v. Reed, 503 P.2d 1265 (Okla. 1972).

By invoking the power and authority of the judicial system to adjust its relations with Williams [former employee] . . . the School Board concomitantly waived any immunity from suit it may have possessed.

11.3 INSURING TORT LIABILITY

When a school district purchases insurance, it is often argued that, in so doing, the district waives its governmental immunity. The weight of authority does not support this contention, although there is authority to the contrary.

The purchase of liability insurance by a school district entails the use of tax money to pay insurance premiums. It must be remembered that a school district has no legal power to spend public funds to purchase insurance unless such expenditures have been authorized by the legislature, either specifically or by necessary implication. If the authority is expressly granted, there is no doubt that school districts may purchase liability insurance.[114] However, an Idaho court indicated that school districts may not purchase coverage in excess of the amount authorized by the legislature.[115]

Statutes which create a liability risk by abrogating common-law immunity imply that school districts may purchase insurance against potential losses.[116] Such statutes may take the form of a broad removal of immunity, as in California, or the abrogation of immunity may be limited, e.g., "save-harmless" statutes, "safe-place" statutes, or statutes imposing liability for injuries sustained in certain aspects of the school program such as pupil transportation.

Where no statutes abrogate a school district's common-law immunity from tort liability, the authority of school boards to purchase liability insurance cannot be implied, since the district has no liability to insure. A West Virginia case touched this point directly. It was held[117] that a statute vesting a district board of education with the general management of the schools and authorizing it to provide for the transportation of pupils did not, by implication, authorize the board to purchase liability insurance.

The recent decisions which have removed the immunity from tort liability of school districts in some states raise the question of whether such decisions imply that school districts in those states have authority to purchase liability insurance. In spite of the fact that the common-law immunity rule has been abrogated in a more limited way by court decisions in several states, the issue of whether such decisions imply authority to purchase liability insurance apparently has not come before the higher courts. However, one might conjecture that their answer would be in the affirmative, since in several cases the courts have noted that the availability of liability insurance removes the validity of the argument that retention of the immunity rule is essential to prevent the dissipation of school funds in the payment of damages to injured parties.[118] It also should be noted that, following the decisions abrogating immunity, state legislatures generally have enacted laws specifically authorizing the purchase of general liability insurance and limiting the recovery of injured parties to the extent of the liability insurance coverage.

11.3a Effect on common-law immunity

The courts are in some disagreement as to whether school districts waive their governmental immunity from tort liability when they purchase liability insurance. The weight of authority is to the effect that the mere purchase of liability insurance does not constitute a waiver of immunity.[119] Courts holding this view have said that statutes permitting a district to purchase liability insurance do not necessarily imply that the defense of governmental immunity has been removed. Their reasoning is illustrated in a decision by a federal court in a case in which the defendant school district had purchased insurance covering the liability of its employees and was named as an insured in the policy. The court held that

---

[114]Standard Accident Insurance Co. v. Perry County Board of Education, 72 F.Supp. 142 (Ky. 1947); Brown v. City of Oakland, 124 P.2d 369 (Cal. 1942).

[115]Anneker v. Quinn-Robbins Co., 323 P.2d 1073 (Ida. 1958).

[116]Hughes v. Hartford Accident & Indemnity Co., 134 So. 461 (Ala. 1931); Rogers v. Butler, 92 S.W.2d 414 (Tenn. 1936).

[117]Board of Education v. Commercial Casualty Insurance Co., 182 S.E. 87 (W.Va. 1935).

[118]Marion County v. Cantrell, 61 S.W.2d 477 (Tenn. 1933); Thomas v. Broadlands Community Consolidated School District, 109 N.E.2d 636 (Ill. 1952); Sawaya v. Tucson High School District No. 1, 281 P.2d 105 (Ariz. 1955).

[119]Rittmiller v. School District No. 84, 104 F.Supp. 187 (Minn. 1952); Hughes v. Hartford Accident & Indemnity Co., 134 So. 461 (Ala. 1931); Wallace v. Laurel County Board of Education, 153 S.W.2d 915 (Ky. 1941); Bradfield v. Board of Education, 36 S.E.2d 512 (W.Va. 1945); Hummer v. School City of Hartford City, 112 N.E.2d 891 (Ind. 1953); Thompson v. Board of Education, 94 A.2d 206 (N.J. 1953); Supler v. School District of North Franklin Township, 182 A.2d 535 (Pa. 1962); Sayers v. School District No. 1, 114 N.W.2d 191 (Mich. 1962).

this action did not impose direct liability on the school district:

> . . . the fact that the insurance policy herein by its terms insured the School District as well as its employees, does not result in any waiver of its immunity. In the absence of a clear intention on the part of the Legislature to impose liability for tort, a municipality which takes our insurance under such statutory authority does not waive its immunity.[120]

It also has been held[121] that the existence of liability insurance does not make a school district liable when persons are injured in school buildings or on school premises even if the injury was due to the negligence of the district or its officers, agents, or employees.

Not all courts agree that the purchase of liability insurance has no effect on a school district's common-law immunity from tort liability. Although there is general agreement that a statute authorizing school districts to obtain liability insurance does not abrogate the immunity doctrine,[122] a number of cases have come before the courts in which injured parties have been allowed to recover damages to the limit of a school district's liability insurance coverage.[123] In a Kentucky case, for example, it was held[124] that a statute permitting school districts to purchase liability insurance against the negligence of school bus drivers did not make a district liable for torts but did permit the district to be sued and a judgment against it obtained which would establish the insurance carrier's liability. Courts in Tennessee have ruled[125] that pupils injured in the course of pupil transportation activities may recover damages up

to the limit of the district's liability insurance coverage. They reason that funds devoted to education will not be depleted if recovery to the limit of the district's insurance coverage is allowed. This reasoning also was followed in an earlier Illinois case. A child was injured on the school premises and suit was brought to recover damages, alleging that negligence was responsible for the injury. It also was alleged that the district had purchased liability insurance, and the appellant offered to accept the limit of the insurer's liability as the extent of recovery. The court held that when insurance was carried the district's immunity was waived to the extent of the insurance coverage. The court reasoned:

> The only justifiable reason for the immunity of quasi-municipal corporations from suit for tort is the sound and unobjectionable one that it is the public policy to protect public funds and public property, to prevent the diversion of tax monies, in this case school funds, to the payment of damage claims. There is no justification or reason for absolute immunity if the public funds are protected. Their protection has been the real and historical reason for the absolute immunity both elsewhere and in Illinois accorded quasi-municipal corporations, and similarly, municipal corporations in the exercise of a governmental function. Liability insurance, to the extent that it protects the public funds, removes the reason for, and thus the immunity to, suit. . . . If the public funds are protected by liability insurance, the justification and reason for the rule of immunity are removed.[126]

Some courts have said, it also should be noted, that by enacting legislation authorizing school districts to obtain insurance policies the legislature has seen fit to waive the district's immunity from tort liability to the extent of the money available from insurance coverage.[127]

11.4 WORKMEN'S COMPENSATION INSURANCE

For many years school employees had no claim to compensation for injuries sustained in the course of their employment. Public employees, including teachers, could not sue for damages when injured in line of duty, since districts could not be sued in tort unless such action was permitted by statute. With the advent of coverage by workmen's compensation laws,

[120]Rittmiller v. School District No. 84, 104 F.Supp. 187 (Minn. 1952).

[121]Hummer v. School City of Hartford City, 112 N.E.2d 891 (Ind. 1953); Thompson v. Board of Education, 94 A.2d 206 (N.J. 1953); Michael v. School District of Lancaster, 137 A.2d 456 (Pa. 1958); Kobylanski v. Chicago Board of Education, 317 N.E.2d 714 (Ill. 1974).

[122]Taylor v. Knox County Board of Education, 167 S.W.2d 700 (Ky. 1942); Hummer v. School City of Hartford City, 112 N.E.2d 891 (Ind. 1953); Maffei v. Incorporated Town of Kemmerer, 338 P.2d 808 (Wyo. 1959).

[123]General Insurance Co. v. Gilliam County High School District, 234 F.Supp. 109 (Ore. 1964); Tracy v. Davis, 123 F.Supp. 160 (Ill. 1954); Rogers v. Butler, 92 S.W.2d 414 (Tenn. 1936); Thomas v. Broadlands Community Consolidated School District, 109 N.E.2d 636 (Ill. 1952); McBride v. North Carolina State Board of Education, 125 S.E.2d 393 (N.C. 1962).

[124]Taylor v. Knox County Board of Education, 167 S.W.2d 700 (Ky. 1942).

[125]Marion County v. Cantrell, 61 S.W.2d 477 (Tenn. 1933); Rogers v. Butler, 92 S.W.2d 414 (Tenn. 1936); Taylor v. Cobble, 187 S.W.2d 648 (Tenn. 1945).

[126]Thomas v. Broadlands Community Consolidated School District, 109 N.E.2d 636 (Ill. 1952).

[127]Maffei v. Incorporated Town of Kemmerer, 338 P.2d 808 (Wyo. 1959).

employees of a school district no longer need look to the courts to recover damages for work injuries. Workmen's compensation statutes rest on the assumption that accidents are inevitable and should be regarded as a necessary cost of doing business. Thus, the cost of work accidents should be reflected in the price paid for goods and services and be borne by society.

Workmen's compensation laws negate the question of negligence by providing compensation for all workers who are injured in the course of their employment, regardless of fault. Although every state has adopted workmen's compensation laws, coverage of public employees is not compulsory in all states. The specific provisions of the various workmen's compensation laws must be ascertained from the laws of the several states, since, as Kulp has remarked, "their most striking feature is their dissimilarity."[128]

The constitutionality of laws making workmen's compensation insurance applicable to school district employees has been contested on the ground that such laws authorize the expenditure of public funds for a private purpose. Although this contention was sustained by one court,[129] the weight of authority indicates that such statutes are not unconstitutional.[130] Many of the cases dealing with this issue have cited with approval a statement by the Wisconsin Supreme Court in an early case bearing on the constitutionality of the Wisconsin workmen's compensation law:

> Again, it is said that the act compels municipalities to levy taxes for other than public purposes, since all workmen injured in the employ of the public are to be compensated, and thus taxpayers will be deprived of their property without due process of law. . . . We shall only say that the manner in which the state or the public shall treat its workmen is peculiarly a matter for the Legislature to determine. . . . We know of no reason why the public, acting by its law making power, may not provide that its employees shall have as part of their compensation certain indemnities in case of accidental injury in the public service. When a law does so provide, the raising of the funds to discharge those indemnities becomes plainly a proper public purpose.[131]

The Supreme Court of Utah has held[132] that a school board may spend funds to pay for workmen's compensation insurance for teachers when a statute authorizes it to do so, even when the law does not specifically provide for raising funds for such a purpose.

11.5 PERSONAL LIABILITY OF SCHOOL OFFICERS

Since members of boards of education seldom receive more than a modest pecuniary reward for their services, the extent of their personal liability for their actions as school board members is of vital concern. The general rule, followed by most American courts, is that school board members will not be held personally liable for a loss or injury resulting from an act which is within the scope of their authority and within their discretion.[133] If school board members were held liable for their errors in judgment, it would tend to discourage able persons from seeking the office and to interfere with the judicious exercise of the duties of the office. This is implicit in the following statement by the court in the case of *McCormick v. Burt:*

> In such cases the law seems to be well settled there can be no action maintained against school officers where they act without malice.
>
> The rule is certainly a reasonable one. A mere mistake in judgment, either as to their duties under the law or as to facts submitted to them, ought not to subject such officers to an action. They may judge wrongly, and so may a court or other tribunal, but the party complaining can have no action when such officers act in good faith and in the line of what they think is honestly their duty. Any other rule might work great hardship to honest men who, with the best of motives, have faithfully endeavored to perform the duties of these inferior offices. Although of the utmost importance to the public, no considerable emoluments are attached to these minor offices, and the duties are usually performed by persons sincerely desiring to do good for their neighbors, without

---

[128]See C. A. Kulp, *Casualty Insurance* (New York: The Ronald Press Company, 3d ed., 1956), pp. 89–92.

[129]Floyd County v. Scoggins, 139 S.E. 11 (Ga. 1927).

[130]School District No. 1 v. Industrial Commission, 185 Pac. 348 (Col. 1919); Kroncke v. Caddo Parish School Board, 183 So. 86 (La. 1938); Clauss v. Board of Education, 30 A.2d 779 (Md. 1943).

[131]Borgnis v. Falk Co., 133 N.W. 209 (Wis. 1911).

[132]Woodcock v. Board of Education, 187 Pac. 181 (Utah 1920).

[133]De Levay v. Richmond County School Board, 284 F.2d 340 (4th Cir. 1960); Consolidated School District No. 1 v. Wright, 261 Pac. 953 (Okla. 1927); Medsker v. Etchison, 199 N.E. 429 (Ind. 1936); Betts v. Jones, 166 S.E. 589 (N.C. 1932); Board of Education of Oklahoma City v. Cloudman, 92 P.2d 837 (Okla. 1939); Wood v. Farmer, 29 N.W. 440 (Iowa 1886); Roschen v. Packard, 81 Atl. 174 (Md. 1911); Kenmare School District No. 28 v. Cole. 161 N.W. 542 (N.D. 1917); Stewart v. Southard, 17 Ohio 402 (1848); Lemon v. Girardot, 65 P.2d 1427 (Col. 1936); Board of Education of Mountain Lakes v. Maas, 152 A.2d 394 (N.J. 1959); Smith v. Hefner, 68 S.E.2d 783 (N.C. 1952).

any expectation of personal gains, and it would be a very harsh rule that would subject such officers to an action for damages for every mistake they may make in the honest and faithful discharge of their official duties as they understand them.[134]

There are, however, situations where school board members are not immune from liability. In the recent case of *Wood v. Strickland*, the United States Supreme Court limited the immunity of school officials in civil rights cases where an infringement of constitutional rights was involved.[135] While the Court acknowledged that generally school officials are entitled to a qualified good faith immunity from liability for damages under the Civil Rights Act, it held that in the context of school discipline, a school official is not immune from liability for damages under Section 1983 of the Civil Rights Act if the official knew or reasonably should have known that the action which was taken violated the constitutional rights of the student involved, or if such action was taken with the malicious intention of causing a deprivation of constitutional rights or other injury to the student. With regard to damages, the Court stated:

A compensatory award will be appropriate only if the school board member has acted with such impermissible motivation or with such disregard of the student's clearly established constitutional rights that his action cannot reasonably be characterized as being in good faith.[136]

Likewise, protection from liability does not extend to situations in which loss or injury is sustained by another person as the result of an act by a school official which is outside the scope of official authority or beyond the powers conferred upon the official by statutes.[137] Although occasionally it has been said that school board members are immune from liability in the performance of official duties, even if they act maliciously,[138] the weight of authority is

that a school board member will be held liable for loss or injury caused by willful or wanton acts[139] or by acts tinged with malice or undertaken with corrupt motives.[140]

Questions also arise as to whether a school board member may be held liable for loss or injury sustained because of the failure to perform a duty. It has been decided[141] that a school board member may be held personally liable for failure to perform a duty which is owed to an individual who has a unique interest separate and apart from that of the general public—such as the duty of a school district treasurer to pay the salary due a teacher when payment has been duly authorized, the money has been properly appropriated, and sufficient funds are available in the district treasury. A different view prevails, however, if the duty is one which the school officer owes to the general public. It has been held[142] that a school officer is not personally liable for failure to perform a duty owed to the general public, as opposed to one owed to a specific person.

Another question which often is of concern is that of the personal liability of individual school board members for acts of the board as a corporate body. It has been held[143] consistently that the individual members of a board of education are not personally liable for injury or damage sustained as a result of the board's negligence in performing its duties or as a result of the board's failure to perform a duty.

Statutory provisions relative to the personal liability of members of boards of education are controlling. A school board member may be made liable by statute for actions which result in injury or damage to others, or for injury or damage sustained by others as a result of the member's failure to act.[144]

---

[134]McCormick v. Burt, 95 Ill. 263 (1880).

[135]Wood v. Strickland, 421 U.S. 997, 95 S.Ct. 992, 44 L.Ed.2d 664 (Ark. 1975); *see also* Thonen v. Jenkins, 517 F.2d 3 (4th Cir. 1975).

[136]*Ibid.*

[137]Burroughs v. Mortenson, 143 N.E. 457 (Ill. 1924); Fulk v. School District No. 8 of Lancaster County, 53 N.W.2d 56 (Neb. 1952); Parish Board of School Directors v. Alexander, 51 So. 906 (La. 1910); Sweeney v. Young, 131 Atl. 1955 (N.H. 1925); Elder v. Anderson, 205 Cal.App.2d 326 (1962).

[138]Lipman v. Brisbane Elementary School District, 359 P.2d 465 (Cal. 1961); Van Buskirk v. Bleiler, 368 N.Y.S.2d 88 (1974).

[139]Fertich v. Michener, 14 N.E. 68 (Ind. 1887); Board of Education of Oklahoma City v. Cloudman, 92 P.2d 837 (Okla. 1939); Gorski v. School District of Borough of Dickson City, 113 A.2d 334 (Pa. 1955); Campbell v. Jones, 264 S.W.2d 425 (Tex. 1954).

[140]Medsker v. Etchison, 199 N.E. 429 (Ind. 1936); Betts v. Jones, 166 S.E. 589 (N.C. 1932); Roschen v. Packard, 81 Atl. 174 (Md. 1911); Spruill v. Davenport, 100 S.E. 527 (N.C. 1919); Stewart v. Southard, 17 Ohio 402 (1848).

[141]Edson v. Hayden, 18 Wis. 657 (1864).

[142]Robbins v. Scarborough, 181 Ill.App. 58 (1913).

[143]Herman v. Board of Education, 137 N.E.24 (N.Y. 1922); Dawson v. Tulare Union High School District, 276 Pac. 424 (Cal. 1929); Reese v. Isola State Bank, 105 So. 636 (Miss. 1925); Perkins v. Trask, 23 P.2d 982 (Mont. 1933); Gilbert v. Harlan County Board of Education, 309 S.W.2d 771 (Ky. 1958).

[144]Medsker v. Etchison, 199 N.E. 429 (Ind. 1936); Gilbert v. Harlan County Board of Education, 309 S.W.2d 771 (Ky. 1958).

11.5a Ministerial duties

It is important to distinguish between discretionary duties and ministerial duties when considering the personal liability of school board members. The distinction has been drawn judicially as follows:

Discretion in the manner of the performance of an act arises when the act may be performed in one of two or more ways, either of which would be lawful, and where it is left to the will or judgment of the performer to determine in which way it shall be performed. But when a positive duty is enjoined, and there is but one way in which it can be performed lawfully, then there is no discretion.[145]

Although school officers are not held personally liable for injury or loss resulting from their performance of discretionary duties if they act without malicious intent, a different situation obtains when ministerial duties are involved. The general rule is that a school officer will be held personally liable for injury or loss suffered by other persons as a result of the improper performance of ministerial duties or the failure to perform such duties.[146] As stated by one court, "it is well settled that when the law casts any duty upon a person which he refuses or fails to perform, he is answerable in damages to those whom his refusal or failure injures."[147]

In an Indiana case individual school board members were held personally liable for injuries sustained by spectators at a field day when temporary stands collapsed. The court distinguished between the liability of the individual board members for discretionary acts and their liability for ministerial acts:

. . . we hold that . . . members of the school board, in determining that there should be field day exercises in connection with their school were acting within their jurisdiction, and that such act, together with their action in determining the manner in which such exercises should be conducted, was discretionary, and that for injuries resulting therefrom they were not liable; but that the duties performed in making preparation for such field day exercises and the general management thereof were ministerial acts, for the negligent performance of which, if so performed, whether performed by themselves,

by their agent, or by an independent contractor, they were liable for damages for injuries suffered by reason thereof.[148]

When a ministerial duty is imposed on the board of education as a corporate body, rather than upon the individual members of the board, the courts disagree as to whether the individual board members are to be held personally liable for the board's failure properly to perform the duty. In a number of jurisdictions the individual board members have been held personally liable in such cases.[149] For example, individual board members were held[150] personally liable for damages sustained by a third party in a school bus accident where the board of education had failed to procure school bus insurance as required by statute. The court ruled that the statute imposed a ministerial duty on the board of education, thus permitting them no discretion in the matter. The weight of authority, however, supports the view that school board members will not be held individually liable for their failure to perform properly a ministerial duty where that duty has been imposed upon the board as a corporate body.[151] Courts holding this view reason that, where the statutes impose a duty upon a corporate body, the corporation, not its individual members, should be held responsible for improper performance of that duty. Their reasoning is exemplified by the court's statement in *Basset v. Fish:*

. . . it is not seen how a member of a corporate body, upon which body a duty rests, can be held individually liable for the neglect of its duty by that body. There is no duty upon him to act individually. His duty is as a corporator, and it is to act in the corporation in the way prescribed for its action, and by the use of its powers and meanings. And if there is neglect to exert its powers or all its means, it is the neglect of the body and not the individuals composing it.[152]

---

[148] Adams v. Schneider, 124 N.E. 718 (Ind. 1919).

[149] Owen v. Hill, 34 N.W. 649 (Mich. 1887); Bronaugh v. Murray, 172 S.W.2d 591 (Ky. 1943); Boyce v. San Diego High School District, 10 P.2d 62 (Cal. 1932); Commonwealth v. Fahey, 40 A.2d 167 (Pa. 1944); Gilbert v. Harlan County Board of Education, 309 S.W.2d 771 (Ky. 1958).

[150] Bronaugh v. Murray, 172 S.W.2d 591 (Ky. 1943).

[151] Bassett v. Fish, 75 N.Y. 303 (1878); Consolidated School District No. 1 v. Wright, 261 Pac. 953 (Okla. 1927); Herman v. Board of Education, 137 N.E. 24 (N.Y. 1922); Reese v. Isola State Bank, 105 So. 636 (Miss. 1925); Blanchard v. Burns, 162 S.W. 63 (Ark. 1913); Daniels v. Board of Education of City of Grand Rapids, 158 N.W. 23 (Mich. 1916); Lemon v. Girardot, 65 P.2d 1427 (Col. 1936); Medsker v. Etchison, 199 N.E. 429 (Ind. 1936); Perkins v. Trask, 23 P.2d 982 (Mont. 1933); Noland Co. Inc. v. Board of Trustees of Southern Pines School, 129 S.E. 577 (N.C. 1925).

[152] Bassett v. Fish, 75 N.Y. 303 (1878).

---

[145] Blalock v. Johnston, 185 S.E. 51 (S.C. 1936).

[146] First National Bank of Key West v. Filer, 145 So. 204 (Fla. 1933); Commonwealth v. Zang, 16 A.2d 741 (Pa. 1940); Bronaugh v. Murphy, 172 S.W.2d 591 (Ky. 1943); Burton Machinery Company v. Ruth, 186 S.W. 737 (Mo. 1916); Adams v. Schneider, 124 N.E. 718 (Ind. 1919).

[147] Owen v. Hill, 34 N.W. 649 (Mich. 1887).

11.5b Torts

Pupils, teachers, or members of the general public occasionally sustain injury or loss as a result of school activities. In seeking compensation they frequently bring suit against members of the board of education, as well as all those in any way connected with the administration of the school system. Whether they are personally liable for the torts of officers, agents, or employees of the district can be a question of great concern to school board members.

School board members enjoy broad immunity from personal liability for torts committed by the board of education and by its officers, agents, and employees. In general, it may be said that school board members, acting within the scope of their authority in the performance of powers and duties involving the exercise of judgment and discretion, will not be held personally liable for the negligent acts of employees of the district.[153] A distinction is drawn between employees of the district, who are personally liable for their own torts, and school board members, who, as public officers, are not liable for the negligent acts of their employees. In a number of cases persons injured through the negligence of an employee of a school district have sought to invoke the doctrine of *respondeat superior,* i.e., the masters are responsible for the acts of their servants. It has been held[154] that no master-servant relationship exists between the individual members of a board of education and the employees of the district. An Oregon case is illustrative. The plaintiff, who suffered from paralysis after sustaining a broken neck while playing in a high school football game, sought to recover damages from the members of the board of education (among others). In holding that the members of the board of education were not individually liable, the court said:

> ... the individual members of the district school board, the district superintendent, and the district principal do not stand in the relation of master and servant with persons subordinate to themselves; consequently the doctrine of respondeat superior *cannot operate to impose vicarious liability upon these persons for the negligence of their subordinates.*[155]

It should be noted that in the same case a master-servant relationship was indicated to exist between a school *district* and its employees.

Personal Negligence

In some cases school board members may be held personally liable for loss or damage which results from their own negligent acts, as well as for the negligent acts of agents or employees who are acting under their direct supervision.[156] The liability in such cases results not from the fact that the individual is a school board member but from the fact that that individual did the negligent act or was directly responsible for its doing.[157] In at least one case, however, the individual members of a board of education were held[158] not personally liable for injuries to a third party resulting from the collapse of a pile of concrete blocks which had been stacked by employees under the immediate direction of members of the board of education. The court reasoned that the members of the board were engaged in official acts involving the exercise of discretion and thus could not be held personally liable for negligence involved in such acts.

Willful Acts

A further restriction on the freedom from personal liability for torts which is enjoyed by school board members is found in the familiar rule that school board members will be held liable for their willful, wanton, or malicious acts. For example, members of a school board were not immune from personal liability in a case[159] in which a pupil was killed in a school bus accident; the driver, who was the son of one member of the board, was known to be a reckless and incompetent driver, and his hiring had been protested by patrons of the district.

[153]Medsker v. Etchison, 199 N.E. 429 (Ind. 1936); Perkins v. Trask, 23 P.2d 982 (Mont. 1933); Donovan v. McAlpin, 85 N.Y. 185 (1881); Daniels v. Board of Education of City of Grand Rapids, 158 N.W. 23 (Mich. 1916); Consolidated School District No. 1 v. Wright, 261 Pac. 953 (Okla. 1927); Antin v. Union High School District No. 2 of Clatsop County, 280 Pac. 664 (Ore. 1929); Herman v. Board of Education, 137 N.E. 24 (N.Y. 1922); Smith v. Hefner, 68 S.E.2d 783 (N.C. 1952); Lipman v. Brisbane Elementary School District, 359 P.2d 465 (Cal. 1961); Hall v. Columbus Board of Education, 290 N.E.2d 580 (Ohio 1972).

[154]Antin v. Union High School District No. 2 of Clatsop County, 280 Pac. 664 (Ore. 1929); Donovan v. McAlpin, 85 N.Y. 185 (1881); Vendrell v. School District No. 26C, 360 P.2d 282 (Ore. 1961).

[155]Vendrell v. School District No. 26C, 360 P.2d 282 (Ore. 1961).

[156]School District No. 11 v. Williams, 38 Ark. 454 (1882); Luce v. Board of Education, 157 N.Y.S.2d 123 (1956); Betts v. Jones, 181 S.E. 334 (N.C. 1935); Whitt v. Reed, 239 S.W.2d 489 (Ky. 1951); Stokes v. Newell, 165 So. 542 (Miss. 1936).

[157]Bassett v. Fish, 75 N.Y. 303 (1878).

[158]Smith v. Hefner, 68 S.E.2d 783 (N.C. 1952).

[159]Betts v. Jones, 181 S.E. 334 (N.C. 1935); See also Hall v. Columbus Board of Education, 290 N.E.2d 580 (Ohio 1972).

Defamation of Character

Defamation of character involves statements to third parties which have a tendency to reduce the esteem, respect, confidence, or good will in which a person is held. Defamatory statements tend to injure a person's reputation or good name and involve an element of personal disgrace. Defamation in written or printed form is libel; in spoken form it is slander.

The law encourages freedom of discussion by public officials where such freedom is necessary to the conduct of public business. One such situation is at official meetings of school board members. As long as all remarks relate to legitimate business of the board and are not maliciously made, a school board member is immune from liability for statements made at a board meeting, even though they may be shown to be untrue and damaging to the character or reputation of the complainant. This doctrine of law is known as "qualified privilege." The doctrine of qualified privilege is applicable when it is reasonably necessary that certain information be communicated for the protection of one's own interests, the interests of third parties, or the interests of the public. For example, the doctrine of qualified privilege has been found[160] to extend to a communication to the school board by a school principal that rumors concerning a pupil were being circulated among students and teachers. To insure that they enjoy the protection of qualified privilege, school board members should confine any remarks of a delicate or derogatory nature about a teacher, a pupil, or anyone else connected with the school system to a legally called meeting of the school board and then should relate the matter only if it is relevant to what is under discussion or if it is so important that they have a duty to introduce the subject as new matter.

The question of whether school board members themselves may be held personally liable for defamation of character has been before the courts in several recent cases.[161] There is general agreement that school board members are not personally liable for defamation of character which occurs in the course of discretionary acts

within the scope of their authority.[162] No immunity exists, however, if the defamatory acts complained of are beyond the scope of their authority.[163] Since boards of education frequently must deal with potentially defamatory information concerning teachers, administrators, and pupils, it is important to determine the point at which they exceed their authority or discretion.

In a California case, for example, a school superintendent sought damages from three school trustees, among others, claiming that they had maliciously engaged in conduct designed to discredit her reputation and force her from her position. It was held[164] that the trustees were within the scope of their authority when asking questions about the superintendent's fitness for her position in order to determine whether a cause for dismissal existed. However, the trustees went beyond the scope of their authority when they made allegations about the superintendent's competence to other persons, including newspaper reporters. In making such allegations, they forfeited their immunity from liability because they did not enjoy the protection of qualified privilege, and if the allegations were false, the trustees could be held liable for defamation of character. In another California case it was decided[165] that members of a board of education would not be immune from liability if statements about two pupils contained in an announcement of a meeting to discuss "the serious violation of manners, morals and discipline" by the two pupils, and mailed to many members of the general public, were false and defamatory.

In a New York case a board of education adopted a resolution placing the district's superintendent on permanent leave of absence for the best interests of the educational program. The resolution was published in the official minutes of the board meeting. The superintendent brought suit against the members of the board, claiming that publication of the resolution constituted defamation of character. In holding that the members of the board were not personally liable the Court said:

[160]Forsythe v. Durham, 200 N.E. 674 (N.Y. 1936).

[161]De Levay v. Richmond County School Board, 284 F.2d 340 (4th Cir. 1960); Elder v. Anderson, 205 Cal.App.2d 326 (1962); Lipman v. Brisbane Elementary School District, 359 P.2d 465 (Cal. 1961); Smith v. Helbraun, 251 N.Y.S.2d 533 (1964); Ranous v. Hughes, 141 N.W.2d 251 (Wis. 1966).

[162]De Levay v. Richmond County School Board, 284 F.2d 340 (4th Cir. 1960); Lipman v. Brisbane Elementary School District, 359 P.2d 465 (Cal. 1961); Elder v. Anderson, 205 Cal.App.2d 326 (1962); Smith v. Helbraun, 251 N.Y.S.2d 533 (1964).

[163]Lipman v. Brisbane Elementary School District, 359 P.2d 465 (Cal. 1961); Elder v. Anderson, 205 Cal.App.2d 326 (1962); Ranous v. Hughes, 141 N.W.2d 251 (Wis. 1966).

[164]Lipman v. Brisbane Elementary School District, 359 P.2d 465 (Cal. 1961).

[165]Elder v. Anderson, 205 Cal.App.2d 326 (1962).

In executing their duties, the members [of the board of education] perform a state function of high importance to the people at large and within the city. Hence, the defendants are clothed with an absolute privilege for what is said or written by them in discharging their responsibilities.[166]

In a Wisconsin case, however, the court stated[167] that school board members enjoyed only a qualified privilege, not an absolute privilege. It further said that the defense of qualified privilege would be lost if a school board member did not believe, or had no reasonable grounds to believe, that the defamatory material was true; if the defamatory material was published by a school board member for purposes other than those for which the qualified privilege was given; if publication of the defamatory material was made to some person not reasonably necessary to accomplish the purpose of the qualified privilege; or if the publication of information included defamatory material not reasonably necessary to accomplish the purposes of the qualified privilege.

11.5c Acts other than torts

In addition to possibly becoming personally liable as a result of torts, school officers may become liable because of their improper acts, or their failure to act, in other areas of school operation. In the interest of providing a complete discussion of the personal liability of school officers, liability arising from acts other than torts will be considered briefly in the following sections.

Loss of School Funds

Boards of education are responsible for authorizing the expenditure of vast sums of money. Furthermore, the district treasurer and other district officers are responsible for safeguarding and properly disbursing school funds. Since the opportunities for irregular or illegal expenditure of school funds are many, the personal liability of school board members when school funds are lost or expended irregularly is of real concern.

Considering first those school officers responsible for the handling and safeguarding of school funds, the general rule is that a school officer is absolutely liable for all school funds which come into that officer's custody.[168] Thus a school board treasurer, and any other school board member who has custody of school funds, is personally liable for funds which either are disbursed without authorization or are misappropriated.[169] A school officer is not liable, however, if school funds are misapplied or misappropriated by a co-officer, providing that officer takes no part in the transaction.[170]

State statutes may permit or require that school funds be deposited in a bank or in a designated public depository. When the statutes require them to be deposited in a bank, a school officer is relieved of liability for their loss through failure or insolvency of the bank so long as prudence and good faith were exercised in selecting it.[171] However, if the school officer knows, or has reason to believe, that the bank selected as the depository for school funds is failing or in danger of failing, depositing school funds in such a bank will not relieve the officer of personal liability for their loss.[172] Where statutes do not require that school funds be deposited in a bank, a school officer cannot escape liability for the loss of such funds by depositing them in a bank, even if directed to do so by the board of education.[173] The school officer remains the insurer of such funds and is liable for their loss. Thus it has been said that "a public officer is an insurer of public funds lawfully in his possession, and therefore liable for losses which occur without his fault. . . . The liability is absolute, admitting of no excuse, except perhaps the act of God or the public enemy."[174]

In determining the personal liability of

[166]Smith v. Helbraun, 251 N.Y.S.2d 533 (1964).
[167]Ranous v. Hughes, 141 N.W.2d 251 (Wis. 1966).

[168]Thurston County v. Chmelka, 294 N.W. 857 (Neb. 1940); Thunder Hawk School District No. 8 v. Western Surety Co., 235 N.W. 921 (S.D. 1931).
[169]Fulk v. School District No. 8 of Lancaster County, 53 N.W.2d 56 (Neb. 1952); Superior Grade School District No. 110 v. Rhodes, 75 P.2d 251 (Kan. 1938); Board of Trustees v. Indemnity Insurance Company of North America, 280 Ill. App. 86 (1935); Borger Independent School District v. Dickson, 52 S.W.2d 505 (Tex. 1932); Board of Education of Town of Ellington v. Town of Ellington, 193 A.2d 466 (Conn. 1963).
[170]State v. Julian, 93 Ind. 292 (1883).
[171]American Surety Company of New York v. Independent School District No. 18, 53 F.2d 178 (8th Cir. 1931); Thunder Hawk School District No. 8 v. Western Surety Co., 235 N.W. 921 (S.D. 1931).
[172]Benton School District No. 26 v. Woodard, 231 N.W. 288 (S.D. 1930); Edgemont Independent School District v. Wickstrom, 223 N.W. 948 (S.C. 1929).
[173]Thurston County v. Chmelka, 294 N.W. 857 (Neb. 1940); School District No. 64 v. Hand, 257 Pac. 931 (Kan. 1927); Rushing v. Alabama National Bank, 148 So. 306 (Ala. 1933).
[174]American Surety Company of New York v. Ne Smith, 174 S.E. 262 (Ga. 1934).

school board members for money illegally or irregularly expended, a distinction is drawn between those expenditures which are expressly forbidden by statutory or constitutional provisions and those which are within the power of the board but which have not been made in accordance with statutory requirements. The weight of authority clearly indicates that school board members will be held personally liable for expenditures which are expressly forbidden or which are completely beyond the power of the board, i.e., *ultra vires*.[175] It should be noted, however, that two members of a board of education who voted against an expenditure later held to be *ultra vires* were excluded from personal liability for the funds which had been expended illegally; only those board members who voted in favor of the expenditure were held personally liable.[176] It has been held[177] in several cases that school officers who vote for or permit the misapplication of school funds are personally liable for the amount of money which has been misused.

When an expenditure is within the authority of the board of education but is illegal because of the board's failure to follow the proper mode or procedure, board members will not be held personally liable for the expenditure if they have acted in good faith, especially if the district retains the benefits of the expenditure.[178] The reasoning of the courts in regard to such expenditures was succinctly expressed in a Kentucky case:

... *where the thing is authorized to be done, and is done by the party charged with doing it, but done in a manner contrary to that directed by the statute, the court will not compel the official to pay back the money and let the public continue to enjoy the benefits of its expenditure. If it is made to appear that the expenditure was in good faith, and the public has got that which it was entitled to, good*

conscience forbids the recovery. The law therefore denies it.[179]

Similar reasoning was followed in a case in which it was held[180] that school board members were not personally liable for expenditures for the construction of a schoolhouse which exceeded the district's legal limit of indebtedness.

Although the general principles concerning the personal liability of school board members for irregular or illegal expenditures are quite clear, it should be noted that the courts are not in complete agreement when applying these principles in similar cases. Thus, where school board members have let contracts without advertising for bids as required by statute, they have been held personally liable in some jurisdictions[181] but not in others.[182] Similarly, school board members in some jurisdictions have been held personally liable for expenditures which were beyond the board's authority but not expressly prohibited,[183] while in other jurisdictions they have not been held personally liable for such expenditures.[184]

A final question to be considered is whether a school officer who is liable for the loss or misapplication of school funds may be "excused" by the board of education or the electorate of the district. Unless the power to grant such relief is conferred by statute, it does not exist. Without statutory authority, neither the school board nor the electorate can relieve a school officer from liability for the loss of school funds.[185] Full restitution must be made.

Contracts

In order to maintain and operate the schools of a district, a board of education frequently must enter into contracts on the assumption that it has implied authority to do so. When they misjudge or go beyond their authority, are board members personally liable for payment due under the contract? The general rule is that the individual

[175]Fulk v. School District No. 8 of Lancaster County, 53 N.W.2d 56 (Neb. 1952); Flowers v. Logan County, 127 S.W. 512 (Ky. 1910).

[176]Fulk v. School District No. 8 of Lancaster County, 53 N.W.2d 56 (Neb. 1952).

[177]Quattlebaum v. Busbea, 162 S.W.2d 44 (Ark. 1942); Johnson v. Independent School District of Virginia, 249 N.W. 177 (Minn. 1933); Borger Independent School District v. Dickson, 52 S.W.2d 505 (Tex. 1932).

[178]Board of Education of Oklahoma City v. Cloudman, 92 P.2d 837 (Okla. 1939); Kenmare School District No. 28 v. Cole, 161 N.W. 542 (N.D. 1917); State v. Farris, 150 N.E. 18 (Ind. 1925); People v. Rea, 57 N.E. 778 (Ill. 1900); Ryszka v. Board of Education, 214 N.Y.S. 264 (1926); Miller v. Tucker, 105 So. 774 (Miss. 1925).

[179]Flowers v. Logan County, 127 S.W. 512 (Ky. 1910).

[180]Kenmare School District No. 28 v. Cole, 161 N.W. 542 (N.D. 1917).

[181]Commonwealth v. Zang, 16 A.2d 741 (Pa. 1940); Appeal from Auditor's Report, 19 Cambria 83 (Pa. 1957).

[182]State v. Farris, 150 N.E. 18 (Ind. 1925).

[183]Fulk v. School District No. 8 of Lancaster County, 53 N.W.2d 56 (Neb. 1952).

[184]Board of Education of Oklahoma City v. Cloudman, 92 P.2d 837 (Okla. 1939).

[185]Taylor District Township v. Morton, 37 Iowa 550 (1873); Board of Education of the City of Pine Island v. Jewell, 46 N.W. 914 (Minn. 1890).

members of a board of education are not personally liable on contracts made in behalf of the district.[186] The familiar requirement that the members act in good faith and without fraudulent intent must, of course, be met.

There is a fundamental difference between the school board member who acts as an agent of the district and the individual who acts as the agent of a private party. Agents of private parties derive all of their authority from the principal and are bound to know the limits of their authority. School officers, on the other hand, derive all of their authority from the statutes. The statutes are public documents which are open to everyone, and all are presumed to know the law. Consequently, those who contract with a board of education are presumed to know the limits of its authority. If they misjudge the extent of the board's power, they must bear the consequences of their error.[187] From this reasoning it follows that school board members who have acted in good faith and without fraudulent intent will not be held personally liable for damages sustained by those who contract with the board.

The rule is well established that school board members cannot claim immunity from personal liability on contracts if they have expressly agreed to assume personal liability.[188] The issue which arises most frequently in this regard is whether school officers act to bind themselves or the district in a contract. The presumption is always that school officers intended to bind the district, not themselves, when entering into contracts in their official capacity, and parol evidence may be admitted to clarify the intent of the parties where their intent is not clear from the contract itself.[189] A written contract constitutes prima facie evidence of the intent of the parties. Thus, if a contract

shows on its face that a school officer is acting in an official capacity, that officer is not bound personally.[190] However, a designation of the official position following a school official's signature on a contract does not, in itself, constitute sufficient evidence of a clear intent to bind the district.[191] A clear intent to bind the district must be expressed in the contract. By the same token, where a contract plainly shows on its face the intent of school officers to be bound personally, they will be held personally liable.[192] Furthermore, they will not be permitted to introduce parol evidence which contradicts the terms of a clear and unambiguous contract. The importance of the form of a contract should be apparent from the foregoing discussion. School board members who sign a contract on behalf of the district should exercise great care to insure that the contract clearly shows they are acting in their official capacity with the intention of binding the district.

Under certain circumstances school board members may be held personally liable for the salary due a teacher under a contract. For example, it has been held[193] that where a board of education reemployed a teacher, but refused her permission to teach, the board members were personally liable for her salary. In discussing the personal liability of school board members in a case involving the attempted abrogation of a teacher's contract by a board of education, the Mississippi Supreme Court noted:

It is true that officers are not liable for the honest exercise of discretionary powers confided to them, but when they go outside their powers and commit wrongs under the color of office, there is liability. They are not given immunity from willful wrongs or malicious acts.[194]

It has been noted previously that school board members may be held personally liable for expenditures expressly forbidden by statute or *ultra vires*. Consequently, board members may incur personal liability for school funds paid out on an *ultra vires*

[186]Sanborn v. Neal, 4 Minn. 83 (1860); Gherardi v. Board of Education of City of Trenton, 147 A.2d 535 (N.J. 1958); Campbell v. Jones, 264 S.W.2d 425 (Tex. 1954); Oppenheimer v. Greencastle School Township, 72 N.E. 1100 (Ind. 1905); Robinson v. Howard, 84 N.C. 151 (1881); Reid v. McKinney Independent School District, 322 S.W.2d 647 (Tex. 1959).

[187]Jennes v. School District No. 31, 12 Minn. 337 (1867); First National Bank v. Adams School Township, 46 N.E. 832 (Ind. 1897); Floyd County Board of Education v. Slone, 307 S.W.2d 912 (Ky. 1957); School District of Philadelphia v. Framlaw Corp., 328 A.2d 866 (Pa. 1974).

[188]Sanborn v. Neal, 4 Minn. 83 (1860); Wing v. Glick, 9 N.W. 384 (Iowa 1881); State Bank of Reeseville v. Kienberger, 122 N.W. 1132 (Wis. 1909).

[189]Sanborn v. Neal, 4 Minn. 83 (1860); Wabash Railroad Co. v. People, 66 N.E. 824 (Ill. 1903).

[190]Coberly v. Gainer, 72 S.E. 790 (W.Va. 1911); MacKenzie v. Board of School Trustees of Edinburg, 72 Ind. 189 (1880); Grady v. Pruit, 63 S.W. 283 (Ky. 1901).

[191]Wing v. Glick, 9 N.W. 384 (Iowa 1881); Sharp v. Smith, 32 Ill.App. 336 (1889).

[192]State Bank of Reeseville v. Kienberger, 122 N.W. 1132 (Wis. 1909); Western Publishing House v. Murdick, 56 N.W. 120 (S.D. 1893); Wing v. Glick, 9 N.W. 384 (Iowa 1881).

[193]Cooksey v. Board of Education of Fairview Independent School District, 316 S.W.2d 70 (Ky, 1957).

[194]Stokes v. Newell, 165 So. 542 (Miss. 1936).

contract, e.g., a contract with a person who does not possess a teacher's certificate where the statutes require such a certificate as a prerequisite for employment as a teacher.

11.6 TORT LIABILITY OF TEACHERS AND OTHER PROFESSIONAL EMPLOYEES

Teachers and other school employees, unlike the district which employs them, do not enjoy immunity from tort liability. A teacher, principal, superintendent, or any other school employee is liable for his or her own negligence.[195] Teachers stand *in loco parentis*, i.e., in the place of the parent, to pupils who are in their care and will be held liable for any injuries which pupils sustain as a result of their negligence. Teachers, and any other school district employees, are required to exercise the same degree of care for the pupils in their charge that a reasonable and prudent person would have exercised in similar circumstances.[196] It also has been said[197] that the standard of care owed to pupils by a teacher is that standard of care which a parent of ordinary prudence would observe in comparable circumstances.

The fact that a pupil sustains an injury in a school-related activity does not, in itself, mean that the teacher in charge of the activity will be held liable for the injury. Injuries to pupils may result from pure accidents, i.e., accidents which occur without negligence.[198] A pure accident is one which a reasonably prudent person could not have foreseen and avoided by the exercise of reasonable precautions. Thus, the question of whether the possibility of an accident should have been foreseen by the teacher in connection with a given activity is an important one. It should be emphasized that the law requires only that a teacher act in the same manner as a reasonable person of ordinary intelligence and foresight would have acted under the same circumstances.

Application of the rule that a teacher is expected to exercise reasonable foresight is illustrated by a case in which a pupil was

crushed by a log at a beach while on a school outing. The teacher in charge of the outing was assisted by several other adults, including the mother of the injured child. Several children climbed upon a large log lying on the beach some distance from the water's edge. While the teacher was taking a picture of the children on the log, a large wave suddenly surged up the beach causing the log to roll over. The injured child fell to the seaward side of the log, and when the wave receded it drew the log over the child. The court ruled that the injury was foreseeable and that the teacher was negligent in failing to take action to avoid the injury. The court commented:

The first proposition asks this court to hold, as a matter of law, that unusual wave action on the shore of the Pacific Ocean is a hazard so unforeseeable that there is no duty to guard against it. . . . On the contrary, we agree with the trial judge, who observed that it is common knowledge that accidents substantially like the one that occurred in this case have occurred at beaches along the Oregon coast. Foreseeability of such harm is not so remote as to be ruled out as a matter of law. . . .

Foreseeability of harm gives rise to a duty to take reasonable care to avoid the harm.[199]

In other cases involving the question of foreseeability it has been held that a teacher was negligent in permitting a boy to weld an automobile gasoline tank, which exploded, killing one pupil and seriously injuring another,[200] and that a teacher was negligent in failing to take proper precautions in demonstrating the production of explosive gas to a chemistry class, where a pupil was injured when an explosion occurred.[201]

In other cases, however, it has been ruled that an accident which resulted in injury to a pupil could not reasonably have been foreseen by the teacher. In a Michigan case, for example, a pupil was injured while watering plants used in a nature study class. The pupil, with the teacher's knowledge, stood on a chair to water some plants and was severely cut when she fell from the chair and landed on a broken bottle in which she had been carrying water. In ruling that the teacher had not been negligent, the Supreme Court of Michigan said:

[195]Esposito v. Emergy, 249 F.Supp. 308 (Pa. 1965); Kersey v. Harbin, 351 S.W.2d 76 (Mo. 1975); but see Weinstein v. Evanston Tp. Community Consolidated School District, 351 N.E.2d 236 (Ill. 1976).

[196]Brooks v. Jacobs, 31 A.2d 414 (Me. 1943); Luna v. Needles Elementary School District, 316 P.2d 773 (Cal. 1957); Eastman v. Williams, 207 A.2d 146 (Vt. 1965); County School Board of Orange County v. Thomas, 112 S.E.2d 877 (Va. 1960); DeGooyer v. Harkness, 13 N.W.2d 815 (S.D. 1944); Guerrieri v. Tyson, 24 A.2d 468 (Pa. 1942).

[197]Lawes v. Board of Education of City of New York, 213 N.E.2d 667 (N.Y. 1965).

[198]Wire v. Williams, 133 N.W.2d 840 (Minn. 1965).

[199]Morris v. Douglas County School District No. 9, 403 P.2d 775 (Ore. 1965).

[200]Dutcher v. Santa Rosa High School District, 290 P.2d 316 (Cal. 1955).

[201]Damgaard v. Oakland High School District, 298 Pac. 983 (Cal. 1931).

There was nothing in the nature of the act itself or the instrumentalities with which plaintiff was permitted to perform the act which would lead a reasonably careful and prudent person to anticipate that the child's safety or welfare was endangered in the performance of the act. The mere fact that an accident happened, and one that was unfortunate, does not render defendant liable. [202]

It also has been ruled that a teacher could not be expected to anticipate that a paper bag which she asked a pupil to pick up would contain a broken soda bottle upon which the pupil would cut herself,[203] and that a teacher could not be expected to anticipate that a pupil would be injured by a pencil thrown by a classmate while the teacher was temporarily absent from the classroom performing her usual duties.[204]

11.6a Inadequate supervision

Both teachers and administrators may become liable for injuries sustained by pupils as a result of improper or inadequate supervision of school-related activities. When it is alleged that a pupil was injured because of inadequate supervision, it is necessary to determine whether the supervision provided was inadequate and, if so, whether negligence in supervision was the proximate cause of the pupil's injury. Where such negligence is the proximate cause of the injury, the teacher or administrator responsible will be held liable because, as one jurist has stated, "Parents do not send their children to school to be returned to them maimed because of the absence of proper supervision or the abandonment of supervision."[205]

A number of cases[206] have arisen in which teachers have been held liable for injuries sustained by pupils as a result of improper or inadequate supervision. The circumstances in one case were particularly ironic in that the instructor was giving a lecture on safety at the time the pupil was injured. The pupils were seated on the lawn in a semicircle around the teacher while he gave the lecture. One boy started flipping a homemade knife into the ground. After this had continued for about thirty minutes, the knife was deflected by a drawing board and injured the eye of another pupil so severely that the eye had to be removed. The court ruled[207] that, under the circumstances, the teacher either knew or should have known that the knife-flipping activity was going on and that proper supervision by the teacher could have prevented the accident. In another case a teacher was found[208] to be negligent, and therefore liable, when a boy was accidentally electrocuted in an initiation ceremony being supervised by the teacher.

The question of whether a teacher's absence from the classroom constitutes negligence in supervision has been before the courts several times. In a New York case a teacher was temporarily absent from her classroom while storing instructional supplies in an adjacent closet. During her absence a pupil was struck in the eye by a pencil thrown by a classmate. The court ruled[209] that the teacher's absence was not the proximate cause of the injury and that a reasonable person could not have foreseen that the pencil-throwing episode would occur during the teacher's absence. In a later New York case, however, it was ruled that a teacher's absence from the classroom was the proximate cause of a pupil's injury and that the school was liable for damages. In this case the teacher was absent when the pupils reported to their classroom at 8:30 A.M. and still had not appeared when the bell rang signaling the start of class at 8:45 A.M. Shortly thereafter, one of the pupils pulled out a knife and after several minutes suddenly stabbed another boy in the hand. In ruling that the teacher's absence was the proximate cause of the injury, the court said:

There was legal causation between the failure to provide supervision and the injury to the plaintiff. It is true that the efficient cause of the plaintiff's injury was the wrongful act of an intervening third party, a mischievous boy. However, under all the circumstances here—the dangerous instrumentality, the warning period of five to ten minutes—the stabbing of the plaintiff was an act which could have been reasonably foreseen by a teacher if he were present in the classroom. It was an act which could easily have been

---

[202]Gaincott v. Davis, 275 N.W. 229 (Mich. 1937).

[203]West v. Board of Education of City of New York, 187 N.Y.S.2d 88 (1959).

[204]Ohman v. Board of Eduation, 90 N.E.2d 474 (N.Y. 1949).

[205]Feuerstein v. Board of Education of City of New York, 202 N.Y.S.2d 524 (1960); see also Castro v. Los Angeles Board of Education, 126 Cal. Rptr. 537 (1976).

[206]Bruenn v. North Yakima School District No. 7, 172 Pac. 569 (Wash. 1918); Lilienthal v. San Leandro Unified School District, 293 P.2d 889 (Cal. 1956); Feuerstein v. Board of Education of City of New York, 202 N.Y.S.2d 524 (1960); DeGooyer v. Harkness, 13 N.W.2d 815 (S.D. 1944).

[207]Lilienthal v. San Leandro Unified School District, 293 P.2d 889 (Cal. 1956).

[208]DeGooyer v. Harkness, 13 N.W.2d 815 (S.D. 1944).

[209]Ohman v. Board of Education, 90 N.E.2d 474 (N.Y. 1949).

anticipated in the reasonable exercise of the teacher's legal duty to each classmate. The third party act was not an event which could occur equally as well in the presence of the teacher as during his absence. The act producing the injury might have been prevented by the presence of a teacher. [Emphasis supplied by the court.][210]

Thus, it would appear that absence from the classroom which a teacher is responsible for supervising is inadvisable, no matter how short its duration. The reasoning in the above cases illustrates that the question of negligence hinges on whether or not the teacher could have foreseen the possibility of injury to a pupil as a result of a given activity and taken positive steps to prevent the injury.

The possibility of injury, and hence the need for adequate supervision, is greater in some school-related activities than in others. Shops, laboratories, and playgrounds are fraught with more hazards than are most other areas of the school. Thus, teachers responsible for supervision of activities in these areas need to be particularly alert. For example, in a Louisiana case a science teacher was found to be negligent in leaving eighth grade students unsupervised while they were using alcohol-burning devices. The students were unfamiliar with the device and one girl was injured when she attempted to relight a defective burner. The court observed that an extraordinary degree of care is required of those who deal in, handle, or distribute inherently dangerous objects, and that the duty is particularly heavy where children are exposed to a dangerous condition which they do not appreciate.[211] This is not to say, however, that specific supervision of each piece of equipment or each game is generally required.[212] Where the supervision of activities in such areas is adequate and reasonable, a teacher will not be held liable if injuries occur.[213] Of course, the teacher is expected to take into consideration both the age of the child and the nature of the activity when supervising playground activities.

A teacher may be negligent in permitting pupils of disparate weight and height to compete in a highly competitive game such as soccer.[214]

A teacher generally will not be held liable for injuries sustained by pupils as a result of physical assault by other pupils,[215] particularly if the teacher is unaware that a pupil has a propensity to commit physical assault on others.[216] Misbehavior of this type is likely to occur whether the teacher is present in or absent from the classroom. However, if a pupil is known to possess such tendencies, the teacher would probably be expected to exercise a greater degree of care to prevent misconduct.

School administrators, like teachers, may be held liable for injuries sustained by others as a result of their personal negligence. As a rule, school administrators will not be held liable for the negligence of teachers or other subordinates. Administrators will not be held liable for the acts of omission or commission of subordinates unless they personally participated in such acts or ordered them to be done.[217] A school administrator may be held liable for injuries resulting from the acts of an incompetent subordinate if the administrator knowingly employed such a person.[218] However, a school administrator will not be held liable for the acts of a competent teacher; an administrator's duty is to employ competent teachers, not to supervise personally their every act.[219]

In most instances the school administrator has only a general duty of supervision rather than a duty to supervise specific activities. If it is found that the administrator has a duty to supervise specific activities, however, the administrator may be held liable because of failure to supervise them adequately. Thus, it has been ruled[220] that an administrator may be liable for failure to give pupils adequate supervision or establish rules and regulations for their safety.

[210]Christofides v. Hellenic Eastern Orthodox Christian Church, 227 N.Y.S.2d 946 (1962).

[211]Station v. Travelers Insurance Co., 292 So.2d 289 (La. 1974).

[212]Miller v. Board of Education Union Free School District No. 1, 291 N.Y.S. 633 (1936); Cordaro v. Union Free School District No. 22, 220 N.Y.S.2d 656 (1962); Passafaro v. Board of Education, 353 N.Y.S.2d 178 (1974).

[213]Pirkle v. Oakdale Union Grammar School District, 253 P.2d 1 (Cal. 1953); Graff v. Board of Education of New York City, 15 N.Y.S.2d 941 (1939), *affirmed,* 27 N.E.2d 438 (N.Y. 1940).

[214]Brooks v. Board of Education of City of New York, 205 N.Y.S.2d 777 (1960).

[215]Doktor v. Greenberg, 155 A.2d 793 (N.J. 1959).

[216]Ferraro v. Board of Education of City of New York, 212 N.Y.S.2d 615 (1961); Doktor v. Greenberg, 155 A.2d 793 (N.J. 1959); But see Korenak v. Curative Workshop Adult Rehabilitation Center, 237 N.W.2d 43 (Wis. 1976).

[217]Payne v. Bennion, 3 Cal.Rptr. 14 (1960).

[218]Whitt v. Reed, 239 S.W.2d 489 (Ky. 1951).

[219]Vendrell v. School District No. 26C, 360 P.2d 282 (Ore. 1961); Smith v. Consolidated School District No. 2, 408 S.W.2d 50 (Mo. 1966).

[220]Selleck v. Board of Education, 94 N.Y.S.2d 318 (1949); Ohman v. Board of Education, 90 N.E.2d 474 (N.Y. 1949).

11.6b Inadequate instruction

Teachers have a legal duty to provide adequate instruction to their pupils and to warn them of the dangers which are associated with a given activity. This duty is exceedingly important where pupils use inherently dangerous equipment or where the activity itself is inherently dangerous, e.g., machines found in school shops, or sports such as boxing, wrestling, football, and gymnastics. A teacher may be held personally liable for injuries sustained by a pupil as a result of inadequate instruction by the teacher. A case in which a pupil was injured in the course of a chemistry laboratory experiment affords an excellent example. The pupil was injured by an explosion when he used the wrong ingredients and failed to follow the method described in the textbook. In discussing the teacher's responsibility, the court said:

It is not unreasonable to assume that it is the duty of a teacher of chemistry, in the exercise of ordinary care, to instruct students regarding the selection, mingling, and use of ingredients with which dangerous experiments are to be accomplished, rather than to merely hand them a text-book with general instructions to follow the text. This would seem to be particularly true when young and inexperienced students are expected to select from similar containers a proper harmless substance rather than another dangerous one which is very similar in appearance. [221]

In another case a teacher directed two boys who were untrained in the skills of boxing to box three one-minute rounds. The teacher did not give the pupils any instruction in boxing prior to the bout. One of the boys sustained a cerebral hemorrhage as a result of a blow to his temple, and the teacher was held[222] guilty of negligence for allowing the pupils to engage in the activity without adequate instruction. Teachers also have been ruled guilty of failing to give adequate instruction to a pupil injured while playing line soccer[223] and a pupil injured while attempting a headstand.[224]

It should be noted, however, that where adequate instruction has been given and pupils have been warned of the dangers involved in a given activity, a teacher generally will not be held liable for injuries sustained by a pupil. In a New Jersey case, for example, a pupil suffered a broken arm in a jump over a gymnasium horse. Evidence substantiated that the teacher had instructed the pupil on the use of the horse, had demonstrated the jump, had warned the pupil of the possible dangers, and had advised the pupil not to attempt the jump if he thought that he could not perform it. The court held[225] that the teacher was not responsible for the pupil's injury.

11.6c Medical treatment of pupils

The question often arises regarding what action should be taken when a child becomes ill or is injured while at school. Obviously, if a school nurse or school physician is available, the child should be referred to such a person for care. It is important to note, however, that, while a school district may employ doctors, dentists, and nurses,[226] they generally are permitted to perform only inspectorial and diagnostic duties; they may not provide pupils with any medical treatment except that which might be required in an emergency.[227]

Unless an emergency exists, a teacher or principal should never treat a sick or injured child except to render the first aid that a reasonable and prudent person would render under similar circumstances. Only a competent person, i.e., one trained in the practice of medicine, should treat a pupil who is ill or who has sustained an injury. It has been said that in regard to the treatment of injuries the teacher or principal stands *in loco parentis* to the pupil only in an emergency, and that an emergency exists only when there is proof that the decision to secure medical aid cannot safely await the decision of the parent.[228] It was ruled[229] in a Pennsylvania case that where an emergency does not exist a teacher has no right to exercise judgment (as a parent may) in treating an injury or disease suffered by a pupil. In this case a ten-year-old boy had an infected finger, although the infection was not serious enough to prevent him from playing ball during the noon recess. Two teachers took it upon themselves to treat the infected finger. They detained the boy after school, heated a pan of water to the boiling point, and immersed the boy's hand in the water for about ten minutes. The "treatment" resulted in permanent disfigurement of the

[221]Mastrangelo v. West Side Union High School District, 42 P.2d 634 (Cal. 1935).
[222]LaValley v. Stanford, 70 N.Y.S.2d 460 (1947).
[223]Keesee v. Board of Education of City of New York, 235 N.Y.S.2d 300 (1962).
[224]Gardner v. State, 22 N.E.2d 344 (N.Y. 1939).

[225]Sayers v. Ranger, 83 A.2d 775 (N.J. 1951).
[226]Hallett v. Post Printing & Publishing Co., 192 Pac. 658 (Col. 1920); State v. Brown, 128 N.W. 294 (Minn. 1910).
[227]McGilvra v. Seattle School District No. 1, 194 Pac. 817 (Wash. 1921).
[228]Duda v. Gaines, 79 A.2d 695 (N.J. 1951).
[229]Guerrieri v. Tyson, 24 A.2d 468 (Pa. 1942).

boy's hand. The teachers were sued for damages and were held liable. The court pointed out that there was no emergency, that neither of the teachers had medical training or experience, and that the situation did not justify substituting the teachers' judgment for that of the parent in regard to the treatment of the infected finger.

Failure to take proper action also can cause a teacher to be ruled negligent where pupils are injured in school-related activities. Thus, a coach was found[230] to have acted negligently when he permitted a pupil injured in a football scrimmage to be carried off the playing field without the use of a stretcher, seriously aggravating the player's injuries.

It should be emphasized, however, that teachers are not expected to possess expert medical knowledge concerning the treatment of injuries. They are only required to take that action which a reasonable and prudent layman untrained in the practice of medicine would have taken. This principle is illustrated by a case in which a pupil was struck in the abdomen during a touch football game. The teacher had the boy rest after the accident, and about two hours later the boy was taken home. It later developed that the boy had sustained an injury so serious that it was necessary to remove his spleen and one kidney. The teacher was found[231] not to be negligent in a suit for damages. Testimony by medical experts established that a layman could not reasonably have been expected to know the nature of the injury and that the delay in discovering the nature and extent of the injury did not result in aggravation of the injury. In another case a boy who sustained a broken arm while jumping over a gymnasium horse was taken to the supervisor's office, given first aid, and then taken to a hospital. The parents sued the teacher for damages, claiming that he was negligent in having the pupil walk to the supervisor's office after being injured. The court ruled[232] that the teacher was not negligent and that the steps which were taken to aid the pupil were proper.

11.6d Defamation of character

The legal principles involved in defamation of character have been discussed in a preceding section.[233] Teachers and school administrators should be aware of these principles, since they may be in possession of potentially defamatory material concerning pupils or school employees. The question of whether such information can be communicated to others under the protection of the doctrine of qualified privilege is of considerable importance.

As a general rule, potentially defamatory material should be communicated only to a person who has a legitimate interest in it and who is in a position to act upon the information. In a Georgia case the president of a college, during an investigation into a theft which occurred in a girls' dormitory, made certain defamatory oral accusations which allegedly were overheard by another faculty member who was assisting with the investigation. The Supreme Court of Georgia aptly expressed the obligations of faculty members in regard to the communication of defamatory material:

> . . . the right of members of the faculty of a college, who are entrusted with the supervision, regulation and training of boys and girls, to speak freely with each other in the performance of those duties is involved. No one, and certainly no parent of those students would wish that the faculty abdicate or even half heartedly perform their duties in this respect. It would be nonsense to require them to maintain discipline and moral conduct, and at the same time deny them the right to freely confer with each other revealing facts, circumstances, and suspicions of wrongdoing by any student. . . . Any legal restraint of . . . faculty in the reasonable discharge of duty, not only would not be beneficial to the child or student but might well be disastrous to them.[234]

It must be recognized, however, that in the teacher-pupil relationship the pupil is an involuntary party, and that this creates a confidential relationship between the pupil and teacher which imposes a higher standard of conduct upon the teacher than would exist if the two parties were dealing as equals. Because of this relationship the teacher is obligated to exhibit the utmost good faith in discharging the duty to the pupil. Good faith requires that the teacher refrain from taking advantage of the pupil; act honestly with good motives and intent, and without fraud, collusion, or deceit; and make a concerted effort to ascertain and act upon the truth in any matter involving the pupil. Disclosure of defamatory information concerning a pupil can be made in good

---

[230]Welch v. Dunsmuir Joint Union High School District, 326 P.2d 633 (Cal. 1958).
[231]Pirkle v. Oakdale Union Grammar School District, 253 P.2d 1 (Cal. 1953).
[232]Sayers v. Ranger, 83 A.2d 775 (N.J. 1951).
[233]Supra, under Section 11.5b.
[234]Walter v. Davidson, 104 S.E.2d 113 (Ga. 1958).

faith only if it is made to a person to whom the teacher has a duty to disclose the information (such as a school principal) or if it is made to one who is professionally qualified to assist the pupil (such as a counselor or social worker). Good faith requires that rumors or suspicions concerning a pupil be communicated only to a person to whom the teacher has a positive duty to report such information.

Teachers and administrators frequently receive requests for information about pupils from prospective employers or from colleges or universities which pupils wish to attend. Such information generally is covered under the doctrine of qualified privilege, particularly when it is supplied in response to a specific request rather than volunteered. It is well to require that such requests be made in writing in order that the legitimacy of the request can be ascertained and that the student authorized release of the information.

In a Kentucky case the doctrine of qualified privilege was extended to include a discussion at a PTA meeting concerning an allegation that the principal of the school was guilty of immoral conduct with girl pupils in the school. The court explained the considerations involved in the doctrine of qualified privilege as follows:

> Appellant was the principal of the school in question, and if rumors were abroad concerning his conduct and morality and fitness to teach young girls, it was entirely proper that the same should be discussed at a meeting of an organization of this kind. Under such circumstances, a discussion of a teacher's conduct and moral fitness, if made in good faith, and without actual malice, and with reasonable or probable grounds for believing them to be true, would be privileged, since it would be upon a subject-matter in which the members of such an association would have a vital, public, moral, and social interest as it involves their children.

> Although the law presumes malice, where the publication is libelous or slanderous per se, yet if the publication is made under circumstances which disclose a qualified privilege, it is relieved of the presumption of malice, and the burden is then on the plaintiff to prove actual malice. [235]

The question of defamation of character also may arise in regard to recommendations provided by a school administrator concerning the professional qualifications of a former employee. In Wisconsin it has

been ruled[236] that a public school official expressing an opinion as to the qualifications of a former employee who had submitted an application for employment as a teacher has the benefit of qualified privilege. In this case a school superintendent was sued for libel by a former teacher in the system who had listed him as a reference when applying for a job elsewhere. The superintendent gave the teacher a negative recommendation in response to the prospective employer's letter of inquiry. The negative recommendation was based on the fact that six principals of schools in which the teacher had taught had recommended to the superintendent that, on the basis of their analysis of the teacher's qualifications, his contract should not be renewed. Public policy, the court ruled, requires that malice not be imputed in such a situation, for otherwise one who enjoys a qualified privilege might be reluctant to give a sincere, yet critical, response.

11.7 TORT LIABILITY OF SCHOOL BUS OPERATORS

A review of tort actions involving school districts soon leads one to conclude that more of these actions involve injuries resulting from the transportation of pupils than from any other school-related activity. Consequently, it is worthwhile to discuss some of the legal principles involved in such actions. Subject to whatever limitations are imposed by the statutes and court decisions discussed previously, a school district, school board, or other governmental agency is usually immune from tort liability for the personal injury or death of pupils or other persons resulting from the operation of school buses,[237] or from failure to furnish pupils with safe and suitable

---

[235]Thompson v. Bridges, 273 S.W. 529 (Ky. 1925).

[236]Hett v. Ploetz, 121 N.W.2d 270 (Wis. 1963).
[237]Standard Accident Insurance Co. v. Perty County Board of Educatijon, 72 F.Supp. 142 (Ky. 1947); Thurman v. Consolidated School District No. 128, 94 F.Supp. 616 (Kan. 1950); Turk v. County Board of Education, 131 So. 436 (Ala. 1930); Roberts v. Baker, 196 S.E. 104 (Ga. 1938); Wallace v. Laurel County Board of Education, 153 S.W.2d 915 (Ky. 1941); McKnight v. Cassidy, 174 Atl. 865 (N.J. 1934); Benton v. Board of Education of Cumberland County, 161 S.E. 96 (N.C. 1931); Wright v. Consolidated School District No. 1, 19 P.2d 369 (Okla. 1933); Rankin v. School District No. 9, 23 P.2d 132 (Ore. 1933); Kesman v. School District of Fallowfield Township, 29 A.2d 17 (Pa. 1942); Schornack v. School District No. 17-2 of Brown County, 266 N.W. 141 (S.D. 1936); Chackness v. Board of Education of Harford County, 120 A.2d 392 (Md. 1956); Wilson v. Maury County Board of Education, 302 S.W.2d 502 (Tenn. 1957); Mire v. Lafourche Parish School Board, 62 So.2d 541 (La. 1952); Campbell v. Hillsboro Independent School District, 203 S.W.2d 663 (Tex. 1947); Bradfield v. Board of Education, 36 S.E.2d 512 (W.Va. 1945).

means of transportation to and from school.[238]

While a school district may enjoy immunity from tort liability, the school bus operator is not absolved from liability for personal negligence, assuming all essential elements of actionable negligence are present.[239] To avoid liability for injuries sustained by pupils, the school bus operator must exercise the degree of caution and prudence expected of a person who is in charge of young children.

11.7a Standard of care

The fact that children usually cannot and do not exercise the same degree of prudence for their own safety as adults, and that they are inclined to be careless and impulsive, imposes on those dealing with children a duty to exercise proportionately greater vigilance and caution to assure their safety. Some authorities hold that the school bus operator must exercise ordinary care for the safety of school children.[240] This is the degree of care that a person of ordinary prudence would exercise under similar circumstances. Other authorities hold that the school bus operator is to be treated as a carrier of passengers for hire[241] and must exercise extraordinary care and diligence[242] or the highest degree of care.[243] It also has been ruled[244] that in view of the tender age of the passengers a school bus operator must exercise a high degree of vigilance and caution to assure their safety.

The current status of the law seems to be that, when a common carrier contracts to render a special service for a group of individuals or a public agency, it thereupon becomes, with few exceptions, a private rather than a common carrier.[245] That is, the carrier must render only "ordinary care" rather than the "highest degree of care" normally expected of common carriers. Thus, when a cab company contracted to transport pupils to and from their schools, and to carry only pupils during these hours, the company ceased to be a common carrier while transporting pupils and was held only to the duty of exercising ordinary care for their safety.[246]

11.7b Pickup and discharge of passengers

A school bus operator ordinarily has a duty to pickup and discharge riders at a reasonably safe place.[247] The operator also has an obligation to warn passengers of an approaching vehicle.[248] In some cases it has been held[249] that the operator's duty to discharge passengers safely continues until the child is safely off the highway. It was held,[250] for example, that when a seven-year-old child was killed when struck by a bus from which he had just alighted the driver was negligent in failing to ascertain whether or not all children had crossed the road and in moving the bus so quickly that all children did not have adequate time to pass in front of it. In another case a school bus operator was held[251] to have been negligent where it appeared that he had allowed a twelve-year-old boy to serve as "flagman" without giving him sufficient instruction concerning the assignment. A school bus operator was also held[252] negli-

[238]Harris v. Salem School District, 57 Atl. 332 (N.H. 1904); Girard v. Monrovia City School District, 264 P.2d 115 (Cal. 1953).

[239]Wynn v. Gandy, 197 S.E. 527 (Va. 1938); Roberts v. Baker, 196 S.E. 104 (Ga. 1938); Tipton v. Willey, 191 N.E. 804 (Ohio 1934); Cartwright v. Graves, 184 S.W.2d 373 (Tenn. 1944). *Contra*, Hibbs v. Independent School District of Green Mountain, 251 N.W. 606 (Iowa 1933); Holmes v. School Board of Orange County, 301 So.2d 145 (Fla. 1974).

[240]Pendarvis v. Pfeifer, 182 So. 307 (Fla. 1938); Krametbauer v. McDonald, 104 P.2d 900 (N.M. 1940); Gaudette v. McLaughlin, 189 Atl. 872 (N.H. 1937); Cartweight v. Graves, 184 S.W.2d 373 (Tenn. 1944); Mire v. Lafourche Parish School Board, 62 So.2d 541 (La. 1952).

[241]McVeigh v. Harrison, 22 S.E.2d 752 (Ga. 1942); Eason v. Crews, 77 S.E.2d 245 (Ga. 1953); Adams v. Great American Indemnity Co., 116 So.2d 307 (La. 1959).

[242]McVeigh v. Harrison, 22 S.E.2d 752 (Ga. 1942); Davidson v. Horne, 71 S.E.2d 464 (Ga. 1952); Roberts v. Baker, 196 S.E. 104 (Ga. 1938).

[243]Lincoln City Lines v. Schmidt, 245 F.2d 600 (8th Cir. 1957); Earl W. Baker & Co. v. Lagaly, 144 F.2d 344 (10th Cir. 1944); Van Cleave v. Illini Coach Co., 100 N.E.2d 398 (Ill. 1951); Roberts v. Baker, 196 S.E. 104 (Ga. 1938); Webb v. City of Seattle, 157 P.2d 312 (Wash. 1945); Norris V. American Casualty Co., 176 So.2d 677 (La. 1965).

[244]Cartwright v. Graves, 184 S.W.2d 373 (Tenn. 1944).

[245]Lincoln City Lines v. Schmidt, 245 F.2d 600 (8th Cir. 1957); Hopkins v. Yellow Cab. Co., 250 P.2d 330 (Cal. 1952); Shannon v Central-Gaither Union School District, 23 P.2d 769 (Cal. 1933); Hunt v. Clifford, 209 A.2d 182 (Conn. 1965).

[246]Hopkins v. Yellow Cab Co., 250 P.2d 330 (Cal. 1952).

[247]Davidson v. Horne, 71 S.E.2d 464 (Ga. 1952); Mire v. Lafourche Parish School Board, 62 So.2d 541 (La. 1952); Tipton v. Willey, 191 N.E. 804 (Ohio 1934); Hunter v. Boyd, 28 S.E.2d 412 (S.C. 1943); Chackness v. Board of Education of Harford County, 120 A.2d 392 (Md. 1956).

[248]Cartwright v. Graves, 184 S.W.2d 373 (Tenn. 1944).

[249]Greene v. Mitchell County Board of Education, 75 S.E.2d 129 (N.C. 1953); Reeves v. Tittle, 129 S.W.2d 364 (Tex. 1939); Mikes v. Baumgartner, 152 N.W.2d 732 (Minn. 1967).

[250]Greene v. Mitchell County Board of Education, 75 S.E.2d 129 (N.C. 1953).

[251]County School Board of Orange County v. Thomas, 112 S.E.2d 877 (Va. 1960).

[252]Mire v. Lafourche Parish School Board, 62 So.2d 541 (La. 1952).

gent for failing to see a passing automobile in a rearview mirror, and a pupil who had just alighted from the bus was injured when she was struck by the passing car. It should be noted, however, that in several cases it has been ruled[253] that a school bus operator need not assist a child off the bus or across the highway unless there is a specific need for it. It also has been ruled[254] that a school bus operator did not owe a duty to a child to protect her from injury while she was walking from her home to the point where the bus stopped to pick her up, and that a school district did not have a duty to route a school bus so that no child who rode the bus would need to cross a highway to board it.

To avoid liability for negligence, the operator of a school bus must substantially comply with statutes regulating the place where a school bus may stop to pickup or discharge passengers. However, under a statute providing for pickup and discharge of children "at the edge of the road," it was decided[255] that a school bus operator was not required to drive the bus out on the shoulder of the road. It also has been ruled[256] that a statute prohibiting parking on the near side of the highway adjacent to a schoolhouse did not prohibit parking a school bus in such a position for a short period of time while waiting for school children.

11.7c Other motorists

The duty of a school bus operator to observe reasonable precaution to safeguard passengers is not negated by the negligence of the driver of another vehicle.[257] Thus, where a child was struck by another vehicle, and the bus operator's negligence was one of two proximate causes of her injuries, both drivers could be held jointly liable.[258] In this case the intervening negligence of the driver of the other vehicle did not relieve the negligence of the bus operator where, by exercising reasonable care, the bus operator could have foreseen the accident. However, where the original negligence of the school bus operator is not the

proximate cause of an injury, the driver will not be held liable.[259]

The school bus operator's duty is not affected by a statute requiring certain precautionary acts on the part of other motorists in regard to school buses. A statute requiring all vehicles to stop when a school bus is taking on or discharging passengers is not to be construed as completely abolishing the hazards of traffic on public highways and is not intended to relieve the school bus operator of any duty the violation of which would constitute negligence. The violation of such a statute has been held[260] to constitute negligence per se and is an immediate cause of the injury which results, but it does not conclusively, or as a matter of law, constitute an independent cause of action so as to preclude recovery based on the negligence of the bus operator.

11.8 EDUCATIONAL MALPRACTICE

A new and somewhat unusual type of legal action involving the liability of the school district and perhaps school personnel for lack of pupil achievement is coming to the courts. One decision has been handed down in this area and other cases are pending. In the case decided on this issue, the school district was sued on the basis that the pupil who was graduated from high school had not been trained in the basic skills at a level that would permit him to function in adult society. The court held that failing to receive instruction to achieve the desired educational level was not an "injury" within the meaning of tort law. The court pointed out that many factors account for educational achievement or lack of it, and they are not all within the responsibility or control of the school. Thus, the court refused to hold the school district liable.[261]

11.9 SUMMARY

A tort is a wrong committed against the person or property of another for which a court will award damages. A tort involves loss or damage sustained by a person as a result of another person's failure to protect such person from unreasonable risk. Torts arise from negligence, i.e., failure to exercise the degree of care for the safety of others that a reasonable and prudent person would have exercised under similar circumstances. Because children ordinarily

---

[253]Greeson v. Davis, 9 S.E.2d 690 (Ga. 1940); Dickerhooff v. Bair, 6 N.E.2d 990 (Ohio 1936); Hunter v. Boyd, 28 S.E.2d 412 (S.C. 1943); Adams v. Great American Indemnity Co., 116 So.2d 307 (La. 1959).

[254]Price v. York, 164 N.E.2d 617 (Ill. 1960); accord, Vogt v. Johnson, 153 N.W.2d 247 (Minn. 1967); Pratt v. Robinson, 336 N.Y.S.2d 612 (1972).

[255]Gholston v. Richards, 169 S.W.2d 846 (Tenn. 1943).

[256]Swenson v. Van Harpen, 283 N.W. 309 (Wis. 1939).

[257]Ibid.; Adams v. Great American Indemnity Co., 116 So.2d 307 (La. 1959); Mikes v. Baumgartner, 152 N.W.2d 732 (Minn. 1967).

[258]Reeves v. Tittle, 129 S.W.2d 364 (Tex. 1939).

[259]Adams. v. Great American Indemnity Co., 116 So.2d 307 (La. 1959).

[260]Reeves v. Tittle, 129 S.W.2d 364 (Tex. 1939).

[261]Doe v. San Francisco Unified School District, 131 Cal. Rptr. 854 (1976).

lack the foresight and prudence of adults, one who cares for children is expected to exercise greater care for their safety than would be expected if one were caring for adults.

An invitee (one who is on premises by invitation) is in a more advantageous position than a licensee (one who is on premises by permission or sufferance). The owner must exercise reasonable care for the safety of invitees, but need only refrain from willfully or wantonly injuring a licensee. The distinction is particularly important when field trips involving pupils are undertaken.

Persons who through their own negligence contribute to their injuries are guilty of contributory negligence and, under the common law, are barred from recovering damages for their injuries. A school-age child cannot be charged with contributory negligence unless he or she is old enough to understand and appreciate the dangers involved in a given activity. In a number of states the common-law rule of contributory negligence has been modified by statutes which provide for recovery by the injured party on the basis of the comparative negligence of the parties involved in the accident.

One who voluntarily exposes oneself to known dangers assumes the risk of injury from these dangers and cannot recover damages for injuries caused by them. For example, pupils who voluntarily participate in such sports as football and basketball assume the risk of injuries normally associated with them.

The tort liability of school districts in the United States depends upon the common law, state statutes, and judicial rulings. Under the common law, a school district, as an agency of the state, is immune from tort liability. Some states—for example, California—have enacted legislation making a school district liable for the torts of its officers, agents, and employees. Other states have removed a portion of their immunity from tort liability by enacting "safe-place" and "save-harmless" statutes.

The common-law immunity from tort liability has been either altered or completely removed by judicial rulings in some states. The courts in New York consistently have held that a school board is liable for its own negligence. In some states, school districts have been held liable for damages caused by nuisance or trespass; in others, school districts have been held liable for torts committed while engaging in a proprietary function. In Illinois, Wisconsin, Minnesota, and Arizona the immunity doctrine has been ab-

rogated completely by the courts. However, the legislatures in these states generally have enacted statutes limiting the amount of recovery which may be had by one injured as a result of the negligence of a school district or its officers, agents, or employees.

Where it is granted such authority by statute, or where immunity from liability has been modified or removed by legislative action or by judicial rulings, a school district may purchase liability insurance. The mere purchase of liability insurance does not remove a school district's common-law immunity from tort liability. In some cases, however, the courts have permitted injured parties to recover damages to the limit of the district's liability insurance coverage.

School district employees generally are covered by workmen's compensation laws. Such laws provide compensation for workers injured in the course of their employment without regard to negligence.

As a general rule, school officers are not personally liable for loss or injury resulting from an act which is within the scope of their authority or discretion. They will be held liable for injuries caused by acts which are beyond their discretion, by their willful or wanton acts, or by their malicious acts. School board members are not personally liable for the negligent acts of the board as a corporate body, but they are personally liable for their own negligent acts. Individual school board members have been held personally liable for failure properly to perform ministerial duties, although the weight of authority indicates that they are not personally liable for improper performance of ministerial duties imposed on the board as a corporate body.

School officers are not personally liable for injuries which result from negligent acts of employees of the district unless they participated in negligent acts or directed them to be done. In regard to defamation of character, school board members have the protection of qualified privilege within the scope of their authority and discretion. They may be held liable for defamation of character, however, if they publish or communicate defamatory material in acts which are beyond the scope of their authority.

In regard to acts other than torts, school officers are absolutely liable for all school funds which come into their individual custody unless they have been deposited in a designated bank or other public depository. School board members will be held personally liable for expenditures which are expressly forbidden or which are completely beyond the authority of the school board. They also will be held personally liable on contracts in which they have expressly agreed to assume personal liability, but not on contracts which they have entered into on behalf of the district.

Teachers and other school employees will be held liable for injuries sustained by pupils as a result of their failure to exercise the same degree of care for the pupils' safety and well-being that a reasonable and prudent person would have exercised under similar circumstances. A teacher is expected to foresee sources of potential danger to pupils and to take appropriate action to prevent pupils from being injured. Teachers may become liable for damages as a result of their improper or inadequate supervision of pupils who are under their care. They also may be held liable for injuries sustained by pupils as a result of the teacher's failure to provide adequate instruction or to warn pupils of the dangers inherent in certain activities.

Teachers and administrators should not attempt to treat pupils who become ill or who are injured while at school. They should make decisions concerning the medical treatment to be obtained for a pupil only when an emergency requires that such decisions be made. They are not expected to possess an expert knowledge of medicine but are expected to act as a reasonable and prudent person untrained in the practice of medicine would act under similar circumstances.

The doctrine of qualified privilege will usually protect teachers and administrators from liability for defamation of character. However, they will become liable for defamation of character if they indiscriminately communicate to others defamatory material concerning either pupils or other school employees. To guard against such liability, potentially defamatory material should be communicated only to one to whom is owed a duty of reporting such information or to one who is qualified to act upon it.

A high proportion of the tort cases involving school districts and/or school employees arise from accidents which occur in the course of transporting pupils to and from school. Unless it has been abrogated by statute or judicial ruling, the common-law rule of immunity from tort liability protects school districts from liability for such injuries. School bus operators, however, will be held liable if their negligence results in injuries to pupils who are in their care. The operator of a school bus has a duty to pickup and discharge passengers at a reasonably safe place and to warn them of dangers such as approaching vehicles. The fact that a child is injured as a result of the negligence of another motorist does not relieve the bus operator of liability if the bus driver's negligence also was a proximate cause of the pupil's injury. While damage suits have been initiated against school districts when graduates have failed to acquire the basic skills, to date none has been successful.

Admission and Attendance of Pupils

12.0 INTRODUCTION

Public education operates within an established legal framework, and educational activities are regulated and controlled by constitutions and laws at both the federal and state level, as well as by rules and regulations of local boards of education. If the meaning of constitutions, legislative provisions, and local regulations were clear and unmistakable, not in conflict with each other, and administered in good faith, court interpretations and judicial decisions would be minimal. This obviously is not the case in the area of admissions and attendance of pupils, for a large and important source of school law is found in court decisions and judicial interpretation on this topic.

12.1 CONSTITUTIONAL
PROVISIONS FOR PUBLIC EDUCATION

Constitutional provisions as interpreted in court decisions on educational issues are of utmost importance. They guarantee personal educational rights and represent the floor or level below which no state may go in providing educational programs and facilities. They in no sense are to be interpreted as a limitation prohibiting legislatures from doing more. The legislature may go as far beyond constitutional requirements as it desires to achieve the intent or goals of the framers of the constitution. It may not do less.

Constitutional guarantees are not to be eliminated or set aside by enactments of Congress, the legislature, or local boards of education. Constitutions, both federal and state, frequently have been described as "the highest law of the land." Thus, where there is conflict between statutes and constitutions, statutes must give way to constitutional mandate.[1] Decisions to this effect apply not only to education but to constitutional guarantees in all other fields.[2] Constitutional rights extend not only to citizens of the United States but also to persons living in the United States who owe allegiance to foreign countries.[3]

Indirectly the federal Constitution determined that education is a state rather than a federal function. For example, it was held[4] in Kentucky at an early date that the power of the states to establish and maintain systems of common schools, to raise money by taxation, and to govern, control, and regulate schools when established are powers not delegated to the United States by the Constitution or prohibited by it to the states and are therefore reserved to the states respectively or to the people.

The relationship of the state legislature to local school districts also is determined by constitutional provisions. According to an early Iowa constitutional provision, the educational interest "shall be under the management of a board of education" subject to certain restrictions by the legislature. Under this provision it was held[5] that the legislature could not originate school measures but could act in the premises only after the local school board of education had been organized and taken action. This case is in no sense a declaration that education is a local and not a state function; rather, it is an indication that if certain rights and responsibilities are vested in an official local body by the constitution, the legislature is without authority in the matter.

Since the legal authority of the constitution is so controlling, constitutional provisions regarding age for admission to school are of great consequence. When the state constitution guarantees free public education within certain ages, the courts usually have held that education at least for these ages must be provided. The legislature, if not restricted by the constitution, may provide additional education. However, two limitations relative to constitutional age limits are to be noted. Constitutional guarantees probably are not applicable to the specified age group attending colleges or universities, and constitutional provisions are not self-executing.

In a Wisconsin case the plaintiff contended that constitutional provisions guaranteeing free public education for all persons between the ages of four and twenty applied to students at the university and fees and tuition were not collectible. The court held[6] that the specified constitutional provision when read together with the section requiring the establishment of free public education for elementary and secondary schools as nearly uniform as practicable, clearly indicated that it was the intent of the constitution to guarantee free public education in elementary and secondary schools but not in institutions of higher learning.

On the issue of whether constitutional provisions are self-executing, it was held[7]

[1]Almond v. Gilmer, 49 S.E.2d 431 (Va. 1948).
[2]Murray v. Hoboken Land Company, 59 U.S. (How.) 272, 15 L.Ed. 372 (N.J. 1855).
[3]In re Tiburcio Parrott, I Fed. 481 (C.C.C.D. Cal. 1880).
[4]Marshall v. Donovan, 73 Ky. (10 Bush.) 681 (1874).

[5]District Township v. City of Dubuque, 7 Iowa 7 (Clarke) 262 1858).
[6]State v. Regents of University, 11 N.W. 472 (Wis. 1882).
[7]State v. Board of Education, 42 N.W.2d 168 (Neb. 1950).

in a Nebraska case that, although, according to the constitution, the legislature must provide free instruction for all children between the ages of five and twenty-one, it was the duty of the legislature to implement such provisions if the language was directed to the legislature or if action by the legislature was contemplated. Since the legislature had not provided for kindergarten education under the described circumstances, it was stated in the syllabus by the court that "a court has no power by mandamus to control the decision of those matters which are left by statutes to the discretion of the governing body of a governmental agency." Thus, the court refused to require a local board of education to establish kindergartens in spite of the constitutional stipulation that the legislature shall provide free instruction in the common schools of the state for all persons between the specified ages.

A very common constitutional provision is to the effect that the legislature shall establish a system of free public education for all residents of the state. Thus, the constitution anticipates that the legislature will enact statutes to implement constitutional provisions. A number of state constitutions also specify the ages between which the legislature must provide free public education.[8]

12.2 CONSTITUTIONAL PROVISIONS REGARDING SCHOOL ATTENDANCE AGE

The Missouri constitution has the most extensive age range of any state, requiring that public schools be provided for all children not in excess of twenty-one years of age as prescribed by law. Other state constitutions designating specific ages for free public education give a prescribed lower and upper age limit. Wisconsin has the lowest specified age of any state—four years. Its constitution states that schools are to be free and without charge for tuition for all children ages four to twenty. Nebraska's constitutional provisions include all children between the ages of five and twenty-one. Free public education is to be supplied for all children six to twenty-one (or between the ages of six and twenty-one) in Arizona, Arkansas, Colorado, Mississippi, Montana, and North Carolina. The designated age span in New Jersey is five to eighteen years, and in Pennsylvania free public schools must be provided for all

children above six years of age. Public education for all children of school age is required by the New Mexico constitution.

Louisiana appears to have detailed the educational requirements more specifically in its constitution than any other state, embodying features that are usually statutory enactments. Its constitution provides that public schools are to be available for all children between the ages of six and eighteen years, but children must attain the age of six within four months of the beginning of the term to be eligible for admission. Kindergartens may be authorized for children between the ages of four and six, and parish or municipality schools may provide that only children reaching five on or before December 31 may enter kindergarten and only those attaining age six by that date may enter "regular" school.

The majority of states do not specify ages or age ranges in their constitutions. Rather, the state constitutions include a general declaration to the effect that the legislature shall establish and maintain a system of free public schools. The legislature then specifies the ages for school attendance.

12.3 LEGISLATIVE AUTHORITY BEYOND CONSTITUTIONAL AGES

When age ranges are specified in state constitutions, the states are not thereby prohibited from providing education for groups outside the specified range. It has been held in a number of cases that the legislature may go beyond the constitutional provisions and provide free public schools for groups not included in the constitutional guarantee of free public education. As an example, the Colorado constitution provides for free public education for children ages six to twenty-one. The legislature provided for the establishment of kindergartens for children below the age of six. The courts held[9] that the legislature had the authority to establish kindergartens, asserting that the constitution in no way prohibited or limited the power of the legislature to provide education for children outside the constitutional age range.

A New Jersey decision involving the upper constitutional age limit was of the same import. Although the state constitution provided only for education of children between the ages of five and eighteen, the legislature enacted a statute providing for free public education between the ages of five and twenty-one. In upholding the authority of the legislature to go beyond the

---

[8]Information is for the most part from *Constitutions of the United States, National and State,* Legislative Drafting Research Fund of Columbia University (Oceana Publications, 1962).

[9]*In re Kindergarten Schools,* 32 Pac. 422 (Col. 1893).

constitutionally mandated age to provide more extensive education, the court said, "There is nothing in the constitution to forbid the legislature from providing for better school facilities than the constitution itself requires."[10]

A Wisconsin decision again demonstrated the authority of the legislature to provide free public education beyond the age range specified in the constitution. Although the Wisconsin constitution guarantees free public education between the ages of four and twenty, the legislature authorized the establishment of vocational schools for adults. The law required communities not providing vocational schools to pay the tuition of adults attending neighboring city vocational schools. Taxpayers in the Town of Manitowoc Rapids objected to the statute on the grounds that the constitution provided for free public education between the ages of four and twenty and this statute provided education in excess of the ages guaranteed in the constitution. The court sustained the statute, holding that the legislature must do as much as the constitution required but may provide education beyond the constitutional requirements. In the words of the court:

The constitutional provision [that] the Legislature shall provide for establishment of district schools and that such schools shall be free to all children between the ages of four and twenty years does not impliedly prohibit free education for persons beyond the age of twenty and under the age of four.[11]

Statutes are unconstitutional only when they attempt what is contrary to and prohibited by the constitution. They are not unconstitutional when they go beyond, furthering the intent of the constitution either by providing additional free public education or furthering other rights guaranteed by the constitution.

12.4 RULES OF BOARDS OF EDUCATION—ADMISSION AND ATTENDANCE

In addition to constitutional and statutory provisions, admission and attendance at school are governed by rules and regulations of state and local boards of education. Local boards in all states are vested with extensive authority by the state in educational matters as long as they act within

constitutional provisions and in accordance with state and federal statutes. Their actions will not be overruled by the courts as long as they act within their jurisdiction, in a reasonable manner, and in good faith. This applies to admission and attendance of pupils as well as to all other educational considerations.

12.5 RIGHTS OF PUPILS TO ATTEND SCHOOL

The right to attend a public school is not a private right but a privilege held in common by all members of the community within specified ages. It is a privilege conditioned on the acceptance of certain obligations which have been spelled out by the statutes and the courts over a period of time in most states.

The right to attend a public school cannot be demanded on the basis of citizenship alone and is not a right guaranteed by the federal constitution.[12] It is subject to appropriate, reasonable regulations by the legislature and local boards of education. The right cannot be insisted upon when it will deprive others of their constitutional right of school attendance in an atmosphere where pupils can study and learn without distractions. When necessary, the courts have not hesitated to apply "police power" to guarantee the greatest good to the greatest number, as subsequently cited cases on admission and attendance will demonstrate.

12.6 ESTABLISHMENT OF ATTENDANCE AREAS AND ASSIGNMENT OF PUPILS

The courts will not determine boundary lines for the attendance area of a particular school.[13] Boards of education have the right to establish boundary lines for attendance areas and determine the schools which pupils shall attend.[14] Pupils must attend the schools to which they are assigned, assuming the board has acted in a reasonable manner and has not abused its discretion. To quote directly from the Ohio court: "Boards of education may make such assignments of the youth of their respective districts to the schools established by them as in their opinion will best promote the interests of education in their districts."[15]

[12]Trustees of Columbia Academy v. Board of Trustees of Richland County School District No. 1; 202 S.E.2d 860 (S.C. 1974); Bell v. Town of North Reading, 295 N.E.2d 894 (Mass. 1973).

[13]McEwan v. Brod, 91 N.Y.S.2d 565 (1949).

[14]Howell School Board v. Hubbartt, 70 N.W.2d 531 (Iowa 1955).

[15]State ex rel. Lewis v. Board of Education of Wilmington School District, 28 N.E.2d 496 (Ohio 1940).

[10]In re Newark School Board, 70 Atl. 881 (N.J. 1907).

[11]Manitowoc v. Manitowoc Rapids, 285 N.W. 403 (Wis. 1939).

In determining the attendance area, the board of education may not assign a child to a school so far removed from the child's home as to make the walking distance unreasonable when no transportation is provided.[16] This requirement should not be interpreted to mean that a child must be assigned to the nearest school or the school most conveniently located.[17] This principle is illustrated in a Mississippi case in which the school code provided that the board "shall have the power to specify attendance areas and designate the school each pupil shall attend." Acting under this statute the board assigned some pupils to schools which were not the closest to their homes. In the opinion of the court the board had authority to so assign the pupils if it had not acted arbitrarily or capriciously.

Boards of education must be reasonable in their assignment of pupils to a particular school. They may not, for example, assign pupils to a school the route to which is so hazardous that the children are daily exposed to danger to life and limb. Distance to be traveled, amount of time necessary for the journey, availability of public transportation for pupils who wish to stay after school, age of children involved, traffic hazards, and incidence of crime along the route are all factors which must be considered in establishing attendance areas.[18]

A North Dakota court held[19] that a local board of education, with the approval of the county superintendent, could close its school and transport the children to a neighboring school if the children's tuition was paid and educational opportunities were greater. Where discretion to establish boundary lines is vested in a public official, i.e., the county superintendent, the courts will not control that discretion.[20] They will seek only to determine whether the discretion has been abused or whether the public official has acted in good faith and in a reasonable manner.

In Missouri, where the county superintendent was authorized under certain circumstances to assign a pupil to an adjacent school district more convenient to the pupil, it was held[21] that the assignment legally could be made effective at some future date. A child living in a county school district in Mississippi was not authorized to attend the city district schools without the approval of both the city and the county school district.[22]

When statutes require boards of education to pay tuition to another district if children live more than five miles from the nearest school in their own district by way of the nearest publicly traveled road and no bus service is provided, there is no option or exercise of discretion or judgment. A mandamus action will compel the implementation of the provision of the statute if administrative remedies have been exhausted and time for appeal has not expired.[23]

When parents are dissatisfied with the action of the board because a pupil objectionable to their child has been assigned to a school which their own child attends, their action is to request the reassignment of their own child. They have no legal basis for requesting that the other pupil be reassigned.[24]

12.7 SCHOOL ATTENDANCE AND CLEANLINESS

To enjoy the privilege of school attendance, parents and their children must assume certain basic obligations normally imposed on all members of a civilized society. Children so physically unclean as to be unfit to associate with other children may be denied admission to school. As a case in point, school authorities have been empowered to make judgments and exercise discretion in excluding children afflicted with head lice from school. If the board's action is characterized by good faith, it is not reviewable by the courts.[25]

12.8 SCHOOL ATTENDANCE AND HEALTH REGULATIONS

In a Colorado case it was held[26] that the board of education had undoubted power to exclude from school pupils not meeting reasonable health requirements and to employ persons competent to advise on health questions. In this case the statute authorized school boards to employ teachers, mechanics, and laborers. It was argued that boards were restricted by the statutes and

[16]State v. Hall, 64 Atl. 1102 (N.H. 1906).

[17]County Board of Education of Jones County v. Smith, 121 So.2d 139 (Miss. 1960); Commonwealth v. School Directors, 4 Pa.Dist.Rep. 314 (1895); Freeman v. Board of Education, 26 Ill. App. 476 (1888).

[18]School Committee of Springfield v. Board of Education, 287 N.E.2d 438 (Mass. 1972).

[19]Herman v. Medicine Lodge School District, 71 N.W.2d 323 (N.D. 1955).

[20]Moles v. Daland, 264 N.W. 74 (Iowa 1935).

[21]School District of Mexico, Mo. v. Maple Grove School District, 324 S.W.2d 369 (Mo. 1959).

[22]Hinze v. Winston County Board of Education, 103 So.2d 353 (Miss. 1958).

[23]Olson v. Pulaski Common School of Faulk County District, 92 N.W.2d 678 (S.D. 1958).

[24]Thompson v. County School Board, 159 F.Supp. 567 (Va. 1957).

[25]Carr v. Inhabitants of Town of Dighton, 118 N.E. 525 (Mass. 1918).

[26]Hallett v. Post Printing and Publishing Co. 192 Pac. 658 (Col. 1920).

were precluded from employing doctors and nurses to inspect children and advise as to their physical condition. The issue did not include providing medical and surgical treatment for diseases since doctors and nurses were not employed for that purpose. The court was of the opinion that the power of school boards to exclude from school pupils who did not meet reasonable health standards clearly implied authority to employ persons to provide expert advice on which the judgment of the school board could be based.

In a North Dakota case a survey revealed a substantial number of positive and suspected cases of trachoma in the county and all children suspected of having trachoma were excluded from school. The court refused to hold[27] the exclusions unreasonable.

Boards of education may require all pupils to pass a physical examination as a condition of school attendance,[28] even though parental objection is based on religious grounds or right of conscience. This principle is illustrated in a Minnesota case in which a six-year old girl was excluded from school because of a sore throat. She was required to furnish a report of a negative throat culture to the division of public health of the city and either to obtain a certificate from a physician indicating a negative throat culture or to submit to a physical examination by a school physician or nurse as a condition of school attendance. The girl, who was a Christian Scientist, refused. The court upheld the exclusion, saying, "All authority exercised in the protection of the public health is to be liberally construed."[29] Because matters of health are delegated to public health authorities, it does not follow that school boards are denied the exercise of power in this area. The protection of the health of other pupils may furnish grounds for exclusion of pupils even when no misconduct is involved.[30]

Control during school hours extends to health, and parental authority may be temporarily superseded.[31] Children may be required to remain on the school grounds at recess and eat lunch at the school cafeteria or bring it from home. In a case dealing directly with this issue a board action was upheld against the charge that this regulation interfered with prerogatives of parents to prescribe diet and select food for their children. The court held[32] that the board was empowered to adopt reasonable rules and regulations for the management of the school, and these rules extended to health, proper surroundings, necessary discipline, promotion of morality, and other wholesome influences.

Schools are authorized to maintain medical inspection and health programs in schools and to establish health departments. They are not, however, authorized to provide remedial treatment of a surgical, medical, or dental nature unless the statutes so stipulate. In the absence of statutes they are not authorized to maintain clinics or employ physicians. This principle is illustrated in a suit brought against the city of Dallas, Texas, to restrain the board of education from maintaining and operating a health department in the public schools. The program included instruction in physical culture and health in the curriculum, maintaining a health department employing doctors and nurses, and prescribing health regulations including periodic health examinations except where parents objected. No medical or surgical treatment was involved. The court ruled[33] that the above program, as part of an efficient school system, was an exercise of discretion of the board which the courts would not control.

When authorized by statutes, the city board of health may close schools during an epidemic.[34] School boards, too, have the authority to adopt reasonable health regulations for the benefit of the pupils and the general public.[35]

12.9 VACCINATION AS A CONDITION OF SCHOOL ATTENDANCE

12.9a State statutes

Whether vaccination or immunization can legally be required by state statutes as a condition of school attendance has been before the courts in California,[36] Connecticut,[37] Georgia,[38] Kentucky,[39] New Hamp-

[27]Martin v. Craig, 173 N.W. 787 (N.D. 1919).

[28]Streich v. Board of Education of Independent School District of City of Aberdeen, 147 N.W. 779 (N.D. 1914).

[29]Stone v. Probst, 206 N.W. 642 (Minn. 1925); See also Matter of Gregory S. 380 N.Y.S.2d 620 (1976).

[30]Commonwealth v. Johnson, 35 N.E.2d 801 (Mass. 1941); Hammond v. Hyde Park, 80 N.E. 650 (Mass. 1907); Carr v. Inhabitants of Town of Dighton, 118 N.E. 525 (Mass. 1918).

[31]Richardson v. Braham, 249 N.W. 557 (Neb. 1933).

[32]Bishop v. Independent School District, 29 S.W.2d 312 (Tex. 1930).

[33]Moseley v. City of Dallas, 17 S.W.2d 36 (Tex. 1929).

[34]Globe School District No. 1 v. Board of Health, City of Globe, 179 Pac. 55 (Ariz. 1919).

[35]Duffield v. Williamsport School District, 29 Atl. 742 (Pa. 1894).

[36]French v. Davidson, 77 Pac. 663 (Cal. 1904).

[37]Bissell v. Davison, 32 Atl. 348 (Conn. 1894).

[38]Anderson v. State, 65 S.E.2d 848 (Ga. 1951).

[39]Mosier v. Barren County Board of Health, 215 S.W.2d 967 (Ky. 1948)

shire,[40] New Jersey,[41] New York,[42] Ohio,[43] Pennsylvania,[44] Texas,[45] and Washington.[46] It also was adjudicated in the Supreme Court of the United States in a case originating in Massachusetts,[47] where the statutes authorized boards of health to require vaccination as a condition of school attendance whenever they felt it was necessary. In every case in which the statutes authorized or required vaccination as a condition of school attendance the statutes have been upheld. This was equally true whether the statutes authorized boards of education or boards of health to require vaccination as a condition of school attendance. Statutory enactments now are providing more precise direction relative to immunizations. The Michigan statute (Michigan Compiled Laws 340.376 of 1970) is an example of the more comprehensive enactments. Here the statutes provide that:

All children enrolling in any public, private or parochial or denominational school in Michigan for the first time shall submit either a statement signed by a physician that they have been immunized or protected against smallpox, diphtheria, tetanus, pertussis, rubella, measles and poliomyelitis and tuberculin tested to determine the presence of infection from tuberculosis; a statement signed by a parent or guardian to the effect that the child has not been immunized and tuberculin tested because of religious convictions or other objections to immunization; or a request signed by a parent or guardian that the local health department give the needed protective injections and diagnostic test.

12.9b Authority of boards of education

In the absence of statutory authority, vaccination may be required in a number of states if epidemics exist in the community. It has been held that boards of education may require vaccination when an epidemic exists in Arkansas,[48] Illinois,[49] Pennsyl-

vania,[50] South Dakota,[51] and Texas.[52] When no epidemic exists, vaccination may be required by a board of education in Missouri,[53] North Carolina,[54] and New York.[55] An exception is noted for pupils who have a physical disability which may contraindicate smallpox vaccination; then the vaccination may be omitted until such condition is removed.[56] In the absence of an epidemic, boards of education may not require vaccination as a condition of school attendance in several states, including Illinois[57] and Michigan.[58]

12.9c Authority of boards of health

Boards of health have wide authority in health matters in schools as well as in the community. If an epidemic exists, they may order all unvaccinated pupils excluded from school in Arkansas,[59] Illinois,[60] Indiana,[61] Michigan,[62] Minnesota,[63] Utah,[64] and Washington.[65] They may order school boards to exclude unvaccinated pupils in Indiana,[66] Kentucky,[67] and Michigan.[68] In Minnesota[69] both the boards of health and the school boards may exclude children who are a menace to the health of others.

In Arkansas[70] and Texas[71] it has been held that boards of health may require all children attending a public or private school to be vaccinated, even in the absence of an epidemic. In several states it has been held that boards of health may not, in the

[40]Barber v. School Board of Rochester, 135 Atl. 159 (N.H.1926).
[41]Sadlock v. Board of Education of Carlstadt in Bergen County, 58 A.2d 218 (N.J. 1948).
[42]Viemeister v. White, 72 N.E. 97 (N.Y. 1904).
[43]State v. Board of Education, 81 N.E. 568 (Ohio 1907).
[44]Field v. Robinson, 48 Atl. 873 (Pa. 1901).
[45]Zucht v. King, 225 S.W. 267 (Tex. 1920) Itz. v. Penick, 493 S.W.2d 506 (Tex. 1973).
[46]State v. Shorrock, 104 Pac. 214 (Wash. 1909).
[47]Jacobson v. Commonwealth of Massachusetts, 197 U.S. 11, 25 S.Ct. 358, 49 L.Ed 643 (Mass. 1905).
[48]Auten v. Board of Directors, 104 S.W. 130 (Ark. 1907).
[49]Hagler et al. v. Larner, 120 N.E. 575 (Ill. 1918).

[50]Duffield v. School District of City of Williamsport, 29 Atl. 742 (Pa. 1894).
[51]Glover v. Board of Education of Lead, 84 N.W. 761 (S.D. 1900).
[52]Zucht v. San Antonio School Board, 170 S.W. 840 (Tex. 1914).
[53]In the matter of Rebenack, 62 Mo.App. 8 (1895).
[54]Hutchins v. School Committee of the Town of Durham, 49 S.E. 46 (N.C. 1904).
[55]Pierce v. Board of Education of City of Fulton, 219 N.Y.S.2d 519 (1961).
[56]Seubold v. Fort Smith Special School District, 237 S.W.2d 884 (Ark. 1951).
[57]Burroughs v. Mortenson, 143 N.E. 457 (Ill. 1924).
[58]Mathews v. Kalamazoo Board of Education, 86 N.W. 1036 (Mich. 1901).
[59]State v. Martin, 204 S.W. 622 (Ark. 1918).
[60]Hagler v. Lorner, 120 N.E. 575 (Ill. 1918).
[61]Blue v. Beach, 56 N.E. 89 (Ind. 1900).
[62]People v. Board of Education of City of Lansing, 195 N.W. 95 (Mich. 1923).
[63]State v. Zimmerman, 90 N.W. 783 (Minn. 1902).
[64]State v. Board of Education of Salt Lake City, 60 Pac. 1013 (Utah 1900).
[65]State v. Partlow, 205 Pac. 420 (Wash. 1922).
[66]State v. Beil, 60 N.E. 672 (Ind. 1901).
[67]Board of Trustees of Highlands Park Graded Common School District No. 46 v. McMurtry, 184 S.W. 390 (Ky. 1916).
[68]People v. Board of Education of Lansing, 195 N.W. 95 (Mich. 1923).
[69]Stone v. Probst, 206 N.W. 642 (Minn. 1925).
[70]State v. Martin, 204 S.W. 622 (Ark. 1918).
[71]Zucht v. King, 225 S.W. 267 (Tex. 1920).

absence of statutory authority, require vaccination as a condition of school attendance unless there is an epidemic in the community. These states include Kansas,[72] Illinois,[73] North Dakota,[74] and Wisconsin.[75] In Oregon[76] boards of health may not order schools closed unless they are authorized to do so specifically by statutes.

12.10 METHODS OF VACCINATION

What constitutes satisfactory vaccination is a frequent legal issue. In some early cases parents objected to the approved method of vaccination and attempted to have another method substituted. In an illustrative case a parent attempted to substitute medicine taken internally for the medically accepted method of scarification. The courts refused to sustain this substitution.[77] In every case coming to the courts, boards of education have been sustained in requiring vaccination for smallpox by the medically accepted method, i.e., injection of cowpox in the human system and evidence of scarification.[78]

12.11 DEFENSES AGAINST REQUIRED VACCINATION

A variety of defenses against vaccination have been presented to the courts. In answer to these defenses the courts have held that vaccination is not an unreasonable restraint upon personal liberty, not a violation of the right of conscience, not an illegal delegation of legislative power, and not class legislation.

In a case involving the charge of unreasonable restraint a boy of ten was excluded from school for refusing to be vaccinated as required by state law. The law provided that "no child or person not vaccinated shall be admitted or received in any public school of the state and the trustees ... shall cause this provision of the law to be enforced." No smallpox was prevalent in the community at the time, and the appellant claimed that the law placed an unreasonable restriction on the right of the child to attend school as well as violating the constitutional and general guarantees of rights, privileges, and liberties of citizens. The court held that the law imposed no un-

reasonable restraint and that rights conferred by the constitution were not violated either by the law or by action of school authorities. The law and its enforcement were held[79] to be a reasonable exercise of police power.

A number of cases relating to whether vaccination was a violation of the right of conscience have arisen.[80] In a Kentucky case[81] in which the appellants charged a violation of the right of conscience one of them pleaded that his religious and conscientious beliefs prevented him from subjecting his children to vaccination by injecting foreign substances into their veins; consequently to compel him to have his children vaccinated would interfere with his religious freedom. In answer, the court quoted the United States Supreme Court: "Religious freedom embraces two conceptions, freedom to believe and freedom to act. The first is absolute but in the nature of things the second cannot be."[82] A 1959 case involved a statute which provided that the "board may exempt pupils from vaccination" if the parents object. The parent, a Christian Scientist, objected on religious grounds. The court held[83] that the word "may" permitted the board to use its discretion. It did not require the board to exempt anyone. The fact that there had been neither smallpox nor diphtheria in the community for almost ten years did not invalidate the board's action.

In a 1966 case in Arkansas the parents were members of a religious sect who believed that vaccination was against the will of God. The church conducted a parochial school which did not require vaccination. The court found[84] that the vaccination requirement was applicable to parochial schools and the parents were guilty of neglect for failure to have their children vaccinated.

Several vaccination cases have related to the charge of illegal delegation of power.[85]

[72]Osborn v. Russell, 68 Pac. 60 (Kan. 1902).

[73]Burroughs v. Mortenson, 143 N.E. 457 (Ill. 1924).

[74]Rhea v. Board of Education of Devil's Lake Special School District, 171 N.W. 103 (N.D. 1919).

[75]State v. Burdge, 70 N.W. 347 (Wis. 1897).

[76]Crane v. School District No. 14, 188 Pac. 712 (Ore. 1920).

[77]Lee v. Marsh, 79 Atl. 564 (Pa. 1911).

[78]State v. Cole, 119 S.W. 424 (Mo. 1909); Abney v. Fox, 250 S.W. 210 (Tex. 1923); Allen v. Ingolls, 33 S.W.2d 1099 (Ark. 1931).

[79]Viemeister v. White, 72 N.E. 97 (N.Y. 1904); Cram v. School Board of Manchester, 136 Atl. 263 (N.H. 1927).

[80]Staffel v. San Antonio School Board, 201 S.W. 413 (Tex. 1918); Commonwealth v. Green, 168 N.E. 101 (Mass. 1929); State v. Miday, 140 S.E.2d 325 (N.C. 1965); Cude v. State, 377 S.W.2d 816 (Ark. 1964).

[81]Mosier v. Barren County Board of Health, 215 S.W.2d 967 (Ky. 1948).

[82]United States v. Ballard, 322 U.S. 78, 64 S.Ct. 882, 88 L.Ed. 1148 (Cal. 1944).

[83]Board of Education of Mountain Lake v. Maas, 152 A.2d 394 (N.J. 1959).

[84]Mannis v. State, 398 S.W.2d 206 (Ark. 1966).

[85]Zucht v. King, 225 S.W. 267 (Tex. 1920); Blue v. Beach, 56 N.E. 89 (Ind. 1900); State v. Board of Education of Salt Lake City, 60 Pac. 1013 (Utah 1900); Hagler v. Lorner, 120 N.E. 575 (Ill. 1918).

In one, the law vested authority in the city commission (city council) to require vaccination. No legislative power or authority was vested in the board of health. The appellants maintained that the city council did not have power to delegate legislative power to the board of health or anyone else. The court held that "the board of health is the public agency through which the city council acts to determine the necessity arising to put the ordinance into effect . . . and that is no delegation of legislative power."[86]

Against the charge that required vaccination of public school pupils is class legislation it was held[87] that even though vaccination affected only one class of citizens—pupils—it was not class legislation. Any legislation which applies equally to all children of school age is not special or discriminatory. Nor is required vaccination unconstitutional on the basis that it is required in some public schools and not in others and is not applicable to children attending private schools. Required vaccination is a valid exercise of police power.

When vaccination is made a condition of school attendance in public and private schools, it cannot be avoided by operating a parochial school. A parochial school is a private school within the meaning of the term *private school.*[88]

As noted previously, many of the decisions relating to required vaccination are found in earlier cases. Recent statutes are much more explicit and are written with sufficient clarity to permit a much greater reliance on their wording, eliminating in many instances the necessity of court interpretation.

12.12 ADMISSION AND ATTENDANCE OF HANDICAPPED CHILDREN

In the past many statutes authorized teachers and administrators to exclude handicapped children from school. Even in the absence of such statutes it was frequently held that boards of education had authority to exclude handicapped children under the general grant of authority to administer schools and court decisions generally had the effect of excluding handicapped children from school.[89] Statutory enactments and court decisions of this nature were understandable in a situation where no special classes were provided for handicapped children and they were placed in a regular classroom, where frequently the teacher was already instructing a larger number of normal children than could be taught effectively.

More recently, with the establishment of special education opportunities for the handicapped, both statutory enactments and judicial interpretations have extended educational opportunities to more handicapped children.[90] It has been held[91] that to ignore educating the handicapped is a denial of equal protection and due process guaranteed by the Constitution. Parents, too, are granted rights in connection with the placement of their handicapped children. A 1973 case held parents were entitled to a hearing regarding placement of their child.[92]

A handicapped child is entitled to attend a private school and have the district pay the tuition when no public facilities are available. The fact that notice of such attendance was not filed during the year, as required by statutes, did not justify nonpayment of tuition.[93] A town is not excused from its obligation to pay for the special education of handicapped pupils on the ground that it had never identified the child as requiring special education. This identification was a function of the Welfare Commission and not of the town.[94]

However, provisions for education of the handicapped are subject to reasonable limits. In a New York case it was held that the level of educational support for programs of handicapped children must be commensurate with the level of support of other educational and governmental activities. In the view of the court, the financing of a near ideal situation for one segment of society is not justifiable without consideration being given to other societal needs. In this instance, substantial progress was being made to improve the situation for the handicapped. In another New York case the father of a seventeen-year-old retarded girl brought action to require the board to con-

[86]French v. Davidson, 77 Pac. 663 (Cal. 1904).

[87]Board of Education of Mountain Lake v. Maas, 152 A.2d 394 (N.J. 1959); French v. Davidson, 77 Pac. 663 (Cal. 1904).

[88]Mannis v. State, 398 S.W.2d 206 (Ark. 1966), *cert. denied,* 384 U.S. 972 (1966).

[89]Stone v. Probst, 206 N.W. 642 (Minn. 1925); Martin v. Craig, 173 N.W. 787 (N.D. 1919).

[90]*In re* Kirkpatrick, 354 N.Y.S.2d 499 (1972); Harrison v. Michigan, 350 F.Supp. 846 (Mich. 1972); Penn. Ass'n. for Retarded Children v. Commonwealth of Pennsylvania, 343 F.Supp. 279 (Pa. 1972); Panitch v. State of Wis., 371 F.Supp. 955 (Wis. 1974); *In interest of* G. H., 218 N.W.2d 441 (N.D. 1974); State *ex rel.* Warren v. Nusbaum, 219 N.W.2d 577 (Wis. 1974).

[91]Mills v. Board of Education of District of Columbia, 348 F.Supp. 866 (D.C. 1972); *In matter of* Jessup, 379 N.Y.S.2d 626 (1975).

[92]Lebank v. Spears, 60 F.R.D. 135 (La. 1973).

[93]*In the matter of Arthur K.,* 347 N.Y.S.2d 271 (1973).

[94]The Children's Center v. Town of East Windsor, 313 A.2d 430 (Conn. 1973).

tinue to keep her in school until she was twenty-one. A statute had been enacted in 1957 requiring districts having ten or more retarded children from ages five to twenty-one to establish special classes for them. In this instance the board provided classes for all retarded children until age seventeen or completion of the junior high school. Only those pupils who could profit by further schooling were continued in school until age twenty-one. The court sustained the board's program, holding that schools were not obligated to keep a person for what would be only custodial care.[95]

12.13 KINDERGARTEN ADMISSION AND ATTENDANCE

The question of whether children are entitled to attend kindergarten when they are within the constitutional age span for free public education is of major educational importance. The specific question has not come to the court's attention in a manner that has produced a definitive answer. Thus, whether children within the constitutional age span are entitled to free kindergarten education still awaits judicial determination.

In Nebraska the constitution required the legislature to provide for the free instruction in the common schools of all persons between the ages of five and twenty-one. The statutes provided that the district school "shall not admit any child to the first grade unless the child has reached the age of six years or will reach such age before October 15 of the current year...." A number of parents maintained that, since the constitution provided for the establishment by the legislature of free schooling from ages five to twenty-one, the establishment of kindergartens was mandatory. The court ruled[96] to the contrary, holding that constitutional guarantees were not self-executing and the legislature had not acted to provide public kindergartens. The court was not asked to determine the constitutionality of the law restricting first-grade entrance to six-year-olds where no kindergarten was provided and where five-year-olds were within the constitutional guarantee of free public education.

In Wisconsin, where the state constitution provided for the establishment of schools without charge for tuition for all children ages four to twenty, a case was brought to compel the school board to provide kindergarten instruction. The parent proceeded under a statute then in force which required the signatures of the parents of twenty-five children within the four- to six-year range on a petition requesting the establishment of a kindergarten. A petition signed by one parent of each of the twenty-five pupils was submitted to the board of education on August 11. The court in passing on this petition held[97] that to guarantee satisfactory attendance the petition must be signed by both parents, if living, of each eligible child. If sufficient attendance was assured, it was the duty of the district to establish a kindergarten. The board of education was entitled to a reasonable length of time to secure the necessary facilities, supplies, equipment, and a qualified teacher for the kindergarten.

In New York a child who would not be five until January 12 was admitted to kindergarten although the usual cutoff date was age five by December 1. One of the parents signed a form indicating "that the child would be expected to remain in kindergarten 2 years." This the court indicated by way of dicta "would probably not be effective as a waiver, or bar the infant from any right accorded by law." The child attended only 128 of 191 days and, in view of his poor attendance and perhaps because of the agreement signed by the parent was not tested for placement in first grade. The parent brought suit to compel attendance of the child in the first grade. The statute provided for education for all persons over five and under twenty-one. The court held[98] that inasmuch as the kindergarten was a part of the public school system the child could be required to attend there as his right under the statutory guarantee of free public education. The court would not require the board of education to register a five-year-old in the first grade.

A kindergarten issue of a somewhat different and perhaps conflicting nature recently came before the courts in the same state. In this instance a child had attended a kindergarten for most of a year, losing a small amount of time because of illness. At the end of the year the child was given a reading readiness test and failed to demonstrate the ability necessary for first-grade work. She did not attend school the following year but entered kindergarten again a year later and was again given the

[95]Elgin v. Silver, 182 N.Y.S.2d 669 (1958); New York State Association for Retarded Children v. Rockefeller, 357 F.Supp. 752 (N.Y. 1973).
[96]State v. Board of Education, 42 N.W.2d 168 (Neb. 1950).
[97]State ex rel. Mueller v. Common School Board of Joint School District No. 2 of City of Princeton, 242 N.W. 574 (Wis. 1932).
[98]Isquith v. Levitt, 137 N.Y.S.2d 493 (1954).

reading readiness test. On the basis of the test the parents were informed that the child would not be admitted to first grade but must continue in kindergarten. She attended kindergarten twenty days and withdrew from school because she was not permitted to attend first grade. Action was started under the compulsory attendance law to compel the child to attend school. The court held[99] that a child could not be compelled to attend kindergarten (school) under these circumstances, and the parents, willing to send the child to first grade, were not in violation of the compulsory attendance law. An implication of this case is that a child cannot be required to attend kindergarten under the compulsory attendance statutes even though it is part of the public school system.

12.14 ADMISSION TO FIRST GRADE

Boards of education have the power to establish the age for entrance to school. This is implied from the general authority to operate and maintain schools. They must, of course, establish an admission age that conforms to state statutes and may not establish regulations that are in violation of or prohibited by the state or federal Constitution.[100]

With the educational conviction that children generally are better prepared to profit by first-grade instruction when they are six years of age or older, a trend toward establishing higher first-grade entrance ages by state statutes and/or school board regulations is apparent. The ages established for entrance to first grade, in some cases, are higher than the age of guaranteed public education under the constitution. This does not necessarily render the statute or board rule unconstitutional, since free public education and entrance to first grade are not necessarily identical. In Montana, for example, the constitution required that education be provided for all children between the ages of six and twenty-one while the statutes required that a child to be admitted to the first grade be six on or before October 31. Under unusual circumstances children were admitted if they became six prior to November 15. A child who became six after the designated date attempted to enter school under his constitutional guarantee of free public education. When he reached age six, he and his parents contested the rule of the board of education as unconstitutional. The court ruled[101] that the

board of education had the legal authority to establish cutoff dates for entrance into first grade and that the above regulation was reasonable and valid.

In West Virginia the legality of a statute was questioned which provided that children who reached age six subsequent to the first day of November "shall not be admitted for the remainder of the term." When tested by court action, it was held[102] that such a law was neither unreasonable nor arbitrary. While the constitution of West Virginia was silent on the minimum age for free public education, the state statutes provided that schools should be open for the full school term to all children ages six to twenty-one.

In an early Illinois case it was held[103] that boards of education could adopt reasonable rules regarding the admission of children to school which would prevent children from entering first grade immediately after becoming six years of age. The regulation under consideration provided that children were entitled to enter school if they arrived at school age (six years) during the first month of school. This was held to be reasonable. However, another part of the rule provided that a child who arrived at school age a month after the opening of the fall term was not entitled to attend school during either the fall term or the winter term. An exclusion of this length of time the court held was unreasonable. It must be understood that each term was separate and distinct. Illinois does not specify an age for admission to schools in its constitution. The statutes in Illinois provide for free public education for all children over six and under the age of twenty-one.

In an early Massachusetts case it was held[104] that the legal definition of a scholar under the compulsory attendance law was not to be interpreted as the legal definition of a scholar for purposes of school attendance. Scholars under compulsory attendance would be limited to children between the ages of eight and fourteen. Scholars for school attendance purposes under the statute would include all children as soon as they had sufficient scholastic ability to profit by instruction until age twenty-one.

In another Massachusetts case it was held[105] that the board of education could

---

[99]In re Beverly Winters, 146 N.Y.S.2d 107 (1955).
[100]In re Kindergarten Schools, 32 Pac. 422 (Col. 1893).
[101]State v. School District of Fergus County, 348 P.2d 797 (Mont. 1960).

[102]Detch v. Board of Education, 117 S.E.2d 138 (W.Va. 1960).
[103]Board of Education v. Bolton, 85 Ill.App. 92 (1899).
[104]Inhabitants of Needham v. Inhabitants of Wellesley, 31 N.E. 732 (Mass. 1885).
[105]Alvord v. Inhabitants of Town of Chester, 61 N.E. 263 (Mass. 1901).

exclude from school a child under age seven unless he began in the fall term or within four weeks thereafter, or unless he was qualified to enter existing classes. No specified age for enrolling in free public education appeared in the Massachusetts constitution at the time.

In an Arizona case where statutes vested in school trustees the authority to exclude children under age six from primary grades it was held[106] that the statutes necessarily implied the power to admit children under that age. The Arizona constitution provides free public education for all children between the ages of six and twenty-one.

Whether boards of education may refuse admission to pupils transferring from another district who are younger than children admitted from their own district was at issue in Colorado and New York cases. It was held[107] that a school district requiring a child to attain the age of six by a specified date could not refuse to admit a transfer pupil even if the pupil was younger than the designated age. It was the opinion of the courts that the age of admission and the acceptance of transfer pupils were two distinct legal issues.

The Board of Regents of New York adopted a resolution that a child who was five years and eight months old who had attended a registered nonpublic kindergarten would be admitted to first grade. The same resolution provided that a child of the same age from a nonregistered nonpublic kindergarten would be admitted at the discretion of the administrator. This type of resolution, according to the courts,[108] was discriminatory and unconstitutional.

12.15 ADMISSION BY EXAMINATION

In a Kansas case it was held[109] that school boards have the right to require examinations for admission of children to high school from private and parochial schools while admitting children from public schools without examination. The court agreed that an examination to ascertain academic competence is a necessary aspect of the proper gradation of pupils, which is vested in the boards of education. The court also indicated, although this was not at issue, that a school board could require

elementary graduates from other public schools to take an examination. A Missouri case was to the same effect.[110] Thus, school boards may require examinations of pupils from some elementary schools while accepting a certificate of graduation from others without being guilty of discrimination.

12.16 ADMISSION OF OLDER PUPILS

The question of whether older pupils are entitled to free public education is determined by the wording and intent of state constitutions and/or state statutes as exhibited either by direct expression or by clear implication. The courts in interpreting the constitution or statutes will attempt to ascertain the intent of the makers. Unless an intent to provide free public education for the specific age group can be found, the courts have no alternative but to rule against free public education for the particular person or persons in the specified age group. Since age twenty-one is the highest age found in any constitutional guarantee, legislatures must make statutory provisions for free public education of persons beyond that age if it is to be granted.

Statutes may extend the privilege of free public education beyond high school and beyond twenty-one years of age. This was a court's interpretation[111] in a Washington, D.C., case in which a federal law provided that pupils whose parents were employed in that city were entitled to attend public schools without payment of tuition. A girl was permitted to continue to attend Wilson Teachers College without payment of tuition although she was over twenty-one years of age. The court decided that this was the intent of Congress since no age limit was specified.

It was held[112] in a Vermont case that a person who had reached the age of twenty-one was entitled to free public secondary education and to have his tuition paid. From a review of the statutes it was decided that it was the intent of the legislature to provide free secondary education without an age limit.

In North Dakota a boy who had failed to obtain sufficient credits for high school graduation in four years returned for a fifth year. The board of education had enacted a rule charging tuition to pupils who had already spent four years in high school. The

[106]Harkins v. School District No. 4, 288 P.2d 777 (Ariz. 1955).
[107]Simonson v. School District No. 14, 258 P.2d 1128 (Col. 1953); Fogel v. Goulding, 273 N.Y.S.2d 554 (1966); But see O'Leary v. Wisecup, 364 A.2d 770 (Pa. 1976).
[108]Jokinen v. Allen, 183 N.Y.S.2d 166 (1958).
[109]Creyhon v. Board of Education of City of Parsons, 163 Pac. 145 (Kan. 1917).
[110]Kayser v. Board of Education, 201 S.W. 531 (Mo. 1918).
[111]Cavanagh v. Ballou, 36 F.Supp. 445 (D.C. 1941).
[112]Town School District of St. Johnsbury v. Town School District of Topsham, 169 A.2d 352 (Vt. 1961).

court held[113] the rule unreasonable. However, it was held[114] in a New York case that a pupil who had graduated from the primary department earlier could not claim admission to the same department in the same school, particularly if there was no room for him.

The Wisconsin court in an early case held[115] that an overage pupil was not entitled to attend a manual training school without payment of tuition. Wisconsin statutes have subsequenty been amended to provide free high school education for overage pupils under certain conditions. However, the Supreme Court of Wisconsin held[116] that free public education does not extend to the university.

12.17 COMPULSORY ATTENDANCE

Compulsory attendance statutes have abrogated the common law which gave parents complete control over the education of their child or, indeed, the right to determine that the child should have no education at all. Parental control of a child's education was adopted from the English common law, which said in an early case, "a father is bound by every social tie to give his children an education suitable to their rank, but it is the duty of imperfect obligation, and could not be enforced in a court of law."[117]

In the United States it was held[118] that parents have control of their child except as modified by statute. This principle was restated in a later Oklahoma case.[119]

The constitutionality of compulsory attendance laws is now settled beyond dispute.[120] It repeatedly has been held that the natural rights of parents over their children in educational matters may be properly regulated and controlled by law. Compulsory attendance laws are a valid exercise of the police power of the state.[121] The obligation of parents to educate their children is one of the parents' most important duties, and they

may be forced by statutes to fulfill this obligation.[122]

Free public education has been established and enforced less as a right of children or their parents than as a demand imposed for the good of society. This concept has been expressed in a variety of ways in a number of states.[123] In essence the concept is: The purpose of establishing and supporting schools and requiring school attendance is not primarily to benefit the child or the parent. It is for the well-being and safety of the state itself. Its major purpose is the benefit of society.

12.17a Enforcement

However strongly the courts have endorsed and supported compulsory attendance statutes, they always have sustained the proposition that such laws must be enforced with reason. Courts always will consider the sufficiency of the reasons presented and determine whether they justify noncompliance with compulsory attendance statutes. Thus, parents may establish the defense that there was sufficient reason for keeping their children out of school. For example, parents are not required to send their children to school if the route is so dangerous that they have a genuine and justifiable concern for the safety of the children.[124] It was held[125] that a mother could not be prosecuted for violation of compulsory attendance laws when she taught the child at home in lieu of sending the child to a school which would have necessitated traveling a lonely road poorly maintained and unfenced. Pupils may be excused from compulsory attendance if they live a long distance from school and no transportation is provided.[126] Illness is an incontestable excuse for nonattendance under compulsory attendance laws,[127] and if a child is, in fact, ill and the parent withdraws the child from school in good faith and believing it necessary for the child's health and welfare, compulsory attendance is excused.

Parents may not establish the defense under compulsory attendance laws that they intended to send their child to a pri-

---

[113]Batty v. Board of Education of City of Williston, 269 N.W. 49 (N.D. 1936).

[114]People v. Board of Education, 4 N.Y.S. 102 (1888).

[115]Maxcy v. City of Oshkosh, 128 N.W. 899 (Wis. 1910).

[116]State v. Regents of University, 11 N.W. 472 (Wis. 1882).

[117]Hodges v. Hodges, Peake Add.Cas. 79, 170 Eng.Rep. 201 (1796).

[118]School Board District No. 18 v. Thompson, 103 Pac. 578 (Okla. 1909).

[119]Sheppard v. State, 306 P.2d 346 (Okla. 1957).

[120]State v. Bailey, 61 N.E. 730, 59 L.R.A. 435 (Ind. 1901); Sheehan v. Scott, 520 F.2d 825 (7th Cir. 1975).

[121]Commonwealth v. Bey, 70 A.2d 693 (Pa. 1950); State v. Jackson, 53 Atl. 1021, 60 L.R.A. 739 (N.H. 1902); State v. Garber, 419 P.2d 896 (Kan. 1966).

[122]State v. Bailey, 61 N.E. 730 (Ind. 1901).

[123]Bissell v. Davison, 32 Atl. 348 (Conn. 1894); State v. Bailey, 61 N.E. 730 (Ind. 1901); State v. McCaffrey, 37 Atl. 234 (Vt. 1896).

[124]Williams v. Board of Education, 99 Pac. 216 (Kan. 1908).

[125]Directors of School District No. 302 v. Libby, 237 Pac. 505 (Wash. 1925); In re Richards, 7 N.Y.S.2d 722 (1938).

[126]State v. Hall, 64 Atl. 1102 (N.H. 1906); In re Richards, 7 N.Y.S.2d 722 (1938).

[127]State v. Jackson, 53 Atl. 1021 (N.H. 1902).

vate school later.[128] Where the statute requires attendance beginning with the opening of school and continuing for a specified number of weeks, parents must send their child to some school either public or private immediately, at the opening of the school term. The courts will not countenance undue procrastination. There must be compliance at the earliest practicable date. The religious belief of parents who consider it their duty to teach their children themselves does not exempt the parents from compliance with reasonable civil requirements imposed by statutes.[129] In the same case it was decided that where statutes required the attendance of children in school, parents have no constitutional right to avail themselves of free public education during a portion of the week and refuse to have their children attend school on Fridays because it is a religious holiday.

In 1972 the United States Supreme Court was required to determine whether Amish children within the compulsory school age could be compelled to attend school beyond the eighth grade. While the Court affirmed the constitutionality of compulsory attendance laws, it held[130] that for the Amish people, compulsory school laws must give way to the free exercise of religion. The basis of the decision was that to deny the free exercise of religion required a state interest of sufficient magnitude to override the free exercise clause of the United States Constitution. Such a degree of state interest was not shown.

Where parents took a child out of school one afternoon a week for ballet lessons, they were adjudged[131] guilty of violating the compulsory attendance statutes. In Pennsylvania a father violently opposed daylight saving time and showed his opposition by directing his children to arrive at school every day one hour after the usual starting time. Action to force prompt attendance was brought under the compulsory attendance law, and the court held[132] that the parent was in violation of compulsory attendance by this practice of delayed attendance.

However, a resolution of the board of education in Chicago authorizing the superintendent to excuse pupils one hour per day for religious instruction off the school grounds was held[133] not to violate compulsory attendance laws. It was reasoned that school authorities have discretionary power to determine what constitutes a satisfactory excuse for absence from school.

To conform to the requirements of compulsory attendance children must be sent to schools where their grade placement and instruction are suitable to their attainments. In Indiana a father whose child had already graduated from the eighth grade attempted to send the child to an elementary school in an adjoining township. The court held[134] that inasmuch as the child had already graduated from the elementary school the parent was required to send his child to high school. This case affirmed an earlier decision of the same court which held[135] that an unemployed eighth-grade graduate under age fourteen (the age for compulsory attendance) could be required to attend high school since the high school was part of the common school system. However, a New York court reached a contrary conclusion. It held[136] that parents who were willing to send their daughter to first grade could not be prosecuted under the compulsory attendance law for failure to send her to kindergarten where tests indicated she should be placed.

12.18 ATTENDANCE AT PRIVATE SCHOOLS

An early leading case settled in the United States Supreme Court[137] established the principle that children cannot be compelled to attend public schools exclusively. The statute in Oregon requiring attendance in public schools, without exception was declared unconstitutional. Standards for nonpublic schools cannot be made so strict as to virtually eliminate all such schools. More recent cases have continued to hold that efforts to eliminate nonpublic schools are unconstitutional.[138] The basis for these decisions was found in the Fourteenth Amendment of the United States Constitution which provides that no person shall be

---

[128]State v. McCaffrey, 37 Atl. 234 (Vt. 1896).

[129]State v. Bailey, 61 N.E. 730 (Ind. 1901).

[130]Wisconsin v. Yoder, 406 U.S. 205, 92 S.Ct. 1526, 32 L.Ed.2d 15 (Wis. 1972).

[131]Commonwealth v. Rapine, 88 Pa. D.& C. 453 (1954).

[132]Commonwealth v. Schrock, 77 Pa. D.& C. 258 (1951).

[133]People v. Board of Education of the City of Chicago, 68 N.E.2d 305 (Ill. 1946).

[134]Miller v. State, 134 N.E. 209 (Ind. 1922).

[135]State v. ODell, 118 N.E. 529 (Ind. 1918).

[136]Re Beverly Winters, 146 N.Y S.2d 107 (1955).

[137]Pierce v. Society of Sisters, 268 U.S. 510, 45 S.Ct. 571, 69 L.Ed. 1070 (Ore. 1925).

[138]Roman Catholic Welfare Corporation v. City of Piedmont, 289 P.2d 438 (Cal. 1955); Special District for Education and Training of Handicapped Children of St. Louis County v. Wheeler, 408 S.W.2d 60 (Mo. 1966); State v. Whisner, 351 N.E.2d 750 (Ohio 1976).

deprived of property without due process of law. The right of parents to select their children's school is "property" within the meaning of the Fourteenth Amendment. The right to operate a school, private as well as parochial, also was held to be a "property" right. This decision clearly established the principle that states may not enact statutes which would have the effect of abolishing private schools. It is also clear that compulsory attendance statutes may be met by attendance at educationally recognized private and parochial schools.[139]

There are, however, certain limitations or restrictions on private school attendance. In a number of states, to meet compulsory attendance requirements the quality of education in the private school must be shown to be essentially equivalent to that in the public schools. An Ohio case involved the old order of the Amish Mennonite church which operated a one-room school in a frame building with no artificial lighting and heated by a coal stove. The school consisted of all eight grades, taught by one teacher who was not an eighth-grade graduate and who had no previous teaching experience. The court ruled[140] that compulsory attendance was not met by attendance at this type of school since the instruction was not equivalent to that in the public schools.

In Illinois several children of compulsory school age were not in public school attendance. When the parents were prosecuted under the compulsory attendance laws they claimed they had organized a private, parochial school which their children were attending. Since the law in Illinois requires that education in private schools or at home be equivalent to that offered in the public schools, the facts of the case were reviewed. The evidence indicated that the school was disorganized, lacked system, and had for the most part inexperienced teachers who taught without textbooks. On the basis of these facts the parents were found guilty of violation of the compulsory attendance statute.[141]

If parents insist on sending their child to a school which the school committee does not approve, they are within their rights if they can show that the school is, in fact, a satisfactory one. The purpose of the compulsory attendance law is to guarantee that all children be educated, not that they be educated in a specific manner in a specific type of school.[142] However, enrollment in correspondence courses does not meet the requirements of compulsory attendance in California. Here it was held[143] that this type of instruction was not a public or private school, or instruction by a qualified private tutor, as the law required. Statutes on compulsory attendance are to be liberally construed, but they must be complied with, and education not within the purview of the statutes is not acceptable.

12.19 EDUCATION AT HOME

Frequently parents will attempt to educate their children at home instead of sending them to a public or private school. In a number of states home instruction is permissible if the educational program provided is essentially equivalent to that offered in the public schools[144] and is effective.[145] In some cases in which education outside public and private schools is legally acceptable, the burden of proof that the education provided is not satisfactory is on school authorities. In Oklahoma,[146] and in two Missouri cases,[147] in the absence of proof that children were not receiving the same type of education at home as in a public or private school, the courts refused to hold the parents guilty of violating the compulsory attendance law. However, according to the weight of authority, the burden of proof is on the parents to show that an educational program is provided outside the regularly organized school and that it is substantially equivalent to that offered in the public schools.[148] Whether the facilities for education outside the public schools are equivalent to those afforded by the state is a question of fact for the jury.[149]

When tutoring is provided, it need not be in the same branches of learning as those taught in the public schools if a pupil has achieved a satisfactory degree of competence in those areas, according to a Massachusetts decision.[150] In England, where

[139]Special District for Education and Training of Handicapped Children of St. Louis County v. Wheeler, 408 S.W.2d 60 (Mo. 1966).
[140]State v. Hershberger, 144 N.E.2d 693 (Ohio 1955).
[141]People v. Harrell, 180 N.E.2d 889 (Ill. 1962).

[142]Commonwealth v. Roberts, 34 N.E. 402 (Mass. 1893); People v. Levisen, 90 N.E.2d 213 (Ill. 1950).
[142]Shinn v. People, 195 Cal.App.2d 683 (1961).
[144]State v. Peterman, 70 N.E. 550 (Ind. 1904).
[145]Ibid.; Commonwealth v. Roberts, 34 N.E. 402 (Mass. 1893); Wright v. State, 209 Pac. 179 (Okla. 1922); People v. Levisen, 90 N.E.2d 213 (Ill. 1950).
[146]Sheppard v. State, 306 P.2d 346 (Okla. 1957); Wright v. State, 209 Pac. 179 (Okla. 1922).
[147]State v. Cheney, 305 S.W.2d 892 (Mo. 1957); State v. Pilkimton, 310 S.W.2d 304 (Mo. 1958).
[148]Commonwealth v. Roberts, 34 N.E. 402 (Mass. 1893); People v. Levisen, 90 N.E.2d 213 (Ill. 1950).
[149]Wright v. State, 209 Pac. 179 (Okla. 1922).
[150]Commonwealth v. Roberts, 34 N.E. 402 (Mass. 1893).

parents are accorded greater freedom of choice in subjects pursued by their children, it was held[151] that children were not required to study the same subjects as are offered in the public schools to meet the requirements of compulsory attendance.

In some states social contact with other children has been held[152] to be so important that the child must attend a school, either public or private. This is especially true where the compulsory attendance statutes require attendance at a public or private school and make no mention of tutoring or instruction at home.[153] In Washington, where the statute demands attendance of all children between the ages of eight and sixteen at a public or private school, instruction at home by a mother not qualified as a teacher did not meet the statutory requirement. In Virginia, where the statutes specified that teachers of children at home have the qualifications prescribed by the state board of education and be approved by the division superintendent, the question of sufficiency of the teaching and of the quality of the education received was immaterial,[154] since the statutory qualification requirement had not been met in the instant case.

In Kansas the law required "that every parent or other person . . . having control or charge of any child . . . shall require such child to attend continuously a public school or a private, denominational or parochial school taught by a competent instructor . . . for such periods as the public school of the district in which the child resides is in session." Under this statute instruction in a correspondence course approved for certain purposes by the United States Office of Education and attendance one morning a week in a school instructed by an unqualified teacher did not suffice.[155]

12.20 COMPULSORY ATTENDANCE OF MARRIED PUPILS

Whether a married child is subject to the provisions of the compulsory attendance act has been before the court on a number of occasions. It commonly has been held that the marriage relationship, regardless of the age of the person, imposes obligations inconsistent with school attendance. In

Louisiana cases it was held[156] that fourteen- and fifteen-year-old married women were not "children" under the compulsory attendance act and could not be compelled to attend school. The court also held that the obligations of a married woman are inconsistent with school attendance. The same decision was rendered[157] in a case regarding the compulsory attendance of a fourteen-year-old married woman in New York. These decisions seem to imply that if circumstances were different, i.e., if there were no obligations inconsistent with school attendance and married persons were not specifically excluded under compulsory attendance statutes, they might be required to attend school until they had attained the required age. This was the opinion of the Attorney General under an earlier Wisconsin statute.[158]

12.21 SPECIAL ASPECTS OF COMPULSORY ATTENDANCE

When parents objected to public school attendance on religious grounds, they were not upheld in a Kansas case.[159] In a Pennsylvania case[160] exemption from compulsory attendance was sought on religious ground and because of dire financial necessity. The court reiterated the principle that the right to believe is absolute but the freedom to act is not and that religious beliefs are not legal justification for violation of positive law. While the child might have been excused from attendance because of "dire financial circumstances," this was not established by the parents.

Virginia cases touched upon a number of specific points related to compulsory attendance: whether the reasons given in statutes were exhaustive; whether the fact that parents did not intend to violate the law was material; whether the adequacy of instruction was material; whether a tutor must have designated qualifications; and whether religious beliefs were justification for nonattendance. In these cases it was held[161] that enumeration of valid reasons in the statutes for not sending a child to school was deemed exhaustive and precluded submitting another reason to the jury for determination of validity. The fact that the

---

[151]Bevan v. Shears, 2 K.B. 936 (1911).

[152]State v. Counort, 124 Pac. 910 (Wash. 1912); State v. Lowry, 383 P.2d 962 (Kan. 1963); *Matter of* Franz, 378 N.Y.S.2d 317 (1976).

[153]State v. Counort, 124 Pac. 910 (Wash. 1912); State Superior Court v. King County Juvenile Court, 346 P.2d 999 (Wash. 1960); *In re* Davis, 318 A.2d 151 (N.H. 1974).

[154]Rice v. Commonwealth, 49 S.E.2d 342 (Va. 1948).

[155]State v. Garber, 419 P.2d 896 (Kan. 1966).

[156]In re State in Interest of Goodwin, 39 So.2d 731 (La. 1949); State v. Priest, 27 So.2d 173 (La. 1946).

[157]In re Rogers, 234 N.Y.S.2d 172 (1962).

[158]Opinion of Wisconsin Attorney General cited as 37 OAG 8 (1948).

[159]State v. Garber, 419 P.2d 896 (Kan. 1966).

[160]Commonwealth v. Smoker, 110 A.2d 740 (Pa. 1955).

[161]Dobbins v. Commonwealth, 96 S.E.2d 154 (Va. 1957); Rice v. Commonwealth, 49 S.E.2d 342 (Va. 1948).

parents did not intend to violate the law and commit a crime in not sending their children to school was immaterial. If compulsory education statutes require children to be in school or to be taught by a tutor of designated qualifications, the adequacy of instruction is immaterial. The fact that the parents interpreted the Bible as compelling them to teach their own children did not excuse them from compliance with compulsory attendance laws.

Dual enrollment programs whereby a child enrolls part time in the public schools and part time in parochial schools meet the requirement of compulsory attendance.[162] In this connection the court restated the accepted judicial opinion that the object of compulsory attendance is to guarantee that all children be educated, not that they be educated in a particular way.

In the enforcement of compulsory attendance laws in some situations the courts appear to have been unusually lenient. In one case it was held[163] that parents had the right to temporarily excuse a child from school attendance if there were good reasons. Leniency was again shown in a somewhat unusual case which held[164] that the lower court had erred in placing a child in the custody of the court when truancy was not extreme and had taken place with the knowledge and acceptance of the mother. Actually, many absences from school due to truancy are within the knowledge of the parents. Other states have not considered parents' knowledge that pupils were not in school an excuse under compulsory attendance laws.

The father of a black child was prosecuted for violation of the compulsory attendance law when he refused to send his daughter to a black school which had inferior facilities and lacked educational advantages. He had attempted to enroll his daughter in a school for white children but was refused permission to do so. The Virginia court held[165] that under these circumstances he was not guilty of violating the compulsory attendance law.

12.22 RESIDENCE FOR SCHOOL PURPOSES

12.22a Determination of
Whether a child is entitled to be admitted to the schools of a district and to attend free of tuition depends on whether the child has a domicile in the district and/or is a resident for school purposes. For a clear understanding of the decisions of the courts it is necessary to understand what is meant by residence and domicile of pupils and their parents. These terms are legally defined as follows:[166] a *domicile* is a person's true, fixed and permanent home and principal establishment, to which, when absent, the person intends to return, not for a mere special or temporary purpose, but with the present intention of making a permanent home, for an unlimited or indefinite period. A *residence* is a factual place of abode or living in a particular locality. It requires only bodily presence as an inhabitant of a place.

The domicile of children ordinarily follows that of the parents. When parents are separated, the domicile of the children is normally with the father. However, if the mother or some other person has been given legal custody of the children, the domicile of the children is where the person having legal control over them resides. When there has been no legal separation or legal custody awarded, the children may be able to gain domicile for school purposes when living with the mother or in a home in which the children have been placed by the mother.

12.22b Residing in district for nonschool purposes
As a general rule, the children will be able to attend school without payment of tuition in the district where their parents or legal guardians reside. If parents need to be in the school district even temporarily for purposes other than school attendance of their children, i.e., if their work is there or if their business requires them to live there, their children are entitled to attend school free of tuition. Three cases illustrate this principle.

In a Missouri case a person leased a building for three years for use as an office and home and moved the family in from a farm in another district for most of the year. Other circumstances indicated that the family considered it their home. The place was adjudged[167] the person's legal domicile and no tuition was chargeable. In a Nebraska case where the statute provided free public education for all children who "lived" in the district, it was held[168] that the governor and state superintendent were entitled to send their children to school tuition free in

[162]Morton v. Board of Education of City of Chicago, 216 N.E.2d 305 (Ill. 1966).
[163]Holmes v. Nester, 306 P.2d 290 (Ariz. 1957).
[164]*In re* Miller, 209 N.Y.S.2d 964 (1961).
[165]Dobbins v. Commonwealth of Virginia, 96 S.E.2d 154 (Va. 1957).

[166]Adapted from *Black's Law Dictionary* (St. Paul, Minn.: West Publishing Co., 1951).
[167]Northern v. McCow, 175 S.W. 317 (Mo. 1915).
[168]State v. Sellech, 107 N.W. 1022 (Neb. 1906).

the capital city even though they maintained their legal domicile elsewhere. In a New Hampshire case a mother had been given custody of the son in a divorce agreement some years earlier. The son did not live with the father during the summer but lived with him during the school year. The major reason why the son lived with the father was that the humidity where the mother lived affected the boy's asthma. Under these circumstances the court held[169] that the son was entitled to have his tuition to a high school paid by the school district of the father's residence. The law required school districts which did not maintain a high school to pay the tuition of the resident children desiring to attend high school. A number of recent cases reiterate the above principles.[170] The controlling element in these cases was that the parents or children had not moved into the school district for the primary purpose of securing school privileges.

12.22c Residing in
district for school purposes
If parents move into the district for the sole or primary purpose of taking advantage of the school district's educational facilities, they are not entitled to education for their children without payment of tuition. The courts have been required to adjudicate a number of cases related to this principle.

Parents who attempt to avoid payment of tuition by moving into the school district after school has begun and a legal controversy over payment of tuition has started will be required to pay tuition, as will people who have moved into the district without intention of living there with any degree of permanency.[171] When each autumn a father moved his family and a portion of his household goods to a district and returned to the farm at the end of the school year, the evidence indicated that the move to the district was primarily for school purposes and the family was liable for tuition.[172]

In Kansas a mother moved with her children from the family farm to town in the fall

so the children could attend school there and back to the farm during the summer. The father remained on the farm except for weekends. The children were ruled nonresidents of the town district and were not entitled to attend school tuition free.[173]

12.22d Residing in
district from physical necessity
When there is a genuine physical necessity for a child to live with a relative or some person other than a parent, tuition generally is not chargeable. A number of cases substantiate this principle.

In Michigan it was held[174] that the following children were entitled to instruction in the public schools without payment of tuition: Two orphans residing with their sister; a child living with an aunt; an orphan living with a woman, not a relative; a child living with a grandfather. In none of the instances had the children been adopted, nor had the persons having custody been appointed legal guardians.

In a Missouri case it was held[175] that a child, living continuously with a grandfather who had control of the child, whose parents did not contribute anything to the child's support, was entitled to attend school without payment of tuition. In establishing the fact that the child was not residing in the district primarily for school purposes, the court took judicial notice of the fact that there were good schools in the district where the parents lived. In this case the court commented that statutes relating to school attendance should be liberally construed, "so as to open and not close the doors of the school against the children of the state."

In a case decided in Nebraska it was held[176] that a girl who lived with her brother-in-law under an agreement that she would reside with his family until she became of age was entitled to free schooling in the district. In another Nebraska case[177] a motherless child left with a relative who had agreed to raise, educate, and treat the child in all respects as her own was entitled to free education. Legal adoption was not necessary in either of the above cases.

A Pennsylvania statute provided that when a child was supported gratis in a

[169]Luoma v. Union School District, 214 A.2d 120 (N.H. 1965).

[170]Hanson v. Unified School District No. 500, 364 F.Supp. 300 (Kan. 1973); State ex rel. Doe v. Kingery, 203 S.E.2d 258 (W.Va. 1974); Brownsville Independent School District v. Gamboa, 498 S.W.2d 448 (Tex. 1973).

[171]School District v. Matherly, 84 Mo.App. 140 (1900); See also School District v. Matherly, 90 Mo.App. 403 (1901); Barnard School District v. Matherly, 76 S.W. 1109 (Mo. 1903); Smith v. Binford, 256 Pac. 366 (Ida. 1972).

[172]State v. School District, 75 N.W. 855 (Neb. 1898).

[173]Sulzen v. School District No. 36, 62 P.2d 880 (Kan. 1936).

[174]Public Schools of City of Muskegon v. Wright, 141 N.W. 866 (Mich. 1913).

[175]State v. Clyner, 147 S.W. 1119 (Mo. 1912).

[176]Mizner v. School District, 96 N.W. 128 (1901) and 96 N.W. 1006 (Neb. 1903).

[177]McNish v. State, 104 N.W. 186 (Neb. 1905).

home he was entitled to free public education. In a case[178] considered under this statute a child who was housed, clothed, fed, and supported by an aunt was entitled to attend school without the payment of tuition.

Children have been held to be entitled to free public education in circumstances similar to those described above in Connecticut,[179] Illinois,[180] Iowa,[181] Kansas,[182] Kentucky,[183] a later Nebraska case,[184] North Dakota,[185] Ohio,[186] South Dakota,[187] West Virginia,[188] and Wisconsin.[189]

Admittedly, there are cases in which children living with relatives were charged tuition. Cases in New York and Illinois dealt with this issue.[190] In New York it was held that in the absence of evidence that the parents had actually released control and custody of the child to the aunt who was caring for the child free schooling could not be compelled. The court indicated that a putative residence of a child in a district, established for the purpose of taking advantage of school facilities, does not require that the child receive an education at the expense of resident taxpayers. The court did indicate that a child could have a residence for school purposes other than where the child's parents resided, but not in this case. In Illinois, where a child lived in a district different from his parents for the purpose of attending school there, he was not considered a resident for school purposes. However, the weight of authority and humanitarian considerations argue for tuition-free education for children in the unfortunate circumstances of being forced by necessity to live with persons other than their own parents.

12.22e Residing in private and boarding homes

The principles which apply to children living with relatives are also applicable to children living in boarding and private homes apart from relatives. When it is clear that the child is not primarily in the district to receive the advantage of public schools but is there for arrangements of living and livelihood, the child is generally entitled to free education. The arrangements must be such that the person having custody of the child does in fact have parental responsibility which must be more than of a temporary nature. Where resident children are entitled to free bus transportation, this right belongs equally to children living in private homes, where they have been so placed to provide them with a "good home."[191] Where children are placed in a private home by a children's aid society, they are entitled to free schooling in the district.[192] However, where a child is boarded in the district during the week and returns home weekends the child is not entitled to free schooling.[193] Nor are inmates of a boarding school residents for school purposes[194] where there is no evidence that the parent has surrendered control of the children.[195] When money for custody and upkeep of children is paid by parents or custodians, or agencies of some other district, those responsible for support of the children are also responsible for the payment of their tuition.[196]

12.22f Residing in institutions

Whether children living in an institution are entitled to attend the local school without payment of tuition has been questioned in many jurisdictions. It has been held that these children are entitled to free schooling in Illinois,[197] Iowa,[198] Kansas,[199] Ken-

---

[178]Confluence Borough School District v. Ursina Borough School District, 88 Pa.Super. 299 (1926).

[179]Yale v. West Middle School District, 22 Atl. 295 (Conn. 1890).

[180]Board of Education v. Lease, 64 Ill.App. 60 (1895) People v. Board of Education, 206 Ill. App. 381 (1917).

[181]Mt. Hope School District v. Hendrickson, 197 N.W. 47 (Iowa 1924).

[182]Mariadahl Children's Home v. Bellegarde School District, 180 P.2d 612 (Kan. 1947).

[183]Board of Trustees of Stanford Graded School District v. Powell, 140 S.W. 67 (Ky. 1911).

[184]Martins v. School District, 162 N.W. 631 (Neb. 1917).

[185]Anderson v. Breithbarth, 245 N.W. 483 (N.D. 1932).

[186]Board of Education v. Dille, 165 N.E.2d 807 (Ohio 1959).

[187]Independent School District v. Bordewyk, 241 N.W. 619 (S.D. 1932).

[188]Morrison v. Smith Pocahontas Coal Co., 106 S.E. 448 (W.Va. 1921).

[189]State v. Thayer, 41 N.W. 1014 (Wis. 1889).

[190]Drayton v. Baron, 276 N.Y.S.2d 924(1967); Turner v. Board of Education of North Chicago Community H.S. District 123, 294 N.E.2d 264 (Ill. 1973).

[191]Fangman v. Mayers, 8 P.2d 762 (Col. 1932).

[192]Dean v. Board of Education District No. 89, 53 N.E.2d 875 (Ill. 1944); People v. Hendrickson, 90 N.E. 1163 (N.Y. 1908).

[193]State v. School District No. 12, Niobrara County, 18 P.2d 1010 (Wyo. 1933).

[194]Mansfield Township Board of Education v. State Board of Education, 129 Atl. 765 (N.J. 1925).

[195]Horowitz v. Board of Education, 216 N.Y.S. 646 (1926).

[196]Black v. Graham, 86 Atl. 266 (Pa. 1913); Dumpson v. Board of Education, 214 N.Y.S.2d 196 (1961).

[197]Ashley v. Board of Education, 114 N.E. 20 (Ill. 1916); Logsdon v. Jones, 143 N.E. 56 (Ill. 1924); Dean v. Board of Education of School District No. 89, 53 N.E.2d 875 (Ill. 1944).

[198]Salem Independent School District v. Kiel, 221 N.W. 519 (Iowa 1928); School Township 76 of Muscatine County v. Nicholson, 288 N.W. 123 (Iowa 1939).

[199]Mariadahl Children's Home v. Bellegarde School District No. 23, 180 P.2d 612 (Kan. 1947).

tucky,[200] Michigan,[201] Minnesota,[202] New Hampshire,[203] South Dakota,[204] and West Virginia.[205] In Wisconsin, a child in a licensed child welfare agency is eligible to participate in the benefits of the school district despite the fact that the institution is of a proprietary nature.[206] In Ohio,[207] Pennsylvania,[208] and Vermont[209] and in other states it has been held that children living in an institution are not entitled to attend school without payment of tuition. Where children have not been entitled to attend school in the district tuition free, there have been exceptional circumstances in each case. The following are typical:

1. The institution had agreed in its charter to provide an education for the children.
2. The charter was silent on education and the home had made ample provisions.
3. The state provided a teacher for the home.
4. The district of legal residence of the child was required by law to pay the tuition.

One of the best analyses of the apparent conflict of cases relating to tuition of children living in children's homes and exceptions to the general rule of tuition-free attendance is that of Garber.

The exceptions to the general rule are, on the whole, more apparent than real. For example, two of the Ohio cases appear to have been decided in terms of a statute that made the school district in which a child had formerly resided liable for his tuition when he became an inmate of a home of the sort involved there. Also, one of the Pennsylvania cases involved

an interpretation of two statutes. One provided that the residence of a child who has no parents or guardian shall be considered to be in the district in which the person who sustains a parental relationship toward the child resides. Another provided that a board of school directors of a district in which an orphans' home was located could permit children who were inmates of the home, but who were not residents, to attend school with or without payment of tuition. It also provided that if tuition was charged it was to be paid for by the district from which the child had come.

Again, in one Pennsylvania and in one Michigan case, at least one decisive factor influencing the court's opinion was the fact that the charitable institution or home was created in part for the purpose of educating the children admitted. It should also be pointed out that the Vermont case has a slightly different angle than most of the other cases. Here, the court held that where a town supported its pauper children in a poorhouse operated jointly with other towns, the education of the child remained the responsibility of the town from which the child came and did not shift to the town in which the poorhouse was located.

If these cases, just commented upon, are ignored, it is apparent that the exceptions to the general rule—minor inmates of charitable institutions are entitled to attend schools tuition-free in the districts in which the institutions are located—are comparitively few in number.[210]

12.22g Residing on government land

Originally there was serious question as to whether children living on federal government land such as army posts, Indian reservations, defense areas, and public housing projects were entitled to free public education. Early cases in Massachusetts,[211] Ohio,[212] and South Dakota[213] held that the children were not entitled to attend local schools without payment of tuition. Pennsylvania cases of a more recent date have rendered the same decision.[214] However, most recent cases go in the opposite direction. The decisions seem to hinge on the question of whether the federal govern-

[200]Crain v. Walker, 2 S.W.2d 654 (Ky. 1928); Jefferson County Board of Education v. Goheen, 207 S.W.2d 567 (Ky. 1947); Wirth v. Board of Education of Jefferson County, 90 S.W.2d 62 (Ky. 1936); Board of Education of Louisville v. Board of Education of Jefferson County, 97 S.W.2d 11 (Ky. 1936).

[201]Child Welfare Society v. Kennedy School District, 189 N.W. 1002 (Mich. 1922).

[202]State v. School Board of Consolidated School District No. 3, 287 N.W. 625 (Minn. 1939).

[203]School District No. 2 v. Pollard, 55 N.H. 503 (1875).

[204]State v. Cotton, 289 N.W. 71 (S.D. 1939).

[205]Grand Lodge I.O.O.F. of West Virginia v. Board of Education, 110 S.E. 440 (W. Va. 1922); State ex rel. Doe v. Kingery, 203 S.E.2d 358 (W.Va. 1974).

[206]Browndale International v. Board of Adjustment, 208 N.W.2d 121 (Wis. 1973).

[207]State v. Sherman, 135 N.E. 625 (Ohio 1922); State v. Eveland, 158 N.E. 169 (Ohio 1927); State v. Board of Education, 138 N.E. 865 (Ohio 1922).

[208]School District of Borough of Ben Avon v. School District of Pittsburgh, 77 Pa.Super. 75 (1921); Commonwealth v. Directors of Upper Swataro Township School District, 30 Atl. 507 (Pa. 1894).

[209]Sheldon Poor House Association v. Town of Sheldon, 47 Atl. 542 (Vt. 1900).

[210]Lee O. Garber, *School Pupils and the Law*, School of Law, Duke University, Vol. 20, No. 1, Winter 1955, chap. 2, p. 43.

[211]Opinion of Justice, 42 Mass. (1 Met.) 580 (1840).

[212]State v. Board of Education, 57 N.E.2d 118 (Ohio 1944).

[213]School District No. 20 v. Steele, 195 N.W. 448 (S.D. 1923); Rockwell v. Independent School District, 202 N.W. 478 (S.D. 1925).

[214]Schwartz v. O'Hara Twp. School District, 100 A.2d 621 (Pa. 1953). See also Volpe v. O'Hara, 101 Pittsburgh Leg.J. 223 (Pa. 1953).

ment has taken exclusive jurisdiction. Unless exclusive jurisdiction has been taken by the federal government, children are entitled to attend the local schools without payment of tuition.[215] Recent instances of the federal government's taking exclusive jurisdiction are exceedingly rare.

12.22h Emancipated minors

Emancipated minors are entitled to attend school without payment of tuition in the district in which they reside. An emancipated minor is one who is self-sufficient and has no intention of returning to the parents' residence. These minors may acquire legal residence in the same manner as adults. In a Wisconsin case[216] a boy took up his residence and attended school in a different district with no intention of living at home after his father told him he would be unable to help him secure a high school education, and it was agreed he would be his own master and seek his own livelihood. Under the laws of Wisconsin this boy was entitled to attend school tuition free if he was an emancipated minor. In this case the court defined an emancipated minor as one who is released and set free from the care, custody, control and service of a parent. The relinquishing of control and authority over the child by the parent conferred on him the right to his earnings and terminated the parent's legal duty to support the child. This was done, informally, in the judgment of the court, and the boy was entitled to attend school tuition free. While courts have upheld the right of emancipated minors to attend school free of tuition, they would not permit two young girls living with a 21-year old man to attend school tuition-free in the district where he resided.[217] Emancipation of minors need not be an expressed act of parents; it may be inferred from circumstances and conduct of the parties.[218]

12.22i Ownership of property or business

The fact that parents conduct a business or own property and pay taxes in a school district does not make the children residents of that district for school purposes un-

less the statutes so provide.[219] This is illustrated in a case[220] in which a parent lived in one district and operated a restaurant in another. The children were not entitled to attend school without payment of tuition in the district where the restaurant was located since they did not live there. The only exception to the rule that ownership of property in a district does not grant tuition-free education is found where state statutes specifically provide that children acquire school residence in districts in which their parents own property. Where the statutes so provide, it is immaterial that property is acquired for this specific purpose or that the property acquired is of little relative value.[221]

12.22j Tuition-free status

The principle developed in the preceding tuition cases may be summarized by stating that it is the intention of the state for all children within its borders to have free education, and to assure this privilege school residence is to be liberally construed.[222]

An early Tennessee case carried this interpretation to an extreme. Children in this state could attend school tuition free when the statutes so provided, even though they were not residents of the district, according to one court decision.[223] Needless to say, this does not represent the weight of authority. Other jurisdictions have held that "the rule of taxation shall be uniform" and taxpayers in one school district may not be required through local taxation to provide for the education of children from neighboring districts.

12.22k Admission of nonresidents

Whether a school district is required to admit nonresidents if it does not desire to do so depends on statutes. Most states, of which Michigan,[224] Ohio,[225] Washington,[226] and Wisconsin[227] are examples, make admission of nonresident pupils optional with local districts. In a Pennsylvania

---

[215]McGwinn v. Board of Education of Cleveland City School District, 69 N.E.2d 381 (Ohio 1946); Tagge v. Gulzow, 271 N.W. 803 (Neb. 1937); Rolland v. School District, 271 N.W. 805 (Neb. 1937).

[216]Kidd v. Joint School District, 216 N.W. 499 (Wis. 1927); Wirsig v. Scott, 112 N.W. 655 (Neb. 1907).

[217]Clark v. Green, 290 A.2d 836 (Conn. 1971).

[218]Wurth v. Wurth, 322 S.W.2d 745 (Mo. 1959).

[219]Cape Girardeau School District No. 63 v. Frye, 225 S.W.2d 484 (Mo. 1949); Logan City School District v. Kowallis, 77 P.2d 348 (Utah 1938); Ferndale Area School District v. Shawley, 313 A.2d 366 (Pa. 1973).

[220]State v. Rogers, 77 N.E.2d 594 (Ind. 1948).

[221]Mosely v. Welch, 62 S.E.2d 313 (S.C. 1950).

[222]Yale v. West Middle School District, 22 Atl. 295 (Conn. 1890).

[223]Edmonson v. Board of Education, 108 Tenn. 557 (Pickle 24) (1902).

[224]Michigan Compiled Laws, 340.582 (1970).

[225]Page's Ohio Revised Code Annotated, Title 33, 33.13.64 (1972).

[226]Revised Code of Washington, 28A.58.240 (1970).

[227]Wisconsin Statutes 121.77(1) (1972).

case it was held[228] that, under a statute which provided that pupils residing in a school district with no high school could attend the nearest or most convenient high school, the receiving high school was required to accept the students.

12.23 SCHOOL ATTENDANCE AND SEGREGATION

12.23a Introduction

On May 17, 1954, the United States Supreme Court in the case of *Brown v. Board of Education* made obsolete the doctrine of "separate but equal" for the different races.[229] The "separate but equal" doctrine, which had influenced court decisions and served as precedent since 1849,[230] was overruled. In the Brown case the Supreme Court declared that segregated public school facilities were inherently unequal and violated the "equal protection" clause of the Fourteenth Amendment to the United States Constitution. On the same day the United States Supreme Court ruled[231] that segregation of children in public schools in the District of Columbia violated the "due process" clause of the Fifth Amendment. These decisions now constitute the "law of the land," and when state constitutional provisions and state legislation are in conflict they must give way.

Cases on segregation decided before 1954 are now of only historical significance and will not be cited. "The law" is found in decisions since that date. In view of the volume of cases, many of them touching on the same or nearly the same point, it appears more fruitful to attempt to identify legal principles and authoritative statements and to document them with citations from federal and state court decisions than to present a historical review.

12.23b Segregation prohibited

Since 1954 the courts have left no doubt that segregation must end. Black children must be permitted to attend integrated schools and to participate in all aspects of the school program including extracurricular activities on a nondiscriminatory basis.[232] Boards of education are not permit-

ted to classify pupils by race, and it is immaterial whether such classification is sought from sentiment, tradition, caprice, or the exercise of police power.[233] Nor are school districts permitted to discontinue the operation of some public schools to avoid integration. To allow some children to attend public schools in a state while other children are denied the right to attend school at public expense because schools are closed to avoid desegregation is discriminatory.[234]

The fact that state statutes or constitutional provisions regarding racial segregation are declared unconstitutional does not make related provisions requiring the operation of a uniform system of public schools unconstitutional.[235] It is not legally permissible to use public funds to pay the tuition of pupils attending nonsectarian private schools to avoid integration.[236] Nor may school districts sell buildings to be used as an all-white academy.[237] It also has been held to be improper for a state board of education to furnish textbooks and supplies to a segregated private academy.[238] However, in two decisions it was held[239] that kindergartens are not subject to overall desegregation plans.

A city district may not educate its white children in its own schools and contract with a neighboring county district to educate its black children.[240] Neither may a county district operate a high school for white children and assign black children to high schools outside the county.[241]

Segregated schools may not be maintained even if done so by the expressed desire of black people or the mutual consent of blacks and whites.[242] Even if the board of education maintains a school attended by both races, it may not legally maintain other

[228]School District of Chester Township v. School District of City of Chester, 210 A.2d 501 (Pa. 1965).

[229]Brown v. Board of Education of Topeka, Kansas, 347 U.S. 483, 74 S.Ct. 686, 98 L.Ed. 873 (Kan. 1954).

[230]Roberts v. City of Boston, 59 Mass. 198 (1849).

[231]Bolling v. Sharpe, 347 U.S. 497, 74 S.Ct. 693, 98 L.Ed. 884 (D.C. 1954).

[232]Monroe v. Board of Commissioners, 244 F.Supp. 353 (Tenn. 1965).

[233]Orleans Parish School Board v. Bush, 242 F.2d 156 (5th Cir. 1957).

[234]James v. Almond, 170 F.Supp. 331 (Va. 1959)

[235]Harrison v. Day, 106 S.E.2d 636 (Va. 1959).

[236]Ibid.

[237]Wright v. City of Brighton, 441 F.2d 447 (5th Cir. 1971); McNeil v. Tate City School District, 460 F.2d 568 (5th Cir. 1971).

[238]Graham v. Evangeline Parish School Board, 484 F.2d 649 (5th Cir. 1973).

[239]Davis v. Board of Education of North Little Rock School District, 362 F.Supp. 730 (Ark, 1973); Thompson v. School Board of City of Newport News, 363 F.Supp. 458 (Va. 1973).

[240]Goins v. County School Board, 186 F.Supp. 753 (Va. 1960).

[241]Griffith v. Board of Education, 186 F.Supp. 511 (N.C. 1960).

[242]Cameron v. Board of Education, 318 P.2d 988 (Kan. 1957).

schools exclusively for blacks and exclusively for whites.[243]

While it is not mandatory for all the children from the same attendance area to go to the same school, the maintenance of two attendance areas, one for black children and one for white children, is not permissible.[244] This clearly is segregation and discrimination. Where the statutes make different provisions for white and for black children, black children may bring action for the same privileges granted white children.[245] Educational opportunities which the state has undertaken to provide must be available to all on equal terms. This right is guaranteed not only by the United States Constitution, but by the Civil Rights Act of 1964.[246]

Boards of education are not permitted to establish reasons for failure to proceed with integration even if the reasons seem sufficient to them. For example, overcrowded conditions are not a legally acceptable reason for the exclusion of children from some schools on the basis of race.[247] Nor may school districts avoid desegregation on the plea of poverty or lack of funds.[248] However, where most of the schools of the district have been segregated, the courts will not require desegregation of every school where the cost of transportation, time of pupils involved, etc., appears excessive.[249]

12.23c Pupil assignment and classification

Many states concerned with the problems of assignment of black pupils to white schools after the Supreme Court decision outlawing segregation enacted pupil classification or assignment laws. Criteria for assignment included, among other items, pupil achievement, intelligence quotients, mental maturity, and health. If these laws were reasonable and not designed to perpetuate segregation, they were held to be constitutional.[250] If tests were not employed in a manner to perpetuate racial segregation, they were given the Court's approval.[251] Thus, courts have held[252] that psychological testing in the elementary schools is acceptable. Ability and achievement tests may be used to determine which children have learning problems and which ones are to be assigned to schools for mentally retarded children.[253] However, such tests cannot be utilized to assign pupils to classroooms in recently desegregated schools if the practice tends to perpetuate segregated classes.[254]

An academic high school with high standards of admission and achievement legally may be operated,[225] as may separate schools for academic and vocational students even if racial separation results, as long as they are operated in a nondiscriminatory manner.[256] However, a system of "tracking" where pupils are assigned to an academic or "blue color" track and which results in a preponderance of blacks in the "blue color" track and few in the academic track is unreasonable.[257] The courts have made it clear that if tests are to be permitted, the administration must be convenient for the children and not be so cumbersome as to deny children their constitutional right to attend desegregated schools.[258] Often past records of the ability and achievement of pupils which may be used to determine a pupil's academic ability are not available. In these instances boards of education are permitted to use their previous knowledge and judgment in determining the ability of the children. In making this judgment they may give more weight to achievement than intelligence scores.[259] During the transition period tests may be given to children desiring to integrate and need not be given to other children. The plan, however, cannot be so administered as to permit only black children of exceptional ability to attend schools enrolling white children or to constitute discrimina-

---

[243]Kelly v. Board of Education, 159 F.Supp. 272 (Tenn. 1958).

[244]Wheeler v. Durham City Board of Education, 196 F.Supp. 71 (N.C. 1961).

[245]Robinson v. Board of Education of St. Mary's County, 143 F.Supp. 481 (Md. 1956).

[246]Natonabah v. Board of Education of Gallup-McKinley County School District, 355 F.Supp. 716 (N.M. 1973).

[247]Borders v. Rippy, 247 F.2d 268 (5th Cir. 1957); Clemons v. Board of Education, 228 F.2d 853 (6th Cir. 1956).

[248]Cato v. Parham, 297 F.Supp. 403 (Ark. 1969).

[249]Northcross v. Board of Education of Memphis City Schools, 489 F.2d 15 (6th Cir. 1973).

[250]Joyner v. McDowell County Board of Education, 92 S.E.2d 795 (N.C. 1956).

[251]Borders v. Rippy, 247 F.2d 268 (5th Cir. 1957).

[252]Murray v. West Baton Rouge Parish School Board, 472 F.2d 438 (5th Cir. 1973).

[253]Copeland v. School Board, 464 F.2d 932 (4th Cir. 1972).

[254]Moses v. Washington Parish School Board, 456 F.2d 1283 (5th Cir. 1972).

[255]Berkelman v. San Francisco Unified School District, 501 F.2d 1264 (9th Cir. 1972).

[256]Boykins v. Fairfield Board of Education, 457 F.2d 1091 (5th Cir. 1972).

[257]Hobson v. Hansen, 269 F.Supp. 401, upheld, Smuck v. Hobson, 408 F.2d 175 (D.C. 1969).

[258]Beckett v. School Board of City of Norfolk 181 F.Supp. 870 (Va. 1959).

[259]Jones v. School Board of the City of Alexandria, 179 F.Supp. 280 (Va. 1959).

tion in other ways.[260] Tests of academic achievement, mental ability, etc., may not be applied differently to the two races[261] to discriminate or negate desegregation.[262]

12.23d Basis for pupil assignment
What is a reasonable basis for assignment of pupils has frequently been a question before the courts. From the many decisions it is possible to identify specific provisions which provide reasonable bases for pupil assignment.

Reasonable Basis
Residence and distance from school have been considered by the courts as acceptable criteria for assigning pupils.[263] Assignment of pupils by race may be made where the objective and effect is the reduction or elimination of segregation and discrimination.[264] All children in the same family may be placed in the same school except under unusual circumstances.[265]

Racial quotas are useful as a starting point, but the constitution does not require that pupils be assigned so every school reflects the racial composition of the district as a whole.[266] Schools once desegregated are not required to make yearly adjustments in the racial composition of the student body.[267] There is no affirmative duty to change attendance areas because of a shift in population which increases or decreases the number of either black or white students.[268] School boards may legally order pairing of schools to achieve integration.[269] School districts must permit a student who is attending a school in which his or her race is in majority to attend a school in which that race is in minority.[270] However,

where an approved desegregation plan was thwarted by the flight of white students who had been assigned to previously all-black schools, the court did not require the assignment of additional white students to replace those who had fled.[271]

12.23e Pupil assignment procedures
Pupil assignment criteria are assumed to be valid and are sustained unless it appears that they are used to perpetuate segregation.[272] Pupils, parents, or guardians are responsible for filing an application for placement in the desired school. If no application is filed as required by statute, there is no evidence to show that the children would not have been admitted.[273] If admission is denied, the board must show that the denial was unrelated to race, that no discrimination existed,[274] and that the plan for integration was objective and realistically could be expected to eliminate segregation.[275] A school district may not appeal a court order prematurely, i.e., before the date it is to be put into effect.[276]

When children have been erroneously excluded from an integrated school and are qualified by admission criteria, they are later entitled to attend the integrated school if they desire and enroll in the academic curriculum.[277] Assignment procedures must be operated objectively and without racial discrimination. A child's constitutional rights are not dependent upon state legislative action.[278]

12.23f "With all deliberate speed"
While the phrase "with all deliberate speed" appeared time and again in the early cases, the concept is now dead and the courts no longer countenance deliberate speed in desegregation. They require prompt and effective action.[279] In the strongest possible language the highest court in the land has stated that it wants

[260]Dove v. Parham, 181 F.Supp. 504 (Ark. 1960).

[261]Allen v. School Board, 203 F.Supp. 225 (Va. 1961); Dodson v. School Board, 289 F.2d 439 (4th Cir. 1961).

[262]Taylor v. Board of Education, 195 F.Supp. 231 (N.Y. 1961).

[263]Allen v. School Board, 203 F.Supp. 225 (Va. 1961); Evans v. Buchanan, 195 F.Supp. 321 (Del. 1961); Jackson v. School Board, 201 F.Supp. 620 (Va. 1962).

[264]Jipping v. Manning, 166 N.W.2d 472 (Mich. 1968); Pride v. Community School Board of Brooklyn, N.Y. No. 18, 488 F.2d 321 (1973), *affirmed*, 482 F.2d 257 (2d Cir. 1973).

[265]Ross v. Dyer, 203 F.Supp. 124 (Tex. 1962).

[266]Swann v. Charlotte Mecklenburg Board of Education, 402 U.S. 1, 91 S.Ct. 1267, 28 L.Ed.2d 554 (N.C. 1971).

[267]*Ibid.*; Brinkman v. Gilligan, 539 F.2d 1084 (6th Cir. 1976).

[268]United States v. School District of Omaha, 367 F.Supp. 179 (Neb. 1973).

[269]Lee v. Macon County Board of Education, 429 F.2d 1218 (5th Cir. 1970); Northcross v. Board of Education, 466 F.2d 890 (6th Cir. 1972).

[270]Singleton v. Jackson Municipal Separate School District, 419 F.2d 1211 (5th Cir. 1970), *cert. denied*, 396 U.S. 1032, 90 S.Ct. 612, 24 L.Ed.2d 530 (Fla. 1970).

[271]United States v. Choctaw County Board of Education, 339 F.Supp. 901 (Ala. 1971).

[272]Jones v. School Board, 278 F.2d 72 (4th Cir. 1960).

[273]DeFebio v. County School Board, 100 S.E.2d 760 (Va. 1957).

[274]Aaron v. Tucker, 186 F.Supp. 913 (Ark. 1960); Calhoun v. Members of Board of Education, 188 F.Supp. 401 (Ga. 1959); Dove v. Parham, 183 F.Supp. 389 (Ark. 1960).

[275]Dove v. Parham, 282 F.2d 256 (8th Cir. 1960).

[276]Swann v. Charlotte Mecklenburgh Board of Education, 489 F.2d 966 (4th Cir. 1974).

[277]Pettit v. Board of Education, 184 F.Supp. 452 (Md. 1960).

[278]Evans v. Buchanan, 195 F.Supp. 321 (Del. 1961).

[279]School Committee of Springfield v. Board of Education, 311 N.E.2d 69 (Mass. 1974); Morgan v. Kerrigan, 523 F.2d 917 (1st Cir. 1975).

desegregation and it wants it now. In the words of the Court in Green: "The burden on a school board today is to come forward with a plan that promises realistically to work and promises realistically to work now."[280] School boards are required to formulate plans that promise to work immediately and realistically. The view of the courts is well summarized in an Arkansas case:

However, the time has lapsed for experimental policies proved ineffective. The Board is under an immediate and absolute constitutional duty to afford non-racially operated school programs and it has been given judicial and executive guidelines for the performance of that duty. . . . The time is coming to an end when recalcitrant state officials can force unwilling victims of illegal discrimination to bear the constant and crushing expense of enforcing their constitutionally accorded rights.[281]

12.23g "Freedom of choice" laws

In an effort to achieve desegration for all pupils who desire to attend an integrated school, "freedom of choice" of schools has been provided in a number of states. Under this system pupils and their parents may select the school to be attended, and black children may go to schools attended by white children and vice versa. This plan originally had the support of the United States Office of Education and the courts asserted in a number of cases the constitutionality of the plan as an instrument of desegregation.[282]

As early as 1965, however, the Court in the Fourth circuit had some question about the effectiveness of the freedom of choice policy. In a decision on this issue it held that while the policy was reasonable, it was acceptable only if applied in a reasonable manner.[283] In the following year another federal court held[284] that it was desirable for the district court to retain jurisdiction to be certain that a constitutionally acceptable plan would be adopted and operated in a constitutionally permissible manner so the goals of a desegregated, nonracially operated school system would be rapidly achieved. In other jurisdictions it was held[285] that boards adopting "freedom of choice" regulations as a plan for ending segregation must adhere in good faith to the spirit as well as the letter of this type of plan and affirmatively take all necessary action to afford constitutional guarantees of equal protection to all pupils. Over a period of time it was increasingly apparent that "freedom of choice" plans in and of themselves were not eliminating segregation.

In June of 1968 the Department of Health, Education and Welfare which had originally supported "freedom of choice" laws called for their modification or elimination.[286] The United States Supreme Court ruled[287] in 1968 that "freedom of choice" desegregation plans are inadequate when school districts are not desegregated as rapidly as by other available methods. By this decision "freedom of choice" plans alone are deemed unsatisfactory.

12.23h De Facto Segregation

While the United States Supreme Court has not indicated under what precise circumstance *de facto* segregation is constitutionally acceptable, it did state in a case on this issue that *de facto* segregation is not unconstitutional per se.[288] However, it held in the same case that if school authorities divide a substantial part of the district into clearly unrelated units, a duty evolves on the board of education to desegregate the entire district.

A federal court held[289] in 1972 that school segregation based solely on residential

[280]Green v. County Board of Education of New Kent County, 391 U.S. 430, 88 S.Ct. 1689, 20 L.Ed.2d 716 (Va. 1968); Alexander v. Holmes County Board of Education, 396 U.S. 802, 90 S.Ct. 14, 24 L.Ed.2d 59 (Miss. 1972).

[281]Clark v. Board of Education of Little Rock School District, 369 F.2d 661 (8th Cir. 1966).

[282]Broussard v. Houston Independent School District, 262 F.Supp. 266 (Tex. 1966); Bradley v. School Board of City of Richmond, 345 F.2d 310 (4th Cir. 1965); Davis v. Parish School Board, 269 F.Supp. 60 (La. 1967); Franklin v. Barbour County Board of Education, 259 F.Supp. 545 (Ala. 1966); Steele v. Board of Public Instruction of Leon County, 371 F.2d 395 (5th Cir. 1967); Clark v. Board of Education of Little Rock School District, 360 F.2d 661 (8th Cir. 1966); United States v. Natchez Special Municipal Separate District, 267 F.Supp. 614 (Miss. 1966); Miller v. School District No. 2, Clarendon County, 256 F.Supp. 370 (S.C. 1966).

[283]Felder v. Harnett County Board of Education, 349 F.2d 366 (4th Cir. 1965).

[284]Clarke v. Board of Education of Little Rock School District, 369 F.2d 661 (8th Cir. 1966).

[285]Bowman v. County School Board of Charles City County, 382 F.2d 326 (4th Cir. 1967); United States v. Haywood County Board of Education, 271 F.Supp. 460 (Tenn. 1967); Hobson v. Hansen, 260 F.Supp. 401 (D.C. 1967).

[286]*Nation's Schools*, Vol. 82, No. 1, July 1968.

[287]Green et al. v. County School Board, 391 U.S. 430, 88 S.Ct. 1689, 20 L.Ed.2d 716 (Va. 1968); Rancy et al., v. Board of Education, 391 U.S. 443, 88 S.Ct. 1697, 20 L.Ed.2d 727 (Ark. 1968).

[288]Keyes v. School District No. 1, 413 U.S. 189, 93 S.Ct. 1278, 37 L.Ed.2d 548 (Col. 1973).

[289]United States v. Board of Education, 459 F.2d 720 (10th Cir. 1972).

segregation is not unconstitutional. This decision was based on the assumption that governmental authorities had not caused the residential segregation. If school policies have contributed even to a minor degree to segregation, and even if the basic cause is the residential housing pattern, desegregation is required.[290]

Cases from California, Pennsylvania and Illinois involving de facto segregation have recently come to the courts. In the California case, the state appellate court held[291] that school districts were required to alleviate racial imbalance regardless of the cause if it denied minority groups equal educational opportunities. In the Pennsylvania case, it was held[292] that while school boards may not constitutionally be required to integrate schools which are segregated because of housing patterns, if schools are not integrated they are held to a high standard of equality. In the Illinois case, the court upheld[293] a state statute which prohibited de facto segregation.

12.23i Neighborhood schools

Courts have uniformly held that attending a neighborhood school is not a constitutional right.[294] However, it has been held[295] that neighborhood schools are acceptable even though they result in de facto segregation. In Ohio, the court refused to order any change in the pattern of neighborhood schools which were allegedly de facto segregated.[296] In this instance, a black child could attend any school in the city as long as the child lived in the neighborhood that fed into the school.

While there is evidence to the contrary,[297] the prevailing view appears to be that neighborhood schools are not unconstitutional, even if de facto segregation results, particularly if the school is operated without segregative intent.[298]

Recognizing the efforts that some local districts are making to correct racial imbalance, the courts uphold most actions of boards aimed in this direction, particularly if a plan has been approved by the state commissioner of education who is interested in securing better racial balance.[299] School boards have been supported in contracting with outside districts to achieve better racial balance,[300] as in plans of voluntary transfer from city to suburban schools on a limited basis. In the judgment of the courts such action is not unconstitutional, arbitrary, or capricious.

While school districts are prohibited from drawing boundary lines which will perpetuate segregation, they may consider race in drawing boundary lines. Actions aimed at elimination of segregation, de facto or otherwise, do not violate the constitutional rights of white parents.[301] The duty to desegregate is clear[302] and boards will be upheld in any reasonable and lawful activity to achieve integration even if neighborhood schools are eliminated in the process.

12.23j Abolishment of public schools

Whether any state or subdivision of a state may abolish its public school system to avoid desegregation has been a thorny legal question which has required adjudication by the United States Supreme Court. With limited exceptions states submitted a plan for public education in requesting statehood. Whether this proposed and accepted plan of public education represented a contractual agreement of the federal government with the state upon admission of the state into the Union has been difficult to determine, since no court of record has adjudicated this issue.

The closed-school issue was a vexing one in Prince Edward County, Virginia, and the decision was long in coming. An action was

[290]Kelly v. Gwinn, 456 F.2d 100 (9th Cir. 1972); Booker v. Special School District No. 1, 351 F.Supp. 799 (Minn. 1972).

[291]People v. San Diego Unified School District, 96 Cal.Rptr. 658, cert. denied, 405 U.S. 1016, 92 S.Ct. 1288, 31 L.Ed.2d 478 (Cal. 1972); Crawford v. Board of Education of City of Los Angeles, 130 Cal.Rptr. 724 (1976); N.A.A.C.P. v. San Bernardino Unified School District, 130 Cal.Rptr. 744 (1976):

[292]Husband v. Commonwealth of Pennsylvania, 359 F.Supp. 925 (Pa. 1973).

[293]Tometz v. Board of Education, 237 N.E.2d 498 (Ill. 1968).

[294]Lawlor v. Board of Education of Chicago, 458 F.2d 660 (7th Cir. 1972); Linker v. Unified School District No. 259, 344 F.Supp. 1187 (Kan. 1972); Balsbaugh v. Rowland, 290 A.2d 85 (Pa. 1972).

[295]Bell v. School City of Gary, 324 F.2d 209 (7th Cir. 1963).

[296]Deal v. Cincinnati Board of Education, 419 F.2d 1387 (6th Cir. 1969).

[297]Downs v. Board of Education, 336 F.2d 988 (10th Cir. 1964); Lynch v. Renston School District, 299 F.Supp. 740 (Ohio 1964); Hobson v. Hansen, 260 F.Supp. 401 (D.C. 1967).

[298]Barksdale v. Springfield School Committee, 237 F.Supp. 543 (Mass. 1965); Blocker v. Board of Education of Manhasset, 229 F.Supp. 709 (N.Y. 1964); Board of Education of Oklahoma City Public Schools Independent District No. 89 v. Dowell, 327 F.2d 158 (10th Cir. 1967); Diaz v. San Jose Unified School District, 412 F.Supp. 310 (Cal. 1976).

[299]Vetere v. Allen, 206 N.E.2d 174 (N.Y. 1966); Booker v. Board of Education, 212 A.2d 1 (N.J. 1965).

[300]Etter v. Littwitz, 262 N.Y.S.2d 924 (1965); Etter v. Littwitz, 268 N.Y.S.2d 885 (1966).

[301]Offerman v. Nitkowski, 278 F.2d 32 (2nd Cir. 1967).

[302]Offerman v. Nitkowski, 248 F.Supp. 129 (N.Y. 1965).

brought to require the appropriate officials to reopen and maintain the public schools.[303] When the federal court was assured that suit would be brought in the state court, the federal court deferred ruling on the question of whether a county could close its schools to avoid desegregation until after the state court had reached a decision. The Supreme Court of Appeals of Virginia ruled[304] that the Board of Supervisors was not required to levy or appropriate funds for educational purposes. "Neither state constitution providing for raising sums by local taxation for maintenance of public free schools nor statutes implementing it, impose mandatory duty upon county boards to levy local taxes and appropriate money for their support." While the above ruling is understandable in the existing emotional climate, it is impossible to reconcile with the many decisions rendered over a long period of time in other states. This decision denies the principle that education is a state function and responsibility and sets aside or ignores decisions in many other states that have required local boards to levy necessary taxes to operate the public schools.

In its decision the United States Supreme Court held[305] that the public schools of Prince Edward County could not continue legally to be kept closed to avoid desegregation. Immediate action to open them and to make the necessary tax levy to support them was ordered.

In the same state (Virginia) it was held[306] that under a constitutional mandate to maintain public schools it was unconstitutional to close a particular school or grade to avoid desegregation while permitting other public schools in the state to remain open. In this respect local districts are bound by the same principles of law as state boards of education.

In Louisiana it was held[307] that the state could not close schools in one area and permit them to remain open in another. This, according to the court, was a clear case of discrimination.

The courts will require school boards to make plans for desegregation while its schools are closed so that plans will be available and can be put into effect when the schools are reopened.[308]

12.23k Lines of responsibility

In segregation, as in other matters, there is a clear line of legal responsibility for the operation of schools. The board of education has the responsibility for the local administration of schools, and city authorities have no power to determine which schools are to be opened and which schools are to be closed.[309] While the state may close a local school temporarily because of disturbances such as bringing in federal troops, local school authorities may not be divested of their control of the schools.[310]

Where statutes make state boards of education responsible for maintaining public schools, this body will not be excused from its responsibility on the grounds that the courts have failed to prohibit local boards of education from practicing segregation.[311] State legislatures may not enact statutes to prohibit desegregation or to harass and frustrate local boards of education in their efforts to desegregate schools.[312]

While acknowledging that education is a state function, the federal courts will take jurisdiction when schools are operated in such a manner that federal constitutional provisions are violated.[313] They will prohibit boards of education from evading federal court orders and denying pupils their constitutional rights.[314] Federal courts will enforce desegregation in the District of Columbia as elsewhere. There segregation violates the "due process" provision of the Fifth Amendment.[315]

12.23l Administrative remedy

In earlier cases involving desegregation, it was held that constitutional rights were individual rights and were to be asserted by individuals, not by members of a group.[316] Later, class action suits were permitted for blacks suffering discrimination and denial of constitutional rights.[317] Currently, class action suits are somewhat restricted, with

---

[303]Allen v. County School Board, 198 F.Supp. 497 (Va. 1961).

[304]Griffin v. Board of Supervisors, 124 S.E.2d 227 (Va. 1962).

[305]Griffin v. County School Board of Prince Edward County, 377 U.S. 218, 84 S.Ct. 1226, 12 L.Ed.2d 256 (Va. 1964).

[306]James v. Almond, 170 F.Supp. 331 (Va. 1959).

[307]Hall v. St. Helena Parish School Board, 197 F.Supp. 649 (La. 1961).

[308]Allen v. County School Board, 198 F.Supp. 497 (Va. 1961).

[309]James v. Duckworth, 170 F.Supp. 342 (Va. 1959).

[310]Harrison v. Day, 106 S.E.2d 636 (Va. 1959).

[311]Evans v. Buchanan, 256 F.2d 688 (3rd Cir. 1958).

[312]Bush v. Orleans Parish School Board, 187 F.Supp. 42 (La. 1960).

[313]Cooper v. Aaron, 358 U.S. 1, 78 S.Ct. 1401, 3 L.Ed.2d 3 (Ark. 1958).

[314]James v. Duckworth, 170 F.Supp. 342 (Va. 1959).

[315]Bolling v. Sharpe, 347 U.S. 497, 74 S.Ct. 693, 98 L.Ed. 884 (D.C. 1954).

[316]Aaron v. Tucker, 186 F.Supp. 913 (Ark. 1960); Evans v. Ennis, 281 F.2d 385 (3rd Cir. 1960).

[317]Hackett v. Kincade, 36 F.R.D. 442 (Miss. 1964).

the requirement that members of the class be clearly identified. To facilitate desegregation and assist individuals in establishing their rights to an integrated education, the Attorney General of the United States is now authorized to bring suits to desegregate public schools and colleges on behalf of individuals who cannot afford such action or who hesitate to bring suit for fear of personal safety, employment, or economic reasons.[318] Federal legislation also provides that no person can be excluded because of race, color, or national origin from any benefit, program, or activity receiving federal assistance.[319]

It is well-established policy that, where the state law provides an administrative remedy, aggrieved persons must exhaust their administrative remedy before they appeal to the court.[320] For example, when it is required by statute that the decision of a local board be appealed to the state superintendent, a person must first appeal to the state superintendent before attempting to secure court action. Likewise, where a pupil assignment plan has been approved, one complaining of the manner in which it is administered must first exhaust any administrative remedies before taking the case to the federal court.[321] Where the law provides that specific action regarding enrollment, etc., must be taken, persons aggrieved by alleged deprivation of constitutional rights must first attempt to follow the required procedure before appealing to the courts.[322]

There are, however, exceptions to the requirement that a person must exhaust administrative remedies, as follows:

1. Where state action allegedly denies a citizen rights guaranteed by the United States Constitution, the citizen may appeal such matters directly to the federal courts,[323] and it is not necessary to resort to the state courts before taking the case to the federal court.[324]

2. Where the remedy provided in the statutes is a resort to the state courts, the remedy is a judicial and not an administrative procedure. Thus, the administrative remedy need not be exhausted by appeal to the state court before resort to the federal courts may be had.[325]

3. Administrative remedies must be both adequate and appropriate.[326] When it is apparent that regulations are such that an appeal to an administrative body is useless, the courts generally have permitted a direct judicial appeal.[327] Administrative remedies need not be sought if they are inherently inadequate or are so applied as to deny constitutional rights.[328]

4. Where an attack is upon board policy, a pupil is not required to apply for admission to a particular school before taking the case to court.[329] This applies to an action against segregation rather than a case to secure assignment to a particular school.[330]

5. When it is undisputed that a board of education is operating a racially segregated school, all administrative remedies need not be exhausted before suing for an injunction.[331]

6. Where administrative remedies have been followed initially, they are not required a second time.[332] Thus, applications filed by black children for admission to a white school did not need to be refiled in a situation in which black children applied for admission to a white school and shortly thereafter all white children and teachers were assigned to another school and were replaced by black children and staff.

7. In action under the Civil Rights Act (42 U.S.C.A., para 1983) a federal court indicated disapproval of a general or automatic requirement that administrative rem-

[318]Civil Rights Act of 1964, Title IV.
[319]Civil Rights Act of 1969, Title VI.
[320]Dove v. Parham, 176 F.Supp. 242 (Ark. 1959); Dove v. Parham, 181 F.Supp. 504 (Ark. 1960); Gibson v. Board of Public Instruction of Dade County, 272 F.2d 763 (5th Cir. 1959); McKissick v. Durham City Board of Education, 176 F.Supp. 3 (N.C. 1959); Parham v. Dove, 271 F.2d 132 (8th Cir. 1959).
[321]McKissick v. Durham City Board of Education, 176 F.Supp. 3 (N.C. 1959).
[322]Aaron v. Tucker, 186 F.Supp. 913 (Ark. 1960).
[323]Bush v. Orleans Parish School, 188 F.Supp. 916 (La. 1960); Bush v. Orleans Parish School Board, 190 F.Supp. 861 (La. 1960).
[324]Aaron v. Tucker, 186 F.Supp. 913 (Ark. 1960); Dove v. Parham, 282 F.2d 256 (8th Cir. 1960); Norwood v. Tucker, 287 F.2d 798 (8th Cir. 1961).

[325]Ibid.
[326]Carson v. Warlick, 238 F.2d 724 (4th Cir. 1956); Moore v. Board of Education of Harford County, 146 F.Supp. 91 (Md. 1956); Orleans Parish School Board v. Bush, 242 F.2d 156 (5th Cir. 1957); Robinson v. Board of Education of St. Mary's County, 143 F.Supp. 481 (Md. 1956).
[327]Borders v. Rippy, 247 F.2d 268 (5th Cir. 1957); Gibson v. Board of Public Instruction, 246 F.2d 913 (5th Cir. 1957); Kelly v. Board of Education, 159 F.Supp. 272 (Tenn. 1958); School Board v. Atkins, 246 F.2d 325 (4th Cir. 1957); Thompson v. County School Board, 159 F.Supp. 567 (Va. 1957).
[328]McCoy v. Greensboro City Board of Education, 283 F.2d 667 (4th Cir. 1960).
[329]Gibson v. Board of Public Instruction, 246 F.2d 913 (5th Cir. 1957); Kelley v. Board of Education, 159 F.Supp. 272 (Tenn. 1958).
[330]Orleans Parish School Board v. Bush, 242 F.2d 156 (5th Cir. 1957).
[331]East Baton Rouge Parish School Board v. Davis, 287 F.2d 380 (5th Cir. 1961).
[332]McCoy v. Greensboro City Board of Education, 283 F.2d 667 (4th Cir. 1960).

edies be exhausted before appealing to the courts. It did, however, state that some definitive administrative or institutional action was necessary before court action was appropriate under para 1983 of the Civil Rights Act.[333]

A number of cases involving desegregation and the busing of pupils have been adjudicated by the courts at all levels. These will be considered in Chapter 15. Additional cases relating to various aspects of desegregation have come to the courts recently causing considerable confusion relative to the exact legal status of desegregation.[334]

12.24 SUMMARY

In school admission and attendance, boards of education have extensive discretionary authority unless constitutional rights are denied. They are empowered by law to establish and maintain standards for admission, placement, and gradation of pupils based on the pupils' level of ability and achievement. The courts will not interfere with a board's action in the admission and placement of pupils as long as its discretion is exercised in a reasonable manner.

Both statutory enactments and constitutional provisions give boards of education direction in the formulation and execution of policy concerning the admission and attendance of pupils. Statutes frequently establish the conditions under which pupils may avail themselves of the educational program, and constitutional provisions guarantee educational rights which may not be abrogated by statutes or board regulations.

Education is a state function under control of the state legislature. The federal courts will not control education except to assure pupils of rights guaranteed by the federal Constitution. Local boards of education have control of education only to the extent that authority is delegated to them by state legislatures.

While constitutional guarantees of education for children at the lower end of the age scale have not been clearly determined, one point is clear: State legislatures may go as much beyond the constitutional guarantees in providing free public education as they desire. They may establish educational programs for age groups below and above the ages specified in state constitutions.

School attendance is a privilege which imposes obligations on children and their parents. They must submit to reasonable health and vaccination requirements. The "police power" of the state will be employed to prohibit pupils from attendance if their presence adversely affects the school and/or the program of other children.

In recent years, increased attention has been given to education of handicapped children. In both legislative enactments and constitutional interpretation, evidence is found to support the proposition that handicapped children are entitled to educational opportunities fitted to their abilities and needs.

Boards of education may establish reasonable cutoff dates for age for admission to first grade, but they may be required to admit transfer students who are younger than the required age of their own pupils in some cases. Examinations may be given as a condition of admittance to children from private, parochial, or other public schools.

Compulsory attendance laws must be complied with unless the child has a satisfactory excuse. The courts will always consider the sufficiency of the excuse presented. Illness of a pupil is an incontestable excuse for nonattendance. Pupils may not be required to attend school if the route is so dangerous that parents have a well-founded fear for the physical safety of their children. Religious beliefs are no excuse for noncompliance with compulsory attendance laws. Attendance at private schools generally meets the requirements of compulsory attendance, as does home instruction by a qualified tutor. The education provided must be essentially equivalent to that in the public schools. The burden of proof that the education is of essentially the same quality is usually placed on the parents who seek other means of instruction.

It is commonly held that a married child cannot be compelled to attend school since the obligation of a married person is inconsistent with school attendance. This is the

[333]Raper v. Lucey, 488 F.2d 748 (1st Cir. 1973).

[334]Morgan v. Kerrican, 509 F.2d 580 (1st Cir. 1974), cert. den. 421 U.S. 963, 95 S.Ct. 1950, 44 L.Ed.2d 449 (1975); Cincinnati v. Department of Health Education and Welfare, 369 F.Supp. 203 (Ohio 1975); Arthur v. Nyquist, 415 F.Supp. 904 (N.Y. 1976); Armstrong v. O'Connell, 416 F.Supp. 1347 (Wis. 1976); Evans v. Buchanan, 416 F.Supp. 328 (Del. 1976); Hills v. Gautreaux, 96 S.Ct. 1538 (Ill. 1976); Robinson v. Vollert, 411 F.Supp. 461 (Tex. 1976); Lasby v. Estes, 412 F.Supp. 1192 (Tex. 1976); United States v. Board of School Commissioners of City of Indianapolis, 541 F2d 1211 (7th Cir. 1976); Remanded 97 S.Ct. 802 (Ind. 1977); Washington v. Davis, 426 U.S. 229, 96 S.Ct. 2040, 48 L.Ed.2d 597 (D.C. 1976); Metropolitan School District v. Buckley, 97 S.Ct. 800, 801 (Ind. 1977); Board of Education of Jefferson County v. Newbury Area Council Inc., 510 F.2d 1358; 541 F.2d. 538; cert. den. 97 S.Ct. 82 (Ky. 1977); Village of Arlington Heights v. Metropolitan Development Corporation, 97 S.Ct. 555, 48 L.Ed.2d 597 (Ill. 1976); The Regents of the University of California v. Allan Bakke, No. 76–811 (Hearing Oct. 12, 1977).

case regardless of the age of the married pupil.

A child normally may attend school where the parents reside without payment of tuition even though it is not the parents' legal domicile. Children usually may attend school without payment of tuition when living with relatives or in a private home if they are not living in the district primarily for the purpose of school attendance. Children living on federal land generally may attend the schools in the district tuition free, unless the federal government has taken exclusive jurisdiction. Emancipated minors are entitled to attend school in the district in which they reside without payment of tuition.

A review of cases relating to ages of admission to the first grade indicates that it is within the jurisdiction of boards of education, in accordance with statutes and constitutions, to designate the age for admission to the first grade. Since entrance to school and entrance to the first grade are not the same, the age of entrance to the first grade need not conform to the entrance age for free public education established in the constitution. It is generally agreed that boards of education may establish a cutoff age for entrance to the first grade, such as requiring the sixth birthday by a given date. Pupils may not demand entrance to the first grade at any time during the school year, but only at the beginning of the term. Boards may not discriminate between pupils from different types of kindergartens or schools in admission of transfer pupils.

In 1954 the long-accepted doctrine of "separate but equal" school facilities for both black and white races was superseded, and desegregation of schools was ordered by the United States Supreme Court. At the outset, courts were extremely lenient in permitting schools to develop plans leisurely, start desegregation gradually, and move slowly. The courts clearly stated that they required only a plan for gradual integration and a start in desegregation. Desegregating one grade at a time was satisfactory. Pupil assignment plans, which applied equally to both races, were held constitutional until their administration showed them to be discriminatory.

Recently there has appeared a disposition on the parts of the courts to reevaluate their earlier definition of "all deliberate speed," and a growing impatience with the delays in integration is apparent. It is evident that long delays will no longer be countenanced by federal courts and recent court decisions indicate that the courts require desegregation immediately.

Local schools were permitted to remain closed until ordered reopened by a decision of the United States Supreme Court. This decision is in line with others which have held that failure to provide schools is unconstitutional. The decisions recognize education as a state function and that local districts may be compelled to levy taxes and operate schools. This has been the conclusion of the courts in practically every jurisdiction in the United States.

In each segregation case the federal courts have made it clear that they will insist on guaranteeing black children their constitutional rights and will issue the necessary injunctions and mandates to assure them "equal protection" under the law. Where local or state administrative remedies are inadequate or incapable of providing relief, appeal may be taken directly to the federal courts.

While there was some early conflict on the issue, the weight of authority now indicates that boards of education may take race into consideration in drawing school district boundaries to correct racial imbalance.

While the courts are still having difficulty defining their precise stand on de facto segregation and neighborhood schools, it appears that where de facto segregation results entirely from the housing patterns, the court will accept de facto segregation and permit the continued operation of neighborhood schools. The opposite is true of de jure segregation. The courts are determined that it must end, and at an early date.

Instruction of Pupils

13.0 INTRODUCTION

Instructional programs for pupils in every state are circumscribed by constitutional provisions, statutory enactments, and decisions of boards of education at the state, intermediate, and local level. Constitutional provisions, because of their stability and resistance to change, have had a marked influence on educational programs over an extended period of time. Statutory enactments provide the framework for the day-by-day operation of schools within which regulations of boards of education must be formulated. States are granted wide latitude of operation within their constitutions and boards of education have been granted extensive authority in instructional programing by state statutes.

In this chapter some constitutional and statutory provisions will be presented. Information will also be provided on the legal framework within which the several agencies controlling and directing the instructional program operate. These include:

1. State-level agencies—the legislature, the state board of education, and the state department of education.
2. Intermediate-level agencies—the county superintendent and the county board of education.
3. Local-level agency—the local board of education.

Because of their massive influence on public education, the legal rights of pupils and their parents to control the instructional program will be considered, as well as the influence of religion on public school instruction.

13.1 CONSTITUTIONAL PROVISIONS

Perhaps more than in any other field, the framers of the constitutions have jealously safeguarded the guarantees of public education, and funds for its support. Constitutions have provided state legislatures with directions for the establishment and operation of many phases of the educational program. In every interpretation of the constitution the courts have made it clear that constitutional provisions are to be heeded and may not be set aside by legislative acts.

Sometimes the delineation of what is encompassed by the school system is not explicit. In these instances the courts have been asked to determine the extent of the system of public education. They have held[1] that the legislature is not limited to providing only for the common schools in fulfilling the constitutional requirements to establish a school system but may establish other programs as well.

While the language varies from state to state, the intent of constitutional provisions is to require that schools and education be encouraged and that a uniform system of schools be established as soon as practical. Some states, for example, California, define public education to include a comprehensive program including kindergarten, elementary, secondary, technical schools, and state colleges. Utah provides for an agricultural college and a university as well as primary, grammar grades, and high schools in its constitution. Most state constitutions do not define the scope of the educational program.

Provisions relative to textbooks are found in the constitutions in some states. Only rarely do constitutions require the legislature to furnish textbooks free of cost in the public schools as is true in Oklahoma. The more general provision directs the state board of education to provide for the selection and adoption of the textbooks to be used in the public schools. A directive not to change the textbooks more often than once in six years occasionally appears. In most states neither the state constitution nor state statutes provide for state adoption of textbooks. In these states the legislature has generally empowered the local district to select the textbooks to be used, generally without standards or restrictions. Where this function is vested in the local board of education the people of the district are without legal authority in this matter.[2]

State constitutions often designate some of the subjects to be taught. These are not necessarily the subjects generally regarded as essential, such as reading, arithmetic, spelling, etc., but rather those for which special interest groups have been able to generate support. These may be subjects supported by patriotic groups, such as instruction in state and federal constitutions and duties of citizenship, or they may embody the teaching of character traits such as truthfulness, temperance, purity, public spirit, and respect for honest labor. The practical arts have had their share of support and constitutional direction includes instruction in elements of agriculture, horticulture, stock raising, and domestic science.

[1]Associated Schools of Independent District No. 63 v. School District No. 83, 142 N.W. 325 (Minn. 1913).

[2]Schlake v. Board of Education of Fort Thomas, 42 S.W.2d 526 (Ky. 1931); Grosser v. Woolett, 341 N.E.2d 356 (Ohio 1974).

Instruction in the English language is a requirement in a number of states. However, instruction in the English language alone is not sufficient in some states or school districts. New Mexico has attempted to guarantee that teachers will be able to instruct Spanish-speaking children who have no knowledge of English. Its constitution requires that the legislature provide training for teachers so they may be proficient in both English and Spanish to qualify them to teach Spanish-speaking pupils.

In one aspect of education state constitutions are in almost complete agreement. With the exception of two states, Maine and North Carolina, constitutional provisions prohibit any sectarian instruction in the public schools and/or the spending of public funds to support sectarian instruction.

13.2 STATE-LEVEL AGENCIES

In considering the state's obligation to educate, the courts have held[3] that the furnishing of education is a state function, duty, and an indispensable obligation. In fulfilling this obligation the state operates through the legislature, state boards of education, and state departments of education. The operation of each of these agencies is presented in the following sections.

13.2a State legislatures

The authority of the state legislature in educational matters, including direction and control of the instructional program of pupils, is succinctly described in *Corpus Juris Secundum:*

> Subject to constitutional provisions, the power of the legislature as to the management, operation and regulation of school districts is plenary; local regulations and charter provisions as to school matters must conform to constitutional and statutory provisions.[4]

The courts have interpreted this to mean that any reasonable legislative act will be upheld unless it is in violation of the state or federal constitutions. It also means that authority for local action must be granted by the legislature either by specific provision or by clear implication.

Court decisions on a number of specific issues provide additional information concerning state legislatures' authority and responsibility in education. The courts have stated that a statutory method of carrying out a certain act takes precedence over all other methods.[5] Other methods may not be employed by either state agencies or local school districts when statutory methods are prescribed.

The division of the territory of the state into school districts, the conduct of schools, the instruction of pupils, the qualification of teachers, the curricula, and provision for textbooks, are all within the control of the legislature.[6] Selected subdivisions related to instruction of pupils are discussed in the following sections.

13.2b State boards of education

Constitutional clauses provide for state boards of education in several states. Their powers and duties as set forth in state constitutions are generally those "prescribed by law." However, in a few instances the constitution indicates specific responsibilities of state boards of education. Examples are given below:

> Supervision of schools of higher grade vested in state board of education as law shall provide. (Florida, XII, 3.)

> Supervision of state educational institutions vested in state board of education. (Idaho, IX, 2.)

Missouri provides that the state board of education shall appoint the professional staff of the department of education and fix its compensation. (Missouri, IX, 2.)

Supervision of schools is vested by constitutional acts in state boards of education in Colorado (IX, 1), Hawaii (IX, 3), Idaho (IX, 2), Louisiana (XII, 6), Missouri (IX, 2a), North Carolina (IX, 9), New Mexico (XII, 6), Oklahoma (XIII, 5), Utah (X, 8), and Virginia (IX, 130). It is vested in a state board of education, a state superintendent of public instruction, county school superintendents, and governing boards of state institutions as provided by law in Arizona (XI, 2). Since the powers of state boards of education are defined by constitutional requirements in some states and by statutory requirements in others, there have been few judicial decisions involving state boards of education in relation to the instruction of pupils.

However, occasionally the power of a state board of education has been contested. A New Jersey court was called upon to determine whether the state board of education had authority to supervise and control

---

[3]State v. D'Aulisa, 52 A.2d 636 (Conn. 1947).
[4]78 Corpus Juris Secundum, *Schools and School Districts,* p. 812, sec. 83a.

[5]State v. Hendrix, 107 P.2d 1078 (Ariz. 1940).
[6]Sturgis v. Allegan County, 72 N.W.2d 56 (Mich. 1955).

education.[7] In Washington it was held[8] that state boards of education may prescribe a state course of study and local boards may not adopt a program which conflicts with it. In Kentucky the authority of the state board of education to determine general educational policies was tested.[9] In each of the above cases it was determined that the state board had the designated authority provided either through statute or through constitutional enactment. In Montana it was held[10] that state boards of education could not be compelled to grant accreditation unless it could clearly be shown that the denial of the application was an arbitrary and capricious act. In Nebraska it was held[11] that the purpose of accreditation was to provide better educational opportunities and the state could legally authorize freeholders to transfer their land from a nonaccredited to an accredited district. Some states, for example, New Mexico, vest in the state board of education authority over the inclusion of subjects not required by the statutes. State boards are then authorized to designate the course of study.

While not related to instruction a case[12] involving a state board of education points out clearly the rule that is applied to any actions of state boards of education, i.e., the findings of fact of an administrative board will not be set aside unless they are arbitrary, capricious, or unreasonable. When there are two possible interpretations of the law, a board does not act in an arbitrary, capricious, or unreasonable manner in selecting one rather than the other interpretation. Needless to say state officials may not interfere with city or county boards of education in their efforts to comply with the law.[13]

13.2c State commissioners and departments of education

In several states the commissioner of education or the state superintendent is charged by the constitution with supervision of the public schools. In other states this is a duty imposed by statute. Whether granted by constitution or statute, the authority of the commissioner is conclusive in all matters relating to the supervision and control of the public school system.[14]

Although in the field of instruction the state commissioner or superintendent is seldom involved in litigation, a few such cases have occurred. It has been held[15] that, when authority has been delegated by the legislature to the state department of education, the department may not delegate the power conferred upon it to others. It also has been found[16] to be within the authority of the state department of education to promote vocal music in the kindergarten and the first two grades and to accept a gift (by will) to further this objective.

State departments of education exert extensive influence on the instructional program through the authority of judicial review in most states. This power is exercised to a marked degree in New Jersey and New York where the commissioner's office decides many educational cases. While the decisions of the commissioner may be and frequently are appealed to the courts, they have almost universally upheld the decisions of the commissioners. Cases in which the decisions have been set aside are those where the commissioners have acted without full knowledge of the law or with an erroneous interpretation of it, acted without regard for the facts in an arbitrary, capricious, or unreasonable manner, or failed to accord the complainants a full and complete hearing embodying the elements of due process.[17]

13.3 INTERMEDIATE-UNIT AGENCIES

The intermediate unit of operation has had so little direct responsibility for the enforcement of constitutions and statutory enactments relative to the instructional program that few court cases have been adjudicated involving this administrative unit. Primarily responsible for the paucity of cases is the fact that the intermediate unit is and should be a promoter of good education rather than a unit which promulgates rules and regulations and enforces them.

Cases coming to the courts involving intermediate unit agencies generally have not related to instruction of pupils. Rather they have involved questions of detachment of territory from one school district and at-

---

[7]Rankin v. Board of Education of Egg Harbor Township, 51 A.2d 194 (N.J. 1947).

[8]Wagner v. Royal, 78 Pac. 1094 (Wash. 1904).

[9]Board of Education of Bath County v. Goodpaster, 84 S.W.2d 55 (Ky. 1935).

[10]State v. Cooney, 59 P.2d 48 (Mont. 1936).

[11]Application of Pribil, 129 N.W.2d 356 (Neb. 1966).

[12]School District of Omaha v. State Board of Education, 181 N.W.2d 861 (Neb. 1970).

[13]Lee v. Macon County Board of Education, 231 F.Supp. 743 (Ala. 1964).

[14]O'Connor v. Emerson, 188 N.Y.S. 236 (1921) affirming 185 N.Y.S. 49 (1920) affirmed 134 N.E. 572 (N.Y. 1921).

[15]Ibid.

[16]Eckles v. Lounsberry, 111 N.W.2d 638 (Iowa 1961).

[17]Jenkins v. Township of Morris School District, 279 A.2d 619 (N.J. 1971); DeHarried v. Ewald B. Nyquist, 318 N.Y.S.2d 650 (1971); Board of Education of City of N.Y. v. Nyquist, 322 N.Y.S.2d 370 (1971).

tachment to another,[18] legal consequences of enacting a grandfather clause related to educational qualifications,[19] posting of notices of meetings,[20] determination of its legal status,[21] election of members,[22] and assumption of legality when its own actions are reviewed.[23]

13.3a County boards of education

County boards of education have been established in a large number of states. In states with county units the county board of education is in reality the *local* board of education and its responsibilities were considered when those of local boards of education were presented.

Selected constitutional provisions relative to different types of county board organizations are given below. It is clear from these provisions that in several states county boards of education are constitutional agencies.

Legislature may constitute as judicial officers members of county school boards . . . ; may provide that all school action taken by them requiring exercise of discretion or judgment be judicial action. (Alabama, VI, 139 Am. CXI.)

Legislature shall provide for [county boards] in all counties. (California, IX, 7.)

Establishment of county boards (terms of election, number, etc.). (Georgia, VIII, sec. V, 1.)

Legislature has power to increase, diminish, consolidate, or abolish named county officers, including county superintendents. (Nevada, IV, 32.)

In cities of the first and second class, city boards of education to control separate and apart from counties in which located. (Utah, X, 6.)

Study of cases in courts of record does not reveal that the instructional function of county boards of education, operating as intermediate units, has been legally questioned.

13.3b County superintendents of schools

The county superintendent of schools in intermediate units is often a constitutional

officer. The duties of the officer, however, while assumed to be related to the improvement of instruction, are seldom spelled out. The specific responsibilities of the office may rest with the legislature or be subject to change by it even when it is a constitutional office. The following constitutional provisions make this clear:

Legislature to have power to increase, diminish, consolidate or abolish named county officers, including county superintendent of schools. (Nevada, IV, 32.)

Office created subject to change by legislature for each organized county. (Arizona, XII, 3; Oklahoma, XVII, 2.)

Legislature may provide for county superintendent of schools. (West Virginia, XII, 3.)

In states with county unit districts the county superintendent has broad instructional responsibilities, akin to the responsibilities of local superintendents of schools. These responsibilities will be considered later in connection with local educational agencies. (Cases related to employment problems of county superintendents of schools are included in Chapter 17.)

13.4 LOCAL BOARDS OF EDUCATION

In contrast with state and intermediate educational agencies, which have only limited legal involvement related to instruction, local boards of education have been involved in extensive litigation. Their heavy responsibility for the operation of the educational program and for the formulation and adoption of policies and regulations makes them vulnerable to legal attack. Court decisions pertaining to the length of term, courses of study, and other aspects of the instructional program related to local boards of education will now be considered.

13.5 INSTRUCTIONAL ISSUES

A large number of educational issues come to focus in the instruction of pupils. They evolve from constitutional guarantees, statutory enactments, and rules and regulations of boards of education at all levels. These are viewed in the courts against the desires and rights of the constituency, parents and pupils. Issues and court decisions on a variety of conflicts will be considered in the following sections.

13.5a Length of school term

In practically all states the legislatures now require a minimum length of school

[18]Warner Independent School District No. 230 Brown Co. v. Co. Board of Education Brown Co., 179 N.W.2d 6 (S.D. 1970)

[19]Black v. Blanchard, 179 S.E.2d 288 (Ga. 1971).

[20]Lipscomb Independent School District v. County School Trustees, 498 S.W.2d 364 (Tex. 1973).

[21]Harrison County School Board v. State Highway Commission, 284 So.2d 50 (Miss. 1973).

[22]Fetterman v. Cope, 364 F.Supp. 79 (Tenn. 1973).

[23]Mitchell v. Garrett, 510 S.W.2d 894 (Tenn. 1974).

term. Although the prescribed term is of substantial duration, in some instances no local school authorities have contested these laws in court. The authority of the state legislature over the length of the school year is apparently so firmly established and so well accepted that it is not challenged.

In the absence of constitutional or statutory restrictions the decision concerning the length of the school term is within the discretion of the school board.[24] Even in the presence of constitutional provisions the board has extensive discretion since constitutional requirements are minimal[25] and districts are not restricted to the length of term designated in the constitution.[26] The length of the school year may be influenced by the amount of money available and other factors. When authority to determine the length of the school term is vested in the electors, they obviously exercise this authority. However, they may determine the length of the term only for the year in which they are given control and may not determine the length of term vested in another annual meeting.[27] When the legislature is silent it has been held[28] that the determination of the length of the school term is vested in the local school committee (board). Within the limits established by the constitution or statutes, local boards may exercise their discretion in the opening and closing dates of the school year. Discretion in this instance, as in others, is not consumed by use, nor can it be bargained away.[29] However, there is judicial opinion that the school calendar is negotiable by the teachers' bargaining agency and the board of education.[30] Boards of education may change their minds after having adopted a particular school calendar. Holidays and the school calendar are to be determined by the body in which the legislature has placed this responsibility. Local boards of education also have the authority at the beginning of the school year to designate the termination date.[31]

13.5b Course of study

The state legislature has the authority, frequently exercised, to prescribe courses which must be taught in the public schools. As long as the designated courses appear to be in the interest of the welfare and safety of the country and its citizens, the courts have sustained legislative acts related to course requirements. Even acts which may appear unwise to the court have been sustained. Only those actions which are arbitrary, capricious, unreasonable, or in violation of state or federal constitutions have been declared invalid.

All required courses in the state course of study obviously must be offered. Where state rules and regulations for the offering of the course are promulgated, they too must be followed. However, the requirements do not serve as a limitation on the local district, and activities beyond those required may be instituted by the local school district.[32]

The legislature may forbid any immoral or dangerous teaching even though taught as a moral or religious duty.[33] Likewise it may prohibit any subversive (un-American) teaching in the schools.[34]

The extent to which the courts will support the legislature's designated courses of study is illustrated in an early Tennessee case. In this instance a statute prohibited the teaching of evolution in the schools. This statute was upheld[35] by the courts even under a state constitution which made it the "duty of the legislature to cherish literature and science." (Tennessee, XI, 12). In Arkansas it was held[36] that the enactment of a statute prohibiting the teaching of evolution was an unconstitutional exercise of power, rather than a constitutionally permissible exercise of the state's power to specify the curriculum in public schools.

The Mississippi Supreme Court in 1970 held[37] unconstitutional a statute which prohibited the teaching of evolution. In the view of the court such a statute violated the free exercise of religion guaranteed by the First Amendment. Courts will not sustain a complaint that evolution is being taught to the exclusion of other theories of creation. It is not practical to expect schools to teach all theories of the evolution of man. Failure to

[24]Morley v. Power, 10 Lea (Vol. 78 Tenn.) 219 (1882).
[25]Coe v. Surry County, 36 S.E.2d 910 (N.C. 1946); Hallyburton v. Board of Education of Burke Co., 195 S.E.21 (N.C. 1938).
[26]Bridges v. City of Charlotte, 20 S.E.2d 825 (N.C. 1942).
[27]Matney v. Boydston, 27 Mo.App. 36 (1887).
[28]Weymouth Ninth School District v. Loud, 12 Gray 61 (Mass. 1858).
[29]Monroe County Board of Education v. Thurmond, 132 S.E. 427 (Ga. 1926).
[30]Jt. School District No. 8, City of Madison v. Wisconsin Employment Relations Board and Madison Teachers Inc., 155 N.W.2d 78 (Wis. 1967).
[31]State v. Board of Education, Pleasant Local School District, 124 N.E.2d 721 (Ohio 1955).

[32]Smith v. Consolidated School District No. 2, 408 S.W.2d 50 (Mo. 1966).
[33]People v. Stanley, 255 Pac. 610 (Col. 1927).
[34]Board of Education v. Jewett, 68 P.2d 404 (Cal. 1937); Joyce v. Board of Education, 60 N.E.2d 431 (Ill. 1945).
[35]Scopes v. State of Tennessee, 289 S.W. 363 (Tenn. 1927).
[36]Epperson v. Arkansas, 393 U.S. 97, 89 S.Ct. 266, 272 L.Ed. 2d 228 (Ark. 1968).
[37]Smith v. State, 242 So.2d 692 (Miss. 1970).

do so does not constitute establishment of a religion or deny equal protection.[38]

The legislature may not enact statutory provisions in violation of rights guaranteed by a state or federal constitution. however, attempts have been made by legislatures to prohibit the teaching of a foreign language or instruction in foreign language in the schools. Iowa's legislature enacted a statute which prohibited the teaching of a foreign language to any child who had not passed the eighth grade. This enactment was held[39] unconstitutional. Hawaii's legislature attempted to prohibit teaching of any language other than English to children who had not passed the fourth grade. This, too, was declared[40] unconstitutional. Another bitterly contested case arose in Nebraska, where a statute prohibited teaching in German in public or private schools below the eighth grade. This was appealed to the United States Supreme Court, where the act was ruled[41] unconstitutional as it related to private schools. Basic in this decision was the determination that this type of legislation deprived persons of property (rights) without due process of law.

The state has the power to prescribe the curriculum and studies in the public schools and when a uniform program of study has been adopted by the state, local boards of education must follow it.[42] Some states have detailed the subjects to be studied while others have left the decisions on curriculum to local district control. Wisconsin is typical of states specifying much of the curriculum in the statutes. In this state subjects required by the statutes include: reading, writing, spelling, English grammar and composition, geography, arithmetic, elements of agriculture and conservation of natural resources, history and civil government of the United States and of Wisconsin, citizenship, physiology and hygiene, physical education, morals, animal life, fire prevention, cooperatives, and conservation and value of dairy products. The extent to which a number of these subjects are to be taught is also specified.[43]

The courts will also require a school district to provide instruction in English for children of Chinese descent who, because of lack of knowledge of English, cannot understand the directions and teaching in the regular classroom. In the opinion of the court a child is entitled to an education in a language he or she can understand.[44]

In the absence of such prescription the local board of education has discretion to provide for the teaching of whatever subjects it deems best.[45] Where the county board has the duty to prescribe the courses of instruction approved by the state board and fails to do so, the local board is not excused from meeting standards.[46]

When specific subjects are required by the state, local school boards may not fail to offer the required subjects.[47] However, the local school board has authority to determine the scope of the course and the method to be employed in teaching it.[48]

Unless there are constitutional or statutory prohibitions, the control of the instructional program is within the jurisdiction of local boards of education. Boards of education have been upheld in including the German language,[49] music,[50] Latin and Greek,[51] manual training,[52] and thrift instruction[53] in the school program. It is not necessary to submit the question of whether a course is to be offered to the voters of the district,[54] and a determination of the amount of time devoted to a subject is a prerogative of the board of education.[55] Literary events, musical recitals and entertainments, dramatics, dances, lecture courses, and similar activities have been held[56] to be educational activities, within the province of the board of education. In its decision the court indicated that it would not substitute a different definition of education from that held by the board.

---

[38]Wright v. Houston Independent School District, 366 F.Supp. 1208, *affirmed*, 486 F.2d 137 (5th Cir. 1972); Steele v. Waters, 527 S.W.2d 72 (Tenn. 1975).

[39]Bartels v. Iowa, 262 U.S. 404, 43 S.Ct. 628, 67 L.Ed. 1047 (Iowa 1923).

[40]Mo Hock Ke Lok Po v. Stainback, 336 U.S. 368, 60 S.Ct. 606, 93 L.Ed. 741 (Hawaii 1949).

[41]Meyer v. Nebraska, 262 U.S. 390, 43 S.Ct. 625, 67 L.Ed. 1042 (Neb. 1923).

[42]Westland Publishing Co. v. Royal, 78 Pac. 1096 (Wash. 1904).

[43]Wisconsin Statutes 118.01 sec. 1-10 (1972).

[44]Lau v. Nichols, 414 U.S. 563, 94 S.Ct. 786, 39 L.Ed.2d 1 (Cal. 1974).

[45]79 Corpus Juris Secundum *Schools and School Districts*, p. 429, sec. 485a.

[46]Board of Education of Aberdeen-Huntington Local School District v. State Board of Education, 189 N.E.2d 81, *appeal dismissed*, 189 N.E.2d 86 (Ohio 1962).

[47]Jones v. Board of Trustees, 47 P.2d 804 (Cal. 1935).

[48]Neilan v. Board of Directors, 205 N.W. 506 (Iowa 1925).

[49]Powell v. Board of Education, 97 Ill. 375 (1881).

[50]W. P. Myers Pub. Co. v. White River School Township, 62 N.E. 66 (Ind. 1901); State v. Webber, 8 N.E. 708 (Ind. 1886).

[51]Newman v. Thompson, 4 S.W. 341 (Ky. 1887).

[52]People v. Board of Education, 176 Ill.App. 491 (1912).

[53]Security National Bank v. Bagley, 210 N.W. 946 (Iowa 1926).

[54]People v. Board of Education, 176 Ill.App. 491 (1912).

[55]Epley v. Hall, 155 Pac. 1083 (Kan. 1916).

[56]State Tax Commission v. Board of Education, 73 P.2d 49 (Kan. 1937).

Additional cases have indicated that in the absence of mandatory statutes a board of education has complete discretion in determining what courses shall be offered, continued, or discontinued; its discretion will not be interfered with by the court.[57]

The most hotly debated curricular issue in recent years has been the offering of sex education courses. The courts have sustained the schools in providing this type of instruction. In a Michigan case the court held[58] that where attendance in a sex education course was not compulsory, the offering of the course authorized by state statutes was not unconstitutional, nor was the statutory authorization for offering instruction in this area an illegal delegation of authority. A New Jersey court witnessed an attack on required attendance at sex education courses.[59] The complaint later was dismissed[60] on the technical grounds that the plaintiffs had failed to exhaust their administrative remedy. A Connecticut court also rejected[61] an attack on compulsory sex education courses. Freedom of choice of the education to be provided the children, as long as what is taught is not immoral or clearly inimical to the existence of society, may not be denied under the police power of the state.[62] Courts may not judge the propriety of the school curriculum, methods of teaching, or demonstrations which school officials deem proper and necessary.[63] The courts will not interfere in courses of study prescribed by a school board acting within the scope of its authority.[64] However, under certain circumstances the courts will require specific programs. For example, in a plan for desegregation of schools a remedial education program was required.[65] The courts have also held[66] that compensatory educational programs will be required to provide as nearly as possible equal educational opportunity where, because of the density of residential segregation, integration is impossible.

In all cases the courts will assure that constitutional rights of black children must be upheld to the greatest extent possible. However, the courts recognize that the educational offerings of all school districts cannot be the same. It was held[67] recently that every school district is not compelled to offer all the subjects and classes offered in other school districts. Thus, a student's constitutional rights are not violated if his or her school district has a less extensive curricular offering than another district.

The establishment of departments such as high schools, kindergartens, or night schools[68] is governed by local school authorities. It has been held[69] that authority to establish kindergartens is implied from statutes authorizing the establishment of branches, grades, and supplementary departments as well as from "authority to prescribe other studies."[70] Boards of education may determine whether or not to provide driver education for adults over twenty-one years of age. However, unless the statutes provide for reimbursement, it cannot be made.[71]

The authority of boards of education regarding the curriculum extends beyond the usual academic subjects. It has been held[72] that organized sports are properly included in the school program under management of the board of education. Athletics have been held[73] to be a part of the regular school program. A Montana court held[74] that a local board of education had legal authority to build and equip an outdoor gymnasium and athletic field as part of the facilities needed to produce good citizens. However, physical education credits are not such an indispensable aspect of education to justify prohibiting a girl from graduating when, because of illness, she failed to acquire the required number of credits in physical education.[75]

While a board of education may require

---

[57]State v. Board of Education of City of St. Louis, 233 S.W.2d 697 (Mo. 1950).

[58]Hobalt v. Greenway, 218 N.W.2d 98 (Mich. 1974).

[59]Valent v. State Board of Education, 274 A.2d 832 (N.J. 1971).

[60]Valent v. State Board of Education, 288 A.2d 52 (N.J. 1972).

[61]Hopkins v. Hamden Board of Education, 289 A.2d 914 (Conn. 1971).

[62]Packer Collegiate Institute v. University of State of New York, 76 N.Y.S.2d 1499 (1948); reversed 81 N.E.2d 80 (1948).

[63]State v. Avoyelles Parish School Board, 147 So.2d 729 (La. 1962).

[64]Ritz v. School District of Hazle Township, 51 Luz. L.Rag. 269 (Pa. 1961).

[65]Miller v. School District No. 2, Clarendon County, S.C. 256 F.Supp. 370 (S.C. 1966).

[66]Hobson v. Hanson, 269 F.Supp. 401 (D.C. 1967).

[67]Board of Education of Okay Independent School District v. Carroll, 513 P.2d 872 (Okla. 1973).

[68]Cusack v. New York Board of Education, 66 N.E. 667 (N.Y. 1903).

[69]State v. Board of Education, 42 N.W.2d 168 (Neb. 1950).

[70]Sinnott v. Colombet, 40 Pac. 329 (Cal. 1895).

[71]Acorn Auto Driving School Incorporated v. Board of Education of Leyden High School District No. 212, 187 N.E.2d 722 (Ill. 1963).

[72]Mathias v. School District of Trafford Borough, 35 West. 143 (Pa. 1953).

[73]Appeal of Ganapaski, 2 A.2d 742 (Pa. 1938); Alexander v. Phillips, 254 Pac. 1956 (Ariz. 1927); Woodson v. School District No. 26, 274 Pac. 728 (Kan. 1929).

[74]McNair v. School District No. 1, 288 Pac. 188 (Mont. 1930).

[75]Matter of O'Brien, 13 Ed. Dept. Report, N.Y. Commissioner's Decision 8828.

pupils to attend physical education classes and participate in the program, it may not require pupils to wear prescribed uniforms deemed immodest by the pupils or their parents. In passing on these issues the court held[76] that required participation did not abrogate constitutional rights as long as the pupil was not required to perform any exercise which would be immodest when performed in ordinary wearing apparel.

An interesting case related to athletics arose in Illinois in 1963. A high school student in a school holding membership in the Illinois High School Athletic Association attempted to restrain the association from preventing his participation in athletic contests. There was some dispute about the date of his birth which was controlling since it was the basis of his declared ineligibility and restraint from participation in athletic contests. After three hearings the association determined that the student was ineligible. The Illinois Appellate Court upheld[77] the association on the ground that there was no evidence of fraud or collusion or that the association had acted unreasonably or arbitrarily. It was the position of the court that an athletic association must be permitted to enforce its rules for member schools. Certiorari for review of the case was denied by the United States Supreme Court.

In a Missouri case it was held[78] that a rule prohibiting 19-year-old students from participating in athletics was not unreasonable, arbitrary, and unfair. In another case from the same state it was held[79] that the State Activities Association could lawfully impose a regulation which provided that a secondary school student, who attended a summer camp specializing in one sport for more than two weeks, would lose eligibility for the following year.

Where a high school principal admitted responsibility for fighting among spectators after a football game, the State Athletic Association was within its rights to impose sanctions on the school.[80] Regulations of state athletic or activities associations have not been upheld universally. A regulation which permitted only four years of continuous eligibility from the time the student entered the 9th grade was held[81] unreasonable since it provided no opportunity for the student to present a hardship case. Such a regulation was a denial of due process. Where a boy was removed from an undesirable environment and attended school in another district the rule of the state athletic association that he was ineligible for competition for a year was held to be unreasonable.[82] Nor may a school board delegate its rule-making power to a state athletic association. Thus, the court refused to uphold[83] a rule of a state athletic association which made ineligible for athletic competition a boy who used or transported alcoholic beverages or drugs or who was aware that they were being transported.

One of the most perplexing legal problems is the extent to which girls may participate on boys' athletic teams. A Minnesota court held girls were entitled to participate in a boys' interscholastic athletic program where it was shown that they could compete effectively on these teams and there were no alternate competitive teams for girls.[84] In the view of the court, discrimination by sex in interscholastic athletics constitutes discrimination in education. In this instance the court did not concern itself with the broader question of whether the Minnesota State High School League's rule prohibiting girls from participating on boys' teams was unconstitutional. The above decision is in accord with a ruling with application outside schools which held[85] that the refusal of the Little League Baseball, Inc., to permit girls to play on boys' baseball teams was discriminatory and violated civil rights laws.

In an Illinois case female high school students challenged the limitation placed on girls' contests which were not applicable to boys' contests and prevented them from participating on the boys' swimming team solely because of their sex. The discrimination was ordered by a rule of the Illinois High School Association. The court held[86]

[76]Mitchell v. McCall, 143 So.2d 629 (Ala. 1962).

[77]Robinson v. Illinois High School Association, 195 N.E.2d 38 (Ill. 1963), *cert. denied*, 379 U.S. 960 (1965).

[78]State *ex rel.* Missouri State H.S. Activities Association v. Schoenlaub, 507 S.W.2d 354 (Mo. 1974).

[79]Art Gaines Baseball Camp, Inc. v. Houston, 500 S.W.2d 735 (Mo. 1973).

[80]School District of City of Harrisburg v. Pennsylvania Interscholastic Athletic Association, 309 A.2d 353 (Pa. 1973).

[81]State *ex rel.* Missouri State Activities Association v. Schoenlaub, 507 S.W.2d 354 (Mo. 1974).

[82]Sturrup v. Mahan, 290 N.W.2d 64 (Ind. 1972).

[83]Bunger v. Iowa H.S. Athletic Association, 197 N.W.2d 555 (Iowa 1972).

[84]Brenden v. Independent School District, 342 F.Supp. 1224 (Minn. 1972). For additional cases on this subject see: Commonwealth v. Pennsylvania Interscholastic Athletic Ass'n. 334 A.2d 839 (Pa. 1975); Gelpin v. Kansas State H. S. Activities Ass'n., Inc., 377 F.Supp. 1233 (Kan. 1974); Ruman v. Eskew, 333 N.E.2d 138 (Ind. 1975); Carnes v. Tennessee Secondary School Athletic Association, 415 F.Supp. 569 (Tenn. 1976).

[85]National Organization for Women, Essex County Chapter v. Little League Baseball, Inc., 318 A.2d 33 (N.J. 1974).

[86]Bucha *et al.* v. Illinois H. S. Association, 351 F.Supp. 69 (Ill. 1972).

that there are physical and psychological differences between male and female athletes and refused to order participation of girls on the boys' teams. From decisions to date it appears that if there are no competitive teams for girls they are entitled to participate on boys' teams in noncontact sports.[87] Athletic rules prohibiting mixing of sexes in contact or collision sports have been upheld in one jurisdiction has having a rational basis for a legitimate purpose, and separate but equal athletic programs for boys and girls and have been legally sanctioned.[88]

School dances have not always been given the court's approval as an educational activity. In one case the majority of the court held[89] that they were for recreation and pleasure. One of the justices wrote a strong dissent holding that supervised dances were a definite part of the educational program of any school system.

13.5c Organization of instruction

Local boards of education have the authority to determine the organization for instructional purposes in local school districts. Where the number of pupils in each grade is unevenly distributed, the board may employ another teacher or revert to ungraded rooms so that all pupils may be taught by the teachers employed.[90] A board of education has the power to reduce the number of classes if desired.[91] Grades may be grouped together; i.e., the high school may have four or six grades in one building or may spread over several buildings at the discretion of the board.[92]

In the interest of better education it is sometimes decided to organize schools in a grade-1-through-6 pattern. This action was taken by a local board in Texas upon recommendation of the state superintendent. When objection was raised by the patrons of the district, it was held[93] that the action was not arbitrary as a matter of law and specific arbitrary action must be shown if the action was to be halted. It also was held[94] that, since instruction in graded schools is the preferred method in the United States, courts will not interfere when school boards direct that instruction be given by this method and children are sent from a one-teacher school to a larger, graded school.

It is the function of a local board of education to determine what grades are most appropriately taught in the school district. Thus, it was held[95] that the school board (committee) could, with the approval of the state department of education, discontinue grades 10, 11, and 12 and send the pupils to another high school on a tuition basis. When each county is required to provide twelve grades of education, it is not obligatory to teach all twelve grades in every school district of the county. Decisions concerning services to be provided, and where, are within the sound discretion of the board of education.[96]

It has been held[97] that high school grades are part of a common school system. The county board of education, at its discretion, may establish one or more high schools or junior high schools.[98] The question of continuing or not continuing a department is primarily for the school board to decide, and its discretion, properly exercised, is final.[99] "Public schools" within the statutes providing that all persons over five years old are entitled to attend school include kindergartens when they are available. Authority to determine the class in which a child is to be enrolled, including enrollment in the kindergarten, is within the authority of the school board.[100]

In all cases it is the function of the local board of education to determine within statutory and constitutional requirements what grades and schools are to be operated, and whether in a common school district or a city district. School directors (board members) are permitted discretion to adapt their courses to local conditions.[101] The city council has no voice in determining what schools or grades are to be operated since it is without legal authority in this matter.[102]

---

[87]Morris v. Michigan State Board of Education, 472 F.2d 1207 (6th Cir. 1973); Lee v. Florida H.S. Activities Association, 291 So.2d 636 (Fla. 1974).

[88]Ritacco v. Norwin School District, 361 F.Supp. 930 (Pa. 1973); See also Gilpin v. Kansas State H.S. Activities Association, Inc., 377 F.Supp. 1233 (Kan. 1974).

[89]State Tax Commission v. Board of Education, 73 P.2d 49 (Kan. 1937).

[90]In re Washington Township School, 15 Pa.Co. 509 (Pa. 1894).

[91]Bates v. Board of Education of City and County of San Francisco, 72 Pac. 907 (Cal. 1903).

[92]Hathaway v. New Baltimore, 12 N.W. 186 (Mich. 1882).

[93]District Trustees of District No. 46 of Freestone County v. County Trustees of Freestone County, 197 S.W.2d 579 (Tex. 1946).

[94]Ashton v. Jones, 47 Lack.Jur. 229 (Pa. 1946).

[95]Dowd v. Town of Dover, 133 N.E.2d 501 (Mass. 1956).

[96]Wilson v. Alsip, 76 S.W.2d 288 (Ky. 1934).

[97]Irwin v. Crawford, 78 S.E.2d 609 (Ga. 1953).

[98]Patterson v. Boyd, 87 S.E.2d 861 (Ga. 1955).

[99]Isquith v. Levitt, 137 N.Y.S.2d 497 (1955).

[100]Paden v. Lake Township School District, 42 Luz. L.Reg. 73 (Pa. 1952).

[101]Longauer v. Olyphant Borough School District F, 61 Lack.Jur. 57 (Pa. 1960).

[102]James v. Duckworth, 170 F.Supp. 342 (Va. 1959).

13.5d Gradation of pupils

Local boards of education have authority to determine the level of instruction to be offered and the grades and classes to which pupils are assigned.[103] They may double-promote a pupil if in their judgment the educational interest of the child is best served by doing so.[104] They may refuse to promote a pupil if they do not believe the pupil should be in a higher grade because of age even though the evidence showed the pupil probably was capable of doing the required work.[105] Establishment and maintenance of classes and gradation of pupils are prerogatives of the local board of education, and classifications made in good faith are valid.[106] In conducting schools, boards of education may establish standards for promotion of pupils from one grade to the next and for continuing pupils as members of any particular grade or class.[107] The only limitation is that rules and decisions must be made in good faith and be reasonable.[108]

The preceding general declaration of board power established in litigation summarizes the extent of the authority of the board of education with respect to grade designation of students. This authority to determine the placement of pupils was again affirmed in a New York case. Parents insisted that their son be admitted to the first grade since he was of appropriate age and had already spent a portion of a year in kindergarten. The board placed the student in kindergarten because his attendance at kindergarten the previous year had been inadequate and because the board doubted that his scholarship was sufficient for first-grade work. In considering the parents' petition that their son be placed in first grade the court said:

After a child is admitted to a public school, boards of education have the power to provide rules and regulations for promotion from grade to grade based, not on age, but on training, knowledge and ability.

A board of education is within its legal right in placing children in the kindergarten or 1st or 2nd or any other grade in accordance with its judgment based upon the mental attainment of the child.[109]

The above case not only bears directly on grade-by-grade promotional authority vested in boards of education but also delineates the authority vested in a board to permit pupils to "skip" grades.

An Ohio case supported the authority of the board of education to determine both the methods of normal promotion and those by which a child may be permitted to skip a grade. In this instance a child successfully completed the sixth grade. During the summer he was tutored so that he would be prepared to enter the eighth grade at the beginning of the next school year. That fall he attempted to enter the eighth grade but was refused admission because he had not been authorized by school officials to skip grade 7. Although there was some conflicting testimony, the evidence was substantial that the child was able to meet the scholarship standards necessary for admission to the eighth grade. The Supreme Court of Ohio denied mandamus to compel the district to allow the student to skip the seventh grade because the board of education's prescribed method of requesting permission to skip a grade had not been followed and the board of education refused to authorize promotion in this case. In denying mandamus the court said:

A rule which provides for proper examination at the end of the school year of pupils jointly by teacher of the grade and the superintendent of schools; and for the promotion of pupils to the next higher grade upon recommendation of such teacher and superintendent, the same based on merit, is a reasonable rule. Without proper application, even if a child is mentally able and properly trained, the board will not be compelled to allow the child to skip a grade. Double promotion of a pupil from one grade to the second higher grade is discretionary with the board of education, and in the absence of evidence of permission by the board the court will not order it to be done. . . .[110]

The weight of authority clearly supports the right of the board of education to exercise wide discretionary power in establishing policies and procedures for the retention, demotion, and promotion of pupils.[111] However, one case has held[112] to the contrary. Here the parents of a child were not deemed guilty of violation of the compulsory attendance law when they refused to

[103]Corpus Juris Secundum, op. cit., p. 427, sec. 484c.
[104]Sycamore Board of Education v. State, 88 N.E. 412 (Ohio 1909).
[105]Ibid.
[106]State v. Board of Education, 42 N.W.2d 168 (Neb. 1950).
[107]Creylion v. Board of Education, 163 Pac. 145 (Kan. 1917).
[108]47 American Jurisprudence Schools, p. 403, sec. 147.
[109]Isquith v. Levitt, 137 N.Y.S.2d 497 (1955).

[110]Sycamore Board of Education v. State, 88 N.E. 412 (Ohio 1909).
[111]State v. Ghrist, 270 N.W. 376 (Iowa 1936); State v. Board of Education of the City of Antigo, 172 N.W. 153 (Wis. 1919); Cameron v. Lakeland Class "A" School District, Kootenai County, 353 P.2d 652 (Ida. 1960).
[112]In re Beverly Winters, 146 N.Y.S.2d 107 (1955).

send their child, who was seven years old, to kindergarten a second time after she had been refused admission to the first grade. The child had been denied admittance to the first grade because she had failed to attain the required score on a readiness test administered and interpreted by school authorities. While recognizing that the kindergarten was a regular part of the public school system, the court decided the child could not be compelled to attend there. This decision seems to be a contradiction of the earlier-cited New York case of *Isquith v. Levitt.*

13.5e Lack of scholarship or achievement

Earlier cases held[113] that schools were not required to attempt to instruct pupils who demonstrated a lack of scholarship although it was ruled earlier in California[114] and Ohio[115] that lack of proficiency in subject matter was not grounds for dismissal from a normal school. In both of these cases it was the opinion of the court that exclusion would amount to deprivation of educational opportunities to which the students were entitled. When the board of education attempted to exclude an Illinois boy from high school because he had not satisfactorily passed a grammar test, the court held[116] in favor of the boy. The fact that the father did not wish his child to study grammar weighed in the decision. A recent case has sustained dismissal from school for failure to maintain satisfactory scholastic ratings, absent an abuse of discretionary authority.[117]

13.5f Subversive teaching and learning

From the early 1950s state legislatures, boards of education and laymen have exhibited grave concern lest subversive teaching and learning would take place in the schools. Numerous state laws and local regulations were enacted in an effort to curb such activities. These laws were generally of two types. One was a simple affirmation that teachers or other school employees would uphold the Constitution of the United States and of the state in which they taught or worked. Laws of this type were generally upheld by the courts. The other

type of law or regulation not only required an oath to uphold the Constitution of the United States and the state but prohibited membership in any subversive organization. These laws and regulations were almost universally held to be unconstitutional. Since subversive cases, by and large, resulted in efforts to dismiss teachers, the details of these cases are presented in Chapter 18.

13.5g Instruction of handicapped children

The right to attend school and receive instruction is not a private right held by an individual separate and distinct from the community at large; it is a civil right or political privilege held in common with all others in the same community.[118] The privilege, however, does not appertain to a citizen of the United States as such, and therefore cannot be demanded on the mere status of citizenship.[119] Thus it has been held[120] in several cases that no pupil will be privileged to attend school if the pupil's mental or physical condition is such as to be unduly detrimental to the welfare and progress of the other children in the class or school.

On the other hand, although the board of education has the right to assign mentally retarded pupils to a particular school and in some instances exclude mentally retarded pupils from school altogether, a New York case indicated[121] that school boards are not duty bound to do either. This ruling was made in spite of the recognition in the case of the board's duty to promote the best interest of the school.

It also has been held[122] that boards of education having the option under statutes of establishing special schools for the mentally retarded have the implied power to discontinue such classes.

While the courts generally continue to sustain the rights of schools to classify pupils and place handicapped children in special classes, there is increasing statutory support for the concept that handicapped children are entitled to receive instruction best fitted to their needs. An enactment[123] of the 1973 session of the Wisconsin legislature is indicative of the more recent think-

---

[113]Barnard v. Shelburne, 102 N.W. 1095 (Mass. 1913); Ward v. Flood, 48 Cal. 36, 17 Am.Rep. 405 (1874).

[114]Volume 50 Lawyers' Reports Annotated. (N.S.) P.268 (1914).

[115]*Ibid.*

[116]Trustees of School v. People, 87 Ill. 303, 29 Am.Rep. 55 (1877).

[117]Navato v. Slettern, 415 F.Supp. 312 (Mo. 1976).

[118]Zavilla v. Masse, 147 P.2d 823 (Col. 1944).

[119]Ward v. Flood, 48 Cal. 36, 17 Am.Rep. 405 (1874).

[120]Watson v. Cambridge, 32 N.E. 864 (Mass. 1893).

[121]Hines v. Board of Education of New York City, 10 N.Y.S.2d 840 (1939).

[122]Schwalback v. Board of Education of San Luis Obispo High School District, 60 P.2d 984 (Cal. 1936).

[123]Wisconsin Chapter 89, Laws of 1973.

ing in this area. A number of excerpts make this thinking clear:

SECTION 1. LEGISLATIVE POLICY. (1) *It is the policy of this state to provide, as an integral part of free public education, special education sufficient to meet the needs and maximize the capabilities of all children with exceptional educational needs.*

(2) Furthermore, it is the policy of this state to ensure that each child who has exceptional educational needs is provided with the opportunity to receive a special education at public expense suited to his individual needs. To obtain this end, the legislature recognizes the necessity for a flexible program of special education and for frequent reevaluation of the needs, capabilities and progress of a child with exceptional educational needs.

(3) The legislature also recognizes that it is the responsibility of the school district in which a child with exceptional educational needs resides to ensure that the child is able to receive an education at public expense which is tailored to his needs and capabilities. Special assistance, services, classes or centers shall be provided whenever necessary.

(4) Preference is to be given, whenever appropriate, to education of the child in classes along with children who do not have exceptional educational needs. Where it is not desirable to educate the child who has exceptional educational needs with children who do not have such needs, the child shall be provided with whatever special education is appropriate.

Judicial interpretations of recent years have also upheld the right of handicapped children to an education. In New York in 1973 the Court upheld[124] a statute which required that a physically handicapped child be placed in a suitable institution with expenses paid by the school district. The impact of decisions in Michigan,[125] the District of Columbia,[126] and Pennsylvania[127] are impressive in upholding the rights of handicapped children to an education at public expense. Some of the New York cases,[128] however, are less certain of establishing this right.

The question of whether public funds to provide education for handicapped children could be paid directly to a private school was answered in a Kentucky case. In this instance a statute authorized the payment of public funds to private educational institutions. The court first declared that the statute was primarily for a welfare rather than an educational purpose and then upheld[129] the constitutionality of the statute. A Missouri case established a number of restrictions on the use of public funds in private schools, e.g., prohibiting public school teachers from going into private schools to provide instruction.[130]

13.5h Required homework

Boards of education may control conduct both within and outside the school which has a direct and immediate bearing on the achievement of pupils and may impose reasonable regulations regarding homework. In a Texas case it was held[131] that a teacher could legally punish a pupil for refusing to do an arithmetic assignment at home. In Georgia it was held[132] that the school could prohibit pupils from attending movies or social functions except on Friday or Saturday nights to permit more time for evening study and homework.

However, rules related to homework must be reasonable. A rule which required all pupils to remain in their homes and study from 7:00 to 9:00 every evening was not upheld.[133] In this instance the court held that the school had invaded the home and wrested from the parents the right to control their child.

13.5i Parental rights in instruction

The history of the public school system in this country has been accompanied by acceptance of the principle that local school authorities must have broad, explicit, and implied powers if they are to fulfill their purpose successfully. Generally, if no constitutional or statutory provisions exist to the contrary, boards of education have the right and the responsibility to exercise discretion in formulating rules and taking action which they believe to be educationally sound and in the best interests of the school system.

[124]*In the matter of* Richard C. 348 N.Y.S.2d 42 (1973).
[125]Harrison v. Michigan, 350 F.Supp. 846 (Mich. 1972).
[126]Mills v Board of Education of District of Columbia, 348 F.Supp. 866 (D.C. 1972).
[127]Pennsylvania Association of Retarded Children v. Commonwealth of Pennsylvania, 343 F.Supp. 279 (Pa. 1972).
[128]McMillan v. Board of Education of State of New York, 430 F.2d 1145 (2d Cir. 1970); New York State Association for Retarded Children, Inc. v. Rockefeller, 357 F.Supp. 752 (N.Y. 1973); Aspira of New York v. Board of Education of City of New York, 48 F.R.D. 62 (N.Y. 1973).

[129]Butler v. United Cerebral Palsy of Northern Kentucky, Inc., 352 S.W.2d 203 (Ky. 1961).
[130]Barrera v. Wheeler, 475 F.2d 1338 (8th Cir. 1973), *affirmed,* 417 U.S. 402, 94 S.Ct. 2274, 41 L.Ed.2d 159 (1974).
[131]Balding v. State, 4 S.W. 579 (Tex. 1887).
[132]Mangum v. Keith, 95 S.E. 1 (Ga. 1918).
[133]Hobbs v. Germany, 49 So. 515, 22 L.R.A. (N.S.) 983 (Miss. 1909).

Although it is recognized that boards of education have the same broad discretionary power in establishing rules and making decisions in matters related to the instructional program as they have in other educational matters, parents have often challenged this exercise of discretionary power. The underlying reasons that parents have contested the school board's authority appear to grow out of (1) the lack of explicitly stated applicable constitutional or statutory authority, (2) the inherent conflict between the common-law principles of family autonomy and state welfare, and (3) the uncertainty that exists with reference to the extent to which the state may exercise police power without infringing on rights guaranteed by the Constitution of the United States.

The first area relates to the fact that neither the constitution nor the statutes have provided specific, clearly enunciated operational directives. As a result, the legal question has generally revolved around whether school officers have acted reasonably and in good faith. When personally involved, many parents find this a difficult question to answer objectively.

Perhaps an even more basic reason why controversies arise is a divergence of belief inherent in two fundamental common-law principles, namely, the right of parents to guide their child's education, with primary concern presumably directed at the welfare of the child, and the right of the board of education, as an arm of the state, to direct the child's education for the primary purpose of enhancing the welfare of the state. The courts, when called upon to determine what balance should exist between these two principles, have weighed their decisions in light of the influence the decisions would have on the overall welfare and safety of the state as against an undue encroachment on the right of the parents to rear their children in their own way.

The final but nonetheless important reason that controversies arise from board action in instruction of pupils hinges on the extent to which the state may exercise its police power. This reason for controversy is closely related to the preceding issue in that the police power of the state means that power which the state inherently possesses to restrict the rights of the individual for the general welfare of the people of the state. Since the Constitution of the United States, especially the Fourteenth Amendment, guarantees certain basic rights to the individual, how far the state may go in usurping these rights often must be determined by the courts.

Within the broad framework of individual rights and state welfare, specific rights of parents regarding the education of their children will be presented.

13.5j Selection of subjects

Parents are given considerable latitude in selecting subjects to be studied by their children. This is one of the liberties guaranteed by the Fourteenth Amendment.[134] The courts hold[135] that parents have a deep and abiding interest in the education of their children, deeper even than the interest of the teacher. Thus, it is agreed[136] that parents may make a reasonable selection from the prescribed studies for their child provided that such selection does not interfere with the organization or system of instruction in the particular school. If there are reasonable grounds, it has been held that parents may require the board to excuse their child from physical exercises[137] or from pursuing certain subjects.[138]

Within the broad scope of authority of parents to determine the subjects to be pursued, it has been held[139] that children may not be compelled, over the objection of their parents, to study grammar or geography,[140] domestic science,[141] or to attend sessions devoted to the reading of the Bible.[142] In considering whether a child could be compelled to study a subject to which the parent objected the court explained its position as follows:

> The policy of the school law is only to withdraw from the parent the right to select the branches to be studied by the child, to the extent that the exercise of that right would interfere with the system of instruction prescribed for the school, and its efficiency in imparting education to all entitled to share in its benefits.

> . . . Conceding that all the branches of study decided to be taught in the school shall not necessarily be pursued by every pupil, we are unable to perceive how it can, in any wise, prejudice the school, if one branch rather than

[134]People v. Stanley, 255 Pac. 610 (Col. 1927).
[135]State v. School District No. 1, 48 N.W. 393 (Neb. 1891).
[136]Corpus Juris Secundum, op. cit., p. 430, sec. 485c.
[137]Hardwick v. Fruitridge School District, 205 Pac. 49 (Cal. 1921).
[138]State v. Ferguson, 144 N.W. 1039, 50 A.L.R. (N.S.) 266 (Neb. 1914).
[139]State v. School District No. 1, 48 N.W. 393 (Neb. 1891). See also Trustees of School v. People, 87 Ill. 303, 29 Am.Rep. 55 (1877).
[140]Morrow v. Wood, 35 Wis. 59, 17 Am.Rep. 471 (1874).
[141]State v. Ferguson, 144 N.W. 1039 (Neb. 1914).
[142]People v. Stanley, 255 Pac. 610 (Col. 1927).

another be omitted from the course of study of a particular pupil.[143]

Parents may likewise forbid participation of their children in social dancing in class when the objection is on religious grounds.[144] The dancing in this case was performed in couples, boys and girls dancing together.

The reasonable selection of courses which may be made by the parent[145] does not entitle parents to insist that their child be taught courses not in the curriculum of the school.[146]

Even though the above decisions represent the weight of authority, they have not been upheld universally. In some jurisdictions pupils have been required to pursue a particular subject regardless of the wishes of their parents. Pupils have been required against the wishes of their parents to study music,[147] to prepare written exercises and declamations,[148] to study rhetoric when it is a prescribed part of the curriculum,[149] to write compositions and enter into debates,[150] and even to take the part of an Irish character at a commencement exercise.[151]

While parents generally may select subjects to be studied, it is the function of the school and the professional staff to determine the proper mode of instruction, and the courts have consistently held[152] this a prerogative of the school. Pupils may not refuse to study a subject because the parent objects to the method of instruction used by the teacher.[153] Nor may parents insist that their child use a textbook different from that of the others or follow a method of study that interferes with the study of other pupils.[154]

13.5k Inspection of records

In recent years, by both statutory enactments and court decisions, parents and students over 18 have been given increased access to their children's and/or their own records. The Family Education Rights and Privacy Act of 1974 and the Buckley Amendments[155] provide that all schools must review their record-keeping policies and develop criteria to determine appropriate content of student records. Violation may lead to loss of federal educational funds. In addition, the Act provides that parents or any student over 18 years of age or attending a postsecondary institution may inspect "any and all official records, files and other data directly related to their children" or to them. A hearing is also provided where parents and students may challenge the inclusion of inaccurate, misleading, or inappropriate materials. No one except a school official or a teacher with a legitimate educational interest may see such records without written consent of the parent. Some clarifying amendments to the Act have made certain limited information, such as letters of recommendation, confidential information. Students may also waive their rights to see confidential financial statements submitted to colleges by their parents and permit colleges to send to parents grades of students classified as dependent.

To date few states have statutes dealing with the right of privacy of student records and this area in the past has been left almost exclusively to local rules and regulations. In some judicial decisions it has been held[156] that the right of examination extends to all public records bearing on the decision about the child. Other cases limit the information which a school district may collect. In a case decided in the United States Supreme Court it was held[157] that schools are not authorized to collect information relating to marriage, procreation, contraception, family relationship, and child rearing. In another Supreme Court case it was held[158] that parents can have removed from the files and bar collection of data that impose on a child a negative label of doubtful validity.

[143]Trustees of School v. People, 87 Ill. 303, 29 Am.Rep. 55 (1877).

[144]Hardwick v. Fruitridge School District, 205 Pac. 49 (Cal. 1921).

[145]Garvin County School Board District No. 18 v. Thompson, 103 Pac. 578, 24 L.R.A. (N.S.) 221 (Okla. 1909).

[146]Trustees of School v. People, 87 Ill. 303, 29 Am.Rep. 55 (1877).

[147]State v. Webber, 8 N.E. 708, 58 Am.Rep. 30 (Ind. 1886).

[148]Kidder v. Chellis, 59 N.H. 473 (1880).

[149]Sewell v. Board of Education, 29 Ohio St. 89 (1876).

[150]Samuel Benedict Memorial School v. Bradford, 36 S.E. 920 (Ga. 1900).

[151]Cross v. Board of Trustees, 110 S.W. 346 (Ky. 1908).

[152]Wulff v. Inhabitants of Wakefield, 109 N.E. 358 (Mass. 1915); Guernsey v. Pitkin, 32 Vt. 224, 76 Am.Dec. 171 (1859).

[153]Ibid.

[154]School Trustees v. People, 87 Ill. 303, 29 Am.Rep. 55 (1877).

[155]Public Law 93-380 Family Educational Rights and Privacy Act of 1974; But see Chappell v. Commissioner of Education of N.J. 343 A.2d 811 (N.J. 1975).

[156]Mills v. Board of Education of District of Columbia, 348 F.Supp. 866 (D.C. 1972).

[157]Roe v. Wade, 410 U.S. 113, 93 S.Ct. 705, 35 L.Ed.2d 147, rehearing denied, 410 U.S. 959, 93 S.Ct. 1409, 35 L.Ed.2d 694 (Tex. 1973).

[158]Wisconsin v. Constantineau, 400 U.S. 433, 91 S.Ct. 507, 27 L.Ed.2d 515 (Wis. 1971).

In a Pennsylvania case it was held[159] that information which is of a private nature is protected by several amendments of the Constitution.

13.6 TEXTS, LIBRARY BOOKS, AND INSTRUCTIONAL MATERIAL

The authority to select textbooks must be pursuant to statutes. The legislature has the authority to provide terms under which textbooks may be selected, and local school districts must comply with such terms.[160] Where a uniform system of textbooks is required, the state may implement its operation with the least expense and inconvenience.[161] The fact that the constitution authorizes free textbooks in the elementary grades provides no authorization for free textbooks in high schools.[162] A legislative act that stipulates the furnishing of free textbooks without reference to private schools is construed to apply to the public schools only.[163] If the legislature provides for the use of uniform adopted textbooks, such textbooks must be used in local school districts.[164]

While an earlier case held[165] that unless the constitution or statutes provided for free textbooks they could not be furnished, this situation no longer prevails. The question of whether free textbooks are included in the guarantee of free public education has been before the courts on numerous occasions and the courts are in serious disagreement on this issue. The disagreement is explained to some degree by differences in the wording of constitutional guarantees and statutory provisions, but much of the difference cannot be reconciled. Decisions in Michigan[166] and Idaho[167] have held that textbooks and/or supplies are to be included in the guarantee of free public education. In Michigan the court held that the provision for free education included both books and

school supplies. In Idaho the court held a fee could not be charged for textbooks nor could extracurricular fees be imposed on all students whether or not they participated. Other states have taken a contrary point of view: In Arizona and Colorado it has been held[168] that the state's constitutional guarantee of free public education does not mandate free textbooks for high school students. In Indiana it was held[169] that the constitutional provisions for free public education do not include the provision of free textbooks. In this case it was also held that the constitutional provision of free public education in no way invalidated the school book rental policy of a district. The case did, however, hold that pupils could not be suspended merely because their parents had not paid school fees or executed an "ability to pay" form. In Illinois it was decided[170] that at the time of adoption of the state constitution it was not envisioned that textbooks would be provided at public expense. Therefore, the court upheld constitutional and statutory provisions which authorized school boards to purchase textbooks and rent them to pupils. A related case tested the constitutionality of a New York law which provided state financial aid to any district for the purchase of textbooks to be loaned free to students in grades 7–12 but not in grades 1–6. The court upheld[171] the statute, indicating that it did not constitute a denial of equal protection of the law. After the United States Supreme Court granted certiorari to review this decision, the school district voted to provide free textbooks in grades 1–6. Subsequently the Supreme Court decided not to review the case.

In deciding whether a fee could be charged for textbooks as well as a variety of other instructional items, both curricular and extracurricular, a Montana court set the following criterion to determine if it was to be provided free: "Is a given course or activity reasonably related to a recognized academic or educational goal. . . ." If this criterion is met, it constitutes part of the public school system commanded to be free by the Montana Constitution. In its decision the court pointed out that it was considering only activities offered during the school

---

[159]Merriken et al. v. Cressman et al., 364 F.Supp. 913 (Pa. 1973). See also United States v. Kalish, 271 F.Supp. 968 (Puerto Rico 1967).

[160]State v. Haworth, 23 N.E. 946, 7 L.R.A. 240 (Ind. 1890).

[161]Duncan v. Heyward, 54 S.E. 760 (S.C. 1906).

[162]Macmillan Co. v. Clarke, 194 Pac. 1030, 17 A.L.R. 288 (Cal. 1921).

[163]Smith v. Donahue, 195 N.Y.S. 715 (1922); Haas v. Independent School District No. 1 Yankton, 9 N.W.2d 707 (S.D. 1943).

[164]Schlake v. Board of Education of Fort Thomas, 42 S.W.2d 526 (Ky. 1931).

[165]Haas v. Independent School District No. 1, 9 N.W.2d 707 (S.D. 1943).

[166]Bond v. Public School of Ann Arbor School District, 178 N.W.2d 484 (Mich. 1970).

[167]Paulson v. Minidoka County School District No. 31, 463 P.2d 935 (Idaho 1970).

[168]Carpio v. Tucson High School District No. 1, 517 P.2d 1288 (Ariz. 1974); Marshall v. School District RE 3 Morgan County, 553 P.2d 784 (Col. 1976).

[169]Chandler v. South Bend Community School Corporation, 312 N.E.2d 914 (Ind. 1974).

[170]Hamer v. Board of Education of School District No. 109, 265 N.E.2d 616 (Ill. 1970).

[171]Johnson v. New York State Education Department, 449 F.2d 871 (2nd Cir. 1971).

year.[172] Thus, fees may be charged for summer school. This later statement is at variance with the law in other states, such as Wisconsin.[173] In New York the Commissioner of Education upheld school districts in charging an annual swimsuit fee and prohibited students from bringing their own swimsuits on the basis of health and safety.[174] However, charging of fees has not been universally held.[175]

In the absence of constitutional or statutory directives local boards of education have wide latitude in selection of text and library books. However, local pressure groups exert extensive unofficial pressure in this area. Virtually every literary work of any importance in this century has been banned somewhere in the United States, the American Library Association reports.[176] The books most often banned, according to Kenneth Donelson of Arizona State University, are Salinger's *Catcher in the Rye*, Steinbeck's *The Grapes of Wrath*, and Vonnegut's *Slaughterhouse Five*. Other books which have been banned include *Jonathan Livingston Sea Gull*, *Silas Marner*, *Moby Dick*, *Brave New World*, *1984*, and *Fahrenheit 451*.

Cases of this type infrequently come to the attention of the courts, but when they do the authority of the board to determine the books to be used is usually upheld.[177] One illustration of this authority is found in a New York case in which a taxpayer attempted to force a board of education to desist from using *Oliver Twist* and *The Merchant of Venice* in the public schools because it was claimed that they portrayed Jewish characters in an unfavorable light. The court refused to sustain the objection to the use of the books, holding that, except where a book has been maliciously written for the apparent purpose of promoting and fomenting a bigoted and intolerant hatred of a particular racial or religious group, public interest in a free and democratic society

does not warrant its suppression. Discretion of administrative officers of public schools in their choice of books must not be interfered with by the courts in the absence of proof of actual malevolent intent. The use of the book *Slaughterhouse Five* was also upheld[178] against the charges that it contained reference to religious matters and was obscene. The book was used as an elective in a contemporary literature course.

The power delegated to local boards of education to select textbooks is a continuous legislative power and is not to be interfered with by the courts except on grounds of abuse or fraud. In a Wisconsin case it was held[179] that the school board was not subject to the common council's approval or disapproval of textbooks. Another Wisconsin case decided[180] that the board had the right to rescind previous action adopting certain textbooks in favor of choosing other books. The selection and adoption of school books was to be exercised in accordance with the good judgment and discretion of the board and was not to be dictated or controlled by the courts.

It should be understood that all constitutional and statutory restrictions must be obeyed. Many states prohibit textbooks that are sectarian or denominational in nature.[181] It has been held that the Bible is a sectarian book and may not be used in the public schools. However, a Michigan court in an early decision approved[182] reading from a book containing passages from the Bible. The book was made up almost entirely of passages from the Bible but emphasized moral precepts, calculated to inculcate good morals to be practiced by all citizens. In a 1962 case[183] a Florida court refused to prohibit religious art work displays in public schools. When this case was appealed to the United States Supreme Court, the state court was upheld on this issue but deemed in error in upholding reading of the Bible in the public schools.[184]

The statutes of a number of states have the

---

[172]Granger v. Cascade County School District, 499 P.2d 780 (Mont. 1972).

[173]Wisconsin Statutes Annotated 118.04 (1973).

[174]Matter of Posman, Education Department N.Y. Commissioner's Decision 8524 (1972).

[175]Young v. Trustees of Fountain Inn Graded School, 41 S.E. 824 (S.C. 1902); Paulson v. Minedoka County School District, 463 P.2d 935 (Ida. 1970); Bond v. Public Schools of Ann Arbor School District, 178 N.W.2d 484 (Mich. 1970).

[176]*Phi Delta Kappa*, Bloomington, Indiana, January, 1975, p. 376; See also National Education Association, *Today's Education*, January-February 1975 p. 22-26.

[177]Rosenberg v. Board of Education of City of New York, 92 N.Y.S.2d 344 (1949); But see Minarcini v. Strongsville City School District, 541 F.2d 577 (6th Cir. 1976).

[178]Todd v. Rochester Community Schools, 200 N.W.2d, 90 (Mich. 1972).

[179]Madden v. Kinney, 93 N.W. 535 (Wis. 1903).

[180]Ginn v. Wilson, 99 N.W. 336 (Wis. 1904).

[181]State v. District Board, City of Edgerton, 44 N.W. 967, 7 L.R.A. 330 (Wis. 1890); State v. Scheve, 91 N.W. 846, 93 N.W. 169, 50 L.R.A. 927 (Neb. 1902); But see Williams v. Board of Education City of Kanawha, 388 F.Supp. 93 (W.Va. 1975).

[182]Pfeiffer v. Board of Education, 77 N.W. 250 (Mich. 1898).

[183]Chamberlin v. Dade County Board of Public Instruction, 143 So.2d 21 (Fla. 1962).

[184]Chamberlin v. Dade County Board of Public Instruction, 377 U.S. 402, 84 S.Ct. 1272, 12 L.Ed.2d 407 (Fla. 1964).

intent of prohibiting subversive textbooks in the schools. A section of the Wisconsin statute is specific in this regard and reads as follows:

> No book shall be adopted for use or be used in any public school which falsifies the facts regarding the history of our nation, or which defames our nation's founders, or misrepresents the ideals and causes for which they struggled and sacrificed, or which contains propaganda favorable to any foreign government.[185]

Statutory regulations such as the above have full force regardless of any local regulations to the contrary.

13.7 RELIGIOUS INFLUENCE IN EDUCATION

Religious instruction in the public schools is not of recent origin; controversy over its rightful place has been voiced from the earliest days of public education in the United States. Horace Mann was forced to defend himself against the charge of being antireligious when he attempted to restrict religious instruction in the public schools to Bible reading without interpretation and comment. The early issue was not whether religion should be taught in the public schools. It was an accepted part of the curriculum and its teaching was a fact. Actually, the major purpose of education was to teach reading so the Bible could be read, as witnessed by the "Old Deluder Satan" Act of Massachusetts in 1647. The issue was which particular sectarian religion was to be taught in the public schools and to what extent.

13.7a Bible reading and prayers

Over the years Bible reading has been required by constitutional enactments or statutory provisions in a number of states. These provisions often require the recitation of the Lord's Prayer.

Bible reading in the public schools together with religious and moral instruction has had a long history of court approval. An early, precedent-setting case[186] interpreted mandatory Bible reading as authority to compel the reading of the King James Version. The large majority of state courts, over the years, have held that reading of the King James Version of the Bible without comment did not violate any constitutional provisions nor interfere with any rights of religious freedom. This same position was taken in three cases decided between 1950 and 1962.[187]

The *Chamberlin* case critically referred to decisions in the United States federal court and rendered a decision at variance with that of the federal court. The federal court decision prohibiting Bible reading was later sustained by the United States Supreme Court.

Over a period of years there have been important exceptions to approved Bible reading or saying of prayers in the public schools. A minority of states have ruled that reading from the King James Version of the Bible was sectarian instruction and prohibited by their constitutions. Cases in Illinois,[188] Louisiana,[189] Pennsylvania,[190] Nebraska,[191] New Jersey,[192] and Wisconsin[193] have ruled against the practice, generally holding that the Bible was a sectarian book. Illinois ruled on a combination of Bible reading and recitation of the Lord's Prayer in its decision, holding the combined activities unconstitutional. In Missouri it was held[194] that boards of education may not use their power to enforce religious worship in the public schools even in the faith of the parents.

13.7b United States Supreme Court and subsequent cases

The focal issue of saying prayers in the public schools came to the United States Supreme Court in 1963 when the Regents of the State of New York formulated a prayer and recommended that it be recited in the public schools of the state. The formulated prayer was as follows: "Almighty God, we acknowledge our dependence upon Thee, and we beg Thy blessings upon us, our parents, our teachers and our country."

Union Free School District No. 9, New Hyde Park, New York, adopted the prayer, and parents objected on the grounds that the use of the state-formulated prayer vio-

---

[185]Wisconsin Statutes 118.03(2) (1972).
[186]Donahoe v. Richards, 38 Me. 376 (1854).

[187]Doremus v. Board of Education, 75 A.2d 880 (N.Y. 1950); Chamberlin v. Dade County Board of Public Instruction, 143 So.2d 21 (Fla. 1962); Carden v. Bland, 288 S.W.2d 718 (Tenn. 1956).
[188]People v. Board of Education of District 24, 92 N.E. 251 (Ill. 1910).
[189]Herold v. Parish Board, 68 So. 116 (La. 1915).
[190]Schempp v. School District of Abington Township, 201 F.Supp. 815 (Pa. 1962).
[191]State v. Scheve, 91 N.W. 846 (Neb. 1902).
[192]Tudor v. Board of Education, 100 A.2d 857 (N.J. 1953).
[193]State v. District Board of Edgerton, 44 N.W. 967 (Wis. 1890).
[194]Harfst v. Hoegen, 163 S.W.2d 609, 141 A.L.R. 1136 (Mo. 1942).

lated the First Amendment of the United States Constitution since it related to the establishment of a religion. The school district argued that, since the prayer was non-denominational and pupils could remain silent or be excused from the room, there was no establishment of a religion. The United States Supreme Court by a six-to-one vote sustained the parents' charges and prohibited the use of the prayer in the public schools.[195]

On June 17, 1963, the United States Supreme Court rendered a more far-reaching decision regarding religious activities in the public schools. While in *Engel v. Vitale (supra)* the United States Supreme Court had before it the question of the use of a state-formulated prayer, which could more easily be decided, it now was faced with the broader issue of whether the Lord's Prayer and Bible reading could be used in the public schools under any circumstances.

The decision was in response to two appeals: one from Maryland,[196] the other from Pennsylvania.[197] The cases differed only slightly. In the *Murray* case (Maryland) the facts were not subjected to trial. The Baltimore school board demurred to the facts, i.e., indicated that even if the facts as alleged were true there was no cause for legal action. The school board required the "reading, without comment, of a chapter in the Holy Bible and/or the use of the Lord's Prayer." In the *Schempp* case (Pennsylvania) testimony was taken and considered. In this instance the King James Version of the Bible was read by the students, without comment. Following the reading of the Bible, the Lord's Prayer was recited in unison.

In consolidating these cases, the Supreme Court determined that for all practical purposes the essential points for decision were the same. The decision was composed of the majority opinion, three concurring opinions, and one dissent. The majority and concurring opinions held[198] that both the reading of the Bible and recitation of the Lord's Prayer were unconstitutional. It was held that these practices violate both the clause of the First Amendment which prohibits the establishment of a religion and the clause which guarantees the free exercise thereof. While it was recognized by the

Supreme Court that the school did not compel children to join in the religious activities if their parents objected, the social forces exerted on a pupil were excessive. Thus, the argument of the voluntary attendance feature was looked upon by the court as lacking in substance, and voluntary and compulsory provisions were held to be identical.

It is to be noted that the court did say in the dicta of the case that the study of comparative religion, the history of religion, and the relationship of religion to civilization were not prohibited by this decision. It would appear from the dicta that, although the Bible may not be used to teach religion, if objectively presented, passages from it may be used in several different areas of study, e.g., history, civics, literature, etc.

The several decisions of the United States Supreme Court reported above did not end litigation regarding Bible reading and saying of prayers in public schools. As expected, most subsequent decisions have held Bible reading and/or the saying of prayers unconstitutional. Decisions to this effect have been rendered in Delaware,[199] Florida,[200] Idaho,[201] Massachusetts,[202] New Hampshire,[203] New Jersey,[204] and New York.[205] In a number of these cases the statutes of the state provided for compulsory daily reading of the Bible and/or saying of the Lord's Prayer or other types of devotionals. State statutes, as well as local regulations of this nature, were held unconstitutional.

In Alabama a state statute requiring daily Bible reading in the schools was declared[206] unconstitutional in 1971 as violating the Establishment Clause of the United States Constitution. The third circuit enjoined[207] a school district in Pennsylvania from permitting voluntary Bible reading and non-denominational mass prayers in the public

[195]Engel v. Vitale, 370 U.S. 421, 82 S.Ct. 1261, 8 L.Ed.2d 601 (N.Y. 1962).

[196]Murray v. Curlett, 179 A.2d 698 (Md. 1962).

[197]Schempp v. School District of Abington Township, 201 F.Supp. 815 (Pa. 1962).

[198]School District of Abington Township v. Schempp, 374 U.S. 203, 83 S.Ct. 1560, 10 L.Ed.2d 844 (Pa. 1963).

[199]Johns v. Allen, 231 F.Supp. 852 (Del. 1964).

[200]Chamberlin v. Dade County Board of Public Instruction, 377 U.S. 402, 84 S.Ct. 1272, 12 L.Ed.2d 407 (Fla. 1964).

[201]Adams v. Engelking, 232 F.Supp. 666 (Ida. 1964).

[202]Attorney General v. School Committee of North Brookfield, 199 N.E.2d 553 (Mass. 1964); Waite v. School Committee of Newton, 202 N.E.2d 297 (Mass. 1964).

[203]Opinion of the Justices, 228 A.2d 161 (N.H. 1967).

[204]Sills v. Board of Education of Hawthorne, 200 A.2d 615 (N.J. 1963).

[205]Stein v. Oshinsky, 348 F.2d 999 (2d Cir. 1965), cert. denied, 382 U.S. 957 (1966).

[206]Alabama Civil Liberties Union v. Wallace, 331 F.Supp. 966 (Ala. 1971).

[207]Mangold v. Albert Gallatin School District, 438 F.2d 1194 (3rd Cir. 1971).

schools. In West Virginia and New Jersey the court prohibited[208] use of school facilities to permit high school pupils to hold voluntary group prayer meetings. More recently courts appear to be upholding periods of silent meditation when provided by statutes.[209]

In a related prayer case the children in an Illinois kindergarten class recited the following verse:

We thank you for the flowers so sweet;
We thank you for the food we eat;
We thank you for the birds that sing;
We thank you for everything.

Prior to recitation of this verse it was alleged that the children folded their hands in their laps, closed their eyes, and assumed a prayerful attitude. The parents maintained these activities constituted a prayer in violation of the federal Constitution. School authorities maintained that this exercise taught the children politeness, good manners, and gratitude and helped prepare the children for life. The lower court held[210] the activity acceptable since no government law or regulation authorized the verse. It was the choice of an individual teacher and was a "mere shadow rather than a real threat" to constitutional guarantees. Thus the complaint of the parents was dismissed. However, on appeal the decision was reversed and the prayer prohibited.[211]

In an opinion of the Justices in New Hampshire it was indicated that a proposed bill requiring periods of meditation in the first class each day in all public schools would be constitutional. The opinion also stated that requiring every public school classroom to display a suitable plaque bearing the words, "In God We Trust" would not violate the Establishment Clause of the First Amendment.[212]

13.7c Purchase and distribution of Bibles

Whether Bibles may be purchased by the public schools and kept in the school library appears to depend both on the word-ing of the constitution and on the courts' interpretation of it.

In Wisconsin, as in several other states, the Bible has been held[213] to be a sectarian book. Since public funds may not be spent for a sectarian purpose, it seems to follow that they may not be spent to purchase the Bible or to provide facilities for its safekeeping (library). In an early California case it was held[214] that the board of education could purchase copies of both the King James and the Douay Version of the Bible since neither was considered a sectarian book. Obviously if the Bible is not held to be a sectarian book, the constitutional prohibitions against spending money for a sectarian purpose do not apply to either the purchase of the Bible or keeping it in the library.

A related problem is whether the professional staff of a school district may assist the Gideon Society in distribution of the King James Version of the Bible. In states where the Bible is held to be a sectarian book and there is a constitutional prohibition against spending public funds for a sectarian purpose, any assistance provided by tax-supported funds in the distribution would be illegal. It was so held[215] in one case where this issue was adjudicated.

13.7d Religious instruction

Direct religious instruction in the public schools generally is held to be sectarian instruction and is not permitted by the courts. Public school teachers may not place religious pamphlets in schoolrooms.[216]

Where certain nuns and brothers of the Roman Catholic Church employed in the public schools knowingly taught sectarian religion during regular school hours in violation of statutes, they were permanently enjoined from teaching in the public schools.[217]

13.7e Released time in public schools

Closely related to the issue of religious instruction in the public schools is that of released time. The first case on this issue in New York in 1925 held[218] that the furnishing of registration cards for a released-time program violated the constitutional provision prohibiting use of funds to aid sectar-

---

[208]Hunt v. Board of Education, 321 F.Supp. 1263 (W.Va. 1971); State Board of Education v. Board of Education, 262 A.2d 21, *affirmed*, 270 A.2d 412, *cert. denied*, 401 U.S. 1013, 91 S.Ct. 1253, 28 L.Ed.2d 550 (N.J. 1971).
[209]Gaines v. Anderson, 421 F.Supp. 337 (Mass. 1976); Opinion of the Justices, 228 A.2d 161 (N.H. 1967).
[210]DeSpain v. DeKalb County Community School District 428, 255 F.Supp. 655 (Ill. 1966).
[211]DeSpain v. DeKalb County Community School District 428, 384 F.2d 836 (7th Cir. 1967), *cert. denied*, 390 U.S. 906 88 S.Ct. 815 19 L.Ed.2d 873 (1968).
[212]Opinion of the Justices, 228 A.2d 161 (N.H. 1967).

[213]State v. District Board, City of Edgerton, 44 N.W. 967, 7 L.R.A. 330 (Wis. 1890).
[214]Evans v. Selma High School District, 222 Pac. 801, 31 A.L.R. 1121 (Cal. 1924).
[215]Tudor v. Board of Education, 100 A.2d 857 (N.J. 1953), cert. denied, 348 U.S. 816 (1954).
[216]Miller v. Cooper, 244 P.2d 520 (N.M. 1952).
[217]Zellers v. Huff, 236 P.2d 949 (N.M. 1951).
[218]Stein v. Brown, 211 N.Y.S. 822 (1925).

ian instruction. Two years later, in New York, released time was upheld[219] when other agencies furnished the cards.

In 1946 the issue of released time was again before the courts, this time in Illinois. In its decision the court permitted[220] the board of education to excuse children at the request of the parents for one hour each week before the regular closing of school.

In 1947 a California court ruled[221] that a statute which permitted the board to release children for religious instruction was constitutional.

The released-time issue has been adjudicated twice in the United States Supreme Court. The first case was on appeal from the Supreme Court of Illinois in 1948. The Board of Education of Champaign, Illinois, by cooperative agreement with a local religious educational association, allowed religious teachers, employed by private religious groups, to come weekly into the school buildings during the hours in which school was regularly in session. Students whose parents so desired and so signified in writing could attend these classes, which were conducted in regular rooms of the school. Students who did not choose to take religious instructions were required to leave their classrooms and study elsewhere. The court's decision held[222] that, in view of the provisions of the First and Fourteenth Amendments of the United States Constitution, a state could not utilize its tax-supported public schools to aid any or all religious faiths or sects in the dissemination of their doctrines and ideals. This was what was being done, in the opinion of the court.

Four years later the second major released-time case came to the United States Supreme Court from the state of New York. The New York City schools conducted a program which permitted students to leave the school buildings and grounds during the school day to gather at religious centers for religious instruction or devotional exercises. A student was released on written request of his or her parents. Those not released stayed in the classrooms. The churches made weekly reports to the schools, sending a list of children who, though released from public school, had not reported for religious instruction. The program involved neither the use of public

school classrooms nor the direct use of public funds.

In its opinion that this type of program was constitutional the court held[223] that it did not establish a religion. The criteria used by the majority as the basis of decision were that (1) the state must be neutral in religion—it may not favor one sect over another—and (2) no public funds may be spent to aid sectarian instruction in any way. Both of these conditions, in the opinion of the majority, were met in the New York program. The majority opinion expressed the view that the encouragement of religious instruction and cooperation with religious authorities by adjusting school schedules followed the best of our American traditions.

In a more recent decision the Oregon Supreme Court in 1960 held[224] that, where the statutes provide for excusing of pupils to attend religious instruction, released time is mandatory so that a child must be excused upon application of the parent. The released-time statute was not unconstitutional even though it failed to designate clearly to whom the application for released time was to be made.

In 1970 a federal district court invalidated[225] a released-time program in Virginia similar to that operated in the *McCollum* case. The school permitted teachers from a private organization to provide religious instruction in the elementary schools. Children whose parents objected were permitted to go to special study rooms. In dicta the court noted that a school program for all children without indoctrination —such as a course in comparative religion or history of religion—would be constitutional.

Several state supreme courts have ruled[226] released time constitutional: California, Illinois, New York, Oregon, and Washington. In 1973 Wisconsin enacted a statute providing for released time in the public schools. The program operated here has been held constitutional as was a more recent released-time program in Virginia.[227]

[219]Lewis v. Graves, 156 N.E. 663 (N.Y. 1927).
[220]People v. Board of Education, 68 N.E.2d 305 (Ill. 1946).
[221]Gordon v. Board of Education, City of Los Angeles, 178 P.2d 488 (Cal. 1947).
[222]McCollum v. Board of Education, 333 U.S. 203, 68 S.Ct. 461, 92 L.Ed. 648 (Ill. 1948).

[223]Zorach v. Clauson, 343 U.S. 306, 72 S.Ct. 679, 96 L.Ed. 954 (N.Y. 1952).
[224]Dilger v. School District 24 C.J., 352 P.2d 564 (Ore. 1960).
[225]Vaughn v. Reed, 313 F.Supp. 431 (Va. 1970).
[226]Lewis v. Spaulding, 85 N.Y.S.2d 682 (1948); Gordon v. Board of Education, City of Los Angeles, 178 P.2d 488 (Cal. 1947); People v. Board of Education, 68 N.E.2d 305 (Ill. 1946); Dilger v. School District 24 C.J., 352 P.2d 564 (Ore. 1960); Perry v. School District No. 81, Spokane, 344 P.2d 1036 (Wash. 1960).
[227]Holt v. Thompson, 225 N.W.2d 678 (Wis. 1975); Smith v. Smith, 523 F.2d 121 (4th Cir. 1975).

13.7f Nuns in public schools

Religious issues coming before the courts at the present time are more likely to involve tangential issues than the direct question of religious instruction. One such issue is the employment of "sectarian" oriented teachers wearing religious garb. Generally the wearing of religious garb has not been considered[228] a direct sectarian influence apart from some overt act of religious influence. Thus, it was deemed unjust to deny an otherwise qualified teacher who wears religious garb the right to teach in the public schools. However, Missouri, New York, and New Mexico do not permit the wearing of religious garb in the public schools; it was held[229] that the wearing of religious garb was indicative of sectarian instruction. Two states have permitted nuns teaching in the public schools to donate their earnings to their religious order; it was held[230] that this did not constitute the use of public funds for sectarian purposes.

13.7g Related religious issues

A number of other religious issues with varying degrees of relationship to public school instruction has been brought to the courts: shared time or dual enrollment, free textbooks for parochial school children, rental of instructional space from sectarian groups, graduation and baccalaureate exercises in churches, distribution of religious pamphlets, and censorship of films (religious). Each of these issues will be treated briefly.

13.7h Shared time or dual enrollment

Shared time or dual enrollment is defined as an arrangement which contemplates the enrollment of a pupil in two regularly constituted and maintained educational institutions for varying portions of the school day (e.g., a half-day at each school), the one owned, directed, and maintained as a tax-supported institution, the other as a religious institution. Pupils may attend either institution only with the expressed consent of their parents, and no direction or control is to be exerted by either institution upon the other. In each instance attendance con-

stitutes part-time enrollment in each of the two institutions.

The specific issue of the constitutionality and other aspects of shared time or dual enrollment came to the Appellate Court of Illinois in 1966 when the dual enrollment program of the city of Chicago was challenged. The court upheld the program, indicating that it complied with the compulsory attendance statute and was not in violation of statutory or constitutional provisions. The same decision was rendered in Michigan.[231]

In a related case in Missouri the court arrived at a somewhat different conclusion. Here the public school district provided speech therapy for children in the parochial schools. During the first year of the program the speech teachers went to the parochial schools. The following year the district changed its program and provided speech therapy for parochial school children in a public school building. Parochial school children desiring to receive such therapy were released from their parochial schools for part of the regular school day. This type of program, the court held,[232] violated the section of the Missouri constitution which provides that state funds are to be appropriated to free public schools and for no other uses or purposes whatsoever.

Usually the courts have held that school boards may enact such reasonable rules and regulations as may be necessary for the satisfactory administration of the school. Under these decisions a board of education may enact a rule authorizing pupils to be enrolled for less than a full day. This is a common practice in a variety of circumstances at the present time. If part-time attendance is legal regardless of what pupils do during the balance of the school day, it would appear that a shared-time program would be legally possible, assuming that local boards of education deemed such a practice desirable and approved the necessary regulations for part-time attendance in public schools.

13.7i Free textbooks for parochial school children

Few cases have come into litigation challenging the constitutionality of statutes providing free textbooks in parochial

[228]Hysong v. Gallitzin Borough School Dist., 30 Atl. 482 (Pa. 1894); State v. Boyd, 28 N.E.2d 256 (Ind. 1940); Rawlings v. Butler, 290 S.W.2d 801 (Ky. 1956); Gerhardt v. Heid, 267 N.W. 127 (N.D. 1936); Moore v. Board of Education of Southwest Local School District, 212 N.E.2d 833 (Ohio 1965).

[229]Berghorn v. Reorganized School District No. 8, 260 S.W.2d 573 (Mo. 1954); O'Connor v. Hendrick, 77 N.E. 612 (N.Y. 1906); Zellers v. Huff, 236 P.2d 949 (N.M. 1951).

[230]Gerhardt v. Heid, 267 N.W. 127 (N.D. 1936); Zellers v. Huff, 236 P.2d 949 (N.M. 1951).

[231]Morton v. Board of Education of the City of Chicago, 216 N.E.2d 305 (Ill. 1966); Citizens to Advance Public Education v. Porter, 237 N.W.2d 232 (Mich. 1975).

[232]Special District for Education and Training of Handicapped Children of St. Louis County v. Wheeler, 408 S.W.2d 60 (Mo. 1966); See also Committee for Public Education and Religious Liberty v. Levitt, 414 F.Supp. 1174 (N.Y. 1976).

schools. A very early case tried in Maine resulted in a ruling[233] against the provision of free textbooks for all students regardless of the school attended.

Mississippi's constitution provides that "no religious or other sect shall ever control any part of the school or other educational funds of this state, nor shall any funds be appropriated toward the support of any sectarian school, or to any school that at the time it is receiving such appropriation is not conducted as a free school." A statute passed in 1940 provided funds for the purchase of textbooks, which were to be loaned to private and sectarian schools. The state court ruled that this was legal because the books belonged to and were controlled by the state. They were merely loaned to the individual pupils, and compensation would be taken if the books were lost or damaged. This practice, ruled the courts, did not place the parochial school in control of any part of the school or educational funds of the state. Loans, the court said, are not direct or indirect aids to the respective schools which the students attend.[234]

The issue of furnishing free textbooks in all schools came to the United States Supreme Court from Louisiana in 1930 in *Cochran v. Board of Education*. The facts were as follows: The Louisiana state legislature passed a statute in 1928 providing that the severance tax fund of the state should be used to supply school books to the school children of the state. Books were to be furnished to all school children free of cost. The Louisiana Supreme Court held[235] that the books could be provided to students in all schools of the state, both public and private, and such "aid" was not repugnant to either the state or the federal constitution.

In delivering the opinion of the United States Supreme Court, Justice Hughes quoted approvingly from the Louisiana Supreme Court:

One may scan the acts in vain to ascertain where any money is appropriated for the purchase of school books for the use of any church, private, sectarian, or even public school. The appropriations were made for the specific purpose of purchasing school books for the use of the school children of the state, free of cost to them. It was for their benefit and the resulting benefit to the state that the appropriations were made.[236]

A statute is viewed as having the effect attributed to it, and the taxing power of the state is exerted for a public purpose. Thus the theory of "child benefit" was enunciated in the United States Supreme Court.

Five textbook cases have reached appellate courts since *Cochran v. Board of Education*, and have arrived at a different decision. The first case was in Oregon, where the statute providing free textbooks to children in parochial schools was declared unconstitutional.[237] The second case contested a New York law which made it the duty of boards of education to purchase textbooks and lend them to private and parochial school pupils in grades 7–12. While other issues became involved in this case, the appellate court stated[238] that it was satisfied that the textbook loan statute did not contravene the federal and state constitutions. This decision was upheld[239] by the United States Supreme Court. Following the New York case three cases of a similar nature were contested in Rhode Island, Ohio and South Dakota.[240] In Rhode Island a statute that provided that textbooks be furnished to students attending nonpublic schools was upheld. In its decision the supreme court of that state held that the holding of the United States Supreme Court in *Allen* (New York) was controlling on the issues presented. An Ohio decision in 1976 held that a statute providing secular textbooks, supplies, and diagnostic texts was constitutional. However, it was held in South Dakota that free textbooks to children in parochial schools violated the constitution of that state.

13.7j Rentals from sectarian organizations

An early Wisconsin case ruled upon the legality of the public school district's renting instructional space from the parochial school. In this instance the school board had rented space in a parochial school for some twenty years, paying rent and upkeep with full knowledge of the voters, who were almost 100 percent Catholic. In effect a parochial school was maintained by nuns in religious garb who gave religious instruction, etc. Suit was brought to enjoin the practice and to regain all funds which had

[233]Donahoe v. Richards, 38 Me. 376 (1854).
[234]Chance v. Mississippi State Textbook Rating and Purchasing Board, 200 So. 706 (Miss. 1941).
[235]Cochran v. Board of Education, 123 So. 664 (La. 1929).
[236]Cochran v. Board of Education, 281 U.S. 370, 50 S.Ct. 335, 74 L.Ed. 913 (La. 1930).

[237]Dickman v. School District 62C, 363 P.2d 533 (Ore. 1961).
[238]Board of Education of Central School District No. 1 v. Allen, 276 N.Y.S. 234 (1966).
[239]Board of Education of Central School District No. 1 v. Allen 392 U.S. 236, 88 S.Ct. 1923, 20 L.Ed.2d 1060 (N.Y. 1968).
[240]Bowerman v. O'Connor, 247 A.2d 82 (R.I. 1968); McDonald v. School Board of Yankton, 246 N.W.2d 93 (S.D. 1976); Walman v. Essex, 417 F.Supp. 1113 (Ohio 1976).

been paid out by the school board. The Wisconsin Supreme Court affirmed the action of the lower courts and held[241] that the acts of the board were within their power in the rental of the building. The precise issue of sectarian instruction was not raised in this case.

Decisions to the same effect have been handed down in a later Wisconsin case[242] and in cases in Illinois,[243] Indiana,[244] Iowa,[245] and Missouri.[246] The essence of these decisions is that a board of education in paying rent to a sectarian group for instructional facilities is using public funds not to aid sectarian instruction but solely for the purpose of public education. Clearly, however, sectarian instruction may not legally be offered in the facilities so rented.

13.7k Graduation and baccalaureate exercises in churches

In an early case the Wisconsin Supreme Court ruled[247] that holding graduation exercises in a church or saying prayers did not constitute sectarian instruction. However, in 1974 under slightly different circumstances a federal district court in a Wisconsin case ruled[248] that holding graduation exercises in a Catholic school, even though approved by the great majority of seniors, was unconstitutional. In a case on related issues it was held[249] that inclusion of an invocation and a benediction at public high school graduation ceremonies where attendance was voluntary did not offend the constitutional guarantee of freedom of religion or give preference to any religion. The U.S. Supreme Court refused to review this case, thus allowing the decision of the state court to stand.

In 1965 the Supreme Court of Florida reaffirmed its previous judgment that parents had no standing to complain of religious and sectarian baccalaureate programs and related religious activities. Reading from the Bible and saying of prayers, also involved in this case, were declared uncon-

stitutional[250] by the United States Supreme Court.

In New Mexico baccalaureate services were held in a Baptist church. Graduation exercises were held in the Presbyterian church. These were the only buildings of sufficient size to adequately accommodate persons desiring to attend. The court held[251] that the activities did not violate the principle of separation of church and state or constitute sectarian instruction.

13.7l Religious pamphlets and films

A New Mexico case related to distribution of Presbyterian pamphlets and literature in the public schools. The pamphlets were kept in plain sight of the pupils and the pupils apparently took some of them from time to time. In spite of a statute prohibiting any use of sectarian material in the school and providing penalties, the penalties were not assessed. However, the court ordered[252] the display and distribution of the literature discontinued.

Since films are a major phase of education both within and without public schools, the censorship of films is of utmost importance. In New York the department of education was required by statute to examine all films prior to their first showing and to license them unless they were "obscene, indecent, immoral, inhuman, sacrilegious" or would corrupt morals or invite crime. When Catholics objected to the showing of The Miracle, it was pronounced sacrilegious by the state court. The United States Supreme Court overruled[253] the state court and declared the censorship statute unconstitutional.

13.8 SUMMARY

The framers of state constitutions, in their efforts to guarantee the continuing growth of public education, provided among other activities for the establishment of public schools, minimum school terms, teacher qualifications, selection of textbooks, and the teaching of English. To safeguard tax funds for the support of public schools, nearly every state constitution prohibited the use of public funds for sectarian instruction.

State legislatures have spelled out the

[241]Dorner v. School District No. 5, Town of Luxemberg, 118 N.W. 353 (Wis. 1908).

[242]State v. Joint School District, 156 N.W. 477 (Wis. 1916).

[243]Millard v. Board of Education, 10 N.E. 669 (Ill. 1887).

[244]State v. Boyd, 28 N.E.2d 256 (Ind. 1940).

[245]Scripture v. Burns, 12 N.W. 760 (Iowa 1882).

[246]Harfst v. Hoegen, 163 S.W.2d 609, 141 A.L.R. 1136 (Mo. 1942).

[247]State v. Joint School District, 156 N.W. 477 (Wis. 1916).

[248]Lemke v. Black, 376 F.Supp. 87 (Wis. 1974).

[249]Wiest v. Mt. Lebanon School District, 320 A.2d 362 (Pa. 1974).

[250]Chamberlin v. Dade County Board of Public Instruction, 377 U.S. 402, 84 S.Ct. 1272, 12 L.Ed.2d 407 (Fla. 1964).

[251]Miller v. Cooper, 244 P.2d 520 (N.M. 1952).

[252]Ibid.

[253]Burstyn v. Wilson, 343 U.S. 495, 72 S.Ct. 777, 96 L.Ed. 1098 (N.Y. 1952). For a comprehensive discussion of cases on religion see: 37 L.Ed.2d 1147-1221.

broad educational concepts embodied in state constitutions and have vested the administration and control of education in state, intermediate, and local educational agencies. These agencies have authority to carry on activities specifically granted by statutes or clearly implied from them. While state legislatures generally have delegated the administration of public education to these agencies, they also have attempted to control subversive teachings directly by restricting the teaching of undemocratic foreign theories of government or the violent overthrow of government and by prohibiting teacher membership in subversive organizations.

State-level agencies, i.e., state boards of education and state departments of education, are seldom involved in legal controversies over the instruction of pupils except as arbitrators of local disputes. When the authority of the state commissioner has been questioned, the courts have held that the officer's authority is conclusive in all matters relating to the supervision and control of the public schools.

The intermediate units and county superintendents of intermediate units likewise seldom have been involved in court cases related to instruction of pupils.

Local boards, however, are frequently involved in legal controversy. In these disputes the courts have given the following interpretations of the local district's authority in selected areas of instruction:

Local boards of education may set the school calendar, and designate the date for the beginning and closing of school, unless this authority is vested in some other body. Boards may change their minds and set new dates in the school calendar since discretion is not exhausted by use. While the school calendar is negotiable its final determination is a function of the board of education.

Unless the state prescribes a uniform program, the local board may provide for the teaching of any subject it deems desirable. The establishment of departments such as kindergartens and night school usually are matters for local authorities.

Athletics have been held to be a part of the regular school program, and public funds legally may be spent for athletic equipment, facilities, etc. However, the state athletic association may determine whether a student is eligible to participate in athletics in member schools.

Local boards of education have full authority in the promotion and gradation of pupils. They may "double promote" pupils, retain them in the same grade another year, or demote them. They may assign mentally or physically handicapped children to special rooms or classes or place them in regular classrooms.

Unless the authority is vested in some other body such as the state board of education, local boards may determine the textbooks to be used. School boards, like other boards, are subject to the laws of obscenity.

Homework may be required of pupils, and those who refuse to do their homework may be punished. However, homework assignments must be reasonable.

While the subjects to be taken generally are prescribed by the school, all pupils may not be compelled to take the designated courses. Parents may make a reasonable selection of courses if it does not adversely affect the education of the other children. The child must, however, use the same textbooks as the other children in the class. The teacher and not the parent determines the method of instruction to be followed. In some instances pupils have been compelled to do certain types of schoolwork over the objections of their parents. These have included the preparation of written exercises and declamations, the study of rhetoric when it was part of the prescribed curriculum, the preparation of compositions, participation in debates, and the presentation of a designated character at commencement exercises.

Religious instruction in the public schools has provoked extensive litigation. This generally has involved Bible reading, reciting the Lord's Prayer, and released-time programs. These issues have been adjudicated in the United States Supreme Court. It has been held unconstitutional to require the reciting of the Lord's Prayer or the reading of the Bible even without comment. Released-time programs are legal only if they are held away from school property and if no public funds are used.

In related religious issues it generally has been held that nuns may wear religious garb while teaching in the public schools. They also may donate their salaries to their religious orders. The purchase of free textbooks for children in private and parochial schools in Louisiana was upheld by the United States Supreme Court. However, Oregon and South Dakota more recently have held unconstitutional the practice of providing free textbooks in parochial schools. The rental of facilities for public school use from sectarian organizations has been universally upheld. The practice of holding public school graduation and baccalaureate exercises in churches generally has been sustained.

CHAPTER 14

Control of Pupil Conduct

14.7 SEARCH OF PUPILS

The authority of schools to search pupils' person or lockers is a difficult problem, not resolved in a like manner by all courts. The basic issue is to balance the constitutional guarantees of the Fourth Amendment, which guarantees that a person will be free from unreasonable search, against the need of the schools to maintain discipline and instruct students in a manner calculated to produce effective and productive citizens. In arriving at decisions a number of courts have resorted to the concept of *in loco parentis* much utilized in earlier years. In a review of the cases it is well to keep in mind that a search includes not only the actions commonly understood to be in encompassed in this activity but also includes prying into hidden places for things which may be concealed.[146]

In a Tennessee case[147] a pupil attempted to collect damages for being searched for $21.00 stolen from the teacher's pocketbook. The hall teacher took the girl from her class and into an unused room. After examining the contents of her pockets, which the pupil showed her, and finding no money, the teacher directed her to take off her clothing, including her outer clothing and bloomers. While the hall teacher was searching the girl, the principal was searching a boy who was also suspected of the theft. Neither found the missing money. Later it was discovered that another boy had taken the money. Neither the teacher nor the principal had indicated the purpose of the search. In the court action which followed, it was alleged that the girl pupil was maliciously assaulted and cruelly treated while being searched, but evidence did not sustain these allegations. Thus the issue was clearly centered on the right of a teacher to search a pupil for missing money. The lower court dismissed the case, but the appellate court held there was a cause for action and remanded the case to the circuit court for a new trial.

In a second Tennessee case[148] involving punishment and searching of a pupil, it was maintained by the teacher that the primary purpose of the punishment was for a falsehood on the part of the pupil and only incidentally a search for a lost dime. Here the teacher was not held liable; the court distinguishing the second case from the earlier one on the basis that the proof indicated the

search was only a secondary part of the punishment. It was primarily to clear the child from suspicion and was for the benefit of the child. It is interesting to note that the earlier case considered this argument on the part of the teacher and rejected it. Thus it appears that search of a pupil by teachers when of secondary importance will be sustained in the courts of Tennessee but not if it is of primary importance.

In any type of action, if a student asserts a right which the court recognizes as protected by the First Amendment, it will not permit infringement unless the state can show a *compelling* state interest. This also is presumably true of other amendments including those which protect the right of privacy.[149]

However, the courts must always balance the rights of the students against the state's interest in providing an educational atmosphere conducive to good learning. The following cases exemplify this type of balancing, where the courts most frequently arrive at decisions upholding the action of school officials.

In a California case the principal, acting without a warrant but on information from a student informer and the observable intoxicated behavior of a student, ordered him to empty his pockets. The student protested. In its decision the court considered the guarantees of the Fourth Amendment but found[150] no constitutional violation. The search had not been unreasonable in the opinion of the court.

The court in a Texas case refused to suppress the evidence obtained in a search by a principal without a warrant. In this instance the student was sent to the principal's office because of absences. The principal noticed a bulge in the student's pockets and ordered him to empty them. Under protest the student did so and produced 37 LSD tablets. The search was upheld.[151]

In a Delaware case the court upheld[152] the search of a student by a vice-principal. Although the student resisted, the principal took the student's coat, searched it, and found ten packets of hashish. The court ruled that a principal stands *in loco paren-*

[146]Deering v. State, 284 N.E.2d 533 (Ind. 1972); State v. Beck, 85 S.W.2d 1026 (Mo. 1935).
[147]Phillips v. Johns, 12 Tenn.App. 354 (1931).
[148]Marlar v. Bill, 178 S.W.2d 634 (Tenn. 1944).

[149]Griswold. v. Connecticut, 381 U.S. 479, 85 S.Ct. 1678, 14 L.Ed.2d 510 (Conn. 1965); *See also* Skelton v. Tucker, 364 U.S. 479, 81 S.Ct. 247, 5 L.Ed.2d 231 (Ark. 1960).
[150]*In re* G., 90 Cal.Rptr. 361 (1970).
[151]Ranniger v. State, 460 S.W.2d 181 (Tex. 1970).
[152]State v. Baccino, 282 A.2d 869 (Del. 1971), *See also* Mercer v. State, 450 S.W.2d 715 (Tex. 1970); Burdeau v. McDowell, 256 U.S. 465, 41 S.Ct. 474, 65 L.Ed. 1048 (Pa. 1921); Picha v. Wielgos, 410 F.Supp. 1214 (Ill. 1976).

tis and a "reasonable suspicion" was sufficient to justify the search of the student.

A discipline coordinator noted a suspicious bulge in a student's pocket while he was taking him to his office. The student ran from the school and the coordinator caught him several blocks from school. The coordinator took possession of drugs and drug apparatus from the student's pocket. The court held[153] that school authorities must have power to control, restrain, and correct students to accomplish the purpose of education.

In a Pennsylvania case the court was asked to determine what constitutional rights, if any, were violated by a search down to bra and panties in an effort to locate a lost ring. The court held[154] that there was sufficient evidence of Fourth Amendment violations to find school personnel, as well as police, proper defendents in a suit for damages.

While it is generally conceded that students have Fourth Amendment rights, not all courts hold that they apply in school relationships. A New York criminal court held[155] that it is the duty of school officials to investigate when they have reasonable suspicion that a student possesses drugs. Since the school official who investigated was considered a private person, it was the judgment of the court that the Fourth Amendment did not apply.

A tendency for courts to permit search of student lockers in elementary and secondary school is found in a review of court cases. In one of the earlier cases on this issue the court held[156] that the vice-principal, without a search warrant, was authorized to search a student's locker for the following reasons:

1. The school stands *in loco parentis* in matters of school discipline.
2. The vice-principal is not a governmental official within the meaning of the Fourth Amendment but rather is a private party.
3. The school retained the combinations of the lockers and entered them from time to time to search for bombs, intoxicating liquor, and stolen articles. Thus the lockers were as much or more school lockers as student lockers.

The Supreme Court of Kansas sustained[157] a school principal in opening and searching a student's locker. In this decision the Court pointed out that the *Miranda*[158] rule requiring a warning and explanation of rights was not applicable.

In a New York case with a legal history spanning several years, it was held[159] that a vice-principal's voluntary search without a warrant was valid. In the opinion of the court, schools have an affirmative duty to supervise students and thus control access to student lockers which permits them to freely search or consent to a search of the lockers.[160]

An assistant principal, upon being informed by four students that another student had marijiuana in his locker, searched it and found the drug. The court upheld[161] the action of the assistant principal after subjecting it to two criteria:

1. Was the search within the scope of the school official's duties?
2. Was the search reasonable within the facts and circumstance of the case?

In its decision the court noted that *in loco parentis* is limited by Fourth Amendment rights.

A new dimension of Fourth Amendment rights is now being set forth—the concept of a "reasonable expectation of privacy." Constitutionally protected areas include the legitimate boundaries of "expectation of privacy."[162]

Cooperation with police in search of students' persons or lockers presents a more difficult problem. Unless school officials have the right to make the search themselves they have no authority to consent to a search to be made by another party.[163] Any evidence obtained from a search made with the consent of school officials will be excluded unless they had sufficient control over the property to give consent.[164] A police officer in school or out is clearly a person who must accord any student searched the full extent of rights guaranteed by the Fourth Amendment. When the school cooperated with the police in the strip search of eight high school girls after a classmate reported a lost ring the case was

[153]People v. Jackson, 319 N.Y.S.2d 731 (1971).
[154]Potts v. Wright, 357 F.Supp. 215 (Pa. 1973).
[155]People v. Stewart, 313 N.Y.S.2d 253 (1971).
[156]*In re* Donaldson, 75 Cal.Rptr. 220 (1969).
[157]State v. Stein, 456 P.2d 1 (Kan. 1971).

[158]Arizona v. Miranda, *on retrial mandated by* 384 U.S. 436, 85 S.Ct. 1602, 16 L.Ed.2d 694 (Ariz. 1969).
[159]Overton v. Rieger, 311 F.Supp. 1035, *cert. denied,* 401 U.S. 1003, 91 S.Ct. 1230, 28 L.Ed.2d 539 (N.Y. 1971).
[160]*Ibid.*
[161]In the matter of Christofer W., 105 Cal.Rptr. 775 (1973).
[162]People v. Stewart, 110 Cal.Rptr. 227 (1973); Brown v. State, 292 A.2d 767 (Md. 1972).
[163]People v. Barbat, 212 N.W.2d 318 (Mich. 1973). *But see In re* Fred C., 102 Cal.Rptr. 682 (1972).
[164]Commonwealth v. Rhoads, 310 A.2d 406 (Pa. 1973).

dismissed against the county, the city, and the school board. However, the court refused to dismiss it against the chief of police, the police department, the superintendent of schools, the principal, and the assistant principal. They were held[165] to be proper defendents in a suit for damage for illegal search.

14.8 SMOKING, ALCOHOLIC BEVERAGES AND DRUGS

School authorities may control and prohibit the use of tobacco and alcoholic beverages in school. In cases on this issue the court did not question the school board's authority.[166] However, in the intoxicating beverage case the court of appeals discovered that the school board made its decision without evidence since no one had checked to see if the punch which the girls had spiked with two twelve-ounce cans of malt liquor was actually intoxicating.

The United States Supreme Court requires that students be given due process in school discipline cases. In one case it requested the Eighth Circuit Court of Appeals to clarify the immunity status of public officials to determine if they had wrongfully violated the constitutional rights of students.[167]

More severe and troublesome than the problem of alcoholic beverages has been the use of drugs in schools. From the court cases dealing with possession and use of drugs several directives to teachers and school administrators can be formulated.

A school board may formulate rules and regulations against possession and distribution of drugs and expel students for violations.[168] However, a student may not be expelled for having been *charged* in court action with possession of drugs.[169] Several cases have upheld school authorities in their search and seizure of drugs. In one case a girl who was selling drugs in the restroom was searched by a female teacher. The search and the penalty imposed by the school were upheld.[170] In another case the assistant principal required the student to come to his office, empty his pockets and take off his shoes. No *Miranda* type warning

was given. A bottle of capsules was found. The court held[171] there was no constitutional violation since the search was made by a private person and not a governmental official. In a third case the vice-principal of the high school was upheld[172] in searching on reasonable suspicion. The evidence found was admissible. The court reasoned that the vice-principal stood in *loco parentis*. In an effort to identify possible drug users both students and teachers were asked to identify students who made unusual remarks, got into fights, made inappropriate responses during school activities, or who had to be coaxed or forced to work with others. The court held collection of data of this nature was illegal.[173]

14.9 CARRYING FIREARMS

In a Texas case a teacher forced a pupil by use of corporal punishment to surrender a pistol which he had brought to school. The teacher was upheld[174] in applying such physical force as was necessary to make the child surrender the pistol. In this case the court determined that the teacher applied only such force as was necessary and when the pupil gave up the pistol the teacher ceased to apply force. It is the legal consensus that a teacher has not only the right but the duty to remove dangerous objects from students which threaten the safety of students and school personnel.

14.10 CONTROL OF CONDUCT OFF THE SCHOOL GROUNDS

It has long been held[175] that the nature of the act and not the place where the act was committed determines the right to punish the perpetrator of an act. The act for which punishment is inflicted must be related to and have a direct and substantial bearing on the good conduct of the school. In an imposing array of cases it has been decided[176] that

[171]Commonwealth v. Dingfelt, 323 A.2d 145 (Pa. 1974).
[172]State v. Baccio, 282 A.2d 869 (Del. 1971).
[173]Merrikan et al. v. Cressman et al., 364 F.Supp. 913 (Pa. 1973).
[174]Metcalf v. State, 17 S.W. 142 (Tex. 1886).
[175]Stebens v. Fassett, 27 Me. 266 (1847); State v. Mizner, 50 Iowa 145, 24 Am.Rep. 769 (1878).
[176]Lander v. Seaver, 32 Vt. 114, 76 Am.Dec. 156 (1859); Burdick v. Babcock, 31 Iowa 562 (1871); Kinzer v. Independent School District of Marion, 105 N.W. 686 (Iowa 1906); State v. District Board of School District No. 1, 116 N.W. 232 (Wis. 1908); Sherman v. Charlestown, 8 Cush. 160 (Mass. 1851); O'Rourke v. Walker, 128 Atl. 25 (Conn. 1925); Mangum v. Keith, 95 S.E. 1 (Ga. 1918); Deskins v. Gose, 85 Mo. 485, 55 Am.Rep. 387 (1885); Douglas v. Campbell, 116 S.W. 211 (Ark. 1909); Jones v. Cody, 92 N.W. 495 (Mich. 1902); Sweeney v. Young, 131 Atl. 155 (N.H. 1925); Guethler v. Altman, 60 N.E. 355 (Ind. 1901); Balding v. State, 4 S.W. 579 (Tex. 1887).

[165]Potts v. Wright, 357 F.Supp. 215 (Pa. 1973).
[166]Randal v. Newberg Public School Board, 542 P.2d 938 (Ore. 1975). Strickland v. Inlow, 485 F.2d 186 (8th Cir. 1973).
[167]Wood v. Strickland, 420 U.S. 308, 95 S.Ct., 992, 43 L.Ed.2d 214 (Ark. 1975).
[168]Kelley v. Martin, 490 P.2d 836 (Ariz. 1971); Fisher v. Burkburnett Independent School District, 419 F.Supp. 1200 (Tex. 1976).
[169]Howard v. Clark, 299 N.Y.S.2d 65 (1969).
[170]State in Interest of G.C., 296 A.2d 102 (N.J. 1972).

a board of education may discipline a pupil for any act, no matter where or when committed, if the act tends immediately and directly to destroy the discipline of the school or make it less effective. The jurisdiction of the teacher extends to acts committed away from the school as well as those committed on the school grounds.[177]

An early Iowa case summarizes the authority of the school to control acts committed outside school hours and away from the school:

> If the effects of acts done out of school hours reach within the school room during school hours and are detrimental to good order and the best interests of the pupils, it is evident that such acts may be forbidden. . . . The view that acts, to be within the authority of the school board and teachers for discipline and correction, must be done within the school hours, is narrow, and without regard to the spirit of the law and the best interests of our common schools.[178]

In an early Arkansas case the court held[179] that the board of education had authority to suspend from school a pupil who was drunk and disorderly on the streets of the village on Christmas day. This decision was recognized in a later New Hampshire case.[180]

In a New York case[181] a pupil under age sixteen was declared a delinquent after being found guilty of disorderly conduct on a school bus. She repeatedly disobeyed the instructions of the school bus driver and resisted efforts to remove her from the bus. Since her acts disturbed and annoyed other pupils in the bus, she was judged guilty of disorderly conduct. In the course of its discussion the court clearly recognized the school's authority to maintain order on the school bus and in pupil transportation.

The courts have sustained regulations prohibiting fighting and using profane language while going to and from school[182] and requiring pupils to go directly home from school at the close of the school day.[183] The court has also sustained a teacher who punished a pupil found guilty of annoying small girls on their way home from school. The fact that the offense was committed after the refractory pupil had reached home and was on the premises of his parents did not negate the teacher's authority.[184]

The leading case and the one most frequently quoted in support of the authority of the teacher to punish for acts committed off the school ground is a Vermont case, nostalgically referred to as the "old Jack Seaver case."[185] In this instance a pupil after going home went to get the family cow. While passing the teacher's house with another pupil he made disparaging remarks about the teacher. The next morning at school the teacher gave the pupil a whipping with a rawhide. The action of the teacher was upheld by the court against the charge of assault and battery. Authority to punish acts committed off the school ground was directly upheld.

Iowa decisions relating to the discipline of pupils off the school grounds may at first glance appear contradictory. In one case the court held[186] that the board was without authority to expel a pupil for publishing an article in a local newspaper which ridiculed the board of education. In a later case it was held[187] that the board had full authority to punish acts committed outside school hours when the influence of the act reached within the school. It is to be noted that in the first case the court concerned itself with provisions of the statutes which established gross immorality or persistent violation of a rule of the board as legitimate grounds for dismissal. Since the student was guilty of neither of these acts, the court did not sanction dismissal. The second case asserted the more general principle of law which is usually applicable in other states, i.e., the board has full authority to punish pupils for acts committed away from the school which adversely affect discipline in the school. Recent cases have been to the same effect. In one such case disciplining a student who made vulgar remarks about a teacher both on and off the school ground was upheld.[188]

14.11 SCHOOL
CONTROL OF PUPILS AT HOME

The circumstances of each case determine the extent to which the school may control pupils' time and activities at home. In this area two opposite opinions were rendered in seemingly similar cases, but the details revealed differences.

---

[177]Balding v. State, 4 S.W. 579 (Tex. 1887); Lander v. Seaver, 32 Vt. 114, 76 Am.Dec. 156 (1859); O'Rourke v. Walker, 128 Atl. 25 (Conn. 1925).

[178]Burdick v. Babcock, 31 Iowa 562 (1871).

[179]Douglas v. Campbell, 116 S.W. 211 (Ark. 1909).

[180]Sweeney v. Young, 131 Atl. 155 (N.H. 1925).

[181]In re Neal, 164 N.Y.S.2d 549 (1957).

[182]Hutton v. State, 5 S.W. 122 (Tex. 1887); Deskins v. Gose, 85 Mo. 485, 55 AmRep. 387 (1885).

[183]Jones v. Cody, 92 N.W. 495 (Mich. 1902).

[184]O'Rourke v. Walker, 128 Atl. 25 (Conn. 1925).

[185]Lander v. Seaver, 32 Vt. 114, 76 Am.Dec. 156 (1859).

[186]Murphy v. Independent District of Marengo, 30 Iowa 429 (1870).

[187]Burdick v. Babock, 31 Iowa 562 (1871).

[188]People v. De Caro, 308 N.E.2d 196 (Ill. 1974).

In one case the board of education was sustained[189] in prohibiting pupils from attending any show, movie, or social function except on Friday nights and Saturday. Pupils were not progressing at an acceptable rate, and school authorities determined that homework was necessary to insure satisfactory progress of the pupils.

In the other case the Supreme Court of Mississippi seems to have taken the opposite position. Here it was held[190] that a rule requiring all children to remain in their homes and study from seven to nine in the evening invaded the authority of the parent and was not upheld. The fact that the regulation prohibited a child from accompanying his parent to church seemed to the court an invasion of parental responsibility to an extent that it would not sanction. This does not mean that pupils may not be assigned homework. That is a different proposition. In a case[191] involving this issue the teacher was sutained in punishing a pupil who refused to do his homework in arithmetic.

One state avidly guards the rights of parents to control their children while at home. Missouri has held on two occasions that the school was without authority to control the social life of students. In the first decision the court held[192] that the board of education was without authority to prohibit pupils from attending social parties during the school term. In the other case[193] the faculty of a state normal school prohibited students from attending parties, entertainments, or places of public amusement without permission. The court held that this rule was unenforceable against a student living at home and attending a social function with parental consent.

14.12 FRATERNITIES, SORORITIES, AND SECRET SOCIETIES

As assiduously as some courts guard parental rights to control the activities of their children, they have not, with few exceptions, extended this control to a determination of whether their children may be members of fraternities, sororities, and secret societies. Nor is this issue of ancient vintage only; it continues to be before the courts. It usually takes the form of whether a child can be excluded from participating in extracurricular activities for holding membership in a secret society. The regulations are either mandated by statute, or promulgated by local board regulation, and occasionally both.

14.12a Statutory provisions

The courts, including the United States Supreme Court, have held[194] that schools may with statutory authority control membership in fraternities, sororities, and secret societies in the public schools. Statutes may authorize school boards to deprive pupils maintaining membership from participation in extracurricular activities or even to exclude them from school. A statute requiring school boards to expel pupils who are members is not void because it is discriminatory since it does not discriminate against pupils in similar situations.[195] The constitutionality of this type of statute was tested in California courts, which held[196] that prohibiting membership in secret societies was not special or class legislation and did not abridge the privileges and immunities of citizens in violation of the Fourteenth Amendment. An Iowa court held[197] that a statute prohibiting public school pupils from belonging to a fraternity or secret society was a valid exercise of the legislative authority of the state. In a more recent case the constitutionality of a statute prohibiting fraternities and secret societies in the public schools was upheld.[198]

14.12b Board of education prohibition

While the number of states prohibiting membership in high school fraternities, sororities, or secret societies by statute is impressive, it still is far from all inclusive. In many states regulation of membership is by local school board rule. Since boards of education have only such authority as is granted by statute or clearly implied from statutes, the question of the authority of the board to regulate membership in frater-

---

[189]Mangum v. Keith, 95 S.E. 1 (Ga. 1918).

[190]Hobbs v. Germany, 49 So. 515 (Miss. 1909).

[191]Balding v. State, 4 S.W. 579 (Tex. 1887).

[192]Dritt v. Snodgrass, 66 Mo. 286, 27 Am.Rep. 343 (1877).

[193]State v. Osborne, 24 Mo.App. 309 (1887).

[194]Robinson v. Sacramento City Unified School District, 53 Cal.Rptr. 781 (1966). Sutton v. Board of Education, 183 N.E. 131 (Ill. 1923); Lee v. Hoffman, 166 N.W. 565 (Iowa 1918); Bradford v. Board of Education, 121 Pac. 929 (Cal. 1912); Steele v. Sexton, 234 N.W. 436 (Mich. 1931); Satan Fraternity v. Board of Public Instruction for Dade County, 22 So.2d 892 (Fla. 1945); Antell v. Stokes, 191 N.E. 407 (Mass. 1934); Hughes v. Caddo Parish School Board 232 U.S. 685, 65 S.Ct. 562, 89 L.Ed. 555 (La. 1945).

[195]Sutton v. Board of Education, 138 N.E. 131 (Ill. 1923).

[196]Bradford v. Board of Education, 121 Pac. 929 (Cal. 1912); Robinson v. Sacramento City Unified School District, 53 Cal.Rptr. 781 (1966).

[197]Lee v. Hoffman, 166 N.W. 565 (Iowa 1918).

[198]Passel v. Fort Worth Independent School District, 453 S.W.2d 888, *cert. denied*, 402 U.S. 968, 91 S.Ct. 1667, 29 L.Ed.2d 133 (Tex. 1971), *rehearing denied*, 403 U.S. 941, 91 S.Ct. 2250, 29 L.Ed.2d 721.

nities, sororities, and secret societies in the absence of statute is of obvious significance. This issue was raised when schools attempted to limit the privileges of pupils who maintained membership in fraternities. A large number of states have held that regulation of membership in a fraternity comes within the board's grant of authority to manage the school.[199] A leading case relating to denial of the privilege of representing the school in any literary or athletic contest or in any other public capacity was adjudicated in Illinois. Here the court ruled[200] that the school board had not abused its discretion. It had simply permitted the pupils to determine whether they preferred membership in the secret societies to representing their schools. In this case the court again emphasized that it was within the province of the board, and not the courts, to determine how the schools should be managed.

Missouri's courts stand alone in holding[201] that a board of education may not prohibit pupils who are members of a fraternity from representing the school in any capacity. The court refused to sustain a school board rule in the absence of evidence that fraternity membership was detrimental to the operation and control of the school. From the dicta of the case it may be concluded that the decision might have been different if evidence of the harmful effect of fraternity membership had been presented or if the rule had not also included a provision that members of the fraternity were prohibited from participating in graduation exercises.

14.13 DRESS CODES AND HAIR STYLES

Seldom has a school issue required the legal attention demanded by dress codes and hair styles. The demand on the time of the courts has been so great as to cause United States Supreme Court Justice Hugo L. Black to observe that he did not believe "the federal Constitution imposed on the United States Courts the burden of supervising the length of hair that public school students should wear."[202] In the same case

he added "surely the federal judiciary can perform no greater service to the Nation than to leave the states unhampered in the performance of purely local affairs. Surely few policies can be thought of that states are more capable of deciding than the length of the hair of schoolboys." Reflecting this attitude, the United States Supreme Court has consistently refused to review the decisions of the lower courts.[203]

It is the opinion of other courts that high school dress codes which regulate the length of hair of males and prohibit females from wearing jeans raise no issue of constitutional dimensions.[204] Numerous other cases hold to the contrary.[205] Fortunately, the number of cases related to hair styles continues to decline. Whether students may wear the clothes they desire or their hair of any length they wish has not been satisfactorily answered. The answer appears to depend on the circuit court of appeals to which the specific case is brought. In the Fifth,[206] Sixth,[207] Ninth,[208] and Tenth[209] Circuits it has been held that a male student has no constitutionally protected right to wear his hair in the manner he chooses. The First,[210] Third,[211] Fourth,[212] Seventh,[213] and Eighth[214] Circuits have ruled otherwise. In the Third Circuit it was held, in part, that schools could regulate hair length where safety was involved, not otherwise. State courts have also come to opposite opinions, generally reflecting the decision of the circuit court of appeals in their region. A brief review of a number of selected recent state and federal court cases sets forth the issues and decisions.

Generally at issue is a dress code which

---

[199]Wilson v. Board of Education, 84 N.E. 697 (Ill. 1908); Wayland v. Board of School Directors, 86 Pac. 642 (Wash. 1906); Coggins v. Board of Education, 28 S.E.2d 527 (N.C. 1944); Isgrig v. Srygley, 197 S.W.2d 39 (Ark. 1946); Burkitt v. District No. 1, 246 P.2d 566 (Ore. 1952); Wilson v. Abilene Independent School District, 190 S.W.2d 406 (Tex. 1945); Holroyd v. Eibling, 188 N.E.2d 797 (Ohio 1962).

[200]Wilson v. Board of Education, 84 N.E. 697, 15 L.R.A. (N.S.) 1136, 13 Ann.Cas. 330 (Ill. 1908).

[201]Wright v. Board of Education, 246 S.W. 43 (Mo. 1922).

[202]Karr v. Schmidt, 401 U.S. 1201, 91 S.Ct. 592, 27 L.Ed.2d 797 (Tex. 1972).

[203]Cert. denied, 404 U.S. 1042 (1972); 400 U.S. 957 (1970); 400 U.S. 850 (1970); 398 U.S. 937 (1970); 404 U.S. 1042 (1972); 405 U.S. 1032 (1972); 404 U.S. 979 (1972).

[204]Dunkerson v. Russell, 502 S.W.2d 64 (Ky. 1973).

[205]See, e.g., Richard V. Thurston, 304 F.Supp. 449 (Mass. 1969), affirmed, 424 F.2d 1281 (1st Cir. 1970); Crosson v. Fatsi, 309 F.Supp. 114 (Conn. 1970).

[206]Karr v. Schmidt, 460 F.2d 609 (5th Cir.), motion to vacate denied, 401 U.S. 1201, 91 St.Ct. 592, 27 L.Ed.2d 797 (Tex. 1973).

[207]Jackson v. Dorrier, 424 F.2d 213 (6th Cir. 1970), cert. denied, 400 U.S. 850, 91 S.Ct. 55, 27 L.Ed.2d 88 (Tenn. 1971).

[208]Olff v. East Side Union High School, 445 F.2d 932 (9th Cir.. 1971), cert denied, 404 U.S. 1042, 92 S.Ct. 703, 30 L.Ed.2d 736 (Cal. 1972).

[209]Freeman v. Flake, 448 F.2d 258 (10th Cir. 1971), cert. denied, 405 U.S. 1032, 92 S.Ct. 1292, 31 L.Ed.2d 489 (Utah, Cal., N.M. 1972).

[210]Richards v. Thurston, 424 F.2d 1281 (1st Cir. 1970).

[211]Stull v. School Board, 459 F.2d 339 (3rd Cir. 1972).

[212]Massie v. Henry, 455 F.2d 778 (4th Cir. 1972).

[213]Arnold v. Carpenter, 459 F.2d 939 (7th Cir. 1972).

[214]Bishop v. Colaw, 450 F.2d 1069 (8th Cir. 1971).

attempts to regulate both dress and hair length. However, a few cases have dealt with dress only. A New York case,[215] made it clear that a school board may regulate dress only to the extent necessary to protect the safety of the wearer or to control distractions or disturbances which interfere with the educational process. On this basis a rule was invalidated which prohibited wearing of slacks except when permitted by the principal or when warranted by inclement weather. In a New Hampshire case the court held[216] that dress was a matter of personal liberty. While a school had a duty to exclude persons who were unsanitary, or scantily or obscenely dressed, it could not prohibit the wearing of blue jeans. There was no showing that the wearing of jeans inhibited the educational process. A decision by the Commissioner of Education of New Jersey invalidated[217] a school board regulation which prohibited the wearing of slacks by female students.

However, there are many cases where school regulations of dress have been upheld. In an Arkansas case the court upheld[218] that portion of a dress code which prohibited excessively tight skirts, or pants or skirts that were more than six inches above the knee. In a Texas case the federal district court also upheld[219] a dress code which prohibited girls from wearing pant suits to school. The court held that wearing pant suits is not a freedom of expression within the meaning of the Constitution and expressed a determination not to become involved in what was basically a state issue.

While most dress codes relate to both dress and hair styles, a few codes relate to hair styles only. While there are many cases on both sides of the hair style issue, there appears to be an increasing tendency for the courts to permit students to select their own hair style and strike down regulations which penalize students who do so.

In an Ohio case it was held[220] that a student who was penalized because of his hair style was entitled to:

1. Reinstatement as president of student council
2. Permission to participate in extracurricular activities

3. Deletion of point reduction in grades
4. Expungement of notation on his school record

The student was not, however, entitled to recover damages from the school board members, absent a showing of malice. In Michigan students have the right to choose their own hair style. To be upheld[221] school board regulations must bear some relationship to the purpose of education. In the Fourth Circuit it is constitutionally impermissible for the coach to attempt to regulate the length of hair not only during the football season, but throughout the school year.[222]

Two states which have invalidated hair style regulations have not settled the question on federal constitutional grounds. Oregon, in invalidating a hair style regulation, held[223] that under state law schools had no authority to regulate hair style. In Alaska the court held[224] a hair style regulation illegal as a violation of the state constitution.

A number of states have upheld the constitutionality of restrictive regulations on hair styles. In a Missouri case the regulation on hair style was upheld.[225] The Kansas Supreme Court also upheld[226] a hair regulation on the ground that it promoted safety in shop classes and avoided potential disruption. (For an illustrative listing of cases in which the board has been upheld in its hair style regulations, see footnote [227]. For a more extensive list of cases see The Yearbook of School law, 1969[228] and subsequent volumes.)

The same degree of confusion regarding hair style regulations in extracurricular activities is found in court decisions.[229] How-

[215]Scott v. Board of Education, 305 N.Y.S.2d 601 (1969).
[216]Bannister v. Paradis, 316 F.Supp. 185 (N.H. 1970).
[217]S.V. by Parents and Guardian, ad litem v. Board of Education of Borough of Sea Girt et al., Decision of New Jersey Commissioner of Education (1974).
[218]Wallace v. Ford, 346 F.Supp. 156 (Ark, 1972).
[219]Press v. Pasadena Independent School District, 326 F.Supp. 550 (Tex. 1971).
[220]Jacob v. Benedict, 301 N.E.2d 723 (Ohio 1973).

[221]Graber v. Kniola, 216 N.W.2d 925 (Mich. 1974).
[222]Long v. Zopp, 476, F.2d 180 (4th Cir. 1973).
[223]Neuhaus v. Federico, 505 P.2d 939 (Ore. 1973).
[224]Breeze v. Smith, 501 P.2d 159 (Alaska, 1972).
[225]Kraus v. Board of Education of City of Jennings, 492 S.W.2d 783 (Mo. 1973).
[226]Blaine v. Board of Education, 502 P.2d 693 (Kan. 1972).
[227]Gere V. Stanley, 453 F.2d 205 (3rd Cir. 1971); Pound v. Holaday, 444 F.2d 234 (5th Cir. 1971); Gfell v. Rickelman, 441 F.2d 444 (6th Cir. 1971); Whitsell v. Tampa Independent School District, 439 F.2d 1198 (5th Cir. 1971); Kraus v. Board of Education of City of Jennings, 492 S.W.2d 783 (Mo. 1973); Karr v. Schmidt, 460 F.2d 609 (5th Cir.), motion to vacate denied 401 U.S. 1201, 91 S.Ct. 592, 27 L.Ed.2d 797 (Tex. 1973).
[228]National Organization on Legal Problems in Education, The Yearbook of School law 1969, 1970, 1971, 1972, 1973, 1974, 1975, and 1976. (Topeka, Kan.: National Organization on Legal Problems in Education).
[229]Corley v. Daunhauer, 312 F.Supp. 811 (Ark. 1970); Cordova v. Chonko, 315 F.Supp. 953 (Ohio 1970); Neuhaus v. Torrey, 310 F.Supp. 192 (Cal. 1970); Dunham v. Pulsifer, 312 F.Supp. 411 (Vt. 1970); Jacobs v. Benedict, 301 N.E.2d 723 (Ohio, 1973).

ever, recent cases appear to grant more freedom in pupil determination of hair styles.

While the diversity of decisions on dress code and hair style cases is impossible to reconcile, some explanation is found in an analysis of the basis on which decisions have been made. Some courts place major emphasis on the First Amendment to the Constitution; others look to the Ninth or the Fourteenth Amendments; others prefer to utilize state statutes and the state constitution. Sometimes the case revolves on questions of due process, or on the question of whether a rule has in fact been violated. In other instances it has been a question of whether the regulation is over-broad or constitutionally vague. Frequently the reasonableness of the rule and the discretion of the school board is given major consideration. As long as judges may utilize any criteria they desire, diversity of decisions, not only on hair styles and dress code issues, but in other school operation areas as well, will continue.

14.14 REGULATIONS REGARDING MARRIAGE

Any law, regulation, or agreement in restraint of marriage is against public policy and unenforceable whether inside or outside the field of education.[230] This policy does not extend to "child marriages," which have been held[231] to be against public policy. However, girls of high school age are not considered to come within the category of children, and their marriages have not been held to be against public policy.

A 1929 Mississippi case posed a direct question of whether a regulation excluding a girl from school solely because of marriage was reasonable and enforceable. The court held[232] the regulation unreasonable, indicating that marriage is a relation highly favored in the law, and pupils in school associating with a married person would be benefited, not harmed. It further declared that since a married person could not be compelled to attend school it was laudatory for a person to continue in school without compulsion to be better fit for the duties of life.

A Tennessee case, while not permitting exclusion from school on a permanent basis, did approve temporary exclusion

from school because of marriage. The board formulated a rule that all pupils who married during the year would be automatically expelled for the remainder of the term and those marrying during the summer would not be permitted to attend school during the next succeeding term. When the rule was contested in court, the high school principals of the county testified that pupil marriages occasioned confusion and disorder at school, especially in the period immediately following the marriage. On the basis of the judgment of experts in the field (the principals), the court determined[233] that the rule was reasonable and enforceable. It indicated that it was the sole function of the court to determine whether the rule was reasonable or whether the board in adopting the rule had acted arbitrarily or unreasonably. The court held that the board had acted in a reasonable manner.

The courts have held[234] invalid a school board regulation requiring married students to withdraw for a year after marriage. The regulation of the board compelled any student who married to leave school immediately and remain out of school for a year. Admission then would be permitted only with the approval of the principal. A female student who married April 10, 1964, was allowed to remain until April 24 to enable her to complete the six-week term. The student and her parents asked the board to readmit her, but the request was refused. In the case which ensued the court held the exclusion regulation arbitrary and unreasonable and therefore void, especially in its administration. The board argued that the most disruptive time was immediately before and after marriage, yet the girl was permitted to attend school during these periods and then prohibited from attendance for a year afterward. Two 1967 Texas cases were to the same effect. Even though the board argued that the suspension was only temporary the court held[235] the rule suspending pupils from school solely because of marriage was unreasonable.

A 1973 New York case summarized the present legal status on regulations related to marriage in the United States. Here the court held[236] that students may not be expelled from school because of marriage, ab-

[230]*In re* Burnside's Estate, 27 N.Y.S.2d 78 (1941); *In re* Seaman's Will, 112 N.E. 576 (N.Y. 1916).
[231]Ohio v. Gans. 151 N.E.2d 709 (Ohio 1958), *cert denied*, 359 U.S. 945, 79 S.Ct. 722, 3 L.Ed.2d 678 (1958).
[232]McLeod Trustees Moss Point Public School v. State, 122 So. 737 (Miss. 1929).

[233]State v. Marion County Board of Education, 302 S.W.2d 57 (Tenn. 1957).
[234]Board of Education v. Bentley, 383 S.W.2d 677 (Ky. 1965).
[235]Anderson v. Canyon Independent School District, 412 S.W.2d 387 (Tex. 1967); Carrollton-Farmers Branch Independent School District v. Knight, 418 S.W.2d 535 (Tex. 1967).
[236]O'Neill v. Dent, 364 F.Supp. 565 (N.Y. 1973).

sent a showing of misconduct, of immorality, or a clear showing that the welfare or discipline of the other pupils was injuriously affected by the presence of the married students.

14.15 RULES RELATED TO PREGNANCY AND PARENTHOOD

In a Kansas case the board of education attempted to exclude from school a married girl whose child had been conceived out of wedlock. She had married before the child was born and after a very short period was abandoned by her husband. After her child was born she attempted to reenter school. The court ruled that the board of education had acted in an unreasonable manner in excluding her from school. It held[237] that she should not be prevented from gaining an education, which would better fit her to meet the problems of life.

In a 1966 case it was held[238] that a sixteen-year-old mother could not be excluded from school. In this instance the statutes provided that children over six and not over twenty-one were entitled to the benefits of the public schools.

In an Ohio case the courts were asked to decide whether a school board could require a married pregnant pupil to withdraw from school. In this instance a board rule required pupils to withdraw immediately after discovery of pregnancy. The board excluded the pregnant girl but provided her with instruction for the homebound. The board maintained that the rule was for the protection of the pregnant girl and not punitive. Largely on the basis of the contention of protection of the pregnant girl and because the rule was not designed to be punitive, the court held[239] the regulation reasonable.

In a 1969 Mississippi case the court had already held[240] that schools could not exclude unwed mothers. This, the court decided, was a violation of the equal protection clause of the Fourteenth Amendment. A 1973 Georgia case also upheld[241] the provision of alternate education for a fifteen-year-old mother. Here the mother was required to attend night school, where she had to pay for her tuition and textbooks. The court invalidated the tuition and textbook charge but permitted the atten-

dance at night school regulation to stand. In arriving at its decision, the court did not require the state to show "a compelling state interest" but only a "rational basis" for infringement on the girl's right to procreation. This basis is at variance with a decision of the United States Supreme Court a year later which held[242] that the right to procreate is a fundamental right to be infringed upon or curtailed only by showing a "compelling state interest."

In view of the decisions of the past few years, and particularly the recent decisions of the United States Supreme Court, one may assume that pregnant girls and mothers, whether wed or not, are entitled to an education. It appears that under certain circumstances this may be an alternate, but equal, education.

14.16 MARRIAGE AND PARENTHOOD RELATED TO EXTRACURRICULAR ACTIVITIES

Courts have exhibited a complete reversal in their decisions on whether students who are married, pregnant, or parents could participate in extracurricular activities. In the earlier cases, participation in extracurricular activities was considered a privilege rather than a right and the restrictions on participation in extracurricular activities were upheld by the courts. In a Texas case the school prohibited from participation in athletics a boy who had played football previously and was married before the rule was enacted. When he was not permitted to continue playing football, he challenged the rule on several grounds, one of which was the violation of Article I, Section 16 of the Constitution, which prohibits the enactment of retroactive laws. Another ground for challenging the rule was that he was denied the potential of an athletic scholarship at college. The court ruled against him on all counts[243] by holding that the rule was reasonable, that the retroactive aspect prohibited by the Constitution was not applicable, and that the potential scholarship was speculative and not particularly pertinent to the case. Other earlier cases came to the same conclusions.[244] A Michigan court was less positive in its decision. A trial

[237]Nutt v. Board of Education, 278 Pac. 1065 (Kan. 1929).
[238]Alvin Independent School District v. Cooper, 404 S.W.2d 76 (Tex. 1966).
[239]State v. Chamberlain, 175 N.E.2d 539 (Ohio 1962).
[240]Perry v. Grenada Municipal Separate School District, 300 F.Supp. 748 (Miss. 1969).
[241]Houston v. Prosser, 361 F.Supp. 295 (Ga. 1973).

[242]La Fleur v. Cleveland Board of Education, 414 U.S. 632, 94 S.Ct. 791, 39 L.Ed.2d 52 (Ohio 1974).
[243]Kissick v. Garland Independent School District, 330 S.W.2d 708 (Tex. 1961).
[244]Baker v. Stevenson, 189 N.E.2d 181 (Ohio 1962); Starkey v. Board of Education of Davis County School District 381 P.2d, 718 (Utah 1963); Board of Directors of Independent School District of Waterloo v. Green, 147 N.W.2d 854 (Iowa 1967).

court had sustained the board action and on appeal one judge voted to sustain on the basis that the case was moot, three other judges upheld the rule, while four held for the student.[245]

Beginning in 1972, restrictions have been universally invalidated in courts of record. In Tennessee, where a married student challenged a regulation prohibiting married students from participation in extracurricular activities, the court held[246] that the regulation infringed upon the fundamental right of marriage. In an Ohio case, the court invalidated[247] a rule which prohibited married students from participation in extracurricular activities on the basis that it was an invasion of the right of (marital) privacy, a violation of the Constitution. In a Montana case the court granted[248] an injunction against a rule prohibiting married students from participation in football competition. In a slightly different situation a school attempted to bar a divorced student from engaging in extracurricular activities. The court granted[249] a permanent injunction against the rule. Two recent Texas cases[250] have invalidated a board of education regulation prohibiting married students from engaging in extracurricular activities. In *Bell* the court recognized that "our holding is in direct opposition to *Kissick*" (*Supra* footnote 243).

14.17 EXCLUSION FOR IMMORALITY

In a very early case involving alleged immoral sexual behavior, a Massachusetts court was required to determine whether a girl who allegedly had been guilty of gross immorality manifested by licentious propensities could be excluded from school. It was alleged that the girl was guilty of immoral acts bordering on, if not actually constituting, prostitution. She also was allegedly guilty of loud, obnoxious language and disgraceful manners. The plaintiff maintained that these allegations, even if proved, were not legal justification for exclusion from school as long as there was neither violation of any rule of the school nor any misconduct in school. The court did not agree with this contention and held[251] that a pupil could be excluded from

school for immoral acts off the school grounds and outside of school hours.

In a 1973 case, which dealt not with the issue of immorality, but rather with attempted exclusion because of marriage, the court used language which indicated[252] that in its judgment a student could be expelled for immoral acts. Whether the act took place on or off the school grounds did not appear to be of any consequence. These holdings are in conformity with other decisions which have sustained exclusions for other offenses committed off the school ground and outside of school hours.

14.18 CONTROL OF PROTESTS

Early forms of protests were exhibited in the wearing of insignias and emblems. In a 1966 case the court upheld the wearing of buttons bearing the letters "SNCC," signifying support for the Student Nonviolent Coordinating Committee, and buttons reading "One Man One Vote." In this instance the students' activities caused no commotion but were merely the subject of curiosity. Under these circumstances prohibition against wearing the buttons was arbitrary and unreasonable and constituted an unnecessary stifling of free speech.[253]

When students joining a peaceful parade for civil rights were arrested because the group had not obtained a license as required by law, they could not be expelled from school for the balance of the school term without a hearing. In this instance a restraining order was issued against expulsion. the court reasoning[254] that prohibition of school attendance unless restrained would work an irreparable loss of an asserted right.

However, school authorities were upheld[255] in prohibiting the wearing of buttons where the record showed an unusual degree of commotion, boisterous conduct, and infringement on the rights of others. In this instance, the principal banned the buttons when the noisy talk about the buttons created a disturbance and the students were in the halls when they were scheduled to be in classes.

The major case in this area *(Tinker)* came to the United States Supreme Court in 1969. Students were prohibited from wearing black armbands protesting the United States' engagement in the war in Vietnam and supporting a truce. The court invali-

[245]Cochrane v. Board of Education of Misick Consolidated School District, 103 N.W.2d 569 (Mich. 1960).
[246]Holt v. Shelton, 341 F.Supp. 821 (Tenn. 1972).
[247]Davis v. Meek, 344 F.Supp. 298 (Ohio 1972).
[248]Moran v. School District No. 7, 350 F.Supp. 1180 (Mont. 1972).
[249]Romans v. Crenshaw, 354 F.Supp. 868 (Tex. 1972).
[250]Hollon v. Mathis Independent School District, 491 F.2d 92 (5th Cir. 1974); Bell v. Lone Oak Independent School District, 507 S.W.2d 636 (Tex. 1974).
[251]Sherman v. Charlestown, 8 Cush. 160 (Mass. 1851).

[252]O'Neill v. Dent, 364 F.Supp. 565 (N.Y. 1973).
[253]Burnside v. Byars, 363 F.2d 744 (5th Cir. 1966).
[254]Woods v. Wright, 334 F.2d 369 (5th Cir. 1964).
[255]Blackwell v. Issaquena County Board of Education, 363 F.2d 749 (5th Cir. 1966).

dated[256] the regulation of the board of education. In so doing, the court pointed out that it did not question the comprehensive authority of boards of education to prescribe rules for the conduct of the schools. However, such rules may not abridge students' First Amendment rights. This same point of view was again expressed[257] by the United States Supreme Court in 1972.

In line with the decision and dicta in *Tinker* cited above, subsequent cases have upheld regulations of the board of education on the one hand and students on the other. If the insignias cause severe tension which in the past has resulted in disruptions or are clearly anticipated to do so, the board may prohibit the wearing of the insignia according to the holding[258] in several cases. In two Texas cases where the evidence did not justify or support the contention of disruption, the students were upheld[259] in wearing of armbands.

Cases relating to control of racial symbols have presented a difficult question. Because of the high emotional overtones of racial issues, the likelihood of conflict and disruption is nearly always imminent. Within this framework, a number of courts have held[260] that racial symbols, insignias, or emblems which create racial tension and impede integration may be banned from the schools. However, the Seventh Circuit has held[261] it was not illegally discriminatory toward black students to use symbols which some blacks found offensive.

14.19 PUBLICATION AND DISTRIBUTION OF PUBLICATIONS

During the past decade the question of whether or to what extent school authorities may control publications and the distribution of publications has been before the courts on numerous occasions. One of the very difficult questions is whether school authorities may impose prior restrictions on materials to be included in a school publication. The Seventh Circuit, in two separate cases,[262] saw prior restraint as preventing First Amendment rights. The Second, Fourth, and Fifth Circuits have held[263] that some prior restraints are legal under certain conditions. The Second Circuit observed that the United States Supreme Court has upheld certain procedural safeguards in a film censorship case. To be legal, however, prior restraints may not deny students their First Amendments rights.

Equally difficult, and frequently involved in prior restraint regulations, is the distribution of publications on or near the school grounds. The general proposition that schools may control the time, place, and manner of the expression of ideas and of publications is well supported.[264] However, the regulations may not be such as to stifle free expression.[265] Nor may regulations require that students obtain prior approval of every proposed distribution. The board must set forth the regulations applicable to all distributions.[266] Other circuits have given additional directives in distribution cases. The Second Circuit has indicated[267] that it would be wise for a school board to specify areas of school property where appropriate materials could be distributed. Another court held[268] that a board could provide that all leaflets be distributed outside the school buildings or in the student lounge. It could prohibit distribution in a manner which would disrupt or interfere with classroom activities. However, regulation may not be over-broad or vague. A regulation which prohibited any distribution while classes were being conducted was

[256]Tinker v. Des Moines Independent Community School District, 393 U.S. 503 89 S.Ct. 733, 21 L.Ed.2d 731 (Iowa 1969).

[257]Healy v. James, 408 U.S. 169, 92 S.Ct. 2338, 33 L.Ed.2d 266 (Conn. 1972).

[258]Guzick v. Drebus, 431 F.2d 594 (6th Cir. 1970), cert. denied 401 U.S. 948, 91 S.Ct. 941, 28 L.Ed.2d 231 (Ohio 1971); Hill v. Lewis, 323 F.Supp. 55 (N.C. 1971); Hernandez v. School District No. 1, Denver, Col., 315 F.Supp. 289 (Col. 1970); Wise v. Sauers, 345 F.Supp. 90 (Pa. 1972).

[259]Aguirre v. Tahoka Independent School District, 311 F.Supp. 664 (Tex. 1970); Butts v. Dallas Independent School District, 436 F.2d 728 (5th Cir. 1971).

[260]Melton v. Young, 465 F.2d 1332 (6th Cir. 1972), cert. denied 411 U.S. 951, 93 S.Ct. 1926, 36 L.Ed.2d 414 (Tenn. 1973); Smith v. St. Tammany Parish School Board, 448 F.2d 414 (5th Cir. 1971); Augustus v. School Board of Escambia County, 361 F.Supp. 383 (Fla. 1973); Tate v. Board of Education of Jonesboro, 453 F.2d 975 (8th Cir. 1972).

[261]Banks v. Muncie Community Schools, 433 F.2d 292 (7th Cir. 1970).

[262]Fujishima v. Board of Education, 460 F.2d 1355 (7th Cir. 1972); Jacobs v. Board of School Commissioners, 490 F.2d 601 (7th Cir. 1973), cert. granted 417 U.S. 929, 94 S.Ct. 2638, 41 L.Ed.2d 232 (Ind. 1974).

[263]Eisner v. Stamford Board of Education, 440 F.2d 803 (2d Cir. 1971); Quarterman v. Byrd, 453 F.2d 54 (4th Cir. 1971); Baughman v. Freienmuth, 478 F.2d 1345 (4th Cir. 1973); Shanley v. Northeast Independent School District, 462 F.2d 960 (5th Cir. 1972).

[264]Grayned v. City of Rockford, 408 U.S. 104, 92 S.Ct. 2294, 33 L.Ed.2d 222 (Ill. 1972).

[265]Stanley v. Northeast Independent School District, 462 F.2d 960 (5th Cir. 1972).

[264]Grayned v. City of Rockford, 408 U.S. 104, 92 S.Ct. 2294, 33 L.Ed.2d 222 (Ill. 1972).

[265]Shanley v. Northeast Independent School District, 462 F.2d 960 (5th Cir. 1972).

[266]Fujishima v. Board of Education, 460 F.2d 1355 (7th Cir. 1972).

[267]Eisner v. Stamford Board of Education, 440 F.2d 803 (2d Cir. 1971).

[268]Vail v. Board of Education of Portsmouth School District, 354, F.Supp. 592 (N.H. 1973).

held[269] to be in that category. The courts require[270] that boards establish both criteria to be employed to determine whether to grant permission to distribute, and an expeditious review of the decision of the board.

While criticism by students of school officials, administrators, teachers, and other personnel may be distasteful to those criticized, the courts have held[271] this to be a form of guaranteed free speech. As long as publications of this type do not promote disruption, materially interfere with school activities, or intrude into school affairs or the lives of others, they cannot be banned. Even an article which indicated that the Dean was "the product of a sick mind," considered a disrespectful and tasteless attitude toward authority, was held legal by the court. In another case, where the court found[272] the criticism of school officials to be on a mature and intelligent level, the students were upheld.

In a number of other instances, students have been upheld in relation to controversial issues. They were upheld[273] in the distribution of an antiwar leaflet and a "High School Bill of Rights". School authorities were unsuccessful[274] in an effort to control in-school advertising and promotional efforts of nonschool organizations. The right of high school students to have inserted in the school newspaper an advertisement opposing the war in Vietnam has been upheld.[275] Students were also upheld[276] in their advocacy of offering information on birth control and of review of laws regarding marijuana. Schools may not promulgate regulations which bar the distribution of materials not written by a student, teacher, or other school employee.[277] In most of these decisions, the underlying concept of the *Tinker* decision is apparent. The statement from that case that personal intercommunication among students is pro-

tected not only in the classroom, but elsewhere, is most relevant.

Strongly as the courts have protected the right of free speech and communication, this right has not been expanded to include obscenity and vulgarity. There is no question of the school's authority to ban such materials, even materials which could not be banned from the public streets.[278] The question for the determination of the courts is: what are obscenity and vulgarity? The legal concept of obscenity is an appeal for prurient sexual interest.[279] Thus, the word "fucked" in a statement, "High school is fucked," has no reference to sex, but rather connotated the high school was in bad shape, and was not considered obscene.[280] Likewise, a joke about sex was held permissible,[281] as were words relating to body functions and sexual intercourse.

Prior restraint, where a principal is authorized to make a determination of whether material is obscene, is not sufficiently precise and understandable to be an acceptable criticism. Thus, the court held[282] material could be banned by a postpublication sanction if it was actually obscene, but not before. The same point of view was expressed[283] in a Fourth Circuit case.

The above cases should not be interpreted to indicate that students are always upheld in obscenity and vulgarity cases. Where a court found disruption caused by the distribution of an off-campus newspaper containing profanity and vulgarities it upheld[284] a ten-day suspension of the student responsible for the distribution.

In contrast with earlier cases which upheld[285] school board regulations against publication of off-campus newspapers, more recent cases have held these activities within the rights of students. The Fifth Circuit declared unconstitutional[286] a school

[269]Jacobs v. Board of School Commissioners, 490 F.2d 601 (7th Cir. 1973), *cert. granted* 417 U.S. 929, 94 S.Ct. 2638, 41 L.Ed.2d 232 (Ind. 1974).

[270]Quarterman v. Byrd, 453 F.2d 54 (4th Cir. 1971).

[271]Scoville v. Board of Education of Joliet Township High School District 204, 452 F.2d 10 (7th Cir. 1970), *cert. denied* 400 U.S. 826, 91 S.Ct. 51, 27 L.Ed.2d 55 (Ill. 1970).

[272]Sullivan v. Houston Independent School District, 305 F.Supp. 1328 (Tex. 1969).

[273]Riseman v. School Committee of City of Quincy, 439 F.2d 148 (1st Cir. 1971).

[274]*Ibid.*

[275]Zucker v. Panitz, 299 F.Supp. 102 (N.Y. 1969).

[276]Shanley v. Northeast Independent School District, 462 F.2d 960 (5th Cir. 1972).

[277]Jacob v. Board of School Commissioners, 490 F.2d 601 (7th Cir. 1973), *cert. granted* 417 U.S. 929, 94 S.Ct. 2638, 41 L.Ed.2d 232 (Ind. 1974).

[278]Ginsberg v. New York, 390 U.S. 629, 88 S.Ct. 1274, 20 L.Ed.2d 1975 (N.Y. 1967).

[279]Fujishima v. Board of Education, 460 F.2d 1355 (7th Cir. 1972); Koppell v. Levine, 347 F.Supp. 456 (N.Y. 1972).

[280]Sullivan v. Houston Independent School District, 475 F.2d 1071 (5th Cir. 1973).

[281]Scoville v. Board of Education of Joliet Township High School District 204, 425 F.2d 10 (7th Cir. 1970), *cert. denied* 400 U.S. 826, 91 S.Ct. 51, 27 L.Ed.2d 55 (Ill. 1970).

[282]Baughman v. Freienmuth, 478 F.2d 1345 (4th Cir. 1973).

[283]*Ibid.*

[284]Baker v. Downey City Board of Education, 307 F.Supp. 517 (Cal. 1969).

[285]Burdick v. Babcock, 31 Iowa 562 (1871); State v. District Board of School District No. 1, 116 N.W. 232 (Wis. 1908); Morrison v. Lawrence, 72 N.E. 91 (Mass. 1904).

[286]Shanley v. Northeast Independent School District, 462 F.2d 960 (5th Cir. 1972).

board policy which provided for punishment of students for off-campus publication and distribution for materials. The policy in the opinion of the court punished the exercise of a constitutionally guaranteed right.

In a number of cases the courts have adjudicated the issue of solicitation and sales of newspapers in schools or to students. The courts have invalidated a rule against exchange of money for literature on school premises except for the benefit of the school,[287] and against the prohibition of a "counter-culture" newspaper distribution on a free or donation basis by unpaid volunteers, some of whom were not students. Where the board made no attempt to prevent the free distribution of any papers, the court upheld[288] a ban on formation of a club to sell newspapers of all viewpoints on public school property. The court viewed this case as a commercial transaction rather than a First Amendment issue. A rule of long standing was invoked to prohibit the distribution of a leaflet requesting contributions to pay for the defense of the "Chicago eight." The rule, which the court upheld,[289] prohibited all solicitation of public school pupils.

14.20 REQUIRED FLAG SALUTE AND PLEDGE OF ALLEGIANCE

Whether pupils can be compelled to salute the flag and recite the pledge of allegiance in violation of religious beliefs is a question which has long vexed the courts in many states. From 1937 to 1943 the issue was in constant litigation, and in six instances the state courts upheld the flag salute statutes as constitutional. In additional cases the courts refused to compel the board of education to reinstate pupils who had been expelled for refusal to salute the flag. The flag salute issue was appealed twice to the United States Supreme Court within a three-year period. In spite of the differences in the issues considered and in spite of a different basis for each decision, for all practical purposes the Court did a complete reversal in these two cases. In the first one it was held[290] that the power existed in the state to impose a flag salute requirement upon school children and a local rule could

require all children to salute the flag. Thus, the required flag salute was upheld. In the second, the Court held[291] that the flag salute required by state law violated the religious beliefs of Jehovah's Witnesses, who considered the flag an "image" and thus could not salute it without violating their conscience. Three of the justices dissented from the majority opinion in this case. On the basis of this decision of the United States Supreme Court it may be concluded (1) that the flag salute cannot be compelled if it is in violation of religious belief or conscience and (2) that statutes and regulations compelling *all* pupils to salute the flag are unconstitutional.

While the second of the above flag salute cases also required a pledge of allegiance, this fact appears to have been overlooked in most discussions of the findings. Since this case was closely linked to saluting the flag, it may be assumed that the pledge of allegiance cannot be required under the 1943 Supreme Court decision. Subsequent cases have substantiated this assumption.

In 1966 a flag salute case involving a religious and/or political issue came to the Supreme Court of New Jersey. Students who believed in the Islamic religion and were sometimes called Muslims or Black Muslims refused to salute the flag although they were willing to stand at attention while the flag salute exercise was held. The school board maintained that their refusal to salute the flag was more political than religious. According to the state commissioner, the children could not be compelled to salute the flag and it was not necessary to determine whether from religious or political motives or both. The New Jersey Supreme Court accepted[292] both the reasoning and the decision of the state commissioner.

Not only has the required flag salute been invalidated, but students have been permitted to remain seated[293] while the pledge of allegiance is being said. In a New York case it was held[294] that a student could not be required to stand or leave the classroom during a flag salute exercise in which the student did not participate. In a related case, it was held[295] that pupils cannot be suspended or expelled for exhibiting disre-

[287]Jacobs v. Board of School Commissioners, 490 F.2d 601 (7th Cir. 1973), *cert. granted* 417 U.S. 929, 94 S.Ct. 2638, 41 L.Ed.2d 232 (Ind. 1974).

[288]Cloak v. Cody, 449 F.2d 781 (4th Cir. 1971).

[289]Katz v. McAulay, 438 F.2d 1058 (2d Cir. 1971), *cert. denied* 405 U.S. 933, 92 S.Ct. 930, 30 L.Ed.2d 809 (N.Y. 1972).

[290]Board of Education of Minersville School District v. Gobitis, 310 U.S. 586, 60 S.Ct. 1010, 84 L.Ed. 998, 1375 (Pa 1940).

[291]West Virginia State Board of Education v. Barnette, 319 U.S. 624, 63 S.Ct. 1178, 87 L.Ed. 1628 (W.Va. 1943).

[292]Holden v. Board of Education, 216 A.2d 387 (N.J. 1966).

[293]Frain v. Baron, 307 F.Supp. 27 (N.Y. 1969).

[294]Goetz v. Ansell, 477 F.2d 636 (2d Cir. 1973). *See also* State v. Lindquist, 278 A.2d 263 (Md. 1971).

[295]Banks v. Board of Public Instruction of Dade County, 314 F.Supp. 285 (Fla. 1970), *affirmed per curiam* 450 F.2d 1103 (5th Cir. 1971).

spect for flag and country. At the college level, the courts have held unconstitutional statutes which prohibit desecration and defiling of the American flag.[296]

In a case relating to another form of patriotic expression, the courts also sustained[297] the students' point of view. In this instance it was held that a pupil could not be suspended from school for failure to stand while the National Anthem was being played and/or sung. The student had objected to participation based on religious beliefs.

14.21 DENIAL OF
CREDITS FOR POOR DEPORTMENT

Whether a student may be denied credits because of poor deportment is not an easy question to answer. The courts are very reticent about permitting boards to withhold credits which the students have earned. An Iowa court ordered a school district to grant the credits and diplomas earned to pupils who declined to wear caps and gowns at graduation exercises.[298] Another court refused[299] to permit the board to withhold the diploma of a pupil accused of cheating when the cheating was not satisfactorily proved.

In two more recent cases, lowering grades for poor deportment was not permitted.[300] In the first instance, the New Jersey Commissioner of Education held that the use of grades as a means of punishment was improper. In Ohio, where a student's grades were lowered (among other forms of punishment) for refusing to adhere to a "hair code" the court ordered the grades restored. In two recent cases, however, reduction of grades and loss of credit because of poor deportment were permitted.[301]

14.22 STUDENT
RECORDS IN DISCIPLINE CASES

Because student records are sometimes a legal issue in relation to student conduct, several cases are included at this point rather than in Chapter 13 (Instruction of Pupils), where major consideration is given

to this topic. In decisions of recent origin, courts have held[302] that the right of examination extends to all public records bearing on a decision about the child. The United States Supreme Court has held[303] that schools are not entitled to collect all information they may desire. Information may not be collected relating to marriage, procreation, contraception, family relationship, or child rearing. Parents can have removed from the files and bar collection of data that impose upon the child a negative image of dubious validity.[304] Where a child has a long discipline history, a substitute teacher is entitled to examine the student's record so as to be better prepared to take precautionary action that will protect the other children.[305] While an anecdotal record may be used in a disciplinary hearing, it may not be introduced at the last minute, giving the student little or no opportunity to prepare a defense.[306] Where a student is expelled illegally, the courts will require that the notation on the student's record arising from the offense be expunged.[307] The same decision was arrived at[308] in a case involving a student suspended from school for distribution of controversial literature. In a university case, where a student attended a party where marijuana was smoked, suspension was illegal and the court required[309] the record to be expunged.

14.23 DESTRUCTION
OF SCHOOL PROPERTY

Courts have been unanimous in holding that pupils may not be required to pay for property accidentally destroyed.[310] This issue came before the courts of Indiana, Iowa, and Michigan, and in each case it was held that to require payment for property accidentally destroyed would exclude from

---

[296]Crosson v. Silver, 319 F.Supp. 1084 (Ariz. 1970); Korn v. Elkins, 317 F.Supp. 138 (Md. 1970).
[297]Sheldon v. Fannin, 221 F.Supp. 766 (Ariz. 1963).
[298]Valentine v. Casey Independent School District, 183 N.W. 434 (Iowa 1921).
[299]Ryan v. Board of Education, 257 Pac. 945 (Kan. 1927); See also State v. Wilson, 297 S.W. 419 (Mo. 1927).
[300]New Jersey Commissioner of Education, Decision March 24, 1972.
[301]Knight v. Board of Education of Tri-Pt. Community Unified School District No. 6J. 348 N.E.2d 299 (Ill. 1976); Fisher v. Burkburnett Independent School district, 419 F.Supp. 1200 (Tex. 1976).

[302]Mills v. Board of Education of D.C., 348 F.Supp. 866 (D.C. 1972).
[303]Merriken et al. v. Cressman et al., 364 F.Supp. 913 (Pa. 1973). See also Roe v. Wade, 410 U.S. 113, 93 S.Ct. 705, 35 L.Ed.2d 147 (Tex. 1973).
[304]Wisconsin v. Constantineau, 400 U.S. 433, 91 S.Ct. 507, 27 L.Ed.2d 515 (Wis. 1971). See also United States v. Kalish, 271 F.Supp. 968 (Puerto Rico, 1967).
[305]Ferraro v. Board of Education of City of New York, 212 N.Y.S.2d 615, affirmed, 221 N.Y.S.2d 279 (1961).
[306]Matter of the Appeal of Watson, N.Y. Commissioner of Education Decision January 5, 1971.
[307]Sims v. Colfax, 307 F.Supp. 485 (Iowa 1970); Church v. Board of Education of Saline Area, 399 F.Supp. 538 (Mich. 1972).
[308]Joy v. Yankowski, U.S.D.C. New York Case No. 71C.489, July 12, 1971.
[309]Stewart v. Reng, 321 F.Supp. 618 (Ark. 1970).
[310]Holman v. Trustees of Avon, 43 N.W. 996, 6 L.R.A. 534 (Mich. 1889); State v. Vanderbilt, 18 N.E. 266 (Ind. 1888); Perkins v. Independent School District of West Des Moines, 9 N.W. 356 (Iowa 1880).

school the youths most in need of education.

A different situation prevails when textbooks or library books are carelessly destroyed or lost. On the issue of retaining the deposit which students had made for the use of textbooks an Illinois court held[311] that the board was authorized to retain the deposit when books were lost or damaged.

It was established early that when property is accidentally destroyed pupils are not held liable.[312] If it is deliberately destroyed by acts of vandalism the contrary is true. Statutes frequently are enacted holding the parents absolutely liable or liable within specified limits for property deliberately destroyed. In several states, including New Jersey, the statutes provide[313] that where a pupil injures school buildings or other property the pupil and/or parents or guardians shall be liable for the damage. It was held[314] in New Jersey that the statute was in derogation of common law and was to be strictly construed but was applicable both during and outside school hours. When it is realized that the destruction of a school building (in this case the damage was $344,000) could involve a million dollars or more in damages, the responsibility parents carry for the acts of their children when property is deliberately destroyed is immediately apparent.

14.24 IDENTIFICATION OF PUPILS

A school board may require students as well as faculty and staff to carry identification cards and present them to school officials upon request. In the opinion[315] of the court such a requirement is reasonably related to the orderly conduct of schools and the educational process.

A requirement that pupils be fingerprinted is reasonable under certain circumstances. Where a class ring was found near the body of a homicide victim and fingerprints other than the victim's were found on the victim's vehicle when it was recovered, the court upheld[316] the require-

ment that all members of the eighth grade class be fingerprinted.

14.25 REASONABLE AND UNREASONABLE RULES AND ACTIONS

Examples of reasonable and unreasonable rules regarding pupil conduct have been cited at many points in this chapter, but a succinct statement of court decisions regarding the reasonableness or unreasonableness of rules seems appropriate for ready reference. Additional documentation and case citations are provided. The decisions obviously were based on the facts of each specific case; hence the necessity of reading the case for details before a decision can be applied to a given set of facts in a local school situation.

The following actions and rules of boards of education have been held reasonable:

Expulsion of a girl for immoral conduct off school ground and outside of school hours.[317]

Expulsion of a boy who deliberately injured another pupil and refused to accompany him home when requested to do so by the teacher.[318]

Expulsion of pupil for insulting the teacher.[319]

Expulsion of a pupil who refused to tell who had written an obscene statement on the schoolhouse.[320]

Suspension of a pupil for the violation of a rule prohibiting pupils from leaving the school grounds without permission during the noon period.[321]

Suspension of a pupil for violation of a rule requiring prompt and constant school attendance.[322]

Formulation of a rule requiring pupils either to bring their lunches from home or eat them in the school lunchrooms,[323] and suspension of a pupil for violation of the regulation.[324]

Requiring that students write composi-

---

[311]Segar v. Rockford Board of Education, 148 N.E. 289 (Ill. 1925).

[312]Holman v. Trustees of Avon, 43 N.W. 996, 6 L.R.A. 534 (Mich. 1889); State v. Vanderbilt, 18 N.E. 266 (Ind. 1888); Perkins v. Independent School District of West Des Moines, 9 N.W. 356 (Iowa 1880).

[313]New Jersey Statutes Annotated 18A:7-3 (1968–1976 Supplement).

[314]Board of Education of Borough of Palmyra v. Hansen, 153 A.2d 393 (N.J. 1959).

[315]La Porte v. Escanaba Area Public Schools, 214 N.W.2d 840 (Mich. 1974).

[316]In the matter of the Finger Printing of M.B. et al., 309 A.2d 3 (N.J. 1973).

[317]Sherman v. Charlestown, 8 Cush. 160 (Mass. 1851).

[318]State v. Randall, 79 Mo.App. 266 (1898).

[319]Board of Education v. Booth, 62 S.W. 872, 53 L.R.A. 787 (Ky. 1901).

[320]Board of Education v. Helston, 32 Ill.App. 300 (1890).

[321]Flory v. Smith, 134 S.E. 360, 48 A.L.R. 654 (Va. 1926).

[322]King v. Jefferson City School Board, 71 Mo. 628, 36 Am.Rep. 499 (1880); Ferriter v. Tyler, 48 Vt. 444, 21 Am.Rep. 133 (1876); Burdick v. Babcock, 31 Iowa 562 (1871); Churchill v. Fewkes, 13 Ill.App. 520 (1883).

[323]Casey County Board of Education v. Luster, 282 S.W.2d 333 (Ky. 1955).

[324]Bishop v. Independent School District, 29 S.W.2d 312 (Tex. 1930).

tions and enter into debates[325] and prepare rhetoric exercises.[326]

Requiring all pupils to study music.[327]

Requiring all children to stay on the school grounds between 9 AM and 3:05 PM except for children living close to the school whose parents requested that they be permitted to come home for lunch.[238]

Requiring pupils to park their cars in a parking lot when they arrived at school and leave them there until 3:45 PM unless granted permission to use them.[329]

Disciplining of pupils who as directed by their father arrived at school one hour late in protest of daylight saving.[330]

Requiring pupils in grades 4–12 to serve in the cafeteria without compensation and against their will.[331]

While the courts have appeared to "lean over backward" to uphold boards of education in rules promulgated for the operation of the schools, in a number of instances they have held that school board rules were unreasonable and unenforceable.

In a case of ancient origin it was held that a pupil could not be expelled for refusal to bring in a stick of wood each time he passed the woodshed on his way to the schoolhouse. The court held[332] this activity to be menial labor and not related to education of pupils or discipline of the school. Neither could pupils be compelled to address envelopes for a circular advancing the nomination of candidates for election to school committees. The court decided[333] that addressing these envelopes had nothing to do with the regular school assignment. In this case the teachers, and not the pupils, were subject to disciplinary action.

14.26 SUMMARY

The courts will uphold a board of education unless it acts in an unreasonable and arbitrary manner. The courts will not substitute their own discretion for that of the board. They will not review the facts of a situation unless it can be shown that school authorities have acted maliciously or in bad faith.

Until recently, school board members were not held personally liable for damages caused by mistakes in the exercise of discretion unless they acted maliciously or refused to perform acts made mandatory by statutes. Now, however, by enactments of the civil rights acts school board members may be liable if they deny pupils or school personnel their constitutional rights. To date, the damages assessed have been nominal.

Teachers and school administrators are expected to enforce rules of the board of education. They also have authority to make reasonable rules on their own and to enforce discipline when no rules have previously been made. The authority of teachers extends to all pupils in school, not only to those in the teacher's classes.

A teacher may inflict reasonable corporal punishment unless prohibited by statute or school board rules. Punishment must be reasonable in terms of the offense, the age of the child, etc. The previous conduct of the child may be considered in determination of punishment. There can be no legal punishment, regardless of how moderate, when actuated by malice.

Teachers generally are held liable when permanent injury results from corporal punishment or when punishment is excessive. Principals may administer corporal punishment, but the authority of the superintendent to do so is questionable.

Pupils generally are entitled to the elements of due process before they may be suspended (except under emergency situations) or expelled. While not all the elements of due process of criminal procedure are required, sufficient elements must be present to assure a fair and impartial hearing. A hearing need not be public unless the statutes require it, particularly if the pupil desires a private hearing.

Pupils may legally be detained after school as an appropriate discipline measure. They may be punished for misconduct off the school grounds if the act has a substantial bearing on the good conduct of the school. Some courts have extended the school's control of pupils into the home, but other courts have refused to do so.

Where membership in fraternities, sororities, and secret societies is prohibited by statutes, such statutes are universally upheld. School board rules prohibiting membership are generally, but not universally, upheld.

[325] Samuel Benedict Memorial School v. Bradford, 36 S.E. 920 (Ga. 1900); Guernsey v. Pitkin, 32 Vt. 224, 76 Am.Dec. 171 (1859).

[326] Sewell v. Board of Education, 29 Ohio St. 89 (1876).

[327] State v. Webber, 8 N.E. 708, 58 Am.Rep. 30 (Ind. 1886).

[328] Richardson v. Braham, 249 N.W. 557 (Neb. 1933); Haffner v. Braham, 249 N.W. 560 (Neb. 1933).

[329] McLean Independent School District v. Andrews, 333 S.W.2d 886 (Tex. 1960).

[330] Commonwealth v. Schrock, 77 D.S.C. 258 (Pa. 1951).

[331] Bobilin v. Board of Education State of Hawaii, 403 F.Supp. 1095 (Hawaii 1975).

[332] State v. Board of Education, 23 N.W. 102, 53 Am.Rep. 282 (Wis. 1885).

[333] Bray v. Barry, 160 A.2d 577 (R.I. 1960); Royal v. Barry, 160 A.2d 572 (R.I. 1960).

Schools may not control the clothing worn by students unless it is immodest or disruptive. Whether a grooming code controlling the hair style of students is legal appears to depend on the jurisdiction. Increasingly, schools are permitting students to wear their hair in the style desired unless it is unsafe or creates a disturbance.

If wearing of armbands or freedom buttons is accompanied by unruly demonstrations, pupils may be suspended or expelled. However, quietly wearing an armband or freedom button is a symbol of free speech guaranteed by the Constitution.

Pupils may not be required to salute the flag if it is against their religion, conscience, or other beliefs. They may not be compelled to pledge allegiance to the flag or to stand while the pledge is being said or the National Anthem is being played. They may not be compelled to leave the room when they refuse to participate in the exercise. Statutes which prohibit desecration or defiling of the flag have been held unconstitutional.

Reduction of grades or loss of credits for poor deportment does not always find judicial approval. Other forms of discipline, such as detention and reasonable corporal punishment, are more acceptable.

Pupils may not be required to pay for school property accidentally destroyed, with the possible exception of books, but they may be required to pay for wanton destruction of school property. Such payment is required by law in some jurisdictions.

Students, as well as adults, enjoy Fifth Amendment constitutional rights and cannot be compelled to divulge information which may be self-incriminatory. However, it has been held that a pupil may be required to provide information of an unauthorized or illegal act if the pupil is not personally involved.

Pupils may not be forced to do noneducational tasks. These include carrying in firewood and addressing envelopes for a circular advancing the nomination of candidates for election to a school committee.

School Transportation

15.0 INTRODUCTION

Transportation of pupils to the public schools is a major function of education in terms of funds required, number of pupils transported, and responsibilities of the school district. The magnitude of the task has increased dramatically and will continue to grow as additional districts are reorganized and consolidated.

Pressure has risen sharply in recent years for transportation of children to private and parochial schools at public expense. As a result, sixteen states by statutory enactments require public school districts to provide transportation for private and parochial school pupils. Nine additional states have by statutory enactments permitted but not required local school districts to provide transportation for private and parochial school pupils.[1]

With the development of this auxiliary program of major scope, not unexpectedly numerous legal issues arose on a variety of problems which required adjudication by the courts. This chapter presents decisions rendered with cases categorized by major areas.

15.1 TRANSPORTATION IN
ABSENCE OF STATUTORY AUTHORITY

Although all states now have school transportation statutes, the need for pupil transportation developed in many regions before it was recognized by legislative enactments. As a result, early cases were concerned with the school district's right to provide transportation in the absence of authorizing statutes. Since school districts are empowered to carry on only those activities clearly stated or implied in statutory enactments, authority to transport pupils, in the absence of transportation statutes, generally has not been approved by the courts. Thus, the courts have almost universally held[2] that expressed statutory enactments are necessary to authorize school districts to expend money for the transportation of school pupils, and transportation at public expense is authorized only in the manner and to the extent permitted by statute.[3] No

authority to transport pupils has been implied from the duty imposed on the school trustees to secure for the children of the district the right and opportunity of equal education,[4] or from a statute authorizing boards to do "all things needful and necessary for the maintenance, prosperity and success of the schools of the district and the promotion of the thorough education of children thereof."[5]

15.2 TRANSPORTATION
AUTHORITY BY IMPLICATION

The authority to transport children has been implied under statutes granting a school district "the usual powers of corporations for school purposes" and providing that common school district electors shall have authority to instruct the board in matters pertaining to the management of the school.[6] Where the children lived an excessive walking distance from school, the board was held[7] to have the implied authority to provide transportation. Authority to provide transportation has been implied from statutes authorizing consolidation[8] and where centralization of schools imposes such a necessity.[9]

A Kansas court (prior to integration of the schools) held[10] that a board of education had the implied authority (1) to transport black children to school where the limited number of schools for black children placed some children a great distance from the school they were authorized to attend and (2) to transport undernourished children to special schools. A Connecticut court held[11] that the failure of a town to provide transportation which is reasonable and desirable is failure to furnish "school accommodations" within the statute imposing upon each town the duty of furnishing school accommodations. However, a more recent case in the same state held[12] that without statutory enactments school districts have

[1]*The Law and the School Superintendent*, 2d ed. (Cincinnati, Ohio: National Organization on Legal Problems of Education, 1971), p. 127.

[2]State v. Board of Education of Portsmouth City, 25 N.E.2d 317 (Ohio 1939); Bruggeman v. Independent School District No. 4, 289 N.W. 5 (Iowa 1939); Harwood v. Dysart Consolidated School District, 21 N.W.2d 334 (Iowa 1946); Hendrix v. Morris, 191 S.W. 949 (Ark. 1917); Mills v. School Directors, Consolidated District No. 532, 154 Ill.App. 119 (1910); State v. Jackson, 81 N.E. 62 (Ind. 1907); Carothers v. Board of Education of City of Florence, 109 P.2d 63 (Kan. 1941); St. Louis-San Francisco Railway Co. v. Bryan County, 97 P.2d 77 (Okla. 1939).

[3]Galstan v. School District of City of Omaha, 128 N.W.2d 790 (Neb. 1964); O'Neal v. School District No. 15 School Board, 451 P.2d 791 (Wyo. 1969); Knauff v. Board of Education, 293 N.Y.S.2d 133 (1968).

[4]Mills v. School Directors, Consolidated District No. 532, 154 Ill.App. 119 (1910).

[5]Township School District of Bates, Stambaugh and Iron River v. Elliott, 268 N.W. 744 (Mich. 1936).

[6]Dahl v. Independent School District No. 2 of Lawrence County, 187 N.W. 638 (S.D. 1922); Almond v. Day, 97 S.E.2d 824 (Va. 1957).

[7]Malounek v. Highfill, 131 So. 313 (Fla. 1930); People v. Graves, 153 N.E. 49 (N.Y. 1926).

[8]People v. Graves, 153 N.E. 49 (N.Y. 1926).

[9]Williams v. Board of Public Instruction for Holmes County, 182 So. 837 (Fla. 1938).

[10]Foster v. Board of Education of City of Topeka, 289 Pac. 959 (Kan. 1930).

[11]Town of Waterford v. Connecticut State Board of Education, 169 A.2d 891 (Conn. 1961).

[12]Murray v. Eagan, 256 A.2d 844 (Conn. 1969).

no authority to expend school funds to bus underprivileged children to special schools.

15.3 CONSTITUTIONALITY OF TRANSPORTATION STATUTES

As the necessity for providing transportation became more apparent and the several state legislatures enacted statutes authorizing school districts to provide transportation at public expense, persons opposing free transportation and objecting to providing the tax revenue necessary to support this service attacked the constitutionality of the laws.

Statutes providing for free transportation of school children have been universally upheld against the charge of unconstitutionality. In an early Tennessee case[13] legislation authorizing school officers to provide transportation for pupils residing too far from school to attend without transportation was sustained. This legislation was held not to be violative of the state constitution since it did not involve an invalid diversion of school funds and/or discrimination even though some pupils were not transported. Since members of a community could bring themselves within the provision of the law by changing residence, the charge of discrimination was not sustained. In California an act which required a school district to provide transportation was sustained[14] against the charge that transportation was a gift of public money to private individuals in violation of the constitution. Nor was the use of school funds for the transportation of pupils a diversion of educational funds for noneducational purposes in violation of the state constitution in Mississippi.[15] Over a long period of time the courts in many states have upheld[16] the constitutionality of statutes expressly providing for transportation of public school pupils against a variety of legal contentions.

However, authorization of boards of education to provide transportation is generally interpreted to mean transportation only within the district under the jurisdiction of the board. In an Illinois case it was held[17] that boards of education authorized to provide transportation within the high school district were not authorized to provide free transportation for pupils residing outside the district. A number of states, however, have empowered high school districts to transport nonresident pupils attending their high school on a tuition basis. No legal obstacles to provisions of this type exist unless a discriminatory financial burden is placed on the transporting school district.

15.4 EXCLUSIVE AUTHORITY OF SCHOOL DISTRICTS IN TRANSPORTATION

Whether school districts have exclusive authority to transport or whether this authority is vested in municipalities obviously depends on the wording of the statutes. It is clear that in the absence of constitutional restraint the state legislature may vest any public body with any educational function it desires. The state has frequently vested transportation responsibilities in school districts as agencies of the state. When this is the case, transportation is a governmental and not a proprietary function.[18] Where the state has taken over the field of legislation pertaining to transportation, municipalities cannot enter the field or interfere in its operation. When the transportation of pupils in the county school system is by statutes under the jurisdiction and control of county boards of education, the state board of education is without authority to furnish, control, or direct transportation activities.[19]

15.5 DISCRETIONARY TRANSPORTATION

Early statutory enactments generally made transportation optional with the local districts; i.e., a district could elect to transport or not transport pupils at its discretion. A statute providing that a school board "may" provide for the free transportation of pupils to and from school at the expense of the school district is merely permissive, with determination vested in the school board.[20] It has been held[21] in numerous cases that the decision of a board acting

[13]Cross v. Fisher, 177 S.W. 43 (Tenn. 1915).

[14]Pasadena City High School District of Los Angeles County v. Upjohn, County Superintendent of Schools et al., 276 Pac. 341 (Cal. 1929). Note: Court stated that the California education code does not provide unconstitutional classification, though some pupils within the city may be farther from school than pupils living outside the city.

[15]Bufkin v. Mitchell, 63 So. 458 (Miss. 1913).

[16]Nichols v. Henry, 191 S.W.2d 930 (Ky. 1946); Carey v. Thompson, 30 Atl. 5 (Vt. 1894); County Board of Education of Bath County v. Goodpaster, 84 S.W.2d 55 (Ky. 1935); School District No. 3 of Atchison County v. Atzenweiler, 73 Pac. 927 (Kan. 1903); Johnson v. Sabine Parish School Board, 140 So. 87 (La. 1932); Seiler v. Gelher, 209 N.W. 376 (N.D. 1926); Lichty v. Board of Education of Crane Township Rural School District of Paulding Co., 171 N.E. 846 (Ohio 1929); Minshall v. State, 176 N.E. 888 (Ohio 1931).

[17]Steele v. Board of Education of Haw Creek Township High School, 2 N.E.2d 118 (Ill. 1936).

[18]City of Bloomfield v. Davis County Community School District, 119 N.W.2d 909 (Iowa 1963), citing 101 C.J.S., Zoning, sec. 10.

[19]Opinion of the Justices, 160 So.2d 648 (Ala. 1964).

[20]State v. School District No. 70, Otter Tail County, 283 N.W. 397 (Minn. 1939).

[21]White v. Jenkins, 209 S.W.2d 457 (Ark. 1948); Muehring v. School District No. 31 of Stearns County, 28 N.W.2d 655 (Minn. 1947); Salter v. Board of Education, 159 So. 78 (Ala. 1935); Scott v. Mattingly, 182 So. 24 (Ala. 1938).

under discretionary power is not subject to judicial control. Only when discretion has been abused[22] will the court intervene.[23] This proposition was reiterated in a 1965 case which stated that courts have no general supervisory power over school districts in school bus transportation and will not seek to control actions even though boards have exercised faulty judgment. They will interfere only if acts of boards of education are infected with fraud, bad faith, or gross abuse of discretion.[24]

If transportation is discretionary, boards may provide it[25] or abolish it[26] or regulate it as they see fit, even though the pupil denied free transportation is unable to walk because of a physical infirmity[27] or even though unintentional and unavoidable discrimination is found in the adoption of bus schedules.[28] A number of courts have supported the school board's discretion in determining not to furnish transportation or financial reimbursement in lieu thereof, where it has not been practicable or reasonable.[29]

A school board was found[30] not to have abused its discretion by refusing payment to a parent entitled to compensation for transportation of his children to school when he chose to send them to a school in an adjacent district which was farther away than the one in his own district. The court did suggest[31] that the decision might have been different if the adjacent school had been closer and more convenient than the one in the district in which the children lived since the parent would then have come under the statute providing that parents owning property in an adjoining district may send their children there without expense, if it is more convenient by reason of distance.

Inequalities in transportation constitute discrimination and an abuse of discretion and, with the few exceptions previously noted, are not permitted by the courts. For example, it has been held[32] that when a district votes to transport pupils and allocates tax funds for this purpose, the transportation furnished must be for all the children living more than a prescribed distance from school. When children are legally transferred to a new district, they become entitled to the transportation under the same conditions as children who are resident in the district.[33]

15.6 DISCRETIONARY-MANDATORY TRANSPORTATION

A school district has no duty to supply transportation to its pupils except as provided by statute.[34] The statutes may make the provision of transportation mandatory, discretionary, or both. A Kentucky statute is typical of laws combining mandatory and discretionary aspects. It provides that the board of education "shall" furnish transportation to grade school pupils and "may" provide transportation to high school pupils subject to reasonable regulations of the board of education as to the latter. The court sustained this statute, holding[35] that it is permissible to make transportation of grade school youngsters obligatory and transportation of high school pupils optional.

Statutes sometimes provide that pupils living on the regular bus route may or shall be transported. This stipulation is cited to indicate that children will not be picked up at their homes and obviously does not mean that only the resident children living on the route will be entitled to free transportation. Resident children who can walk, or are privately transported, to the bus route obviously can claim free transportation. To hold otherwise would be arbitrary and unreasonable.[36]

15.7 MANDATORY TRANSPORTATION

Statutes in most jurisdictions at present provide mandatory transportation by school authorities for children living specified distances from school. Under such statutes it is well accepted that the required transportation does not apply to children in private schools.[37] The county board of education,[38]

---

[22]Schmidt v. Payne, 199 S.W.2d 990 (Ky. 1947); Fogg v. Board of Education, 82 Atl. 173 (N.H. 1912).

[23]Douglas v. Johnson County Board of Education, 138 S.E. 226 (Ga. 1927).

[24]Ex parte Perry County Board of Education, 180 So.2d 246 (Ala. 1965).

[25]Brown v. Allen, 256 N.Y.S.2d 106 (1965); Steinberg v. Donovan, 257 N.Y.S.2d 306 (1965).

[26]Landerman v. Churchill Area School District, 200 A.2d 867 (Pa. 1964).

[27]Berry v. Barrington School Board, 95 Atl. 952 (N.H. 1915).

[28]Woodlawn School District No. 6 v. Brown, 223 S.W.2d 818 (Ark. 1949).

[29]State v. Mostad, 148 N.W. 831 (N.D. 1914). Contra, Manjares v. Newton, 411 P.2d 901 (Cal. 1966).

[30]Richey v. School District No. 52, 275 Pac. 1076 (Kan. 1929).

[31]Ibid.

[32]Fogg v. Board of Education, 82 Atl. 173 (N.H. 1912); State v. Smith, 196 S.W. 115 (Mo. 1917).

[33]Wellston v. Consolidated School District No. 1 v. Matthews, 230 Pac. 739 (Okla. 1924).

[34]Raymond v. Paradise Unified District of Butte County, 218 Cal.App.2d 1 (1963).

[35]Japs v. Board of Jefferson County, 291 S.W.2d 825 (Ky. 1956).

[36]State v. Nusbaum, 115 N.W.2d 761 (Wis. 1962).

[37]Schmidt v. Payne, 199 S.W.2d 990 (Ky. 1947); Silver Lake Consolidated School District v. Parker, 29 N.W.2d 214 (Iowa 1947).

[38]Madison County Board of Education v. Skinner, 187 S.W.2d 268 (Ky. 1945); Hines v. Pulaski County Board of Education, 166 S.W.2d 37 (Ky. 1942).

as well as independent districts, may be assigned the mandatory duty to furnish transportation to children in the district who live beyond the prescribed distance from the school. Statutes making it a mandatory duty to provide transportation in consolidated schools confer no authority or obligation to provide transportation in any other type of district.[39]

The mandatory duty to transport pupils living more than the specified distance from school has been upheld[40] even though it may be costly and burdensome to the district.[41] This principle was reiterated in a 1966 California case, which held[42] that society has a compelling interest in affording children an opportunity to attend school since an education has become the *sine qua non* of a useful existence.

Under an Illinois statute which required free public transportation for children residing a mile and a half or more from school, except where adequate public transportation was available, the children were required to walk three-quarters of a mile to the public bus stop and half a mile from the bus stop to the school. Under these conditions the court upheld[43] the school board's ruling that free mandatory transportation by the school district was not required since adequate public transportation was available.

Where school districts are required by statute to provide transportation beyond a given distance, the distance is the legal yardstick. Hazards of the route are not relevant unless the legislature has made them so.[44] Under appropriate state statutes it is mandatory upon school authorities to furnish transportation to pupils from abandoned schools[45] and those which have been closed for lack of pupils.[46] However, districts must not be subjected to any more expense in the provision of transportation than is necessary and reasonable.[47]

15.8 DETERMINATION OF DISTANCE TO SCHOOL

A pupil's right to transportation usually is based on how far from school the pupil lives. Thus the administration of transportation laws requires the measurement of the distance from home to school. How this distance should be measured has precipitated many court fights, in which the terms of the statutes have been subjected to judicial interpretation. Where the statute provided for measurement by the "nearest traveled highway," the route included a private highway leading to a pupil's home.[48] Another court held[49] that the distance is properly measured on the nearest public route or on one which has been duly authorized or exists by law. A Kansas decision[50] interpreted "usually traveled road" to include the distance from the pupil's house to the public road and from the public road to the schoolhouse itself. The court pointed out that pupils do not live in the middle of the road, nor do they attend school in the center of the road in front of the schoolhouse; therefore, the distance should be measured from the pupil's home to the schoolhouse. However, in at least one jurisdiction the distance was measured to the point where the highway touched the school grounds.[51] In 1947 a Pennsylvania court stated[52] that the distance must be measured over the nearest passable highway, which excluded a public road abandoned as impassable though not formally vacated by judicial proceeding. The court brushed aside the fact that it was still a public road and pointed out that it was no longer passable by adult pedestrians, let alone by vehicles or school children. The evidence showed that the area was a mass of stones with two-foot gullies, bearing no resemblance to a road. The board, therefore, was required to furnish transportation since, with this road voided, the children lived beyond the mile-and-a-half distance specified by the statute.

Under statutes providing that no child shall be required to walk more than one mile to school the court held[53] that the distance should be measured by the nearest traveled road from the point at school where

[39]Conecuh County Board of Education v. Campbell, 162 So.2d 233 (Ala. 1964).

[40]Mumm v. Troy Township School District, 38 N.W.2d 583 (Iowa 1949); Flowers v. Independent School District of Tama, 16 N.W.2d 570 (Iowa 1944); Harwood v. Dysart Consolidated School District, 21 N.W.2d 334 (Iowa 1946); Gordon v. Wooten, 152 So. 481 (Miss. 1934); Schmidt v. Blair, 213 N.W. 593 (Iowa 1927).

[41]Mumm v. Troy Township School District, 38 N.W.2d 583 (Iowa 1949).

[42]Manjares v. Newton, 411 P.2d 901 (Cal. 1966).

[43]People v. School Directors of District No. 108, 208 N.E.2d 301 (Ill. 1965).

[44]Studley v. Allen, 261 N.Y.S.2d 138 (1965).

[45]Boone v. Carter, 187 N.E. 357 (Ind. 1933).

[46]Riecks v. Independent School District of Danbury, 257 N.W. 546 (Iowa 1934).

[47]Walters v. State, 248 N.W. 777 (Wis. 1933); State v. Mostad, 148 N.W. 831 (N.D. 1914); Flowers v. Independent School District of Tama, 16 N.W.2d 570 (Iowa 1944).

[48]Pagel v. School District No. 1 of Town of Concord, 199 N.W. 67 (Wis. 1924).

[49]Eastgate v. Osage School District of Nelson County, 171 N.W. 96 (N.D. 1919).

[50]Purkeypyle v. School District No. 101, 275 Pac. 146 (Kan. 1929).

[51]Tillotson v. Leroy Township School District, 8 Pa. Dist. & Co. 220 (1926).

[52]Thompson v. Findley Township School Directors, 58 Pa. Dist. & Co. 615 (1947).

[53]Madison County Board of Education v. Grantham, 168 So.2d 515 (Miss. 1964).

pupils are unloaded from the bus in the morning or loaded into the bus in the afternoon to the home of the pupil.

A statute providing that transportation for school pupils shall be provided up to a distance of ten miles, the distance in each case to be measured by the nearest available route from home to school, does not require transportation to or from the pupil's home to a school more than ten miles away.[54]

Interpretations relative to measurement of distances are not easily reconciled. However, courts generally consider transportation statutes beneficial, with all doubts resolved in favor of the person to be transported. This construction is applied in school transportation cases particularly in resolving any doubt as to whether a road is a private road or a public highway.[55]

15.9 REASONABLE
WALKING DISTANCE TO SCHOOL

Determination of a "reasonable walking distance" rests with the board of education subject to review by the courts to determine if the board has acted unreasonably and abused its discretion.[56]

In determination of a satisfactory walking distance, it was held[57] earlier that a distance of two and one-fourth miles was not unreasonable for elementary pupils where school safety patrol and county traffic patrol assisted them across busy streets and where children could ride to school on common carrier buses for less than seven cents. Decisions as to *reasonable* walking distance must recognize the hazards and conditions of the roads[58] and safety factors in general[59] as well as the distance.

A Kentucky court required[60] a school district to furnish transportation where pupils would otherwise have been compelled to walk along a crooked, winding, heavily traveled road, crossing a narrow bridge, a railroad, and a main federal highway. However, two miles on a gravel road over which only fifty cars a day traveled was considered a reasonable walking distance for elementary school children even though the road had no shoulder or walkways. In this case the school board was held[61] to be legally justified in refusing to furnish transportation. When transportation is only for children living more than a mile from school, the school district has no responsibility for the safety of children living less than one mile from school. This is parental and not school district responsibility.[62]

15.10 REASONABLE
WALKING DISTANCE TO SCHOOL BUS

When legislation requires transportation "to and from school," the board of education usually has considerable leeway in determining the distances pupils must walk to the bus as long as there is no abuse of discretion.[63] An early decision upheld[64] the practice of requiring several boys to walk one-quarter of a mile and cross a frozen river in order to meet the school wagon on the other side of the river. Otherwise, the wagon would have had to travel four miles to pick up the boys.

A school was discontinued in Indiana, and a uniform route was established along which pupils were picked up at designated points, no child being required to walk more than five-eighths of a mile each way to the wagon. Transportation by this plan could be accomplished in one and one-half hours. It would have taken six hours a day and necessitated starting at an unreasonably early hour as well as additional expenditures for wagons and drivers if the school board had been required to pick up and discharge each pupil at home as requested by the parents. The board was upheld[65] in the above transportation plan. Although the above decisions (North Dakota and Indiana) were early cases and involved transportation by horse-drawn school wagons, the legal principles upon which they were based are applicable to transportation by present-day motor buses.

A regulation requiring the school bus to come only to a point about three-eighths of a mile from the child's home, and in in-

[54]Perry v. Board of Education of Union Free School District No. 8, 233 N.Y.S.2d 454 (1962).

[55]Commonwealth v. Ferguson Township School District, 22 Pa.Dist. 592 (1913); Purkeypyle v. School District No. 101, 275 Pac. 146 (Kan. 1929); Peterson v. School District, 246 N.W. 723 (Neb. 1933); Derichs v. Lake Creek School District No. 62, 234 N.W. 527 (S.D. 1931).

[56]Schmidt v. Payne, 199 S.W.2d 990 (Ky. 1947); Bowen v. Meyer, 255 S.W.2d 490 (Ky. 1953); Japs v. Board of Education of Jefferson County, 291 S.W.2d 825 (Ky. 1956).

[57]Bowen v. Meyer, 255 S.W.2d 490 (Ky. 1953).

[58]Madison County Board of Education v. Skinner, 187 S.W.2d 268 (Ky. 1945); Schmidt v. Payne, 199 S.W.2d 990 (Ky. 1947); Board of Education of Clay County v. Bowling, 229 S.W.2d 769 (Ky. 1950).

[59]Town of Waterford v. Connecticut State Board of Education, 169 A.2d 891 (Conn. 1961); Hoefer v. Hardin County Board of Education, 441 S.W.2d 418 (Ky. 1969); School Committee of Springfield v. Board of Education, 287 N.E.2d 438 (Mass. 1972).

[60]Schmidt v. Payne, 199 S.W.2d 990 (Ky. 1947).

[61]Board of Education of Clay County v. Bowling, 229 S.W.2d 769 (Ky. 1950).

[62]Studley v. Allen, 261 N.Y.S.2d 138 (1965).

[63]Lyle v. State, 88 N.E. 850 (Ind. 1909); State v. Miller, 141 N.E. 60 (Ind. 1923).

[64]State v. Mostad, 148 N.W. 831 (N.D. 1914).

[65]Lyle v. State, 88 N.E. 850 (Ind. 1909).

clement weather only to a point about two miles from a child's home, was considered reasonable under Missouri law (Mo. R.S.A., sec. 10326), and mandamus would not lie[66] to compel free transportation to and from the child's home. In Wisconsin the school district was upheld[67] in requiring pupils to walk one-half mile to an enclosed shelter, at the site of a discontinued school which they formerly attended, where they boarded an automobile provided by the school district. The court reasoned that since the statute called for transportation only for children living over two miles from school, and those living less than two miles were not furnished transportation, it was not unreasonable to require pupils who were transported to walk one-half mile to the pickup point. The Pennsylvania Supreme Court held[68] that it was reasonable for pupils to be required to walk up to one and a half miles to the shelter where they were picked up. Where a twelve-year-old boy had to walk one and a half miles to the pickup point on the bus route, the court pointed out that this was no farther than he had walked to his old school and upheld[69] the board's finding that such partial transportation was all that was reasonably necessary to enable the boy to attend school. However, an Illinois court held that requiring a child to walk one and one-half miles to a pick up point was not reasonable where the statute made provision of transportation mandatory for pupils who lived more than one and one-half miles from school.[70]

In two instances it was held reasonable to require parents to transport their children to a point which connected with the regular school bus route. However, the school board could allow reasonable compensation for this transportation. The statutory provision in the above Vermont case was as follows:

A board of school directors shall have control of and regulate transportation . . . of pupils in the schools under its charge . . . and contracts therefore shall be made by it. . . . Each legal pupil . . . may be furnished with such total or partial transportation to such school . . . as is in the opinion of the board of school directors reasonable and necessary to enable him to attend such school, as required by law. Such compensation may be paid to parents or guardians, and shall be payable only in return

for such actual transportation . . . as shall be stipulated by the school directors.[71]

A Wisconsin decision indicated[72] that a school board did not act arbitrarily in determining that buses need not enter long driveways to pick up and return children, where the distance from the house to the road never exceeded seven-tenths of a mile and where children in similar situations were treated in the same manner.

Children residing in an abandoned school district have been required to walk as far as one-half mile to the main route where the school bus passed, even though they had to cross railroad tracks each day on foot and were not provided with a shelter at a place where they met the bus.[73] High school students have been obliged to walk up to one mile to their former grade school where they were picked up and transported the remaining four miles.[74] In substantiation of this decision, the court cited an earlier Pennsylvania decision which stated very generally that "under certain conditions the pupils may be required to walk one and one-half miles to meet a public conveyance when stations are maintained."[75]

15.11 ESTABLISHMENT OF BUS ROUTES

The authority of school districts to establish bus routes is usually specifically provided by statute. The Kansas statute, which reads in part, "The governing body . . . may establish regular routes for the transportation of such pupils,"[76] is typical.

Within limits of reasonableness in compliance with statutes requiring school districts to provide transportation for pupils, the board may determine routes and times and places for gathering up pupils as long as there is no discrimination.[77] The Wisconsin statutes exemplify those specifically vesting wide discretion in boards of education in matters of pupil transportation: "The School Board of each district shall make and be responsible for all necessary provisions for the transportation of pupils, including the establishment, administration and scheduling of school bus routes."[78] The

---

[66]State v. Tompkins, 203 S.W.2d 881 (Mo. 1947).
[67]Walter v. State, 248 N.W. 777 (Wis. 1933).
[68]Commonwealth v. Benton Township School District, 120 Atl. 661 (Pa. 1923).
[69]Proctor v. Hufnail, 16 A.2d 518 (Vt. 1940).
[70]People ex rel. Schuldt v. Schimanski, 266 N.E.2d 409 (Ill. 1971); See also Wiswell v. Pembroke School District, 348 A.2d 347 (N.H. 1975).

[71]Lamphier v. Tracy Consolidated School District, 277 N.W. 740 (Iowa 1938); Proctor v. Hufnail, 16 A.2d 518 (Vt. 1940).
[72]State v. Joint District No. 1, 92 N.W.2d 232 (Wis. 1958).
[73]State v. Miller, 141 N.E. 60 (Ind. 1923).
[74]Lehman Township School District v. Lake Township School District, 17 Pa. Dist. & Co. 555 (1931).
[75]Jones v. Boulter, 61 Pa.S.Ct. 73 (1915).
[76]K.S.A. 72-617 (1972).
[77]Walters v. State, 248 N.W. 777 (Wis. 1933); Sand Point Academy v. Board of Education, 311 N.Y.S.2d 588 (1970).
[78]Wis. Stat., 121.56 (1972).

statutes put no superior or equal power to determine bus routes in the district meeting. Thus, discretion exercised with regard to school bus routes is that of the school board, and the board is not bound to follow preferences expressed by district meetings.[79] Where a resolution of a school district meeting provided for picking up children at their *homes*, which would have required school buses to enter long driveways to pick up and return children, the resolution of the district meeting was not controlling.

Even contractual provisions may be modified to conform to changing conditions and to the discretionary judgment of school boards regarding bus routes to be followed. A 1955 case involved a contract for transportation with a private carrier. The court held[80] that the school district was justified in withholding money from the contract price of a driver who refused to adjust his route when the need arose. The driver contended that he was following the language of the signed contract, which had specified the route. The court determined, however, that under the terms of a three-year contract the plaintiff contractor was under a duty to travel such routes and to pick up such pupils as the defendant school district determined from time to time. It was recognized by the court that families move and pupils graduate, with the result that transportation may be required over a certain route one year and over different routes the next year. The school district could not, however, require the contractor to travel excess mileage over less desirable roads.

15.12 CHARACTERISTICS OF SAFE CONVEYANCES

Typically statutes requiring safe transportation read as follows: "The sending school board shall provide for the safe and comfortable transportation of such children in an enclosed conveyance or conveyances, properly heated, or shall compensate parents for transporting their children. . . ."[81] Similar statutes earlier were made applicable to special types of districts (consolidated) in Kansas:

The district board of consolidated school districts shall provide for the comfortable transportation of the pupils of said district who live two or more miles from the schoolhouse by the usually traveled road, in a

safe and enclosed conveyance or conveyances. . . .[82]

In 1914 the use of a "top buggy, closed with side curtains, and drawn by a horse," was sufficient compliance with a provision of an Indiana statute that "such transportation shall be in comfortable and safe conveyance."[83] A 1924 Wisconsin case held[84] that an open buggy was "safe, comfortable, and convenient" and was sufficient to satisfy the requirements of the statute.

Although this case was not tried by a jury, due to a technical point of no witnesses, the judge indicated that there was sufficient evidence to indicate that an old-fashioned canopy-top platform wagon, with a wood box about nine feet by three feet without side or wheel guards and an inattentive woman driving two gentle horses, was not a "reasonably safe mode of conveyance" as required by statute and presented a cause of action.[85] A nine-year-old girl fell over a wheel and was injured, and in subsequent court action the conveyance was ruled unsafe.[86]

15.13 PROVISION OF SHELTERS

When a statute authorizes boards of education to designate places as depots from which to collect pupils for transportation, and provides that these places shall be comfortable during inclement weather, school boards are vested with discretion as to whether or not depots shall be designated.[87] There is no abuse of discretion in refusing to designate a depot and erect a shelter to accommodate one pupil. However, when shelter locations are designated, boards are under a duty to provide shelters.[88] It is not necessary that they be heated.[89]

15.14 TRANSPORTATION IN ABANDONED DISTRICTS

After abandonment, discontinuance, or suspension of a school or school district, transportation of pupils to other schools may or must be furnished in accordance

[79]State v. Joint School District No. 1, 92 N.W.2d 232 (Wis. 1958).
[80]Yocum v. Smithfield-Juniata Joint School District, 3 Pa. Dist. & Co. 541 (1955).
[81]Kans. Stat. An. 72-701 (2) (1972).

[82]Kans. Stat. An. 72-602 (1936).
[83]Greenlee v. Newton School Township, 104 N.E. 610 (Ind. 1914).
[84]Andrews v. School District No. 1, 197 N.W. 813 (Wis. 1924).
[85]Williams v. Eaton District No. 1, 198 N.Y.S. 476 (1923).
[86]Williams v. Eaton District No. 1, 205 N.Y.S. 742 (1924).
[87]State v. Board of Education of Lykens Township, 132 N.E. 16 (Ohio 1921).
[88]Ibid.
[89]Waller v. Mehoopany Township School District, 26 Pa.Dist. 1017 (1917); Walters v. State, 248 N.W. 777 (Wis. 1933).

with the terms of the statutes. In the absence of statutory requirements, when a school is consolidated and the school house is located in another town pupils are not entitled to have their transportation paid by their town of residence to the district in which they attend school.[90] Even though a school building had been destroyed by fire and legally abandoned and never rebuilt and the school district had been providing transportation and then discontinued it, transportation could not be compelled.[91] The court by way of a dictum suggested that this was an administrative problem, and the relators should have petitioned for the establishment of a new school district where they would doubtless find a remedy for their grievance.

Pupils are not entitled as a matter of right to transportation where a statute gives the school trustees discretionary power to transport after the closing of a school.[92] The board may, however, provide transportation[93] to a neighboring school under the following type of statute:

> Whenever the number of children between the ages of six and sixteen years, in any district school shall be fewer than six, it shall be lawful for the directors of such district to arrange for them to attend a neighboring school. Such transfer and free transportation shall be held to be in compliance with paragraph nine of Section 114 of this act, entitling said district to receive its share of the funds distributed in accordance with Section 35 of this act.[94]

Where a statute requires transportation to be furnished in abandoned, suspended, or discontinued school districts, pupils who live beyond the distance limits fixed by statutes are entitled to transportation.[95] Which school they will be transported to is primarily within the discretion of school authorities.[96]

Acting under a Kentucky statute, all subdistrict schools were abolished by the school board. Several students were refused admission to a school less than two miles from their homes because of overcrowded conditions. They then attended a school six miles from home, and were furnished free transportation for three years before the district discontinued transportation payments. An action followed in which the court entered judgment[97] requiring the school board to enroll children in a school within reasonable walking distance of their home or furnish free transportation to another school. The board in the exercise of its reasonable discretion could select the school in which the children could enroll.

It was clearly pointed out[98] in an Iowa decision that an independent school district had no duty to provide transportation for pupils from another district whose school was closed, unless the school was closed for lack of pupils, in which case statutory provisions for transportation was a mandatory duty. The district could perform this duty by furnishing transportation facilities or by allowing reasonable compensation to the parents or guardians of the pupils.

In a Michigan case it was held[99] that the duty of the trustees to transport was mandatory after discontinuance of a school where the statute provided that the pupils "shall be sent" to another school and that the trustees shall have authority to use the school fund for transportation. This was the decision under circumstances where the trustees had discretionary power under the statute to discontinue the school or keep it open.[100] In Indiana it was not necessary to have a formal order transferring the pupils from the abandoned district or school to the new school.[101] The situation could be established from the facts.

It is well settled[102] under the Montana law that, where the school board has closed the school, the board must either furnish transportation to another school or provide board and rent for pupils residing in the closed district. It should be noted, however, that when schools are closed the statutes relating to assigning of pupils to other schools and providing for transportation at the expense of the district refer only to public school pupils.[103]

---

[90]State v. Widolff, 167 N.E. 633 (Ind. 1929).

[91]Nelson v. State, 81 N.E. 486 (Ind. 1907).

[92]Bacon v. Delmar Township School Directors, 16 Pa.Dist. 495 (1906).

[93]People v. McKinstry, 42 N.E.2d 68 (Ill. 1942).

[94]Ill. Rev. Stat., ch. 122, § 129 (1959).

[95]Jackson School Township v. State, 183 N.E. 657 (Ind. 1932); Boone v. Carter, 187 N.E. 357 (Ind. 1933); Hines v. Pulaski County Board of Education, 166 S.W.2d 37 (Ky. 1942).

[96]Jackson School Township v. State, 183 N.E. 657 (Ind. 1932); Nishna Valley Community School District v. Malvern Community School District, 121 N.W.2d 646 (Iowa 1963).

[97]Hines v. Pulaski County Board of Education, 166 S.W.2d 37 (Ky. 1942).

[98]Riecks v. Independent School District of Danbury, 257 N.W. 546 (Iowa 1934).

[99]Dennis v. Wrigley, 141 N.W. 605 (Mich. 1913).

[100]Ibid.

[101]Patterson v. Middle School Township, 98 N.E. 440 (Ind. 1912).

[102]State v. School District No. 73 of Stillwater County, 76 P.2d 330 (Mont. 1938).

[103]Connell v. Board of School Directors of Kennett Township, 52 A.2d 645 (Pa. 1947).

15.15 TRANSPORTATION TO SCHOOLS IN ANOTHER DISTRICT

Under appropriate statutory provisions children of one school district may be transported by school authorities to schools in other districts,[104] but this power cannot be implied from a statute which provides only for transportation of pupils to schools within their own district.[105] In Kansas resident taxpayers of a consolidated school district were empowered to maintain an action to enjoin the district board from using the school bus to transport students living outside the district.[106] If the statute forbids use of vehicles to transport pupils in another district without the consent of the county board, operation of the school bus outside the school district owning the bus is not authorized except upon approval of the county board.

In Arkansas, where it was not legal to operate school buses outside district boundaries, it was held[107] that the district was authorized to pick up nonresident pupils at the boundary lines of the district and to return them to the district boundary lines after school. This action was found not to discriminate against the nonresident (transferred) pupils since transportation within the district was the only transportation right held by pupils resident in the district.

In New York the statute prohibits transferring children in central districts in grades below the seventh to another school district without approval of legal voters.[108]

School authorities may contract for the education and transportation of children of other districts under appropriate constitutional and statutory provisions.[109] However, when a pupil resides in one district and is educated in another the costs must be divided fairly.[110]

A school board may be authorized by statute to transport pupils to another district if in its judgment the education of the pupils will be improved,[111] or where the school is nearer, or more accessible.[112] The authority granted to a county school board to approve or disapprove attendance and transportation of pupils in a district other than the one of their residence must be carefully exercised for the promotion of the school system and the best welfare of the children, according to a Florida court.[113]

Where parents transported a deaf child 200 miles round trip each day to a district with special educational facilities, the court ruled[114] that they were not entitled to more than the statutory maximum of $300 per year for pupil transportation. The cost to the parents obviously far exceeded this amount.

15.16 TRANSPORTATION TO EXTRACURRICULAR ACTIVITIES

Whether school districts are authorized to provide transportation to extracurricular activities at public expense is dependent on the wording of the statutes or on the existence of any statutory provisions. In most states this power is extended by statutes and may be exercised. Unless it is granted, it does not exist according to an Iowa court in 1927 which prohibited[115] transportation of students to basketball games outside the district. North Carolina in 1961 took a much more liberal attitude. Here the court held[116] that school districts had the implied power to transport to extracurricular activities.

15.17 REIMBURSEMENT FOR TRANSPORTATION BY PARENTS

Parents have been permitted to send their children to a school in another district and have been allowed reimbursement for transportation of their children under a variety of circumstances. The following are typical:

1. A bus was not available to them.
2. Educational opportunities in the other district were greater.
3. The school in the district of their residence was five miles from the family home over an almost impassable road while the distance

[104]Parrish v. Menz School District No. 5, Sioux County, 223 N.W. 693 (N.D. 1929).

[105]Carothers v. Board of Education of City of Florence, 109 P.2d 63 (Kan. 1941); Board of Directors of Gould Special School District v. Holdtoff, 285 S.W. 357 (Ark. 1926); Brawley School District No. 38 v. Knight, 173 S.W.2d 125 (Ark. 1943); White v. Jenkins, 209 S.W.2d 457 (Ark. 1948).

[106]Carothers v. Board of Education of City of Florence, 109 P.2d 63 (Kan. 1941).

[107]Brawley School District No. 38 v. Knight, 173 S.W.2d 125 (Ark. 1943).

[108]McKinney's Consolidated Laws of New York Annotated, Education Law, sec. 1805 (1953); See also Levert v. Central School District No. 6, 202 N.Y.S.2d 248 (1960).

[109]Snipes v. Anderson, 175 S.E. 650 (Ga. 1934); Downer v. Stevens, 22 S.E.2d 139 (Ga. 1942).

[110]Ravenna Public School District v. Big Springs School District, 169 N.W.2d 183 (Mich. 1969).

[111]Keever v. Board of Education of Gwinnett County, 3 S.E.2d 886 (Ga. 1939); Pass v. Pickens, 51 S.E.2d 405 (Ga. 1949); Herman v. Medicine Lodge School District No. 8, 71 N.W.2d 323 (N.D. 1955).

[112]Stoops v. Hale, 14 P.2d 491 (Col. 1932); Fitzpatrick v. Johnson, 163 S.E. 908 (Ga. 1932); Harris v. School District No. 48 of Pennington County, 143 N.W. 898 (S.D. 1913).

[113]Reaves v. Sadler, 189 So. 41 (Fla. 1939).

[114]Christman v. Board of Education, 106 N.E.2d 846 (Ill. 1952).

[115]Schmidt v. Blair, 213 N.W. 593 (Iowa 1927).

[116]State of North Carolina v. McKinnon, 118 S.E.2d 134 (N.C. 1961).

was only three miles over a good road to the school of the adjoining district.[117]

4. The rural school district board honestly exercised its discretion and believed that it was for the best interest of the children.[118]

15.18 TRANSPORTATION IN CONSOLIDATED SCHOOL DISTRICTS

Statutory or constitutional provisions may expressly or impliedly authorize or require the transportation of pupils in consolidated districts. However, in the absence of statutory requirements trustees of a consolidated school district in most states are under no obligation to provide free transportation for pupils to and from school. The duty will not be implied from a statute authorizing transportation of a pupil to a nearer school in the adjoining district. Unless there is a specific statute requiring that transportation be provided, it cannot be compelled by mandamus.[119] It has been held,[120] however, that the power and duty to furnish transportation may be implied from a constitutional provision wherever the refusal to transport would deny any child constitutional rights. It also has been implied from the following constitutional provision: "Legislature shall provide for the maintenance and support of a system of free common schools, wherein all the children of this state may be educated."[121] It is within the power of the state commissioner of education to compel the trustees of a consolidated school district to perform this duty (provide transportation) and to levy taxes for this purpose[122] even against the vote of the taxpayers.[123]

Since, in each instance, decisions on pupil transportation in consolidated districts are closely related to the specific statutes of a state, generalizations are difficult. However, some decisions appear to be of nearly universal import. These are recounted briefly in the following section.

15.18a State statutes

In jurisdictions in which the statutes authorize but do not require the school board to transport the pupils in consolidated districts, the power of the board is discretionary. In the absence of evidence of discretionary abuse the board's action will not be reviewed by the courts.[124] The board operating under a statute authorizing a county board to consolidate schools and arrange transportation is functioning in a quasi-legislative capacity.[125]

School boards in consolidated districts may arrange for children living in a consolidated district to attend school in another district under certain circumstances. If this procedure is followed and tuition is paid by the consolidated district, the district is obligated for transportation costs also when the children live beyond walking distance (five miles) from the school attended.[126]

Where the statutes place discretion relative to provision of transportation in the voters, affirmative action on their part places a duty on the school trustees to carry out the voters' mandate.[127] Unless transportation is authorized by a majority of the voters union districts have been held[128] to be without authority to furnish transportation.

Statutes obligating consolidated districts to provide transportation to the consolidated school have been held[129] constitutional. Thus a board of education can be compelled to furnish transportation to the consolidated school[130] or, if it has not yet been built, to a school in another district[131] in accordance with statutory obligations.

A consolidated district is not required to transport pupils to a high school in another district when the districts which were consolidated never had a high school.[132] Transportation laws relating to consolidated schools are not applicable to newly formed regular school districts.[133] A district in Iowa was not authorized to send elementary pupils to a school outside the district when school facilities were provided within the district and all children lived within two miles of currently operated schools.[134]

---

[117]Stoops v. Hale, 14 P.2d 491 (Col. 1932).
[118]Herman v. Medicine Lodge School District No. 8, 71 N.W.2d 323 (N.D. 1955).
[119]State v. Hackson, 81 N.E. 62 (Ind. 1907).
[120]People v. Graves, 153 N.E. 49 (N.Y. 1926).
[121]N.Y. Const., art. XI, § 1.
[122]People v. Graves, 153 N.E. 49 (N.Y. 1926).
[123]Ibid.

[124]Keever v. Board of Education of Gwinnett Co., 3 S.E.2d 886 (Ga. 1939); Connell v. Board of School Directors of Kennett Township, 52 A.2d 645 (Pa. 1947).
[125]Shores v. Elmore Co. Board of Education, 3 So.2d 14 (Ala. 1941); Lauderdale County Board of Education v. Alexander, 110 So.2d 911 (Ala. 1959).
[126]Dermit v. Sergeant Bluff Consolidated Independent School District, 261 N.W. 636 (Iowa 1935).
[127]State v. Smith, 196 S.W. 115 (Mo. 1917).
[128]Reynolds v. Tankersley, 29 P.2d 976 (Okla. 1934); St. Louis-San Francisco Railway Co. v. Bryan County, 97 P.2d 77 (Okla. 1939).
[129]Bufkin v. Mitchell, 63 So. 458 (Miss. 1913); Cross v. Fisher, 177 S.W. 43 (Tenn. 1915).
[130]Tow v. Dunbar Consolidated School District, 206 N.W. 94 (Iowa 1925).
[131]State v. School District No. 44, 231 N.W. 782 (Neb. 1930).
[132]Tow v. Dunbar Consolidated School District, 206 N.W. 94 (Iowa 1925).
[133]State v. School District No. 44, 231 N.W. 782 (Neb. 1930).
[134]Manders v. Consolidated Independent School District of Community Center, 43 N.W.2d 714 (Iowa 1950).

In this instance the consolidated district continued to operate existing facilities in the district after electors refused to vote funds for a central building.

When children living in a consolidated district were transported if they lived two miles or more from school, a pupil legally transferred from another district was also entitled to transportation at the expense of the district. The court indicated[135] that the child was entitled to transportation from the point where his route intersected the route of the children being transported, at a point two miles or more from the school building.

A consolidated school district has authority to receive elementary pupils from an adjoining union graded district on a tuition basis under agreement between parents and the consolidated school district. In this instance a legal transfer of pupils had been refused by the union graded district. Although the union graded district maintained comparable educational facilities, the consolidated district was permitted[136] to go into the union graded district to transport pupils as long as it did not violate transportation statutes.

Where a county board effects consolidation, the board may provide for transportation out of the general fund when consolidation is more economical than creation of an emergency school or when some emergency makes the operation of a subdistrict impossible.[137] In this case a large number of pupils lived beyond a reasonable walking distance, and the board of education had acted unreasonably in its failure to provide transportation for them. In a related case it was held[138] that the county board of education could pay for transportation of pupils out of the general fund without the required vote of the people. In this case three subdistricts each had an average daily attendance of less than twenty-five pupils, and the evidence indicated that it was a wise exercise of discretion to consolidate the subdistricts and provide transportation.

A statute providing that pupils not entitled to transportation before consolidation are not entitled to it after consolidation, if consolidation placed them no farther from school, is superseded by one authorizing transportation of all children living a stated distance from school. Thus, a consolidated school may not deny transportation privileges to children living beyond the stated distance merely because they lived no farther from school than they did before consolidation.[139]

15.19 PAYMENT IN LIEU OF TRANSPORTATION

Statutes in several states authorize payments under varying circumstances in lieu of providing transportation. The amount, to whom payable, and when payable are governed by the terms of the statute as specifically expressed and reasonably interpreted.

15.19a Payments to parents

The constitutionality of an act providing for compensation in lieu of transportation was established at the turn of the century, when the courts ruled[140] that allowing parents to be paid out of public funds for conveying their children to a public school was not diverting public funds to private and individual use. Under statutes requiring a school board to furnish transportation for pupils living a stated distance from school or to allow monetary compensation in lieu thereof, the board has the option of selecting the alternative.[141] It may supply pupils with fares to ride such conveyances as are available to the general public as common carriers, including cabs.[142] It may provide transportation for some pupils while tendering a monetary allowance to others.[143] It may provide a conveyance for part of the distance and a monetary allowance for the balance.[144] As long as the board acts within its statutory jurisdiction and in good faith, its actions will not be disturbed.

In Kansas a school bus was not required to go three miles off the route to an "out-of-the-way place" to pick up pupils, and an allowance of forty cents per day per pupil transported these three miles was not an exercise of bad faith on the part of the board.[145] A North Dakota court, interpreting legislation on compensation in lieu of providing transportation, declared[146] that the

---

[135]Wellston Consolidated School District No. 1 v. Matthews, 230 Pac. 739 (Okla. 1924).

[136]Consolidated School District No. 12 v. Union Graded School District No. 3, 94 P.2d 549 (Okla. 1939).

[137]Knox County Board of Education v. Fultz, 43 S.W.2d 707 (Ky. 1931).

[138]Audas v. Logan County Board of Education, 55 S.W.2d 341 (Ky. 1932).

[139]State v. Smith, 196 S.W. 115 (Mo. 1917).

[140]School District No. 3 of Atchison County v. Atzenweiler, 73 Pac. 927 (Kan. 1903); Seiler v. Gelhar, 209 N.W. 376 (N.D. 1926).

[141]Schumaker v. School District No. 141, 22 P.2d 441 (Kan. 1933); Harkness v. School Board of District No. 3, 175 Pac. 386 (Kan. 1918).

[142]Hopkins v. Yellow Cab Company, 250 P.2d 330 (Cal. 1952).

[143]Reich v. Dietz School District No. 16 of Grant County, 55 N.W.2d 638 (N.D. 1952); Harkness v. School Board of District No. 3, 175 Pac. 386 (Kan. 1918).

[144]Park v. McKinney, 245 Pac. 1021 (Kan. 1926).

[145]Ibid.

[146]Seiler v. Gelhar, 209 N.W. 376 (N.D. 1926).

legislature did not intend to pay every patron the actual value or cost of the service of transporting children to school, and where parents lived in remote areas they were expected to share part of this financial burden.

Where a statute provided for transportation of pupils, the board was warranted in applying money, which would have been used for such purposes, equitably among children's parents providing transportation in a sparsely settled district.[147] However, a statute authorizing the board to "arrange with any person outside the board for the transportation" of pupils did not give parents the right to recover for their services in transporting their child to school without prior arrangements, even though the district had a mandatory duty under the statute to provide transportation.[148] In this case there was no allegation that the board had consented to, approved of, or ratified the transportation furnished by the parent although the district knew of it. Under these circumstances the district was not liable for compensation on a contract implied in law, and the proper remedy of the appellant to obtain transportation services was an action of mandamus.[149] Nor may a board compensate a parent for transportation in the absence of contract where the statute contemplates a contract or at least an understanding between the board and the person furnishing transportation.[150] Hence, where pupils attended a school in another district farther from their residence than the school in the district in which they resided, the district was not liable for transportation allowance in the absence of any previous arrangements between the two school boards.[151]

Other statutory interpretations are more favorable to the parents. Under a statute which provided that, if the board failed to transport, parents could transport or provide for transportation of their child and be paid by the district, the court held in favor of the complaining parent even though there was no contract.[152] The same point was considered in an Iowa case[153] involving a father who transported his children five

miles to a school in Nebraska rather than driving twenty-five miles to his own Iowa district school. His own district had been paying tuition to the Nebraska school for some years. Since the school district paid the tuition, it also was held liable for the transportation charges. On a similar issue in Vermont the court held[154] the parents were not entitled to collect for transportation. Here the distance was much shorter and partial transportation had been offered by the district and rejected by the parents.

The fact that a school board failed to list transportation funds in its budget, to include certain costs of transportation which could have been anticipated at the time the budget was adopted in its general fund, or to secure funds obtainable for school transportation purposes did not relieve the school board of its statutory liability to compensate a parent for transporting pupils. The pupils did not in fact reside two and one-half miles from the school by the usually traveled road at the time the defendant prepared and adopted its budget, but during the school year the road traveled became impassable. The shortest usually traveled road capable of being used, and used for the rest of the year, was four miles long, and the court held[155] that the parent was entitled to compensation at five cents a mile as specified in the statute. In this instance the statute[156] obligated the school district board to compensate persons transporting the children at a specified rate when a school district did not provide transportation. Payment of at least fifteen cents a day in lieu of furnishing transportation was held[157] to require the payment of at least fifteen cents a day for each child conveyed, and not fifteen cents for each family, when more than one child in the family was being transported.

A Wisconsin statute[158] providing for compensation to parents transporting children living more than two miles from school, if they attended not less than five months while being transported, did not require 100 percent consecutive attendance. Where the children attended school more than 100 days, the court, giving a liberal construction to this beneficent statute, found[159] substantial compliance. The court pointed out that 100 percent consecutive at-

[147]Stoops v. Hale, 14 P.2d 491 (Col. 1932).

[148]Bruggeman v. Independent School District No. 4, 289 N.W. 5 (Iowa 1939).

[149]*Ibid.*

[150]Proctor v. Hufnail, 16 A.2d 518 (Vt. 1940).

[151]Harris v. School District No. 48 of Pennington County, 143 N.W. 898 (S.D. 1913); Richey v. School District No. 52, Cheyenne County, 275 Pac. 1076 (Kan. 1929).

[152]Rysden v. School District No. 67 of Union County, 58 P.2d 614 (Ore. 1936).

[153]Dermit v. Sergeant Bluff Consolidated School District, 261 N.W. 636 (Iowa 1935).

[154]Proctor v. Hufnail, 16 A.2d 518 (Vt. 1940).

[155]Kimminau v. Common School District No. 1, 223 P.2d 689 (Kan. 1950).

[156]Kansas general statutes supplement 72-621 (1947).

[157]Waits v. Kelley, 236 Pac. 827 (Kan. 1925).

[158]Wisconsin statutes 40.16 (1921).

[159]Andrews v. School District No. 1, Town of Knapp, 197 N.W. 813 (Wis. 1924).

tendance is rather unusual, especially in rural districts, and a law which assumes to compensate a parent or guardian for transporting children to school conditioned upon a 100 percent attendance would savor of irony rather than beneficence.

15.20 RIGHT OF TRUSTEES TO RECEIVE COMPENSATION FOR TRANSPORTATION

A school board may contract with one of its members for transportation of his or her own children despite statutes which state that "it shall be unlawful for any school trustee to have any pecuniary interest, either directly or indirectly. . . to receive or accept any compensation or reward for services rendered as trustees."[160] A Kentucky court permitted subdistrict trustees to receive compensation for transporting other pupils as well:

> Neither of these sections seems to prohibit or embrace the entering into a contract by the board of education with a person holding the office of a subdistrict trustee for the transportation of pupils to and from the schools in a consolidated district. A subdistrict trustee is prohibited from being financially interested in a contract to buy land for the school or repair of the school house or for equipment or supplies for the school, but the Legislature has not seen proper to make unlawful by such trustees the receipt of compensation for transporting pupils to a consolidated school, and it is not unlawful if the arrangement is unmixed with graft or corruption.[161]

The Supreme Court of Washington has permitted transportation contracts with some of the members of the board of education, but not other contracts in which the board member or spouse had a pecuniary interest.[162]

15.21 DETERMINATION OF ALLOWANCE FOR TRANSPORTATION

Under some statutes the amount of compensation payable in lieu of transportation is based on the mileage traveled in excess of a stated distance over the "nearest practicable traveled road." A road cannot be considered a "practicable traveled road" within the meaning of the statute unless it is publicly maintained and it is not located on private property, or where it is necessary to open and close gates to prevent the escape of cattle and over which travel is precarious.

It has been held[163] that the authority of the board to establish a route which is the basis of computation does not permit it to direct or compel travel by a specified route. Routes established must be along section lines or regular highways properly maintained and cannot be over private lands.[164] Where the distance over the nearest passable public route exceeds the distance beyond which transportation is required, the parent is entitled to compensation even though the child follows a shorter route through pastures and private lands on occasion.[165]

When it has been determined, in accordance with the statute,[166] that no school shall be maintained in a school district because of the small number of pupils, and provision is made for sending the children to another district, it is within the discretion of the school board to provide for transportation a sum not in excess of that which would otherwise have been spent.[167] Where parents are directed to transport their children, the amount to be paid is within the sound discretion of the board unless determined by statute. The fact that the school board allowed the parents the statutory minimum of fifteen cents per pupil per day for transporting their children two miles to school was not so unreasonably inadequate as to indicate fraud or bad faith.[168] Where a parent voluntarily transported his own children to school after refusing several offers by the school district to furnish vehicular transportation or its equivalent, it was held[169] that he could recover only compensation fixed by the statute authorizing school districts to pay transportation charges, since there was no implied contract with the school district for reasonable value of the parent's services. It also was held[170] that transportation of children to high school by a member of their own family cannot be arranged at the expense of the common school district with contributions from state appropriations where a bus route is already established and functioning. Here, the school bus traveled within a mile of plaintiff's home. It was pointed out that the larger the loads, the lower the per pupil costs would be to the school district.

---

[163]Derichs v. Lake Creek School District No. 62, 234 N.W. 527 (S.D. 1931).
[164]Ibid.
[165]Ibid.
[166]Kans. Gen. Stat. 72-701 (1923).
[167]Schumaker v. School District No. 141, 22 P.2d 441 (Kan. 1933).
[168]Ibid.
[169]Reich v. Dietz, School District No. 16 of Grant County, 55 N.W.2d 638 (N.D. 1952).
[170]Perszyk v. School District No. 32, 4 N.W.2d 321 (Minn. 1942).

---

[160]State v. School District No. 73 of Stillwater County, 76 P.2d 330 (Mont. 1938).
[161]Keenon v. Adams, 196 S.W. 173 (Ky. 1917).
[162]Cunningham v. Union High School District No. "O," 228 Pac. 855 (Wash. 1924); Director of School District No. 302 v. Libby, 237 Pac. 505 (Wash. 1925).

Further, it was considered safer to transport the pupils on regular school buses than to have several autos each carrying only a few pupils to and from school.

Where the school has been closed for lack of pupils, under most state statutes a school board is authorized to furnish transportation for pupils to neighboring school districts. However, parents cannot compel a school board to furnish transportation for their child but are entitled to an allowance as provided by the statutes.[171] Thus, under many transportation statutes a mandamus action will not lie to compel school boards to provide transportation for school children where the board fails to furnish transportation; rather, the parents will be compensated by the district for providing the transportation.[172] Compensation is recoverable on proof that the children transported lived more than the stated number of miles from school over the usually traveled route,[173] and the fact that a parent permitted his son, who was under the lawful age to drive an auto, to drive to school occasionally did not preclude recovery of statutory compensation for transporting children to school.[174] However, a parent could not recover costs of transportation which he incurred and paid without previous demand on the board,[175] but his suit to recover was held to constitute a demand for transportation authorizing recovery of reasonable costs of transportation after the date on which the suit was filed.[176]

Parents who never filed or attempted to file any written claims with the school board or with any member thereof, when the board consistently refused to recognize the validity of oral demands of parents for allowance for transportation, were not entitled to recover transportation allowance from the school district. They had failed to comply with the statutes requiring the filing of written demands for transportation.[177] The court pointed out in this case that, where a statute provides the manner and form in which a right may be exercised,

these provisions are mandatory; if they are not complied with, no right exists. A similar decision was handed down[178] in Kansas, denying a parent compensation after his oral demand was refused and he failed to present a duly verified voucher as required by statute.

15.22 PROVISIONS FOR BOARD AND ROOM

School authorities may pay for room and board of pupils in lieu of transportation under permissive statutes. Where the statute states that the school board shall make such provisions for schooling of children not satisfactorily transported as shall be determined by the county superintendent, or by the state board of education, the state board[179] or the county superintendent[180] has the designated power to arrange details for the boarding of such children and to order the school district board to carry them out. It becomes the legal duty of the board to comply with the orders. The constitutionality of such statutes has been upheld.[181]

In the absence of a statute, school directors are without authority to pay board and room for a pupil who lives beyond walking distance from school. Thus, it was declared[182] that the board had abused its discretion in unlawfully and unnecessarily paying $2.00 a week for the board and lodging of a pupil. The statute authorizing school directors of a discontinued school to pay for transportation cannot be implied to authorize payment for board and/or room.

A statute[183] provided that if the school board closed the school, it must then either supply the pupils residing in the district with transportation to another school or with board and rent. The court ordered[184] the board to exercise its discretion in determining which to do, and asserted that a school trustee under the law[185] could not be considered to have an illegal pecuniary interest in the arrangements even though he was the parent of the children to be transported. Under a statute making it mandatory for local boards of education to transport high school pupils whose homes are a specified distance from the school or to furnish board and lodging near the school, and

[171]Bender v. Palmer, 48 N.W.2d 65 (Neb. 1951).
[172]Hein v. Luther, 221 N.W. 386 (Wis. 1928); Bender v. Palmer, 48 N.W.2d 65 (Neb. 1951).
[173]Heldebrand v. School District No. 59 in Trego County, 15 P.2d 412 (Kan. 1932); Gandt v. Joint School District No. 3 of Town of Oconto Falls, 90 N.W.2d 549 (Wis. 1958).
[174]Heldebrand v. School District No. 59 in Trego County, 15 P.2d 412 (Kan. 1932).
[175]Warren v. Knox County Board of Education, 79 S.W.2d 681 (Ky. 1935); Christman v. Board of Education, 106 N.E.2d 846 (Ill. 1952).
[176]Warren v. Knox County Board of Education, 79 S.W.2d 681 (Ky. 1935).
[177]George v. School District No. 24 of Red Willow County, 61 N.W.2d 401 (Neb. 1953).

[178]Harlow v. School District No. 19 of Seward County, 53 P.2d 467 (Kan. 1936).
[179]State v. Keaster, 266 Pac. 387 (Mont. 1928).
[180]Mendenhall v. Slim Buttes School District No. 4, Harding County, 196 N.W. 97 (S.D. 1923).
[181]State v. Keaster, 266 Pac. 387 (Mont. 1928).
[182]Peiffer v. Reno, 14 Pa.Dist. 47 (1904).
[183]Mont. Revised Codes, 1010 (1935).
[184]State v. School District No. 73 of Stillwater County, 76 P.2d 330 (Mont. 1938).
[185]Mont. Revised Codes S1016 (1935).

TABLE 1 §   Statutory Provisions for Parochial Pupil Transportation in the Fifty States.

Provision	Alabama	Alaska	Arizona	Arkansas	California	Colorado	Connecticut	Delaware	Florida	Georgia	Hawaii	Idaho	Illinois	Indiana	Iowa	Kansas	Kentucky	Louisiana	Maine	Maryland	Massachusetts
PERMISSIVE					x	x					x ‡						x	x	x		
Same service as to public schools					x	x					x						x	x	x		
Along established routes					x																
Using non-educational funds																	x				
Requires approval of voters							x											x			
MANDATORY									x		x	x				x				x *	x
Same service as to public schools									x			x									x
Along established routes											x	x				x					x

*Required by legislation in twelve counties. Some counties are permitted to establish additional routes.
**Parents or guardian must pay proportionate share of cost.
+Opinion of Attorney General casts doubt on application of statute to non-public schools.
‡Of doubtful validity due to ruling of state supreme court.
§*Law and the School Superintendent*, 2d ed. (Cincinnati, Ohio: National Organization on Legal Problems of Education, 1971), p. 127.

further providing that if the district board fails to do so the county board shall transport or furnish board and lodging, a mandatory duty rests on the county board of education to perform this service if it is not performed by local boards.[186] Under such a statute there is an implied obligation imposed on the pupil to make a demand on the board for the service, and a casual conversation between the parent of the pupil and a member of the board is not a legal equivalent of the demand contemplated by the statute.[187]

15.23 SPECIAL TRANSPORTATION

Where statutes do not specifically provide, it is necessarily implied[188] that a school district has the power to educate not only the physically well pupils but also those who are less fortunate physically and mentally. Public welfare demands that pupils who are physically handicapped have an opportunity to gain an education the same as more favored children.[189] Thus, it was held[190] that a board of education had the implied power to furnish transportation to undernourished children to a special school when it was shown that they were unable to mingle in the regular grade schools or to carry the work load of the physically normal child.

However, parents, before qualifying for reimbursement of transportation expenses, must consult with the proper school officials and have a determination made that the child is physically handicapped; they must make mutually satisfactory arrangements with the school officials for attendance at and transportation to a school where special facilities are available.[191] Thus, parents were able to recover only a fraction of their actual cost and no more than the $300 per year maximum stipulated

[186]State v. Beamer, 141 N.E. 851 (Ohio 1923).
[187]Board of Education of Swan Township v. Cox, 159 N.E. 479 (Ohio 1927).
[188]Foster v. Board of Education of City of Topeka, 289 Pac. 959 (Kan. 1930).

[189]Hopkins v. Yellow Cab Company, 250 P.2d 330 (Cal. 1952).
[190]Foster v. Board of Education of City of Topeka, 289 Pac. 959 (Kan. 1930).
[191]Christman v. Board of Education, 106 N.E.2d 846 (Ill. 1952).

Michigan	Minnesota	Mississippi	Missouri	Montana	Nebraska	Nevada	New Hampshire	New Jersey	New Mexico	New York	No. Carolina	North Dakota	Ohio	Oklahoma	Oregon	Pennsylvania	Rhode Island	So. Carolina	South Dakota	Tennessee	Texas	Utah	Vermont	Virginia	Washington	W. Virginia	Wisconsin	Wyoming
																										+		
									x			x														x		
																										x		
									x			x																
									x																			
				*																								
				*																								
x				x			x	x		x			x			x	x	x									x	
							x	x		x			x					x									x	
				x														x	x									

by the state superintendent of public instruction when they failed to make arrangements for transportation of their deaf child, although the district had no facilities for the education of deaf children.[192] The court pointed out that the statute did not permit parents to determine that their child was physically handicapped, select the school of their choice, and incur liability against the school district without first consulting with school officials. "To hold otherwise would lead to the absurd but equally logical conclusion that a child could be transported by plane to school some three hundred miles away at an intolerable expense to the district." The legislative intent in another case was interpreted to limit the transportation of handicapped children to the confines of the local school district, and when the state had paid the maximum set forth in the statute, it had met its obligation: "If the legislature intended the expense of transportation of a temporary residence should be paid for by the district or the state, it would have so provided

in certain and definite language as it did for the education of deaf-blind children."[193]

15.24 TRANSPORTATION TO NONPUBLIC SCHOOLS

It now appears well established that in the absence of statutory authority children may not be transported to private and/or parochial schools. Where courts have faced the issue directly, as in Wisconsin,[194] the answer was a direct prohibition against such transportation. As a result intense pressure has been exerted on state legislators to enact legislation to authorize the provision of such transportation. These efforts have been quite successful. As shown in Table 1, nine states have enacted statutory provisions permitting school districts to transport children to private or parochial schools at public expense. School districts in sixteen states are required by statute to provide transportation for children attend-

[192]Ibid.

[193]Schutte v. Decker, 83 N.W.2d 69 (Neb. 1957).
[194]Van Straton v. Milquet, 192 N.W. 392 (Wis. 1923); Costigan v. Hall, 23 N.W.2d 495 (Wis. 1946).

TABLE 2 State Constitutional Provisions Related to the Use of Public Funds for Sectarian Purposes

STATE	CONSTITUTIONAL REFERENCE
Alabama	XIV, 263
Alaska	VII, 1; IX, 6
Arizona	IX, 10
Arkansas	XIV, 2
California	IX, 8
Colorado	IX, 7
Connecticut	VII, 1; VIII, 2
Delaware	X, 3; X, 4
Florida	XII, 13
Georgia	VIII, 1 See Private Schools
Hawaii	IX, 1
Idaho	IX, 5
Illinois	VIII, 3
Indiana	VII, 3, 7
Iowa	IX, 3
Kansas	VI, 6(c)
Kentucky	S. 189
Louisiana	XII, 13
Maine	1, 3
Maryland	VIII, 3. Art. 36
Massachusetts	III, 4
Michigan	I, 2
Minnesota	VIII, 3
Mississippi	VIII, 208
Missouri	XI, 11
Montana	XI, 8
Nebraska	VII, 4, 11
Nevada	XI, 10
New Hampshire	II, 83
New Jersey	I, 5; VII, 4 (2)
New Mexico	XII, 3
New York	XI, 3
North Carolina	IX, 6, 7
North Dakota	VIII, 152
Ohio	VI, 2
Oklahoma	II, 5; XI, 5
Oregon	I, 5
Pennsylvania	III, 15
Rhode Island	I, 3
South Carolina	XI, 9
South Dakota	VI, 3; VIII, 16
Tennessee	XI, 12
Texas	I, 7
Utah	X, 13
Vermont	I, Art. 3
Virginia	I, 16
Washington	IX, 4; XXVI
West Virginia	III, 15
Wisconsin	X, 3
Wyoming	VII, 8

15.24a State constitutional provisions

With regard to the enactment of statutes providing for transportation of children to private and parochial schools, the provisions of state constitutions are determinants of whether or not such statutes may be implemented. Thus, a brief review of relevant constitutional provisions is essential. Constitutional prohibitions against the use of public funds for support of aspects of private or parochial school programs are stated in a variety of ways but may be classified into four major categories. To the extent that states have more than one constitutional prohibition they appear in more than one category:

1. Prohibiting the use of public funds by sectarian institutions or for any sectarian purpose
2. Prohibiting the use of public funds for sectarian or nonstate schools
3. Prohibiting the use of public school funds for other than public school purposes
4. Prohibiting the enactment of laws respecting the establishment of religion or requiring support of religious denominations.

States with one or more of the above prohibitions, together with the references to their constitutional provision(s), are shown in Table 2.

15.24b Court decisions

In view of the prohibitions against the use of public funds to aid sectarian schools, an appropriate question is: Does transportation of parochial school pupils aid the schools? This question was answered by the United States Supreme Court relative to the federal Constitution when it ruled[195] in *Everson* that neither the First nor the Fourteenth Amendment prohibited the use of public tax funds for transportation of children to parochial schools. In this decision the "child-benefit" theory was enunciated, the court holding that the provision of the law benefited the child and not sectarian instruction. It is of interest to note that this decision divided the court 5 to 4 and Justice Douglas, who voted to uphold the statute, has since indicated that in light of recent judgments he would not have done so if the issue were before the Court today.

In interpreting their own constitutions a number of states had previously declared such laws unconstitutional. Following the *Everson* decision some states adopted the child-benefit theory while others have held

ing private and parochial schools. Nine of these states require that transportation of private and parochial school pupils be provided on the same basis as for public school pupils, and seven states require transportation to be provided along the routes established for public school pupils.

[195]Everson v. Board of Education, 330 U.S. 1, 67 S.Ct. 504 91 L.Ed. 711 (N.J. 1947).

TABLE 3   **Cases Since Everson (1947) in Which Statutes Were Held Unconstitutional**

STATE	YEAR	CASE REFERENCE
Alaska	1962	Mathews v. Quinton, 362 P.2d 932 appeal dismissed, 368 U.S. 517, 82 S.Ct. 530, 7 L.Ed.2D 522.
Delaware	1966	Opinion of the Justices, 216 A.2d 668
Hawaii	1968	Spears v. Honda, 449 P.2d 130
Idaho	1971	Epeldi v. Engelking, 488 P.2d 860 certiorari denied, 406 U.S. 957, 92 S.Ct. 2058, 32 L.Ed.2d 343
Iowa	1947	Silverlake Consolidated School District v. Parker, 29 N.W.2d 214*
Missouri	1953	McVey v. Hawkins, 258 S.W.2d 927; Luetkemeyer v. Kaufman, 364 F. Supp. 376 (Mo. 1973)**
Oklahoma	1963	Board of Education v. Antone, 384 P.2d 911
Washington	1949	Visser v. Nooksack Valley School District, 207 P.2d 198

*Case pending at the time of the *Everson* decision
**Upheld statutes which provided transportation to public schools only

statutes providing public funds for transportation of children to private and parochial schools to be in violation of their state constitution. Cases in which this issue has been adjudicated since *Everson* (1947) and in which the enabling statutes were held unconstitutional are shown in summary form in Table 3.

In both New York and Wisconsin statutes providing public support for transportation to parochial schools were declared unconstitutional.[196] However, their constitutions have now been changed to permit the use of public expenditures for this purpose.[197]

Prior to the decision in *Everson* statutes providing transportation at public expense for children attending private and parochial schools had been upheld in Kentucky,[198] Maryland,[199] and California.[200] Subsequent to the *Everson* decision transportation of parochial school pupils by public schools was again challenged in Kentucky. In this case the Court ruled[201] that public school tax money could not be used for that purpose but that the fiscal courts could pay for such transportation. After *Everson* statutes authorizing transportation of pupils to private and parochial schools have been upheld in Connecticut,[202] Massachusetts,[203]

Michigan,[204] New Jersey,[205] Ohio,[206] Pennsylvania,[207] and Rhode Island.[208]

Courts have also been involved in the interpretation of related statutes and school board policies in the operation of transportation programs to private and parochial schools. In these decisions the courts have held:

1. A school board may not discontinue bus service for all pupils on Catholic religious days which are not state or national holidays.[209]
2. A school board may curtail transportation of public and nonpublic school children due to a reduction in funds.[210]
3. A high school district may provide transportation for elementary parochial pupils on a secondary school bus.[211]
4. Where statutes authorize transportation of parochial school pupils on public school bus routes new routes for parochial school children may not be established.[212]
5. Under New York statutes a school district is not required to transport parochial school children to a school in another district over 10 miles from the pupils' residence,[213] or eight miles outside the district.[214]

[196]Judd v. Board of Education, 15 N.E.2d 576 (N.Y. 1938); State v. Nusbaum, 115 N.W.2d 761 (Wis. 1962).
[197]New York Constitution XI, 3; Wisconsin Constitution I, 23.
[198]Nichols v. Henry, 191 S.W.2d 930 (Ky. 1944).
[199]Board of Education v. Wheat, 199 Atl. 628 (Md. 1938); See also Adams v. County Commissioners, 26 A.2d 377 (Md. 1942).
[200]Bowker v. Baker, 167 P.2d 256 (Cal. 1946).
[201]Rawlings v. Butler, 290 S.W.2d 801 (Ky. 1956).
[202]Snyder v. Newton, 161 A.2d 770, *appeal dismissed*, 364 U.S. 299 81 S.Ct. 692, 5 L.Ed.2d 688 (Conn. 1960).
[203]Quinn v. School Committee, 125 N.E.2d 410 (Mass. 1955).

[204]Alexander v. Bartlett, 165 N.E.2d 445 (Mich. 1968).
[205]McCanna v. Sells, 247 A.2d 691 (N.J. 1968).
[206]Honohan v. Holt, 244 N.E.2d 537 (Ohio 1968).
[207]Rhoades v. School District, 226 A.2d 53, *cert. denied* 389 U.S. 11, 88 S.Ct. 61, 19 L.Ed.2d 7 (Pa. 1967).
[208]Chevas v. School Committee, 211 A.2d 639 (R.I. 1965).
[209]Wooley v. Spalding, 293 S.W.2d 563 (Ky. 1956).
[210]Cartwright v. Sharpe, 162 N.W.2d 5 (Wis. 1968).
[211]Board of Education v. State Board of Education, 141 A.2d 542 (N.J. 1959).
[212]Fox v. Board of Education, 226 A.2d 471 (N.J. 1967); Rawdin v. Bristol Township School District, 44 D.&C.2d 713 (Pa. 1968).
[213]Brown v. Allen, 256 N.Y.S.2d 106 (1965).
[214]Application of Board of Union Free School District No. 18, 198 N.Y.S.2d 151 (1960).

15.25 NONDISCRIMINATION
IN PUPIL TRANSPORTATION

More emotionalism has been evoked relative to school bus transportation to avoid discrimination than any other educational issue of recent years. This issue has involved not only transportation to achieve racial balance but also urban-rural transportation. On the latter issue, it was held that when there are two statutes, one requiring transportation of all children residing two miles or more from school and another denying it to children who lived in cities, the statutes are to be liberally construed so as not to discriminate against city children.[215]

The many cases related to transportation of pupils involving questions related to desegregation have delineated a number of legal principles which may be summarized as follows:

1. A plan to desegregate schools must include a plan to desegregate pupil transportation wherein black children are transported on the same basis and terms as white children.[216]
2. Under "freedom of choice" laws black children must be accorded transportation to the extent possible and reasonable.[217]
3. While under "freedom of choice" laws children may select their schools, they may not select their buses.[218]
4. Where a court's desegregation order has been effectively implemented without free bus transportation a district is not required to provide free transportation.[219]
5. Bussing is a permissible device for elimination of *de jure* segregation.[220] However, involuntary bussing may not be of such time and distance as to be a hazard to health or impinge on the educational program.[221]
6. A state statute which would make the right to attend a neighborhood school an absolute right is unconstitutional,[222] as is one

which prohibits bussing to achieve racial balance in the schools.[223]
7. School boards have authority to provide for extensive transportation of pupils to achieve racial balance.[224]
8. The Civil Rights Act of 1964 does not prohibit transportation within a district to achieve racial balance.[225]
9. School districts may not be required to operate a multidistrict desegregation plan, transporting pupils across district boundary lines, or to consolidate with other districts to achieve racial balance.[226]
10. A state may not provide transportation grants to a private school to which only white children are admitted; such a provision violates the Fourteenth Amendment.[227]
11. Transportation of children to achieve desegregation of schools is an extraordinary remedy to be employed only when appreciable results may be anticipated and when other alternatives have been exhausted.[228]

15.26 PURCHASE AND
OWNERSHIP OF SCHOOL BUSES

A general power conferred on a school board to provide transportation for pupils impliedly commits the methods of transportation to the discretion of the board[229] on a racially nondiscriminatory basis.[230] Where statutes do not specify, it is within the discretion of the board to provide its own vehicles[231] or to contract with persons who pro-

---

[215]Morrissette v. DeZonia, 217 N.W.2d 377 (Wis. 1974).

[216]Vick v. County Board of Education of Obion County, 205 F.Supp. 436 (Tenn. 1962); Harris v. Crenshaw County Board of Education, 259 F.Supp. 167 (Ala. 1966); Franklin v. Barbour County Board of Education, 259 F.Supp. 545 (Ala. 1966); Kelly v. Public School District No. 22, 378 F.2d 483 (8th Cir. 1967); Boomer v. Beaufort County Board of Education, 294 F.Supp. 179 (N.C. 1968).

[217]Franklin v. Barbour County Board of Education, 259 F.Supp. 545 (Ala. 1966).

[218]Kelly v. Public School District No. 22, 378 F.2d 483 (8th Cir. 1967).

[219]Quarles v. Oxford Municipal Separate School District, 487 F.2d 824 (5th Cir. 1973); Bradley v. Milliken, 402 F.Supp. 1096 (Mich. 1975).

[220]Smuck v. Hobson, 408 F.2d 175 (4th Cir. 1969); United States v. School District, 404 F.2d 1125 (7th Cir. 1969).

[221]Opinion of the Justices, 298 N.E.2d 840 (Mass. 1973).

[222]*Ibid.*

[223]Lee v. Nyquist, 318 F.Supp. 710 (N.Y. 1970), affirmed, 402 U.S. 935, 91 S.Ct. 1618, 29 L.Ed.2d 105 (1971); Swan v. Charlotte-Mecklenburg Board of Education, 312 F.Supp. 503 (N.C. 1970), affirmed, 403 U.S. 912, 91 S.Ct. 2200, 29 L.Ed.2d 689 (1971).

[224]Strippoli v. Bickal, 209 N.E.2d 123 (N.Y. 1984); Bablabin v. Rubin, 250 N.Y.S.2d 281 (1964); Van Blerkom v. Donovan, 259 N.Y.S.2d 825 (1965); Bradley v. Milliken, 519 F.2d 679 (6th Cir. 1975).

[225]United States v. Jefferson County Board of Education, 372 F.2d 836 (5th Cir. 1966).

[226]Bradley v. School Board of City of Richmond, 462 F.2d 1058 (4th Cir. 1972); Bradley v. Milliken, 418 U.S. 717, 94 S.Ct. 3112, 41 L.Ed.2d 1087 (Mich. 1974); United States v. Board of School Commissioners of Indianapolis, 474 F.2d 81 (7th Cir. 1973), cert. denied, 421 U.S. 929, 95 S.Ct. 1654, 44 L.Ed.2d 86 (Ind. 1975); But see Evans v. Buchanan, 416 F.Supp. 328 (Del. 1976); Metropolitan School District v. Buckley, 541 F.2d 1211 (7th Cir. 1976); affirmed 97 S.Ct. 800, 801 (Ind. 1977).

[227]Pettaway V. County School Board, 230 F.Supp. 480 (Va. 1964).

[228]Bradley v. Milliken, 402 F.Supp. 1096 (Mich. 1975); Morgan v. Kerrigan, 401 F.Supp. 216 (Mass. 1975). See also Morgan v. Kerrigan, 523 F.2d 917 (1st Cir. 1975).

[229]Johnson v. Sabine Parish School Board, 140 So. 87 (La. 1932).

[230]Evans v. Buchanan, 195 F.Supp. 321 (Del. 1961).

[231]Herman v. Medicine Lodge School District No. 8, 71 N.W.2d 323 (N.D. 1955); Shores v. Elmore County Board of Education, 3 So.2d 14 (Ala. 1941); Smith v. Rose, 169 S.W.2d 609 (Ky. 1943); Leslie v. School District No. 1, Mason Township, 239 N.W. 270 (Mich.

vide their own vehicles.[232] The Alabama court has said that the county board of education has the right to purchase buses in such numbers as are reasonably necessary to accommodate the pupils and, incidental to such authority, is the right to determine the type of buses to the end that the welfare and safety of the pupils may best be conserved, notwithstanding the poor financial condition of the district.[233] Other courts generally have approved the right of school districts to buy and sell buses. A statute which authorized transportation of school pupils gave the county board of education discretionary power to determine whether the board would furnish the bus and hire the driver or contract for the bus and driver.[234] A North Dakota statute provided that "School boards shall have the power to purchase a bus body, a chassis, or a complete motor bus" using money from the general fund.[235] Under a statute which provided that school conveyances should be by "electric railways, school conveyances, and other public transportation," conveyance by common carriers only was not required,[236] and transportation could be furnished in a bus owned by a school.

A person who had been recommended by the superintendent to receive the contract to furnish a bus and driver was not entitled to recover damages from the school board when he failed to receive the contract. A recommendation by the school superintendent gave him no "vested right" to the contract or employment.[237]

15.27 SCHOOL BUS STANDARDS

Increasingly the necessity of school bus standards is recognized in the law. For example, according to a North Dakota statute,[238] such bus "shall meet the standards set up by the superintendent of public instruction and the highway commissioner." Other states have comparable provisions, and many states require that national school bus safety standards be met.

15.28 QUALIFICATION OF BUS DRIVERS

School bus drivers' qualifications are also enumerated in the statutes in many states. Those stated in the North Dakota statute are an example:

15–34.2–14. Qualifications, character, and age of school bus drivers.—The driver of a school bus shall be in good physical and mental health, able-bodied, free from communicable diseases, and shall have normal use of both hands, both feet, both eyes, and both ears. It shall be the duty of school boards to designate reputable physicians to examine each driver annually. It shall be the duty of each driver to present the physician's certificate of physical fitness to the employing school board before a contract is signed. Such driver shall possess a good moral character, shall be at least eighteen and not more than sixty-five years of age, and shall be required to have a North Dakota driver's license. However, the school board, in its discretion, may extend the maximum age of a driver to age sixty-seven. Any driver reaching the age of sixty-seven during the school year may be allowed to drive until the completion of that school year. All drivers over the age of sixty-five must submit to a physical examination once every six months and present the physician's certificate of physical fitness to the school board after each examination. The term school bus as used in this section shall mean a passenger motor vehicle having an actual seating capacity of seventeen or more passengers.[239]

15.29 BIDS FOR TRANSPORTATION SERVICES

Normally school districts are not required to take bids for transportation services when an individual or corporation provides school transportation under contract. When the taking of bids is required, all the usual procedures in accepting bids must be followed. Both quality of service and price are to be considered in accepting the bidder. Thus, it was held[240] that a bid could be refused where it appeared that the bidder had bid four specific routes at less than cost to take the contract away from another satisfactory bidder and where the low bidder had been involved in previous difficulties with the board over mileage on its routes.

15.30 SUMMARY

School districts generally may not provide transportation for school pupils unless so authorized by statutes. Authority to transport derived from statutory implica-

1931); McKnight v. Cassady, 174 Atl. 865 (N.J. 1934); Homestead Bank v. Best, 178 S.E. 143 (S.C. 1935).
[232]Shores v. Elmore County Board of Education, 3 So.2d 14 (Ala. 1941); Boone v. Carter, 187 N.E. 357 (Ind. 1933); Smith v. Rose, 169 S.W.2d 609 (Ky. 1943); McKnight v. Cassady, 174 Atl. 865 (N.J. 1934).
[233]Scott v. Hattingly, 182 So. 24 (Ala. 1938).
[234]Board of Education of City of Muskogee v. Baldwin, 137 P.2d 932 (Okla. 1943).
[235]Herman v. Medicine Lodge School District No. 8, 71 N.W.2d 325 (N.D. 1955).
[236]Commonwealth v. Benton School District, 120 Atl. 661 (Pa. 1923).
[237]Smith v. Rose, 169 S.W.2d 609 (Ky. 1943).
[238]North Dakota Century Code, 15-34-18 (1973).

[239]North Dakota Century Code, 15-34.2-14 (1975 Supplement).
[240]Hahn v. Palmerton Area School District, 32 Pa. Dist. & Co. 2d 91 (1963).

tions, while sustained in certain circumstances, is comparatively rare. Statutes providing for transportation of public school pupils have now been enacted in all states.

Statutes providing for free transportation of school children have been universally held to be constitutional against all manner of charges. Transportation generally has been limited to transportation of students within the school district although extension of authority to transport students outside the district has been approved in some circumstances. The authority to transport is usually vested by the state in the school district; when it is so vested, municipalities or state boards of education may not interfere or invade the field.

Statutes frequently give boards of education wide discretionary power relative to all aspects of the transportation program, and when such discretion is granted, its use will not be interfered with by the courts. Courts will control the discretion of school boards only when they act arbitrarily, capriciously, fraudulently. or maliciously.

Several methods of measuring how far a child lives from school have been sustained by the courts. A sound method was provided by a Kansas court which held that the distance should be measured from the pupil's home to the schoolhouse over the usually traveled road. It was stated that a child does not live in the middle of the road in front of a house nor is a child taught in the road in front of the school.

Children transported may be required to walk a reasonable distance to meet the bus. The courts of the several states have held various distances up to two miles under certain circumstances to be reasonable. School buses cannot be compelled to enter private driveways or pick up children at their homes unless the statutes so provide.

If statutes require safe, comfortable conveyances, these conditions must be met. Statutes also require shelters in some instances. However, it is not necessary that the shelters be heated unless specifically required by law.

Parents may be reimbursed in a number of instances for transporting their children in lieu of the district's providing transportation. When there is a choice, the option is to be exercised by the school board not the parents. When a given amount of money per mile is provided by statute, it is applicable to each child in the family unless otherwise specified.

The fact that a school board fails to anticipate its transportation costs and to include funds for them in the budget does not relieve it of its obligation to parents. The fact that children lived within walking distance of school when the budget was formulated is irrelevant.

A school board may normally contract with members of the board for the transportation of their children as long as the compensation paid is reasonable and corresponds to the statutory amounts.

When granted authority to provide transportation for school children, boards of education may also transport mentally retarded and physically handicapped children. In some states boards have not only the right but the obligation to transport handicapped children.

Most state constitutions prohibit use of public funds for sectarian purposes. Where courts have viewed transportation to private and parochial schools as an aid to sectarian education it has been prohibited. Where such transportation is viewed as a "child-benefit" it has been permitted. The United States Supreme Court held in *Everson* that the use of public funds to provide transportation to private and parochial schools does not violate the United States Constitution. A number of states have accepted the "child-benefit" theory enunciated in *Everson* and have permitted the use of public funds to provide transportation to children attending private and parochial schools. A number of other state supreme courts have interpreted their constitution as prohibiting public assistance for transportation to private and parochial schools. Even when not prevented by constitutional provisions, districts may not transport children to nonpublic schools unless specially authorized by statutes. Even statutes providing for transportation of *all* children do not authorize transportation of children to parochial schools.

When boards of education are authorized to provide transportation and the method is not specified, it is within the discretion of the board to provide transportation by any reasonable means, including the operation of its own vehicles or contracting with others to supply the transportation.

Racial discrimination is not permitted, and where freedom of choice of schools is allowed, transportation must be furnished to the extent that it is reasonable and practicable. School districts may transport children to achieve racial balance and may be compelled by the courts to do so. However, school districts may not be required to operate multidistrict desegregation plans transporting pupils across district boundaries, nor be compelled to consolidate with other districts to achieve racial balance except under unusual circumstances.

Bids for bus transportation, when required, must follow accepted procedure in calling for and accepting bids. However, the low bid need not be accepted if there is a factual basis for judging that it would be unsatisfactory.

Most state statutes establish safety standards for school buses and call for regular inspections. Most states also require qualifications for school bus drivers to insure a high degree of safety in pupil transportation.

Certification of Professional Personnel

16.0 INTRODUCTION

The prima facie evidence of a teacher's qualifications and eligibility for employment in certain capacities in the public schools is a license or certificate. One who holds oneself out as such is not a teacher unless and until the certificate has been granted. As stated in the *Harvard Journal on Legislation*:

> The primary purpose of teacher certification is to insure that only qualified persons teach in a state's public school system. It is necessary for the state to carry this burden because local school boards often are not equipped or in a position to check adequately the qualifications of teachers in their schools.[1]

State responsibility in this field has largely been delegated to state boards of education and state departments of education. They establish and revise the qualifications required to receive a certificate according to the changing needs of the profession and the demand for teachers. Standards for certification are constantly reevaluated in the light of changing demands upon teachers. Qualifications for teachers' certificates are published from time to time so that the prospective teacher has advance knowledge of them and can plan a preparation program accordingly. The objective of certification procedure is to assure local school boards that persons who hold a teaching certificate possess certain educational qualifications.

16.1 STATE
PROCEDURES AND REQUIREMENTS

The state has a legitimate interest in prescribing standards designed to improve the quality of teaching in the public schools. As was observed in a Connecticut case:

> It is axiomatic that schools can be no better than the teachers employed in them. A board has the right to demand that a teacher know his subject and that he be capable of arousing and holding the interest of his pupils and maintaining discipline.[2]

Each state has adopted its own procedures and requirements for certification. In some the application must be individually processed (secured through the personal efforts of the teacher); in others it is granted automatically upon completion of the approved program and upon recommendation of the preparing institution; in still others employment is required before the certificate is issued.

The initial certificate is usually valid for a few years only. It is the teacher's professional responsibility to keep it renewed. Sometimes the teacher must show evidence of professional growth as well as teaching experience in order to qualify for renewal of a certificate of longer duration. By 1975 every state except Nebraska required a baccalaureate degree for certification of elementary teachers; some states, however, still grant substandard certificates for teachers below the prescribed educational level.[3] A fifth year of preparation is required for high school teachers in a few states and eighteen states require completion of a fifth year within a specified time after the initial certification.[4]

Regardless of professional preparation, teachers usually are not eligible for certification unless they meet certain additional requirements, such as good moral character, a minimum age, and citizenship. A number of states require the passage of an oral interview and a written examination for certain certificates. Since the qualifications for various teaching and supervisory positions differ, several types of certificates have been devised.

Procedure related to teachers' certificates in each state is governed by statutes and regulations of the agency to which the administration of teacher certification has been delegated. In the process of administering this program, the constitutional and legal rights of candidates for certificates, or of teachers seeking renewal or new certification, are involved. Consequently, the courts in effect play a vital supervisory and adjudicatory role in preserving these rights from legislative and administrative abuse.

---

[3]National Education Association, *Manual for School Certification Requirements for Secondary and Elementary School Personnel* (Washington D.C.: National Education Association, 1975). By 1975 all states required a baccalaureate degree of secondary school teachers. In addition, most states require supervised practice teaching for certification. With the rise in the number of certified teachers, the use of substandard certificates has decreased substantially. Such certificates are primarily issued only in specialized fields such as industrial arts, special education, and library science.

[4]National Education Association, *Manual for School Certification Requirements for Secondary and Elementary School Personnel* (Washington, D.C.: National Education Association, 1975). *See also* Elizabeth H. Woellner, *Requirements for Certification for Elementary Schools, Secondary Schools, and Junior Colleges*, 40th ed. (Chicago, Ill.: University of Chicago Press, 1976).

[1]2 Harvard Journal Legislation (1965), p. 150.
[2]Devlin v. Bennett, 213 A.2d 725 (Conn. 1965).

16.2 DELEGATION OF AUTHORITY TO STATE AGENCY

The administration of a teacher certification program requires expertise and a day-by-day application of specialized knowledge which are beyond the capability of a legislative body. A state legislature can, as it must, establish the standards, the policies, and the guidelines for teacher certification, but their actual implementation must, of necessity, be delegated to an administrative agency, usually to the state board of education. Normally, the legislature authorizes the state board to adopt rules and regulations consistent with the legislative standards which delineate the procedures for administering teacher certification. The legislature creates the framework; the board provides the details and the implementation.[5] In issuing, denying, suspending, or revoking certificates the state board often serves in a quasi-judicial as well as in an administrative capacity. Within the limitations of its delegated authority it establishes certain requirements which must be met by each applicant and determines whether they have been satisfied.

An appeal is often permitted from a decision of the board either to the state superintendent of education or directly to the courts, depending upon the practice in the particular state. In either case substantial weight is given to the factual findings and determinations of the board in recognition of the special competence and experience of its personnel. Thus courts have declared that a board's decision will be upheld unless it is "clearly erroneous" or is not supported by "substantial evidence."

16.3 PROCEDURE FOR OBTAINING A CERTIFICATE

As previously indicated, procedures are governed by state statutes and board regulations, which vary from state to state. Under the procedure followed by many states the applicant is required to complete a form which includes scholastic background, a transcript of college grades, recommendations from the college or its dean, and past employment record. If there has been no actual teaching experience, the candidate may, depending upon the law of the particular state, be issued a probationary or temporary certificate for a two- to five-year period.

16.4 TYPES OF CERTIFICATES

The need for teachers in a state often determines the types of certificates which are issued: temporary or limited, emergency or special, permanent, and advance or supervisory.[6]

16.4a Temporary or limited

The temporary certificate is useful for realistically determining the qualifications of an applicant for a permanent certificate. The issuance of a temporary certificate provides an opportunity for local school authorities to observe and evaluate the applicant's teaching ability over an extended period of time;[7] enables an applicant to demonstrate ability; permits some relaxation of the regular certification standards (provided they are fulfilled by the time the permanent certificate is issued); allows the certifying agency to examine the applicant's actual teaching record, as well as periodic reports from the applicant's immediate supervisor and superintendent, in addition to considering the educational background; and facilitates a simplified initial certification procedure since a fuller and more reliable evaluation of the applicant's qualifications for a more permanent certificate can be made at a later date. The preliminary period of observation made possible by a one- to five-year temporary certificate reduces the likelihood that a disqualified or undesirable person will be given a permanent certificate.[8]

The limited certificate permits qualified applicants to teach particular courses or at specified grade levels. Under this certificate it has consistently been held[9] by state boards and the courts that the holder has no authorization to teach beyond the areas stated in the certificate. However, an Indiana court ruled[10] that a teacher was wrongfully discharged for failure to have a license to teach physics where he had ob-

[5]People v. Kerstein, 108 N.E.2d 915 (Ill. 1952).

[6]The study in support of an Alternative Standard for Teacher Certification reported in 2 Harvard Journal Legislations (1965), describes the many types of certificates on p. 153: "In 1959 the states issued a total of 630 different certificates, ranging from one in West Virginia (with one or more forms) to 65 in New Jersey. Of these 88 were issued on preparation below a bachelor's degree."

[7]Application of Myerson, 264 N.Y.S.2d 986 (1965).

[8]Under Section 24(11) of the Illinois School Code a teacher before acquiring "contractual continued service" status must serve a two-year probationary period consisting of two consecutive school terms as a full-time teacher. In commenting upon the objective of this provision the Appellate Court of Illinois stated in Elder v. Board of Education of School District No. 127½, 208 N.E.2d 423 (Ill. 1965).

[9]People v. Kerstein, 108 N.E.2d 915 (Ill. 1952), concerning a limited supervisory certificate.

[10]Union School Township of Gibson County v. Sellers, 12 N.E.2d 508 (Ind. 1939). It was held that the issuance of the permit fully completed the qualifications of the teacher to teach physics.

tained a permit to teach the subject (in addition to his regular license to teach social subjects and mathematics).

16.4b Emergency or special

The emergency certificate is designed to provide needed flexibility where there is an insufficient number of regularly certificated teachers to meet current demands. While the number of college graduates prepared to teach has increased substantially in recent years, there are still teacher shortages in some regions of the country and in many specialized subjects.[11] The Kentucky statute providing for emergency certification is typical:

> When a district board of education satisfies the State Board of Education that it is impossible to secure qualified teachers for a position in a school under the control of the district board, the State Board of Education may, on approval of the Superintendent of Public Instruction, issue emergency certificates to persons who meet the qualifications determined by the State Board of Education for emergency certificates.[12]

Emergency certificates are ordinarily renewable on an annual basis. If the emergency has ended, a state board may (and should) reject renewal.[13] As the Pennsylvania court correctly reasoned,[14] the legislature intended that the authority to employ substitutes as a wartime emergency measure should not extend beyond a period of absolute necessity, and this necessity ended when fully qualified teachers became available. A renewal of an emergency certificate may also be denied where the holder has failed to complete the requirements for a first-class certificate during the prescribed period.[15] The legislature may permit local school districts to issue special certificates to meet a local shortage of teachers. In such cases the certificates are valid only in the district where issued.[16] State laws may place a time limit upon the length of certification or eligibility for employment in a particular capacity—as one year for a substi-

tute teacher[17] or eight years for a principal's eligibility list.[18]

16.4c Conditional

It is not uncommon to grant certificates on condition that certain prescribed requirements be satisfied before a first-class or permanent certificate will be issued. In an Illinois case[19] the board required each teacher who had less than a bachelor's degree to earn six additional semester hours of acceptable college credits by a specified date. In upholding the regulation the court said, "Irrespective of legislative fiat we conclude that Boards of Education may require continued professional growth of its teachers as a condition of continued tenure so long as the requirement is reasonable in the light of the object to be obtained." Although the above is a tenure case, the general principle announced is applicable, namely, that a board of education may impose reasonable conditions in granting teachers' certificates.

A New York case[20] is more directly in point. A teacher was permitted to take an examination for a teaching position upon condition that the requirements be met by a specified date, although he was ineligible for the position at the time. It was held that the license granted was a conditional one and temporary in nature, and was subject to revocation in the event the teacher did not meet the eligibility requirements by the date fixed. In another New York case[21] the petitioner received a permanent appointment "subject to meeting preparation requirements in full by February 15, 1964." The court held that the teacher was entitled to a hearing before her contract could be terminated for failure to meet the conditions.

16.4d Permanent

Apart from its authority to impose reasonable conditions as indicated above, and from its power to exercise a sound discretion, a board of education cannot issue permanent certificates to teachers unless they fulfill the prescribed requirements.

[11]Graybeal, *Teacher Surplus and Teacher Shortage,* 37th Education, Digest 13 (1972.)

[12]Kentucky Revised Status, 161.100 (1967).

[13]Bloom v. Pike Township School District, 56 A.2d 348 (Pa. 1948).

[14]*Ibid.*

[15]Starling v. Board of Education for County of Mingo, 175 F.Supp. 703 (W.Va. 1959).

[16]Union High School District No. 2 v. Paul, 95 P.2d 5 (Col. 1939). The case also holds that a certificate is void if the agency has no authority to issue it.

[17]Matthews v. Board of Education of City of San Diego, 18 Cal.Rptr. 101 (1962).

[18]Bauer v. Board of Education of City of New York, 250 N.Y.S.2d 2 (1964).

[19]Last v. Board of Education of Community Unit School District, 185 N.E.2d 282 (Ill. 1962).

[20]Glass v. Board of Education of City of New York, 241 N.Y.S.2d 890 (1963).

[21]Mannix v. Board of Education of City of New York, 260 N.Y.S.2d 811 (1965).

Accordingly, it has been held[22] that the board may vacate a permanent certificate issued through error. In a New York case the limitation of the board was recognized as follows:

> The appointment which she received necessarily had to be measured by the license which she had and accordingly at best it was an appointment for a temporary basis only. No regular appointment could have been awarded to her at that time nor, unless she fulfilled the requirements for the position, could a regular appointment be awarded to her in the future since under Education Law, §2573, subd. 9, no teacher may be so appointed unless she possesses the necessary qualifications. It thus was not within the power of the Board of Education, since the requirement for eligibility for the position had not been fulfilled, to make petitioner's appointment permanent. . . .[23]

While a teacher with tenure may be compelled by a state board of education to fulfill reasonable requirements for professional growth,[24] the Kentucky court declared[25] that a county board of education cannot impose requirements of scholastic training greater than those fixed by the statute under which the permanent certificate was issued. In a Pennsylvania decision the court held[26] that a teacher holding a permanent supervising principal's certificate "in any Public School District of the third or fourth class" was qualified to be the principal of a four-year high school, which position was created after her certification. The court held that her certificate was unlimited and unconditional, and in the absence of any changes of the standards and requirements for the position by the state council of education she was qualified for it. Higher standards may be required of a permanent teacher than of a substitute.[27]

16.4e Advance or supervisory
As with other teaching positions, a teacher must hold the proper certificate to be qualified for an advanced or supervisory position. Many states demand a valid supervisory certificate as a prerequisite to filling a supervisory position. In a *quo war-*

ranto proceeding to remove from office a county superintendent of schools, it was held[28] that he was properly ousted because he could not show possession of a valid supervisory certificate.

16.5 QUALIFICATIONS FOR CERTIFICATE
The qualifications for each type of certificate are established in the statutes of the particular state and/or in the regulations of its state board of education or similar body. They therefore vary from state to state. In determining the question of qualifications the state board must compare all that is known about the applicant with the composite requirements for the certificate for which application is made.

A classic statement appears in an early Massachusetts case:

> The committee might find an applicant to be really a person of good character, and yet of such reputation as would prevent the attendance of the scholars. A teacher might have personal habits or manners so offensive or peculiar as to make his influence upon the scholars injurious. He might be too severe in his requirements; inclined to devote too much time to the older or better scholars, at the expense of the younger or more ignorant; a person of strong prejudices; a decided partisan and propagandist in politics or history; unskillful in imparting knowledge, or unable to appreciate the difficulties of beginners; and still be a person of sound morals, great learning, and undoubted capacity to govern. Yet all these considerations might very properly be regarded by the committee in determining his "qualifications to teach."[29]

As previously mentioned, persons must meet the qualifications for the requested license before they can complain if it is not issued to them. In New York, where the maximum age for an applicant was forty-six years of age, an applicant forty-seven years old took and passed the examination for a regular license as a laboratory assistant in day high schools. In this instance it was held[30] that the applicant had knowledge of her ineligibility and therefore could not be heard to complain when her application was denied.

16.5a Good moral character
Every state expects applicants for teaching certificates to be of good moral character. Whether an applicant meets this re-

[22]Mare v. Dillion, 70 N.Y.S.2d 376 (1947), *affirmed*, 80 N.E.2d 665.
[23]Glass v. Board of Education of New York, 241 N.Y.S.2d 890 (1963).
[24]Last v. Board of Education of Community Unit School District, 185 N.E.2d 282 (Ill. 1962).
[25]Simpson County Board of Education v. Bradley, 56 S.W.2d 34 (Ky. 1933).
[26]Appeal of Dugan, 59 A.2d 888 (Pa. 1948).
[27]Meyerson v. Allen, 264 N.Y.S.2d 986 (1965).

[28]People v. Kerstein, 108 N.E.2d 915 (Ill. 1952).
[29]School District No. 10 in Uxbridge v. Rich. D. Mowry, 91 Mass. 94 (1864).
[30]Sobel v. Bogen, 190 N.Y.S.2d 562 (1959).

quirement is a question of fact and depends upon an evaluation of all relevant evidence available to the state board. The evidence includes information contained in the written application form, which inquires into past criminal records and prosecutions, testimony of witnesses and the applicant, and recommendations or reports from local school authorities and others. As with the findings of fact of administrative agencies generally, the courts will give considerable weight to the findings of the state board since it has the benefit of hearing the testimony and observing the conduct of the applicant or any witnesses. An appellate court cannot effectively judge such "demeanor" evidence even when it has received a record of the proceedings before the board. The Oregon Supreme Court in a 1963 case affirmed the deference shown by courts to the decisions of administrative agencies when it said:

> The extent to which a reviewing court should review the action of an administrative agency has been expressed by this court, as follows:
>
> . . . Generally, they go no further than to determine whether the agency (1) acted impartially; (2) performed faithfully the duties delineated in the legislative acts which conferred jurisdiction upon it; (3) stayed within its jurisdiction; (4) committed no error of law; (5) exercised discretion judiciously or capriciously; and (6) arrived at no conclusion which was clearly wrong.
>
> Whether or not the Board arrived at a conclusion which was clearly wrong depends upon whether a review of the entire record discloses any facts from which the conclusion drawn by the Board could be reached by reasonable minds.[31]

Determining whether an applicant possesses good moral character is difficult.[32] Here, as in other areas, a great deal of the responsibility is placed on the local school board, which periodically reviews the subsequent teaching record before a teacher's contract is renewed or the teacher is placed on tenure.[33] State boards too are required to rule in this sensitive area. In a number of decisions state boards' rulings against good

character have been upheld in the courts. The following are typical:

> Illicit relations with a female student resulting in pregnancy.[34]

> A crime covered by the education code.[35] Several acts of grand larceny committed while serving in a position of trust as a night policeman.[36]

> Falsely including the names of nonstudents on attendance records.[37]

> Pleading guilty to presenting false claims against the United States.[38]

> Writing two letters to the mayor derogatory of members of the school board, which were considered intemperate and libelous.[39]

> Using illegal means to bring about social or legal changes going beyond the First and Fourteenth amendments.[40]

16.5b Minimum educational requirements

At present, every state except one requires applicants to have a college degree including a certain number of hours in a prescribed curriculum. Determination of whether or not specific courses meet the established requirements is generally within the province of the state board. Where an applicant had completed only five courses totaling twelve hours rather than the twenty-four hours required, the board correctly ruled[41] that the applicant was ineligible for a license as an assistant director of community education. Applicants for advanced certificates may be required to earn a master's degree or complete a given number of years of successful teaching.[42]

16.5c Recommendations

Another common requirement is one or more recommendations from specified persons, such as staff members at the college

---

[31]Application of Bay, 378 P.2d 558 (Ore. 1963). In this case the court distinguished between "character" and "reputation" as follows: "Character is what a man or woman is morally, while reputation is what he or she is reputed to be."

[32]School District No. 10 in Uxbridge v. Rich. D. Mowry, 91 Mass. 94 (1864).

[33]Crawford v. Lewis, 186 S.W. 492 (Ky. 1916).

[34]Ibid.

[35]Vogulkin v. State Board of Education of the State, 15 Cal.Rptr. 335 (1961).

[36]Application of Bay, 378 P.2d 558 (Ore. 1963).

[37]People v. Flaningham, 179 N.E. 823 (Ill. 1932).

[38]Huff v. Anderson, 90 S.E.2d 329 (Ga. 1955).

[39]Steger v. Board of Examiners of Board of Education, 12 N.Y.S.2d 263 (1939).

[40]Christmas v. Board of Education of Harford County, Maryland, 231 F.Supp. 331 (Md. 1964). The mere engaging in civil rights demonstrations is not evidence of bad character providing the means used are not illegal or unconstitutional.

[41]Klot v. Wilson, 156 N.Y.S.2d 425 (1956).

[42]Antell v. Board of Education of City of New York, 195 N.Y.S.2d 959 (1959).

of his blindness, and the decision of the board was sustained. Recent legislation on employment of handicapped persons grant them greater employment opportunities.

It has been decided that a teacher may be required to procure a biennial chest x-ray to show freedom from tuberculosis[70] and a vaccination for smallpox.[71] As early as 1939 it was ruled by an Oregon court "that the district has implied power to determine by physical examination whether an applicant is affected with any communicable disease or is incapable of discharging his or her duties as a teacher."[72]

16.6 ISSUANCE OF CERTIFICATES

If the applicant meets the prescribed requirements for the certificate applied for, the board must issue it and cannot arbitrarily withhold it. After exhausting any administrative procedures which may be provided the applicant has recourse to the courts to set aside the board's findings and compel the issuance of the certificate.[73]

16.6a Discretion in issuing agency

It has been said repeatedly that fitness to teach depends upon a broad range of factors, many of which require the exercise of good judgment by the members of the issuing agency. A certain degree of discretion must be vested in such members in determining whether the applicant has met the qualifications for the certificate sought, particularly in the administration and grading of competitive and qualifying examinations.[74] The exercise of this discretion will be upset by the courts only where an abuse has been shown, as by unreasonable, arbitrary, capricious, or discriminatory action. Most state constitutions include a provision, similar to the Fourteenth Amendment to the United States Constitution, which prohibits unreasonable and arbitrary discrimination by agencies of the state government. Even in the absence of such a provision, a board charged with issuing teachers' certificates must act fairly, reasonably, in good faith, and must treat alike persons who are similarly situated. An examining board must apply the same criteria in evaluating each candidate, but formal rigid-

ity is not required, nor is exactness of treatment beyond reason. Each case must be judged on its own facts.

16.7 DENIAL OF CERTIFICATES

To the same extent that the board has an obligation to issue a certificate to a qualified applicant, it has a duty to deny one to an unqualified candidate. In the latter instance, as previously explained, a conditional or temporary certificate may be appropriate. In granting or denying a certificate it is the duty of the board to make a fair, reasonable, and honest judgment on the basis of the available relevant information before it.[75]

16.7a Privilege and not a right

A license to teach is said to be a privilege and not an absolute right.[76] In the words of a federal district judge in South Carolina, "No individual as a matter of right has a constitutional privilege to be in the public employ as a school teacher, and all teachers in public schools are subject to reasonable rules and regulations by state and local school officials."[77] This means that an unqualified person has no right to be a teacher. However, an applicant meeting all the prescribed qualifications and conditions for a certificate has a right to receive one. The South Carolina judge added, "State or local officials cannot, however, deprive a teacher of any constitutional right, by imposing unreasonable or unlawful conditions as a necessary adjunct to employment; nor should such rights be denied because of race or color."[78]

Courts often speak in terms of a privilege and not a right in upholding revocations of certificates for incompetence, immorality, or unprofessional conduct, or in permitting the enactment of additional regulations after the issuance of a license. A more rational explanation would be that the profession of teaching is interlaced with the public interest and is subject to reasonable regulation. The question is better stated in terms of "reasonableness" or "unreasonableness" than as a "right" or a "privilege." Of course, no one has an absolute right to teach or to teach on his or her own terms, but all prospective teachers have an absolute right to have their qualifications to

which the student attended.[43] The objective, unbiased opinion of a school superintendent in appraising a teacher's ability is entitled to great weight.[44] However, the superintendent's recommendation of a tenure appointment does not foreclose the board of education's denying it.[45] By furnishing references for recommendations the applicant authorizes the board to inquire directly of them.[46]

16.5d Prior experience

For certain certificates prior specific experience is a prerequisite. In New Jersey it was held,[47] for example, that service as a dean of boys could not substitute for three years of experience as vice-principal while "properly certified as a principal." In New York an applicant for an assistant principal's license was required to teach two of the five years in "special service" elementary and junior high schools.[48] This requirement obviously had to be met before the candidate could receive the license.

16.5e By types of examinations

Some states grant certificates on the basis of examinations, written or oral, competitive or noncompetitive. For example, the examination for a license as chairman of the speech department in the day high schools "consisted of four tests—(1) a written test; (2) an interview test; (3) a supervision test; (4) a teaching test. In addition thereto there was an appraisal of record, a rating of training and experience and a physical and medical examination."[49]

16.5f Competitive and noncompetitive examinations

For the competition to be fair, a competitive examination itself must be fair and meet "objective standards," as was remarked by the New York court:

An examination cannot be classed as competitive unless it conforms to measures or standards which are sufficiently objective to be capable of being challenged and reviewed,

when necessary, by other examiners of equal ability and experience.[50]

Another New York case correctly described the nature of a noncompetitive examination, such as may be given to determine eligibility for employment to certain positions:

Noncompetitive examination does not restrict the appointing officer to the name highest on the list. He may reject any on the list, or all, if their personal qualities or associations seem to render them ineligible. Noncompetitive examination is merely an assurance that along with personal qualities or associations satisfactory to the appointing officer there shall also be the attainment of some standard of efficiency established as a minimum.[51]

In both competitive and noncompetitive examinations the examiners have considerable discretion in framing the questions as long as they reasonably relate to the necessary qualifications for the position and are not designed to favor one applicant over another.

An excellent comment on this point is found in a New York case:

It would be impossible to formulate a standard by which such qualities may be defined or measured with entire objectivity. The law does not require the impossible or forbid the reasonable. . . . Exact definition of the qualities which are essential or desirable may be impossible; exact formula or standard by which such qualities may be measured has never been achieved; mechanical application of any standard is certainly not practicable. Much must be left to the judgment of the examiners.[52]

Examining boards have greater discretion in the administration of noncompetitive then competitive examinations. In either case good examination practices should be observed; however, in the former the examining board has greater latitude in changing announced ratings or rules.[53] A noncompetitive examination is required to be a reasonable test of merit and fitness, but no advance notice need be given, and no advanced standards fixed, as in the case of

[70]Conlon v. Marshall, 59 N.Y.S.2d 52 (1945).
[71]Cude v. State, 377 S.W.2d 816 (Ark. 1964).
[72]School District No. 1 v. Teachers' Retirement Fund Association, 95 P.2d 720, 723 (Ore. 1939).
[73]Cheasty v. Board of Examiners of Board of Education of City of New York 230 N.Y.S.2d 234 (1961).
[74]Abrahamson v. Commissioner of Education of State, 150 N.Y.S.2d 270 (1956).

[75]Devlin v. Bennet, 213 A.2d 725 (Conn. 1965).
[76]Stone v. Fritts, 82 N.E. 792 (Ind. 1907); Hodge v. Stegall, 242 P.2d 720 (Okla. 1952).
[77]Bradford v. School District No. 20, 244 F.Supp. 768, 771 (S.C. 1965).
[78]Ibid.

[43]Epstein v. Board of Examiners of Board of Education of City of New York, 295 N.Y.S. 796 (1936), affirmed, 6 N.Y.S.2d 872 (1938), motion for leave to appeal denied 18 N.E.2d 866 (1939).
[44]Chambers v. Hendersonville City Board of Education, 245 F.Supp. 759 (N.C. 1965).
[45]Gunthorpe v. Board of Education, 246 N.Y.S.2d 462 (1963).
[46]Barnett v. Fields, 92 N.Y.S.2d 117 (1949).
[47]In re Masiello, 138 A.2d 393 (N.J. 1958).
[48]Antell v. Board of Education of City of New York, 195 N.Y.S.2d 959 (1959).
[49]Cheasty v. Board of Examiners of Board of Education of City of New York, 230 N.Y.S.2d 234 (1961).

[50]Fink v. Finegan, 1 N.E.2d 462, 465 (N.Y. 1936), quoted with approval in Barnett v. Fields, 92 N.Y.S.2d 117, 127 (1949).
[51]Ottinger v. Civil Service Commission, 148 N.E. 627, 629 (N.Y. 1925), quoted with approval in Barnett v. Fields, 92 N.Y.S.2d 117, 127 (1949).
[52]Sloat v. Board of Examiners of Board of Education of City of New York, 9 N.E.2d 12, 112 A.L.R. 660 (N.Y. 1937).
[53]Barnett v. Fields, 92 N.Y.S.2d 117 (1949).

competitive examinations.[54] It has been held[55] that a constitutional provision to the effect that appointments are to be made by competitive examination does not require a written examination.

16.5g Written examinations

Written examinations are employed not only to determine eligibility for certification but for employment or reemployment. However, in recent years employment tests in all fields have been scrutinized critically. The equal protection guarantee of the Fourteenth Amendment requires that such tests be "reasonably related to the purpose for which they are designed." In the case of teachers' exams, they must be reasonably related to teaching qualifications. In a recent case, the Fifth Circuit concluded[56] that the Graduate Record Examination was not a reliable or valid measure for choosing good teachers. The test was not designed to measure nor could it measure the competency of a teacher, nor could it indicate future effectiveness. The standard used in grading exams must also be reasonable. Where such standards are announced in advance for a competitive exam, they cannot be changed. In a New York case the board of examiners was held[57] to be without authority to raise the passing mark from 60 to 65 percent after the announcement of the passing mark had been made. However, in another case[58] the board was permitted to grant a five percent credit to all applicants where it determined the test was too difficult.

16.5h Oral interviews

When the applicant applies for an advance or supervisory certificate, the interview examination becomes both more useful and more widely used. The opportunity of the board personally to observe the candidate is invaluable. However, the proper evaluation of the results of oral interviews places a greater burden upon the board than grading written examinations. Subjective reactions are difficult to suppress. For this reason it is required that each board member be disinterested and unbiased. As was remarked in a 1961 New York case, in which one of the examiners herself had expressed an interest in the position:

Not only were the petitioner and persons similarly situated entitled to a fair and impartial examination by the examiners, but public interest demands that such examination should at all times have the appearance of fairness. Not only should an examiner be unbiased, impartial and disinterested in fact, but equally essential is that all doubt or suspicion to the contrary should be jealously guarded against and eliminated. The mere fact that Miss Giroux questioned the propriety of her acting as examiner indicates that even though she believed she could be objective, she recognized that her position might be construed as being in conflict.[59]

In this case the board was directed to give the applicant a new "teaching test" before different examiners with "no possible conflict of interest."

By the nature of an oral examination, judicial review is limited, for the court has no adequate record before it to question the findings of the examining board. However, as previously noted, courts will pass upon the fairness, objectivity, and impartiality of the procedure, as well as upon any claim of bad faith or fraud in the conduct of the interview examination. The courts recognize that such oral tests cannot be applied in exactly the same form to each applicant, but they will consider contentions by one failing the test that the board acted arbitrarily.[60] If an announcement is made as to the qualities to be measured in the interview, the board must state them fairly.[61]

Where the court finds the procedure to be fair, it will rarely disturb the conclusion of the examiners, as is demonstrated in a New York decision.[62] The applicant had failed an "Interview (Content)" test. The court's opinion reflected a hands-off policy where no evidence was found of arbitrariness or capriciousness. The applicant contended that the discussions during his test were of so controversial a nature that his failure reflected an arbitrary attitude by the board since his opinions were supported by eminent authorities. In rejecting this argument the court concluded that the board had been chosen as experts in their field and that their appraisal of the applicant's views must prevail.

An Illinois decision was similar. The applicant objected to an oral examination given by the board of examiners on the

ground that it failed to apply an objective standard in determining her qualifications. The trial court had ordered the board of examiners to give her a new examination without considering her "poise or other personal factors" and to give her the same tests as other candidates. In reversing, the appellate court held that it is impossible for a board of examiners to formulate.

. . . a standard by which certain qualities may be defined or measured with entire objectivity, and that the evaluation of results must depend in a great measure upon the opinion of the Examiners. Professional knowledge alone of the candidate as tested in a written examination does not suffice to determine general fitness. The candidate's personality is a paramount and controlling factor.[63]

One of the problems of providing a broader judicial review than merely inquiring into possible fraud, collusion, discrimination, conflict of interest, honesty, and good faith is that an adequate record of the proceedings before the examiners is not available to the courts. In many jurisdictions the examining board's only action is a letter notifying the applicant that the application has been denied, with no reason stated for the denial.

16.5i Medical examination

Applicants may be required to have a medical examination prior to receiving a certificate in order to determine whether they possess any communicable disease or whether their health will permit them to discharge their duties effectively.[64] Unless the appointing board's evaluation of the results in a particular case and the standards it applies "are so clearly irrelevant and unreasonable as to palpably be arbitrary and improper," its findings will be sustained.[65] Thus, it was held[66] in a New York case that an extension of a substitute teacher's license could be refused on the ground that she was

not fit for service because of obesity. In an earlier New York case the board of examiners was upheld[67] in failing to certify that a high school teacher of economics and economic geography had passed the physical examination. In this case expert medical opinions differed as to the seriousness of the applicant's heart condition. In the course of its opinion the court said:

Petitioner contends that it is only his present physical fitness that may be inquired into. He takes the position that, because he is at present capable of teaching, he may not be rejected because the doctors have determined as a matter of prognosis that disability will develop in a short time. Of course, the scope of a physical examination should not include mere speculation as to the span of life, but it seems reasonable to permit it to include inquiry into the question as to whether a recognized disease, presently existing, will render the applicant unable to perform his duties in a short time. To this extent, the inclusion of prognosis by the medical staff of the Board is not the use of standards which are improper. The public's interests are sufficiently involved to permit consideration of the element of prognosis within reasonable limitations on the question of fitness. Teachers attain tenure of office and pension rights after permanent appointment and service in the public schools. Those in charge of children in the classroom may be required to be reasonably fit to meet various emergencies. We cannot say because an applicant may engage in physical exercise today, that the advice of medical science may not be availed of to ascertain whether a present infirmity will disable him in the near future. At least it may not be held arbitrary for the Board to take heed of such advice.[68]

Section 3004 of the New York Education Law provides that

The commissioner of Education shall prescribe . . . regulations governing . . . certification of teachers employed in all public schools of the state, except that no such regulation . . . shall hereafter prohibit, prevent or disqualify any person, who is otherwise qualified . . . solely by reason of his or her blindness.

It was held[69] that this law did not apply to the Board of Education of the City of New York and that its regulation requiring 20/30 vision in one eye, with or without glasses, was reasonable. The applicant was denied a license as a regular teacher of music in the New York City junior high schools because

[54]*Ibid.*

[55]Koltun v. Board of Education of City of New York, 242 N.Y.S.2d 246 (1963).

[56]Armstead v. Starkville Municipal Separate School District, 461 F.2d 276 (5th Cir. 1972).

[57]Gilburt v. Kroll, 144 N.Y.S.2d 270 (1956).

[58]Abrahamson v. Commissioner of Education of State, 150 N.Y.S.2d 270 (1956).

[59]Cheasty v. Board of Examiners of Board of Education of City of New York, 230 N.Y.S.2d 234 (1961).

[60]Sloat v. Board of Examiners of Board of Education of City of New York, 9 N.E.2d 12 (N.Y. 1937).

[61]Fink v. Finegan, 1 N.E.2d 462 (N.Y. 1936).

[62]Weinberg v. Fields, 114 N.Y.S.2d 238 (1932).

[63]People v. Board of Education of City of Chicago, 97 N.E.2d 615 (Ill. 1951).

[64]Strauss v. Hanning, 11 N.Y.S.2d 102 (1939); School District No. 1 v. Teachers' Retirement Fund Association, 95 P.2d 720 (Ore. 1939); Conlon v. Marshall, 59 N.Y.S.2d 52 (1945).

[65]Tripp v. Board of Examiners of City of New York, 255 N.Y.S.2d 526 (1964); Anonymous v. Board of Examiners of the Board of Education, 318 N.Y.S.2d 163 (1970). However, where there is no evidence to support the conclusion that a teacher is physically unfit, the denial of a certificate is arbitrary and unreasonable and will not be sustained. Corsover v. Board of Examiners of the City of New York, 298 N.Y.S.2d 757 (1968).

[66]*Ibid.* The obesity must be found to impair ability to teach or to maintain discipline. Parolisi v. Board of Examiners of City of New York, 258 N.Y.S.2d 936 (1967).

[67]Strauss v. Hanning, 11 N.Y.S.2d 102 (1939).

[68]*Ibid.*, pp. 105, 106.

[69]Chavich v. Board of Examiners of Board of Education of City of New York, 258 N.Y.S.2d 677 (1965).

teach reasonably evaluated in accordance with reasonable standards. It has been held[79] that reasonable regulations or statutes adopted after the issuance of a license may be applied to the holder even though the holder may have expended money in reliance on the license. In accepting the license the applicant impliedly assents to all existing restrictions and to those which may reasonably be imposed subsequently.

16.7b Prejudice of examining board

A candidate for a teaching certificate is entitled to have an application passed on by an unbiased and objective examining board. Thus, where a member of the board seeks the same position as the applicant, that member should voluntarily leave the board until the position has been filled or withdraw application for the position. Where an examiner fails to take such action, the applicant has been held[80] to be entitled to a new examination before an impartial panel. However, any charge of prejudice must be supported by substantial evidence.[81]

16.7c Right to a hearing

An applicant is entitled to a hearing only to the extent provided by statute or by the regulations of the board. The Education Law of New York provides an appeal or petition to the state commissioner of education. Under this statute it was held[82] that the commissioner determined the nature of the appeal and that the petitioner was not entitled to a hearing with a stenographic reporter and an opportunity to cross-examine supervisors who made adverse comments about the petitioner.

16.7d Administrative review

The disappointed applicant usually can obtain some review of the denial of an application for a certificate where the board has acted in bad faith or arbitrarily or has determined erroneously that the applicant failed to meet a prescribed requirement which obviously has been met. If the statutes of the particular state provide a review by an administrative officer or agency, this review must be exhausted before recourse may be had to the courts.[83] In New York, for example, where the appropriate board has denied an applicant's request for an advance certificate or a permanent license, the applicant generally can appeal to the state superintendent of education.[84] The administrative review normally is based on the proceedings and records made by the issuing board in passing on the application and is not a trial at which witnesses may be examined.[85] The courts will not prescribe the procedure to be followed by the reviewing officer or agency so long as a procedure is followed which does not offend the statutes and which gives the petitioner an opportunity fully to present the grievance.[86]

16.7e Correction of mistakes

Prior to the issuance of a certificate the board ordinarily has authority to review the matter and correct any mistakes in evaluating the applicant's qualifications which it may have made. In an Illinois case the board of education found that the applicant did not possess the necessary qualifications to teach in the intermediate and upper grades of the elementary schools of Chicago, in that he lacked two years of successful teaching experience. It discovered this fact after the board of examiners had reported that he had passed the written and oral examinations and had recommended that he be issued the certificate. However, the certificate had not yet been issued to him. The court said:

> Plaintiff had no right to teach in the public schools of Chicago until he obtained a certificate. Until that time the Board of Examiners had authority to review any former action in respect to plaintiff and correct whatever errors had been made. Had a certificate to teach been issued to plaintiff, a different question would be presented.[87]

16.7f Judicial review

After exhausting whatever administrative remedies have been provided, an applicant generally is permitted to appeal to the courts. If the statutes of the state provide for such an appeal, the prescribed procedures must be followed for taking the appeal. Even where no statutory right of appeal is expressly given, resort may be had to the courts by use of one or more of the so-called "extraordinary actions," such as injunction

[79]Hodge v. Stegall, 242 P.2d 720 (Okla. 1952).

[80]Cheasty v. Board of Examiners of Board of Education of City of New York, 230 N.Y.S.2d 234 (1961).

[81]Measels v. Owens, 46 S.W.2d 40 (Ark. 1932).

[82]Liebman v. Van Denburg, 6 N.Y.S.2d 428 (1938).

[83]Nestler v. Board of Examiners of Board of Education of City of New York, 80 N.Y.S.2d 747 (1948); Pinto v. Wynstra, 255 N.Y.S.2d 536 (1964).

[84]Cochran v. Levy, 25 N.Y.S.2d 960 (1940).

[85]Liebman v. Van Denburg, 6 N.Y.S.2d 428 (1938).

[86]Ibid.

[87]People v. Board of Education, 94 N.E.2d 74p, 745 (Ill. 1960).

or mandamus.[88] In such cases a successful recourse to the courts may be had only where the alleged action is arbitrary or unreasonable.[89] A court will then enjoin or prohibit a board from taking the arbitrary action or will compel it to do whatever the law requires. However, the courts are extremely reluctant to interfere on a matter within the discretion of the board. They will not substitute their judgment for that of the board and will act only upon a clear showing of abuse of discretion.

16.8 EXPIRATION AND RENEWAL OF CERTIFICATES

This section does not concern permanent certificates but only those of a temporary nature: emergency, substitute, conditional, and temporary certificates. The rights of a teacher holding any certificate to a renewal thereof depend upon the terms of the certificate, state statutes, regulations of the board, and federal and state constitutions. Although it was in a tenure case,[90] the general principles announced in a recent New Jersey case are applicable:

Today, the powers of a board of education in appointment, transfer or dismissal are not so broad. They are limited by the Fourteenth Amendment of the United States Constitution. For example, in Morris v. Williams, 149 F.2d 703, 708-09 (8 Cir. 1945), the court held that a custom or usage of a school board in discriminating against Negro teachers in Little Rock in respect to salaries solely on account of color violates the Fourteenth Amendment. The board's powers are also limited not only by the terms of the contract of employment but also by the New Jersey Constitution, by the Teacher's Tenure Act, and by other statutory provisions such as the Law against Discrimination. . . . Except as provided by the

above limitations or by contract the board has the right to employ and discharge its employees as it sees fit.[91]

Renewal of a conditional appointment for a limited period may be denied if teachers fail to overcome the deficiencies in their qualifications.[92] A statute has been found[93] constitutional which provided that limited supervisory certificates of teachers could be renewed at their expiration or within a specified time thereafter at the option of the county superintendent and on certified evidence that the holder had completed all requirements for renewal. In a West Virginia case[94] the court reversed the state superintendent for failing to renew the certificate of a first-grade teacher where without further hearing the county superintendent had been permitted to withdraw his recommendation. Renewal cannot be denied on the basis of race, color, or national origin.[95] Neither may the issuance of the certificate in the first instance be determined by any of these factors.

16.9 EFFECT OF FAILURE TO HAVE CERTIFICATE

State educational laws commonly prescribe that no person may be employed as a teacher who does not hold the proper certificate or license to teach. Under such statutes it generally is held[96] that the teacher's contract is void, regardless of actual qualifications, if that teacher has not obtained the prescribed license or certificate which has been made a prerequisite of teaching. The requirement of a certificate cannot be waived, dispensed with, or circumvented,[97] except perhaps where necessity demands.[98] Whether a person who holds no certificate at the time of employment but has secured one prior to entering upon teaching duties is a qualified teacher has been vigorously debated by the courts. The wording of the

---

[88]In Gilburt v. Kroll, 144 N.Y.S.2d 219 (1955), an action of mandamus was successfully brought to compel the board to rate petitioners as having passed the supervision test and to administer to them the remaining tests. The board had changed the passing score from 60 percent to 65 percent after the test had been announced. In Marrs v. Matthews, 270 S.W. 586 (Tex. 1925), an injunction was sought against the state superintendent of public instruction to enjoin him from canceling plaintiff's certificate. Plaintiff contended in part that the use of the word *unworthy* in the state statute was too vague and uncertain to define a disqualification to further hold a teacher's certificate. However, the appellate court found the term to be sufficiently specific and denied the injunction.

[89]Nestler v. Board of Examiners of Board of Education of City of New York, 80 N.Y.S.2d 747 (1948).

[90]A distinction must be recognized between tenure contracts of employment and certificates. A certificate is a condition precedent to employment but is no guarantee of employment.

[91]Zimmerman v. Board of Education of Newark, 183 A.2d 25 (N.J. 1962).

[92]Glass v. Board of Education of City of New York, 241 N.Y.S.2d 890 (1963).

[93]People v. Kerstein, 108 N.E.2d 915 (Ill. 1952).

[94]Copley v. Trent, 188 S.E.138 (W.Va. 1936).

[95]Buford v. Morganton City Board of Education, 244 F.Supp. 437 (N.C. 1965); United States v. Ramsey, 353 F.2d 650 (5th Cir. 1965).

[96]Buchanan v. School District No. 134, Elk County, 54 P.2d 930 (Kan. 1936); Union High School District No. 2 v. Paul, 95 P.2d 5 (Col. 1939); Pearson v. School District No. 8, 129 N.W. 940 (Wis. 1911); Gormley v. Board of Education, 129 N.Y.S. 153 (1911).

[97]Catlin v. Christie, 63 Pac. 328 (Col. 1900); Perkins v. Inhabitants of Town of Standish, 62 A.2d 321 (Me. 1948).

[98]Hale v. Risely, 37 N.W. 570 (Mich. 1888).

statute in the particular state often determines the answer. If the words *shall employ* are used, the courts will generally hold[99] a qualified teacher has been legally employed if the teacher secures the certificate prior to employment, i.e., before beginning to teach. But if the statutes provide that the board shall contract only with legally qualified teachers, the courts may deny[100] that a valid contract is held unless the teacher has a certificate at the time of contracting. Where the certificate expires and another is not procured, the teacher does not remain eligible to teach.[101] However, that teacher continues to be eligible where another certificate or a renewal is obtained upon expiration of the existing certificate.[102] A gap between certificates is not disqualifying where it occurs during a period when the teacher is not teaching, as during summer vacation.[103]

A mother teaching a child at home is required to have a teacher's certificate[104] in some states. Attendance at a private school not taught by qualified teachers constitutes a violation of the compulsory school attendance law.[105]

In the absence of special circumstances teachers may not recover compensation for periods they teach without a valid certificate.[106] They are considered volunteers during such period, their employment contracts being regarded as void.[107] If the teacher procures a certificate at a later date, the teaching contract cannot be ratified so as to make it valid from the beginning but only from the time that the certificate is received.[108] A school district has been permitted to recover the salary paid to a teacher for teaching during a period when that person did not hold a license to teach.[109] A teacher may be properly dismissed upon the expiration of a certificate where there is no renewal thereof and no procurement of another certificate and where a teacher's certificate is voided, he or she may properly be dismissed for failure to meet prerequisites.[110]

16.10 REVOCATION OF CERTIFICATE

Revocation of a teaching certificate must be distinguished from dismissal by a local school board. When a license is revoked, the teacher's conduct has been found to justify the termination of the right to teach in the state whereas dismissal by a local school system in no way affects the right to apply for and be employed in another school district.

16.10a Grounds for

Normally a revocation of a certificate will be based upon grounds set out in the educational laws of the state or in the regulations of the appropriate board or agency adopted pursuant thereto. An Indiana court has said:

> It is generally accepted doctrine that where a statute or ordinance authorizes the revocation of a license for causes enumerated, such license cannot be revoked upon any ground other than one of the causes specified.[111]

In the state of Washington the statutes provide:

> Any certificate to teach authorized under the provisions of this chapter of rules and regulations promulgated thereunder may be revoked by the authority authorized to grant the same under complaint of any school district superintendent, or intermediate school district superintendent for immorality, violation of written contract, intemperance, crime against the law of the state, or any

---

[99]Lee v. Mitchell, 156 S.W. 450 (Ark. 1913); Shaler v. Jones, 137 N.W. 481 (N.D. 1912); Board of Education for Logan County v. Akers, 47 S.W.2d 1046 (Ky. 1932); Reynolds v. Spurlock, 78 S.W.2d 787 (Ky. 1935); Swinford v. Chasteen, 87 S.W.2d 373 (Ky. 1935); Martin v. Knott County Board of Education, 122 S.W.2d 98 (Ky. 1938); Cottingham v. Stewart, 127 S.W.2d 149 (Ky. 1939); State ex rel. Lawson v. Cherry, 47 So.2d 768 (Fla. 1950).

[100]O'Connor v. Francis, 59 N.Y.S. 28 (1899); Jenness v. School District No. 31, 12 Minn. 448 (1867).

[101]People ex rel. Christie v. Board of Education, 67 N.Y.S. 836 (1900).

[102]Tate v. School District, 23 S.W.2d 1013 (Mo. 1929).

[103]Wabbeseka School District No. 7 v. Johnson, 286 S.W.2d 841 (Ark. 1956), where the teacher lacked a valid license between September 1 and September 11 but the teaching duties did not begin until September 15.

[104]State v. Superior Court, 346 P.2d 999 (Wash. 1959).

[105]Ibid.

[106]State v. Gettinger, 105 N.E.2d 161 (Ind. 1952); Falanry v. Barrett, 143 S.W. 38 (Ky. 1912); Harrodsburg Educational District v. Adams, 154 S.W. 44 (Ky. 1913); Kimball v. School District No. 122, 63 Pac. 213 (Wash. 1900); Bryan v. Fractional School District No. 1, 69 N.W. 74 (Mich. 1896).

[107]Floyd County Board of Education v. Sloane, 307 S.W.2d 912 (K. 1957).

[108]State v. Gettinger, 105 N.E.2d 161 (Ind. 1952); Hosmer v. Sheldon School District No. 2, 59 N.W. 1035 (N.D. 1894); Richard v. Richardson, 168 S.W. 50 (Tex. 1914); Zevin v. School District No. 11 of City of Cozad, 12 N.W.2d 634 (Neb. 1944).

[109]Vick Consolidated School District No. 21 v. New, 187 S.W.2d 948 (Ark. 1945).

[110]Perkins v. Inhabitants of Town of Standish, 62 A.2d 321 (Me. 1948); Seamonds v. School District No. 14, Fremont County, 68 P.2d 149 (Wyo. 1937) In the Matter of Feingold, 299 N.Y.S.2d 606 (1969).

[111]Stone v. Fritts, 82 N.W. 792 (Ind. 1907).

unprofessional conduct, after the person whose certificate is in question has been given an opportunity to be heard. [112]

Under the Kentucky statute it is provided that:

> *Any certificate . . . may be revoked by the state board of education, on the written recommendation of the superintendent of public instruction, for immorality, misconduct in office, incompetency or willful neglect of duty. Before the certificate is revoked the defendant shall be given a copy of the charges against him and an opportunity, upon not less than ten (10) days notice, to be heard in person or by counsel.* [113]

False swearing to a loyalty oath or in the application for a certificate may be a ground for revocation. [114] A license may not be revoked because of race, religion, scruples against nuclear warfare, or other invasion of the holder's constitutional rights. [115] However, refusal to obey an order of the school and civil defense authorities to conduct air-raid shelter drills was held [116] not to be protected under the First Amendment. The Court said:

> *Accordingly, while one may think and believe as he will without interference, conduct resulting from the exercise of said right is not safeguarded by the First Amendment if it violates a reasonable nondiscriminatory regulation by governmental authority which has as its purpose the promotion of public good and safety.* [117]

It was found in this case that petitioner's insubordination warranted the cancellation of his license.

In addition to the above, the revocation of certificates has been upheld on the following grounds:

> *Finding that petitioner did not meet the qualifications for the license.* [118]

> *Finding that a teacher had paranoid schizophrenic type mental illness.* [119]

Cheating on recertification examination. [120]

Neglecting teaching duties, as by reporting late, failing to make daily preparation, refusal to attend monthly institutes, etc. [121]

Willful violation of state law. [122]

Illicit relations with a female student. [123]

Drunkenness. [124]

Immoral or unprofessional conduct. [125]

Immoral or Unprofessional Conduct

The most common grounds for revocation of a license are immoral activities and unprofessional conduct or incompetence. A revocation of license generally requires a petition to be filed before the state board, and often local authorities prefer to manage the matter in some other way, such as by a "covered up" resignation in order to avoid exposure.

Where a teacher is charged with immoral or unprofessional conduct or conduct involving moral turpitude, generally the misconduct must be such as indicates an unfitness to teach. In a leading California case, the court stated:

> *In determining whether the teacher's conduct thus indicates unfitness to teach the board may consider such matters as the likelihood that the conduct may have adversely affected students or fellow teachers, the degree of such adversity anticipated, the proximity or remoteness in time of the conduct, the type of teaching certificate held by the party involved, the extenuating or aggravating circumstances, if any, surrounding the conduct, the praiseworthiness or blameworthiness of the motives resulting in the conduct, the likelihood of the recurrence of the questioned conduct, and the extent to which disciplinary action may inflict an adverse impact or chilling effect upon the constitutional rights of the teacher involved or other teachers. These factors are relevant to the extent that they assist the board in determining a teacher's fitness to teach, i.e., in determining whether*

---

[112]Revised Statutes of Washington, 28A 70.160 (1970).

[113]Kentucky Revised Statutes, 161.120 (1969).

[114]Mack v. State Board of Education, 36 Cal.Rptr. 677 (1964).

[115]Council v. Donovan, 244 N.Y.S.2d 199 (1963).

[116]Ibid.

[117]Ibid., p. 206.

[118]Adelson v. Board of Education of City of New York, 98 N.Y.S.2d 763 (1950).

[119]Alford v. Department of Education, 91 Cal.Rptr. 843 (1970).

[120]Shirer v. Anderson, 88 F.Supp. 858 (D.C. 1950). However, a single instance of assistance to another teacher during a certification examination was held not to be sufficient ground for revoking a license in Superintendent of Common Schools of Daviess County v. Taylor, 49 S.W. 38 (Ky. 1899).

[121]Stone v. Fritts, 82 N.E. 792 (Ind. 1907).

[122]Hodge v. Stegall, 242 P.2d 720 (Okla. 1952).

[123]Crawford v. Lewis, 186 S.W. 492 (Ky. 1916).

[124]Bowman v. Ray, 80 S.W. 516 (Ky. 1904).

[125]Tringham v. State Board of Education, 326 P.2d 850 (Cal. 1958); Bowman v. Ray, 80 S.W. 516 (Ky. 1904).

the teacher's future classroom performance and overall impact on his students are likely to meet the board's standards.[126]

The court went on to observe that a teacher may be removed only upon a showing "that his retention in the profession poses a significant danger of harm to either students, school employees, or others who might be affected by his actions as a teacher."[127]

A showing of such harm may be based on adverse inferences drawn from past conduct as to the teacher's probable future ability as well as upon the likelihood that the publicity surrounding the incident may substantially impair his or her function as a teacher.[128]

Where a teacher is charged with immoral or unprofessional conduct, the charge must relate to actions occurring within a reasonable time of its filing and must specify the times and nature of the acts with reasonable certainty.[129] As was declared in an early Kentucky case:

There is no intimation as to the date of these alleged acts of intemperance. So far as the notices go, they may have occurred many years before he obtained his certificate as a teacher, and might not have affected either his moral character or competency at the date of the notice. Unless the alleged intemperance was subsequent to the date of his certificate as a teacher, or was so close thereto in point of time as to affect his moral standing at that time, they would not be sufficient to authorize the revocation of the certificate, or their investigation to that end by the appellee.[130]

Where a county superintendent of schools had pleaded guilty to presenting false claims against the federal government in violation of a federal criminal statute, the court upheld a revocation of his license on the ground that he had been "convicted of a crime involving moral turpitude."[131] A plea of guilty was found to be tantamount to a conviction. The fact that the superintendent did not personally benefit from his mis-

deeds or commit them with ulterior motives was held to be immaterial. The paramount interest of the community in licensing teachers of good character justifies the revocation of a license for serious misconduct outside the duties of teaching.

The rule or regulation which establishes the conduct to be followed must be in existence and published before the alleged violation. In the words of the Oklahoma court:

Obviously, if it was sought to revoke for a willfull violation of one of the rules or regulations of the State Board of Education, such rule or regulation would have to be promulgated prior to the violation. Also, under the fourth provision, that it might be revoked for "other proper cause," such other proper cause must be established by some rule or regulation of the State Board promulgated prior thereto so that the teacher may know of the rules of conduct under which his license may be revoked.[132]

16.10b Right to notice and hearing

As has already been shown in Section 16.10a, state statutes dealing with revocation of certificates provide the procedures to be followed by the board in consummating the revocation and by the teacher in protesting the board's action. Clearly the holder of a certificate is entitled to all the protection granted by statutes or regulations enacted in that state.[133] Revocations have been set aside by the courts where the board failed to appoint an investigating committee as required by statute to determine the probable cause[134] or failed to prefer charges and to hold a hearing as provided in the statute.[135] Where the statutes do not state how a preliminary investigation is to be made, the board has considerable discretion in the matter so long as it does not act arbitrarily.[136] The teacher need not be given notice of the investigation, nor is it essential that the teacher be present.[137]

While a board may have a good deal of latitude in determining the details or nature of a hearing where these are not specified, it must meet minimum due process standards.[138] Such hearings must be fair, give

---

[126]Morrison v. State Board of Education, 461 P.2d 375 (Cal. 1969). In this case the board failed to establish the unfitness of a teacher who had been involved in a single noncriminal relationship of a homosexual nature.

[127]Ibid.

[128]Pettit v. State Board of Education, 513 P.2d 889 (Cal. 1973).

[129]Bowman v. Ray, 80 S.W. 516 (Ky. 1904).

[130]Ibid., p. 517.

[131]Huff v. Anderson, 90 S.E.2d 329 (Ga. 1955). The case defines "moral turpitude" at length. *See also* Sarac v. State Board of Education, 57 Cal.Rptr. 69 (1967), where a revocation based on an arrest for homosexual behavior was upheld.

[132]Hodge v. Stegall, 242 P.2d 720, 723 (Okla. 1952).

[133]Neal v. Bryant, 149 So.2d 529 (Fla. 1962).

[134]Ibid.

[135]Matteson v. State Board of Education, 136 P.2d 120 (Cal. 1943).

[136]Crawford v. Lewis, 186 S.W. 492 (Ky. 1916).

[137]Ibid.

[138]Pordum v. Board of Regents of the State of New York, 491 F.2d 1281 (2d Cir. 1974); Huntley v. North Carolina State Board of Education, 493 F.2d 1016 (4th Cir. 1974).

teachers adequate notice thereof and indicate charges against them, be held within a reasonable time, provide opportunity for teachers to present their cases fully, and be held before an impartial tribunal.[139] The court's comments in a 1965 Connecticut case on contract renewal are equally applicable to license revocation:

> The fundamental purpose of the hearing is to give a probationary teacher who has already been acquainted with the reasons why a board of education has decided not to renew his contract a full and fair opportunity to persuade and convince the board that it is mistaken in that decision. The teacher may attempt to answer or rebut the reasons given. He may attempt to show that the reasons given are mistaken in fact or are insufficient to justify the decision not to renew, and that it should be reversed and the teacher's contract renewed. It might well be that the teacher may be able to present to the board information or knowledge that it did not possess at the time of its original decision not to renew, and that such information or knowledge might materially affect the thinking of board members and the decision of the board.[140]

Complaints setting out charges against teachers must be sufficiently definite as to time, place, and description to inform them of the misconduct with which they are charged.[141] A teacher may be suspended pending a hearing provided the teacher's salary is not interrupted.[142] It may be permissible according to the practice in a particular state for a teacher to move that specified charges be made more definite or be stricken as too vague and indefinite.[143] A hearing was upheld[144] in which only two members of the board (less than a quorum) conducted the hearing, took testimony, and reported a summary thereof to the whole board, which made the decision. The petitioner's attorney had been allowed to cross-examine the witness.

16.10c Summary procedure

Some state statutes permit a summary procedure for the revocation of a certificate in a situation where the grounds therefor are clear, as where the teacher has been convicted of a crime involving moral turpitude or a sex offense. A California statute authorizes a summary revocation upon conviction of a sex offense. It was decided[145] that a hearing was nevertheless required where the conviction occurred prior to the enactment of the statute. In other words, the statute authorizing the summary procedure was not to be applied retroactively. The procedure of summary dismissal for conviction for sex offenses has been held[146] not to violate a teacher's constitutional rights. In this case the state board of education had adopted a resolution revoking the certificates of several teachers who had pleaded guilty to sex offenses. The court found that the statute imposed a mandatory duty upon the board to revoke summarily the licenses of such teachers.

A summary procedure is often authorized in the termination of the certificates of substitute or probationary teachers.[147] The Board of Education of the City of New York adopted bylaws which permitted the termination of a substitute teacher's license "at any time." Under this provision the New York court held[148] that there was no judicial review of the case on its merits. The bylaw authorized the board to terminate such license "at any time." The judicial issue involved would be whether the bylaw itself was arbitrary or unreasonable.

While the summary revocation procedure is admittedly harsh, its harshness is mitigated by the fact that its use normally is limited to clear-cut issues or to probationary, temporary, or substitute teachers. The trend is, however, to greater protection for the teacher, and some statutes now provide a hearing even in the case of probationary teachers.[149]

A summary procedure also was upheld[150] where the board discovered its mistake and revoked a certificate issued to a disqualified applicant.

---

[139]Horner v. Board of Trustees of Excelsior Union High School District of Los Angeles, 389 P.2d 713 (Cal. 1964); Huntley v. North Carolina State Board of Education, 493 F.2d 1016 (4th Cir. 1974).

[140]Hodge v. Stegall, 242 P.2d 720 (Okla. 1952).

[141]Huntley v. North Carolina State Board of Education, 493 F.2d 1016 (4th Cir. 1974).

[142]Pordum v. Board of Regents of the State of New York, 491 F.2d 1281 (2d Cir. 1974).

[143]Stone v. Fritts, 82 N.E. 792 (Ind. 1907).

[144]Pettiford v. S.C. Board of Education, 62 S.E.2d 780 (S.C. 1950).

[145]Fountain v. State Board of Education, 320 P.2d 899 (Cal. 1958).

[146]Di Genova v. State Board of Education, 288 P.2d 862 (Cal. 1955).

[147]Giangrande v. Board of Education of City of New York, 254 N.Y.S.2d 643 (1964).

[148]*Ibid.*

[149]Griggs v. Board of Trustees of Merced Union High School District, 37 Cal.Rptr. 194 (1964).

[150]Glass v. Board of Education of City of New York, 241 N.Y.S.2d 890 (1963); People ex rel. Latimer v. Board of Education of Chicago, 94 N.E.2d 742 (Ill. 1950); Marrs v. Matthews, 270 S.W. 586 (Tex. 1925); Adelson v. Board of Education of City of New York, 98 N.Y.S.2d 763 (1950).

16.10d Judicial remedies

The form, nature, and extent of judicial review of administrative action in revoking a certificate is determined by the statutes of each state. A person has no constitutional right to an appeal to the courts from the final decision of an administrative body. As noted by a United States district court in upholding the summary revocation of certificates for cheating on a recertification examination:

Aside from this, the teacher's certificate relates only to the right to teach in the service of the state; and it cannot be a denial of due process for the state to provide for revocation of such certificate by administrative action without provision for judicial review. The idea that due process requires judicial approval of matters relating to the hiring or discharge of a public employee is one which has no foundation either in reason or authority.[151]

The above quotation refers to a direct appeal from the decision of the board (after all prescribed administrative remedies have been exhausted) in which the court reviewed the board's decision on the merits. In such a proceeding the court determines on the basis of the record or evidence before it whether the revocation is justified on the facts of the case.

If a direct review is not provided by the statutes of the particular state, this does not mean that the courts are closed to the teacher. In almost all cases the teacher will have available one or more of the so-called extraordinary remedies, such as injunction or mandamus. The former is used to enjoin the board from revoking the certificate and to reinstate it if revoked. The latter is appropriate to direct public officials to do their duty, namely, to conduct the certification of teachers according to law. However, when either an injunction or mandamus is sought, the question before the court is not precisely the same as on direct review although the practical result is often the same. The question is not ordinarily on the merits as to whether the certificate should have been revoked; rather the inquiry concerns the means, methods, and procedures used to revoke it. Thus, it is often said that a board cannot act arbitrarily, capriciously, unreasonably, in bad faith, or contrary to the established procedures. If the court finds that the board has done so in a particular case, it usually will grant relief by injunction, mandamus, or similar remedy, even though no direct appeal to the courts

has been provided. But if a direct appeal exists, its procedure is to be followed since, as a general rule, an injunction, mandamus, or other extraordinary remedy cannot be used as a substitute for appeal.

16.10e Loyalty oath, discrimination, and other constitutional issues

Even where no direct appeal to the courts is provided from a final decision revoking a teacher's certificate, the courts, through the use of one of the extraordinary remedies discussed in the preceding section, will protect the constitutional rights of a teacher. Thus, a license cannot be revoked because of race, religion, or beliefs protected by the First Amendment.[152] The United States Supreme Court in *Shelton v. Tucker*[153] declared unconstitutional an Arkansas statute which compelled every teacher, as a condition of employment in a state-supported school or college, to file annually an affidavit listing without limitation every organization to which the teacher belonged or regularly contributed within the preceding five years.

In a five-to-four decision the United States Supreme Court also struck down as unconstitutionally vague a New York law which required the removal of teachers for uttering any treasonable or seditious words or for doing any treasonable or seditious act. This is one of the most recent expressions of the Supreme Court on the question of loyalty oaths. It strikes down specifically two types of laws. The first is a statute or regulation drafted in broad terms without defining precisely the subversive activity which it seeks to proscribe. Such laws, like the New York law in question, are held to be unconstitutionally vague. The New York statute read:

A person employed as superintendent of schools, teacher or employee in the public schools, in any city or school district of the state, shall be removed from such position for the utterance of any treasonable or seditious word or words or the doing of any treasonable or seditious act or acts while holding such position.[154]

---

[151]Shirer v. Anderson, 88 F.Supp. 858, 862 (D.C. 1950).

[152]Council v. Donovan, 244 N.Y.S.2d 199 (1963); Rackley v. School District No. 5, 258 F.Supp. 676 (S.C. 1966).

[153]364 U.S. 479, 81 S.Ct. 247, 5 L.Ed.2d 231 (Ark. 1960).

[154]Keyishian v. Board of Regents of University of State of New York, 385 U.S. 589, 87 S.Ct. 675, 17 L.Ed.2d 629 (N.Y. 1967). In a one-sentence per curiam decision the Supreme Court affirmed the decision of the United States District Court of New York upholding the following oath: "I do solemnly swear (or affirm) that I will support the constitution of the United States of America

The majority of the Court strongly suggested that the statute would have been constitutional if it had contained definitions of "treasonable" or "seditious." It cited with apparent approval the definitions of such terms found in Subsection 3 of Section 105 of the New York Civil Service Law.

The second type of statute which a majority of the Court held to be unconstitutional is one barring employment or granting of a teacher's certificate to a person who simply holds membership or who has been a member of a listed organization. The majority concluded:

> We therefore hold that Civil Service Law, Section 105 (1) (c) and Education Law, Section 3022 (2) are invalid insofar as they sanction mere knowing membership without any showing of specific intent to further the unlawful aims of the Communist Party of the United States or of the State of New York.

On this point the majority cited the Smith Act as a good example since it condemns only persons shown to have an "intent to cause the overthrow or destruction of any such government."

16.10f Recovery of salary after wrongful revocation

The laws of each state need to be examined to determine the extent to which money damages may be recovered for the wrongful revocation of a certificate. In New York a substitute teacher sued for lost salary when her certificate was restored following an appeal to the state commissioner of education. Her claim was disallowed since it was found that the cancellation was not negligent, in bad faith, or without due process, and was done by competent authority.[155] It must be noted that a substitute teacher in New York City has very limited rights. In a recent Second Circuit case the court stated[156] that a teacher might be entitled to back pay if found to be fit after the certificate has been revoked.

16.11 SUMMARY

A proper certificate is to teachers what a license to practice is to the lawyer, physi-

cian, or dentist. It is the document which attests to their qualifications for the teaching or supervisory position in question. These qualifications are established by state law, and the procedure for the issuance, renewal, or revocation of teacher certificates is established by that law. These functions are customarily delegated to the state board of education or other governmental agency. Since it is an administrative body, the general principles of administrative law apply. Decisions within its discretion can be successfully challenged only by showing an abuse in the exercise of that discretion. Judicial review in this instance, whether by appeal or by extraordinary remedy (injunction, prohibition, mandamus), is limited to such questions as whether the agency acted arbitrarily, with prejudice or discrimination, in excess of its jurisdiction, contrary to the great weight of the evidence, or fraudulently. Where appeal to an administrative agency is permitted, all administrative remedies must be exhausted before review may be sought in the courts. Where an application for a certificate has been denied, the applicant is entitled to a hearing only to the extent provided by statute or by the regulations of the board.

Since the qualifications for different positions in the educational system differ and since it is usually desirable to provide a trial period for the beginner, numerous types of certificates have been devised. The temporary certificate is normally issued to the inexperienced teacher, and an emergency or special permit is granted during times of serious teacher shortages to individuals who fall short of the usual qualifications. The latter type of certificate is not to be used where a sufficient number of properly qualified teachers can be employed. A conditional certificate is utilized where a teacher fails to satisfy fully all of the qualifications or it is desired to require continued professional growth. The permanent certificate usually is issued when the teacher has met all of the requirements prescribed therefor and has reached the stage of tenure. Advance or supervisory certificates are granted to teachers who qualify for the position of principal or other supervisory responsibility.

The qualifications for each type of certificate customarily differ. They normally include a baccalaureate degree, good moral character, a minimum age, satisfactory health, and citizenship. For certain certificates satisfactory experience may be a prerequisite, as well as an oral interview and written examination.

The rights of a teacher to a certificate, or

and the constitution of the State of New York, and that I will faithfully discharge, according to the best of my ability, the duties of the position of ———— to which I am now assigned." Knight v. Board of Regents of University of New York, 390 U.S. 36, 88 S.Ct. 816, 19 L.Ed.2d 812 (1968). *See also* Whitehall v. Elkins, 389 U.S. 35 88 S.Ct. 184, 19 L.Ed.2d 35 (Md. 1967).

[155]Warner v. Board of Education of City of New York, 220 N.Y.S.2d 795 (1961).

[156]Pordum v. Board of Regents of the State of New York, 491 F.2d 1281 (2d Cir. 1974).

of one holding a certificate, are dependent upon the terms of state statutes, regulations of the issuing agency, and federal and state constitutions. Relief from certain requirements is being sought increasingly on the basis of the First and Fourteenth amendments to the United States Constitution. These amendments prohibit discrimination in the issuance or renewal of certificates on the basis of race, color, or creed. They also require a fairness and reasonableness in the procedure or in the requirements since they may not offend "due process of law" or the "equal protection of the laws." Loyalty oaths required for certification in some states will be stricken down by the United States Supreme Court if they are unconstitutionally vague or if they prohibit the mere membership in a subversive organization without any showing of specific intent to further its unlawful aims.

The Employment Contract and Professional Negotiation

PART TWO: LABOR UNIONS AND PROFESSIONAL NEGOTIATIONS

which the student attended.[43] The objective, unbiased opinion of a school superintendent in appraising a teacher's ability is entitled to great weight.[44] However, the superintendent's recommendation of a tenure appointment does not foreclose the board of education's denying it.[45] By furnishing references for recommendations the applicant authorizes the board to inquire directly of them.[46]

16.5d Prior experience

For certain certificates prior specific experience is a prerequisite. In New Jersey it was held,[47] for example, that service as a dean of boys could not substitute for three years of experience as vice-principal while "properly certified as a principal." In New York an applicant for an assistant principal's license was required to teach two of the five years in "special service" elementary and junior high schools.[48] This requirement obviously had to be met before the candidate could receive the license.

16.5e By types of examinations

Some states grant certificates on the basis of examinations, written or oral, competitive or noncompetitive. For example, the examination for a license as chairman of the speech department in the day high schools "consisted of four tests—(1) a written test; (2) an interview test; (3) a supervision test; (4) a teaching test. In addition thereto there was an appraisal of record, a rating of training and experience and a physical and medical examination."[49]

16.5f Competitive and noncompetitive examinations

For the competition to be fair, a competitive examination itself must be fair and meet "objective standards," as was remarked by the New York court:

An examination cannot be classed as competitive unless it conforms to measures or standards which are sufficiently objective to be capable of being challenged and reviewed,

when necessary, by other examiners of equal ability and experience.[50]

Another New York case correctly described the nature of a noncompetitive examination, such as may be given to determine eligibility for employment to certain positions:

Noncompetitive examination does not restrict the appointing officer to the name highest on the list. He may reject any on the list, or all, if their personal qualities or associations seem to render them ineligible. Noncompetitive examination is merely an assurance that along with personal qualities or associations satisfactory to the appointing officer there shall also be the attainment of some standard of efficiency established as a minimum.[51]

In both competitive and noncompetitive examinations the examiners have considerable discretion in framing the questions as long as they reasonably relate to the necessary qualifications for the position and are not designed to favor one applicant over another.

An excellent comment on this point is found in a New York case:

It would be impossible to formulate a standard by which such qualities may be defined or measured with entire objectivity. The law does not require the impossible or forbid the reasonable. . . . Exact definition of the qualities which are essential or desirable may be impossible; exact formula or standard by which such qualities may be measured has never been achieved; mechanical application of any standard is certainly not practicable. Much must be left to the judgment of the examiners.[52]

Examining boards have greater discretion in the administration of noncompetitive then competitive examinations. In either case good examination practices should be observed; however, in the former the examining board has greater latitude in changing announced ratings or rules.[53] A noncompetitive examination is required to be a reasonable test of merit and fitness, but no advance notice need be given, and no advanced standards fixed, as in the case of

---

[43]Epstein v. Board of Examiners of Board of Education of City of New York, 295 N.Y.S. 796 (1936), *affirmed*, 6 N.Y.S.2d 872 (1938), *motion for leave to appeal denied* 18 N.E.2d 866 (1939).

[44]Chambers v. Hendersonville City Board of Education, 245 F.Supp. 759 (N.C. 1965).

[45]Gunthorpe v. Board of Education, 246 N.Y.S.2d 462 (1963).

[46]Barnett v. Fields, 92 N.Y.S.2d 117 (1949).

[47]In re Masiello, 138 A.2d 393 (N.J. 1958).

[48]Antell v. Board of Education of City of New York, 195 N.Y.S.2d 959 (1959).

[49]Cheasty v. Board of Examiners of Board of Education of City of New York, 230 N.Y.S.2d 234 (1961).

[50]Fink v. Finegan, 1 N.E.2d 462, 465 (N.Y. 1936), quoted with approval in Barnett v. Fields, 92 N.Y.S.2d 117, 127 (1949).

[51]Ottinger v. Civil Service Commission, 148 N.E. 627, 629 (N.Y. 1925), quoted with approval in Barnett v. Fields, 92 N.Y.S.2d 117, 127 (1949).

[52]Sloat v. Board of Examiners of Board of Education of City of New York, 9 N.E.2d 12, 112 A.L.R. 660 (N.Y. 1937).

[53]Barnett v. Fields, 92 N.Y.S.2d 117 (1949).

competitive examinations.[54] It has been held[55] that a constitutional provision to the effect that appointments are to be made by competitive examination does not require a written examination.

16.5g Written examinations

Written examinations are employed not only to determine eligibility for certification but for employment or reemployment. However, in recent years employment tests in all fields have been scrutinized critically. The equal protection guarantee of the Fourteenth Amendment requires that such tests be "reasonably related to the purpose for which they are designed." In the case of teachers' exams, they must be reasonably related to teaching qualifications. In a recent case, the Fifth Circuit concluded[56] that the Graduate Record Examination was not a reliable or valid measure for choosing good teachers. The test was not designed to measure nor could it measure the competency of a teacher, nor could it indicate future effectiveness. The standard used in grading exams must also be reasonable. Where such standards are announced in advance for a competitive exam, they cannot be changed. In a New York case the board of examiners was held[57] to be without authority to raise the passing mark from 60 to 65 percent after the announcement of the passing mark had been made. However, in another case[58] the board was permitted to grant a five percent credit to all applicants where it determined the test was too difficult.

16.5h Oral interviews

When the applicant applies for an advance or supervisory certificate, the interview examination becomes both more useful and more widely used. The opportunity of the board personally to observe the candidate is invaluable. However, the proper evaluation of the results of oral interviews places a greater burden upon the board than grading written examinations. Subjective reactions are difficult to suppress. For this reason it is required that each board member be disinterested and unbiased. As was remarked in a 1961 New York case, in which one of the examiners herself had expressed an interest in the position:

Not only were the petitioner and persons similarly situated entitled to a fair and impartial examination by the examiners, but public interest demands that such examination should at all times have the appearance of fairness. Not only should an examiner be unbiased, impartial and disinterested in fact, but equally essential is that all doubt or suspicion to the contrary should be jealously guarded against and eliminated. The mere fact that Miss Giroux questioned the propriety of her acting as examiner indicates that even though she believed she could be objective, she recognized that her position might be construed as being in conflict.[59]

In this case the board was directed to give the applicant a new "teaching test" before different examiners with "no possible conflict of interest."

By the nature of an oral examination, judicial review is limited, for the court has no adequate record before it to question the findings of the examining board. However, as previously noted, courts will pass upon the fairness, objectivity, and impartiality of the procedure, as well as upon any claim of bad faith or fraud in the conduct of the interview examination. The courts recognize that such oral tests cannot be applied in exactly the same form to each applicant, but they will consider contentions by one failing the test that the board acted arbitrarily.[60] If an announcement is made as to the qualities to be measured in the interview, the board must state them fairly.[61]

Where the court finds the procedure to be fair, it will rarely disturb the conclusion of the examiners, as is demonstrated in a New York decision.[62] The applicant had failed an "Interview (Content)" test. The court's opinion reflected a hands-off policy where no evidence was found of arbitrariness or capriciousness. The applicant contended that the discussions during his test were of so controversial a nature that his failure reflected an arbitrary attitude by the board since his opinions were supported by eminent authorities. In rejecting this argument the court concluded that the board had been chosen as experts in their field and that their appraisal of the applicant's views must prevail.

An Illinois decision was similar. The applicant objected to an oral examination given by the board of examiners on the

---

[54]*Ibid.*

[55]Koltun v. Board of Education of City of New York, 242 N.Y.S.2d 246 (1963).

[56]Armstead v. Starkville Municipal Separate School District, 461 F.2d 276 (5th Cir. 1972).

[57]Gilburt v. Kroll, 144 N.Y.S.2d 270 (1956).

[58]Abrahamson v. Commissioner of Education of State, 150 N.Y.S.2d 270 (1956).

[59]Cheasty v. Board of Examiners of Board of Education of City of New York, 230 N.Y.S.2d 234 (1961).

[60]Sloat v. Board of Examiners of Board of Education of City of New York, 9 N.E.2d 12 (N.Y. 1937).

[61]Fink v. Finegan, 1 N.E.2d 462 (N.Y. 1936).

[62]Weinberg v. Fields, 114 N.Y.S.2d 238 (1932).

ground that it failed to apply an objective standard in determining her qualifications. The trial court had ordered the board of examiners to give her a new examination without considering her "poise or other personal factors" and to give her the same tests as other candidates. In reversing, the appellate court held that it is impossible for a board of examiners to formulate.

> . . . a standard by which certain qualities may be defined or measured with entire objectivity, and that the evaluation of results must depend in a great measure upon the opinion of the Examiners. Professional knowledge alone of the candidate as tested in a written examination does not suffice to determine general fitness. The candidate's personality is a paramount and controlling factor. [63]

One of the problems of providing a broader judicial review than merely inquiring into possible fraud, collusion, discrimination, conflict of interest, honesty, and good faith is that an adequate record of the proceedings before the examiners is not available to the courts. In many jurisdictions the examining board's only action is a letter notifying the applicant that the application has been denied, with no reason stated for the denial.

16.5i Medical examination

Applicants may be required to have a medical examination prior to receiving a certificate in order to determine whether they possess any communicable disease or whether their health will permit them to discharge their duties effectively. [64] Unless the appointing board's evaluation of the results in a particular case and the standards it applies "are so clearly irrelevant and unreasonable as to palpably be arbitrary and improper," its findings will be sustained. [65] Thus, it was held [66] in a New York case that an extension of a substitute teacher's license could be refused on the ground that she was

not fit for service because of obesity. In an earlier New York case the board of examiners was upheld [67] in failing to certify that a high school teacher of economics and economic geography had passed the physical examination. In this case expert medical opinions differed as to the seriousness of the applicant's heart condition. In the course of its opinion the court said:

> Petitioner contends that it is only his present physical fitness that may be inquired into. He takes the position that, because he is at present capable of teaching, he may not be rejected because the doctors have determined as a matter of prognosis that disability will develop in a short time. Of course, the scope of a physical examination should not include mere speculation as to the span of life, but it seems reasonable to permit it to include inquiry into the question as to whether a recognized disease, presently existing, will render the applicant unable to perform his duties in a short time. To this extent, the inclusion of prognosis by the medical staff of the Board is not the use of standards which are improper. The public's interests are sufficiently involved to permit consideration of the element of prognosis within reasonable limitations on the question of fitness. Teachers attain tenure of office and pension rights after permanent appointment and service in the public schools. Those in charge of children in the classroom may be required to be reasonably fit to meet various emergencies. We cannot say because an applicant may engage in physical exercise today, that the advice of medical science may not be availed of to ascertain whether a present infirmity will disable him in the near future. At least it may not be held arbitrary for the Board to take heed of such advice. [68]

Section 3004 of the New York Education Law provides that

> The commissioner of Education shall prescribe . . . regulations governing . . . certification of teachers employed in all public schools of the state, except that no such regulation . . . shall hereafter prohibit, prevent or disqualify any person, who is otherwise qualified . . . solely by reason of his or her blindness.

It was held [69] that this law did not apply to the Board of Education of the City of New York and that its regulation requiring 20/30 vision in one eye, with or without glasses, was reasonable. The applicant was denied a license as a regular teacher of music in the New York City junior high schools because

[63]People v. Board of Education of City of Chicago, 97 N.E.2d 615 (Ill. 1951).

[64]Strauss v. Hanning, 11 N.Y.S.2d 102 (1939); School District No. 1 v. Teachers' Retirement Fund Association, 95 P.2d 720 (Ore. 1939); Conlon v. Marshall, 59 N.Y.S.2d 52 (1945).

[65]Tripp v. Board of Examiners of City of New York, 255 N.Y.S.2d 526 (1964); Anonymous v. Board of Examiners of the Board of Education, 318 N.Y.S.2d 163 (1970). However, where there is no evidence to support the conclusion that a teacher is physically unfit, the denial of a certificate is arbitrary and unreasonable and will not be sustained. Corsover v. Board of Examiners of the City of New York, 298 N.Y.S.2d 757 (1968).

[66]Ibid. The obesity must be found to impair ability to teach or to maintain discipline. Parolisi v. Board of Examiners of City of New York, 258 N.Y.S.2d 936 (1967).

[67]Strauss v. Hanning, 11 N.Y.S.2d 102 (1939).

[68]Ibid., pp. 105, 106.

[69]Chavich v. Board of Examiners of Board of Education of City of New York, 258 N.Y.S.2d 677 (1965).

of his blindness, and the decision of the board was sustained. Recent legislation on employment of handicapped persons grant them greater employment opportunities.

It has been decided that a teacher may be required to procure a biennial chest x-ray to show freedom from tuberculosis[70] and a vaccination for smallpox.[71] As early as 1939 it was ruled by an Oregon court "that the district has implied power to determine by physical examination whether an applicant is affected with any communicable disease or is incapable of discharging his or her duties as a teacher."[72]

16.6 ISSUANCE OF CERTIFICATES

If the applicant meets the prescribed requirements for the certificate applied for, the board must issue it and cannot arbitrarily withhold it. After exhausting any administrative procedures which may be provided the applicant has recourse to the courts to set aside the board's findings and compel the issuance of the certificate.[73]

16.6a Discretion in issuing agency

It has been said repeatedly that fitness to teach depends upon a broad range of factors, many of which require the exercise of good judgment by the members of the issuing agency. A certain degree of discretion must be vested in such members in determining whether the applicant has met the qualifications for the certificate sought, particularly in the administration and grading of competitive and qualifying examinations.[74] The exercise of this discretion will be upset by the courts only where an abuse has been shown, as by unreasonable, arbitrary, capricious, or discriminatory action. Most state constitutions include a provision, similar to the Fourteenth Amendment to the United States Constitution, which prohibits unreasonable and arbitrary discrimination by agencies of the state government. Even in the absence of such a provision, a board charged with issuing teachers' certificates must act fairly, reasonably, in good faith, and must treat alike persons who are similarly situated. An examining board must apply the same criteria in evaluating each candidate, but formal rigid-

ity is not required, nor is exactness of treatment beyond reason. Each case must be judged on its own facts.

16.7 DENIAL OF CERTIFICATES

To the same extent that the board has an obligation to issue a certificate to a qualified applicant, it has a duty to deny one to an unqualified candidate. In the latter instance, as previously explained, a conditional or temporary certificate may be appropriate. In granting or denying a certificate it is the duty of the board to make a fair, reasonable, and honest judgment on the basis of the available relevant information before it.[75]

16.7a Privilege and not a right

A license to teach is said to be a privilege and not an absolute right.[76] In the words of a federal district judge in South Carolina, "No individual as a matter of right has a constitutional privilege to be in the public employ as a school teacher, and all teachers in public schools are subject to reasonable rules and regulations by state and local school officials."[77] This means that an unqualified person has no right to be a teacher. However, an applicant meeting all the prescribed qualifications and conditions for a certificate has a right to receive one. The South Carolina judge added, "State or local officials cannot, however, deprive a teacher of any constitutional right, by imposing unreasonable or unlawful conditions as a necessary adjunct to employment; nor should such rights be denied because of race or color."[78]

Courts often speak in terms of a privilege and not a right in upholding revocations of certificates for incompetence, immorality, or unprofessional conduct, or in permitting the enactment of additional regulations after the issuance of a license. A more rational explanation would be that the profession of teaching is interlaced with the public interest and is subject to reasonable regulation. The question is better stated in terms of "reasonableness" or "unreasonableness" than as a "right" or a "privilege." Of course, no one has an absolute right to teach or to teach on his or her own terms, but all prospective teachers have an absolute right to have their qualifications to

---

[70]Conlon v. Marshall, 59 N.Y.S.2d 52 (1945).

[71]Cude v. State, 377 S.W.2d 816 (Ark. 1964).

[72]School District No. 1 v. Teachers' Retirement Fund Association, 95 P.2d 720, 723 (Ore. 1939).

[73]Cheasty v. Board of Examiners of Board of Education of City of New York 230 N.Y.S.2d 234 (1961).

[74]Abrahamson v. Commissioner of Education of State, 150 N.Y.S.2d 270 (1956).

[75]Devlin v. Bennet, 213 A.2d 725 (Conn. 1965).

[76]Stone v. Fritts, 82 N.E. 792 (Ind. 1907); Hodge v. Stegall, 242 P.2d 720 (Okla. 1952).

[77]Bradford v. School District No. 20, 244 F.Supp. 768, 771 (S.C. 1965).

[78]Ibid.

teach reasonably evaluated in accordance with reasonable standards. It has been held[79] that reasonable regulations or statutes adopted after the issuance of a license may be applied to the holder even though the holder may have expended money in reliance on the license. In accepting the license the applicant impliedly assents to all existing restrictions and to those which may reasonably be imposed subsequently.

16.7b Prejudice of examining board

A candidate for a teaching certificate is entitled to have an application passed on by an unbiased and objective examining board. Thus, where a member of the board seeks the same position as the applicant, that member should voluntarily leave the board until the position has been filled or withdraw application for the position. Where an examiner fails to take such action, the applicant has been held[80] to be entitled to a new examination before an impartial panel. However, any charge of prejudice must be supported by substantial evidence.[81]

16.7c Right to a hearing

An applicant is entitled to a hearing only to the extent provided by statute or by the regulations of the board. The Education Law of New York provides an appeal or petition to the state commissioner of education. Under this statute it was held[82] that the commissioner determined the nature of the appeal and that the petitioner was not entitled to a hearing with a stenographic reporter and an opportunity to cross-examine supervisors who made adverse comments about the petitioner.

16.7d Administrative review

The disappointed applicant usually can obtain some review of the denial of an application for a certificate where the board has acted in bad faith or arbitrarily or has determined erroneously that the applicant failed to meet a prescribed requirement which obviously has been met. If the statutes of the particular state provide a review by an administrative officer or agency, this review must be exhausted before recourse may be had to the courts.[83] In New York, for example, where the appropriate board has denied an applicant's request for an advance certificate or a permanent license, the applicant generally can appeal to the state superintendent of education.[84] The administrative review normally is based on the proceedings and records made by the issuing board in passing on the application and is not a trial at which witnesses may be examined.[85] The courts will not prescribe the procedure to be followed by the reviewing officer or agency so long as a procedure is followed which does not offend the statutes and which gives the petitioner an opportunity fully to present the grievance.[86]

16.7e Correction of mistakes

Prior to the issuance of a certificate the board ordinarily has authority to review the matter and correct any mistakes in evaluating the applicant's qualifications which it may have made. In an Illinois case the board of education found that the applicant did not possess the necessary qualifications to teach in the intermediate and upper grades of the elementary schools of Chicago, in that he lacked two years of successful teaching experience. It discovered this fact after the board of examiners had reported that he had passed the written and oral examinations and had recommended that he be issued the certificate. However, the certificate had not yet been issued to him. The court said:

> Plaintiff had no right to teach in the public schools of Chicago until he obtained a certificate. Until that time the Board of Examiners had authority to review any former action in respect to plaintiff and correct whatever errors had been made. Had a certificate to teach been issued to plaintiff, a different question would be presented.[87]

16.7f Judicial review

After exhausting whatever administrative remedies have been provided, an applicant generally is permitted to appeal to the courts. If the statutes of the state provide for such an appeal, the prescribed procedures must be followed for taking the appeal. Even where no statutory right of appeal is expressly given, resort may be had to the courts by use of one or more of the so-called "extraordinary actions," such as injunction

[79]Hodge v. Stegall, 242 P.2d 720 (Okla. 1952).
[80]Cheasty v. Board of Examiners of Board of Education of City of New York, 230 N.Y.S.2d 234 (1961).
[81]Measels v. Owens, 46 S.W.2d 40 (Ark. 1932).
[82]Liebman v. Van Denburg, 6 N.Y.S.2d 428 (1938).
[83]Nestler v. Board of Examiners of Board of Education of City of New York, 80 N.Y.S.2d 747 (1948); Pinto v. Wynstra, 255 N.Y.S.2d 536 (1964).

[84]Cochran v. Levy, 25 N.Y.S.2d 960 (1940).
[85]Liebman v. Van Denburg, 6 N.Y.S.2d 428 (1938).
[86]Ibid.
[87]People v. Board of Education, 94 N.E.2d 74p, 745 (Ill. 1960).

or mandamus.[88] In such cases a successful recourse to the courts may be had only where the alleged action is arbitrary or unreasonable.[89] A court will then enjoin or prohibit a board from taking the arbitrary action or will compel it to do whatever the law requires. However, the courts are extremely reluctant to interfere on a matter within the discretion of the board. They will not substitute their judgment for that of the board and will act only upon a clear showing of abuse of discretion.

16.8 EXPIRATION AND RENEWAL OF CERTIFICATES

This section does not concern permanent certificates but only those of a temporary nature: emergency, substitute, conditional, and temporary certificates. The rights of a teacher holding any certificate to a renewal thereof depend upon the terms of the certificate, state statutes, regulations of the board, and federal and state constitutions. Although it was in a tenure case,[90] the general principles announced in a recent New Jersey case are applicable:

Today, the powers of a board of education in appointment, transfer or dismissal are not so broad. They are limited by the Fourteenth Amendment of the United States Constitution. For example, in Morris v. Williams, 149 F.2d 703, 708-09 (8 Cir. 1945), the court held that a custom or usage of a school board in discriminating against Negro teachers in Little Rock in respect to salaries solely on account of color violates the Fourteenth Amendment. The board's powers are also limited not only by the terms of the contract of employment but also by the New Jersey Constitution, by the Teacher's Tenure Act, and by other statutory provisions such as the Law against Discrimination. . . . Except as provided by the

above limitations or by contract the board has the right to employ and discharge its employees as it sees fit.[91]

Renewal of a conditional appointment for a limited period may be denied if teachers fail to overcome the deficiencies in their qualifications.[92] A statute has been found[93] constitutional which provided that limited supervisory certificates of teachers could be renewed at their expiration or within a specified time thereafter at the option of the county superintendent and on certified evidence that the holder had completed all requirements for renewal. In a West Virginia case[94] the court reversed the state superintendent for failing to renew the certificate of a first-grade teacher where without further hearing the county superintendent had been permitted to withdraw his recommendation. Renewal cannot be denied on the basis of race, color, or national origin.[95] Neither may the issuance of the certificate in the first instance be determined by any of these factors.

16.9 EFFECT OF FAILURE TO HAVE CERTIFICATE

State educational laws commonly prescribe that no person may be employed as a teacher who does not hold the proper certificate or license to teach. Under such statutes it generally is held[96] that the teacher's contract is void, regardless of actual qualifications, if that teacher has not obtained the prescribed license or certificate which has been made a prerequisite of teaching. The requirement of a certificate cannot be waived, dispensed with, or circumvented,[97] except perhaps where necessity demands.[98] Whether a person who holds no certificate at the time of employment but has secured one prior to entering upon teaching duties is a qualified teacher has been vigorously debated by the courts. The wording of the

---

[88]In Gilburt v. Kroll, 144 N.Y.S.2d 219 (1955), an action of mandamus was successfully brought to compel the board to rate petitioners as having passed the supervision test and to administer to them the remaining tests. The board had changed the passing score from 60 percent to 65 percent after the test had been announced. In Marrs v. Matthews, 270 S.W. 586 (Tex. 1925), an injunction was sought against the state superintendent of public instruction to enjoin him from canceling plaintiff's certificate. Plaintiff contended in part that the use of the word *unworthy* in the state statute was too vague and uncertain to define a disqualification to further hold a teacher's certificate. However, the appellate court found the term to be sufficiently specific and denied the injunction.

[89]Nestler v. Board of Examiners of Board of Education of City of New York, 80 N.Y.S.2d 747 (1948).

[90]A distinction must be recognized between tenure contracts of employment and certificates. A certificate is a condition precedent to employment but is no guarantee of employment.

[91]Zimmerman v. Board of Education of Newark, 183 A.2d 25 (N.J. 1962).

[92]Glass v. Board of Education of City of New York, 241 N.Y.S.2d 890 (1963).

[93]People v. Kerstein, 108 N.E.2d 915 (Ill. 1952).

[94]Copley v. Trent, 188 S.E.138 (W.Va. 1936).

[95]Buford v. Morganton City Board of Education, 244 F.Supp. 437 (N.C. 1965); United States v. Ramsey, 353 F.2d 650 (5th Cir. 1965).

[96]Buchanan v. School District No. 134, Elk County, 54 P.2d 930 (Kan. 1936); Union High School District No. 2 v. Paul, 95 P.2d 5 (Col. 1939); Pearson v. School District No. 8, 129 N.W. 940 (Wis. 1911); Gormley v. Board of Education, 129 N.Y.S. 153 (1911).

[97]Catlin v. Christie, 63 Pac. 328 (Col. 1900); Perkins v. Inhabitants of Town of Standish, 62 A.2d 321 (Me. 1948).

[98]Hale v. Risely, 37 N.W. 570 (Mich. 1888).

statute in the particular state often determines the answer. If the words *shall employ* are used, the courts will generally hold[99] a qualified teacher has been legally employed if the teacher secures the certificate prior to employment, i.e., before beginning to teach. But if the statutes provide that the board shall contract only with legally qualified teachers, the courts may deny[100] that a valid contract is held unless the teacher has a certificate at the time of contracting. Where the certificate expires and another is not procured, the teacher does not remain eligible to teach.[101] However, that teacher continues to be eligible where another certificate or a renewal is obtained upon expiration of the existing certificate.[102] A gap between certificates is not disqualifying where it occurs during a period when the teacher is not teaching, as during summer vacation.[103]

A mother teaching a child at home is required to have a teacher's certificate[104] in some states. Attendance at a private school not taught by qualified teachers constitutes a violation of the compulsory school attendance law.[105]

In the absence of special circumstances teachers may not recover compensation for periods they teach without a valid certificate.[106] They are considered volunteers during such period, their employment contracts being regarded as void.[107] If the teacher procures a certificate at a later date, the teaching contract cannot be ratified so as to make it valid from the beginning but only from the time that the certificate is received.[108] A school district has been permitted to recover the salary paid to a teacher for teaching during a period when that person did not hold a license to teach.[109] A teacher may be properly dismissed upon the expiration of a certificate where there is no renewal thereof and no procurement of another certificate and where a teacher's certificate is voided, he or she may properly be dismissed for failure to meet prerequisites.[110]

16.10 REVOCATION OF CERTIFICATE

Revocation of a teaching certificate must be distinguished from dismissal by a local school board. When a license is revoked, the teacher's conduct has been found to justify the termination of the right to teach in the state whereas dismissal by a local school system in no way affects the right to apply for and be employed in another school district.

16.10a Grounds for

Normally a revocation of a certificate will be based upon grounds set out in the educational laws of the state or in the regulations of the appropriate board or agency adopted pursuant thereto. An Indiana court has said:

> It is generally accepted doctrine that where a statute or ordinance authorizes the revocation of a license for causes enumerated, such license cannot be revoked upon any ground other than one of the causes specified.[111]

In the state of Washington the statutes provide:

> Any certificate to teach authorized under the provisions of this chapter of rules and regulations promulgated thereunder may be revoked by the authority authorized to grant the same under complaint of any school district superintendent, or intermediate school district superintendent for immorality, violation of written contract, intemperance, crime against the law of the state, or any

---

[99]Lee v. Mitchell, 156 S.W. 450 (Ark. 1913); Shafer v. Jones, 137 N.W. 481 (N.D. 1912); Board of Education for Logan County v. Akers, 47 S.W.2d 1046 (Ky. 1932); Reynolds v. Spurlock, 78 S.W.2d 787 (Ky. 1935); Swinford v. Chasteen, 87 S.W.2d 373 (Ky. 1935); Martin v. Knott County Board of Education, 122 S.W.2d 98 (Ky. 1938); Cottingham v. Stewart, 127 S.W.2d 149 (Ky. 1939); State ex rel. Lawson v. Cherry, 47 So.2d 768 (Fla. 1950).

[100]O'Connor v. Francis, 59 N.Y.S. 28 (1899); Jenness v. School District No. 31, 12 Minn. 448 (1867).

[101]People ex rel. Christie v. Board of Education, 67 N.Y.S. 836 (1900).

[102]Tate v. School District, 23 S.W.2d 1013 (Mo. 1929).

[103]Wabbeseka School District No. 7 v. Johnson, 286 S.W.2d 841 (Ark. 1956), where the teacher lacked a valid license between September 1 and September 11 but the teaching duties did not begin until September 15.

[104]State v. Superior Court, 346 P.2d 999 (Wash. 1959).

[105]Ibid.

[106]State v. Gettinger, 105 N.E.2d 161 (Ind. 1952); Falanry v. Barrett, 143 S.W. 38 (Ky. 1912); Harrodsburg Educational District v. Adams, 154 S.W. 44 (Ky. 1913); Kimball v. School District No. 122, 63 Pac. 213 (Wash. 1900); Bryan v. Fractional School District No. 1, 69 N.W. 74 (Mich. 1896).

[107]Floyd County Board of Education v. Sloane, 307 S.W.2d 912 (K. 1957).

[108]State v. Gettinger, 105 N.E.2d 161 (Ind. 1952); Hosmer v. Sheldon School District No. 2, 59 N.W. 1035 (N.D. 1894); Richard v. Richardson, 168 S.W. 50 (Tex. 1914; Zevin v. School District No. 11 of City of Cozad, 12 N.W.2d 634 (Neb. 1944).

[109]Vick Consolidated School District No. 21 v. New, 187 S.W.2d 948 (Ark. 1945).

[110]Perkins v. Inhabitants of Town of Standish, 62 A.2d 321 (Me. 1948); Seamonds v. School District No. 14, Fremont County, 68 P.2d 149 (Wyo. 1937) In the Matter of Feingold, 299 N.Y.S.2d 606 (1969).

[111]Stone v. Fritts, 82 N.W. 792 (Ind. 1907).

unprofessional conduct, after the person whose certificate is in question has been given an opportunity to be heard.[112]

Under the Kentucky statute it is provided that:

Any certificate . . . may be revoked by the state board of education, on the written recommendation of the superintendent of public instruction, for immorality, misconduct in office, incompetency or willful neglect of duty. Before the certificate is revoked the defendant shall be given a copy of the charges against him and an opportunity, upon not less than ten (10) days notice, to be heard in person or by counsel.[113]

False swearing to a loyalty oath or in the application for a certificate may be a ground for revocation.[114] A license may not be revoked because of race, religion, scruples against nuclear warfare, or other invasion of the holder's constitutional rights.[115] However, refusal to obey an order of the school and civil defense authorities to conduct air-raid shelter drills was held[116] not to be protected under the First Amendment. The Court said:

Accordingly, while one may think and believe as he will without interference, conduct resulting from the exercise of said right is not safeguarded by the First Amendment if it violates a reasonable nondiscriminatory regulation by governmental authority which has as its purpose the promotion of public good and safety.[117]

It was found in this case that petitioner's insubordination warranted the cancellation of his license.

In addition to the above, the revocation of certificates has been upheld on the following grounds:

Finding that petitioner did not meet the qualifications for the license.[118]

Finding that a teacher had paranoid schizophrenic type mental illness.[119]

Cheating on recertification examination.[120]

Neglecting teaching duties, as by reporting late, failing to make daily preparation, refusal to attend monthly institutes, etc.[121]

Willful violation of state law.[122]

Illicit relations with a female student.[123]

Drunkenness.[124]

Immoral or unprofessional conduct.[125]

Immoral or Unprofessional Conduct

The most common grounds for revocation of a license are immoral activities and unprofessional conduct or incompetence. A revocation of license generally requires a petition to be filed before the state board, and often local authorities prefer to manage the matter in some other way, such as by a "covered up" resignation in order to avoid exposure.

Where a teacher is charged with immoral or unprofessional conduct or conduct involving moral turpitude, generally the misconduct must be such as indicates an unfitness to teach. In a leading California case, the court stated:

In determining whether the teacher's conduct thus indicates unfitness to teach the board may consider such matters as the likelihood that the conduct may have adversely affected students or fellow teachers, the degree of such adversity anticipated, the proximity or remoteness in time of the conduct, the type of teaching certificate held by the party involved, the extenuating or aggravating circumstances, if any, surrounding the conduct, the praiseworthiness or blameworthiness of the motives resulting in the conduct, the likelihood of the recurrence of the questioned conduct, and the extent to which disciplinary action may inflict an adverse impact or chilling effect upon the constitutional rights of the teacher involved or other teachers. These factors are relevant to the extent that they assist the board in determining a teacher's fitness to teach, i.e., in determining whether

---

[112]Revised Statutes of Washington, 28A 70.160 (1970).

[113]Kentucky Revised Statutes, 161.120 (1969).

[114]Mack v. State Board of Education, 36 Cal.Rptr. 677 (1964).

[115]Council v. Donovan, 244 N.Y.S.2d 199 (1963).

[116]Ibid.

[117]Ibid., p. 206.

[118]Adelson v. Board of Education of City of New York, 98 N.Y.S.2d 763 (1950).

[119]Alford v. Department of Education, 91 Cal.Rptr. 843 (1970).

[120]Shirer v. Anderson, 88 F.Supp. 858 (D.C. 1950). However, a single instance of assistance to another teacher during a certification examination was held not to be sufficient ground for revoking a license in Superintendent of Common Schools of Daviess County v. Taylor, 49 S.W. 38 (Ky. 1899).

[121]Stone v. Fritts, 82 N.E. 792 (Ind. 1907).

[122]Hodge v. Stegall, 242 P.2d 720 (Okla. 1952).

[123]Crawford v. Lewis, 186 S.W. 492 (Ky. 1916).

[124]Bowman v. Ray, 80 S.W. 516 (Ky. 1904).

[125]Tringham v. State Board of Education, 326 P.2d 850 (Cal. 1958); Bowman v. Ray, 80 S.W. 516 (Ky. 1904).

the teacher's future classroom performance and overall impact on his students are likely to meet the board's standards.[126]

The court went on to observe that a teacher may be removed only upon a showing "that his retention in the profession poses a significant danger of harm to either students, school employees, or others who might be affected by his actions as a teacher."[127]

A showing of such harm may be based on adverse inferences drawn from past conduct as to the teacher's probable future ability as well as upon the likelihood that the publicity surrounding the incident may substantially impair his or her function as a teacher.[128]

Where a teacher is charged with immoral or unprofessional conduct, the charge must relate to actions occurring within a reasonable time of its filing and must specify the times and nature of the acts with reasonable certainty.[129] As was declared in an early Kentucky case:

There is no intimation as to the date of these alleged acts of intemperance. So far as the notices go, they may have occurred many years before he obtained his certificate as a teacher, and might not have affected either his moral character or competency at the date of the notice. Unless the alleged intemperance was subsequent to the date of his certificate as a teacher, or was so close thereto in point of time as to affect his moral standing at that time, they would not be sufficient to authorize the revocation of the certificate, or their investigation to that end by the appellee.[130]

Where a county superintendent of schools had pleaded guilty to presenting false claims against the federal government in violation of a federal criminal statute, the court upheld a revocation of his license on the ground that he had been "convicted of a crime involving moral turpitude."[131] A plea of guilty was found to be tantamount to a conviction. The fact that the superintendent did not personally benefit from his mis-

deeds or commit them with ulterior motives was held to be immaterial. The paramount interest of the community in licensing teachers of good character justifies the revocation of a license for serious misconduct outside the duties of teaching.

The rule or regulation which establishes the conduct to be followed must be in existence and published before the alleged violation. In the words of the Oklahoma court:

Obviously, if it was sought to revoke for a willfull violation of one of the rules or regulations of the State Board of Education, such rule or regulation would have to be promulgated prior to the violation. Also, under the fourth provision, that it might be revoked for "other proper cause," such other proper cause must be established by some rule or regulation of the State Board promulgated prior thereto so that the teacher may know of the rules of conduct under which his license may be revoked.[132]

16.10b Right to notice and hearing

As has already been shown in Section 16.10a, state statutes dealing with revocation of certificates provide the procedures to be followed by the board in consummating the revocation and by the teacher in protesting the board's action. Clearly the holder of a certificate is entitled to all the protection granted by statutes or regulations enacted in that state.[133] Revocations have been set aside by the courts where the board failed to appoint an investigating committee as required by statute to determine the probable cause[134] or failed to prefer charges and to hold a hearing as provided in the statute.[135] Where the statutes do not state how a preliminary investigation is to be made, the board has considerable discretion in the matter so long as it does not act arbitrarily.[136] The teacher need not be given notice of the investigation, nor is it essential that the teacher be present.[137]

While a board may have a good deal of latitude in determining the details or nature of a hearing where these are not specified, it must meet minimum due process standards.[138] Such hearings must be fair, give

---

[126]Morrison v. State Board of Education, 461 P.2d 375 (Cal. 1969). In this case the board failed to establish the unfitness of a teacher who had been involved in a single noncriminal relationship of a homosexual nature.

[127]*Ibid.*

[128]Pettit v. State Board of Education, 513 P.2d 889 (Cal. 1973).

[129]Bowman v. Ray, 80 S.W. 516 (Ky. 1904).

[130]*Ibid.*, p. 517.

[131]Huff v. Anderson, 90 S.E.2d 329 (Ga. 1955). The case defines "moral turpitude" at length. See also Sarac v. State Board of Education, 57 Cal.Rptr. 69 (1967), where a revocation based on an arrest for homosexual behavior was upheld.

[132]Hodge v. Stegall, 242 P.2d 720, 723 (Okla. 1952).

[133]Neal v. Bryant, 149 So.2d 529 (Fla. 1962).

[134]*Ibid.*

[135]Matteson v. State Board of Education, 136 P.2d 120 (Cal. 1943).

[136]Crawford v. Lewis, 186 S.W. 492 (Ky. 1916).

[137]*Ibid.*

[138]Pordum v. Board of Regents of the State of New York, 491 F.2d 1281 (2d Cir. 1974); Huntley v. North Carolina State Board of Education, 493 F.2d 1016 (4th Cir. 1974).

teachers adequate notice thereof and indicate charges against them, be held within a reasonable time, provide opportunity for teachers to present their cases fully, and be held before an impartial tribunal.[139] The court's comments in a 1965 Connecticut case on contract renewal are equally applicable to license revocation:

> The fundamental purpose of the hearing is to give a probationary teacher who has already been acquainted with the reasons why a board of education has decided not to renew his contract a full and fair opportunity to persuade and convince the board that it is mistaken in that decision. The teacher may attempt to answer or rebut the reasons given. He may attempt to show that the reasons given are mistaken in fact or are insufficient to justify the decision not to renew, and that it should be reversed and the teacher's contract renewed. It might well be that the teacher may be able to present to the board information or knowledge that it did not possess at the time of its original decision not to renew, and that such information or knowledge might materially affect the thinking of board members and the decision of the board.[140]

Complaints setting out charges against teachers must be sufficiently definite as to time, place, and description to inform them of the misconduct with which they are charged.[141] A teacher may be suspended pending a hearing provided the teacher's salary is not interrupted.[142] It may be permissible according to the practice in a particular state for a teacher to move that specified charges be made more definite or be stricken as too vague and indefinite.[143] A hearing was upheld[144] in which only two members of the board (less than a quorum) conducted the hearing, took testimony, and reported a summary thereof to the whole board, which made the decision. The petitioner's attorney had been allowed to cross-examine the witness.

16.10c Summary procedure

Some state statutes permit a summary procedure for the revocation of a certificate in a situation where the grounds therefor are clear, as where the teacher has been convicted of a crime involving moral turpitude or a sex offense. A California statute authorizes a summary revocation upon conviction of a sex offense. It was decided[145] that a hearing was nevertheless required where the conviction occurred prior to the enactment of the statute. In other words, the statute authorizing the summary procedure was not to be applied retroactively. The procedure of summary dismissal for conviction for sex offenses has been held[146] not to violate a teacher's constitutional rights. In this case the state board of education had adopted a resolution revoking the certificates of several teachers who had pleaded guilty to sex offenses. The court found that the statute imposed a mandatory duty upon the board to revoke summarily the licenses of such teachers.

A summary procedure is often authorized in the termination of the certificates of substitute or probationary teachers.[147] The Board of Education of the City of New York adopted bylaws which permitted the termination of a substitute teacher's license "at any time." Under this provision the New York court held[148] that there was no judicial review of the case on its merits. The bylaw authorized the board to terminate such license "at any time." The judicial issue involved would be whether the bylaw itself was arbitrary or unreasonable.

While the summary revocation procedure is admittedly harsh, its harshness is mitigated by the fact that its use normally is limited to clear-cut issues or to probationary, temporary, or substitute teachers. The trend is, however, to greater protection for the teacher, and some statutes now provide a hearing even in the case of probationary teachers.[149]

A summary procedure also was upheld[150] where the board discovered its mistake and revoked a certificate issued to a disqualified applicant.

---

[139]Horner v. Board of Trustees of Excelsior Union High School District of Los Angeles, 389 P.2d 713 (Cal. 1964); Huntley v. North Carolina State Board of Education, 493 F.2d 1016 (4th Cir. 1974).

[140]Hodge v. Stegall, 242 P.2d 720 (Okla. 1952).

[141]Huntley v. North Carolina State Board of Education, 493 F.2d 1016 (4th Cir. 1974).

[142]Pordum v. Board of Regents of the State of New York, 491 F.2d 1281 (2d Cir. 1974).

[143]Stone v. Fritts, 82 N.E. 792 (Ind. 1907).

[144]Pettiford v. S.C. Board of Education, 62 S.E.2d 780 (S.C. 1950).

[145]Fountain v. State Board of Education, 320 P.2d 899 (Cal. 1958).

[146]Di Genova v. State Board of Education, 288 P.2d 862 (Cal. 1955).

[147]Giangrande v. Board of Education of City of New York, 254 N.Y.S.2d 643 (1964).

[148]Ibid.

[149]Griggs v. Board of Trustees of Merced Union High School District, 37 Cal.Rptr. 194 (1964).

[150]Glass v. Board of Education of City of New York, 241 N.Y.S.2d 890 (1963); People ex rel. Latimer v. Board of Education of Chicago, 94 N.E.2d 742 (Ill. 1950); Marrs v. Matthews, 270 S.W. 586 (Tex. 1925); Adelson v. Board of Education of City of New York, 98 N.Y.S.2d 763 (1950).

16.10d Judicial remedies

The form, nature, and extent of judicial review of administrative action in revoking a certificate is determined by the statutes of each state. A person has no constitutional right to an appeal to the courts from the final decision of an administrative body. As noted by a United States district court in upholding the summary revocation of certificates for cheating on a recertification examination:

Aside from this, the teacher's certificate relates only to the right to teach in the service of the state; and it cannot be a denial of due process for the state to provide for revocation of such certificate by administrative action without provision for judicial review. The idea that due process requires judicial approval of matters relating to the hiring or discharge of a public employee is one which has no foundation either in reason or authority. [151]

The above quotation refers to a direct appeal from the decision of the board (after all prescribed administrative remedies have been exhausted) in which the court reviewed the board's decision on the merits. In such a proceeding the court determines on the basis of the record or evidence before it whether the revocation is justified on the facts of the case.

If a direct review is not provided by the statutes of the particular state, this does not mean that the courts are closed to the teacher. In almost all cases the teacher will have available one or more of the so-called extraordinary remedies, such as injunction or mandamus. The former is used to enjoin the board from revoking the certificate and to reinstate it if revoked. The latter is appropriate to direct public officials to do their duty, namely, to conduct the certification of teachers according to law. However, when either an injunction or mandamus is sought, the question before the court is not precisely the same as on direct review although the practical result is often the same. The question is not ordinarily on the merits as to whether the certificate should have been revoked; rather the inquiry concerns the means, methods, and procedures used to revoke it. Thus, it is often said that a board cannot act arbitrarily, capriciously, unreasonably, in bad faith, or contrary to the established procedures. If the court finds that the board has done so in a particular case, it usually will grant relief by injunction, mandamus, or similar remedy, even though no direct appeal to the courts

has been provided. But if a direct appeal exists, its procedure is to be followed since, as a general rule, an injunction, mandamus, or other extraordinary remedy cannot be used as a substitute for appeal.

16.10e Loyalty oath, discrimination, and other constitutional issues

Even where no direct appeal to the courts is provided from a final decision revoking a teacher's certificate, the courts, through the use of one of the extraordinary remedies discussed in the preceding section, will protect the constitutional rights of a teacher. Thus, a license cannot be revoked because of race, religion, or beliefs protected by the First Amendment.[152] The United States Supreme Court in *Shelton v. Tucker*[153] declared unconstitutional an Arkansas statute which compelled every teacher, as a condition of employment in a state-supported school or college, to file annually an affidavit listing without limitation every organization to which the teacher belonged or regularly contributed within the preceding five years.

In a five-to-four decision the United States Supreme Court also struck down as unconstitutionally vague a New York law which required the removal of teachers for uttering any treasonable or seditious words or for doing any treasonable or seditious act. This is one of the most recent expressions of the Supreme Court on the question of loyalty oaths. It strikes down specifically two types of laws. The first is a statute or regulation drafted in broad terms without defining precisely the subversive activity which it seeks to proscribe. Such laws, like the New York law in question, are held to be unconstitutionally vague. The New York statute read:

A person employed as superintendent of schools, teacher or employee in the public schools, in any city or school district of the state, shall be removed from such position for the utterance of any treasonable or seditious word or words or the doing of any treasonable or seditious act or acts while holding such position. [154]

[151]Shirer v. Anderson, 88 F.Supp. 858, 862 (D.C. 1950).

[152]Council v. Donovan, 244 N.Y.S.2d 199 (1963); Rackley v. School District No. 5, 258 F.Supp. 676 (S.C. 1966).
[153]364 U.S. 479, 81 S.Ct. 247, 5 L.Ed.2d 231 (Ark. 1960).
[154]Keyishian v. Board of Regents of University of State of New York, 385 U.S. 589, 87 S.Ct. 675, 17 L.Ed.2d 629 (N.Y. 1967). In a one-sentence per curiam decision the Supreme Court affirmed the decision of the United States District Court of New York upholding the following oath: "I do solemnly swear (or affirm) that I will support the constitution of the United States of America

The majority of the Court strongly suggested that the statute would have been constitutional if it had contained definitions of "treasonable" or "seditious." It cited with apparent approval the definitions of such terms found in Subsection 3 of Section 105 of the New York Civil Service Law.

The second type of statute which a majority of the Court held to be unconstitutional is one barring employment or granting of a teacher's certificate to a person who simply holds membership or who has been a member of a listed organization. The majority concluded:

> We therefore hold that Civil Service Law, Section 105 (1) (c) and Education Law, Section 3022 (2) are invalid insofar as they sanction mere knowing membership without any showing of specific intent to further the unlawful aims of the Communist Party of the United States or of the State of New York.

On this point the majority cited the Smith Act as a good example since it condemns only persons shown to have an "intent to cause the overthrow or destruction of any such government."

16.10f Recovery of salary after wrongful revocation

The laws of each state need to be examined to determine the extent to which money damages may be recovered for the wrongful revocation of a certificate. In New York a substitute teacher sued for lost salary when her certificate was restored following an appeal to the state commissioner of education. Her claim was disallowed since it was found that the cancellation was not negligent, in bad faith, or without due process, and was done by competent authority.[155] It must be noted that a substitute teacher in New York City has very limited rights. In a recent Second Circuit case the court stated[156] that a teacher might be entitled to back pay if found to be fit after the certificate has been revoked.

16.11 SUMMARY

A proper certificate is to teachers what a license to practice is to the lawyer, physi-

cian, or dentist. It is the document which attests to their qualifications for the teaching or supervisory position in question. These qualifications are established by state law, and the procedure for the issuance, renewal, or revocation of teacher certificates is established by that law. These functions are customarily delegated to the state board of education or other governmental agency. Since it is an administrative body, the general principles of administrative law apply. Decisions within its discretion can be successfully challenged only by showing an abuse in the exercise of that discretion. Judicial review in this instance, whether by appeal or by extraordinary remedy (injunction, prohibition, mandamus), is limited to such questions as whether the agency acted arbitrarily, with prejudice or discrimination, in excess of its jurisdiction, contrary to the great weight of the evidence, or fraudulently. Where appeal to an administrative agency is permitted, all administrative remedies must be exhausted before review may be sought in the courts. Where an application for a certificate has been denied, the applicant is entitled to a hearing only to the extent provided by statute or by the regulations of the board.

Since the qualifications for different positions in the educational system differ and since it is usually desirable to provide a trial period for the beginner, numerous types of certificates have been devised. The temporary certificate is normally issued to the inexperienced teacher, and an emergency or special permit is granted during times of serious teacher shortages to individuals who fall short of the usual qualifications. The latter type of certificate is not to be used where a sufficient number of properly qualified teachers can be employed. A conditional certificate is utilized where a teacher fails to satisfy fully all of the qualifications or it is desired to require continued professional growth. The permanent certificate usually is issued when the teacher has met all of the requirements prescribed therefor and has reached the stage of tenure. Advance or supervisory certificates are granted to teachers who qualify for the position of principal or other supervisory responsibility.

The qualifications for each type of certificate customarily differ. They normally include a baccalaureate degree, good moral character, a minimum age, satisfactory health, and citizenship. For certain certificates satisfactory experience may be a prerequisite, as well as an oral interview and written examination.

The rights of a teacher to a certificate, or

---

and the constitution of the State of New York, and that I will faithfully discharge, according to the best of my ability, the duties of the position of ———— to which I am now assigned." Knight v. Board of Regents of University of New York, 390 U.S. 36, 88 S.Ct. 816, 19 L.Ed.2d 812 (1968). *See also* Whitehall v. Elkins, 389 U.S. 35 88 S.Ct. 184, 19 L.Ed.2d 35 (Md. 1967).

[155]Warner v. Board of Education of City of New York, 220 N.Y.S.2d 795 (1961).

[156]Pordum v. Board of Regents of the State of New York, 491 F.2d 1281 (2d Cir. 1974).

of one holding a certificate, are dependent upon the terms of state statutes, regulations of the issuing agency, and federal and state constitutions. Relief from certain requirements is being sought increasingly on the basis of the First and Fourteenth amendments to the United States Constitution. These amendments prohibit discrimination in the issuance or renewal of certificates on the basis of race, color, or creed. They also require a fairness and reasonableness in the procedure or in the requirements since they may not offend "due process of law" or the "equal protection of the laws." Loyalty oaths required for certification in some states will be stricken down by the United States Supreme Court if they are unconstitutionally vague or if they prohibit the mere membership in a subversive organization without any showing of specific intent to further its unlawful aims.

The Employment Contract and Professional Negotiation

PART ONE: TEACHER CONTRACTS

17.0 INTRODUCTION

17.1 CONTRACTING WITH TEACHERS
17.1*a* Period of Employment
17.1*b* Form of Board Action
17.1*c* Compensation When Schools are
    Closed
       Periods of Illness and
        Epidemics
       Reasons Other Than Illness
        and Epidemics
17.1*d* Responsibility of Teachers When
    Schools Are Closed

**17.2 BREACH OF CONTRACT
BY THE BOARD OF EDUCATION**
17.2*a* Payment of Salary
17.2*b* Compromising Claims

**17.3 BREACH OF
CONTRACT BY TEACHER**
17.3*a* Involuntary Breach
17.3*b* Voluntary Breach
17.3*c* Liquidated Damages
17.3*d* Actual Damages
17.3*e* Inducements to Comply

17.3*f* Revocation of Certificate
17.3*g* Withholding Salary

**17.4 TERMINATION
CLAUSES IN TEACHERS' CONTRACTS**

17.5 EMPLOYMENT OF RELATIVES

**17.6 COMPATIBILITY OF
PUBLIC OFFICE AND TEACHING**

**17.7 INCREASED SALARY
WITHIN TERM OF EMPLOYMENT**

**17.8 SALARY
PAYMENT DURING LEAVE**

**17.9 TEACHER
CONTRACT PROVISIONS**
17.9*a* Curriculum Assignments
17.9*b* Extracurricular Assignments
17.9*c* Extra Pay for Extra Work

**17.10 NATURE
OF SALARY SCHEDULES**

**17.11 COMPLIANCE
WITH CONDITIONS PRECEDENT**

17.12 MISCELLANEOUS PROVISIONS

**17.13 PROFESSIONAL AND
IN-SERVICE REQUIREMENTS**

PART TWO: LABOR UNIONS AND PROFESSIONAL NEGOTIATIONS

PART ONE
Teacher contracts

17.0 INTRODUCTION

Many people are of the opinion that a teacher's contract is different from other personal service contracts. They believe that it is a one-sided contract favoring the teacher and permitting the teacher to breach the contract while requiring the board of education to fulfill it. Actually this is not the case. The general legal principles governing contracts are also applicable to teaching contracts.[1] It must be understood, however, that teaching contracts are for personal services and are to be interpreted and treated in this light. For example, teaching contracts apply to the entire period and are not divisible.[2]

Like other persons, teachers are free agents and cannot be compelled to enter into contracts for their services if they elect otherwise. Nevertheless, because of the public nature of the teacher's employment, there are some differences between the contracts of teachers and those of nongovernmental employees. Teachers' rights and duties are largely defined by state statutes and by rules and regulations of state and local boards of education. They are not as free to join in concerted action to enforce their economic demands through strikes as are private employees in industrial or business enterprises.[3] Even though they may bargain in part through a professional organization, unlike their counterparts in private industry they are given or have individual contracts.

Since teachers,[4] supervisors,[5] and city superintendents[6] generally have been adjudged by the courts to be employees[7] rather than public officers, the terms and conditions of their employment are dependent upon their contracts. While the contract may be oral, in most cases it will be written or expressed in law.[8] These last types of contract are found in tenure and continuing contract laws and will be discussed in detail in Chapter 18. It should be pointed out here, however, that even though no formal contract is issued under tenure, and in some instances under continuing contract legislation, the teachers do have contracts and are considered to be contractual employees. By the nature of their employment all teachers have contracts of employment, which either are specifically issued or can be deduced from statutory enactments.

17.1 CONTRACTING WITH TEACHERS

Teaching contracts, with some of the exceptions noted above, are considered and interpreted in the same manner as other contracts for personal services. The essential elements for such contracts, rules for their interpretation, and their enforceability are discussed in Chapter 6. The present chapter will be devoted to specific problems involved in teacher contracts.

17.1a Period of employment

The question of the length of time teachers or administrators may be employed has been subject to some litigation. On this issue state statutes and the motives of the parties are controlling. If there is no evidence of fraud or no statute to the contrary, a board of education may employ a teacher or superintendent for any reasonable period of time.[9] However, a statute limiting the term of a contract must be respected. Thus, if a statute provides for one-year contracts, obviously contracts for two or more years will be illegal. Likewise, if the law says that a teacher may not be employed until the new board is elected, any contract with the outgoing board is void.[10]

In states requiring that employment be restricted to the life of the board of education, a board cannot make a contract with a teacher for services to be performed after its official life.[11] However, the law generally

---

[1] See generally 17 Am.Jur.2d Contracts, pp. 319 et seq.

[2] Hong v. Independent School District, No. 245, 232 N.W. 329, 72 A.L.R. 280 (Minn. 1930).

[3] United States v. United Mine Workers, 330 U.S. 258, 67 S.Ct. 677, 91 L.Ed 884 (1947); Norwalk Teachers Association v. Board of Education of City of Norwalk, 83 A.2d 482 (Conn. 1951); see also Pruzen v. Board of Education, 209 N.Y.S.2d 966 (1961).

[4] Board of Education of Doerun v. Bacon, 95 S.E. 753 (Ga. 1918); Alexander v. School District No. 1, 164 Pac. 711 (Ore. 1917).

[5] State v. Martin, 163 S.E. 850 (W.Va. 1932); Cross v. Fisher, 177 S.W. 43 (Tenn. 1915).

[6] Seeb v. City of Racine, 187 N.W. 989 (Wis. 1922). Contra, Cottingim v. Stewart, 142 S.W.2d 171 (Ky. 1940); Eason v. Majors, 196 N.W. 133, 30 A.L.R. 1419 (Neb. 1923).

[7] Gardner v. North Little Rock Special School District, 257 S.W. 73 (Ark. 1923); Davis v. Public Schools of the City of Escanaba, 140 N.W. 1001 (Mich. 1913).

[8] Unless, as in most states, the statute requires that contracts with professional employees be in writing. See Gordon v. Board of Directors of West Side Area Vocational Technical School, 347 A.2d 347 (Pa. 1975).

[9] Smith v. School District No. 57 in Sussex County, 42 Atl. 368 (Del. 1898).

[10] Chittenden v. School District No. 1, 56 Vt. 549 (1882); Burkhead v. Independent School District of Independence, 77 N.W. 491 (Iowa 1898); Independent School District of Liberty v. Pennington, 165 N.W. 209 (Iowa 1917).

[11] State ex rel Campe v. Board of Education of Loudon Dist., 118 S.E. 877 (W.Va. 1923).

provides that the board of education is a continuous corporate body, its actions not controlled by the term of office of any individual. A board of education may not repudiate a valid contract made by its predecessors in office.[12] Unless restricted by statute, the board of education, acting in good faith, may employ administrators or teachers for a period extending beyond the term of office of all members of the board.[13] According to a 1963 decision,[14] a board of education also may terminate the contract of a superintendent by mutual consent one year before its completion and issue the superintendent a new five-year contract. In this instance the issuance of the new five-year contract was held to be within the province of the board, and the subsequently elected board was not permitted to repudiate it.

Where it has been necessary to interpret the meaning of "one year" as the duration of a teacher's contract, it has been judged to be the balance of the current year and the next ensuing school year.[15] Thus, a teacher in Wisconsin may contract for the next ensuing school year any time during the current school year. In the absence of fraud such a contract is legal.

17.1b Form of board action

As has been emphasized in a preceding chapter, a board of education legally can take action only when its members are meeting in a legally called session. Actions taken by members of the board of education acting as individuals do not bind the district. Consequently, contracts with teachers must be acted upon by the board as a corporate body. However, it has been held[16] that two members of a three-member board may bind the district in a teaching contract at a meeting at which the third member was present or of which he had legal notice. The fact that he refused to act or to vote on any motion was irrelevant.

When all the terms of a contract have been agreed upon, it is not necessary that it be signed at a legal meeting of the board.[17] Nor is it necessary that it be signed by all board members at the same time.[18] However, where the statute requires that a contract be signed by the teacher and the president of the board of education, no contract can obtain legality until signed by the latter, even though it is voted by the board, prepared by the principal, and signed by the teacher.[19] It is not necessary that all parties attach their names to the written memorandum at the same time.[20]

The power of appointment requires the exercise of judgment, which cannot be delegated. The duty of appointment generally is placed in the board of education, which has a responsibility to perform it.[21] It is the collective judgment of the members of the board of education which must be exercised. Authority vested in the board of education to contract with teachers cannot be delegated to the superintendent or to a committee of the board unless this is specifically authorized by legislation.[22] However, the legislature can vest authority to carry on any educational function in whomsoever it deems appropriate. In states where the authority to employ teachers is vested in the superintendents, they legally may employ teachers.[23]

17.1c Compensation when schools are closed

Occasionally schools are closed because of contingencies in the community. Teachers are, of course, interested in knowing whether they will be paid, and every board member desires to know the legal obligation of the district in these circumstances.

In some jurisdictions, the question of the school district's liability for teachers' wages is covered by statute. For example, the Pennsylvania statute provides:

[12]Wilson v. East Bridgeport School District, 36 Conn. 280 (1869); People ex rel. Davidson v. Bradley, 47 N.E.2d 93 (Ill. 1943).

[13]School Town of Milford v. Zeigler, 27 N.E. 303 (Ind. 1891); Sparta School Township v. Mendell, 37 N.E. 604 (Ind. 1894); Webster v. School District No. 4, 16 Wis. 336 (1862).

[14]Sharon v. Spalding Township School District No. 1, 121 N.W.2d 849 (Mich. 1963).

[15]Rulings of Wisconsin Attorney General, 30 O.A.G. 279 (Wis. 1941).

[16]School District No. 42 v. Bennett, 13 S.W. 132 (Ark. 1890).

[17]Faulk v. McCartney, 22 Pac. 712 (Kan. 1889); Cloverdale Union High School District v. Peters of Sonoma County, 264 Pac. 273 (Cal. 1928).

[18]School District No. 16 v. Barnes, 144 Pac. 1046 (Okla. 1914); School Town of Milford v. Zeigler, 27 N.E. 303 (Ind. 1891); Holloway v. Ogden School District No. 9, 28 N.W. 764 (Mich. 1886).

[19]Potts v. School District of Penn Township, 193 Atl. 290 (Pa. 1937).

[20]School District No. 16 v. Barnes, 144 Pac. 1046 (Okla. 1914).

[21]Taggart v. School District No. 1 of Multnomah County, 188 Pac. 908 (Ore. 1920).

[22]Ibid.; State ex rel. Milligas v. Jones, 224 S.W. 1041 (Tenn. 1920); Andrews v. Union Parish School Board, 184 So. 552 (La. 1938).

[23]National Education Association, The Teacher and the Law, Research Monograph 1959-M3 (Washington, D.C.: The Association, 1959), p. 13.

When a board of school directors is compelled to close any school or schools on account of contagious disease, the destruction or damage of the school building by fire or other causes, the school district shall be liable for the salaries of the teachers of said school or schools for the terms for which they were engaged. Whenever a teacher is prevented from following his or her occupation as a teacher, during any period of the school term, for any of the reasons in this section specified, the school district shall be liable for the salary of such teacher for such period, at the rate of compensation stipulated in the contract between the district and the teacher, in addition to the time actually occupied in teaching by such teacher.[24]

In the absence of a statute, teachers must look to their contracts, past practice, and court decisions to determine what their rights and obligations are under these circumstances.

Periods of Illness and Epidemics

If the school is legally closed by the board of education,[25] there appears to be no question that teachers are entitled to receive their pay unless otherwise provided in their contract.[26] The board could have protected the district against the liability of payment if it had so desired, either by a clause to that effect inserted in the teachers' contracts or by board regulation made known to the teacher at the time of signing the contract.

Where the school is legally closed by the board of health, there is some difference of opinion among the courts on the right of teachers to collect their salaries. The courts of Nebraska[27] and Indiana[28] have held that in such instances the teacher is not authorized to collect salary. The crux of these decisions is that both parties were ready, willing, and able to fulfill the terms of the contract. A third party prohibited them from doing so. Consequently, one party (the board) should not be penalized to the benefit of the other party (the teacher).

It would appear that the decision of the court in the Nebraska case overlooked a sound principle of contract interpretation, i.e., they who draw the contract should have any doubts resolved against them in favor of the other party. It should have been evident that schools on some occasions might be closed because of illness or epidemics in the community. The school board could have protected itself by specifying that teachers were not to be paid under these circumstances. Therefore, the doubts should have been resolved against the party drawing the contract (the board) and in favor of the other party (the teacher).

A close examination of the above-cited Indiana case indicates that the facts upon which the decision was rendered are easily distinguishable from present-day practice. There, the teacher was employed to teach for a stipulated wage per day. He was not, therefore, to be paid for days he did not teach since his contract called for payment only for days he actually taught. Although the Indiana court held that the teacher could not collect his salary, it clearly acknowledged the general rule that, when schools are closed by the proper authorities because of illness or an epidemic, teachers employed on annual contract are entitled to compensation. This principle represents the weight of authority and has been stated in numerous decisions.[29]

A number of other states, including Illinois,[30] Kansas,[31] Massachusetts,[32] Michigan,[33] Ohio,[34] Oregon,[35] and Utah,[36] have held that teachers are entitled to pay when schools are closed by the school board or board of health. This is an equitable result since teachers are required to keep themselves available to teach in fulfillment of their contract. The courts of Oklahoma[37] and Texas[38] specifically have held that teachers are to receive their salaries during

[24]Pennsylvania Statutes Annotated, 11-1153 (1962).

[25]Phelps v. School District No. 109, 134 N.E. 312, 21, A.L.R. 737 (Ill. 1922).

[26]Dewey v. Union School District of the City of Alpena, 5 N.W. 646 (Mich. 1880); Libby v. Inhabitants of Douglas, 55 N.E. 108 (Mass. 1900); McKay v. Barnett, 60 Pac. 1100, 50 A.L.R. 371 (Utah 1900); Smith v. School District No. 64 of Marion County, 131 Pac. 557 (Kan. 1913); Crane v. School District No. 14, 188 Pac. 712 (Ore. 1920).

[27]School District No. 16 of Sherman County v. Howard, 98 N.W. 666 (Neb. 1904).

[28]Gregg School Township, Morgan County v. Hinshaw, 132 N.E. 586, 17 A.L.R. 1222 (Ind. 1921).

[29]School District v. Gardner, 219 S.W. 11 (Ark. 1920); Phelps v. School District No. 109, Wayne County, 134 N.E. 312 (Ill. 1922).

[30]Phelps v. School District No. 9, Wayne County, 134 N.E. 312 (Ill. 1922).

[31]Smith v. School District No. 64, 131 Pac. 557 (Kan. 1913).

[32]Libby v. Inhabitants of Douglas, 55 N.E. 808 (Mass. 1900).

[33]Dewey v. Union School District of the City of Alpena, 5 N.W. 646 (Mich. 1880).

[34]Montgomery v. Board of Education of Liberty Tp, Union County, 131 N.E. 497 (Ohio 1921).

[35]Crane v. School District No. 14, 188 Pac. 712 (Ore. 1920).

[36]McKay v. Barnett, 60 Pac. 1100, 50 A.L.R. 371 (Utah 1900).

[37]Board of Education v. Couch, 162 Pac. 485 (Okla. 1917).

[38]Randolph v. Sanders, 54 S.W. 621 (Tex. 1899).

the period schools are closed by the board of health.

A local board of education may not refuse to pay the teacher when schools are closed because of illness and then assert the defense of "act of God," which made it impossible for it to consummate the contract. An epidemic is not generally considered to be an "act of God" excusing a board of education from its contractual obligations.[39] It is not so considered since it is a foreseeable event.

Reasons Other Than Illness and Epidemics

Schools occasionally are closed for such reasons as holidays, inclement weather which makes bus transportation extremely hazardous, or the destruction of a school building by fire, tornado, or other disaster. While there is some authority to the contrary, the weight of authority indicates that teachers may recover salaries for the time that schools are closed for these reasons,[40] unless, of course, the school board has protected itself by including an appropriate provision in the teacher's contract excusing payment if the schools are closed for the specified reasons.

The courts have never decided[41] that inability to hold school because of inclement weather or destruction of property was "an act of God" excusing performance of contract. This conclusion is sound, since neither the storm nor the destruction of property itself is the real reason for closing school. In case of inclement weather it is the inability of the community to clear the highways and to operate the buses. Likewise the destruction of school buildings may not be the major reason for closing the school. The cause may be found in the board of education's inability to locate immediately other adequate or acceptable facilities. In any case it is legally impossible to attribute the failure to hold school to "an act of God" when societal responsibility is not completely met in coping with the emergency. As a general rule, where schools are closed because of contagion, or destruction of school buildings by fire or tornado, and where teachers are ready and willing to continue their duties under the contracts, no deduction from their salaries can be made.[42]

Teaching contracts are frequently drawn in a way that makes it difficult to determine whether a teacher is entitled to pay for recognized holidays. When nothing is said in the contract regarding this item, it has been held[43] that teachers are entitled to their salary on such holidays. However, if the teacher has made up the days, compensation for such days cannot legally be recovered.

17.1d Responsibility of teachers when schools are closed

The courts have had little to say about the responsibility of teachers when schools are closed for illness, epidemics, destruction of school buildings, intemperate weather, etc.[44] As a result, close examination of the teacher's contract is necessary to determine what responsibility, if any, a teacher may have. In general, a teacher is under obligation to be at school between given hours for a certain number of days per week. A teacher is responsible for teaching and carrying on other professional duties, including extracurricular activities.[45] These obligations are implied in school board regulations and contractual relations. Thus, a teacher, while being paid, can be expected to be at school and to carry on professional activities related to teaching during the hours and days the school normally would be in session. A teacher cannot be required to perform clerical and other activities unrelated to teaching, since the contract calls for the rendition of professional teaching services. Except in an emergency, a teacher cannot be required to assume custodial functions.[46]

[39]Dewey v. Union School District, 5 N.W. 646, 38 Am.Rep. 206 (Mich. 1880).

[40]Clune v. School District No. 3, Town of Buchanan, 166 N.W. 11, 6 A.L.R. 736 (Wis. 1918). However, teachers may not receive salary for a period during which they are absent from work on a strike. School Committee of the City of Pawtucket v. State Board of Education, 237 A.2d 713 (R.I. 1968). A board of education may question the authenticity of physicians' certificates where there has been a mass absence due to illness. Farmer v. Board of Education of Camden, New Jersey Commissioner of Education, October 10, 1967.

[41]Charlestown School Township v. Nay, 74 Ind. 127 (1881); School Directors v. Crews, 23 Ill.App. 367 (1887); Corn v. Board of Education, 39 Ill.App. 446 (1890); Hall v. School District No. 10, 24 Mo.App. 213 (1887).

[42]Gear v. Gray, 37 N.E. 1059 (Ind. 1894); Dewey v. Union School District, 5 N.W. 646, 38 Am.Rep. 206 (Mich. 1880); Libby v. Inhabitants of Douglas, 55 N.E. 808 (Mass. 1900); Randolph v. Sanders, 54 S.W. 621 (Tex. 1899); Smith v. School District No. 64, 131 Pac. 557 (Kan. 1913); Board of Education v. Couch, 162 Pac. 485 (Okla. 1917); McKay v. Barnett, 60 Pac. 1100, 50 A.L.R. 371 (Utah 1900).

[43]School District No. 4 of Township of Marathon v. Gage, 39 Mich. 484, 33 Am.Rep. 421 (1878).

[44]6 A.L.R. 746, 17 A.L.R. 1224, and 21 A.L.R. 741.

[45]McGrath v. Burkhard, 280 P.2d 864 (Cal. 1955); Parrish v. Moss, 106 N.Y.S.2d 577, 200 Misc. N.Y. 375, affirmed, 107 N.Y.S.2d 580 (1951).

[46]School District No. 25 of Elaine County v. Bear, 233 Pac. 427, 38 A.L.R. 1413 (Okla. 1925).

17.2 BREACH OF CONTRACT
BY THE BOARD OF EDUCATION

While it is not a frequent occurence a board of education sometimes breaks a contract with a teacher—in some instances because of outright dissatisfaction with the teacher's work; in others, on account of misunderstandings; and in still others, because of a decreased need for teachers due to reorganization of school districts. Whatever the cause, both teachers and boards of education are interested in ascertaining their rights and obligations under the contract. Fortunately, the courts have spelled out answers in some detail where these issues have been adjudicated.

When teachers are dismissed, the question of whether they are entitled to a hearing may arise. The answer normally depends upon the law of the particular state and whether teachers are entitled to due process. In some states teachers who are dismissed are entitled to a hearing since boards of education are held[47] to be acting in a quasi-judicial capacity in the dismissal of teachers, thus entitling teachers to be heard. In other states it has been held[48] that a teacher is not entitled to a public hearing but may be dismissed without a hearing if the grounds for dismissal are sufficient. In Wisconsin, for example—if teachers are dismissed, or if their contracts are not renewed, they are entitled to a hearing before an employment relations board or similarly designated agency to determine whether dismissal or nonrenewal of contract was due to "union" activities. The Wisconsin Education Association has been found to be a union. Thus, a hearing before the employment relations board may be held where it is charged that dismissal or nonrenewal of contract is related to activities in local units of the Wisconsin Education Association as well as in teachers' unions.

In a Wisconsin case[49] the supreme court decided that a school board's authority in regard to the retention or dismissal of teachers was restricted by Section 111.70 of the Wisconsin Statutes; that failure to offer a teacher another contract because of his activities as chairman of the bargaining committee of the local education association

was an unfair labor practice, even though he may not have been a particularly effective teacher; and that the superintendent, principal, etc., were agents of the school board as far as labor relations were concerned. The court affirmed the order of the Wisconsin Employment Relations Board directing the school board to reemploy the teacher.

17.2a Payment of salary

Teachers who have been unjustly dismissed are not automatically entitled to their full salary or to the full balance due under their contract. There is a familiar principle of law which requires innocent parties to use reasonable means to reduce or mitigate their damages. The general rule was articulated by the California Court of Appeals in a case involving the wrongful dismissal of a school bus driver:

The familiar rule requiring a plaintiff in a tort or contract action to mitigate damages embodies notions of fairness and socially responsible behavior which are fundamental to our jurisprudence. Most broadly stated, it precludes the recovery of damages which, through the exercise of due diligence, could have been avoided. Thus, in essence, it is a rule requiring reasonable conduct in commercial affairs. This general principal governs the obligations of an employee after his employer has wrongfully repudiated or terminated the employment contract. Rather than permitting the employee simply to remain idle during the balance of the contract period, the law requires him to make a reasonable effort to secure other employment.[50]

This rule is equally applicable to school teachers.[51] While teachers are obligated to search for other employment, they need not, in order to comply with the legal duty to mitigate damages, accept a dissimilar position, or one materially inferior to the one from which they were dismissed,[52] or one

---

[47]Clark v. Wild Rose Special School District No. 90, 182 N.W. 307 (N.D. 1921); Trustees of State Normal School v. Cooper, 24 Atl. 348 (Pa. 1892).

[48]State ex rel. Board of Directors of School District No. 306 v. Preston, 208 Pac. 47 (Wash. 1922); Ewin v. Independent School District No. 8, 77 Pac. 222 (Ida. 1904); Bump v. Union High School District No. 3, 24 P.2d 330 (Ore. 1933).

[49]Muskego-Norway Consolidated School Dist. v. Wis. Employment Relations Bd., 151 N.W.2d 617 (Wis. 1967).

[50]California School Employees Association v. Personnel Commission of the Pajaro Valley Unified School District of Santa Cruz County, 106 Cal.Rptr. 283 (1973).

[51]Shiffer v. Board of Education of Gibralter School District, 224 N.W.2d 255 (Mich. 1974); Byrne v. Independent School District of Struble, 117 N.W. 983 (Iowa 1908); Cable v. School District of the Township of Metal, 116 A.2d 113 (Pa. 1955); Ayers v. Western Line Consolidated School District, 404 F.Supp. 1225 (Miss. 1975); Beebee v. Haslett Public Schools, 239 N.W.2d 724 (Mich. 1976).

[52]State ex rel. Freeman v. Sierra County Board of Education, 157 P.2d 234 (N.M. 1945); Shiffer v. Board of Education of Gibralter School District, 224 N.W.2d 255 (Mich. 1974).

in another geographical area.[53] They are not obliged to accept another position until they are unemployed, i.e., until after the school term has started.[54] Even when teachers are ill, they have been allowed to collect under contracts from which they had been illegally dismissed.[55] Furthermore, teachers may properly refuse employment which would conflict with their efforts to obtain reinstatement.[56]

If teachers secure other employment, they may be able to collect something from the district from which they were illegally dismissed. For example, if the salary in the newly acquired position is less, the teacher should receive the difference. The teacher may have secured a position through a commercial teachers' agency. If so, the teacher will be able to collect the amount paid in commission since this is a necessary expense. The teacher will also be able to obtain the amount spent for a personal interview, travel, meals, lodging, etc. The teacher is not, however, entitled to collect the expense of securing long-term (two-year) employment.[57] If required to move to secure employment, the amount spent in moving may be included in computing the damage which a teacher has suffered. If the cost of living is substantially higher in the new community, these added costs may also be recovered.[58] All necessary additional expenses of securing and carrying on the work in the new position are properly included in the amount which a dismissed teacher should be awarded in damages, provided they do not exceed the unpaid balance under the original contract.

If the dismissed teacher, in spite of a diligent search, is unable to obtain other employment, the dismissing board will be required to pay the teacher's salary in full. The burden of proof is on the board of education to show that the teacher could have obtained and accepted other comparable

employment.[59] The fact that the person was able to reduce expenses while not teaching is immaterial. When suspended and later legally dismissed, a teacher is not entitled to pay during the period between suspension and dismissal.[60]

When a teacher is dismissed illegally and the school district has gone out of existence because of a reorganization of school districts, the new district comprising the territory of the original district is obligated for the amount of any damages awarded the teacher or for salary.[61] Under specific statutes, by implications of statutes, or by court decisions, new districts created from other districts inherit both the assets and the liabilities of the territory of the original district.

Where the board is required to pay the teacher in full, it is entitled to the services as provided for in the contract. The courts have permitted some variation from the obligations specified therein, such as being transferred to another school within the system. However, they have held[62] that the assignment must be to services of a professional nature.

17.2b Compromising claim

Settlement of claims or avoidance of litigation is always to be encouraged when a board of education is presented with a claim by a teacher. Since cases of this type are settled out of court, few precedents directly indicate the authority of the board in this area. Answers must be drawn from an examination of general legal principles and those which may be applied by analogy from other cases.

In the final analysis a settlement is the modification of the contract by mutual consent. School boards have been held[63] to possess power to modify a contract by agreement with the teacher. Whether or not

---

[53]Byrne v. Independent School District of Struble, 117 N.W. 983 (Iowa 1908); Shiffer v. Board of Education of Gibraltar School District, 224 N.W.2d 255 (Mich. 1974).

[54]Farrell v. School District No. 2 of Township of Rubicon, 56 N.W. 1053 (Mich. 1893).

[55]School District No. 21 v. Hudson, 277 S.W. 18 (Ark. 1925).

[56]Edgecomb v. Traverse City School District, 67 N.W.2d 87 (Mich. 1954); George v. School District of 8R of Umatilla County, 490 P.2d 1009 (Ore. 1971).

[57]Gardner v. North Little Rock Special School District, 257 S.W. 73 (Ark. 1923).

[58]School District No. 3 in Clear Creek County v. Nash, 140 Pac. 473 (Col. 1914).

[59]Tate v. School District No. 11 of Gentry County, 28 S.W.2d 1013 (Mo. 1929); Newton v. Calhoun County School District, 341 S.W.2d 30 (Ark. 1960); California School Employees Association v. Personnel Commission of the Pajaro Valley Unified School District of Santa Cruz County, 106 Cal.Reptr. 283 (1973); Shiffer v. Board of Education of Gibraltar School District, 224 N.W.2d 255 (Mich. 1974).

[60]Kaplan v. School District of Philadelphia, 130 A.2d 672 (Pa. 1957).

[61]Shirley v. School Board of School District No. 58, 332 P.2d 267 (Kan. 1958); Independent School District No. 65 of Wagner County v. Stafford, 257 P.2d 1092 (Okla. 1953); But see Beckett v. Roderick, 251 A.2d 427 (Me. 1969).

[62]Ryan v. Mineral County High School District, 146 Pac. 792 (Col. 1915).

[63]Seeb v. City of Racine, 187 N.W. 989 (Wis. 1922); Johnson v. Rapp, 229 P.2d 414 (Cal. 1951).

people in the district approve of the settlement is of no legal concern. The board of education, and not the people of the district, is charged with the responsibility of contracting with teachers.

17.3 BREACH OF CONTRACT BY TEACHER

Teachers may breach their contracts either of necessity or by choice. The contract has been breached if the teacher is unable to be on hand to assume teaching duties when school starts, or when the teacher is absent excessively while school is in session. However, it was held[64] that temporary delay in arriving at school because of floods and disruption of rail service did not justify dismissal of a teacher. The delay in reporting under these circumstances was beyond the teacher's control. Frequent tardiness has been held[65] to be a breach of contract. But it is not sufficient to allege frequent tardiness; tardiness must be proved. A Louisiana case held[66] that it was essential that a teacher first be warned by her superior and given an opportunity to correct the alleged tardiness before she could be dismissed. In the view of the court tardiness is remediable and with warning and direction may be overcome.

17.3a Involuntary breach

A teacher who has breached a contract because of illness or for reasons beyond human control is not likely to be sued for damages. However, the teacher may be replaced. In some instances the teacher may sue for all or part of the salary under the terms of the contract. Recovery is dependent upon whether the court decides that temporary absence from the position was justified or was just cause for dismissal. A teacher whose illness extended beyond the sick-leave period and who was unable to assume the duties and responsibilities of his position had not fulfilled his contract.[67] When a teacher has been ill beyond the sick-leave period, some courts have held that the contract has been broken and that the teacher legally may be dismissed. However, there is a growing tendency for the courts to take a more liberal point of view depending upon the terms of the particular

employment contract and any applicable statute or regulation.[68]

17.3b Voluntary breach

Voluntary breach of contract by teachers in recent years has caused increased concern in both educational and legal circles. In an effort to curb breaching of contracts by teachers, the Code of Ethics of the National Education Association states that the members of the teaching profession have an inescapable obligation with respect to employment. In fulfilling the Code of Ethics a teacher must adhere to the conditions of a contract until service thereunder has been performed, secure its termination by mutual consent, or otherwise legally terminate the contract. By implication, if not by direct statement of the National Education Association, a teacher who breaks a contract is guilty of an unethical practice. Many state associations have similar provisions in their codes of ethics.

17.3c Liquidated damages

To decrease breaking of contracts by teachers some boards of education have at times inserted so-called "penalty" or "liquidated damages" clauses in the contract. These clauses provide that if the teacher does not fulfill the terms of the contract the teacher agrees to pay a specified amount of money to the school district. While such provisions may be a deterrent to the breaching of contracts, their enforcement has not been without legal difficulty. An Iowa case on this point appears sufficiently important to present in some detail. The essential facts of the case were as follows:

The teacher agreed to teach for 36 weeks, the full period of the contract. The contract stated that the teacher guaranteed the fulfillment of the contract except for reason of illness or death or release by the board of education. If the teacher failed to fulfill the contract, she agreed to forfeit all sums remaining due and unpaid under the contract plus the sum of $200.00 designated as "liquidated damages."[69]

The teacher, upon being offered a position in another school district, resigned and ac-

[64]Turner v. Hampton, 97 S.W. 761 (Ky. 1906).
[65]School Directors v. Birch, 93 Ill.App. 499 (1900).
[66]Lewing v. De Soto Parish School Board, 113 So.2d 462 (La. 1959).
[67]Hong v. Independent School District No. 245, 232 N.W. 329 (Minn. 1930); Stowers v. Board of Education of Lincoln County, 198 S.E. 522 (W.Va. 1938); Auran v. Mentor School District, 233 N.W. 644 (N.D. 1930).

[68]Special School District of Fort Smith v. Lynch, 413 S.W.2d 880 (Ark. 1967); Campbell v. Wishek Public School District, 150 N.W.2d 840 (N.D. 1967); Garber v. Board of Education of City of New York, 271 N.Y.S.2d 329 (1966).
[69]Independent School Dist. of Manchester v. Dudley, 192 N.W. 261 (Iowa 1923).

cepted the offered position. The resignation was not accepted, and the board sued for the $200. The question for the court was whether the amount of $200 was "liquidated damages" or constituted a penalty, which the policy of the law does not permit to be exacted. Reasoning that the use of the term *liquidated damages* in the contract was not conclusive, the court determined on the basis of all of the relevant facts that the amount was a penalty and therefore uncollectible.

For a "liquidated damage" provision to be enforceable, the amount must bear a reasonable relationship to the actual damage; i.e., it must be a reasonable estimate of the actual damages which the school district would suffer if the teacher refused to complete the contract. Where such a provision is not included in the contract, the school district is not without a remedy, since it may recover the actual damages which it sustained by reason of the breach of contract by the teacher. However, for policy reasons the board of education may decide to include a "liquidated damage" clause. This clause has the advantage of obviating the necessity of proving the actual damages, but unless a low sum is specified, it may be construed as a penalty clause and be unenforceable.

17.3d Actual damages

A lower Nebraska court had before it the question of the amount of damages sustained by a school district when a teacher broke his contract. It limited recovery to the value of the time and expense of the superintendent in employing another teacher. Other items of damages were disallowed.[70]

If a larger salary is paid to the teacher who replaces the one breaching the contract, the question of whether this is to be recognized in assessing damages has not been settled and is currently a matter of legal speculation. It would appear reasonable to include the increased salary as damages where it is shown that it was necessary in the exercise of prudent management to pay a higher salary because of changes in salary levels or in the availability of qualified teachers.

It is a well-established principle of law that when a person induces another to break a contract for personal services that person commits a tort and is equally liable with the person breaking the contract for any damages suffered as a result of the breach. This

liability obviously would apply to superintendents, principals, supervisors, teachers, and school board members acting in their official capacity who induce teachers to breach contracts.

17.3e Inducements to comply

Instead of inserting a penalty clause or requiring payment if the teacher does not complete the terms of the contract, a few school systems have attempted to encourage teachers to fulfill the terms of their contracts by providing a cash bonus for those who do so. Although this procedure may appear desirable from an administrative point of view, it probably is illegal. It violates the provisions of many constitutions which prohibit the payment of additional compensation for services already performed. The wording of the Wisconsin constitution on this point is typical: "The legislature shall never grant any extra compensation . . . after the services have been rendered. . . ."[71]

In a case involving additional payment to retired teachers it was held[72] that the legislature was without authority to grant compensation for services already performed. The same principle appears applicable to bonus payments to teachers. In payments of bonuses school boards would be making a "gift" of public funds to the teacher in violation of the constitutions of several states.

17.3f Revocation of certificate

When a teacher breaches a contract, the question of whether the teaching certificate may be revoked is pertinent. The answer is found in the statutes of the respective states, which may cover the point either directly or by implication, i.e., provision that the teacher's certificate may be revoked for breach of contract or for unethical activities, or some similar statement. However, any revocation by implication must be by *clear* implication, since such important action must be firmly grounded in the law. The majority of states do not revoke teaching certificates for breach of contract when teachers accept another position.

17.3g Withholding salary

Unless it has been agreed in the contract, or provided for by statute, a board is acting illegally in withholding any part of the salary a teacher has already earned. In the absence of a contractual provision permitting

---

[70]National Education Association, transcription of record of lower court (Edgar, Nebraska case).

[71]Wisconsin Constitution, Article IV, Section 26.
[72]State *ex rel.* Thomson v. Giessel, 53 N.W.2d 726 (Wis. 1952).

such withholding as liquidated damages, the proper legal procedure is to pay all money then due the teacher and, if desired, to institute suit for damages suffered. A compromise settlement is legally possible. By proceeding in this manner boards of education minimize legal involvements.

17.4 TERMINATION
CLAUSES IN TEACHERS' CONTRACTS

More often than is supposed, a termination clause is inserted in teachers' contracts. Typically it provides that either party may terminate the contract by giving thirty, sixty, or eighty days' notice. Whether such clauses are legal depends upon the statutes of the state. If they require an annual contract, contracts of shorter duration obviously are in violation of statutes. If, on the other hand, they permit boards of education to contract with teachers for any period they desire, such a clause is valid. It was so held[73] in a Wisconsin case. The same decision also was reached[74] in Pennsylvania.

In earlier teacher contracts, clauses like the following were frequently found: "We reserve the right to terminate this contract at any time," or "This contract may be terminated at any time if we are dissatisfied with the services of the teacher." In reviewing such contracts courts generally have expressed the opinion that teachers under contract can be dismissed only when there is some legitimate reason. To dismiss them arbitrarily for a flimsy excuse or for no reason at all is in violation of public policy.[75]

17.5 EMPLOYMENT OF RELATIVES

The question of whether relatives of the superintendent or of members of the board of education legally may be employed arises on some occasions. The legality of employing relatives of the superintendent is easily determined. Since in most states the superintendent does not employ teachers, the superintendent is not employing a relative but is merely recommending the employment to the board. The board of education makes the final decision and, unless prohibited by statute, may employ any qualified teacher, including a relative of the superintendent, regardless of any interest which the superintendent may have in the earnings of the relative. However, if legally authorized to employ staff, the superintendent is not permitted to hire a relative in whose earnings there is a personal financial interest. Such employment would be contrary to public policy.

With few exceptions, board members may not employ relatives in whose earnings they have a direct pecuniary interest.[76] The California Education Code is typical of those statutes which prohibit conflicts of interest. It provides: "No member of the governing board of any school district shall be interested in any contract made by the board of which he is a member."[77] While this statute would normally prevent the employment of a spouse or child of a board member, there is an exception in the statute which provides that such contracts are valid where (1) the interest is disclosed, (2) the contract is approved in good faith by a vote sufficient for the purpose without counting the vote of the interested member, and (3) the contract is just and reasonable.[78] Accordingly, a teacher who is married to a member of the board may be employed by a board of education if the requirements of the statute are met.[79]

Even in the absence of a statutory exception, there are circumstances where a board may employ relatives. For example, a board member would normally be assumed to have an interest in the earnings of a minor child. Nevertheless, this assumption may be rebutted where it is shown that the minor child has become emancipated from the parents and is no longer dependent upon them.[80] Where the husband has no legal control over his wife's earnings, which is true in non-community property states, the wife of a board member legally may be employed.[81] School board members may not employ themselves as teachers or in other capacities for pay except to the extent permitted by statutes, even though they are well qualified for the position.[82]

---

[73]Kuebler v. City of Two Rivers, 257 N.W. 591 (Wis. 1934).

[74]Tishock v. Tohickon Valley Joint School Board, 124 A.2d 148 (Pa. 1956).

[75]School Directors v. Ewington, 26 Ill.App. 379 (1887); Tripp v. School District No. 3, 7 N.W. 840 (Wis. 1881); Public School District No. 11 of Maricopa County v. Holson, 252 P. 509 (Ariz. 1927).

[76]Brewer v. Howell, 299 S.W.2d 851 (Ark. 1957). See also, Shoreman v. Burgess, 412 F.Supp. 831 (Ill. 1976); Whately v. Leonia Board of Education, 538 A.2d 826 (N.J. 1976).

[77]California Education Code, 1174 (West 1969).

[78]California Education Code, 1174.5 (West 1969).

[79]Coulter v. Board of Education of Temple City Unified School District, 114 Cal.Rptr. 271 (1974).

[80]State ex rel. Swann v. Burchfield, 12 Lea (Tenn.) 30 (1883).

[81]Thompson v. District Board of School District No. 1 of Moorland Township, 233 N.W. 439, 74 A.L.R. 790 (Mich. 1930).

[82]Scott v. School District No. 9 in Williamstown, 31 Atl. 145, 27 A.L.R. 588 (Vt. 1894).

A number of states have nepotism laws prohibiting the employment of specified relatives. These laws generally are applicable to other contracts as well as to teaching contracts and are held to be a valid exercise of legislative power. Thus, statutes prohibiting the employment of specific relatives of members of the board of education are enforceable.[83] But when certain relatives are mentioned and those mentioned do not include spouses, the prohibition will not be extended to them.[84]

17.6 COMPATIBILITY OF PUBLIC OFFICE AND TEACHING

Two positions held by teachers simultaneously may be incompatible because they have been made so by statute or by public policy because of the nature of the positions. If one position controls another in some direct manner, the two positions are held to be incompatible.[85] Thus, it is assumed that a teacher may not serve as the mayor or as a member of the city council when the mayor and city council approve the school budget. However, the relationship of the legislature to the teacher is not sufficiently direct to prohibit teachers or principals from serving as members of the state legislature.[86] This decision was rendered in Oklahoma, where it was held[87] that the teacher-legislator could collect his past salary. But he could not collect any part of his salary paid in part by legislative appropriations made when he was a member of the legislature.

Teachers have been entitled to hold a variety of county and municipal offices in which there is no incompatability. For example, no incompatability was found between the position of bus driver and membership on a county school committee which reorganized schools and approved bus routes.[88] However, because of the interest of school districts in reorganization and enlargement of their local school districts, membership on county school committees by school board members, superintendents, and teachers would probably represent a conflict of interest rendering the two responsibilities incompatible.

17.7 INCREASED SALARY WITHIN TERM OF EMPLOYMENT

With contracts extending for longer periods of time and inflation shrinking the value of the teacher's dollars, recent years have witnessed many requests for salary adjustments above the amount specified in the contracts originally signed. Although it is impossible under most state constitutions and statutes to increase the salary of an officer during the term of office, the restrictions do not apply to employees such as most city or district superintendents of schools, supervisors, or teachers.[89] Salary contracts with employees of the board of education may legally be modified by mutual consent.

17.8 SALARY PAYMENT DURING LEAVE

The courts of Massachusetts in an early case went so far as to hold[90] that granting a leave of absence with pay constituted a gift and was beyond the power of the board. Since it is now commonly accepted that school systems profit by the added learning, vigor, and enthusiasm of persons returning from leaves of absence, probably no court would now hold that a leave with pay is a "gift." In fact, the exact opposite has been held. In Louisiana it was specifically ruled[91] that teachers could be granted sabbatical leaves with pay. But when teachers are absent without leave, the board unquestionably has authority to deduct an appropriate amount from their salary for the time lost.[92]

17.9 TEACHER CONTRACT PROVISIONS

17.9a Curriculum assignments

Teachers sometimes believe that their contracts call for a different type of teaching responsibility from what they are assigned to perform, which misinformation causes misunderstandings. For example, a teacher expecting to teach second grade may be assigned to teach first grade, or one anticipating a complete teaching load in mathematics may be assigned to teach a section in biology. Whether such shifts can legally be made depends upon the wording of the teacher's contract. Without consent, a school board cannot compel a teacher to teach subjects or grades other than those

[83] Keckeiser v. Independent School District, 509 F.2d 1062 (8th Cir. 1975).

[84] Board of Education of Zaleski School Dist. v. Boal, 135 N.E. 540 (Ohio 1922).

[85] State v. Jones, 110 N.W. 431 (Wis. 1907); State *ex rel.* Johnson v. Nye, 135 N.W. 126 (Wis. 1912).

[86] Board of Trustees of Fairview Graded Common School District v. Renfore, 83 S.W.2d 27 (Ky. 1935).

[87] Settles v. Board of Education, 389 P.2d 356 (Okla. 1964).

[88] Rulings of Wisconsin Attorney General, 40 O.A.G. 433 (1951).

[89] Alexander v. School District No. 1 in Multinomah County, 164 Pac. 711 (Ore. 1917); Board of Education of Doerun v. Bacon 95 S.E. 753 (Ga. 1918).

[90] Whittaker v. City of Salem, 104 N.E. 359 (Mass. 1914).

[91] State *ex rel.* Scroggens v. Vernon Parish School Board, 44 So.2d 385 (La. 1950).

[92] 38 L.R.A. (N.S.) 513.

called for in the contract of employment. If a contract states that a teacher is employed to teach second grade, the teacher cannot be made to teach first; if it states that a teacher is to teach mathematics, he or she cannot be required to teach biology. However, if the contract specifies teaching in the primary grades, the teacher may be required to teach in first, second, or third grade. The fact that it was understood that the teacher was to teach second grade is of no legal consequence. Preliminary understandings are merely part of the negotiations unless specifically embodied in the contract.

If the contract simply calls for teaching in a school system, teachers legally may be required to teach any subject for which they are qualified whether they desire to teach the particular subject or not. Actually, it must be assumed that a person is legally qualified to teach any subject for which a "permit" to teach can be secured. Thus, persons who have signed contracts "to teach in the school system" may be required to teach any subject for which they are qualified either by certificate or by permit. They may not, however, be assigned to teach subjects for which they have no qualifications[93] even under a contract which reads "to teach in the public schools of said township, in such building, grade and room as said trustees might designate."

Where qualified to teach only one subject, teachers may not be assigned to teach other subjects even if their services are no longer required to teach the subject for which they are qualified.[94] However, where teachers are employed to teach physical education, they also may be required to coach football and basketball.[95]

While teachers may be transferred to schools other than the one in which they agreed to teach, the transfers can be made only in cases of emergencies. They may not be made simply because a transfer is expedient.[96]

Under terms of teaching contracts teachers cannot be compelled to do their own janitor work unless this is specifically required in the contract.[97]

From the point of view of the board of

education it is desirable to have contract flexibility so all subjects and grades can be taught by teachers best qualified to offer them. In carefully drawn contracts it should be possible to guarantee teachers that they will teach in the field of their specialty and also to guarantee the board that all essential offerings can be adequately supplied.

17.9b Extracurricular assignments

Teachers' contracts generally make only vague reference to extracurricular activities if they mention them at all. Consequently teachers may be unaware that they will be assigned to extracurricular responsibilities such as supervising athletic events on weekends or sponsoring after-school activities. Teachers frequently request relief from such responsibilities and on occasions have challenged the authority of the board to make such assignments. In most cases, extracurricular assignments have been held to be proper, even where not specifically mentioned in the teacher contract, as long as they are reasonable and distributed impartially among the teachers.

In *Parrish v. Moss*[98] it was decided that the extracurricular assignment must be related to the teacher's field of specialty. But the court went on to observe:

> The broad grant of authority to fix 'duties' of teachers is not restricted to classroom instruction. Any teaching duty within the scope of the license held by a teacher may properly be imposed. The day in which the concept was held that teaching duty was limited to classroom instruction has long since passed. Children are being trained for citizenship and the inspiration and leadership in such training is the teacher.

The only requirement in *McGrath v. Burkhard*[99] was that no particular teacher should be discriminated against in the assignment of extracurricular activities, i.e., that the extracurricular assignment of each teacher be comparable to that of other teachers. In this case a teacher in the Sacramento senior high school sued to prohibit the board of education from assigning him extracurricular responsibilities in athletics or at social functions. His refusal to accept extracurricular assignments had resulted in his being assigned an extra class. He contended that such assignments were police work, unprofessional in nature, foreign to his field of

[93]Jefferson School Township v. Graves, 150 N.E. 61 (Ind. 1926).

[94]Funston v. District School Board for School Dist. No. 1 in Multonomah County, 278 Pac. 1075, 63 A.L.R. 1410 (Ore. 1929).

[95]Appeal of Ganaposki, 2 A.2d 742, 119 A.L.R. 815 (Pa. 1938).

[96]White v. Board of Education of Lincoln County, 184 S.E. 264, 103 A.L.R. 1376 (W.Va. 1936).

[97]School District No. 25 of Blaine County v. Bear, 233 Pac. 427, 38 A.L.R. 1413 (Okla. 1925).

[98]Parrish v. Moss, 106 N.Y.S.2d 577, *affirmed*, 107 N.Y.S.2d 580 (1951).

[99]McGrath v. Burkhard, 280 P.2d 864 (Cal. 1955).

instruction, and unreasonable in the number of hours they added to his duties which were not contemplated in his contract. It was held that a board of education has authority to assign teachers to extracurricular activities so long as such assignments are impartial and without discrimination in relation to other teachers in the school system. These activities, it was reasoned, are part of a total school program; they are in the interest of students, parents, and community; they need to be carried on; they can best be conducted under the auspices of a school; teachers are expected to assist with them; and there is nothing unreasonable in a fair assignment of extracurricular responsibilities. Likewise, in *District 300 Education Association v. Board of Education*[100] it was held that supervision of athletic events was a necessary adjunct to normal school activities, was reasonably related to teaching duties, and was neither demeaning in character nor unreasonably burdensome. Therefore, the court concluded that it was within the discretion of the school authorities to assign teachers to such extracurricular duties.

17.9c Extra pay for extra work

The issue of extra pay for extra work was before the Pennsylvania court in a case[101] involving a person who had served first as a teacher, in which position he acquired tenure, then as principal. His first principalship was in the high school, and later he was transferred to the junior high school. In the latter position he sued for an extra month's salary on the basis that he was required to work in the aggregate an extra month. The court held that he was not entitled "to be paid additional for every fragmentary hour he applies to his responsibilities. . . ."

17.10 NATURE OF SALARY SCHEDULES

Teachers occasionally elect to teach in a school system with a salary schedule in preference to accepting a higher-paying position in school districts without a schedule. Under these circumstances the teacher assumes that the salary schedule will continue in force and usually it does. However, a salary schedule has no contractual status. It is merely a statement of pol-

icy, to be continued or withdrawn at the school board's option. Sometimes this conclusion is explicit in the statute, but more often it is not specifically expressed. A 1956 court decision confirmed[102] the noncontractual nature of salary schedules. Accordingly, boards of education may alter, amend, or repeal salary schedules.[103] In addition, salary schedules may be adopted which will increase salaries for some teachers and decrease them for others.[104]

17.11 COMPLIANCE WITH CONDITIONS PRECEDENT

When certain acts must be performed before a contract becomes effective, or before it requires performance from the other party, they are referred to as conditions precedent. The courts uniformly uphold the necessity of complying with conditions precedent. Two decisions, from among many, illustrate this principle of law. In one instance teachers' contracts which had not been approved by the county superintendent as the law required were held[105] to be illegal, and any time taught under them was ruled not to count in fulfilling the time requirement under tenure.

In the second case,[106] where prior recommendation of the county superintendent was prescribed by statute, it was found to be necessary for boards of education to appoint only teachers who had been so recommended. In such instances the board could exercise discretion in selecting teachers from the recommended list but could not appoint teachers who had not been recommended.

Where superintendents are required to recommend teachers before they may legally be employed, superintendents may put their own name on the list. An appointment by the board of a superintendent from such a list is valid.[107]

17.12 MISCELLANEOUS PROVISIONS

Provision may be made for paying teachers for time spent at an institute or conference, especially if authorized ex-

[100]District 300 Education Association v. Board of Education, 334 N.E.2d 165 (Ill. 1975). *See also* Pease v. Millcreek Township School District, 195 A.2d 104 (Pa. 1963).
[101]Taggart v. Board of Directors of Canon-McMilland Joint School System, 185 A.2d 332 (Pa. 1962).

[102]Frisk v. Board of Education of the City of Duluth, 75 N.W.2d 504 (Minn. 1956).
[103]Federbush v. Board of Education of Borough of Carteret, Middlesex County, 70 A.2d 88 (N.J. 1949).
[104]San Diego Federation of Teachers, Local 1278 AFL-CIO v. Board of Education of City of San Diego, 31 Cal.Rptr. 146 (1963).
[105]State ex rel. Wilder v. Adams, 74 S.2d 65 (Fla. 1954).
[106]Cochran v. Trussler, 89 S.E.2d 306 (W.Va. 1955).
[107]White v. Board of Education of Lincoln County, 184 S.E. 264, 103 A.L.R. 1376 (W.Va. 1936).

pressly by statute.[108] However, if the teachers then fail to attend the institute or conference, it is doubtful that they can be paid unless they render other services for the board during the period or participate in some other program intended to improve their ability or knowledge. Obviously, school boards may not make gifts of public money or pay out money unless there is some value received either at present or in the future.

Health regulations and requirements are increasingly common in teachers' contracts. It has been held[109] that teachers may be required to meet any reasonable regulations pertaining to their health that are established by a board of education. Thus, they may be asked to furnish a health certificate as a condition of employment. They also may be required to submit to a physical examination.[110]

A board of education may not discriminate against a teacher because of marital status[111] or because of creed or religious beliefs.[112] Neither can there be differentiation in the salaries paid teachers based solely on their race or sex.[113]

To continue in a teaching position it is not necessary that every teacher be an outstanding one, desirable as that would be. Teachers must, however, possess average qualifications and ability.[114] They also may be required to possess good moral character.[115]

Teachers may not employ their own substitutes;[116] they may only recommend to the board of education that certain persons be employed. Neither is a board of education bound by an agreement made by one of its members to accept a certain person as a substitute teacher during the regular teacher's illness.[117]

Boards of education are authorized to grant teachers leaves of absence due to illness.[118] In some instances a teacher may be placed on leave-of-absence status without requesting it.[119] However, it must be understood that tenure teachers on leave retain their tenure rights.[120]

Teachers' contracts generally do not authorize teachers to purchase school supplies and charge them to the district, no matter how necessary the supplies may be. When teachers purchase school supplies without securing proper authorization to do so, they cannot recover from the board of education money they have spent on them.[121] Their actions in making such purchases are considered to be those of volunteers. Consequently, they are not permitted to recover money they may have spent.

17.13 PROFESSIONAL AND IN-SERVICE REQUIREMENTS

There appears to be no question of the authority of boards of education to enact reasonable rules and regulations intended to improve the educational or professional qualifications of the teaching staff. Such regulations automatically become part of a teacher's contract. A local board of education may require the teachers it employs to meet qualifications which are higher than those set by the state itself as long as such requirements are reasonable. This pattern has been followed consistently in a large number of states including Kentucky,[122] Illinois,[123] Missouri,[124] Pennsylvania,[125] and New York.[126] Teachers may also be required to join one or more teacher associations—local, state, or national—as a condition for enjoying the benefits held[127] to be of professional value to teachers and the school system in that it assists in educational improvement.

---

[108]Sandry v. Brooklyn School District No. 78 of Williams County, 182 N.W. 689, 15 A.L.R. 719 (N.D. 1921).

[109]Tate v. School District of Gentry County, 23 S.W.2d 1013, 70 A.L.R. 771 (Mo. 1930).

[110]School District No. 1, Multnomah County v. Teacher Retirement Fund Association, 95 P.2d 720, 96 P.2d 419, 125 A.L.R. 720 (Ore. 1939).

[111]133 A.L.R. 1437.

[112]Hysong v. School District of Gallitzin Borough, 30 Atl. 482, 26 L.R.A. 203 (Pa. 1894).

[113]Alston v. School Board of City of Norfolk, 112 F.2d 992, 130 A.L.R. 1506 (4th Cir. 1940); cert. denied, 311 U.S. 693, 61 S.Ct. 75, 85 L.Ed. 448 (Va. 1940).

[114]Neville v. District No. 1 School Directors, 36 Ill. 71 (1864).

[115]Board of Education of Galesburg v. Arnold, 1 N.E. 163 (Ill. 1884).

[116]School Directors v. Hudson, 88 Ill. 563 (1878).

[117]Auran v. Mentor School District No. 1 of Divide County, 233 N.W. 644 (N.D. 1930).

[118]People ex rel. Patterson v. Board of Education of City of Syracuse, 54 N.Y.S.2d 80, appeal denied, 56 N.Y.S.2d 196. See also 62 N.E.2d 491 (1945).

[119]Noble v. Williams, 150 S.W. 507, 42 L.R.A. (N.S.) 1177 (Ky. 1912).

[120]Cooke v. Board of Education, 161 F.2d 877 (4th Cir. 1947).

[121]Ibid.

[122]Daviess County Board of Education v. Vanover, 293 S.W. 1063 (Ky. 1927).

[123]People ex rel. Fursman v. City of Chicago, 116 N.E. 158 (Ill. 1917).

[124]Crabb v. School District No. 1, 93 Mo.App. 254 (1902).

[125]Commonwealth ex rel. Sherry v. Jenks, 26 Atl. 371 (Pa. 1893).

[126]Lena v. Raftery, 50 N.Y.S.2d 565 (1944).

[127]Magenheim v. Board of Education of School District of Riverview Gardens, 347 S.W.2d 409 (Mo. 1961).

PART TWO
Labor unions and professional negotiations

17.14 INTRODUCTION

One of the most discussed topics in educational circles is the extent to which teacher organizations may conduct professional negotiations or bargain collectively with boards of education.[128] Initial efforts by teachers to organize and bargain collectively met with severe criticism. The principal arguments against unionization of teachers were: that collective bargaining is unprofessional; that collective bargaining means strikes; that the rights of teachers are largely circumscribed by legislation and budgetary procedures which do not permit wide-range bargaining; that boards of education are charged with the responsibility of decision making and cannot bargain away their responsibility; that the legislature and boards of education are public bodies, imbued with a spirit of dealing justly with public employees; and that collective bargaining by public employees is therefore unnecessary. However, in recent years, the public's attitude toward collective bargaining by public and professional employees has changed considerably and it is now widely accepted. Nevertheless, it must be recognized that because of the very nature of the employment relationship, there are vast differences between the rights of public employees and those employed by private industry, particularly with regard to the right to strike. As the Connecticut Supreme Court observed:

> Under our system, the government is established by and run for all of the people, not for the benefit of any person or group. The profit motive, inherent in the principle of free enterprise, is absent. It should be the aim of every employee of the government to do his or her part to make it function as efficiently and economically as possible. The drastic remedy of organized strike to enforce the demand of unions of government employees is in direct contravention of this principle.[129]

17.15 THE RIGHT OF TEACHERS TO JOIN A COLLECTIVE BARGAINING ORGANIZATION

The National Labor Relations Act[130] confers upon certain employees the right to organize and bargain collectively through organizations of their choice as determined through supervised elections. However, this act does not apply to public school teachers because it exempts from its coverage employees of the United States, or of any state, or of any political subdivision thereof.

The general rule at common law was that public employees were not entitled to bargain collectively and public employers were without the power to enter into such agreements.[131] Over the years, states have come to recognize the importance of maintaining orderly and constructive relationships between public employees and their employers and in many jurisdictions teachers and other public employees have been granted collective bargaining rights by the legislature.[132] The Rhode Island statute is typical:

> It is hereby declared to be the public policy of this state to accord to certified public school teachers the right to organize, to be represented, to negotiate professionally and to bargain on a collective basis with school committees covering hours, salary, working conditions and other terms of professional employment, provided, however, that nothing contained in this chapter shall be construed to accord to certified public school teachers the right to strike.[133]

In the absence of a statute either authorizing or prohibiting collective bargaining by teachers, the prevailing view today seems to be that teachers have that right.[134] In a 1965 opinion, the Attorney General of Kentucky observed:

---

[128] For a fuller discussion see Rezney, *Legal Problems of School Boards* (Cincinnati: The W. H. Anderson Co., 1966), chap. 6; Stinnett, Kleinmann, and Ware, *Professional Negotiation in Public Education* (New York: The Macmillan Company, 1966); "Collective Bargaining in the Public Schools: Discussion and Criticism of Some Recent Developments," *Chicago-Kent Law Review* 106 (1975); Edwards, "The Developing Labor Relations Law in the Public Sector," 10 *Duquesne Law Review* 357 (1972).

[129] Norwalk Teachers' Association v. Board of Education, 83 A.2d 482 (Conn. 1951).

[130] 29 U.S.C.A., 152.

[131] State v. American Federation of State, County and Municipal Employees, 298 A.2d 362 (Del. 1972); *See also* 48 Am. Jur. 2d, Labor and Labor Relations, 1142.

[132] See e.g., California Government Code 3501 (West 1966); Connecticut General Statutes Annotated, 179.61 (Supp. 1976); Florida Statutes Annotated, 839,221 (1965); Illinois Annotated Statutes, ch. 127, 63b 109 (7) (Smith-Hurd Supp. 1976); Minnesota Statutes Annotated, 179.61 (Supp. 1976); Rhode Island General Statutes Annotated, 28-9.3-1 (1968 Reenactment); Wisconsin Statutes Annotated, 111.70 (1974).

[133] Rhode Island General Stautes Annotated, 28-9.3-1 (1968 Reenactment).

[134] Norwalk Teachers' Association v. Board of Education, 83 A.2d 482 (Conn. 1951).

In the absence of prohibitory statute or regulation, there seems to be no reason why teachers and other employee groups in the public schools may not legally organize and bargain in a collective manner with their employer, the board of education. In fact, this office has previously advised that the courts in other jurisdictions are in general agreement that a teacher has a right to join a union.

There are states where a teacher's right to organize has been limited by statute. Missouri, for example, specifically excludes teachers from the statute which grants public employees the right to form and join labor organizations and to present proposals to any public body relative to salaries and other conditions of employment.[135] While the statute limits the right of teachers to join unions and bargain collectively, it is not as restrictive as it would appear. The Supreme Court of Missouri has held[136] that the statute does not prohibit negotiations between a voluntary teachers' association and a board of education regarding proposals for a revision of existing policies. In so holding, the court recognized the constitutional right to peacefully assemble and organize for any proper purpose and to speak freely and present grievances to any public officer or legislative body.

It must be recognized that even though a public school teacher may have the right to join a teacher's organization and meet with school officers regarding conditions of employment, teachers are not on equal footing with their counterparts in private industry. As a general rule, teachers are limited in both the scope of collective bargaining and in the means available to them to secure their demands.

17.16 REPRESENTATION ELECTIONS

Generally, before a school board is obligated to meet with a collective bargaining organization or union, it must be sure that the organization actually represents a majority of the teachers. Procedures for elections and certification are frequently set out in state statutes. As has been previously noted, teachers in Rhode Island have the statutory right to bargain collectively and to be represented by an association or labor organization. For a particular association or union to be recognized in Rhode Island as the bargaining representative of teachers in

the district, 20 percent of the certified teachers must file a petition with the state labor relations board stating that they wish to be represented by a particular union. The state labor relations board then holds an election and certifies the association or union selected by the majority as the representative of such teachers.[137] Once certified, that association or union is the sole and exclusive bargaining agent for all public school teachers in the district until such time as recognition is withdrawn.[138] While the procedure varies from state to state, the general rule is that, unless prohibited by law, the board of education may negotiate with a teachers' organization where it has received a majority vote of those eligible to vote in a representation election.[139] Generally, the organization receiving the majority of votes is recognized as the exclusive bargaining agent for the teachers.

17.17 EXTENT OF COLLECTIVE BARGAINING

Having concluded that, unless prohibited by statute, teachers may organize and bargain collectively, the next step is to examine the scope or proper subjects of collective bargaining. At the outset it must be recognized that the scope of collective bargaining in the public sector is not nearly as broad as it is in the private sector. While it is necessary to look to the statutes and case law in a particular jurisdiction to determine the precise limits of collective bargaining in that state, there are some general rules which have developed. Among the limitations commonly accepted are (1) that teachers may not bargain under the threat of strike, (2) that the public body (board of education) is charged with the responsibility of administering the affairs of the school system and some of those responsibilities cannot legally be delegated, and (3) that limitations of tax revenues and other funds restrict the benefits which can be granted to teachers.

---

[135]Missouri Annotated Statutes, 105.510 (1976 Supp.).

[136]Peters v. Board of Education of Reorganized School District, 506 S.W.2d 429 (Mo. 1974).

[137]Rhode Island General Statutes Annotated, 28-9.3-5 (1968 Reenactment); *See also* Wisconsin Statutes Annotated, 111.70 (4) (d) (1974).

[138]Rhode Island General Statutes Annotated, 28-9.3.3 (1968 Reenactment).

[139]Minnesota Federation of Teachers Local 59 v. Obermeyer, 147 N.W.2d 358 (Minn. 1966); Norwalk Teachers' Association v. Board of Education, 83 A.2d 482 (Conn. 1951). A board of education may conduct a representation election even in the absence of statutory authority. New Haven Federation of Teachers v. New Haven Board of Education, 237 A.2d 373 (Conn. 1967); *See also* City of Madison v. Wisconsin Employment Relation Commission,——U.S.——,97 S.Ct. 421 50 L.Ed. 2d 376 (Wis. 1976); Memphis American Federation of Teachers Local 2032 v. Board of Education, 534 F.2d 699 (6th Cir. 1976).

When teachers organize for the purpose of collective bargaining, a meaningful type of negotiation and bargaining is essential. Little is gained by friendly discussions about pleasant, but relatively insignificant, matters. Unless prohibited by law in the particular state, representatives of teacher organizations may meet with representatives of the board of education to discuss and bargain about matters of genuine substance—salary schedules, conditions of work, extra compensation for supplemental work, personnel policies, grievance procedures, sick leave, disability benefits, health programs, the school calendar, and similar issues.[140] It must be understood, however, that public employers need not capitulate to every demand and that the final decision on each item ultimately rests with the board of education in the discharge of the responsibility imposed upon it by law.[141] Usually, teacher representatives may furnish information and reports to representatives of the board, may present a list of proposals or demands to them, may discuss with them fully each of the items, and may argue vigorously for their adoption.

17.17a Threat of strike

In private industry, the most common method of enforcing recognition and collective bargaining is to strike. But, as has been previously observed, public employees generally do not have this right and they may not use the threat of strike as a method of enforcing their demands.[142]

17.17b Delegation

A teachers' association or union may organize and bargain collectively only for those items which are within the power of the board of education to grant. It is well recognized that a school board may not negotiate a contract which involves surrender of the board's legal discretion, is contrary to law, or is otherwise *ultra vires*.[143] Obviously, the answer to the question of whether or not there has been an improper exercise of the board's discretion will depend upon the particular state law which vests the school board with its power. For this reason, it is difficult to establish absolute rules concerning what are and are not proper subjects for collective bargaining. Furthermore, the law in this area is still in its infancy and there is considerable conflict between jurisdictions. Nevertheless, a few examples may serve to illustrate the problems.

Matters such as determination of teacher qualifications and the hiring and dismissal of teachers are usually regarded as being within the exclusive control of the board and are not proper subjects for collective bargaining. Under the New Jersey law, for example, public employers are obligated to meet and negotiate with employee representatives with respect to terms and conditions of employment. A teachers' association and a board of education negotiated a collective bargaining agreement which included a teachers' salary guide providing salary increments for each year of service. The board then passed a resolution which stated that such increments were not automatic and would only be granted to teachers who had rendered satisfactory service. This resolution was consistent with a state statute which provided that such increments could be withheld for inefficiency or other good cause. In upholding the board's right to withhold increments, the Superior Court observed:

> The statute authorized the board to withhold an increment for good cause and establishes a statutory policy which cannot be frustrated by the mere promulgation of a salary guide as part of a contract between the board and the association. . . . To accept the plaintiff's contention would destroy the inherent right of the board to exercise its preeminent function to pass upon the quality of teacher performance—a function which is manifestly a management prerogative beyond the reach of negotiations.[144]

Similarly, the Court of Appeals of Arizona has held[145] that the Board of Regents may not enter into a contract with a collective bargaining representative which would deprive it of its statutory duty to make decisions relating to appointments, employment, salaries, and removal of officers and employees. The decision was based in part on the fact that collective bargaining was not authorized by either the state constitution or by statute.

---

[140]*Ibid*. The school calendar is a negotiable item. Joint School District No. 8 v. Wisconsin Employment Relations Board, 155 N.W.2d 78 (Wis. 1967).

[141]Fibreboard Paper Products Corp. v. National Labor Relations Board, 379 U.S. 203, 85 S.Ct. 398, 13 L.Ed.2d 339 (D.C. 1964).

[142]Norwalk Teachers' Association v. Board of Education, 83 A.2d 482 (Conn. 1951).

[143]*Ibid*.

[144]Clifton Teachers' Association, Inc. v. Board of Education, 346 A.2d 107, 108 (N.J. 1975; *See also* Board of Education South Stickney School District III v. Johnson, 315 N.E.2d 634 (Ill. 1974).

[145]Communication Workers of America v. Arizona Board of Regents, 498 P.2d 472 (Ariz. 1972); *See also* Board of Education v. Scottsdale Education Association, 498 P.2d 587 (Ariz. 1972).

In an Illinois case a probationary teacher challenged the nonrenewal of his contract on the ground that the board failed to comply with the terms of the collective bargaining agreement which required the board to advise him of his deficiencies and afford him a hearing. The court recognized the general rule that the school board may not delegate matters of discretion, including the power to appoint and discharge teachers. It concluded, however, that the agreement in this case did no more than establish certain procedures consistent with the ordinary concept of fairness which the board agreed to follow and these procedures did not limit the power of the board to exercise its absolute discretion.[146]

One of the most frequently litigated questions is whether or not a contract provision which requires arbitration of disputes constitutes an improper delegation by the board. A recent Illinois case represents one line of thought on this problem. There, a teacher attempted to use the contractual arbitration procedure to challenge her involuntary transfer to another school. The arbitration provision was challenged on the ground that it constituted an improper delegation authority under the school code. The court in that case agreed with the district and held[147] that matters of teacher evaluation and appointment were specifically reserved to the board and could not be delegated or limited by contract. The court went on to distinguish between major and minor disputes and concluded that arbitration of minor disputes was permissible. This is not to say that arbitration has no place in a teacher's contract, for there are many jurisdictions where it is proper under the applicable state statute. In Pennsylvania, for example, it was held[148] that a school district could agree to submit the question of the propriety of a discharge to an arbitrator. The court relied, in part, on the fact that state law authorized arbitration of public employee disputes. Further, it emphasized the importance of providing an orderly mechanism for resolving disputes so as to avoid the use of economic force which is costly to the general public and may result in interruption of public services.

17.17c Fiscal limitations

There are certain financial limitations which restrict the power of the board in negotiating contract provisions relating to wages and fringe benefits. Generally, the board cannot commit funds which have not been appropriated or which are not within the limits of the estimated revenues of the district. The general rule was stated by the court in a Delaware case:

> ... at least one limitation upon the collective bargaining statute, and upon any agreement entered into thereunder, is that the State or any of its agencies cannot be bound to the expenditure of funds which have not been properly appropriated. This condition would pertain whether or not the parties formally recognized it by including it in the negotiated agreement.[149]

17.18 GOOD FAITH BARGAINING

Where a board of education bargains with representatives of a teacher organization, whether under compulsion of law or voluntarily, it should do so in good faith. Good faith bargaining generally requires a give-and-take discussion, the making of counterproposals, statement of the reasons for rejecting a demand, and the maintenance of a flexible position. The United States Supreme Court in a number of cases has interpreted the requirements of "good-faith bargaining" as they are applicable to private employers.[150] These same standards have frequently been cited as the rule in public employment collective bargaining. In a case involving the Winton Act (California's "meet-and-confer" statute), the California Court of Appeals outlined the school board's obligations with regard to good faith bargaining. Relying upon the holding

---

[146]Illinois Education Association v. Board of Education of School District No. 218, Cook County, 320 N.E.2d 240 (Ill. 1974). *Note:* "Non-Salary Provisions in Negotiated Teacher Agreements: Delegation and the Illinois Constitution, Article VII, Section 10," 24 *DePaul Law Review* 731 (1975).

[147]Board of Education, South Stickney School District III v. Johnson, 315 N.E.2d 634 (Ill. 1974); Board of Education v. Rockford Education Association, Inc., 280 N.E.2d 286 (Ill. 1972).

[148]Board of Education of the School District of Philadelphia v. Philadelphia Federation of Teachers, 346 A.2d 35 (Pa. 1975).

[149]State v. American Federation of State, County and Municipal Employees, 298 A.2d 362 (Del. 1972); *See also* Norwalk Teachers' Association v. Board of Education, 83 A.2d 482 (Conn. 1951).

[150]National Labor Relations Board v. American National Insurance Co., 343 U.S. 395, 72 S.Ct. 824, 96 L.Ed. 1027 (Tex. 1952); National Labor Relations Board v. Wooster Division of Borg-Warner Corporation, 356 U.S. 342, 78 S.Ct. 718, 2 L.Ed.2d 823 (Ohio 1958); National Labor Relations Board v. Truitt Mfg. Co., 351 U.S. 149, 76 S.Ct. 753, 100 L.Ed. 1027 (N.C. 1956); National Labor Relations Board v. Katz, 369 U.S. 736, 82 S.Ct. 1107, 8 L.Ed.2d 230 (N.Y. 1962); National Labor Relations Board v. Insurance Agents' International Union AFL-CIO, 361 U.S. 477, 80 S.Ct. 419, 4 L.Ed.2d 454 (1960); Fibreboard Paper Products Corp. v. National Labor Relations Board, 379 U.S. 203, 85 S.Ct. 398, 13 L.Ed.2d 339 (D.C. 1964).

in a case decided under the Labor Management Relations Act, the court stated:

> The statutory duty to bargain collectively . . . imposes upon the parties the obligation to meet . . . and confer in good faith with respect to wages, hours and other terms and conditions of employment with a view to the final negotiation and execution of an agreement. The statute states specifically that this obligation "does not compel either party to agree to a proposal or require the making of a concession." Thus the adamant insistence on a bargaining position is not necessarily a refusal to bargain in good faith. "If the insistence is genuinely and sincerely held, if it is not mere window dressing, it may be maintained forever though it produces a stalemate." . . . The determination as to whether negotiations which have ended in stalemate were held in the spirit demanded by the statute is a question of fact which can only be answered by a consideration of all the "subtle and elusive factors" that, viewed as a whole, create a true picture of whether or not a negotiator has entered into discussion with a fair mind and a sincere purpose to find a basis of agreement.[151]

17.19 THE RIGHT TO STRIKE

Although there are some states where public school teachers do have the right to strike,[152] these states are the exception rather than the rule and it has been held that if the legislature wishes to give public school teachers the right to strike it must do so in clear and unmistakable language.[153] Most states have enacted statutes which specifically prohibit teachers from striking.[154] The Wisconsin statute is typical in providing that "nothing contained in this subchapter [Municipal Employment Relations Act] shall constitute a grant of the right to strike by any county or municipal employee and such strikes are hereby expressly prohibited."[155]

Even in the absence of such a statute, courts generally hold[156] that public employees may not strike. The reasons are that there is no right to public employment, that the interest of the public is paramount, and that a strike by public employees is in effect a strike against the government and hence is against public policy. As the Supreme Court of Illinois observed: "the underlying basis for the policy against strikes by public employees is the sound and demanding notion that governmental functions may not be impeded or obstructed . . ."[157]

There have been numerous constitutional challenges to the prohibition against strikes by public employees and they have been almost unanimously unsuccessful. Even though employees in private industry have such a right, in no case has it been held that public employees have a constitutional right to strike. As the Rhode Island Supreme Court has observed:

> . . . the equal protection afforded by the Fourteenth Amendment does not guarantee perfect equality. There is a difference between a private employee and a public employee, such as a teacher who plays such an important part in enabling the state to discharge its constitutional responsibility. The need of preventing governmental paralysis justifies the "no strike" distinction we have drawn between the public employee and his counterpart who works for the private sector within our labor force.[158]

There have, however, been cases where school board policies or statutes have been held unconstitutional because, in addition to prohibiting strikes, they also prohibited constitutionally protected speech.[159]

17.19a Penalties

Even where teachers are prohibited from striking, slowdowns, walkouts, and strikes do occur. The school board's response to such collective activities will depend on the tools afforded by the law of the particular state. In many instances the board will seek

[151]San Juan Teachers Association v. San Juan Unified School District, 118 Cal.Rptr. 662 (Cal. 1975).

[152]Arizona Revised Statutes Annotated, 23-1303 (1973); Hawaii Revised Statutes, 89-12 (1972 Supp.); Louisiana Revised Statutes Annotated, 23:876 (1969); Nebraska Revised Statutes, 48-836 (1968); Pennsylvania Statutes Annotated, title 43, 1101-1101-4 (1971 Supp.).

[153]School Committee of Town of Westerly v. Westerly Teachers Association, 299 A.2d 441 (R.I. 1973).

[154]Minnesota Statutes Annotated, 179.64 (1976 Supp.); North Carolina General Statutes, 95-36-1 (1974); Rhode Island General Statutes Annotated 28-9.3-1 (1968 Reenactment); Wisconsin Statutes Annotated, 111.70 (4) (1974).

[155]Wisconsin Statutes Annotated, 111.70 (41) (1974).

[156]Head v. Special School District No. 1, 182 N.W.2d 887 (Minn. 1970); School Committee of Town of Westerly v. Westerly Teachers Association, 299 A.2d 441

(R.I. 1973); Jefferson County Teachers Association v. Board of Education, 463 S.W.2d 627 (Ky. 1970); Norwalk Teachers' Association v. Board of Education, 83 A.2d 482 (Conn. 1951); See also 37 A.L.R.3d 1147 (1971) and State v. Barshay, 364 A.2d 830 (Del. 1976).

[157]Board of Education v. Redding, 207 N.E.2d 427 (Ill. 1965).

[158]School Committee of Town of Westerly v. Westerly Teachers Association, 299 A.2d 441 (R.I. 1973).

[159]Aurora Educational Association v. Board of Education of Aurora Public School District, 490 F.2d 431 (7th Cir. 1974) declaring unconstitutional a school regulation which precluded a teacher from receiving full salary if, as a matter of dogma, he or she believed a teacher should be free to strike; See also Dause v. Bates, 369 F.Supp. 139 (Ky. 1973).

to enjoin the strike.[160] If the teachers violate the injunction by continuing the strike, they may be held in contempt of court. Furthermore, under some statutes the union or teacher association may be held in contempt and fined.[161]

In New York the law provides that for each day a teacher participates in an illegal strike, an amount equal to twice the person's daily rate of pay shall be deducted from his or her salary.[162] The ultimate penalty is discharge or nonrenewal of a teacher's contract. Such penalties are imposed in some states and have been upheld.[163]

17.20 ALTERNATIVES TO THE STRIKE

Recognizing that teachers usually do not have the benefit of economic pressure to enforce their demands, they must find effective substitutes for the right to strike. Publicizing undesirable situations by teacher organizations and accrediting agencies is one substitute. Another means frequently used is that of turning to an impartial third party or agency to assist in the resolution of disputes or impasses. Such procedures may result in binding decisions or in some cases merely advisory opinions. In either event, the primary goal is to bring about an orderly settlement of the dispute within a relatively short period of time.

Wisconsin's Municipal Employment Relations Act establishes a comprehensive scheme for the resolution of labor disputes in the public sector.[164] The act provides for mediation by the state employment relations commission if the parties so request. The function of the mediator is to encourage voluntary settlement by the parties; the mediator does not have the power of compulsion. Under the act the parties may agree to submit disputes pertaining to the meaning and application of the terms of a written collective bargaining agreement to an arbitrator. The act also provides for fact-finding. Fact-finding may be initiated by either party if the dispute has not been settled within a reasonable period of time and the parties have exhausted all available settlement pro-

cedures. If the commission determines that a deadlock does exist and decides that fact-finding should be initiated, it appoints a qualified, disinterested person or panel to serve as fact-finder. The fact-finder holds a hearing and issues written findings of fact and recommendations for solution of the dispute. Each party must then notify the other as to whether it will accept or reject the fact-finder's recommendations. Plans similar to that used in Wisconsin are being employed more and more frequently by public employers and employees in the settlement of labor disputes.

17.21 THE TREND

There is a definite trend toward greater use and acceptance of collective bargaining by public employees. An increasing number of states have recognized the value of good employee relations and have adopted statutes authorizing negotiation with teachers and other public employees. In addition, school boards and teacher organizations are seeking viable alternatives to strikes in order to bring about peaceful settlement of disputes.

17.22 SUMMARY

Teachers should be aware of the special requirements of the state in which they are employed regarding the making of a legal teacher contract. They should also understand that they may not be compensated for their services if they do not meet the specified requirements.

A teacher's contract is subject to the general provisions of the law relating to personal services. Thus, to be valid, the contract must be definite. It must contain a statement of the salary to be paid and the period of time the teacher is to work. Many of the rules governing the employer-employee relationship are embodied in statutes or regulations and a contractual provision which is in conflict with the statute is void. The contract cannot compel the teacher to agree to provisions which are not in accord with the law, i.e., to accept less than the minimum salary or to forgo sick leave or other benefits provided by state law. It must embody all "agreements" between the board of education and the teacher made in advance of signing the contract. Otherwise, they are "mere negotiations" and not enforceable.

Teachers may be employed for any period designated in the statutes. When the statutes are silent, the contract may be for any reasonable period agreed to by the teacher and the board. Unless it is specified otherwise in the teacher's contract, the teacher

[160]See, e.g., Joint School District No. 1, City of Wisconsin Rapids v. Wisconsin Rapids Education Association, 234 N.W.2d 289 (Wis. 1976).

[161]Kenosha Unified School District No. 1 v. Kenosha Education Association, 234 N.W.2d 311 (Wis. 1975).

[162]Wilson v. Board of Education, Union Free School District, 333 N.Y.S.2d 828 (1972).

[163]See, e.g., Dause v. Bates, 369 F. Supp. 139 (Ky. 1973) and Hortonville Joint School District No. 1 v. Hortonville Education Association, 423 U.S.821, 96 S.Ct. 2308, 49 L.Ed.2d 1 (Wis. 1976).

[164]Wisconsin Statutes Annotated, 111.70 (1974).

usually may collect salary for the period during which a school is legally closed, as for an epidemic. However, teachers may be required to carry on professional activities related to teaching while the school is closed. If a teacher holds a contract with a district which goes out of existence through reorganization, the teacher generally has a contract with the new district which embraces the territory of the original district.

The usual rules regarding damages for breach of contract apply to the teacher's contract. Thus, penalty clauses are unenforceable, but provisions for liquidated damages (a reasonable estimate of the actual damages) are enforceable. Teachers who are illegally dismissed must make a reasonable effort to secure other comparable employment to mitigate the damages. They are allowed to recover any expenses incurred in obtaining new employment or any added cost in carrying on the employment secured.

Most contracts give boards of education wide latitude in assigning teaching and other responsibilities. Teachers may be required to carry their fair share of extracurricular duties. If the teacher is willing to teach only certain subjects or grades, the contract should specify the subjects or grades the person is willing to teach.

Salary schedules are not contractual but are merely statements of policy which the board legally may modify at any time. Since teachers are employees and not officers, their salaries may be increased during the contract period.

A school contract in which a school board member has a direct pecuniary interest usually is void or at least voidable. A number of states prohibit school board members from employing relatives. Similarly, many states prohibit teachers from holding public office.

Teachers may join teachers' organizations and, unless prohibited by law, the organization may negotiate or bargain collectively with the board of education regarding salaries, working conditions, and other items. However, there are certain inherent limitations on the ability of teachers to secure their demands through collective bargaining. It must be recognized that in the majority of states teachers may not bargain under the threat of strike, that the board has the ultimate responsibility for operating the schools and some of its public responsibilities legally cannot be delegated, and that the limitations of public funds restrict the board's ability to agree to certain demands. While the parties must bargain in good faith, the school board need not capitulate to every demand made by the teachers' organization.

Generally teachers are prohibited from striking and such a restriction is constitutionally permissible as long as it does not prohibit teachers from exercising their rights under the First Amendment. When teachers violate the no-strike rule, they may be subject to certain penalties which may be imposed by statutes, the court, or the board.

While teachers do not enjoy all of the rights of private employees, the field of public employment labor relations is developing rapidly and teachers now have many rights not previously granted them.

Security of Employment of Professional and Classified Staff

18.0 INTRODUCTION

Over the years the extension of legal tenure to teachers has been a major issue in public education. It has been stoutly defended by teachers' organizations and professional groups; it has been strongly criticized by boards of education and many members of the lay public. More court cases involve tenure than any other teacher-related problem. Likely subjects of judicial review are the rights of a tenure teacher who has been dismissed, suspended, removed, or reassigned.

Security of employment of professional staff is anchored in four major categories of the law. The first two are found in state laws providing tenure or continuing contract status for teachers. The third is found in civil rights laws[1] guaranteeing freedom from discrimination based on race, sex, age, marital status, and other factors unrelated to job performance. The fourth category relates to rights guaranteed by federal and state constitutions. Judicial interpretations of these rights prohibit dismissal for exercising the constitutional rights of free expression, symbolic speech, etc. Cases based on each of the above categories will be presented in subsequent sections of this chapter.

In reviewing cases concerning tenure of teachers, principals, and superintendents, no effort has been made to exhaustively treat the multitudinous array of cases on the subject, many of which interpret specific statutory provisions and do not involve general principles of the law relating to tenure. In this chapter cases enunciating general principles must, of necessity be stressed.

18.1 HISTORY OF TEACHER TENURE

Teacher tenure is essentially civil service extended to teachers.[2] Thus, the history of teacher tenure actually started on January 16, 1883, when the first civil service act was passed by the United States government. In 1885 the National Education Association appointed a committee to study the question of tenure for school officials. The committee recommended that the principle of civil service be extended to the teaching profession. In 1886 Massachusetts enacted a law relating to tenure which permitted school districts to enter into contracts with teachers for a period longer than one year. In 1889 the Committee on Rules of the Boston School Community proposed a tenure law providing for a probationary period of one year, four years of annual elections, and thereafter permanent tenure subject to removal for cause after a proper hearing.

After the turn of the century teacher tenure spread rapidly through the United States, at first in larger cities and later on a statewide basis. In the 1930s, when jobs were scarce and contracts were not renewed for trivial or irrelevant reasons, a major effort was expended to attain the enactment of tenure laws and regulations. In the 1950s and 1960s, however, when teachers were scarce and jobs plentiful, the need for such laws subsided and fewer proposals for tenure legislation were introduced. Currently nearly all states have tenure or continuing contract laws for some or all teachers. In some states the laws are optional with local districts, or apply only to school systems of a given size, or exempt rural areas.

While historically it has been assumed that the legislature must enact laws pertaining to tenure to empower districts to adopt it, in at least one state it has been held[3] that a board of education was authorized to adopt a tenure system in the absence of state legislation.

18.2 NATURE OF TENURE

The National Education Association, one of the staunchest defenders of tenure, has set forth the objectives of tenure through its Committee on Tenure and Academic Freedom, as follows:

1. To protect the classroom teacher and other members of the teaching profession against unjust dismissal of any kind—political, religious, or personal;
2. To prevent the management or domination of the schools by political or noneducational groups for selfish and other improper reasons;
3. To secure for the teacher employment conditions which will encourage him to grow in the full practice of his profession, unharried by constant pressure and fear;
4. To encourage competent, independent thinkers to enter and to remain in the teaching profession;
5. To permit school management to devote more time to the cause of education and less time to personnel problems;
6. To set up honest, orderly, and definite procedures by which undesirable people may be removed from the teaching profession;

[1] Teachers commonly rely on the provisions of 42 U.S.C.A. 1983 as a basis for action, although Title VII as well as other Titles of the 1964 Civil Rights Act and subsequent amendments are increasingly utilized.

[2] McSherry v. City of St. Paul, 277 N.W. 541 (Minn. 1938); Johnson v. Board of Education, 419 P.2d 52 (Ariz. 1966); Pickering v. Board of Education of Township High School District, 225 N.E.2d 1 (Ill. 1967).

[3] Ironside v. Tead, 28 N.E.2d 399 (N.Y. 1940).

7. To protect educators in their efforts to promote the financial and educational interests of public school children;
8. To protect teachers in the exercise of their rights and duties of American citizenship; and
9. To enable teachers, in spite of reactionary minorities, to prepare children for life in a republic under changing conditions.[4]

School board members, and often members of the lay public, have denied that tenure accomplishes the stated objectives and have charged that any advantages afforded by tenure are offset by the greater difficulty of dismissing incompetent teachers. This difficulty is genuine, and frequently less aggressive administrators prefer to continue to employ an incompetent teacher rather than to fight a long, drawn-out legal battle for dismissal. If this were not a fact, an even greater number of tenure cases probably would be before the courts.

Whatever its shortcomings, it is generally agreed that tenure does achieve two desirable objectives: it protects good teachers from unjust dismissal and it provides an orderly procedure to be followed in the dismissal of incompetent members of a professional staff. These are objectives of major dimensions in the administration of staff personnel.

18.3 DISTINCTION BETWEEN NONRENEWAL AND DISMISSAL

In discussion of security of employment of teachers the terms nonrenewal or nonretention and dismissal are sometimes used interchangeably. While the net result of such actions may be the same, there is a substantial legal difference in the manner in which the termination operates. If not protected by tenure and no constitutional question is involved, a teacher may be nonrenewed without stating a reason, except as required by statute. In fact, some courts have held that a teacher may be nonrenewed for any reason or for no reason at all.[5] Most courts handing down decisions in this area reason that the contract has simply terminated and there is no expectation of future employment. Dismissal, on the other hand, whether under tenure or contract, is permissable only for a cause related to the teacher's performance or efficiency. The

stated cause must be proven by the board of education by relevant, sufficient evidence and the board has the burden of proof in establishing the unfitness of a teacher.[6] A dismissed tenured teacher is entitled to a due process hearing embodying all elements of fair procedure.[7]

Teachers under continuing contract laws have such rights as the statutes provide. Typically their termination of employment is by nonrenewal or nonretention and cases arise where boards of education have failed to accord the rights or follow the procedures detailed in the continuing contract statutes.

18.4 JUDICIAL ATTITUDE TOWARD TENURE LAWS

In the considerable litigation and interpretation of tenure laws by the courts there appear to be at least three basic ways in which tenure statutes have been interpreted.

1. Tenure statutes have been construed[8] strictly in favor of boards of education on the grounds that such statutes create a new liability on the part of boards and also are in dorogation of certain common-law rights.
2. Tenure statutes have been construed[9] in favor of the teachers who constitute the class designated as the primary beneficiaries of such legislation.
3. Tenure statutes have been construed[10] liberally to effect the general purpose of the legislation. That is, the courts have given major emphasis to promoting fundamental public policy in obtaining better education for the children of the state.

In the interpretation of tenure laws certain specific objectives of tenure have been recognized by the courts. An early California case indicated[11] that it was the purpose of teacher tenure legislation to protect competent and qualified teachers in the security of their positions. Similarly, an Ohio court

---

[4]National Education Association, *Trends in Teacher Tenure Through Legislation and Court Decisions* (Washington, D.C.: The Association, 1957), p. 8.

[5]Buhr v. Buffalo School District No. 39, 364 F.Supp. 1225 (N.D. 1973); *See also* DeLong v. Board of Education of Southwest School District, 303 N.E.2d 890 (Ohio 1973).

[6]Mass v. Board of Education of San Francisco Unified School District, 39 Cal.Rptr. 739 (1964).

[7]Wagner v. Elizabethton City Board of Education, 496 S.W.2d 468 (Tenn. 1973). *See also* Waller v. Board of Education, 328 N.E.2d 604 (Ill. 1975); Lovelass v. Ingram, 518 P.2d 1102 (Okla. 1973).

[8]Eveland v. Board of Education of Paris Union School District, 92 N.E.2d 182 (Ill. 1950); Anderson v. Board of Education of School District No. 91, 61 N.E.2d 562 (Ill. 1945).

[9]Andrews v. Union Parish School Board, 184 So. 552 (La. 1938).

[10]Swick v. School District of Borough of Tarentum, 14 A.2d 898 (Pa. 1940); Board of Education, Tucson H.S. Dist. No. 1 v. Williams, 403 P.2d 324 (Ariz. 1965).

[11]Mitchell v. Board of Trustees, 42 P.2d 397 (Cal. 1935).

determined[12] that the purpose of tenure legislation was to assure teachers of their employment during competence and good behavior. A Michigan court stated[13] that the purpose of tenure legislation was to protect teachers, after an adequate probationary period, against removal for unfounded, flimsy, or political reasons. Other interpretations of the purposes of teacher tenure statutes also have been given: to secure permanency in the teaching force;[14] to protect teachers and improve the school system;[15] to provide stability, certainty, and permanency of employment to those who demonstrate their fitness;[16] and to assure teachers that their employment depends upon merit and not upon the personal whims of individual citizens.[17]

Courts generally have viewed teacher tenure legislation in broader aspects and have judged it to be fundamentally in the public interest. They have ruled that it is the purpose of tenure laws to achieve permanency in the teaching staff and insure an efficient school system. The ultimate objective of this legislation, in the view of the courts, is to secure a better education for all children.

It is of interest, by way of contrast, to note what the courts have not considered to be the purpose of teacher tenure laws. It is not the purpose of tenure to interfere with the administration and control of the school with respect to policy and curricular offerings. This was the ruling[18] in an early Pennsylvania case involving the dismissal of a teacher because of decreasing enrollments in some areas of the curriculum and increasing enrollments in commercial courses. The dismissed teacher, although unable to teach in the commercial area, appealed under the tenure laws to retain his position. The courts denied the appeal. In another case the court ruled[19] that it was not the function of the tenure law to destroy or alter a district's financial plan. Involved here was the decision of a board of educa-

tion to discontinue kindergarten classes for economic reasons. A kindergarten teacher appealed under the tenure law to retain her position but the court ruled against her.

18.5 CONSTITUTIONALITY OF TENURE LAWS

When no limiting constitutional provision applies, state legislatures have plenary power over education. This principle applies to teacher tenure.[20] Even where relevant constitutional provisions exist, the courts have universally ruled in favor of tenure statutes.

For example, an early Indiana case held[21] that the tenure law did not violate the section of the constitution prohibiting discrimination or class legislation. Similarly, in a later case involving an interpretation of the Ohio Teachers' Tenure Act, it was held[22] that the act did not interfere with the constitutional principle of freedom to contract. In Pennsylvania it was found[23] that the tenure act did not contravene the constitution by creating offices for life or for terms longer than good behavior. Finally, in a case testing the validity of the teacher tenure law in Florida, it was held[24] that the law was not unconstitutional on the ground that the legislature was required to provide for a uniform system of free public schools in spite of the fact that the tenure law covered only one county. The constitutionality of tenure laws is now so well established that this issue is seldom litigated.

18.6 CONTRACTUAL NATURE OF TENURE

The question of whether a tenure law is contractual in nature is of considerable import to teachers. If a law is contractual in nature, it may not be repealed or amended except by mutual assent, and any rights once granted teachers may not be withdrawn unilaterally by the legislature. Mutual assent means agreement between the state and each individual teacher; therefore, the assent of every teacher must be obtained to amend a contractual tenure law.

Because of the permanency of contractual agreements, it is the legal presumption that the legislative enactments are not contractual, and anyone asserting the creation of a contract has the burden of overcoming this

[12]State ex rel. Weekly v. Young, 47 N.E.2d 776 (Ohio 1943).

[13]Rehberg v. Board of Education of Melvindale, 48 N.W.2d 142 (Mich. 1951).

[14]Pickens County Board of Education v. Keasler, 82 So.2d 19 (Ala. 1955).

[15]Donahoo v. Board of Education, 109 N.E.2d 787 (Ill. 1953).

[16]Frisk v. Board of Education of City of Duluth, 75 N.W.2d 504 (Minn. 1956).

[17]Hankenson v. Board of Education, 141 N.E.2d 5 (Ill. 1956).

[18]Jones v. Holes, 6 A.2d 102 (Pa. 1939).

[19]Ehert v. School District of Borough of Kulpmont, 5 A.2d 188 (Pa. 1939). But see Spencer v. Laconia School District, 218 A.2d 437 (N.H. 1966).

[20]Taylor v. Board of Education of City of San Diego, 89 P.2d 148 (Cal. 1939).

[21]McQuaid v. State ex rel. Sigler, 6 N.E.2d 547 (Ind. 1937).

[22]State v. Board of Education, 40 N.E.2d 913 (Ohio 1942).

[23]Malone v. Hayden, 197 Atl. 344 (Pa. 1938).

[24]State ex rel. Glover v. Holbrook, 176 So. 99 (Fla. 1937).

presumption. However, the presumption may be rebutted by evidence, as has been done in regard to teacher tenure laws in some states. The United States Supreme Court determined[25] that the language of the Indiana teacher tenure law created a preferential right of employment which was construed as being contractual in nature. In making this decision the court noted that, while the principal function of a legislative body is to make laws which declare public policy for the state, nevertheless a legislative enactment may contain provisions which become a contract between individuals and the state or its political subdivisions. The court noted too the number of times the word *contract* was used in the Indiana tenure law and held it was to be implied from the repeated use of the word that the legislature had intended to create a contract between the teacher and the state. The Alabama tenure law also was held[26] to be worded in a manner which created a contract between teachers and the state. Tenure statutes have been held contractual in Montana[27] and Nevada.[28]

In other states where this issue has been tested, tenure statutes[29] have been found merely to declare public policy for the regulation of the conduct of school officials in dismissing teachers. Rights under noncontractual statutes are not immune from modification and repeal by the legislatures, and they frequently have been amended and occasionally repealed in their entirety by legislative action. As a general rule, statutory tenure terms may be changed by the legislature but not by a board of education,[30] and a provision in a teacher's contract at variance with the teacher tenure law normally is held to be invalid.[31]

The reasoning in decisions holding tenure laws to be statements of legislative policy is that it is the business of the legislature to make laws, and generally not to make contracts which will bind the hands of future legislatures. Another reason why tenure legislation is not presumed to be con-

tractual was set forth[32] by the Wisconsin Supreme Court, which declared that the tenure statute granted gratuities, required nothing of the teacher as a requisite to acquiring tenure, involved no agreement, and consequently created no vested rights. However, ordinarily it is held that a tenure law in effect at the time of the signing of the contract becomes part of the contract between the teacher and the school district.[33]

18.7 ATTAINMENT OF TENURE-PROBATIONARY PERIOD

Tenure is attained only by complying with specific conditions prescribed by legislation. The nature of these conditions varies considerably among the several states, but certain provisions are included in most satisfactory enactments. Nearly all statutes require that teachers serve a period of probationary service before permanent tenure becomes effective, although two states do not require a probationary period. The usual probationary period is three years, during which time a teacher is employed on an annual contract. The final year of the probationary period must be completed before tenure begins. During the probationary period teachers are subject to the same regulations as any other teacher under contract. A school superintendent is ordinarily without authority to waive the probationary period.[34] Unless statutory enactment provides, unless there is expectation of continued employment, or unless nonrenewal is for a constitutionally impermissible reason there is no obligation on the part of the board to reemploy a teacher at the end of any probationary contract period, and seldom is there any requirement that the reasons for nonrenewal of contract be made known to the teacher. After completion of the probationary period and the awarding of the next contract, a teacher attains tenure and then is entitled to the rights and is subject to the responsibilities of the tenure law. It has been held[35] that tenure is acquired even though a permanent appointment is subject to the completion of certain preparation requirements.

The courts sometimes are obliged to determine what is meant by a year under the requirement that a teacher serve a specified number of years of probation before attain-

[25]Indiana *ex rel.* Anderson v. Brand, 303 U.S. 95, 58 S.Ct. 641, 82 L.Ed. 1123, 113 A.L.R. 1482 (Ind. 1938).

[26]Faircloth v. Fulmer, 40 So.2d 697 (Ala. 1949).

[27]State *ex rel.* Keeney v. Ayers, 92 P.2d 306 (Mont. 1939).

[28]Richardson v. Board of Regents, 261 P.2d 515 (Nev. 1954).

[29]Phelps v. Board of Education of West New York, 300 U.S. 319 65 S.Ct. 68, 89 L.Ed. 542 (N.J. 1937).

[30]Mannix v. Board of Education of City of New York, 260 N.Y.S.2d 811 (1965).

[31]Spencer v. Laconia School District, 218 A.2d 437 (N.H. 1966); See also State v. Hardy, 206 N.E.2d 589 (Ohio 1965).

[32]Morgan v. Potter, 298 N.W. 763 (Wis. 1941).

[33]Maxey v. Jefferson County School District, 408 P.2d 970 (Col. 1965).

[34]Elder v. Board of Education of School District No. 127½, 208 N.E.2d 423 (Ill. 1965). As to the right of a probationary teacher to a hearing, see Butler v. Allen, 287 N.Y.S.2d 197 (1968).

ing tenure. When the statutes fail to define the number of teaching days in a year, contractual provisions govern, and a year is held to be the school year. In Illinois[36] and New York,[37] however, the courts have interpreted a teaching year as a calendar year.

Service prior to the effective date of a tenure statute sometimes has been computed as a part of the probationary period. Such service generally must encompass the period immediately preceding the time when the statute took effect. Teachers in Colorado were not permitted to count prior service toward fulfillment of the probationary period unless they were reelected after the law became effective.[38]

Teachers may acquire tenure by estoppel or by inaction of the school board when they teach beyond the probationary period with the full knowledge and consent of the board and when the board continues to pay them.[39]

18.8 PART-TIME AND SUBSTITUTE TEACHERS

Part-time and permanent substitute teachers generally have been held to come within the provisions of the tenure statutes, as is illustrated by an early Indiana case[40] involving an art teacher employed to teach for twelve days in each school month. The board of education reduced the teacher's salary (legally comparable to dismissal), contending that the teacher was not on tenure status and hence as a "part-time" teacher was not protected by the tenure law. The court ruled that the tenure law did not require a teacher to teach every day or every hour of every day, and that the teacher was regularly employed and entitled to tenure. Similarly, in Minnesota the court ruled[41] that a substitute teacher who had to keep in constant readiness to teach when called upon was a regular teacher as defined under the Minnesota Teacher Tenure Act. More recently the Montana court ruled[42] that a

teacher who was requested by the board to teach only in the morning for seventeen hours per week had tenure rights. However, substitute teachers in many states do not acquire tenure.[43]

18.9 UNCERTIFICATED TEACHERS

A somewhat different question was presented in a 1958 Florida case.[44] Here a teacher taught for three years outside the field in which she was certified. She then was certificated in the field in which she was teaching (elementary) and appointed to teach for a fourth year. In proceedings to compel the board of education to acknowledge the teacher's tenure status and to issue the teacher a contract, the court ruled that the three years of teaching outside the field counted toward the statutory probationary period. However, it was held[45] in Louisiana that a teacher who did not qualify for a regular certificate but taught under a temporary certificate did not acquire a tenure status.

18.10 TERMINATION OF EMPLOYMENT PRIOR TO THE EFFECTIVE DATE OF TENURE

When a teacher's employment was terminated prior to the effective date of a tenure act, it was held[46] that the teacher was not entitled to permanent status even though the dismissal was wrongful and she had served longer than the probationary period. On the other hand, where employment was not terminated until after the effective date of the legislation, it was held[47] that tenure was established even though notice of dismissal was given prior to the effective date of the legislation.

18.11 TENURE OF OTHER PROFESSIONAL EMPLOYEES

In some jurisdictions the statutes quite clearly define which school employees are entitled to the benefits of tenure legislation; in others they are not so clear. Consequently, there is some question as to whether certain supervisory or administrative personnel come under tenure laws.

---

[35]Mannix v. Board of Education of City of New York, 260 N.Y.S.2d 811 (1965).

[36]Wilson v. Board of Education, 68 N.E.2d 257 (Ill. 1946).

[37]Grace v. Board of Education, 241 N.Y.S.2d 429 (N.Y. 1963).

[38]Dugan v. School District No. 1, Arapahoe County, 265 P.2d 998 (Col. 1954).

[39]Gunthorpe v. Board of Education, 246 N.Y.S.2d 462 (1963); Wooten v. Byers School District No. 32J, 396 P.2d 964 (Col. 1964).

[40]Sherrod v. Lawrenceburg School, 12 N.E.2d 944 (Ind. 1938).

[41]McSherry v. City of St. Paul, 277 N.W. 541 (Minn. 1938).

[42]State *ex rel.* Saxtroph v. District Court, Fergus County, 275 P.2d 209 (Minn. 1954).

[43]Council v. Donovan, 244 N.Y.S.2d 199 (1963); Brodie v. School Committee of Easton, 324 N.E.2d 922 (Mass. 1975).

[44]State *ex rel.* Alderman v. Board of Public Instruction of Palm Beach County, 105 So.2d 510 (Fla. 1958).

[45]State *ex rel.* Sibley v. Ascension Parish School Board, 64 So.2d 221 (La. 1953).

[46]Walter v. Topper, 11 A.2d 649 (Pa. 1940).

[47]Shaffer v. Johnson, 5 A.2d 157 (Pa. 1939).

18.11a Supervisors

In Louisiana a parish supervisor of classroom instruction holding a teacher's certificate is a "teacher" within the meaning of the tenure laws.[48] In Tennessee it was held[49] that a supervisor of public schools for a county was a teacher under the meaning of the Tennessee tenure laws. Similarly, under the tenure laws of Pennsylvania, which specify tenure protection for professional employees, the courts held[50] that the term *professional employees* included principals and other supervisory personnel.

18.11b Principals

In California it was decided[51] that principals do not secure tenure in that capacity. If a person has previously gained tenure as a teacher, that person retains the classification of permanent teacher when promoted to the position of principal. A similar result also has been obtained in tenure regulations in some city systems, but in most states having teacher tenure laws the principal is able to secure tenure as a principal. Needless to say, one must be legally qualified for the position of principal to attain tenure at this rank. In two states (New York and Kentucky) a principal may not acquire tenure except on recommendation of the superintendent. As is true of teachers, the principal normally must serve a probationary period, and is generally subject to dismissal for the same reasons as are teachers.

If principals gain tenure rights as teachers, they may be removed from the principalship and assigned teaching responsibilities. However, if tenure is attained as a principal, a person cannot be reassigned to a teaching position except under unusual conditions, such as closing of the school of which that person is principal,[52] because a principal usually does not retain tenure rights as a teacher after leaving the classroom and attaining tenure rights as a principal. However, a principal may be directed to do some teaching, and refusal to comply with the request is insubordination, justifying dismissal.[53]

18.11c Administrative assistants

Whether a person who abandoned teaching duties and accepted the position of administrative assistant had tenure was at issue in a Minnesota case. Here it was held[54] that leaving the position of teacher for the administrative post did not constitute abandonment of tenure rights.

18.11d Superintendents

While principals normally may acquire tenure either as teachers or as principals in states having teacher tenure laws, the same is not true of superintendents. In most states their right to tenure has not been upheld by the courts. However, tenure is granted to superintendents in New Jersey[55] and, if the superintendent spends a given amount of time per day in the classroom, also in Colorado.[56] The Indiana Supreme Court ruled[57] that the superintendent was a teacher within the teacher tenure act. An Illinois case held[58] that the character of the service of superintendents and their relationship to the board of education would require a clear declaration of intent to bring them under the tenure act. A few years later the Illinois Supreme Court declared[59] that the tenure law covered all school district employees required to be certified, and since superintendents were certified, they were covered by the tenure law.

Even if superintendents have acquired tenure in one district, they are not covered when they move to other districts. Like teachers and principals, they must establish tenure in the new district by serving a probationary period. However, statutes may provide for a shorter period than the original probationary requirement. The court of Minnesota held[60] that with a liberal construction the tenure act could be construed to embrace the superintendent within its provisions but it refused to so liberally construe the tenure statute. Likewise in Ohio a discharged county superintendent's claim to a position of elementary supervisor based on tenure was denied,[61] the court finding

[48]State ex rel. Parker v. Vernon Parish School Board, 62 So.2d 111 (La. 1952).

[49]Mayes v. Bailey, 352 S.W.2d 220 (Tenn. 1961).

[50]Hautz v. School District of Borough of Coraopolis, 55 A.2d 375 (Pa. 1947).

[51]Board of Education, City of Los Angeles v. Swan, 261 P.2d 261 (Cal. 1953).

[52]Smith v. School District of Township of Darby, 130 A.2d 661 (Pa. 1954); Jantzen v. School Committee of Chelmsford, 124 N.E.2d 534 (Mass. 1955); Verrett v. Calcasieu Parish School Board, 103 So.2d 560 (La. 1958).

[53]Shockley v. Board of Education of Laurel Special School District, 149 A.2d 331 (Del. 1959).

[54]Board of Education, City of Minneapolis v. Sand, 34 N.W.2d 689 (Minn. 1948).

[55]New Jersey Statutes Annotated, 18A:28-5 (4) (1969).

[56]Colorado Revised Statutes, 22-63-102(9) (1973).

[57]School, City of Lafayette v. Highley, 12 N.E.2d 927 (Ind. 1938).

[58]Biehn v. Tess, 91 N.E.2d 1960 (Ill. 1950).

[59]McNely v. Board of Education of Community Unit District No. 7, 137 N.E.2d 63 (Ill. 1956); See also Lester v. Board of Education of School District No. 119, 230 N.E.2d 893 (Ill. 1967).

[60]Eelkema v. Board of Education, 11 N.W.2d 76 (Minn. 1943).

[61]State ex rel. Saltsman v. Burton, 103 N.E.2d 740 (Ohio 1952).

that the Ohio tenure laws do not cover those in an administrative capacity. Tenure rights under the Rhode Island tenure laws are limited to those described in the act, which does not include superintendents.[62]

18.12 PROCEDURE IN NONRENEWAL AND DISMISSAL

The question of the proper procedure to be followed in dismissal of teachers and other professional employees is most important. It has been established that, within the legal framework of tenure statutes, the board of education determines what in its opinion is cause for dismissal.[63] It need not conduct a hearing prior to reaching a decision to recommend that dismissal proceedings be begun.[64] Where a teacher's contract is nonrenewed or terminated at the end of the contract period the procedure to be followed is dictated largely by state statutes and/or the expectation of continued employment. Judicial interpretation of the status of probationary teachers and those under continuing contracts appear to vary by jurisdictions. In Nebraska, for example, nonrenewal of the contract of a teacher under the continuing contract law may be for "any cause whatsoever or for no cause at all."[65] Under Missouri law the school board may legally notify a teacher that his or her contract will not be renewed without providing the teacher a statement of alleged deficiencies or an opportunity to correct them.[66] In Oregon a nontenured teacher is not entitled to a pretermination hearing[67] and a simple notice is all that is required in nonrenewal of the contract of a nontenured teacher.[68] In Delaware a school board is not required to account for its decision not to renew the contract of a teacher who has not acquired tenure.[69] Even when the statute requires a notice of nonrenewal for nontenured teachers, it does not create a property right requiring a due process hearing.[70]

Other states and jurisdictions have accorded the nontenured teacher more rights.

In Arkansas, for example, a teacher with fifteen years of experience is entitled to a due process hearing. A meeting of the teacher and school officials does not constitute such a hearing.[71] In California probationary teachers are vested with the right of continued employment. Therefore the rule which permits nonrenewal where the board believes it has substantial evidence to justify its action must be replaced by the independent review rule, i.e., the court must make an independent review of the evidence to determine if nonrenewal is justified.[72] Where the statutes provide that probationary teachers may be nonrenewed only upon an adverse recommendation of the superintendent this is a prerequisite to termination and a collective bargaining agreement to the contrary is void.[73] Under Oklahoma law a notice of nonrenewal which contains no statement of reasons for nonrenewal is ineffective to terminate employment.[74]

Teachers who are entitled to a due process hearing must be notified in advance of the nature of the testimony to be given against them and the names of the witnesses. They are also entitled to a copy of the supervisors' memoranda which will be used against them in the hearing.[75] Teachers must be given sufficient time to prepare for a hearing to meet the requirements of due process. When a teacher requested a hearing on March 29 and it was scheduled at 4:00 P.M., March 30, the teacher was not accorded due process.[76] Teachers under tenure have the right to cross-examine witnesses,[77] this being a right of due process guaranteed by the Fourteenth Amendment.

Teachers may not be dismissed for political reasons or for exercising their constitutional rights. However, when a teacher claims that dismissal is based on the exercise of constitutional rights the burden of proof is on the teacher.[78] Where a teacher is dismissed for engaging in rights protected by the First Amendment the case may be taken directly to the federal courts without

---

[62]Irish v. Collins, 107 A.2d 455 (R.I. 1954).

[63]Jepsen v. Board of Education, 153 N.E.2d 417 (Ill. 1958).

[64]Board of Education, Tucson H.S. Dist. No. 1 v. Williams, 403 P.2d 324 (Ariz. 1965).

[65]Schultz v. Board of Education of Dorchester, 222 N.W.2d 578 (Neb. 1974).

[66]White v. Scott County School District No. R-V, 503 S.W.2d 35 (Mo. 1973).

[67]Hawkins v. Linn County School District, 517 P.2d 330 (Ore. 1973).

[68]Irby v. McGowan, 380 F.Supp. 1024 (Ala. 1974).

[69]Newman v. Board of Education of Pleasant School District, 324 A.2d 387 (Del. 1974).

[70]Shirck v. Thomas, 486 F.2d 691 (7th Cir. 1973).

[71]Wagnor v. Little Rock District, 373 F.Supp. 876 (Ark. 1974).

[72]Young v. Governing Board of Oxnard School District, 115 Cal.Rptr. 456 (1974); Pendray v. Board of Trustees of Lodi Unified School District, 116 Cal.Rptr. 695 (1974).

[73]Johnson v. Nyquist, 361 N.Y.S.2d 431 (1974).

[74]Lovelace v. Ingram, 518 P.2d 1102 (Okla. 1973).

[75]Parker v. Letson, 380 F.Supp. 280 (Ga. 1974).

[76]Fisher v. Independent School District No. 118, 215 N.W.2d 65 (Minn. 1974).

[77]Forman v. Creighton School District No. 11, 351 P.2d 165 (Ariz. 1960).

[78]Amburgey v. Cassady, 607 F.2d 728 (6th Cir. 1974).

exhaustion of state administrative remedies.[79]

A letter from a superintendent of schools recommending dismissal of a teacher cannot be used as a substitute for notice to the teacher and a hearing where such is required by the statutes.[80] The board is also the proper tribunal to determine whether a teacher is to be dismissed for cause, and it may conduct an independent inquiry to verify such cause prior to a formal hearing.[81] Courts will not set aside decisions of boards of education unless the decisions are without foundation or evidence.[82]

Most tenure laws prescribe procedures for dismissing a teacher. The procedures generally include the service of notice, the right of the teacher to a hearing, the right to be represented by counsel, and similar provisions. When the statutes expressly provide that removal or dismissal is to follow certain procedures, at least all essential steps must be substantially complied with to make the action legal.[83]

The board has the burden of proof in establishing the unfitness of the teacher.[84] It may not automatically place a teacher who has been found to be physically unfit on the inactive list. The regular procedure for dismissal must be followed, including a hearing if one is required by law.[85] A teacher on tenure is normally entitled to a hearing before being retired for disability.[86]

The power to dismiss or remove a teacher may be exercised by the proper school authorities as specified in the statutes. However, such power may also be implied from the power to employ. In either case the power to dismiss or remove is subject to the limitations imposed by the statutes. Teacher tenure statutes are considered as imposing restrictions on the former power of the board of education to renew or not to renew contracts at will. If the statutes provide for the dismissal of a teacher by a particular officer or board, this authority may not be exercised by anyone else, since the statutory power to dismiss cannot be delegated.[87] Where the power to conduct the proceedings has been divided between the local board of education and a state agency, this statutory division of responsibility must be respected.[88]

It is the obligation of the teacher to take notice of all statutory provisions with respect to dismissal or removal since they are automatically incorporated as terms of the contract.[89] A teacher should also note all rules of the board of education which may affect the board's power to dismiss the teacher.[90]

A teacher who was denied tenure was not permitted an appeal to a public grievance board in New York since the denial of tenure is not a grievance contemplated by the statute. Here it was held[91] that the tenure statutes were controlling, and since the teacher had no case under the tenure provisions, she had no cause of action.

In dismissal of tenured teachers as a general rule seniority must be recognized. When a teacher is dismissed because of having less seniority in a given department, the teacher is entitled to employment in other areas in which he or she is competent and has greater seniority than other teachers.[92] Where written notice is required in cases of dismissal, sending the minutes of the board meeting to all teachers affected is not sufficient.[93] It was held in one instance that a tenured teacher may not be removed as coach without a due process hearing.[94] However, in other cases the right of school boards to relieve a tenured teacher of coaching responsibilities while continuing as a teacher has been upheld.[95] Even where the facts indicate that sufficient reasons for

[79]Plano v. Baker, 502 F.2d 595 (2d Cir. 1974).

[80]State v. Jefferson Parish School Board, 188 So.2d 143 (La. 1966); Hankenson v. Board of Education of Waukegan Tp., 134 N.E.2d 356 (Ill. 1956).

[81]Griggs v. Board of Trustees of Merced Union High School District, 389 P.2d 722 (Cal. 1964).

[82]Last v. Board of Education, Com. Unit School District, 185 N.E.2d 282 (Ill. 1962).

[83]Tempe Union High School District v. Hopkins, 262 P.2d 387 (Ariz. 1953); Boyd v. Collins, 182 N.E.2d 610 (N.Y. 1962).

[84]Mass v. Board of Education of San Francisco Unified School District, 39 Cal.Rptr. 739 (1964).

[85]Brown v. Board of Education of City of New York, 254 N.Y.S.2d 60 (1964); Stone v. Gross, 269 N.Y.S.2d 81 (1966); Munter v. Gross, 248 N.Y.S.2d 717 (1964).

[86]Munter v. Gross, 248 N.Y.S.2d 717 (1964); Stone v. Gross, 269 N.Y.S.2d 81 (1966); Brown v. Board of Education of City of New York, 254 N.Y.S.2d 60 (1964).

[87]Davis v. School Committee of Somerville, 30 N.E.2d 401 (Mass. 1940).

[88]In re Fulcomer, 226 A.2d 30 (N.J. 1967); Neal v. Bryant, 149 So.2d 529 (Fla. 1962).

[89]Chehock v. Independent School District, 228 N.W. 585 (Iowa 1930).

[90]Hendryz v. School District No. 4, 35 P.2d 235 (Ore. 1934).

[91]Pinto v. Wynstra, 250 N.Y.S.2d 1012 (1964).

[92]Amos v. Union Free School District No. 9, 364 N.Y.S.2d 640 (1975).

[93]Glover v. Board of Education, 316 N.E.2d 534 (Ill. 1974).

[94]Davis v. Barr, 373 F.Supp. 740 (Tenn. 1973).

[95]Richards v. Board of Education, Jt. School District No. 1, 206 N.W.2d 597 (Wis. 1973); Hennessey v. Grand Forks School District, 206 N.W.2d 876 (N.D. 1973); See also Lukac v. Acocks, 466 F.2d 577 (6th Cir. 1972); Chiodo v. Board of Education of Special School District No. 1, 215 N.W.2d 806 (Minn. 1974).

nonrenewal existed, a trial court has discretion to award the teacher reasonable attorney fees and some costs.[96] Teachers are entitled to remuneration for periods in which they are suspended pending a hearing to determine whether dismissal is justified.[97] Where the judgment to dismiss a teacher made by the local board is based on a comprehensive professional evaluation made by the county superintendent the state board of education may not overrule the local board.[98]

In situations involving the dismissal or nonretention of teachers, efforts often have been made to evaluate their competence to determine which teachers are to be continued in employment. If the tests or evaluations utilized are racially motivated or biased they may not be employed.[99] The board has responsibility for developing objective and nondiscriminatory criteria.[100] Once proper criteria have been established, merit qualifications may be applied.[101] In some instances the National Teachers Examination (NTE) has been used in an effort to develop objective criteria. In Mississippi[102] where the use of the NTE scores together with other data resulted in dismissal of a large number of black teachers and only a few white teachers, use of the tests was not permissable. In Texas the court held the use of the NTE scores was incompatible with "Affirmative Action" in hiring, promotion, and dismissal.[103] However, the NTE was held to be a reasonable criterion in teacher selection in Virginia.[104] Here the minimum score for unacceptability fell in the bottom tenth to fifteenth percentile. The court reasoned that the board is not prevented

from upgrading its faculty by employing the best qualified applicants.

18.12a Notice of charges

The statutory procedure of giving notice to the teacher of the alleged grounds for dismissal must be followed. Even when there is no statutory requirement of notice of charges, such notice must be given to fulfill the requirements of due process. The notice normally must be in writing and it must be served upon or otherwise given to the teacher. Unless some other mode of service is expressly authorized, as by registered or certified mail, personal delivery of the notice to the teacher is contemplated.[105] The notice should fix the date and place of hearing as well as specify the charges against the teacher.[106] A teacher is entitled to bring witnesses to the hearing and to have legal counsel present.[107] A teacher may waive a failure to receive notice in the prescribed mode or form by appearing at the hearing and making no objection to any discrepancy in procedure.

Where statutes provide that charges against a teacher may be filed by patrons of the school district, the charges may be so filed.[108] Generally, however, the duty of bringing charges against the teacher is vested in the board of education.[109] The filing of charges need not follow the strict practice of the courts with respect to form and language, but the charges must be in writing if the statutes so stipulate.[110] They must also be filed within the time prescribed by the statute.[111]

Where notification of dismissal must be given by a specified date, and a hearing is required, the hearing does not have to be held by the date specified. It is sufficient if it is held within a reasonable time. However, it is not reasonable to schedule the hearing at 4:00 P.M. the day after the teacher is notified of the date of the hearing; ample time must be allowed to permit the teacher

[96]Goodman v. Bethel School District No. 403, 524 P.2d 918 (Wash. 1974); See also Campbell v. Gadsen County School Board, 534 F.2d 650 (5th Cir. 1976); de Groat v. Newark Unified School District 133 Cal.Rptr. 225 (1976); Black v. School Committee of Malden, 341 N.E.2d 896 (Mass. 1976).

[97]Jerry v. Board of Education, 354 N.Y.S.2d 745 (1974); Hodgkins v. Central School District No. 1, 355 N.Y.S.2d 932 (1974).

[98]Zeitschel v. Board of Education of Carroll City, 332 A.2d 906 (Md. 1975).

[99]Perry v. Sindermann, 408 U.S. 593, 92 S.Ct. 2694, 33 L.Ed.2d 578 (Tex. 1972); Karstetter v. Evans, 350 F.Supp. 528 (Tex. 1971); See also Nichols v. Echert, 504 P.2d 1369 (Alaska 1973).

[100]Smith v. Concordia Parish School Board, 445 F.2d 285 (5th Cir. 1971).

[101]Carter v. West Feliciana Parish School Board, 432 F.2d 285 (5th Cir. 1971).

[102]Baker v. Columbus Municipal Separate School District, 329 F.Supp. 706 (Miss. 1971), 462 F.2d 1112 (5th Cir. 1972).

[103]United States v. State, 330 F.Supp. 235 (Tex. 1971).

[104]United States v. Nansemond County School Board, 351 F.Supp. 196 (Va. 1972).

[105]Robel v. Highline Public Schools, District No. 401, 398 P.2d 1 (Wash. 1965).

[106]Belen Municipal Board of Education v. Sanchez, 405 P.2d 229 (N.M. 1965).

[107]Springfield School District v. Shellem, 328 A.2d 535 (Pa. 1974).

[108]Schrader v. Cameron Tp. School District No. 6, 266 N.W. 473 (Iowa 1936).

[109]Gaderer v. Grossmont Union High School Dist., 13 P.2d 401 (Cal. 1932).

[110]Harrison v. State Board of Education, 48 A.2d 579 (N.J. 1946); Devlin v. Bennett, 213 A.2d 725 (Conn. 1965).

[111]Eidenmiller v. Board of Education, 170 N.E.2d 792 (Ill. 1960).

to organize a defense against the charges.[112] The court is the judge of what period of time is reasonable.[113] It was held[114] that a notice of nonemployment required to be sent at least thirty days before the end of the school year was timely when sent thirty days before the last day teachers were required to be present even though classes had ended several days earlier.

Earlier, a variety of statements met the statutory requirement that a board of education give the reason for dismissal in its notice of nonemployment. For example, (1) the board desires a change of person in the position;[115] (2) complaints from parents;[116] (3) the interest of the school requires the teacher's dismissal.[117] More recently, the charges must relate more specifically to educational practices if the dismissal of the teacher is to be upheld. Several reasons were set forth in a 1974 case.[118] They included (1) leaving the classroom unattended; (2) making interracial sexual statements in class; (3) failing to provide the substitute teacher with lesson plans and the classbook for roll call; (4) walking in the hall during a free period making notes which upset other teachers and pupils; and (5) refusing to accept professional criticisms and suggestions for improvement. Stating the reason for dismissal in a reasonably clear way constitutes substantial compliance with the statutory requirements. Tenure provisions do not call for a greater exactness in the written complaint than in a civil complaint.[119] The charges must give fair notice of their essential nature. If they are not sufficiently specific to enable the teacher to prepare a case, the teacher should be able to obtain the particulars by a timely demand.[120] An Illinois case stated that the notice "must fairly apprise the teacher of the alleged deficiency upon which the employer-school board bases its action, and with sufficient specificity to enable the teacher to refute the charge."[121]

18.12b Hearing

With teachers entitled to both substantive and procedural due process, in many situations they are entitled to a hearing whether provided by statutes or not. If the teacher is deprived of liberty or property,[122] or if dismissal is alleged to be for exercise of constitutional rights of free speech or other constitutional guarantees, including the right of privacy, the teacher is entitled to due process. When the teacher alleges expectation of continued employment or dismissal because of activities related to representing the local teacher's association as an official, the teacher is entitled to a hearing.[123] The teacher may still be dismissed if dismissal is warranted, but a fair hearing is required. The board may not circumvent the requirement of a hearing by holding a hearing devoid of the aspects which make it a fair and adequate hearing.[124] A teacher must be given an opportunity to present evidence and call witnesses.[125] Likewise, the hearing must be held at a reasonable time and in a reasonable place.[126] It must be borne in mind, however, that there are many situations, not included in the above categories, where teachers are not entitled to a hearing.[127]

18.12c Decision of the board

In dismissal of teachers the board's action must be supported by relevant, probative, and sufficient evidence.[128] The courts gen-

---

[112]Fisher v. Independent School District No. 118, 215 N.W.2d 65 (Minn. 1974).

[113]Horner v. Board of Trustees of Excelsior Union High School District of Los Angeles, 389 P.2d 713 (Cal. 1964); Mesna v. Dawson, 389 P.2d 721 (Cal. 1964).

[114]State ex rel. Brown v. Board of Education, 124 N.E.2d 721 (Ohio 1955).

[115]State ex rel. Bohanon v. Wanamaker, 289 P.2d 647 (Wash. 1955).

[116]State ex rel. Knight School District v. Wanamaker, 281 P.2d 846 (Wash. 1955).

[117]Pearson v. Board of Education, 138 N.E.2d 326 (Ill. 1956).

[118]Simon v. Jefferson Davis Parish School Board, 289 So.2d 511 (La. 1974).

[119]Board of Education of Ashland School District v. Chattin, 376 S.W.2d 693 (Ky. 1964).

[120]Ibid.

[121]Wade v. Granite City Community Unit School District No. 9, 218 N.E.2d 19 (Ill. 1966).

[122]Perry v. Sindermann, 408 U.S. 593, 92 S.Ct. 2694, 33 L.Ed.2d 578 (Tex. 1972).

[123]Johnson v. Fraley, 470 F.2d 179 (4th Cir. 1972); Schnellhaase v. Woodbury Central Community School District, 439 F.Supp. 988 (Iowa 1972); Pardue v. Livingston Parish School Board, 251 So.2d 833 (La. 1970); Hostrop v. Board of Junior College District No. 515, 337 F.Supp. 955 (Ill. 1972), 471 F.2d 488 (7th Cir. 1972).

[124]Bates v. Hinds, 334 F.Supp. 528 (Tex. 1971).

[125]Rehberg v. Board of Education of Melvindale, 77 N.W.2d 131 (Mich. 1956); Anderson v. Westwood Community School District, 212 N.W.2d 232 (Mich. 1973).

[126]Wagner v. Little Rock School District, 373 F.Supp. 876 (Ark. 1973). See also Hardy v. Independent School District No. 694, 223 N.W.2d 124 (Minn. 1974); Letson v. Parker 380 F.Supp. 280 (Ga. 1974).

[127]Hix v. Tulaso-Midway Independent School District, 489 S.W.2d 706 (Tex. 1972); Gibson v. Butler, 484 S.W.2d 356 (Tenn. 1972).

[128]Tipton v. Board of Education of Blount County, 165 So.2d 120 (Ala. 1962); Tessier v. Board of Education, 260 N.Y.S.2d 789 (1965); Brummitt v. Board of Education, 250 N.Y.S.2d 937 (1964); Watts v. Seward School Board, 421 P.2d 586 (Alaska 1966); Morey v. School Board of Independent School District No. 492, 148 N.W.2d 370 (Minn. 1967).

erally will sustain boards of education if their judgment is based on substantial evidence. This is frequently referred to as the "substantial evidence rule." However, some courts insist that the proper basis, particularly in cases involving constitutional rights, is the "independent judgment rule." These two bases determine whether a court will accept the judgment of the board if it is not unreasonable, capricious, or arbitrary,[129] or whether the court will itself review the evidence and make an independent judgment.[130]

Since any appeal to or review by the court on the merits will be based on the record made at the hearing, it is desirable, if not essential, for a court reporter to be present to make a record of the proceedings. It is also desirable for the board's decision to take the form of written findings of fact. In some states, this is required.[131] The court in a Minnesota case remanded the matter back to the school board to make proper findings of fact. It said:

> In a case such as the present one, where the school board, acting in a quasi-judicial capacity, might have based its resolution on any or all of several grounds, findings of fact are vital to prevent substitution of the reviewing court's judgment for that of the school board's. Without findings of fact, the trial court had no way of knowing upon which of the four charges the school board based its decision. If the trial court were to review the merits of the case without findings of fact, there would be no safeguard against judicial encroachment on the school board's function since the trial court might affirm on a charge rejected by the school board.[132]

Usually it is sufficient if the majority of the quorum at a school board meeting votes for dismissal. However, the statutes may require that the decision be by majority of the full membership of the board.[133] Where the affirmative vote of four members of the board of education is required for dismissal, it is not legally sufficient that only three members vote for dismissal.[134]

In California the statutes provide that the school board shall assume all expenses of the hearing. However, it was held[135] that this prescription did not extend to the payment of attorney's fees for the teacher. In this case the court upheld the discharge, finding that proper procedure had been followed in determining that the teacher was incompetent on several counts—lack of self-control, inability to discipline pupils, lack of courtesy and cooperativeness with fellow workers, poor classroom procedures, and lack of emotional stability, among others.

The board may find that the evidence does not sustain the charges and dismiss the proceedings. The teacher is then restored to former status. The board also may voluntarily withdraw the charges prior to hearing.[136]

18.12d Judicial review

The primary purpose of judicial review of a decision of an administrative agency is to keep the agency within the jurisdictional and judicial bounds prescribed by law and to guard the rights of the parties which are guaranteed to them by the constitution or the statutes.[137] In the exercise of this responsibility the court has a duty to review the record of the hearing to satisfy itself that relevant, probative, and substantial evidence supports the board's findings and conclusions.[138] The court may determine whether evidence received in an executive session following the adjournment of the hearing was prejudicial to the teacher.[139] It will review the fairness of the proceedings, but the fact that the same board acted as an investigative body, as a prosecutor, and as the adjudicator does not ordinarily constitute a denial of due process[140] and it generally has been held[141] that the board of edu-

[129]Ray v. Minneapolis Board of Education, 202 N.W.2d 375 (Minn. 1972); Hickey v. Board of School Directors of Pennsylvania Manor School, 328 A.2d 549 (Pa. 1974); Beverlin v. Board of Education of Lewis County, 216 S.E.2d 554 (W.Va. 1975).

[130]Francisco v. Board of Directors of Bellevue Public Schools, 537 P.2d 789 (Wash. 1975).

[131]Morey v. School Board of Ind. School District No. 492, 136 N.W.2d 105 (Minn. 1965).

[132]Morey v. School Board of Ind. School District No. 492, 128 N.W.2d 302 (Minn. 1964).

[133]Wisconsin Statutes 118.22(2) (1972).

[134]Agner v. Smith, 167 So.2d 86 (Fla. 1964).

[135]Griggs v. Board of Trustees of Merced Union High School District, 389 P.2d 722 (Cal. 1964).

[136]McFerran v. Board of Education, Central School Dist. No. 1, 251 N.Y.S.2d 48 (1964).

[137]Hankenson v. Board of Education of Waukegan Tp., 134 N.E.2d 356 (Ill. 1956).

[138]Ibid.

[139]Moffett v. Calcasieu Parish School Board, 179 So.2d 537 (La. 1965).

[140]Griggs v. Board of Trustees of Merced Union High School District, 389 P.2d 722 (Cal. 1964).

[141]Leach v. Board of Education, 295 A.2d 582 (Del. 1972). See also Duke v. North Texas State University, 469 F.2d 829 (5th Cir. 1972); Bates v. Hinds, 334 F.Supp. 528 (Tex. 1971); White v. Board of Education, 501 P.2d 358 (Hawaii, 1972). Contra, King v. Caesar Rodney School District, 380 F.Supp. 1112 (Del. 1974); Francisco v. Board of Bellvue Public Schools, 525 P.2d 278 (Wash. 1974); See also Hortonville Jt. School District No. 1 et al. v. Hortonville Education Association, 423 U.S. 821, 96 S.Ct. 2308, 49 L.Ed.2d 1 (Wis. 1976); Schneider v. McLaughlin Independent School District No. 21, 241 N.W.2d 574 (S.D. 1976).

cation is an impartial tribunal in cases involving the dismissal of teachers. A trial de novo before the court is normally not permitted.[142] New evidence usually should not be received at the judicial hearing.[143] On this point the New Mexico Supreme Court observed:

> However, at the conclusion of the reception of the evidence, the court announced that none of such evidence would be considered, and that the decision would be based solely upon the record of the proceedings before the local and state boards. We think that the court was able to disregard the additional evidence and that no prejudice resulted to the local board.[144]

Of course, the appeal or review procedure from the findings of the board must be taken in accordance with the law of the particular state. Where administrative remedies are provided, they must first be exhausted.[145]

18.13 REASONS FOR TERMINATION OF SERVICE

Because of the great amount of litigation relating to the dismissal of teachers broad generalizations are difficult relative to causes which (either under statutes, contract, or proper exercise of discretionary power) have been held to be sufficient to constitute grounds for dismissal. However, certain principles can be deduced from court cases. A teacher may not be removed or dismissed for any other cause when the statutes specifically enumerate the causes for which a teacher may be discharged.[146] Nevertheless, in some cases the legislature clearly intended that other causes may also serve as bases for dismissal by including the provision that dismissal may be for any other good or just cause. But even in these instances the cause must be of a character similar to those enumerated, i.e., the doctrine of ejusdem generis applies.[147] In a 1965 Mississippi case the court said:

> The phrase, "or other good cause," in the statute must be considered in connection with the specific causes preceding it. It is a well recognized rule of law that where in a statute general words follow a designation of particular charges, the meaning of the general words will be presumed to be restricted by the particular designation, and to include only things of the same kind, class, or nature as those specifically enumerated, unless there is a clear manifestation of a contrary purpose.[148]

The legal provision of dismissal for any good or just cause refers to the teacher's fitness or capacity to discharge teaching duties.[149] Any grounds put forward by a board of education must be in good faith and not arbitrary, irrational, unreasonable, or irrelevant to the board's task of building an efficient school system.[150] "Good cause" vests a discretion trammeled only by proof of abuse.[151]

Where the statutes do not specify what constitutes good cause, the power to determine this question is in the hands of the board of education. This power may not be exercised unreasonably or arbitrarily.[152] A contract may specify grounds for dismissal where the statutes are silent or where it is clear that the grounds expressed by statutes are not intended to be exclusive of all others.[153]

A variety of reasons for dismissal have appeared over a period of time, some of them of recent origin. Among them are: condition of health, both physical and mental; age; causing or supporting disruption; engaging in illegal activities; using offensive language; personal appearance; sex-related activities; insubordination; incompetency or inefficiency; neglect of duty; unprofessional conduct; subversive activities; decreased need for services; marriage; civil rights activities; political activities; and, reasons such as intoxication and use of drugs. While some overlapping appears in the above classification, it seems desirable to treat these reasons for dismissal as separate categories and court cases related to them are presented in the following sections.

18.13a Health—physical and mental

Dismissal for physical illness has not been a source of extensive litigation. With at least some sick leave provisions almost universally granted, teachers usually are cov-

---

[142]Parker v. Board of Trustees of Centinela Val. U. H.S. District, 51 Cal.Rptr. 653 (1966); Foster v. Carson School District No. 301, Skamania County, 385 P.2d 367 (Wash. 1963).

[143]Belen Municipal Board of Education v. Sanchez, 405 P.2d 229 (N.M. 1965).

[144]Ibid., p. 231.

[145]Board of Public Instruction of Taylor County v. State, 171 So.2d 209 (Fla. 1964).

[146]City of Elwood v. State, 180 N.E. 471 (Ind. 1932).

[147]Stiver v. State ex rel. Kent, 1 N.E.2d 1006 (Ind. 1936).

[148]Madison County Board of Education v. Miles, 173 So.2d 425, 427 (Miss. 1965).

[149]Ibid.

[150]Davis v. School Committee of Somerville et al., 30 N.E.2d 401 (Mass. 1940).

[151]Muehle v. School District No. 38, 100 N.E.2d 805 (Ill. 1951).

[152]Eveland v. Board of Education, 92 N.E.2d 182 (Ill. 1950).

[153]Consolidated School District v. Millis, 139 P.2d 138 (Okla. 1943).

ered during short periods of illness. In some instances teachers with prolonged illnesses are covered under a "sick-leave bank" established by other teachers or by board action. Such provisions have been upheld[154] by the courts. When teachers are ill, boards often exhibit a degree of leniency, thus eliminating the need for court action. However, in earlier cases the courts upheld[155] dismissal for reaons of physical illness. Courts have not permitted dismissal for illness related to pregnancy.[156]

Currently the issue of dismissal because of mental illness or disorder has engaged the attention of the courts. Sometimes mental illness is also associated with physical unfitness and related problems. In a New York case a teacher who became a drug user as a result of admitted psychological problems was legally dismissed on the basis of mental and physical unfitness.[157] In a California case, where a teacher was hospitalized for mental illness and a psychiatric test showed the teacher unfit to teach, dismissal was upheld.[158] In a similar situation a New York court upheld[159] the dismissal of a teacher who received an unfavorable psychiatric report indicating that there was sufficient evidence of impaired psychological health to render him incapable of effective service as a teacher. A teacher who in public view dressed and undressed a mannequin in a lewd and suggestive manner was considered mentally unbalanced and was legally dismissed.[160] Teachers dismissed for alleged mental disorder, and thus deprived of reputation and good name, are entitled to a due process hearing with full opportunity to rebut the charges. This is true whether or not a teacher has acquired tenure.[161]

18.13b Age

With federal regulations prohibiting discrimination because of age[162] and similar state regulations clearly stated, boards of education are rarely involved in court action on this issue. However, a few cases involving dismissal for age have been adjudicated. It has been well established that either the state or boards of education may establish a retirement age.[163] A mandatory retirement age that does not apply to other state employees may be established for elementary and secondary teachers. Such a regulation or statute does not violate the equal protection clause of the Fourteenth Amendment.[164] Where a tenured principal was refused a contract following his 65th birthday, neither the statutes prohibiting discrimination because of age nor any constitutional rights were violated.[165]

On a somewhat different issue, a board of education found it necessary to reduce the number of teachers and terminated a teacher at age 62 who was rated as barely satisfactory. The courts upheld[166] the termination even though other teachers age 62 and older who performed in a more proficient manner were retained.

18.13c Causing or supporting disruption

While the courts are assiduous in guarding teachers' civil and constitutional rights to demonstrate peacefully, wear armbands, and petition for rights, teachers may not incite or cause disruptions. Thus, the dismissal of a teacher who was involved with a group creating disruption was upheld.[167] A teacher may also be dismissed for inviting students to participate in disruptive activities if the disruption actually occurs.[168] In this instance the teacher also suggested to the students that they should get ROTC off the campus and made remarks to an ROTC sergeant that disrupted classes and the orderly operation of the school. In Ohio a teacher was dismissed legally after contesting the school administrator's orders to return to classes.[169] Two additional cases

[154]Syracuse Teachers Association v. Board of Education of Syracuse, 345 N.Y.S.2d 239 (1973).

[155]Riggins v. Board of Education, 300 P.2d 848 (Cal. 1956).

[156]Paxman v. Wilkerson, 390 F.Supp. 442 (Va. 1975).

[157]Anonymous v. Board of Examiners, 318 N.Y.S.2d 163 (1973).

[158]Alford v. Department of Education, 91 Cal.Rptr. 843 (1971).

[159]Coriou v. Nyquist, 304 N.Y.S.2d 486 (1969). See also Appeal of Watson, 105 A.2d 576 (Pa. 1954).

[160]Bleint v. Marion County School Board, 366 F.Supp. 727 (Mass. 1973); Wishart v. McDonald, 500 F.2d 1110 (1st Cir. 1974).

[161]Lombard v. Board of Education of City of New York, 502 F.2d 631 (2d Cir. 1974).

[162]See Civil Rights Amendment, 1967.

[163]Frantz v. Baldwin-Whitehall School District, 331 A.2d 484 (Pa. 1975); Harren v. Middle Island Central School District No. 12, 373 N.Y.S.2d 20 (1975); King v. Cochran, 419 F.Supp. 53 (Ark. 1976); Monnier v. Todd County Independent School District, 245 N.W.2d 503 (S.D. 1976).

[164]Lewis v. Tucson School District No. 1, 531 P.2d 199 (Ariz. 1975).

[165]Kennedy v. Community Unified School District No. 7, 319 N.E.2d 243 (Ill. 1974).

[166]Frantz v. Baldwin-Whitehall School District, 331 A.2d 484 (Pa. 1975).

[167]Vanderzandon v. Lowell School District No. 71, 369 F.Supp. 67 (Ore. 1973).

[168]Birdwell v. Hazelwood School District, 491 F.2d 490 (8th Cir. 1974).

[169]Whitsel v. Southeast Local School District, 484 F.2d 1222 (5th Cir. 1973).

occured at the university level which upheld the dismissal of professors who aided disruption.[170] In a number of cases teachers have been terminated or dismissed for causing friction and disruption among the professional staff. However, since these cases more directly involved issues related to civil rights they will be presented in Section 18.13o.

18.13d Illegal activities

Whether or not a person charged or convicted of illegal activities can be dismissed has sometimes been the subject of court action. A criminal offense in some instances may by statute be made the basis for dismissal action against teachers.[171]

A person who has been charged with a criminal act may be dismissed from a teaching position even though the charges later are dropped. The evidence required for a dismissal action may be less than that required in criminal court proceedings.[172] If the action is long delayed or unproven, the teacher is entitled to a due process hearing.[173] There are numerous cases where teachers have engaged in illegal activities related to a strike action in states where public employees are prohibited from engaging in work stoppage or strikes. Leading cases in this area are presented in Chapter 17.

18.13e Offensive language

While teachers are guaranteed the same freedom of speech as are other citizens, this freedom is not absolute. The courts will always balance the teacher's right to constitutional guarantees against the rational relationship of a given rule to school operation.[174] In some situations the courts have adjudicated the right of teachers to use language considered by others to be offensive.[175] In one case a tenured teacher was discharged for using offensive language and applying corporal punishment which had been prohibited by superiors after an earlier encounter with pupils. The federal district court upheld[176] the dismissal. In another

situation an emotionally disturbed teacher kicked students, used obscene language, and committed other offenses. After a voluntary leave and extensive litigation, the question of dismissal revolved around the teacher's right to a due process hearing. The teacher was held[177] to be entitled to the hearing. In a Colorado case a teacher-assistant principal concocted offensive stories about people with Spanish surnames, which embarrassed some of his students. After a hearing and collection of facts the teacher-assistant principal was reinstated but his contract was not renewed. The board's action was sustained.[178] The contract of a teacher who made remarks in a class relative to sex activities of blacks and whites was properly terminated.[179] It was also held[180] that a tenured teacher could be dismissed for requiring fifth grade pupils to write vulgar four-letter words. In Florida a nontenured teacher was offered a tenure contract if he would refrain from discussing his personal experiences with prostitutes, masturbation, and homosexuals. The teacher brought suit holding that these restrictions violated his right of free speech. The court held[181] that freedom of speech did not extend to this type of discussion in classes composed of fifteen-year olds. The teacher had a clear choice: accept the terms of the contract or seek other employment.

In a rather unusual case a teacher was dismissed for writing allegedly obscene letters to a boy who had graduated from the high school the previous year. The boy's mother found the letters among his personal effects and turned them over to the police. Local newspapers learned of the letters and ran stories about them. The court ruling[182] in the teacher's favor, said that although the letters contained language that some adults would find gross, vulgar, and offensive, an eighteen-year old male would find them unsurprising and fairly routine. In any case it was not the teacher who made the letters public; that was the action of others for which the teacher was not responsible.

[170]Dougherty v. Walker, 349 F.Supp. 629 (Mo. 1972); Rozman v. Elliot, 335 F.Supp. 1086 (Neb. 1971); See also Shields v. Watrel, 333 F.Supp. 260 (Pa. 1971).

[171]California Statutes Education: 13206 (1975).

[172]Board of Education of El Monte School District v. Calderson, 110 Cal.Rptr. 915 (1973).

[173]Moore v. Knowles, 482 F.2d 1069 (5th Cir. 1973).

[174]Cook v. Hudson, 365 F.Supp. 855 (Miss. 1973).

[175]Board of Directors of Kennewick School District v. Coates, 287 P.2d 102 (Wash. 1955); Palo Verde School District v. Hensey, 88 Cal.Rptr. 570 (1970); Wood v. Goodman, 381 F.Supp. 413 (Mass. 1974).

[176]Wood v. Goodman, 381 F.Supp. 413 (Mass. 1974).

[177]Lombard v. Board of Education of City of New York, 502 F.2d 631 (2d Cir. 1974); See also Stevenson v. Wheeler County Board of Education, 426 F.2d 1154 (6th Cir. 1970).

[178]Merritt v. Consolidated School District No. 8, 522 P.2d 137 (Col. 1974).

[179]Simon v. Jefferson Davis Parish School District, 289 So.2d 511 (La. 1974).

[180]Celestine v. Lafayette Parish School Board, 284 So.2d 250 (La. 1973).

[181]Moore v. School Board of Gulf City, 364 F.Supp. 355 (Fla. 1973).

[182]Jarvella v. Willoughly East Lake School District, 233 N.E.2d 143 (Ohio 1967).

18.13f Personal appearance

The early 1970s witnessed considerable controversy relative to regulation of the personal appearance of members of the teaching staff. The courts were torn between the authority of boards of education to adopt reasonable rules concerning the operation of schools and the right of self-expression guaranteed, or at least implied, in the Constitution. The decisions often attempted to distinguish between those aspects of appearance (dress) which could be applied to the schoolroom only and which would leave teachers free to appear as they desired at other times, and those aspects of appearance which must necessarily be the same both in school and out, such as haircuts and beards. However, this distinction appeared superficial in consideration of constitutional guarantees.

The furor over teachers' appearances has subsided, perhaps as a result of the general acceptance by society of varying life styles and appearance in the total population. However, as late as 1974 a case was decided on this issue in which it was held[183] that, since the appearance of the faculty affects both students' appearance and the educational process, it could properly be controlled by the board. The court did not view the wearing of a beard or sideburns as presenting a significant constitutional issue.

In other cases related to the personal appearance of teachers the court decided[184] in a Tennessee case that a teacher may be dismissed for failure to follow a school dress code and refusing to shave. On the other hand, a Mississippi case held[185] that a dress code violated the teacher's constitutional rights. The court did point out, however, that if the teacher's grooming detracted from the ability to teach or the students' ability to learn, the board could take reasonable action to rectify the situation. In a Louisiana case it was held[186] that a male teacher could be compelled to wear a necktie while in school. In California a teacher was upheld[187] in wearing a beard. The court held this to be one of the liberties protected by the Fourteenth Amendment. In another case a teacher of French, who was considered a superior teacher, was not reappointed because he wore a goatee. The

teacher was black and wore the goatee as a matter of racial pride. He claimed that the nonretention violated his constitutional rights and the court agreed.[188] In a Massachusetts case it was held[189] that a teacher who was dismissed for wearing a beard was entitled to back pay and $1000 damages. The case was not decided upon the substantive issue but on the bases that the teacher was not informed of the charges or told that refusal to shave off his beard would result in his dismissal, nor was he given the rights of due process to which he was entitled.

18.13g Sex-related activities

While increasing evidence indicates that life styles of teachers which vary from the norm are less likely to result in their dismissal than formerly, teachers may not engage in activities which are clearly detrimental to classroom teaching and the sound operation of the school. Courts still hold that the right of teachers to teach does not depend solely on their conduct in the classroom.[190] Offensive actions outside the school can pervade the classroom and make effective instruction impossible. The courts have so held in a number of cases related to sexual activities. In some instances the teacher's acts have resulted in dismissal or transfer from teaching assignments. In other instances teachers have been separated from teaching by revocation of their license to teach. Since the net results is the same, all leading cases related to termination of employment are treated together.

In a New Jersey case a male teacher who exhibited abnormal behavior, underwent sex reassignment, and became a woman was legally dismissed. The court agreed[191] that retention of the teacher in the school system could result in potential emotional harm to the students. A number of cases related to homosexual activities have been adjudicated in recent years and the decisions are difficult to reconcile. In a 1967 California case the court upheld[192] the revocation of a teacher's credentials on the basis that he made sexual advances to another male on a public beach. Two years later a California court refused[193] to revoke the license of a

[183]Miller v. School District No. 167, 495 F.2d 658 (7th Cir. 1974).

[184]Morrison v. Hamilton County Board of Education, 494 S.W.2d 770 (Tenn. 1973).

[185]Conard v. Goolsby, 350 F.Supp. 713 (Miss. 1972).

[186]Blanchet v. Vermilion Parish School Board, 220 So.2d 534 (La. 1969).

[187]Finot v. Pasadena City Board of Education, 250 C.A.2d 189 (1967).

[188]Braxton v. Board of Public Instruction of Duval County, 303 F.Supp. 958 (Fla. 1969).

[189]Lucia v. Duggan, 303 F.Supp. 112 (Mass. 1969).

[190]Meinhold v. Clark County School District, 506 P.2d 420 (Nev. 1973). See also Moore v. Knowles, 482 F.2d 1069 (5th Cir. 1973); Erb v. Iowa State Board of Public Instruction, 216 N.W.2d 339 (Iowa 1974).

[191]Re Grossman, 316 A.2d 39 (N.J. 1974).

[192]Sarac v. State Board of Education, 57 Cal.Rptr. 69 (1967); See also Board of Education of Long Beach v. Millette, 133 Cal.Rptr. 275 (1976).

[193]Morrison v. Board of Education, 461 P.2d 375 (Cal. 1969).

teacher for a homosexual act which occurred in the private apartment of another male. In a 1977 case (Gaylord v. Tacoma School District No. 10, 559 P.2d 1340 [Wash. 1977]) the State Supreme Court upheld the dismissal of a homosexual teacher. The U.S. Supreme Court refused Certiorari, thus permitting the decision to stand (C.C.H. U.S. Supreme Court Bulletin page B 35).

At the college level, the Minnesota Supreme Court upheld[194] the right of the Board of Regents to refuse to approve the employment of a librarian who was a member of FREE (Fight Repression of Erotic Expression) and who planned to secure a license to marry a homosexual friend. However, a person may not be transferred from a teaching position for making public statements about homosexuality, although in this case deliberate concealment of significant information about his participation in a homosexual club was held against him.[195]

In a California case a teacher and her husband were members of a "swinger's club" which engaged in "wife swapping". The teacher engaged in two acts of sexual relations with other men which were viewed by her husband. The court upheld[196] the revocation of the teacher's license. In this instance the building principal found the teacher's work satisfactory and the board had agreed to rehire her.

A California court upheld[197] the dismissal of a teacher for oral copulation in a doorless toilet stall in a downtown store. Even though the evidence was obtained in an unconstitutional manner and was not admissible in a criminal case, the court justified the dismissal as necessary to protect pupils from an undesirable moral influence. In another California case it was held[198] that a teacher could be dismissed for a sex offense even if the charges were not proven in criminal court.

The courts have been unanimous in upholding the dismissal of teachers for having sexual relations with a student or a former student. In Washington a junior high school teacher was dismissed for having engaged in sexual relations with a student. Such ac-

tivity was deemed detrimental to the best interest of the school.[199] A school board may conduct an investigation into allegations that a school counselor slept with an eighteen-year-old former student for approximately two months after counseling her. Such an investigation was upheld against a claim that it violated the right of privacy and suspension of the teacher without pay was sustained.[200] It was stated that a teacher-counselor must be held to a strict standard of conduct and the likely presumption was that the affair started when the girl was his counselee. An Illinois court affirmed[201] the dismissal of a teacher who admitted being partially undressed in a car with an eighteen-year-old high school student. The board had not erred in limiting the number of character witnesses or in failing to receive evidence that the criminal prosecution growing out of the incident had resulted in acquittal. In a case at the junior college level a teacher, after class, drove a female student to a dark street near the college and parked. A deputy sheriff seeing the parked car investigated and found the couple apparently engaged in sexual relations. The teacher shouted at the deputy to get away and then knocked him down by opening the car door. The deputy later apprehended the teacher after a high speed chase. On the basis of the above facts the teacher was dismissed and the court sustained[202] the action of the board.

However, dismissal of teachers for sexual activities and alleged immoral activities has not always been sustained by the courts. It was held[203] in Alabama that an unmarried pregnant teacher's contract could not be cancelled based on a charge of immorality. The evidence to sustain the board's case was solicited by the superintendent from the teacher's physician, thus violating the teacher's right to privacy. It has also been held[204] that a teacher eight and one-half months pregnant, married one month, could not be dismissed legally. Nor could a teacher be dismissed for having frequent overnight guests, friends of her son, which

[194]McConnell v. Anderson, 451 F.2d 193 (8th Cir. 1971).
[195]Acanfora v. Board of Education of Montgomery City, 491 F.2d 498 (4th Cir. 1974); See also Ferndale Education Association v. School District for City of Ferndale, 242 N.W.2d 481 (Mich. 1976).
[196]Pettit v. State Board of Education, 513 P.2d 889 (Cal. 1973).
[197]Governing Board of Mountain View School District v. Metcalf, 36 Cal.3d 546 (1974).
[198]Board of Education of El Monte School District v. Calderon, 35 Cal.3d 490 (1973).

[199]Denton v. South Kitsap School District No. 402, 516 P.2d 1080 (Wash. 1973).
[200]Goldin v. Board of Education, 357 N.Y.S.2d 867 (1974).
[201]Yang v. Special Charter School District No. 150, 296 N.E.2d 74 (Ill. 1973); See also Wishert v. McDonald, 367 F.Supp. 336 (Mass. 1973).
[202]Board of Trustees of Compton Junior College District v. Stubblefield, 94 Cal.Rptr. 318 (1971).
[203]Drake v. Covington County Board of Education, 371 F.Supp. 974 (Ala. 1974); But see Brown v. Bathke, 416 F.Supp. 1194 (Neb. 1976).
[204]Reinhardt v. Board of Education, 311 N.E.2d 710 (Ill. 1974).

resulted in inferences against her moral character. The board failed to show that the inferences made her incapable of instructing or maintaining discipline.[205] It also has been held[206] that barring a teacher from employment in public schools merely because she had previously had an illegitimate child is illegal.

18.13h Insubordination

Insubordination is a recognized cause for dismissal.[207] Teachers are required to obey reasonable rules and regulations of the board of education, whether they were in force at the time of employment or enacted later. Reasonableness requires that the teacher be given adequate notice of such rules.

Two Louisiana cases are illustrative of what has been held to be insubordination or lack of cooperation. In one instance a teacher refused to allow supervisory personnel to enter his classroom even when advised that this was a regulation of the board of education. In the opinion of the court dismissal was justified.[208] Similarly, dismissal was upheld[209] when a high school industrial arts teacher refused to obey an order from his superiors to build, with his students' assistance, certain forms needed for paving a sidewalk at the school. Failure to complete financial records as required by the superintendent also was held[210] to be sufficient reason for discharge. A teacher was guilty of insubordination for refusal to obey a school board directive to take a general aptitude test.[211] In this instance the teacher had not met certification requirements and could be dismissed at any time. A teacher who refuses to complete forms to be used in evaluation of the foreign language and social studies department is guilty of insubordination and legally may be dismissed.[212] Such action does not violate the teacher's constitutional right of free speech. A teacher who refused the superintendent's request for information of a reasonable nature, i.e., whether the teacher planned to return the following year, and urged other teachers not to provide the information requested, was subject to dismissal.[213] A teacher guilty of distribution of flyers in violation of board policy was guilty of insubordination.[214] Such action is not protected by the constitutional guarantee of freedom of speech.

Teachers must conform to reasonable policies of the board and follow designated procedures. A Pennsylvania teacher who was unable to cope with the students and was unwilling to conform to procedures required by the board was dismissed legally.[215] Boards of education may require an annual physical examination of teachers to be performed by a physician of the teacher's choice, and teachers who refused to comply are guilty of insubordination.[216] Refusal of a teacher to conform to a grooming code which required male teachers to be clean shaven constituted insubordination in a Tennessee case.[217] A teacher supposedly out on sick leave was seen taking a walk and apparently in good health. When the teacher refused to explain the situation or submit evidence of his illness, the court upheld[218] his dismissal for insubordination. Teachers may be compelled to send their children to public rather than private schools. Such a requirement does not violate the teacher's constitutional rights under the Fourteenth Amendment, although earlier it was so held.[219] Such a policy had a rational relationship to the quality of education in the opinion of the court.

It was held,[220] however, that a teacher need not obey the rules of the superintendent which are not rules of the board of

[205]Fisher v. Snyder, 476 F.2d 375 (8th Cir. 1973).

[206]Andrews v. Drew Municipal Separate School District, 371 F.Supp. 27 (Miss. 1973).

[207]Johnson v. United School District, 191 A.2d 897 (Pa. 1963); Stiver v. State ex rel. Kent, 1 N.E.2d 1006 (Ind. 1936); Yuen v. Board of Education of School District No. U-46, 222 N.E.2d 570 (Ill. 1966).

[208]Tichenor v. Orleans Parish School Board, 144 So.2d 603 (La. 1962).

[209]State ex rel. Williams v. School Board, 147 So.2d 729 (La. 1962).

[210]Board of Education of Ashland School District v. Chattin, 376 S.W.2d 693 (Ky. 1964).

[211]Garner v. Louisiana State Board of Education, 277 So.2d 492 (La. 1973).

[212]Ray v. Minneapolis Board of Education, 202 N.W.2d 375 (Minn. 1972); See also Leach v. Board of Education, 295 A.2d 582 (Del. 1972); Drown v. Portsmouth School District, 451 F.2d 1106 (1st Cir. 1971), cert. denied, 402 U.S. 972, 91 S.Ct. 1659, 29 L.Ed.2d 137 (N.H. 1971); Doran v. Board of Education, 285 N.E.2d 825 (Ind. 1972).

[213]Pietrunti v. Board of Education of Brick Township, 319 A.2d 262 (N.J. 1974).

[214]Gilbertson v. McAlister, 383 F.Supp. 1107 (Conn. 1974).

[215]Stroman v. Board of School Directors, 300 A.2d 286 (Pa. 1973).

[216]Pitcher v. Iberia Parish School Board, 280 So.2d 603 (La. 1973).

[217]Morrison v. Hamilton County Board of Education, 494 S.W.2d 770 (Tenn. 1973).

[218]Peterkin v. Board of Education, 360 N.Y.S.2d 53 (1974).

[219]Cook v. Hudson, 511 F.2d 744 (5th Cir. 1975). Contra, Berry v. Macon City Board of Education, 380 F.Supp. 1244 (Ala. 1971).

[220]Hovland v. School District No. 152, 278 P.2d 211 (Mont. 1954).

education. In a slightly different aspect of tenure the court in Washington ruled that dismissal for insubordination was not justified when the conduct was provoked by actions of the board and the teacher momentarily lost self-control. In this case, involving a highly controversial discharge of a school superintendent, the court said[221] that, while teachers are expected to exercise a high degree of patience and self-control when dealing with students, their relationship with adults (including school board members) should be judged by ordinary standards.

18.13i Incompetence or inefficiency

Another cause for dismissal relates to the teacher's ability, competence, or efficiency in teaching.[222] It is not always clear what constitutes incompetence or the degree of proof of incompetence required. Administrators, the board, and the general public have often complained bitterly that it is impossible to discharge or nonretain an incompetent teacher but the facts do not support this contention. In recent years the courts have increasingly sustained the action of a school board when factual evidence to the buttress case has been presented.

Since the teacher holds a valid certificate, there is a presumption of competence before the law, and the burden of proof of incompetence rests on the board of education. A Connecticut court declared[223] that teachers are guilty of gross inefficiency when their efforts are failing to an intolerable degree to produce the effect intended so that they are manifestly incompetent or incapable persons. In a North Dakota case the court commented:

> . . . it becomes important to distinguish
> between a cause for discharge and termination
> of a contract based on a rule and a cause for
> discharge and termination of a contract not
> based on a rule. In the latter case, the
> misconduct must be of such a serious nature
> that, standing alone, it would constitute
> cause.[224]

In a leading and often cited Illinois case, it was established[225] that the highest qualifications are not necessary in order to be judged competent. The law requires only average qualifications and ability.

It is also the opinion of several courts that examples of inefficient or incompetent teaching behavior which can be remedied are not sufficient cause for dismissal. A teacher may be issued a warning (without being given a written notice and hearing) that, unless the quality of his or her performance improves, dismissal will be recommended.[226] The warning notice should be tendered at such time as would allow the teacher a reasonable period to correct the alleged deficiencies.[227] In two Illinois cases it was ruled[228] that the board of education had discretion to determine whether or not the causes for which a teacher was dismissed were remediable, and in the absence of prior warning remediable causes were not sufficient for discharge. Specific examples of remediable behavior given by the court included failure to require sufficient schoolwork, improper grading of papers and tests, and allowing students to change answers on papers. A teacher dismissed for causes which are remediable must be reinstated.[229] In one instance it was held[230] that use of corporal punishment, use of improper language, and exhibiting uncontrollable temper were remediable. In Louisiana it was held[231] that charges against a school principal for an alleged violation of school-lunch regulations related to trivial and immediately corrected incidents and did not constitute sufficient cause for discharge.

Previous incompetent behavior may not be used to justify dismissal of a teacher. In

---

[221]Board of Directors of Kennewick School District v. Coates, 287 P.2d 102 (Wash. 1955).

[222]Horosko v. School District of Mt. Pleasant Tp., 6 A.2d 866 (Pa. 1939); State ex rel. Cochrane v. Peterson, 294 N.W. 203 (Minn. 1940).

[223]Conley v. Board of Education of City of New Britain, 123 A.2d 747 (Conn. 1956).

[224]In Miller v. South Bend Special School District No. 1, 124 N.W.2d 475, 479 (N.D. 1963).

[225]Neville v. School Directors of District No. 1, 36 Ill. 71 (1864).

[226]Board of Education, Tucson H.S. District No. 1 v. Williams, 403 P.2d 324 (Ariz. 1965).

[227]Miller v. Board of Education of School District No. 132, 200 N.E.2d 838 (Ill. 1964). No prior warning need be given where the cause of dismissal is irremediable. Wells v. Board of Education of Community Consolidated School District No. 64, 230 N.E.2d 6 (Ill. 1967).

[228]Werner v. Community Unit School District No. 4, 190 N.E.2d 184 (Ill. 1963); Miller v. Board of Education of School District No. 132, 200 N.E.2d 838 (Ill. 1964).

[229]Yesinowski v. Board of Education, 328 N.E.2d 23 (Ill. 1975); Gilliland v. Board of Education of Pleasant View Consolidated School District No. 622, 343 N.E.2d 704 (Ill. 1976).

[230]Miller v. Board of Education of School District No. 132, 200 N.E.2d 838 (Ill. 1964).

[231]Johra v. Jefferson Davis Parish School Board, 154 So.2d 581 (La. 1963). Failure of an experienced teacher to maintain classroom discipline has been held to constitute sufficient cause for the nonrenewal of her contract. Robel v. Highline Public Schools, District No. 401, 398 P.2d 1 (Wash. 1965); See also Griggs v. Board of Trustees of Merced Union High School District, 389 P.2d 722 (Cal. 1964).

New Mexico it was held[232] that a teacher who met the educational standards established by the board of education during the probationary period could not be dismissed after qualifying for tenure when the educational qualifications fixed by the board were lacking in quality and substance. Likewise, in a Louisiana case it was held[233] that a teacher transferred from one curricular area to another could not be discharged more than a year later for alleged incompetence in the former position.

Since 1970 the courts have sustained dismissal of teachers for incompetency for the following reasons:(1) teacher's pupils were below average in scholastic accomplishment;[234] (2) teacher, with 19 years of experience, was ineffective in team-teaching and individualized instruction which the school inaugurated;[235] (3) teacher's performance was unsatisfactory;[236] (4) teacher was given a substantiated unsatisfactory rating based on failure to conduct classes conducive to learning, failure to maintain discipline, and employing an arbitrary grading system;[237] (5) teacher lacked emotional self-control, i.e., had an uncontrollable temper which failed to improve in spite of repeated conferences; lacked proper relations with the administration, students, and parents; and the science courses suffered;[238] (6) teacher failed to control students and maintain an orderly classroom;[239] and (7) teacher failed to maintain discipline, keep adequate records, develop lesson plans, and follow suggestions of the principal.[240]

In a number of instances the legality of dismissal or nonretention for incompetence revolved around the procedure employed rather than incompetence *per se*. For example, when the contract of a nontenured teacher was not renewed on charges of poor classroom performance and lack of pupil control, the teacher charged the evaluation was not objective and violated constitu-

tional rights. The court held[241] for the board and against the teacher. In Pennsylvania the contract of a teacher who received unsatisfactory ratings during his last four months of service was not renewed. The teacher raised the issue of whether his hearing satisfied due process and whether the board's decision was arbitrary and capricious. The court held[242] that the board hearing did satisfy due process and that the unsatisfactory ratings were substantiated. When an Ohio teacher failed to improve in spite of assistance the board did not renew her contract. The teacher charged that failure to rehire her without giving the reasons violated procedural and substantive due process. The court disagreed and held[243] the teacher had other legal recourses if her rights were denied. When a superintendent informed a teacher of the board's intention to dismiss him for incompetence the teacher alleged that the charges were vague and sought judicial review. The court held[244] the teacher had not exhausted his administrative remedies and required that this be done.

It should not be interpreted from the foregoing decisions that boards of education have always been successful in their efforts to dismiss teachers for incompetency. Boards have failed frequently in their attempt to dismiss teachers, especially where charges have not been substantiated,[245] where time for remedial action has not been given in situations where the cause of dismissal was remediable,[246] or where the wrong dismissal procedure has been employed.[247] The cases cited do point out, however, that the courts will sustain boards of education in the dismissal of incompetent teachers where the charges are substantiated by sufficient evidence and proper procedures are employed.

[232]McCormick v. Board of Education, Hobbs School District, 274 P.2d 299 (N.M. 1954).

[233]Herbert v. Lafayette Parish School Board, 146 So.2d 848 (La. 1962).

[234]Scheelhaase v. Woodbury Central Community School District, 488 F.2d 237 (7th Cir. 1973).

[235]Cannady v. Person County Board of Education, 375 F.Supp. 689 (N.C. 1974).

[236]Manchester v. Lewis, 507 F.2d 289 (5th Cir. 1974).

[237]Glover v. Board of Education, 316 N.E.2d 534 (Ill. 1974).

[238]Kallas v. Board of Education, 304 N.E.2d 527 (Ill. 1973).

[239]Phillips v. Board of Education, 330 A.2d 151 (Del. 1975).

[240]Merideth v. Board of Education, 513 S.W.2d 740 (Mo. 1974).

[241]Pickens v. Okolona Municipal Separate School District, 380 F.Supp. 1036 (Miss. 1974).

[242]Acitelli v. Westmont Hilltop School District, 325 A.2d 490 (Pa. 1974).

[243]Burkett v. Tuslaw School District Board of Education, 380 F.Supp. 812 (Ohio 1974).

[244]Lovett v. School District City and County of Denver, 523 P.2d 152 (Col. 1974).

[245]Elwood City Area School District v. Secretary of Education, 308 A.2d 635 (Pa. 1973); See also Kallas v. Board of Education, 304 N.E.2d 527 (Ill. 1973); Wojt v. Chimacum School District No. 49, 516 P.2d 1099 (Wash. 1973).

[246]Yesinowski v. Board of Education, 328 N.E.2d 23 (Ill. 1975).

[247]Amos v. Union Free School District No. 9, 364 N.Y.S.2d 640 (1975); Gardner v. Hollinfield, 533 P.2d 730 (Idaho 1975); Estill County Board of Education v. Rose, 518 S.W.2d 341 (Ky. 1975); Board of Education of Union Free School District No. 3 v. Association of Teachers of Huntington, 319 N.Y.S.2d 469 (1971); See also Blue Springs Reorganized School District IV v. Landuyt, 499 S.W.2d 33 (Mo. 1973).

18.13j Neglect of duty

Neglect of duty, either purposeful or inadvertent, is an adequate reason for termination of a teacher's contract or tenure.[248] Like other causes, neglect of duty is often difficult to define and to prove. Examples of neglect of duty are found in cases under contract as well as cases under tenure. It is assumed that neglect of duty which justifies dismissal under contract would justify dismissal under tenure and vice versa.

Neglect of duty may result from outside employment[249] or continued illness.[250] An unavoidable delay of short duration in reporting for duty does not justify dismissal for neglect of duty. A teacher visiting in Europe missed the ship that would have allowed her to report to her position in time for the opening of school. This unavoidable delay was not sufficient to terminate her contract.[251] A Kentucky teacher who was prevented by floods from reaching her teaching position could not be dismissed legally for neglect of duty.[252] However, willfull absence from duty is ground for dismissal.[253]

A ruling by the Tenure Commission of Michigan indicates that minor neglect of duty does not justify dismissal of tenure teachers. A teacher upset over a discipline problem and an unrelated reprimand by the assistant superintendent turned his keys and classbook over to another teacher. Two days later when he apologized and indicated his willingness to return, he was informed that he was no longer employed. The Tenure Commission of Michigan held that the teacher was wrongfully dismissed and that he did not in fact quit. However, the Michigan Supreme Court held[254] that the Tenure Commission was without authority to decide the case and that the board of education was authorized to appeal the case to the courts. In Colorado a teacher who was absent for church holy days and assemblies was guilty of neglect of duty and was legally dismissed.[255] When a person

calls in and reports illness, is later seen out for a walk in apparent good health, and refuses to substantiate the illness, that person is guilty of neglect of duty as well as insubordination.[256]

18.13k Unprofessional conduct

Improper or unprofessional conduct of a teacher is grounds for dismissal.[257] Definition of such conduct is difficult. To assist in clarifying it, cases involving professional personnel under contract, as well as under tenure, are cited.

It is not necessary that a teacher be found guilty of an immoral or improper act to be dismissed. A teacher may be dismissed for a bad reputation.[258] A teacher was discharged for immorality and improper conduct for misusing money received from pupils. The court defined[259] immorality to include any conduct that offends the morals of the community and is inconsistent with moral rectitude. An Illinois teacher was dismissed for her outside activities when she appeared on the streets in an intoxicated condition, even though there was no question of her competence as a teacher.[260]

It was held[261] that a principal charged in criminal proceedings could be dismissed for conduct against morality and good order even though the verdict had been not guilty. A teacher convicted of a criminal act was dismissed under the California tenure law, and removal from the classroom was required.[262] A California teacher who falsified attendance records was legally dismissed on the grounds of unprofessional conduct.[263]

Where the teacher was guilty of unprofessional conduct in 1971–72 and was employed in 1972–73, the district could use as evidence in the termination of the contract the misconduct of 1971–72.[264]

[248]Hamberlin v. Tangipahoa Parish School Board, 27 So.2d 307 (La. 1946); West Mahanoy Tp. School District v. Kelly, 41 A.2d 344 (Pa. 1945).

[249]Meredith v. Board of Education of Community Unit School District, 130 N.E.2d 5 (Ill. 1955).

[250]Riggins v. Board of Education, 300 P.2d 848 (Cal. 1956).

[251]School District No. 1 v. Parker, 260 Pac. 521 (Col. 1927).

[252]Turner v. Hampton, 97 S.W. 761 (Ky. 1906).

[253]Board of Public Instruction v. State, 171 So.2d 209 (Fla. 1965).

[254]School District of City of Benton Harbor v. Michigan State Tenure Commission, 126 N.W.2d 102 (Mich. 1964).

[255]School District No. 11 v. Unberfield, 512 P.2d 1166 (Col. 1973).

[256]Peterkin v. Board of Education, 360 N.Y.S.2d 53 (1974).

[257]Cadman v. School Directors of School District No. 14, 6 N.E.2d 246 (Ill. 1937); Goldsmith v. Sacramento City High School, 225 Pac. 783 (Cal. 1924); Watts v. Seward School Board, 421 P.2d 586 (Alaska 1966); Jarvella v. Willoughby-Eastlake City School District, 233 N.E.2d 143 (Ohio 1967).

[258]Freeman v. Town of Bourne, 49 N.E. 435 (Mass. 1898). See also Watts v. Seward School Board, 381 U.S, 126, 85 S.Ct. 1321 14 L.Ed.2d 261 (Alaska 1965).

[259]Appeal of Edward F. Flannery, 178 A.2d 751 (Pa. 1962). See also Jarvella v. Willoughby-Eastlake City School District, 233 N.E.2d 143 (Ohio 1967).

[260]Scott v. Board of Education of Alton, 156 N.E.2d 1 (Ill. 1959).

[261]Jenkyns v. Board of Education, District of Columbia, 294 F.2d 260 (D.C. 1961).

[262]DiGenova v. State Board of Education, 288 P.2d 862 (Cal. 1955).

[263]Board of Education of San Francisco v. Weiland, 4 Cal.Rptr. 286 (Cal. 1960).

[264]Vick v. Board of Education of Los Angeles Unified School District, 132 Cal.Rptr. 506 (1976).

In a Nevada case a teacher who persistently authorized and encouraged his daughters to refuse to attend school in violation of state law was dismissed for unprofessional conduct.[265] In New York a teacher who had been granted an extended leave to serve in the state legislature was convicted of conspiracy to promote bribery of public officials. When he was considered for reemployment the Commissioner of Education directed the board not to reemploy him. The court sustained[266] the Commissioner in withholding the person's teaching certificate and breaking his tenure. In the same state a teacher requested a leave of absence of 21 days to attend the New York University Senate as a member. When the board refused to grant the leave, the teacher attended the meetings, falsely certified that he was ill, and received sick-leave pay. The court sustained[267] the teacher's dismissal. In a Missouri case the court upheld[268] the board of education in dismissing two tenured teachers who were responsible for supervising auditorium programs because they permitted racially inflamatory and obscene programs to be presented in the school auditorium.

Not all cases where boards charge a teacher with unprofessional conduct have resulted in dismissal of the teacher. In one instance a drama coach was removed from her position because the play she had selected was objectionable to the superintendent. However, the teacher was able to convince the court that the language and other aspects of the play were characteristic of the life being portrayed, and that the school had no policy prohibiting plays of this type.[269]

A number of other cases in which unprofessional conduct has been charged have come before the courts. These cases involved activities related to sex, use of offensive language, use of corporal punishment, etc. Since these cases were treated under these specific categories, they are not repeated here.

18.13l Subversive activities

In 1952 the United States Supreme Court upheld the constitutionality of New York's "Feinberg law," which provided for the dismissal of teachers who held membership in an organization advocating the forceful overthrow of the government.[270] Fifteen years later, however, the court held that ". . . constitutional doctrine which has emerged since that decision has rejected its major premise. That premise was that public employment, including academic employment, could be conditioned upon the surrender of constitutional rights which could not be abridged by direct government action."[271]

Since the 1952 decision numerous loyalty cases have come to the courts, generally from the colleges. However, a number of decisions of major significance involving secondary schools have been adjudicated and are reported in this section.

In a 1971 case it was held[272] that an oath to support the state and federal constitution was valid against the charges that it denied freedom of speech, religion, and association. In this case a teacher who was a Quaker refused on religious grounds to sign an oath or affirmation to support the state or federal constitution. Her refusal resulted in her dismissal, which was affirmed with the court holding that she was not denied the position because of her religion but because she refused to avow her support of the state and federal constitutions.

In earlier cases courts, including the United States Supreme Court, upheld statutes which required affirmation of support for the state and federal constitutions. In a New York case[273] teachers were required to take the following oath: "I do solemnly swear (or affirm) that I will support the Constitution of the United States of America and the Constitution of the State of New York, and that I will faithfully discharge, according to the best of my ability, the duties of the position of ——— to which I am assigned." Lower court decisions upholding statutes of this type were affirmed by the Supreme Court of the United States without written opinion.

In two subsequent Colorado cases loyalty oaths of a similar nature were upheld.[274] In a Florida case the section of the law relating to membership in the Communist party was

[265]Meinhold v. Clark County School District, 506 P.2d 420 (Nev. 1973).

[266]Pordum v. Board of Regents of the State of New York, 491 F.2d 1281 (2d Cir. 1974).

[267]Pell v. Board of Education, 313 N.E.2d 321 (N.Y. 1974).

[268]Harrod v. Board of Education, City of St. Louis, 500 S.W.2d 1 (Mo. 1973).

[269]Webb v. Lake Mills Community School District, 344 F.Supp. 791 (Iowa 1972).

[270]Adler v. Board of Education, 342 U.S. 485, 72 S.Ct. 380, 96 L.Ed. 517 (N.Y. 1952).

[271]Keyishan v. Board of Regents, 385 U.S. 589, 87 S.Ct. 675, 17 L.Ed.2d 629 (N.Y. 1967).

[272]Biklen v. Syracuse Board of Education, 333 F.Supp. 902 (N.Y. 1971).

[273]Knight v. Board of Regents, 269 F.Supp. 876 (N.Y. 1967).

[274]Hosack v. Smiley, 276 F.Supp. 876 (Col. 1967); Ohlson v. Phillips, 304 F.Supp. 1152 (Col. 1969).

declared unconstitutional while the section which required teachers to affirm that they do not believe in overthrow of the government by force and violence was upheld.[275]

While the courts generally have upheld loyalty oaths which require a simple affirmation to support and uphold the constitution of the state and the United States, they have not supported oaths prohibiting membership in societies or parties alleged to be unfriendly to the United States. A number of decisions, several by the United States Supreme Court, have struck down[276] statutes of this type. Typical of the laws which have been found objectionable are those containing vague and uncertain terms requiring teachers to refrain directly or indirectly from subscribing to or teaching any theory of government, economics, or social relations which is inconsistent with the fundamental principles of patriotism and high ideals of Americanism. An early United States Supreme Court case held loyalty oaths of this type to be vague and unenforceable.[277]

In a somewhat different factual situation a teacher objected to taking a loyalty oath which was required as a condition of securing a teaching certificate. The oath not only required support of the state and federal constitution and laws, but required the teacher to promote respect for the flag, respect for law and order, and allegiance to the government of the United States. Such a statute was held[278] indistinguishable from those declared unconstitutional by the United States Supreme Court and thus was unenforceable.

Another case related to the loyalty of a teacher but did not involve a loyalty oath. In this instance a teacher who refused to profess her loyalty by saluting the flag and reciting the pledge of allegiance was dismissed. She objected particularly to the phrase "with liberty and justice for all," indicating that she did not believe this rep-

resented the true situation in contemporary American life. There was no evidence that she attempted to influence her students to follow her example. She brought suit charging that her dismissal was a violation of her First Amendment right of freedom of expression. The court agreed[279] with the teacher, recognizing that she was entitled to the protection of free speech and could not be dismissed for exercising her First Amendment rights. A similar decision was handed down in New York two years later.[280]

For a time it was thought that loyalty oaths and related issues might be settled, but a 1972 case reopened the issue. In this instance a lower court had held a Massachusetts statute which required a public employee to swear to oppose overthrow of the government by violence or illegal means to be unconstitutionally vague. However, the United States Supreme Court disagreed. It held[281] the clause meant only to assure that public employees were willing to support the Constitution and suggested that the oath in this case was really "no more than an amenity." Whether this decision signals that the Court may not scrutinize loyalty oaths as carefully in the future remains to be seen.

18.13m Decreased need for services

With the establishment of unified school systems, school district reorganization and consolidation, and levy failures and lack of revenue resulting in reduction of staff, the problem of which teachers to dismiss has created problems of major proportions. In accordance with statutory provisions, a teacher may be dismissed for reasons of economy[282] or when certain services are no longer needed.[283]

When school districts change from a segregated to a unified system it is often necessary to reduce the number of personnel employed by the system, an action which the courts will sustain. However, a nonracial and objective basis of evaluation must be employed to determine the persons who will be released.[284] Where valid, objec-

[275]Cornell v. Higginsbotham, 305 F.Supp. 445 (Fla. 1969).

[276]Elfbrandt v. Russell, 384 U.S. 11, 86 S.Ct. 1238, 16 L.Ed.2d 321 (Ariz. 1966); Haskett v. Washington, 294 F.Supp. 912 (D.C. 1968); Brush v. State Board of Higher Education, 422 P.2d 268 (Ore. 1966); Whitehall v. Elkins, 389 U.S. 54, 88 S.Ct. 184, 11 L.Ed.2d 228 (Md. 1967); Gallagher v. Smiley, 270 F.Supp. 86 (Col. 1967); Gilmore v. James, 274 F.Supp. 75 (Tex. 1968); Pedlosky v. Massachusetts Institute of Technology, 224 N.E.2d 414 (Mass. 1967); Opinion of the Justices, 228 A.2d 165 (N.H. 1967); Cramp v. Board of Public Instruction, 368 U.S. 278, 82 S.Ct. 275, 7 L.Ed.2d 285 (Fla. 1961).

[277]Baggett v. Bullitt, 377 U.S. 360, 84 S.Ct. 1316, 12 L.Ed.2d 377 (Wash. 1964); See also Whitehall v. Elkins, 389 U.S. 54, 88 S.Ct. 184, 11 L.Ed.2d 228 (Md. 1965).

[278]MacKay v. Rafferty, 321 F.Supp. 177 (Cal. 1970).

[279]Hanover v. Northrup, 325 F.Supp. 170 (Conn. 1970).

[280]Russo v. Central School District No. 1, 469 F.2d 623 (2d Cir. 1972).

[281]Cole v. Richardson, 405 U.S. 676, 92 S.Ct. 1332, 31 L.Ed.2d 593 (Mass. 1972).

[282]Downs v. Board of Education of Hoboken District, 171 Atl. 528 (N.J. 1934); Palone v. Jefferson Parish School Board, 306 So.2d 679 (La. 1974).

[283]Jones v. Hales, 6 A.2d 102 (Pa. 1939).

[284]Gay v. Wheeler, 363 F.Supp. 764 (Tex. 1973); See also United States v. Coffeeville Consolidated School District, 513 F.2d 244 (5th Cir. 1975).

tive methods of evaluation are utilized, refusal to reemploy black teachers with the lowest ratings is justifiable and does not deprive teachers of their civil rights.[285] A person who held the position of teacher-principal before schools were desegregated legally may be assigned to full-time teaching after the schools are reorganized on a unitary basis.[286] However, when a school is desegregated it may not refuse to employ less qualified teachers who were employed by the original district while employing new teachers who are better qualified.[287]

Layoffs and nonrenewals may result from other types of school district reorganization, from lack of funds, and for other reasons. The courts have sustained boards of education in reduction of staff in many situations. In one such instance teachers were dismissed because of a decrease in enrollment. The board refused to place them in positions for which they were unqualified, and new teachers were employed instead.[288] In a case where a teacher's position was abolished for reasons of economy and her duties distributed among the other teachers, the court determined that the board had acted in good faith and held[289] that it would not disturb the action of the board unless its acts were "purely arbitrary." Where the school board abolishes a position and so informs the teacher, termination is not automatic. The teacher may reasonably expect a transfer, since specific action is required to terminate the employment of a teacher.[290]

An impending financial crisis is a sufficient reason for dismissal.[291] Where the school board had adopted comprehensive criteria for elimination of positions to reduce expenditures, the court sustained dismissals based on objective application of these criteria, only one of which related to seniority, and concluded: "School boards should have broad discretionary power free from judicial interference in the absence of a finding that their actions were arbitrary and capricious."[292] In a Pennsylvania case a

reading coordinator's position was abolished and she was assigned as a reading teacher at a reduced salary. The evidence failed to show that the board had acted capriciously or arbitrarily. The fact that the teacher was president of the district's employees' association and had questioned school board action which related to abolition of the position did not invalidate the board's action.[293] The assignment of the director of elementary art to a teaching position at a lower salary in a bona fide reorganization of the school system has been upheld.[294] The Chicago Board of Education was upheld[295] in a reorganization of staff which resulted in reassignment of approximately 640 nonteaching, nontenured personnel to teaching positions. Where it is likely that a number of administrators may lose their positions due to lack of funds, the board may notify a large number of them (1700) that they may be terminated if insufficient funds make this action necessary. Those who actually will be terminated must then be given a legal notice.[296] A decision of the board of education to decrease the working time and compensation of principals and assistant principals as an economy measure was held[297] not to be arbitrary or capricious. Principals in Oregon whose positions were eliminated in a reorganization plan were entitled to a hearing.[298] However, in Michigan a statutory requirement of 60 days notice was not applicable to teachers whose positions were abolished because of financial exigency.[299]

The question of the weight to be given seniority when making reductions in staff is a vexing problem. Some states, e.g., New York, make seniority the highest (if not the only) criterion in retention of staff.[300] Other states consider seniority to be much less important. For example, the courts in the state of Washington have indicated that teachers need not be terminated according to their seniority and that it is not necessary

---

[285]Ibid.

[286]Celestain v. Vermillion Parish School Board, 364 F.Supp. 618 (La. 1973).

[287]Adams v. Rankin County Board of Education, 485 F.2d 324 (5th Cir. 1973).

[288]Smith v. Board of School Directors of Harmony School District, 328 A.2d 883 (Pa. 1974).

[289]Beers v. Nyquist, 338 N.Y.S.2d 745 (1972); See also Mann v. Nyquist, 336 N.Y.S.2d 270 (1972).

[290]Lazette v. Board of Education, Hudson City School District, 319 N.E.2d 189 (N.Y. 1974).

[291]Pierce et al. v. Lake Stevens School District No. 4, 529 P.2d 810 (Wash. 1974).

[292]Jordal v. Independent School District No. 129, 225 N.W.2d 224 (Minn. 1975).

[293]Bilotta v. Secretary of Education, 304 A.2d 190 (Pa. 1973).

[294]Kaplan v. School Community of Melrose, 294 N.E.2d 209 (Mass. 1973).

[295]Chicago Teachers Union v. Board of Education, 301 N.E.2d 833 (Ill. 1973).

[296]Council of Directors and Supervisors v. Los Angeles Unified School District, 35 Cal.3d 147 (1973).

[297]Kempt v. Jefferson Parish School Board, 305 So.2d 744 (La. 1974).

[298]Schaaf v. Eugene School District No. 5, 529 P.2d 943 (Ore. 1974).

[299]Steby v. School District of Highland Park, 224 N.W.2d 97 (Mich. 1975).

[300]New York Statutes Education Law. 2510 (2) (3) (1975); See also Dreyfus v. Board of Education, 345 N.Y.S.2d 836 (1973).

for the board to offer a nonrenewed teacher another position at the expense of a teacher who has less seniority.[301] In a similar situation in Texas the court held[302] in favor of a school board that continued in employment teachers who had less seniority but more instructional skills than those who were dismissed.

Boards of education have not been universally successful in terminating employees when the need for their services has ended. When a tenured supervisor of instruction was reassigned to a teaching position at a reduced salary the trial court required her reinstatement. However, when she was transferred to an assistant principalship in the high school at no salary reduction the board's action was upheld.[303] Where a tenured teacher of French with the least seniority was dismissed it was held[304] that she was entitled to teach in other areas in which she was competent where the board had retained teachers with less seniority, and that she could not be removed except through tenure procedures. It also has been held[305] that a school board may not abolish the position of second assistant principal without the recommendation of the superintendent where such an action was necessary to conform to the teacher tenure statute.

If the board of education of a consolidated district attempts to dismiss a teacher who has acquired tenure in the original district the efforts generally will not be successful.[306] In accordance with other decisions in cases of this type, a New Mexico court stated the situation clearly: A teacher who has acquired tenure in the original district can not be dismissed without cause by the board of the consolidated district. A teacher does not lose tenure as the result of merger or consolidation of school districts and is entitled to all of the benefits of tenure acquired in the original district.[307]

18.13n Marriage

Cases of dismissal or nonretention of female teachers on the basis of marriage are now only of historical significance. The various state and federal statutes dealing with discrimination based on sex make it clear that such actions will not be tolerated. The changed attitude toward married women working has permeated the thinking of school board members nationwide to the point where dismissal of female teachers because of marriage is no longer an issue.

18.13o Civil rights and constitutional guarantees

Civil rights are based on both constitutional guarantees and statutory enactments. These include the provisions of the First, Fifth, Ninth, and Fourteenth Amendments, the provisions of the Civil Rights Acts of 1871 and 1964 and their amendments, and other enactments at both the state and federal levels. Taken together, these provisions guarantee freedom of speech, press, and peaceful assembly; the right to petition and the right of privacy; protection against self-incrimination; and protection from discrimination because of race, sex, age, or other reasons. The right of due process also is assured, including not only the usually understood elements of substantive and procedural due process but also relief from actions which are unreasonable, arbitrary, or capricious.

Several aspects of civil rights have been considered elsewhere under such topics as racial segregation, sexual activities, maternity leaves, etc., and will not be repeated here. The discussion in this section will center on the rights of freedom of speech and writing, both actual and symbolic, both outside and inside the classroom. The accompanying right of teachers to academic freedom will also be considered.

A teacher may not be nonrenewed for exercising a constitutional right.[308] When teachers claim to have been denied tenure because they exercised their constitutional rights, it is their responsibility to present evidence to substantiate this allegation.[309] Likewise, a teacher who claims to have been dismissed for exercising constitutional rights carries the burden of proving that this was the real reason for dismissal.[310] The courts will not disturb the discretion of a board in nonrenewal cases unless it can be

[301]Peters v. South Kitsap School District No. 402, 509 P.2d 67 (Wash. 1973); Pierce et al. v. Lake Stevens School District No. 4, 529 P.2d 810 (Wash. 1974); Black v. Jt. School District No. 401-100, 535 P.2d 135 (Wash. 1975); Hill v. Dayton School District No. 2, 532 P.2d 1154 (Wash. 1975).

[302]Davis v. Winters Independent School District, 359 F.Supp. 1065 (Tex. 1973).

[303]Mitchell v. Garrett, 510 S.W.2d 894 (Tenn. 1974).

[304]Amos v. Union Free High School District No. 9, 364 N.Y.S.2d 640 (1975).

[305]Palone v. Jefferson Parish School Board, 306 So.2d 679 (La. 1975).

[306]State ex rel. Tittle v. Covington Community Consolidated Schools, 96 N.E.2d 334 (Ind. 1951); Simpson v. School District, 76 A.2d 385 (Pa. 1950).

[307]Hensley v. State Board of Education, 376 P.2d 968 (N.M. 1962).

[308]Needlemann v. Bohlen, 386 F.Supp. 741 (Mass. 1974).

[309]Bergstein v. Board of Education, 313 N.E.2d 767 (N.Y. 1974).

[310]Amburgey v. Cassady, 370 F.Supp. 571 (Ky. 1974).

shown that the board's decision was based on constitutionally impermissible reasons.[311] Thus, a teacher who questioned policy decisions, made suggestions and recommendations for change, and sought information on reasons for administrative decisions was entitled to a hearing to determine whether the decision not to renew her contract was based on her exercise of freedom of speech.[312] Similarly, a teacher charged with being a racist was entitled to a hearing on the charges.[313]

A leading case involving the freedom of teachers to criticize superiors (Pickering) has been decided by the United States Supreme Court.[314] In this instance the Court upheld the right of the teacher to write a letter to the editor of the local paper criticizing the superintendent of schools and the board of education for their manner of raising money for new schools and their expenditures for athletic purposes. In spite of the fact that some of the statements in the letter were inaccurate, the Court was of the opinion that the teacher's letter was protected by his constitutional rights. The Court did not believe that the teacher's statements were of the type it had condemned in an earlier case when it held[315] that "the knowingly false statement and the false statement made with reckless disregard for the truth do not enjoy constitutional protection." The Court noted that the persons criticized in the letter were not the teacher's immediate superiors with whom he worked on a day-to-day basis.

While reckless disregard for the truth is not protected by the First Amendment, indiscreet bombast in a letter which does not damage the operation of the school is protected. To hold otherwise, according to one court, would discourage others from criticizing or cause them to express their criticism in terms so innocuous that the criticism would be ineffective or obsequious.[316] A teacher's right to criticize the city council and board of trustees relative to community and economic problems affecting students and teachers was upheld by the

court in a Texas case.[317] When the discharge of a tenured teacher is based on allegations which are both grounds for dismissal under the tenure law and grounds that are constitutionally impermissible, it has been held[318] that the teacher may be dismissed if the charges under the tenure law are proven.

In a case somewhat similar to Pickering, but differing in certain essential aspects, the court upheld[319] the dismissal of two teachers who wrote a controversial "open letter" to the school board. The letter charged that certain actions of the superintendent were detrimental to the morale of the teaching staff and the effectiveness of the school system. Ten incidents were cited to substantiate these charges. Several of the allegations were false. In deciding this case the court pointed out several important differences from Pickering. First, the statement concerned the teachers' immediate superior; second, the false statement could easily have been corrected from public records; third, rather than being greeted by massive apathy as was true in Pickering, the letter led to intense public controversy; and fourth, the accusations were made in reckless disregard of the truth. Another case involved a tenured teacher who, in a speech at an orientation meeting, referred to the dismissal of two nontenured teachers, the superintendent's involvement in politics, and removal of books from the English curriculum. He called the superintendent a "villain" and described the school system as a "snake pit." This type of attack, in the opinion of the court, justified his dismissal.[320] While these two cases may not appear to differ sufficiently from Pickering to warrant the opposite decision, it must be kept in mind that all cases involving constitutional rights of necessity either implicitly or explicitly involve a balancing process. Namely, does the good society gains by denying an individual's constitutional rights over-balance the loss of the individual rights? The values and beliefs of the judge(s) in the case inevitably will be factors in decisions of this type.

The pronouncements and activities

[311]Rottenberg v. Cartwright School District No. 83, 528 P.2d 859 (Ariz. 1974).

[312]Winston v. Board of Education, 319 A.2d 226 (N.J. 1974).

[313]Wellner v. Minnesota State Junior College Board, 487 F.2d 153 (8th Cir. 1973).

[314]Pickering v. Board of Education, 391 U.S. 563, 88 S.Ct. 1731, 20 L.Ed.2d 811 (Ill. 1968).

[315]Garrison v. Louisiana, 375 U.S. 900, 84 S.Ct. 195, 11 L.Ed.2d 142 (La. 1964).

[316]Puentes v. Board of Education, 250 N.E.2d 232 (N.Y. 1969).

[317]Lusk v. Estes, 361 F.Supp. 653 (Tex. 1973); Adcock v. Board of Education, 513 P.2d 900 (Cal. 1973).

[318]Gilbertson v. McAllister, 383 F.Supp. 1107 (Conn. 1974).

[319]Watts v. Seward School Board, 454 P.2d 732 (Alaska 1969); See also Doscher v. Seminole Consolidated School District No. 1, 377 F.Supp. 1170 (Tex. 1974).

[320]Pietrunti v. Board of Education, 319 A.2d 262 (N.J. 1974).

which occur within the classroom are no easier to judge. However, because of the United States Supreme Court's commitment to freedom of inquiry and study, courts most frequently appear to support teachers. A quotation from the United States Supreme Court makes this commitment to academic freedom explicit: "Teachers and students must always remain free to inquire, to study, and to evaluate to gain new maturity and understanding. . . ."[321] While academic freedom is not specifically mentioned as a constitutionally protected right, the language of the First Amendment is sufficiently broad to encompass its attributes. Though seldom applied, it would appear that the Fourteenth Amendment's guarantee that no person shall be deprived of liberty or property without due process of law also has implications for academic freedom, i.e., the liberty of teachers to teach the truth as they see it by the method they deem best.

Whatever the basis used, the courts have sustained teachers in many types of activities to which the community and the school administration have objected. In Alabama, for example, a teacher assigned a comic satire entitled *Welcome to the Monkey House*. The principal and the associate superintendent both expressed their displeasure, describing the work as literary garbage condoning free sex and the killing of the elderly. Applying the balancing process, the court stated that to restrict a person's First Amendment rights it must be shown that the forbidden conduct would substantially interfere with appropriate discipline and the satisfactory operation of the school. The court found that the assignment in question did not do this and required that the teacher be reinstated.[322]

In another case a teacher of civics and political science at the twelfth grade level included in his assignments controversial subjects such as race relations and the war in Vietnam. Following complaints by parents he was dismissed. In the view of the district court, the teacher had the right under the First and Fourteenth Amendments to choose the proper teaching methods as long as they served a demonstrated educational purpose. However, the court refused to reinstate the teacher on the grounds that parents would be antagonized. Instead, the court levied judgment against the board members of $20,000

plus 6 percent interest, plus $5000 for attorney fees and court costs. The Fifth Circuit Court of Appeals affirmed that the dismissal was arbitrary but vacated the remedy on the basis that the fact that parents would be antagonized was an impermissible ground for dismissal and remanded the case.[323]

In an Arkansas case a teacher's contract was not renewed because the board objected to her "Think and Do" program. In this exercise she encouraged her second grade pupils to express their feelings, through drawing and writing, on matters relating to the health and welfare of the pupils. Some pupils drew pictures of inoperative water fountains, an unsafe incinerator, and poor nutritional planning in the lunchroom at the school. The teacher was upheld[324] and the program was judged to be related to the protection of the health and safety of her pupils.

In a number of other cases associated with civil rights teachers have been successful in securing reinstatement. A teacher who had been dismissed for wearing a black arm band was ordered reinstated and was awarded back pay and court costs because no educational or disciplinary disruption was shown as a result of the teacher's activity.[325] A Mississippi teacher was successful in a suit for reemployment when the court concluded[326] she would have been reemployed had she not been the wife of a local activist.

Numerous other cases have come to the courts in which teachers have claimed that their dismissal was based on the exercise of their constitutional rights.[327] However, the evidence presented in these cases showed that the teachers were dismissed for other reasons which were accepted by the courts as good and sufficient, and the dismissals were upheld.

18.13p Political activities

In earlier years the regulations of many school districts, and even the laws of some states, prohibited teachers from participat-

---

[321]Sweezy v. New Hampshire, 354 U.S. 234, 77 S.Ct. 1203, 1 L.Ed.2d 1311 (N.H. 1957).
[322]Parducci v. Rutland, 316 F.Supp. 352 (Ala. 1970).

[323]Sterzing v. Fort Bend Independent School District, 496 F.2d 92 (5th Cir. 1974).
[324]Downs v. Conway School District, 328 F.Supp. 338 (Ark. 1971).
[325]James v. Board of Education, 385 F.Supp. 209 (N.Y. 1974).
[326]Randel v. Indianola Municipal Separate School District, 373 F.Supp. 766 (Miss. 1974).
[327]Calvin v. Rupp, 334 F.Supp. 358 (Mo. 1971); Doscher v. Seminole Consolidated School District No. 1, 377 F.Supp. 1170 (Tex. 1974); Amburgey v. Cassady, 507 F.2d 728 (6th Cir. 1974); Simon v. Jefferson Davis Parish School District, 289 So.2d 511 (La. 1974).

ing in any type of political activity other than voting and teachers could be dismissed for failure to comply. More recently, as a result of a changing concept of the teacher's role, teachers have been encouraged to participate actively in politics. State statutes[328] and constitutional mandates[329] now guarantee teachers the right to engage in political activities and to be candidates for public office, and several court decisions have been to the same effect.[330] However, the courts will not sustain[331] being employed full-time in teaching and being a candidate for a full-time office at the same time. Nor may a teacher take a partisan stand in the classroom, campaigning for a particular candidate.[332]

18.13q Miscellaneous reasons—drugs, intoxication, etc.

The courts have upheld dismissal of teachers and other professional personnel for a variety of other reasons. Some of the most common are: using and praising the use of drugs and failure to report the use of marijuana;[333] being intoxicated;[334] being guilty of shoplifting;[335] and swearing.[336]

Whether or not the use of marijuana is grounds for dismissal appears to depend on the circumstances of the case. Two cases from California,[337] which were heard together on appeal, arrived at opposite conclusions. In the first case, the teacher, while in Hawaii, was arrested and charged with possession of marijuana. Pursuant to his plea of *nolo contendere* he was convicted as charged, fined and granted probation. Based on extended testimony by the assistant principal of the adverse effect that this

incident would have on the pupils and the educational program of the school, the court sustained dismissal. In the other case the teacher was in possession of marijuana while in San Diego and was arrested and convicted. Revocation of his license and loss of his position was not upheld because proof of the allegations of adverse effects on the school system was negligible. The dicta did indicate, however, that with more convincing proof the certificate would have been revoked.

18.14 TRANSFER OF PROFESSIONAL STAFF

As a general rule, a school district has a right to transfer a tenured teacher to any position of equal rank, dignity, and compensation.[338] It may transfer or reassign a teacher from one public school to another public school within the school district[339] and from one position to another so long as there is no element of demotion, or lowering of professional standing, or any reduction in salary.[340] Thus, a principal may be transferred to the position of director of guidance services and supervisor of adult education[341] and a mathematics teacher to full-time study hall supervision.[342] The general rule was stated in a New Mexico case, as follows:

We do not see in our tenure statute any guaranty that a teacher must be retained in any particular school or given any particular assignment. Nothing can be found in the statute giving a teacher a vested right to teach in any one school or any one class. Our tenure law, as is true of most tenure laws, does not purport to limit the right or power of the governing school authorities to exercise their discretion in making assignments of tenure teachers.[343]

It has been held[344] that pay may be reduced proportionately where a teacher is transferred from a calendar-year to an academic-

[328]See e.g., Texas Civil Statutes, Article 2922-21a (1969).

[329]e.g., Oregon adopted a constitutional amendment in 1958 providing that an employee of any school board "shall be eligible to a seat in the Legislative Assembly. . . ."

[330]Johnson v. Branch, 374 F.2d 177 (4th Cir. 1966); Williams v. Sumter School District, 255 F.Supp. 397 (S.C. 1966); See also Rackley v. School District, 258 F.Supp. 676 (S.C. 1966).

[331]Jones v. Board of Control, 131 So.2d 713 (Fla. 1961).

[332]Goldsmith v. Board of Education, 225 Pac. 783 (Cal. 1924).

[333]Brubaker v. Board of Education of School District No. 49, 502 F.2d 973 (7th Cir. 1974); Calvin v. Rupp, 334 F.Supp. 358 (Mo. 1971).

[334]Bradford v. School District No. 20, 244 F.Supp. 768 (S.C. 1975).

[335]Caravello v. Board of Education of Norwich City School District, 369 N.Y.S.2d 829 (1975).

[336]MacKenzie v. School Committee of Ipswich, 174 N.E.2d 657 (Mass. 1975).

[337]Jefferson Union High School District v. Jones and Comings v. State Board of Education, 100 Cal.Rptr. 73, 47 A.L.R.3d 742 (1972).

[338]State v. Jefferson Parish School Board, 188 So.2d 143 (La. 1966); Goodwin v. Bennet City High School District, 226 N.W.2d 166 (S.D. 1975); McMullen v. District School Board, 533 P.2d 812 (Ore. 1975).

[339]Opinion of the Justices, 160 So.2d 648 (Ala. 1964); Wheeler v. Durham City Board of Education, 363 F.2d 738 (4th Cir. 1966).

[340]Aswell v. Jackson Parish School Board, 176 So.2d 741 (La. 1965); Maxey v. Jefferson County School District, 408 P.2d 970 (Col. 1965).

[341]Aswell v. Jackson Parish School Board, 176 So.2d 741 (La. 1965).

[342]VanHeusen v. Board of Education of City School District, 271 N.Y.S.2d 898 (1966).

[343]State v. Montoya, 386 P.2d 252, 256 (N.M. 1963).

[344]Diggs v. Orleans Parish School Board, 161 So.2d 433 (La. 1964).

year position. The Kentucky Court of Appeals decided[345] that a teacher who received compensation in addition to her base pay for her various additional responsibilities as principal of an elementary school was entitled to continue to receive additional compensation when she was removed from her position as principal and assigned to teaching duties. It was held that her salary under the tenure law could be reduced only as part of a uniform plan affecting the entire district or as cause existed for demotion.

Recent cases have held that tenured teachers are not required to accept inferior employment or employment in a different location.[346] However, transfer from high school teaching to eighth grade at the same salary was not considered a demotion. The courts upheld[347] such a transfer even though the school board retained nontenured teachers at the high school level.

When the position of supervisor of instruction and materials was eliminated the board acted properly, according to the court,[348] in transferring the person holding that position to a position of assistant principal at the same salary. When the position of guidance counselor was discontinued and the counselor was assigned as classroom teacher, the action involved no loss of a constitutional right.[349] However, transfers must conform to the provisions of a collective bargaining agreement.[350] The transfer of a principal is not a denial of due process[351] and transfer of principals who supported an unlawful teacher strike did not deny them any constitutional right.[352]

Under the civil rights acts the power to reassign or transfer teachers may not be exercised in a discriminatory manner.[353]

18.15 RESIGNATION OF PROFESSIONAL STAFF

As a general rule, if a tenured teacher resigns and the resignation is not accepted, or if accepted, the acceptance is rescinded, or is withdrawn, the tenure rights of the teacher upon resuming teaching are restored, provided no new rights have intervened. In an Ohio case the teacher resigned on April 20, 1963, during his third year of teaching, the resignation to be effective at the end of that year. The resignation was accepted. At a meeting of the school board on June 15, 1963, its action accepting resignation was rescinded. The school board then offered the teacher a one-year, limited contract, which he accepted. The court held[354] in an action of mandamus that the teacher was entitled to a continuing contract for the fourth year and thereafter. His action in accepting the one-year contract was held not to be a waiver of his rights under the tenure law. In a somewhat similar situation the court held for the teacher where the teacher resigned November 19, effective November 23. On November 20 she attempted to withdraw her resignation but the board refused to permit her to do so. On the same day the personnel officer or his secretary changed the effective date of the resignation to November 20. Such a resignation was invalid and the court held[355] the teacher had not resigned. Although it has been held in limited instances that a known right, including teacher tenure, may be voluntarily waived by mutual consent, whether or not a voluntary waiver has occurred can only be ascertained from the facts in a particular case.[356]

A teacher's right to continue in employment is not barred by a written statement of intention to retire at the close of the school year since such a statement is not a resignation.[357] A teacher on sabbatical leave who

[345]Board of Education of Nelson County v. Lawrence, 375 S.W.2d 830 (Ky. 1963).

[346]Kenaston v. School Administrative District No. 40, 17 A.2d 7 (Me. 1974).

[347]DeCarlo v. Tarrant City Board of Education, 291 So.2d 155 (Ala. 1974).

[348]Mitchell v. Garrett, 510 S.W.2d 894 (Tenn. 1974).

[349]Mohr v. Dade County School Board, 287 So.2d 337 (Fla. 1973).

[350]Classroom Teachers Association v. Board of Education, 304 N.E.2d 516 (Ill. 1973).

[351]Coe v. Bogart, 377 F.Supp. 302 (Tex. 1974).

[352]Bates v. Dause, 502 F.2d 865 (6th Cir. 1974).

[353]Christmas v. Board of Education of Harford County, Md., 231 F.Supp. 331 (Md. 1964); Price v. Deneson Independent School District Board of Education, 348 F.2d 1010 (5th Cir. 1965); Rogers v. Paul, 345 F.2d 117 (8th Cir. 1965); Bradley v. School Board of City of Richmond, Virginia, 345 F.2d 310 (4th Cir. 1965); Franklin v. County School Board of Giles County, 242 F.Supp. 371 (Va. 1965); Kier v. County School Board of Augustus County, Virginia, 249 F.Supp. 239 (Va. 1966).

[354]State v. Hardy, 206 N.E.2d 589 (Ohio 1965). A resignation, unsupported by consideration, may be withdrawn at any time prior to its acceptance by the school board. Eberle v. Joint School District No. 1 of Towns of Ithaca, Etc., 155 N.W.2d 573 (Wis. 1968). Where the resignation has been accepted by the board, it cannot be withdrawn even though the attempt is made before its effective date. State v. Cameron Parish School Board, 200 So.2d 34 (La. 1967). A teacher who resigned under threat of dismissal for homosexual activities was unable to secure a rescission of the resignation in Odorizzi v. Bloomfield School District, 54 Cal.Rptr. 533 (1966).

[355]Wiljamace v. Board of Education of City of Flint, 213 N.W.2d 830 (Mich. 1974).

[356]Perry v. Independent School District No. 696, 210 N.W.2d 283 (Minn. 1973).

[357]Schwartz v. Board of Education, 358 N.Y.S.2d 48 (1974).

fails to follow the approved program is not entitled to compensation. Such action, however, does not constitute a resignation from the school system.[358]

18.16 CONTINUING CONTRACT LAWS

States not granting teachers tenure status have developed an intermediate level of security between annual contracts and tenure through continuing contract statutes. Under provision of such laws teaching contracts are automatically renewed unless notice of termination of the contract is given by a specific date. By either statutory language or court interpretation three distinct operational categories of continuing contract provisions have emerged. In the first category the board is not required to state the reasons for nonretention or to afford the teacher a hearing on the charges. In these instances teachers are entitled only to a notice by a specified date that they will not be retained. In the second category a teacher not only must be notified of nonretention by a given date, but also must be given the reasons for nonretention. The teacher is not entitled to a hearing unless the reasons given for nonretention are constitutionally impermissible. In the third category are statutes and/or court interpretations which require both the giving of specific reasons for nonretention and the holding of a hearing on the charges. Teachers may request a private hearing in most of these situations.

In a number of states no mention is made in the statutes of any specific action concerning nonrenewal. In these situations a requirement that reasons be given will not be inferred, although there are some exceptions, e.g., New Jersey. A number of states refer to notification of nonretention but do not require boards of education to provide reasons. Examples of states not requiring boards to give reasons include Alabama, Colorado, Michigan, New Hampshire, Ohio, and Wisconsin. If boards are not required to give notice of nonrenewal then no hearing can be required, since the reasons given in the notice are the issues on which a hearing is held.[359]

A number of states specifically require that the reasons for dismissal be given a teacher who is not retained. Examples of statutes of this type are found in Alaska, Arizona, California, Connecticut, Delaware,

and Illinois. Some of these states require that reasons be given but do not require a hearing. Others require both reasons and a hearing. Arizona is typical of the states which provide for a statement of the reasons for nonretention but no hearing. The Arizona statute provides that "notice of the board's intention not to reemploy a probationary teacher shall be by delivering it personally to the teacher or sending it by certified mail . . . on or before April 15. . . . The notice shall incorporate a statement of the reasons for not reemploying the teacher."[360]

In California, where both the reasons for nonrenewal and a hearing are required, the statute reads as follows:

> (b) The employee may request a hearing to determine if there is cause for not reemploying him for the ensuing year.

> (d) The governing board's determination not to reemploy a probationary employee for the following year shall be for cause only. The determination of the governing board as to the sufficiency of the cause shall relate solely to the welfare of the schools and the pupils thereof. . . .[361]

In the majority of continuing contract laws the term *teacher* includes all full-time employees whose employment requires a certificate and who hold a teacher's certificate. However, emergency part-time employees and/or substitutes are usually not covered unless their employment is of a continuous nature or unless coverage is specifically provided by statutes.[362]

18.17 SECURITY OF CLASSIFIED STAFF

An increasing number of cases involving civil service employees of school districts are being adjudicated in courts of records. Because the bases of termination of the employee's rights closely parallel those of the professional staff only a limited discussion of this topic is presented.

Female custodians must be paid the same salary as male custodians and no discrimination in hiring or dismissal is permitted.[363] Discharge and refusal to employ applicants as teacher aides because they are unwed

---

[358]Lindbergh School District v. Syrewicz, 516 S.W.2d 507 (Mo. 1974).

[359]See e.g., Wisconsin Statutes 118.22 (1972). The teacher is entitled to a private conference with the board after the initial notice that nonretention is contemplated, but no hearing is provided by statutes.

[360]See, e.g., Arizona Revised Statutes. Education 15-252 (1975); See also Rottenburg v. Cartwright School District No. 83, 528 P.2d 859 (Ariz. 1974).

[361]See e.g., California Statutes. Education 13443 (b) (d) (1975).

[362]Council v. Donovan, 244 N.Y.S.2d 199 (1963); Brodie v. School Committee of Easton, 324 N.E.2d 922 (Mass. 1975).

[363]Brennan v. Board of Education of Jersey City, 374 F.Supp. 817 (N.J. 1975).

mothers is legally impermissible.[364] A civil servant who is reinstated with lost salary and benefits has no grounds for an action for punitive damages and cannot sue the school board members in their individual capacity for malicious intent.[365]

A construction worker who pleaded guilty to receiving illegal gratuities legally could be dismissed.[366] Dismissal also was upheld[367] for a classified employee who was absent from work 31 percent of the time over a five-year period. A school secretary does not have a reasonable expectation of permanent employment and as a consequence is not entitled to a due process hearing on dismissal.[368] However, if discharge deprives an employee of some liberty, broadly interpreted, including a stigma or potential disability in securing future employment, the employee is entitled to a hearing.[369] When an employee is dismissed, evidence of the employee's prior misconduct is admissable.[370]

18.18 REMEDIES FOR WRONGFUL DISMISSAL

A teacher who alleges that a dismissal or termination is illegal usually claims either (1) the denial of procedural due process, i.e., the procedure followed in the dismissal has denied the teacher constitutional rights; (2) the denial of substantive due process, i.e., the reasons for dismissal are not related to his or her effectiveness as a teacher, or (3) the denial of both procedural and substantive due process. Where dismissal is attempted for reasons of incompetency, insubordination, neglect of duty, and other shortcomings related to teaching, the burden is on the board of education to prove that the teacher is, in fact, incompetent, insubordinate, or neglectful of duty. However, when the teacher alleges that dismissal has resulted from the exercise of constitutional rights, the burden is on the teacher to show that this was, in fact, the case. It should be noted in this regard that the right of

teachers and other school employees to live outside the school district in which they are employed is not a constitutionally protected right.[371]

In the past it generally has been held that school board members are not personally liable when acting in a discretionary capacity unless malice can be shown. The United States Supreme Court, in considering a student's rights case, now has fashioned a different definition in cases involving the denial of constitutional rights under the civil rights acts. It has determined[372] that school board members may be held personally liable if they knew, or could have known, that they were depriving any individual of constitutional rights. The school board, as a legal entity, is not a "person" under civil rights acts and is immune from damages in most jurisdictions,[373] but individual school board members may be held liable. As in the past, board members may be held personally liable for injury caused by their wrongful acts while carrying on ministerial functions.

The remedy for wrongful dismissal is generally limited to reinstatement with back pay. However, some of the more recent cases have awarded payment of court costs and attorney fees[374] and damages in addition to salary lost because of dismissal.[375] Interest on the back pay of the teacher has also been authorized.[376] The teacher is, of course, expected to mitigate damages by searching for and accepting comparable employment.[377] However, wages earned in dissimilar employment, such as working for

[371]Wardwell v. Board of Education of Cincinnati, 529 F.2d 625 (6th Cir. 1976); *See also* McCarthy v. Philadelphia Civil Service Commission, 424 U.S. 645, 96 S.Ct. 1154, 47 L.Ed.2d 366 (Pa. 1976); Mogle v. Sevier County School District, 540 F.2d 478 (10th Cir. 1976); Park v. Lansing School District, 233 N.W.2d 592 (Mich. 1975); Pittsburgh Federation of Teachers Local 400 American Federation of Teachers, AFL-CIO v. Aaron, 417 F.Supp. 94 (Pa. 1976).
[372]Wood v. Strickland, 420 U.S. 308, 95 S.Ct. 992, 43 L.Ed.2d 214 (Ark. 1975).
[373]Howell v. Winn Parish School Board, 377 F.Supp. 815 (La. 1974); Thomas v. Ward, 374 F.Supp. 206 (N.C. 1974).
[374]Doherty v. Wilson, 365 F.Supp. 35 (Ga. 1973); James v. Board of Education of Central District No. 1, 385 F.Supp. 209 (N.Y. 1974); Conrad v. Goolsby, 350 F.Supp. 713 (Miss. 1972). *Contra,* Waller v. Board of Education of Century Community Unit School District No. 100, 328 N.E.2d 604 (Ill. 1975). *See also* footnote 96.
[375]Woodward v. England School District No. 2, 479 F.2d 671 (8th Cir. 1973); *See also* Jackson v. Wheatley School District No. 28, 489 F.2d 608 (5th Cir. 1973).
[376]Williams v. Albemarle City Board of Education, 508 F.2d 1242 (4th Cir. 1974).
[377]Mass v. Board of Education of San Francisco Unified School District, 394 P.2d 579 (Cal. 1964).

[364]Andrews v. Drew Municipal Separate School District, 371 F.Supp. 27 (Miss. 1974).
[365]Van Buskirk v. Bleir, 354 N.Y.S.2d 93 and 360 N.Y.S.2d 88 (1974).
[366]Pell v. Board of Education of Union Free School District No. 1, 313 N.E.2d 32 (N.Y. 1974).
[367]California School Employee Association v. Jefferson Elementary School District, 119 Cal.Rptr. 668 (1975).
[268]Crampton v. Harmon, 533 P.2d 364 (Ore. 1975).
[369]Williams v. Civil Service Commission, 329 A.2d 556 (N.J. 1974); Mescia v. Berry, 40 F.Supp. 1181 (S.C. 1974); *See also* Owen v. City of Independence, Mo. 421 F.Supp. 1110 (Mo. 1976).
[370]Daggs v. Boonville School District, 508 S.W.2d 46 (Ark. 1974).

the highway department, are not to be deducted as mitigated damage payments.[378]

As one reviews the court decisions handed down during the 1960s and in most of the 1970s, assiduous protection of the constitutional rights of teachers is readily apparent. However, teachers are held to a rigid standard in proving that their constitutional rights have been violated. The assertion of dismissal for exercise of constitutional rights or the proof of activities in constitutionally protected areas is not sufficient. Evidential substantiation of the causal relationship of the exercise of constitutional rights and dismissal must be presented.

18.19 SUMMARY

Originally teachers had little security in employment. The contract, of course, had to be fulfilled, but contracts were of short duration; one year in most instances. At the end of the contract period the teacher's services could be terminated for any reason or no reason at all. Under these circumstances efforts were first made to assure some degree of security as early as 1885 and a form of tenure was enacted in Boston in 1889. Tenure spread rapidly in the twentieth century and was most desired during the 1930s when jobs were scarce and teachers' contracts frequently were not renewed, often for flimsy reasons. In the 1950s and early 1960s, with the scarcity of teachers, some of the pressure for teacher tenure subsided and has not resurfaced in any marked degree. Other enactments have provided additional means to assure job security, thus reducing the need for tenure statutes.

Proponents of tenure hold that it is the principle of civil service extended to teachers and that it is essential to protect good teachers from arbitrary and unwarranted dismissal, particularly in periods of job scarcity. The opponents counter with the argument that tenure protects incompetent and objectionable teachers and, since incompetence is almost impossible to prove in a court of law, perpetuates the incompetents in service. The proponents appear to have argued more effectively. Since tenure is enjoyed in the more populous cities and states, a substantial majority of all teachers now have tenure rights.

The constitutionality of tenure laws has been upheld universally against all types of contention. In essence it has been held that tenure is for the improvement of education

and not for the special benefit of any one class (teachers).

Teacher tenure laws may be written in a manner making them contractual. This is the situation in at least four states—Alabama, Indiana, Montana and Nevada. Generally they are expressions of legislative policy which may be changed by future legislatures. Under the policy type of tenure laws no rights are vested and tenure may be withdrawn from any or all teachers at the direction of the legislature.

Nearly all tenure laws require that teachers serve a probationary period. During this period contracts may or may not be renewed at the option of the board, except as recent statutes and court decisions have required the board to give the teacher reasons for nonretention and/or provide for a hearing on the reasons. Teachers may gain tenure if employed regularly, even on a part-time basis. In some instances regular substitutes may acquire tenure. If conditions precedent are required before tenure can be gained, such as the issuance of a fourth contract, recommendations of the superintendent, etc., tenure cannot be achieved until these conditions have been met.

Principals, supervisors, and administrative assistants generally may attain tenure in states having teacher tenure laws although in some instances they attain tenure only as teachers. Superintendents usually are not granted tenure but may acquire it by direct statutory enactment or indirectly as teachers because they hold teacher's certificates.

Causes for dismissal must be substantial and not easily remediable. They must be related to those set forth in the law. If "other just causes" are stipulated as reasons for dismissal, they must be directly related to the causes enumerated and to the teacher's efficiency. The reasons for dismissal stated in the tenure laws or interpreted by the courts include (1) insubordination, (2) incompetence or inefficiency, (3) neglect of duty, (4) conduct unbecoming a teacher, (5) subversive activities, (6) retrenchment or decreased need for services, (7) physical and/or mental health, (8) age, (9) causing or encouraging disruption, (10) engaging in illegal activities, (11) using offensive language, (12) personal appearance, (13) sex-related activities (14) political activities, and (15) use of drugs or intoxicants.

Where tenure statutes have been enacted, the courts enforce their provisions rigorously and anyone dealing with tenure laws must follow the requirements precisely since substantial compliance is not ac-

---

[378]Spencer v. Laconia School District, 218 A.2d 437 (N.H. 1966).

cepted. The requirements of tenure statutes apply with equal force to teachers and to school boards. In lieu of tenure statutes teachers in recent years have been granted additional security in employment in one or more of the following ways:

1. Enactment of continuing contract laws
2. Requirements that teachers be given the reasons for nonretention under continuing contract and/or probationary status
3. Provision for a hearing on the reasons for nonrenewal; such hearings to provide the elements of due process
4. Protection under civil rights acts, both federal and state, voiding nonretention if it involves any form of discrimination
5. Judicial interpretations voiding any dismissal or nonretention based on exercise by the teacher of guaranteed constitutional rights
6. Provisions regarding nonretention in collective bargaining agreements
7. Expectation of continued employment

While the above list, together with teacher tenure, would appear to provide a high degree of security of employment for teachers, this has not always been the case. Some states have no tenure statutes for many teachers. Many continuing contract and probationary teachers can be nonretained without being given a reason and no hearing is provided. While the majority of teachers have a high degree of security in employment the minority have little. However, all teachers are assured that they will not be dismissed or nonretained for exercising their constitutionally guaranteed rights.

An increasing number of cases involving nonprofessional employees of school districts are being adjudicated. If a school employee has a reasonable expectation of continued employment, he or she is entitled to a due process hearing. The legal principles governing the employment and dismissal of classified staff personnel closely parallel those that apply to the professional employees.

Nontenured teachers currently are contesting dismissal or nonrenewal primarily on two bases, both of relatively recent origin: (1) violation of rights guaranteed under the civil rights acts, and (2) denial of their constitutional rights. Teachers may not be dismissed for exercising the rights accorded them by the various civil rights acts. They may not be discriminated against because of age, race, sex, or religious affiliation. They are entitled to due process when such issues are raised and are protected against unreasonable, arbitrary, and capricious actions by a board of education or an administrator. When a teacher alleges dismissal for exercise of constitutional rights the burden of proof is on the teacher to show that dismissal was, in fact, the result of exercising constitutional rights and not for some other reason. If the reason for dismissal is incompetency, inefficiency, insubordination, or other instructionally relevant causes, the burden of proof is on the board of education to show that the instruction-related causes justified dismissal. The courts are reluctant to permit dismissal for a remediable reason unless remedies have been attempted and have failed.

Workmen's Compensation, Fringe Benefits, Retirement, and Social Security

PART THREE: RETIREMENT BENEFITS

PART FOUR: SOCIAL SECURITY BENEFITS

PART ONE
Workmen's compensation

19.0 INTRODUCTION

Prior to the adoption of workmen's compensation laws, it was extremely difficult for an employee who was injured while working to collect compensation. Remedy was limited to that provided by common law, which normally required a showing of negligence on the part of the employer. Even when negligence could be established, the employer had available three important defenses which often defeated claims by the injured employees. First, if the *employee* was negligent, such contributory negligence would bar any recovery. Second, an employee who had voluntarily accepted the unsafe working conditions involved was held to have assumed the risk. And third, if the employer could show that it was actually the negligence or other acts of a co-worker which caused the injuries, recovery was disallowed under the "fellow servant" rule. Even when employees were successful in prosecuting their claims, they often placed their jobs in jeopardy since a lawsuit against their employers was involved. The uncompensated employee, of course, had to bear the loss alone or become an object of public charity.

Workmen's compensation laws introduced a new philosophy of compensation, which was well summarized in a 1953 Missouri case:

> The fundamental purpose of the Legislature in enacting the Workmen's Compensation Law was, as a matter of public welfare, to place upon industry the losses sustained by workmen and their dependents by reason of injuries and death arising out of and in the course of employment—the theory being that compensation for such losses should be paid by industry rather than to leave the injured employee or his dependents to bear such loss alone.[1]

19.1 COMPARISON WITH COMMON LAW

Workmen's compensation laws change the common-law remedies in several important respects. They abolish the old defenses of contributory negligence, assumption of risk, and fellow servant. While an employee generally may not recover for a self-inflicted injury, the only inquiries made under workmen's compensation laws are:

1. Is there an employment relationship?
2. Are the employee and the employer covered by the law?
3. If so, has the employee sustained an injury or an occupation disease covered by the law?
4. If so, was such injury or disease incurred as a result of accident arising out of the course and scope of that employment?
5. In case of death, are there surviving dependents?

Under workmen's compensation the employee may be careless and still recover. The employee may have willingly and without protest worked under the unsafe conditions causing the injury or occupational disease. The employer may not have been at fault in any way. The injury may have been caused by the carelessness or intentional actions of a co-worker.

19.1a Change in procedure for litigating claims

At common law, if the matter could not be settled amicably, a lawsuit had to be brought by the injured employee against the employer charging the latter with negligence or, in some instances, breach of contract in failing to provide the employee with a safe place to work. The employer seldom carried insurance to protect against such claims. Today, under workmen's compensation, it is expected that an employee will be compensated for injuries received on the job, and the employer carries insurance for this purpose or is capable of self-insurance.

Normally, injured employees receive the compensation and benefits to which they are entitled quickly and without controversy. When disputes arise, they usually concern either the extent of injuries or disability or whether at the time of injury the employee was acting within the course and scope of the employment. In the case of disagreement the employee presents the claim to a state workmen's compensation board or other agency. An ultimate appeal is allowed to the courts, but the initial proceedings are held before an administrative agency.

19.2 LIBERAL INTERPRETATION OF WORKMEN'S COMPENSATION LAWS

Workmen's compensation laws are to receive a liberal construction and application in order to effectuate their purpose of providing compensation to employees.[2] This is

---

[1]Hickey v. Board of Education of City of St. Louis, 256 S.W.2d 775, 777 (Mo. 1953).

[2]Jacobs v. Bob Eldridge Construction Co., 393 S.W.2d 33 (Mo. 1965).

the situation even though such laws are in derogation of the common law. The objective is to carry out the legislative intent of providing a new remedy for injured employees. In Kentucky, for example, the statute specifically provides that the workmen's compensation laws shall be liberally construed and that the general rule which requires strict construction of statutes in derogation of the common law does not apply.[3]

19.3 AUTHORITY TO SPEND SCHOOL FUNDS FOR WORKMEN'S COMPENSATION

In a Missouri case[4] the court had squarely before it the question of whether school district funds could be used to purchase workmen's compensation insurance. Plaintiffs' action was to restrain by means of an injunction the proposed expenditure. Citing a long list of cases from many jurisdictions on the same point, the court concluded, "The weight of authority is that expenditures of public moneys for workmen's compensation for public employees are for public purposes and are not 'grants' of public money."[5] If the state legislature authorizes public employees, including school teachers, to be included under workmen's compensation, by implication it empowers school districts to secure workmen's compensation insurance.

In a mandamus action a teacher may compel a school district to pay a compensation claim, even though such a district is immune from tort suits.[6]

19.4 COVERAGE OF SCHOOL TEACHERS

It has been said that all states provide some kind of coverage of employees under workmen's compensation.[7] Workmen's compensation laws apply to "employers" and "employees." It is generally held that school districts are employers within the meaning of such laws[8] and that teachers are employees.[9] The following persons also

have been held to be employees: instructor of dairying,[10] football coach of grade school,[11] part-time manual arts teacher,[12] secretary of board of school commissioners,[13] and manual arts teacher in a separate building.[14]

19.4a Employee or independent contractor

The law makes a distinction between "employees" and "independent contractors." The former are covered by an employer's workmen compensation coverage; the latter are not. In order to be an employee, an employment contract between the employer and employee must exist wherein the latter agrees to perform specified services directly to the former (and not a third person) and to work under the former's supervision and control.[15] An independent contractor is one exercising an independent employment who contracts to do a piece of work according to independent methods without being subject to the control of the employer except as to the results thereof.[16] Painters who were redecorating a high school building were held[17] to be employees of the contractor, not of the school district, where they received their pay from the former and the contractor determined when and where they were to work.

A question sometimes arises as to the status of a "loaned employee." The general rule was stated by the Iowa court:

The rule recognizes a class of cases where a workman is employed by one employer from whom he received his wages, and has been by such general employer loaned to another employer for some special work or job. Under that rule if injury occurs to the employee while working for and under the direction and control of the special employer, such special employer is liable to such employee for such injuries under the Workmen's Compensation Act, because in such case it is said that the worker is in the actual employ of the special

[3]Kentucky Revised Statutes 242.044 (1969).

[4]Hickey v. Board of Education of City of St. Louis, 256 S.W.2d 775 (Mo. 1953).

[5]*Ibid.*, p. 777; State v. Krueger, 72 N.W.2d 734 (Wis. 1955); City of Red Wing v. Eichinger, 203 N.W. 622 (Minn. 1925). *Contra,* Georgia Casualty Co. v. Lackey, 294 S.W. 276 (Tex. 1927).

[6]Woodcock v. Board of Education, 187 Pac. 181, 10 A.L.R. 181 (Utah 1920).

[7]Hickey v. Board of Education of City of St. Louis, 256 S.W.2d 775 (Mo. 1953).

[8]Bailey v. School Dist. No. 5, 198 N.Y.S. 247 (1923); Nevada Industrial Commissions v. Leonard, 68 P.2d 576 (Nev. 1937). *Contra,* Ponca City Board of Education v. Beasley, 11 P.2d 466 (Okla. 1932).

[9]Whitney v. Rural Independent School Dist. No. 4, 4 N.W.2d 394 (Iowa 1942); Nevada Industrial Commission v. Leonard, 68 P.2d 576 (Nev. 1937).

[10]Crowley v. Idaho Industrial Training School, 26 P.2d 180 (Ida. 1933).

[11]Perdue v. State Board of Equalization, 172 S.E. 396 (N.C. 1934).

[12]Evans v. Louisiana State Board of Education, 85 So.2d 669 (La. 1956).

[13]Reissner v. Board of School Commissioners, 4 N.E.2d 581 (Ind. 1936).

[14]Board of Education v. Industrial Commission, 134 N.E. 70 (Ill. 1922).

[15]Hoover v. Independent School Dist., 264 N.W. 611 (Iowa 1936). School District No. 4 v. Industrial Commission, 216 N.W. 844 (Wis. 1927).

[16]Montgomery v. Mine LaMotte Corp., 304 S.W.2d 885 (Mo. 1957).

[17]Hoover v. Independent School District, 264 N.W. 611 (Iowa 1936).

employer at the time the injury is sustained. This is held to be true even though the contract of employment was entirely with the general employer, and the wage was paid by the general employer.[18]

19.4b Employees or public officers

Some workmen's compensation laws distinguish between employees and officers or supervisory personnel. The Massachusetts law extended coverage to "laborers, workmen and mechanics." It was found in a 1954 case[19] that the chief of police of Harvard University was not included within such terms and hence was not covered. The court cited with approval a 1917 Massachusetts case[20] holding that a teacher at an annual salary in a vocational school was not a "laborer, workman, or mechanic" and therefore was not covered by the workmen's compensation law.

An Ohio case has held[21] that a county superintendent of schools is an employee and not an official within the meaning of a statutory provision excluding "any official of ... school district." Since the superintendent was answerable to the county board of education, it was found that he did not exercise "certain independent public duties, a part of the sovereignty of the state" in order to make him an "official."

19.4c Number of employees

State statutes frequently prescribe that a certain minimum number of employees is required before there is automatic or mandatory coverage under the workmen's compensation law. According to a Michigan statute, "This act excepting section I hereof shall not apply to employers who regularly employ less than 8 employees at 1 time nor to domestic servants or farm laborers." In a Michigan case the plaintiff, a school teacher, was the only employee of a school district. It was held[22] that the district was not liable to her for compensation since it was not covered by the law.

19.5 INJURIES ARISING OUT OF AND IN THE COURSE OF EMPLOYMENT

In order for an injury to be compensable under the workmen's compensation law it must arise out of and in the course of the employment. When the injury occurs while the teacher is engaged in the performance of regular duties at the usual work station, there is likely to be no question. However, if the injury occurs at some other time and place, as en route from home to school or to a school meeting, or at a function off the school premises, or at home, a problem is presented as to whether the injury arose out of and in the course of employment.

The words *arising out of* and *in the course of* have been the subject of numerous court decisions. The Supreme Court of North Carolina has defined them as follows:

The words "arising out of" refer to the cause or origin of the accident; they involve the idea of causal connection between the employment and the injury, and impose the condition that an injury in order to be compensable must spring from or have its origin in the employment. ...

The term "in the course of" relates more particularly to the time, the place, and the circumstances under which the injury occurs.[23]

19.6 INJURIES OCCURRING AT SCHOOL DURING PERFORMANCE OF DUTIES

Proof standing alone that an employee was at the place of employment and was doing the usual work at the time of injury is insufficient. Although such evidence establishes that the injury occurred in the course of employment, it must also be shown that the injury arose out of the employment. In a North Carolina case[24] the principal of a high school was murdered by an enraged person in his office sometime after 9:30 P.M. It was agreed "that he was at the place of his employment and was about the performance of his usual duties as principal." The question was whether there was any causal connection between the murderous assault and his employment as high school principal. The principal had earlier in the evening reprimanded his assailant, who was a boarding student of an orphanage, for the violation of a rule of the orphanage. The Industrial Commission found that the reprimand was not administered by the deceased in the performance of his duties as principal and hence that his death did not arise out of his employment.

In the following instances compensation was allowed:

18*Ibid.*, p. 612.

19Randall's Case, 119 N.E.2d 189 (Mass. 1954).

20Lesuer v. City of Lowell, 116 N.E. 483 (Mass. 1917).

21Anderson v. Industrial Commission, 57 N.E.2d 620 (Ohio 1943).

22Wickham v. Carlton Township School District 2, 37 N.W.2d 770 (Mich. 1949).

23Sweatt v. Rutherford County Board of Education, 75 S.E.2d 738, 742 (N.C. 1953).

24*Ibid.*

An injury received by a manual training teacher while instructing a student how to operate a circular saw.[25]

An injury sustained after regular hours by a substitute teacher who voluntarily assisted a student organization.[26]

An injury sustained by a part-time manual arts teacher while assisting a student on a class project during a time when the other students had been released to attend a class play.[27]

An injury received by a rural school teacher who was struck in the eye by a toy tractor wheel thrown by a pupil.[28]

A back injury sustained by a teacher in shoving a heavy desk so that she could get a book from the bookcase.[29]

An injury incurred by slipping on a polished floor in a schoolroom.[30]

Death caused by a cyclone which destroyed a school building where it was found that the building was located on an eminence and the teacher's duties in supervising the safety of the pupils exposed her to greater danger from the "act of God" than the general public.[31]

19.7 INJURIES RECEIVED ON SCHOOL PREMISES OUTSIDE THE CLASSROOMS

Injuries are sometimes compensable even though they do not occur at the teacher's usual place of employment and during the performance of customary duties. However, the teacher must be performing work for the employer, and the injury must be caused by such work. In an Indiana case[32] an injury to a teacher was held to arise out of and to be in the course of the employment where she slipped and fell on the sidewalk outside the school building one-half hour before the start of classes. It was shown that it was customary for one of the teachers to be on the playground early and to supervise students marching along the sidewalk to an adjoining church for religious instruction. The teacher was at the head of the line of students when she slipped and fell.

---

[25]Board of Education v. Industrial Commission, 134 N.E. 70 (Ill. 1922).
[26]Maurice v. Orleans Parish School Board, 295 So.2d 184 (La. 1974).
[27]Evans v. Louisiana State Board of Education, 85 So.2d 669 (La. 1956).
[28]Whitney v. Rural Independent School District No. 4, 4 N.W.2d 394 (Iowa 1942).
[29]Elk Grove Union High School District v. Industrial Accident Commission, 168 Pac. 392 (Cal. 1917).
[30]Lowman v. Industrial Commission, 96 P.2d 405 (Ariz. 1939).
[31]Scott County School Board v. Carter, 159 S.E. 115 (Va. 1931).
[32]Kunkel v. Arnold, 158 N.E.2d 660 (Ind. 1959).

In a North Carolina case[33] the coach of a school football team was found to be in the course of his employment when he died from a blow struck by the referee during the course of an argument at a game.

19.8 INJURIES SUSTAINED GOING TO AND FROM SCHOOL

Unless the teacher is on a special mission for or otherwise performing service of benefit to the employer, injuries sustained while going to and returning from school are not compensable. The general rule is against compensation. In the words of the Illinois Supreme Court, "The general rule is that employment does not begin until the employee reaches the place of employment, and does not continue after he has left the place of employment."[34] The general rule was followed and no compensation was allowed in the following cases:

Where a teacher slipped on ice while going to work even though the superintendent had required the teacher to carry various school supplies with her.[35]

Where a teacher suffered injuries in falling on the steps of her home en route to school while carrying a kettle to be used in school.[36]

Where a teacher fell on the sidewalk in front of the school steps while returning from lunch.[37]

However, in recent years there has been some erosion of the "going and coming" rule and a number of exceptions have developed. Of particular importance to teachers is the so called "twofold purpose" or "dual purpose" doctrine which allows an employee to recover when injured furthering the employer's business even though the employee's own interests are furthered as well. This doctrine is frequently relied upon by teachers who are injured while traveling to and from school. Compensation was awarded in the following cases:

Where a teacher was injured while driving home from work and it was shown that she was transporting materials that were "difficult to handle" (report cards, books, and teaching

---

[33]Perdue v. State Board of Equalization, 172 S.E. 396 (N.C. 1934).
[34]Board of Education v. Industrial Commission, 64 N.E.2d 374 (Ill. 1945); Burchett v. Delton-Kellogg School, 144 N.W.2d 337 (Mich. 1966).
[35]Board of Education v. Industrial Commission, 64 N.E.2d 374 (Ill. 1945).
[36]Industrial Commission of Ohio v. Harkrader, 3 N.E.2d 61 (Ohio 1935).
[37]Strahlendorff v. Board of Education, 4 A.2d 848 (N.J. 1939).

materials) and that she could not fulfill her professional responsibility at the level required without taking work home.[38]

Where a teacher was injured while traveling to her home and it was established that she had no time to prepare lessons and correct papers during regular working hours.[39]

Where a teacher was injured while walking home and her duties included supervision of pupils on their way to and from school and on the playground.[40]

It is apparent that courts are not in total agreement on the applicability of the dual purpose doctrine. In an attempt to clarify the Michigan law, the Supreme Court of that state posed the following questions to determine if recovery should be awarded for injuries sustained on the way home from school:

Does the employer expect or command teachers to transport papers home for correction? Does the employer provide time and facilities for doing this work on the employer's premises? Or, alternatively, is the teacher transporting these papers home for her own convenience? Finally, the all conclusive question: If the teacher failed to transport the papers, would the employer find it necessary to hire someone else to complete this task?[41]

19.9 INJURIES OCCURRING DURING SPECIAL MISSIONS OR DUTIES

Teachers may and do perform duties related to their employment away from their usual place of work. If a teacher is injured during the course of a special mission or duty, and the injury arises therefrom, the injury is covered by workmen's compensation. Thus, an injury sustained by a school janitor was compensable where he was struck by an automobile when crossing a street to buy cleaning material which he was instructed to buy,[42] or when he was struck by an automobile while returning to the schoolhouse in the evening in response to the principal's call to turn on the lights for a basketball game in the gymnasium.[43]

Similarly, a teacher was held[44] to be covered for an injury she received on the way to the city to purchase graduation supplies, when permission to purchase them had been granted by the school board. However, where a teacher and a superintendent were injured in an automobile accident as they were returning from making an unauthorized and unlawful purchase of school supplies, their injuries were held[45] not to have arisen "out of and in course of employment."

The Iowa court permitted[46] an elderly teacher to recover compensation for a broken hip which she sustained in a fall on an icy highway about one block from school, which highway she was inspecting to see if it was safe for the school buses and for the school teachers to travel. (Actually, the buses had left a few minutes before she ventured out to check the condition of the highway.) In another case[47] a teacher in the English department of a junior high school was inspecting a gun in the home of its owner to determine whether it was suitable for use as a needed "property" in a dramatic production. She was injured when the gun went off. The injury was held to be compensable. She had been directed to examine the gun by the teacher in charge of dramatics. However, an assault upon a teacher as she entered her parked car at night after attending a Christmas party of a student club of which she was the faculty adviser was found[48] not to arise out of her employment. It was not shown that she was assaulted because she was a teacher or because of any events growing out of her teaching duties.

Some school personnel, as superintendents and supervising teachers, have no one place of work and often no fixed hours of employment. They may be engaged in performing the duties of their employment, or something incidental thereto, at various times and places, including travel from one place to another. In a South Dakota case[49] a school superintendent, who had no fixed hours of work and who often performed work at his home, was permitted to recover for injuries sustained on his way from his home to the high school on a snowy day.

[38]Wilson v. Workmen's Compensation Appeals Board, 120 Cal.Rptr. 113 (1975).

[39]Burchett v. Delton-Kellogg School, 144 N.W.2d 337 (Mich. 1966).

[40]Nevada Industrial Commission v. Leonard, 68 P.2d 576 (Nev. 1937).

[41]Burchett v. Delton-Kellogg School, 144 N.E.2d 337 (Mich. 1966).

[42]Massey v. Board of Education of Mecklenburg County, 167 S.E. 695 (N.C. 1933).

[43]Kyle v. Greene High School, 226 N.W. 71 (Iowa 1939).

[44]England v. Fairview School District No. 16 of Power County, 77 P.2d 655 (Ida. 1938).

[45]Babcock v. School District No. 107, Cedar Bluffs, 243 N.W. 831 (Neb. 1932).

[46]Crowe v. DeSoto Consolidated School District, 68 N.W.2d 63 (Iowa 1955).

[47]Maynard v. Board of Education, School District No. 4, 7 N.Y.S.2d 714 (1938).

[48]Bobertz v. Board of Education of Hillside Tp., 52 A.2d 827 (N.J. 1947).

[49]Lang v. Board of Education, 17 N.W.2d 695 (S.D. 1945).

One of his duties was to determine whether weather conditions required the closing of the school. After his fall he called off classes for the afternoon. In a Wisconsin case a supervising teacher on her way home from conducting an evening meeting ran off the road into a river and was drowned. It was held[50] that she was on the highway incidental to her duties and therefore was covered by workmen's compensation.

Whether injuries sustained by teachers in participating in patriotic activities arise out of or in the course of their employment depends upon the degree of school involvement. Teachers assisting during World War II in the issuance of war ration books were held[51] not to be covered by workmen's compensation. However, a teacher was allowed[52] compensation where she was injured while riding on a jeep with school children during a war bond drive sponsored by the school. The accident occurred on school property.

19.10 INJURIES SUSTAINED IN TRAVELING TO OR FROM AND AT MEETINGS, INSTITUTES, AND SPEAKING ENGAGEMENTS

Injuries sustained while attending functions which teachers are expected to attend as part of their duties, or which they are directed to attend by proper authority, normally are compensable. Recovery of workmen's compensation benefits was allowed in the following situations:

Travel connected with attendance at a teachers' institute.[53]

Death of a school superintendent in an automobile collision which occurred while he was on a trip to attend a meeting devoted to a discussion of school affairs and to interview a teaching prospect.[54]

Injury sustained in an automobile collision on the way to a teachers' meeting held during school hours.[55]

Falling and breaking a leg while at a meeting of a teachers' association.[56]

Injury sustained by a principal in an automobile accident while on the way to attend a state directors' convention, which he had been instructed to attend by the school board.[57]

Death of a principal resulting from travel to a state university at its invitation to confer with graduates of his high school.[58]

Injury sustained by a teacher in an automobile accident while traveling to the residence of the chairman of the board of trustees to make a customary report.[59]

In an Indiana case, however, a teacher who was injured while traveling from a state teacher's convention to a cheerleader workshop was denied compensation apparently because she was not required to attend the workshop.[60]

Injuries sustained in connection with speaking engagements were held compensable in two cases and denied in another. In an Ohio case[61] the traveling representative of a university died as a result of a pinprick received while pinning on a rose at a lecture he delivered to the graduating class of a high school. The lecture was held to be part of his duties and compensation was allowed. The wearing of the rose presented to him was incidental thereto. A special errand by a librarian to attend a ceremony at another library to deliver a short talk, and to discuss book purchases, was held[62] to be covered in a California case. However, in a Colorado case a widow of a law school dean was not permitted to recover compensation for her husband's death from a heart attack sustained while addressing a local law fraternity.[63]

19.11 ARISING FROM ACCIDENT

In order to be compensable, the injury or death must be caused by accident (or in

[50]Racine County v. Industrial Commission, 246 N.W. 303 (Wis. 1933).

[51]Burton v. Board of Education, 31 A.2d 337 (N.J. 1943); Bituminous Casualty Co. v. Industrial Commission, 13 N.W.2d 925 (Wis. 1944).

[52]Worthington v. Plainfield Board of Education, 40 A.2d 9 (N.J. 1944).

[53]Bower v. Industrial Commission, 22 N.E.2d 840 (Ohio 1939).

[54]Williams v. School City of Winchester, 10 N.E.2d 314 (Ind. 1937); Anderson v. Industrial Commission, 57 N.E.2d 620 (Ohio 1943).

[55]Bradley v. Frazier, 233 N.Y.S.2d 894 (1962).

[56]Dearing v. Union Free School District No. 1, 70 N.Y.S.2d 418 (1947).

[57]Howell v. Kingston Tp. School District, 161 Atl. 559 (Pa. 1932).

[58]Mann v. Board of Education of City of Detroit, 253 N.W. 294 (Mich. 1934).

[59]Scrivner v. Franklin School Dist. No. 2, 293 Pac. 666 (Ida. 1930).

[60]Weeks v. Wa-Nee Community Schools, 250 N.E.2d 258 (Ind. 1969).

[61]Industrial Commission v. Davison, 160 N.E. 693 (Ohio 1928).

[62]Los Angeles Jewish Community Council v. Industrial Accident Commission, 209 P.2d 991 (Cal. 1949).

[63]University of Denver-Colorado Seminary v. Johnston, 378 P.2d 830 (Col. 1963).

some instances by occupational disease) arising out of and in the course of employment. The word *accident* generally is construed to mean "an unexpected or unforeseen event, happening suddenly and violently, with or without human fault and producing at the time, injury to the physical structure of the body."[64] In most cases the question of accident poses no difficulty, as where a teacher is injured by a fall, by a thrown object, by a machine or piece of equipment, or in an automobile collision. Questions do arise as to whether heart attacks, eye hemorrhages, hernias, and the like are caused by accident. If the event could have occurred outside of as well as during employment, such as a heart attack, the claimant has the difficult burden of establishing an employment-connected accident. However, there are instances when the unusual stress, or strain, or shock of the job may produce the condition which under other circumstances would not have occurred. In two cases in which teachers have died of heart attacks at a school or school-related event no "accident" was found and consequently compensation was denied. In both cases the teachers were aware of a preexisting condition. As the Pennsylvania court put it:

> To constitute a compensable "accident" it must be shown that the work in which he was engaged at the time of the occurrence was of a different nature and required a materially greater amount of exertion, risk or exposure, than that to which he was ordinarily subjected, so as to justify a conclusion that the increased severity of the work was the cause of, and not merely coincidental with, the aggravation of the previously existing infirmity.[65]

The court found "the guiding principle for the disposition of [such] cases" in a quotation from an earlier Pennsylvania court decision: "Death or disability from a natural cause overtaking an employee while engaged in his accustomed work in the usual manner cannot be considered as accidental, though hastened by his work." In the above case a physical education instructor died while participating in the annual exhibition basketball game between the varsity and the faculty.

In the above Colorado case the court affirmed[66] the finding of the Industrial Commission of that state that the law school dean's heart attack did not arise from "accident," even though it was shown that the dean fretted and worried over each speech.

19.12 SELF-INFLICTED INJURY

Under most, if not all, state workmen's compensation laws, a claimant cannot recover for a self-inflicted injury. The intentional doing of an act which produces injury, such as shoving a heavy desk,[67] does not in itself fall within the prohibition. An intent to cause the injury in question must also be shown.

19.13 EFFECTS OF BENEFITS OR PAYMENTS RECEIVED FROM THIRD PERSONS

Unless made with the purpose of compromising or settling a compensation claim, payments or the value of benefits received from another source are not deductible from the compensation to be paid. Thus, a teacher was allowed to retain, in addition to her full compensation benefits, the sum of $1027.25 paid to her by the mother of a boy who accidentally shot her,[68] and a janitor was permitted to receive a $15-per-month pension.[69]

Sometimes a teacher will return to work too soon or take another job before returning to teaching. Earnings in this situation are not deductible, nor do they disprove the disability where it is shown that the teacher worked out of necessity and suffered pain while doing so.[70]

19.14 TIMELY FILING OF CLAIM

Workmen's compensation laws specify that a claim for compensation must be filed with the administrative agency within a prescribed period of time after the accident occurred, often one year. In addition, prompt notice of the accident must be given to the employer. Where compensation payments are begun and then are discontinued, the statute of limitations usually begins to run from the receipt of the last payment.[71]

---

[64]See the statutory definition in State v. District Court, 168 N.W. 555 (Minn. 1918).

[65]McFeeley v. School District, 47 A.2d 925, 926 (Pa. 1946).

[66]University of Denver-Colorado Seminary v. Johnston, 378 P.2d 830 (Col. 1963).

[67]Elk Grove Union High School District v. Industrial Accident Commission, 168 Pac. 392 (Cal. 1917).

[68]Maynard v. Board of Education, School District No. 4, 7 N.Y.S.2d 714 (1938).

[69]Rhodus v. American Employers Insurance Company, 9 So.2d 821 (La. 1942).

[70]Scott v. Caddo Parish School Board, 12 So.2d 823 (La. 1943).

[71]Morrow v. Industrial Commission, 56 P.2d 35 (Col. 1936).

PART TWO
Fringe benefits

19.15 GENERALLY

As part of the total "money package," private and public employers are providing an ever expanding program of "fringe benefits" to their employees. These may consist of group life insurance, health and accident insurance, major medical insurance programs, paid holidays, sick leave, paid vacations, sabbatical leaves, and the like. The programs vary greatly and cannot be examined in detail here. However, there are two legal questions which arise frequently with regard to such fringe benefit programs. The initial question involves the authority of the school district to participate in whole or in part in defraying the cost of such fringe benefits. The second problem relates to fringe benefits which may in some way be discriminatory and violate either state or federal law.

19.16 AUTHORITY TO USE
PUBLIC FUNDS FOR FRINGE BENEFITS

The authority to use public funds for fringe benefits depends on the state constitution, statutes, and applicable regulations. Cases involving the authority generally fall in three categories: (1) those where a state constitution or statute prohibit such an expenditure; (2) those where the legislature has passed a statute expressly authorizing such expenditure; and (3) those where neither a restriction nor an express authorization is present, and the question is whether the school district may incur such expenditure under its implied powers.

19.16a Constitutional limitations

A decision by the United States Court of Appeals for the Fifth Circuit illustrates the first situation. Polk County, Georgia, joined with its employees under a contributory plan wherein both the county and the employees paid the premiums for life insurance and for health, accident, sickness, and hospital insurance for employees of the county. Relying on an earlier decision of the Georgia Supreme Court (as it was bound to do), a federal court held[72] that under the Georgia constitution counties could levy taxes only for the enumerated purposes, and

paying premiums to insurance companies was not one of them. The United States Court of Appeals acknowledged:

> The district court found and the appellee here asserts that the weight of authority is contrary to the conclusion we have reached. Decisions of courts of other jurisdictions are cited to sustain the proposition that counties may supplement the wages of employment by paying part of insurance premiums for employees. It is said that the county could obtain better employees, that employees would have a sense of security, that an injured employee would receive his wages from the insurance company and not from the county. These are, in substance, the arguments which were rejected by the Supreme Court of Georgia in the Scoggins case [the earlier decision relied upon].[73]

It must be stressed that this decision was based upon a very restrictive provision in the Georgia constitution.

In a Tennessee case the court held that the payment of premiums by the City of Memphis on a group insurance policy covering its water department employees did not violate a constitutional prohibition against the appropriation of public funds for private purposes. The court reasoned:

> It could hardly be contended but that the governing powers would have the right to increase the annual wages of each employee of the water department $18 per annum, if justified by existing conditions. This, in effect, is what it did when it took out said policy of group insurance, but from an economic basis it concluded that better results would be obtained as to both parties by investing it in insurance instead of paying the money to the employee. Ordinarily what can be done indirectly can be done directly. . . .[74]

> The large enterprises of this country have reached a wonderful condition of economic efficiency, and, according to the stipulation, they are adopting the group insurance system for the benefit of their employees. If it is beneficial to them, why would it not be beneficial to our municipalities?[75]

---

[72]Polk County, Georgia v. Lincoln National Life Insurance Company, 262 F.2d 486 (5th Cir. 1959).

[73]Ibid.
[74]State v. City of Memphis, 251 S.W. 46 (Tenn. 1923).
[75]Ibid., p. 50.

19.16b Express statutory authorization

In many jurisdictions legislatures have enacted statutes which specifically authorize state or local units to purchase group life or medical insurance for their employees. Such statutes control unless they are in conflict with the state constitution. For example, some state constitutions direct that the salary of certain officers may not be increased or decreased during their term of office. Assuming that fringe benefits are considered as part of an individual's salary or compensation, then new benefits cannot be granted to such an employee during that term of office. However, in an early New Mexico case, it was decided that such a limitation had no application to a city official who had no fixed tenure of office but served during the pleasure of the appointing power.[76] School boards must also be sure that they comply with the statutory bidding requirements if they are applicable to insurance contracts.

19.16c Implied powers

In the absence of either a constitutional or statutory restriction or express authority, the question may arise as to whether a governmental body has the implied power to provide certain fringe benefits for its employees. In another New Mexico case, the court held that the authority to defray "all other expenses connected with the proper conduct of the public schools in their respective districts" was sufficient to confer this authority.[77] It was reasoned that furnishing group insurance "for the teachers enables the board of education to procure a better class of teachers, and prevents frequent changes in the teaching force." There is, however, authority to the contrary which suggests that in the absence of specified statutory authority a governmental body has no authority to secure insurance for its employees since it does not directly relate to a public purpose.[78] Because of the apparent conflict of opinion on this point, it seems desirable for state legislatures which have not already done so to adopt enabling legislation expressly authorizing the expenditure of public funds by school districts for usual fringe benefits.

19.17 DISCRIMINATORY APPLICATION OF BENEFITS

In recent years there have been a number of suits against various governmental units, including school boards, for alleged discrimination in the application of policies and benefits. The majority of these cases have involved maternity benefits and were brought under the due process or equal protection provision of the Fourteenth Amendment or the various civil rights statutes. For example, in *Cleveland Board of Education v. LaFleur*[79] a teacher challenged the constitutionality of the school board's mandatory maternity leave policy. The policy in question required a teacher to take leave some five months before the expected birth of her child and not return to teaching until the child was at least three months old. The Supreme Court stated that ". . . the arbitrary cutoff dates embodied in the mandatory leave rules before us have no rational relationship to the valid state interest of preserving continuity of instruction." The Court observed that the rule contained an irrefutable presumption of physical incompetency, and that the presumption applied even where the medical evidence as to a particular teacher was wholly contrary. Such a rule was arbitrary and denied the teacher due process as guaranteed by the Fourteenth Amendment.

Similar suits have been brought under Title VII of the Civil Rights Act of 1964 which, among other things, prohibits discrimination in employment on the basis of sex. School board policies which deny teachers the use of accumulated "sick leave" while recovering from childbirth have been declared invalid under Title VII.[80] School boards must treat pregnancy-related disabilities the same as other temporary disabilities.[81]

---

[76]Bowers v. City of Albuquerque, 200 P.421 (N.M. 1921; *See also* Opinion of the Justices, 30 S.W.2d 14 (Ala. 1947).

[77]Nohl v. Board of Education of City of Albuquerque, 199 P.373 (N.M. 1921); *See annotations in* 16 A.L.R. 1089 and 27 A.L.R. 1267.

[78]Opinion of the Justices, 30 So.2d 14, 16 (Ala. 1947); People v. Dibble, 189 N.Y.S. 29 (1921).

[79]Cleveland v. LaFleur, 414 U.S. 632, 94 S.Ct. 791, 39 L.Ed.2d 52 (Ohio 1974); *See also* Paxman v. Wilkerson, 390 F.Supp. 442 (Va. 1975).

[80]Hutchison v. Lake Oswego School District, 519 F.2d 961 (9th Cir. 1975); Liss v. School District of the City of Ladue, 396 F.Supp. 1035 (Mo. 1975); Vineyard v. Hollister Elementary School, 64 F.R.D. 580 (Cal. 1974).

[81]Holthaus v. Compton and Sons, Inc., 514 F.2d 651 (8th Cir. 1975).

PART THREE
Retirement benefits

19.18 RELATIONSHIP
TO SOCIAL SECURITY

Retirement plans, whether or not in conjunction with social security, are intended to provide three types of benefits: (1) superannuation or retirement, (2) disability, and (3) death. By 1950, when social security first became available to public employees, all full-time teachers in the public schools of the United States were covered by state or local retirement programs. The 1950 extension of social security to employees of state and local governments excluded those protected by retirement systems. Public school teachers therefore could not avail themselves of social security until this restriction was removed in 1954. Owing to the comity existing between federal and state governments, coverage of public employees was not made mandatory but depended upon special arrangements or voluntary agreements between each state and the Secretary of the Department of Health, Education, and Welfare. Groups of public employees, such as the employees of a school district, under an existing retirement system were required to elect to come under social security by majority vote. Some teacher groups rejected social security, fearing that it would weaken their existing retirement plans. However, by 1960 social security had been added as a supplement to the retirement programs of about two-thirds of all public school teachers. In a few additional states the existing retirement programs were modified with the advent of social security, so that the amount of retirement allowance was reduced by the amount received under social security.

Some problems have arisen in the coordination of a state's teacher retirement system with social security. In Iowa a statute was enacted permitting boards of education to liquidate their retirement systems, place teachers under federal social security, and return the contributions of teachers in five annual installments without interest. The constitutionality of the statute was upheld.[82] In New Jersey the statute directed an offset of retirement allowances by the amount received under federal social security except that teachers who were born prior to January 1, 1900, could receive both the full pension allowance and social security benefits if they filed an application for retirement prior to January 1, 1963. A

teacher otherwise qualifying filed her application on February 4, 1963. The court held[83] that she had substantially complied with the law, especially since she had informally advised the pension fund of her intent to retire as early as December 1, 1962.

19.19 AUTHORITY
TO SPEND PUBLIC FUNDS FOR
TEACHERS' RETIREMENT PROGRAMS

Occasionally someone challenges the authority of the state or local board to expend public funds for teachers' retirement programs. In a 1937 case, the Rhode Island Court observed, "It has repeatedly been held by courts of last resort that providing for retirement pay to public school teachers is a proper public function in aid of free education."[84] It also has been held repeatedly that the legislature may improve the benefits for teachers in the system. However, there is a conflict of authority as to whether benefits may be increased for teachers already in retirement. In an early Illinois case, it was held that extending additional benefits to the latter group did not violate a constitutional provision prohibiting the granting of extra compensation for services already rendered.[85] Such teachers form a distinct class and may properly be treated differently from other persons. In a 1951 case that same court observed:

The State legislature is charged with the duty of providing the residents of this State a free and public educational system. Such a system requires qualified and competent teachers. The legislature requires these teachers to have certain qualifications. The legislature, by tax laws, provides the means by which these teachers are paid during their teaching careers and thereby, at least indirectly, fixes the amount of their compensation. Under these circumstances, for the legislature to determine that the welfare of the public-school system required that a system of retirement allowances be set up for them as a group does not seem unreasonable, and there seems ample justification to distinguish them as a class for that purpose. The legislature may have determined that under all these circumstances the State had a moral obligation to them and we have held that the

---

[82]Nelson v. Board of Directors, Etc., 70 N.W.2d 555 (Iowa 1955).

[83]Swiney v. Department of Treasury, Division of Pensions, 201 A.2d 392 (N.J. 1964).

[84]Powers v. Home for Aged Women, 192 Atl. 770, 773 (R.I. 1937).

[85]Ridgley v. Board of Trustees, 21 N.E.2d 286 (Ill. 1939).

expenditure of public money for a moral obligation is an expenditure for a public purpose. . . . They are reasonably classified as a group for the purpose of providing retirement allowances, and an increase of such allowances. . . .[86]

In some jurisdictions, the granting of increased benefits after retirement has been held to violate state constitutional provisions prohibiting the granting of extra compensation.[87] In most jurisdictions, however, the use of public funds for retirement benefits does not constitute the bestowal of gratuities but is deemed to be deferred compensation to promote and reward long-continued and faithful services.[88] However, the statute which increases the benefits must clearly indicate that teachers already retired are to be included, since legislative enactments are generally presumed to operate prospectively and not retrospectively. In this connection a Utah court observed:

However, increases in the benefits to teachers who have already retired do not substantially tend to attract qualified persons to the system or to induce members of the system to remain therein. Increases in benefits of persons who have previously retired do not substantially aid in the fulfillment of the purposes of the act.[89]

19.20 CREDIT FOR PRIOR TEACHING

Credit may be given for various types of prior service. It has been held constitutional to allow "prior service" credit for teaching in parochial schools.[90] Credit has also been allowed in some cases for service prior to the establishment of the retirement system.[91] Most retirement programs allow some type of credit for out-of-state teaching service. Kentucky is typical in its requirement:

1. Out of state service credit will be given if a comparable position would have been covered in Kentucky;
2. a maximum of eight (8) years credit will be allowed;
3. the teacher must make the required contribution, plus interest; and
4. no credit will be permitted where the service will be used to qualify the teacher for another retirement program financed by state funds.[92]

Regardless of the basis of prior service credit, a teacher who disagrees with the board's computation of prior service must promptly notify the board if changes are requested.[93]

19.21 ELIGIBILITY FOR PARTICIPATION

A teacher's eligibility to participate in a retirement program depends on the state law and/or applicable regulations. While full-time public school teachers are always covered, the status of part-time teachers, other professional staff, and administrators varies by system. In New York City, for example, a substitute teacher does not qualify for membership in the retirement system.[94] In Wisconsin substitute teachers have an optional right to such membership,[95] if they comply with the terms and conditions of membership. In Washington the court held[96] that all years during which a substitute teacher actually taught were to be counted in computing the thirty-year period. In Arizona prior service credit was allowed to teachers serving under temporary emergency teaching permits.[97]

Under the New York City retirement system, retirement service credit may be withheld during the period of a teacher's suspension when no services are rendered,[98] and a resignation constitutes a complete break in the service. Upon resigning, the teacher is to be paid forthwith the accumulated contributions standing to his or her credit.[99] Upon withdrawal of a resignation and reemployment the teacher may regain

[86]Krebs v. Board of Trustees of Teachers' Retirement System, 102 N.E.2d 321 (Ill. 1951). *See also* Voigt v. Board of Education of City of Chicago, 108 N.E.2d 426 (Ill. 1952).

[87]State v. Giessel, 53 N.W.2d 726 (Wis. 1952).

[88]Anderson v. Board of Education, 165 N.Y.S.2d 908 (1957); Bridges v. City of Charlotte, 20 S.E.2d 825 (N.C. 1942); McCord v. Iowa Employment Security Commission, 56 N.W.2d 5 (Iowa 1952). *But see* Opinion of the Justices, 150 A.2d 816 (N.H. 1959).

[89]McCarrey v. Utah State Teachers' Retirement Board, 177 P.2d 725 (Utah 1947). *See also* Mattson v. Flynn, 13 N.W.2d 11 (Minn. 1944), holding that the rights of a teacher coming into the system in 1918 and retiring in 1931 were governed by the 1915 act and not the 1931 act.

[90]Gubler v. Utah State Teachers' Retirement Board, 192 P.2d 580 (Utah 1948).

[91]Opinion of the Justices, 151 A.2d 777 (N.H. 1959).

[92]Kentucky Revised Statutes 161.515 (1976 Cumulative Issue). *See also* Ohio Revised Statutes 3307.01 (1976 Supplement).

[93]Application of Schein, 138 N.Y.S.2d 321 (1954).

[94]Winkel v. Teachers' Retirement System, 149 N.Y.S.2d 443 (1956).

[95]Blau v. City of Milwaukee, 285 N.W. 347 (Wis. 1939).

[96]Charters v. Board of Trustees of Seattle Teachers' Retirement Fund, 73 P.2d 508 (Wash. 1937).

[97]Montgomery v. Crawford, 220 P.2d 853 (Ariz. 1950).

[98]Douglas v. Teachers' Retirement Board of City of N.Y., 244 N.Y.S.2d 173 (1963).

[99]Winkel v. Teachers' Retirement System, 149 N.Y.S.2d 443 (1956).

membership in the retirement program.[100] Under certain circumstances special credit may be allowed for summer school teaching.[101]

In Iowa the time a claimant served as county superintendent of schools was excluded since he was then considered a public officer and not an employee.[102] A Colorado case held[103] that a teacher may waive or release her right to a pension.

19.22 PERIODS OF MILITARY SERVICE

Teachers are frequently allowed retirement credit for time spent in the military service, but such rights are totally dependent upon state law and applicable regulations. In some states the board of education contributes to the retirement program while the teacher is in the military service. In New Jersey the statute integrating the retirement acts with the federal Social Security Act provided that a veteran should receive a refund of "accumulated deductions." It was held[104] that such refund was limited to the veteran's own actual contributions and did not include those made for the veteran by the board of education during the period of military service.

The applicable statute may also limit the amount of credit for which an individual may be eligible. Under the New York State Retirement System, it has been held that the military duty credit was intended to aid career teachers who take temporary leave to serve their country and was not intended to aid career military personnel who happen to teach before and after their military careers. Consequently, a career military officer was not eligible for credit during the twenty-two years spent in the military.[105]

Likewise, military credit may be limited to particular types of service. In Washington it was held[106] that a teacher was not entitled to wartime service credit for time spent on active duty with the Civil Air Patrol.

19.23 DISTINCTION BETWEEN ANNUITY AND PENSION FUNDS

Where deductions are made from a teacher's salary and are paid into a segregated retirement fund, in most states the teacher acquires contractual rights therein, the terms of which are ascertained by reference to the applicable statutes or regulations. An Illinois case makes a distinction between a pension fund and an annuity fund. It describes the former as "in the nature of a bounty springing from the appreciation and graciousness of the sovereign, and may be given, withheld, distributed, or recalled at its pleasure"; "the money is not first segregated from the public fund so as to become private property and then turned over to the pension fund, but is set aside or transferred from one public fund to another, and remains public money over which the person from whose salary it is deducted has no control, and in which he has no right." It defines an annuity fund as one which is kept separate from other public moneys, and one into which a teacher, after electing to participate, must make contributions as a condition of employment. The teacher acquires rights and an interest in an annuity fund.[107]

When the retirement program is established as a fund separate and segregated from other public moneys, and participating teachers as a condition of their employment make contributions to the fund, usually by payroll deductions, the fund is normally referred to as "an annuity fund" or "an annuity reserve fund." A pension is normally paid from public funds or the contributions made by government to the fund. An annuity is usually based on the accumulated contributions of the teacher or on the joint contributions of teacher and employer.[108] What distinctions may exist between the two terms in a particular case are dependent upon the laws of the particular state. The terms *pension* and *annuity* are often used interchangeably.

A true pension is considered a gratuity payable at the discretion of the public authority from public funds. A teacher has contractual rights in an annuity fund but not in a true pension fund. As was observed by the Kansas court:

It is generally held that a pension granted by the public authorities is not a contractual obligation, but a gratuitous allowance in the continuance of which the pensioner has no vested right. By the great weight of authority the fact that a pensioner has made compulsory

[100]*Ibid.*

[101]Mantell v. Teachers' Retirement System, 160 N.Y.S.2d 502 (1957).

[102]Eller v. Iowa Employment Security Commission, 100 N.W.2d 417 (Iowa 1960).

[103]School District No. 1 v. Faker, 105 P.2d 406 (Col. 1940).

[104]Bruder v. Teachers' Pension & Annuity Fund, 142 A.2d 225 (N.J. 1958). As to the right of a New Jersey teacher to receive a veteran's pension, see Race v. Board of Education, 117 A.2d 312 (N.J. 1955).

[105]Newcomb v. New York State Teachers' Retirement System, 336 N.Y.S.2d 298 (1972).

[106]Carpenter v. Butler, 201 P.2d 704 (Wash. 1949).

[107]Raines v. Board of Trustees, 7 N.E.2d 489 (Ill. 1936).

[108]Birnbaum v. New York State Teachers' Retirement System, 152 N.E.2d 241 (1958).

contributions to the fund does not give him a vested right in the pension.[109]

A Montana case found[110] that contributions made by a teacher were to an annuity fund and therefore she had contractual rights in the fund which could not be impaired. It declared void a legislative act paying upon withdrawal of accumulated contributions three-fourths of the interest on the account to the pension accumulation fund and not to the teacher.

19.24 UNAUTHORIZED EXPENDITURES FROM RETIREMENT FUNDS

In a Wisconsin case a declaratory judgment suit was brought by the State Teachers' Retirement Board against the director of the budget to test the legality of a state statute requiring the fund to reimburse the state for a portion of the cost of making a study of retirement systems. The amount involved was $18,312.02. In holding that such an expenditure from the teachers' retirement fund was invalid, the Supreme Court of Wisconsin said:

> It is argued that the plaintiff board is required to pay out funds according to law and appropriations from the earnings of the fund have been made by law each year, and therefore there is no vested right in the gross earnings of the fund. We do not agree. The teacher's right, based on contract, extends to the retirement system. The earnings on investments, part of which represent contributions made by the teachers and part contributed by the state under the contract with them, constitute assets of the system. The reserve for contingencies set up by the board is a part of the system. . . . However, the legislature and the plaintiff board are not free to spend or appropriate the earnings of the fund except in a manner authorized by statute relating to the state teacher's retirement system.[111]

The Wisconsin Supreme Court concluded that "teachers have a contractual relationship with the state and a vested right in the state teacher's retirement system."

19.25 COMPUTATION OF BENEFITS

In most cases, benefits will be based on the teacher's average monthly earnings prior to retirement. In some states the retirement allowance is based on earnings during the final year while in others it is based on an averaging of certain years or the highest years. Regardless of the plan adopted in a particular jurisdiction, questions frequently arise as to what types of compensation should be included in this computation. For example, the New York statute excludes lump sum payments for sick leave, annual leave, or any form of termination pay in the computation of "final average salary." It has been held[112] that under this system, a 12 percent salary increase received by a teacher upon giving notice of her intent to retire was a form of termination pay and could not be included in the computation of average salary computation. Similarly, in a New Jersey case the court upheld[113] the decision of the board of trustees of the Teachers' Pension and Annuity Fund in disallowing extra compensation received by certain teachers during their final year of employment in computating their retirement allowances.

However, in a Georgia case, where the statute made no specific exclusions, the court construed[114] the statute liberally in favor of the pensioner and allowed the inclusion of $1194.00 in accumulated sick pay in the computation of her average monthly salary. Similarly, under the Massachusetts plan, extra pay received for coaching has been included.[115]

19.26 DIMINUTION OF BENEFITS

May a teacher challenge action which may ultimately adversely affect the amount of retirement benefits? The New York Court of Appeals in a 1958 case answered this question in the affirmative. In that case[116] plaintiffs, on behalf of themselves and other teachers similarly situated, brought an action of declaratory judgment to challenge the validity of the action of the New York State Teachers Retirement System in adopting a new actuarial table which they claimed would reduce their annuities upon retirement by 5 percent. Plaintiffs had neither resigned nor applied for retirement.

[109]State v. Board of Education of City of Topeka, 129 P.2d 265 (Kan. 1942).

[110]Clarke v. Ireland, 199 P.2d 965 (Mont. 1948), in which the court observed (p. 969):

The courts have also recognized the difference between a pension fund into which the potential beneficiaries only make token payments and the bulk of which is made up by legislative appropriations, and annuity funds whereby the prospective beneficiary makes payments on an insurance basis computed by experienced actuaries and receives benefits in direct proportion to the payments made.

[111]State Teachers' Retirement Board v. Giessel, 106 N.W.2d 301, 305 (Wis. 1960).

[112]Simonds v. New York State Teachers' Retirement System, 349 N.Y.S.2d 140 (1973).

[113]Board of Trustees of Teachers' Pension and Annuity Fund v. LaTronica, 196 A.2d 7 (N.J. 1963).

[114]Purdie v. Jarrett, 152 S.E.2d 749 (Ga. 1966).

[115]Murphy v. City of Boston, 150 N.E.2d 542 (Mass. 1958).

[116]Birnbaum v. New York State Teachers' Retirement System, 152 N.E.2d 241 (1958).

Nevertheless, they were found to have a standing to sue, the court stating:

> The value of retirement benefits and prospective rate of payment, especially in the face of continued inflation, is of vital concern to the plaintiffs and might as well be the determining factor in their decision to continue in the teaching profession, or seek more lucrative employment.[117]

In holding that the actuarial table could not be changed, the court relied upon a 1938 amendment to the New York constitution which provided:

> After July first, nineteen hundred forty, membership in any pension or retirement system of the state or of a civil division thereof shall be a contractual relationship, the benefits of which shall not be diminished or impaired.[118]

Under this constitutional amendment the minimum rights of teachers become fixed at the time they become members of the system.

In the absence of constitutional restriction, the United States Supreme Court has held that a state legislature may reduce the amounts of annuity payments to teachers without violating the "impairment of contracts" and the "due process" clauses of the United States Constitution.[119] Again the question turns upon the form of the state law and upon whether such law confers upon teachers contractual rights in the fund.

The court in *Taylor v. Board of Education*[120] articulated the general rule relating to noncontributory plans:

> The unquestionable general rule is that a pension granted by the public authorities is not a contractual obligation but a gratuitous allowance in the continuation of which the pensioner has no vested right and that a pension is accordingly terminable at the will of the grantor, either in whole or in part. And

> since there is no contract on the part of the state to continue the payment of a benefit or annuity, a change in the law affecting such benefits or annuity does not impair the obligation of a contract or deprive the petitioner of property within the constitutional meaning. [Citing 40 Am.Jur., Pensions, Section 24].

There is an exception to the general rule, and that is where any particular payment becomes due, the pensioner has a vested right to that payment. This does not mean that there is a vested right in any future payments, but only that pensioners have a right to payments which have accrued to them.[121]

Where, however, the pension plan provides for contribution to the fund by the teacher, his or her rights vest at the time of retirement. In such cases the benefits provided by such plan may not be diminished or otherwise affected by subsequent legislation unless such right is reserved by the statute or authority creating the plan.[122]

19.27 ELECTION OF ANNUITY OPTIONS

At the time of applying for a superannuation retirement allowance, the teacher may have several plans of payment from which to choose. One plan, for example, will pay a "maximum annuity" throughout the teacher's life, but all payments will cease upon death. In a Pennsylvania case a teacher elected to receive such maximum annuity. He retired on June 30, 1958, and before receiving his first monthly retirement check he died, on August 19, 1958. His contributions plus interest amounted to over $12,500. The court upheld[123] the decision of the retirement board that his estate was entitled to receive only two monthly retirement payments for July and August. It was pointed out that the deceased could have elected a different option which upon his death would have paid his estate the balance of his superannuation retirement allowance.

In a New York case[124] a teacher elected

---

[117]*Ibid.*, p. 243. The acceptance of the lesser amount by beneficiaries did not bar them from seeking relief. Ayman v. Teachers' Retirement Board of City of N.Y., 193 N.Y.S.2d 2 (1959); 172 N.E.2d 571 (N.Y. 1961). In Ostrove v. New York State Teachers' Retirement System, 247 N.Y.S.2d 212 (1963), a declaratory judgment action was brought to determine whether two sets of mortality tables could be used in computing mortality allowances. *See also* Garvin v. Teachers' Retirement Bd. of City of N.Y., 204 N.Y.S.2d 293 (1960).

[118]Section 7 of Article V. Haupt v. Teachers' Retirement Board of N.Y., 210 N.Y.S.2d 337 (1960).

[119]Dodge v. Board of Education, 302 U.S. 74, 58 S.Ct. 98, 82 L.Ed. 57 (Ill. 1937).

[120]Taylor v. Board of Education of the County of Cabell, 166 S.E.2d 150 (W.Va. 1969).

[121]Bender v. Anglin, 60 S.E.2d 756, cert. denied, 340 U.S. 878, 71 S.Ct. 125, 95 L.Ed. 838 (Ga. 1950).

[122]Klamm v. State ex rel. Carlson, 126 N.E.2d 487 (Ind. 1955); Clarke v. Ireland, 199 P.2d 965 (Mont. 1948); State ex rel. Phillip v. Public School Retirement System of City of St. Louis, 262 S.W.2d 569 (Mo. 1953); Driggs v. Utah State Teachers Retirement Board, 142 P.2d 657 (Utah 1943).

[123]Ogden v. Public School Employees' Retirement Board, 182 A.2d 228 (Pa. 1962).

[124]Schwartzberg v. Teachers' Retirement Board of N.Y., 83 N.E.2d 146 (N.Y. 1948); *See also* Ortelere v. Teachers' Retirement Board of the City of New York, 303 N.Y.S.2d 362 (1969); Keith v. New York State Teachers' Retirement System, 362 N.Y.S.2d 231 (1974).

the option which would pay the balance to her estate. A number of years after her retirement, after becoming incompetent, she revoked this plan and elected another option giving her the maximum allowance during her life but providing no payment to her estate upon her death. After her death the court set aside the last-elected option on the ground of mental incapacity.

Some states provide that if death occurs shortly after retirement, such as within thirty days, any option selected shall be ineffective and the deceased shall be treated as though in active service at the time of death.[125]

19.28 RETIREMENT BENEFITS

Ordinarily, little problem is experienced in applying for and receiving monthly annuity payments following retirement. The matter involves only the teacher's preparation of an application with whatever supporting proof as to age, etc., may be required, and perhaps also a formal resignation from the teaching position. The application may be submitted by another on behalf of the teacher where that person has been authorized to do so, as by a power of attorney.[126] The election to take an early retirement after completing the requisite number of years of service may invoke a somewhat more complicated procedure.[127] In some cases a teacher may have been dismissed for cause, or the contract may not have been renewed leaving the teacher ineligible for retirement benefits. Such action is likely to be challenged in the courts[128] but normally will be sustained if the school board has acted in good faith and with justification.

Sometimes a question arises as to when a teacher must retire under a compulsory retirement law. This will, of course, depend upon the wording of each law or regulation. In a case in Chicago the law required a teacher to retire at the end of the semester in which the age sixty-five years was attained. It was held[129] that a teacher could be retired at the end of the first semester if he became sixty-five on the first day of the second semester. In another case it was decided[130]

that a teacher who was granted a leave of absence until his fifty-fifth birthday, the minimum age of retirement, qualified for superannuation benefits.

Retirement payments normally cease when a teacher returns to teaching and receives a salary therefor.[131] The teacher may thereby become eligible to retire under a more generous retirement act adopted during the reemployment.[132]

A teacher whose contributions to the fund were not deducted through error and who knew about the mistake was required to pay to the fund, before she could obtain retirement benefits, what she would have paid if proper deductions had been made.[133]

19.29 DEATH BENEFITS

Death benefits may be payable in two situations: death before retirement and death after retirement. In the latter instance whether a payment is to be made will depend upon the annuity option elected by the deceased at the time of retirement. In either case a question may arise as to whether the death benefit should be paid to the decedent's estate or to a named beneficiary. The problem is complicated where the teacher has not changed beneficiaries following a divorce from the designated beneficiary,[134] marriage and children,[135] remarriage after the death of the named beneficiary,[136] and the like. Marriage may be considered as in effect a revocation of the earlier designation of a mother or brother. It has been held[137] that the estate has a claim superior to that of the spouse where the latter's rights were extinguished in a property settlement. However, in a Florida case[138] the divorced wife prevailed over the second wife where death occurred during active service and the former was designated as the beneficiary to receive such payment. In an earlier Wisconsin

[125]Maillet v. Board of Trustees, Teachers' Retirement System, 176 So.2d 7 (La. 1965); 183 So.2d 321 (La. 1966).
[126]People v. Graves, 45 N.E.2d 161 (N.Y. 1942).
[127]Deibert v. Board of Trustees of Teachers' Pension, 200 A.2d 325 (N.J. 1964).
[128]Driver v. Independent School District of Sioux City, 276 N.W. 37 (Iowa 1937).
[129]People v. Board of Education of City of Chicago, 99 N.E.2d 592 (Ill. 1951).
[130]Bartlett v. Duluth Teachers' Retirement Fund Association, 28 N.W.2d 740 (Minn. 1947).

[131]State v. Foraker, 323 P.2d 1107 (N.M. 1958); Baumgartner v. Michigan Public School Employee Retirement Fund Board, 41 N.W.2d 328 (Mich. 1950).
[132]Baumgartner v. Michigan Public School Employee Retirement Fund Board, 41 N.W.2d 328 (Mich. 1950).
[133]Board of Education of City of Linden v. Liebman, 153 A.2d 385 (N.J. 1956).
[134]Gallaher v. State Teachers' Retirement System, 47 Cal.Rptr. 139 (1965); First Western Bank and Trust Co. v. Omizzolo, 1 Cal.Rptr. 758 (1959). See also Di Dio v. Board of Trustees, 156 N.W.2d 418 (Wis. 1968).
[135]Bergin v. Board of Trustees of Teachers' Retirement System, 198 N.E.2d 527 (Ill. 1964); 202 N.E.2d 490 (Ill. 1964).
[136]Watenpaugh v. State Teachers' Retirement System, 336 P.2d 165 (Cal. 1959).
[137]First Western Bank and Trust Co. v. Omizzolo, 1 Cal.Rptr. 758 (1959). Contra: Wolf v. Jebe, 9 N.W.2d 124 (Wis. 1943).
[138]Rogers v. Rogers, 152 So.2d 183 (Fla. 1963).

case[139] a divorce settlement terminated the wife's right in her husband's property, but it was held that she was still entitled to retirement benefits since her designation as beneficiary had not been changed. A will has been held[140] to effect a revocation of a designation of a named beneficiary. A sister drawing retirement benefits from the same fund may be designated as the beneficiary.[141]

19.30 DISABILITY BENEFITS

Normally, if disability benefits are to be obtained, the disability must occur during active service and before retirement.[142] After a teacher has been declared disabled and has been retired for physical disability,

it has been held[143] that the teacher is no longer entitled to receive a salary. It also has been decided[144] that a retirement board was without authority to adopt an administrative regulation providing that a disability retirement would not become effective until thirty days from the time the request has been received. The disability must usually be established by competent medical evidence.[145]

In a New Jersey case the Teachers' Pension and Annuity Fund had granted a teacher an accidental disability retirement allowance. It was held[146] that it could not deduct the amount of a workmen's compensation award paid by the board of education for the same injuries.

[139]Wolf v. Jebe, 9 N.W.2d 124 (Wis. 1943).
[140]Lyles v. Teachers' Retirement Board, 33 Cal.Rptr. 328 (1963).
[141]Kirkland v. Kirkland, 359 S.W.2d 651 (Tex. 1962).
[142]Katz v. New York City Teachers' Retirement Board, 52 N.E.2d 902 (N.Y. 1943).

[143]Tilton v. Board of Education, 78 P.2d 474 (Cal. 1938).
[144]Frigiola v. Board of Education, 95 A.2d 491 (N.J. 1953).
[145]Weisman v. Teachers' Retirement Board of City of N.Y., 258 N.Y.S.2d 946 (1965).
[146]Sevan v. Board of Trustees of Teachers' Pension, Etc., 204 A.2d 371 (N.J. 1964).

PART FOUR
Social Security benefits

19.31 HISTORICAL
DEVELOPMENT OF SOCIAL SECURITY

The original Social Security Act was signed into law by President Franklin D. Roosevelt on August 14, 1935. It established a twofold program of old-age benefits for retired workers and a federal-state system of unemployment insurance. Since then the act has been amended repeatedly to enlarge benefits and coverage. In 1956 the program was significantly broadened by the addition of disability insurance. The Medicare features of the plan were adopted in 1965.

19.32 FINANCIAL
ASPECTS OF SOCIAL SECURITY

Social security, often called Old-Age, Survivors, and Disability Insurance (OASDI),[147] is self-supporting since the benefits and costs are financed from the social security taxes paid by employees, employers, and self-employed people. All receipts go into federally administered trust funds[148] which are used exclusively to finance the various social security programs. Surplus funds are invested in interest-bearing securities of the United States government.

19.33 MANDATORY INCLUSION OF
EMPLOYEES UNDER SOCIAL SECURITY

Once the employees of a school district are included under social security, as will be explained more fully later, they all must participate. Little or no choice is afforded the individual teacher in this regard. If the program were not compulsory, many employees might elect greater present take-home pay, undiminished by the social security taxes, in preference to retirement and possible disability benefits to be received later in life. The deductions from a teacher's salary of the social security taxes are therefore mandatory once one has been brought under social security coverage. However, certain public employee groups are now entitled to withdraw from social security and establish their own system.

19.34 ADMINISTRATION
OF THE SOCIAL SECURITY PROGRAM

The Secretary of Health, Education, and Welfare is responsible for administering all aspects of the old-age, survivors, and dis-ability insurance programs except (1) the collection of social security taxes (which is performed mainly by the Internal Revenue Service), (2) the preparation and mailing of benefit checks (which is done by the Department of the Treasury), and (3) the management of the trust funds (which is handled by the Secretary of the Treasury as Managing Trustee). The Social Security Administration, a division of the Department of Health, Education, and Welfare, has been delegated responsibility for the actual administration of the programs.

19.35 SOCIAL SECURITY
ADMINISTRATION FIELD OFFICES

The Administration has field offices throughout the country which assist the public by offering advice and information and processing applications for benefits. The field offices also have available copies of explanatory bulletins and printed forms which are most helpful. They are there to be of service and should be consulted by anyone having questions or problems concerning entitlement to social security benefits. These benefits are not charity. They are rights which have been paid for by the employee and the employer through payment of the social security taxes.

19.36 SUMMARY OF
BENEFITS UNDER SOCIAL SECURITY

There are four different kinds of programs, all of which require application for benefits:

1. *Monthly retirement benefits* in full begin at age sixty-five (unless a person continues to work and earn above the permitted level), or reduced benefits begin as early as age sixty-two. A widow or dependent widower may qualify for benefits as early as age sixty.
2. *Monthly survivors benefits* are payable to
   a. A widow or dependent widower,[149] or in certain cases a dependent divorced wife, if she is sixty years of age or older.

---

[147]For the act of Congress relating to federal old-age, survivors and disability benefits, see 42 U.S.C.A., 401–425.

[148]42 U.S.C.A., 401.

[149]The requirement that a widower be "dependent" has been challenged in four recent cases: Goldfarb v. Secretary of Health Education and Welfare, 396 F.Supp. 308 (N.Y. 1975); Silbowitz v. Secretary of Health Education and Welfare, 397 F.Supp. 862 (Fla. 1975); Jablon v. Secretary of Health Education and Welfare, 399 F.Supp. 118 (Md. 1975); and Coffin v. Secretary of Health Education and Welfare, 400 F.Supp. 953 (D.C. 1975) have all held that to require a widower to be "dependent" while not placing the same requirement on a widow is constitutionally impermissable. These cases have all been appealed to the Supreme Court.

b. Children who are under age eighteen (twenty-two in the case of unmarried, full-time students).

c. Children who are eighteen years of age, or older children if they became disabled before age twenty-two.

d. A widow or widower caring for a child of the deceased spouse, unless the child is receiving benefits solely because he or she is a student.

e. Dependent parents sixty-two years of age or over.

f. In addition, a lump sum for funeral expenses is payable either to a spouse, to the person who pays funeral expenses, or directly to the funeral director.

3. *Monthly disability benefits*, if one is disabled.

4. *Medicare benefits*, consisting of (a) basic Medicare which covers up to 90 days of hospitalization for any period of illness, posthospital care of up to 100 days for any period of illness in a "skilled nursing facility," and up to 100 home health visits after discharge from a hospital in which the patient has stayed at least three days; (b) voluntary "supplementary" medicare covering doctor's bills and other medical and health services, for which there is an additional charge; and (c) a combined federal-state medicare program for the needy supported by general taxes, the benefits of which vary from state to state. In addition, payments are made by social security under the Supplemental Security Income program to persons with very limited income.

19.37 MONTHLY RETIREMENT BENEFITS

Since there are a number of variables, such as average monthly wage and size of family, and since retirement benefits are subject to periodic revisions, no attempt is made here to set them forth. Interested parties may obtain a brochure from a field office of the Social Security Administration containing a table showing the current monthly benefits.

19.37a Outside earnings[150]

As of January 1, 1977, no benefits are withheld if an individual earns less than $3,000 in a year. If more than $3,000 is earned, the general rule is that $1.00 in benefits is withheld for every $2.00 in earnings above that amount. There are three exceptions to this rule:

1. If in any month one neither earns more than $250 working for someone else nor does substantial work in a business of one's own, there will be no deduction from one's benefit for that month no matter how much one earns in the balance of the year.

2. Royalties received after age sixty-five from copyrights or patents derived from one's own efforts (and obtained before reaching sixty-five) are excepted.

3. After age seventy-two there is no deduction from benefits because of outside earnings.

19.37b Application for

It must be stressed that application must be made for all benefits for which one is eligible under social security and that benefits may be lost by reason of late filing of an application, although a person may be entitled to receive benefits retroactively for as many as twelve months before the month in which application for benefits was filed.[151] For example, if a person reaches age sixty-five in June 1967 and is then fully insured but does not file an application for old-age insurance benefits until June 1968, that person can receive retroactive benefits back to June 1967. However, if the applicant had become sixty-five in June 1966, payments from June 1966 to June 1967 would be lost. Application forms may be obtained from and filed with a district or field office of the Social Security Administration.

Proof of age may be established by a birth certificate, baptismal record, early school record, census record (a search for such a record may be obtained for a fee of $4.00 for a regular search or $5.00 for an expedited search by writing to the Personal Service Branch, Bureau of the Census, Pittsburg, Kansas), or by such evidence of age as may be found in a family Bible, a marriage certificate, immigration or naturalization records, insurance policies, employment and military records, and the like.

19.38 COMBINATION OF RETIREMENT AND SOCIAL SECURITY

In 1950 social security was extended to cover employees of state and local governments by special arrangements provided they were not protected by public employee retirement systems. The 1954 amendments to the Social Security Act removed this restriction and made it possible for state and local employees covered by retirement systems (except for policemen and firemen in some states) to come under the act.[152]

It must be emphasized that state and local government employees, including employees of school districts, are covered by social security only if a special arrangement or voluntary agreement with the Secretary of Health, Education, and Welfare has been entered into by the state. Each unit of government employees included in the

[150]See 42 U.S.C.A., 403.

[151]*Ibid.*, 402(j).
[152]*Ibid.*, 418.

agreement is known as a "coverage group," which may include the employees of an individual school district. There are two basic types of coverage groups: (1) groups composed of employees of the state or one of its political subdivisions whose positions are not under a state or local retirement system, and (2) retirement system coverage groups, i.e., groups composed of employees whose positions are covered by a state or local retirement system. Generally, to secure social security coverage a majority of the employees in a unit or group under a retirement system must vote for coverage in a referendum held under authorization of the state. Where a majority of teachers under a state or local retirement system vote in favor of participation in social security and their unit is included as a retirement system coverage group in the agreement entered into between the state and HEW, the teachers will be covered by both their retirement plan and social security, unless the state legislature liquidates its plan when social security is adopted. If the majority so votes, the balance of the teachers in the group also are brought under social security. Of course, in such event teachers will have their share of social security taxes deducted from their salaries. As part of its agreement with the Department of Health, Education, and Welfare, a state obligates itself to pay the employer's share of social security taxes to the Secretary of the Treasury.[153]

19.39 DISABILITY
BENEFITS UNDER SOCIAL SECURITY

Social security pays monthly disability benefits to disabled teachers or other employees under the age of sixty-five as long as the disability lasts or until they begin to receive old-age insurance benefits. Social security also pays monthly benefits to certain dependents of disabled workers. The term *disability* as used in the Social Security Act is defined as:

A. inability to engage in any substantial gainful activity by reason of any medically determinable physical or mental impairment which can be expected to result in death or which has lasted or can be expected to last for a continuous period of not less than 12 months; or

B. in the case of an individual who has attained the age of 55 and is blind (within the meaning of "blindness' as defined in Section 416 (i) (1) of this title), inability by reason of such blindness to engage in substantial gainful activity in which he has

previously engaged with some regularity and over a substantial period of time.[154]

19.40 PROOF OF DISABILITY

The burden is upon the social security claimants to establish their claims of disability. They meet this burden when they show their inability to perform their usual occupation, such as school teaching, and the burden then shifts to the Social Security Administration to prove that they are able to engage in some other substantial gainful activity.[155] The testimony of physicians is helpful but not controlling.[156] "Substantial gainful employment" must be both substantial and gainful and within the claimant's capability, realistically measured by education, training, and experience. The question is, what employment opportunities are there for a person who can do only what the claimant can do? Mere theoretical ability to engage in substantial gainful activity is not enough if no reasonable opportunity for that activity is available.[157] There must be a reasonable possibility of employment as opposed to theoretical employability.[158] The test for disability consists of two parts: (1) a determination of the extent of the claimant's physical or mental impairment and (2) a determination of whether or not that impairment results in inability to engage in any substantial activity.[159] There are four elements of proof to be considered in making a finding of claimant's ability or inability to engage in any substantial gainful activity:[160] (1) objective medical facts which are clinical findings of examining or treating physicians divorced from their expert judgments or opinion as to significance of these clinical findings; (2) diagnosis of expert medical opinions of these physicians; (3) subjective evidence of pain and disability testified to by claimant, and corroborated by claimant's family and neighbors; (4) claimant's educational background, work history, and present age.

Few court decisions relating to disability under the social security law are directly applicable to teachers. Most cases concern persons of limited education or background who find it difficult, if not impossible, to shift to another line of work upon receiving

[153]*Ibid.*, 418(e).

[154]*Ibid.*, 423(c) (2).
[155]Ihnen v. Gardner, 253 F.Supp. 541 (S.D. 1966).
[156]*Ibid.*
[157]Hodgson v. Celebrezze, 357 F.2d 750 (3d. Cir., 1966).
[158]*Ibid.*
[159]Morgan v. Gardner, 254 F.Supp. 977 (Okla. 1966).
[160]Pendergraph v. Celebrezze, 255 F.Supp. 313 (N.C. 1966).

a disability which prevents them from continuing in their usual occupation. Thus, a coal miner doing physical labor who possesses a second-grade education and who injures his back has great difficulty in finding other employment. In a case which came before the United States Court of Appeals it was suggested that a fifty-eight-year-old man who had worked as a coal miner for thirty-one years could return to school teaching. The court rejected[161] the suggestion and found him to be disabled. He had a high school education, in 1929 had been issued a teacher's certificate, and had taught school for two years until be became an underground coal miner.

19.41 SUMMARY

Teachers and other school employees generally enjoy retirement and other benefits comparable to those received by employees in other fields of employment.

Teachers now generally are covered by workmen's compensation. If a teacher sustains an injury, and the teacher and district are covered by the law, the teacher will be covered if the accident or occupational disease arose during and within the scope and course of employment. Only in exceptional cases may a teacher recover workmen's compensation for injuries received off the school premises. Exceptions include injuries incurred as a result of a special mission or assignment for the benefit of the school and attendance at functions which the teacher has a duty to attend.

Unless restrictive provisions are found in state constitutions or statutes, school funds may be expended for retirement, workmen's compensation, sick leave, and other fringe benefit programs. Naturally, such benefits must be administered in a nondiscriminatory manner.

Many states provide retirement benefits in combination with or as a supplement to social security. Social security payments are based upon federal statutes, whereas the rights of teachers in a retirement fund are dependent upon the statutes of a particular state. Where the state retirement program is deemed contractual, certain rights in the fund are acquired which cannot be divested from the teacher although they are usually subject to reasonable change by state legislation.

Under most retirement programs, as well as under social security, three types of benefits are provided—retirement, death, and disability. In most cases, teachers have certain options or elections as to retirement payments. Normally, if disability benefits are to be obtained the disability must occur during active service and before retirement. Upon reaching retirement age, the disabled person is entitled to retirement benefits. In most states, a teacher is covered by social security and receives the same benefits as employees in private industry. Social security and some retirement programs require the beneficiary to make formal application for the particular benefits sought. Benefits may be lost if no application is made or if it is improper or untimely.

---

[161]Polly v. Gardner, 364 F.2d 969 (6th Cir. 1966).

Law Books in School Law Research

20.0 INTRODUCTION

The objective of legal research is to locate authoritative statements of the law which would be considered binding or highly persuasive to the court or other body which must make the ultimate decision on the particular matter in issue. Law emanates from one of the branches of government; but as there are multiple governments, the law of one may not be binding upon a transaction subject to the jurisdiction of another. It is axiomatic, however, that law stemming from a superior government is controlling upon lesser governments and their inhabitants. Thus, the law of the United States, wherever it applies, is considered the supreme law of the land and cannot be superseded by any contrary state or local law. Similarly, the law of a state, apart from any overriding federal law, is supreme throughout the state and applies to inhabitants and occurrences in any of its counties and cities. However, the laws of state A are not considered binding upon the people of state B, and the ordinances of city X are not applicable to activities within city Y. It must be understood that the rules of law are not universally accepted, as are the principles of mathematics.

In looking up the law to determine the answer to a legal question, the beginning point is to ascertain the governing law and the law books in which it may be found. A wider search of source books of law is often indicated, but statements found therein will be considered only persuasive and not binding upon the ruling body or court. As with most problems, legal questions divide themselves into easy ones and hard ones. The former often may be answered by the simple reading of a state statute or of an applicable government regulation; the latter may be troublesome even for the Supreme Court of the United States. Sometimes the best answer which can be given to a knotty legal question of first impression is a prophecy of what the courts will do when the matter is presented to them.

School law problems run the gamut of the whole body of the law and involve laws emanating from all levels and branches of government. Accordingly, the researcher must be familiar with the publications found in a good law library and with the best methods for their use. Such publications will include constitutions and statutes, court decisions, administrative rules and regulations, textbooks, legal encyclopedias, legal periodicals, attorney general opinions, and the like.

The nature of the particular problem to be resolved largely determines the books to be searched and the procedure to be followed. On questions involving the constitutionality of federal aid to education, for example, the beginning point will be the Constitution of the United States and court decisions construing its applicable provisions. In resolving questions relating to the power of a board of education, the search will be devoted primarily to a careful examination of the statutes of the state and to court decisions interpreting them since the authority of the board is derived from the state legislature. Problems concerning the administration locally of programs based on federal assistance will require a check of the applicable acts of Congress together with any rules and regulations which may have been adopted by the agencies charged with implementation of the acts. Other questions, such as the disciplinary authority of a teacher, may not be governed by legislation; here the search will be confined principally to court decisions. In these instances it is customarily said that the question is controlled by the common law, a term that is used to describe judge-made law.

20.1 CLASSIFICATION OF LAW BOOKS

Law books are commonly classified as primary authority, secondary authority, and books of index. Primary authority is either binding upon courts or highly persuasive. It represents the authority of government and emanates from its three branches (executive, legislative, and judicial) at federal, state, and local levels. The executive branch of government and its various agencies, such as the United States Department of Health, Education, and Welfare, or a state department of education, promulgates rules and regulations which have the persuasiveness of primary authority. Legislative bodies enact laws. At the federal and state level these are called statutes. Local enactments are termed ordinances. Statutory materials, as used in the above classification, also include constitutions, treaties, and court rules. The judicial branch of government consists of the federal, state, and local courts. However, only the published opinions of the appellate courts (as distinguished from the trial and local courts) are normally regarded as primary authority. Rules and regulations of the executive branch of government and enactments of the legislative branch seek to control future conduct and apply to the public generally. A court decision, on the other hand, pronounces a rule settling a present or past dispute between the parties to the litigation. Since a court can be expected to decide a similar question in the same manner, court decisions serve as precedents in future cases and hence are classified as primary authority.

Commentaries by private authors on the law are referred to as secondary authority. They are found in legal encyclopedias, textbooks, treatises, and legal periodicals.

Books of index are used to find primary authority. Besides the books listed above as secondary authority, they include the digests; the various annotated sets, such as the annotated statutes and the *American Law Reports* (A.L.R.); and *Words and Phrases*.

20.2 BOOKS CONTAINING GOVERNMENT RULES AND REGULATIONS

Administrative rules and regulations consist of executive orders (such as those issued by the President of the United States), rules and regulations promulgated by boards and agencies (including those of school boards), and decisions of such bodies. Orders issued by the President and rules and regulations of federal departments and agencies are published, as they are made, in the *Federal Register* and at the end of each year are compiled in the *Code of Federal Regulations*. For example, many of the regulations of the Department of Health, Education, and Welfare pertaining to education are contained in Title 45 of the *Code of Federal Regulations*.

Regulations of state agencies are often published in one or more bound volumes. In Kentucky, for instance, they are found in the *Kentucky Administrative Regulations Service*. Rules of city agencies are customarily published in the same volumes as are the ordinances. Generally, the clerk of each school board must be consulted concerning its rules and regulations. Copies of regulations of a governmental agency may often be obtained from an office of the agency. In the case of federal agencies they may also be purchased from the U.S. Government Printing Office, Washington D.C., 20402. Upon request it will mail a list of its publications and their purchase prices.

20.3 CONSTITUTIONS, WHERE FOUND

A constitution, whether state or federal, is the supreme law of the jurisdiction and, among other matters, defines the authority of each of its three branches of government. Frequently, the constitutionality of a statute, regulation, or other governmental action will be at issue. Constitutions are normally found in the law library in the sets of books containing the statutes of the federal government or of the particular state. One of the best sources to consult as to the United States Constitution is the *United States*

Code Annotated. It provides an easy method for obtaining a list of the court decisions interpreting the sections of the federal Constitution in which the researcher is interested. Following each section the court decisions construing it are set forth in digest form. This is one of the features of "annotated" codes or statutes.

Annotated sets of the constitutions and statutes exist also for many of the states. One example is *Vernon's Annotated Missouri Statutes*. The statute books published by an agency of the state normally also contain citations and summaries of court decisions as well as helpful historical data.

20.4 TREATIES

Treaties extend to all proper subjects of negotiation between governments. Until 1950 treaties to which the United States was a party were published in the *United States Statutes at Large* (vols. 1-64). Since then they have been published officially in the *United States Treaties and Other International Agreements Series*.

20.5 PUBLICATIONS CONTAINING STATUTES

Legislation is a definitive expression of governmental policy. It is adopted by a legislative body, i.e., the Congress of the United States, a state legislature or general assembly, or a board of aldermen. The publication of legislation usually involves several steps. First, at the close of each session of a state legislature or of the United States Congress, its enactments are published in books which are variously called Session Laws, General Laws, or Public Acts. For example, the *United States Statutes at Large* contains the enactments of each session of Congress, while the *Missouri Session Laws* publishes the enactments of each session of the Missouri General Assembly.

Periodically, the session laws will be incorporated in the sets containing a compilation of the statutes passed by earlier legislatures. Such compilations are normally called codes or revised statutes. They group together all laws relating to a particular topic in the form of chapters. The chapter (or chapters) of state statutes setting out the statutes relating to schools is often entitled "Schools and School Districts." The statutes are indexed to facilitate the search for laws pertaining to a particular problem.

Statutes of the United States have been codified in two publications: one, the official governmental publication, called the *United States Code*, and the other, an unofficial publication of a private publisher, entitled the *United States Code Annotated*.

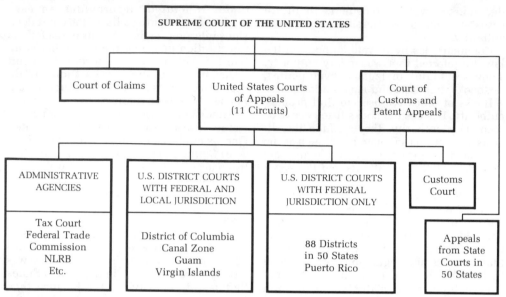

(From "The United States Courts." House Document No. 180. 88th Congress. 1st Session.)

The latter is of greater value in research since it contains historical notes and a digest of the court decisions construing each statute and constitutional provision.

The statutes of many of the states also are published officially (i.e., by an agency of the state) and unofficially (i.e., by a private publisher). The latter normally takes the form of an annotated set of many volumes. The *Missouri Revised Statutes* of 1959 together with its supplement provides an example of an official publication, whereas *Vernon's Annotated Missouri Statutes* illustrates an unofficial publication. In practice, citations to unofficial statutes are accepted by the courts. The numbers of the statutes are the same in both publications.

20.6 MUNICIPAL ORDINANCES

In the smaller cities the clerk or some other municipal officer must be consulted for a copy of the ordinances. However, the ordinances and administrative regulations of large cities are customarily published in bound or loose-leaf volumes commonly known as "The Ordinances of ——", (name of city).

20.7 COURT RULES

These rules govern the practice and procedures of the courts to which they apply. They are normally promulgated by the highest court in the federal or state judiciary and are published in the volumes containing the federal or state statutes.

20.8 ORGANIZATION OF THE FEDERAL COURTS

The Constitution of the United States and the Congress have established a system of federal courts consisting of the Supreme Court of the United States, the eleven United States courts of appeals, the 88 United States district courts, which also are the courts of bankruptcy, the Tax Court, the Court of Claims, the Customs Court, the Court of Customs and Patent Appeals, and the courts martial, including the United States Court of Military Appeals. The chart above shows the organization of the federal courts.

20.9 ORGANIZATION OF STATE COURTS

The names and organizations of the courts vary from state to state. Normally, a state's court system consists of appellate, trial, and inferior courts. The highest state court is usually called the supreme court or the court of appeals. It primarily hears and decides appeals from lower courts. Its decisions are published and are considered binding upon the courts throughout the state.

A number of states have a system of intermediate appellate courts, most of whose decisions are final. Their decisions are customarily published and are considered the law of the state except as they are inconsistent with a later statute or a decision of the highest appellate court.

The trial courts in a state are usually called circuit or district courts. They hear witnesses, receive other evidence, conduct jury trials where appropriate, and decide the case in the first instance.

Inferior courts consist of police, small claims, probate, juvenile, etc. Lower and inferior court decisions are not published and are not regarded as precedent or binding on other courts.

20.10 PUBLICATION OF COURT DECISIONS—THE NATIONAL REPORTER SYSTEM

Decisions of the lower federal courts were published in the *Federal Cases* from 1789 to 1880. Since then decisions of the United States courts of appeals have been published in the *Federal Reporter*, First and Second Series, and opinions of the United States district courts in the *Federal Supplement*. The *Federal Rules Decisions* report district court decisions involving the Federal Rules of Civil Procedure and the Federal Rules of Criminal Procedure.

Opinions of the United States Supreme Court may be found in three different sets of books: the *United States Reports*, the *Supreme Court Reporter*, and the *Lawyers' Edition of the Supreme Court Reports*. The last work, in addition to reporting all of the decisions of the United States Supreme Court, annotates many of them on a selective basis. These annotations discuss the points of law involved in the particular case and also review other cases relating thereto.

The decisions of the highest state courts (including the intermediate court of appeals) are usually published in two places: in the state reports (for example, the *Missouri Reports*) and in the National Reporter System published by the West Publishing Company. The latter system was begun in 1879. The National Reporters contain the decisions of all state appellate courts. They are now divided into nine regional reporters: the *Atlantic Reporter*, the *California Reporter*, the *New York Supplement*, the *North Eastern Reporter*, the *North Western Reporter*, the *Pacific Reporter*, the *South Eastern Reporter*, the *Southern Reporter*, and the *South Western Reporter*. The *New York Supplement* originally contained all of the lower appellate court decisions of the state of New York. It has since been expanded to include the decisions of the New York Court of Appeals. A recent addition to the National Reporter System is the *California Reporter*. Reported therein are decisions of the following California courts: Supreme Court, District Courts of Appeal, and the Appellate Department of the Superior Court.

The complete National Reporter System also includes the *Federal Reporter*, the *Federal Supplement*, the *Federal Rules Decisions*, and the *Supreme Court Reporter*. Recent decisions are first published in the advance sheets for each of the reporters, prior to their inclusion in the bound volumes. Like the National Reporters, the advance sheets feature headnotes or syllabi summarizing the holding of each case, each paragraph of which begins with the appropriate key number. As will be explained later, the same key number can be used to locate other court decisions on the same point in the digests.

20.11 THE ANNOTATED REPORTS

Court decisions of specialized or particular interest are published in the annotated reports. Each report sets out the court decision and follows it with an annotation or commentary exhaustively reviewing statutes and other court decisions on the same point. The report may also include summaries of briefs filed by counsel, library references, and other research aids. If such an annotation is found, the work of the researcher is greatly simplified. The *American Law Reports* (A.L.R.) is the annotated publication of a general nature. *Wage and Hour Cases*, *Labor Cases*, and *Negligence Compensation Cases Annotated* are examples of some of the specialized reporters.

20.12 METHOD OF CITING COURT DECISIONS

Where a court decision is published in more than one reporter, it is customary to show all sources in a citation of the case. A citation includes (in this order) the name or title of the case (i.e., the names of the plaintiff and the defendant), the number of the volume, the abbreviated name of the reporter, the page number, and the year in which the case was decided. When more than one reporter is listed for a single case, the official report is cited first. For example, the United States Reports (U.S.) or the Indiana Reports (Ind.) would precede reference to national reporters such as Supreme Court Reporter (S.Ct.) or North Eastern Reporter (N.E.). As will be noted later, many states have ceased publication of state reports and have adopted the National Reporter as the official report. The following examples will illustrate proper citation form:

1. *A U.S. Supreme Court case*. The full citation of the famous prayer decision is: *Engel v. Vitale*, 370 U.S. 421, 82 S.Ct. 1261, 8 L.E.2d 601, 86 A.L.R.2d 1285 (1962). This means that the parties in the case were Engel and Vitale and that the case may be found in four different places: first in Vol-

ume 370 of the *United States Reporter* at page 421; second in Volume 82 of the *Supreme Court Reporter* at page 1261; third in Volume 8 of the *Lawyers' Edition of the Supreme Court Reporter, Second Series*, at page 601; and fourth in Volume 86 of the *American Law Reports, Second Series*, at page 1285. Finally, the year in which the case was decided is shown in parentheses.

2. *An Oregon case.* The complete citation of the 1957 decision of the Supreme Court of Oregon holding that teachers are employees of the board of education is: *Monaghan v. School District*, 211 Ore. 360, 315 P.2d 797 (1957). This decision may be found in Volume 211 of the *Oregon Reports* at page 360 and also in Volume 315 of the *Pacific Reporter, Second Series*, at page 797. (The abbreviation Pac. or P. would be used if the case were reported in the First Series of the *Pacific Reporter*.).

3. *An early Indiana case.* The citation to the 1879 Indiana Supreme Court case deciding that a teacher must possess a teacher's certificate at the time of signing the contract is: *Putnam v. School Town of Irvington*, 69 Ind. 80 (1879). This case may be found only in the *Indiana Reports*. The *North Eastern Reporter*, in which Indiana cases are now also reported, had not yet begun publication.

4. *A recent Kentucky case.* A case similar to the Indiana one above is the 1957 decision of the Court of Appeals of Kentucky: *Floyd County Board of Education v. Slone*, 307 S.W.2d 912 (Ky. 1957). Like some other states, Kentucky no longer publishes decisions in state reports. They are now reported only in the *South Western Reporter*. The name of the state is shown in parentheses together with the year in which the case was decided.

The abbreviations of the National and Regional Reporters are:

Atlantic—Atl. and (or A) and A.2d
California—Cal.Rptr.
New York Supplement—N.Y.Supp. (or N.Y.S.) and N.Y.S.2d
North Eastern—N.E. and N.E.2d
North Western—N.W. and N.W.2d
Pacific—Pac. (or P.) and P.2d
South Eastern—S.E. and S.E.2d
South Western—S.W. and S.W.2d
Southern—So. and So.2d
Supreme Court—S.Ct.
Federal—Fed. or F and F.2d
Federal Rules Decisions—F.R.D.
Federal Supplement—F.Supp.

20.13 LEGAL ENCYCLOPEDIAS

Legal encyclopedias, along with the digests and the annotated statutes, are among the most popular tools of the legal researcher. They serve two main purposes: one, they are an excellent means, through their indexes and footnotes, of locating primary authority (court decisions, statutes, and government regulations); and two, their narrative statements of the law are generally highly accurate and easily used. They are often cited in opinions rendered by attorneys or in briefs submitted to courts. However, such statements are not binding on judges or other ruling bodies.

There are two types of encyclopedias: unrestricted and restricted. The former incorporates all court decisions in its extensive text and footnotes. The *Cyclopedia of Law and Procedure* was the first major publication of this type. It was replaced by *Corpus Juris*, which in turn was succeeded by *Corpus Juris Secundum*. The latter represents a complete rewriting of the text of *Corpus Juris*, but it cites only the more recent cases. For earlier cases it is necessary to consult the corresponding sections of *Corpus Juris*.

A restricted encyclopedia contains the same general subject matter and topics as an unrestricted one. However, it does not purport to refer to all of the reported cases but only to those considered important or leading. *Ruling Case Law* was the first of the restricted encyclopedias. It has been replaced by *American Jurisprudence*, now replaced by *American Jurisprudence, Second Series*. One of its most useful features is its footnote references to the annotations in *American Law Reports*. When in point such annotations in A.L.R. should be examined.

20.14 TEXTBOOKS AND TREATISES ON SCHOOL LAW

Like legal encyclopedias and law journals, textbooks and treatises are narrative treatments of the law by private authors. A textbook or treatise normally deals in depth with a particular area of the law. It is helpful because it brings together in one place court decisions, statutes, government regulations, and other legal writings relating to the subject and discusses current problems, some of which may not have been answered authoritatively by the courts. A sizable number of textbooks relating to various aspects of school law have been published.

20.15 OTHER TEXTBOOKS AND LEGAL PERIODICALS

There are other legal textbooks which are helpful to the research of a problem in school law. If the problem concerns a teacher's liability for a personal injury sustained by a student, for example, Prosser's[1] textbook on the law of torts should prove useful. On a contract question a standard work is Corbin's[2] treatise on contracts.

The law journals or legal periodicals published by law schools often contain articles of interest, such as Professor Bolmeier's "A Board of Education's Right to Regulate Married Students," appearing in the *Journal of Family Law* (1961) published by the University of Louisville. The *Journal of Law and Education* and the *NOLPE School Law Journal* are specialized journals which contain useful articles on school law.

20.16 THE DIGESTS

Digests contain short summaries of court decisions under alphabetically arranged topic headings, of which "Schools and School Districts" is one. Those published by the West Publishing Company preface each heading with the proper "key number" except in the Century and the First Decennial Digest where paragraph numbers are used. Once the key or paragraph number is found, it permits a speedy search throughout all of the digests for court decisions on the point.

The *American Digest* consists of several sets and digests all of the cases, federal and state. The *Century Digest* covers the years prior to 1896. Court decisions for each succeeding ten-year period are found in the Decennial Digests, of which there are now seven: the First, Second, Third, Fourth, Fifth, Sixth, and Seventh Decennial Digests. The volumes of the *General Digest*, Fourth Series, cover the years since 1966, pending publication of the Eighth Decennial Digest.

If only decisions of federal courts are sought, the *Federal Digest* may be used instead of the bulkier *American Digest*. The various state digests, such as the *Missouri Digest*, are also more convenient than the *American Digest* for locating court decisions of a particular state.

20.17 FINDING THE KEY NUMBERS

The appropriate key number or numbers may be located by using:

1. The descriptive word index to the digest.
2. The topical analysis at the beginning of each topic in the digest.
3. The headnotes to a case in point appearing in the national or regional reporter.

[1]Prosser, *Handbook on the Law of Torts*, 4th ed. (St. Paul, Minn.: West Publishing Co., 1971).
[2]Corbin, *The Law of Contracts* (St. Paul, Minn.: West Publishing Co., 1952).

4. The Table of Cases to the digest where the name of a case in point is known.

To illustrate the method for ascertaining the key number or key numbers, assume that we are interested in researching the question of the power of a school board to regulate the attendance of married students. Assume further that we know that one of the cases in point is *Kissick v. Garland Independent School District*, 330 S.W.2d 708. Finding the case in Volume 330 of the *South Western Reporter*, Second Series, at page 708, we search the headnotes to the case for the one which relates to our question. This search discloses that the point of law in which we are interested may be found under the topic "Schools and School Districts," and the key number is 172. The same result could be obtained by finding the case in the Table of Cases and checking the various topics and key numbers given. Since the Kissick case was decided on December 18, 1959, it will be found digested and in the table of cases in the volume containing "Schools and School Districts" in the Seventh Decennial Digest. One of the topics and key numbers shown after the name of the case in the Table of Cases is "Schools, 172."

If a case in point is not known, but the topic of "Schools and School Districts" is known, the key number may be located by looking through the analysis at the beginning of the topic. Doing so, we find Division H, "Pupils, and Conduct and Discipline of Schools," and the heading opposite number 172, "Rules and Regulations—Reasonableness and Validity." If the Descriptive Word Index were used, the index under the heading "Schools and School Districts" and the subhead "Rules and regulations relating to pupils" would refer one to the index heading "Pupil." A reference thereto locates the heading "Rules and Regulations—Reasonableness," followed by "Schools, 172."

20.18 TECHNIQUES FOR RESEARCHING THE LAW

Law may be defined as the application of legal principles and rules to particular fact situations. The preceding sections have described the various law books in which legal principles and rules may be found. The basic techniques for their use in locating the principles and rules applicable to a given problem will be developed in the succeeding sections. Each attorney or experienced researcher has a preferred method. However, any method should involve the following steps:

1. Ascertaining the essential facts.
2. Analyzing the problem.
3. Framing the question to be researched.
4. Identifying key words or the proper topical heading or headings.
5. Using an appropriate search method.
6. Studying the primary and secondary authorities found.
7. Checking the subsequent history of primary authorities in *Shepard's Citations.*

20.19 ANALYZING THE PROBLEM

It is often helpful to break down the problem in terms of (1) the parties or persons, (2) the subject matter or property involved, (3) the nature of the claim, and (4) the object or remedy sought to be obtained.

The parties may be important because one or more may belong to a class governed by special rules (such as infants), or to a particular occupation (teaching), or because a special relationship may exist between them (guardian and ward, parent and child, teacher and student).

The subject matter or property comprises the essential things and places involved in the problem (for example, a teacher's contract, a school bus, a playground).

The nature of the claim or issue may consist of an act of commission (assault and battery, libel and slander, embezzlement or conversion of school funds), of an act of omission (failure to inspect the condition of playground equipment or to employ a competent bus driver), or of a violation of a statutory provision (disregarding a teacher's tenure rights).

The object or the remedy sought in a civil case may be money damages, an injunction, specific performance of a contract, a declaration of rights, etc.

As an illustration of the above analysis, assume that a married high school student has been dropped from the football team pursuant to a resolution of the school board restricting married students to classroom work. Through his parent (as next friend) the boy seeks to enjoin the application of the resolution to him by bringing an injunction action against the school district. He contends that the resolution is discriminatory and unreasonable and therefore unconstitutional. Analyzing the facts of this case in the light of the rules heretofore mentioned, one finds that the parties are a pupil and a school district, the subject matter is the resolution of the school board, the nature of the claim is the contention that the resolution is unreasonable, and the remedy sought is an injunction against the enforcement of the resolution.

20.20 FRAMING THE QUESTION TO BE RESEARCHED

After a careful analysis of the problem, the next step is to frame the question to be researched or to identify the legal issue or issues involved. If two or more points are raised, a separate question should be framed on each point. In stating the issue or framing the question, it may be helpful to assume that it will be turned over to someone else for research. It should be stated with sufficient fullness so that the researcher will understand it but narrowly enough to be confined to the single issue involved. This does not mean that the issue or question as originally stated becomes final. Further research and the ascertainment of additional facts may require that it be restated.

If the above suggestions were applied to the facts hypothesized in the preceding section, the question to be researched may be stated as follows: May a school district be enjoined from enforcing its regulation prohibiting a married high school student from participating in nonclassroom activities, such as playing football?

20.21 IDENTIFYING APPROPRIATE CATCHWORDS OR TOPICAL HEADINGS

As will be explained in the succeeding sections, the material in the principal legal research books (the digests, statutes, and encyclopedias) is organized alphabetically by topic. It is necessary at the outset to gain a working knowledge of the main topics used therein and also of the main index headings. The latter are often referred to as "catchwords." Before an index may be used effectively, the catchwords for the problem must be identified.

20.22 USING AN APPROPRIATE SEARCH METHOD

There are four basic methods for legal research: (1) the analytical or law chart approach, (2) the descriptive word index approach, (3) the table of cases approach, and (4) the words and phrases approach.

20.23 THE ANALYTICAL RESEARCH METHOD (AN ILLUSTRATION)

The analytical approach is the most scholarly and least mechanical of the four methods. The digests and encyclopedias divide the law into about four hundred topics. These are listed in the law chart at the beginning of the first volume of *Corpus Juris Secundum* under the seven grand divisions of the law: persons, property, contracts, torts, crimes, remedies, and government.

In using the analytical method the appropriate grand division must first be selected. In the illustration of the married high school student prohibited from playing football, it would appear to be "Government." We are concerned with a school district, which is a unit of government. This division of the law chart should then be consulted to determine the topic within the grand division which embraces our problem. Looking through it, we find the topic "Schools and School Districts" to be the most appropriate.

At this point, it should be reemphasized that the editors of the digests and encyclopedias have arranged the topics in alphabetical order. For example, Volume 1 of *Corpus Juris Secundum* covers topics "A"to "Adjective Law," Volume 2, topics "Adjoin" to "Agency," Sections 1-137, and so on.

To turn again to our illustrative problem, it is found that the topic "Schools and School Districts" is treated in Volumes 78 and 79 of *Corpus Juris Secundum*. Referring to the index to that topic at the end of Volume 79, we notice under "Pupils" the heading "Athletic Activities" and the subhead "Validity of rules forbidding participation," with a reference to Section 500. In this section appears the following statement:

It has been held that a rule of a school board forbidding pupils to play football under the auspices of the school is not unreasonable or in excess of the authority of the board, although applied to conduct on holidays and away from the school grounds.

Many law books, including the volumes in *Corpus Juris Secundum*, are kept up to date through supplements or pocket parts, so named because they are inserted in a "pocket" in the inside back cover of the book. It is essential to refer to the supplement or pocket part for developments in the law occurring after publication of the volume. Searching through the pocket part to Volume 79 of *Corpus Juris Secundum* under the topic "Schools and School Districts," Section 500, we see the statement "Married students prohibited from participation in athletics" and a citation to the Texas case of *Kissick v. Garland Independent School District*, 330 S.W.2d 708. In legal citations, as previously mentioned, the first number is the number of the volume and the second is the number of the page in the volume. An examination of the Kissick case reveals that a similar resolution to the one in question, namely, a resolution of a school board prohibiting a married high school student from

playing football, was found to be reasonable and enforceable.

However, it must be stressed that the Kissick case is not the law outside of Texas, except as it is found persuasive by courts in other states. Normally, research should not end until all of the available law books have been examined on the point in question. Among other works, the legal encyclopedia *American Jurisprudence* and *American Jurisprudence, Second Series*, should also be consulted, especially since its footnotes contain citations to annotations in the *American Law Reports*. Volume 47 of *American Jurisprudence* includes a comprehensive section on "Schools." By referring to this topic in the index at the end of the volume, we find that Section 155 applies to our problem. In this section we read, "However, a pupil may not be excluded from school because married, where no immorality or misconduct of the pupil is shown. . . ." Authority for the statement is given in footnote 10, referring to a court decision and to an annotation in Volume 63 of the *American Law Reports* at page 1164. One is fortunate in research whenever an A.L.R. annotation is found on the problem at hand, for it reviews and comments upon all the existing court decisions relating thereto. Periodically, the earlier annotations are updated by supplemental annotations appearing in later volumes. The annotation referred to in 63 A.L.R. 1164 analyzes all court decisions then existing on the subject: "Marriage or other domestic relations as ground for exclusion of pupil from public school." More recent court decisions and annotations on the same general subject may be located by referring to the supplements of A.L.R. under the heading "Schools," Section 50.

20.24 THE DESCRIPTIVE WORD INDEX SEARCH METHOD (AN ILLUSTRATION)

The descriptive word index approach involves an examination of the facts and issues to ascertain the outstanding words or phrases, commonly called catchwords. The descriptive word indexes, which comprise either the first or the last volume or volumes of most digests, list the numerous catchwords in alphabetical order. When the word is located in the index, reference is made to a particular volume and page, section, or key number wherein the matter is treated.

The use of the descriptive word index can be demonstrated by searching the index in an attempt to find the law applicable to this problem: A taxpayer questions the right of a school district to purchase liability insurance, contending that it enjoys an immunity from suit and hence there is no liability to insure. The precise question to be researched may be framed as follows: May a school district, which enjoys immunity from tort liability, purchase liability insurance? An appropriate catchword must be selected. It would seem to be *insurance*. A good beginning place is to use the descriptive word index to the Fifth Decennial of the *American Digest*.

The catchword *insurance* is found on page 823 of the first volume. Looking alphabetically under this heading, the subtitle "School property" is found and below it the line, "Authority of district to purchase insurance," followed by "Schools, 78." This means that all court decisions on this point will be digested in the volumes containing the topic "Schools and School Districts" under the key number 78.

The use of the descriptive word index of one of the state digests, such as the *Missouri Digest*, would have produced the same result for that particular state. However, unless research is limited to a single state, an exhaustive search would require an examination of the various volumes in the *American Digest* containing the topic "Schools and School Districts." Since there are currently seven decennial editions, at least seven separate volumes, together with the recent supplementary volumes, must be examined. For purposes of this illustration the search will be limited to the Fifth, Sixth, and Seventh Decennial Digests.

In the Fifth Decennial the topic "Schools and School Districts" is found in Volume 39. Although the appropriate key number could have been located by using the analysis at the beginning of this topic, since key number 78 was previously found in the descriptive word index, it may be turned to directly. Here we find a 1942 California decision, the digest note of which says, "School boards are liable as such in the name of the school district for judgments against the district for injury to persons or property, and may insure against liability for damages." The digest note cites the California School Code, Section 2.990, and the case of *Brown v. City of Oakland*, 124 P.2d 369. Checking for more recent cases, we see that the topic "Schools and School Districts" is found in Volume 26 of the Sixth Decennial Digest. A search of court decisions under key number 78 reveals no case directly in point, but a Kansas case is of interest in that it confirms the general rule that "the power of a school district to contract is only such as is conferred by express

statute or by fair implication from the statute." Volume 27 of the Seventh Decennial must also be examined. Again we would look under the topic "Schools and School Districts" and the key number 78. This search discloses a 1959 Idaho case of interest holding that a school district and a liability insurer may not contract for liability coverage in excess of that legislatively authorized.

20.25 SEARCHING THE
STATUTES AND THE LEGAL PERIODICALS

The preceding two sections have demonstrated the use of the legal encyclopedias (*Corpus Juris Secundum* and *American Jurisprudence*) and the digests. The use of *American Jurisprudence* also revealed a method of locating annotations in the *American Law Reports* (A.L.R.). However, in all school law questions research should include a careful check of the statutes of the particular state. Normally, the search should begin with them, particularly on questions concerning the authority of school boards since it is derived from the state legislature.

The state statutes relating to education and schools will ordinarily have been assembled together in several chapters. The sections included in each chapter are shown in numerical order at the beginning of the chapter. Normally, however, the detailed index to the statutes is consulted. Suppose research on the problem considered in the preceding section was continued in the Illinois statutes. An examination of the index to Illinois statutes under the heading "School Board" discloses that the power of a school board to purchase liability insurance is covered by Chapter 122, Section 10, Subsection 22.3. Turning to this subsection we find that an Illinois school board has authority "to insure against any loss or liability of the school district or of any agent, employee, teacher, officer or member of the supervisory staff thereof resulting from the wrongful or negligent act of such agent, employee, teacher, officer or member of the supervisory staff."

The various indexes to the legal periodicals or law journals published by the law schools and bar associations should also be checked. Again materials on school law are generally found under the index heading "Schools and School Districts." A search of the *Index to Legal Periodicals* for the years 1958-1961 reveals an article in the *University of Kansas Law Review* on the subject "Liability and Authority of School Districts and of Members of Boards of Education," which may be helpful. Further on in the same index we find an article in the *University of Notre Dame Law Journal* analyzing the Kissick case concerning the legality of regulations of married high school students, previously discussed. Of course, the other volumes to the *Index to Legal Periodicals* should also be examined.

20.26 THE TABLE OF CASES APPROACH

If the names of the parties to a court decision and its approximate date are known, the volume and page where it is reported may be found by using the appropriate volume of the digest containing the Table of Cases. Even where the citation of the case is known, the Table of Cases may be used to locate the sections in the digest where it has been summarized. This is one of the recognized methods for locating similar cases by obtaining the proper key number or key numbers.

20.27 THE WORDS AND PHRASES SEARCH METHOD

If the objective is to ascertain the court decisions construing a particular word or phrase, such as *in loco parentis, tenure* or *good faith,* the simplest and most effective method is to consult the set of books entitled *Words and Phrases,* wherein words and phrases which have been subject to judicial interpretation are alphabetically listed. A summary of the holding in each case is also set out.

20.28 CHECKING THE SUBSEQUENT HISTORY OF CASES AND STATUTES (SHEPARDIZING THE CASE)

A court decision or statute cannot be relied upon with confidence unless its subsequent history has been checked to determine whether it has been overruled, modified, or repealed. This involves the use of the proper volume of *Shepard's Citations,* which also is a method of finding additional cases and articles since all of them are listed that apply, interpret, or otherwise cite the court decision or statute under investigation. A separate *Shepard's Citation* exists for each reporter, including reporters of the states. Thus, federal decisions and statutes are covered in *Shepard's United States Citations,* cases reported in the *South Western Reporter* in *Shepard's South Western Citation,* and Missouri decisions and statutes in *Shepard's Missouri Reporter and Statutory Citations.*

To illustrate the use of *Shepard's Citations,* assume that we wish to check the subsequent history of the case of *Joseph Triner Corporation v. McNeil,* reported in 2 N.E.2d 929, dealing with the constitutionality of the Illinois Fair Trade Act. Consulting the 1945 volume of *Shepard's North Eastern Reporter Citations,* we first locate the volume number in which the Triner case is reported, namely, 2 N.E.2d. The second step is to find the page number, namely, 929. By the use of symbols, the key to which appears at the beginning of the volume, *Shepards's* sets out the history of our case.

On the page referring to the Triner case, the first line cites additional reports in which the case may be found. We discover that it is also reported in Volume 363 of the *Illinois Supreme Court Reports* at page 559 and in Volume 104 of the *American Law Reports* at page 1435. The next three citations, preceded by the letter *a,* indicate that the case was affirmed by the United State' Supreme Court and that its opinion may be found in the references given to the *United States Reports,* the *Lawyer's Edition of the Supreme Court Reports,* and the *Supreme Court Reporter.* The next citation, preceded by the letter *s,* denotes a previous decision in the same case. Later citations, preceded by *f,* signify that the principles of law summarized in the designated paragraphs of the headnotes in the Triner case were followed in the cited cases. The small superior number in the citation indicates the paragraph number of the headnote.

We also observe that the Triner case has been cited by a lower federal court and in notes of the *American Law Reports.* The latter is evidenced by the letter *n* following the particular citations. Further citations reveal additional cases wherein the Triner case was referred to and also indicate that it was commented upon in the *Harvard Law Review,* the *Boston University Law Review,* and the *Massachusetts Law Quarterly.* Most important for our purposes, the above use of *Shepard's Citations* establishes that the Triner case has not been overruled or modified and that it is therefore still good authority.

Shepardizing the Kissick married high school student case, we find it has been followed in 333 S.W.2d 891, and has been referred to in 356 S.W.2d 185, 103 N.W.2d 578, and 189 N.E.2d 184. It was later reversed in 507 S.W.2d 636 and in 491 F.2d 92.

Shepard's Citations is used in much the same manner in connection with statutory materials. It shows every instance in which a particular statute or constitutional provision has been cited, applied, construed, or changed by subsequent legislation. The symbols used in this division are somewhat different, but their key is easily found at the beginning of the particular volume.

Where there is more than one volume in the *Shepard* unit, each volume and the cumulative supplement must be consulted.

20.29 SUMMARY

Each of the preceding chapters concludes with a summary of its contents. The subject matter of this chapter does not lend itself to such treatment. In essence the entire chapter is a summary: first, of the books found in a law library and second, of their use in legal research.

BIBLIOGRAPHY

Alexander, Kern, Ray Corns, and Walter McCann. *Public School Law: Cases and Materials.* St. Paul, Minnesota: West Publishing Company, 1969. 734 pp. (This work has been updated with a fall 1972 supplement.)

Alexander, Kern and K. Forbis Jordan. *Legal Aspects of Educational Choice: Compulsory Attendance and Student Assignment.* Topeka, Kansas: National Organization on Legal Problems of Education, 1973. 75 pp.

Alexander, Kern and Erwin S. Solomon. *College and University Law.* Charlottesville, Virginia: The Michie Company, 1972. 776 pp.

Anson, Ronald J. and Peter J. Kuriloff (eds.). *Student's Right to Due Process: Professional Discretion and Liability.* Washington, D.C.: Capitol Publications, Inc., 1975. 177 pp.

Bolmeier, Edward C. *Legality of Student Disciplinary Practices.* Charlottesville, Virginia: The Michie Company, 1975. 194 pp.

Bolmeier, Edward C. *Sex Litigation and the Public Schools.* Charlottesville, Virginia: The Michie Company, 1975. 215 pp.

Bolmeier, Edward C. *Landmark Supreme Court Decisions on Public School Issues.* Charlottesville, Virginia: The Michie Company, 1973. 233 pp.

Bolmeier, Edward C. *School in the Legal Structure,* Second Edition. Cincinnati, Ohio: W. H. Anderson Company, 1973. 346 pp.

Browning, R. Stephen (ed.). *From Brown to Bradley: School Desegregation 1954–1974.* Cincinnati, Ohio: Jefferson Law Book Company, 1975. 220 pp.

Buss, William G. *Legal Aspects of Crime Investigation in the Public Schools.* Topeka, Kansas: National Organization on Legal Problems of Education, 1971. 73 pp.

Butler, Henry E., K. D. Moran, and Floyd A. Vanderpool. *Legal Aspects of Student Records.* Topeka, Kansas: National Organization on Legal Problems of Education, 1972. 62 pp.

Center for Law and Education. *The Constitutional Rights of Students.* Cambridge, Massachusetts: Center for Law and Education, Harvard University, 1976. 413 pp.

Chambers, M. M. *The Colleges and the Courts: Faculty and Staff Before the Bench.* Danville, Illinois: The Interstate Printers and Publishers, 1973. 260 pp.

Delon, Floyd G. *Substantive Legal Aspects of Teacher Discipline.* Topeka, Kansas: National Organization on Legal Problems of Education, 1972. 63 pp.

Duscha, Julius and Thomas Fischer. *The Campus Press: Freedom and Responsibility.* Washington, D.C.: American Association of State Colleges and Universities, 1973. 115 pp.

Fischer, Louis and David Schimmel. *The Civil Rights of Teachers.* New York: Harper & Row, 1973. 220 pp.

Flygare, Thomas J. *Legal Rights of Teachers.* Bloomington, Indiana: The Phi Delta Kappa Educational Foundation, 1976. 45 pp.

Gaddy, Dale. *Rights and Freedoms of Public School Students: Directions from the 1960's.* Topeka, Kansas: National Organization on Legal Problems of Education, 1970. 60 pp.

Gatti, Daniel J. and Richard D. Gatti. *The Teacher and the Law.* West Nyack, New York: Parker Publishing Company, 1972. 206 pp.

Goldstein, Stephen R. *Law and Public Education.* Indianapolis, Indiana: Bobbs-Merrill Company, 1974. 965 pp.

Holmes, Grace W. (ed.). *Student Protest and the Law.* Ann Arbor, Michigan: The Institute of Continuing Legal Education, 1969. 403 pp.

Hudgins, H. C., Jr. *The Warren Court and the Public Schools.* Danville, Illinois: The Interstate Printers and Publishers, Inc., 1970. 178 pp.

Hudgins, H. C., Jr. and Marshall Gorodetzer. *Public School Desegregation: Legal Issues and Judicial Decisions.* Topeka, Kansas: National Organization on Legal Problems of Education, 1973. 78 pp.

Kallen, Laurence. *Teachers' Rights and Liabilities Under the Law.* New York: Arco Publishing Company, 1971. 144 pp. (Summary of laws governing pupil management in the 50 states.)

Kurland, Philip B. *Politics, the Constitution, and the Warren Court.* Chicago, Illinois: The University of Chicago Press, 1970. 222 pp.

LaMonte, Michael W., Harold W. Gentry, and D. Parker Young. *Students' Legal Rights and Responsibilities.* Cincinnati, Ohio: W. H. Anderson, 1971. 241 pp.

LaNoue, George R. *Educational Vouchers: Concepts and Controversies.* Teachers College Press, Columbia University, 1234 Amsterdam Avenue, New York, 1972. 176 pp.

Miller, Dean F. *School Health Programs: Their Basis in Law.* South Brunswick, New Jersey: A. S. Barnes, 1972. 161 pp.

Mills, Joseph L. *Legal Rights of College Students and Administrators: A Handbook.* Washington, D.C.: Lerner Law Book Publishing Company, 1971. 177 pp.

Missouri Bar, The. *Due Process of Law.* Jefferson City, Missouri: The Missouri Department of Education, 1970. 70 pp.

Morris, Arval A. *The Constitution and American Education.* St. Paul, Minnesota: West Publishing Company, 1974. 883 pp.

National Education Association, Research Division, School Law Series. *The Student's Day in Court.* Washington, D.C. (published annually).

National Education Association, Research Division, School Law Series. *The Teacher's Day in Court.* Washington, D.C. (published annually).

National Organization on Legal Problems of Education. *Yearbooks of School of Law.* Topeka, Kansas. (published annually from 1972).

National Organization on Legal Problems of Education. *Proceedings of National Conference.* Topeka, Kansas. (published annually since 1964).

National Organization on Legal Problems of Education. *School Law Journal.* Topeka, Kansas. (published semiannually from 1970).

Nolte, M. Chester (ed.). *Law and the School Superintendent.* Second Edition. Cincinnati, Ohio: Jefferson Law Book Company, 1971. 295 pp.

Nolte, M. Chester. *Status and Scope of Collective Bargaining in Public Education.* Eugene, Oregon: ERIC Clearinghouse in Educational Administration, 1970. 62 pp.

Nunnery, Michael Y. and Ralph B. Kimbrough. *Politics, Power, Polls, and School Elections.* Berkeley, California: McCutchan Publishing Corporation, 1971. 169 pp.

Nygaard, Joseph M. *The Counselor and Students' Legal Rights.* Boston, Massachusetts: Houghton-Mifflin Company, 1973. 86 pp.

O'Hara, William T. and John G. Hill, Jr. *The Student—The College—The Law.* New York: Teachers College, Columbia University Press, 1972, 220 pp.

Phay, Robert E. *The Law of Suspension and Expulsion.* Topeka, Kansas: National Organization of Legal Problems of Education, 1975. 66 pp.

Phay, Robert E. and Jasper L. Cummings, Jr. *Teacher Dismissal and Nonrenewal of Teacher Contracts.* Chapel Hill, North Carolina: Institute of Government, University of North Carolina, 1972. 41 pp.

Piele, Philip K. and James R. Forsberg. *School Property: The Legality of its Use and Disposition.* Topeka, Kansas: National Organization on Legal Problems of Education, 1974. 47 pp.

Punke, Harold H. *The Teacher and the Courts.* Danville, Illinois: The Interstate Printers and Publishers, 1971. 781 pp.

Remmlein, Madaline Kinter and Martha L. Ware. *School Law,* Third Edition. Danville, Illinois: Interstate Publishers, Inc., 1970. 388 pp.

Reutter, E. Edmund, Jr. *The Courts and Student Conduct.* Topeka, Kansas: National Organization on Legal Problems of Education, 1975. 93 pp.

Reutter, E. Edmund, Jr. and Robert R. Hamilton. *The Law of Public Education,* Second Edition. Mineola, New York: The Foundation Press, Inc., 1976. 747 pp.

Rubin, David. *The Rights of Teachers.* New York: Hearst Corporation, Discus Books, Division of Avon, 1972. 176 pp.

Schimmel, David and Louis Fischer. *The Legal Rights of Students.* New York: Harper & Row, 1975. 348 pp.

Seitz, Reynolds C. (ed.). *School Law Reporter.* Topeka, Kansas: National Organization on Legal Problems of Education. (published bimonthly).

Smith, Michael R. and Joseph E. Bryson. *Church-State Relations: The Legality of Using Public Funds for Religious Schools.* Topeka, Kansas: National Organization on Legal Problems of Education, 1972. 89 pp.

Strahan, Richard D. *The Courts and the Schools.* Lincoln, Nebraska: Professional Educators Publications, 1973. 148 pp.

Van Der Smissen, Betty. *Legal Liability of Cities and Schools for Injuries in Recreation and Parks.* Cincinnati, Ohio: The W. H. Anderson Company, 1968. 402 pp.

Von Brock, Robert C., James G. Bailey, and Godfrey C. Albert. *A Survey of Court Decisions Affecting Student Dress and Appearance.* Baton Rouge, Louisiana: Bureau of Educational Materials and Research, College of Education, LSU, 1972. 26 pp.

Young, D. Parker (ed.). *Conference on Higher Education: The Law and Student Protest.* Athens, Georgia: University of Georgia, Institute of Higher Education, 1970. 51 pp. (proceedings of seminar).

Young, D. Parker (ed.). *Higher Education: The Law and Campus Issues.* Athens, Georgia: The University of Georgia, Institute of Higher Education, Center for Continuing Education, 1972. 52 pp. (proceedings of seminar).

Young, D. Parker (ed.). *Higher Education: The Law and Individual Rights and Responsibilities.* Athens, Georgia: Institute of Higher Education, University of Georgia, 1971. 51 pp. (proceedings of seminar).

Young, D. Parker and Donald D. Gehring. *Briefs of Selected Court Cases Affecting Student Dissent and Discipline in Higher Education.* Athens, Georgia: Institute of Higher Education, University of Georgia, 1970. 49 pp.

Ziegler, Carol L. *Struggle in the Schools: Constitutional Protection for Public High School Students.* Princeton, New Jersey: Woodrow Wilson School of Public and International Affairs, Princeton University, 1970. 47 pp.

Also See: Phi Delta Kappa, Bloomington, Indiana, for monthly articles on school law; *Journal of Law and Education,* Washington, D.C. (published quarterly).

SUMMARY OF CIVIL RIGHTS ACTS

Civil Rights Act of 1865, 42 U.S.C.A. §1972, prohibited members of the armed forces from interfering with the freedom of elections.

Civil Rights Act of 1866, 42 U.S.C.A. §1982, granted to all citizens the rights of white citizens in the ownership, sale, and leasing of real and personal property.

Civil Rights Act of 1870, 42 U.S.C.A. §1981, 18 U.S.C.A. §§241 and 242, specified that all persons shall have the same rights as white citizens to make and enforce contracts, to be a party to litigation, and to the full and equal benefit of all laws pertaining to security of person and property; also provides criminal penalties.

Civil Rights Act of 1871, 42 U.S.C.A. §1983, created a cause of action in favor of a person who has been injured by being deprived of any rights, privileges, or immunities against any person who has done so while acting under color of law.

Civil Rights Act of 1875, 42 U.S.C.A. §1984, 18 U.S.C.A. §243, qualified persons for jury service regardless of race, color, or previous condition of servitude.

Civil Rights Act of 1957, as amended in 1970 and 1975, 42 U.S.C.A. §§1975–1975e, created the Civil Rights Commission and the Civil Rights Division of the United States Department of Justice, gave these agencies authority to enforce civil and criminal remedies for violation of voting rights, permitted the Attorney General to seek injunctive relief, and prohibited the use of threats intended to hinder the right to vote in federal elections.

Civil Rights Act of 1960, 42 U.S.C.A. §§1974–1974e, provided for federal voting referees and prohibited certain discriminatory practices against black persons.

Civil Rights Act of 1964, 28 U.S.C.A. §1447, 42 U.S.C.A. §§1971, 1975a–1976d, 2000a-2000h-6, provided comprehensive protection of the important civil rights of voting, public accommodations, use of public facilities, public education, and employment; extended the life of the Civil Rights Commission; and created the Equal Employment Opportunity Commission and Community Relations Service.

Civil Rights of Act of 1965, 42 U.S.C.A. §§1973–1973p, provided a long list of remedies for those discriminated against as to voting rights, among them, suspension of literacy tests, assignment of federal examiners to list qualified applicants, appointment of poll watchers, and excusal from accumulated poll taxes.

Civil Rights Act of 1968, 82 Stats. 73 et. seq., Public Law 90-284, approved April 11, 1968, contained 12 titles, several of which extended civil rights protection to Indians and Titles VIII and IX which established a fair housing code.

Civil Rights Act of 1970, 42 U.S.C.A. §§1973aa–1973aa-4, 1973bb–1973bb-4, eliminated tests as a prerequisite for voting, regulated residential requirements in presidential elections, and reduced the voting age to 18 in federal, state, and local elections.

INDEX OF UNITED STATES SUPREME COURT DECISIONS

NOTE: Numbers in parentheses after page numbers are footnote numbers.

INDEX